SIXTH EDITION

DIGITAL BUSINESS AND E-COMMERCE MANAGEMENT

STRATEGY, IMPLEMENTATION AND PRACTICE

DAVE CHAFFEY

PEARSON

Harlow, England • London • New York • Boston • San Francisco • Toronto • Sydney • Auckland • Singapore • Hong Kong
Tokyo • Seoul • Taipei • New Delhi • Cape Town • São Paulo • Mexico City • Madrid • Amsterdam • Munich • Paris • Milan

Pearson Education Limited
Edinburgh Gate
Harlow CM20 2JE
United Kingdom
Tel: +44 (0)1279 623623
Web: www.pearson.com/uk

First published 2002 (print)
Second edition published 2004 (print)
Third edition published 2007 (print)
Fourth edition published 2009 (print)
Fifth edition published 2011 (print)
Sixth edition published 2015 (print and electronic)

Pearson Education is not responsible for the content of third-party internet sites.

ISBN: 978-0-273-78654-2 (print)
        978-0-273-78657-3 (PDF)
        978-0-273-78655-9 (eText)

British Library Cataloguing-in-Publication Data
A catalogue record for the print edition is available from the British Library

Library of Congress Cataloging-in-Publication Data
A catalog record for the print edition is available from the Library of Congress

10 9 8 7 6 5 4 3 2 1
18 17 16 15 14

Print edition typeset in 10/12pt MinionPro by 75
Print edition printed and bound by L.E.G.O.S.p.A., Italy

Brief contents

Contents

Part 3

Implementation   467

Lecturer Resources

For password-protected online resources tailored to support the use of this textbook in teaching, please visit **www.pearsoned.co.uk/chaffey**

ON THE WEBSITE

Preface

In 1849, a group of settlers travelling west towards the promised land, California, entered a then unnamed valley. The valley presented a harsh environment with a barrier of mountains to the west making the way forward unclear. Some of the settlers lost their lives as they sought to find a route west before eventually reaching California and what was to become one of the most prosperous places on earth. As the group left the valley, one of the women in the group turned and said, 'Goodbye, Death Valley', and hence the valley got its name.

Today, flagship digital businesses with headquarters in California, such as eBay, Facebook and Google, are now leading global brands with turnovers of billions of dollars, yet this has happened in a few short years, less than 300 years after the first modern settlers arrived.

Likewise for other businesses, the road to digital business success is not straightforward and fraught with difficulties of selecting the correct strategic direction and surviving in an increasingly harsh competitive environment. Not all who follow the route survive. But whether it's the start-up businesses or an existing business, what they have in common is that those who prosper learn to optimise to take the right strategic decisions about digital technology, digital marketing and supply chain management.

This book is intended to equip current and future managers with some of the knowledge and practical skills to help them navigate their organisation towards digital business.

A key aim of this book is to identify and review the key management decisions required by organisations moving to digital business and consider the process by which these decisions can be taken. Key questions include: What approach to digital business strategy do we follow? How much do we need to invest in digital business? Which processes should be our digital business priorities? Should we adopt new business and revenue models? What are the main changes that need to be made to the organisation to facilitate digital business?

Given the broad scope of digital business, this book takes an integrative approach drawing on new and existing approaches and models from many disciplines, including information systems, strategy, marketing, supply chain management, operations and human resources management.

What is digital business management?

Digital business
how businesses apply digital technology and media to improve the competitiveness of their organisation through optimising internal processes with online and traditional channels to market and supply.

As we will see in Chapter 1, digital business is aimed at enhancing the competitiveness of an organisation by deploying innovative digital technologies throughout an organisation and beyond, through links to partners and customers and promotion through digital media. It does not simply involve using technology to automate existing processes, but is about digital transformation by applying technology to help change these processes to add value to the business and its customers. To be successful in managing digital business, a breadth of knowledge is needed of different business processes and activities from across the value chain, such as marketing and sales, through new product development, manufacturing and

Supply chain management (scm)
The coordination of all supply activities of an organisation from its suppliers and partners to its customers.

Value chain
A model for analysis of how supply chain activities can add value to products and services delivered to the customer.

inbound and outbound logistics. Organisations also need to manage the change required by new processes and technology through what have traditionally been support activities such as human resources management.

From this definition, it is apparent that digital business involves looking at how electronic communications can be used to enhance all aspects of an organisation's supply chain management. it also involves optimising an organisation's value chain, a related concept that describes the different value-adding activities that connect a company's supply side with its demand side. the digital business era also involves management of a network of interrelated value chains or value networks.

What is e-commerce management?

Value networks
The links between an organisation and its strategic and non-strategic partners that form its external value chain.

Electronic commerce (e-commerce)
All electronically mediated information exchanges between an organisation and its external stakeholders.

Buy-side e-commerce
E-commerce transactions between an organisation and its suppliers and other partners.

Sell-side e-commerce
E-commerce transactions between an organisation and its customers.

To set the scope of this book, in its title we reference both 'digital business' and 'e-commerce'. Both these terms are applied in a variety of ways; to some they mean the same, to others they are quite different. As explained in Chapter 1, what is most important is that they are applied consistently within organisations so that employees and external stakeholders are clear about how the organisation can exploit electronic communications. The distinction made in this book is to use electronic commerce (e-commerce) to refer to all types of electronic transactions between organisations and stakeholders, whether they are financial transactions or exchanges of information or other services. These e-commerce transactions are either buy-side e-commerce or sell-side e-commerce and the management issues involved with each aspect are considered separately in Part 2 of the book. 'Digital business' is applied as a broader term encompassing e-commerce but also including all electronic transactions within an organisation.

Management of e-commerce involves prioritising buy-side and sell-side activities and putting in place the plans and resources to deliver the identified benefits. These plans need to focus on management of the many risks to success, some of which you may have experienced when using e-commerce sites, from technical problems such as transactions that fail, sites that are difficult to use or are too slow, through to problems with customer service or fulfilment, which also indicate failure of management. Today, the social media or peer-to-peer interactions that occur between customers on company websites, blogs, communities and social networks have changed the dynamics of online commerce. Likewise, the frenzied consumer adoption of mobile technology platforms via mobile sites and mobile apps offers new platforms to interact with customers which must be evaluated and prioritised. Deciding which of the many emerging technologies and marketing approaches to prioritise and which to ignore is a challenge for all organisations!

How is this book structured?

Social media
A category of media focussing on participation and peer-to-peer communication between individuals, with sites providing the capability to develop user-generated content (ugc) and to exchange messages and comments between different users.

The overall structure of the book, shown in Figure P.1, follows a logical sequence: introducing the foundations of digital business concepts in Part 1; reviewing alternative strategic approaches and applications of digital business in Part 2; and how strategy can be implemented in Part 3. Within this overall structure, differences in how electronic communications are used to support different business processes are considered separately. This is achieved by distinguishing between how electronic communications are used, from buy-side e-commerce aspects of supply chain management in Chapters 6 and 7, to the marketing perspective of sell-side e-commerce in Chapters 8 and 9. Figure P.1 shows the emphasis of perspective for the particular chapters.

Mobile technology platforms

Devices and services used by consumers to interact with other consumers and companies including smartphones, tablets and wearable technology.

Mobile apps

A software application that is designed for use on a mobile phone or tablet, typically downloaded from an app store. Iphone apps are best known, but all smart phones support the use of apps which can provide users with information, entertainment or location-based services such as mapping.

Part 1: Introduction (Chapters 1–4)

Part 1 introduces digital business and e-commerce. It seeks to clarify basic terms and concepts by looking at different interpretations of terms and applications through case studies.

- **Chapter 1: Introduction to digital business and e-commerce**. Definition of the meaning and scope of digital business and e-commerce. Social media, social commerce and mobile apps are also introduced. Introduction to business use of the internet – what are the benefits and barriers to adoption and how widely used is it?
- **Chapter 2: Marketplace analysis for e-commerce**. Introduction to new business models and marketplace structures enabled by electronic communications.
- **Chapter 3: Managing digital business infrastructure**. Background on the hardware, software and telecommunications that need to be managed to achieve digital business.
- **Chapter 4: E-environment**. Describes the macro-environment of an organisation, which presents opportunities and constraints on strategy and implementation.

Part 2: Strategy and applications (Chapters 5–9)

In Part 2 of the book, approaches to developing digital business strategy and applications are reviewed for the organisation as a whole (Chapter 5) and with an emphasis on buy-side e-commerce (Chapters 6 and 7) and sell-side e-commerce (Chapters 8 and 9).

- **Chapter 5: Digital business strategy**. Approaches to developing digital business strategy. Differences from traditional strategic approaches. Relation to IS strategy.
- **Chapter 6: Supply chain management**. A supply chain perspective on strategy with examples of how technology can be applied to increase supply chain and value chain efficiency.
- **Chapter 7: E-procurement**. Evaluation of the benefits and practical issues of adopting e-procurement.
- **Chapter 8: Digital marketing**. A sell-side e-commerce perspective to digital business, reviewing differences in marketing required through digital media. Structured around developing a digital marketing plan.
- **Chapter 9: Customer relationship management**. Reviews marketing techniques that apply e-commerce for acquiring and retaining customers.

Part 3: Implementation (Chapters 10–12)

Management of digital business implementation is described in Part 3 of the book in which we examine practical management issues involved with creating and maintaining digital business solutions.

- **Chapter 10: Change management**. How to manage the organisational, human and technology changes required in the move to digital business.
- **Chapter 11: Analysis and design**. We discuss the main issues of analysis and design raised by e-commerce systems that need to be discussed by managers and solutions providers.
- **Chapter 12: Digital business implementation and optimisation**. How should e-commerce systems be managed and monitored once they are live?

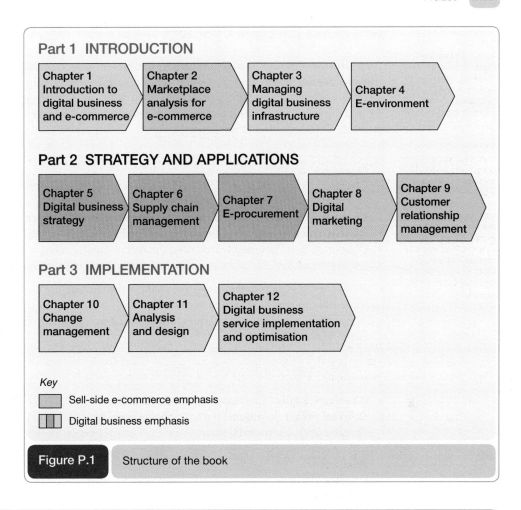

Part 1 INTRODUCTION

Chapter 1
Introduction to
digital business
and e-commerce

Chapter 2
Marketplace
analysis for
e-commerce

Chapter 3
Managing
digital business
infrastructure

Chapter 4
E-environment

Part 2 STRATEGY AND APPLICATIONS

Chapter 5
Digital business
strategy

Chapter 6
Supply chain
management

Chapter 7
E-procurement

Chapter 8
Digital
marketing

Chapter 9
Customer
relationship
management

Part 3 IMPLEMENTATION

Chapter 10
Change
management

Chapter 11
Analysis
and design

Chapter 12
Digital business
service implementation
and optimisation

Key

☐ Sell-side e-commerce emphasis

☐ Digital business emphasis

Figure P.1 Structure of the book

Who should use this book?

Students

This book has been created as the main student text for undergraduate and postgraduate students taking specialist courses or modules which cover digital business, e-commerce information systems or digital marketing. The book is relevant to students who are:

- *undergraduates on business programmes* which include modules on the use of the Internet and e-commerce; this includes specialist degrees such as electronic business, electronic commerce, internet marketing and marketing or general business degrees such as business studies, business administration and business management;
- *undergraduate project students* who select this topic for final-year projects or dissertations – this book is an excellent resource for these students;
- *undergraduates completing work placement* involved with different aspects of digital business such as managing an intranet or company website;
- *postgraduate students on specialist masters degrees in electronic commerce, electronic business or digital marketing and generic MBA, Certificate in Management or Diploma in Management Studies* which involve modules or electives for electronic commerce and digital marketing.

What does the book offer to lecturers teaching these courses?

The book is intended to be a comprehensive guide to all aspects of deploying digital business and e-commerce within an organisation. The book builds on existing theories and concepts and questions the validity of these models in the light of the differences between the internet and other media. The book references the emerging body of literature specific to digital business, e-commerce and digital marketing. As such, it can be used across several modules. Lecturers will find that the book has a good range of case studies, activities and exercises to support their teaching. These activities assist in using the book for student-centred learning as part of directed study. Web links given in the text and at the end of each chapter highlight key information sources for particular topics.

Practitioners

There is also much of relevance in this book for the industry professional, including:

- *senior managers and directors* seeking to apply the right digital business and e-commerce approaches to benefit their organisation;
- *information systems managers* who are developing and implementing digital business and e-commerce strategies;
- *marketing managers* responsible for defining a digital marketing strategy and implementing and maintaining the company website;
- *supply chain, logistics and procurement managers* wanting to see examples of best practice in using e-commerce for supply chain management;
- *technical project managers or webmasters* who may understand the technical details of building a site, but have a limited knowledge of business or marketing fundamentals.

Student learning features

A range of features have been incorporated into this book to help the reader get the most out of it. They have been designed to assist understanding, reinforce learning and help readers find information easily. The features are described in the order you will encounter them.

At the start of each chapter

- *Chapter at a glance*: a list of main topics, 'focus on' topics and case studies.
- *Learning outcomes*: a list describing what readers can learn through reading the chapter and completing the activities.
- *Management issues*: a summary of main issues or decisions faced by managers related to the chapter topic area.
- *Web support*: additional material on the companion website.
- *Links to other chapters*: a summary of related topics in other chapters.
- *Introductions*: succinct summaries of the relevance of the topic to marketing students and practitioners together with content and structure.

In each chapter

- *Activities*: short activities in the main text that develop concepts and understanding, often by relating to student experience or through reference to websites. Model answers to activities are provided at the end of the chapter where applicable.

- *Case studies*: real-world examples of issues facing companies that implement digital business. Questions at the end of the case study highlight the main learning points from that case study.
- *Real-world digital business experiences*: interviews with e-commerce managers at a range of UK, European and US-based organisations concerning the strategies they have adopted and their approaches to strategy implementation.
- *Digital trends updates*. References to relevant statistical sources to update information on the latest consumer and business adoption of digital technology.
- *Box features*: these explore a concept in more detail or give an example of a principle discussed in the text.
- *'Focus on' sections*: more detailed coverage of specific topics of interest.
- *Questions for debate*: suggestions for discussion of significant issues for managers involved with the transformation required for digital business.
- *Definitions*: when significant terms are first introduced the main text contains succinct definitions in the margin for easy reference.
- *Web links*: where appropriate, web addresses are given for further information, particularly those that update information.
- *Chapter summaries*: intended as revision aids and to summarise the main learning points from the chapter.

At the end of each chapter

- *Self-assessment exercises*: short questions which will test understanding of terms and concepts described in the chapter.
- *Discussion questions*: require longer essay-style answers discussing themes from the chapter, and can be used for essays or as debate questions in seminars.
- *Essay questions*: conventional essay questions.
- *Examination questions*: typical short-answer questions found in exams and can also be used for revision.
- *References*: these are references to books, articles or papers referred to within the chapter.
- *Further reading*: supplementary texts or papers on the main themes of the chapter. Where appropriate a brief commentary is provided on recommended supplementary reading on the main themes of the chapters.
- *Web links*: these are significant sites that provide further information on the concepts and topics of the chapter. All website references within the chapter, for example company sites, are not repeated here. The website address prefix 'http://' is omitted from www links for clarity.

At the end of the book

- *Glossary*: a list of all definitions of key terms and phrases used within the main text.
- *Index*: all key words and abbreviations referred to in the main text.

Learning techniques

The book is intended to support a range of learning styles. It can be used for an active or student-centred learning approach whereby students attempt the activities through reflecting on questions posed, answering questions and then comparing their answer to a suggested answer at the end of the chapter. Alternatively, students can proceed straight to suggested answers in a more traditional learning approach, which still encourages reflection about the topic.

Module guide

Table B presents one mapping of how the book could be used in different weekly lectures and seminars through the core eleven weeks of a module where the focus is on management issues of digital business and e-commerce.

A full set of PowerPoint slides and accompanying notes to assist lecturers in preparing lectures is available for download at www.pearsoned.co.uk/chaffey.

Enhancements for the sixth edition

The effective chapter structure of previous editions has been retained, but many other changes have been incorporated based on lecturer and student feedback. We now refer to digital business throughout rather than the dated term e-business which we had included from the first edition in 2002. The rationale is that the term e-business is less used now in industry; instead companies increasingly reference management of digital technologies, channel strategies, digital marketing and digital transformation.

You will see from the listing of updates below that the most significant additions to the content reflect the growth in importance of mobile marketing and commerce and inbound marketing, including content marketing and social media marketing.

Each chapter has been rationalised to focus on the key concepts and processes recommended to evaluate capability and develop digital business strategies. The main updates for the sixth edition on a chapter-by-chapter basis are:

- *Chapter 1.* The chapter starts by introducing the major trends now determining selection of digital services which are a major theme in the book: *inbound marketing* (*content, search and social media marketing*), Google's *Zero Moment of Truth* (ZMOT) and *mobile commerce.*

  Paid, owned, earned (POE) media options for reaching audiences are introduced and a new mini case study on Tatu Couture shows how small and larger businesses can use these techniques to reach new audiences. All other cases have been updated, as is the case for the majority in the book.

  Dated Internet adoption data has been removed and replaced by a new 'Trends update' feature and activities directing students via Dave Chaffey's *SmartInsights.com* site to the best data sources in their country for reviewing adoption of digital technologies.
- *Chapter 2.* Increased emphasis on online start-up businesses, of particular interest to students. Mini case study on *Ecomum* added to give a recent example of an e-retail failure with serious consequences. New case at start of chapter on Blackcircles.com.

  Updated review of *online ecosystem* to explain the increasing role of *mobile platform usage* and *multiscreening.*

  Business model canvas introduced. A useful new tool for students to review online business models for case studies and assignments.
- *Chapter 3.* A new introductory section on the growing range of *digital business technology platforms*, focussing on *mobile platforms*, has been added at the start. Decisions on implementing mobile design such as responsive vs adaptive design are covered in Chapter 11. An example of setting objectives and strategies for mobile platforms is given.

  In this chapter we now focus on the management decisions involved with creating an effective technology infrastructure rather than explaining the technology in detail. We explained the technology such as TCP/IP and XML in more detail in previous editions, when it was less familiar. Research and feedback from users of the book have shown that this knowledge usually exists from other courses, modules or during work, so there is little value in duplicating it. The chapter has been simplified and restructured to reflect this change.

- *Chapter 4*. Data on consumer and business adoption and usage of different digital platforms updated. Sections on changes in *privacy law* updated.
- *Chapter 5*. This chapter has remained much the same, since the fundamental processes of strategy creation are similar. It has been simplified and the examples updated, including examples of vision setting.

  Discussion of mobile value propositions is added in Mini-case study 5.1.
- *Chapter 6*. A mini case study on the launch of the Pebble watch on *crowdfunding* site Kickstarter shows how digital business potentially makes it easier to set up new supply chains to manufacture and distribute products. A new case study on the implementation of SCM showing the impact on outbound logistics at 3 Suisses France is included.

  US Department of Commerce (2013) data used to illustrate the aim of reducing inventory holding across the supply chain. Review of the concept of inventory turnover as applied to supply chain management.

  Development of the Internet of Things and machine-to-machine (M2M) applications is introduced and briefly reviewed.

  PriceWaterhouseCoopers (PWC)'s 2013 global supply chain survey data are reviewed at end of chapter.
- *Chapter 7*. Mini-case study 7.1 added. This gives an example of how one UK business has created a solution to help its customers worldwide with e-procurement. IFO-Basware (2012) study of the global adoption of e-invoicing summarised. Alibaba.com case study updated.
- *Chapter 8*. Chapter renamed *digital marketing* in place of *E-marketing* to reflect common industry usage describing this activity. Interview reviewing how the marketing mix strategy can change with the adoption of digital media added. Concepts of inbound and content marketing introduced at the start of the chapter, with a new activity introduced around the content marketing matrix to audit and improve content quality. Five different classes of interactive online feedback tools which digital businesses can use to understand and identify customer needs and perceptions added.
- *Chapter 9*. Sections on content marketing, social CRM and social media marketing expanded.
- *Chapter 10*. The new interview at the start of the chapter shows how many companies are now continuously improving their digital services through *conversion rate optimisation*. *Growth hacking* is a related concept that is particularly relevant to online startups, but can be applied to existing businesses too. A section on transformation to the *Social Business* has been added at the end of the chapter.
- *Chapter 11*. Box 11.2 explains the *Big Data* concept and gives examples of the application of big data. The concept of *Social Sign-in* is introduced briefly.

  The move from designing a user experience (UX) on a single device to the more complex challenge of *customer experience management* (CXM) across multiple devices, including smartphones and tablets, and physical locations is described.

  Today, the increasing importance of mobile design means that designing for mobile devices is a key consideration, so we have added a separate section on design for mobile platforms reviewing five alternative approaches that managers need to discuss, including responsive and adaptive design.

  Security breaches data updated and 10 security guidelines for business added.
- *Chapter 12*. New section on the process and tools needed for managing content marketing updates. Section added within analytics on evaluating social media.

Table A	In-depth case studies in Digital Business and E-Commerce Management, 6th edition

Chapter	Case study	
1 Introduction to digital business and e-commerce	1.1	The Facebook business model
	1.2	eBay – the world's largest online business?
2 Marketplace analysis for e-commerce	2.1	i-to-i – a global marketplace for a start-up company
3 Managing digital business infrastructure	3.1	Innovation at Google
4 E-environment	4.1	The implications of globalisation for consumer attitudes
5 Digital business strategy	5.1	Debenhams creates value through mobile commerce
	5.2	Setting the Internet revenue contribution at Sandvik Steel
	5.3	Boo hoo – learning from the largest European dot-com failure
6 Supply chain management	6.1	Shell Chemicals redefines its customers' supply chains
	6.2	Argos uses e-supply chain management to improve customer convenience
	6.3	RFID: keeping track starts its move to a faster track
7 E-procurement	7.1	Cambridge Consultants reduce costs through e-procurement
	7.2	Covisint – a typical history of a B2B marketplace?
8 Digital marketing	8.1	The evolution of easyJet's online revenue contribution
	8.2	Dell gets closer to its customers online
9 Customer relationship management	9.1	Tesco.com increases product range and uses triggered communications to support CRM
10 Change management	10.1	Process management: making complex business simpler
	10.2	Using collaborative tools to support knowledge management at Janssen-Cilag Australia
11 Analysis and design	11.1	Providing an effective online experience for local markets
12 Digital business service implementation and optimisation	12.1	Learning from Amazon's culture of metrics

Table B	Module guide

Week	Lecture topic		Seminar or tutorial topics		Notes
1	LI	Introduction to digital business and e-commerce	Activity 1.1	Introduction	Chapter 1 and Chapter 3 (technical introduction)
			Case study 1.2	eBay	
			Debate 1.1	**How new is the Digital business concept?**	
2	L2	E-commerce micro-environment	Activity 2.1	Introduction	Chapter 2
			Case study 2.1	i-to-i	
			Debate 2.1	**Countermediation**	
			Debate 2.2	**Innovative business models**	
3	L3	E-commerce macro-environment	Activity 4.1	Introduction	Chapters 3 and 4
			Case study 4.1	Globalisation	
			Debate 4.1	Opt-in	
4	L4	Digital business strategy: (a) Situation analysis and objective setting	Activity 5.2	Digital channels	Chapter 5
			Case study 5.1	Debenhams	
			Debate 5.1	Digital business responsibility	
5	L5	Digital business strategy: (b) Strategy and tactics	Activity 5.3	Digital business strategies	Chapter 5
			Case study 5.3	Boo.com	
			Debate 5.2	Board-level representation	
6	L6	Digital business applications: (a) Supply chain management	Activity 6.1	Introduction	Chapter 6
			Case study 6.1	Shell Chemicals	
			Case study 6.2	Argos	
			Debate 6.1	Value chain	
7	L7	Digital business applications: (b) E-procurement	Activity 7.1	Introduction	Chapter 7
			Case study 7.1	Cambridge Consultants	
			Case study 7.2	Covisint	
			Debate 7.2	B2B marketplaces	
8	L8	Digital business applications: (c) Digital marketing	Activity 8.3	Competitor benchmarking	Chapter 8
			Case study 8.1	easyJet	
			Debate 8.1	Digital marketing planning	
9	L9	Digital business applications: (d) E-CRM	Activity 9.1	Introduction	Chapter 9
			Case study 9.1	Tesco.com	
			Debate 9.1	Permission marketing	

Table B	Continued			
Week	**Lecture topic**	**Seminar or tutorial topics**		**Notes**
10	L10 Change management	Activity 10.1	Introduction	Chapter 10
		Case study 10.1	Process management	
		Case study 10.2	Janssen-Cilag	
		Debate 10.1	Organising for digital business	
11	L11 Evaluation and maintenance	Activity 12.1	Introduction	Chapters 11 and 12
		Case study 11.1	i-to-i	
		Case study 12.1	Amazon	
		Debate 12.1	Standards control	

Table C	The author's timeline	
		1960
1963	Born	Black and white television
		1970
1976		Colour television
		1980
1982		First used computer-programmed mainframe using punched cards
1985	BSc, Imperial College, London	
1988	PhD, University of Leeds	Wrote PhD on mainframe
1989	Project Manager in software house developing GIS for marketing planning	First used PC
		1990
1991	Software Engineering Manager for company producing packaged and bespoke engineering software	Sent first email
1994	Project Manager for customer-facing financial services systems	Started using World Wide Web
1995	Senior Lecturer, Business Information Systems, Derbyshire Business School, University of Derby	First ordered book online
1997	Delivering CIM Internet Marketing seminars	Built first website
1998	*Groupware, Workflow and Intranets* published	Mobile phone
1999	*Business Information Systems* published	
		2000
2000	*Internet Marketing* published	Interactive digital TV
2000	MSc E-commerce course launched at Derby	WAP phone
2003	Nominated by CIM as one of 50 'gurus' to have 'shaped the future of marketing' along with Philip Kotler and Michael Porter!	
2004	Recognised by the Department of Trade and Industry, NOP World and E-consultancy as one of the 'Top 100 people commended by the industry as key influencers and drivers, who have driven the development and growth of e-commerce in the UK over the last ten years'	
2005	Second edition of *E-marketing Excellence* published	Blogging and RSS on www.davechaffey.com
2006	Third edition of *Digital business and E-Commerce Management* published	Participating in social networks such as Facebook and Linked-In
2008	E-consultancy Managing Digital Channels research report published	Using Twitter to stay up to date with technology innovation

This timeline considers the diffusion of technological innovation at home and in the workplace. The author first started using a computer regularly when he was 18, yet his 4-year-old daughter is already an internet user. Readers can compare their own adoption of computer technology at home and at work. How do you think the use of the internet and its successors for e-commerce and e-entertainment will change as successive generations become increasingly computer literate?

Guided tour

Part introduction Each part of the book is summarized with a brief list of chapter contents and 'focus on' issues.

Chapter at a glance This feature summarizes the main topics of the chapter and the case studies.

Learning outcomes These are set out clearly at the start of each chapter.

Management issues These list the strategic and practical implications of each topic and case study.

Links to other chapters To highlight the connections between chapters.

Web support To highlight additional support material on the website.

Focus on 'Focus on' sections contain more detailed coverage of key areas.

Mini Case Study Extra smaller case studies have been added to give students more examples of e-commerce within business.

Activity To test students' understanding of key topics.

Essay, Discussion and Examination questions These provide engaging activities for students and lecturers in and out of the classroom.

'Real-world Digital Business' Interviews with industry leaders in the e-commerce world to give personal insight to students.

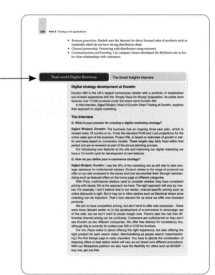

Case Study Integrated throughout the text with many taken from the *Financial Times*, illustrating current examples of e-commerce and its applications.

About the author

Dave Chaffey BSc, PhD, FCIM, HIDM

Dave manages his own digital business, Smart Insights (www.smartinsights.com), an online publisher and analytics company providing advice and alerts on best practice and industry developments for digital marketers and e-commerce managers. The advice is also created to help readers of Dave's books. The most relevant information is highlighted at www.smartinsights.com/book-support.

Dave also works as an independent Internet marketing trainer and consultant for Marketing Insights Limited. He has consulted on digital marketing and e-commerce strategy for companies of a range of sizes from larger organisations like 3M, Barclaycard, HSBC, Mercedes-Benz and Nokia to smaller organisations like Arco, Confused.com, Euroffice, Hornbill and i-to-i.

Dave's passion is educating students and marketers about the latest and best practices in digital marketing, so empowering businesses to improve their online performance through getting the most value from their web analytics and market insight. In other words, making the most of online opportunities and avoiding waste.

He is proud to have been recognised by the Department of Trade and Industry as one of the leading individuals who have provided input to, and influence on, the development and growth of e-commerce and the internet in the UK over the past 10 years. Dave has also been recognised by the Chartered Institute of Marketing as one of 50 marketing 'gurus' worldwide who have helped shape the future of marketing. He is also proud to be an Honorary Fellow of the IDM.

Dave is a visiting lecturer on e-commerce courses at different universities, including Birmingham, Cranfield, Derby, Manchester Metropolitan and Warwick. He is a tutor on the IDM Diploma in Digital Marketing, for which he is also senior examiner.

In total, Dave is author of five best-selling business books, including *Internet Marketing: Strategy, Implementation and Practice*, *eMarketing eXcellence* (with PR Smith) and *Total Email Marketing*. Many of these books have been published in new editions since 2000 and translations include Chinese, Dutch, German, Italian and Serbian.

When offline he enjoys fell-running, indie guitar music and travelling with his family.

Acknowledgements

The author would like to thank the team at Pearson Education in Harlow, in particular Catharine Steers, David Harrison, Eileen Srebernik, Kelly Miller, Tim Parker, Angela Hawksbee, Annette Abel and David Hemsley for their help in the creation of this book. I would particularly like to thank the reviewers who undertook detailed reviews for the second, third and fourth editions – these reviews have been important in shaping the book: Magdy Abdel-Kader, University of Essex; Poul Andersen, Aarhus Business School, Denmark; Michelle Bergadaa, University of Geneva, Switzerland; Bruce Bowhill, University of Portsmouth; Yaw Busia, University of Middlesex; Hatem El-Gohary, Bradford University; Janet French, Barking College; Andy Gravell, University of Southampton; Ulf Hoglind, Örebro University, Sweden; Judith Jeffcoate, University of Buckingham; Britt-Marie Johansson, University of Jönköping, Sweden; Matthias Klaes, Keele University; Mette P. Knudsen, University of Southern Denmark; Tuula Mittila, University of Tampere, Finland; Barry Quinn, University of Ulster; Gerry Rogers, EdExcel Qualifications Leader; Chandres Tejura, University of North London; Ian Watson, University of Northumbria; Steve Wood, Liverpool John Moores University.

Thanks also to these reviewers who were involved at earlier stages with this book: Fintan clear, Brunel University; Neil Doherty, Loughborough University; Jean-Noel Ezingeard, Henley Management College; Dr Felicia Fai, University of Bath; Lisa Harris, Brunel University; Sue Hartland, Gloucestershire Business School at Cheltenham and Gloucester College of Higher Education; Mike Healy, University of Westminster; Eric Van Heck, Rotterdam School of Management, The Netherlands; Dipak Khakhar, Lund University, Sweden; Robert Proops, University of Westminster; Professor Michael Quayle, University of Glamorgan; Richard Riley, University of Central England; Gurmak Singh, University of Wolverhampton; John Twomey, Brunel University; Gerry Urwin, Coventry University.

Publisher's acknowledgements

We are grateful to the following for permission to reproduce copyright material:

Figures

Figure 1.10 adapted from Nova Spivack blog posting. How the WebOS Evolves? 9 February, 2009, http://novaspivack.typepad.com/nova_spivacks_weblog/2007/02/steps_towards_a.html, Nova Spivack, www.novaspivack.com; Figure 3.9 from http://www.google.com/about/datacenters/gallery/index.html#/locations/hamina/2, Google, Photo credit: Connie Zhou/Google, AlamyCelebrity/Alamy; Figure 4.7 from http://ec.europa.eu/information_society/digital-agenda/documents/edcr.pdf (no longer available), European Commission (2010), © European Union, 1995–2012; Figure 4.9 from Blogpulse (no longer available) (www.blogpulse.com), © 2013 The Nielsen Company; Figure 4.11 from From International E-Economy: Benchmarking the World's Most Effective Policy for the E-Economy, report published 19th November, London, www.e-envoy.gov.uk/oee/nsf/sections/summit_benchmarking/$file/indexpage.htm, Crown copyright; Figure 4.13 from Report summary, http://www.gartner.com/it/page.jsp?id=1447613., Gartner, Inc.; Figure 5.9 from Towards a manager's model of e-business strategy decisions, *Journal of General Management*, 30 (4) (Perrott, B. Summer 2005), The Braybrooke Press; Figure 5.12 from *Mastering Information Management*, Financial Times Prentice Hall, Harlow

(D. Marchand, T. Davenport and T. Dickson (editors) 1999) pp. 187–92., Pearson; Figure 5.18 from E-consultancy, 2008. Managing digital channels research report by Dave Chaffey, reprinted with permission; Figure 6.3 from Towards the inter-organisational product information supply chain – evidence from the retail and consumer goods industries. *Journal of the Association for Information Systems,* 9(3/4) ed. Special Issue, 119-50 (Legner, C. and Schemm, J. 2008), Association for Information Systems,. Used with permission from Association for Information Systems, Atlanta, GA; 404-413-7444; www.aisnet.org. All rights reserved; Figure 6.8 adapted from *Executive's Guide to Digital business. From Tactics to Strategy.* Wiley, New York (Deise, M., Nowikow, C., King, P. and Wright, A. 2000) figure 6.4(b), Wiley; Figure 6.9 adapted from *Executive's Guide to Digital business. From Tactics to Strategy.* Wiley, New York (Deise, M., Nowikow, C., King, P. and Wright, A. 2000) Wiley, New York.; Figure 6.12 from European Commission, 2008, i2010 Annual Information Society Report 2008, mid-term report, published at http://ec.europa. eu/information_society/eeurope/i2010/mid_term_review_2008/index_en.htm (c) European Communities, 1995–2008; Figure 7.2 from An e-valuation framework for developing net-enabled business metrics through functionality interaction. *Journal of Organisational Computing and Electronic Commerce,* 17 (2) ed., pp.175–203 (Riggins, F. and Mitra, S. 2007), Taylor and Francis; Figure 8.1 from Managing digital teams. Integrating digital marketing into your organisation. Author: Dave Chaffey. Available at http://econsultancy.com, reprinted with permission; Figure 8.7 from Smith, PR (1990, 2012) The SOSTAC ® Guide To Writing The Perfect Plan, published by www.PRSmith.org; Figure 8.11 from www. bowencraggs.com, Bowen Craggs & Co.; Figure 9.5 adapted from Are the drivers and role of online trust the same for all web sites and consumers? A large-scale exploratory empirical study. Reprinted with permission from Journal of Marketing, published by the American Marketing Association, (Bart, Y., Shankar, V., Sultan, E. and Urban, G.), 2005, October edition, pp.133–52; Figure 9.6 from research originally published at, www.brandnewworld.co.uk, AOL UK / Anne Molen (Cranfield School of Management)/ Henley Centre; Figure 9.12 from Social CRM: The New Rules of Relationship Management. White Paper published April 2010, By R 'Ray' Wang and Jeremiah Owyang with Christine Tran. Editor Charlene Li., www.altimetergroup.com/2010/03/altimeter-report-the-18-use-cases-of-social-crm-the-new-rules-of-relationship-management.html., Altimeter Group; Figure 9.16 adapted from 'Putting the service-profit chain to work' *Harvard Business Review,* March-April (Heskett, J., Jones, T., Loveman, G., Sasser, W. and Schlesinger, E 1994), Harvard Business; Figures 10.2, 10.10 from Managing an E-commerce team. Integrating digital marketing into your organisation. Author: Dave Chaffey., Available from www.e-consultancy.com, reprinted with permission; Figures 10.3, 10.8 from Managing an E-commerce team. Integrating digital marketing into your organisation. Author: Dave Chaffey. Available from www.e-consultancy.com, reprinted with permission; Figures 10.4, 10.5 from E-Consultancy, 2007, Web project management. The practices behind successful web projects. Research report by Sonia Kay available from http://econsultancy.com, reprinted with permission; Figure 10.9 adapted from Organizing for digital marketing, *McKinsey Quarterly,* No. 4, pp. 183–192 (Parsons, A., Zeisser, M. and Waitman, R. 1996), www.mckinsey-quarterly.com, McKinsey & Co., Inc.; Figure 11.2 adapted from *Groupware, workflow and intranets—Re-engineering the enterprise with collaborative software,* 1 ed., Digital Press, Woburn, MA (Chaffey, D. 1998) Elsevier, reprinted by permission of Elsevier Science; Figure 11.25 from UK Department of Business, Enterprise and Regulatory Reform (BERR). Crown copyright; Figure 11.27 from UK Department of Business, Enterprise and Regulatory Reform (BERR) (2008). Crown copyright; Figure 12.1 adapted from *The Art of Agile Development,* O'Reilly, Sebastopol, CA. (Shore, J. and Warden, S. 2008) O'Reilly Media, Inc.; Figure 12.2 from Port80 software, www.port80software.com/surveys/top1000appservers; Figure 12.10 from Framework: The Social Media ROI Pyramid. December 13, 2010. Author: Owyang, Jeremiah, http://www.web-strategist.com/ blog/2010/12/13/framework-the-social-media-roi-pyramid, Altimeter Group.

Screenshots

Screenshot 1.1 from Google circa 1998 Source: Wayback machine archive: http://w6eb.archive.org/ web/19981111183552/google.stanford.edu. Google; Screenshot 1.6 from https://www.yammer.com/ about/case_studies., Microsoft Office Division, Microsoft product screenshots reprinted with permission from Microsoft Corporation; Screenshot 1.9 from www.tatucouture.com, Tatu Couture; Screenshot 2.2 from www.Blackcircles.com, Black Circles Ltd.; Screenshot 2.3 from FT.com/ Business School, www. ft.com, Financial Times, © The Financial Times Limited. All Rights Reserved; Screenshot 2.13 from www.firebox.com, Copyright Firebox; Screenshot 3.1 from www.magiq.com, MAGIC (part of the Speed-Trap Group of companies); Screenshot 3.2 adapted from South Korea subway virtual store, http://www. tescoplc.com/index.asp?pageid=69&mediacategory=27, Tesco PLC; Screenshot 3.8 from www.salesforce. com, Salesforce.com UK; Screenshot 5.3 from www.britishairways.com, British Airways; Screenshot 5.13

from www.arenaflowers.com, Arena Online Ltd; Screenshot 6.1 from www.kickstarter.com, Kickstarter, Inc.; Screenshot 6.4 from www.bluescopesteelconnect.com, BlueScope Steel Ltd; Screenshot 6.6 from www.elemica.com, Elemica, London. UK; Screenshot 6.11 from www.e2open.com, E2open, Inc.; Screenshot 6.13 from www.3suisses.fr/, Otto Group; Screenshot 7.6 from FT.com/View from the Top, http://www.ft.com/cms/8a38c684-2a26-11dc-920, Financial Times, © The Financial Times Limited. All Rights Reserved; Screenshot 7.6 from FT.com, reprinted with permission; Screenshot 8.3 from www.spinebreakers.co.uk, Penguin Books Ltd; Screenshot 8.4 from www.Kampyle.com, Kampyle Ltd; Screenshot 8.13 from www.easyjet.com, easyJet plc, copyright permission of easyJet Airline Company Limited.; Screenshot 9.10 from google.com, reprinted by permission of Google, Inc. Google Analytics™ search engine is a trademark of Google, Inc.; Screenshot 9.15 from www.toptable.co.uk, OpenTable International Limited, Inc; Screenshot 9.20 from www.zappos.com, Zappos IP, Inc.; Screenshot 11.11 from Let's Colour Interactive Magazine, http://www.dulux.co.uk/, AkzoNobel Ltd; Screenshot 11.13 from www.rswww.com, Screenshot of RS Components homepage supplied courtesy of RS Components (http://rswww.com); Screenshot 11.22 from www.app.ft.com Financial Times, © The Financial Times Limited. All Rights Reserved; Screenshot 11.26 from The geographic spread of the 'Slammer' worm, http://www.caida.org/research/security/code-red/coderedv2_analysis.xml, Copyright 2003 The Regents of the University of California; Screenshot 12.11 from uberVU via HootSuite, app.ubervu.com, HootSuite Media Inc.; Screenshot 12.15 from www.nationalexpress.com, National Express Group PLC.

Tables

Table 2.3 adapted from *The New Marketing: Transforming the Corporate Future,* Butterworth-Heinemann, Oxford. (McDonald, M. and Wilson, H 2002) Copyright Elsevier, and adapted from Electronic commerce: three emerging strategies. *McKinsey Quarterly,* 1 ed., pp. 152–9 (Berryman, K., Harrington, L., Layton-Rodin, D. and Rerolle, V. 1998), McKinsey and Co. ; Table 7.7 adapted from E-hubs: the new B2B marketplaces, *Harvard Business Review,* May-June, 2000, p.99 (Kaplan, S. and Sawhney, M.,), Harvard Business School Publishing Corporation; Table 9.1 from Efficient Frontier, www.efficientfrontier.com, reprinted with permission; Table 9.2 adapted from Interactive Advertising Bureau XMOS is a registered trademark of the IAB, www.iab.net Interactive Advertising Bureau; Table 9.4 adapted from Your secret weapon on the web, *Harvard Business Review,* July-August (Reichheld, F. and Schefter, P., 2000), Harvard Business; Table 10.6 adapted from How risky is your company?, *Harvard Business Review,* May-June, p. 87 (Simon, R. 1999), Harvard Business; Table 11.6 adapted from *Internet Marketing,* Wiley, New York (Hofacker, C. 2001) Wiley, USA; Table 12.3 adapted from *Software Testing: A Craftsman's Approach.* CRC Press, Boca Raton, FL (Jorgensen, P. 1995) Taylor and Francis Group; Table 12.5 from ABC Electronics, www.abce.org.uk.

Text

Box 3.7 adapted from Member Briefing Paper, August, 2008 Published by the Intranet Benchmarking Forum www.ibforum.com, Digital Workplace Group; Box 3.8 from The International Communications Market 2007. Report published December 2007., www.ofcom.org.uk/research/cm/icmr07/overview/landscape/., Ofcom copyright 2006–11.; Case Study 6.1 from Did IT work? Service was paramount when enhancing supply chain. *Financial Times,* 30/01/2008 (Pritchard, S.), Financial Times, © The Financial Times Limited. All Rights Reserved; Case Study 6.3 from Keeping track starts its move to a faster track *The Financial Times,* 20/04/2005 (Nairn,G.), reprinted with permission; Case Study 9.2 from Blog posting, 9 September 2008, www.arenaflowers.com/blog/2008÷09/09/wiser-about-web-from-a-flowers-website-to-academic-text/#comment-4361. Arena Online Ltd; Extract on page 493 from 'Scalability': the paradox of human resources in e-commerce. *International Journal of Service Industry Management,* 12(1), 34–43 (Hallowell, R. 2001), Emerald Group Publishing Limited; Case Study 10.1 from Process Management: Making complex business a lot simpler? *The Financial Times,* 14/05/2008 (Cane A.), FT, © The Financial Times Limited. All Rights Reserved; Case Study 10.2 from e-gineer.com blog by Nathan Wallace, Associate Director – Information Technology (i.e. CIO) for Janssen-Cilag Australia, www.e-gineer.com/v2/blog/2007÷08/our-intranet-wiki-case-study-of-wiki.htm., Janssen-Cilag Australia; Extract on page 574 from Information Security Breaches Survey 2013, managed by Pricewaterhouse-Cooper for UK Department of Business, Enterprise and Regulatory Reform (BERR).

In some instances we have been unable to trace the owners of copyright material, and we would appreciate any information that would enable us to do so.

Part 1

Introduction

Part 1 introduces digital business and e-commerce and their relevance to organisations and consumers. It clarifies terms and concepts such as online business, revenue and technology models by reviewing alternative applications through activities and case studies.

1 Introduction to digital business and e-commerce p. 3

- The impact of electronic communications on traditional businesses
- What is the difference between digital business and e-commerce?
- Digital business opportunities
- Risks and barriers to digital business adoption
- Barriers to consumer Internet adoption

2 Marketplace analysis for e-commerce p. 41

- Online marketplace analysis
- Location of trading in the marketplace
- Business models for e-commerce

Focus on . . .
- Online start-up companies – the 'dot-coms'

3 Managing digital business infrastructure p. 77

- Digital business infrastructure components
- A short introduction to Internet technology
- Management issues in creating a new customer-facing digital service
- Managing internal digital communications through intranets and extranets
- Web presentation and data exchange standards

Focus on . . .
- Web services, SaaS and service-oriented architecture (SOA)
- Internet governance

4

E-environment p. 127

- Social and legal factors
- Environmental and green issues related to Internet usage
- Taxation
- Economic and competitive factors

- Political factors
- E-government
- Technological innovation and technology assessment

Introduction to digital business and e-commerce

Web support

The following additional case studies are available at **www.pearsoned.co.uk/chaffey**

→ SME adoption of sell-side e-commerce

→ Death of the dot-com dream

→ Encouraging SME adoption of sell-side e-commerce

The site also contains a range of study material designed to help improve your results.

Scan code to find the latest updates for topics in this chapter

Learning outcomes

After completing this chapter the reader should be able to:

● Define the meaning and scope of digital business and e-commerce and their different elements

● Summarise the main reasons for adoption of digital business and barriers that may restrict adoption

● Outline the ongoing business challenges of managing digital business in an organisation, paticularly online start-up businesses

Management issues

The issues for managers raised in this chapter include:

● How do we explain the scope and implications of digital business to staff?

● What is the full range of benefits of introducing digital business and what are the risks?

● How do we evaluate our current digital business capabilities?

Links to other chapters

The main related chapters are:

● *Chapter 2* examines the principal e-commerce business and marketplace models in more detail

● *Chapter 3* introduces the technical infrastructure of software and hardware that companies must incorporate to achieve e-commerce

● *Chapter 5* describes approaches to digital business strategy introduced in *Chapter 1*

Introduction

The Internet

'The Internet' refers to the physical network that links computers across the globe. It consists of the infrastructure of network servers and wired and wireless communication links between them that are used to hold and transport data between the client devices and web servers.

World Wide Web (WWW)

The most common technique for publishing information on the Internet. It is accessed through desktop or mobile web browsers which display interactive web pages of embedded graphics and HTML/XML-encoded text.

Wireless communications

Electronic transactions and communications conducted using mobile devices such as laptops and mobile phones (and fixed access platforms) with different forms of wireless connection.

Disruptive digital technologies

Technologies which offer opportunities for business for new products and services for customers and can transform internal business processes. Danneels (2004) defined disruptive technologies as 'a technology that changes the bases of competition by changing the performance metrics along which firms compete. Customer needs drive customers to seek certain benefits in the products they use and form the basis for customer choices between competing products'.

Organisations have now been applying technologies based on **the Internet**, **World Wide Web** and **wireless communications** to transform their businesses for over 20 years since the creation of the first website (http://info.cern.ch) by Sir Tim Berners-Lee in 1991. Deploying these **disruptive digital technologies** has offered many opportunities for innovative businesses to transform their services. Table 1.1 highlights some of the best-known examples and in Activity 1.1 you can explore some of the reasons for success of these companies.

In *Digital Business and E-Commerce Management* we will explore approaches managers can use to assess the relevance of different digital technologies and then devise and implement strategies to exploit these opportunities. We will also study how to manage more practical risks such as delivering a satisfactory service quality, maintaining customer privacy and managing security. In this chapter we start by introducing the scope of digital business and e-commerce. Then we review the main opportunities and risks of digital business together with the drivers and barriers to adoption.

For the author, e-commerce and digital business is an exciting area to be involved with, since many new opportunities and challenges arise yearly, monthly and even daily. Innovation is a given, with the continuous introduction of new technologies, new business models and new communications approaches. For example, Google innovates relentlessly. Its service has developed a long way since 1998 (Figure 1.1) with billions of pages now indexed and other services such as web mail, pay-per-click adverts, analytics and social networks all part of its offering. Complete Activity 1.1 or view Table 1.1 to see other examples of the rate at which new innovations occur.

Figure 1.1   Google circa 1998
Source: Wayback machine archive: http://web.archive.org/web/19981111183552/google. stanford.edu. Google and the Google logo are registered trademarks of Google Inc., used with permission.

Table 1.1	Timeline of websites indicating innovation in business model or marketing communications approach	

Year founded	Company/site	Category of innovation and business model
1994	Amazon	Retailer
1995 (March)	Yahoo! (yahoo.com)	Directory and portal
1995 (Sept)	eBay	Online auction
1995 (Dec)	AltaVista (altavista.com)	Search engine
1996	Hotmail (hotmail.com)	Web-based email Viral marketing (using email signatures to promote service) Purchased by Microsoft in 1997
1998	GoTo.com (goto.com) Overture (2001)	Pay-per-click search marketing Purchased by Yahoo! in 2003
1998	Google (google.com)	Search engine
1999	Blogger (blogger.com)	Blog publishing platform Purchased by Google in 2003
1999	Alibaba (alibaba.com)	B2B marketplace with $1.7 billion IPO on Hong Kong stock exchange in 2007 (see case in Chapter 7)
1999	MySpace (myspace.com) Formerly eUniverse	Social network Purchased by News Corp. in 2005
2001	Wikipedia (wikipedia.com)	Open encyclopaedia
2002	Last.fm	A UK-based Internet radio and music community website, founded in 2002
2003	Skype (skype.com)	Peer-to-peer Internet telephony VoIP – Voice over Internet Protocol Purchased by eBay in 2005
2003	Second Life (secondlife.com)	Immersive virtual world
2004	Facebook (facebook.com)	Social network applications and groups
2005	YouTube (youtube.com)	Video sharing and rating
2009	Foursquare (foursquare.com)	A location-based social media website designed for mobile access.
2011	Pinterest	Social network offering image sharing
2014	Google Glass	An example of a wearable computing device
??	The future	??

Activity 1.1	Innovative digital businesses

Purpose

To illustrate innovation in online business models and communications approaches.

Questions

1 Think about the innovation that you have witnessed during the time you have used the Internet and World Wide Web. What would you say are the main sites used in your country which have changed the way we spend our time or buy online?

> 2 We talk about these businesses being 'successful', but what is success for a start-up business?
>
> 3 What do these services have in common that you think has made them successful?
>
> *Answers to activities can be found at* www.pearsoned.co.uk/chaffey

The impact of electronic communications on traditional businesses

Digital business transformation

Significant changes to organisational processes, structures and system implemented to improve organisational performance through increasing the use of digital media and technology platforms.

During the period shown in Table 1.1 managers at established businesses have had to determine how to apply new electronic communications technologies to transform their organisations. As we will see later in this chapter, existing businesses have evolved their approaches to digital business through a series of stages. Innovation is relentless, with the continuous introduction of new technologies, new business models and new communications approaches. So all organisations have to review new electronic and Internet-based communications approaches for their potential to make their business more competitive and also manage ongoing risks such as security and performance. For example, many businesses are reviewing the benefits, costs and risks of digital business technologies they are currently implementing as part of **digital business transformation** projects.

At the time of writing, there are two key opportunities of digital transformation open to most businesses, which we focus on in this book: inbound marketing and mobile marketing.

Inbound marketing

Zero Moment of Truth (ZMOT)

A summary of today's multichannel consumer decision-making for product purchase where they search, review ratings, styles, prices and comments on social media before visiting a retailer.

Inbound marketing

The consumer is proactive in actively seeking out information for their needs, and interactions with brands are attracted through content, search and social media marketing.

Content marketing

The management of text, rich media, audio and video content aimed at engaging customers and prospects to meet business goals, published through print and digital media including web and mobile platforms, which is repurposed and syndicated to different forms of web presence such as publisher sites, blogs, social media and comparison sites.

On the Internet it is often the customer who initiates contact and is seeking information through researching information on a website. In other words, it is a 'pull' mechanism where it is particularly important to have good visibility in search engines when customers are entering search terms relevant to a company's products or services. Amongst marketing professionals this powerful new approach to marketing is now commonly known as **inbound marketing** (Shah and Halligan, 2009). Google have referred to this consumer decision-making before they visit a retailer as the **Zero Moment of Truth (ZMOT)** in a handbook by Lecinski (2012). This describes the combination of online and offline influences on purchase as shown in Figure 1.2.

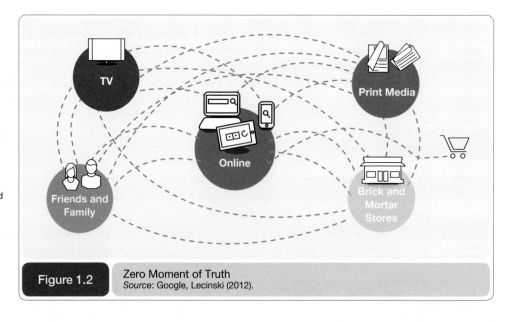

Figure 1.2	Zero Moment of Truth
	Source: Google, Lecinski (2012).

Search marketing
Companies seek to improve their visibility in search engines for relevant search terms by increasing their presence in the search engine results pages.

Inbound marketing is powerful since advertising wastage is reduced. **Search marketing, content marketing** and **social media marketing** can be used to target prospects with a defined need – they are proactive and self-selecting. But this is a weakness, since marketers may have less control than in traditional communications where the message is pushed out to a defined audience and can help generate awareness and demand. Advocates of inbound marketing such as Dharmesh Shah and Brian Halligan argue that content, social media and search marketing do have a role to play in generating demand.

Social media marketing
Monitoring and facilitating customer–customer interaction and participation throughout the web to encourage positive engagement with a company and its brands. Interactions may occur on a company site, social networks and other third-party sites.

Social media marketing

The growth in popularity of **social media** is a major trend in digital business. In particular **social network sites (SNS)** such as Facebook, Google+, Twitter and for business-to-business users LinkedIn and **RSS feeds**. Some niche social media sites are independent from the social networks, including **virtual worlds** such as Habbo Hotel, and **blogs** created by many individuals and businesses. Social media marketing also includes **rich media** such as online video and interactive applications featured on specialist social networks such as YouTube or embedded into websites.

Trends update	Social media usage
	The popularity of different social platforms in different countries constantly changes. Visit this compilation to find out the latest in your region or country: http://bit.ly/smartsocialstats.

Social media
A category of media focussing on participation and peer-to-peer communication between individuals, with sites providing the capability to develop user-generated content (UGC) and to exchange messages and comments between different users.

It's important for all businesses to understand the business and revenue models of the major social networks and platforms which are today so influential in shaping people's opinions about brands. Figure 1.3 summarises the main types of social sites that companies need to consider.

Since there are so many types of social presence, it is helpful to simplify the options to manage them. For this we recommend these six categories based on chapters in Weinberg (2010). You can see there's more to social media than social networks:

Really Simple Syndication (RSS) feeds
Blog, news or other content is published by an XML standard and syndicated for other sites or read by users in RSS reader software services. Now typically shortened to 'feed', e.g. news feed or sports feed.

1 **Social networking.** The emphasis here is on listening to customers and sharing engaging content. Facebook tends to be most important for consumer audiences and LinkedIn for business audiences.
2 **Social knowledge.** These are informational social networks like Yahoo! Answers, where you can help an audience by solving their problems and subtly showing how your products have helped others. Wikipedia is another site in this category, although it has relatively little application for marketing.
3 **Social sharing.** These are social bookmarking sites like Delicious (www.delicious.com) which can be useful for understanding the most engaging content within a category.
4 **Social news.** Twitter is the best-known example.
5 **Social streaming.** Rich and streaming media social sites for sharing photos, video and podcasting.
6 **Company user-generated content and community.** Distinct from the other types of social presence which are independent of companies, these are the company's own social space which may be integrated into product content (reviews and ratings), a customer support community or a blog.

Virtual world
An electronic environment which simulates interactions between online characters known as avatars. Also known as Massively Multiplayer Online Roleplaying Games (MMORPG).

Blog
An online diary or news source prepared by an individual or a group of people.

Rich media
Digital assets such as ads are not static images, but provide animation, audio or interactivity as a game or form to be completed.

Case study 1.1 considers the growth of Facebook, the largest consumer social network in many countries.

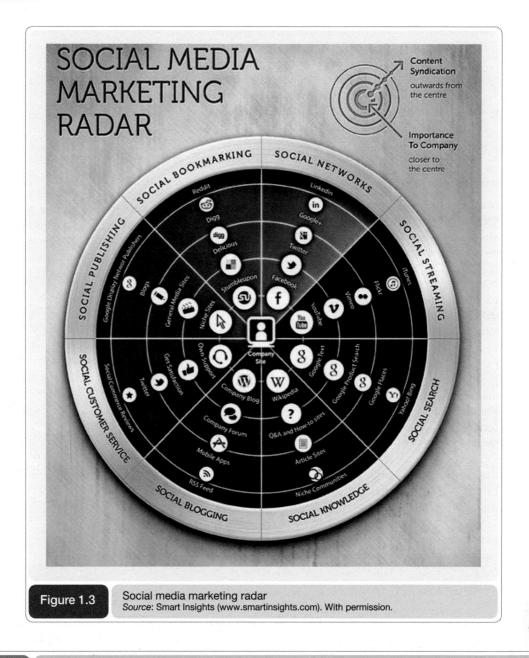

Figure 1.3	Social media marketing radar *Source*: Smart Insights (www.smartinsights.com). With permission.

Case Study 1.1   The Facebook business model

Context

This case is about the social network Facebook which hardly needs an introduction, but when we first featured it in an earlier edition of *E-Business and E-Commerce Management* it was a niche service mainly used in colleges and universities. It is still a good case study in that it shows many of the success factors needed for launch of a new digital business, but also the risks of alienating users when their privacy needs are not listened to. It's incredible that it now has more than a billion users active monthly worldwide, yet has fewer than 5,000 employees.

In line with other case studies in the book, the case study features a summary using the key categories of the Business Model Canvas (which is introduced in the business models section in Chapter 2).

Value proposition

In 2013, the Facebook mission is simply to 'make the world more open and connected'. Previously,

Facebook described itself as 'a social utility that helps people communicate more efficiently with their friends, family and coworkers. The company develops technologies that facilitate the sharing of information through the social graph, the digital mapping of people's real-world social connections. Anyone can sign up for Facebook and interact with the people they know in a trusted environment'.

Consumer value proposition

You have probably seen the 2010 film 'The Social Network' which describes how Facebook was founded while Mark Zuckerberg was a student at Harvard University. Initially membership was limited to Harvard students. The initial viral effect of the software was indicated since more than half of the undergraduate population at Harvard registered on the service within the first month! Zuckerberg used open-source software PHP and the MySQL database to create the original 'TheFacebook.com' site and these technologies are still in use today. The film also describes the long-running dispute over ownership of Facebook, in which another Harvard-originated social networking site, 'HarvardConnection', which later changed its name to ConnectU, alleged in September 2004 that Zuckerberg had used its source code to develop Facebook when it originally contracted him to help in building its site.

When Facebook first launched in February 2004, there were just three things that users could do on the site, which are still core to the functionality of the site. Users could create a profile with their picture and information, view other people's profiles and add people as friends.

Facebook (2013) explains these core consumer benefits defined by the company:

Connect and Share with your friends. Staying connected is the core feature as we would expect, but note the more emotional underpinnings of the other elements of the value proposition.

Discover and Learn. Facebook references public figures and organisations that interest them – available through Facebook company pages.

Express yourself. A fundamental need. Facebook does this through its key features which it describes as the Timeline, News Feed, Photos and Videos, and messaging through Email, Chat and Text.

Stay connected everywhere. Referencing the importance of mobile use and use on other sites to Facebook's users and business model: **People can access Facebook through our website, mobile sites, smartphone apps, and feature phone products**.

Value proposition for marketers and businesses

Facebook works hard to monetise its audience, particularly since Facebook held its initial public offering (IPO) on 18 May 2012. This was the biggest IPO for an Internet company, with a peak market capitalisation of over $104 billion. Facebook describes its offer to business as follows:

Marketers can engage with more than one billion monthly active users on Facebook or subsets of our users based on information people have chosen to share with us such as their age, location, gender, or interests. We offer marketers a unique combination of reach, relevance, social context, and engagement to enhance the value of their ads.

Commercial companies or not-for-profit organisations (e.g. www.facebook.com/joinred) can also create their own Facebook Pages for their company (currently free). Facebook users can then express their support by adding themselves as a fan, writing on the company Wall, uploading photos, and joining other fans in discussion groups. When users become fans, they can optionally agree to be kept up to date about developments, and updates then appear in their newsfeeds.

To encourage companies to advertise, Facebook uses an algorithm known as EdgeRank which determines the percentage of company status updates that appear in a user's newsfeed. Marketers need to work hard to maintain the relevance of their posts using the techniques described by Page (2012).

Revenue model

Facebook has an ad-based revenue model. Some of the features of Facebook Ads (www.facebook.com/ads) include:

- Targeting by age, gender, location, interests, and more.
- Alternative payment models: cost per click (CPC) or impression based (CPM).
- 'Trusted Referrals' or 'Social Ads' – ads can also be shown to users whose friends have recently engaged with a company's Facebook page or engaged with the company website.

At the time of the launch of ads, the Facebook blog made these comments, which indicate the delicate balance between advertising revenue and user experience. They said, first of all, 'what's not changing':

- 'Facebook will always stay clutter-free and clean.
- Facebook will never sell any of your information.
- You will always have control over your information and your Facebook experience.
- You will not see any more ads than you did before this.'

And what is changing:

- 'You now have a way to connect with products, businesses, bands, celebrities and more on Facebook.
- Ads should be getting more relevant and more meaningful to you.'

Facebook's strategy

Facebook describes the key elements of its strategy in its SEC filing as:

1 **Expand global community.** Facebook names specific 'relatively less-penetrated, large markets' such as Brazil, India, Mexico and Japan.
2 **Develop social products to provide the most compelling user experience.** As with many SEC filings of successful Internet businesses, there is a clear commitment to user experience. Facebook's approach is based on Insight: 'To provide the most compelling user experience, we continue to develop products and technologies focused on optimizing our social distribution channels to deliver the most useful content to each user by analyzing and organizing vast amounts of information in real time.' Smart Insights (2012) quotes Andrew (Boz) Bosworth, who is the Director of Engineering at Facebook, as saying:

Every day, we run hundreds of tests on Facebook, most of which are rolled out to a random sample of people to test their impact. For example, you may have seen a small test for saving newsfeed stories last week.

Other products might require network effects to be properly tested, so in those cases we launch to everyone in a specific market, like a whole country.

3 **Mobile Products.** Facebook is seeking to make these more engaging and more easily available. By the end of 2012 Facebook had more than 680 million average monthly users of mobile services. The acquisition of photo sharing app Instagram in August 2012 was part of this strategy.
4 **Facebook Platform.** Facebook notes the importance of developing an open system through apps and websites built by developers using the Facebook Platform, including Application Programming Interfaces (API) and Social Plugins (for example, Like and Share buttons) to help integration with other services such as websites. The Facebook Platform was introduced in 2007 and by January 2008, over 18,000 applications had been built on it, with 140 new applications added per day. More than 95% of Facebook members have used at least one application built on Facebook Platform. Facebook Platform for mobile applications was launched in October 2007, although many

Facebook users already interacted with their friends through mobile phones

5 **Improve ad products.** With the IPO this is a vital aim for Facebook, but it has to be balanced against the other elements of the strategy, particularly number 2 above. Facebook states: 'Our advertising strategy centers on the belief that ad products that are social, relevant, and well-integrated with other content on Facebook can enhance the user experience while providing an attractive return.'
6 **Build a scalable infrastructure.** Facebook describes its investment in software and hardware infrastructure that enables their aim to provide a 'unique, personalized experience to each of our users around the world'. To do this, Facebook explains its technology investments as focussing on analytics and development in areas including content optimisation and delivery, graph query, media storage and serving, large-scale data management, and software performance.

Facebook's competitors

Although it seems curious to think of a company as large as Facebook having competitors, it has new global rivals and local rivals. It mentions: Google+, which Google has integrated with certain of its products, including search and Android, as well as other, largely regional, social networks that have strong positions in particular countries, such as Mixi in Japan and vKontakte and Odnoklassniki in Russia. It also describes companies that offer microblogging (Twitter), developers of platforms such as Apple iOS and Google Android, and games developers as key competitors. It has taken the decision not to create a competing mobile platform, instead in 2013 launching Facebook Home on Android to increase usage of Facebook on these devices.

Risk factors

Today Facebook states that: 'Trust is a cornerstone of our business' and they now dedicate significant resources to the goal of building user trust through developing and implementing programs designed to protect user privacy, promote a safe environment, and assure the security of user data. Facebook has to some extent learnt this lesson from early mistakes, with incidents including:

Initial concerns about privacy of member data – 14 December 2005. Two MIT students downloaded over 70,000 Facebook profiles from four schools (MIT, NYU, the University of Oklahoma, and Harvard) using an automated script, as part of a research project on Facebook privacy.

New feed functionality launched – September 2006. New information feeds were launched in mid-2006 which show the challenges of balancing the benefit of new functionality against disrupting existing user habits. Writing in the Facebook blog in September 2006 Mark Zuckerberg said: 'We've been getting a lot of feedback about Mini-Feed and News Feed. We think they are great products, but we know that many of you are not immediate fans, and have found them overwhelming and cluttered. Other people are concerned that non-friends can see too much about them. We are listening to all your suggestions about how to improve the product; it's brand new and still evolving.' Later, in an open letter on the blog dated 8 September 2006, Zuckerberg said: 'We really messed this one up. When we launched News Feed and Mini-Feed we were trying to provide you with a stream of information about your social world. Instead, we did a bad job of explaining what the new features were and an even worse job of giving you control of them. I'd like to try to correct those errors now.'

Privacy concerns sparked by 'Beacon technology' – November 2007. Facebook received a lot of negative publicity on its new advertising format related to the 'Beacon' tracking system. Mark Zuckerberg was forced to respond on the Facebook blog (5 December 2007). He said:

About a month ago, we released a new feature called Beacon to try to help people share information with their friends about things they do on the web. We've made a lot of mistakes building this feature, but we've made even more with how we've handled them. We simply did a bad job with this release, and I apologize for it. While I am disappointed with our mistakes, we appreciate all the feedback we have received from our users. I'd like to discuss what we have learned and how I have improved Beacon.

When we first thought of Beacon, our goal was to build a simple product to let people share information across sites with their friends. It had to be lightweight so it wouldn't get in people's way as they browsed the web, but also clear enough so people would be able to easily control what they shared. We were excited about Beacon because we believe a lot of information people want to share isn't on Facebook, and if we found the right balance, Beacon would give people an easy and controlled way to share more of that information with their friends.

But we missed the right balance. At first we tried to make it very lightweight so people wouldn't have to

touch it for it to work. The problem with our initial approach of making it an opt-out system instead of opt-in was that if someone forgot to decline to share something, Beacon still went ahead and shared it with their friends. It took us too long after people started contacting us to change the product so that users had to explicitly approve what they wanted to share. Instead of acting quickly, we took too long to decide on the right solution. I'm not proud of the way we've handled this situation and I know we can do better.

Privacy setting concerns – Autumn to 2009 to Spring 2010. In December 2009, Facebook implemented new privacy settings. This meant that some information, including 'lists of friends', was 'publicly available', when it was previously possible to restrict access to this information. Photos and some personal information were also public unless users were sufficiently knowledgeable and active to limit access. Privacy campaigners, including the Electronic Frontier Foundation and American Civil Liberties Union, criticised the changes. In May 2010 further changes were made to give users greater control and simplify the settings.

Facebook lists some of its other key risk factors as:

- 'users increasingly engage with other products or activities;
- we fail to introduce new and improved products or if we introduce new products or services that are not favorably received;
- users feel that their Facebook experience is diminished as a result of the decisions we make with respect to the frequency, prominence, and size of ads that we display;
- we are unable to continue to develop products for mobile devices that users find engaging, that work with a variety of mobile operating systems and networks, and that achieve a high level of market acceptance;
- we are unable to manage and prioritize information to ensure users are presented with content that is interesting, useful, and relevant to them;
- users adopt new technologies where Facebook may not be featured or otherwise available.'

Key sources for the latest information on Facebook

All Facebook (www.allfacebook.com) and Inside Facebook (www.insidefacebook.com) are sites specialising in reporting all developments at Facebook.

Key Facts – updated quarterly at close of year: http://newsroom.fb.com/Key-Facts

SEC updates – Security and Exchange Commission annual report filings give great insights into how Facebook positions itself and what it sees as its risk factors: http://investor.fb.com/

Smart Insights Facebook updates and advice: www.smartinsights.com/social-media-marketing/facebook-marketing/ covers the major developments that marketers need to be aware of

Social Bakers (www.socialbakers.com/facebook-statistics/) – Facebook statistics by country and brand popularity

Wikipedia (2013) Wikipedia Pages for Facebook (http://en.wikipedia.org/wiki/Facebook)

Questions

1 As an investor in a social network such as Facebook, which financial and customer-related metrics would you use to assess and benchmark the current business success and future growth potential of the company?

2 Complete a situation analysis for Facebook focussing on an assessment of the main business risks which could damage the future growth potential of the social network.

3 For the main business risks to Facebook identified in Question 2, suggest approaches the company could use to minimise these risks.

Mobile commerce (m-commerce)

Electronic transactions and communications conducted using mobile devices such as smartphones and tablets, and typically with a wireless connection.

Mobile apps

A software application that is designed for use on a mobile phone, typically downloaded from an app store. iPhone Apps are best known, but all smartphones support the use of apps which can provide users with information, entertainment or location-based services such as mapping.

Mobile commerce

The potential of **mobile commerce** (m-commerce) is evident from the predictions of Mary Meeker, an analyst at Kleiner Perkins Caufield Byers who shares her insights about the current state of the Internet in a presentation called Internet Trends (see the link to her insights at the end of this chapter). One of Meeker's bravest predictions from 2008 was that mobile web use would surpass desktop web use by 2014, and this is currently on plan to occur at a global level.

The growth in popularity of **mobile apps** (Chapter 3), from the iPhone store, Google Android Play, Microsoft Windows app store and other handset vendors, is another significant development in mobile communications. Flurry (2013) released a summary of categories of app usage across smartphones and tablets and it showed that 80% of mobile time was in apps rather than the browser. You do have to be careful in interpreting this, though, since Facebook, games and utility apps will naturally have the greatest time spent and browser use is still significant.

Location-based use of mobile devices is another significant trend as users may use apps or browsers while shopping, for example. Related to this activity is location-based tracking of goods and inventory as they are manufactured and transported.

Trends update   Mobile usage

Mobile usage was forecast to overtake desktop usage in 2014. Find out the latest statistics on mobile and app usage at: http://bit.ly/smartmobilestats.

Mini case study 1.1   Qype and Yelp provide location-based review services

An example of the popularity of location-based mobile services is Qype (www.qype.com). Founded in 2006, Qype is Europe's largest site for user-generated reviews and recommendations of places, events and experiences. Qype allows users to search for and read reviews about a restaurant, shop, service or experience and, with the Qype app, users can read and add reviews on their phone and use the application as a personal satnav to find places nearby. Available in seven different languages, Qype is a pan-European local review site with 3 million reviews covering more than 900,000 places worldwide. In 2013 it merged with Yelp, a US-based site with 102 monthly unique visitors and 39 million local reviews across the US, Europe and Asia Pacific. Although Facebook and Google offer similar services, it shows that there are opportunities for other companies that focus on this niche.

This can be completed individually or as a group activity comparing popular apps for different mobile handsets. Review the most popular apps today, using either the app store for your mobile phone or a compilation from an information provider such as Flurry, comScore (comScore, 2010) or Nielsen (Nielsen, 2010).

Questions

1 Identify the most popular categories of apps from the top 10 or 20 most popular apps, including browser apps such as Google's Chrome or Apple's Safari.

2 Discuss the opportunities for companies to promote their brands or services using apps in comparison with mobile sites delivered through web browsers.

What is the difference between digital business and e-commerce?

The rapid advancement of technology and its application to business has been accompanied by a range of new terminology and jargon such as e-CRM, e-retail and e-procurement. Do we need to be concerned about the terminology? The short answer is no; Mougayer (1998) noted that it is understanding the services that can be offered to customers and the business benefits that are obtainable through digital technology that is important. However, labels are convenient in defining the *scope* of the changes we are looking to make within an organisation through using electronic communications. Managers within an organisation need to agree and communicate the digital transformation they are proposing through using digital technologies to employees, customers and partners.

E-commerce defined

Electronic commerce (e-commerce)
All electronically mediated information exchanges between an organisation and its external stakeholders.

The scope of **electronic commerce (e-commerce)** is narrower than digital business. It's often thought simply to refer to buying and selling using the Internet; people immediately think of consumer retail purchases from companies such as Amazon. But e-commerce should be considered as *all* electronically mediated transactions between an organisation and any third party it deals with. By this definition, non-financial transactions such as customer support and requests for further information would also be considered to be part of e-commerce. Kalakota and Whinston (1997) referred to a range of different perspectives for e-commerce which are still valid today:

1 A *communications perspective* – the delivery of information, products or services or payment by electronic means.
2 A *business process perspective* – the application of technology towards the automation of business transactions and workflows.
3 A *service perspective* – enabling cost cutting at the same time as increasing the speed and quality of service delivery.
4 An *online perspective* – the buying and selling of products and information online.

These definitions show that electronic commerce is not solely restricted to the actual buying and selling of products, but also includes pre-sale and post-sale activities across the supply chain.

Trends update	E-commerce growth rates

There is an annual growth rate of around 10–20% in e-commerce sales in most countries: http://bit.ly/smartetailstats.

When evaluating the strategic impact of e-commerce on an organisation, it is useful to identify opportunities for buy-side and sell-side e-commerce transactions as shown in Figure 1.4, since systems with different functionalities will need to be created in an organisation to accommodate transactions with buyers and with suppliers. **Buy-side e-commerce** refers to transactions to procure resources needed by an organisation from its suppliers. In Chapter 6, Case Study 6.1 reviews how Shell has developed a digital business capability that enables buy-side e-commerce for its customers. **Sell-side e-commerce** refers to transactions involved with selling products to an organisation's customers.

Social commerce is an increasingly important part of e-commerce for site owners since incorporating reviews and ratings into a site and linking to social networking sites can help understand customers' needs and increase conversion to sale. It can also involve group buying, using a coupon service like Groupon.

Digital business defined

Debate 1.1

How new is the digital business concept?

'Digital business is just a new label – there is no distinction between the role of digital business and traditional information systems management.'

Digital business is broader in its scope than e-commerce. It is similar to the term e-business (which was first coined by IBM), who described it in 1997 as:

e-business (e'biz'nis) – the transformation of key business processes through the use of Internet technologies.

In the sixth edition of this book we have changed from using the term e-business to using digital business since it reflects the current usage in industry and research on the impact of digital technologies on business.

Figure 1.4   The distinction between buy-side and sell-side e-commerce

Key:
- Suppliers
- Suppliers' suppliers
- Organisational processes and functional units
- Intermediaries
- Customers
- Customers' customers

Social commerce
A subset of e-commerce which encourages participation and interaction of customers in rating, selecting and buying products through group buying. This participation can occur on an e-commerce site or on third-party sites.

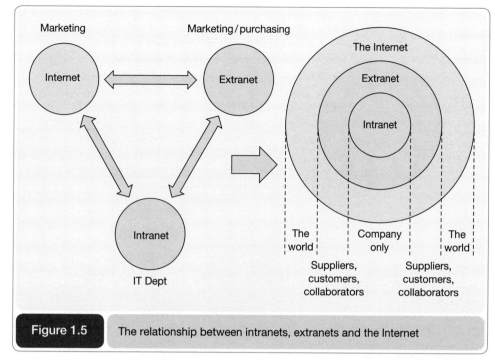

Figure 1.5 The relationship between intranets, extranets and the Internet

Digital business (digital business)
How businesses apply digital technology and media to improve the competitiveness of their organisation through optimising internal processes with online and traditional channels to market and supply.

Intranet
A private network within a single company using Internet standards to enable employees to access and share information using web publishing technology.

Enterprise social media software
Systems used inside organisations to enable real-time collaboration between employees and other stakeholders such as customers and suppliers to support business processes such as customer service, supply chain management and new product development. Collectively these tools are sometimes referenced as Enterprise 2.0.

In Figure 1.4 the key digital business processes are the organisational processes or units in the centre of the figure. They include research and development, marketing, manufacturing, and inbound and outbound logistics. The buy-side e-commerce transactions with suppliers and the sell-side e-commerce transactions with customers can also be considered to be key digital business processes.

Intranets and extranets

The majority of Internet services are available to any business or consumer that has access to the Internet. However, many digital business applications that access sensitive company information require access to be limited to qualified individuals or partners. If information is restricted to employees inside an organisation, this is an **intranet**, as is shown in Figure 1.5.

Today, the term intranet is still used, but software services similar to Twitter and Facebook are being implemented within companies to achieve similar goals of information sharing and collaboration. Mini case study 1.2 shows an example of one such **enterprise social media software** tool, Yammer (Figure 1.6).

Mini Case Study 1.2 | Suncorp implement an internal social network

The Suncorp financial services group manages 25 brands in Australia and New Zealand spanning banking, insurance, investment and superannuation. Suncorp has over 219,000 shareholders, over 16,000 employees and around 7 million customers.

Suncorp has used enterprise social networking tool Yammer to help geographically dispersed people and teams to connect, share, discuss and innovate. It has also helped Suncorp create a culture where collaboration is more natural by enabling people to interact online in an open, informal and transparent way.

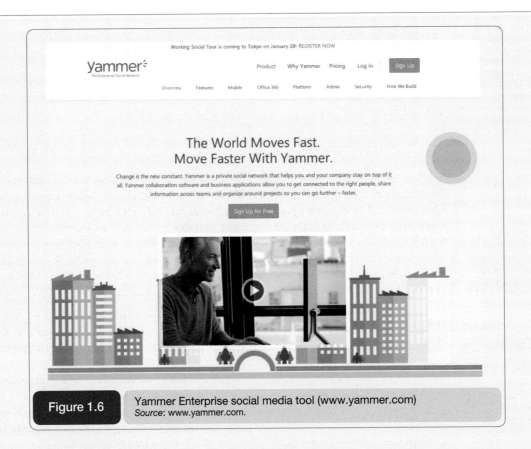

| Figure 1.6 | Yammer Enterprise social media tool (www.yammer.com)
Source: www.yammer.com. |
|---|---|

Within a matter of months, Yammer membership grew from a handful of early adopters to over 1,700 users and continues to grow.

Jeff Smith, Suncorp, the Chief Information Office of Yammer, explains the benefits as follows:

> Yammer has enabled us to harness the wisdom of our people who are spread across multiple teams, geographies and brands to help achieve our purpose of delivering business solutions for competitive advantage.

Brian Robbins, Chief Marketing Office (CMO), added:

> We recently signed up for Yammer and are seeing it spread virally among our employees. It is helping us accelerate collaboration and internal communications across our 20,000 employees in 300 offices in 30 countries. We're seeing all kinds of serendipitous connections across projects, cultures and time zones.

The benefits of applying a tool like Yammer to Suncorp can be summarised as:

- Increased informal knowledge flow across the organisation through microblogging.
- Overcome barriers to collaboration, providing instant connection for people, teams, informal networks, communities of practice and other shared interest groups.
- Improved alignment between executives and employees by use of broadcast message to communicate messages and quickly crowdsource to get ideas, suggestions and answers to questions.
- Helped stimulate greater sharing and discussion amongst common role groups, e.g. developers, architects and testers.

Source: Adapted from Yammer (2010).

Extranet
A service provided through Internet and web technology delivered by extending an intranet beyond a company to customers, suppliers and collaborators.

If access to an organisation's web services is extended to some others, but not everyone beyond the organisation, this is an **extranet**. Whenever you log on to an Internet service such as that for an e-retailer or online news site, this is effectively an extranet arrangement, although the term is most often used to mean a business-to-business application such as the Shell SIMON capability described in Case Study 6.1 where certain customers or suppliers are given shared access. We look at examples of intranets and extranets in Chapter 3, including the Dell Premier extranet.

Different types of sell-side e-commerce

Sell-side e-commerce doesn't only involve selling products online, but also involves using digital technologies to market services using a range of techniques (which we will explore in Chapters 8 and 9). Not every product is suitable for sale online, so the way in which a website is used to market products will vary. It is useful to review these five main types of online presence for sell-side e-commerce, each of which has different objectives and is appropriate for different markets. These are not clear-cut website categories since any company may combine these types, but with a change in emphasis according to the market they serve. As you review websites, note how organisations have different parts of the site focussing on these five functions:

1 **Transactional e-commerce sites.** These enable purchase of products online. The main business contribution of the site is through sale of these products. The sites also support the business by providing information for consumers who prefer to purchase products offline. These include retail sites, travel sites and online banking services.

2 **Services-oriented relationship-building websites.** Provide information to stimulate purchase and build relationships, particularly where products are not suitable for sale online. Information is provided through the website and e-newsletters to inform purchase decisions. The main business contribution is through encouraging offline sales and generating enquiries or leads from potential customers, known as lead generation.

3 **Brand-building sites.** Provide an experience to support the brand. Products are not typically available for online purchase. Their main focus is to support the brand by developing an online experience of the brand. They are typical for low-value, high-volume fast-moving consumer goods (FMCG brands).

4 **Publisher or media sites.** Provide information, news or entertainment about a range of topics. This is information both on the site and through links to other sites. Media sites have a diversity of options for generating revenue, including advertising, commission-based sales and sale of customer data (lists).

Social network sites (SNS)
A site that facilitates peer-to-peer communication within a group or between individuals through providing facilities to develop user-generated content (UGC) and to exchange messages and comments between different users.

5 **Social network sites (SNS).** Social networks could be considered to be in the previous category since they are often supported by advertising, but the influence of social networks such as Facebook, LinkedIn and Twitter on company and customer communications suggests they form a separate category.

Complete Activity 1.3 to consider examples of these different types of site.

Activity 1.3	Understanding different types of online presence

Purpose

To help you assess how different types of online presence are used for marketing.

Activity

Review the popularity of the different site types in your country or globally. The recommended information sources are:

- Similar Web (www.similarweb.com) or Compete (www.compete.com) site comparison services.

- The Hitwise Data Centers (e.g. www.hitwise.com/us/resources/data-center) available for Australia, Canada, France, Hong Kong, Singapore, New Zealand, UK, and US.

Visit each of the sites below and then indicate which of the five categories of online presence are their primary and secondary focus:

1 Transactional e-commerce site.

2 Services-oriented relationship-building website.

3 Brand-building site.

4 Portal or media site.

5 Social network.

Example sites

- Business media site: The Financial Times (www.ft.com) or Mashable (www.mashable.com)
- Bank, e.g. HSBC (www.hsbc.com)
- Lingerie manufacturer, e.g. Gossard (www.gossard.com)
- Management consultants such as PricewaterhouseCoopers (www.pwc.co.uk) and Accenture (www.accenture.com)
- Beverage manufacturers, e.g. Bacardi.com (www.bacardi.com) and Guinness (www.guinness.com)
- Travel company, e.g. Thomas Cook (www.thomascook.com)
- An end-product manufacturer such as Vauxhall (www.vauxhall.co.uk)
- Consumer site, e.g. Yahoo! (www.yahoo.com)
- Online retailer such as Amazon (www.amazon.com)

Answers to activities can be found at www.pearsoned.co.uk/chaffey

Digital marketing

Digital marketing
This has a similar meaning to 'electronic marketing' – both describe the management and execution of marketing using electronic media such as the web, email, IP TV and mobile media in conjunction with digital data about customers' characteristics and behaviour.

Digital marketing, e-marketing or Internet marketing is yet another field that is closely related to e-commerce. 'Digital marketing' is the term increasingly used which we use in this book (and explore in more detail in Chapters 8 and 9).

To help explain the scope and approaches used for digital marketing the author developed a more detailed definition with training organisation The IDM (www.theidm.com):

Digital marketing involves:

Applying these technologies which form online channels to market:

Web, email, databases, plus mobile/wireless and digital TV.

To achieve these objectives:

Support marketing activities aimed at achieving profitable acquisition and retention of customers . . . within a multichannel buying process and customer lifecycle.

Through using these marketing tactics:

Recognising the strategic importance of digital technologies and developing a planned approach to reach and migrate customers to online services through e-communications and traditional communications. Retention is achieved through improving our customer knowledge (of their profiles, behaviour, value and loyalty drivers), then delivering integrated, targeted communications and online services that match their individual needs.

Let's now look at each part of this description in more detail. The first part of the description illustrates the range of access platforms and communications tools that form the online channels which marketers use to build and develop relationships with customers.

Podcasts
Individuals and organisations post online media (audio and video) which can be viewed in the appropriate players (including the iPod which first sparked the growth in this technique). The latest podcast updates can be automatically delivered by really simple syndication.

Social network
A site facilitating exchange of text, audio or video content.

Different access platforms deliver content and enable interaction through a range of different online communication tools or media channels. Some are well-established techniques which will be familiar to you, like websites, search engines, email and text messaging. One of the most exciting things about working in digital media is the introduction of new tools and techniques which have to be assessed for their relevance to a particular marketing campaign.

Recent innovations (which we discuss further in Chapters 8 and 9) include blogs, feeds, **podcasts** and **social networks**. The growth of social networks has been documented by Boyd and Ellison (2007) who describe social networking sites as:

Web-based services that allow individuals to (1) construct a public or semi-public profile within a bounded system, (2) articulate a list of other users with whom they share a connection, and (3) view and traverse their list of connections and those made by others within the system.

The interactive capabilities to post comments or other content and rate content are surprisingly missing from this definition.

Trends update   Social network usage http://bit.ly/smartsocialstats

Social media accounts for a significant amount of online usage, particularly on mobile devices. This update shows varying use in different countries.

Options for companies to reach their audience online

For companies to be successful in their digital communications they must decide how they invest their time and budget in the sometimes bewildering range of online communications tools. In Chapters 8 and 9 we review these tools in detail, but here is a summary of the main options for investment options.

Owned, earned and paid media options

To help develop a strategy to reach and influence potential customers online it has become commonplace today to refer to three main types of media channels marketers need to consider (Figure 1.7):

1 **Paid media.** These are bought media where there is investment to pay for visitors, reach or conversions through search, display advertising networks or affiliate marketing. Offline, traditional media like print and TV advertising and direct mail remain important, accounting for the majority of paid-media spend.

2 **Earned media.** Traditionally, earned media has been the name given to publicity generated through PR invested in targeting influencers to increase awareness about a brand. Now earned media also includes word-of-mouth that can be stimulated through viral and social media marketing and includes conversations in social networks, blogs and other communities. It's useful to think of earned media as developed through different types of partners such as publishers, bloggers and other influencers, including customer advocates. Another way of thinking about earned media is as different forms of conversations between consumers and businesses occurring both online and offline.

3 **Owned media.** This is media owned by the brand. Online, this includes a company's own websites, blogs, email list, mobile apps or their social presence on Facebook, LinkedIn or Twitter. Offline, owned media may include brochures or retail stores. It's useful to think of a company's own presence as media in the sense that they are an alternative investment to other media and they offer opportunities to promote products using similar ad or editorial formats to other media. It emphasises the need for all organisations to become multichannel publishers.

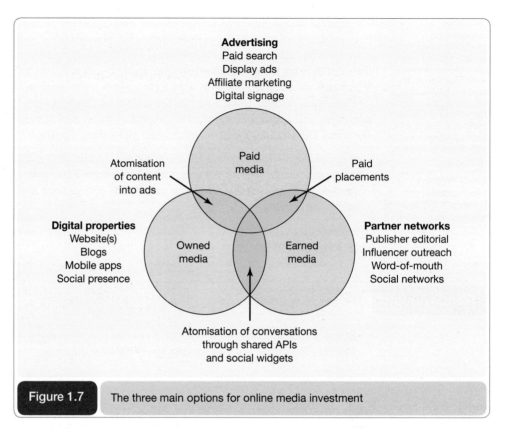

Widget

A badge or button incorporated into a site or social network space by its owner, with content or services typically served from another site making widgets effectively a mini-software application or web service. Content can be updated in real time since the widget interacts with the server each time it loads.

Digital media channels

Online communications techniques used to achieve goals of brand awareness, familiarity, favourability and to influence purchase intent by encouraging users of digital media to visit a website to engage with the brand or product and ultimately to purchase online or offline through traditional media channels such as by phone or in-store.

Pay-per-click (PPC) search marketing

Refers to when a company pays for text ads to be displayed on the search engine results pages as a sponsored link (typically above, to the right of or below the natural listings) when a specific key phrase is entered by the search users. It is so called since the marketer pays for each time the hypertext link in the ad is clicked on. If a link is clicked repeatedly, then this will be detected by the search engine as click fraud and the marketer will not be charged.

Search engine optimisation (SEO)

A structured approach used to increase the position of a company or its products in search engine natural or organic results listings (the main body of the search results page) for selected keywords or phrases.

Figure 1.7 — The three main options for online media investment

You can see in Figure 1.7 that there is overlap between the three different types of media. It is important to note this, since achieving this overlap requires integration of campaigns, resources and infrastructure. Content on a content hub or site can be broken down (atomised) and shared between other media types through widgets powered by program and data exchange APIs such as the Facebook API.

The six key types of digital media channels

There are many online communications techniques which marketers must review as part of their digital business communications strategy or as part of planning an online marketing campaign. To assist with planning, Chaffey and Smith (2012) recommend reviewing the six main types of digital media channels for reaching audiences shown in Figure 1.8. Note that offline communications should also be reviewed for their role in driving visitors to a company website or social network presence.

1 **Search engine marketing.** Placing messages on a search engine to encourage clickthrough to a website when the user types a specific keyword phrase. Two key search marketing techniques are: paid placements or sponsored links using pay-per-click, and placements in the natural or organic listings using search engine optimisation (SEO).

2 **Online PR.** Maximising favourable mentions and interactions with a company's brands, products or websites using third-party sites such as social networks or blogs that are likely to be visited by your target audience. It also includes responding to negative mentions and conducting public relations via a site through a press centre or blog. It is closely related to social media marketing.

3 **Online partnerships.** Creating and managing long-term arrangements to promote your online services on third-party websites or through email communications. Different forms of partnership include link building, affiliate marketing, aggregators such as price comparison sites like MoneySuperMarket (www.moneysupermarket.com), online sponsorship and co-branding.

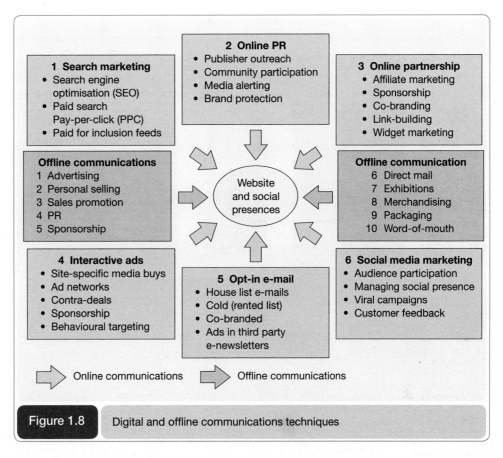

Figure 1.8 Digital and offline communications techniques

4 **Interactive advertising.** Use of online ads such as banners and rich media ads to achieve brand awareness and encourage clickthrough to a target site.

5 **Opt-in email marketing.** Renting email lists or placing ads in third-party e-newsletters or the use of an in-house list for customer activation and retention.

6 **Social media marketing.** Social media marketing is an important category of digital marketing which involves encouraging customer communications on a company's own site, or a social presence such as Facebook or Twitter, or in specialist publisher sites, blogs and forums. It can be applied as a traditional broadcast medium, for example companies can use Facebook or Twitter to send messages to customers or partners who have opted in. However, to take advantage of the benefits of social media it is important to participate in customer conversations. These can be related to products, promotions or customer service and are aimed at learning more about customers and providing support, so improving the way a company is perceived. (In Chapter 9 we identify six main applications of social media.)

Mini case study 1.3 gives an illustration of how a small start-up business can use the combination of marketing tools illustrated in Figure 1.8.

Mini case study 1.3	Tatu uses paid, owned and earned media to expand its global reach

Start-up brand Tatu Couture designs and manufactures luxury British lingerie which is sold through stockists in the UK, Paris and New York. Tatu Couture has a unique vision to push the boundaries of design and innovation with its trend-setting luxury lingerie and designer body wear. All its goods are manufactured and hand finished in the UK.

Figure 1.9	Tatu Couture
	Source: from www.tatucouture.com, Tatu Couture.

Overview and digital strategy

Agency Tonica supported Tatu Couture by creating a four-stage strategy to increase digital presence. In addition to the stockist route, Tatu Couture was keen to increase its own direct sales, so it had two simple objectives for the work – to increase visits to tatucouture.com and increase sales from the site. The steps to develop the reach of the company are explained by the agency as:

Step 1 – Take Control

Like many small to medium-sized enterprises (SMEs), Tatu Couture had employed a web designer to create their site, but were unfamiliar with some of the standard tools that could help them track success. In this phase of work, we focussed on empowering Tatu Couture to take control so that they could cost-effectively develop their site without spending budget on external resource:

- Suggesting Tatu Couture gain full account control of their Shopify website
- Assisting Tatu Couture in having Google Webmaster Tools access in order to access information about the health of their site
- Setting up Google Analytics in order to track website performance.

Step 2 – Make the Most of your Contacts

In this phase, we were keen to ensure that Tatu Couture could conduct their own email campaigns using free provider, Mailchimp. During this process we also consolidated their contact data into a new Tatu Couture Mailchimp account, and set up a website 'sign up' so that new prospects could be captured.

Step 3 – Promote (for free when possible!)

In addition to the email campaigns, we identified several low-cost or no-cost promotion options:

- Google Merchant (aka Google Shopping/Google Product Search). In order to increase online presence we were keen to feed Tatu Couture products into Google Shopping, particularly as this was still a free service in the UK (prior to March 2013). Luckily Shopify had a fairly easy integration option for this, so we were able to activate the integration and add a few settings (such as Shipping) for products to be regularly submitted.

- Google Places – a free local service which helps Tatu Couture stand out regionally.
- Google AdWords (pay-per-click advertising). Since the launch campaign, low-cost Google Adwords campaigns have been used at key events in the calendar, continuing to lower the cost per click, increase click-through rates and utilise the best-performing keywords. We have also used micro-geographic targeting in Google AdWord campaigns as a proxy for income – for example, targeting South Kensington and Chelsea postcodes.
- Facebook. Tatu Couture is using this investment to reach the most likely recipients to purchase. The challenge in promoting a luxury product online is reaching an audience likely to purchase and this is where the beauty of Facebook could help. By targeting Facebook profiles who already liked other luxury or designer products, our Facebook campaign could reach a more tailored market than using Google alone. During the campaign we were able to double Facebook likes for Tatu Couture. In the last three months, Facebook has driven 16% of the traffic to the site.

Step 4 – Search Engine Optimisation

As well as suggesting search engine optimisation changes along the way, we suggested a more formal SEO review as Step 4. Tatu Couture has begun to implement these SEO changes in an effort to drive more organic traffic to the site. The changes included incorporating more keywords into the product descriptions in addition to the unique Tatu Couture copy.

Source: Smart Insights (2013)

Multichannel and omnichannel marketing
Customer communications and product distribution are supported by a combination of digital and traditional channels at different points in the buying cycle. Omnichannel references the importance of social media and mobile-based interactions in informing purchase.

Multichannel marketing strategy
Defines how different marketing channels should integrate and support each other in terms of their proposition development and communications based on their relative merits for the customer and the company.

The second part of the definition of digital marketing shows that it should not be the technology that drives digital marketing, but the business returns from gaining new customers and maintaining relationships with existing customers. It also emphasises how digital marketing does not occur in isolation, but is most effective when it is integrated with other communications channels such as phone, direct mail or face-to-face. The role of the Internet in supporting **multichannel and omnichannel marketing** and **multichannel marketing strategy** is another recurring theme in this book. (Chapters 2 and 5 in particular explain its role in supporting different customer communications channels and distribution channels.) Online channels should also be used to support the whole buying process or **customer journey** from pre-sale to sale to post-sale and further development of customer relationships. This clarifies how different marketing channels should integrate and support each other in terms of their proposition development and communications based on their relative merits for the customer and the company.

The final part of the description summarises approaches to **customer-centric marketing**. It shows how success online requires a planned approach to migrate existing customers to online channels and acquire new customers by selecting the appropriate mix of e-communications and traditional communications. Gaining and keeping online customers needs to be based on developing **customer insight** by researching their characteristics and behaviour, what they value and what keeps them loyal, and then delivering tailored, relevant web and email communications.

Web 2.0 and user-generated content

From 2004, the **Web 2.0 concept** increased in prominence amongst website owners and developers. The main technologies and principles of Web 2.0 have been explained in an influential article by Tim O'Reilly (O'Reilly, 2005). Behind the label 'Web 2.0' lies a bewildering range of interactive tools and social communications techniques such as blogs, podcasts and social networks which are still in use today.

Web 2.0 also references methods of exchanging data between sites in standardised formats, such as the feeds that merchants use to supply shopping comparison sites with data about products offered and their prices. The main characteristics of Web 2.0 that are still key characteristics of successful online brands typically involves:

(i) Web services or interactive applications hosted on the web such as Flickr (www.flickr.com), Google Maps™ (http://maps.google.com) or blogging services such as Blogger.com or Wordpress (www.wordpress.com).

(ii) Supporting participation – many of the applications are based on altruistic principles of community participation best represented by the most popular social networks such as Bebo, MySpace and Facebook.

(iii) Encouraging creation of user-generated content – blogs are the best example of this. Another example is the collaborative encyclopaedia Wikipedia (www.wikipedia.org).

(iv) Enabling rating of content and online services – for example social commerce on e-retail sites.

(v) Ad funding of neutral sites – web services such as Google GMail™ and many blogs are based on contextual advertising such as Google AdSense™.

(vi) Data exchange between sites through XML-based data standards. RSS is based on XML, but has relatively little semantic mark-up to describe the content. Data can also be exchanged through standard **microformats** such as hCalendar and hReview which are used to incorporate data from other sites into the Google listings (see www.microformats.org for details). New classes of content can also be defined and **mashups** created.

(vii) Use of rich media or creation of rich Internet applications (RIA) which provide for a more immersive, interactive experience. These may be integrated into web browsers or may be separate applications like that downloaded for Second Life (www.secondlife.com).

(viii) Rapid application development using interactive technology approaches known as 'Ajax' (Asynchronous JavaScript and XML). The best-known Ajax implementation is Google Maps which is responsive since it does not require refreshes to display maps.

Figure 1.10 summarises the evolution of digital and web-related technologies. Note that the terms Web 2.0, 3.0 and 4.0 are not terms commonly used today, yet it's useful to understand the principles of Web 2.0 in particular since they are important to creating interactive, integrated desktop and mobile experiences (as explained in Chapter 11). Many sites still don't have these characteristics.

Supply chain management

When distinguishing between buy-side and sell-side e-commerce we are looking at different aspects of managing an organisation's supply chain. **Supply chain management (SCM)** is the coordination of all supply activities of an organisation from its suppliers and delivery of products to its customers. (The opportunities for using e-commerce to streamline and restructure the supply chain are described in more detail in Chapter 6.) The **value chain** is a related concept that describes the different value-adding activities that connect a company's supply side with its demand side. We can identify an *internal* value chain within the boundaries of an organisation and an *external* value chain where these activities are performed by partners. Note that in the era of digital business a company will manage many interrelated value chains, so we also consider the concept of a **value network** (see Chapter 6).

Business or consumer models of e-commerce transactions

It is now commonplace to describe e-commerce transactions between an organisation and its stakeholders according to whether they are primarily with consumers (**business-to-consumer – B2C**) or other businesses (**business-to-business – B2B**).

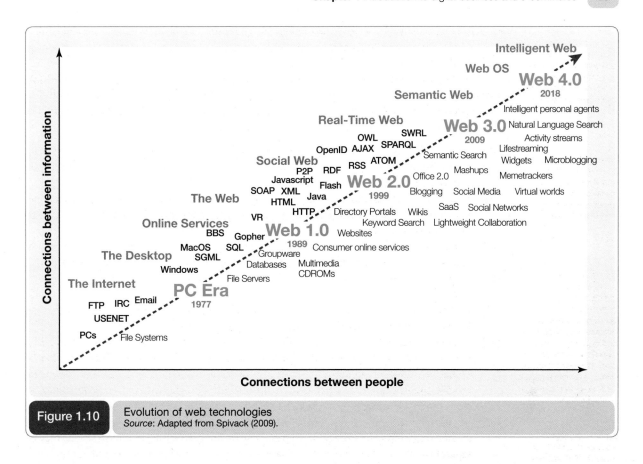

Figure 1.10   Evolution of web technologies
Source: Adapted from Spivack (2009).

Web 3.0 concept

A description of the web around 2009 incorporating high-speed connectivity, complex cross-community interactions, full range of digital media (text, voice, video) and an intelligent or semantic web where automated applications can access data from different online services to assist searchers to perform complex tasks of supplier selection.

Supply chain management (SCM)

The coordination of all supply activities of an organisation from its suppliers and partners to its customers.

Value chain

A model for analysis of how supply chain activities can add value to products and services delivered to the customer.

Value network

The links between an organisation and its strategic and non-strategic partners that form its external value chain.

Figure 1.11 gives examples of different companies operating in the business-to-consumer (B2C) and business-to-business (B2B) spheres. Often companies such as BP or Dell Computer will have products that appeal to both consumers and businesses, so will have different parts of their site to appeal to these audiences.

Referring to the well-known online companies in Table 1.1 initially suggests that these companies are mainly focussed on B2C markets. However, B2B communications are still important for many of these companies since business transactions can drive revenue, as for example eBay Business (http://business.ebay.com/), or the B2C service may need to be sustained through advertising provided through B2B transactions; for example, Google's revenue is largely based on its B2B AdWords (http://adwords.google.com/) and advertising service, and advertising-based revenue is also important to sites such as YouTube, MySpace and Facebook.

Figure 1.11 also presents two additional types of transaction, those where consumers transact directly with other consumers (**C2C**) and where they initiate trading with companies (**C2B**). These monikers are less widely used (e.g. *Economist*, 2000), but they do highlight significant differences between Internet-based commerce and earlier forms of commerce. Consumer-to-consumer interactions (also known as peer-to-peer or person-to-person, P2P) were relatively rare, but are now very common in the form of social networks. Hoffman and Novak (1996) suggested that C2C interactions are a key characteristic of the Internet that is important for companies to take into account, but it is only in recent years with the growth of always-on broadband connections and mobile access to the web that these have become so popular. P2P transactions are also the main basis for some online business models for digital businesses such as Betfair (see Mini case study 1.4) and eBay (www.ebay.com, see Case study 1.2) which are still run on a business basis, and some blogs which are not run by companies but by individuals.

Finally, the diagram also includes government and public services organisations which deliver online or e-government services. As well as the models shown in Figure 1.11, it has also been suggested that employees should be considered as a separate type of consumer through the use of intranets; this is referred to as employee-to-employee or E2E.

	From: Supplier of content/service		
	Consumer or citizen	*Business (organisation)*	*Government*
Consumer or citizen	**Consumer-to-Consumer (C2C)** • eBay • Peer-to-Peer (Skype) • Blogs and communities • Product recommendations • Social networks: MySpace, Bebo	**Business-to-Consumer (B2C)** • Transactional: Amazon • Relationship-building: BP • Brand-building: Unilever • Media owner – News Corp • Comparison intermediary: Kelkoo, Pricerunner	**Government-to-Consumer (G2C)** • National government transactional: Tax – inland revenue • National government information • Local government services
Business (organisation)	**Consumer-to-Business (C2B)** • Priceline • Consumer-feedback, communities or campaigns	**Business-to-Business (B2B)** • Transactional: Euroffice • Relationship-building: BP • Media Owned: Emap business publications • B2B marketplaces: EC21	**Government-to-Business (G2B)** • Government services and transactions: tax • Legal regulations
Government	**Consumer-to-Government (C2G)** • Feedback to government through pressure group or individual sites	**Business-to-Government (B2G)** • Feedback to government businesses and non-governmental organisations	**Government-to-Government (G2G)** • Inter-government services • Exchange of information

To: Consumer of content/service

Figure 1.11 Summary and examples of transaction alternatives between businesses, consumers and governmental organisations

---

Mini case study 1.4   Betfair profits with C2C online gambling service

Betfair provides a great example of the creation of a digital business with an innovative business model. It holds licences to operate in the UK, US, Australia, Austria, Germany, Italy and Malta with just under 50% of all new registrations coming from outside the UK and Ireland. Its 2012 Annual Report notes that it has identified Italy and Spain as priority markets attractive in terms of scale, growth potential and regulatory outlook. It is looking to achieve a top-three position in this market. In this year it had around 744,000 active customers with average revenue per user (ARPU) of £360. Twenty-three per cent of customers made an overall profit in the year. Commercial and marketing spend was £87.5 million representing 25% of revenue. Technology and product development costs were £67.2 million.

Betfair is the world's biggest online sports betting company and pioneered the first successful betting exchange in 2000. Driven by cutting-edge technology, Betfair enables customers to choose their own odds and bet even after the event has started. The company now processes over 6 million transactions a day from its 3 million registered customers around the world (the 3 million mark was passed in 2010).

Betfair introduced a novel form of betting which replaces the typical role of the bookmaker such as Ladbrokes or William Hill who provide fixed odds and take their own risk on the outcome. With Betfair, all bets placed are with other Betfair customers rather than with Betfair, which has no risks on the outcome. As with all forms of gambling, there is a risk of corruption 'throwing the bet'; to reduce this risk Betfair has a transparent approach where evidence of corruption may be shared with the governing body of a sport.

Through providing an online service, there are additional aspects of its proposition:

- You can either place bets conventionally or request your own odds.
- You can choose the odds you want to play at.
- You can bet while the game is in play.

Betfair's revenue model

Betfair charges a commission (typically 5%) on each player's net winnings on a market. If a player loses, there is no commission. There is a discount on commission; when you place more bets this rewards regular punters.

Betfair's growth

This outline history of Betfair shows how it has extended its product range and partnerships to support its growth:

1 2000 – The Sporting Exchange Ltd launches Betfair.com from Russell Square, London. At launch, funds were limited, so the company used 'guerrilla marketing' to promote it, such as a procession through the City of London with coffins with banners 'death of the bookmaker' and fake demonstrations with 'Betfair – unfair' banners.
2 2001 – Betfair matches £1 million in seven days for the first time.
3 2002 – Betfair announces a merger with competitor Flutter and sponsorship of Fulham Football Club.
4 2003 – Betfair launches sites in German, Danish, Greek, Italian, Swedish, Norwegian, Finnish and Chinese.
5 2004 – Betfair launches Betfair poker, which today has 60,000 registered players. Betfair signs joint venture with Australia's Publishing and Broadcasting Limited.
6 2005 – Betfair sponsors the Channel 4 Ashes Cricket coverage and records the highest-ever single market turnover, matching £36 million on the Fifth Ashes Test Match alone! Betfair signs exclusive deal

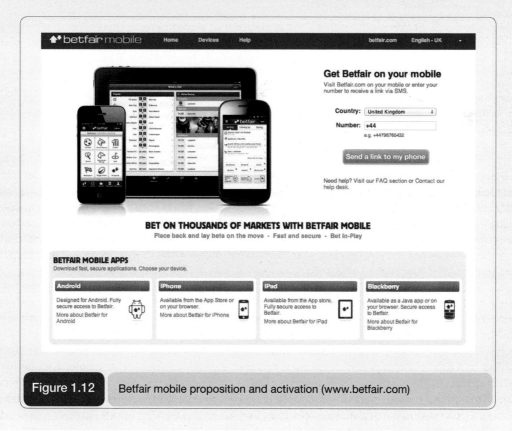

| Figure 1.12 | Betfair mobile proposition and activation (www.betfair.com) |

with Yahoo! UK and Ireland to launch a simplified betting exchange as well as a co-branded betting exchange.

7   Betfair's key performance indicators are suggested by an annual report for year ending 30 April 2007 when it had an annual turnover in excess of £180 million with operating profit of £35 million based on 18 million 'active player-days', which is a key performance measure derived from the 433,000 active customers and an average 9 player-days per month per active customer. International revenues grew most rapidly and contributed 23% of exchange revenues compared with 18 per cent in the previous year.

8   By 2010 Betfair employed over 1,700 people globally. Its headquarters are in Hammersmith in West London, while its international business is based in Malta. It also has large operational bases in the UK in Stevenage and Australia in Tasmania and Melbourne, a software development hub in Romania and offices in Los Angeles and San Francisco.

9   Technology challenges are indicated by the 6 million transactions a day processed, equating to 360 bets a second. Using Oracle database technology, Betfair processes 99.9 per cent of bets in less than one second.

10 In April 2010 an iTunes app was released, with Betfair noting that their registered mobile users increased 40% in 2009 with a 50% increase in year-on-year mobile revenues.

11 Betfair's API allows customers or software developers to interact with, and develop applications linked to, the Exchange directly, without the need to use its website. The first site to go live with an app cloud betting service was Manchester United's official website, manutd.com.

12 Mobile bets doubled between 2011 and 2012, to 44 million in total in 2012 based on apps and the mobile site (Figure 1.12).

Source: Corporate site (www.betfaircorporate.com).

Business-to-consumer (B2C)
Commercial transactions between an organisation and consumers.

Business-to-business (B2B)
Commercial transactions between an organisation and other organisations (inter-organisational marketing).

Consumer-to-business (C2B)
Consumers approach the business with an offer.

E-government
The application of e-commerce technologies to government and public services for citizens and businesses.

E-government defined

E-government refers to the application of e-commerce technologies to government and public services. In the same way that e-business can be understood as transactions with customers (citizens), suppliers and internal communications, e-government covers a similar range of applications:

- *Citizens* – facilities for dissemination of information and use of online services at local and national levels. For example, at a local level you can find out when refuse is collected and at national level it is possible to fill in tax returns.
- *Suppliers* – government departments have a vast network of suppliers. The potential benefits (and pitfalls) of electronic supply chain management and e-procurement (described in Chapters 6 and 7) are equally valid for government.
- *Internal communications* – this includes information collection and dissemination and email and workflow systems for improving efficiency within government departments.

E-government is now viewed as important within government in many countries. The European Union set up 'i2010' (*European Information Society in 2010*) whose aims included

> *providing an integrated approach to information society and audio-visual policies in the EU, covering regulation, research, and deployment and promoting cultural diversity. (eEurope, 2005)*

Digital business opportunities

Digital business has introduced new opportunities for small and large organisations to compete in the global marketplace. As we observed at the start of this chapter, many commentators have noted that one of the biggest changes introduced by electronic communications is how approaches to transmitting and transforming information can be used for competitive advantage. A significant commentary on the disruptive, transformational nature of electronic communications is provided in Box 1.1.

The Internet also provides significant opportunities for many businesses to build closer relationships with their existing customers and suppliers online to help achieve customer retention. Encouraging use of online, digital business services by customers and suppliers can significantly reduce costs while providing a new, convenient channel for purchase and customer service. Through providing high-quality online services, organisations can build lasting relationships with their stakeholders. While it is sometimes said that '*online, your customers are only a mouse click away from your competitors*', this is a simplification, and encouraging use of online services can help achieve '**soft lock-in**'. This means that a customer or supplier continues to use a service since they find the service valuable, they have invested time in learning the service or integrating it with their systems and there are some costs in switching. Think of online services you use for different purposes. How often do you switch between them? Of course, the ideal is that the service meets the needs of its users so well and delivers value such that they are satisfied and do not consider switching.

Soft lock-in
Customers or suppliers continue to use online services because of the switching costs.

Box 1.1   Evans and Wurster on the impact of disruptive Internet technologies

Evans and Wurster of Harvard argue in their classic 1997 paper 'Strategy and the new economics of information' that there are three characteristics of information which, when combined with disruptive Internet technologies, can have a major impact on a marketplace. These characteristics of information are reach, richness and affiliation:

1 *Reach*. Conventionally, 'reach' refers to the potential number of customers a business can interact with. The Internet enables reach to be increased nationally and internationally at low cost through making content available via search engines. 'Reach' also refers to the number of different categories and products a consumer interface (e.g. store, catalogue or website) can cover: witness the large range of products available through digital businesses such as Amazon, eBay and Kelkoo.com and existing companies such as easyJet.com and Tesco.com which have used the web to extend their product range.
2 *Richness*. This is a characteristic of the information itself. The Internet enables more detailed information about products, prices and availability to be made available. It also enables more interactivity and customisation to engage customers and to provide more up-to-date information. But, Evans and Wurster also note that richness is limited by bandwidth (the volume of information that can be transmitted using a communications link in a given time), the accuracy or reliability of information and its security.
3 *Affiliation*. This refers to the effectiveness of links with partners. In an online context, an organisation which has the most and richest links with other compatible organisations will be able to gain a larger reach and influence. Consider how digital businesses such as eBay, Google and Yahoo! have successfully formed partnerships or acquired other companies to provide new diverse information services such as social networking, mapping, voice communications and online photography, to name just a few.

In markets such as car sales which have been transformed by the Internet, understanding how to improve reach, richness and affiliation is crucial. This is not because a large proportion of people buy cars online, but rather the majority research online their preferred make, model and supplier.

Business adoption of digital technologies for e-commerce means that as managers, we need to assess the impact of e-commerce and digital business on our marketplace and organisation. What are the drivers of changed consumer and business behaviour? How should we respond? How much do we need to invest? What are our priorities and how quickly do we need to act? Answering these questions is an essential part of formulating a digital business and digital marketing strategy (and is considered in more detail in Part 2). To answer these questions, marketing research will need to be conducted (as described in Chapters 2 to 4) to determine the current levels of adoption of the Internet for different activities amongst customers and competitors in our market sector and in other sectors.

Drivers of digital technology adoption

Business adoption of e-commerce and digital business is driven by benefits to different parts of the organisation. First and foremost, businesses are concerned about how the benefits of digital business will impact on profitability or generating value to an organisation. The two main ways in which this can be achieved are:

- Potential for increased revenue arising from increased reach to a larger customer base and encouraging loyalty and repeat purchases amongst existing customers.
- Cost reduction achieved through delivering services electronically. Reductions include staff costs, transport costs and costs of materials such as paper.

At an early point in digital technology adoption, a government report (DTI, 2000) identified two main categories of drivers which remain relevant today for introducing new technology:

Cost/efficiency drivers

1 Increasing speed with which supplies can be obtained
2 Increasing speed with which goods can be dispatched
3 Reduced sales and purchasing costs
4 Reduced operating costs

Competitiveness drivers

5 Customer demand
6 Improving the range and quality of services offered
7 Avoiding losing market share to businesses already using e-commerce

More recently, in interviews with Australian businesses, Perrott (2005) identifies four key areas driving performance: cost–benefit, competitive pressures, market advantage and value-adding, i.e. improving customer satisfaction while building strong relationships.

When reviewing potential benefits, it is useful to identify both tangible benefits (for which monetary savings or revenues can be identified) and intangible benefits (for which it is more difficult to calculate cost savings). The types of potential benefits are summarised in Table 1.2.

Doherty *et al.* (2003) researched the drivers and barriers to retailers' adoption of Internet technologies to determine the most important factors. Table 1.3 summarises the ranking in importance for different degrees of Internet adoption from static **brochureware** (A), through an active website containing product information (B) to a transactional site where items can be purchased (C). You can see that the two most important factors which correlate with adoption are 'Internet target segment', i.e. customers in their market are typically adopters of the Internet, and 'Internet strategy', i.e. a defined Internet strategy is in place. This suggests, as would be expected, that companies that do not have a coherent Internet or digital business strategy are less likely to use higher levels of Internet services. Many larger organisations that have responded to the challenge of digital business have created a separate

Brochureware
Brochureware describes a website to which a company has migrated its existing paper-based promotional literature without recognising the differences required by this medium.

Table 1.2	Tangible and intangible benefits from e-commerce and digital business

Tangible benefits	Intangible benefits
• Increased sales from new sales leads giving rise to increased revenue from: – new customers, new markets – existing customers (cross-selling) • Marketing cost reductions from: – reduced time in customer service – online sales – reduced printing and distribution costs of marketing communications • Supply chain cost reductions from: – reduced levels of inventory – shorter cycle time in ordering • Administrative cost reductions from more efficient routine business processes such as recruitment, invoice payment and holiday authorisation	• Corporate image communication • Enhancement of brand • More rapid, more responsive marketing communications, including PR • Faster product development lifecycle enabling faster response to market needs • Improved customer service • Learning for the future • Meeting customer expectations to have a website • Identifying new partners, supporting existing partners better • Better management of marketing information and customer information • Feedback from customers on products

e-commerce plan and separate resources to implement it. This book covers what needs to go into such a plan and the issues to consider when implementing it.

Case study 1.2 illustrates the benefits of setting up an online operation for an SME. It also highlights some of the challenges of managing an online business and highlights the need for continued investment to refine online services and the marketing needed to attract visitors to the website.

Table 1.3	Summary of factors most important in encouraging Internet adoption amongst e-retailers

Factor influencing adoption		A	B	C
1	Internet target segment	3	2	1
2	Internet strategy	1	1	6
3	Internet marketplace	4	5	2
4	Infrastructure and development capability	2	3	5
5	Internet communications	5	6	4
6	Cost of Internet trading	8	9	10
7	Internet cost opportunity	6	8	7
8	Market development opportunity	7	4	3
9	Concerns	9	10	9
10	Consumer preferences	10	7	8

A = Internet adoption (static website), B = active website, C = online sales (transactional site)
Based on a compilation from separate tables in Doherty *et al.* (2003)

Risks and barriers to digital business adoption

Opportunities have to be balanced against the risks of introducing digital business services, which include strategic and practical risks. One of the main strategic risks is making the wrong decision about digital business investments. In every business sector, some companies have taken advantage of digital business and gained a competitive advantage. But others have invested in digital business without achieving the hoped-for returns, either because the execution of the plan was flawed, or simply because the approaches were inappropriate. The impact of the Internet and technology varies by industry. Andy Grove, Chairman of Intel, one of the early adopters of digital business, noted that every organisation needs to ask whether, for them:

The Internet is a typhoon force, a ten times force, or is it a bit of wind? Or is it a force that fundamentally alters our business? (Grove, 1996)

This statement still seems to encapsulate how managers must respond to different digital technologies; the impact will vary through time from minor for some companies to significant for others, and an appropriate response is required.

There are also many practical risks to manage which, if ignored, can lead to bad customer experiences and bad news stories which damage the reputation of the company. In the section on digital business opportunities, we reviewed the concept of soft lock-in; however, if the customer experience of a service is very bad, they will stop using it, and switch to other online options. Examples of poor online customer experience include:

- Websites that fail because of a spike in visitor traffic after a peak-hour TV advertising campaign.
- Hackers penetrating the security of the system and stealing credit card details.
- A company emails customers without receiving their permission, so annoying customers and potentially breaking privacy and data protection laws.
- Problems with fulfilment of goods ordered online, meaning customer orders go missing or are delayed.
- Email customer service enquiries from the website don't reach the right person and are ignored.

The perception of these risks may result in limited adoption of digital business in many organisations, which is suggested by the data in Figure 1.11. This is particularly the case for SMEs. (We study adoption levels and drivers in this type of business further in Chapter 4.)

Another approach to reviewing the strategy issues involved with implementing digital business is the classic McKinsey 7S strategy instrument (Waterman *et al.*, 1980) which is summarised in Table 10.1.

Debate 1.2

Limited SME adoption of digital business

'Adoption of digital business by established SMEs is generally less than that in larger businesses. This is principally a consequence of the negative attitude of managing directors and CEOs to the business benefits of information and communication technology (ICT).'

Evaluating an organisation's digital business capabilities

Assessment of an organisation's existing digital business capabilities is a starting point for the future development of their digital business strategy. We will see in Chapter 5 how different forms of **stage models** can be used to assess digital business capability. An example of a basic stage model reviewing capabilities for sell-side and buy-side e-commerce is shown in Figure 1.13. This shows how companies will introduce more complex technologies and extend the range of processes which are digital business-enabled. Stage 5 includes social commerce.

Stage models
Used to review how advanced a company is in its use of information and communications technology (ICT) to support different processes.

Drivers of consumer technology adoption

To determine investment in sell-side e-commerce, managers need to assess how to adopt new services such as web, mobile and interactive TV and specific services such as blogs,

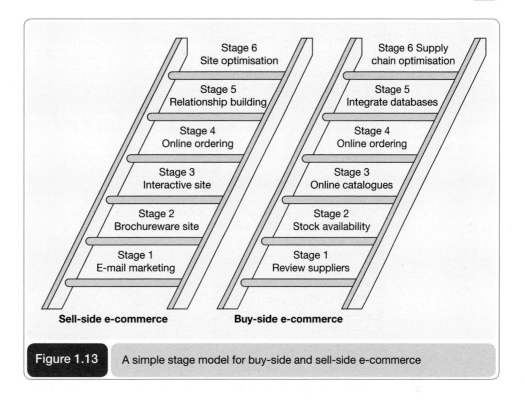

Figure 1.13   A simple stage model for buy-side and sell-side e-commerce

Online value proposition (OVP)
A statement of the benefits of online services reinforces the core proposition and differentiates from an organisation's offline offering and those of competitors.

social networks and feeds. (In Chapter 4, we see how such demand analysis is conducted in a structured way.)

We will see (in Chapter 5 on strategy development for digital business) how it is important that companies offering e-commerce services create a clear **online value proposition (OVP)** to encourage customers to use their specific online services. Typical benefits of online services are summarised by the 'Six Cs', a simple mnemonic to show different types of customer value:

1 *Content* – In the mid-1990s it was often said that 'content is king'. Well, relevant rich content is still king. This means more detailed, in-depth information to support the buying process for transactional or relationship-building sites or branded experiences to encourage product usage for FMCG brands.

2 *Customisation* – In this case mass customisation of content, whether received as website pages such as 'Amazon recommends' or email alerts, and commonly known as 'personalisation'.

3 *Community* – The Internet liberates consumers to discuss anything they wish through forums, chat-rooms and blog comments. (We will explore these techniques more in Chapters 2 and 3.)

4 *Convenience* – This is the ability to select, purchase and in some cases use products from your desktop at any time: the classic $24 \times 7 \times 365$ availability of a service. Online usage of products is, of course, restricted to digital products such as music or other data services. Amazon has advertised offline using creative ads showing a Christmas shopper battling against a gale-swept street clutching several bags to reinforce the convenience message.

5 *Choice* – The web gives a wider choice of products and suppliers than via conventional distribution channels. The success of online intermediaries such as Kelkoo (www.kelkoo.com) and Reevoo (www.reevoo.com) is evidence of this. Similarly, Tesco.com provides Tesco with a platform to give consumers a wider choice of products (financial, travel, white goods) with more detailed information than are physically available in-store.

6 *Cost reduction* – The Internet is widely perceived as a relatively low-cost place of purchase. Often customers expect to get a good deal online as they realise that online traders have

a lower cost-base as they have lower staff and distribution costs than a retailer that runs a network of high-street stores. A simple price differential is a key approach to encouraging usage of online services. In the late 1990s, low-cost airline easyJet encouraged the limited change behaviour required to move from phone booking to online booking by offering a £2.50 discount on online flight bookings.

Note that the 7Cs of Rayport and Jaworski (2003) provide a similar framework of Context, Content, Community, Customisation, Communication, Connection and Commerce.

Barriers to consumer Internet adoption

An indication of some of the barriers to using the Internet, in particular for consumer purchases, is clear from a survey (Booz Allen Hamilton, 2002) of perceptions in different countries. It noted that consumer barriers to adoption of the Internet included:

- No perceived benefit
- Lack of trust
- Security problems
- Lack of skills
- Cost

This lack of demand for Internet services still present in every country needs to be taken into account when forecasting future demand.

To complete this chapter, read Case study 1.2 for the background on the success factors which have helped build one of the world's biggest digital businesses.

Case Study 1.2	eBay – the world's largest online business?

This case summarises the strategic approach used by eBay to take advantage of increased consumer adoption of the Internet. It summarises its objectives, strategy and proposition and key risks that need management. You will see that many of its success factors are similar to those for smaller retailers.

Context

It's hard to believe that one of the most celebrated dot-coms has now been established nearly 20 years. Pierre Omidyar, a 28-year-old French-born software engineer living in California, coded the site while working for another company, eventually launching the site for business on Monday, 4 September 1995 with the more direct name 'Auction Web'. Legend reports that the site attracted no visitors in its first 24 hours. The site became eBay in 1997. By 2012, eBay had 112 million active users globally, defined as users who have bid, bought or listed an item during the preceding 12-month period, with the total worth of goods sold on eBay $60 billion, which is equivalent to $2,000 every second. Total revenue was $8.7 billion.

Mission

eBay describes its purpose as to 'pioneer new communities around the world built on commerce, sustained by trust, and inspired by opportunity'.

At the time of writing eBay comprises three major businesses:

1 The eBay marketplaces (approximately 50% of net revenues in 2012). Originally only offering auctions, by 2012, the fixed-price listing format accounted for approximately 66% of eBay's gross merchandise volume, or GMV, with the auction-style format accounting for the remaining 34% of GMV. Marketplaces also include other sites like comparison site Shopping.com and StubHub (event tickets). The mission for the core eBay business is to 'create the world's online marketplace'. eBay has also created vertical formats, such as Classifieds, Daily Deals, Fashion, Motors (vehicles, parts and accessories) and Electronics.

The marketplace platforms had more than 112 million active users at the end of 2012, compared to

100 million at the end of 2011. In 2012, nearly $13 billion was transacted on mobile platforms, more than double the mobile commerce volume from the previous year, and expected to increase to $20 billion. In 2007, eBay's SEC filing noted the success factors for this business, for which eBay sought to manage the functionality, safety, ease of use, and reliability of the trading platform. In 2010 the strategic priorities had changed to trust, value, selection and convenience.

2 PayPal (approximately 43% of net revenues in 2012). The mission is to 'create the new global standard for online payments'. This company was acquired in 2003 and is now a significant contributor to eBay revenue, with the service incorporated in many other e-commerce sites.

3 GSI (accounting for 7% of revenues in 2012) was acquired by eBay in June 2011. GSI is a provider of e-commerce and interactive marketing services, including websites and fulfilment centres, to enterprise clients that include some of the world's leading brands and retailers covering merchandise categories including apparel, sporting goods, toys & baby, health & beauty and home.

Revenue model

The vast majority of eBay's revenue is for the listing of and commission on completed sales. For PayPal purchases an additional commission fee is charged. Margin on each transaction is phenomenal, since once the infrastructure is built, incremental costs on each transaction are tiny – all eBay is doing is transmitting bits and bytes between buyers and sellers.

Advertising and other non-transaction net revenues represent a relatively small proportion of total net revenues and the strategy is that this should remain the case. Marketing services and other revenues accounted for an additional $2 billion in 2012.

Another part of the business, Skype Internet telephony, was acquired in 2005 by eBay and sold to an investor group in November 2009, with a 30% share retained by eBay.

Proposition

The eBay marketplace is well known for its core service which enables sellers to list items for sale on an auction or fixed-price basis, giving buyers the opportunity to bid for and purchase items of interest.

Software tools are provided, particularly for frequent traders, including Turbo Lister, Seller's Assistant, Selling Manager and Selling Manager Pro, which help automate the selling process, plus the Shipping Calculator, Reporting tools, etc. Today, over 60% of listings are facilitated by software, showing the value of automating posting for frequent trading.

According to the SEC filing, eBay summarises the core messages to define its proposition as follows:

For buyers:

● Trust
● Value
● Selection
● Convenience

In 2007, eBay introduced Neighborhoods (http://neighborhoods.ebay.com), where groups can discuss brands and products with which they have a high involvement.

For sellers:

● Access to broad global markets
● Efficient marketing and distribution
● Opportunity to increase sales

In January 2008, eBay announced significant changes to its marketplaces business in three major areas: fee structure, seller incentives and standards, and feedback. These changes have been controversial with some sellers, but are aimed at improving the quality of experience. Detailed Seller Ratings (DSRs) enable sellers to be reviewed in four areas: (1) item as described, (2) communication, (3) delivery time and (4) postage and packaging charges. This is part of a move to help increase conversion rate by increasing positive shopping experiences, for example by including more accurate descriptions with better pictures and avoiding excessive shipping charges. Power sellers with positive DSRs will be featured more favourably in the search results pages and will gain additional discounts.

Risk factors

Fraud is a significant risk factor for eBay. The BBC (2005) reported that around 1 in 10,000 transactions within the UK were fraudulent; 0.0001% is a small percentage, but scaling this up across the number of transactions, this is a significant volume. To counter this, eBay has developed 'Trust and Safety Programs' which are particularly important to reassure customers since online services are prone to fraud. For example, the eBay feedback forum can help establish credentials of sellers and buyers. Every registered user has a feedback profile that may contain compliments, criticisms and/or other comments by users who have conducted business with that user. The Feedback Forum requires feedback to be related to specific transactions and Top Seller status was introduced in 2010 to increase trust in the service. There is also a Safe Harbor data protection method and a standard purchase protection system.

The fees model that eBay uses is often changed and this can cause problems with users, but the impact is calculated such that it does not affect overall sales. In their 2012 SEC filing eBay note:

> We regularly announce changes to our Marketplaces business intended to drive more sales and improve seller efficiency and buyer experiences and trust. Some of the changes that we have announced to date have been controversial with, and led to dissatisfaction among, our sellers, and additional changes that we announce in the future may also be negatively received by some of our sellers. This may not only impact the supply of items listed on our websites, but because many sellers also buy from our sites, it may adversely impact demand as well.

In common with other global platforms like Amazon, Facebook and Google, eBay note the potential threat of the shift to tablet and smartphone platforms, stating that one risk factor is: 'Our ability to manage the rapid shift from online commerce and payments to mobile and multichannel commerce and payments.'

There is also the common risk factors for online pureplays of retaining an active user base, attracting new users and encouraging existing users to list items for sale, especially when consumer spending is weak.

Competition

Although there are now few direct competitors of online auction services in many countries, there are many indirect competitors. eBay (2013) describes competing channels as including online and offline retailers, distributors, liquidators, import and export companies, auctioneers, catalogue and mail-order companies, classifieds, directories, search engines, products of search engines, virtually all online and offline commerce participants, and online and offline shopping channels and networks.

In their SEC filing, eBay states that the principal competitive factors for the Marketplaces business include the following:

- ability to attract, retain and engage buyers and sellers;
- volume of transactions and price and selection of goods;
- trust in the seller and the transaction;
- customer service; and
- brand recognition.

Although eBay is one of the largest e-commerce businesses, these factors also need to be actively managed by the smallest online e-retailer. For their online and mobile competition, they describe additional competitive factors, including:

- community cohesion, interaction and size;
- website or mobile application ease-of-use and accessibility;

- system reliability;
- reliability of delivery and payment;
- level of service fees; and
- quality of search tools.

Before the advent of online auctions, competitors in the collectables space included antique shops, car boot sales and charity shops. Anecdotal evidence suggests that all of these are now suffering. Some have taken the attitude of 'if you can't beat 'em, join 'em'. Many smaller traders who have previously run antique or car boot sales are now eBayers. Even charities such as Oxfam now have an eBay service where they sell high-value items contributed by donors. Other retailers such as Vodafone have used eBay as a means to distribute certain products within their range.

Objectives and strategy

The overall eBay aims are to increase the gross merchandise volume and net revenues from the eBay marketplace. More detailed objectives are defined to achieve these aims, with strategies focussing on:

1 *Acquisition* – increasing the number of newly registered users on the eBay marketplace.
2 *Activation* – increasing the number of registered users that become active bidders, buyers or sellers on the eBay marketplace.
3 *Activity* – increasing the volume and value of transactions that are conducted by each active user on the eBay marketplace.

The focus on each of these three areas will vary according to strategic priorities in particular local markets.

eBay marketplace growth was driven by defining approaches to improve performance in these areas. First, category growth was achieved by increasing the number and size of categories within the marketplace, for example Antiques, Art, Books, and Business and Industrial. Second, formats for interaction. eBay Stores was developed to enable sellers with a wider range of products to showcase their products in a more traditional retail format, including the traditional 'Buy-It-Now' fixed-price format. eBay has constantly explored new formats, often through acquisition of other companies, for example through the acquisition in 2004 of mobile. de in Germany and Marktplaats.nl in the Netherlands, as well as investment in craigslist, the US-based classified ad format. Another acquisition is Rent.com, which enables expansion into the online housing and apartment rental category. In 2007, eBay acquired StubHub, an online ticket marketplace, and it also owns comparison marketplace Shopping.com. Finally, marketplace growth is achieved through delivering specific sites localised for different geographies as follows. You can see there is still potential for greater localisation, for example in parts of Scandinavia, Eastern Europe and Asia.

Localised eBay marketplaces:

- Australia
- Austria
- Belgium
- Canada
- Singapore
- South Korea
- Spain
- France
- Germany
- Hong Kong
- India
- Ireland
- Sweden
- Switzerland
- Italy
- Malaysia
- Netherlands
- New Zealand
- Philippines
- United Kingdom
- United States

In addition, eBay has a presence in Latin America through its investment in MercadoLibre.

eBay's growth strategy

In its SEC filing, success factors eBay believes are important to enable it to compete in its market include:

- ability to attract buyers and sellers;
- volume of transactions and price and selection of goods;
- customer service; and
- brand recognition.

This implies that eBay believes it has optimised these factors, but its competitors still have opportunities for improving performance in these areas which will make the market more competitive. According to its 2010 SEC filing: 'Our growth strategy is focused on reinvesting in our customers by improving the buyer experience and seller economics by enhancing our products and services, improving trust and safety and customer support, extending our product offerings into new formats, categories and geographies, and implementing innovative pricing and buyer retention strategies.'

Updates on eBay case study information

eBay company pages (http://pages.ebay.co.uk/aboutebay.html)

eBay investor relations (http://investor.ebay.com/index.cfm)

eBay SEC filings (http://investor.ebayinc.com/financial_releases.cfm)

eBay Wikipedia page (http://en.wikipedia.org/wiki/EBay)

Question

Assess how the characteristics of the digital media and the Internet together with strategic decisions taken by its management team have supported eBay's continued growth.

Summary

1 Electronic commerce traditionally refers to electronically mediated buying and selling.

2 Sell-side e-commerce or digital marketing involves all electronic business transactions between an organisation and its customers, while buy-side e-commerce involves transactions between an organisation and its suppliers. Social commerce encourages customers to interact to support sales goals.

3 'Digital business' or e-business is a broader term, referring to how technology can benefit all internal business processes and interactions with third parties. This includes buy-side and sell-side e-commerce and the internal value chain.

4 Digital marketing involves investment in paid, owned and earned media across the six key digital marketing media channels of search engine marketing, online PR and social media, partnerships, display advertising, email marketing and viral marketing. Inbound marketing describes the use of integrated content, social media and search marketing to influence consumers as they select products, sometimes referred to as the Zero Moment of Truth.

5 Web 2.0 is used to refer to web services that facilitate interaction of web users with sites to create user-generated content and encourage behaviours such as community or social network participation, mashups, content rating, use of widgets and tagging.

6 The main business drivers for introducing e-commerce and digital business are opportunities for increased revenues and reducing costs, but many other benefits can be identified that improve customer service and corporate image.

7   Consumer adoption of the digital technology is limited by lack of imperative, cost of access and security fears. Business adoption tends to be restricted by perceptions of cost, making return on investment difficult to quantify.

8   Introducing new technology is not all that is required for success in introducing e-commerce and digital business. Clearly defined objectives, creating the right culture for change, mix of skills, partnerships and organisational structure are arguably more important.

Exercises

Answers to these exercises are available online at www.pearsoned.co.uk/chaffey

Self-assessment questions

1   Distinguish between e-commerce and digital business.

2   Explain what is meant by buy-side and sell-side e-commerce.

3   Explain the scope and benefits of social media and social commerce to an organisation of your choice.

4   Summarise the consumer and business adoption levels in your country. What seem to be the main barriers to adoption?

5   Outline the reasons why a business may wish to adopt e-commerce.

6   What are the main differences between business-to-business and business-to-consumer e-commerce?

7   Summarise the impact of the introduction of digital business on different aspects of an organisation.

8   What is the relevance of intermediary or influencer sites to a B2C company?

Essay and discussion questions

1   Suggest how an organisation can evaluate the impact of digital technology on its business. Is it a passing fad or does it have a significant impact?

2   Explain the concepts of social media and social commerce and how they can assist organisations in reaching their objectives.

3   Similar benefits and barriers exist for the adoption of sell-side e-commerce for both B2B and B2C organisations. Discuss.

4   Evaluate how social media marketing techniques can be applied within an organisation and with its stakeholders.

5   The web presence of a company has similar aims regardless of the sector in which the company operates.

Examination questions

1   Explain the relationship between the concepts of e-commerce and digital business.

2   Distinguish between buy-side and sell-side e-commerce and give an example of the application of each.

3   Summarise three reasons why a company may wish to introduce e-commerce.

4   Describe three of the main barriers to adoption of e-commerce by consumers and suggest how a company could counter these.

5 Outline the internal changes a company may need to make when introducing digital business.

6 Summarise the benefits of applying social media marketing approaches to an organisation.

7 Name three risks to a company that introduces buy-side e-commerce.

8 Name three risks to a company that introduces sell-side e-commerce.

References

BBC (2005) eBay's 10-year rise to world fame. By Robert Plummer. Story from BBC News, 2 September. **http://news.bbc.co.uk/1/hi/business/4207510.stm**.

Booz Allen Hamilton (2002) International E-Economy: Benchmarking the World's Most Effective Policies for the E-Economy. Report published 19 November 2002, London.

Boyd, D. and Ellison, N. (2007) Social network sites: definition, history, and scholarship. *Journal of Computer-Mediated Communication*, 13 (1), 210–30.

Chaffey, D. and Smith, P.R. (2012) *Emarketing Excellence: Planning and Optimizing Your Digital Marketing*, 4th edn. Routledge, London.

comScore (2010) comScore Media Metrix Ranks Top-Growing Properties and Site Categories for April 2010. Press release, 10 May: **www.comscore.com/Press_Events/ Press_Releases/2010/5/comScore_Media_Metrix_Ranks_Top-Growing_Properties_ and_Site_Categories_for_April_2010**.

Danneels, E. (2004) Disruptive technology reconsidered: a critique and research agenda. *Journal of Product Innovation Management*, 21 (4), 246–58.

Doherty, N., Ellis-Chadwick, F. and Hart, C. (2003) An analysis of the factors affecting the adoption of the Internet in the UK retail sectors. *Journal of Business Research*, 56, 887–97.

DTI (2000) *Business in the Information Age – International Benchmarking Study 2000*. UK Department of Trade and Industry.

eBay (2013) Annual SEC filing 2013. **http://investor.ebayinc.com/sec.cfm**.

Economist (2000) E-commerce survey. Define and sell. *Supplement*, 26 February, 6–12.

eEurope (2005) Information Society Benchmarking Report. From eEurope (2005) initiative. Published at: **http://europa.eu.int/information_society/eeurope/i2010/docs/bench-marking/051222%20Final%20Benchmarking%20Report.pdf**.

Evans, P. and Wurster, T.S. (1997) Strategy and the new economics of information. *Harvard Business Review*, September–October, 70–82.

Facebook (2013) Annual SEC filing 2013: **http://investor.fb.com/sec.cfm**.

Flurry (2013) Flurry Five-Year Report: It's an App World. The Web Just Lives in It. Blog post by Simon Khalaf, 3 April 2013: **http://blog.flurry.com/bid/95723/ Flurry-Five-Year-Report-It-s-an-App-World-The-Just-Web-Lives-in-It**.

Grove, A. (1996) *Only the Paranoid Survive*. Doubleday, New York.

Hoffman, D.L. and Novak, T.P. (1996) Marketing in hypermedia computer-mediated environments: conceptual foundations. *Journal of Marketing*, 60 (July), 50–68.

Kalakota, R. and Whinston, A. (1997) *Electronic Commerce: A Manager's Guide*. Addison-Wesley, Reading, MA.

Lecinski, J. (2012) Winning the Zero Moment of Truth. Published by Google, available from **www.zeromomentoftruth.com/**.

Mougayer, M. (1998) E-commerce? E-business? Who e-cares? *Computer World* website (**www.computerworld.com**), 2 November.

Nielsen (2010) The State of Mobile Apps, June 2010: **http://blog.nielsen.com/nielsenwire/ online_mobile/the-state-of-mobile-apps/**.

O'Reilly, T. (2005) What Is Web 2? Design Patterns and Business Models for the Next Generation of Software. Web article, 30 September. O'Reilly Publishing, Sebastopol, CA.

Page, M. (2012), How to improve Edge Rank. Blog post, 7 July 2012, Smart Insights: **www.smartinsights.com/social-media-marketing/facebook-marketing/ how-to-improve-edgerank-part-2/**.

Perrott, B. (2005) Towards a manager's model of e-business strategy decisions. *Journal of General Management*, 30 (4), Summer.

Rayport, J. and Jaworski, B. (2003) *Introduction to E-Commerce*, 2nd edn. McGraw-Hill, New York.

Shah, D. and Halligan, B. (2009) *Inbound Marketing: Get Found Using Google, Social Media and Blogs*. John Wiley & Sons, Hoboken, NJ.

Smart Insights (2012) Ship Early, Ship Often. By Dave Chaffey, 4 September 2012. Blog post: **www.smartinsights.com/goal-setting-evaluation/web-analytics-strategy/ ship-early-ship-often/**.

Smart Insights (2013) A Digital Campaign Example of a Startup Fashion Brand. Blog post, 25 April 2013: **www.smartinsights.com/traffic-building-strategy/campaign-planning/ startup-fashion-brand-campaign-example/**.

Spivack (2009) How the WebOS Evolves? Nova Spivack blog post, 9 February: **www. novaspivack.com/?s=How+the+WebOS+Evolves%3F**.

Waterman, R.H., Peters, T.J. and Phillips, J.R. (1980) Structure is not organization. *McKinsey Quarterly* in-house journal, McKinsey & Co., New York.

Weinberg, T. (2010) *The New Community Rules: Marketing on The Social Web*. John Wiley & Sons, Hoboken, NJ.

Yammer (2010) Suncorp case study, accessed May 2010, Yammer website: **https://about. yammer.com/customers/suncorp/**.

Web links

Sites giving general information on market characteristics of digital business:

ClickZ Stats (**www.clickz.com/stats/**) The definitive source of news on Internet developments, and reports on company and consumer adoption of the Internet and characteristics in Europe and worldwide. A searchable digest of most analyst reports.

European Commission Information Society Statistics (**http://ec.europa.eu/information_ society/digital-agenda/index_en.htm**) Reports evaluating digital business activity and consumer adoption across the European Union.

Econsultancy.com (**www.econsultancy.com**) Research, best practice reports and supplier directory for online marketing.

Mary Meeker (**www.kpcb.com/insights**) An analyst at Kleiner Perkins Caufield Byers who presents trends and forecasts on digital technology yearly with a focus on mobile channels.

Ofcom (**http://stakeholders.ofcom.org.uk/**) The Office of Communication has an annual Communications Market report on the adoption of digital media including telecommunications and the Internet (including broadband adoption), digital television and wireless services.

Smart Insights (**www.smartinsights.com**) Guidance on digital marketing best practice from Dave Chaffey to help businesses succeed online. It includes alerts on the latest developments in applying digital technology and templates to create marketing plans and budgets.

2

Marketplace analysis for e-commerce

Web support

The following additional case studies are available at
www.pearsoned.co.uk/chaffey

→ Dynamic pricing at GlaxoSmithKline
→ Ahold explores new ways to reach customers
→ The implications of broadband access
→ Learning from the dot-coms

The site also contains a range of study material designed to help improve your results.

Scan code to find the latest updates for topics in this chapter

Learning outcomes

After completing this chapter the reader should be able to:

- Complete an online marketplace analysis to assess competitor, customer, and intermediary use of digital technologies and media as part of strategy development
- Identify the main business and marketplace models for electronic communications and trading
- Evaluate the effectiveness of business and revenue models for online businesses, paticularly online start-up businesses

Management issues

The fundamentals of e-commerce imply these questions for managers:

- What are the implications of changes in marketplace structures for how we trade with customers and other partners?
- Which business models and revenue models should we consider in order to exploit the Internet?
- What will be the importance of online intermediaries and marketplace hubs to our business and what actions should we take to partner these intermediaries?

Links to other chapters

The main related chapters are:

- *Chapter 3* explains the hardware and software infrastructure enabling these new business models
- *Chapters 4* and *5* consider appropriate strategic responses to these new models and paradigms
- *Chapter 6* explores new models of the value chain in more detail
- *Chapter 7* explores the effect of new intermediaries and marketplaces on procurement
- *Chapter 9* discusses models of online customer behaviour which is another aspect of environment analysis

Introduction

Online marketplace
Exchanges of information and commercial transactions between consumers, businesses and governments completed through different forms of online presence such as search engines, social networks, comparison sites and destination sites.

Path to purchase
The different sites, channels, devices and information sources that consumers use to inform their purchase decision for a product or service. Also known as conversion pathways on a site.

Multiscreening
A term used to describe simultaneous use of devices such as digital TV and tablets.

Destination site
Typically a retailer or manufacturer site with sales and service information. Intermediaries such as media sites may be destination sites for some.

Online intermediaries
Websites which help connect web users with content they are seeking on destination sites. Includes new online intermediaries such as search engines and shopping comparison sites and traditional brokers, directories and newspaper and magazine publishers that now have an online presence.

In the first part of Chapter 2 we show how companies can review their presence in the **online marketplace** to increase their visibility across different customer touchpoints The **path to purchase** is now much complex since purchase decisions are influenced by many more touchpoints today. For example, decisions are influenced when accessing social media sites via desktop and mobile sites plus communications in traditional channels. Increasingly multiple devices are used simultaneously, for example when using smartphones or tablets while watching TV, the process known as **multiscreening**.

To determine the best way to influence purchasers requires careful consideration. Businesses must collect and review insights that help them understand this behaviour and then improve their visibility and communications on different channels to improve this. Consider a B2B organisation. Traditionally it will have sold its products through a network of distributors. With the advent of e-commerce, it now has the opportunity to bypass distributors and trade directly with customers via a destination website, and it also has the opportunity to reach customers through new types of online sites such as blogs and B2B marketplaces. Similarly, for B2C organisations such as an e-retail **destination site** there is the opportunity to market its products through **online intermediaries** or influencers such as search engines, price comparison sites, social networks, blogs and other publisher sites. We will show you how different information sources can be used to assess customer usage of different types of intermediary. We then look at how electronic communications have facilitated restructuring of the relationships between members of the electronic marketplace – a key feature of e-commerce.

Business and revenue models for e-commerce

Electronic communications have also given rise to many exciting new business and revenue models that we evaluate in the second part of this chapter. We will use the Business Model Canvas which is an excellent framework for reviewing the business models for both online start-up businesses and existing businesses who are developing new propositions. Throughout this chapter we mainly consider the sell-side elements of e-commerce rather than the digital business as a whole. (A review of the entire supply chain is completed in Chapter 6.)

Our *Digital business in Practice interview* with Michael Welch of online start-up Blackcircles.com gives an example of what a well-managed, customer-focussed online business can deliver.

Online marketplace analysis

Situation analysis
Collection and review of information about an organisation's external environment and internal processes and resources in order to inform its strategies.

Environmental scanning and analysis
The process of continuously monitoring the environment and events and responding accordingly.

Understanding the online elements of an organisation's environment, which are shown in Figure 2.1, is a key part of **situation analysis** for digital business strategy development. There is also the need for a process to continually monitor the environment, which is often referred to as **environmental scanning**.

Knowledge of the opportunities and threats presented by these marketplace changes is essential to those involved in defining business, marketing and information systems strategy (which we cover in Chapter 5). In this chapter we introduce a number of frameworks for analysing the immediate marketplace of the micro-environment.

To inform e-commerce strategy, the most significant influences are those of the immediate marketplace of the micro-environment that is shaped by the needs of customers and how services are provided to them through competitors and intermediaries and via upstream suppliers. (In Chapter 4 we examine the issues of the broader e-commerce environment in more detail using the SLEPT framework to examine Social, Legal, Economic, Political and Technological issues.)

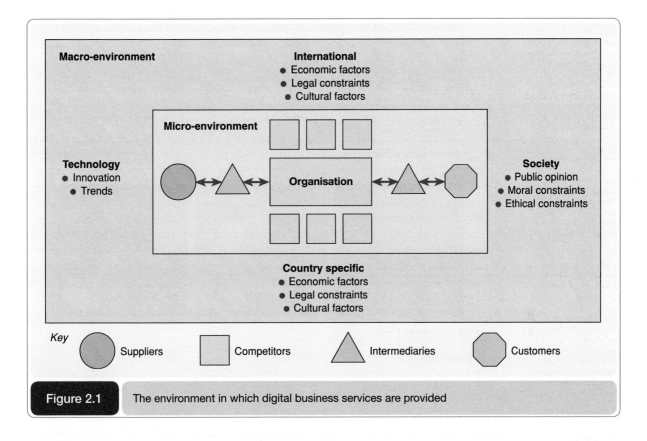

| **Figure 2.1** | The environment in which digital business services are provided |

Michael Welch of Blackcircles.com on creating a new online business

Overview and concepts covered

Michael Welch created Blackcircles.com (Figure 2.2) as a new way for consumers to buy tyres at competitive prices either over the Internet or on the telephone. From the site, consumers can find the best deal from a network of over 1,400 local dealerships.

Blackcircles.com now has a turnover of £30 million and is growing rapidly, so we thought it would be interesting to learn the approaches its founder, Michael Welch, has used to grow and sustain the business.

Q. Which factors were important to the initial success of Blackcircles.com?

Michael Welch, Blackcircles.com: At the very beginning it was mainly about hard work, determination and not 'taking no for an answer'. If I'm honest there was no real difference between me and the next guy walking down the street – I just wanted it more.

A key factor in the company getting to where it is today, though, was also having a strong USP (unique selling point). There were a couple of other companies around at the same time with a similar USP and there are now countless smaller operations that seem to have modelled their USP on ours.

| Figure 2.2 | BlackCircles.com
Source: Black Circles Ltd. |

Providing a culture of excellent customer service is an obvious way to go; back when you are a new company – at times – it is all you have. When brand awareness is zero to slim, you have to work as hard as possible to show the customers at first use that you – and in reality you are taking a gamble – that you give a damn and that their gamble has paid off. I worked hard to make sure customers came first.

Q. Which marketing activities are important to your continued growth?

Michael Welch, Blackcircles.com: The base of our continued growth actually hasn't altered much from those early days. Customer satisfaction is still very much key, the desire to make the company a success is there and our USP is just as strong as it was back at the start of the last decade.

I suppose there has been a shift in that we were once the underdogs and now we are leading the pack. Implementing new ideas and technologies has played a major part in helping us to stay on top, i.e. making sure we are up to date with the best SEO techniques, embracing the world of social media and continually trying to offer more attractive services to our customers – the launch of car servicing being one such evolution on the original 'tyre retailer' tag that Blackcircles.com started with.

Underneath all that, though the company is supported by a foundation of 'getting the basics right'.

Q. How do you manage and improve service quality?

Michael Welch, Blackcircles.com: It's a vital ongoing process. The most obvious way in which we check on the site's service quality is through customer feedback. This has been the backbone of many changes we've made over the years. Our customers are a great resource and I'm often surprised at the number of people I meet who don't listen to what their customers are saying to them – it's free advice, why wouldn't you take it?

We recently placed Trustpilot on our website which is the online retail industry's equivalent of Trip Advisor. This shows independent customer reviews and an overall rating. This is a further commitment from us and a great message to customers that we will be doing everything possible to give them a great service. We are passionate about great service.

On top of listening to what our customers are saying we also actively take part in user-testing. We've been working with a company recently which records anonymous users (which you can define, i.e. British person in mid-30s who doesn't often use the Internet to shop) on our site.

Not only are we able to see what they are doing, but they also giving a narration of their thoughts. Its early days but we've already discovered areas of the site that can be improved due to this.

The newest form of testing we're just beginning to get involved with is a heat-map-style technology. Seeing where users are clicking and where they are not is great. It makes you ask why certain areas of a page are receiving attention while the rest is being ignored.

Q. How do you review the success of your site, which approaches do you use?

Michael Welch, Blackcircles.com: As far as I'm concerned, if you don't include web analytics in your marketing plan, then quite simply, you don't have a marketing plan.

Gone are the days when all website owners ever worried about was visitor numbers – good riddance too as it means we don't have to put up with those horrible 'visitor counters' that you used to see bandied about everywhere.

Understanding not just how many visitors you have, but also how they are using your site is invaluable. We actively check out this information on a regular basis. A quick example would be: what percentage of our visitors search for tyres? From this, what percentage then adds a set of tyres to their basket and then how many actually end up on the payment confirmation page?

Looking at these stats we can see at what point in an order process people exit our site. Then we ask ourselves what content is on each page, are there enough calls to actions? Is there enough information? Is it easy to navigate? Could we add in new content to encourage people to buy? If we come up with a potential change that we believe will help a page perform better, we then track to see the difference. If conversions go up, great – but how can we improve it further? If they drop – back to the drawing board.

Not only do we see the importance on an 'order process'-based analysis, but also using it for certain technical aspects. For instance, customers with one browser end up buying in greater percentages than those with a different browser. OK, so is there a piece of code on a page that is affecting the customers' experience? Or is it even a demographic thing?

All this is just scratching the surface. Web analytics can answer so many questions you didn't even know you needed to ask. The trick is not getting overawed – it is too easy to get lost in an ocean of statistics.

Q. Which new approaches in the marketplace are you reviewing currently?

Michael Welch, Blackcircles.com: The use of video is an interesting avenue that we are keenly pursuing at the moment. Audio and visual are right up there in terms of brand development and with the sheer number of opportunities available on the web online videos have never been more exciting. We're still testing the water at the moment with a new 'Blackcircles.com TV' channel on YouTube, but I'm pleased with the results so far.

In a bit of a more traditional sense we are also enhancing our email campaigns. However, I'm very wary of over saturating our customers with information that they will just mark as spam. The key goal for us at the moment is engaging our customers with the brand. Social media is playing a large role in this as well, as you would expect.

Strategic agility
The capability to innovate and so gain competitive advantage within a marketplace by monitoring changes within an organisation's marketplace and then to efficiently evaluate alternative strategies and select, review and implement appropriate candidate strategies.

Strategic agility

The capacity to respond to these environmental opportunities and threats is commonly referred to as strategic agility. **Strategic agility** is a concept strongly associated with knowledge management theory and is based on developing a sound process for reviewing marketplace opportunities and threats and then selecting the appropriate strategy options.

Mini Case Study 2.1 | The Marine Corps demonstrates strategic agility

Professor Donald N. Sull is an Associate Professor of Management Practice in the Strategy and International Management faculty at the London Business School.

In the first video tutorial, 'Fog of the Future' on strategic agility (visit www.ft.com/multimedia and search for 'London Business School'), he asserts that traditional management models of creating a long-term vision are flawed since our knowledge of the future is always imperfect and marketplace conditions are changing continuously (Figure 2.3). Rather than being the captain of a ship surveying the far horizon, analogous with the top-down model of strategy, the reality for managers is that their situation is more akin to that of a racing car driver on a foggy day, constantly looking to take the right decisions based on the mass of information about their

Figure 2.3 | Professor Donald Sull of London Business School talks about strategic agility
Source: www.ft.com.

surroundings coming through the fog. He believes that having a clear long-term vision, particularly where it isn't based on environment analysis, isn't practical in most industries. Instead he says that companies should '*keep vision fuzzy but current priorities clear*'.

In a second video tutorial, 'Strategic Agility', Sull explains the basis for strategic agility. He explains that all knowledge of the future is based on uncertainty, but that managers must act now, so they need to put in place US Marine Corps-style reconnaissance missions as an army would in order to make their battle plans. He gives the example of Dell, explaining how they spend relatively little on research and development, but are instead constantly probing the marketplace, trialling new ideas with multiple probes into the approach. He stresses the importance of finding anomalies in the marketplace where it doesn't appear as expected and that these may represent learnings or opportunities. Detailed customer insights and business performance are necessary to identify these anomalies. Finally, he makes the point of the need to act rapidly to have scalability to 'swarm the gap in the defences of the enemy' where there is a strong opportunity.

In a digital business context, we can see that strategic agility requires these characteristics and requirements for an organisation to be successful in its strategy development:

1 Efficient collection, dissemination and evaluation of different information sources from the micro- and macro-environment.
2 Effective process for generating and reviewing the relevance of new strategies based on creating new value for customers.
3 Efficient research into potential customer value against the business value generated.
4 Efficient implementation of prototypes of new functionality to deliver customer value.
5 Efficient measurement and review of results from prototypes to revise further to improve proposition or to end trial.

A process for online marketplace analysis

Click ecosystem

Describes the customer behaviour or flow of online visitors between search engines, media sites, other intermediaries to an organisation and its competitors.

Analysis of the online marketplace or 'marketspace' is a key part of developing a long-term digital business plan or creating a shorter-term digital marketing campaign. Completing a marketplace analysis helps to define the main types of online presence that are part of a '**click ecosystem**' which describes the customer journeys or flow of online visitors between search engines, media sites and other intermediaries to an organisation and its competitors. Prospects and customers in an online marketplace will naturally turn to search engines to find products, services, brands and entertainment. Search engines act as a distribution system which connects searchers to different intermediary sites for different phrases, so the flow of visits between sites must be understood by the marketer in their sector.

Online market ecosystem

describes the customer behaviour or flow of online visitors between search engines, media sites, other intermediaries to an organisation and its competitors.

Major online players such as Facebook, Google and Salesforce have developed their own infrastructure or online market ecosystem which connects websites through data exchange, giving opportunities to enhance the customer experience and extend their reach and influence. For example, Facebook has developed the Facebook platform API to enable exchange of data between websites and applications, including mobile apps. This enables other site owners to incorporate information about consumer Facebook interactions into their own websites and apps and share social objects across the Facebook ecosystem to extend their reach. Google has developed its own ecosystem related to search marketing and mobile – the Android ecosystem. As part of marketplace analysis, companies have to evaluate the relative importance of these ecosystems and the resources they need to put into integrating their online services with them, to create a plan.

Analysing the impact of different ecosystems on online consumer behaviour or customer journeys is, today, as important as observing their physical behaviour in the real world.

Activity 2.1   Online ecosystems

Purpose

To explore the increasing importance of facilitating communications through online platforms and service providers.

Activity

Discuss in a group, or make notes to identify, the main companies (e.g. Facebook) and platforms (e.g. tablet devices) used by consumers that are important for companies to review their presence on. Once you have identified the main company or service types, group them together so that their overall importance can be reviewed.

Answers to activities can be found at www.pearsoned.co.uk/chaffey

---

Mini Case Study 2.2   Using real-time experience tracking (RET) to assess the impact of omnichannel communications on customer touchpoints

Real-time experience tracking involves asking a consumer panel to send text messages on their cellphones every time they see a message or reference to a given brand or one of its competitors over a period of a week to a month, depending on the length of the purchase process. The structured four-character message captures the brand, the touchpoint type (Saw a tweet about it? Saw it in a shop window?), how positive the customer felt about the encounter, and how persuasive it was. Respondents add further detail online, and fill in surveys at the start and end of the study to record brand attitude changes.

Examples of RET in action

RET can be used to assess how consumers perceive brands in different markets; for example, Unilever could not understand why a campaign for Axe body spray wasn't working in Italy when it was performing well in Poland. In both countries, TV advertising was positively received. But whereas in Poland the ads were followed by high-street touchpoints such as the 'Axe Police' – attractive women who would 'arrest' young men and spray them with Axe – such reminders close to potential purchase moments were missing in Italy. RET can also diagnose how attitudes lead to the next step in the chain, as one major international charity discovered. The charity, which relies on a large network of stores selling both second-hand and new goods to raise both revenue and awareness, recently applied RET in an effort to understand why direct donations (as opposed to store profits) to the charity were falling. The RET project revealed that the in-store experience of customers was rather mixed; quite a few people felt that the stores were poorly organised and deduced from this that the charity probably wasn't very good at helping its beneficiaries either.

RET can also help highlight the relative influence of channels, including those that are less easy to track than online channels. In another example, PepsiCo used RET to fine-tune its re-launch of Gatorade in Mexico, repositioning the brand around sports nutrition. They soon found that experiences in gyms and parks (seeing posters or seeing other people drinking Gatorade, for instance) were twice as effective in shifting brand attitudes as similar encounters elsewhere. They were able to quickly shift more ad and distribution resources into these touchpoints and pass on what they learnt as Gatorade was re-launched in other Latin American countries.

Source: MacDonald *et al.* (2012).

| Figure 2.4 | An online marketplace map |

The main elements of the online marketplace map presented in Figure 2.4 which should be reviewed as part of the process of marketplace analysis are:

1 **Customer segments**

   The marketplace analysis should identify and summarise different target segments for an online business in order to then understand their online media consumption, buyer behaviour and the type of content and experiences they will be looking for from intermediaries and your website. (We cover customer analysis further in Chapter 9.)

2 **Search intermediaries**

   These are the main search engines in each country. Typically they are Google, Yahoo!, Microsoft Live Search and Ask, but others are important in some markets such as China (Baidu), Russia (Yandex) and South Korea (Naver). You can use audience panel data from different providers indicated in Box 2.1 to find out their relative importance in different countries. The Google Trends tool (Figure 2.5) is a free tool for assessing site popularity and the searches used to find sites and how they vary seasonally, which is useful for student assignments. The example in Figure 2.5 shows relative preference for three social networks.

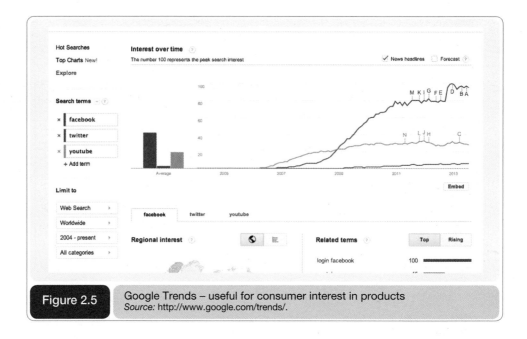

Figure 2.5 Google Trends – useful for consumer interest in products
Source: http://www.google.com/trends/.

Choi and Varian (2009) note that Google Trends data on search volumes through time is very useful for predicting levels of spending. They argue that 'because Google Trends data are practically available in real time, any statistical relationship between actual sales and Google Trends can be exploited to produce more timely estimates of consumer demand'.

Companies need to know which sites are effective in harnessing search traffic and either partner with them or try to obtain a share of the search traffic using the search engine marketing and affiliate marketing techniques explained in Chapter 9. Well-known, trusted brands which have developed customer loyalty are in a good position to succeed online since a common consumer behaviour is to go straight to the site through entering a URL, a bookmark, email or searching for the brand or URL. Hitwise provides this type of insight, as shown in Table 2.1. Through evaluating the type and volume of phrases used to search for products in a given market it is possible to calculate the total potential opportunity and the current share of search terms for a company. '**Share of search**' can be determined from web analytics reports from the company site which indicate the precise key phrases used by visitors to actually reach a site.

3 Intermediaries, influencers and media sites

Media sites and other intermediaries such as aggregators, affiliates and influencers such as blogs are often successful in attracting visitors via search or direct since they are mainstream brands. Companies need to assess potential online media and distribution partners in the categories shown in Figure 2.4 such as:

(a) **Mainstream news media sites or portals.** Include traditional, e.g. FT.com or Times, or pureplay e.g. Google news, an aggregator.

(b) **Social networks,** e.g. Facebook, Google+, Twitter and LinkedIn.

(c) **Niche or vertical media sites,** e.g. SmartInsights.com, SearchEngineLand.com, ClickZ.com coveringB2B marketing.

(d) **Price comparison sites** (also known **aggregators**), e.g. Moneysupermarket, Kelkoo, Shopping.com, uSwitch.

(e) **Superaffiliates. Affiliates** gain revenue from a merchant they refer traffic to using a commission-based arrangement based on the proportion of sale or a fixed amount. They are important in e-retail markets, accounting for tens of per cent of sales.

Share of search
The audience share of Internet searches achieved by a particular audience in a particular market.

Aggregators
An alternative term for price comparison sites. Aggregators include product, price and service information, comparing competitors within a sector such as financial services, retail or travel. Their revenue models commonly include affiliate revenues (CPA), pay-per-click advertising (CPC) and display advertising (CPM).

Affiliate
A company promoting a merchant typically through a commission-based arrangement either directly or through an affiliate network.

Table 2.1	Search terms			
Search Term	**Food retailers**	**Volume of search relative to the top term**	**Textiles clothing and footware**	**Volume of search relative to the top term**
1 Top term	Tesco	100	Shoes	100
2	ASDA	50	Boots	75
3	Tesco Direct	15	Dress	55
4	Morrisons	10	Clothes	45
5	Sainsbury's	10	Next	40
6	Aldi	5	Dresses	35
7	Clubcard	5	Nike	35
8	George ASDA	5	River island	35
9	Ocado	5	Watches	35
10	Sainsbury	5	New look	30

Source: Chamberlin (2010).

(f) **Niche affiliates, influencers or bloggers.** These are often individuals, but they may be important; for example, in the UK, Martin Lewis of Moneysavingexpert.com receives millions of visits every month. Smaller affiliates and bloggers can be important collectively.

Again, the relative importance of these site types can be assessed using the services summarised in Box 2.1.

4 **Destination sites**

Online value proposition (OVP)

A statement of the benefits of e-commerce service that ideally should not be available in competitor offerings or offline offerings.

These are the sites that the marketer is trying to generate visitors to, whether these are transactional sites, like retailers, financial services or travel companies or manufacturers or brands. Figure 2.4 refers to OVP or **online value proposition** which is a summary of the unique features of the site (see Chapters 4 and 8). The OVP is a key aspect to consider within marketplace analysis – marketers should evaluate their OVPs against competitors' as part of competitor analysis and think about how they can refine them to develop a unique online experience. (Competitor analysis is also covered in Chapter 8.)

Box 2.1	Resources for analysing the online marketplace

There is a wealth of research about current Internet usage and future trends which strategists can use to understand their marketplace. In Table 2.2, we summarise a selection of free and paid-for services which can be used for online marketplace analysis to assess the number of people searching for information and the popularity of different types of sites measured by the number of **unique visitors**.

E-consultancy (www.e-consultancy.com) provides a summary of much of the latest research from these sources together with its own reports such as the Internet Statistics compendium. The pages I curate on Smart Insights link to the latest sources on online consumer behaviour which we introduced in Chapter 1 (www.smartinsights. com/book-support).

Unique visitors

Individual visitors to a site measured through cookies or IP addresses on an individual computer.

Table 2.2	Research tools for assessing your digital marketplace

Service	Usage
1 Google tools Mainly included within their Adwords service (http://adwords.google.com)	Google is one of the best sources of accurate tools for marketplace analysis including: • Placement tool (this Adwords tool shows relative size and audience of publishers in the Google programme) • Google Trends – variation through time of search volume by country – no sign-in required Keyword Planner – this tool available within AdWords gives additional detail.
2 Alexa (www.alexa.com). Free tool, but not based on a representative sample, see also www.similarweb.com. The Google Trends for Websites (http://trends.google.com/websites, Figure 2.5) gives this information using a larger sample size.	Free service owned by Amazon which provides traffic ranking of individual sites compared to all sites. Works best for sites in top 100,000. Sample dependent on users of the Alexa toolbar. Compete.com provides another alternative.
3 Hitwise (www.hitwise.com). Paid tool, but free research available at http://weblogs.hitwise.com and Data centres.	Paid service available in some countries to compare audience size and search and site usage. Works through monitoring IP traffic to different sites through ISPs.
4 Nielsen (www.nielsen.com). Paid tool. Free data on search engines and intermediaries available from press-release section.	Panel service based on at-home and at-work users who have agreed to have their web usage tracked by software. Top rankings on-site give examples of most popular sites in several countries.
5 ComScore www.comscore.com. Paid tool. Free data on search engines and intermediaries available from press-release section.	A similar panel service to Netratings, but focusing on the US and UK. A favoured tool for media planners.
6 Google Analytics	Free and paid-for services, which provide insight into website audience behaviour.
7 Forrester (www.forrester.com). Paid research service. Some free commentary and analysis within blogs (http://blogs.forrester.com).	Offers reports on Internet usage and best practice in different vertical sectors such as financial services, retail and travel. Free research summaries available in press-release section and on its Marketing blog (http://blogs.forrester.com).
8 Smart Insights Digital Marketing Statistics (http://bit.ly/smartstatistics).	A regularly updated compilation of statistics including the top 10 recommended statistics sources.
9 Internet or Interactive Advertising Bureau (IAB) US: www.iab.net, UK: iab.uk.net, Europe: www.iabeurope.eu (see also www.eiaa.net).	Research focussing on investment in different digital media channels, in particular display ads and search marketing.
10 Internet Media in Retail Group (IMRG) www.imrg.org.	The IMRG has compilations on online e-commerce expenditure and most popular retailers in the UK.

Location of trading in the marketplace

Electronic marketplace
A virtual marketplace such as the Internet in which no direct contact occurs between buyers and sellers.

While traditional marketplaces have a physical location, an Internet-based market has no physical presence – it is a virtual marketplace. Rayport and Sviokla (1996) used this distinction to coin a new term: **electronic marketplace**. This has implications for the way in which the relationships between the different actors in the marketplace occur.

The new electronic marketplace has many alternative virtual locations where an organisation needs to position itself to communicate and sell to its customers. Managers need to understand the relative importance of different types of sites and consumer and business interactions and information flows. In this section we will review how marketplace channel structures, the location of trading and multichannel marketing models can be assessed to inform digital business strategy. Finally, we will review commercial arrangements for transactions.

Review of marketplace channel structures

Marketplace channel structures describe the way a manufacturer or organisation delivers products and services to its customers. Typical channel structures between business and consumer organisations are shown in Figure 2.6.

Disintermediation
The removal of intermediaries such as distributors or brokers that formerly linked a company to its customers.

A distribution channel will consist of one or more intermediaries such as wholesalers and retailers. The relationship between a company and its channel partners shown in Figure 2.6 can be dramatically altered by the opportunities afforded by the Internet. This occurs because the Internet offers a means of bypassing some of the channel partners. This process is known as **disintermediation** or 'cutting out the middleman'. For example, a music company today can distribute digital tracks straight to sites such as iTunes and Napster, a major change to their channel strategy which has led to the closure of many music stores. Bands can even bypass retailers and sell direct; for example, in 2008 Radiohead released their *In Rainbows* album direct from their site, allowing purchasers to name their own price!

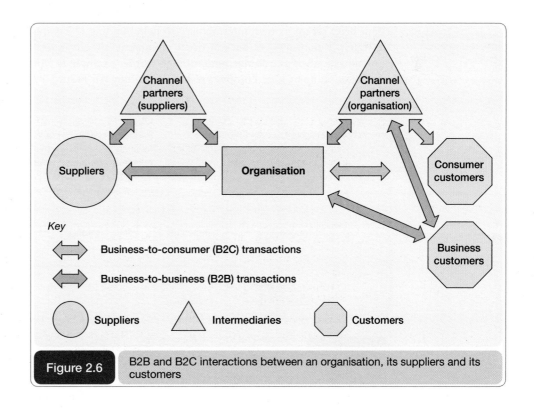

Figure 2.6 B2B and B2C interactions between an organisation, its suppliers and its customers

Figure 2.7 illustrates disintermediation in a graphical form for a simplified retail channel. Further intermediaries such as additional distributors may occur in a business-to-business market. Figure 2.7(a) shows the former position where a company marketed and sold its products by 'pushing' them through a sales channel. Figure 2.7(b) and Figure 2.7(c) show two different types of disintermediation in which the wholesaler (b) or the wholesaler and retailer (c) are bypassed, allowing the producer to sell and promote direct to the consumer. The benefits of disintermediation to the producer are clear – it is able to remove the sales and infrastructure cost of selling through the channel. Benjamin and Weigand (1995) calculated that, using the sale of quality shirts as an example, it is possible to make cost savings of 28 per cent in the case of (b) and 62 per cent for case (c). Some of these cost savings can be passed on to the customer in the form of cost reductions.

Reintermediation
The creation of new intermediaries between customers and suppliers providing services such as supplier search and product evaluation.

Although disintermediation has occurred, **reintermediation** is perhaps a more significant phenomenon resulting from Internet-based communications. Figure 2.8 illustrates this concept. Figure 2.8(a) shows the traditional situation in which many sales were through brokers such as the Automobile Association (www.theaa.co.uk). With disintermediation (Figure 2.8(b)) there was the opportunity to sell direct, initially via call centres as with Direct Line (www.directline.co.uk) and then more recently by their transactional website. Purchasers of products still needed assistance in the selection of products and this led to the creation of new intermediaries, the process referred to as reintermediation (Figure 2.8(c)).

In the UK MoneySupermarket.com and Confused.com are examples of a new intermediary providing a service for people to find online insurance at a competitive price. Esurance.com and Insurance.com are US examples.

Debate 2.1

Countermediation

'The advent of e-commerce means that marketers cannot rely on the online presence of existing intermediaries – instead they must create their own online intermediaries.'

What are the implications of reintermediation for the e-commerce manager? First, it is necessary to make sure that your company, as a supplier, is represented on the sites of relevant new intermediaries operating within your chosen market sector. This implies the need to integrate databases containing price information with those of different intermediaries. Forming partnerships or setting up sponsorship with some intermediaries can give better online visibility compared to competitors. Second, it is important to monitor the prices of other suppliers within this sector (possibly by using the intermediary website). Third, it may be appropriate to create your own intermediary; for example, DIY chain B&Q set up its own intermediary to help budding DIYers, but formerly positioned separately from its owners. Such tactics to counter or take advantage of reintermediation are sometimes known as **countermediation**. A further example is Opodo (www.opodo.com) which was set up by nine European airlines, including Air France, BA, KLM and Lufthansa.

Countermediation
Creation of a new intermediary such as a publisher or comparison site by an established company. May be a new site or acquired through purchase or partnering.

Figure 2.7
Disintermediation of a consumer distribution channel showing (a) the original situation, (b) disintermediation omitting the wholesaler, and (c) disintermediation omitting both wholesaler and retailer

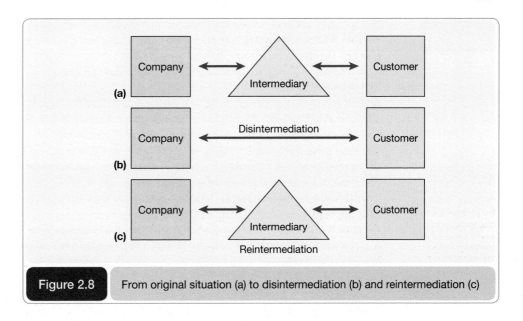

| Figure 2.8 | From original situation (a) to disintermediation (b) and reintermediation (c) |

Location of trading in the marketplace

Another perspective on the configuration of the marketplace relates to the position of trading and relative strength between different players within the marketplace.

Berryman *et al.* (1998) created a useful framework for this, identifying three different types of location. Seller-controlled sites are the main home page of the company and are e-commerce enabled. Buyer-controlled sites are intermediaries that have been set up so that the buyer initiates the market-making. In procurement posting, a purchaser specifies what they wish to purchase, and a message is sent by email to suppliers registered on the system and then offers are awaited. Aggregators involve a group of purchasers combining to purchase a multiple order, thus reducing the purchase cost. Neutral sites are independent evaluator intermediaries that enable price and product comparison.

The framework of Berryman *et al.* (1998) has been updated by McDonald and Wilson (2002) who introduce two additional locations for purchase which are useful (Table 2.3).

We will see in Chapter 7 that the most successful procurement intermediaries are often those which are not independent, but are seller-orientated or seller-controlled.

As noted in Chapter 1, Evans and Wurster (1999) have argued that there are three aspects of navigation that are key to achieving competitive advantage online. These are Reach, Richness and Affiliation.

The importance of multichannel marketplace models

Online purchasers typically use a combination of channels as they follow their **customer journeys**. As they select products and interact with brands, they do not use the Internet in isolation – they consume other media such as print, TV, direct mail and outdoor ads. It follows that an effective approach to using the Internet is as part of a **multichannel marketing strategy**. This defines how different marketing channels should integrate and support each other in terms of their proposition development and communications based on their relative merits for the customer and the company.

Developing 'channel chains' to help us understand multichannel behaviour is a powerful technique recommended by McDonald and Wilson (2002) for analysing the changes in a marketplace introduced by the Internet. A channel chain shows alternative customer

Customer journey
A description of modern multichannel buyer behaviour as consumers use different media to select suppliers, make purchases and gain customer support.

Multichannel marketing strategy
Defines how different marketing channels should integrate and support each other in terms of their proposition development and communications based on their relative merits for the customer and the company.

Table 2.3	Different places for online representation

Place of purchase	Examples of sites
A Seller-controlled	• Vendor sites, i.e. home site of organisation selling products, e.g. www.dell.com
B Seller-oriented	• Intermediaries controlled by third parties to the seller such as distributors and agents, e.g. Opodo (www.opodo.com) represents the main air carriers
C Neutral	• Intermediaries not controlled by buyer's industry, e.g. Alibaba (www.alibaba.com) • Product-specific search engines, e.g. CNET (www.cnet.co.uk/) • Comparison sites, e.g. MoneySupermarket (www.moneysupermarket.com) • Auction space, e.g. eBay (www.ebay.com)
D Buyer-orientated	• Intermediaries controlled by buyers, e.g. Covisint used to represent the major motor manufacturers (www.covisint.com), although they now don't use a single marketplace, but each manufacturer uses the technology to access its suppliers direct • Purchasing agents and aggregators
E Buyer-controlled	• Website procurement posting on company's own site, e.g. Deutsche Telekom Corporate Procurement portal (www.einkauf.telekom.de), which controls part of the company's purchasing budget

Source: Adapted from McDonald and Wilson (2002).

journeys for customers with different channel preferences. It can be used to assess the current and future performance of these different customer journeys. An example of a channel chain is shown in Figure 2.9. A market map can show the flow of revenue between a manufacturer or service provider and its customers through intermediaries and new types of intermediaries. Thomas and Sullivan (2005) give the example of a US multichannel retailer that used cross-channel tracking of purchases through assigning each customer a unique identifier to calculate channel preferences, as follows: 63% bricks-and-mortar store only, 12.4% Internet-only customers, 11.9% catalogue-only customers, 11.9% dual-channel customers and 1% three-channel customers.

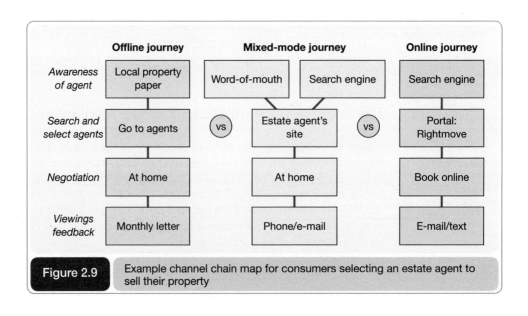

Figure 2.9	Example channel chain map for consumers selecting an estate agent to sell their property

Commercial arrangement for transactions

Markets can also be considered from another perspective – that of the type of commercial arrangement that is used to agree a sale and price between the buyer and supplier. The main types of commercial arrangement are shown in Table 2.4.

Debate 2.2

Innovative business models

'The new business models associated with the dot-com era were, in fact, existing models in an online context. Business models and revenue models have not changed.'

Each of these commercial arrangements is similar to traditional arrangements. Although the mechanism cannot be considered to have changed, the relative importance of these different options has changed with the Internet. Owing to the ability to publish new offers and prices rapidly, auction has become an important means of selling on the Internet. A turnover of several billion dollars has been achieved by eBay from consumers offering items such as cars and antiques.

An example of a completely new commercial mechanism that has been made possible through the web is provided by priceline.com (www.priceline.com). This travel site is characterised by its unique and proprietary 'Name Your Own Price™' buying service. Here, users enter the price they wish to pay for airline tickets, hotel rooms or car hire together with their credit card details. If priceline.com can match the user's price and other terms with inventory available from its participating suppliers, the deal will go ahead. The brand has also been licensed in the UK and Asia.

Different types of online intermediary and influencers

As we showed through Figure 2.4, identifying different types of online intermediary as potential partners to promote an online business is a key part of marketplace analysis. In this section, we take a more in-depth look at the different types of intermediaries and the business and revenue models they adopt.

Table 2.4	Commercial mechanisms and online transactions

Commercial (trading) mechanism	Online transaction mechanism of Nunes *et al.* (2000)
1 **Negotiated deal** *Example:* can use similar mechanism to auction, as on Commerce One (www.commerceone.net)	Negotiation – bargaining between single seller and buyer. Continuous replenishment – ongoing fulfilment of orders under pre-set terms
2 **Brokered deal** *Example:* intermediaries such as Compare The Market (www.comparethemarket.com)	Achieved through online intermediaries offering auction and pure markets online
3 **Auction** *Examples:* C2C: eBay (www.ebay.com); B2B: Industry to Industry (http://business.ebay.co.uk/)	Seller auction – buyers' bids determine final price of sellers' offerings. Buyer auction – buyers request prices from multiple sellers. Reverse – buyers post desired price for seller acceptance
4 **Fixed-price sale** *Examples:* all e-tailers	Static call – online catalogue with fixed prices. Dynamic call – online catalogue with continuously updated prices and features
5 **Pure markets** *Example:* electronic share dealing	Spot – buyers' and sellers' bids clear instantly
6 **Barter** *Examples:* www.intagio.com and www.bartercard.co.uk	Barter – buyers and sellers exchange goods. According to the International Reciprocal Trade Association (www.irta.com), barter trade was over $9 billion in 2002

Sarkar *et al.* (1996) identified many different types of new intermediaries (mainly from a B2C perspective) which we can still recognise today:

- Directories (such as Yahoo!, Excite).
- Search engines (AltaVista, Infoseek).
- Malls (BarclaySquare, Buckingham Gate).
- Virtual resellers (own-inventory and sell-direct, e.g. Amazon, CDNow).
- Financial intermediaries (offering digital cash and cheque payment services, such as Paypal).
- Forums, fan clubs and user groups (referred to collectively as 'virtual communities').
- Evaluators (sites which perform review or comparison of services).

Riggins and Mitra (2007) have a more recent evaluation of alternative online marketplace players which we review in Chapter 7. A further type of intermediary is the *virtual marketplace* or virtual trading community of the B2B marketplace. From the supplier's or manufacturer's perspective they provide a new channel for selling their products. The form of these marketplaces is considered in more detail in '*Focus on* B2B marketplaces' in Chapter 7.

Summary of the types of intermediary

Intermediaries vary in scope and the services they offer, so naturally terms have evolved to describe the different types. The main types of intermediary you will identify as part of an online marketplace analysis are shown in Table 2.5. It is useful, in particular for marketers, to understand these typessince they act as a checklist for how their companies can be represented on the different types of intermediaries, online publishers and media owners once known as **portals**, a term that has fallen from favour.

The importance of search engines

Search engines are a key type of intermediary for organisations marketing their services online, since today they are the primary method of finding information about a company and its products. Research compiled by Searchenginewatch (www.searchenginewatch.com) shows that over 90% of web users state that they use search engines to find information online. Their importance can also be seen from their audience sizes by applying the tools in Table 2.2. We will show how search engines can be used for marketing in more detail in Chapter 9. As part of marketplace analysis it is useful for companies to assess demand for products and brand preferences in different countries using tools such as the Google Trends (Figure 2.5) or the Google Keyword Planner. These show the volume of searches by consumers related to clothes in the UK in a one-month period.

Portal

A website that acts as a gateway to information and services available on the Internet by providing search engines, directories and other services such as personalised news or free email.

Search engines, spiders and robots

Automatic tools known as 'spiders' or 'robots' index registered sites. Users search this by typing keywords and are presented with a list of pages.

Online business model

A summary of how a company will generate a profit identifying its core product or service value proposition, target customers in different markets, position in the competitive online marketplace or value chain and its projections for revenue and costs.

Business models for e-commerce

Defining a clear **online business model** is essential for a new start-up online business to be successful. But it's also important for existing businesses thinking about options to refine their business model or add new services to their offerings in the light of new opportunities made possible by the Internet. The Business Model Canvas developed by Osterwald and Pigneur (2010) is a valuable framework for summarising strategy for online businesses. It was published as part of a co-creation project involving 470 practitioners from 45 countries. It's also available as an app and downloadable templates on the Business Model Generation site (www.businessmodelgeneration.com).

Table 2.5	Different types of online intermediary

Type of intermediary	Characteristics	Example
Access portal	Associated with ISP or mobile service provider	• Orange (www.o2.co.uk) • Sky (www.bskyb.com)
Blog	Content updated through time, typically text-based, but can include video or audio delivered by RSS feeds (see Chapter 3 for details)	• Blogger (www.blogger.com) hosts many blogs • Many company blogs are created using Wordpress (www.wordpress.com)
Directory	Listings of sites and businesses details in categories	• Business.com (www.business.com), Yell (www.yell.com)
Geographical (region, country, local)	May be: • horizontal • vertical	• Google country versions • Yahoo! country and city versions • craigslist (www.craigslist.com)
Horizontal or functional portal	Range of services: search engines, directories, news, recruitment, personal information management, shopping, etc.	• Yahoo! (www.yahoo.com) • Microsoft MSN (www.msn.com) • Google (www.google.com) which for a long period just focused on search
Marketplace or auction site	May be: • horizontal • vertical • geographical	• EC21(www.ec21.com) • eBay (www.ebay.com)
Price comparison site or aggregator	Compares products or services on different criteria, including price	• Kelkoo in Europe and Asia (www.kelkoo.com) • Epinions in US (www.epinions.com)
Publisher site	Main focus is on consumer or business news or entertainment	• BBC (www.bbc.co.uk) • Guardian (www.guardian.co.uk) • Information Week (www.informationweek.com)
Search engine	Main focus is on search	• Google (www.google.com) • Ask (www.ask.com) • Baidu in China (www.baidu.com) • Naver in S. Korea (www.naver.com)
Media type	May be: • voice (audio podcasts) • video (video webcasts) Delivered by streaming media or downloads of files	• Audio podcasts, for example Odeo (www.odeo.com) • Video, for example YouTube (www.youtube.com) • Multimedia publisher, e.g. BBC (www.bbc.co.uk)
Vertical intermediary	Covers a particular market or niche audience, such as construction, with news and other services	• Construction Plus (www.constructionplus.co.uk) • Phaidon Atlas of Architecture (www.phaidonatlas.com)

The main sections of the canvas in a logical order to consider them are:

1 **Value proposition.** This is at the heart of what the business offers to its audiences and is arguably most important to success.
2 **Customer segments.** Different target audiences to whom the value propositions will appeal. In the Business Model Canvas the alternatives recommended are mass market, niche market, segmented (broken down further) or a range of diverse segments.
3 **Customer relationships.** The types of relationships that will be formed, for example self-service, automated services, communities or more personal assistance. Co-creation of content may be part of this.

4 **Channels.** The methods by which the organisation's services will be delivered and the audiences reached.
5 **Key partners.** To exploit online and offline value networks, forming partnerships gives an opportunity of expanding reach and taking advantage of existing organisations and online influencers that have built an audience.
6 **Activities.** The main activities that need to be performed to deliver the value proposition to develop revenue.
7 **Resources.** Different types of process and people to complete the activities to create and deliver the value proposition.
8 **Cost structure.** Different cost-elements; these should be checked against activities and resources. Costs are classically broken down into fixed and variable costs and economies of scale.
9 **Revenue stream.** This is the method by which a business derives income. Common online options are: ad revenue, subscription fees, sales of physical or virtual goods or affiliate-based commission arrangements. Licensing and leasing are other alternatives.

An example of how these nine different elements of a business model can be applied is shown in Figure 2.10.

It's a great framework, but it's always worth considering what the missing elements of frameworks are. It's arguably missing a method of specifying key performance indicators (KPIs) for evaluating performance of the business model. I recommend adding these to the relevant sections, in particular for revenue stream, cost structure and key activities. It also

Figure 2.10   Business Model Canvas example
Source: Smart Insights. With permission.

doesn't directly consider the impact of different forms of competitors. To help here, it's also useful to think through how the canvas would look for successful companies already active in this market. (We will look further at how to define elements of the business model such as value proposition and targeting in Chapters 5 and 8.)

A review of the different online business models made available through e-commerce is of relevance to existing companies, but in particular, start-up companies and online intermediaries. Venkatram (2000) pointed out that existing businesses needed to use the Internet to build on current business models, while at the same time experimenting with new business models. New business models may be important to gain a competitive advantage over existing competitors, while at the same time heading off similar business models created by new entrants. More commonly, they may simply offer a different revenue stream through advertising or charging for services in a new way. For Internet start-ups the viability of a business model and in particular their sources of revenue will be crucial to their success and funding from venture capitalists. But what is a business model?

Regardless of the descriptors used, the important point is that as part of strategy development, organisations should identify relevant partners and develop tactics for working with them appropriately.

Finally, Michael Rappa, a professor at North Carolina State University, has a useful compilation of examples of online business models in these and other categories in the link shown at the end of the chapter. At a lower level, Rappa identifies utilities providers that provide online services (such as the Internet service providers and hosting companies we discuss in Chapter 3). Now complete Activity 2.2 to assess whether it is possible to simplify these business models and read Case study 2.1 to see examples of new revenue models that can be used by a forward-looking retailer.

Figure 2.11 suggests a different perspective for reviewing alternative business models. There are three different perspectives from which a business model can be viewed. Any individual organisation can operate in different categories, as the examples below show, but most will focus on a single category for each perspective. Such a categorisation of business models can be used as a tool for *formulating digital business strategy*. The three perspectives, with examples, are:

1 *Marketplace position perspective.* The book publisher here is the manufacturer, Amazon is a retailer and Yahoo! is both a retailer and a marketplace intermediary.
2 *Revenue model perspective.* The book publisher can use the web to sell direct while Yahoo! and Amazon can take commission-based sales. Yahoo! also has advertising as a revenue model.
3 *Commercial arrangement perspective.* All three companies offer fixed-price sales, but, in its place as a marketplace intermediary, Yahoo! also offers alternatives.

Activity 2.2	Exploring business models

Purpose

To explore the different types of business model available on the web and suggest a structure for evaluating business models.

Question

Identify overlap between the different business models identified by Timmers (1999). Can you group the different business models into different types of services? Do you think these business models operate in isolation?

Answers to activities can be found at www.pearsoned.co.uk/chaffey

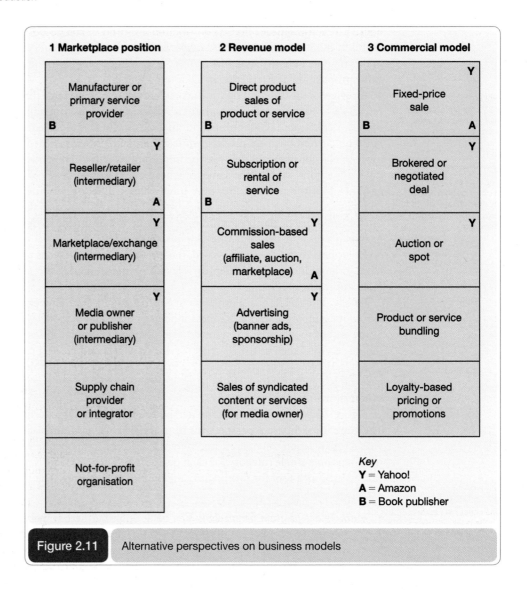

Figure 2.11   Alternative perspectives on business models

Revenue models

Revenue models
Describe methods of
generating income for an
organisation.

Revenue models specifically describe different techniques for generation of income. For existing companies, revenue models have mainly been based upon the income from sales of products or services. This may be either for selling direct from the manufacturer or supplier of the service or through an intermediary that will take a cut of the selling price. Both of these revenue models are, of course, still crucial in online trading. There may, however, be options for other methods of generating revenue; a manufacturer may be able to sell advertising space or sell digital services that were not previously possible.

Online publisher and intermediary revenue models

For a publisher, there are many options for generating revenue online based around advertising and fees for usage of online services. These options, particularly the first four in the list below, can also be reviewed by other types of business such as price comparison sites, aggregators, social networks and destination sites which can also carry advertising to supplement revenue. The main types of online revenue model are:

CPM (cost-per-thousand)

The cost to the advertiser (or the revenue received by the publisher) when an ad is served 1,000 times.

1 **CPM display advertising on-site. CPM** stands for 'cost-per-thousand' where M denotes 'mille'. This is the traditional method by which site owners charge a fee for advertising. The site owner charges advertisers a rate card price (for example £50 CPM) according to the number of times ads are served to site visitors. Ads may be served by the site owner's own ad server or more commonly through a third-party ad network service such as DoubleClick (which is owned by Google).

CPC (cost-per-click)

The cost to the advertiser (or the revenue received by the publisher) of each click of a link to a third-party site.

2 **CPC advertising on-site (pay-per-click text ads). CPC** stands for 'cost-per-click'. Advertisers are charged not simply for the number of times their ads are displayed, but according to the number of times they are clicked upon. These are typically text ads served by a search engine such as Google (www.google.com) on what is known as its content network. Google has its Adsense (http://adsense.google.com) programme for publishers which enables them to offer text- or image-based ads typically on a CPC basis, but optionally on a CPM basis. Typical costs per click can be surprisingly high, i.e. they are in the range £0.10 to £4, but sometimes up to £20 for some categories such as 'life insurance'. The revenue for search engines and publishers from these sources can also be significant: Google's annual reports (http://investor.google.com) show that this is between a quarter and a third of Google's revenue.

3 **Sponsorship of site sections or content types (typically fixed fee for a period).** A company can pay to advertise a site channel or section. For example, the bank HSBC sponsors the Money section on the Orange broadband provider portal (www.orange. co.uk). This type of deal is often struck for a fixed amount per year. It may also be part of a reciprocal arrangement, sometimes known as a 'contra-deal' where neither party pays.

CPA (cost-per-acquisition)

The cost to the advertiser (or the revenue received by the publisher) for each outcome such as a lead or sale generated after a click to a third-party site.

4 **Affiliate revenue (CPA, but could be CPC).** Affiliate revenue is commission-based, for example I display Amazon books on my site SmartInsights.com and receive around 5% of the cover price as a fee from Amazon. Such an arrangement is sometimes known as **cost-per-acquisition (CPA)**. Increasingly, this approach is replacing CPM or CPC approaches where the advertiser has more negotiating power. For example, manufacturing company Unilever negotiates CPA deals with online publishers where it is paid for every email address captured by a campaign rather than a traditional CPM deal. However, it depends on the power of the publisher, who will often receive more revenue overall for CPM deals. After all, the publisher cannot influence the quality of the ad creative or the incentivisation to click which will affect the clickthrough rate and so earnings from the ad.

5 **Transaction fee revenue.** A company receives a fee for facilitating a transaction. Examples include eBay and Paypal who charge a percentage of the transaction cost between buyer and seller.

6 **Subscription access to content or services.** A range of documents can be accessed from a publisher for a fixed period. These are often referred to as premium services on websites.

Digital rights management (DRM)

The use of different technologies to protect the distribution of digital services or content such as software, music, movies or other digital data.

7 **Pay-per-view access to documents.** Here payment occurs for single access to a document, video or music clip which can be downloaded. It may or may not be protected with a password or **digital rights management**. I pay to access detailed best-practice guides on Internet marketing from Marketing Sherpa (www.marketingsherpa.com).

8 **Subscriber data access for email marketing.** The data a site owner has about its customers are also potentially valuable since it can send different forms of email to its customers if they have given their permission that they are happy to receive email from either the publisher or third parties. The site owner can charge for adverts placed in its newsletter or can deliver a separate message on behalf of the advertiser (sometimes known as 'list rental'). A related approach is to conduct market research with the site customers.

Calculating revenue for an online business

Site owners can develop models (Figure 2.11) of potential revenue depending on the mix of revenue-generating techniques from the four main revenue options they use on the site given in the options above.

Consider the capacity of a site owner to maximise revenue or 'monetise' their site – which factors will be important? The model will be based on assumptions about the level of traffic and number of pages viewed plus the interaction with different types of ad unit. Their ability to maximise revenue will be based on these factors which can be modelled in the spreadsheet shown in Figure 2.12:

- *Number and size of ad units.* This is a delicate balance between the number of ad units in each site section or page – too many obtrusive ad units may present a bad experience for site users, too few will reduce revenue. Figure 2.12 has a parameter for the number of ad units or containers in each ad revenue category. There is a tension with advertisers who know that the awareness and response they generate from their ads is maximised when they are as large as practical and in prominent placements. A more accurate revenue model would develop revenue for different page types such as the home page and different page categories, e.g. the money or travel sections.

- *Capacity to sell advertising.* Figure 2.12 also has a parameter for the percentage of ad inventory sold in each category – for example, for the CPM ad display revenue only 40% of inventory may be sold. This is why you may see publisher sites with their own 'house ads' – it is a sign they have been unable to sell all their ad space. A benefit of using the Google AdSense publisher programme is that inventory is commonly all used.

- *Fee levels negotiated for different advertising models.* These will depend on the market competition or demand for advertising space. For 'pay-per-performance' advertising options such as the CPC and CPA models, it also depends on the response. In the first case, the site owner only receives revenue when the ad is clicked upon and in the second case, the site owner only receives revenue when the ad is clicked upon and a product is purchased on the destination merchant site.

- *Traffic volumes.* More visitors equate to more opportunities to generate revenue through serving more pages (which helps with CPM-based advertising) or more clicks to third-party sites (which helps generate revenue from CPC and CPA deals).

- *Visitor engagement.* The longer visitors stay on a site (its 'stickiness'), the more page views that will accumulate, which again gives more opportunities for ad revenue. For a destination site a typical number of page views per visit would be in the range 5 to 10, but for a social network, media site or community the figure could be greater than 30.

Considering all of these approaches to revenue generation together, the site owner will seek to use the best combination of these techniques to maximise the revenue. An illustration of this approach is shown in Figure 2.12.

To assess how effective different pages or sites in their portfolio are at generating revenue using these techniques, site owners will use two approaches. The first is eCPM, or effective cost per thousand. This looks at the total the advertiser can charge (or cost to advertisers) for each page or site. Through increasing the number of ad units on each page this value will increase. The other alternative to assess page or site revenue-generating effectiveness is revenue per click (RPC), also known as 'earnings per click' (EPC). Alternatively, revenue can be calculated as ad revenue per 1,000 site visitors. This is particularly important for affiliate marketers who make money through commission when their visitors click through to third-party retail sites, and then purchase there.

Activity 2.3 explores some of the revenue models that are possible.

Ad revenue option	Measure	Site
	Pages served	100,000
Display advertising (CPM)	CPM (Cost Per Thousand)	£2
	% Inventory served	40%
	Avg. Clickthrough (CTR %)	0.10%
	Ad units served per page	2
	Clicks – CPM ads	80
	Revenue – display ads	**£160**
	Earnings per 100 clicks (EPC)	**£200.0**
	eCPM – display ads	**£1.60**
Fixed run-of-site sponsorship	% Inventory served	100%
	Avg. Clickthrough (CTR %)	0.30%
	Ad units served 1	1
	Clicks – fixed	300
	Revenue – fixed sponsorship	**£3,000**
	Earnings per 100 clicks (EPC)	**£1,000.0**
	eCPM – fixed	**£30.00**
Text ad advertising (CPC)	% Inventory served	100%
	Avg. Clickthrough (CTR %)	1.00%
	Avg. Cost Per Click	£0.30
	Ad units served per page	1
	Clicks – CPC ads	1,000
	Revenue – CPC ads	**£300**
	Earnings per 100 clicks (EPC)	**£30.0**
	eCPM – CPC ads	**£3**
Affiliate commission	% Inventory served	100%
	Avg. Clickthrough (CTR %)	0.50%
	Ad units served per page	1
	Clicks – Affiliates	500
	Desination conversion rate (%)	3%
	Average order value	£100
	Commission %	10%
	Revenue – affiliates	**£150**
	Earnings per 100 clicks (EPC)	**£30.0**
	eCPM – affiliates	**£1.50**
Overall metrics for site	**Clicks – total**	**1,880**
	Revenue – total	**£3,610**
	Earnings per 100 clicks (EPC) – total	**£192.02**
	eCPM – total	**£36.10**

Blue cells = input variables – vary these for 'what-if' analysis

Orange cells = Output variables (calculated – **do not overtype**)

Figure 2.12 Example spreadsheet for calculating a site revenue model
Note: **Available for download at** http://www.smartinsights.com/conversion-model-spreadsheets/

Activity 2.3 | **Revenue models at online media sites**

Purpose

To illustrate the range of revenue-generating opportunities for an online publisher. This site looks at three alternative approaches for publishing, referencing three different types of portal.

Question

Visit each of the sites in this category:

1 Summarise the revenue models which are used for each site by looking at the information for advertisers and affiliates.

2 What are the advantages and disadvantages of the different revenue models for the site audience and the site owner?

3 Given an equivalent audience, which of these sites do you think would generate the most revenue? You could develop a simple spreadsheet model based on the following figures:

- Monthly site visitors: 100,000; 0.5% of these visitors click through to affiliate sites where 2% go on to buy business reports or services at an average order value of 100 CPM.
- Monthly page views: 1,000,000; average of three ads displayed for different advertisers at 20 CPM (we are assuming all ad inventory is sold, which is rarely true in reality).
- Subscribers to weekly newsletter: 50,000; each newsletter broadcast four times per month has four advertisers each paying at a rate of 10 CPM.

Note: These are not actual figures for any of these sites.

The sites are:

- Marketing Profs (www.marketingprofs.com)
- Smart Insights (www.smartinsights.com)
- Marketing Sherpa (www.marketingsherpa.com).

Answers to activities can be found at www.pearsoned.co.uk/chaffey

---

Focus on | **Online start-up companies**

Dot-coms
Businesses whose main trading presence is on the Internet.

Clicks-only or Internet pureplay
An organisation with principally an online presence.

Bricks and mortar or multichannel business
A traditional organisation with limited online presence.

To conclude the chapter, we review how to evaluate the potential of new Internet start-ups. Many 'dot-coms' were launched in response to the opportunities of new business and revenue models opened up by the Internet in the mid-to-late 1990s. We also consider what lessons can be learnt from the dot-com failures. But Table 1.1 showed that innovation and the growth of Internet pureplays did not end in 2000, but rather many successful online companies such as digital publishers and social networks have developed since then.

An Internet 'pureplay' which only has an online representation is referred to as 'clicks-only' as opposed to a 'bricks-and-mortar' or multichannel business'. A pureplay typically has no retail distribution network. It may have phone-based customer service, as is the case with office supplier Euroffice (www.euroffice.co.uk), or not, as is the case with financial services provider Zopa (www.zopa.com), or it may offer phone service for more valuable customers, as is the case with hardware provider dabs.com (www.dabs.com).

Assessing online businesses

As with all new companies, it is difficult for investors to assess the long-term sustainability of start-ups. There are a number of approaches that can be used to assess the success and sustainability of these companies. There have been many examples where it has been suggested that dot-com companies have been overvalued by investors who are keen to make a fast return from their investments. There were some clear anomalies if traditional companies are compared to dot-coms.

Valuing Internet start-ups

Desmet *et al.* (2000) apply traditional discounted cash flow techniques to assess the potential value of Internet start-ups or dot-coms. They point out that traditional techniques do not work well when profitability is negative, but revenues are growing rapidly. They suggest that for new companies the critical factors to model when considering the future success of a company are:

1 The cost of acquiring a customer through marketing.
2 The contribution margin per customer (before acquisition cost).
3 The average annual revenues per year from customers and other revenues such as banner advertising and affiliate revenues. These are often measured as ARPU or average revenue per user, as reported for companies like Betfair, eBay and Facebook in Chapter 1.
4 The total number of customers.
5 The customer **churn rate**.

Churn rate
The proportion of customers (typically subscribers) that no longer purchase a company's products in a time period.

As would be expected intuitively, modelling using these variables indicates that for companies with a similar revenue per customer, contribution margin and advertising costs, it is the churn rate that will govern their long-term success. To look at this another way, given the high costs of customer acquisition for a new company, it is the ability to retain customers for repeat purchases which governs the long-term success of companies. This then forces dot-com retailers to compete on low prices with low margins to retain customers.

A structured evaluation of the success and sustainability of UK Internet start-ups has been undertaken by management consultancy Bain and Company in conjunction with *Management Today* magazine and was described in Gwyther (1999). Six criteria were used to assess the companies as follows.

1 Concept

This describes the strength of the business model. It includes:

• potential to generate revenue including the size of the market targeted;
• superior 'customer value', in other words how well the value proposition of the service is differentiated from that of competitors;
• first-mover advantage (less easy to achieve today).

2 Innovation

This criterion looks at another aspect of the business concept, which is the extent to which the business model merely imitates existing real-world or online models. Note that imitation is not necessarily a problem if it is applied to a different market or audience or if the experience is superior and positive word-of-mouth is generated.

3 Execution

A good business model does not, of course, guarantee success. If there are problems with aspects of the implementation of the idea, then the start-up will fail. Aspects of execution that can be seen to have failed for some companies are:

• Promotion – online or offline techniques are insufficient to attract sufficient visitors to the site.

- Performance, availability and security – some sites have been victims of their own success and have not been able to deliver fast access to the sites or technical problems have meant that the service is unavailable or insecure. Some sites have been unavailable despite large-scale advertising campaigns due to delays in creating the website and its supporting infrastructure.
- Fulfilment – the site itself may be effective, but customer service and consequently brand image will be adversely affected if products are not despatched correctly or promptly.

4 Traffic

This criterion is measured in terms of the number of visitors, the number of pages they visit and the number of transactions they make which control the online ad revenues. Page impressions or visits are not necessarily an indication of success but are dependent on the business model. After the viability of the business model, how it will be promoted is arguably the most important aspect for a start-up. For most companies a critical volume of loyal, returning and revenue-generating users of a service is required to repay the investment in these companies. Promotion from zero base is difficult and costly if there is a need to reach a wide audience. An important decision is the investment in promotion and how it is split between online and offline techniques. Perhaps surprisingly, to reach the mass market, traditional advertising was required to get the message about the service across clearly to the numbers required. For example, Boo had major TV and newspaper campaigns which generated awareness and visits, but didn't translate to sufficient initial or repeat transactions. Some of the other start-up companies such as lastminute.com and Zopa.com have been able to grow without the initial investment in advertising. These have grown more organically, helped by favourable word of mouth and mentions in newspaper features supported by some traditional advertising. Promotion for all these companies seems to indicate that the Internet medium is simply adding an additional dimension to the communications mix and that traditional advertising is still required.

5 Financing

This describes the ability of the company to attract venture capital or other funding to help execute the idea. It is particularly important given the cost of promoting these new concepts.

6 Profile

This is the ability of the company to generate favourable publicity and to create awareness within its target market.

These six criteria can be compared with the other elements of business and revenue models which we discussed earlier in this chapter.

Examples of e-commerce failures

We can learn from examples of failure. They're not written up that commonly since naturally those involved don't want to share their failures.

Boo.com is an interesting case of the potential and pitfalls of an e-commerce start-up and criteria for success, or one could say of 'how not to do it'. The boo.com site was launched in November 1999 following two significant delays in launching and in January 2000 it was reported that 100 of its 400 employees had been made redundant due to disappointing initial revenues of about £60,000 in the Christmas period. Boo faced a high '**burn rate**' because of the imbalance between promotion and site development costs and revenues. As a consequence, it appeared to change its strategy by offering discounts of up to 40 per cent on fashions from the previous season. Closure followed in mid-2000 and the boo.com brand was purchased by an American entrepreneur who still continues to use the brand. (Boo.com features as a case study in Chapter 5.) Investors provided a reported £74 million in capital. This enthusiasm is partly based on the experience of two of the founders in creating bokus. com, a relatively successful online bookseller.

Burn rate
The speed at which dot-coms spent investors' money.

| Case Study 2.1 | i-to-i – a global marketplace for a start-up company |

This case is about a specialist travel and education company, focussing on its online TEFL (Teaching English as a Foreign Language) courses. The case illustrates the importance of marketplace analysis.

i-to-i background

i-to-i (www.i-to-i.com) is an international organisation with offices in the UK, USA, Ireland and Australia. Twenty thousand people have selected i-to-i as they travel on ventures to support 500 worthwhile projects on five continents and it has also trained a further 80,000 people as TEFL teachers. This service is offered through the main site and also through a specialist online TEFL site (www.onlinetefl.com) on which this case focusses.

The history of i-to-i

The founder of i-to-i, Deirdre Bounds, was inspired to create the company following a career break which took her to teach English in Japan, China and Greece and drive a backpackers' bus in Sydney. The company initially started through creating TEFL courses, eventually leading to organising volunteer projects.

Since 2003 the company has supported the i-to-i Foundation, a registered charity committed to providing funds to the most needy community and ecological projects in the i-to-i family. In 2007, i-to-i became part of the TUI travel group.

Proposition

The main features of the i-to-i TEFL proposition are:

- *International accreditation*: i-to-i is externally accredited by the ODLQC in order to ensure that its courses are rigorously monitored and always meet the highest industry standards.
- *World-class reputation*: i-to-i has four offices worldwide and it has over 12 years' experience teaching TEFL.
- *Partnership*: i-to-i is preferred TEFL course provider for STA Travel, Opodo and Lonely Planet.
- *Complete student support*: Students receive advice on how to get work abroad, how best to prepare for their time away and up to the minute advice on current job opportunities.
- *Highly experienced tutors*: All i-to-i tutors have at least three years' overseas teaching experience.

This proposition is backed up by 'the i-to-i TEFL Promise':

1 We will beat any equivalent and cheaper course by 150%.
2 If you're not entirely satisfied after the first seven days, we'll give you a full refund.
3 Our experience, our high academic standards and the quality of our courses mean that i-to-i TEFL certificates are recognised by thousands of language schools worldwide.

Additionally, i-to-i can offer to help students find TEFL jobs abroad.

Audience segmentation

The main segmentation used by i-to-i is geographic:

- UK
- North America
- Europe
- Australia and New Zealand
- Rest-of-world (same as UK)

Different brochures are also available for each geographical area.

Information is also collected on an optional basis about prospects' age and status, although these are not used for targeting emails. Status categories are:

- Student
- Employed
- Self-employed
- Career break
- Unemployed
- Retired

Since optional information is restricted to certain lead tools it is not used to target emails. For weekend TEFL courses, postcode/city is used to target courses to prospects.

Competitors

Some of the main competitors for online TEFL courses based in the UK and Australia include:

- www.cactustefl.com
- www.teflonline.com
- www.eslbase.com

In the US, competitors who also operate in the UK and other countries include:

- www.teflcorp.com/
- ITTP (International Tefl-Tesol-Online) www.tefl-tesol-online.com

Media mix

i-to-i uses a combination of these digital media channels to drive visits, leads and sales:

- Pay per click (PPC) (mainly Google AdWords)
- Social media marketing using Facebook, Twitter and i-to-i's own traveller community
- Natural search
- Affiliate marketing
- Display advertising
- Email marketing

Conversion process

Detailed content to help visitors decide on purchasing a course is available on the site. This includes module outlines and FAQs. Specific landing pages have not been used to convert visitors from paid search or affiliates, for example. Instead, the destination page for visitors from referring sites is the main category page for the product preference indicated by the search performed (for example, online TEFL).

A number of engagement devices are used to generate leads, including brochures, 'TEFL tasters', an email guide and campaign promotions such as winning a course.

Such leads are followed up through a series of welcome emails. Results are monitored, but emails are not proactively followed up on. There is no phone follow-up of leads due to the relative low value of the products, but site visitors are encouraged to ring or set up a callback which often leads to higher conversion rates.

Source: Smart Insights (2012) i-to-i case study. Written by Dave Chaffey and Dan Bosomworth with agreement from the company.

Marketplace challenges

The main marketplace challenges faced by i-to-i are:

1 Increasing its presence and conversion effectiveness in a competitive market in different geographies:

   (a) i-to-i has good exposure in the UK, its primary market, but operates in a cluttered marketplace with price being the main differentiator (products are similar and some competitors are just as established etc.).
   (b) Research suggests that there is good opportunity within the US, but exposure is more limited because of the cost of pay-per-click advertising and because presence in natural search favours the US.
   (c) Rest-of-world sales (outside of UK, USA, Canada, Ireland/Europe, Australia, New Zealand) are increasing and this is believed to be a growing market. i-to-i seeks to penetrate these markets, but in a cost-effective way that will not distract attention from main markets.

2 Increasing demand through reaching and educating those considering travel who are not aware of TEFL courses and the opportunities they unlock. For example, many will look for casual work in other countries, e.g. in bars or in agriculture, but will be unaware of TEFL.

Questions

1 Select one country that i-to-i operates in and summarise the main types of sites and businesses involved using a marketplace map (Figure 2.4).
2 Review the different factors that i-to-i will need to review to gauge the commercial effectiveness of its online presence in different geographic markets.

Mini case study 2.3 gives a more recent example an e-retail failure with serious consequences.

Why dot-coms failed

At the end of Chapter 5 we review the reasons for failed digital business strategies and, in Case study 5.3, we examine the reasons for one of the most spectacular dot-com failures – Boo.com. We will see that in many cases it was a case of an unsound business strategy, or ideas before their time. Many of the dot-coms were founded on innovative ideas which required a large shift in consumer behaviour. A rigorous demand analysis would have shown that, at the time, there were relatively few Internet users, with the majority on dial-up connections, so there wasn't the demand for these services. We see in the Boo.com example that

Mini Case Study 2.3	Ecomum fails to control its revenue model

Ecomom was a small start-up Internet retail company selling earth friendly mum and maternity products including food, toys, apparel, and other baby related items. With headquarters in Las Vegas and San Francisco and a third-party fulfilment in Los Angeles, any volume could be shipped within 24 hours. Founded in 2007, by 2011 it had turnover of just over $1 million, but a further round of investment of $12 million was required further growth, but at what cost?

Business Insider (2013) describes the story of the eventual failure of the company in 2013. With hindsight it's difficult to understand investment in the company, but perhaps this was buoyed by the success story of Tony Hsieh building Las Vegas-based Zappos into an online shoe and retail business that Amazon acquired for $1.2 billion. Of course, investors require growth and Ecomum did achieve revenues of nearly $4 million in 2013. But investors also require a return on their investment and, as you'll read, the way growth was achieved was far from profitable.

Philip Prentiss, who joined the company in 2011 as financial controller, was the first dedicated finance person. As with many start-ups, payroll, tax and accounts are outsourced to third-party bookkeepers. Many company failures are not written up because employees don't want to share the story of failure. But in a candid summary of his time at the failed company, Prentiss (2013) describes the reasons, starting with the lack of financial prudence. Describing Ecomom CEO Jody Sherman, he says:

He was not a numbers guy. I would bring the financial statements to Jody who would glance at them so cursorily and wave me away with 'no one can understand this without extensive analysis'. Critically, he did not understand margin. At the end of December when things were getting truly desperate, he said to me 'Phil, just bring me a forecast that shows how much we need to sell to break even.' He did not understand, after three years of negative margin, that increased sales resulted in increased losses.

In this open letter describing the failure of the company Prentiss shows how the financial presentation format hid a contribution margin of −48% which he identified when he joined the company. In other words, for every additional $60 average order shipped the variable cost was $89 and the company lost $29. This situation was caused by heavy discounting, with common use of 50% discounts on daily deal sites like Groupon. To make matters worse, although discounts were meant to be one time only, the company couldn't limit them by customer, so every discounted order had a 50% reduction regardless of whether they were from a new company or an existing company. The company sales manager was paid based on sales achieved *before* discounting. At the same time, there were no premium lines or own-label items where margin could have been better. In addition, this is a fiercely competitive growing sector with established retail brands such as Whole Foods or general retailers such as Amazon selling similar goods.

By mid-Autumn 2012, a $860K loss for the previous quarter was the result of the discounting strategy. Prentiss notes that no substantive changes were made to the business strategy and, starting from $4.8 million capital raised in August for the five months through 31 December, the company lost $1.1 million after variable cost, spent $1.7 million more on overhead and locked up another $1.2 million in inventory, leaving less than $1 million in the bank.

Sadly, the company closed early in 2013 and shortly afterwards, the CEO, Jody Sherman, took his own life.

In the unsentimental way of business, Ecomom's domain and customer list were purchased by a competitor and the website was planned for reopening later in 2013 with this more than unfortunate legacy.

But the lasting legacy of the company and its founder may be how it has highlighted the pressure of running a start-up. Business Insider quotes Dave McClure, an investor in Ecomom and the entrepreneur behind investment firm 500 Startups, who says:

Oh Jesus, [founding a company] can suck. I can remember facing extremely 'dark days' as an entrepreneur. I went through layoffs, co-founder battles, and wife battles, and not for much gain. It was a hell of a lot of work for not a hell of a lot of return. Then there are days when you sit in a corner and cry. You can't really do anything else. You don't have a social life. You don't really want to interact with family and friends because there's just not much context for them. Your world revolves around your startup and it's all about trying to survive and not look like an idiot in front of employees.

there were also failings in implementation, with technology infrastructure resulting in services that were simply too slow and the consequent poor experience leading to sales conversion rates and returning customer rates that were too low for a sustainable business.

Remember, though, that many companies that identified a niche and carefully controlled their growth did survive, so we finish the chapter on a more positive note with this case study of Firebox.com.

Mini Case Study 2.4	Firebox.com survives the dot-com boom and bust

Firebox.com (Figure 2.13) opened its virtual doors in 1998 as hotbox.co.uk, an Internet retailer which was founded by university flatmates Michael Smith and Tom Boardman. Initially operating out of Cardiff, the company saw rapid initial growth due to the success of the founders' invention, the Shot Glass Chess Set. In the summer of 1999 the company moved to London and re-launched as Firebox.com.

eSuperbrands (2005) described Firebox products as 'unique, unusual and quirky products from around the world'. Examples include unusual gadgets and gifts, such as retro gaming lamps, DIY food and drink kits, and, of course, VW Campervan tents. With many traditional retailers and other niche players operating in this sector now, Firebox positions itself as being one of the first outlets for innovative products. Firebox makes use of the collaborative nature of the web with C2C interactions where Firebox.com customers describe their experiences with products by submitting reviews. Customers are also encouraged to send in photos and videos of them in action via social media channels.

Initially a 'pureplay' Internet-only business, Firebox is now a multichannel retailer, providing a mail-order service via its catalogue and corporate products (including sales promotion and staff incentives for Yahoo!, Oracle, Five, Siemens and Santander plus wholesale and trade suppliers). The trade suppliers then distribute products to other online and offline e-retailers.

Figure 2.13	Firebox
	Source: www.firebox.com, Copyright Firebox.

Firebox received £500,000 of investment from New Media Spark, with further funding from private investors. Sales grew 156% a year from £262,000 in 2000 to £4.4 million in 2003 and £8 million in 2004 from 175,000 orders. In the same year, it received 4.5 million page impressions and 680,000 monthly unique visitors, according to the Nielsen//Netratings panel (eSuperbrands, 2005). Firebox.com became profitable in 2001.

One of the reasons for the success of Firebox is the way it has embraced traditional channels to market. Silicon.com (2004) reports that head of PR Charlie Morgan explained: 'In a marketplace that was fast becoming cluttered there was a strong need to both expand the customer base and ensure that Firebox itself grew as a brand. By building in a programme of catalogue drops, Firebox aimed to recruit many new customers who had not thought of the Internet as a purchasing medium, increase turnover and of course grow the brand.'

In 2009, the company reported that the Firebox.com website attracted nearly 10 million visits in 2009 and served 48 million page impressions according to Google Analytics. The email newsletter is sent twice a week to over 700,000 recipients while over 1 million copies of the catalogue are circulated annually. In 2010, the revenue of the business was £14.4 million. By continuing to look for a niche in the market and playing to its strengths, the company has continued to be a profitable, growing, independently owned company. In 2013 the company continued trading with a mobile responsive site. (See Chapter 11 for more details on this approach.)

Source: Company website, About Us, eSuperbrands (2005) and Silicon.com (2004). With thanks to www.firebox.com.

Summary

1   The constantly changing digital business environment should be monitored by all organisations in order to be able to respond to changes in social, legal, economic, political and technological factors together with changes in the immediate marketplace that occur through changes in customer requirements and competitors' and intermediaries' offerings.

2   The online marketplace involves transactions between organisations and consumers (B2C) and other businesses (B2B). Consumer-to-consumer (C2C) and consumer-to-business categories (C2B) can also be identified.

3   The Internet can cause disintermediation within the marketplace as an organisation's channel partners such as wholesalers or retailers are bypassed. Alternatively, the Internet can cause reintermediation as new intermediaries with a different purpose are formed to help bring buyers and sellers together in a virtual marketplace or marketspace. Evaluation of the implications of these changes and implementation of alternative countermediation strategies are important to strategy.

4   Trading in the marketplace can be sell-side (seller-controlled), buy-side (buyer-controlled) or at a neutral marketplace.

5   A business model is a summary of how a company will generate revenue identifying its product offering, value-added services, revenue sources and target customers. Exploiting the range of business models made available through the Internet is important to both existing companies and start-ups.

6   The Internet may also offer opportunities for new revenue models such as commission on affiliate referrals to other sites or banner advertising.

7   The opportunities for new commercial arrangements for transactions include negotiated deals, brokered deals, auctions, fixed-price sales and pure spot markets, and barters should also be considered.

8   The success of Internet start-up companies is critically dependent on their business and revenue models and traditional management practice.

Exercises

Answers to these exercises are available online at www.pearsoned.co.uk/chaffey

Self-assessment questions

1 Outline the main options for trading between businesses and consumers.
2 Explain the concepts of disintermediation and reintermediation with reference to a particular industry; what are the implications for a company operating in this industry?
3 Describe the three main alternative locations for trading within the electronic marketplace.
4 What are the main types of commercial transactions that can occur through the Internet or in traditional commerce?
5 Digital business involves re-evaluating value chain activities. What types of changes can be introduced to the value chain through digital business?
6 List the different business models identified by Timmers (1999).
7 Describe some alternative revenue models for a website from a magazine publisher.
8 Draw a diagram summarising the different types of online marketplace.

Essay and discussion questions

1 'Disintermediation and reintermediation occur simultaneously within any given market.' Discuss.
2 For an organisation you are familiar with, examine the alternative business and revenue models afforded by the Internet and assess the options for the type and location of e-commerce transitions.
3 For a manufacturer or retailer of your choice, analyse the balance between partnering with portals and providing equivalent services from your website.
4 Contrast the market potential for B2B and B2C auctions.
5 Select an intermediary site and assess how well it makes use of the range of business models and revenue models available to it through the Internet.

Examination questions

1 Explain disintermediation and reintermediation using examples.
2 Describe three different revenue models for a portal such as Yahoo!
3 What is meant by buy-side, sell-side and marketplace-based e-commerce?
4 What are the different mechanisms for online auctions?
5 Describe two alternative approaches for using digital business to change a company's value chain.
6 Explain what a business model is and relate it to an Internet pureplay of your choice.
7 Outline the elements of the digital business environment for an organisation and explain its relevance to the organisation.
8 Give three different transaction types that an industry marketplace could offer to facilitate trade between buyers and suppliers.

References

Benjamin, R. and Weigand, R. (1995) Electronic markets and virtual value-chains on the information superhighway. *Sloan Management Review,* Winter, 62–72.

Berryman, K., Harrington, L., Layton-Rodin, D. and Rerolle, V. (1998) Electronic commerce: three emerging strategies. *McKinsey Quarterly,* no. 1, 152–9.

Business Insider (2013) The Story of a Failed Startup and a Founder Driven to Suicide. Blog post by Alyson Shontell, published by Business Insider.com, 4 April 2013. **www.busi nessinsider.com/jody-sherman-ecomom-2013-4**.

Chamberlin, G. (2010) Googling the Present. *Economic & Labour Review,* December, Office for National Statistics.

Choi, H and Varian, H (2009) Predicting the present with Google Trends, Google Inc, available at **http://googleresearch.blogspot.co.uk/2009/04/predicting-present-with-google-trends.html**.

Desmet, D., Francis, T., Hu, A., Koller, M. and Riedel, G. (2000) Valuing dot coms. *McKinsey Quarterly,* no. 1. Available online at **www.mckinsey.com/insights**.

eSuperbrands (2005) *Your Guide to Some of the Best Brands on the Web.* Superbrands Ltd, London.

Evans, P. and Wurster, T.S. (1999) Getting real about virtual commerce. *Harvard Business Review,* November, 84–94.

Gwyther, M. (1999) Jewels in the web. *Management Today,* November, 63–9.

MacDonald, E. *et al.* (2012) Tracking the Customer's Journey to Purchase. Harvard Business Review Blog by Emma Macdonald, Hugh Wilson and Umut Konus, 17 August: **http:// blogs.hbr.org/2012/08/tracking-the-customers-journey/**.

McDonald, M. and Wilson, H. (2002) *New Marketing: Transforming the Corporate Future.* Butterworth-Heinemann, Oxford.

Nunes, P., Kambil, A. and Wilson, D. (2000) The all-in-one market. *Harvard Business Review,* May–June, 2–3.

Osterwald, A. and Pigneur, Y. (2010) *Business Model Generation Site: A Handbook for Visionaries, Game Changers and Challengers.* **www.businessmodelgeneration.com**. John Wiley & Sons, London.

Prentiss, P. (2013) Implosion at Ecomum. An unedited letter by Phillip Prentiss. Published on Scribd at **www.scribd.com/doc/137629166/Ecomom-Post-Mortem** and later published on Business Insider (2013).

Rayport, J. and Sviokla, J. (1996) Exploiting the virtual value-chain. *McKinsey Quarterly,* no. 1, 20–37.

Riggins, F. and Mitra, S. (2007) An e-valuation framework for developing net-enabled business metrics through functionality interaction. *Journal of Organizational Computing and Electronics Commerce,* 17(2), 175–203.

Sarkar, M., Butler, B. and Steinfield, C. (1996) Intermediaries and cybermediaries. A continuing role for mediating players in the electronic marketplace. *Journal of Computer Mediated Communication,* 1(3). Online-only journal, no page numbers.

Silicon.com (2004) Ecommerce sites: 'Long live. . . the catalogue?' 23 November. Author, Will Sturgeon (**www.silicon.com**).

Smart Insights (2012) In-depth digital marketing case studies. Last updated December 2012. **www.smartinsights.com/guides/digital-marketing-case-studies/**.

Thomas, J. and Sullivan, U. (2005) Managing marketing communications with multichannel customers. *Journal of Marketing,* 69 (October), 239–51.

Timmers, P. (1999) *Electronic Commerce Strategies and Models for Business-to-Business Trading.* Series on Information Systems. John Wiley & Sons, Chichester.

Venkatram, N. (2000) Five steps to a dot-com strategy: how to find your footing on the web. *Sloan Management Review,* Spring, 15–28.

Web links

Adoption of Internet and online services

These sources are listed at the end of Chapter 4 and examples given in that chapter.

Business model development

FastCompany (**www.fastcompany.com**) Also covers the development of business models with a US focus.

Ghost sites (**www.disobey.com/ghostsites**) Steve Baldwin's compilation of failed e-businesses, including the Museum of E-failure!

Paid Content (**www.paidcontent.org**) Covers the development of revenue models for publishers.

Commentators on online business models

Mohansawhney.com (**www.mohansawhney.com**) Papers from e-business specialist, Mohanbir Sawhney of Kellogg School of Management, Northwestern University, Evanston, IL, USA.

Michael Rappa's Business Models page (**http://digitalenterprise.org/models/models.html**) Michael Rappa is a professor at North Carolina State University.

Dave Chaffey's Smart Insights (**www.smartinsights.com**) Discussion on business models and spreadsheets for modelling publishing and e-commerce revenue.

Managing digital business infrastructure

Web support

The following additional case studies are available at
www.pearsoned.co.uk/chaffey

→ Selecting a supplier for hosting website services
→ Achieving integration between different systems through EAI

The site also contains a range of study material designed to help improve your results.

Scan code to find the latest updates for topics in this chapter

Learning outcomes

After completing this chapter the reader should be able to:

● Outline the range of hardware and software technologies used to build a digital business infrastructure within an organisation and with its partners
● Review the management actions needed to maintain service quality for users of digital platforms

Management issues

The issues for managers raised in this chapter include:

● What are the practical risks to the organisation of failure to manage the e-commerce infrastructure adequately?
● How should we evaluate alternative models of delivering web services?

Links to other chapters

This chapter is an introduction to Internet hardware and software technologies. It gives the technical background to Chapters 1 and 2 and to Parts 2 and 3. Its focus is on understanding the technology used but it also gives an introduction to how it needs to be managed. The main chapters that cover management of the digital business infrastructure are:

● *Chapter 10*, Change management
● *Chapter 11*, Analysis and design (including architecture design)
● *Chapter 12*, Implementation and maintenance – this focuses on the issues in selecting the software used for publishing content such as content management systems and blogs

Introduction

Defining an adequate technology infrastructure is vital to all start-up online businesses and existing companies making the transformation to digital business. The infrastructure and support of different types of digital platforms directly affect the quality of service experienced by users of the systems in terms of speed and responsiveness. The range of digital services provided also determines the capability of an organisation to compete through differentiating itself in the marketplace. Mcafee and Brynjolfsson (2008) suggest that to use digital technology to compete, the mantra for the CEO should be:

> *Deploy, innovate, and propagate: First, deploy a consistent technology platform. Then separate yourself from the pack by coming up with better ways of working. Finally, use the platform to propagate these business innovations widely and reliably. In this regard, deploying IT serves two distinct roles – as a catalyst for innovative ideas and as an engine for delivering them.*

Digital business infrastructure
The architecture of hardware, software, content and data used to deliver e-business services to employees, customers and partners.

Digital business infrastructure refers to the combination of hardware such as servers and client desktop computers and mobile devices, the network used to link this hardware and the software applications used to deliver services to workers within the business and also to its partners and customers. Infrastructure also includes the architecture of the networks, hardware and software and where it is located. Finally, infrastructure can also be considered to include the methods for publishing data and documents accessed through applications. A key decision with managing this infrastructure is which elements are located within the company and which are managed externally.

Through being aware of potential infrastructure problems, managers of an organisation can work with their partners to ensure that a good level of service is delivered to everyone, internal and external, who is using the e-business infrastructure. To highlight some of the problems that may occur if the infrastructure is not managed correctly, complete Activity 3.1.

Activity 3.1	Infrastructure risk assessment

Purpose

To indicate potential problems to customers, partners and staff of the e-business if technical infrastructure is not managed adequately.

Activity

Make a list of the potential technology problems faced by customers of an online retailer. Consider problems faced by users of digital business applications which are either internal or external to the organisation. Base your answer on problems you have experienced on a website that can be related to network, hardware and software failures or problems with data quality.

Answers to activities can be found at www.pearsoned.co.uk/chaffey

In this chapter we focus on the management decisions involved with creating an effective technology infrastructure rather than explaining the technology in detail. We explained the technology such as TCP/IP/XML and XML in more detail in previous editions, when it was less familiar to readers. In this edition, the technology introduction is covered through references to other sources and online material taken from other editions. Research and feedback from users of the book have shown that this knowledge usually exists from other courses, modules or from work, so there is little value in duplicating it. Instead, there is a demand to learn more about the management issues of deploying the technology, summarised in Table 3.1.

The interview on Magiq gives an example of how integration of a service into a website can help deliver better results for a business.

Table 3.1	Key management issues of digital business infrastructure	

Main issue	Detail	Where covered?
Which digital access platforms should we support?	Mobile platforms such as tablets and smartphones are rapidly increasing in importance, so the right investment decisions need to be taken here. Other data exchange methods between services such as feeds and APIs also need to be considered.	We introduce the key types of consumer access platforms and data exchange options, and the opportunities of mobile marketing at the start of the chapter.
Setup and selection of services for a new digital service.	Many managers are involved in managing the introduction of a new service where they have to select a platform, suppliers and models for access and data storage.	A section on setup of customer-facing digital service addresses these management decisions, including domain selection, use of hosting providers and cloud services.
How do we achieve quality of service in digital services?	Requirements are: business fit, security, speed, availability and level of errors	Section on ISPs in this chapter, Chapter 11 on design, Chapter 12 on implementation
Where do we host applications?	Internal or external sourcing and hosting via web services	Management issues in creating a new customer-facing digital service in this chapter
Application integration	Integration of digital business solutions with: – legacy systems – partner systems – B2B exchanges and intermediaries	Section on technology options and standards for supply chain management in Chapter 6
How do we publish and manage content and data quality?	How are content and data updated so that they are up to date, accurate, easy to find and easy to interpret?	Web content management, blogs and feeds are introduced in this chapter and in more detail in Chapters 11 and 12
How do we manage employee access to the Internet?	Staff can potentially waste time using the Internet or can act illegally	Covered in Chapter 11 in 'Focus on Security design for digital business'
How do we secure data?	Content and data can be deleted in error or maliciously	Safeguards are described in Chapter 11

Real-world Digital Business	Creating dynamic personalisation software

Q. Give some examples of how Magiq is being used and the benefits it offers

Two of our clients are using Magiq in quite different ways:

Hotel Reservation Service (HRS) is using Magiq to build customer databases from the interactions of the visitors on its website. Magiq records how users interact with the site and logs key information about their behaviour. This includes information about their physical location (town/country), their organisation, any search terms they have used (in reaching the site), other information which helps to characterise their interest (e.g. if they have registered for a newsletter, requested additional information etc.), and it also particularly looks for email addresses that they have entered into the site.

Magiq makes this information available in two forms:

1 as real-time profile information, so that HRS can write Triggers to present specific pieces of content for certain types of user. So for example, if a customer has indicated that they are an SME or procurement manager, then the Trigger can ensure that information relevant to them is injected into the pages presented. By using the Magiq historic customer profile Magiq ensures that the right information is provided on each visit, even if the user does not re-identify themselves.

2 as customer lists. Magiq provides lists of people who are being very active (indicating that they may be 'ready to buy') and would benefit from a call from HRS's sales teams, and it also provides lists of people who look ready to defect (because they were regular users, but have stopped arriving). These lists are downloaded by HRS's sales and customer support teams to help them target their activities and communications to the right people with the right message. Because Magiq provides all the contact information for each visitor (which the visitors provided to the website), together with the data that identifies the customer segment they are in, this communication can be very accurate.

FBTO was one of Magiq's early beta customers. It is an insurance company, and used Magiq's data to personalise the home page for different segments of users. The company identified four stages of engagement in the brand, from users showing an interest in a specific product, to users who had purchased a specific product. For each segment and for each product group FBTO created a small banner which provided specific information for users in that segment on the product group of interest.

By making this simple change, FBTO increased its conversion rates by 15%.

It also used the data to allow its call centre to contact people who looked to be on the point of buying, but had not made their purchase online. Targeting calls in this way produced a campaign that resulted in a sale to one in every three people called.

Q. What are the differences to other similar tools or the well-known Amazon personalisation?

Today, there are behavioural targeting tools that display content on the basis of current behaviour, but we are unaware of any solution that builds and maintains long-term customer behaviour records for every individual visitor, and lets the site owner use that combination of long-term and real-time behaviour to personalise their communications and web page content.

Also, all other approaches to personalisation or recommendation require the site owner to undertake significant tagging activities to collect the data needed, and to add tags to allow content to be added. Magiq by contrast is effectively tag-free, only requiring the inclusion of a static script file into the pages of the site. This can be done via a one-time change to the content management system or can even be done via the web servers or load balancers for the site.

This has several implications. Firstly, deployment of the solution is almost instantaneous, and secondly, a static/flat site or a site or application which the customer is unable to change can be turned into a site with dynamic content and rich media content using Magiq very simply. Moreover, the marketing team can change the content, personalisation rules and content types instantly via Magiq's simple interface.

In actuality, Magiq brings exactly the levels of personalisation and creativity that Amazon has implemented, without needing to spend the millions of pounds in custom development and technology that they had to utilise to implement their solution. In our view, Magiq is really Amazon personalisation in a box!

Privacy issues of personalisation and behavioural targeting

Q. How is the privacy of the user protected and how are possible concerns addressed?

Magiq only uses the data that the users voluntarily enter into the site and link this to location and organisation data derived from their IP addresses . . . . So it's like the message you hear when calling a call centre that says 'this call is being recorded for the purpose of customer service quality improvement'.

Figure 3.1 shows an example of some of the information collected by Maqiq.

Magiq's contracts also require the site owner to disclose the fact that they are collecting data and the purposes for which they will be used, as we believe openness with the visitors is very important.

Magiq's solution also goes to considerable lengths to manage the privacy and security of personal information being collected. For example, all data Magiq collects from the user is encrypted as it is captured, so the transmission of any data is more secure than the data normally passed from the browser to the website. We also provide opt-out functions for the user, allowing people to manage their own data collection and privacy decisions.

Lastly, unlike most 'on-demand' services which are 'multi-tenant', each Magiq customer has his or her own cloud instance – this means that each site's data is in a separate system and the site owner has exclusive access and rights to the data collected.

Figure 3.1	An example of some of the data collected by Magiq
	Source: www.magiq.com.

Moreover, Magiq subscribers can decide if they would prefer their instance to be located in the EU or USA, thus easing data management and privacy compliance.

Q. Which criteria should someone selecting a vendor of personalisation technology consider?

Clearly this will involve the factors affecting the return on investment and cost of ownership on one side and functional issues on the other.

Magiq aims to provide top-notch ROI by reducing deployment costs (via the tag-free deployment) and minimising operating costs by using the latest cloud-computing technology and by allowing users complete control over their expenditure with a simple traffic-banded rate. At the same time it is attempting to provide maximum return by providing usable/actionable data on the individual users and their interests, and by allowing one-to-one real-time personalisation (as opposed to the suck-it-and-see approaches provided by MVT tools and 'herd-behaviour' approaches of product recommendation solutions).

From a functional perspective, each business needs to understand the functions it wants to implement to maximise the effectiveness of its online marketing and communications. This will vary from business to business. Magiq's range of simple-to-use apps attempts to provide powerful personalisation, optimisation and CRM solutions on normal PC and mobile platforms. Other solutions focus on features like product recommendations and simple AB testing which are functions not provided by Magiq today.

Also, the roadmap of a supplier is important as investment in solutions in this area tends to be quite long-term (especially as the value and quality of customer data available grow). So it is important to choose suppliers with long-term commitment to the market, and a vision for the future.

So, for example, Magiq provides a good platform based on individual customer data, and we plan to extend the family of apps to embrace other applications like email campaigns, dynamic pricing, cross-channel data integration etc., and also extend it to embrace Flash, Flex and stand-alone apps created with Adobe AIR.

Q. How would you recommend that a business assesses the value of a tool like Magiq? Which KPIs should be reviewed?

Magiq is focussed on the implementation side of online marketing. While it records all the activity it has undertaken, it does not undertake the analytics part of the process, as most users already have web analytics or customer analytics and reporting tools which we expect users to use to analyse the effectiveness of the campaigns and activities that Magiq implements.

The actual KPIs that should be measured and tracked are clearly customer specific. So for a transactional site these might be focussed on revenue and on conversion rate. For non-transactional sites other metrics are important. Some customers will choose to focus on the visitor retention and engagement factors (duration of engagement, time on site, visit frequency and latency etc.), others will want to analyse the customer data provided by Prospect and Retain to assess the value of the audience that they have in monetary or other ways.

Source: Smart Insights (2010).

Supporting the growing range of digital business technology platforms

If you think of the options to reach and interact with customers or partners online, these interactions have traditionally been via desktop software and browsers. The desktop access platform has been dominant for years and remains so for now, but with mobile Internet access predicted to exceed desktop Internet access by 2014 or 2015, a range of mobile platforms will become available. Combining with these hardware platforms, there are also different software platforms which marketers can use to reach and interact with their audience through content marketing or advertising, so let's look at the range of options that are available:

Desktop, laptop and notebook platforms

1 **Desktop browser-based platform.** This is traditional web access through the consumer's browser of choice, whether Internet Explorer, Google Chrome or Safari.
2 **Desktop apps.** We don't see this platform talked about much, but with the launch of Apple Lion many Apple users are accessing paid and free apps from their desktop too, via the Apple App Store. This gives opportunities for brands to engage via these platforms.
3 **Email platforms.** While email isn't traditionally considered as a platform, it does offer a separate option from browser and app-based options to communicate with prospects or clients, whether through editorial or advertising, and email is still widely used for marketing.
4 **Feed-based and API data exchange platforms.** Many users still consume data through RSS feeds, and Twitter and Facebook status updates can be considered a form of feed or stream where ads can be inserted.
5 **Video-marketing platforms.** Streamed video is often delivered through the other platforms mentioned above, particularly through browsers and plug-ins, but it represents a separate platform. Television channels delivered through streaming over the Internet, known as IPTV, are related to this platform.

It could be argued that the major social networks, Facebook, LinkedIn and Twitter, also provide a form of platform, but these really exist across all of these technology platforms so they haven't been identified separately.

Mobile phone and tablet platforms

Mobile device use has already transformed the way consumers access online content and services for entertainment, socialising and purchase decisions. The options on mobile hardware platforms are similar in many ways to the desktop. Since they can be used in different locations there are many new opportunities to engage consumers through **mobile marketing** and **location-based marketing**. (We cover the design challenges of creating mobile experiences in Chapter 11 where options for responsive web design are reviewed.) Table 3.2 introduces some of these challenges.

Mobile marketing
Marketing to encourage consumer engagement when they're using mobile phones (particularly smartphones) or tablet devices.

Location-based marketing
Location or proximity-based marketing is mobile marketing based on the GPS built into phones or based on interaction with other local digital devices.

Trends update | Mobile usage

Mobile usage was forecast to overtake desktop usage in 2014. Find out the latest statistics on mobile and app usage at: http://bit.ly/smartmobilestats.

The main mobile platforms are:

6 **Mobile operating system and browser.** There are mobile browsers which are closely integrated with the operating system.
7 **Mobile-based apps.** Apps are proprietary to the mobile operating system, whether Apple iOS, Google Android, RIM or Windows. A big decision is whether to deliver content and experience through a browser and/or a specific app which provides an improved experience.

With the growth in mobile platform usage by consumers it becomes important to assess whether companies are gaining similar levels of business from consumers using mobile platforms as from desktop platforms. Table 3.3 shows how companies can assess this using the approach to strategy development from Chapter 5.

The benefits that mobile or wireless connections offer to their users are ubiquity (can be accessed from anywhere), reachability (their users can be reached when not in their normal location) and convenience (it is not necessary to have access to a power supply or fixed-line connection). They

Table 3.2	Five common challenges of creating a mobile web presence

Challenge	Issue	Solution
One site or two? Mobile app	Should you transcode ('screen-scrape') your main website into a standard mobile template to create a separate site, or optimise your site for mobile? Are mobile apps necessary?	Create one site, hosted on one URL, fed by one CMS rather than building a separate site, which requires duplicated content updates. If there is a business case for mobile apps in terms of more revenue from apps compared to mobile sites, these need to be created for the main app stores, or native apps can be created (such as the FT.com example in Chapter 11).
Right content	Agree on a clearly defined content plan (news& info, entertainment, mobile commerce).	Offer content which mobile users want to access on their handsets: maps, info, shopping, social networking and coupons are the most popular mobile Internet activities.
UX	Smaller screen size and lack of keyboard make easy, simple navigation critical.	Use simple navigation; vertical not horizontal navigation. Icons are easier to access than text links, and appear more 'app-like'.
Personalisation	Personalised content maximises page views, extends dwell time, attracts repeat visits.	Build in behavioural, location and time-based components. (See responsive design section in Chapter 11.)
Promotion	Mobile users want to find you quickly and easily on the mobile Internet.	Use all media channels to drive traffic; use trackable links to detect which ones evaluate channel efficiency.

Source: Smart Insights (2013).

Mini Case Study 3.1	Location-based marketing

If you're thinking that location-based marketing is just for corporates with large budgets, the likes of Starbucks and McDonald's, then think again. ClickZ (2010) has reported how AJ Bombers, a speciality burger bar in Milwaukee, attributed a sale increase of 110% to Foursquare. It has 1,400 people on its Foursquare page who have checked in 6,000 times. The mayor gets a free burger, and currently that's 'Amy', who has had to check in 40 times in the last 60 days at the one-location establishment in order to achieve the distinction.

Engagement is also increased through people who add a tip to the restaurant's Foursquare page, getting rewarded with a free cookie when they show it to a waiter or cashier.

The sales increase figure is based on a single campaign which saw 161 check-ins on 28 February, a 110% sales increase when compared to a normal Sunday. Joe Sorge, owner of the restaurant, promoted an AJ Bombers-branded 'Swarm Badge' event to his Foursquare-using regulars. Such a custom badge is awarded to users who check in at a location where at least 50 other users are simultaneously checked in.

The restaurant owner advised that success involves implementing Foursquare as a regular part of operations:

Our staff encourages the use and engagement of Foursquare by virtue of our Foursquare specials being very prominent throughout our business. It encourages our customers to ask questions of our staff. Education of that staff is the key.

Table 3.3	Examples of objectives and strategies to achieve them for mobile platforms

Objectives	Substantiation (informed by situation analysis or insight, for example)	Strategies to achieve goals	Key performance indicators (critical success factors)
1. *Reach objectives.* Deliver 2 million mobile site visitors in year.	Extrapolation of current growth in mobile segments on current site plus +25% increment from promotion in other digital channels.	Start investment in Google AdWords for mobile and mobile display networks. Use device detection to access mobile site. Promotion in-store.	Clickthrough rates from mobile-specific campaigns and impression share delivered by AdWords.
2. *Act objectives.* 4% add-to-basket visit conversion rate from mobile.	This conversion rate is around two-thirds of desktop site conversion. Consistent with reported industry examples.	Develop mobile site-specific search. Mobile site merchandising.	Mobile site search % and add-to-basket rates. Promo clickthrough rates.
3. *Convert objectives.* Mobile AOV = £35 Mobile visit to sale conversion = 2%	This conversion rate is around two-thirds of desktop site conversion. Consistent with reported industry examples.	Initial implementation of mobile checkout. This will be optimised in future years.	Microstep conversion within checkout process. Registration process for new customers.
4. *Engagement objectives.* Customer satisfaction ratings of mobile experience at 80% of online. Reviews placed and repeat-customer conversion at 80% of offline rates.	It is expected with the new mobile site that satisfaction ratings and repeat purchase percentages will be slightly lower, but this is unknown. We need to check thatemails are still successful in generating reviews.	Combination of strategies: Email and mobile messaging specific to mobile site purchasers. Mobile couponing.	% of reviews.

Source: Smart Insights (2013) mobile marketing framework.

also provide security – each user can be authenticated since each wireless device has a unique identification code; their location can be used to tailor content; and they provide a degree of privacy compared with a desktop PC. An additional advantage is that of instant access or being always-on; here there is no need to dial up a wireless connection. Table 3.4 provides a summary of the mobile or wireless Internet access proposition. There are considerable advantages in comparison to PC-based Internet access, but it is still limited by the display limitations.

Other hardware platforms

Apart from desktop and mobile access, there are a host of other and growing platforms through which to communicate with customers. For example:

1 **Gaming platforms.** Whether it's a Playstation, Nintendo or Xbox variety of gaming machine, there are increasing options to reach gamers through ads or placements within games, for example in-game ads.
2 **Indoor and outdoor kiosk-type apps.** For example, interactive kiosks and augmented reality options to communicate with consumers.
3 **Interactive signage.** The modern version of signage, which is closely related to kiosk apps, may incorporate different methods such as touch-screen, Bluetooth or QR codes to encourage interactive.

Table 3.4	Summary of mobile or wireless Internet access consumer proposition

Element of proposition	Evaluation
No fixed location	The user is freed from the need to access via the desktop, making access possible when commuting, for example
Location-based services	Mobiles can be used to give geographically based services, e.g. an offer in a particular shopping centre. Future mobiles will have global positioning services integrated
Instant access/ convenience	The latest General Packet Radio Service (GPRS) and 3G services are always-on, avoiding the need for lengthy connection
Privacy	Mobiles are more private than desktop access, making them more suitable for social use or for certain activities such as an alert service when looking for a new job
Personalisation	As with PC access, personal information and services can be requested by the user, although these often need to be set up via PC access
Security	In the future, mobiles may become a form of wallet, but thefts of mobiles make this a source of concern

Box 3.1	Taking the mobile app vs site decision

Mobile apps
A software application that is designed for use on a mobile phone, typically downloaded from an App store. iPhone apps are best known, but all smartphones support the use of apps which can provide users with information, entertainment or location-based services such as mapping.

Mobile apps are a highly significant development in mobile communications, indeed all digital communications, since they highlight a change in the method of delivering interactive services and content via mobile phones. Until the advent of apps, popularised by Apple iPhone, the web browser had been seen by most people as the main model for delivering content via mobile phones.

The key questions to ask are:

1 **Are apps a strategic priority for us?** The goal of apps for most organisations will be to increase awareness and sales or, for publishers, revenue from advertising or subscriptions. For many companies, this won't be a priority because they will have to put budget into higher-priority areas such as improving the experience of a desktop or mobile site using responsive design or in their social network presence. Owing to the volume of users reached through these other platforms, incremental improvements here are likely to give better returns. But the figures presented above show the potential benefits of apps to marketers in reaching audiences and potentially in selling apps, although the latter will be generally limited to publishers or specialist software developers. For these types of organisation, apps are likely to be a priority.

2 **Do we build our own app and/or leverage existing apps?** Creating an app is only one of the marketing options – advertising and sponsorship options may be a more cost-effective method to build reach and awareness of a brand. A good example of sponsorship fit is the Canon sponsorship of the excellent Guardian Eyewitness photography app. There are also options of new iAds from Apple and Google Adsense mobile display networks.

3 **Free or paid apps?** Retailers will generally offer free apps offering choice and convenience in return for loyalty. Brands offering entertainment will probably also go the free route to increase customer engagement. But for publishers or software houses, a freemium approach of free app showcasing the service and paid app for improved features or content is the standard approach.

4 **Which category of application to target?** As you would expect, accessing social networks and music via apps is popular.

5 **How to best promote mobile apps?** The options for marketing apps were also researched by Nielsen, which found that the most popular methods of app discovery are:

- Searching the appstore
- Recommendations from friends and family
- Mention on device or network carrier page
- Email promotion
- Offline mention in TV and print

6 **How to refine apps in line with feedback.** The success of apps is very dependent on feedback in the appstores and the need to fix bugs and add enhancements to compete shows the need for an ongoing development cycle with frequent updates. A whole new area of app analytics and new solutions will no doubt develop, but a challenge with apps, similar to that of Flash apps before them, is that measurement functionality needs to be specified in advance. Careful review of hurdle rates for the percentage of the user base who are using the app or its different functions is going to be a KPI here.

Augmented reality

Augmented reality (AR)
Blends real-world digital data captured typically with a digital camera in a webcam or mobile phone to create a browser-based digital representation or experience mimicking that of the real world.

Augmented reality (AR) is an exciting concept which can help companies improve their customer experience. It is best explained through examples:

1 Glasses Direct created its 'Video Mirror' app which enabled site visitors to model pairs of glasses using their webcam.

2 BMW used AR within a campaign launching their Z4 model on a 'virtual' test drive around the desk!

3 Layar demonstrated an estate agent application using the camera on a mobile phone while overlaying property information in a similar form to Google Street View.

Mini-case study 3.2 gives a futuristic example.

Mini Case Study 3.2	Tesco Homeplus opens subway virtual store in South Korea

In South Korea, Tesco Home plus has significantly fewer stores than the market leader E-mart. Based on research which showed that many Koreans tend to shop in stores near their homes for convenience, Tesco trialled a virtual store to reach these shoppers.

Virtual displays were implemented in a similar way to actual stores – from the display to merchandise, but with smartphone QR code readers used to shop and after checkout the goods are delivered to the customer's home (Figure 3.2).

Figure 3.2	Tesco virtual store *Source*: adapted from South Korea subway virtual store, http://www.tescoplc.com/index. asp?pageid=69&mediacategory=27, Tesco PLC.

Digital business infrastructure components

Figure 3.3 summarises how the different components of digital business architecture relate to each other. The different components can be conceived of as layers with defined interfaces between each layer. The different layers can best be understood in relation to a typical task performed by a user of a digital business system. For example, an employee who needs to book a holiday will access a specific human resources application or program that has been created to enable the holiday to be booked (Level I in Figure 3.3). This application will enable a holiday request to be entered and will forward the application to the employee's manager and the human resources department for approval. To access the application, the employee will use a web browser such as Microsoft Internet Explorer, Mozilla Firefox or Google Chrome using an operating system such as Microsoft Windows or Apple OS X (Level II). This systems software will then request transfer of the information about the holiday request across a network or transport layer (Level III). The information will then be stored in computer memory (RAM) or in long-term magnetic storage on a web server (Level IV). The information itself, which makes up the web pages or content viewed by the employee, and the data about their holiday request are shown as a separate layer (Level V in Figure 3.3), although it could be argued that this is the first or second level in an e-business architecture.

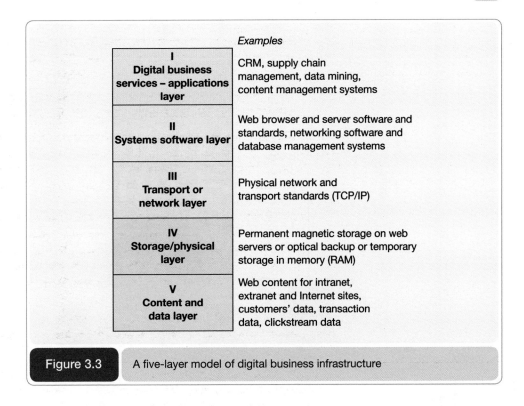

I **Digital business services – applications layer**	CRM, supply chain management, data mining, content management systems
II **Systems software layer**	Web browser and server software and standards, networking software and database management systems
III **Transport or network layer**	Physical network and transport standards (TCP/IP)
IV **Storage/physical layer**	Permanent magnetic storage on web servers or optical backup or temporary storage in memory (RAM)
V **Content and data layer**	Web content for intranet, extranet and Internet sites, customers' data, transaction data, clickstream data

Examples

Figure 3.3   A five-layer model of digital business infrastructure

Kampas (2000) describes an alternative five-level infrastructure model of what he refers to as 'the information system function chain':

1 **Storage/physical.** Memory and disk hardware components (equivalent to Level IV in Figure 3.3).
2 **Processing.** Computation and logic provided by the processor (processing occurs at Levels I and II).
3 **Infrastructure.** This refers to the human and external interfaces and also the network, referred to as 'extrastructure'. (This is Level III, although the human or external interfaces are not shown there.)
4 **Application/content.** This is the data processed by the application into information. (This is Level V.)
5 **Intelligence.** Additional computer-based logic that transforms information to knowledge (Level I).

Each of these elements of infrastructure presents separate management issues which we will consider separately.

A short introduction to Internet technology

Client–server
The client–server architecture consists of client computers, such as PCs, sharing resources such as a database stored on more powerful server computers.

As you will know, the Internet enables communication between millions of connected computers worldwide, but how does the seamless transfer of data happen? Requests for information are transmitted from client computers and mobile devices whose users request services from server computers that hold information and host business applications that deliver the services in response to requests. Thus, the Internet is a large-scale **client–server** system.

Figure 3.4 shows how the client computers within homes and businesses are connected to the Internet via local **Internet service providers (ISPs)** which, in turn, are linked to larger ISPs with connection to the major national and international infrastructure or **backbones**

Figure 3.4	Physical and network infrastructure components of the Internet (Levels IV and III in Figure 3.3)

Internet service provider (ISP)
A provider providing home or business users with a connection to access the Internet. They can also host web-based applications.

Backbones
High-speed communications links used to enable Internet communications across a country and internationally.

which are managed by commercial organisations. These high-speed links can be thought of as the motorways on the 'information superhighway', while the links provided from ISPs to consumers are equivalent to slow country roads.

Globally, many submarine cables form the backbone between countries, and these cables are susceptible to damage. For example, in January 2008 a ship's anchor severed a cable in the Mediterranean, resulting in a dramatic slowdown in Internet access for people in India, Sri Lanka, Pakistan and the Middle East!

Management issues in creating a new customer-facing digital service

In this section we consider some of the issues that managers introducing new services need to be aware of, including:

- Domain name selection
- Selection of hosting services, including cloud providers
- Selection of additional SaaS (Software as a Service) platforms.

Domain name selection

We start with this relatively simple decision, since there is some basic terminology that managers need to be aware of. Companies typically have many digital services located on different domains, particularly for companies with different domains for different countries. The domain name refers to the address of the web server and is usually selected to be the same as the name of the company, and the extension will indicate its type. The extension is commonly known as the generic top-level domain (gTLD). Common gTLDs are:

(i)   **.com** represents an international or American company such as www.travelocity.com.
(ii)   **.org** is for not-for-profit organisations (e.g. www.greenpeace.org).
(iii) **.mobi** – introduced in 2006 for sites configured for mobile phones.
(iv)   **.net** is a network provider such as www.demon.net.

There are also specific country-code top-level domains (ccTLDs):

(v)   **.co.uk** represents a company based in the UK such as www.thomascook.co.uk.
(vi)   **.au, .ca, .de, .es, .fi, .fr, .it, .nl,** etc. represent other countries (the co.uk syntax is an anomaly!).
(vii) **.ac.uk** is a UK-based university or other higher education institution (e.g. www. cranfield.ac.uk).
(viii) **.org.uk** is for a not-for-profit organisation focussing on a single country (e.g. www. mencap.org.uk).

The 'filename.html' part of the web address refers to an individual web page, for example 'products.html' for a web page summarising a company's products.

It is important that companies define a URL strategy which will help customers or partners find relevant parts of the site containing references to specific products or campaigns when printed in offline communications such as adverts or brochures.

Uniform resource locators (URLs)

The technical name for web address is **uniform (or universal) resource locator (URL)**. URLs can be thought of as a standard method of addressing, similar to postcodes or zipcodes, that make it straightforward to find the name of a domain or a document on the domain.

In larger businesses, particularly those with many sites, it's important to develop a **URL strategy** so that there is a consistent way of labelling online services and resources.

There is further terminology associated with a URL which will often be required when discussing site implementation or digital marketing campaigns, as shown in Box 3.2.

Uniform (universal) resource locator (URL)

A web address used to locate a web page on a web server.

URL strategy

A defined approach to forming URLs, including the use of capitalisation, hyphenation and sub-domains for different brands and different locations. This has implications for promoting a website offline through promotional or vanity URLs, search engine optimisation and findability.
A clean URL which fits many of these aims is http://www.domain.com/folder-name/document-name. Care must be taken with capitalisation since Linux servers parse capitals differently from lower-case letters.

Box 3.2	What's in a URL?

A great example of different URL components is provided by Google engineer Matt Cutts (Cutts, 2007). He gives this example:

    http://video.google.co.uk:80/videoplay?docid=-7246927612831078230&hl=en#00
    h02m30s

Here are some of the components of the URL:

- The protocol is http. Other protocols include https, ftp, etc.
- The host or hostname is video.google.co.uk.
- The subdomain is video.
- The domain name is google.co.uk.
- The top-level domain or TLD is uk (also known as gTLD). The uk domain is also referred to as a country-code top-level domain or ccTLD. For google.com, the TLD would be com.
- The second-level domain (SLD) is co.uk.

- The port is 80, which is the default port for web servers (not usually used in URLs when it is the default, although all web servers broadcast on ports).
- The path is /videoplay. Path typically refers to a file or location on the web server, e.g. /directory/file.html.
- The URL parameter is docid and its value is -7246927612831078230. These are often called the 'name, value' pair. URLs often have lots of parameters. Parameters start with a question mark (?) and are separated with an ampersand (&).
- The anchor or fragment is '#00h02m30s'.

Domain name registration

Domain name registration
The process of reserving a unique web address that can be used to refer to the company website.

Most companies own several domains, for different product lines or countries or for specific marketing campaigns. Domain name disputes can arise when an individual or company has **registered** a domain name which another company claims they have the right to. This is sometimes referred to as 'cybersquatting'.

Managers or agencies responsible for websites need to check that domain names are automatically renewed by the hosting company (as most are today). For example, the .co.uk domain must be renewed every two years. Companies that don't manage this process potentially risk losing their domain name since another company could potentially register it if the domain name lapsed.

Mini case study 3.3 shows one example of the value of domains and the need to protect them (which we examine in more detail in Chapter 4).

Mini Case Study 3.3	How much is a domain worth?

One of the highest values attached to a domain in Europe was paid in 2008 when the website cruise.co.uk paid the German travel company NeesReisen £560,000 for the rival name cruises.co.uk. *Guardian* (2008) reported the new owner of cruises.co.uk as saying that he hopes to use the new domain differently – by turning the site into an online intermediary or community for cruising enthusiasts while its existing cruise.co.uk will concentrate on offering the best deals for voyages. Explaining the valuation,cruise.co.uk's managing director, Seamus Conlon, said:

> 'Cruises' is consistently ranked first on Google, with 'cruise' just behind. We wanted the top positions so that when Internet users are searching for cruise deals, reviews or news we are the first port of call.

In the US, the record domain values are higher than when they were exchanged in the late 1990s, including

- Sex.com for $12m
- Business.com for $7.5m
- Beer.com for $7m in 1999.

Managing hardware and systems software infrastructure

Management of the technology infrastructure requires decisions on Layers II, III and IV in Figure 3.3.

Layer II – Systems software

The key management decision is standardisation throughout the organisation. Standardisation leads to reduced numbers of contacts for support and maintenance and can reduce purchase prices through multi-user licences. Systems software choices occur for the client, server and network. On client computers, the decision will be which browser software to standardise on. Standardised plug-ins should be installed across the organisation. The systems software for the client will also be decided on; this will probably be a variant of Microsoft Windows, but open-source alternatives such as Linux may also be considered. When considering systems software for the server, it should be remembered that there may be many servers in the global organisation, both for the Internet and intranets. Using standardised web-server software such as Apache will help maintenance. Networking software will also be decided on.

Managing digital business applications infrastructure

Digital business applications infrastructure
Applications that provide access to services and information inside and beyond an organisation.

Management of the digital business applications infrastructure concerns delivering the right applications to all users of digital business services. The issue involved is one that has long been a concern of IS managers, namely to deliver access to integrated applications and data that are available across the whole company. Traditionally businesses have developed applications silos or islands of information, as depicted in Figure 3.5(a). These silos may develop at three different levels: (1) there may be different technology architectures used in different functional areas, (2) there will also be different applications and separate databases in different areas, and (3) processes or activities followed in the different functional areas may also be different.

Applications silos are often a result of decentralisation or poorly controlled investment in information systems, with different departmental managers selecting different systems from different vendors. This is inefficient in that it will often cost more to purchase applications from separate vendors, and also it will be more costly to support and upgrade. Such a fragmented approach stifles decision-making and leads to isolation between functional units. For example, if customers phone a B2B company for the status of a bespoke item they have ordered, the person in customer support may have access to their personal details but not the status of their job, which is stored on a separate information system in the manufacturing unit. Problems can also occur at tactical and strategic levels. For example, if a company is trying to analyse the financial contribution of customers, perhaps to calculate lifetime values, some information about customers' purchases may be stored in a marketing information system, while the payments data will be stored in a separate system within the finance department. It may prove difficult or impossible to reconcile these different data sets.

To avoid the problems of a fragmented applications infrastructure, companies attempted throughout the 1990s to achieve the more integrated position shown in Figure 3.5(b). Many companies turned to enterprise resource planning (ERP) vendors such as SAP, Baan, PeopleSoft and Oracle.

Enterprise resource planning (ERP) applications
Software providing integrated functions for major business functions such as production, distribution, sales, finance and human resources management.

The approach of integrating different applications through ERP is entirely consistent with the principle of digital business, since digital business applications must facilitate the integration of the whole *supply chain* and *value chain*. It is noteworthy that many of the ERP vendors such as SAP have repositioned themselves as suppliers of digital business solutions! The difficulty for those managing digital business infrastructure is that there is not, and probably never can be, a single solution of components from a single supplier. For example, to gain competitive edge, companies may need to turn to solutions from innovators who, for example, support new channels such as WAP, or provide knowledge management solutions or sales management solutions. If these are not available from their favoured current supplier, do they wait until these components become available or do they attempt to integrate

Figure 3.5   (a) Fragmented applications infrastructure, (b) integrated applications infrastructure
Source: Adapted from Hasselbring (2000).

new software into the application? Thus managers are faced with a precarious balancing act between standardisation or core product and integrating innovative systems where applicable. Figure 3.6 illustrates this dilemma. It shows how different types of applications tend to have strengths in different areas.

ERP systems were originally focussed on achieving integration at the operational level of an organisation. Solutions for other applications such as business intelligence in the form of data warehousing and data mining tended to focus on tactical decision-making based on accessing the operational data from within ERP systems. Knowledge management software (Chapter 10) also tends to cut across different levels of management. Figure 3.7 shows only some types of applications, but it shows the trial of strength between the monolithic ERP applications and more specialist applications looking to provide the same functionality.

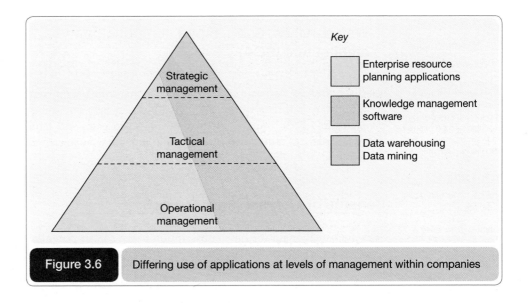

Figure 3.6   Differing use of applications at levels of management within companies

Figure 3.7   Elements of digital business infrastructure that require management

Figure 3.7 summarises some of these management issues and is based on the layered architecture introduced at the start of this section.

Web services, SaaS, cloud computing and service-oriented architecture (SOA)

Web services
Business applications and software services are provided through Internet and web protocols with the application managed on a separate server from where it is accessed through a web browser on an end-user's computer.

Infrastructure as a Service (IaaS)
Hardware used to provide support for end-user applications is outsourced and paid for according to level of usage. The hardware infrastructure used includes servers and networks.

PaaS (Platform as a Service)
Provision of software services for application design, development, data storage, testing and hosting together with messaging tools for collaboration on the development project.

'Web services' or 'Software as a Service (SaaS)' refers to a highly significant model for managing software and data within the digital business age. The web services model involves managing and performing all types of business processes and activities through accessing web-based services rather than running a traditional executable application on the processor of your local computer.

Benefits of web services or SaaS

SaaS are usually paid for on a subscription basis, so can potentially be switched on and off or payments paid according to usage, hence they are also known as 'on demand'. The main business benefit of these systems is that installation and maintenance costs are effectively outsourced. Cost savings are made on both the server and client sides, since the server software and databases are hosted externally and client applications software is usually delivered through a web browser or a simple application that is downloaded via the web.

In research conducted in the US and Canada by Computer Economics (2006), 91% of companies showed a first-year return on investment (ROI) from SaaS. Of these, 57% of the total had economic benefits which exceeded the SaaS costs and 37% broke even in year one. The same survey showed that in 80% of cases, the total cost of ownership (TCO) came in either on budget or lower. There would be few cases of traditional applications where these figures can be equalled. Read Mini case study 3.4 for details on the benefits of a SaaS implementation and how the concept of service usage can also be applied to hardware infrastructure.

Mini Case Study 3.4   How Intel benefits from SaaS, IaaS and PaaS!

CIO (2010) describes how Intel built an intranet for its research and development group. Its aims were to reduce the cost of operations by making more use of existing infrastructure and making users of computing services aware of the cost of their utilisation. Das Kamhout, the project lead, explained the benefits as follows:

Overall, this represents a dramatic change in mindset. On-demand self-service allows IT to get out of the way of the business so we can up-level IT and be a strategic business partner. And with transparent costs, departments across Intel now know what they're costing and what they're consuming.

This approach to server utilisation is known as IaaS (Infrastructure as a Service). Through reduced infrastructure spending and avoiding building new data centre facilities, the company expected to save nearly $200 million. This was achieved through improving its server utilisation rate from 59% in the first half of 2006 to 80% in 2010.

The technical teams within Intel also applied the PaaS (Platform as a Service) concept as part of the initiative. The platform referred to is the specific type of SaaS for developing new software and hardware as part of a systems development project.

Source: Adapted from CIO (2010).

Application programming interfaces (APIs)

Traditionally, organisations have sought to keep proprietary information within their firewalls for security reasons and to protect their intellectual property. But in the Internet era, this strategy may limit opportunities to add value to their services or share information via other online companies and their web services to increase their potential reach. Here are some examples from retail, publishing and software companies where APIs, sometimes known as the 'Programmable Web', have been used to help gain competitive advantage:

- Amazon Web Services (http://aws.amazon.com). One example of AWS allows affiliates, developers and website publishers to use Amazon Product Discovery which enables other sites to incorporate data about Amazon products and pricing.
- Facebook and Twitter use their APIs to help other sites embed social content into their sites.
- The Guardian Newspaper Open Platform (www.guardian.co.uk/open-platform) enables sharing of content and statistics from The Guardian.
- Google APIs exist for a number of its services, most notably Google Maps which, according to this directory (www.programmableweb.com/apis/directory), is one of the most popular mashups created through an API. The Google Analytics API has enabled many businesses and third-party application developers to visualise web performance data in a more tailored way.
- Kayak is an aggregator which allows third-party sites to integrate kayak.com searches and results into their website, desktop application or mobile phone application.

Challenges of deploying SaaS

Although the cost reduction arguments of SaaS are persuasive, what are the disadvantages of this approach? (The pros and cons are similar to the 'make or buy' decision discussed in Chapter 12.) SaaS will obviously have less capability for tailoring to exact business needs than a bespoke system.

The most obvious disadvantage of using SaaS is dependence on a third party to deliver services over the web, which has these potential problems:

Multi-tenancy SaaS
A single instance of a web service is used by different customers (tenants) run on a single server or load-balanced across multiple servers. Customers are effectively sharing processor, disk usage and bandwidth with other customers.

Single-tenancy SaaS
A single instance of an application (and/or database) is maintained for all customers (tenants) who have dedicated resources of processor, disk usage and bandwidth. The single instance may be load-balanced over multiple servers for improved performance.

- Downtime or poor availability if the network connection or server hosting the application or server fails.
- Lower performance than a local database. You know from using Gmail or Hotmail that although responsive, they cannot be as responsive as using a local email package like Outlook.
- Reduce data security since traditionally data would be backed up locally by in-house IT staff (ideally also off-site). Since failures in the system are inevitable, companies using SaaS need to be clear how back-up and restores are managed and the support that is available for handling problems, which is defined within the service level agreement (SLA).
- Data protection – since customer data may be stored in a different location it is essential that it is sufficiently secure and consistent with the data protection and privacy laws discussed in Chapter 4.

These potential problems need to be evaluated on a case-by-case basis when selecting SaaS providers. Disaster recovery procedures are particularly important since many SaaS applications such as customer relationship management and supply chain management are mission-critical. Managers need to question service levels since often services are delivered to multiple customers from a single server in a **multi-tenancy** arrangement rather than a **single-tenancy** arrangement. This is similar to the situation with the shared server or dedicated server we discussed earlier for web hosting. An example of this in practice is shown in Box 3.3.

Box 3.3   Is my SaaS single-tenancy or multi-tenancy?

Smoothspan (2007) has estimated the level of multi-tenancy for different web services, which is also dependent on the number of seats or users per server. He estimates that in 2006 Salesforce was running 40 Dell PowerEdge servers with 6,700 customers (tenants) and 134,000 seats. This is equivalent to 168 tenants per server, and 3,350 seats per server! Although this figure suggests the disadvantage of multi-tenancy, he also estimates that there is a 16:1 cost advantage of multi-tenant over single tenant.

An example of a consumer SaaS, word processing, would involve visiting a website which hosts the application rather than running a word processor such as Microsoft Word on your local computer through starting 'Word.exe'. The best-known consumer service for online word processing and spreadsheet use is Google Docs (http://docs.google.com) which was launched following the purchase in 2006 by Google of start-up Writely (www.writely.com). Google Docs also enables users to view and edit documents offline, through Google Gears, an open-source browser extension. 'Microsoft Office Live' is a similar initiative from Microsoft.

Google Apps enables organisations to manage many of their activities. The basic service is free, with the Premier Edition, which includes more storage space and security, being $50 per user account per year.

Utility computing
IT resources and in particular software and hardware are utilised on a pay-per-use basis and are managed externally as 'managed services'.

A related concept to web services is **utility computing**. Utility computing involves treating all aspects of IT as a commodity service such as water, gas or electricity where payment is according to usage. A subscription is usually charged per month according to the number of features, number of users, volume of data storage or bandwidth consumed. Discounts will be given for longer-term contracts. This includes not only software which may be used on a pay-per-use basis, but also using hardware, for example for hosting. An earlier term is 'applications service providers' (ASP).

Applications service provider
A provider of business applications such as email, workflow or groupware or any business application on a server remote from the user. A service often offered by ISPs.

Figure 3.8 shows one of the largest SaaS or utility providers, Salesforce.com, where customers pay on a per user per month basis according to the facilities used. The service is delivered from the Salesforce.com servers to over 50,000 customers in 15 local languages. Salesforce has added new services through acquisition of other SaaS providers. For example, to create its Marketing Cloud application it acquired social media monitoring tool Radian6 in March 2011for $326 million, advertising service Buddy Media in May 2012 for US$689 million and email marketing service ExactTarget in June 2013 for US$2.5 billion.

Cloud computing

Cloud computing
The use of distributed storage and processing on servers connected by the Internet, typically provided as software or data storage as a subscription service provided by other companies.

In descriptions of web services you will often hear, confusingly, that they access 'the cloud', or you may come across the term '**cloud computing**'. The cloud referred to is the combination of networking and data storage hardware and software hosted externally to a company, typically shared between many separate or 'distributed' servers accessed via the Internet. So, for example, Google Docs will be stored somewhere 'in the cloud' without any knowledge of where it is or how it is managed since Google stores data on many servers. Of course you can access the document from any location. But there are issues to consider about data stored and served from the cloud: 'Is it secure, is it backed up, is it always available?' The size of Google's cloud is indicated by Pandia (2007), which estimated that Google had over 1 million servers running the open-source Linux software. No more recent official figures are available, but Google has been open about individual data centres. In March 2009, it purchased the Summa Mill from Finnish paper company Stora Enso and converted the 60-year-old paper mill into a data centre after investing an initial €200 million. More than 2,000 individuals working for 50 companies (mostly Finnish and from the local area) contributed to the project. One of the server rooms is featured in Figure 3.9.

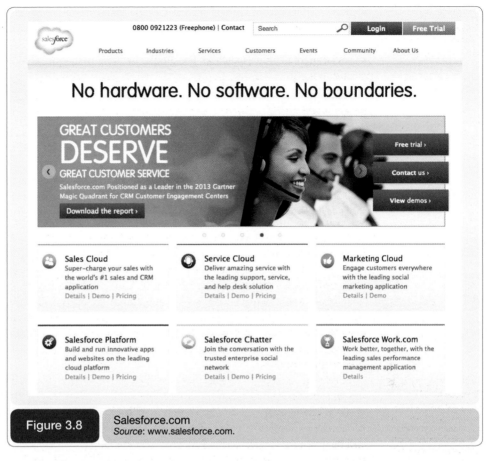

Figure 3.8	Salesforce.com
	Source: www.salesforce.com.

Examples of cloud computing web services

Think of examples of web services that you or businesses use, and you will soon see how important they are for both personal and business applications. Examples include:

- web mail readers;
- e-commerce account and purchasing management facilities such as Amazon.com;

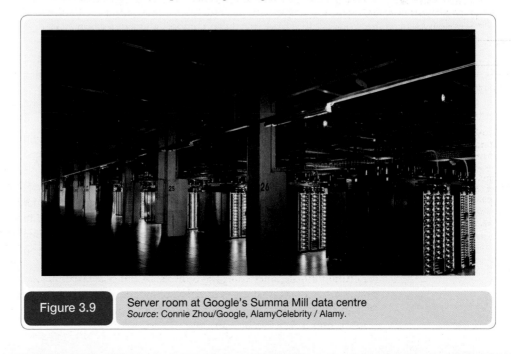

Figure 3.9	Server room at Google's Summa Mill data centre
	Source: Connie Zhou/Google, AlamyCelebrity / Alamy.

- many services from Google such as Google Maps, GMail, Picasa and Google Analytics;
- customer relationship management applications from Salesforce.com and Siebel/Oracle;
- supply chain management solutions from SAP and Oracle;
- social media services such as Facebook, Twitter, Instagram, Google+, Pinterest, Tumblr and LinkedIn.

From the point of view of managing IT infrastructure these changes are dramatic, since traditionally companies have employed their own information systems support staff to manage different types of business applications such as email. Costs associated with upgrading and configuring new software on users' client computers and servers are dramatically decreased.

As seen in Mini case study 3.5, many smaller businesses and start-ups use cloud computing services to provide web-based services at a relatively low cost with the flexibility to meet short-term (high-demand spikes) or longer growth in demand for their services.

Mini Case Study 3.5 — Amazon Web Services supports start-ups through their growth

View the examples at Amazon Web Services (AWS) (http://aws.amazon.com/solutions/case-studies) to gain an idea of the services used by start-up businesses. Here are some examples:

- Application hosting: 99designs' massive design marketplace has received over 3.1 million unique design submissions from over 53,000 designers around the world and runs entirely on AWS.
- Back-up and storage: ElephantDrive turns to Amazon S3 to store client data, expanding their total amount of storage by nearly 20% each week while avoiding increased capital expenses.
- Content delivery: HyperStratus teams with the Silicon Valley Education Foundation to support AWS cloud-based content management serving 13,000 teachers in the Silicon Valley area.
- E-commerce: The Talk Market uses Amazon Flexible Payments Service to power its credit card processing pipeline.
- ERP: Singapore-based Electra is an IT service provider specialising in implementing and running SAP systems for customers across Southeast Asia. Electra uses Amazon Web Services (AWS) to provide customers with a flexible, highly available SAP cloud environment that costs 22% less than on-premises infrastructure.
- High-performance computing: Harvard's Laboratory for Personalized Medicine (LPM) uses customised Oracle AMIs on Amazon EC2 to run genetic testing models and simulations.
- News: Social news site reddit, based in San Francisco, provides an online platform, reddit.com, to post and vote on content. By running on AWS, reddit can scale its platform to support 4 billion page views per month, and was able to quickly double server capacity in minutes for President Obama's live Q&A session in 2012.
- On-demand workforce: Using Amazon Mechanical Turk, Channel Intelligence was able to leverage human intelligence around the globe and decrease task-specific costs by 85%.
- Media streaming: Netflix, a leading online subscription service for watching movies and TV programs, has grown its streaming video business to millions of users globally. By using AWS, Netflix can quickly deploy thousands of servers and terabytes of storage within minutes.
- Social media: HootSuite is a Web and social media dashboard that helps users spread messages, organise conversations, and track results across multiple social networks such as Twitter, Facebook and LinkedIn. Social updates from 2 million users are reliably and securely transmitted around the world by utilising Amazon Elastic Compute Cloud (Amazon EC2), Amazon CloudFront and Amazon Route 53.
- Web hosting: Online mobile commerce provider Gumiyo runs a complete production environment with Amazon Web Services, including web servers, database servers and load balancers.

Activity 3.2	Opportunities for using web services by a B2B company

Purpose

To highlight the advantages and disadvantages of the web services approach.

Question

Develop a balanced case for the managing director explaining the web services approach and summarising its advantages and disadvantages.

Answers to activities can be found at www.pearsoned.co.uk/chaffey

Virtualisation

Virtualisation

The indirect provision of technology services through another resource (abstraction). Essentially one computer is using its processing and storage capacity to do the work of another.

Virtualisation is another approach to managing IT resource more effectively. However, it is mainly deployed within an organisation. VMware was one of the forerunners, offering virtualisation services which it explains as follows (VMware, 2008):

The VMware approach to virtualization inserts a thin layer of software directly on the computer hardware or on a host operating system. This software layer creates virtual machines and contains a virtual machine monitor or 'hypervisor' that allocates hardware resources dynamically and transparently so that multiple operating systems can run concurrently on a single physical computer without even knowing it.

However, virtualizing a single physical computer is just the beginning. VMware offers a robust virtualization platform that can scale across hundreds of interconnected physical computers and storage devices to form an entire virtual infrastructure.

It goes on to explain that virtualisation essentially lets one computer do the job of multiple computers, by sharing the resources of a single computer across multiple environments. Virtual servers and virtual desktops let you host multiple operating systems and multiple applications.

So virtualisation has these benefits:

- Lower hardware costs through consolidation of servers (see Mini case study 3.6).
- Lower maintenance and support costs.
- Lower energy costs.
- Scalability to add more resource more easily.
- Standardised, peronalised desktops can be accessed from any location, so users are not tied to an individual physical computer.
- Improved business continuity.

Mini case study 3.6 gives an example of these benefits.

Mini Case Study 3.6	Virtualisation cuts costs and improves service

The Association of Teachers and Lecturers (ATL) is using virtualisation not only to cut hardware costs, but also to recover quickly from systems failures and maintain business continuity. The ATL is an independent, registered trade union and professional association representing approximately 160,000 teachers, lecturers and support staff in maintained and independent nurseries, schools, sixth forms, and tertiary and further education colleges in the UK.

Ann Raimondo, head of information technology at ATL, is responsible for managing the IT infrastructure for the ever-expanding organisation, including deploying equipment, IT support and training for its

150 employees. In addition to offices in London, Belfast and Cardiff, the ATL has a large volunteer base of remote workers throughout the UK who require IT systems and support. In her role, Raimondo was faced with the following challenges:

- Fifty per cent of the available server storage space was not utilised.
- Seventy-two per cent of the storage space purchased was not being used.
- Storage space could not be reallocated to other systems in need of additional storage.
- Data were physically bound to a server, so if corruption occurred to the operating system or applications, the data on physical drives could not be reattached easily to another server and would need to be restored from back-up.

The implementation resulted in the following benefits:

- Server consolidation. ATL consolidated from 22 servers to 11, reducing hardware requirements and costs by 50 per cent.
- Flexibility and responsiveness. Prior to bringing in ESX Server, deploying a new server would require approximately three weeks for sourcing, ordering and implementing hardware. With VMware virtual infrastructure, this same process takes less than one hour.
- Lowered the cost of disaster recovery. The hardware independence of VMware virtual infrastructure helps mitigate failures caused by hardware and enables recovery from a disaster in a matter of minutes, matching and improving on user downtime expectations.

Source: VMware (2007).

Service-oriented architecture (SOA)

The technical architecture used to build web services is formally known as a '**service-oriented architecture**'. This is an arrangement of software processes or agents which communicate with each other to deliver the business requirements.

The main role of a service within SOA is to provide functionality. This is provided by three characteristics:

Service-oriented architecture
A service-oriented architecture is a collection of services that communicate with each other as part of a distributed systems architecture comprising different services.

1 An interface with the service which is platform-independent (not dependent on a particular type of software or hardware). The interface is accessible through applications development approaches such as Microsoft.Net or Java and accessed through protocols such as SOAP (Simple Object Access Protocol) which is used for XML-formatted messages.
2 The service can be dynamically located and invoked. One service can query for the existence of another service through a service directory – for example an e-commerce service could query for the existence of a credit card authorisation service.
3 The service is self-contained. That is, the service cannot be influenced by other services; rather it will return a required result to a request from another service, but will not change state. Within web services, messages and data are typically exchanged between services using XML.

The examples of web services all imply a user interacting with the web service. But with the correct business rules and models to follow, there is no need for human intervention and different applications and databases can communicate with each other in real time. A web service such as Kelkoo.com exchanges information with all participating merchants through XML using an SOA. The concept of the semantic web mentioned above and business applications of web services such as CRM, SCM and ebXML are also based on an SOA approach.

Selecting hosting providers

While it is possible for companies to manage their own services by setting up web servers within their own company offices, or to use their ISP, it is common practice to use a specialist

Hosting provider
A service provider that manages the server used to host an organisation website and its connection to the Internet backbones.

hosting provider to manage this service. For example, Rackspace (www.rackspace.com), is one of the largest providers of managed servers and cloud services for corporate businesses. According to their site, they have delivered enterprise-level hosting services to businesses of all sizes and kinds around the world since 1998 and had grown to serve more than 205,000 customers by 2014. They were rated a leader in hosting by analysts Gartner (2013) who reviewed the capabilities of different hosting providers.

Managing service quality when selecting Internet service and cloud hosting providers

Service providers who provide access to the Internet are usually referred to as 'ISPs' or 'Internet service providers'. ISPs may also host the websites which publish a company's website content. But many organisations will turn to a separate hosting provider to manage the company's website and other digital business services accessed by customers and partners such as extranets, so it is important to select an appropriate hosting provider.

ISP connection methods

Figure 3.4 shows the way in which companies or home users connect to the Internet. The diagram is greatly simplified in that there are several tiers of ISPs. A user may connect to one ISP which will then transfer the request to another ISP which is connected to the main Internet backbone.

Dial-up connection
Access to the Internet via phone lines using analogue modems.

High-speed broadband is now the dominant home access method rather than the previously popular dial-up connection.

However, companies should remember that there are significant numbers of Internet users who have the slower dial-up access. Ofcom (2010) reported that the proportion of individuals with access to broadband services in the UK is 71% (fixed broadband 65% and mobile broadband 15%).

Broadband connection
Access to the Internet via phone lines using a digital data transfer mechanism.

Broadband commonly uses a technology known as ADSL or asymmetric digital subscriber line, which means that the traditional phone line can be used for digital data transfer. It is asymmetric since download speeds are typically higher than upload speeds. Small and medium businesses can also benefit from faster continuous access than was previously possible.

The higher speeds available through broadband together with a continuous always-on connection have already transformed use of the Internet. Information access is more rapid and it becomes more practical to access richer content such as digital video.

Issues in management of ISP and hosting relationships

The primary issue for businesses in managing ISPs and hosting providers is to ensure a satisfactory service quality at a reasonable price. As the customers and partners of organisations become more dependent on their web services, it is important that downtime be minimised. But severe problems of downtime can occur, as shown in Box 3.4, and the consequences of these need to be avoided or managed.

Speed of access

A site or digital business service fails if it fails to deliver an acceptable download speed for users. In the broadband world this is still important as digital business applications become more complex and sites integrate rich media. But what is acceptable?

Research supported by Akamai (2006) suggested that content needs to load within 4 seconds, otherwise site experience suffers. The research also showed, however, that high product price and shipping costs and problems with shipping were considered more important than speed. However, for sites perceived to have poor performance, many shoppers said they would not be likely to visit the site again (64%) or buy from the e-retailer (62%).

In 2010 Google introduced speed as a signal into its ranking algorithm, effectively penalising slower sites by positioning them lower in its listings. The announcement suggested that this would only affect 1% of sites (Google, 2010). The announcement also summarised more recent research from Akamai which suggested that less than 2 seconds was now an acceptable download speed for e-commerce site users. With Google taking page download speed into account when ranking some particularly slow sites, it's worth comparing your 'page weight' or bloat compared to other sites. The average page size is 320 Kb according to this compilation: http://code.google.com/speed/articles/web-metrics.html.

Box 3.4	How long before you become impatient?

Usability specialist Jakob Nielsen noted (Nielsen, 1994) that the basic advice for response times for human–computer interaction has been about the same for 30 years. He describes these requirements for response:

- 0.1 second is about the limit for having the user feel that the system is reacting instantaneously, meaning that no special feedback is necessary except to display the result.
- 1.0 second is about the limit for the user's flow of thought to stay uninterrupted, even though the user will notice the delay. Normally, no special feedback is necessary during delays of more than 0.1 but less than 1.0 second, but the user does lose the feeling of operating directly on the data.
- 10 seconds is about the limit for keeping the user's attention focussed on the dialogue. For longer delays, users will want to perform other tasks while waiting for the computer to finish, so they should be given feedback indicating when the computer expects to be done. Feedback during the delay is especially important if the response time is likely to be highly variable, since users will then not know what to expect.

Speed of access to services is determined by both the speed of the server and the speed of the network connection to the server. The speed of the site governs how fast the response is to a request for information from the end-user. This will be dependent on the speed of the server machine on which the website is hosted and how quickly the server processes the information. If there are only a small number of users accessing information on the server, then there will not be a noticeable delay on requests for pages. If, however, there are thousands of users requesting information at the same time then there may be a delay and it is important that the combination of web server software and hardware can cope. Web server software will not greatly affect the speed at which requests are answered. The speed of the server is mainly controlled by the amount of primary storage (for example, 1024 Mb RAM is faster than 512 Mb RAM) and the speed of the magnetic storage (hard disk). Many of the search-engine websites now store all their index data in RAM since this is faster than reading data from the hard disk. Companies will pay ISPs according to the capabilities of the server.

Dedicated server
Server contains only content and applications for a single company.

An important aspect of hosting selection is whether the server is **dedicated** or shared (co-located). Clearly, if content on a server is shared with other sites hosted on the same server then performance and downtime will be affected by demand loads on these other sites. But a dedicated server package can cost 5 to 10 times the amount of a shared plan, so many small and medium businesses are better advised to adopt a shared plan, but take steps to minimise the risks with other sites going down.

For high-traffic sites, servers may be located across several computers with many processors to spread the demand load. New distributed methods of hosting content, summarised by Spinrad (1999), have been introduced to improve the speed of serving web pages for very large corporate sites by distributing content on servers around the globe, and the most widely used service is Akamai (www.akamai.com). These are used by companies such as Yahoo!, Apple and other 'hot-spot' sites likely to receive many hits.

The speed is also governed by the speed of the network connection, commonly referred to as the network '**bandwidth**'. The bandwidth of a website's connection to the Internet and the bandwidth of the customer's connection to the Internet will affect the speed with which web pages and associated graphics load. The term is so called because of the width of range of electromagnetic frequencies an analogue or digital signal occupies for a given transmission medium.

As described in Box 3.5, bandwidth gives an indication of the speed at which data can be transferred from a web server along a particular medium such as a network cable or phone line. In simple terms bandwidth can be thought of as the size of a pipe along which information flows. The higher the bandwidth, the greater the diameter of the pipe, and the faster information is delivered to the user. Many ISPs have bandwidth caps, even on 'unlimited' Internet access plans, for users who consume high volumes of bandwidth.

Bandwidth

Indicates the speed at which data are transferred using a particular network medium. It is measured in bits per second (bps).

Box 3.5 — Bandwidth measures

Bandwidth measures are in bits per second where one character or digit, such as the number '1', would be equivalent to 8 bits. So a modem operating at 57,600 bits per second (57.6 kbps) will transfer information at 7,200 characters per second (57,600 ÷ 8). When selecting an ISP or hosting provider it is important to consider the bandwidth of the connection between the ISP and the Internet. Choices may be:

- ISDN – 56 kbps up to 128 kbps
- Frame relay – 56 kbps up to a T1 communications channel (1.55 Mbps)
- Dedicated point-to-point – 56 kbps up to T3 (45 Mbps): connected to the Internet backbone.

  kbps is one kilobit per second or 1,000 bps (a modem operates at up to 56.6 kbps)

  Mbps is one megabit per second or 1,000,000 bps (company networks operate at 10 or more Mbps)

  Gbps is one gigabit per second or 1,000,000,000 bps (fibre-optic or satellite links operate at Gbps).

A major factor for a company to consider when choosing an ISP is whether the server is *dedicated* to one company or whether content from several companies is located on the same server. A dedicated server is best, but it will attract a premium price.

Availability

The availability of a website is an indication of how easy it is for a user to connect to it. In theory this figure should be 100 per cent, but sometimes, for technical reasons such as failures in the server hardware or upgrades to software, the figure can drop substantially below this. Box 3.6 illustrates some of the potential problems and how companies can evaluate and address them.

Box 3.6 — Preventing wobbly shopping carts

The extent of the problem of e-commerce service levels was indicated by *The Register* (2004) in an article titled 'Wobbly shopping carts blight UK e-commerce'. The research showed that failure of transactions once customers have decided to buy is often a problem. As the article said, '*UK E-commerce sites are slapping customers in the face, rather than shaking them by the hand. Turning consumers away once they have made a decision to buy is commercial suicide.*' The research showed this level of problems:

- 20% of shopping carts did not function for 12 hours a month or more.
- 75% failed the standard service level availability of 99.9% uptime.
- 80% performed inconsistently with widely varying response times, time-outs and errors – leaving customers at best wondering what to do next and at worst unable to complete their purchases.

Similarly, SciVisum, a web-testing specialist, found that three-quarters of Internet marketing campaigns are impacted by website failures, with 14% of failures so severe that they prevented the campaign meeting its objectives. The company surveyed marketing professionals from 100 UK-based organisations across the retail, financial, travel and online gaming sectors. More than a third of failures were rated as 'serious to severe', with many customers complaining or unable to complete web transactions. These are often seen by marketers as technology issues which are owned by others in the business, but marketers need to ask the right questions. The SciVisum (2005) research showed that nearly two-thirds of marketing professionals did not know how many users making transactions their websites could support, despite an average transaction value of £50 to £100, so they were not able to factor this into campaign plans. Thirty-seven per cent could not put a monetary value on losses caused by customers abandoning web transactions. A quarter of organisations experienced website overloads and crashes as a direct result of a lack of communication between the two departments.

SciVisum recommends that companies do the following:

1 Define the peak visitor throughput requirements for each customer journey on the site. For example, the site should be able to support at the same time: approximately ten checkout journeys per second, thirty add-to-basket journeys per second, five registration journeys per second, two check-my-order-status journeys per second.
2 Service-level agreement. More detailed technical requirements need to be agreed for each of the transaction stages. Home-page delivery time and server uptime are insufficiently detailed.
3 Set up a monitoring programme that measures and reports on the agreed journeys 24/7.

Service level agreements

Service level agreement (SLA)
A contractual specification of service standards a contractor must meet.

To ensure the best speed and availability a company should check the **service level agreements (SLAs)** carefully when outsourcing website hosting services. The SLA will define confirmed standards of availability and performance measured in terms of the *latency* or network delay when information is passed from one point to the next. The SLA also includes notification to the customer detailing when the web service becomes unavailable with reasons why and estimates of when the service will be restored.

Security

Security is another important issue in service quality. How to control security was referred to in the earlier section on firewalls and is considered in detail in '*Focus on* Security design for digital business' (Chapter 11, p. 572).

Managing internal digital communications through intranets and extranets

In Chapter 1, we introduced the concept of intranets and extranets.

Intranet applications

Intranets are used extensively for supporting sell-side e-commerce from within the marketing function. They are also used to support core supply chain management activities as described in the next section on extranets. Today, they are typically deployed as web-based services supplemented by messages and alerts delivered by email or when users login to a company network. A marketing intranet has the following advantages:

- Reduced product life cycles – as information on product development and marketing campaigns is rationalised we can get products to market faster.
- Reduced costs through higher productivity, and savings on hard copy.
- Better customer service – responsive and personalised support with staff accessing customers over the web.
- Distribution of information through remote offices nationally or globally.

Intranets are also used for internal marketing communications since they can include:

- Staff phone directories.
- Staff procedures or quality manuals.
- Information for agents such as product specifications, current list and discounted prices, competitor information, factory schedules and stocking levels, all of which normally have to be updated frequently and can be costly.
- Staff bulletin or newsletter.
- Training courses.

Total cost of ownership (TCO)
The sum of all cost elements of managing information systems for end-users, including purchase, support and maintenance.

Intranets can be used for much more than publishing information, as shown in Box 3.7. Web browsers also provide an access platform for business applications which were traditionally accessed using separate software programs. This can help reduce the **total cost of ownership (TCO)** of delivering and managing information systems. Applications delivered through a web-based intranet or extranet can be cheaper to maintain since no installation is required on the end-user's PC, upgrades are easier and there are fewer problems with users reconfiguring software. Applications include tools for workgroups to collaborate on projects, self-service human resources (e.g. to book a holiday or arrange a job review), financial modelling tools and a vehicle-build tracking system. Traditional information such as competitive intelligence, company news and manufacturing quality statistics can also be shared.

Box 3.7	Twelve ways to use your intranet to cut your costs

This guidance is from the Intranet Benchmarking Forum (IBF), the world's leading intranet and portal benchmarking group.

1 **Build bridges with internal customers.** Intranet initiatives are driven from the business units that will benefit. They say: 'Where intranets are achieving costsavings, the impetus often comes from business units or functions, not the central intranet team. From HR and finance to manufacturing units and customer service operations, it is these business areas that are best placed to identify inefficient processes and practices in their area, and then approach the intranet team for help.'

2 **Research users' needs.** This is, of course, a prerequisite of any successful information systems project. The IBF advise: 'The leaders in the field carry

out research with the aim of building a picture, for each of their main employee groups, of their working patterns, the processes they follow and where the frustrations, blockages and inefficiencies lie, as well as finding out in detail about how they currently use the intranet and where they think it could help them work more efficiently.'

3 **Implement or expand self-service.** On re-engineering processes to enable self-service, the IBF say: 'The most significant way intranets cut costs for organisations is by enabling administrative processes to be reengineered – particularly in the HR area – and migrated online via the intranet. This can make processes far more cost-efficient (and effective) for the organisation and individual users'. They give the example of how the British Airways intranet has achieved some impressive results following its re-launch as a self-service intranet:

- 100 per cent of internal recruitment is now carried out on the intranet
- 100 per cent of staff travel is booked on the intranet
- 33 per cent of staff training is delivered through the intranet
- 80 per cent of employees update their contact details on the intranet
- The most popular self-service application has been the relatively simple e-Pay tool where employees access their payslip. This alone delivered BA savings of £90,000 per year.

4 **Target further design, print and distribution savings.** Reduction in physical and distribution costs through moving towards a 'paperless office'.

5 **Improve usability.** Making it quicker to find information through improving information architecture and 'findability', i.e. better browsing and searching functionality.

6 **Revamp HR content.** As indicated by the examples given above, improvements to HR functionality often give the biggest benefits to the employees and the business.

7 **Create content for customer-facing staff.** The example is given of the UK-based insurance group Prudential which has used its intranet to provide content and tools that help contact centre staff respond rapidly to telephone, email and postal enquiries from customers.

8 **Create internal helpdesk content.** Costs of internal helpdesks, for example for IT, HR or Finance, can be delivered more efficiently via the intranet. The IBF suggests it costs about £8 to £10 to respond to each request for help by telephone, and about £5 to do so by email.

9 **Enhance the employee directory.** The IBF say: 'A good people search can be a killer app: many intranet experts agree that, more than anything else, staff want to use the intranet to get in touch with one another.'

10 **Put senior leaders online.** Intranets make it easier and more cost-effective for senior leaders to communicate their ideas and 'walk the virtual floor' – for example through blogs that allow staff to comment on posts, or through a regular online webcast or chat Q&A sessions.

11 **Leverage online meetings.** This is web conferencing which, although not directly enabled by the intranet, should facilitate collaboration.

12 **Measure savings.** The IBF state that: 'Few organisations have made progress in measuring the cost savings they can attribute to the intranet, or even to parts of it.' This is partly because it is difficult to measure cause and effect. But the study does give some examples:

- Ford estimates that online training delivered via its portal will drive down training costs to an average of $0.21 per class, down from $300–$2,500 per class.
- Cisco cut the cost of processing employee expense reports from $50.69 with the previous forms-based system to $1.90 three years later. Total corporate savings by that third year were $7m. The average elapsed time for processing each expense report dropped from 21 to 4 days.

> - BT's implementation of e-procurement encompassed 95 per cent of all its goods – including desktop computing, stationery, clothing, travel and agency staff – so reduced the average purchasing transaction cost from £56 to £40 inside a year. Another example is the introduction of an online room booking service some years ago. For a total development cost of £150,000, the service initially reduced direct costs by about £450,000 p.a. The cost savings were achieved through the near elimination of a call centre that previously handled the bookings.
>
> *Source*: Adapted from Member Briefing Paper, August, 2008 Published by the Intranet Benchmarking Forum www.ibforum.com, Digital Workplace Group.

In addition to these 'classical' uses of intranets, intranet developer Odyssey (www.odyssey-i.com) identifies some less common intranet applications:

1 **Employee incentive scheme.** Companies reward the best employees according to anonymous voting by their peers. At the end of each quarter, prizes such as DVD players and televisions are awarded.

SMS (short message services)
The formal name for text messaging.

2 **Text messaging.** A distribution company keeps in touch with its sales staff and drivers through enabling staff to contact colleagues who are 'on the road' using **SMS** text messaging.

3 **Holiday booking.** A workflow system forwards holiday requests to the relevant manager and informs the applicant automatically. Team managers can also check on the intranet to see when people within their group have booked holidays.

4 **Resource booking.** Viewing and making bookings of meeting rooms is another simple application that can save time.

5 **News screen.** Displaying the company's latest news and most recent achievements on a dedicated screen can give a focal point to a waiting room or foyer area.

6 **Integrated external resources.** Route planning, mapping or traffic news sites can be integrated into the intranet to save time for staff. One example of this is a housing authority that stores its list of properties on the intranet. Each house has a link to a mapping site (e.g. Multimap www.multimap.com), which will display the location of the property based on its postcode.

Content management system (CMS)
Software used to manage creation, editing and review of web-based content.

Intranets need to include a suitable technology to enable staff to create and manage their own content. **Content management system (CMS)** features are built into intranet and extranet systems to achieve this (see Chapter 12). For example, Microsoft Sharepoint Server is commonly used for intranet management (http://sharepoint.microsoft.com).

The management challenges of implementing and maintaining an intranet (see *Intranet Journal*, 2009) are similar to those of an extranet. In the next section, we examine five key management issues of extranets.

Extranet applications

Although an extranet may sound complex, from a user point of view it is straightforward. If you have bought a book or CD online and have been issued with a username and password to access your account, then you have used an extranet. This is a consumer extranet. Extranets are also used to provide online services which are restricted to business customers. If you visit the Ifazone (www.ifazone.com) extranet of financial services company Standard Life, which is designed for the independent financial advisers who sell its products, you will see that the website has only three initial options – log-in, register and demonstrations. The Ifazone extranet is vital to Standard Life since 90 per cent of business is now introduced through this source. This usage of the term 'extranet', referring to electronic business-to-business communications, is most typical (see, for example, Vlosky *et al.*, 2000).

Hannon (1998) concurs, and also notes the relationship of extranets with intranets, describing an extranet as

> any network connected to another network for the purpose of sharing information and data. An extranet is created when two businesses connect their respective intranets for business communication and transactions.

Dell Premier is an example of a business customer extranet for a large corporation. You can read how Dell positions the benefits in Mini case study 3.7. The system helps Dell encourage customer loyalty since once integration occurs customers are less likely to change suppliers due to switching costs. It is an example of 'soft lock-in' (which we introduced in Chapter 1). Dell also encourages consumers to make suggestions about new products through its IdeaStorm (www.ideastorm.com) service for which customers have to be registered to add comments, so could be considered as a form of extranet although Dell Premier is a better example since it shows how a service can be provided continuously.

Mini Case Study 3.7   Dell Premier customer extranet provides digital business services

Dell provides Premier.Dell.com (formerly Premier Pages) for its business customers. This is how Dell describes the service to customers:

> Your unique Premier.Dell.com site offers a customized and dedicated interface tailored to your organization's specific technology needs and standards.

- Easy Ordering – A custom online store ensures access to your products at your price.
- Easy Tracking – View real-time order status, online invoices and purchase history details.
- Easy Control – Custom access groups define what users can see and do within Premier.

It explains how Premier.Dell.com can be used for e-procurement as follows:

> Dell integrates a customized Premier catalog with your Enterprise Resource Planning (ERP) system to give you more control over your purchasing process and to help ensure accurate and efficient transactions.
>
> **Aligning with your Procurement System** – Dell can integrate with a variety of ERP applications, including: Ariba, Commerce One, Lawson, Oracle Purchasing, SAP, SciQuest and more.
>
> **Dramatic Savings** – E-Procurement integration can reduce purchasing overhead and order processing time. Consolidating purchase records into one system streamlines administration, while electronic invoicing and payment save employee processing time.
>
> **The Solution for You** – Return your shopping contents to your ERP system electronically as Dell's integrated platform is designed to help improve efficiencies and order accuracy, while reducing product delivery times.

Source: http://premier.dell.com.

Vlosky *et al.* (2000) refer to these business benefits of an extranet:

1 **Information sharing in secure environment.** Information needed to support business through a range of business partners can be shared using an extranet. Vlosky *et al.* (2000) give the example of advertising agency Saatchi using an extranet to allow their advertisers to access draft advertising material during a project. Information for suppliers is often shared by providing a log-in to a database which shows demand for products.

2 **Cost reduction.** Operating processes can be made more efficient through an extranet. The example given by these authors is Merisel, a $3.5 billion computer hardware reseller reducing its order processing costs by 70%. Such cost reductions are achieved by reducing

the number of people involved in placing orders and the need to rekey information from paper documents.

3 **Order processing and distribution.** The authors refer to an 'electronic integration effect'. For example, an extranet can connect a retailer's point of sales terminals to a supplier's delivery system, ensuring prompt replenishment of goods sold. This potentially means fewer lost sales because of out-of-stock items and a lower inventory holding is needed.

4 **Customer service.** Improving levels of service is one of the main benefits of the Premier. Dell.com extranet described above, although it also has the other benefits listed above. Distributors or agents of companies can also find information such as customised pricing or advertising materials. For example, 3M provides open web access to individual customers to find information about its office products such as Post-it notes and transparent films (www.3m.com/uk/office), but it also offers an extranet for distributors such as Spicers (www.spicers.net) and Euroffice (www.euroffice.co.uk).

Many of the management issues involved with managing extranets are similar to those for intranets. These are five key questions that need to be asked when reviewing an existing extranet or when creating a new extranet:

1 **Are the levels of usage sufficient?** Extranets require a substantial investment, so efforts need to be made to encourage usage since we are asking the users of the service to change their behaviour. It is in the organisation's interest to encourage usage, to achieve a return on their investment and achieve the cost efficiencies intended.

2 **Is it effective and efficient?** Controls must be put in place to assess how well it is working and improve its performance. Return on investment should be assessed. For example, visitor levels can be measured for different types of audiences and the level of usage for accessing different types of information can be assessed. The direct and indirect cost savings achieved through each extranet transaction can be calculated to help assess effectiveness. For example, 3M, manufacturer of many products including office products such as Post-it notes, has an extranet to connect to the office supply retailers (see www.3m.com/uk/easy). Retailers download the latest price lists and promotional information such as product pictures. Each digital download represents a significant saving in comparison to shipping physical items to the retailer.

3 **Who has ownership of the extranet?** Functions with an interest in an extranet include IT (technical infrastructure), Finance (setting payments and exchanging purchase orders and invoices), Marketing (providing marketing materials and sales data to distributors or providing services to customers) and Operations Management (exchanging information about inventory). Clearly the needs of these different parties must be resolved and management controls established.

4 **What are the levels of service quality?** Since an extranet will become a vital part of an organisation's operating process, a problem with the speed or availability of the extranet could cause loss of a lot of money; it is arguably more important than the public-facing Internet site.

5 **Is the quality of the information adequate?** The most important attributes of information quality are that it is up to date and accurate. Vlosky *et al.* (2000) point out the importance of liability if information is inaccurate or the extranet crashes.

It will be seen in Chapter 6 that extranets are used extensively to support supply chain management as resources are ordered from suppliers and transformed into products and services delivered to customers. At Marshall Industries, for example, when a new customer order is received across the extranet it automatically triggers a scheduling order for the warehouse (transferred by intranet), an order acknowledgement for the customer and a shipping status when the order is shipped (Mougayer, 1998). To enable different applications on the intranet to communicate, **middleware** is used by systems integrators to create links between organisational applications or between different members of a supply chain. For example, within a supply chain management system, middleware will translate requests from external

Middleware
Software used to facilitate communications between business applications, including data transfer and control.

systems such as a sales order so they are understood by internal systems (relevant fields are updated in the database) and then it will trigger follow-up events to fulfil the order.

Middleware is now also referred to as **enterprise application integration (EAI)** (*Internet World*, 1999). Such applications include a sales-order processing system and a warehousing system. It now also includes software programs from different organisations.

A final example of the use of an extranet on a global basis is that of Mecalux (www.mecalux.com). Mecalux, based in Barcelona, is involved in the design, manufacture and assembly of storage systems. Since it was formed in 1996, the company has expanded and has offices in Argentina, Germany, the UK, France, Portugal, Singapore and Mexico. One of the challenges of this expansion was to improve communications between its representatives around the world and to supply them with the information needed to improve customer service. The management team wanted to create a paperless company where information flows freely in all locations around the world. This makes it easier for the engineers to have the information necessary to respond to any customer's requirements. The extranet created to solve this problem has, for example, enabled representatives in Singapore to tap into data held on the server in Spain to check the availability of the product and get it to a local customer in the shortest possible timeframe. The solution also permits technicians and engineers to collaborate on ideas and work together on future designs from anywhere in the world.

Enterprise application integration (EAI)
Software used to facilitate communications between business applications, including data transfer and control.

Encouraging use of intranets and extranets

Intranets and extranets often represent a change to existing methods of working for business people, so encouraging usage is often a challenge. They may be launched to a great fanfare, but, if their content is neglected, their usage will dwindle. Common warning signs identified in the KM Column (2002) are:

- Staff usage of the intranet is low, and not growing.
- The majority of content is out of date, incomplete or inaccurate.
- The intranet is very inconsistent in appearance, particularly across sections managed by different groups.
- Almost all information on the intranet is reference material, not news or recent updates.
- Most sections of the intranet are used solely to publicise the existence of the business groups within the organisation.

To explore solutions to limited usage of intranets and extranets, complete Activity 3.3.

Activity 3.3	Overcoming limited use of intranets and extranets in a B2B company

Purpose

To illustrate solutions to limited usage of intranets and extranets.

Activity

A B2B company has found that after an initial surge of interest in its intranet and extranet, usage has declined dramatically. Many of the warning signs mentioned in the KM Column (2002) article listed above are evident. Suggest ways in which the digital business manager could achieve the following aims:

1 Increase usage.

2 Produce more dynamic content.

3 Encourage more clients to order (extranet).

Answers to activities can be found at www.pearsoned.co.uk/chaffey

IPTV (Internet TV)

IPTV (Internet Protocol television)
Digital television service is delivered using Internet Protocol, typically by a broadband connection. IPTV can be streamed for real-time viewing or downloaded before playback.

The growth in popularity of **IPTV** or 'Internet TV', where TV and video are streamed via broadband across the Internet, is one of the most exciting developments in recent years. In 2007, services offering streamed viewing of hundreds of channels from providers such as the Europe-based Joost and the US service Hulu (www.hulu.com) launched, and there are many competitors such as Babelgum, Vuze and Veoh. IPTV is sometimes referred to as non-linear TV or on-demand broadcasting.

IPTV is also used to deliver standard channels available on satellite. Then there is also the IPTV option of digital TV downloaded before playback, as is possible with many traditional broadcasters such as the BBC, Sky or ITV using peer-to-peer distribution, where many users download and share small chunks of the programme. Who pays for the large bandwidth required by IPTV is an ongoing debate, covered in the next section on net neutrality.

It will be essential for marketers and ad agencies to learn how to exploit IPTV in order to reach online audiences

Voice over IP (VoIP)

Voice over IP (VOIP)
Voice data is transferred across the Internet – it enables phone calls to be made over the Internet.

Voice over IP (VoIP) can be used for transmitting voice over a LAN or on a wider scale. You will remember that IP stands for Internet Protocol and so VoIP enables phone calls to be made over the Internet. IP enables a single network to handle all types of communications needs of an organisation, i.e. data, voice and multimedia. VoIP (pronounced 'voyp') is proving increasingly popular for reducing the cost of making phone calls within an office and between offices, particularly internationally. IOD (2005) estimates that after initial investment, the cost of managing a converged VoIP communications system could be 50 per cent lower than managing separate voice and data systems. In the longer term, major telecommunications companies such as AT&T and BT will replace their existing voice networks with IP networks.

Other benefits include:

- Click-to-call – users click the number they want from an on-screen directory.
- Call forwarding and conferencing to people at other locations.
- Unified messaging. Emails, voicemails and faxes are all integrated into a single inbox.
- Hot-desking – calls are routed to staff wherever they log in – on-site or off-site.
- Cost control – review and allocation of costs between different businesses is more transparent.

Several options are available:

1 **Peer-to-peer.** The best-known peer-to-peer solution is Skype which offers free calls or video-conferencing between Internet-connected PCs that are enabled with a headset (sometimes called 'softphones'). A service called SkypeOut enables calls to landlines or mobile phones at a reduced cost compared to traditional billing. This service is only really suited to smaller businesses, but could be used in larger businesses for some staff who call abroad frequently to bypass the central system.
2 **Hosted service.** A company makes use of a large centralised IP-based system shared between many companies. This potentially reduces costs, but some companies might be concerned about outsourcing their entire phone directory.

Widgets
A badge or button incorporated into a site or social network space by its owner, with content or services typically served from another site, making widgets effectively a minisoftware application or web service. Content can be updated in real time since the widget interacts with the server each time it loads.

3 **Complete replacement of all telephone systems.** This is potentially costly and disruptive in the short term, but new companies or relocating companies may find this the most cost-effective solution.
4 **Upgrading existing telephone systems to use VoIP.** Typically, the best compromise for existing companies.

Widgets

Widgets are tools made available on a website or on a user's desktop. They either provide some functionality, like a calculator, or they provide real-time information, for example on news or weather.

Site owners can encourage partners to place them on their sites and this will help educate people about your brand, possibly generate backlinks for SEO purposes (Chapter 9) and also engage with a brand when they're not on the brand owner's site. Widgets offer partner sites the opportunity to add value to their visitors through the gadget functionality or content, or to add to their brand through association with you (co-branding).

The main types of widget are:

1 **Web widgets.** Web widgets have been used for a long time as part of affiliate marketing, but they are getting more sophisticated, enabling searches on a site, real-time price updates or even streaming video.
2 **Google gadgets.** Different content can be incorporated onto a personalised Google 'iGoogle' home page.
3 **Desktop and operating system gadgets.** Microsoft Windows makes it easier to create and enable subscription to these widgets and place them into sidebars.
4 **Social media widgets.** These encourage site visitors to subscribe to RSS or to bookmark the page on their favourite social media site such as Delicious, Digg or Technorati.
5 **Facebook applications.** Facebook has opened up its API (application programming interface) to enable developers to create small interactive programs that users can add to their space to personalise it.

Web presentation and data exchange standards

Content
The design, text and graphical information that forms a web page. Good content is the key to attracting customers to a website and retaining their interest or achieving repeat visits.

The information, graphics and interactive elements that make up the web pages of a site are collectively referred to as **content**. Different standards exist for text, graphics and multimedia.

Examples of XML applications

One widely adopted XML application is the Dublin Core Metadata Initiative (DCMI) (www.dublincore.org), so called since the steering group first met in Dublin, Ohio, in 1995, which has been active in defining different forms of metadata to support information access across the Internet. An important part of this initiative is in defining a standard method of referencing web documents and other media resources. If widely adopted this would make it much more efficient to search for a document produced by a particular author in a particular language in a particular date range. Up to now, it has mainly been applied within content management systems to assist in knowledge management for data on intranets and extranets rather than on the public Internet.

The significance of XML is indicated by its use for facilitating supply chain management. For example, Microsoft's BizTalk server (www.microsoft.com/biztalk) for B2B application integration is based on XML. Since this is a proprietary standard, an open standard 'RosettaNet' (www.rosettanet.org) was created by a consortium of many of the world's leading information technology, electronic components and semiconductor manufacturing companies such as Intel, Sony and Nokia. BizTalk server enables different enterprise applications such as SAP and JDEdwards to exchange information as part of improved supply chain management. Microsoft summarises the benefits of BizTalk as:

1 Reduced 'time to value', i.e. development time and cost of application integration.
2 Easy integration with virtually any application or technology.
3 Scalability to any size of application.
4 Support for industry standards such as EDI, XML and Simple Object Access Protocol (SOAP).
5 Reliable document delivery including 'once-only' delivery of documents, comprehensive document tracking, and logging and support for failover (automatic recovery of documents from a back-up system).

6 Secure document exchange – this is not an integral feature of XML but has been built into this application.
7 Automation for complex business processes.
8 Management and monitoring of business processes.
9 Automated trading partner management.
10 Reduced complexity in development.

Another widely adopted application of XML is ebXML (www.ebxml.org). This standard has been coordinated by Oasis (www.oasis-open.org) which is an international not-for-profit consortium for promoting Internet standards. The original project was intended to define business exchange using five standards:

- business processes
- core data components
- collaboration protocol agreements
- messaging
- registries and repositories.

Oasis defines three types of transaction that form business processes:

1 **Business transaction.** A single business transaction between two partners, such as placing an order or shipping an order.
2 **Binary collaboration.** A sequence of these business transactions, performed between two partners, each performing one role.
3 **Multi-party collaboration.** A series of binary collaborations composed of a collection of business partners.

One application developed using ebXML enables different accounting packages to communicate with online order processing systems. This new standard has been recognised by 85% of the accounting industry, the World Wide Web Consortium and the United Nations. Over 120 national and international accounting software vendors have confirmed that they are developing interfaces. Exchequer Software Ltd (www.exchequer.com) is the first company to embed this new technology in its products, which means it receives orders via email directly into its own accounting system. This has resulted in a reduction of 30% in processing costs and a sales increase of 40%. The digital business module of the accounting software can be used to provide a remotely hosted e-commerce shopping cart system with regular updates of stock details, pricing matrices, account information and transactional data, such as outstanding orders and invoices.

Governments are also using XML to standardise data transfer between departments.

Semantic web standards

Semantic web
Interrelated content including data with defined meaning, enabling better exchange of information between computers and between people and computers.

The **semantic web** is a concept promoted by Tim Berners-Lee and the World Wide Web Consortium (www.w3.org) to improve upon the capabilities of the current World Wide Web. Semantics is the study of the meaning of words and linguistic expressions. For example, the word 'father' has the semantic elements male, human and parent and 'girl' has the elements female, human and young. The semantic web is about how to define meaning for the content of the web to make it easier to locate relevant information and services rapidly. As mentioned above, finding information on a particular topic through searching the web is inexact since there isn't a standard way of describing the content of web pages. The semantic web describes the use of metadata through standards such as XML, RDF and the Dublin Core to help users find web resources more readily. Another benefit of the semantic web is that it will enable data exchange between software **agents** running on different server or client computers.

Agents
Software programs that can assist humans by automatically gathering information from the Internet or exchanging data with other agents based on parameters supplied by the user.

Agents are software programs created to assist humans in performing tasks. In this context they automatically gather information from the Internet or exchange data with other agents based on parameters supplied by the user.

The applications of the semantic web are best illustrated through examples. Berners-Lee *et al.* (2001) give the example of a patient seeking medical treatment for a particular condition. They envisage a patient having a personal software agent (effectively a search engine) which is used to find the best source of treatment. The patient's agent will interact with the doctor's agent which will describe the symptoms and search pages from different health-care providers which detail their services. The patient's agent will then give them the different treatment options in terms of cost, effectiveness, waiting time and location. Similarly, a personal agent could be used to find the best flight or a business agent could be used to participate in a reverse auction.

Although the concept of the semantic web has been established for over 10 years, there have been relatively few commercial applications, suggesting the difficulty of implementation together with the lack of demand since the search engines perform well in returning relevant information. The World Wide Web Consortium (www.w3c.org) has compiled some examples which it updates at www.w3.org/2001/sw/sweo/public/UseCases/.

Microformats

Microformats

A simple set of formats based on XHTML for describing and exchanging information about objects, including product and travel reviews, recipes and event information.

Microformats are a practical example of the way the semantic web will develop. Data can be exchanged through standard microformats such as hCalendar and hReview which are used to incorporate data from other sites into the Google listings (see www.microformats.org for details). You can see examples of microformats which Google has incorporated as star ratings from sites it has indexed if you perform a search on movies, hotels or popular products.

Focus on	**Internet governance**

(In Chapter 4 we will look briefly at how governments promote and control, through laws, the use of the Internet in their jurisdiction.) In this section, we look at the growth of the Internet as a global phenomenon and how the standards described in the previous section were devised. The Internet is quite different from all previous communication media since it is much less easy for governments to control and shape its development. Think of print, TV, phone and radio and you can see that governments can exercise a fair degree of control on what they find acceptable.

Internet governance

Control of the operation and use of the Internet.

Esther Dyson (1998) has been influential in advising on the impact of the Internet on society; she describes **Internet governance** as the control put in place to manage the growth of the Internet and its usage. The global nature of the Internet makes it less practical for a government to control cyberspace. Dyson says:

Now, with the advent of the Net, we are privatizing government in a new way – not only in the traditional sense of selling things off to the private sector, but by allowing organizations independent of traditional governments to take on certain 'government' regulatory roles. These new international regulatory agencies will perform former government functions in counterpoint to increasingly global large companies and also to individuals and smaller private organizations who can operate globally over the Net.

Dyson (1998) describes different layers of jurisdiction. These are:

1 Physical space comprising individual countries in which their own laws such as those governing taxation, privacy, and trading and advertising standards hold.
2 ISPs – the connection between the physical and virtual worlds.

There are number of established non-profit-making organisations that control different aspects of the Internet. These are sometimes called 'supra-governmental' organisations since their control is above government level.

The net neutrality principle

Net neutrality

The principle of provision of equal access to different Internet services by telecommunications service providers.

Net (or network) neutrality is based on the organic way in which the Internet grew during the 1980s and 1990s. The principle enshrines equal access to the Internet and the web which is threatened by two different forces. First, and the most common context for net neutrality, is the desire by some telecommunications companies and ISPs to offer tiered access to particular Internet services. The wish of the ISPs is to potentially offer a different quality of service, i.e. speed, to consumers based on the fee paid by the upstream content provider. So potentially ISPs could charge companies such as TV channels more because they stream content such as video content which has high bandwidth requirements.

Concerns over tiered access to services appear strongest in the United States where two proposed Bills to help achieve neutrality, the 2006 Internet Freedom and Nondiscrimination Act and the 2006 Communications Opportunity, Promotion and Enhancement Act, did not become law. The ISPs were strong lobbyists against these Bills and subsequently it has been alleged that provider Comcast has discriminated against users accessing peer-to-peer traffic from BitTorrent (*ArsTechnica*, 2007). In European countries such as the UK, ISPs offer different levels of access at different bandwidths.

The second and less widely applied, but equally concerning, concept of net neutrality is the wish by some governments or other bodies to block access to certain services or content. For example, the government in China limits access to certain types of content in what has been glibly called '*The Great Firewall of China*' (*Wired*, 2007), which describes the development of the Golden Shield which is intended to monitor, filter and block sensitive online content. More recently Google has been criticised for censoring its search results in China for certain terms such as 'Tiananmen Square'. In 2009/2010 Google considered withdrawing its business from China.

Box 3.8	Ofcom on net neutrality in Europe and the United States

Ofcom is the regulator of the Internet in the UK. Its position on net neutrality has a clear description of the potential need for governance on this issue.

The concept of net neutrality

The issue of net neutrality concerns whether and where there should be a principle of non-discrimination regarding different forms of internet traffic carried across networks.

The communications sector is entering a period where there is rapidly increasing traffic on the internet, such as video and peer-to-peer applications (for example, games and VoIP services). This rapid increase in traffic is generating substantial congestion in some parts of the internet. Moreover many of these applications are time-sensitive and are far less tolerant of delay than, say, email or web browsing.

To respond to these new applications and their associated demands, service providers are developing a range of business models that facilitate the prioritisation of different types of traffic. This is enabled by improvements in network technology that are allowing greater identification of internet packets associated with different applications, which can then be prioritised, accordingly.

Ofcom goes on to explain the arguments for and against net neutrality and the current position in Europe.

Arguments for and against net neutrality

Proponents of net neutrality argue that it is fundamental to the protection of consumer choice and innovation on the internet, and advocates in the US have cited the First Amendment to the constitution, arguing that net neutrality is necessary to ensure freedom of speech. Some large internet application and content companies tend to be advocates of net neutrality, alongside some consumer rights groups.

Opponents to net neutrality argue that they should be able to offer different qualities of service, both in order to recover their infrastructure investment costs and to enable quality of service guarantees to improve the consumer experience for services such as VoIP or video streaming. In the United States, cable and incumbent telecom operators have also claimed that the First Amendment supports opposition to net neutrality, arguing that they cannot be compelled to promote speech with which they disagree.

Differences between the European Union and United States

A contrasting set of circumstances exists in the European Union, compared to the United States. Specifically, the net neutrality debate was triggered in the United States by the deregulation of wholesale access services, including access to the internet. In the EU there are obligations to offer unbundled local loops and bitstream access and these continue to be seen as key tools in addressing competition problems.

As part of its proposals to amend the existing EU regulatory framework, the European Commission has proposed a range of measures to ensure that consumers have access to lawful content including proposals to ensure that consumers are made aware of changes to the terms of service offered by their communications provider and the ability to switch contracts with penalty. In addition, the Commission proposed to empower national regulators with the ability to impose minimum quality of service obligations on communications providers subject to a set of standards agreed at European level.

Source: from The International Communications Market 2007. Report published December 2007, www.ofcom.org.uk/research/cm/icmr07/overview/landscape, Ofcom copyright 2006–11.

The Internet Corporation for Assigned Names and Numbers (ICANN, www.icann.org)

The Internet Corporation for Assigned Names and Numbers (ICANN) is the non-profit body formed for domain name and IP address allocation and management. These were previously controlled through US government contract by IANA (Internet Assigned Numbers Authority) and other entities.

According to the ICANN Fact Sheet (http://archive.icann.org/en/cctlds/icann-and-the-global-internet-25feb03.pdf):

In the past, many of the essential technical coordination functions of the Internet were handled on an ad hoc basis by US government contractors and grantees, and a wide network of volunteers. This informal structure represented the spirit and culture of the research community in which the Internet was developed. However, the growing international and commercial importance of the Internet has necessitated the creation of a technical management and policy development body that is more formalized in structure, more transparent, more accountable, and more fully reflective of the diversity of the world's Internet communities.

The independence of such bodies raises several questions, such as who funds them and who they answer to – are they regulated? Incredibly, in 2002 ICANN had just 14 staff and a 19-member volunteer board of directors chaired by Dr Vinton Cerf, who many consider as 'father of the Internet'. Funding is through the fees charged for domain registration by commercial companies. The policy statements on the sites suggest that ICANN policy is influenced by various stakeholders, but the main control is an independent review body of ten.

The Internet Society (www.isoc.org)

The Internet Society (ISOC) is a professional membership society formed in 1992. It summarises its aims as

> *To provide leadership in addressing issues that confront the future of the Internet, and is the organization home for the groups responsible for Internet infrastructure standards, including the Internet Engineering Task Force (IETF) and the Internet Architecture Board (IAB).*

A key aspect of the society's mission statement (www.internetsociety.org/who-we-are/mission) is:

> *To assure the open development, evolution and use of the Internet for the benefit of people throughout the world.*

Although it focuses on technical issues of standards and protocols, it is also conscious of how these will affect global society.

The Internet Engineering Task Force (IETF, www.ietf.org)

This is one of the main technical bodies. It is an international community of network designers, operators, vendors and researchers concerned with the development of the Internet's architecture and its transport protocols such as IP. Significant subgroups are the Internet Architecture Board, a technical advisory group of ISOC with a wide range of responsibilities, and the Internet Engineering Steering Group, which is responsible for overseeing the activities of the IETF and the Internet standards process.

The World Wide Web Consortium (www.w3.org)

This organisation is responsible for web standards. Its director is Tim Berners-Lee. Today, it focuses on improving publishing standards such as HTML and XML. The consortium also aims to promote accessibility to the web for those with disabilities, for instance.

Telecommunications Information Networking Architecture Consortium (TINA-C, www.tinac.com/)

This consortium takes a higher-level view of how applications communicate over communications networks. It does not define detailed standards. Its principles are based on an object-oriented approach to enable easier integration of systems. In its terms:

> *The purpose of these principles is to insure interoperability, portability and reusability of software components and independence from specific technologies, and to share the burden of creating and managing a complex system among different business stakeholders, such as consumers, service providers, and connectivity providers.*

Although it has been established since the 1990s, it has had limited success in establishing solutions which are branded as 'TINA-compliant'.

How can companies influence or take control of Internet standards?

It can be argued that companies seek control of the Internet to gain competitive advantage. For example, Microsoft used what have been judged as anti-competitive tactics to gain a large market share for its browser, Internet Explorer. In a five-year period, it achieved over 75% market share, which has given it advantages in other areas of e-commerce such as advertising revenue through its portal MSN (www.msn.com) and retail through its sites such as travel site Expedia (www.expedia.com). Microsoft has also sought to control standards such as HTML and has introduced rival standards or variants of other standards.

The existence of global Internet standards bodies arguably means that it is less likely that one company can develop proprietary standards, although Microsoft has been successfully using this approach for many years. Today, companies such as Microsoft have to lobby independent organisations to have their input into standards such as XML. Businesses can protect their interests in the Internet by lobbying these organisations or governments, or subscribing as members and having employees involved with development of standards

Many remain worried about the future control of the Internet by companies; the 'World of Ends' campaign (www.worldofends.com) illustrates some of the problems where control can limit consumer choice and stifle innovation. But the future of the Internet is assured because the three core principles espoused in the World of Ends document remain true:

- No one owns it.
- Everyone can use it.
- Anyone can improve it.

Open-source software

Open-source software
Is developed collaboratively, independent of a vendor, by a community of software developers and users.

The selection of **open-source software** to support digital business applications is a significant decision for anyone managing technology infrastructure for a company. Open-source software is now significant in many categories relevant to digital business, including operating systems, browsers, web servers, office applications and content management systems (including blogs).

The Open Source Organisation (www.opensource.org) explains its benefits as follows:

The basic idea behind open source is very simple: When programmers can read, redistribute, and modify the source code for a piece of software, the software evolves. People improve it, people adapt it, people fix bugs. And this can happen at a speed that, if one is used to the slow pace of conventional software development, seems astonishing.

We in the open source community have learned that this rapid evolutionary process produces better software than the traditional closed model, in which only a very few programmers can see the source and everybody else must blindly use an opaque block of bits.

Table 3.5 summarises some of the main advantages and disadvantages of open-source software. To gain an appreciation of the issues faced by a technical manager pondering the open-source dilemma, complete Activity 3.4.

Table 3.5	Three advantages and three disadvantages of open-source software
Advantages of open-source software	**Counter-argument**
1 Effectively free to purchase	Cost of migration from existing systems may be high and will include costs of disruption and staff training
2 Lower cost of maintenance since upgrades are free	There is not a specific counter-argument for this, but see the disadvantages below
3 Increased flexibility	Organisations with the resources can tailor the code. Frequent patches occur through collaborative development
Disadvantages of open-source software	**Counter-argument**
1 Has less functionality than commercial software	Simplicity leads to ease of use and fewer errors. Many functions not used by the majority of users
2 More likely to contain bugs compared to commercial software since not tested commercially	Evidence does not seem to suggest this is the case. The modular design needed by collaborative development enables problems to be isolated and resolved
3 Poor quality of support	Organisations with the resource can fix problems themselves since they have access to the code. Companies such as IBM, SuSe and RedHat do offer support for Linux for a fee. Finding skilled staff for emerging open-source technologies can be difficult

Activity 3.4	Selecting open-source software

Purpose

This activity looks at a common issue facing technical managers: should they adopt standard software promoted by the largest companies or open-source software or cheaper software from other vendors?

Questions

1 For the different alternatives facing a technical manager below, assess:
   (a) Which is most popular (research figures).
   (b) The benefits and disadvantages of the Microsoft solution against the alternatives.

2 Make recommendations, with justifications, of which you would choose for a small–medium or large organisation.
   A Operating system: Microsoft/Windows XP/Server or Linux (open-source) for server and desktop clients.
   B Browser: Internet Explorer browser or rivals such as Mozilla Firefox or Google Chrome which is part based on open-source.
   C Programming language for dynamic e-commerce applications: Microsoft.Net or independent languages/solutions such as the LAMP combination (Linux operating system, Apache server software plus the MySQL open-source database and scripting languages such as PHP, Perl or Python).

Answers to activities can be found at www.pearsoned.co.uk/chaffey

Case Study 3.1	Innovation at Google

Context

In addition to being the largest search engine on Earth, mediating the searches of tens of billions of searches daily, Google is a great example of continuous innovation in its digital services. All involved in managing digital business should follow Google to see the latest approaches its trialling.

Google's mission

Google's mission is encapsulated in the statement 'to organize the world's information. . . and make it universally accessible and useful.' Google explains that it believes that the most effective, and ultimately the most profitable, way to accomplish its mission is to put the needs of its users first. Offering a high-quality user experience has led to strong word-of-mouth promotion and strong traffic growth.

Notable tenets of the Google philosophy are:

● Focus on the user and all else will follow.
● It's best to do one thing really, really well.
● You can make money without doing evil.

Further details on the culture and ethics of Google are available at www.google.com/intl/en/corporate/ten-things.html.

Putting users first is reflected in three key commitments in the Google SEC filing:

1 We will do our best to provide the most relevant and useful search results possible, independent of financial incentives. Our search results will be objective and we will not accept payment for inclusion or ranking in them.

2 We will do our best to provide the most relevant and useful advertising. Advertisements should not be an annoying interruption. If any element on a search result page is influenced by payment to us, we will make it clear to our users.

3 We will never stop working to improve our user experience, our search technology and other important areas of information organization.

In the investor relations SEC filing, the company explains 'How we provide value to our users':

We serve our users by developing products that quickly and easily find, create, organize, and share

information. We place a premium on products that matter to many people and have the potential to improve their lives.

Some of the key benefits which are explained are: Comprehensiveness and relevance; Objectivity; Global access; Ease of use; Pertinent, useful commercial information; Multiple access platforms; and Improving the web.

The range of established Google services is well known and is listed at http://www.google.com/options/.

Google's commitment to innovation is indicated by these more recent services:

- Google TV (announced 2010) as part of a partnership agreement with Sony
- Nexus One Phone using the Google Android mobile operating system launched in January 2010 (www.google.com/phone)
- Google Mobile advertising (although Google has offered text ads for some time, the 2009 acquisition of AdMob enables improvements in sophistication of this approach)
- Google Chrome OS (a lightweight operating system announced in 2009 and targeted initially at Netbooks) and then Google's own Chromebook notebook in 2009.
- Google Chrome (a browser announced as a beta in 2008 and a full product for Windows in 2009)
- Google Glass. A current project to develop wearable technology.

For 2009, Google spent around 12% of its revenue in research and development, an increase from less than 10% in 2005, a larger amount than sales and marketing (8.4%).

Google revenue models

Google AdWords, the auction-based advertising programme that enables advertisers, is the main source of revenue. Advertisers pay on a 'pay-per-click' cost basis within the search engines and within other services such as Gmail, but with cost-per-thousand payment options available on Google Networks members' websites. Google has introduced classified-style ad programmes for other media, including:

- Google Audio Ads (ads are placed in radio programmes)
- Google Print Ads
- Google TV Ads
- Google Promoted Video Ads within YouTube, user-initiated click-to-play video ads.

So, Google's revenues are critically dependent on how many searches it achieves in different countries on desktop and mobile devices and the proportion of searchers who interact with Google's ads. Research by comScore (2008) suggests around 25% of searches

result in an ad click where sponsored search results are included (around 50% of searches). Of course Google is also looking to increase the number of advertisers and invests heavily in this through trade communications to marketers. Increased competition to advertise against a search term will result in increased bid amounts and so increased revenue for Google.

In 2013, according to Google's investors relation site around a third of Google's revenue was from the Google Display Network of content partners, including those who subscribe to the Google Adsense programme. It updated its ad targeting to use an approach called 'Enhanced campaigns' where revenue from mobile devices was improved.

Risk factors

Some of the main risk factors that Google declares include:

1 **New technologies could block Google ads.** Ad-blocking technology could, in the future, adversely affect Google's results, although there has not been widespread adoption of these approaches.
2 **Litigation and confidence loss through click fraud.** Click fraud can be a problem when competitors click on a link, but this is typically small-scale. A larger problem for is structured click fraud where site owners on the Google content network seeks to make additional advertising feeds.
3 **Index spammers could harm the integrity of Google's web search results.** This could damage Google's reputation and cause its users to be dissatisfied with products and services.

Google says:

There is an ongoing and increasing effort by 'index spammers' to develop ways to manipulate our web search results. For example, because our web search technology ranks a web page's relevance based in part on the importance of the web sites that link to it, people have attempted to link a group of web sites together to manipulate web search results.

You can find updates on this case study by searching at SmartInsights.com for 'Google marketing updates'.

Web video explanation: www.google.com/howgoogle works/. (Further information on how Google works is available in Chapter 9 in the section on search engine marketing.)

> ### Question
> Explain how Google generates revenue and exploits innovation in digital technology to identify future revenue growth. You should also consider the risk factors for future revenue generation.

Summary

1   Businesses need to provide a range a digital business infrastructure that can support users on a range of desktop and mobile platforms and is flexible enough to change with different business demands.

2   Mobile platform decisions involve selection of which mobile operating systems to target, provision of mobile-based services and whether additional apps are required.

3   A five-layer model for managing digital business infrastructure is reviewed where Level I is the applications layer, II is the systems software layer, III is the transport layer, IV is the storage or physical layer and V is the content or data layer.

4   Integrating different web services using Cloud Computing can enable business software functions to be added with limited bespoke development.

5   Software as a Service (SaaS) providers are increasingly important as businesses look to reduce infrastructure costs and improve service delivery through external hosting of applications and data outside an organisation.

Exercises

Self-assessment questions

1   What is the difference between the Internet and the World Wide Web?

2   Describe the two main functions of an Internet service provider (ISP). How do they differ from applications service providers?

3   Distinguish between intranets, extranets and the Internet.

4   Describe the standards involved when a web page is served from a web server to a user's web browser.

5   What are the management issues involved with enabling staff access to a website?

6   Explain the following terms: HTML, HTTP, XML, FTP.

7   What is the difference between static web content written in HTML and dynamic content developed using a scripting language such as JavaScript?

8   What software and hardware are required to access the Internet from home?

Essay and discussion questions

1   'Without the development of the World Wide Web by Tim Berners-Lee, the Internet is unlikely to have become a commercial medium.' Discuss.

2   'In the future the distinction between intranets, extranets and the Internet for marketing purposes is likely to disappear.' Discuss.

3   Discuss the merits and disadvantages of locating company digital business services inside a company, in comparison with outsourcing to an ISP or ASP.

4   You are consultant to a small retailer interested in setting up a transactional e-commerce site. Create a summary guide for the company about the stages that are necessary in the creation of a website and the management issues involved.

Examination questions

1   You have been tasked with arranging Internet access for other employees in your company. Summarise the hardware and software needed.

2   How would you explain to a friend what they need to purchase to access the World Wide Web using the Internet? Explain the hardware and software needed.

3   Explain the term 'electronic data interchange'. Is it still relevant to companies?

4 Describe how the following tools would be used by a company hosting a website: HTML, FTP, RSS.

5 The existence of standards such as HTML and HTTP has been vital to the success and increased use of the World Wide Web. Explain why.

6 What benefits to a business-to-business company does the XML standard offer beyond those of HTML?

7 Explain why the digital business coordinator of a company might investigate the use of applications service providers.

8 Explain the differences between intranet, extranet and the Internet from a digital business perspective.

References

Akamai (2006) Akamai and JupiterResearch Identify '4 Seconds' as the New Threshold of Acceptability for Retail Web Page Response Times. Press release, 6 November: www.akamai.com/html/about/press/releases/2006/press_110606.html.

ArsTechnica (2007) Evidence mounts that Comcast is targeting BitTorrent traffic. *ArsTechnica*, The Art of Technology, by Jacqui Cheng, 19 October: http://arstechnica.com/uncategorized/2007/10/evidence-mounts-that-comcast-is-targeting-bittorrent-traffic/.

Berners-Lee, T., Hendler, J. and Lassila, O. (2001) The Semantic Web. *Scientific American*, May. Published online at: www.sciam.com.

ClickZ (2010) Foursquare Marketing Hits and Misses: 5 Case Studies. Christopher Heine, 28 September: www.clickz.com/clickz/news/1735591/foursquare-marketing-hits-misses-case-studies.

CIO (2010) IaaS: Why Intel Dumped the Grid. Article on CIO.com online magazine. By Rick Swanborg, 9 June 2010: www.cio.com/article/596387/IaaS_Why_Intel_Dumped_the_Grid?taxonomyId=3017.

Computer Economics (2006) Software as a Service Shows Attractive Payback. Research Report, June.

comScore (2008) Why Google's surprising paid click data are less surprising. By Magid Abraham, 28 February. Published at: www.comscore.com/Insights/Blog/Why_Google_s_surprising_paid_click_data_are_less_surprising.

Cutts, M. (2007) Talk like a Googler: parts of a url. Blog posting, 14 August: www.mattcutts.com/blog/seo-glossary-url-definitions/.

Dyson, E. (1998) *Release 2.1: A Design for Living in the Digital Age.* Penguin, London.

Google (2010) You and site performance, sitting in a tree . . . Blog posting, Official Google Blog, 2 May: http://googlewebmastercentral.blogspot.com/2010/05/you-and-site-performance-sitting-in.html.

Guardian (2008) Porn? Sex? Britons value cruises much more. *The Guardian*, Richard Wray, 6 February.

Hannon, N. (1998)*The Business of the Internet.* Course Technology, New York.

Hasselbring, W. (2000) Information system integration. *Communications of the ACM,* 43(6), 33–8.

IBF (2008) *12 ways to use your intranet to cut your costs.* Member Briefing Paper, August. Published by the Intranet Benchmarking Forum (www.ibforum.com).

Internet World (1999) Enterprise application integration – middleware apps scale firewalls. *Internet World,* 17 May.

IOD (2005) Voice Over IP. Institute of Directors (www.iod.com), February, London.

Intranet Journal (2009) Creating your SharePoint Governance Plan. Robert Bogue, 4 June, *Intranet Journal* (online magazine). **www.intranetjournal.com/articles/200906/ ij_06_04_09a.html**.

Kampas, P. (2000) Road map to the e-revolution. *Information Systems Management Journal*, Spring, 8–22.

KM Column (2002) September 2002 issue: Sixteen steps to a renewed corporate intranet. Published by Step Two Designs at: **www.steptwo.com.au/papers/kmc_renewintranet/index.html**.

Mcafee, A. and Brynjolfsson, E. (2008) Investing in the IT that makes a competitive difference. *Harvard Business Review*, July–August, 99–107.

Mougayer, W. (1998) *Opening Digital Markets – Battle Plans and Strategies for Internet Commerce*, 2nd edn. CommerceNet Press, McGraw-Hill, New York.

Nielsen, J. (1994) Response Times: The Three Important Limits. Online white paper: **www. useit.com/papers/responsetime.html**.

Ofcom (2007) The International Communications Market 2007. Report published December 2007. Extract from section 1.3, the regulatory landscape: **http://stakeholders. ofcom.org.uk/market-data-research/market-data/communications-market-reports/ icmr07/overview/landscape/**.

Ofcom (2010) The UK Communications Market Report 2010 (August). **http://stakeholders. ofcom.org.uk/market-data-research/market-data/communications-market-reports/ cmr10/**.

Pandia (2007) Google: one million servers and counting. Pandia Search Engine News: **www. pandia.com/sew/481-gartner.html**.

SciVisum (2005) Internet Campaign Effectiveness Study. Press Release, July: **www.scivisum. co.uk**.

Smart Insights (2010) Our interview with Malcolm Duckett about Magiq dynamic personalization. 7 August 2010: **www.smartinsights.com/ecommerce/web-personalisation/ dynamic-personalization-software-maqiq/**.

Smart Insights (2013) Mobile Marketing Strategy Guide by Rob Thurner and Dave Chaffey. April 2013. Published online at: **www.smartinsights.com/mobile-marketing**.

Smoothspan (2007) How Many Tenants For a Multitenant SaaS Architecture? Blog posting, 30 October: **http://smoothspan.wordpress.com/2007/10/30/ how-many-tenants-for-a-multitenant-saas-architecture/**.

Spinrad, P. (1999). The new cool. Akamai overcomes the Internet's hotspot problem. *Wired*, 7 August, 152–4.

The Register (2004) Wobbly shopping carts blight UK e-commerce: *The Register.Co.uk*, 4 June.

Vlosky, R., Fontenot, R. and Blalock, L. (2000) Extranets: impacts on business practices and relationships. *Journal of Business and Industrial Marketing*, 15(6), 438–57.

VMware (2007) Association of Teachers and Lecturers, customer success story: **www. vmware.com/pdf/atl.pdf**.

VMware (2008) Virtualization Basics: **www.vmware.com/virtualization.**

Wired (2007) The Great Firewall: China's Misguided – and Futile – Attempt to Control What Happens Online. *Wired* 15.11, by Oliver August, 23 August.

Web links

A brief history of the Internet (**www.zakon.org/robert/internet/timeline**) An Internet timeline.

CIO Magazine (**www.cio.com/research/intranet**) Intranet and extranet research centre.

Forrester Marketing Blog (**http://blogs.forrester.com/marketing/**) Forrester analysts write about developments in technology.

Google (**www7.scu.edu.au/programme/fullpapers/1921/com1921.htm**) Interesting, but technical, article on Google, 'The anatomy of a large-scale hypertextual web search engine'.

Howstuffworks (**www.howstuffworks.com**) Good explanations with diagrams of many Internet technologies.

Intranet Benchmarking Forum (**www.ibforum.com**). Membership service disseminating intranet best practice from corporate organisations. Their blog (**www.intranetlife.com**) has discussion of topical intranet management issues and extracts of research.

Intranet Focus (**www.intranetfocus.com**) Best-practice guidelines and links on intranets, portals and content management systems.

Intranet Journal (**www.intranetjournal.com**) Articles on intranet management.

ReadWriteWeb (**www.readwriteweb.com**) Site focussing on digital technology trends and developments in content management, web applications and social media.

SmoothSpan (**http://smoothspan.wordpress.com**) Blog by Bob Warfield covering developments in SaaS, Web 2.0 and cloud computing.

XML.com (**www.xml.com**) XML resources.

Mobile marketing resources

- The worldwide Mobile Marketing Association (**www.mmaglobal.com**) has case studies and statistics of adoption.
- Mobile Data Association's text.it (**www.text.it**) focuses on marketing for SMS and picture messaging.
- Mobile Marketing Magazine (**www.mobilemarketingmagazine.co.uk**). An online magazine focussing on emerging approaches and case studies.
- Smart Insights, mobile marketing (**www.smartinsights.com/mobile-marketing**). Examples and the latest developments in mobile marketing.

E-environment

Web support

The following additional case studies are available at **www.pearsoned.co.uk/chaffey**

The site also contains a range of study material designed to help improve your results.

Scan code to find the latest updates for topics in this chapter

Learning outcomes

After completing this chapter the reader should be able to:

- Identify the different elements of an organisation macro-environment that impact on an organisation's digital business and digital marketing strategy
- Assess the impact of legal, privacy and ethical constraints or opportunities on a company
- Assess the role of macro-economic factors such as economics, governmental digital business policies, taxation and legal constraints

Management issues

The issues for managers raised in this chapter include:

- What are the constraints such as legal issues which should be taken into account when developing and implementing a digital business strategy?
- How can trust and privacy be assured for the customer while seeking to achieve marketing objectives of customer acquisition and retention?
- Assessment of the business relevance of technological innovation

Links to other chapters

The main related chapters are:

- *Chapter 2* Marketplace analysis for e-commerce – introduces the different elements of the online marketplace
- The strategic approaches outlined in Part 2 (*Chapters 5, 6 and 8*) require consideration of the constraints placed on strategy by a companies environment

Introduction

Table 4.1 presents the main marketplace or macro-environmental factors and the micro-environmental factors that directly affect an organisation.

In Chapter 2 we introduced the importance of monitoring changes in the online marketplace or micro-environment and how they impact on an organisation. In this chapter we concentrate on the role of the macro-environmental forces using the widely used SLEPT framework. Often, these factors are known as the PEST factors, but we use SLEPT since it is useful to stress the importance of the law in influencing Internet marketing practices. The SLEPT factors are:

- Social factors – these include the influence of consumer perceptions in determining usage of the Internet for different activities.
- Legal and ethical factors – determine the method by which products can be promoted and sold online. Governments, on behalf of society, seek to safeguard individuals' rights to privacy.
- Economic factors – variations in economic performance in different countries and regions affect spending patterns and international trade.
- Political – national governments and transnational organisations have an important role in determining the future adoption and control of the Internet and the rules by which it is governed.
- Technological factors – changes in technology offer new opportunities to the way products can be marketed.

For each factor we look at new issues raised for managers responsible for e-commerce trading.

Now complete Activity 4.1 to reflect on the most important macro-environmental factors that have to be considered by the digital business manager. When completing a review it's important not to give all influences equal weighting, but instead focus on the ones that matter most in the current environment, such as legislation and technology innovation.

The issues identified in Activity 4.1 and others such as economic and competitive pressures tend to change rapidly, particularly dynamic factors associated with advances in technology.

An indication of the challenge of assessing the macro-environment factors is presented in Figure 4.1. This figure of the 'waves of change' shows how fluctuations in the characteristics of different aspects of the environment vary at different rates through time. Managers have

Table 4.1	Factors in the macro- and micro-environment of an organisation
Macro-environment	**Micro-environment (digital marketplace)**
Social	The organisation
Legal, ethical and taxation	Its customers
Economic	Its suppliers
Political	Its competitors
Technological	Intermediaries
Competitive	The public at large

to constantly scan the environment and assess which changes are relevant to their sphere of influence. Changes in social culture and particularly pop culture tend to be very rapid. Introduction of new technologies and changes in their popularity tend to be frequent, too. Governmental and legal changes tend to happen over longer timescales but new laws can be introduced relatively fast. The trick for managers is to identify those factors that are critical to competitiveness and service delivery and monitor these. The technological and legal factors are most important to managing e-commerce, so we focus on these.

Since the law is one of the most important issues for the e-commerce manager to address, the six most important legal issues for managers are introduced in Table 4.2. Each of these is covered in more detail later in the chapter. Organisations that either do not monitor these environmental factors or do not respond to them adequately will not remain competitive and may fail. The process of monitoring the environment is usually referred to as **environmental scanning**. This often occurs as an *ad hoc* process, but if there is no reporting mechanism then some major changes may not be apparent to managers. Environmental analysis is required to evaluate information and respond accordingly.

Environmental scanning
The process of continuously monitoring the environment and events and responding accordingly.

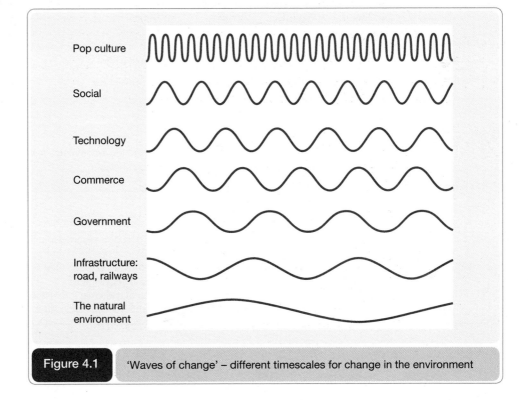

Pop culture

Social

Technology

Commerce

Government

Infrastructure: road, railways

The natural environment

Figure 4.1   'Waves of change' – different timescales for change in the environment

Table 4.2	Significant laws which control digital marketing

Legal issue	Digital marketing activities affected
1 Data protection and privacy law	☑ Collection, storage, usage and deletion of personal information directly through data capture on forms and indirectly through tracking behaviour through web analytics ☑ Email marketing and SMS mobile marketing ☑ Use of viral marketing to encourage transmission of marketing messages between consumers ☑ Use of cookies and other techniques for personalising content and tracking on-site ☑ Use of cookies for tracking between sites, for example for advertising networks and company site using 'behavioural ad targeting' ☑ Use of customer information from social networks ☑ Use of digital assets installed on a user's PC for marketing purposes, e.g. toolbars or other downloadable utilities sometimes referred to as 'malware'

2 Disability and discrimination law	☑ Accessibility of content such as images for the visually impaired within different digital environments:
	  ☑ Website
	  ☑ Email marketing
	  ☑ Mobile marketing
	  ☑ IPTV
	☑ Accessibility affecting other forms of disability including hearing difficulties and motor impairment

3 Brand and trademark protection	☑ Use of trademarks and brand names within:
	  ☑ Domain names
	  ☑ Content on site (for search engine optimisation)
	  ☑ Paid search advertising campaigns (e.g. Google AdWords)
	☑ Representation of a brand on third-party sites, including partners, publishers and social networks
	☑ Defamation of employees

4 Intellectual property rights	☑ Protection of digital assets such as text content, images, audio and sounds through digital rights management (DRM)

5 Contract law	☑ Validity of electronic contracts relevant to:
	  ☑ Cancellations
	  ☑ Returns
	  ☑ Errors in pricing
	☑ Distance-selling law
	☑ International taxation issues where the e-commerce service provider is under a different tax regime from the purchaser

6 Online advertising law	☑ Similar issues to traditional media
7 Social media	☑ Representation of offer ☑ Causing offence (e.g. viral marketing) ☑ Misrepresenting a company by posting a recommendation although the employee works for the company ☑ Defamation – libel against other social network users ☑ Privacy of customer information in social media ☑ Intellectual property – ownership of customer information in social media ☑ Promotions and competitions within social media sites

Social and legal factors

Behavioural ad targeting
Advertisers target ads at a visitor as they move within or between sites dependent on their viewing particular sites or types of content that indicate their preferences.

Malware
Malicious software or toolbar, typically downloaded via the Internet, which acts as a 'trojan horse' by executing unwanted activities such as keylogging of user passwords or viruses which may collect email addresses.

The social and cultural impacts of the Internet are important from an e-commerce perspective since they govern demand for Internet services and propensity to purchase online and use different types of e-commerce services. For example, in Figures 1.11 and 1.15 respectively, we saw how businesses and consumers have adopted different online services.

Complete Activity 4.2 to start to review some of the social issues associated with the Internet.

Factors governing e-commerce service adoption

It is useful for digital business managers to understand the different factors that affect how many people actively use the Internet, so that action can be taken to overcome some of these barriers. For example, marketing communications can be used to reduce fears about the value proposition, ease of use and security. Chaffey *et al.* (2009) suggest that the following factors are important in governing adoption of any e-commerce service:

1 **Cost of access.** This is certainly a barrier for those who do not already own a home computer. The other main costs are the cost of using an ISP to connect to the Internet and the cost of using the media to connect. Free access would certainly increase adoption and usage.

Activity 4.2   **Understanding enablers and barriers to consumer adoption**

Purpose

To identify reasons why businesses or consumers may be encouraged online or may resist.

visit the www

Activity

Access a recent survey of attitudes to the Internet in your country. In particular, you should concentrate on reasons why customers have used the Internet or have not used the Internet at all. Figure 4.2 gives an example for 27 countries in the EU27 in Europe. Note that different activities such as posting updates to social media vary significantly by age, although we see the Internet as ubiquitous.

It's not practical to present the latest data from all countries, so please access the latest data using this compilation of 10 key research resources about the Internet and technology adoption which we have prepared at www.smartinsights.com/digital-marketing-statistics.

Questions

1 Summarise and explain the reasons for the levels of usage of the medium for different activities.

2 What are the main enablers and barriers to higher levels of adoption of these different activities and which actions should organisations take to increase adoption?

Alternatively, devise an *ad hoc* survey to investigate attitudes to, and use of, the Internet using friends, family or classmates as respondents. Example questions might include the following: What have you bought online? If nothing, why not? How many hours do you spend online each month? How many emails do you receive or send? What stops you using the Internet more? What aspects of the Internet are you concerned about?

Answers to activities can be found at www.pearsoned.co.uk/chaffey

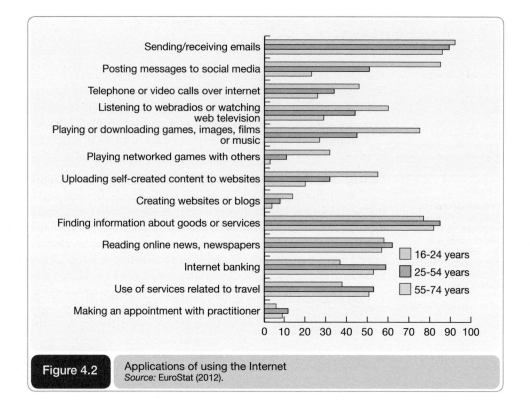

Figure 4.2	Applications of using the Internet
	Source: EuroStat (2012).

2 **Value proposition.** Customers need to perceive a need to be online – what can the Internet offer that other media cannot? Examples of value propositions include access to more supplier information and possibly lower prices.

3 **Ease of use.** This includes the ease of first connecting to the Internet using the ISP and the ease of using the web once connected.

4 **Security.** While this is only, in reality, a problem for those who shop online, the perception may be that if you are connected to the Internet then your personal details may not be secure. It will probably take many years for this fear to diminish.

5 **Fear of the unknown.** Many will simply have a general fear of the technology and the new media, which is not surprising since much of the news about the Internet will concern pornography, fraud and privacy infringements.

The extent of adoption also varies significantly by country – see, for example, EuroStat (2012) where the percentage of individuals who use the Internet daily varies between 30% and 80% across the EU27, showing the value in targeting countries for online investment carefully.

These barriers to access and usage of the web still remain, and governments are concerned about 'social exclusion' where some sectors of society have lower levels of access and opportunity. As expected, there is a strong correlation between Internet use and PC penetration. Countries such as Sweden have encouraged home use most actively through government initiatives. This appears to exert more influence than reduction in cost of access.

Understanding users' access requirements

To fully understand online customer propensity to use online service we also need to consider the user's access location, access device and 'webographics'. 'Webographics' is a term coined by Grossnickle and Raskin (2001), which includes:

- Usage location (from home or work)
- Access device (browser and computer platform including mobile devices)

- Connection speed – broadband versus dial-up connections
- ISP
- Experience level
- Usage type
- Usage level.

Competition in the marketplace amongst broadband providers has caused a great increase in the Internet access options available for consumers and small businesses.

Consumers influenced by using the online channel

Online buyer behaviour

An assessment of how consumers and business people use the Internet in combination with other communications channels when selecting and buying products and services.

To help develop effective online services, we need to understand customers' **online buyer behaviour** and motivation (this topic is considered in more depth in Chapter 9, p. 400). Finding information about goods and services is a common online activity, as shown by Figure 4.2, but each organisation needs to capture data about online influence in the buying process for their own market. Managers also need to understand how different types of media, intermediary and influencer sites introduced in Chapter 2 influence consumers; for example, are blogs, social networks or traditional media sites more trusted?

There is also a wide variation in influence and type of information sought according to type of product, so it is important to assess the role of the web in supporting buying decisions for a particular market. Understanding the potential reach of a website and its role in influencing purchase is clearly important in setting digital marketing budgets. Figure 4.3 shows the variation in number of information sources by sector and Figure 4.4 shows the impact of different forms of online purchase.

Motivation for use of online services

Psychographic segmentation

A breakdown of customers according to different characteristics.

Marketers can also develop **psychographic segmentations** which help explain motivation. Specialised psychodemographic profiles have been developed for web users. See Box 4.1 for an example of this type of segmentation applied to responsiveness to online advertising. Which profile do you fit?

The revised Web Motivation Inventory (WMI) identified by Rodgers *et al.* (2007) is a useful framework for understanding different motivations for using the web. The four motives which cut across cultures are: research (information acquisition), communication (socialisation), surfing (entertainment) and shopping, and these are broken down further below.

1 Community
- Get to know other people
- Participate in an online chat
- Join a group.

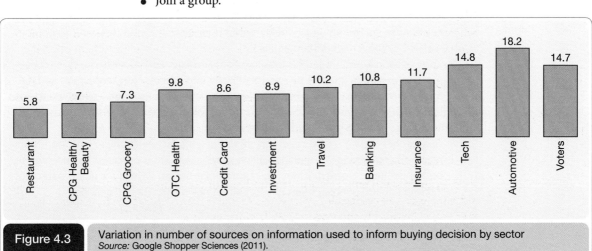

| Figure 4.3 | Variation in number of sources on information used to inform buying decision by sector |

Source: Google Shopper Sciences (2011).

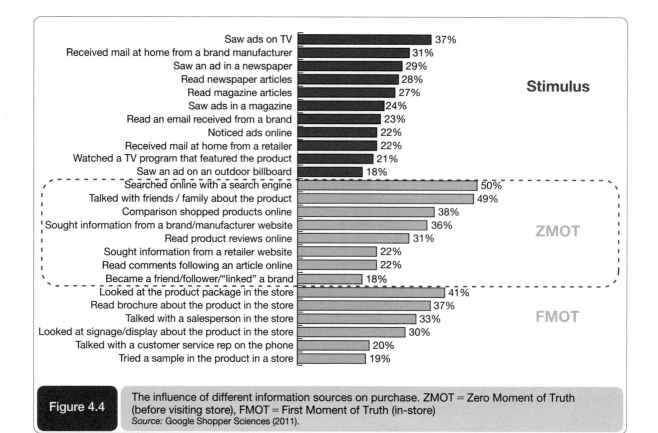

Figure 4.4	The influence of different information sources on purchase. ZMOT = Zero Moment of Truth (before visiting store), FMOT = First Moment of Truth (in-store) *Source:* Google Shopper Sciences (2011).

Box 4.1	Psychographic segmentation for transactional e-commerce

Digital marketing agency Digitas (2007) developed this segmentation to represent different attitudes to online advertising (OLA) and usage of different online services.

1 Casual user (20%) – To the casual user, the Internet is a fun and entertaining way to spend time. Generally, the casual user visits the same small set of sites on a regular basis and does not engage other users online. The oldest of the segments with an average age of 55, this is the segment most likely to subscribe to a daily newspaper, to find value in weekly newspaper circulars, and believe that companies should never send them email.

2 Task-based user (24%) – The task-based user believes that technology is moving too fast and sees Internet usage specifically as a chore. Non-responsive to OLA, this segment is also most likely to feel the need for assistance when using the Internet. Their online behaviours focus on completing a specific task such as online banking or making travel arrangements.

3 Researcher (16%) – The research segment enjoys being online and conducts online research prior to making offline purchases. They consider themselves to be trendsetters. However, they do not transact online. OLA is a trusted source of information and enables them to learn about new products and services.

4 Emerging user (19%) – This segment is the traditional 'sweet spot' for online advertisers. The segment is the most responsive to OLA, and they conduct research online as well as transact online.

> **5** Established user (17%) – The established segment consists of e-commerce veterans who nurture and develop online relationships. They consider themselves to be trendsetters but do not pay attention to online advertising. Rather, they rely on peer reviews to gain information on products and services.
>
> **6** Next Gen user (5%) – The youngest and most affluent of all the segments, the Next Gen segment grew up online and consider their mobile phone a natural extension of their Internet experience. Members of this segment enjoy being online and are the most likely to contribute via social networking tools.

2 Entertainment
- Amuse myself
- Entertain myself
- Find information to entertain myself.

3 Product trial
- Try on the latest fashions
- Experience a product
- Try out a product.

4 Information
- Do research
- Get information I need
- Search for information I need.

5 Transaction
- Make a purchase
- Buy things
- Purchase a product I've heard about.

6 Game
- Play online games
- Entertain myself with Internet games
- Play online games with individuals from other countries.

7 Survey
- Take a survey on a topic I care about
- Fill out an online survey
- Give my opinion on a survey.

8 Downloads
- Download music
- Listen to music
- Watch online videos.

9 Interaction
- Connect with my friends
- Communicate with others
- Instant message others I know.

10 Search
- Get answers to specific questions
- Find information I can trust.

11 Exploration
- Find interesting web pages
- Explore new sites
- Surf for fun.

12 News
- Read about current events and news
- Read entertainment news.

Web advertisers and site owners can use this framework to review the suitability of facilities to meet these needs.

Purchased online

Increasing numbers of consumers are now purchasing online. Figure 4.2 shows that initially Internet users may restrict themselves to searching for information or using email. As their confidence grows, their use of the Internet for purchase is likely to increase. This is often coupled with the use of broadband. For this reason, there is still good potential for e-retail sales, even if the percentage of the population with access to the Internet plateaus.

You can see from Figure 4.5 that Internet users take longer to become confident to purchase more expensive and more complex products. Figure 4.5 shows that the result is a dramatic difference in online consumer behaviour for products according to their price and complexity. For some products such as travel and cinema and theatre tickets, the majority buy online, while fewer people purchase clothes and insurance online. However, there is now less difference between the products than there was two or three years ago. Figure 4.5 suggests that the way companies should use digital technologies for marketing their products will vary markedly according to product type. In some, such as cars and complex financial products such as mortgages, the main role of online marketing will be to support research, while for standardised products there will be a dual role in supporting research and enabling purchase.

Bart *et al.* (2005) have developed a widely referenced conceptual model that links website and consumer characteristics, online trust, and behaviour. We have summarised the eight main drivers of trust from the study in Figure 9.5 in the section on buyer behaviour.

Business demand for digital business services

The B2B market is more complex than B2C in that variation in demand will occur according to different types of organisation and people within the buying unit in the organisation. This analysis is also important as part of the *segmentation* of different groups within a B2B target market. We need to profile business demand according to:

Figure 4.5 Development of experience in Internet usage

1 Variation in organisation characteristics
- Size of company (employees or turnover)
- Industry sector and products
- Organisation type (private, public, government, not-for-profit)
- Division
- Country and region.

2 Individual role

- Role and responsibility from job title, function or number of staff managed
- Role in buying decision (purchasing influence)
- Department
- Product interest
- Demographics: age, sex and possibly social group.

B2B profiles

We can profile business users of the Internet in a similar way to consumers by assessing:

1 **The percentage of companies with access.** In the business-to-business market, Internet access levels are higher than for business-to-consumer. Understanding access for different members of the organisational buying unit amongst their customers is also important for marketers. Although the Internet seems to be used by many companies, it doesn't necessarily reach the right people in the buying unit.
2 **Influenced online.** In B2B marketing, the high level of access is consistent with a high level of using the Internet to identify suppliers. As for consumer e-commerce, the Internet is important in identifying online suppliers rather than completing the transaction online. This is particularly the case in the larger companies.
3 **Purchase online.** This shows the importance of understanding differences in the environment for e-commerce in different countries.

In summary, to estimate online revenue contribution to determine the amount of investment in digital business we need to research the number of connected customers, the percentage whose offline purchase is influenced online and the number who buy online.

Adoption of digital business by businesses

The European Commission reviewed adoption of the digital business services across Europe (EuroStat, 2013), shown in Figure 4.6. It can be seen, perhaps surprisingly, that although most companies now have Internet access, other digital business services such as offering a website or using ERP or CRM are not used so widely, particularly in small business. This certainly shows the opportunities remaining from individuals; indeed, the report states a need for more trained ICT specialists to assist businesses.

Figure 4.7 gives a summary of these barriers. You can see that the lack of relevance or need for e-commerce is the largest barrier, but organisational governance issues are also important.

Daniel *et al.* (2002) researched digital business adoption in UK SMEs and noted four clusters: (1) developers, which were actively developing services, but were limited at the time of research; (2) communicators, which use email to communicate internally and with customers and suppliers; (3) web presence; (4) transactors.

The luxury of sufficient resources to focus on planning and implementing an Internet strategy isn't open to many small businesses and is likely to explain why they have not been such enthusiastic adopters of digital business.

Privacy and trust in e-commerce

Ethical standards
Practice or behaviour which is morally acceptable to society.

Ethical standards are personal or business practices or behaviour generally considered acceptable by society.

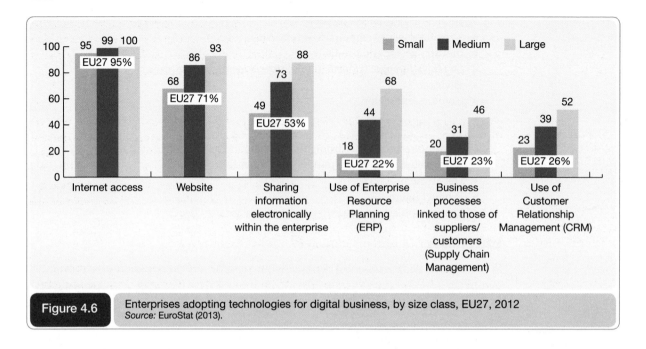

Figure 4.6 Enterprises adopting technologies for digital business, by size class, EU27, 2012
Source: EuroStat (2013).

Ethical issues and the associated laws constitute an important consideration of the Internet business environment for marketers. Privacy of consumers is a key ethical issue that affects all types of organisation regardless of whether they have a transactional e-commerce service. (For example, we saw in Case study 1.1 that Facebook has encountered resistance from its users for its approach to managing their information.)

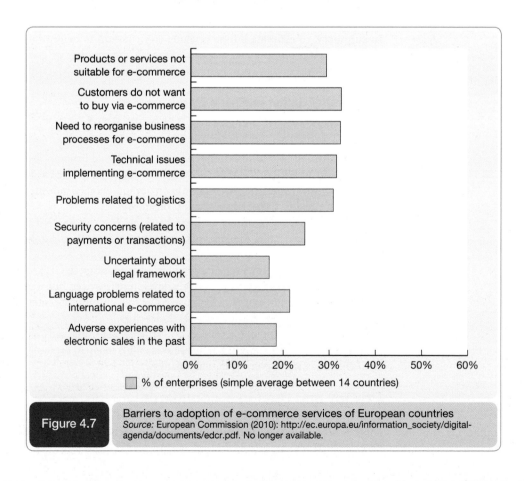

Figure 4.7 Barriers to adoption of e-commerce services of European countries
Source: European Commission (2010): http://ec.europa.eu/information_society/digital-agenda/documents/edcr.pdf. No longer available.

A further ethical issue for which laws have been enacted in many countries is providing an accessible level of Internet services for disabled users. Other laws have been developed for managing commerce and distance-selling online. In many cases, the laws governing e-commerce are in their infancy and lag behind the applications of technology.

Privacy legislation

Privacy

A moral right of individuals to avoid intrusion into their personal affairs.

Identity theft

The misappropriation of the identity of another person without their knowledge or consent.

Privacy refers to a moral right of individuals to avoid intrusion into their personal affairs by third parties. Privacy of personal data such as our identities, likes and dislikes is a major concern to consumers, particularly with the dramatic increase in **identity theft**. This is clearly a major concern for many consumers when using e-commerce services since they believe that their privacy and identity may be compromised. This is not unfounded, as Box 4.2 shows.

While identity theft is traumatic, in the majority of cases the victim will *eventually* be able to regain any lost funds through their financial services providers.

Why personal data are valuable for digital business

While there is much natural concern amongst consumers about their online privacy, information about these consumers is very useful to marketers. Through understanding their customers' needs, characteristics and behaviours it is possible to create more personalised,

---

Box 4.2	Types of identity fraud

Table 4.3 illustrates different types of identity fraud. The data show that it's still a growing problem with a 20% increase in impersonation between 2009 and 2010.

Table 4.3	Identity fraud categories in the UK

Fraud Type	2011	2012	% Change
Identity Fraud – Total	113,259	123,589	+9.1%
Application Fraud – Total	43,263	39,868	−7.8%
False Insurance Claim	396	279	−29.5%
Facility Takeover Fraud	25,070	38,428	+53.3%
Asset Conversion	532	337	−36.7%
Misuse of Facility	53,996	45,824	−15.1%
Victims of Impersonation	96,611	112,179	+16.1%
Victims of Takeover	25,250	38,686	+53.2%

See more at: www.cifas.org.uk/fraudtrendstwentytwelve#sthash.gmmvYOIJ.dpuf

Notes:

Identity fraud cases include cases of false identity and identity theft.

Application fraud/false insurance claim relates to applications or claims with material falsehood (lies) or false supporting documentation where the name has not been identified as false.

Facility takeover fraud occurs where a person (the 'facility hijacker') unlawfully obtains access to details of the 'victim of takeover', namely an existing account holder or policy holder (or of an account or policy of a genuine customer or policy holder) and fraudulently operates the account or policy for their own (or someone else's) benefit.

Asset conversion relates to the sale of assets subject to a credit agreement where the lender retained ownership of the asset (for example a car or a lorry).

Misuse of facility is where an account, policy or other facility is used fraudulently.

Source: CIFAS (2013).

targeted communications, which help increase sales. How should marketers respond to this dilemma? An obvious step is to ensure that marketing activities are consistent with the latest data protection and privacy laws. However, different interpretations of the law are possible and since these are new laws they have not been tested in court. As a result, companies have to take their own business decision based on the business benefits of applying particular marketing practices, against the financial and reputational risks of less strict compliance.

What are the main information types used by the Internet marketer which are governed by ethics and legislation? The information needs are:

1 **Contact information.** This is the name, postal address, email address and, for B2B companies, website address.
2 **Profile information.** This is information about a customer's characteristics that can be used for segmentation. They include age, sex and social group for consumers, and company characteristics and individual role for business customers. (The specific types of information and how they are used is referenced in Chapters 2 and 6.) Research by Ward *et al.* (2005) found that consumers in Australia were willing to give non-financial data if there is an appropriate incentive.
3 **Platform usage information.** Through web analytics systems it is possible to collect information on type of computer, browser and screen resolution used by site users (see Chapter 7).
4 **Behavioural information (on a single site).** This is purchase history, but also includes the whole buying process. Web analytics (Chapter 12) can be used to assess the web and email content accessed by individuals.
5 **Behavioural information (across multiple sites).** This can show how a user accesses multiple sites and responds to ads across sites. Typically these data are collected and used using an anonymous profile based on cookie or IP addresses which is not related to an individual. Complete Activity 4.3 to find out more about behavioural targeting and form an opinion of whether it should be regulated more.

Activity 4.3	Attitudes to behavioural ad targeting

Imagine you are a web user who has just found out about behavioural targeting.

Use the information sources provided by the industry to form an opinion. Discuss with others studying your course whether you believe behavioural ad targeting should be banned (as has been proposed in some countries) or whether it is acceptable.

Suggested information sources:

- Internet Advertising Bureau guide to behavioural advertising and privacy (www.youronlinechoices.com/). If you take a look at this page you will see the number of ad networks that users can potentially you can be targeted on. How many are you targeted by and how do you feel about it? See www.youronlinechoices.com/uk/your-ad-choices.
- Digital Analytics Association (www.digitalanalyticsassociation.org/?page=privacy). A trade association of online tracking vendors.
- Google 'Interest-based advertising': How it works (www.google.com/ads/preferences/html/about.html), which explains the process and benefits as follows:

Many websites, such as news sites and blogs, use Google's AdSense program ('a network of publishers using advertising through Google') to show ads on their sites. It's our goal to make these ads as relevant as possible for you. While we often show you ads based on the content of the page you are viewing, we also developed new

> *technology that shows some ads based on interest categories that you might find useful. The following example explains this new technology step by step:*
>
> *Mary's favourite hobby is gardening. With Google's interest-based advertising technology, Mary will see more relevant gardening ads because she visits many gardening websites. Here's how that works: When Mary visits websites that display ads provided by Google's AdSense program, Google stores a number in her browser (using a 'cookie') to remember her visits. That number could look like this: 114411. Because many of the websites that Mary visits are related to gardening, Google puts her number (114411) in the 'gardening enthusiast' interest category.*
>
> *As a result, Google will show more gardening ads to Mary (based on her browser) as she browses websites that use AdSense.*
>
> *Answers to activities can be found at www.pearsoned.co.uk/chaffey*

Table 4.4 summarises how these different types of customer information are collected and used. The main issue to be considered by the marketer is disclosure of the types of information collection and tracking data used. The first two types of information in the table are usually readily explained through a privacy statement at the point of data collection, which is usually a legal requirement. However, with the other types of information, users would only know they were being tracked if they have cookie monitoring software installed or if they seek out the privacy statement of a publisher which offers advertising.

Ethical issues concerned with personal information ownership have been summarised by Mason (1986) into four areas:

● Privacy – what information is held about the individual?
● Accuracy – is it correct?
● Property – who owns it and how can ownership be transferred?
● Accessibility – who is allowed to access this information, and under which conditions?

Fletcher (2001) provides an alternative perspective, raising these issues of concern for both the individual and the marketer:

● Transparency – who is collecting what information and how do they disclose the collection of data and how it will be used?
● Security – how is information protected once it has been collected by a company?
● Liability – who is responsible if data are abused?

All of these issues arise in the next section, which reviews actions marketers should take to achieve privacy and trust.

Data protection legislation is enacted to protect the individual, to protect their privacy and to prevent misuse of their personal data. Indeed, the first article of the European Union directive 95/46/EC (see http://ec.europa.eu/justice_home/fsj/privacy/) specifically refers to personal data. It says:

> *Member states shall protect the fundamental rights and freedoms of natural persons [i.e. a named individual at home or at work], and in particular their right to privacy with respect to the processing of personal data.*

Notification

The process whereby companies register with the data protection registrar to inform about their data holdings.

In the UK, the enactment of the European legislation is the Data Protection Act 1984, 1998 (DPA). It is managed by the 'Information Commissioner' and summarised at www.ico.gov.uk. This law is typical of what has evolved in many countries to help protect personal information. Any company that holds personal data on computers or on file about customers or employees must be registered with the data protection registrar (although there are some exceptions which may exclude small businesses). This process is known as **notification**.

Table 4.4	Types of information collected online and related technologies

Type of information	Approach and technology used to capture and use information
1 Contact information	• Online forms – online forms linked to customer database • Cookies – are used to remember a specific person on subsequent visits
2 Profile information, including personal information	• Online registration forms collect data on social networks and retail sites • Cookies can be used to assign a person to a particular segment by linking the cookie to a customer database record and then offering content consistent with their segment
3 Access platform usage	• Web analytics system – identification of computer type, operating system and screen characteristics based on http attributes of visitors
4 Behavioural information on a single site	• Purchase histories are stored in the sales order database. Web analytics store details of IP addresses against clickstreams of the sequence of web pages visited • Web beacons in email marketing – a single-pixel GIF is used to assess whether a reader had opened an email • First-party cookies are also used for monitoring visitor behaviour during a site visit and on subsequent visits • Malware can collect additional information such as passwords
5 Behavioural information across multiple sites	• Third-party cookies used for assessing visits from different sources such as online advertising networks or affiliate networks (Chapter 9) • Search engines such as Google use cookies to track advertising through its AdWords pay-per-click program • Services such as Hitwise (www.experian.com/hitwise/) monitor IP traffic to assess site usage of customer groups within a product category

Personal data

Any information about an individual stored by companies concerning their customers or employees.

The guidelines on the eight data protection principles are produced by legal requirements of the 1998 UK Data Protection Act. These principles state that **personal data** should be:

1 Fairly and lawfully processed.

In full: '*Personal data shall be processed fairly and lawfully and, in particular, shall not be processed unless – at least one of the conditions in Schedule 2 is met; and in the case of sensitive personal data, at least one of the conditions in Schedule 3 is also met.*'

The Information Commissioner has produced a 'fair processing code' which suggests how an organisation needs to achieve 'fair and lawful processing'. This requires:

Data controller

Each company must have a defined person responsible for data protection.

Data subject

The legal term to refer to the individual whose data are held.

• Appointment of a **data controller** who has defined responsibility for data protection within a company.
• Clear details in communications such as on a website or direct mail of how a '**data subject**' can contact the data controller or a representative.
• Before data processing 'the data subject has given his consent' or the processing must be necessary either for a 'contract to which the data subject is a party' (for example as part of a sale of a product) or because it is required by other laws.

- Sensitive personal data require particular care,
    - the racial or ethnic origin of the data subject;
    - political opinions;
    - religious beliefs or other beliefs of a similar nature;
    - membership of a trade union;
    - physical or mental health or condition;
    - sexual life;
    - the commission or alleged commission or proceedings of any offence.
- No other laws must be broken in processing the data.

2 Processed for limited purposes.

In full: '*Personal data shall be obtained only for one or more specified and lawful purposes, and shall not be further processed in any manner incompatible with that purpose or those purposes.*'

This implies that the organisation must make it clear why and how the data will be processed at the point of collection. Figure 4.8 suggests some of the issues that should be considered when a data subject is informed of how the data will be used. Important issues are:

- Whether future communications will be sent to the individual (explicit consent is required for this in online channels).
- Whether the data will be passed on to third parties (again explicit consent is required).
- How long the data will be kept.

3 Adequate, relevant and not excessive.

In full: '*Personal data shall be adequate, relevant and not excessive in relation to the purpose or purposes for which they are processed.*'

This specifies that the minimum necessary amount of data is requested for processing. There is difficulty in reconciling this provision between the needs of the individual and the needs of the company. The more details that an organisation has about a customer,

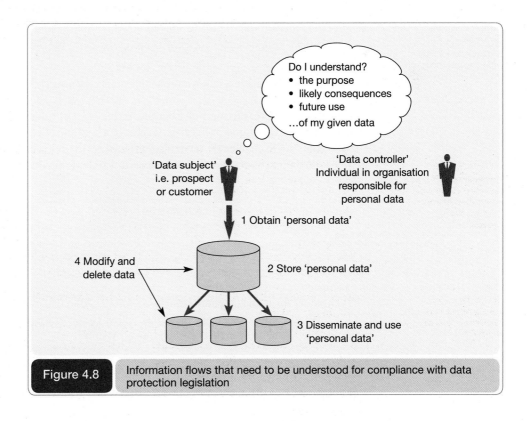

| Figure 4.8 | Information flows that need to be understood for compliance with data protection legislation |

the better they can understand that customer and so develop products and marketing communications specific to that customer.

4 Accurate.

In full: *'Personal data shall be accurate and, where necessary, kept up to date.'*

It is clearly also in the interest of an organisation in an ongoing relationship with a partner that the data are kept accurate and up to date. Inaccurate data are defined in the guidelines as: 'incorrect or misleading as to any matter of fact'.

The guidelines go on to discuss the importance of keeping information up to date. This is only necessary where there is an ongoing relationship and the rights of the individual may be affected if they are not up to date.

5 Not kept longer than necessary.

In full: *'Personal data processed for any purpose or purposes shall not be kept for longer than is necessary for that purpose or those purposes.'*

The guidelines state: *'To comply with this Principle, data controllers will need to review their personal data regularly and to delete the information which is no longer required for their purposes.'*

It might be in a company's interests to 'clean data' so that records that are not relevant are archived or deleted. However, there is the possibility that the customer may still buy again, in which case the information would be useful. For example, a car manufacturer could justifiably hold data for several years.

If a relationship between the organisation and the data subject ends, then data should be deleted. This will be clear in some instances; for example, when an employee leaves a company their personal data should be deleted.

6 Processed in accordance with the data subject's rights.

In full: *'Personal data shall be processed in accordance with the rights of data subjects under this Act.'*

One aspect of the data subject's rights is the option to request a copy of their personal data from an organisation for payment of a small fee such as £10 or £30; this is known as a '**subject access request**'. This includes all information on paper files and on computer.

Subject access request
A request by a data subject to view personal data from an organisation.

Other aspects of a data subject's rights are designed to prevent or control processing which:

- causes damage or distress (for example, repeatedly sending mailshots to someone who has died);
- is used for direct marketing (for example, in the UK consumers can subscribe to the mail, email or telephone preference service to avoid unsolicited mailings, emails or phone calls). This invaluable service is provided by the Direct Marketing Association (www.dmaconsumers.org). Organisations must check against these 'exclusion lists' before contacting you.
- is used for automatic decision taking – automated credit checks, for example, may result in unjust decisions on taking a loan.

7 Secure.

In full: *'Appropriate technical and organisational measures shall be taken against unauthorised or unlawful processing of personal data and against accidental loss or destruction of, or damage to, personal data.'*

(Techniques for managing data security are discussed in Chapter 11.)

Of course, the cost of security measures will vary according to the level of security required. The Act allows for this through this provision:

(i) *Taking into account the state of technological development at any time and the cost of implementing any measures, the measures must ensure a level of security appropriate to: (a) the harm that might result from a breach of security; and (b) the nature of the data to* *be protected. (ii) The data controller must take reasonable steps to ensure the reliability of staff having access to the personal data.*

8 Not transferred to countries without adequate protection.

In full: '*Personal data shall not be transferred to a country or territory outside the European Economic Area, unless that country or territory ensures an adequate level of protection of the rights and freedoms of data subjects in relation to the processing of personal data.*'

Transfer of data beyond Europe is likely for multinational companies. This principle prevents export of data to countries that do not have sound data processing laws. If the transfer is required in concluding a sale or contract or if the data subject agrees to it, then transfer is legal. Data transfer with the US is possible through companies registered through the Safe Harbor scheme (www.export.gov/safeharbor).

Anti-spam legislation

Spam
Unsolicited email (usually bulk-mailed and untargeted).

Laws have been enacted in different countries to protect individual privacy and with the intention of reducing **spam** or unsolicited commercial email (UCE). Spammers rely on sending out millions of emails in the hope that even if there is only a 0.01% response they may make some money, if not get rich.

Anti-spam laws do not mean that email cannot be used as a marketing tool. As explained below, permission-based email marketing based on consent or opt-in by customers and the option to unsubscribe or opt out is the key to successful email marketing.

Before starting an email dialogue with customers, according to law in Europe, America and many countries in the Asia–Pacific region, companies must ask customers to provide their email address and then give them the option of 'opting into' further communications.

Cold list
Data about individuals that are rented or sold by a third party.

Legal opt-in email addresses and customer profile information are available for purchase or rental from a database traditionally known by marketers as a '**cold list**'. Your name will also potentially be stored on an opt-in **house list** where you have given your consent to be contacted by a company you have purchased from or its partners.

House list
Data about existing customers used to market products to encourage future purchase.

Regulations on privacy and electronic communications

While the Data Protection Directive 95 ÷ 46 and Data Protection Act afford a reasonable level of protection for consumers, they were quickly superseded by advances in technology and the rapid growth in spam. As a result, in 2002 the European Union passed the '2002 ÷ 58/EC Directive on Privacy and Electronic Communications' to complement previous data protection law (see Box 4.3). This Act applies specifically to electronic communications such as email and the monitoring of websites using technologies such as cookies.

Worldwide regulations on privacy and electronic communications

In the USA, there is a privacy initiative aimed at education of consumers and business (www.ftc.gov/privacy), but legislation is limited other than for email marketing. In January 2004, a new federal law known as the CAN-SPAM Act (www.ftc.gov/spam) was introduced to assist in the control of unsolicited email. CAN-SPAM stands for 'Controlling the Assault of Non-Solicited Pornography and Marketing' (an ironic juxtaposition between pornography and marketing). The Act requires unsolicited commercial email messages to be labelled (though not by a standard method) and to include opt-out instructions and the sender's physical address. It prohibits the use of deceptive subject lines and false headers in such messages.

Anti-spam legislation in other countries can be accessed:

- Australia enacted a spam Act in 2003 (www.privacy.gov.au)
- Canada has a privacy Act (www.privcom.gc.ca)
- New Zealand Privacy Commissioner (www.privacy.org.nz)
- Summary of all countries (www.privacyinternational.org and www.spamlaws.com).

While such laws are clearly in consumers' interests, some companies see the practice as restrictive. In 2002, ten companies, including IBM, Oracle and VeriSign, who referred to themselves as the 'Global Privacy Alliance (GPA)', lobbied the EU saying that it put too much emphasis on the protection of individuals' privacy, and not enough on ensuring the free flow of information between companies! More positively, the Online Privacy Alliance (www.privacyalliance.org) is a 'group of more than 30 global corporations and associations who have come together to introduce and promote business-wide actions that create an environment of trust and foster the protection of individuals' privacy online'.

| **Box 4.3** | **UK and European email marketing law** |

As an example of European privacy law which covers use of email, SMS and cookies for marketing, we review the implications for managers of the UK enactment of 2002 ÷ 58/EC Directive on Privacy and Electronic Communications. We will contrast this with the law in other European countries.

Privacy and Electronic Communications Regulations Act
A law intended to control the distribution of email and other online communications.

This came into force in the UK on 11 December 2003 as the **Privacy and Electronic Communications Regulations (PECR) Act** (update in force from 2012). Consumer marketers in the UK also need to heed the Code of Advertising Practice from the Advertising Standards Agency (ASA CAP code, www.cap.org.uk/Advertising-Codes.aspx). This has broadly similar aims and places similar restrictions on marketers to the PECR law.

The PECR law is a surprisingly accessible and common-sense document – many marketers will be practising similar principles already. Clauses 22 to 24 are the main clauses relevant to email communications. The PECR law:

1 **Applies to consumer marketing using email or SMS text messages.** 22(1) applies to 'individual subscribers', which currently means consumers, although the Information Commissioner has stated that this may be reviewed in future to include business subscribers as is the case in countries such as Italy and Germany.

   Although this sounds like great news for business-to-business (B2B) marketers, it could be dangerous. The Advertising Standards Agency found against a B2B organisation which had unwittingly emailed consumers from what they believed was a list of B2B customers.

2 **Is an 'opt-in' regime.** The law applies to 'unsolicited communications' (22(1)) and was introduced with a view to reducing spam, although its impact will be limited on spammers beyond Europe. The recipient must have 'previously notified the sender that he consents' (22(2)) or has proactively agreed to receive commercial email. This is **opt-in**. Opt-in can be achieved online or offline through asking people whether they want to receive email. Online this is often done through a tick box. In fact, the PECR law does not mandate a tick box option (except for receiving communications from third parties) provided consent is clearly indicated, such as by pressing a button.

Opt-in
A customer proactively agrees or consents to receive further communications.

The approach required by the law has been used by many organisations for some time, as sending unsolicited emails was thought to be unethical and also not in the best interests of the company because of the risk of annoying customers. In fact, the law conforms to an established approach known as '**permission marketing**', a term coined by US commentator Seth Godin (1999) (see Chapter 9, p. 395)."

Permission marketing
Customers agree (opt in) to be involved in an organisation's marketing activities, usually as a result of an incentive.

| **Debate 4.1** |

How far should opt-in go?
'Companies should always use an opt in privacy policy for
(a) emailing prospects and customers
(b) monitoring website visitors using site analysis software
(c) identifying customer behaviour using cookies.'

Opt-out
A customer declines the offer to receive further information.

3 **Requires an opt-out option in all communications.** An **opt-out** or method of 'unsubscribing' is required so that the recipient does not receive future communications. In a database this means that a 'do not email' field must be created. A 'simple means of refusing' future communications is required both when the details were first collected and in each subsequent communication.

4 **Does not apply to existing customers when marketing similar products.** This common-sense clause (22(3)(a)) states that previous opt-in is not required if the contact details were obtained during the course of the sale or negotiations for the sale of a product or service. This is sometimes known as the 'soft or implied opt-in exception'. This clause is interpreted differently in different European countries, with seven countries, Italy, Denmark, Germany, Austria, Greece, Finland and Spain, not including it. Marketers managing campaigns across Europe need to take the differences into account.

   Clause 22(3)(b) adds that when marketing to existing customers the marketer may market 'similar products and services only'. Case law will help in clarifying this.

5 **Contact details must be provided.** It is not sufficient to send an email with a simple sign-off from 'The marketing team' or 'Web team'. The law requires a name, address or phone number to whom a recipient can complain.

6 **The 'from' identification of the sender must be clear.** Spammers aim to disguise the email originator. The law says that the identity of the person who sends the communication must not be 'disguised or concealed' and that a valid address to which to 'send a request that such communications cease' should be provided.

7 **Applies to direct marketing communications.** The communications that the legislation refers to are for 'direct marketing'. This suggests that other communications involved with customer service, such as an email about a monthly phone statement, are not covered, so the opt-out choice may not be required here.

8 **Restricts the use of cookies.** Some privacy campaigners consider that the user's privacy is invaded by planting **cookies** or electronic tags on the end-user's computer. The concept of the cookie and its associated law is not straightforward, so it warrants separate discussion (see Box 4.4).

Cookies
Small text files stored on an end-user's computer to enable websites to identify them.

Persistent cookies
Cookies that remain on the computer after a visitor session has ended. Used to recognise returning visitors.

| Box 4.4 | Understanding cookies |

A 'cookie' is a data file placed on your computer that identifies the individual computer.

Types of cookies
The main cookie types are:

- **Persistent cookies** – these stay on a user's computer between multiple sessions and are most valuable for marketers to identify repeat visits to sites.
- **Temporary or session cookies** – single session – useful for tracking within pages of a session such as on an e-commerce site.
- **First-party cookies** – served by the site you are currently using – typical for e-commerce sites. These can be persistent or session cookies.
- **Third-party cookies** – served by another site to the one you are viewing – typical for portals where an ad network will track remotely or where the web analytics software places a cookie. These are typically persistent cookies.

Session cookies
Cookies used to manage a single visitor session.

First-party cookies
Served by the site you are currently using – typical for e-commerce sites.

Third-party cookies
Served by another site to the one you are viewing – typical for portals where an ad network will track remotely or where the web analytics software places a cookie.

Cookies are stored as individual text files in a directory on a personal computer. There is usually one file per website. For example: dave_chaffey@british-airways.txt contains encoded information as follows:

```
FLT_VIS`K:bapzRnGdxBYUU`D:Jul-25-1999`    british-airways.
com/0 425259904 293574 26 1170747936 29284034*
```

The information is essentially just an identification number and a date of the last visit, although other information can be stored.

Cookies are specific to a particular browser and computer, so if a user connects from a different computer or starts using a different browser, the website will not identify him or her as a similar user.

Browser suppliers are keen to protect users' online privacy as part of their value proposition. 2008 saw the launch of Internet Explorer 8 and its InPrivate feature and Google Chrome with its Incognito mode. These are intended for temporary use for a session where someone is browsing sites they don't want others in the family or office to know about. They won't delete previous cookies, but new permanent cookies won't be created in these situations.

What are cookies used for?

Common marketing applications of cookies include:

A *Personalising a site for an individual*. Cookies are used to identify individual users and retrieve their preferences from a database.

   For example, I subscribe to the Econsultancy service www.econsultancy.com; each time I return I do not have to log in because it remembers my previous visit. Many sites feature a 'Remember Me' option which implies using a cookie to remember a returning visitor. Retailers such as Amazon can use cookies to recognise returning visitors and recommend related items. This approach generally has benefits for both the individual (it is a hassle to sign in again and relevant content can be delivered) and the company (tailored marketing messages can be delivered).

B *Online ordering systems*. This enables a site such as Tesco.com to track what is in your basket as you order different products.

C *Tracking within a site.* Web analytics software such as Webtrends (www.webtrends. com) relies on persistent cookies to find the proportion of repeat visitors to a website. Webtrends and other tools increasingly use first-party cookies since they are more accurate and less likely to be blocked.

D *Tracking across sites*. Advertising networks use cookies to track the number of times a particular computer user has been shown a particular banner advertisement; they can also track adverts served on sites across an ad network.

Affiliate networks and pay-per-click ad networks such as Google Adwords will also use cookies to track through from a click on a third-party site to a sale or lead being generated on a destination or merchant site. These approaches tend to use third-party cookies. For example, if conversion tracking is enabled in Google Adwords, Google sets a cookie when a user clicks through on an ad. If this user buys the product, then the purchase confirmation page will include script code supplied by Google to make a check for a cookie placed by Google. If there is a match, the sale is attributed to Adwords. An alternative approach is that different online campaigns have different tracking parameters or codes within the links through to the destination site and when the user arrives on a site from a particular source this is identified and a cookie is set. When purchase confirmation occurs, this can then be attributed back to the original source and the particular referrer.

Owing to the large investments now made in pay-per-click and affiliate marketing, this is the area of most concern for marketers since the tracking can become inaccurate. However, sale should still occur even if the cookies are blocked or deleted, so the main consequence is that the ROI of online advertising or pay-per-click marketing may look lower than expected. In affiliate marketing, this phenomenon may benefit the marketer in that payment may not need to be made to the third party if a cookie has been deleted (or blocked) between the time of original clickthrough and sale.

Privacy issues with cookie use

The problem for Internet marketers is that, despite these important applications, blocking by browsers or security software and deletion by users has increased dramatically.

Many distrust cookies since they indicate that 'big brother' is monitoring your actions. Others fear that their personal details or credit card details may be accessed by other websites. This is very unlikely since all that cookies contain is a short identifier or number that is used to link you to your record in a database. In most cases, the worst that someone who gets access to your cookies can do is to find out which sites you have been visiting.

Legal constraints on cookies

The PECR law, particularly its update in May 2012, gives companies guidance on their use of cookies. The original 2003 law states: 'a person shall not use an electronic communications network to store information, or to gain access to information stored, in the terminal equipment of a subscriber or user unless the following requirements are met'.

The requirements are:

(a) the user is provided with clear and comprehensive information about the purposes of the storage of, or access to, that information; and

(b) the user is given the opportunity to refuse the storage of, or access to, that information.

suggests that it is important that there is a clear **privacy statement** and (b) suggests that explicit opt-in to cookies is required – this is what we now see on many sites following the implementation of the law in 2013. In other words, on the first visit to the site, a box has to be ticked to agree to the use of cookies. This was thought by many commentators to be a curious provision since this facility is already available in the web browser.

Privacy statement
Information on a website explaining how and why an individual's data are collected, processed and stored.

Viral email marketing

Viral marketing
In an online context, 'Forward to a friend' email used to transmit a promotional message from one person to another. 'Online word-of-mouth.'

One widespread business practice that is not covered explicitly in the PECR law is '**viral marketing**' (as discussed in Chapter 3 and reviewed in Chapter 9, p. 435).

Several initiatives are being taken by industry groups to reassure web users about threats to their personal information. The first of these is TRUSTe (www.truste.org), sponsored by IBM and with sites validated by PricewaterhouseCoopers and KPMG. The validators will audit the site to check each site's privacy statement to see whether it is valid. For example, a privacy statement will describe:

- how a site collects information;
- how the information is used;
- who the information is shared with;
- how users can access and correct information;
- how users can decide to deactivate themselves from the site or withhold information from third parties.

A UK accreditation initiative aimed at *reassurance* formerly coordinated by the Internet Media in Retail Group is ISIS, a trade group for e-retailers (Internet Shopping Is Safe) (www.imrg.org/ISIS). Another initiative, aimed at *education,* is GetSafeOnline (www.get-safeonline.org), which is a site created by government and business to educate consumers to help them understand and manage their online privacy and security.

Government initiatives will also define best practice in this area and may introduce laws to ensure guidelines are followed.

We conclude this section on privacy legislation with a checklist summary of the practical steps that are required to audit a company's compliance with data protection and privacy legislation. Companies should:

1 Follow privacy and consumer protection guidelines and laws in all local markets. Use local privacy and security certification where available.
2 Inform the user, before asking for information:
   - who the company is;
   - what personal data are collected, processed and stored;
   - what is the purpose of collection.
3 Ask for consent for collecting sensitive personal data, and it is good practice to ask before collecting any type of data.
4 Reassure customers by providing clear and effective privacy statements and explaining the purpose of data collection.
5 Let individuals know when 'cookies' or other covert software is used to collect information about them.
6 Never collect or retain personal data unless it is strictly necessary for the organisation's purposes. If extra information is required for marketing purposes, this should be made clear and the provision of such information should be optional.
7 Amend incorrect data when informed and tell others. Enable correction on-site.
8 Only use data for marketing (by the company, or third parties) when a user has been informed that this is the case and has agreed to this. (This is opt-in.)
9 Provide the option for customers to stop receiving information. (This is opt-out.)
10 Use appropriate security technology to protect the customer information on your site.

Other e-commerce legislation

Sparrow (2000) identified eight areas of law which need to concern online marketers. Although laws have been refined since that time, this is still a useful framework.

1 Marketing your e-commerce business

Domain name
The domain name refers to the name of the web server and it is usually selected to be the same as the name of the company.

Sparrow used this category to refer to purchasing a **domain name** for a website, but other legal constraints now also fall under this category.

A Domain name registration

Most companies are likely to own several domains, perhaps for different product lines, countries or for specific marketing campaigns. Domain name disputes can arise when an individual or company has registered a domain name which another company claims they have the right to (see Chapter 3).

A related issue is brand and trademark protection. Online brand reputation management and alerting software tools offer real-time alerts when comments or mentions about a brand are posted online. Some basic tools are available including:

- Googlealert (www.googlealert.com) and GigaAlerts Google Alerts (www.googlealert.com) which will alert companies when any new pages appear that contain a search phrase such as your company or brand names.
- Copyscape (www.copyscape.com) is used for locating duplicates of content that may arise from plagiarism. Blog Pulse (www.blogpulse.com) gives trends and listings of any phrase (see example in Figure 4.9) and individual postings can be viewed.

B Using competitor names and trademarks in meta-tags (for search engine optimisation)

Meta-tags are used to market websites by enabling them to appear more prominently in search engines as part of search engine optimisation (SEO) (see Chapter 9). Some companies have tried putting a competitor company name within the meta-tags. Case law has found against companies that have used this approach. Privacy law for email marketing was considered in the previous section.

C Using competitor names and trademarks in pay-per-click advertising

Pay-per-click (PPC) search marketing

A company pays for text adverts to be displayed on the search engine results pages when a specific key phrase is entered. The marketer pays for each time the link in the ad is clicked on.

Accessibility legislation

Legislation intended to protect users of websites with disabilities, including visual disability.

A similar approach can potentially be used in **pay-per-click search marketing** (see Chapter 9) to advertise on competitors' names and trademarks. For example, if a search user types 'Dell laptop', can an advertiser bid to place an ad offering an 'HP laptop'? There is less case law in this area and differing findings have occurred in the US and France.

D Accessibility law

Laws relating to discriminating against disabled users who may find it more difficult to use websites because of audio, visual or motor impairment are known as **accessibility legislation**. This is often contained within disability and discrimination Acts. In the UK, the relevant Act is the Disability and Discrimination Act 1995.

Web accessibility refers to enabling all users of a website to interact with it regardless of disabilities they may have or the web browser or platform they are using. The visually impaired or blind are the main audience that designing an accessible website can help. (Coverage of the requirements that accessibility places on web design are covered in Chapter 7.)

Internet standards organisations such as the World Wide Web Consortium have been active in promoting guidelines for web accessibility (www.w3.org/WAI). This site describes such common accessibility problems as:

> *images without alternative text; lack of alternative text for imagemap hot-spots; misleading use of structural elements on pages; uncaptioned audio or undescribed video; lack of*

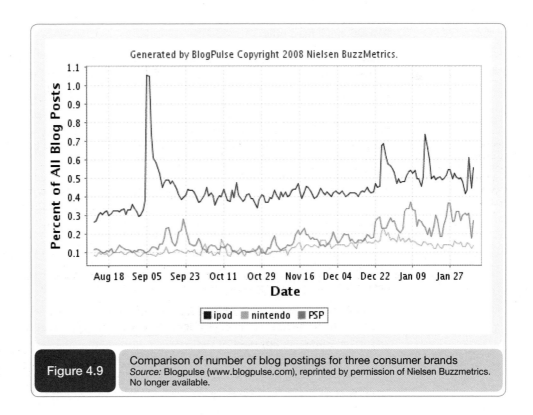

	Comparison of number of blog postings for three consumer brands
Figure 4.9	*Source:* Blogpulse (www.blogpulse.com), reprinted by permission of Nielsen Buzzmetrics. No longer available.

alternative information for users who cannot access frames or scripts; tables that are difficult to decypher when linearized; or sites with poor color contrast.

A tool provided to assess the WWW standards is BOBBY (www.cast.org/learningtools/Bobby/index.html).

In 2000, Bruce Maguire, a blind Internet user who uses a refreshable Braille display, brought a case against the Sydney Organising Committee for the Olympic Games. Maguire successfully demonstrated deficiencies in the site which prevented him using it adequately, which were not successfully remedied. He was protected under the 1992 Australian Disability Discrimination Act and the defendant was ordered to pay AU$20,000. This was the first case brought in the world, and it showed organisations in all countries that they could be guilty of discrimination if they did not audit their sites against accessibility guidelines. Discrimination Acts are now being amended in many countries to specifically refer to online discrimination.

2 Forming an electronic contract (contract law and distance-selling law)

We will look at two aspects of forming an electronic contract: the country of origin principle and distance-selling laws.

Country of origin principle

The contract formed between a buyer and a seller on a website will be subject to the laws of a particular country. In Europe, many such laws are specified at the regional (European Union) level, but are interpreted differently in different countries. This raises the issue of the jurisdiction in which law applies – is it that for the buyer or the seller (merchant)? In 2002, attempts were made by the EU to adopt the '*country of origin principle*', where the law for the contract will be that where the merchant is located. The Out-Law site produced by lawyers Pinsent Mason gives more information on jurisdiction (www.out-law.com/page-479).

Distance-selling law

Sparrow (2000) advises different forms of disclaimers to protect the retailer. For example, if a retailer made an error with the price or the product details were in error, then the retailer is not bound to honour a contract, since it was only displaying the products as 'an invitation to treat', not a fixed offer.

One e-retailer offered televisions for £2.99 due to an error in pricing a £299 product. Numerous purchases were made, but the e-retailer claimed that a contract had not been established simply by accepting the online order, although the customers did not see it that way! Unfortunately, no legal precedent was established since the case did not come to trial.

Disclaimers can also be used to limit liability if the website service causes a problem for the user, such as a financial loss resulting from an action based on erroneous content. Furthermore, Sparrow suggests that terms and conditions should be developed to refer to issues such as timing of delivery and damage or loss of goods.

The distance-selling directive also has a bearing on e-commerce contracts in the European Union. It was originally developed to protect people using mail-order (by post or phone). The main requirements are that e-commerce sites must contain easily accessible content which clearly states:

(i)   The company's identity, including address.
(ii)   The main features of the goods or services.
(iii)   Price information, including tax and, if appropriate, delivery costs.
(iv)   The period for which the offer or price remains valid.
(v)   Payment, delivery and fulfilment performance arrangements.
(vi)   Right of the consumer to withdraw, i.e. cancellation terms.
(vii)   The minimum duration of the contract and whether the contract for the supply of products or services is to be permanent or recurrent, if appropriate.
(viii) Whether an equivalent product or service might be substituted, and confirmation as to whether the seller pays the return costs in this event.

After the contract has been entered into, the supplier is required to provide written confirmation of the information provided. An email confirmation is now legally binding provided both parties have agreed that email is an acceptable form for the contract. It is always advisable to obtain an electronic signature to confirm that both parties have agreed the contract, and this is especially valuable in the event of a dispute. The default position for services is that there is no cancellation right once services begin.

The Out-Law site also gives information on distance selling (www.out-law.com/page-430).

3 Making and accepting payment

For transactional e-commerce sites, the relevant laws are those referring to liability between a credit card issuer, the merchant and the buyer. Merchants need to be aware of their liability for different situations such as the customer making a fraudulent transaction.

4 Authenticating contracts concluded over the Internet

'Authentication' refers to establishing the identity of the purchaser. For example, to help prove a credit card owner is the valid owner, many sites now ask for a three-digit authentication code. This helps reduce the risk of someone who has, for instance, found a credit card number using it to buy fraudulently. Using digital signatures is another method of helping to prove the identity of purchasers (and merchants).

5 Email risks

One of the main risks with email is infringing an individual's privacy. Specific laws have been developed in many countries to reduce the volume of spam, as explained in the previous section on privacy.

A further issue with email is defamation, where someone makes a statement that is potentially damaging to an individual or a company. In 2000, a statement was made on the Norwich Union Healthcare internal email system in England which falsely alleged that rival company WPA was under investigation and that regulators had forced it to stop accepting new business. The posting was published on the internal email system, but it was not contained and became more widespread. WPA sued for libel and the case was settled out of court when Norwich Union paid £415,000 to WPA. Such cases are relatively rare.

6 Protecting intellectual property (IP)

Intellectual property rights (IPR)
Protect the intangible property created by corporations or individuals that is protected under copyright, trade secret and patent laws.

Intellectual property rights (IPR) protect designs, ideas and inventions and include content and services developed for e-commerce sites. Copyright law is designed to protect authors, producers, broadcasters and performers through ensuring that they see some returns from their works every time they are experienced. The European Directive of Copyright (2001 ÷ 29/EC) came into force in many countries in 2003; it covers new technologies and approaches such as streaming a broadcast via the Internet.

IP can be misappropriated in two senses online.

First, an organisation's IP may be misappropriated: it is relatively easy to copy web content and republish it on another site. Reputation management services can be used to assess how an organisation's content, logos and **trademarks** are being used on other websites. Tools such as Copyscape (www.copyscape.com) can be used to identify infringement of content where it is 'scraped' off other sites using 'screenscrapers'.

Trademark
A trademark is a unique word or phrase that distinguishes your company. The mark can be registered as plain or designed text, artwork or a combination.

Secondly, an organisation may misappropriate content inadvertently. Some employees may infringe copyright if they are not aware of the law. Additionally, some methods of designing transactional websites have been patented. For example, Amazon has patented its 'One-click' purchasing option.

7 Advertising on the Internet

Advertising standards that are enforced by independent agencies such as the UK's Advertising Standards Authority Code also apply in the Internet environment. They are traditionally less strongly policed, leading to more 'edgy' creative executions online which are intended to have a viral effect.

The Out-Law site gives more information (www.out-law.com/page-5604).

8 Data protection

Data protection has been referred to in depth in the previous section.

Environmental and green issues related to Internet usage

The future state of our planet is a widely held social concern. Technology is generally seen as detrimental to the environment, but there are some arguments that e-commerce and digital communications can have environmental benefits. Companies can sometimes also make cost savings while positioning themselves as environmentally concerned – see Box 4.6.

Potentially, online shopping can also have environment benefits. Imagine a situation where we no longer travelled to the shops, and 100% of items were efficiently delivered to us at home or at work. This would reduce traffic considerably! Although this situation is inconceivable, online shopping is growing considerably and it may be having an impact. Research by the Internet Media in Retail Group (www.imrg.org) shows the growing importance of e-commerce in the UK where over 10% of retail sales are now online. In 2007 IMRG launched a Go Green, Go Online campaign where it identified six reasons why it believes e-commerce is green:

1 **Fewer vehicle-miles.** Shopping is the most frequent reason for car travel in the UK, accounting for 20% of all trips, and for 12% of mileage. A study by the Swiss online grocer LeShop.ch calculated that each time a customer decides to buy online rather than go shopping by car, 3.5 kg of CO_2 emissions are saved.
2 **Lower inventory requirements.** The trend towards pre-selling online – i.e. taking orders for products before they are built, as implemented by Dell – avoids the production of obsolete goods that have to be disposed of if they don't sell, with associated wastage in energy and natural resources.
3 **Fewer printed materials.** Online e-newsletters and brochures replace their physical equivalent so saving paper and distribution costs.
4 **Less packaging.** Although theoretically there is less need for fancy packaging if an item is sold online, this argument is less convincing, since most items like software or electronic items still come in packaging. At least those billions of music tracks downloaded don't require any packaging or plastic.
5 **Less waste.** Across the whole supply chain of procurement, manufacturing and distribution the Internet can help reduce product and distribution cycles. Some even claim that auction services like eBay and Amazon Marketplace can promote recycling and reuse.
6 **Dematerialisation.** Better known as 'digitisation', this is the availability of products like software, music and video in digital form.

If companies trading online can explain these benefits to their customers effectively, as HSBC has done, then this can benefit these online channels.

But how much could e-shopping reduce greenhouse gas emissions? A study by Finnish researchers Siikavirta *et al.* (2003), limited to e-grocery shopping, has suggested that it is theoretically possible to reduce the greenhouse gas emissions generated by grocery shopping by 18% to 87% compared with the situation in which household members go to the store. The researchers estimated that this would lead to a reduction of all Finland's greenhouse gas emissions by as much as 1%, but in reality the figure is much lower since only 10% of grocery shopping trips are online.

Box 4.6	HSBC customers plant virtual forest

HSBC has committed to improving the environment since it became a climate-neutral company globally in November 2005. Through the use of green technologies and emission-offset trading, HSBC counteracts all CO_2 emissions generated by its building operations and corporate travel. In 2006, 35% of operations in North America were offset by investments in Renewable Energy Certificates from wind power alone.

Another aspect of HSBC green policy is its online banking service, where it encourages paperless billing. For example, in the UK in 2007, over 400,000 customers switched from paper statements to online delivery, creating a virtual tree each time (Figure 4.10), and for every 20 virtual trees, HSBC promised to plant a real one.

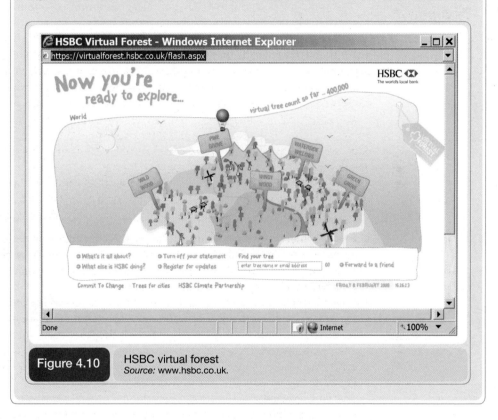

Figure 4.10	HSBC virtual forest *Source:* www.hsbc.co.uk.

Cairns (2005) has completed a study for the UK which shows the importance of grocery shopping – she estimates that car travel for food and other household items represents about 40% of all UK shopping trips by car, and about 5% of all car use. She considers that a direct substitution of car trips by van trips could reduce vehicle-km by 70% or more. A broader study by Ahmed and Sharma (2006) used value chain analysis to assess the role of the Internet in changing the amount of energy and materials consumed by businesses for each part of the supply chain. However, no estimates of savings are made.

Taxation

How to change tax laws to reflect globalisation through the Internet is a problem that many governments have grappled with. The fear is that the Internet may cause significant reductions in tax revenues to national or local governments if existing laws do not cover changes in purchasing patterns. Basu (2007) notes that around a third of government taxation revenue is from domestic consumption tax, with revenue from import taxation around 17%. Governments are clearly keen that this revenue is protected.

Government revenue is normally protected since, taking the UK as an example, when goods are imported from a non-EU territory, an excise duty is charged at the same rate as VAT. While this can be levied for physical goods imported by air and sea, it is less easy to administer for services. Here agreements have to be reached with individual suppliers.

In Europe, the use of online betting in lower-tax areas such as Gibraltar has resulted in lower revenues to governments in the countries where consumers would have formerly paid gaming tax to the government via a betting shop. Large UK bookmakers such as William Hill and Victor Chandler are offering Internet-based betting from 'offshore' locations. Retailers have set up retail operations on Jersey to sell items such as DVDs and CDs which cost less than an £18 Low Value Consignment Relief threshold, so no VAT or excise duty needs to be paid.

This trend has been dubbed LOCI or 'location-optimised commerce on the Internet' by Mougayer (1998).

Since the Internet supports the global marketplace it could be argued that it makes little sense to introduce tariffs on goods and services delivered over the Internet. Such instruments would, in any case, be impossible to apply to products delivered electronically. This position is currently that of the USA. In the document 'A Framework for Global Electronic Commerce', President Clinton stated that:

The United States will advocate in the World Trade Organization (WTO) and other appropriate international fora that the Internet be declared a tariff-free zone.

Tax jurisdiction

Tax jurisdiction determines which country gets tax income from a transaction. Under the pre-electronic commerce system of international tax treaties, the right to tax was divided between the country where the enterprise that receives the income is resident ('residence country') and that from which the enterprise derives that income ('source country'). In 2002, the EU enacted two laws (Council Directive 2002 ÷ 38/EC and Council Regulation (EC) 792 ÷ 2002) on how value added tax (VAT) was to be charged and collected for electronic services. These were in accordance with the principles agreed within the framework of the Organisation for Economic Co-operation and Development (OECD) at a 1998 conference in Ottawa. These principles establish that the rules for consumption taxes (such as VAT) should result in taxation in the jurisdiction where consumption takes place (the country of origin principle referred to above). These laws helped to make European countries more competitive in e-commerce.

The OECD also agreed that a simplified online registration scheme, as now adopted by the European Council, is the only viable option today for applying taxes to e-commerce sales by non-resident traders. The tax principles are as follows in the UK interpretation of this law implemented in 2003 for these electronic services:

- supply of websites or web-hosting services;
- downloaded software (including updates of software);
- downloaded images, text or information, including making databases available;
- digitised books or other electronic publications;
- downloaded music, films or games;
- electronic auctions; or
- Internet service packages.

The UK VAT rules are as follows:

- if the supplier (residence) and the customer (source) are both in the UK, VAT will be chargeable;
- exports to private customers in the EU will attract either UK VAT or local VAT;
- exports outside the EU will be zero-rated (but tax may be levied on imports);

- imports into the UK from the EU or beyond will attract local VAT, or UK import tax when received through customs (for which overseas suppliers need to register);
- services attract VAT according to where the supplier is located. This is different from products and causes anomalies if online services are created. This law has since been reviewed.

Freedom-restrictive legislation

Although governments enact legislation in order to protect consumer privacy on the Internet, some individuals and organisations believe that legislation may also be too restrictive. In the UK, a new Telecommunications Act and Regulation of Investigatory Powers Act (RIP) took several years to enact since it involved giving security forces the ability to monitor all communications passing through ISPs. This was fiercely contested due to cost burdens placed on infrastructure providers and in particular ISPs, and of course many citizens and employees were not happy about being monitored either!

Freedom House (www.freedomhouse.org) is a human rights organisation created to reduce censorship. It notes in a report (Freedom House, 2000) that governments in many countries, both developed and developing, are increasingly censoring online content. Only 69 of the countries studied have completely free media, while 51 have partly free media and 66 countries suffer heavy government censorship. Censorship methods include implementing licensing and regulation laws, applying existing print and broadcast restrictions to the Internet, filtering content and direct censoring after dissemination. In Asia and the Middle East, governments frequently cite protection of morality and local values as reasons for censorship. Even the US government tried to control access to certain Internet sites with the Communications Decency Act in 1996, but this was unsuccessful. Refer to Activity 4.4 to discuss these issues.

Activity 4.4 | **Government and company monitoring of electronic communications**

Purpose

To examine the degree to which governments and organisations should monitor electronic communications.

Activity

Write down the arguments for and against each of these statements, debate individually or as a group to come to a consensus:

1 'This house believes that organisations have no right to monitor employees' use of email or the web.' Use Moreover (www.moreover.com) to research recent cases where employees have been dismissed for accessing or sending emails or web content that is deemed unsuitable. Is this just used as an excuse for dismissing staff?

2 'This house believes that governments have no right to monitor all Internet-based communications passing through ISPs.' Use Moreover (www.moreover.com) to research action taken by the government of your country to monitor and control Internet communications.

What action do you think managers should take with regard to monitoring employee access? Should laws be set at a national level or should action be taken by individual companies?

Answers to activities can be found at www.pearsoned.co.uk/chaffey

Economic and competitive factors

The economic health and competitive environment in different countries will determine their e-commerce potential. Managers developing e-commerce strategies in multinational companies will initially target the countries that are most developed in the use of the technology. A comprehensive framework for assessing an '**e-economy**' has been developed by Booz Allen Hamilton (2002). The report authors define the e-economy as:

Electronic economy (e-economy)

The dynamic system of interactions between a nation's citizens, businesses and government that capitalise upon online technology to achieve a social or economic good.

> *the dynamic system of interactions between a nation's citizens, the businesses and government that capitalise upon online technology to achieve a social or economic good.*

The framework is based upon four layers of environment, readiness, uptake and use, and impact, and three major stakeholder groups: citizens, businesses and government, as shown in Figure 4.11.

A review of how different governments have tried to improve the health of their e-economies is presented later in this chapter.

Knowledge of different economic conditions is also part of budgeting for revenue from different countries. In China there is regulation of foreign ownership of Internet portals and ISPs which could hamper development.

The trend towards globalisation can arguably insulate a company to some extent from fluctuations in regional markets, but is, of course, no protection from a global recession.

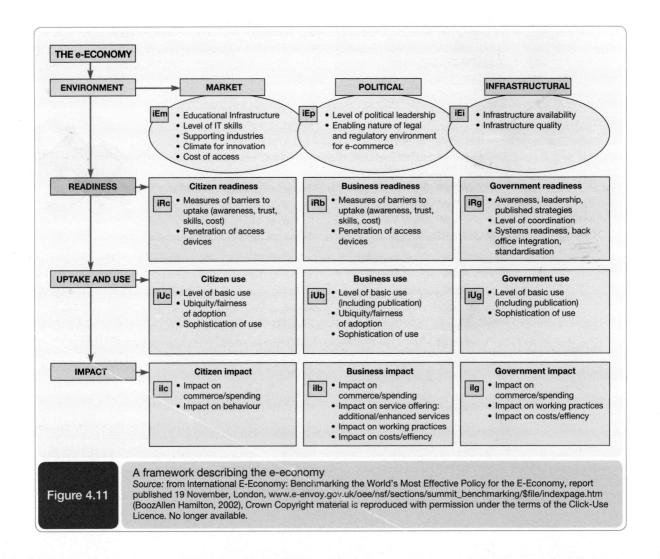

Figure 4.11

A framework describing the e-economy
Source: from International E-Economy: Benchmarking the World's Most Effective Policy for the E-Economy, report published 19 November, London, www.e-envoy.gov.uk/oee/nsf/sections/summit_benchmarking/$file/indexpage.htm (BoozAllen Hamilton, 2002), Crown Copyright material is reproduced with permission under the terms of the Click-Use Licence. No longer available.

Managers can also study e-commerce in leading countries to help predict future e-commerce trends in their own country.

Globalisation refers to the move towards international trading in a single global market-place and also to blurring of social and cultural differences between countries. (We saw in Chapter 1 that for both SMEs and larger organisations, electronic communications give the opportunity for increasing the reach of the company to achieve sales around the world.)

Quelch and Klein (1996) point out some of the obvious consequences for organisations that wish to compete in the global marketplace; they say a company must have:

- *a 24-hour order-taking and customer service response capability;*
- *regulatory and customs-handling experience to ship internationally;*
- *in-depth understanding of foreign marketing environments to assess the advantages of its own products and services.*

Language and cultural understanding may also present a problem and an SME is unlikely to possess the resources to develop a multi-language version of its site or employ staff with sufficient language skills. Similarly, Quelch and Klein (1996) note that the growth of the use of the Internet for business will accelerate the trend of English becoming the lingua franca of commerce. Tailoring e-commerce services for individual countries or regions is referred to as **localisation**. A website may need to support customers from a range of countries with:

- different product needs;
- language differences;
- cultural differences.

The importance of localisation is highlighted by a report by Common Sense Advisory (2002). According to them, for many US Fortune 500 firms, non-US revenue – or what they refer to as 'xenorevenue' – accounts for 20 to more than 50% of their global income. A similar situation is likely to exist for non-US multinational organisations.

It may be necessary to vary:

- The language that content is provided in.
- Tone and style of copy.
- Site design – certain colours or images may be unsuitable or less effective in some countries.
- Range of product offerings.
- Product pricing.
- Promotional offers used to encourage acquisition of customer email address (see Chapter 9). This may be affected by local data protection, taxation and trading laws.
- Local contact points.

Localisation will address all these issues. In order to be effective, a website often needs more than translation, since different promotion concepts may be needed for different countries. For example, Durex (www.durex.com) localises content for many countries since language and the way in which sexual issues can be discussed vary greatly. 3M (www.3m.com), however, only localises content in local language for some countries such as France, Germany and Spain. For large multinational companies, localisation is a significant strategic issue for e-commerce. The decision on the level of localisation will need to be taken on a regional or country basis to prioritise different countries according to the size of the market and the importance of having localisation.

Singh and Pereira (2005) provide an evaluation framework for the level of localisation:

1 **Standardised websites (not localised).** A single site serves all customer segments (domestic and international).
2 **Semi-localised websites.** A single site serves all customers; however, there will be contact information about foreign subsidiaries available for international customers.
3 **Localised websites.** Country-specific websites with language translation for international customers, wherever relevant.

Globalisation
The increase of international trading and shared social and cultural values.

Localisation
Tailoring of web-site information for individual countries or regions.

4 **Highly localised websites.** Country-specific websites with language translation; they also include other localisation efforts in terms of time, date, postcode, currency formats, etc.

5 **Culturally customised websites.** Websites reflecting complete 'immersion' in the culture of target customer segments.

Deciding on the degree of localisation is a difficult challenge for managers, since while it has been established that local preferences are significant, it is often difficult to balance costs against the likely increase or conversion rate. In a survey published in *Multilingual* (2008), 88% of managers at multinational companies stated that localisation is a key issue, with 76% of them saying that it is important specifically for international customer satisfaction. Yet, over half of these respondents also admitted that they allocate only between 1% and 5% of their overall budget for localisation.

An indication of the importance of localisation in different cultures has been completed by Nitish *et al.* (2006) for the German, Indian and Chinese cultures, assessing localised websites in terms not only of content, but of cultural values such as collectivism, individualism, uncertainty avoidance and masculinity. The survey suggests that without cultural adaptation, confidence or flow falls, so resulting in lower purchase intent.

A further aspect of localisation to be considered is search engine optimisation (SEO, see Chapter 9), since sites which have local language versions will be listed more prominently by local versions of the search engines. Many specialist companies have been created to help manage these content localisation issues for companies, for example agency Web Certain maintains a forum advising on localisation (www.multilingual-seo.com).

One example of the effect of localisation on conversion rates is provided by MySpace CEO Mike Katz, who stated in NMA (2008) that: 'All the 27 sites are localised, we don't believe that one size fits all. We know that from the first day we localise in any language, we triple our sign-ups on original users.' In 2008, 45 million of the 130 million MySpace users were outside the US; new sites were planned for Russia, India, Poland and Korea, each requiring a local version.

To explore the implications of globalisation for consumer-orientated companies, refer to Case study 4.1.

Case Study 4.1   The implications of globalisation for consumer attitudes

The article starts by discussing anti-globalisation. It then explores the implications of variations in the characteristics of different cultures on businesses providing services to them. At the end of the article, research about attitudes to globalisation is summarised, along with its implications for businesses trading internationally.

Globalisation, or maybe more specifically, anti-globalisation issues, are never far from the headlines, whether it's coverage of the latest anti-WTO demonstration or news that McDonald's has replaced Ronald McDonald in France with Asterix – in a move to 'appease anti-globalisation protesters'.

But what does globalisation actually mean? Stemming from the application of free market principles it has manifested the belief that the world is small and that consumers are becoming more and more alike, thus allowing companies to use the same advertising and marketing across regions and countries. Such a doctrine has enabled companies to act global and think global, much to the distaste of the anti-globalisation lobbies. Indeed, in 1985 it was Friends of the Earth that coined the slogan 'think global, act local' in its desire to counter such global forces – particularly with regard to environmental issues.

However, such 'glocalisation' [global localisation] makes a lot of sense for multinational companies operating today and planning new market entry, for a number of reasons. Firstly, the term globalisation for many Europeans is virtually synonymous with that of 'Americanisation'. For some this has negative connotations of materialism, loss of native culture and the encroachment of the English language. At its extreme, it drives many of the anti-globalisation activists. Thus there is real risk that companies will damage their brand and reputation if they don't recognise the importance of localisation when considering market entry.

Secondly, consumers are as different as they are similar – local and regional cultures have a profound effect in shaping consumer demand. These differences are potentially more interesting than the similarities, in that they can allow product and service differentiation as well as new approaches to segmentation and marketing communications. To take advantage of such opportunities, businesses have to have a clear insight into how and why consumers in one market may differ from ones in another.

Feelings of anti-Americanisation are a strong undercurrent in Europe. Businesses have to plan how to counter such a groundswell of feeling if planning on entering new markets – given that some 50% of Europeans believe that 'our society is too Americanised' and such an attitude has increased over the past 10 years. While the degree of agreement varies within Europe (e.g. 67% of Spaniards agreeing with the statement, as compared with 44% of Brits), it is a significant influence of customer behaviour. To compound matters, multinational companies are the least trusted of 27 entities when European consumers have been asked to state which they trust to be honest and fair.

As a result, not only have we seen an increase in consumer activism (such as anti-WTO protests, growth of the slow food movement in Europe etc.), but also we have seen global brands coming under threat from emergent local brands which are gaining in currency. We would expect this to continue. This is not to say that there is no room for global brands! Many global brands have successfully tapped into local culture and tastes and recognised the need to either modify the product/ service completely or change different elements of the offer and how it is ultimately marketed. Thus companies expanding into new geographic markets have to ensure that their strategies are based on a real understanding of regional and local markets.

Globalisation is not making the world a smaller, homogeneous place. While this presents many opportunities for businesses, it also implies a need for a clear understanding of what shapes consumer needs and desires in the different nations. Not surprising perhaps that many businesses found the notion of a 'globalised' world compelling, given the significant implications for researching a multitude of different markets in terms of time and money budgets. Similarly, it is easy to understand the temptation of taking well-established national stereotypes and assuming that they are representative of the truth.

Recent attitudinal studies in Europe and the US undertaken by the Henley Centre show the complexity of attempting to categorise consumers on a broad scale. Let's take an example. At one level, results show that all consumers take pride in their family, so a global advertising campaign using the 'family' as a theme may feel like safe territory. To some extent it is. Dig down a bit deeper, however, and you find that different people define 'family' in very different ways, so what people take pride in will be subtly different. At a country level, many more differences expose themselves.

Businesses wanting to broaden their geographic reach have to consider at a strategic level what level of understanding of consumer needs they require. Generalisations are important and are a good place to start, but it is critical to then delve further – national stereotypes are too simplistic. Differences, rather than similarities, have to be considered, and interrogated in terms of how these will impact customer needs.

Source: The Henley Centre.

> **Question**
>
> Based on this article and your experiences, debate the statement: 'Site localisation is essential for each country for an e-commerce offering to be successful in that country.'

The implications of e-commerce for international B2B trading

Hamill and Gregory (1997) highlight the strategic implications of e-commerce for international business-to-business trading. They note that there will be increasing standardisation of prices across borders as businesses become more aware of price differentials. Secondly, they predict that the importance of traditional intermediaries such as agents and distributors will be reduced by Internet-enabled direct marketing and sales.

Larger organisations typically already compete in the global marketplace, or have the financial resources to achieve this. But what about the smaller organisation? Most governments are encouraging SMEs to use electronic commerce to tap into the international market. Hamill and Gregory (1997) identify the barriers to SME internationalisation shown in Table 4.5. Complete Activity 4.5 to look at the actions that can be taken to overcome these barriers.

Activity 4.5	Overcoming SME resistance to international e-commerce

Purpose

To highlight barriers to exporting amongst SMEs and suggest measures by which they may be overcome by governments.

Activity

For each of the four barriers to internationalisation given in Table 4.5, suggest the management reasons why the barriers may exist and actions that governments can take to overcome these barriers. Evaluate how well the government in your country communicates the benefits of e-commerce through education and training.

Table 4.5	Issues in SME resistance to exporting

Barrier	Management issues	How can barrier be overcome?
1 Psychological		
2 Operational		
3 Organisational		
4 Product/market		

Source: Barriers from Hamill and Gregory (1997) and Poon and Jevons (1997).

Answers to activities can be found at www.pearsoned.co.uk/chaffey

More recent research suggests that SMEs have been relatively slow to adopt the Internet. Research by Arnott and Bridgewater (2002) tests the level of sophistication by which SMEs are using the Internet (see stage models in Chapter 5). They find that the majority of firms are using the Internet for information provision rather than interactive, relationship-building or transactional facilities. Smaller firms are using significantly fewer Internet tools than their larger counterparts. Quayle (2002) has assessed issues considered by SMEs to be strategically important. In the UK, 298 SMEs were surveyed. Issues of marketing, leadership and waste reduction were given highest priority, and supplier development, financial management, time to market and supply chain management were medium priority. Perhaps unsurprisingly, the lowest priority was given to technology, research and development, e-commerce, customer management and purchasing – all closely related to e-business. In further research, Meckel *et al.* (2004) analysed e-business adoption by several hundred SMEs in the northwest of England and found that fewer than 15% had formal, documented e-business strategies.

Political factors

The political environment is shaped by the interplay of government agencies, public opinion, consumer pressure groups such as CAUCE (Coalition Against Unsolicited Email – www.cauce.org) and industry-backed organisations such as TRUSTe (www.truste.org) that promote best practice amongst companies.

Political action enacted through government agencies to control the adoption of the Internet can include:

- promoting the benefits of adopting the Internet for consumers and business to improve a country's economic prosperity;
- enacting legislation to protect privacy or control taxation, as described in previous sections;
- providing organisations with guidelines and assistance for compliance with legislation;
- setting up international bodies to coordinate the Internet (see Chapter 3).

Political involvement in many of these activities is intended to improve the economic competitiveness of countries or groups of countries. Quayle (2002) summarises six strands of the UK government strategy for e-commerce which are intended to increase industry competitiveness:

1 Establish a brand in e-commerce both domestically and internationally.
2 Transform existing businesses.
3 Foster e-commerce creation and growth.
4 Expand the e-commerce talent pool (skills).
5 Provide leadership in international e-commerce policy development.
6 Government online should be a priority.

These goals are typical for many countries and specific targets are set for the proportion of people and businesses that have access, including public access points for those who cannot currently afford the technology. Managers who are aware of these initiatives can tap into sources of funding for development or free training to support their online initiatives. Alternatively, there may be incentives such as tax breaks.

The European Commission (EC) provides some other examples of the role of government organisations in promoting and regulating e-commerce:

Information society
A society with widespread access and transfer of digital information within business and the community.

- The EC Information Society initiative was launched in 1998 with the aims of increasing public awareness of the impact of the **information society** and stimulating people's motivation and ability to participate (reducing social exclusion); increasing socio-economic benefits and enhancing the role of Europe in influencing the global information society. Information society was defined by the UK INSINC working party on social inclusion in the information society in 1997 as:

    A society characterised by a high level of information intensity in the everyday life of most citizens, in most organisations and workplaces; by the use of common or compatible technology for a wide range of personal, social, educational and business activities; and by the ability to transmit and receive digital data rapidly between places irrespective of distance.

- UNESCO has also been active in advancing the information society in less developed countries (http://portal.unesco.org/ci).
- The European Community has set up 'i2010' (European Information Society in 2010) whose aims include:

    providing an integrated approach to information society and audio-visual policies in the EU, covering regulation, research, and deployment and promoting cultural diversity. (eEurope, 2005)

- In 1998, new data protection guidelines were enacted to help protect consumers and increase the adoption of e-commerce by reducing security fears. Since 2000, cross-Europe laws have been enacted to control online consumer privacy, electronic selling and taxation.

Booz Allen Hamilton (2002) review approaches used by governments to encourage use of the Internet. They identify five broad themes in policy:

1 **Increasing the penetration of 'access devices'.** Approaches include either home access through Sweden's PC Tax Reform, or in public places, as in France's programme to

develop 7,000 access points by a specific year/target date. France also offers a tax incentive scheme, where firms can make tax-free gifts of PCs to staff for personal use.

2 **Increasing skills and confidence of target groups.** These may target potentially excluded groups, as with France's €150 million campaign to train the unemployed. Japan's IT training programmes use existing mentors.

3 **Establishing 'driving licences' or 'passport' qualifications.** France, Italy and the UK have schemes which grant simple IT qualifications, particularly aimed at low-skilled groups.

4 **Building trust, or allaying fears.** The US 1998 Child Online Protection Act used schemes to provide 'kitemark'-type verification, or certification of safe services.

5 **Direct marketing campaigns.** According to the report, only the UK, with its UK Online campaign, is marketing directly to citizens on a large scale.

Internet governance

Internet governance
Control of the operation and use of the Internet.

Internet governance describes the control put in place to manage the growth of the Internet and its usage (as discussed at the end of Chapter 3).

Dyson (1998) describes the different layers of jurisdiction. These are:

1 Physical space comprising each individual country where its own laws hold.
2 ISPs – the connection between the physical and virtual worlds.
3 Domain name control (www.icann.net) and communities.
4 Agencies such as TRUSTe (www.truste.org).

The organisations that manage the infrastructure also have a significant role in governance.

E-government

Electronic government (e-government)
The use of Internet technologies to provide government services to citizens.

E-government is distinct from Internet governance. (In Chapter 1, we noted that e-government is a major strategic priority for many countries.) To achieve the potential cost savings, some governments have set targets for both buy- and sell-side e-government. In the UK, the government's main target was:

That by 2005, 100% of dealings with Government should be capable of being delivered electronically, where there is a demand.

Although this target is to be applauded, it was not met and we can view this as the UK government's dot-com bubble. Although many services have been created, adoption rates tend to be low and the government is having to invest in marketing usage of these services.

In Australia, the National Office for the Information Economy, NOIE (www.noie.gov.au), has created a strategic framework which has the following themes. This summarises the types of actions that many governments are taking to encourage e-business within their countries.

1 **Access, participation and skills** – Encouraging all sectors of the community to actively participate in the information economy.

2 **Adoption of e-business** – The government is working to provide more efficient communication between businesses to help improve the productivity of the Australian economy.

3 **Confidence, trust and security** – The government is working to build public trust and confidence in going online, and addressing barriers to consumer confidence in e-commerce and other areas of online content and activity.

4 **E-government strategies and implementation** – The use of new technologies for government information provision, service delivery and administration has the potential to transform government, which will improve the lives of Australians.

5 **Environment for information economy firms** – Provide research on the environmental variables that drive innovation and growth in the information economy and underpin its future development.

6 **International dimensions** – NOIE, in cooperation with other government bodies, represents Australia in world forums where decisions are made that may affect national interests in the information economy.

Mini Case Study 4.1	SourceUK

SourceUK (www.sourceuk.net) is a successful e-government initiative that has been responsible for the delivery and management of the busiest electronic communication and e-procurement channels to UK government and wider public-sector departments in line with the Modernising Government Agenda legislation. Approximately 250,000 senior managers, budget holders and decision makers have direct access to the channels for their on-the-minute must-have news and information needs and for the sourcing of their goods and services.

SourceUK is proven to be one of the most accredited, respected, well-known and busiest portals of its sort available to this marketplace. The portal is currently receiving on average 500,000 visits each month.

Source: SourceUK email alert, 2008.

Technological innovation and technology assessment

One of the great challenges of managing e-commerce is the need to be able to assess which new technological innovations can be applied to give competitive advantage – what is 'the next big thing'? The truth is no one can predict the future, and many companies have misunderstood the market for products:

> *This 'telephone' has too many shortcomings to be seriously considered as a means of communication. The device is inherently of no value to us.*
>
> Western Union internal memo, 1876

> *Who the hell wants to hear actors talk?*
>
> H. M. Warner, Warner Brothers, 1927

> *I think there is a world market for maybe five computers.*
>
> Thomas Watson, chairman of IBM, 1943

> *There is no reason for any individual to have a computer in their home.*
>
> Ken Olson (President of Digital Equipment Corporation) at the Convention of the World Future Society in Boston in 1977

I personally believe the best that organisations can do is to analyse the current situation and respond rapidly where appropriate. As the Canadian science-fiction writer William Gibson said:

> *The future is here. It's just not widely distributed yet.*

A slightly different, and more forward-looking, perspective came from Bruce Toganizzi, who founded the Human Interface Team at Apple and developed the company's first interface guidelines (E-consultancy, 2007):

> *Successful technology-predicting is based on detecting discontinuities and predicting the trends that will flow from them.*

He gives the example of the introduction of the Apple iPhone and the other devices based on gestural interfaces that will follow.

In addition to technologies deployed on the website, the suitability of new approaches for attracting visitors to the site must be evaluated – for example, should registration at a paid-for search engine, or new forms of banner adverts or email marketing, be used (Chapter 9)? (Decisions on strategy are covered in Chapter 5.)

When a new technique is introduced, a manager faces a difficult decision as to whether to:

- Ignore the use of the technique, perhaps because it is felt to be too expensive or untried, or the manager simply doesn't believe that the benefits will outweigh the costs – a cautious, 'wait-and-see' approach.
- Enthusiastically adopt the technique without a detailed evaluation since the hype alone convinces the manager that the technique should be adopted – a risk-taking, early-adopter approach.
- Evaluate the technique and then take a decision whether to adopt it according to the evaluation – an intermediate approach.

Early adopter
Company or department that invests in new technologies and techniques.

This diffusion–adoption process (represented by the bell curve in Figure 4.12) was identified by Rogers (1983), who classified those trialling new products as innovators, **early adopters**, early majority, late majority, or laggards.

Figure 4.12 can be used in two main ways as an analytical tool. First, it can be used to understand the stage customers have reached in adoption of a technology, or any product. For example, the Internet is now a well-established tool and in many developed countries we are into the late majority phase of adoption, which suggests that it is essential to use this medium for marketing purposes. Second, managers can look at adoption of a new technique by other businesses – from an organisational perspective. For example, an online supermarket could look at how many other e-tailers have adopted personalisation to evaluate whether it is worthwhile adopting the technique.

An alternative graphic representation of diffusion of innovation has been developed by technology analyst Gartner for assessing the maturity, adoption and business application of specific technologies (Figure 4.13). Gartner (2010) recognises the following stages within a **hype cycle**, an example of which is given in Figure 4.13 for trends current in 2010:

Hype cycle
A graphic representation of the maturity, adoption and business application of specific technologies.

1 **Technology trigger** – The first phase of a hype cycle is the 'technology trigger' or breakthrough, product launch or other event that generates significant press and interest.

1. Innovators (2.5%)
2. Opinion leaders (13.5%)
3. Early majority (34%)
4. Late majority (34%)
5. Laggards (16%)

Conservative adopters

Number of new adopters

Leading edge

1 2 3 4 5

Time

Figure 4.12   Diffusion–adoption curve of a Gartner hype cycle

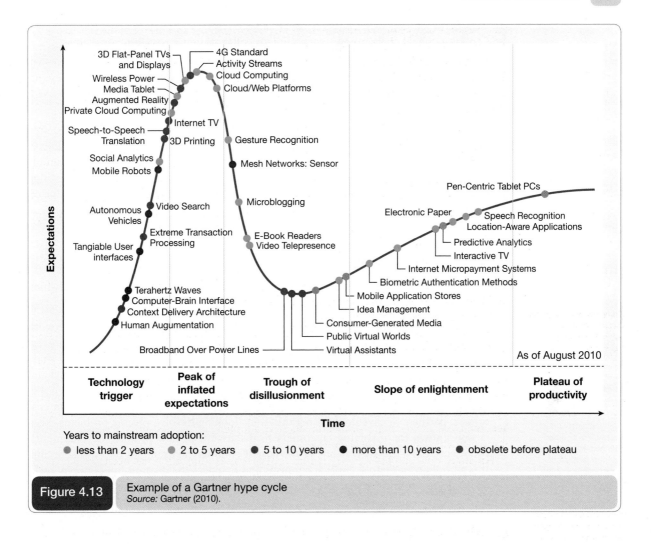

| Figure 4.13 | Example of a Gartner hype cycle
Source: Gartner (2010). |

2 **Peak of inflated expectations** – In the next phase, a frenzy of publicity typically generates over-enthusiasm and unrealistic expectations. There may be some successful applications of a technology, but there are typically more failures.

3 **Trough of disillusionment** – Technologies enter the 'trough of disillusionment' because they fail to meet expectations and quickly become unfashionable. Consequently, the press usually abandons the topic and the technology.

4 **Slope of enlightenment** – Although the press may have stopped covering the technology, some businesses continue through the 'slope of enlightenment' and experiment to understand the benefits and practical application of the technology.

5 **Plateau of productivity** – A technology reaches the 'plateau of productivity' as the benefits of it become widely demonstrated and accepted. The technology becomes increasingly stable and evolves in second and third generations. The final height of the plateau varies according to whether the technology is broadly applicable or benefits only a niche market.

Trott (1998) identifies different requirements that are necessary within an organisation to be able to respond effectively to technological change or innovation:

- Growth orientation – a long-term rather than short-term vision.
- Vigilance – the capability of environment scanning.
- Commitment to technology – willingness to invest in technology.

- Acceptance of risk – willingness to take managed risks.
- Cross-functional cooperation – capability for collaboration across functional areas.
- Receptivity – the ability to respond to externally developed technology.
- Slack – allowing time to investigate new technological opportunities.
- Adaptability – a readiness to accept change.
- Diverse range of skills – technical and business skills and experience.

The problem with being an early adopter (as an organisation) is that the leading edge is often also referred to as the 'bleeding edge' due to the risk of failure. New technologies will have bugs, may integrate poorly with the existing systems, or the marketing benefits may simply not live up to their promise. Of course, the reason for risk taking is that the rewards are high – if you are using a technique that your competitors are not, then you will gain an edge on your rivals.

Approaches to identifying emerging technology

PMP (2008) describes four contrasting approaches to identifying new technologies, which may give a company a competitive edge:

Technology scouting
A structured approach to reviewing technology innovations akin to football scouting.

Crowdsourcing
Utilising a network of customers or other partners to gain insights for new product or process innovations.

1 **Technology networking.** Individuals monitor trends through their personal network and **technology scouting** and then share them through an infrastructure and process that supports information sharing. PMP (2008) explains that Novartis facilitates sharing between inside and outside experts on specific technologies through an extranet and face-to-face events.

2 **Crowdsourcing. Crowdsourcing** facilitates access to a marketplace of ideas from customers, partners or inventors for organisations looking to solve specific problems. Lego is well known for involving customers in discussion of new product developments. InnoCentive (Figure 4.14) is one of the largest commercial examples of crowdsourcing. It is an online marketplace which connects and manages the relationship between 'seekers' and 'solvers'. Seekers are the companies conducting research and development that are looking for new solutions to their business challenges and opportunities. Solvers are the 170,000 registered members of InnoCentive who can win cash prizes ranging from $5,000 to $1,000,000 for solving problems in a variety of domains, including business and technology.

3 **Technology hunting.** This is a structured review of new technology through reviewing the capabilities of start-up companies. For example, British Telecom undertakes a structured review of up to 1,000 start-ups to assess relevance for improving their own capabilities which may ultimately be reduced to five companies with which BT will enter into a formal arrangement each year.

4 **Technology mining.** A traditional literature review of technologies described in published documents. Deutsche Telekom AG use technology to automate the process through software such as Autonomy which searches for patterns indicating potential technology solutions within patents, articles, journals, technological reports and trend studies. A simpler approach is setting up a keyword search for technologies through a free service such as Google Alerts (www.google.com/alerts).

It may also be useful to identify how rapidly a new concept is being adopted. When a product or service is adopted quickly, this is known as 'rapid diffusion'. Access to the Internet is an example of this – in developed countries the use of the Internet has become widespread more rapidly than the use of TV, for example. Internet-enabled mobile phones are relatively slow-diffusion products.

So, what action should e-commerce managers take when confronted by new techniques and technologies? There is no straightforward rule of thumb, other than that a balanced approach must be taken. It would be easy to dismiss many new techniques as fads, or classify them as 'not relevant to my market'. However, competitors will probably be reviewing

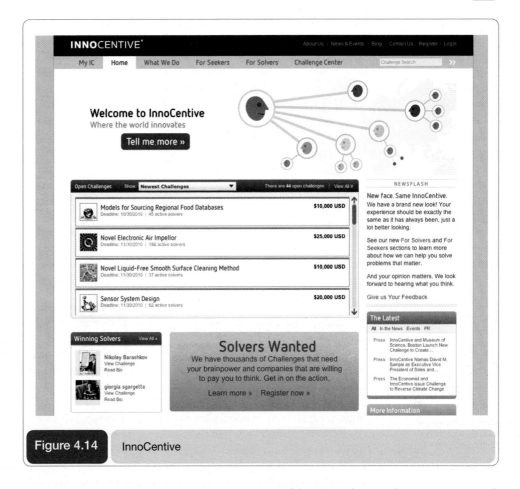

| **Figure 4.14** | InnoCentive |

new techniques and incorporating some, so a careful review of new techniques is required. This indicates that benchmarking of 'best of breed' sites within sectors and in different sectors is essential as part of environmental scanning. However, by waiting for others to innovate and reviewing the results on their website, a company may have already lost 6 to 12 months.

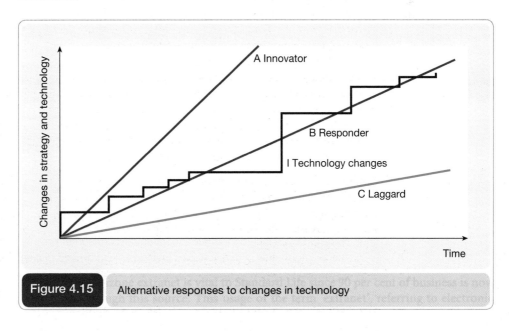

| **Figure 4.15** | Alternative responses to changes in technology |

Figure 4.15 summarises the choices. The stepped curve I shows the variations in technology through time. Some may be small incremental changes such as a new operating system, others such as the introduction of personalisation technology are more significant in delivering value to customers and so improving business performance. Line A is a company that is using innovative business techniques, that adopts technology early, or is even in advance of what the technology can currently deliver. Line C shows the conservative adopter whose use of technology lags behind the available potential. Line B, the middle ground, is probably the ideal situation where a company monitors new ideas as early adopters trial them and then adopts those that will have a positive impact on the business.

Multiscreening
A term used to describe simultaneous use of devices such as digital TV and tablet.

At the time of writing, the growth in use of mobile technology is perhaps the most significant trend in consumer adoption of digital media. **Multiscreening** is a trend that needs to be considered for its impact on consumers. Figure 4.16 shows common uses of mobile platforms introduced in Chapter 3 and considered further in Chapter 11.

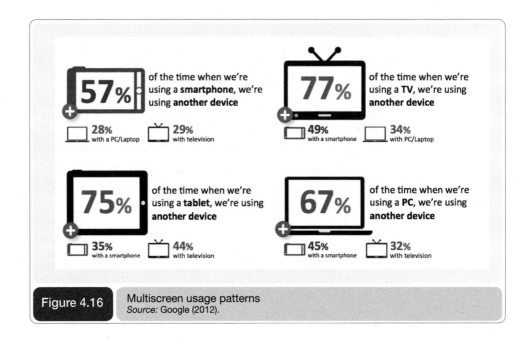

57% of the time when we're using a **smartphone**, we're using **another device**

28% with a PC/Laptop   **29%** with television

77% of the time when we're using a **TV**, we're using **another device**

49% with a smartphone   **34%** with PC/Laptop

75% of the time when we're using a **tablet**, we're using **another device**

35% with a smartphone   **44%** with television

67% of the time when we're using a **PC**, we're using **another device**

45% with a smartphone   **32%** with television

Figure 4.16   Multiscreen usage patterns
Source: Google (2012).

Summary

1   Environmental scanning and analysis are necessary in order that a company can respond to environmental changes and act on legal and ethical constraints on its activities.

2   Environmental constraints are related to the micro-environment variables reviewed in Chapter 5 and the macro-environment variables in this chapter using the SLEPT mnemonic.

3   Social factors that must be understood as part of the move to the Information Society include buyer behaviour characteristics such as access to the Internet and perceptions about it as a communications tool.

4   Ethical issues include the need to safeguard consumer privacy and security of personal information. Privacy issues include collection and dissemination of customer information, cookies and the use of direct email.

5   Legal factors to be considered by e-commerce managers include: accessibility, domain name registration, copyright and data protection legislation.

6   Economic factors considered in the chapter are the regional differences in the use of the Internet for trade. Different economic conditions in different markets are considered in developing e-commerce budgets.

7   Political factors involve the role of governments in promoting e-commerce, but also trying to control it.

8   Rapid variation in technology requires constant monitoring of adoption of the technology by customers and competitors and appropriate responses.

Exercises

Self-assessment questions

1   Why is environmental scanning necessary?

2   Give an example how each of the macro-environment factors may directly drive the content and services provided by a website.

3   Summarise the social factors that govern consumer access to the Internet. How can companies overcome these influences once people venture online?

4   What actions can e-commerce managers take to safeguard consumer privacy and security?

5   What are the general legal constraints that a company acts under in any country?

6   How do governments attempt to control the use of the Internet?

7   Summarise adoption patterns across the continents.

8   How should innovation be managed?

Essay and discussion questions

1   You recently started a job as e-commerce manager for a bank. Produce a checklist of all the different legal and ethical issues that you need to check for compliance on the existing website of the bank.

2   How should the e-commerce manager monitor and respond to technological innovation?

3   Benchmark different approaches to achieving and reassuring customers about their privacy and security using three or four examples for a retail sector such as travel, books, toys or clothing.

4   'Internet access levels will never exceed 50% in most countries.' Discuss.

5   Select a new Internet access technology that has been introduced in the last two years and assess whether it will become a significant method of access.

6   Assess how the eight principles of the UK Data Protection Act (www.gov.uk/data-protection) relate to actions that e-commerce managers need to take to ensure legal compliance of their site.

Examination questions

1   Explain the different layers of governance of the Internet.

2   Summarise the macro-environment variables a company needs to monitor.

3   Explain the purpose of environmental scanning.

4 Give three examples of how websites can use techniques to protect the user's privacy.

5 What are the three key factors which affect consumer adoption of the Internet?

6 Explain the significance of the diffusion–adoption concept to the adoption of new technologies to:

(a) Consumers purchasing technological innovations.

(b) Businesses deploying technological innovations.

7 What action should e-commerce managers take to ensure compliance with ethical and legal standards of their site?

References

Ahmed, N.U. and Sharma, S.K. (2006) Porter's value chain model for assessing the impact of the internet for environmental gains. *International Journal of Management and Enterprise Development,* 3(3), 278–95.

Arnott, D. and Bridgewater, S. (2002) Internet, interaction and implications for marketing. *Marketing Intelligence and Planning,* 20(2), 86–95.

Bart, Y., Shankar, V., Sultan, F., and Urban, G. (2005) Are the drivers and role of online trust the same for all web sites and consumers? A large-scale exploratory empirical study. *Journal of Marketing,* October, 133–52.

Basu, D. (2007) *Global Perspectives on E-commerce Taxation Law.* Ashgate, Aldershot.

Booz Allen Hamilton (2002) *International E-Economy Benchmarking. The World's Most Effective Policies for the E-Economy.* Report published 19 November, London.

Cairns, S. (2005) Delivering supermarket shopping: more or less traffic? *Transport Reviews,* 25(1), 51–84.

Chaffey, D., Mayer, R., Johnston, K. and Ellis-Chadwick, F. (2009) *Internet Marketing: Strategy, Implementation and Practice,* 4th edn. Financial Times Prentice Hall, Harlow.

CIFAS (2013) CIFAS (Credit Industry Fraud Association) Press release: Fraud continues to pose problems in 2012.

Common Sense Advisory (2002) Beggars at the Globalization Banquet. White Paper available at: **www.commonsenseadvisory.com**. Editor: Don Da Palma. No locale given.

'Daniel, L., Wilson, H. and Myers, A. (2002) Adoption of e-commerce by SMEs in the UK. Towards a stage model. *International Small Business Journal,* 20(3), 253–70.

Digitas (2007) Segmenting Internet Users: Implications for online advertising. White Paper published at: **http://digitalhive.blogs.com/digiblog/files/WebDotDigitas.pdf**.

Dyson, E. (1998) *Release 2.1.A Design for Living in the Digital Age.* Penguin, London.

E-consultancy (2007) E-business briefing interview. Bruce Tognazzini on human–computer interaction. Interview published November.

eEurope (2005) Information Society Benchmarking Report. From eEurope (2005) initiative.

EuroStat (2012) Internet use in households and by individuals 2012. *EuroStat,* 50. Published December 2012. Available from: **http://epp.eurostat.ec.europa.eu/portal/page/portal/product_details/publication?p_product_code=KS-SF-12–050**.

EuroStat (2013) Enterprises making slow progress in adopting ICT for e-business integration. Published February 2013: **http://epp.eurostat.ec.europa.eu/portal/page/portal/product_details/publication?p_product_code=KS-SF-13–006**.

Fletcher, K. (2001) Privacy: the Achilles heel of the new marketing. *Interactive Marketing,* 3(2), 128–40.

Freedom House (2000) *Censoring dot-gov report.* 17 April: **www.freedomhouse.org/news/pr041700.html,** New York.

Gartner (2010) Gartner's Hype Cycle: Special Report for 2010. Report summary available at **www.gartner.com/it/page.jsp?id=1447613.**

Godin, S. (1999) *Permission Marketing.* Simon and Schuster, New York.

Google (2012) The New Multiscreen World: Understanding Cross-platform Consumer Behavior. Available at: **http://services.google.com/fh/files/misc/multiscreenworld_final.pdf.**

Google Shopper Sciences (2011) The Zero Moment of Truth Macro Study. Published April 2011: **www.google.com/think/research-studies/the-zero-moment-of-truth-macro-study.html.**

Grossnickle, J. and Raskin, O. (2001) *The Handbook of Online Marketing Research: Knowing Your Customer Using the Net.* McGraw-Hill, New York.

Hamill, J. and Gregory, K. (1997) Internet marketing in the internationalisation of UK SMEs. *Journal of Marketing Management,* 13, 9–28.

Mason, R. (1986) Four ethical issues of the information age. *MIS Quarterly,* March.

Meckel, M., Walters, D. Greenwood, A. and Baugh, P. (2004) A taxonomy of e-business adoption and strategies in small and medium sized enterprises. *Strategic Change,* 13, 259–69.

Mougayer, W. (1998) *Opening Digital Markets – Battle Plans and Strategies for Internet Commerce,* 2nd edn. Commerce Net Press, McGraw-Hill, New York.

Multilingual (2008) Localizing a localizer's website: the challenge. Jan/Feb, 30–33.

Nitish, S., Fassott, G., Zhao, H. and Boughton, P. (2006) A cross-cultural analysis of German, Chinese and Indian consumers' perception of web site adaptation. *Journal of Consumer Behaviour,* 5, 56–68.

NMA (2008) Profile – Travis Katz. Author: Luan Goldie. *New Media Age magazine,* published 31 January.

PMP (2008) Supply Chain& Manufacturing Systems Report. PMP Research Report published at: **www.conspectus.com.** March.

Poon, S. and Jevons, C. (1997) Internet-enabled international marketing: a small business network perspective. *Journal of Marketing Management,* 13, 29–41.

Quayle, M. (2002) E-commerce: the challenge for UK SMEs in the twenty-first century. *International Journal of Operation and Production Management,* 22(10), 1148–61.

Quelch, J. and Klein, L. (1996) The Internet and international marketing. *Sloan Management Review,* Spring, 61–75.

Rodgers, S., Chen, Q., Wang, Y. Rettie, R. and Alpert, F. (2007) The Web Motivation Inventory. *International Journal of Advertising,* 26(4), 447–76.

Rogers, E. (1983) *Diffusion of Innovations,* 3rd edn. Free Press, New York.

Siikavirta, H., Punakivi, M., Karkkainen, M. and Linnanen, L. (2003) Effects of e-commerce on greenhouse gas emissions: a case study of grocery home delivery in Finland. *Journal of Industrial Ecology,* 6(2), 83–97.

Singh, N. and Pereira, A. (2005) *The Culturally Customized Web Site, Customizing Web Sites for the Global Marketplace.* Butterworth-Heinemann, Oxford.

Sparrow, A. (2000) *E-Commerce and the Law. The Legal Implications of Doing Business Online.* Financial Times Executive Briefings, London.

Trott, P. (1998) *Innovation Management and New Product Development.* Financial Times Prentice Hall, Harlow.

Ward, S., Bridges, K. and Chitty, B. (2005) Do incentives matter? An examination of on-line privacy concerns and willingness to provide personal and financial information. *Journal of Marketing Communications,* 11(1), 21–40.

Web links

Smart Insights Digital Marketing Statistics sources (http://bit.ly/smartstatistics/) A compilation of the Top 10 statistics sources and a custom search engine to search them.

Google Think Insights Databoard (http://www.google.com/think/tools/databoard.html) Google's compilation of latest research.

The Oxford Internet Institute (OII) (**www.oii.ox.ac.uk**) Research institute focussed on the study of the impact of the Internet on society.

Government sources on Internet usage and adoption

- European government (**http://ec.europa.eu/eurostat**)
- OECD (**www.oecd.org**). OECD broadband research (**www.oecd.org/sti/ict/broadband**)
- UK government (**www.statistics.gov.uk**)
- Ofcom (**www.ofcom.org.uk**) Ofcom is the independent regulator and competition authority for the UK communications industries, with responsibilities across television, radio, telecommunications and wireless communications services and has in-depth reports on communications markets
- US government reference centre (www.usa.gov)

Online audience panel media consumption and usage data

- These are fee-based data, but contain useful free data within press release sections.
- comScore (**www.comscore.com**). Data from comScore's global consumer panel is available in its blog and press releases section.
- Hitwise (**www.hitwise.com**). Hitwise blog (**http://weblogs.hitwise.com**). Sample reports from Hitwise on consumer search behaviour and importance of different online intermediaries
- Netratings (www.netratings.com)

Other major online research providers

- The European Interactive Advertising Association (**www.eiaa.net**). The EIAA is a pan-European trade organisation with surveys of media consumption and usage across Europe
- International Telecommunications Union (**www.itu.int/ITU-D/icteye**). Adoption of Internet and mobile phone statistics by company
- The Pew Internet & American Life Project (**www.pewinternet.org**). Produces reports that explore the impact of the Internet on families, communities, work and home, daily life, education, healthcare, and civic and political life

Privacy

- **Australian Privacy Commissioner** (**www.privacy.gov.au**). Information on privacy laws in Australia such as the Privacy Act and the Telecommunications Act
- **European Data Protection resources** (http://europa.eu.int/comm/justice_home/fsj/privacy/index_en.htm). These laws are coordinated centrally, but interpreted differently in different countries
- **Federal Trade commission** (www.ftc.gov/privacy). US privacy initiatives
- **GetSafeOnline** (www.getsafeonline.org). Site created by government and business to educate consumers to help them understand and manage their online privacy and security

- **Home Office Identify theft web site (www.identitytheft.org).** An awareness site created by the government
- **iCompli (www.icompli.co.uk).** Portal and e-newsletter about privacy and data protection compliance
- **Information Commissioner (www.ico.org.uk).** Site explaining law for UK consumers and businesses
- **Marketing Law (www.marketinglaw.co.uk).** Useful email update on the latest privacy law developments
- **Outlaw (www.out-law.com).** Compilation of the latest technology-related law
- **Privacy International (www.privacyinternational.org).** A human rights group formed in 1990 as a watchdog on surveillance and privacy invasions by governments and corporations

Part 2

Strategy and applications

In Part 2 of the book approaches to developing digital business strategy and applications are reviewed for the organisation as a whole (Chapter 5), with an emphasis on buy-side e-commerce (Chapters 6 and 7) and sell-side e-commerce (Chapters 8 and 9).

5 — Digital business strategy p. 179

- What is digital business strategy?
- Strategic analysis
- Strategic objectives
- Strategy definition
- Strategy implementation

Focus on . . .
- Aligning and impacting digital business strategies

6 — Supply chain management p. 247

- What is supply chain management?
- Options for restructuring the supply chain
- Using digital business to restructure the supply chain
- Supply chain management implementation

Focus on . . .
- The value chain

7 — E-procurement p. 297

- What is e-procurement?
- Drivers of e-procurement
- Barriers and risks of e-procurement adoption
- Implementing e-procurement
- The future of e-procurement

Focus on . . .
- Estimating e-procurement costs
- B2B marketplaces

8

Digital marketing p. 323

- What is digital marketing?
- Digital marketing planning
- Situation analysis
- Objective setting
- Strategy
- Tactics
- Actions
- Control

Focus on . . .

- Characteristics of digital media communications
- Online branding

9

Customer relationship management p. 387

- What is e-CRM?
- Conversion marketing
- The online buying process
- Customer acquisition management
- Customer retention management
- Customer extension
- Technology solutions for CRM

Focus on . . .

- Marketing communications for customer acquisition
- Social media and social CRM strategy
- Excelling in e-commerce service quality

5

Digital business strategy

Web support

The following additional case study is available at
www.pearsoned.co.uk/chaffey

→ Evolving business models in the Internet car sales market

The site also contains a range of study material designed to help improve your results.

Scan code to find the latest updates for topics in this chapter

Learning outcomes

After completing this chapter the reader should be able to:

- Follow an appropriate strategy process model for digital business
- Apply tools to generate and select digital business strategies
- Outline alternative strategic approaches to achieve digital business

Management issues

Consideration of digital business strategy raises these issues for management:

- How does digital business strategy differ from traditional business strategy?
- How should we integrate digital business strategy with existing business and information systems strategy?
- How should we evaluate our investment priorities and returns from digital business?

Links to other chapters

The main related chapters are:

- *Chapters 6 and 7* review the specific enactment of digital business strategy to supply chain and procurement management processes
- *Chapters 8 and 9* explain how digital marketing and customer relationship management relate to the concept of digital business, and e-commerce and digital marketing planning are approached
- *Chapters 10, 11 and 12* look at practical aspects of the implementation of digital business strategy

Introduction

Developing a digital business strategy requires a fusion of existing approaches to business, marketing, supply chain management and information systems strategy development. In addition to traditional strategy approaches, commentators have exhorted companies to apply innovative techniques to achieve competitive advantage. Around 2000, many articles, fuelled by the dot-com hype of the time, urged CEOs to 'innovate or die'. For many existing companies rapid transformation was neither desirable nor necessary and they have made a more gradual approach to digital business practice. Those companies that have successfully managed the transformation to digital business have done so by applying traditional strategy approaches. At the same time there have been many start-ups featured as cases in previous chapters, such as eBay, Lastminute.com and Zopa.com, that have succeeded through innovative business models. But these companies also have succeeded through applying established principles of business strategy, planning and risk management.

In this chapter we seek to show how a digital business strategy can be created through following these established principles, but also through careful consideration of how to best identify and exploit the differences introduced by new electronic channels. In a nutshell, digital business isn't just about defining *'how to do business online'*; it defines *'how to do business differently by applying digital technology to improve profitability and processes for both customer-facing, partner-facing and internal communications*. The digital business strategy defines how. We look at some examples of business models which need to be developed in the light of the opportunities enabled by digital technology and media in the introductory interview in this chapter.

We start the chapter by introducing digital business strategy and then discuss appropriate strategy process models to follow as a framework for developing digital business strategy. The chapter is structured around this classic four-stage strategy process model:

1 Strategic evaluation.
2 Strategic objectives.
3 Strategy definition.
4 Strategy implementation.

For each of these components of strategy, we cover management actions to review and refine digital business strategy. A recurring theme through this chapter is the need to align digital business strategy with business strategy while also identifying opportunities for digital business strategy to impact business strategy. *'Focus on* Aligning and impacting digital business strategies' at the end of this chapter covers these in more depth.

Development of the social business

With the growing consumer and business adoption of social media (which we discussed in Chapter 4), there has been more focus on creating a social business focussed around customer needs. (Since this requires transformation in the structure of the business we cover this topic in Chapter 10.)

Real-world Digital Business | The Smart Insights interview

Roberto Hortal explains why the marketing mix remains relevant today

Roberto Hortal has worked as head of digital business with many years of experience in different types of businesses operating in different countries. Examples of the UK and global enterprises he has worked for include EDF Energy, RSA insurance group,

MORE TH>N, easyJet and Nokia. Here he shares his experience of how the marketing mix concept is still applicable when taking real-world decisions in companies to shape their online proposition and increase their commercial value.

Q. We often hear that the concept of the marketing mix isn't that useful any longer in this era of 'customer first'. What's your view on its relevance today? Are there any particular aspects of the mix which lend themselves to refining online?

Roberto Hortal: The marketing mix is a conceptual framework, and as such it is useful since it enables a common language to be used in the planning, execution and measurement of a number of coordinated activities that deliver the desired Marketing outcomes. Customer-centricity demands that organisations become a lot better at collecting and reacting to customer insight and adapt their offering to best suit an ever-growing number of narrowing customer segments – ever approaching the ideal of the completely personalised product. As complexity increases exponentially, it is crucial to be able to rely on tried and tested concepts like the marketing mix.

I use the basic components of the marketing mix (such as the Four Ps) at work daily, and as such for me the marketing mix remains a practical tool. In a digital environment routinely identifying and profiling individual consumers over time and adapting to their needs and wants, the 4 Ps become elastic. Is my website a Place, or is it an integral part of the Product? When more efficient digital channels directly influence my ability to Price, do Place and Price become synonymous? This elasticity needs to be managed effectively to avoid the pitfalls of too rigidly applying the model. One must always challenge the validity of every tool in the digital marketing armoury; adding, changing and discarding as business and customers evolve. Proposed evolutions of the marketing mix concept (such as the Four Cs) may ensure it remains relevant today. My personal view is we're still some distance from seeing the end of its useful life.

Q. Could you give some examples of where you applied new ways of applying the mix online?

Roberto Hortal: In my view, the key insight is that digital media can contribute to every element of the mix. Therefore we must avoid a narrow categorisation of digital as contributing solely (or even primarily) to a single component of the mix.

While I haven't come across an organisation that fundamentally disagrees with that view, some organisations find it easier than others to put it into practice. I have worked in organisations where the mix is embedded in the corporate structure with separate Pricing, Product, Distribution (Place) and Marketing (Promotion) departments. Embedding a digital mindset across those silos can be a daunting task.

I've experimented with channel pricing, as pricing is a critical driver of conversion and business value in a services organisation:

- Straight online discounts have proven difficult to justify. Online discounts aren't valued by customers (in the age of price comparison, they focus on the total price, rather than its components) and often do not reflect a real lower cost to the business (lower costs to sell and serve are offset by lower transaction value and lower retention rates).
- Using channel data as a pricing factor has proven a lot more successful: as historical data is accumulated, it is possible to really offer competitive prices to those customers identified as high value at the point of application. An accurate value/propensity model can use the wealth of information available from digital visitors (geography, visit trigger/campaign, past visits, customer history, etc.) to drive truly personalised pricing. In this example, price follows place and both price and promotion reflect the individual customer.

I've successfully extended the data-driven approach to other elements of the mix: dynamic packaging (the creation of a personalised offering from the basis of a modular product) has proven successful many times: at easyJet we built a product that included car hire recommendations based on a predictive model that took destination, seasonality and party size as inputs – increasing car hire uptake very significantly. More recently I've applied the same insight-driven dynamic packaging approach to RSA's Central and Eastern European businesses, increasing sales of optional covers and add-ons very significantly.

Further opportunities exist around selecting which default base products to present: are you more likely to want a cheap energy tariff that tracks price rises or a fixed-price deal that ensures protection against future rises? What we know about you from your digital 'shadow' may provide the clues we need.

Q. Online channels bring great opportunities to test propositions online. Can you advise on approaches to testing propositions?

Roberto Hortal: I have used online channels to test propositions in a couple of ways:

- Assign propositions randomly to visitors on first arrival to test interest/sales. I would typically run this against a large control group (being offered the current main proposition) to both protect commercial results and detect the effect of any external influences that maybe otherwise wrongly influence the experiment. This approach can be extended beyond the site, via randomised allocation of marketing messages on Display, Search etc. to measure a proposition's attractiveness. It's important to test all aspects of the proposition: a very successful proposition at attracting interest may convert badly if it can't be priced at a level that matches customer expectations.
- Provide a modular proposition platform and allow customers to combine proposition elements. We can easily analyse popular combinations as well as secondary correlations such as the propensity to add a certain ancillary product to a particular proposition configuration, and understand the compound impact on profitability, retention and advocacy from what we know about each of the modular components in isolation.

I've found that proposition testing rarely fits neatly an A/B scenario, with tests quickly developing into complex multivariate experiments with a significant number of variables. It is important to ensure the tests are solidly planned, rigorously executed and statistically significant. Free tools like Google Website Optimiser provide information to test and get the best out of website contact. However, such tools will not prevent badly designed experiments from yielding wrong data. In my experience, the only way to ensure valid tests and improved business results is to bring in the best analytical brain you can find. Analytics is the first role I fill when I build a digital team from scratch, it's that important.

Q. Many organisations are now developing social media strategies. How do you see the intersection between social media and the marketing mix since it clearly impacts on product decision-making and service?

Roberto Hortal: If I only had the answer . . . I take a radically different view of social media than many of my peers. While most people see social media as a branding and customer service channel, I see social media's largest potential in the areas of awareness, consideration and acquisition. This is not to say the best way to use social media sites is to advertise in them. Far from it. The social nature of the Internet demands that brands engage in conversation, and identify and incentivise brand ambassadors to help amplify our messages.

There is general acceptance of this, but also a general shyness about steering conversations and seeking to extract immediate commercial value in the form of direct sales. Risk-aversion takes over and anecdotes [are] used to prove the point that there is a risk that poor execution may lead to a social backlash.

The risk is clearly real but there is also an opportunity to execute well and generate significant amounts of business and positive buzz. I recently ran a campaign with Poland's largest social network (Nasza Klassa). A fairly simple personality quiz mechanism was executed beautifully by my Polish team, resulting in what our partners characterised as the country's most successful campaign in terms of reach and engagement, one that generated levels of sales comparable to those contributed by mainstream e-marketing channels.

Social media spaces require nurture and respect, but we must not forget that so do physical locations. In the same way that people like to go to the village's Post Office for a chat but also do their banking, branded social media environments have the potential to merge conversation and commerce in a seamless, altogether better proposition for both consumers and brands.

Q. Many organisations now are looking at providing new mobile propositions. A key decision is whether to implement them as a mobile app or mobile site. How do you approach this platform decision?

Roberto Hortal: I start from the point of view of the user:

- Why would they use this proposition?
- Where would they use the proposition?
- How would they find it first time, and subsequently?
- Would they accept/appreciate the added engagement possibilities of an app (alerts, updates, a permanent place on the home screen)?

Some scenarios where I have used this approach in the past include:

- **Insurance/energy sales.** Website – neither mobile app nor mobile site. In this particular case I think the best option is to provide a solidly usable, accessible web sales capability that works well across devices. Rather than building separate sites/ capabilities for separate devices I prefer to ensure the basis of the experience is optimised – this principle ensures that device-specificity doesn't catch me off-guard: sales websites I have managed worked well on iPhone the day it came out as they were built of solid principles and standards that apply across devices. I do use extensively the principles of progressive enhancement to provide a great experience to segments of people on particular channels/devices such as modern PC browsers and mobile browsers. However, the underlying principle of a solid, accessible, easy to use site has never let me down.
- **Regular/emergency transaction.** Apps – I look at regular events such as submitting an electricity meter reading or unpredictable ones such as registering a motor insurance claim as ideal candidates for a mobile app. Regularity breeds familiarity, and regular events can benefit from app characteristics such as local storage, transparent login, notifications and a permanent place on the user's screen. These same characteristics, together with the reassurance of being completely contained on the device and not requiring uninterrupted Internet access, support the use of apps for functionality perceived as critical. HTML5 may make these distinctions technically irrelevant, but I expect customer behaviour will lag significantly so they will effectively apply for a long while yet.
- **Seamless access vs perceived value.** An app's installation is quite a disruptive process: you need to open the shop interface, confirm credentials, find the app,

start a possibly long download (which may impact on your monthly limits), find the app on the phone screens, start it, watch it initialise (including possibly entering username and password for initial configuration) and finally access it – and from now on it will take space permanently on your device, competing with your music and movies. Quite an expensive process, from a usability point of view. Therefore an app must have quite a high perceived value in order to get installed. On the other hand, if casual use (particularly in conjunction with web searching/browsing) is what is sought, then a mobile site is the best solution.

- **Fragmentation is finally the last of my current worries.** We used to have to contend with the iPhone and the iPad. Two screen sizes in a universal app. Manageable. Suddenly we have myriad versions of iOS, Android, Windows Phone on a continuum of screen sizes and very variable device capabilities (processor speed, camera/s, GPS, NFC, etc.). This is turning into a big argument for HTML5 and mobile sites. Major platform/device combos will continue to be relevant for apps, but I also expect the relative size of this group of devices to shrink in relation to the universe of mobile devices – serving most of which will only be practical through mobile web.

(Options for reviewing the marketing mix are discussed further at the end of Chapter 8 on Digital marketing.)

What is digital business strategy?

Strategy
Definition of the future direction and actions of a company defined as approaches to achieve specific objectives.

Strategy defines the future direction and actions of an organisation or part of an organisation. Johnson and Scholes (2006) define corporate strategy as:

> the direction and scope of an organization over the long-term: which achieves advantage for the organization through its configuration of resources within a changing environment to meet the needs of markets and to fulfil stakeholder expectations.

Lynch (2000) describes strategy as an organisation's sense of purpose. However, he notes that purpose alone is not strategy; plans or actions are also needed.

Digital business strategies share much in common with corporate, business and marketing strategies. These quotes summarising the essence of strategy could equally apply to each strategy:

- 'Is based on current performance in the marketplace.'
- 'Defines how we will meet our objectives.'
- 'Sets allocation of resources to meet goals.'
- 'Selects preferred strategic options to compete within a market.'
- 'Provides a long-term plan for the development of the organisation.'
- 'Identifies competitive advantage through developing an appropriate positioning relative to competitors defining a value proposition delivered to customer segments.'

Johnson and Scholes (2006) note that organisations have different levels of strategy, particularly for larger or global organisations. These are summarised within Figure 5.1. They identify *corporate strategy* which is concerned with the overall purpose and scope of the organisation, *business unit strategy* which defines how to compete successfully in a particular market and *operational strategies* which are concerned with achieving corporate and business unit strategies. Additionally, *functional strategies* describe how the corporate and business unit strategies will be operationalised in different functional areas or business processes. Functional or process strategies refer to marketing, supply chain management, human resources, finance and information systems strategies.

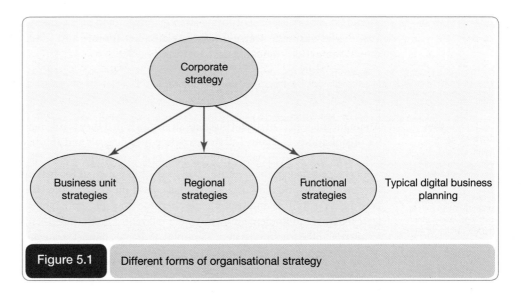

Figure 5.1   Different forms of organisational strategy

Digital business strategy
Definition of the approach by which applications of internal and external electronic communications can support and influence business strategy.

Where does **digital business strategy** fit? Figure 5.1 does not show at which level digital business strategy should be defined, since for different organisations this must be discussed and agreed. We can observe that there is a tendency for digital business strategy to be incorporated within the functional strategies, for example within a marketing plan or logistics plan, or as part of information systems (IS) strategy. A danger with this approach is that digital business strategy may not be recognised at a higher level within organisational planning. A distinguishing feature of organisations that are leaders in digital business, such as Cisco, Dell, HSBC, easyJet and General Electric, is that digital business is an element of corporate strategy development and that transformation to apply digital platforms and media is prioritised and resourced.

There is limited research on how businesses have integrated digital business strategy into existing strategy, although authors such as Doherty and McAulay (2002) and Hughes (2001) have suggested it is important that e-commerce investments be driven by corporate strategies. We return to approaches of alignment later in the chapter.

The imperative for digital business strategy

Think about the implications if digital business strategy is not clearly defined. The following may result:

- Missed opportunities from lack of evaluation of opportunities or insufficient resourcing of digital business initiatives. These will result in more savvy competitors gaining a competitive advantage.
- Inappropriate direction of digital business strategy (poorly defined objectives, for example, with the wrong emphasis on buy-side, sell-side or internal process support).
- Limited integration of digital business at a technical level, resulting in silos of information in different systems.
- Resource wastage through duplication of digital business development in different functions and limited sharing of best practice.

To help avoid these problems, organisations will want digital business strategy to be based on corporate objectives. As Rowley (2002) pointed out, it is logical that digital business strategy should support corporate strategy objectives and it should also support functional marketing and supply chain management strategies.

However, these corporate objectives should be based on new opportunities and threats related to electronic network adoption, which are identified from environment analysis and objectives defined in a digital business strategy. So it can be said that digital business strategy should not only support corporate strategy, but should also influence it. Figure 5.2 explains how digital business strategy should relate to corporate and functional strategies. It also shows where these topics are covered in this book.

Digital channel strategies

Digital channel strategies
Define how a company should set specific objectives and develop specific differential strategies for communicating with its customers and partners through electronic media.

An important aspect of digital business strategies is that they create new '**e-channel strategies**' for organisations. E-channel strategies define specific goals and approaches for using electronic channels. This is to prevent simply replicating existing processes through e-channels, which will create efficiencies but will not exploit the full potential for making an organisation more effective through digital business. We have used the generic 'digital channels' terms since as new digital platforms and technologies become available, companies should implement strategic initiatives to implement them where relevant. These strategies may be buy-side, sell-side or internal infrastructure related. Examples of digital channel strategies include:

- Overarching digital channel or multichannel strategy with specific channel strategies
- Mobile commerce strategy
- Social media strategy
- Social CRM strategy
- Supply chain or enterprise resource planning strategy
- E-procurement strategy.

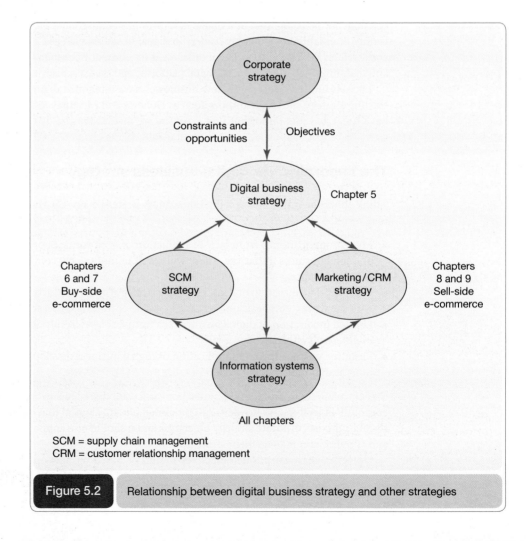

Figure 5.2 Relationship between digital business strategy and other strategies

So at any one time, there will be a lot of potential initiatives which it will be not be financially or operationally practical to implement at the same time. So roadmaps need to be produced and decisions taken over priorities as described at the end of this chapter.

Digital channel strategies also need to define how electronic channels are used in conjunction with other channels as part of a **multichannel digital business strategy**. This defines how different marketing and supply chain channels should integrate and support each other in terms of their proposition development and communications based on their relative merits for the customer and the company. Finally, we also need to remember that digital business strategy also defines how an organisation gains value internally from using electronic networks, such as sharing employee knowledge and improving process efficiencies through intranets. Myers *et al.* (2004) provide a useful summary of the decisions required about multichannel marketing.

The main characteristic of a multichannel digital business strategy is that it is a channel strategy, so it follows that:

Multichannel (omnichannel) digital business strategy
Defines how different marketing and supply chain channels should integrate and support each other to drive business efficiency and effectiveness. As noted in Chapter 1, in 2012–13 the term omnichannel became used, particularly in the retail sector, to reference the importance of customer touchpoints on social media and mobile platforms.

- Specific digital business objectives need to be set to benchmark adoption of e-channels.
- Digital business strategy defines how we should:
  1 *Communicate the benefits of using e-channels*
  2 *Prioritise audiences or partners targeted for e-channel adoption*
  3 *Prioritise products sold or purchased through e-channels*
  4 *Achieve our e-channel targets.*
- Digital channel strategies thrive on creating differential value for all parties to a transaction.
- But digital channels do not exist in isolation, so we still need to manage channel integration and acknowledge that the adoption of digital channels will not be appropriate for all products or services or generate sufficient value for all partners. This selective adoption of e-channels is sometimes referred to as 'right-channelling' in a sell-side e-commerce context (as shown in Table 5.9). Right-channelling can be summarised as:
  – *Reaching the right customer*
  – *Using the right channel*
  – *With the right message or offering*
  – *At the right time.*
- Digital business strategy also defines how an organisation gains value internally from using electronic networks, such as through sharing employee knowledge and improving process efficiencies through intranets.

As an example of how an digital channel strategy was implemented and communicated to an audience, see Mini case study 5.1: BA asks 'Have you clicked yet?' This shows how BA communicates its new digital channel strategy to its customers in order to show them the differential benefits of their using the channel, and so change their behaviour. BA would use 'right-channelling' by targeting a younger, more professional audience for adoption of e-channels, while using traditional channels of phone and post to communicate with less web-savvy customers who prefer to use these media.

Mini Case Study 5.1	BA asks 'Have you clicked yet?'

In 2004, British Airways launched online services which allowed customers to take control of the booking process, so combining new services with reduced costs. BA decided to develop a specific online ad campaign to create awareness and encourage usage of its Online Value Proposition (OVP). BA's UK marketing manager said about the objective:

British Airways is leading the way in innovating technology to simplify our customers' journey through the airport. The role of this campaign was to give a strong message about what is now available online, over and above booking tickets.

The aim of the campaign was to educate and change the way in which BA's customers behave before, while and after they travel. The campaign focussed on the key benefits of the new online services – speed, ease and convenience – and promoted the ability to check in online and print out a boarding pass. The two main target audiences were quite different, early adopters and those who use the web occasionally, but don't rely on it. Early adopters were targeted on sites such as T3.co.uk, Newscientist.com and DigitalHomeMag.com. Occasional users were reached through ads on sites such as JazzFM.com, Vogue.com and Menshealth.com.

Traditional media used to deliver the 'Have you clicked yet?' message included print, TV and outdoor media. The print ad copy, which details the OVP, was:

> *Your computer is now the airport. Check in online, print your own boarding pass, choose your seat, change your booking card and even find hire cars and hotels. Simple.*

A range of digital media were used, including ATMs, outdoor LCD transvision screens such as those in London rail stations which included Bluecasting where commuters could receive a video on their Bluetooth-enabled mobile phone, and digital escalator panels. More than 650,000 consumers interacted with the ATM screen creative. Online ads included overlays and skyscrapers which showed a consumer using their computer, printing out a ticket and walking across the screen to the airport. Such rich-media campaigns generated 17% clickthrough and 15% interaction. The website used in the campaign is shown in Figure 5.3.

Figure 5.3	BA communicates its online value proposition

Source: Based on *Revolution* (2005); wwwbritishairways.com.

Strategy process models for digital business

Before developing any type of strategy, a management team needs to agree the process they will follow for generating and then implementing the strategy. A **strategy process model** provides a framework that gives a logical sequence to follow to ensure inclusion of all key activities of digital business strategy development. It also ensures that digital business strategy can be evolved as part of a process of continuous improvement.

Before the advent of digital business, many strategy process models had been put forward for developing business and marketing strategies. To what extent can management teams apply these models to digital business strategy development? Although strategy process models differ in emphasis and terminology, they all have common elements. Complete Activity 5.1 to discuss what these common elements are.

Debate 5.1

Digital business responsibility

'A single person with specific digital business responsibility is required for every medium-to-large business. It is not sufficient for this to be the responsibility of a non-specialist manager.'

Activity 5.1   Selecting a digital business strategy process model

Purpose

To identify the applicability of existing strategy process models to digital business.

Activity

Review three or four strategy process models that you have encountered. These could be models such as those shown in Table 5.1. Note that columns in this table are independent – the rows do not correspond across models.

Questions

1 What are the strengths and weaknesses of each model?
2 What common features do the models share? List the key elements of an appropriate strategy process model.

Answers to activities can be found at www.pearsoned.co.uk/chaffey

---

Table 5.1   Alternative strategy process models

Jelassi and Enders (2008) Digital business strategy framework	Johnson and Scholes (2006) Parallel corporate strategy model	McDonald (1999) Sequential marketing strategy model	Smith (1999) SOSTAC® Sequential marketing strategy model (see Chapter 8)
SWOT summarising external analysis (e.g. marketplace, customers, competitors); internal analysis (e.g. human, financial and operational)	Strategic analysis (environment, resources, expectations, objectives and culture)	Situation review (marketing audit, SWOT analysis, assumptions)	Situation analysis
Mission and objectives	Strategic choice (generation of options, evaluation of options, selection of strategy)	Goal-setting (mission, corporate objectives)	Objective-setting
Strategy formulation to create and capture value through sustaining competitive advantage and exploring new market spaces	Strategic implementation (resource planning, people and systems, organisation structure)	Strategy formulation (marketing objectives and strategy, estimate expected results, identify alternative plans and mixes)	Strategy

Table 5.1	Continued		
Jelassi and Enders (2008) Digital business strategy framework	**Johnson and Scholes (2006) Parallel corporate strategy model**	**McDonald (1999) Sequential marketing strategy model**	**Smith (1999) SOSTAC® Sequential marketing strategy model (see Chapter 8)**
Strategy implementation including internal organisation, interaction with suppliers and users or customers		Resource allocation and monitoring (budget, first-year implementation plan)	Tactics Actions Control

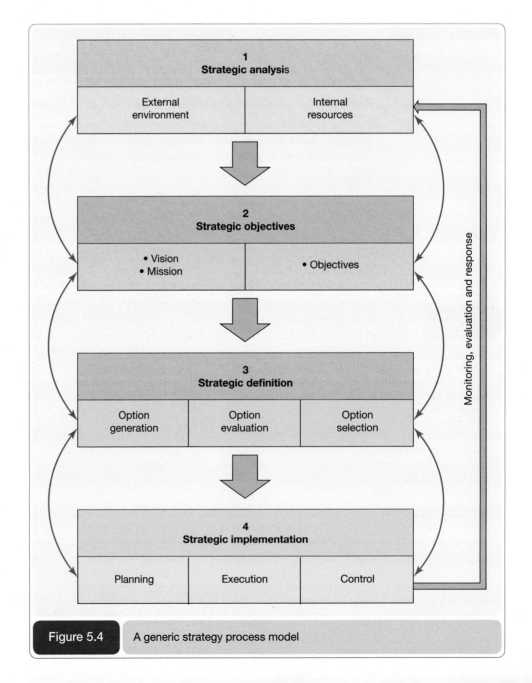

Figure 5.4	A generic strategy process model

Common elements include:

1 Internal and external environment scanning or analysis is needed. Scanning occurs both during strategy development and as a continuous process in order to respond to competitors. Digital business requires a more continuous review of opportunities and threats as new digital platforms are created and adopted by businesses and consumers.
2 A clear statement of vision and objectives is required. Clarity is required to communicate the strategic intention to both employees and the marketplace since digital business requires a major long-term transformation. Objectives are also vital to act as a check as to whether implementation of strategy is on track.
3 Strategy development can be broken down into strategy option generation, evaluation and selection.
4 After strategy development, enactment of the strategy occurs as strategy implementation.
5 Control is required to monitor operational and strategy effectiveness problems and adjust the operations or strategy accordingly. With digital business, optimisation is possible using digital analytics (as described in Chapter 12). This includes tracking of audience behaviour using desktop and mobile services and qualitative feedback via social media. Harnessing this insight is useful to refine the implementation, for example to gain ideas of how to increase conversion rate to sale for e-commerce services.

Although the models suggest that these elements, are generally sequential, in reality they are iterative and require reference back to previous stages.

Jelassi and Enders (2008) suggest that there are three key dimensions for defining an e-commerce strategy:

1 Where will the organisation compete? (That is, which markets within the external micro-environment.)
2 What type of value will it create? (Strategy options to generate value through increased revenue or reduced costs.)
3 How should the organisation be designed to deliver value? (Includes internal structure and resources and interfaces with external companies as discussed in Chapter 10.)

The arrows in Figure 5.4 highlight an important distinction in the way in which strategy process models are applied. Referring to the work of Mintzberg and Quinn (1991), Lynch (2000) distinguishes between prescriptive and emergent strategy approaches. In the **prescriptive strategy** approach, strategic analysis is used to develop a strategy, and it is then implemented. In other words, the strategy is prescribed in advance. Alternatively, in the **emergent strategy** approach, strategic analysis, strategic development and strategy implementation are interrelated.

In reality, most organisational strategy development and planning processes have elements of prescriptive and emergent strategy. The prescriptive elements are the structured annual or six-monthly budgeting process or a longer-term three-year rolling marketing planning process. But, on a shorter timescale, organisations also need an emergent process to enable strategic agility (introduced in Chapter 2) and the ability to respond rapidly to marketplace dynamics. E-consultancy (2008a) has researched approaches used to encourage emergent strategies or strategic agility based on interviews with e-commerce practitioners – see Table 5.2.

Prescriptive strategy
Strategic analysis, strategic development and strategy implementation are linked together sequentially.

Emergent strategy
Strategic analysis, strategic development and strategy implementation are interrelated and are developed together.

Table 5.2	Summary of approaches used to support emergent strategy

Aspect of emergent strategy	Approaches used to support emergent digital strategy
Strategic analysis	• Staff in different parts of organisation encouraged to monitor introduction of new approaches by competitors in-sector or out-of-sector • Third-party benchmarking service reporting monthly or quarterly on new functionality introduced by competitors • *Ad hoc* customer panel used to suggest or review new ideas for site features • Quarterly longitudinal testing of usability to complete key tasks • Subscription to audience panel data (comScore, Netratings, Hitwise) reviews changes in popularity of online services

Table 5.2	Continued

Aspect of emergent strategy	Approaches used to support emergent digital strategy
Strategy formulation and selection	• Budget flexible to reassign priorities • Dedicated or 'ring-fenced' IT budget up to agreed limits to reduce protracted review cycles • Digital channel strategy group meets monthly, empowered to take decisions about which new web functionality to implement
Strategy implementation	• Use of agile development methodologies to enable rapid development • Area of site used to showcase new tools currently under trial (for example Google Labs (http://labs.google.com)). This area no longer exists

Source: E-consultancy (2008a).

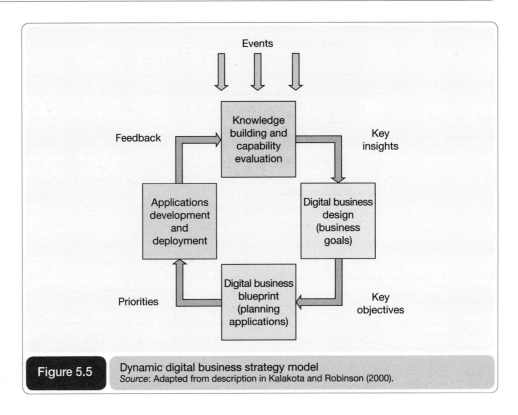

Figure 5.5	Dynamic digital business strategy model *Source*: Adapted from description in Kalakota and Robinson (2000).

Kalakota and Robinson (2000) recommend a dynamic emergent strategy process specific to digital business – see Figure 5.5. It essentially shares similar features to Figure 5.4, but with an emphasis on responsiveness with continuous review and prioritisation of investment in new applications.

Strategic analysis

Strategic analysis
Collection and review of information about an organisation's internal processes and resources and external marketplace factors in order to inform strategy definition.

Strategic analysis or situation analysis involves review of:

- The internal resources and processes of the company to assess its digital business capabilities and results to date in the context of a review of its activity in the marketplace.
- The immediate competitive environment (micro-environment), including customer demand and behaviour, competitor activity, marketplace structure and relationships with suppliers, partners and intermediaries (as described in Chapter 2).

- The wider environment (macro-environment) in which a company operates (this includes the social, legal, economic and political factors reviewed in Chapter 4).

These are summarised in Figure 5.6. For the effective, responsive digital business, as explained earlier, it is essential that situation analysis or environmental scanning be a continuous process with clearly identified responsibilities for performing the scanning and acting on the knowledge acquired.

Resource and process analysis

Resource analysis
Review of the technological, financial and human resources of an organisation and how they are utilised in business processes.

Resource analysis for digital business is primarily concerned with its digital business capabilities, i.e. the degree to which a company has in place the appropriate technological and applications infrastructure and financial and human resources to support it. These resources must be harnessed together to give efficient business processes.

Jelassi and Enders (2008) distinguish between analysis of resources and capabilities:

- Resources are the tangible and intangible assets which can be used in value creation. Tangible resources include the IT infrastructure, bricks and mortar, and financial capital. Intangible resources include a company's brand and credibility, employee knowledge, licences and patents.
- Capabilities represent the ability of a firm to use resources effectively to support value creation. They are dependent on the structure and processes used to manage digital business.

Stage models of digital business development

Stage models are helpful in reviewing how advanced a company is in its use of information and communications technology (ICT) resources to support its processes. Stage models have traditionally been popular in the analysis of the current application of business information systems (BIS) within an organisation. For example, Nolan's (1979) six-stage model referred

Figure 5.6   Elements of strategic situation analysis for the digital business

to the development of use of information systems within an organisation from initiation with simple data processing through to a mature adoption of BIS with controlled, integrated systems. (A simple example of a stage model was introduced in Figure 1.13.)

When assessing the current use of ICT within a company or across a market it is instructive to analyse the extent to which an organisation has implemented the technological infrastructure and support structure to achieve digital business. Quelch and Klein (1996) developed a five-stage model referring to the development of sell-side e-commerce. The stages remain relevant today. Research (referenced in Chapter 1 and Chapter 4) shows that many companies still have limited digital business capabilities and are at an early stage in the model. For existing companies the stages are:

1 **Image and product information** – a basic 'brochureware' website or presence in online directories.
2 **Information collection** – enquiries are facilitated through online forms.
3 **Customer support and service** – 'web self-service' is encouraged through frequently asked questions and the ability to ask questions through a forum or online.
4 **Internal support and service** – a marketing intranet is created to help with support process.
5 **Transactions** – financial transactions such as online sales or the creation of an e-CRM system where customers can access detailed product and order information through an extranet.

Considering sell-side e-commerce, Chaffey and Ellis-Chadwick (2012) suggest there are six options:

- *Level 0.* No website or presence on web.
- *Level 1.* Basic web presence. Company places an entry in a website listing company names. There is no website at this stage.
- *Level 2.* Simple static informational website. Contains basic company and product information, sometimes referred to as 'brochureware'.
- *Level 3.* Simple interactive site. Users are able to search the site and make queries to retrieve information. Queries by email may also be supported.
- *Level 4.* Interactive site supporting transactions with users. The functions offered will vary according to company but they will usually be limited to online buying.
- *Level 5.* Fully interactive site supporting the whole buying process. Provides relationship marketing with individual customers and facilitating the full range of marketing exchanges.

Stage models have also been applied to SME businesses where Levy and Powell (2003) reviewed different adoption ladders which, broadly speaking, have four stages of (1) publish, (2) interact, (3) transact and (4) integrate.

Considering buy-side e-commerce, the corresponding levels of product sourcing applications can be identified:

- *Level I.* No use of the web for product sourcing and no electronic integration with suppliers.
- *Level II.* Review and selection from competing suppliers using intermediary websites, B2B exchanges and supplier websites. Orders placed by conventional means.
- *Level III.* Orders placed electronically through EDI, via intermediary sites, exchanges or supplier sites. No integration between organisation's systems and supplier's systems. Rekeying of orders into procurement or accounting systems necessary.
- *Level IV.* Orders placed electronically with integration of company's procurement systems.
- *Level V.* Orders placed electronically with full integration of company's procurement, manufacturing requirements planning and stock control systems.

(In Chapter 6, the case of BHP Steel (p. 253) is an illustration of such a stage model.)

We should remember that typical stage models of website development such as those described above are most appropriate to companies whose products can be sold online through transactional e-commerce. In fact, stage models could be developed for a range of different types of online presence and business models, each with different objectives. As a summary to this section, Table 5.3 presents a synthesis of stage models for digital business development. Organisations can assess their position on the continuum between stages 1 and 4 for the different aspects of digital business development shown in the column on the left.

Table 5.3	A stage model for digital business development			
	1 Web presence	**2 E-commerce**	**3 Integrated e-commerce**	**4 Digital business**
Services available	Brochureware or interaction with product catalogues and customer service	Transactional e-commerce on buy-side or sell-side	Buy- and sell-side integrated with enterprise resource planning (ERP) or legacy systems. Personalisation of services	Full integration between all internal organisational processes and elements of the value network
Organisational scope	Isolated departments, e.g. marketing department	Cross-organisational	Cross-organisational	Across the enterprise and beyond ('extraprise')
Transformation	Technological infrastructure	Technology and new responsibilities identified for e-commerce	Internal business processes and company structure	Change to digital business culture, linking of business processes with partners
Strategy	Limited	Sell-side e-commerce strategy, not well integrated with business strategy	E-commerce strategy integrated with business strategy using a value-chain approach	Digital business strategy incorporated as part of business strategy

When companies devise the strategies and tactics to achieve their objectives they may return to the stage models to specify which level of innovation they are looking to achieve in the future.

Application portfolio analysis

Analysis of the current portfolio of business applications within a business is used to assess current information systems capability and also to inform future strategies. A widely applied framework within information systems study is that of McFarlan and McKenney (1993) with the modifications of Ward and Griffiths (1996). Figure 5.7 illustrates the results of a portfolio analysis for a B2B company applied within a digital business context. It can be seen that current applications such as human resources, financial management and production-line management systems will continue to support the operations of the business and will not be a priority for future investment. In contrast, to achieve competitive advantage, applications for maintaining a dynamic customer catalogue online, online sales and collecting marketing intelligence about customer buying behaviour will become more important. Applications such as procurement and logistics will continue to be of importance in a digital business context.

Portfolio analysis is also often used to select the most appropriate future Internet projects. A weakness of the portfolio analysis approach is that today applications are delivered by a single digital business software or *enterprise resource planning* application. Given this, it is perhaps more appropriate to define the services that will be delivered to external and internal customers through deploying information systems.

In E-consultancy (2008a) I defined a form of portfolio analysis as the basis for benchmarking current e-commerce capabilities and identifying strategic priorities. The six areas for benchmarking are:

1 **Digital channel strategy.** The development of a clear strategy, including situation analysis, goal-setting, identification of key target markets and audience, and identification of priorities for development of online services.

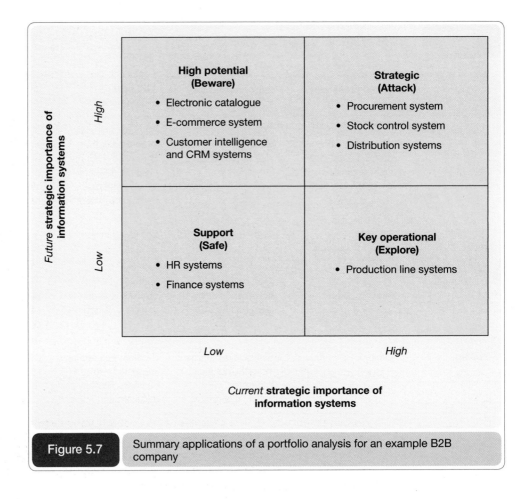

High potential
(Beware)

- Electronic catalogue
- E-commerce system
- Customer intelligence and CRM systems

Strategic
(Attack)

- Procurement system
- Stock control system
- Distribution systems

Support
(Safe)

- HR systems
- Finance systems

Key operational
(Explore)

- Production line systems

Future strategic importance of information systems

High

Low

Low   High

Current **strategic importance of information systems**

Figure 5.7	Summary applications of a portfolio analysis for an example B2B company

2 **Online customer acquisition.** Strategies for gaining new customers online using alternative digital media channels (shown in Figure 1.7), including search engine marketing, partner marketing and display advertising.

3 **Online customer conversion and experience.** Approaches to improve online service levels and increase conversion to sales or other online outcomes.

4 **Customer development and growth.** Strategies to encourage visitors and customers to continue using online services using tactics such as email marketing and personalisation.

5 **Cross-channel integration and brand development.** Integrating online sales and service with customer communications and service interactions in physical channels.

6 **Digital channel governance.** Issues in managing e-commerce services such as structure and resourcing, including human resources and the technology infrastructure such as hardware and networking facilities to deliver these applications.

SWOT analysis
Strengths, weaknesses, opportunities and threats.

Organisational and IS SWOT analysis

You will know that **SWOT analysis** is a relatively simple yet powerful tool that can help organisations analyse their internal resources in terms of strengths and weaknesses and match them against the external environment in terms of opportunities and threats. We recommend that to get the most from SWOT analysis it's of greatest value when it is used not only to analyse the current situation, but also as a tool to formulate strategies. To achieve this it is useful once the strengths, weaknesses, opportunities and threats have been listed to combine them, as shown in Figure 5.8. This can be used to develop strategies to counter the threats and take advantage of the opportunities and can then be built into the digital business strategy.

Figure 5.9 gives an example of a digital marketing SWOT using the approach shown in Figure 5.8.

The organisation	Stengths – S 1 Existing brand 2 Existing customer base 3 Existing distribution	Weaknesses – W 1 Brand perception 2 Intermediary use 3 Technology/skills 4 Cross-channel support
Opportunities – O 1 Cross-selling 2 New markets 3 New services 4 Alliances/co-branding	SO strategies Leverage strengths to maximise opportunities **= Attacking strategy**	WO strategies Counter weaknesses through exploiting opportunities **= Build strengths for attacking strategy**
Threats – T 1 Customer choice 2 New entrants 3 New competitive products 4 Channel conflicts	ST strategies Leverage strengths to minimise threats **= Defensive strategy**	WT strategies Counter weaknesses and threats **= Build strengths for defensive strategy**

Figure 5.8   SWOT analysis

Human and financial resources

Resource analysis will also consider these two factors:

1 **Human resources.** To take advantage of the opportunities identified in strategic analysis the right resources must be available to deliver digital business solutions.
2 **Financial resources.** Assessing financial resources for information systems is usually conducted as part of investment appraisal and budgeting for enhancements to new systems which we consider later in the chapter.

Evaluation of internal resources should be balanced against external resources. Perrott (2005) provides a simple framework for this analysis (Figure 5.9). He suggests that adoption of digital business will be determined by the balance between internal capability and incentives and

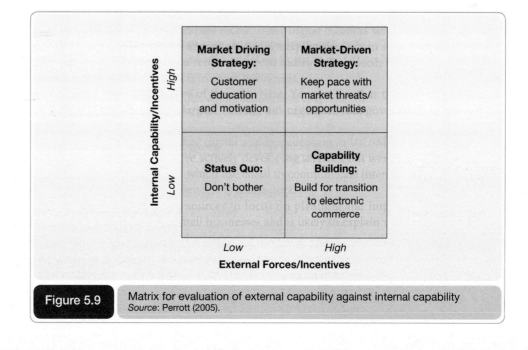

Figure 5.9   Matrix for evaluation of external capability against internal capability
Source: Perrott (2005).

external forces and capabilities. Figure 5.9 defines a matrix where there are four quadrants which businesses within a market may occupy:

- *Market driving strategy* (high internal capabilities/incentives and low external forces/ incentives). This is often the situation for the early adopters.
- *Capability building* (low internal capabilities/incentives and high external forces/ incentives). A later adopter.
- *Market-driven strategy*. Internal capabilities/incentives and external forces/incentives are both high.
- *Status quo*. There isn't an imperative to change since both internal capabilities/incentives and external forces/incentives are low.

An organisation's position in the matrix will be governed by benchmarking of external factors suggested by Perrott (2005), which include the proportion of competitors' products or services delivered electronically, proportion of competitors' communications to customers done electronically, and proportion of different customer segments (and suppliers or partners on the supply side) attracted to electronic activity. Internal factors to be evaluated include technical capabilities to deliver through internal or external IT providers, desire or ability to move from legacy systems and the staff capability (knowledge, skills and attitudes necessary to conduct electronic business). The cost differential of savings made against implementation costs is also included here.

Stage models can also be used to assess internal capabilities and structures. For example, Atos Consulting (2008, Table 5.4) have defined a capability maturity framework. This is based on the well-known capability maturity models devised by Carnegie Mellon Software Engineering Institute (now transferred to the CMMI Institute, http://cmmiinstitute.com/) to help organisations improve their software development practices. (In Chapter 10 there is more detail on how to achieve management of change between these stages.)

Competitive environment analysis

External factors are also assessed as part of strategic analysis. We have already considered how marketplace analysis can be undertaken to identify external opportunities and threats

Table 5.4	Capability maturity model of the adoption of e-business

Carnegie Mellon software development maturity process	Atos Consulting e-business capability framework
Level 1 Initial	*E-business unplanned.* E-business initiatives are ad hoc, unplanned and even chaotic. The organisation lacks the capability to meet commitments consistently.
Level 2 Repeatable	*E-business aware.* Basic e-business processes established necessary to repeat earlier successes but not yet part of planning process. The focus is on developing the capabilities of the organisation.
Level 3 Defined	*E-business enabled.* Central e-business strategy and planning process towards a centralised model (IT and competencies).
Level 4 Managed	*E-business integrated.* E-business part of departmental and business unit planning. Detailed performance measures of e-business process and applications collected and used for control.
Level 5 Optimised	*Extended enterprise.* E-business core part of corporate strategy, with continuous evaluation of digital business improvements enabled by quantitative feedback, piloting innovative ideas and technologies.

for a business in Chapter 2, but here we consider demand analysis and look at competitive threats in more detail.

Demand analysis

A key factor driving digital business strategy objectives is the current level and future projections of customer, partner and internal access and usage of different types of digital technology platforms and e-commerce services, This is **demand analysis**. Using demand analysis is a key activity in producing a digital marketing plan (described in more detail in Chapter 8).

For buy-side e-commerce a company also needs to consider the e-commerce services its suppliers offer: how many offer services for e-commerce and where they are located (Chapter 7, p. 302).

Demand analysis
Assessment of the demand for e-commerce services amongst existing and potential customer segments.

Assessing competitive threats

Michael Porter's classic 1980 model of the five main competitive forces that affect a company still provides a valid framework for reviewing threats arising in the digital business era. Table 5.5 summarises the classic analysis by Michael Porter of the impact of the Internet on business using the five forces framework (Porter, 2001).

Placed in a digital business context, Figure 5.10 shows the main threats updated to place emphasis on the competitive threats applied to digital business. Threats have been grouped into buy-side (upstream supply chain), sell-side (downstream supply chain) and competitive threats. The main difference from the five forces model of Porter (1980) is the distinction between competitive threats from intermediaries (or partners) on the buy-side and sell-side.

Competitive threats

1 Threat of new e-commerce entrants

For traditional 'bricks-and-mortar' companies this has been a common threat for retailers selling products such as books and financial services. For example, in Europe, traditional banks have been threatened by the entry of completely new start-up competitors such as Zopa (www.zopa.com) or traditional companies from a different geographic market that use the Internet to facilitate their entry into an overseas market. ING, an existing financial services group, formed in 1991 and based in the Netherlands, has used the Internet to facilitate

Figure 5.10   Competitive threats acting on the digital business

Table 5.5	Impact of the Internet on the five competitive forces

Bargaining power of buyers	Bargaining power of suppliers	Threat of substitute products and services	Barriers to entry	Rivalry amongst existing competitors
• The power of online buyers is increased since they have a wider choice and prices are likely to be forced down through increased customer knowledge and price transparency, i.e. switching behaviour is encouraged. • For a B2B organisation, forming electronic links with customers may deepen a relationship and it may increase switching costs, leading to 'soft lock-in'.	• When an organisation purchases, the bargaining power of its suppliers is reduced since there is wider choice and increased commoditisation due to e-procurement and digital marketplaces. • The reverse arguments also apply as for bargaining power of buyers. • Commoditisation reduces differentiation of suppliers. • E-procurement can reduce switching costs, although use of preferred systems can achieve lock-in.	• Substitution is a significant threat since new digital products or extended products can be more readily introduced. • The introduction of new substitute products and services should be carefully monitored to avoid erosion of market share. • Internet technology enables faster introduction of products and services. • This threat is related to new business models which are covered in a later section in this chapter.	• Barriers to entry are reduced through lower fixed costs, enabling new competitors, particularly for retailers or service organisations that have traditionally required a high-street presence or a mobile sales force. • New entrants must be carefully monitored to avoid erosion of market share. • Internet services are easier to imitate than traditional services, making it easy for 'fast followers'. The cost of establishing a recognised, trusted brand is a major barrier or cost of entry and new entrants have to encourage customers to overcome switching costs.	• The Internet encourages commoditisation which makes it less easy to differentiate products. • Rivalry becomes more intense as product life cycles shorten and lead times for new product development decrease. • The Internet facilitates the move to the global market with potentially lower cost-base also potentially increasing the number of competitors.

market development. These new entrants have been able to succeed in a short time since they do not have the cost of developing and maintaining a distribution network to sell their products and these products do not require a manufacturing base. In other words, the *barriers to entry* are low. However, to succeed, new entrants need to be market leaders in executing marketing and customer service. The costs of achieving these will be high. This competitive threat is less common in vertical business-to-business markets involving manufacture and process industries such as the chemical or oil industry since the investment barriers to entry are much higher.

2 Threat of new digital products

This threat can occur from established or new companies. The Internet is particularly good as a means of providing information-based services at a lower cost. The greatest threats are likely to occur where digital product fulfilment can occur over the Internet, as is the case with delivering share prices, digital media content or software. This may not affect many business sectors, but is vital in some, such as newspaper, magazine and book publishing, and music and software distribution. In photography, Kodak tried to respond to a major threat of reduced demand for traditional film by increasing its range of digital cameras to enhance this revenue stream and by providing online services for customers to print and share digital photographs. Ultimately these approaches weren't successful. The extent of this threat can be gauged by a review of product in the context of Figure 5.10.

3 Threat of new business models

This threat can also occur from established or new companies. It is related to the competitive threat in that it concerns new methods of service delivery. The threats from existing competitors will continue, with the Internet perhaps increasing rivalry since price comparison is more readily possible and the rival digital businesses can innovate and undertake new product development and introduce alternative business and revenue models with shorter cycle times than previously. This again emphasises the need for continual environment scanning. (See the section on business and revenue models in Chapter 2 for examples of strategies that can be adopted in response to this threat.)

Sell-side threats

1 Customer power and knowledge

This is perhaps the single biggest threat posed by electronic trading. The bargaining power of customers is greatly increased when they are using the Internet to evaluate products and compare prices. This is particularly true for standardised products that can be compared through price comparison engines. For commodities, auctions on business-to-business exchanges can also have a similar effect of driving down price. Purchase of some products that have not traditionally been thought of as commodities may become more price-sensitive. This process is known as '**commoditisation**'. Examples of goods that are becoming commoditised are electrical goods and cars. (The issue of online pricing is discussed in Chapter 8.)

In the business-to-business arena, a further issue is that the ease of use of the Internet channel makes it potentially easier for customers to swap between suppliers – switching costs are lower. With a specific EDI (electronic data interchange) link that has to be set up between one company and another, there may be reluctance to change this arrangement (**soft lock-in** due to switching costs). Commentators often glibly say 'online, your competitor is only a mouse click away', but it should be remembered that soft lock-in still exists on the web – there are still barriers and costs to switching between suppliers since, once customers have invested time in understanding how to use a website to select and purchase a particular type of product, they may not want to learn another service.

2 Power of intermediaries

A significant downstream channel threat is the potential loss of partners or distributors if there is a channel conflict resulting from *disintermediation* (Chapter 2, p. 53). The tensions between intermediaries, and in particular aggregators and strategies to resolve them, are shown by the public discussion between direct insurer Direct Line (www.directline.com) and aggregator Moneysupermarket (www.moneysupermarket.com) in Box 5.1.

Commoditisation
The process whereby product selection becomes more dependent on price than differentiating features, benefits and value-added services.

Soft lock-in
Electronic linkages between supplier and customer increase switching costs.

| **Box 5.1** | The balance of power between brands and aggregator sites |

Guardian (2007) reported on an ongoing spat which saw Direct Line disparaging comparison engines like Moneysupermarket, Confused.com and Go Compare in a multi-million-pound TV campaign. It reported Roger Ramsden, strategy director for Royal Bank of Scotland Insurance, which owns Direct Line, as saying:

> *Direct Line has never been available through a middleman of any sort and never will be, and that's what these [comparison] sites are. They are commercial operations*

> *rather than a public service, and the [advertising] campaign is responding to our customers who tell us they are unaware of this and find the sites confusing.*
>
> His assertion is partially true in that although Moneysupermarket covers approximately 80% of the motor insurance market, it does not list quotes from some large insurers such as Norwich Union or other insurers owned by the Royal Bank of Scotland, including Direct Line, Churchill, Privilege and Tesco Personal Finance.
>
> In a counter-argument, Richard Mason, director of Moneysupermarket.com, said that Direct Line's campaign:
>
> *smacks of complete desperation. We are the new kids on the block and Direct Line don't like it. They have lost their market share since we came on the scene – they were in a position where consumers thought they were competitive and kept renewing their policies. They spent hundreds of millions of pounds on advertising. But now consumers can find cheaper alternatives and are doing so in their droves.*
>
> Data from Hitwise (2006) supports Moneysupermarket's position. It suggests this site achieves around a third of its visits from price-sensitive searchers looking to compare by typing generic phrases such as 'car insurance', 'cheap car insurance' and 'compare car insurance'. It has also invested in traditional advertising through TV, print and outdoor media to increase brand awareness.

An additional downstream threat is the growth in number of intermediaries (another form of partner) to link buyers and sellers. These include consumer portals such as Bizrate (www.bizrate.com) and business-to-business exchanges such as EC21 (www.ec21.com). If a company's competitors are represented on a portal while the company is absent or, worse still, they are in an exclusive arrangement with a competitor, this can potentially exclude a substantial proportion of the market.

Buy-side threats

1 Power of suppliers

This can be considered as an opportunity rather than a threat. Companies can insist, for reasons of reducing cost and increasing supply chain efficiency, that their suppliers use electronic links such as EDI or Internet EDI to process orders. Additionally, the Internet tends to reduce the power of suppliers since barriers to migrating to a different supplier are reduced, particularly with the advent of *business-to-business exchanges*. However, if suppliers insist on proprietary technology to link companies, then this creates 'soft lock-in' due to the cost or complexity of changing suppliers.

2 Power of intermediaries

Threats from buy-side intermediaries such as business-to-business exchanges are arguably fewer than those from sell-side intermediaries, but risks arising from using these services should be considered. These include the cost of integration with such intermediaries, particularly if different standards of integration are required for each. They may pose a threat from increasing commission once they are established.

From the review above, it should be apparent that the extent of the threats will be dependent on the particular market a company operates in. Generally the threats seem to be greatest for companies that currently sell through retail distributors and have products that can be readily delivered to customers across the Internet or by parcel. Case study 5.1 highlights how one company has analysed its competitive threats and developed an appropriate strategy.

Co-opetition

Co-opetition
Interactions between
competitors and
marketplace
intermediaries which
can mutually improve
the attractiveness of a
marketplace.

Jelassi and Enders (2008) note that while the five forces framework focuses on the negative effects that market participants can have on industry attractiveness, the positive interactions between competitors within an industry can have a positive effect on profitability. Examples of interactions encouraged through co-opetition include:

- Joint standards setting for technology and other industry standards. For example, competitors within mobile commerce can encourage development of standard approaches such as 3G, which potential customers can be educated about, and which make it easier to enable customer switching.
- Joint developments for improving product quality, increasing demand or smoothing e-procurement. For example, competing car manufacturers DaimlerChrysler, Ford and General Motors set up Covisint, a common purchasing platform (Chapter 7).
- Joint lobbying for favourable legislation, perhaps through involvement in trade associations.

Competitor analysis

**Competitor analysis
for digital business**
Review of digital
business services offered
by existing and new
competitors and adoption
by their customers.

Competitor analysis is a key aspect of digital business situation analysis. It is also a key activity in producing a digital marketing plan which will feed into the digital business strategy (which is described in more detail in Chapter 8).

Resource-advantage mapping

Core competencies
Resources, including
skills or technologies,
that provide a particular
benefit to customers.

Customer value
Value dependent on
product quality, service
quality, price and
fulfilment time.

It is useful to map the internal resource strengths against external opportunities, to identify, for example, where competitors are weak and can be attacked. To identify internal strengths, definition of core competencies is one approach. Lynch (2000) explains that core competencies are the resources, including knowledge, skills or technologies, that provide a particular benefit to customers, or increase customer value relative to competitors. Customer value is defined by Deise *et al.* (2000) as dependent on product quality, service quality, price and fulfilment time. So, to understand core competencies we need to understand how the organisation is differentiated from competitors in these areas. Benchmarking e-commerce services of competitors (as described in Chapter 8) is important here. The cost-base of a company relative to its competitors' is also important since lower production costs will lead to lower prices. Lynch (2000) argues that core competencies should be emphasised in objective setting and strategy definition.

Strategic objectives

Strategic objectives
Statement and
communication of an
organisation's mission,
vision and objectives.

Defining and communicating an organisation's strategic objectives is a key element of any strategy process model since (1) the strategy definition and implementation elements of strategy must be directed at how best to achieve the objectives, (2) the overall success will be assessed by comparing actual results against objectives and taking action to improve strategy, and (3) clear, realistic objectives help communicate the goals and significance of a digital business initiative to employees and partners. Note that objective setting typically takes place in parallel with strategic analysis, defining a vision and strategy for digital business as part of an iterative process.

Figure 5.11 highlights some of the key aspects of strategic objective setting that will be covered in this section.

Defining vision and mission

Corporate vision is defined in Lynch (2000) as 'a mental image of the possible and desirable future state of the organisation'. Defining a specific company vision for digital business is

| Figure 5.11 | Elements of strategic objective setting for the digital business |

helpful since it contextualises digital business in relation to a company's strategic initiatives (business alignment) and its marketplace. It also helps give a long-term emphasis on digital business transformation initiatives.

Vision or mission statements for digital businesses are a concise summary defining the scope and broad aims of digital channels in the future, explaining how they will contribute to the organisation and support customers and interactions with partners. Jelassi and Enders (2008) explain that developing a mission statement should provide definition of:

Vision or mission statement
A summary of the scope and broad aims of an organisation.

- Business scope (where?). Markets including products, customer segments and geographies where the company wants to compete online.
- Unique competencies (how?). A high-level view of how the company will position and differentiate itself in terms of digital business products or services.
- Values (why?). Less commonly included, this is an emotional element which can indicate what inspires the organisation or its digital business initiative.

Many organisations have a top-level mission statement which is used to scope the ambition of the company and to highlight the success factors for the business. Some examples are shown in Box 5.2.

| Box 5.2 | Example vision or mission statements from digital businesses |

Here are some examples from well-known digital businesses featured in the case studies in this book. Assess how well they meet the criteria we have discussed for an effective vision statement.

Amazon.com Our vision is to be earth's most customer-centric company, to build a place where people can come to find and discover anything they might want to buy online.

Dell Dell listens to customers and delivers innovative technology and services they trust and value.

eBay eBay pioneers communities built on commerce, sustained by trust, and inspired by opportunity. eBay brings together millions of people every day on a local, national and international basis through an array of websites that focus on commerce, payments and communications.

Facebook Facebook is a social utility that helps people communicate more efficiently with their friends, family and co-workers. The company develops technologies that facilitate the sharing of information through the social graph, the digital mapping of people's real-world social connections. Anyone can sign up for Facebook and interact with the people they know in a trusted environment.

Google Google's mission is to organise the world's information and make it universally accessible and useful.

Vision statements can also be used to define a longer-term picture of how the channel will support the organisation through defining strategic priorities. The disadvantage with brief vision statements such as those shown in Box 5.2 is that they can be generic, so it is best to make them as specific as possible by:

- referencing key business strategy and industry issues and goals;
- referencing aspects of online customer acquisition, conversion or experience and retention;
- making them memorable through acronyms or mnemonics;
- linking through to objectives and strategies to achieve them through high-level goals.

Dell expands on the simple vision outlined in the box to explain:

Our core business strategy is built around our direct customer model, relevant technologies and solutions, and highly efficient manufacturing and logistics; and we are expanding that core strategy by adding new distribution channels to reach even more commercial customers and individual consumers around the world. Using this strategy, we strive to provide the best possible customer experience by offering superior value; high-quality, relevant technology; customized systems and services; superior service and support; and differentiated products and services that are easy to buy and use.

Here's a real example of a digital vision statement for a multichannel company that I was working for, summarised to staff as:

$1 \times 2 \times 3$

- Largest online audience share (No. 1) in Europe by XXXX
- By XXXX, 1 in 2 of total sales will be generated online
- 1 in 3 of our people and our customers love our online services and will recommend them to a friend
- 2 in 3 customer service contacts will be electronic by XXXX

You can see that this is simple yet specific enough to link to future targets, unlike many vague mission statements. More generic 'calls to arms' I have heard companies use are '*Digital by Default*', '*Digital First*' and '*Digital DNA*'.

A more detailed vision statement for a multichannel retailer might read:

Our digital channels will make it easy for shoppers to find, compare and select products using a structured approach to merchandising and improving conversion to produce an experience rated as excellent by the majority of our customers.

Different aspects of the vision statement (underlined) can then be expanded upon when discussing with colleagues, for example:

- Digital channels = the website supported by email and mobile messaging.
- Find = improvements to site search functionality.
- Compare and select = using detailed product descriptions, rich media and ratings.
- Merchandising and improving conversion = through delivery of automated merchandising facilities to present relevant offers to maximise conversion and average order value. Additionally, use of structured testing techniques such as AB testing (see Chapter 12) and multivariate testing will be used.
- Experience rated as excellent = we will regularly review customer satisfaction and advocacy against direct competitors and out-of-sector to drive improvements with the website.

Scenario-based analysis
Models of the future environment are developed from different starting points.

Scenario-based analysis is a useful approach to discussing alternative visions of the future prior to objective setting. Lynch (2000) explains that scenario-based analysis is concerned with possible models of the future of an organisation's environment. He says:

The aim is not to predict, but to explore a set of possibilities; scenarios take different situations with different starting points.

Lynch distinguishes qualitative scenario-based planning from quantitative prediction based on demand analysis, for example. In a digital business perspective, scenarios that could be explored include:

1 One player in our industry becomes dominant through use of the Internet.
2 Major customers do not adopt e-commerce due to organisational barriers.
3 **Major disintermediation** (Chapter 2) **occurs in our industry.**
4 B2B marketplaces do or do not become dominant in our industry.
5 New online entrants or substitute products change our industry.

Through performing this type of analysis, better understanding of the drivers for different views of the future will result, new strategies can be generated and strategic risks can be assessed.

Simons (2000a) illustrates the change in thinking required for digital business vision. He reports that to execute Barclays Bank's vision, 'a high tolerance of uncertainty' must be introduced. The group CEO of Barclays (Matt Barrett) at the time said:

our objective is to use technology to develop entirely new business models . . . while transforming our internal structure to make us more efficient and effective. Any strategy that does not achieve both is fundamentally flawed.

In time, it became clear that wholesale changes in business model were often not required. Instead, success in digital business required strategic agility to provide improved propositions through new platforms which could be quickly optimised to make them competitive and maximise customer conversion and customer satisfaction. Speaking at E-metrics 2008, Julian Brewer, Head of Online Sales and Content, Barclays UK Retail Banking, explained how Barclays Bank was using digital technology to make its e-commerce more efficient and effective, including:

- using predictive web analytics (see Chapter 12) which connects online data to effective action by drawing reliable conclusions about current conditions and future events;
- advanced attribution tracking and adoption of different online media across customer touchpoints, in particular paid search such as Google AdWords which accounts for 60% of Barclays' spend on digital media;
- conversion rate optimisation using techniques such as AB and multivariate testing (described in Chapter 12) to boost sales efficiencies.

Benefits in 2006 were a 5% improvement in paid search costs, worth £400k in saved costs (showing that around £8 million annually was spent on paid search and the importance of developing a search engine marketing strategy). An additional 6% of site traffic was generated by applying analytics to improve search marketing, equating to £1.3 million incremental income from this source (Brewer, 2008).

From a sell-side e-commerce perspective, a key aspect of vision is whether the Internet will *complement* or *replace* the company's other channels. It is important to communicate this to staff and other stakeholders.

The impact of digital technology will vary in different industries. Kumar (1999) suggested a way to review the impact when:

1 customer access to the Internet is high (this is now a given in many markets);
2 the Internet can offer a better value proposition than other media (i.e. propensity to purchase online is high);
3 the product can be delivered over the Internet (it can be argued that this is not essential for replacement);
4 the product can be standardised (user does not usually need to view to purchase).

If at least two of Kumar's conditions are met, there may be a replacement effect. For example, purchase of travel services online fulfils criteria 1, 2 and 4. As a consequence, physical outlets for these products may no longer be viable. The extent to which these conditions are met will vary through time, for example as access to the Internet and propensity to purchase online increase. A similar test is de Kare-Silver's (2000) *Electronic Shopping Test* (Chapter 8, p. 352).

A similar vision of the future can be developed for buy-side activities such as procurement. A company can have a vision for how e-procurement and e-enabled supply chain management (SCM) will complement or replace paper-based procurement and SCM.

How can digital business create business value?

As Chaffey and White (2010) have emphasised, much of the organisational value created by digital business is due to more effective use of information and technology to deliver new value-adding services and integrations between processes across the value chain. The strategic importance of business information management in an organisation can be reviewed and communicated as part of the vision using Figure 5.12. This analytic tool, devised by Professor Don Marchand, shows different ways in which digital business can generate value for organisations. The main methods are:

1 **Adding value.** Incremental revenue is delivered through providing better-quality products and services to an organisation's customers. Information can be used to better understand customer characteristics and needs and their level of satisfaction with services. Information is also used to sense and respond to markets. Information about trends in demands, competitor products and activities must be monitored so that organisations can develop strategies to compete in the marketplace. For example, all organisations will use databases to store personal characteristics of customers and details of their transaction history, which shows when they have purchased different products, responded to marketing campaigns or used different online services. Analysis of these databases using data mining can then be used to understand customer preferences and market products that better meet their needs. Companies can use **sense and respond communications**.

> **Sense and respond communications**
> Organisations monitor consumers' preferences indicated by their responses to websites or email communications in order to target them with relevant, personalised and targeted communications.

The classic example of this is the personal recommendations provided by Amazon. The increased use of mobile services is currently a significant way by which companies can generate additional value and they also need to consider how to protect their existing revenue. Digital businesses like Facebook and Google which rely on ad revenue have had to change their advertising services to ensure that their average revenue per user (which we introduced in Chapter 1) from ads is maintained as more users access mobile devices. Other types of business are using mobile to add value. For example, retailers who have a physical presence are using mobile marketing to develop their proposition, as explained in Case study 5.1.

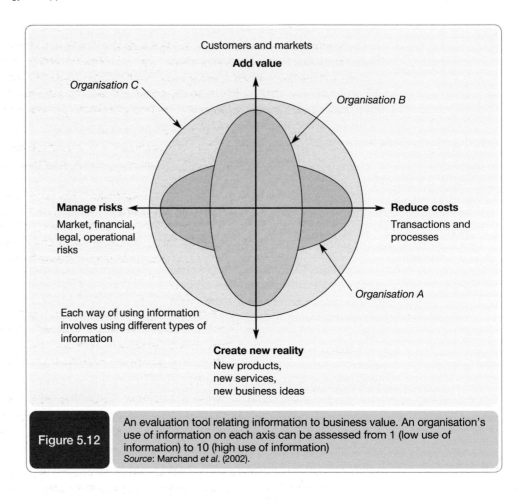

Customers and markets
Add value

Organisation C

Organisation B

Manage risks ← → **Reduce costs**

Market, financial,
legal, operational
risks

Transactions and
processes

Organisation A

Each way of using information
involves using different types of
information

Create new reality
New products,
new services,
new business ideas

Figure 5.12	An evaluation tool relating information to business value. An organisation's use of information on each axis can be assessed from 1 (low use of information) to 10 (high use of information) *Source*: Marchand *et al.* (2002).

2 **Reduce costs.** Cost reduction through information is achieved through making the business processes shown in Figure 10.2 more efficient. Efficiency is achieved through using information to source, create, market and deliver services using fewer resources than previously. Technology is applied to reduce paperwork, reduce the human resources needed to operate the processes through automation and improve internal and external communications.

3 **Manage risks.** Risk management is a well-established use of information within organisations. Marchand (1999) notes how risk management has created functions and professions such as finance, accounting, auditing and corporate performance management.

4 **Create new reality.** Marchand uses the expression 'create new reality' to refer to how information and new technologies can be used to innovate, to create new ways in which products or services can be developed. This is particularly apt for digital business.

Case Study 5.1	Debenhams creates value through mobile commerce

A 2013 survey by EPiserver (an eXommerce and digital marketing solutions company) has revealed that the British high street retailer, Debenhams, was rated best at mobile commerce. 'Mobile Commerce: What Consumers Really Want' looked at customer expectations of thirty of the UK's biggest retailers' apps and mobile sites. It was found that Debenhams scored top marks, as it was able to meet consumer expectations rated at 90%. It was followed by Argos and Expedia, who both scored 85%, and Tesco, whose retail facilities scored 80%.

Debenhams showcases its mobile value proposition at www.debenhams.com/mobile. It offers a choice of a mobile site and apps on iOS (iPhone and iPad), Android (Google Play), Nokia and Blackberry.

You can see from the facilities available on Apple App Store that it has developed specific elements of mobile value to fit the context of use whether at home or in-store and personalise to the individual user:

1 Buy items from the Debenhams app for delivery to home or for collection in-store.
2 Use the barcode scanner like a virtual assistant in-store to see further product details and reviews, to buy items from the phone or to save items to your wish list or gift lists.

3 Personalise the app with 'My Debenhams' by selecting the categories and sizes relevant to you.
4 View product pages with full product details, multiple image views and zoom images, and product reviews and ratings.
5 Add favourite items to a wish list and be notified when stock runs low.
6 Share products with friends on Facebook or by email.
7 Watch the latest videos from Debenhams TV and shop for the products in each video.
8 Find the nearest store with the store finder and check store guides for details of ranges and opening times.
9 Receive alerts on the latest trends and products from Debenhams, and exclusive special offers.

Objective setting

Efficiency
Minimising resources or time needed to complete a process: 'doing the thing right'.

Effectiveness
Meeting process objectives, delivering the required outputs and outcomes: 'doing the right thing'.

An effective strategy development process links general goals, strategies and more specific objectives and performance measures. One method of achieving this linkage is through tabulation, as shown for a fictitious company in Table 5.6. Each of the objectives should have specific KPIs to ensure progress to the more general goal and also a timeframe in which to achieve these objectives. Despite the dynamism of digital business, some of the goals that require processes to be re-engineered cannot be achieved immediately. Prioritisation of goals can help in communicating the digital business vision to staff and also when allocating resources to achieve the strategy. As with other forms of strategic objectives, digital business objectives should be *SMART* (Box 5.3) and include both efficiency and effectiveness measures.

Put simply, **efficiency** is 'doing the thing right' – it defines whether processes are completed using the least resources and in the shortest time possible. **Effectiveness** is 'doing the

Table 5.6	Goals, strategies and objectives, performance indicators for an example B2B company (in order of priority)

Goals	Strategies to achieve goals	Specific objectives (key performance indicators (KPIs))
1 Develop revenue from new geographical markets	1 Create e-commerce facility for standard products and assign agents to these markets	1 Achieve combined revenue of £1m by year-end. Online revenue contribution of 70%
2 Increase revenue from smaller-scale purchases from retailers	2 Create e-commerce facility for standard products	2 Increase sales through retailers from 15% to 25% of total by year 2. Online revenue contribution of 30%
3 Ensure retention of key account customers	3 Attain soft lock-in by developing extranet facilities and continued support from sales reps	3 Retain five key account customers. Online revenue contribution of 100% from these five
4 Improve efficiency of sourcing raw materials	4 Develop e-procurement system	4 Reduce cost of procurement by 5% by year-end, 10% by year 2. Achieve 80% of purchasing online
5 Reduce time to market and costs for new product development	5 Use collaboration and project management tools	5 Reduce cost and time to market by average of 10% by year 3
6 Protect and increase efficiency of distributor and partner network	6 Create partner extranet and aim for paperless support	6 Reduce cost of sales in each of five main geographical markets by 30%

Box 5.3	**Setting SMART objectives**

SMART is used to assess the suitability of objectives set to drive different strategies or the improvement of the full range of business processes.

(i) **Specific.** Is the objective sufficiently detailed to measure real-world problems and opportunities?

(ii) **Measurable.** Can a quantitative or qualitative attribute be applied to create a metric?

(iii) **Actionable.** Can the information be used to improve performance?

(iv) **Relevant.** Can the information be applied to the specific problem faced by the manager?

(v) **Time-related.** Does the measure or goal relate to a defined timeframe?

The key performance indicators column in Table 5.6 gives examples of SMART digital business objectives.

---

right thing' – conducting the right activities, producing the required outputs and outcomes, and applying the best strategies for competitive advantage. When organisations set goals for digital business and e-commerce, there is a tendency to focus on the efficiency metrics but such measures often do not capture the overall value that can be derived. Effectiveness measures will assess how many customers or partners are using the digital business services and the incremental benefits that contribute to profitability. For example, an airline such as BA.com could use its digital channel services to reduce costs (increased efficiency), but could be facing a declining share of online bookers (decreased effectiveness). Effectiveness may also refer to the relative importance of objectives for revenue generation through online sales and improving internal process or supply chain efficiency. It may be more effective to focus on the latter. Some examples of sell-side e-commerce SMART performance indicators for an online flower business are shown in Mini case study 5.2.

Mini Case Study 5.2	**Arena Flowers controls its growth through key performance indicators**

Arena Flowers (Figure 5.13) is an online florist based in London. The business was incorporated in July 2006 and went live with a transactional website in September 2006. The company delivered £2 million net sales in year one and broke even within the first 12 months of trading. At the time of the interview it is forecasting sales of £4 million in year two and making a healthy profit. The head of design and development Sam Barton sees opportunities to keep growing both sales and profitability at a similar rate going forward through various initiatives. For example, the company has developed a Facebook application that provides 15% of the site traffic – an opportunity that has been missed by many of its more established rivals.

Average order values (AOVs) have developed from an initial £30 and have grown month on month. The current level is £42. Ways of increasing AOV have included options to add a vase, make a deluxe bouquet and buy Prestat's chocolates alongside the flowers.

The essence of the Arena Flowers proposition is to cut out all middlemen and buy direct from growers. There are no 'relay' fees and, because of its high stock turnover, it gets fresh flowers in daily and they go straight to the customer, rather than sitting in a hot shop window. Arena Flowers offers free delivery on all its products and was the first online florist in the UK to offer FFP-accredited, ethically sourced flowers. That has been a good 'unique selling point' and enables Arena to offer something different from other suppliers such as supermarkets.

Source: E-consultancy (2008b) Digital business Briefing. Arena Flowers' Sam Barton on web design and development, E-newsletter interview 12 March 2008.

Figure 5.13   Arena Flowers
Source: www.arenaflowers.com.

Performance management systems are needed to monitor, analyse and refine the performance of an organisation. (The use of systems such as web analytics in achieving this is covered in Chapter 12.)

The online revenue contribution

Online or Internet revenue contribution (ORC)
An assessment of the direct or indirect contribution of the Internet to sales, usually expressed as a percentage of overall sales revenue.

By considering the demand analysis, competitor analysis and factors such as those defined by Kumar (1999), an Internet or **online revenue contribution (ORC)** objective can be set. This states the percentage of company revenue directly generated through online transactions. An indirect online contribution can be stated where the sale is influenced by the online presence but purchase occurs using conventional channels. Online revenue contribution objectives can be specified for different types of products, customer segments and geographic markets. They can also be set for different digital channels such as web or mobile commerce.

Conversion modelling for sell-side e-commerce

Conversion marketing
Using marketing communications to maximise conversion of potential customers to actual customers.

Experienced e-commerce managers build conversion or waterfall models of the efficiency of their web marketing to assist with forecasting future sales. Using this approach, the total online demand for a service in a particular market can be estimated and then the success of the company in achieving a share of this market determined. **Conversion marketing** tactics can then be created to convert as many potential site visitors as possible into actual visitors and then convert these into leads, customers and repeat customers. Box 5.4 gives further details.

So, to assess the potential impact of digital channels it is useful to put in place tracking or research which assesses the cross-channel conversions at different stages in the buying process. For example, phone numbers which are unique to the website can be used as an indication of the volume of callers to a contact centre influenced by the website. This insight can then be built into budget models of sales levels such as that shown in Figure 5.14. This shows that of the 100,000 unique visitors in a period we can determine that 5,000 (5%) may actually become offline leads.

E-channel service contribution

The proportion of service-type processes that are completed using electronic channels.

The **e-channel service contribution** gives an indication of the proportion of service-type processes that are completed using electronic channels. Examples include e-service (proportion of customers who use web self-service), e-procurement (proportion of different types of purchases bought online) and administrative process facilities used via an intranet or extranet.

Box 5.4	Conversion modelling

A widely quoted conceptual measurement framework based on the industrial marketing concepts of purchasing decision processes and hierarchy of effects models, which can be applied for conversion marketing, was proposed by Berthon *et al.* (1998). The model assesses efficiency of offline and online communications in drawing the prospect through different stages of the buying decision. The main measures defined in the model are the following ratios:

1 **Awareness efficiency:** target web-users/all web-users.
2 **Locatability or attractability efficiency:** number of individual visits/number of seekers.
3 **Contact efficiency:** number of active visitors/number of visits.
4 **Conversion efficiency:** number of purchases/number of active visits.
5 **Retention efficiency:** number of repurchases/number of purchases.

This model is instructive for improving Internet marketing within an organisation since these different types of conversion efficiency are key to understanding how effective online and offline marketing communications are in achieving marketing outcomes.

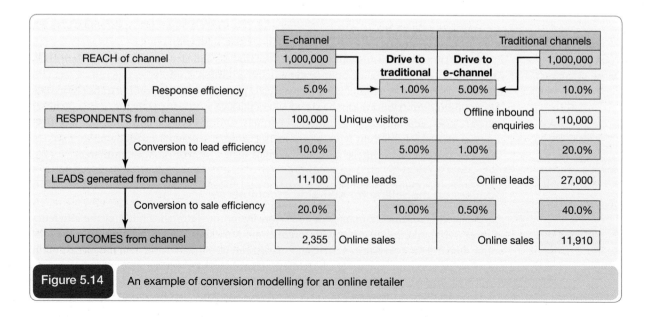

Figure 5.14	An example of conversion modelling for an online retailer

Figure 5.15   Research Online Purchase Online example
Source: Google.

ROPO

Research Online Purchase Offline.

ROPO is a term coined to describe research published by Google (2010) meaning 'Research Online Purchase Offline'. This study reviewed the role of the Internet in the decision process for mobile and broadband contracts involving the Vodafone website and stores in Germany based on a panel of 16,000 web users and questionnaires about their intent and purchase. For both of these services, the contract was signed online by around a third of the audience. However, a significant proportion signed the contract offline. The matrix presented in Figure 5.15 is a good framework for evaluating and summarising multichannel behaviour since it also shows the situation where research is offline and purchase occurs online. This behaviour is particularly common for products such as, in this case, handsets, where consumers want to evaluate their purchase online.

An example of objective setting within a particular company, then at a relatively early stage of adoption, is provided by Case study 5.2 and for different industries in Activity 5.2.

Case Study 5.2   Setting the Internet revenue contribution at Sandvik Steel

Sandvik Steel, a company selling into many international markets, provides a good illustration of how Internet revenue contribution can be used to set objectives for different geographical markets.

When dot-com mania was at its height, so-called old economy companies, such as Sweden's Sandvik, tended to be overshadowed as the brash new online stars took the limelight.

But now that the collapse of Internet and other technology stocks has injected a harsh dose of reality into the stock market and business scene, many established names are back in favour again.

As the experience of Sandvik, founded in 1862, shows, skilful use of the Internet can lead to huge improvements in links with customers and suppliers, bringing considerable cost savings.

Based north of Stockholm in Sandviken, the company's activities seem remote from the virtual world of the Internet. It makes cutting tools, speciality steels and mining and construction equipment.

However, the group is a long-time advocate of IT. Its annual IT budget is some SKr1bn.

'We first formulated our IT strategy in 1969,' says Clas Ake Hedstrom, the chief executive. 'We didn't foresee the Internet.' Only recently, he adds, has IT moved from serving the company to benefiting customers.

Transferring its 30-year-old IT experience to the age of the web requires more than a deep understanding of technology, says Arnfinn Fredriksson, director of Internet business development at the group's Coromant tooling business.

'The major challenges are not IT and systems, but "soft" things such as attitudes, insights and getting people to understand and accept that this is part of their daily work.' This means focussing hard on business needs and cutting through the Internet hype.

Sandvik Steel, the speciality steel operation, also goes beyond transactions to find solutions for its customers. Its extranet enables users to obtain worldwide stock information, catalogues and training aids, as well as take part in online discussions.

At both Coromant and Sandvik Steel, digital business activities are mainly directed towards enhancing links with customers. 'Customer value comes when our product is used, not when it is purchased,' Mr Fredriksson says.

Thus, Coromant allows customers not only to buy tools over the web but also to design their own products – within parameters set by Coromant – and receive advice on how best to use them.

Choosing the right cutting tools and using them effectively can save around 10% of the total cost of manufactured components. The digital business strategy had to take account of this.

It also had to avoid channel conflict, the bypassing of its traditional sales outlets. Most Coromant tools are sold directly to customers, but 40% goes through resellers. Moreover, there are big regional variations: more than 80% of sales in the Nordic region are direct, while most North American sales are indirect.

The company's approach was to work with the traditional sales channels. 'So many companies try to bypass traditional channels and lose sales and relationships,' Mr Fredriksson says.

It is the relationship with the customer – including greater personalisation and an extended reach into global markets – which will be the most important pillar of its digital business strategy in the long term, he says.

This is what provides real competitive advantage. Shifting existing customers to the Internet, winning new ones and saving costs are also important. But other companies will be doing the same.

At present, only a small part of Coromant's orders are transacted over the web. Nordic countries are leading the way. Around 20% of all orders from Denmark are online and 31% of those from Sweden.

The proportion in the US, however, is only 3%, since most business goes through distributors and is conducted by EDI (electronic data interchange), the pre-Internet means of e-commerce.

Over the next six months, the company hopes to raise the US figure to 40%. Mr Fredriksson hopes that in two years, between 40 and 50% of total orders will come via the web.

To enhance its online service to customers, Coromant plans to offer each one a personalised web page. This will enable the company to offer new products, materials and advice on productivity improvements. Training will also be part of this expanded web offering, which Coromant aims to have in place later this year.

For both Coromant and Sandvik Steel, the value of the web lies in strengthening and expanding relationships with customers. In the case of Coromant, with some 25,000 standard products, there are numerous customers buying low volumes. With Sandvik Steel, however, a small number of customers buy a high volume of products.

'Our aims were to have 200 key customers using the extranet by a fixed time; and a confirmation from at least 80% of key customers that they consider the extranet to be a major reason to deal with Sandvik,' says Annika Roos, marketing manager at Sandvik Steel.

By putting the Internet at the heart of its business, the Sandvik group intends to penetrate deeply into the minds and ambitions of its customers. 'The challenge is not just doing digital business, it is becoming a digital business,' she adds.

Source: Andrew Fisher, Sandvik Steel, 4 June 2001.

Questions

1 Summarise Sandvik Steel's digital business strategy as described in the article.
2 Suggest why the proportion of online purchases varies in the different countries in which Sandvik trades.

Activity 5.2	Assessing the significance of digital channels

Purpose

To illustrate the issues involved with assessing the suitability of the Internet for e-commerce.

Activity

For each of the following products and services, assess the suitability of the Internet for delivery of the product or service and position it on the grid in Figure 5.16, with justification, and make estimates in Table 5.7 for the direct and indirect online revenue

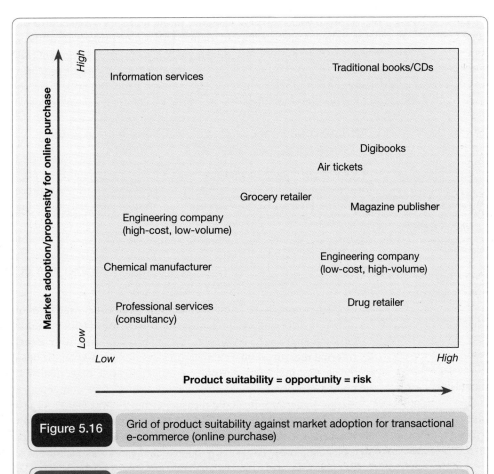

Figure 5.16 Grid of product suitability against market adoption for transactional e-commerce (online purchase)

Table 5.7 Vision of online revenue contribution for a B2B company

Products/services	Now	2 years	5 years	10 years
Example: Cars, US	5%	10%	25%	50%
Direct online sales	50%	70%	90%	95%
Indirect online sales				
Financial services				
Direct online sales				
Indirect online sales				
Clothing				
Direct online sales				
Indirect online sales				
Business office supplies				
Direct online sales				
Indirect online sales				

contribution in two, five and ten years' time for different products in your country. Choose specific products within each category.

No suggested answer supplied.

An equivalent buy-side measure to the online revenue contribution is the proportion of procurement that is achieved online. This can be broken down into the proportions of electronic transactions for ordering, invoicing, delivery and payment (as described in Chapter 7). Deise *et al.* (2000) note that the three business objectives for procuring materials and services should be improving supplier performance, reducing cycle time and cost for indirect procurement, and reducing total acquisition costs. Metrics can be developed for each of these.

The balanced scorecard approach to objective setting

Balanced scorecard
A framework for setting and monitoring business performance. Metrics are structured according to customer issues, internal efficiency measures, financial measures and innovation.

Integrated metrics such as the balanced scorecard have become widely used as a means of translating organisational strategies into objectives and then providing metrics to monitor the execution of the strategy. Since the balanced business scorecard is a well-known and widely used framework, it can be helpful to define objectives for digital business in the categories below.

It was popularised in a *Harvard Business Review* article by Kaplan and Norton (1993). In part, it was a response to over-reliance on financial metrics such as turnover and profitability and a tendency for these measures to be retrospective rather than looking at future potential.

The main areas of the balanced scorecard are:

1 **Customer concerns.** These include time (lead time, time to quote, etc.), quality, performance, service and cost. Example measures from Halifax Bank from Olve *et al.* (1999): satisfaction of mystery shoppers visiting branches and from branch customer surveys.
2 **Internal measures.** Internal measures should be based on the business processes that have the greatest impact on customer satisfaction: cycle time, quality, employee skills, productivity. Companies should also identify critical core competencies and try to guarantee market leadership. Example measures from Halifax Bank: ATM availability (%), conversion rates on mortgage applications (%), arrears on mortgage (%).
3 **Financial measures.** Traditional measures such as turnover, costs, profitability and return on capital employed. For publicly quoted companies this measure is key to shareholder value. Example measures from Halifax Bank: gross receipts (£), mortgage offers (£), loans (£).
4 **Learning and growth:** innovation and staff development. Innovation can be measured by change in value through time (employee value, shareholder value, percentage and value of sales from new products).

For each of these four areas management teams will define objectives, specific measures, targets and initiatives to achieve these targets. For some companies, such as Skandia Life, the

---

Table 5.8	An example of a digital business balanced scorecard for a B2B company

Scorecard component	Objective metric
Customer perspective	Customer acquisition rate (leads generated online) Customer retention rate (% using online services) Customer satisfaction index
Process	Average time for new product development (months) Procurement lead times Sales cycle lead time
Financial	Revenue contribution from online channel Margin from online channel Cost savings from partners using different e-services
Innovation and employee development	Number of new product releases per year Training hours attended per employee: target 30 hours/year

balanced scorecard provides a framework for the entire business strategy process. Olve *et al.* (1999) make the point that a further benefit of the scorecard is that it does not solely focus on outcomes, but also considers performance drivers that should positively affect the outcomes. For example, investments in technology and in employee training are performance drivers.

More recently, it has been suggested that it provides a useful tool for aligning business and IS strategy; see, for example, der Zee and de Jong (1999).

Table 5.8 outlines how the balanced scorecard could be deployed in a B2B organisation to support its digital business strategy. (A more detailed example is given in Chapter 8.)

Strategy definition

Strategy definition
Formulation, review and selection of strategies to achieve strategic objectives.

The **definition of strategy** is driven by the objectives and vision referred to in the previous sections. As strategy is formulated based on vision and objectives, so it is necessary to frequently revisit and revise them.

In this section the key strategic decisions faced by a management team developing digital business strategy are reviewed. For each of the areas of strategy definition that we cover, managers will want to generate different options, review them and select them as shown in Figure 5.17. We start by considering the sell-side-related aspects of digital business and then review the buy-side-related aspects.

Selection of digital business strategy options

When reviewing digital business strategy options, there will be a range of possible strategies and digital business service alternatives to be evaluated. Limited resources will dictate that only some applications are practical. Typical options for an organisation which has a brochureware site might be to implement:

- transactional e-commerce facility;
- online catalogue facility;

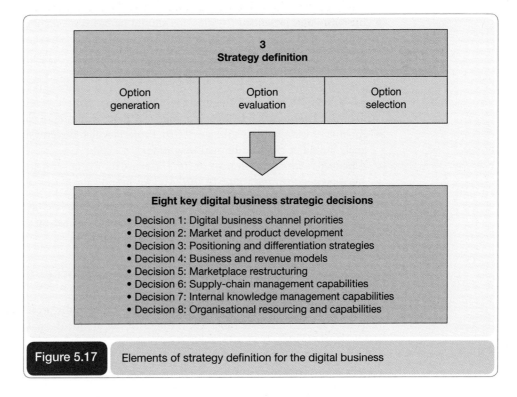

Figure 5.17   Elements of strategy definition for the digital business

- e-CRM system – lead-generation system;
- e-CRM system – customer service management;
- e-CRM system – personalisation of content for users;
- e-procurement system for office supplies;
- partner relationship management extranet for distributors and agents;
- social network or customer forum.

Portfolio analysis can be used to select the most suitable digital business projects. Daniel *et al.* (2001) suggest that potential e-commerce opportunities should be assessed for the value of the opportunity to the company against its ability to deliver. Similarly, McDonald and Wilson (2002) suggest that evaluations should be based on a matrix of attractiveness to customer against attractiveness to company.

Tjan (2001) also suggested a matrix approach of viability (return on investment) against fit (with the organisation's capabilities) for Internet applications. He presents the following metrics for assessing viability of each application. For 'fit' these are:

- Alignment with core capabilities.
- Alignment with other company initiatives.
- Fit with organisational structure.
- Fit with company's culture and value.
- Ease of technical implementation.

For 'viability' the metrics are:

- Market value potential (return on investment).
- Time to positive cash flow.
- Personnel requirement.
- Funding requirement.

When I created the E-consultancy (2008a) report I recommended a form of portfolio analysis (Figure 5.18) as the basis for benchmarking current e-commerce capabilities and identifying strategic priorities. The five criteria used for organisational value and fit (together with a score or rating for their relative effectiveness) are:

- *Business value generated (0–50).* This should be based on *incremental* financial benefits of the project. These can be based on conversion models showing estimated changes in number of visitors attracted (new and repeat customers), conversion rates and results produced. Consideration of lifetime value should occur here.
- *Customer value generated (0–20).* This is a 'softer' measure which assesses the impact of the delivered project on customer sentiment, for example would they be more or less likely to recommend a site, would it increase their likelihood to visit or buy again?
- *Alignment with business strategy (0–10).* Projects which directly support current business goals should be given additional weighting.
- *Alignment with digital strategy (0–10).* Likewise for digital strategy.
- *Alignment with brand values (0–10).* And for brand values.

The cost elements for potential digital business projects are based on requirements for internal people resource (cost/time), agency resource (cost/time), set-up costs and technical feasibility, ongoing costs and business and implementation risks.

Decision 1: Digital business channel priorities

The digital business strategy must be directed according to the priority of different strategic objectives such as those in Table 5.6. If the priorities are for the *sell-side downstream channel,* as are objectives 1 to 3 in Table 5.6, then the strategy must be to direct resources at these objectives. For a B2B company that is well known in its marketplace worldwide and cannot offer products to new markets, an initial investment on *buy-side upstream channel* e-commerce and value chain management may be more appropriate.

Figure 5.18 Matrix for evaluating digital business strategy alternatives
Source: E-consultancy (2008a).

For multichannel businesses with a physical and online sales presence, digital business channel strategy priorities can be summarised in the words of Gulati and Garino (2000): '*Getting the right mix of bricks and clicks*'. This expression usually refers to sell-side e-commerce. The general options for the mix of 'bricks and clicks' are shown in Figure 5.19. This summarises an organisation's commitment to e-commerce and its implication for traditional channels. The other strategy elements that follow define the strategies for how the target online revenue contribution will be achieved.

A similar figure was produced by de Kare-Silver (2000) who suggests that strategic e-commerce alternatives for companies should be selected according to the percentage of the target market who can be persuaded to migrate to use the e-channel and the benefits to the company of encouraging migration in terms of anticipated sales volume and costs for initial customer acquisition and retention.

Although being Internet-only is impractical for many businesses, companies are moving along the curve in this direction. In the UK, the Automobile Association and British Airways have closed the majority of their retail outlets since orders are predominately placed via the Internet or by phone. But both of these companies still make extensive use of the phone channel since its interactivity is needed for many situations. Essentially they have followed a 'bricks and clicks' approach; indeed, most businesses require some human element of service.

The transition to a service that is clicks-only is unlikely for the majority of companies. Where a retailer is selling a product such as a mobile phone or electronic equipment, many consumers naturally want to compare the physical attributes of products or gain advice from the sales person. Even dot-coms such as lastminute.com have set up a call centre and experimented with a physical presence in airports or train stations since this helps them to reach a key audience and has benefits in promoting the brand. Another example of the importance

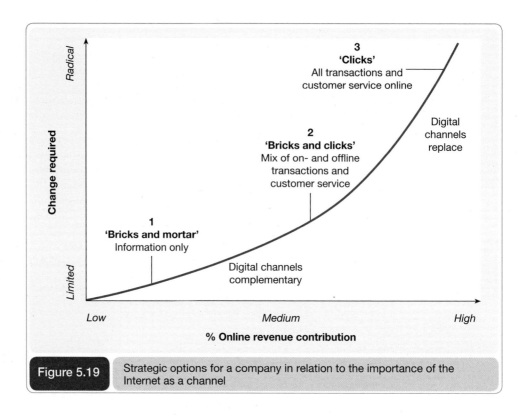

| Figure 5.19 | Strategic options for a company in relation to the importance of the Internet as a channel |

of a physical presence related by Tse (2007) is this quote from the CEO of Charles Tyrwhitt, a London-based shirtmaker that makes heavy use of the online channel:

> *The picture of its Jermyn Street flagship store on our website is worth as much as having the store (in the shoppers' native countries). Jermyn Street meant something to the customers, especially those in the US.*

The diversification of digital platforms

Today, it's no longer simply a question of investment in digital vs traditional channels; businesses have to decide on the prioritisation of investments and support for different digital platforms (introduced in Chapter 1). Decisions have to be taken about which combination of platforms has the highest level of consumer (or channel partner) usage and will give the best commercial rewards (the options are shown in Table 5.9). It's not practical and won't give the best returns to allocate investments individually. Some key prioritisation decisions that need to be taken include:

- Investment and support for desktop vs mobile platform.
- Within mobile platforms, investment in mobile-optimised desktop sites against responsive designs (as discussed in Chapter 3 and 4) and platforms supported for mobile sites (e.g. iOS smartphone and tablet, Android, Windows and Blackberry).
- Investment in social media platform support, i.e. Facebook vs Google+ vs LinkedIn vs Twitter vs Pinterest and other social networks.

Decision 2: Market and product development strategies

Deciding on which markets to target through digital channels to generate value is a key strategic consideration. Managers of digital business strategy have to decide whether to use new technologies to change the scope of their business to address new markets and new products. As for Decision 1, it is a balance between fear of the do-nothing option and fear of poor

Table 5.9	Examples of 'right-channelling' applications

Right-channelling strategy example	Application and tactics to achieve channel adoption	Typical sector and company examples
1 Sell to and serve SMEs through online channels.	Using the Internet for sales and service through an extranet to lower-sales-volume SME customers who cannot be serviced direct through account managers. Customer channel adoption encouraged by convenience and lack of other options.	B2B. Hardware: Dell, software services such as MessageLabs Antivirus; anti-spam and email management services. Commercial banks such as HSBC.
2 Account-managed relationships with larger companies offline, either direct or through partner companies.	The converse of strategy 1. Using face-to-face and phone meetings with large, high-sales-volume clients through account managers. Customer channel adoption encouraged by personal service and capability to negotiate service levels and buying options.	B2B. Account managers at Dell for larger clients. Bank 'relationship managers' who discuss financial management with 'higher-wealth' individuals.
3 Encourage consumers to buy through online channels.	Customers buying online have lower cost of sale. However, there is a risk of customers evaluating competitor offerings and lower conversion rates during the sales process. Customer channel adoption encouraged by reduced 'Internet prices' compared to offline channels and explaining proposition of more choice, more convenience.	Insurance companies such as DirectLine.com and morethan.com. Retailers such as Tesco and Comet.
4 Provide offline conversion to sale options during sales process.	Offer a phone call-back or live chat facility from within web sales process since strategy 3 may involve lower conversion rates than an in-store or call-centre customer interaction. Customer channel adoption encouraged by providing clear contact numbers on-site (but not on home page, when part-way through customer journey).	Insurance companies such as DirectLine.com and morethan.com.
5 Migrate customers to web self-service.	Customers are encouraged to use the web to manage their accounts which results in a lower cost-to-serve for the company. Email notification and e-billing. Customer channel adoption encouraged by marketing campaigns which encourage e-channel adoption, possibly including savings on service.	B2C. Service providers such as mobile phone companies, utility companies, banks and government (tax returns).
6 Selective service levels for different customer types.	With integrated CRM systems (Chapter 9), companies can determine, in real time, the value of customers and then assess where they are placed in queue or which call centre they are directed to.	Most companies would not publicly admit to this, but the practice is common amongst financial services companies, mobile phone network providers and some pureplays.

return on investment for strategies that fail. The model of Ansoff (1957) is still useful as a means for marketing managers to discuss market and product development using electronic technologies. (This decision is considered from a digital marketing perspective in Chapter 8.) The market and product development matrix (Figure 5.20) can help identify strategies to grow sales volume through varying what is sold (the product dimension on the x-axis) and who it is sold to (the market dimension on the y-axis). Specific objectives need to be set for sales generated via these strategies, so this decision relates closely to that of objective setting.

1 **Market penetration.** This strategy involves using digital channels to sell more existing products into existing markets. The Internet has great potential for achieving sales growth or maintaining sales by the market penetration strategy. Figure 5.20 indicates some of the main ways in which the Internet can be used for market penetration:

- **Market share growth** – companies can compete more effectively online if they have websites that are efficient at converting visitors to sale and mastery of online marketing communications techniques.
- **Customer loyalty improvement** – companies can increase their value to customers and so increase loyalty by migrating existing customers online by adding value to existing products, services and brand by developing their online value proposition (see Decision 6).
- **Customer value improvement** – the value delivered by customers to the company can be increased by increasing customer profitability by decreasing cost to serve (and so price to customers) and at the same time increasing purchase or usage frequency and quantity.

2 **Market development.** Here online channels are used to sell into new markets, taking advantage of the low cost of advertising internationally without the necessity for a supporting sales infrastructure in the customer's country.

	Market development strategies	**Diversification strategies**
New markets	Use Internet for targeting: • *New geographic markets* • *New customer segments*	Using the Internet to support: • Diversification into related businesses • Diversification into unrelated businesses • Upstream integration (with suppliers) • Downstream integration (with intermediaries)
Existing markets	**Market penetration strategies** Use Internet for: • *Market share growth* – compete more effectively online • *Customer loyalty improvement* – migrate existing customers online and add value to existing products, services and brand • *Customer value improvement* – increase customer profitability by decreasing cost to serve and increase purchase or usage frequency and quantity	**Product development strategies** Use Internet for: • *Adding value to existing products* • *Developing digital products* (new delivery/usage models) • *Changing payment models* (subscription, per use, bundling) • *Increasing product range* (especially e-retailers)

Market growth (y-axis label)

Existing products   *New products*
Product growth

Figure 5.20   Using the Internet to support different growth strategies

Existing products can also be sold to new market segments or different types of customers. This may happen simply as a by-product of having a website. The Internet may offer further opportunities for selling to market sub-segments that have not been previously targeted. Many companies have found that the audience and customers of their website are quite different from their traditional audience, so this analysis should inform strategy.

3 **Product development.** The web can be used to add value to or extend existing products for many companies. For example, a car manufacture can potentially provide car performance and service information via a website. But truly new products or services that can be delivered by the Internet apply only for some types of products. These are typically digital media or information products. Retailers can extend their product range and provide new bundling options online also.

4 **Diversification.** In this sector, new products are developed which are sold into new markets. The Internet alone cannot facilitate these high-risk business strategies, but it can facilitate them at lower costs than have previously been possible. The options include:

- **Diversification into related businesses** (for example, a low-cost airline can use the website and customer emails to promote travel-related services).
- **Diversification into unrelated businesses** – again the website can be used to promote less-related products to customers.
- **Upstream integration** – with suppliers – achieved through data exchange between a manufacturer or retailer with its suppliers to enable a company to take more control of the supply chain.
- **Downstream integration** – with intermediaries – again achieved through data exchange with distributors such as online intermediaries.

The danger of diversification into new product areas is illustrated by the fortunes of Amazon, which was infamous for limited profitability despite multi-billion-dollar sales. Phillips (2000) reported that for books and records, Amazon sustained profitability through 2000, but it is following a strategy of product diversification into toys, tools, electronics and kitchenware. This strategy gives a problem through the cost of promotion and logistics to deliver the new product offerings. Amazon is balancing this against its vision of becoming a 'one-stop shop' for online shoppers.

Target marketing strategy
Evaluation and selection of appropriate segments and the development of appropriate offers.

A closely related issue is the review of how a company should change its **target marketing strategy**. This starts with segmentation, or identification of groups of customers sharing similar characteristics. Targeting then involves selectively communicating with different segments. (This topic is explored further in Chapter 8.) Some examples of customer segments that are commonly targeted online include:

- *The most profitable customers* – using the Internet to provide tailored offers to the top 20% of customers by profit may result in more repeat business and cross-sales.
- *Larger companies (B2B)* – an extranet could be produced to service these customers, and increase their loyalty.
- *Smaller companies (B2B)* – large companies are traditionally serviced through sales representatives and account managers, but smaller companies may not warrant the expense of account managers. However, the Internet can be used to reach smaller companies more cost-effectively.
- *Particular members of the buying unit (B2B)* – the site should provide detailed information for different interests which supports the buying decision, for example technical documentation for users of products, information on savings from e-procurement for IS or purchasing managers and information to establish the credibility of the company for decision makers.
- *Customers who are difficult to reach using other media* – an insurance company looking to target younger drivers could use the web as a vehicle for this.

- *Customers who are brand-loyal* – services to appeal to brand loyalists can be provided to support them in their role as advocates of a brand as suggested by Aaker and Joachimsthaler (2000).
- *Customers who are not brand-loyal* – conversely, incentives, promotion and a good level of service quality could be provided by the website to try to retain such customers.

Decision 3: Positioning and differentiation strategies

Once segments to target have been identified, organisations need to define how to best position their online services relative to competitors according to four main variables: product quality, service quality, price and fulfilment time.

Chaston (2000) argued that there are four options for strategic focus to position a company in the online marketplace which remain relevant today. He says that these should build on existing strengths, but can use the online facilities to enhance the positioning as follows:

- *Product performance excellence.* Enhance by providing online product customisation or incorporating reviews and detailed product information as with the example of Appliances Online site (www.appliancesonline.com).
- *Price performance excellence.* Offer competitive pricing, of which Amazon is the best-known example. With its buying power and lack of store network, Amazon aims to be price competitive. However, it doesn't aim to deliver this across its whole product range, rather the best-selling products. It has greater productivity on less popular 'long-tail' products.
- *Transactional excellence.* A site such as software and hardware e-tailer Dabs.com (www.dabs.com) offers transactional excellence through combining personalisation and pricing information with dynamic availability information on products.
- *Relationship excellence.* This is related to the creation of an exceptional brand experience (which is described by Figure 11.8). It comprises emotional, design-influenced factors and rational factors based on ease of use, content quality and performance. For example, personalisation features enable customers to review sales order history and place repeat orders such as on the B2B Euroffice (www.euroffice.co.uk) and RS Components site (www.rswww.com). The complexity of the interplay between these factors means that it is important to use the user research and feedback techniques covered in Chapters 11 and 12 to understand the quality of the experience as perceived by customers.

Online value proposition (OVP)
A statement of the benefits of online services reinforces the core proposition and differentiates from an organisation's offline offering and those of competitors.

Marketing mix
Different factors that summarise the customer propositions offered by a business. Marketing mix refers to the 4 core Ps of Price, Product (including branding, Place and Promotion and the 7Ps of the extended Marketing Mix which include People, Process and Physical evidence.

These positioning options remain relevant since they share much in common with Porter's competitive strategies of cost leadership, product differentiation and innovation (Porter, 1980). Porter has been criticised, since many commentators believe that to remain competitive it is necessary to combine excellence in all of these areas. It can be suggested that the same is true for sell-side e-commerce and that the experience of the brand is particularly important. These are not mutually exclusive strategic options, rather they are prerequisites for success.

The type of criteria on which customers judge performance can be used to benchmark the proposition. Table 5.10 summarises criteria typically used for benchmarking. Significantly, the retailers with the best overall score at the time of writing, such as Tesco (grocery retail), smile (online banking) and Amazon (books), are also perceived as the market leaders and are strong in each of the scorecard categories. These ratings have resulted from strategies that enable the investment and restructuring to deliver customer performance.

Plant (2000) also identified four different positional e-strategic directions which he refers to as technology leadership, service leadership, market leadership and brand leadership. The author acknowledges that these are not exclusive. It is interesting that this author does not see price differentiation as important, rather he sees brand and service as important to success online.

Table 5.10	Example scorecard criteria for rating e-tailers

Scorecard category	Scorecard criteria
1 Ease of use	• Demonstrations of functionality • Simplicity of account opening and transaction process • Consistency of design and navigation • Adherence to proper user interaction principles • Integration of data providing efficient access to information commonly accessed by consumers
2 Customer confidence	• Availability, depth and breadth of customer service options, including phone, email and branch locations • Ability to resolve accurately and readily a battery of telephone calls and emails sent to customer service, covering simple technical and industry-specific questions • Privacy policies, service guarantees, fees and explanations of fees • Each ranked website is monitored every 5 minutes, 7 days a week, 24 hours a day for speed and reliability of both public and secure (if available) areas • Financial strength, technological capabilities and independence, years in business, years online and membership of trade organisations
3 On-site resources	• Availability of specific products • Ability to transact in each product online • Ability to seek service requests online
4 Relationship services	• Online help, tutorials, glossary and frequently asked questions • Advice • Personalisation of data • Ability to customise a site • Reuse of customer data to facilitate future transactions • Support of business and personal needs such as tax reporting or repeated buying • Frequent-buyer incentives
5 Overall cost	• A basket of typical services and purchases • Added fees due to shipping and handling • Minimum balances • Interest rates

In Chapter 8 we look further at how segmentation, positioning and creating differential advantage should be integral to digital marketing strategy. We also see how the differential advantage and positioning of an e-commerce service can be clarified and communicated by developing an **online value proposition (OVP)** based on the 7Ps of the **marketing mix**.

To conclude this section on digital business strategies, complete Activity 5.3 for a different perspective on digital business strategies.

Decision 4: Business, service and revenue models

Business model
A summary of how a company will generate revenue, identifying its product offering, value added services, revenue sources and target customers.

Revenue models
Describe methods of generating income for an organisation.

A further aspect of Internet strategy formulation closely related to product development options is the review of opportunities from new **business** and **revenue models** (first introduced in Chapter 2). Constantly reviewing innovation in services to improve the quality of experience offered is also important for digital businesses. For example, innovations at holiday company Thomson (www.thomson.co.uk) have included: travel guides to destinations, video tours of destinations and hotels, 'build your own' holidays and the use of email alerts with holiday offers. Such innovations can help differentiate from competitors and increase loyalty to a brand online.

| Activity 5.3 | Digital business strategies for a B2C company |

Purpose

To evaluate the suitability of different digital business strategies.

Introduction

Many industry analysts such as the Gartner Group, Forrester, IDC Research and the 'big four' consulting firms are suggesting digital business strategies. Many of these will not have been trialled extensively, so a key management skill becomes evaluating suggested approaches from reports and then selecting appropriate measures.

Questions

1 Review the summaries of the approaches recommended by IDC Research below (Picardi, 2000). Which elements of these strategies would you suggest are most relevant to a B2C company?

2 Alternatively, for a company with which you are familiar, review the eight strategy decisions within this section.

Summary of IDC approach to digital business strategies

Picardi (2000) identified six strategies for sell-side e-commerce. The approaches are interesting since they also describe the timeframe in which response is required in order to remain competitive.

1 **Attack e-tailing.** As suggested by the name, this is an aggressive competitive approach that involves frequent comparison with competitors' prices and then matching or bettering them. As customers increasingly use shopping comparison sites, it is important that companies ensure their price positioning is favourable. Shopping sites such as Rakuten.com (www.rakuten.com/) and Even Hotels (http://evenhotels.com) can now find the prices of all comparable items in a category but also guarantee that they will beat the lowest price. These sites have implemented real-time adjustments in prices with small increments based on price policy algorithms that are simply not possible in traditional retailing.

2 **Defend e-tailing.** This is a strategic approach that traditional companies can use in response to 'attack e-tailing'. It involves differentiation based on other aspects of brand beyond price. The IDC research quoted by Picardi (2000) shows that while average prices for commodity goods on the Internet are generally lower, less than half of all consumers purchase the lowest-priced item when offered more information from trusted sources, i.e. price dispersion may actually increase online. Reasons why the lowest price may not always result in the sale are:
   - Ease of use of site and placing orders (e.g. Amazon One-Click makes placing an order with Amazon much easier than using a new supplier).
   - Ancillary information (e.g. book reviews contributed by other customers enhances Amazon service).
   - After-sales service (prompt, consistent fulfilment and notification of dispatch from Amazon increases trust in the site).
   - Trust with regard to security and customer privacy.

   These factors enable Amazon to charge more than competitors and still achieve the greatest sales volume of online booksellers. In summary, trust becomes the means of differentiation and loyalty. As a result, price comparison sites are being superseded by sites that independently rate the overall service, such as Compuware Performance Management (www.compuware.com), or use customers' opinions to rate the service, such as Bizrate (www.bizrate.com) and Epinions (www.epinions.com).

3 **E2E (end-to-end) integration.** This is an efficiency strategy that uses the Internet to decrease costs and increase product quality and shorten delivery times. This strategy is achieved by moving towards an automated supply chain (Chapter 8) and internal value chain.

4 **Market creation.** Picardi (2000) defines market creation as 'the business of supplying market clearing and ancillary services in cyberspace, resulting in the creation of an integrated ecosystem of suppliers'. In tangible terms, this strategy involves integrating and continuously revising supply chains with market-maker sites such as business-to-business exchanges (Chapter 8).

5 **Customer as designer.** This strategy uses the technology to enable customers to personalise products, again as a means of differentiation. This approach is particularly suited to information products, but manufactured products such as cars can now be specified to a fine degree of detail by the customer.

6 **Open-source value creation.** The best-known example of this is the creation and commercial success of the operating system Linux by over 300,000 collaborators worldwide. Picardi (2000) suggests that organisations will make more use of external resources to solve their problems.

Answers to activities can be found at www.pearsoned.co.uk/chaffey

Evaluating new models and approaches is important since if companies do not review opportunities to innovate then competitors and new entrants certainly will. Andy Grove of Intel famously said: '*Only the paranoid will survive*', alluding to the need to review new revenue opportunities and competitor innovations. A willingness to test and experiment with new business models is also required. Dell is another example of a tech company that regularly reviews and modifies its business model, as shown in Mini case study 5.3. Companies at the bleeding edge of technology such as Google and Facebook constantly innovate through acquiring other companies.

Early (first) mover
An early entrant into the marketplace.

These companies also invest in internal research and development and continuously develop and trial new services.

Mini Case Study 5.3	Innovation in the Dell business model

One example of how companies can review and revise their business model is provided by Dell Computer. Dell gained **early-mover** advantage in the mid-1990s when it became one of the first companies to offer PCs for sale online. Its sales of PCs and peripherals grew from the mid-1990s with online sales of $1 million per day to 2000 sales of $50 million per day. Based on this success it has looked at new business models it can use in combination with its powerful brand to provide new services to its existing customer base and also to generate revenue through new customers. In September 2000, Dell announced plans to become a supplier of IT consulting services through linking with enterprise resource planning specialists such as software suppliers, systems integrators and business consulting firms. This venture enabled Dell's Premier B2B customer extranet to be integrated into the procurement component of ERP systems such as SAP and Baan, thus avoiding the need for rekeying and reducing costs. Dell Business Solutions is now an important contributor to its business.

In a separate initiative, Dell launched a B2B marketplace (formerly www.dellmarketplace.com) in mid-2000 aimed at discounted office goods and services procurements including PCs, peripherals, software, stationery and travel. This strategic option did not prove sustainable, but it was able to test a model and then move on – it closed the marketplace after just 4 months! This was Dell's dot-com disaster. However, it does offer Dell Outlet, a relatively low-cost purchase method for returned, refurbished PCs.

More recently, in 2007, Dell launched IdeaStorm (www.ideastorm.com), a site encouraging user participation where anyone can suggest new products and features which can be voted on. Importantly, Dell 'closes the loop' through a separate 'Ideas in Action' section where it updates consumers on actions taken by the company. As well as improvements to customer service, it has explained how it has introduced systems with a non-Windows Linux operating system in response to suggestions on IdeaStorm. In 2008 Dell also had a raft of online options to engage with customers and other partners, including:

- A corporate blog, Direct2Dell (www.direct2dell.com), which is 'a blog about Dell products, services and customers'.
- Studio Dell (www.studiodell.com) 'designed to help you get the most from your Dell experience'.
- A brand channel on YouTube (www.youtube.com/DellVlog).
- Dell Community/Dell Conversations (www.dell.com/conversations) 'interactive ways for you to share and learn with others and with us'.
- Premier (http://premier.dell.com), which is a customised procurement portal (extranet) for larger businesses.

Less radical changes to revenue models that are less far-reaching may nevertheless be worthwhile. For example:

- Transactional e-commerce sites (for example Tesco.com and lastminute.com) can sell advertising space or run co-branded promotions on-site or through their email newsletters or lists to sell access to their audience to third parties.
- Retailers or media owners can sell-on white-labelled services through their online presence such as ISP, email services or photo-sharing services.
- Companies can gain commission through selling products which are complementary (but not competitive to their own). For example, a publisher can sell its books through an affiliate arrangement with an e-retailer.
- Brands who are manufacturers can sell direct or encourage purchase through integrating a marketplace or 'where to buy' service. For example, consumer and B2B manufacturer 3M now offers a store for consumers, but not for its full range of products (Mini case study 5.4). Consumer pet-food brand Royal Canin now offers the option to buy online via its local stores in a marketplace. Similarly, phone manufacturer Nokia has developed an online marketplace for purchase of its products from different phone operators. These systems require deep integration between manufacturer and retailer systems.

Decision 5: Marketplace restructuring

We saw in Chapter 2 that electronic communications offer opportunities for new market structures to be created through *disintermediation*, *reintermediation* and *countermediation* within a marketplace. The options for these should be reviewed.

Decision 6: Supply chain management capabilities

(Supply chain management and e-procurement are discussed further in Chapters 6 and 7.) The main digital business strategy decisions that need to be reviewed are:

- How should we integrate more closely with our suppliers, for example through creating an extranet to reduce costs and decrease time to market?
- Which types of materials and interactions with suppliers should we support through e-procurement?
- Can we participate in online marketplaces to reduce costs?

Mini Case Study 5.4   3M innovates in the digital marketplace

3M was founded in 1902 at the Lake Superior town of Two Harbors, Minnesota, when five businessmen set out to mine a mineral deposit for grinding-wheel abrasives. But the deposits proved to be of little value, and the new Minnesota Mining and Manufacturing Co. was formed to focus on sandpaper products.

Today, 3M is a diversified technology company known for product innovation, with a worldwide presence in consumer and office; display and graphics; electro and communications; healthcare; industrial and transportation; and safety, security and protection services. In 2005 it had a turnover of $21 billion and 69,000 employees. With 3M products sold in nearly 200 countries and over 60% of its turnover occurring outside its US base, 3M has risen to the challenge of using e-channels to distribute its products and services worldwide.

The following are some of the strategies it has pursued to use online channels to change its relationship with its marketplace.

Sell-side

- *Disintermediation (sell-direct) strategy.* 3M has traditionally sold through retail partners, but now offers some products direct through an e-store (www.3mselect.co.uk).
- *Create a new online intermediary (countermediation) strategy.* This is a strategy 3M has not followed due to its diversity of products. Instead it has focussed on its destination site, www.3m.com, which has a tool to help potential customers to research and select products. Localised content is available for many countries, with 'Where to Buy' links to relevant suppliers in these countries. As an example of a countermediation strategy, in the banking sector, banks such as Barclays have created new portals, such as ClearlyBusiness (www.clearlybusiness.com), in this case to reach small, start-up businesses online.
- *Partner with new online or existing intermediary or retailer strategy.* 3M has integrated its product catalogue with online office retailers such as Euroffice (www.euroffice.co.uk). If a customer is on the 3M site and reviewing a product, when they select the 'Where to Buy' option they are linked directly to the relevant page on Euroffice which enables them to buy. Data is exchanged between 3M and Euroffice using XML data feeds.
- *Do nothing!* This is not a realistic strategy for any company, but 3M has gradually made the transition to digital business over a ten-year period. The strength of existing distribution has meant that 3M had to decide when customer usage of the web became such that it needed to offer new online services. This point, of course, varies in different markets.

Buy-side

In keeping with its innovative market position, 3M was one of the first organisations to adopt e-procurement on a large scale. Starting in the mid-1990s, 3M used different e-procurement products to help manage the enormous task of integrating the buying of a wide range of products from suppliers in many countries. (This gave the typical benefits of e-procurement we will see in Chapter 7.) 3M used Ariba's Enterprise Spend Management (ESM) solutions for sourcing and procurement across the entire business.

- *Disintermediation (buy direct, bypassing distributors).* 3M has used its sourcing system to buy more services direct from suppliers. In keeping with exploring new business models and services enabled through digital business, 3M has developed its own HighJump's RFID-enabled product suite (www.highjumpsoftware.com) to help its clients with complex, global supply chains to source, manufacture, develop and distribute products more readily.
- *Buy through new intermediaries such as B2B exchanges.* 3M was involved in the pilot of the Dell B2B marketplace launched in 2000 as a supplier, but it did not prove successful. The use of these marketplaces has not become widespread (as we will see in Chapter 7) since using direct e-procurement with suppliers has proved more sustainable.
- Do nothing!

Decision 7: Internal knowledge management capabilities

Organisations should review their internal digital business capabilities and in particular how knowledge is shared and processes are developed. Questions to ask are:

- How can our intranet be extended to support different business processes such as new product development, customer and supply chain management?
- How can we disseminate and promote sharing of knowledge between employees to improve our competitiveness?

(We reviewed intranet management issues in Chapter 3 and we explore knowledge management issues in more detail in Chapter 10 in the 'Focus on' section.)

Decision 8: Organisational resourcing and capabilities

Once the digital business strategy decisions we have described have been reviewed and selected, decisions are then needed on how the organisation needs to change in order to achieve the priorities set for digital business.

Different aspects of organisational capability that should be reviewed and changed to improve their ability to deliver digital business strategies are shown in Table 5.11. These include:

- *Strategy process and performance improvement.* The process for selecting, implementing and reviewing digital business initiatives.

Table 5.11	Capability maturity model of e-commerce adoption based on E-consultancy (2008a) research

Level	Strategy process and performance improvement	Structure: Location of e-commerce	Senior management buy-in	Marketing integration	Online marketing focus
1 Unplanned	*Limited* Online channels not part of business planning process. Web analytics data collected, but unlikely to be reviewed or actioned	*Experimentation* No clear centralised e-commerce resources in business. Main responsibility typically within IT	*Limited* No direct involvement in planning and little necessity seen for involvement	*Poor integration* Some interested marketers may experiment with e-communications tools	*Content focus* Creation of online brochures and catalogues. Adoption of first style guidelines
2 Diffuse management	*Low-level* Online referenced in planning, but with limited channel-specific objectives. Some campaign analysis by interested staff	*Diffuse* Small central e-commerce group or single manager, possibly with steering group controlled by marketing. Many separate websites, separate online initiatives, e.g. tools adopted and agencies for search marketing, email marketing. E-communications funding from brands or businesses may be limited	*Aware* Management becomes aware of expenditure and potential of online channels	*Separate* Increased adoption of e-communications tools and growth of separate sites and microsites continues. Media spend still dominantly offline	*Traffic focus* Increased emphasis on driving visitors to site through pay-per-click search marketing and affiliate marketing

Table 5.11	Continued

Level	Strategy process and performance improvement	Structure: Location of e-commerce	Senior management buy-in	Marketing integration	Online marketing focus
3 Centralised management	*Specific* Specific channel objectives set. Web analytics capability not integrated to give unified reporting of campaign effectiveness	*Centralised* Common platform for content management and web analytics. Preferred-supplier list of digital agencies. Centralised, independent e-commerce function, but with some digital-specific responsibilities by country, product or brand	*Involved* Directly involved in annual review and ensures review structure involving senior managers from Marketing, IT, operations and finance	*Arm's-length* Marketing and e-commerce mainly work together during planning process. Limited review within campaigns. Senior e-commerce team-members responsible for encouraging adoption of digital marketing throughout organisation	*Conversion and customer experience focus* Initiatives for usability, accessibility and revision of content management system (including search engine optimisation) are common at this stage
4 Decentralised operations	*Refined* Close cooperation between e-commerce and marketing. Targets and performance reviewed monthly. Towards unified reporting. Project debriefs	*Decentralised* Digital marketing skills more developed in business with integration of e-commerce into planning and execution at business or country level. E-retailers commonly adopt direct-channel organisation of which e-commerce is one channel. Online channel profit and loss accountability sometimes controlled by businesses or brands, but with central budget for continuous e-communications spend (search, affiliates, e-communications)	*Driving* Performance Involved in review at least monthly	*Partnership* Marketing and e-commerce work closely together through year. Digital media spend starts to reflect importance of online channels to business and consumers	*Retention focus* Initiatives on analysis of customer purchase and response behaviour and implementation of well-defined touch strategies with emphasis on email marketing. Loyalty drivers well known and managed
5 Integrated and optimised	*Multichannel process* The interactions and financial contribution of different channels are well	*Integrated* Majority of digital skills within business and e-commerce team commonly positioned	*Integral* Less frequent in-depth involvement required. Annual planning and six-monthly	*Complete* Marketing has full complement of digital marketing skills, but calls on specialist resource from	*Optimisation focus* Initiatives to improve acquisition, conversion and retention

Table 5.11	Continued

Level	Strategy process and performance improvement	Structure: Location of e-commerce	Senior management buy-in	Marketing integration	Online marketing focus
	understood and resourced and improved accordingly	within marketing or direct sales operation. 'Front-end' systems development skills typically retained in e-commerce team	or quarterly review	agencies or central e-commerce resource as required. Online potential not constrained by traditional budgeting processes	according to developments in access platform and customer experience technologies. May use temporary multidisciplinary team to drive performance

- *Structure.* Location of e-commerce and the technological capabilities through the software, hardware infrastructure used and staff skills.
- *Senior management buy-in.* Digital business strategies are transformational, so require senior management sponsorship.
- *Marketing integration.* We have stressed the importance of integrated customer and partner communications through right-channelling. Staff members responsible for technology and marketing need to work together more closely to achieve this.
- *Online marketing focus.* Strategic initiatives will focus on the three core activities of customer acquisition (attracting site visitors), conversion (generating leads and sales) and retention (encouraging continued use of digital channels).
- *Partnering with other organisations.* Some services will be best delivered through partnering with other companies.

Within a business there are many issues for changing internal capabilities; these options are considered in more depth in Chapter 10, 'Change management'.

Strategy implementation

Strategy implementation
Planning, actions and controls needed to achieve strategic goals.

Strategy implementation includes all tactics used to achieve strategic objectives. The main tactics and actions required are summarised in Figure 5.21. These actions are described in more detail in the remainder of Part 2 and in Part 3, as indicated in the figure.

Chapter 10 focusses on approaches to managing the change associated with digital business implementation. Figure 10.2 summarises different implementation marketing activities that need to be completed by an online retailer structured according to customer acquisition, conversion and retention activities.

Failed digital business strategies

Unsurprisingly, there are few companies that want to have their mistakes detailed in public, but the names of failures are well known: Boo (clothing retail – see Case study 5.3), eToys (retail), CDNow (retail), Peapod (online grocer), VerticalNet (online B2B marketplaces) and Mondus (B2B marketplaces). Many other Internet companies have failed or merged, and

4 **Strategy implementation**		
Planning	Execution	Control

Implementation issues in later chapters

- Supply chain management strategies (Chs 7 and 8)
- Digital marketing strategies (Chs 8 and 9)
- Planning, scheduling and change management (Ch 10)
- Digital business analysis and design (Ch 11)
- Implementation, maintenance and control (Ch 12)

Figure 5.21 Elements of strategy implementation for the digital business

many existing companies invested in e-commerce without achieving a satisfactory return on investment. (The mini case study on Ecomum at the end of Chapter 2 gives a recent example of an e-retail failure with serious consequences.)

What then can be learnt from these? There are usually more fundamental problems resulting in failure of Internet companies. Miller (2003) has reviewed these misjudgements from an analysis of many Internet failures. He believes that the biggest mistake companies made was to '*massively overestimate the speed at which the marketplace would adopt dot com innovations*'. Furthermore, it was assumed that new innovations would rapidly displace existing product offerings, for example online grocery shopping would rapidly replace conventional grocery shopping. Even Tesco.com, one of the most successful online retailers, achieves a single-digit percentage of its retail sales from the Internet – and this has taken several years to achieve. Other reasons mentioned by Miller include:

- *Timing errors:* for example, services for download of digital entertainment that were offered before high-speed broadband Internet access was widely available. The learning is that insufficient research had been conducted about demand for online products.
- *Lack of creativity:* many services copied existing business models, or other online retail services. The learning is that insufficient research had been conducted about competitor differentiators and capabilities and whether these would be sufficient to encourage consumers to switch providers.
- *Offering free services:* many services were offered free to gain site visitors and registration, and it then became difficult to encourage payment for marginally better services. This is a difficult balance to get right.
- *Over-ambition:* to achieve investor funding amongst many competing companies, some entrepreneurs exaggerated the demand for their products and the growth.

Beyond these reasons, we can also point to classic mistakes that start-up and existing businesses have always made. These include:

- *Situation analysis* – insufficient rigour in researching demand for new products and competitive forces.
- *Objective setting* – setting unrealistic objectives or, worse still, not setting clear objectives.

- *Strategy definition* – poor decisions about business and revenue models, target markets, product differentiation, pricing, distribution, etc.
- *Implementation* – problems with customer service quality, infrastructure and change management (described in Chapter 10).

Digital business strategy implementation success factors for SMEs

An assessment of success factors for digital business strategy implementation in SMEs has been produced by Jeffcoate *et al.* (2002). They suggest these 11 critical success factors, which can also be usefully applied to larger organisations:

1 **Content.** The effective presentation of products or services.
2 **Convenience.** The usability of the website.
3 **Control.** The extent to which organisations have defined processes that they can manage.
4 **Interaction.** The means of relationship building with individual customers.
5 **Community.** The means of relationship building with groups of like-minded individuals or organisations.
6 **Price sensitivity.** The sensitivity of a product or service to price competition on the Internet.
7 **Brand image.** The ability to build up a credible brand name for e-commerce.
8 **Commitment.** A strong motivation for using the Internet and the will to innovate.
9 **Partnership.** The extent to which an e-commerce venture uses partnerships (value chain relationships) to leverage Internet presence and expand its business.
10 **Process improvement.** The extent to which companies can change and automate business processes.
11 **Integration.** The provision of links between underlying IT systems in support of partnership and process improvement.

As a counterpoint to Case study 5.3, consider Mini case study 2.4 which shows how SME Firebox.com has survived and prospered.

Case Study 5.3	Boo hoo – learning from the largest European dot-com failure

Context

'*Unless we raise $20 million by midnight, boo.com is dead.*' So said boo.com CEO Ernst Malmsten on 18 May 2000. Half the investment was raised, but this was too little, too late, and at midnight, less than a year after its launch, Boo.com closed. The headlines in the *Financial Times* the next day read: '*Boo.com collapses as investors refuse funds. Online sports retailer becomes Europe's first big Internet casualty.*'

The Boo.com case remains a valuable case study for all types of business, since it doesn't only illustrate the challenges of managing e-commerce for a clothes retailer, but rather highlights failings in e-commerce strategy and management that can be made in any type of organisation.

Company background

Boo.com was founded in 1998 by three Swedish entrepreneurs, Ernst Malmsten, Kajsa Leander and Patrik Hedelin. Malmsten and Leander had previous business experience in publishing where they created a specialist publisher and had also created an online bookstore, bokus.com, which in 1997 became the world's third largest book e-retailer behind Amazon and Barnes & Noble. They became millionaires when they sold the company in 1998. At Boo.com, they were joined by Patrik Hedelin who was also the financial director at bokus, and at the time they were perceived as experienced European Internet entrepreneurs by the investors who backed them in their new venture.

Company vision

The vision for Boo.com was for it to become the world's first online global sports retail site. It would be a European brand, but with a global appeal. Think of it as a sports and fashion retail version of Amazon. At launch it would open its virtual doors in both Europe and America with a view to 'amazoning the sector'. Note, though, that Amazon did not launch simultaneously in all markets. Rather it became established in the US before providing local European distribution.

The boo.com brand name

According to Malmsten *et al.* (2001), the boo brand name originated from film star Bo Derek, best known for her role in the movie *10*. The domain name 'bo.com' was unavailable, but adding an 'o', they managed to procure the domain 'boo.com' for $2,500 from a domain name dealer. According to Rob Talbot, director of marketing for Boo.com, Boo was '*looking for a name that was easy to spell across all the different countries and easy to remember . . . something that didn't have a particular meaning*'.

Target market

The audience targeted by Boo.com can be characterised as 'young, well-off and fashion-conscious' 18-to-24-year-olds. The concept was that globally the target market would be interested in sports and fashion brands stocked by Boo.com.

The market for clothing in this area was viewed as very large, so the thought was that capture of only a small part of this market was required for Boo.com to be successful. The view at this time on the scale of this market and the basis for success is indicated by *New Media Age* (1999):

> The $60b USD industry is dominated by Gen X'ers who are online and according to market research in need of knowing what is in, what is not and a way to receive such goods quickly. If boo.com becomes known as the place to keep up with fashion and can supply the latest trends then there is no doubt that there is a market, a highly profitable one at that, for profits to grow from.

The growth in market was also supported by retail analysts, with Verdict predicting online shopping in the United Kingdom to grow from £600 million in 1999 to £12.5 billion in 2005.

However, *New Media Age* (2005) does note some reservations about this market, saying:

> Clothes and trainers have a high rate of return in the mail order/home shopping world. Twenty year olds may be online and may have disposable income but they are not the main market associated with mail order. To date there is no one else doing anything similar to boo.com.

The Boo.com proposition

In their proposal to investors, the company stated that 'their business idea is to become the world-leading Internet-based retailer of prestigious brand leisure and sportswear names'. They listed brands such as Polo, Ralph Lauren, Tommy Hilfiger, Nike, Fila, Lacoste and Adidas. The proposition involved sports and fashion goods alongside each other. The thinking was that sports clothing has more standardised sizes with less need for a precise fit than designer clothing.

The owners of Boo.com wanted to develop an easy-to-use experience which re-created the offline shopping experience as far as possible. As part of the branding strategy, an idea was developed of a virtual salesperson, initially named Jenny and later Miss Boo. She would guide users through the site and give helpful tips. When selecting products, users could drag them on to models, zoom in and rotate them in 3D to visualise them from different angles. The technology to achieve this was built from scratch along with the stock control and distribution software. A large investment was required in technology, with several suppliers being replaced before launch which was 6 months later than promised to investors, largely due to problems with implementing the technology.

Clothing the mannequin and populating the catalogue was also an expensive challenge. For 2000, about $6 million was spent on content about spring/summer fashion wear. It cost $200 to photograph each product, representing a monthly cost of more than $500,000.

Although the user experience of Boo.com is often criticised for its speed, it does seem to have had that wow factor that influenced investors. Analyst Nik Margolis, writing in *New Media Age* (1999), illustrates this by saying:

> What I saw at boo.com is simply the most clever web experience I have seen in quite a while. The presentation of products and content are both imaginative and offer an experience. Sure everything loads up fast in an office but I was assured by those at boo.com that they will keep to a limit of 8 seconds for a page to download. Eight seconds is not great but the question is will it be worth waiting for?

Of course, today, the majority of European users have broadband, but in the late 1990s the majority were on dial-up and had to download the software to view products.

Communicating the Boo.com proposition

Early plans referred to extensive 'high-impact' marketing campaigns on TV and newspapers. Public relations were important in leveraging the novelty of the concept and human side of the business – Leander was previously a professional model and had formerly been Malmsten's partner. This PR was initially focussed within the fashion and sportswear trade and then rolled out to publications likely to be read by the target audience. The success of this PR initiative can be judged by the 350,000 email pre-registrations who wanted to be notified of launch. For the launch Malmsten *et al.* (2001) explains that '*with a marketing and PR spend of only $22.4 million we had managed to create a worldwide brand*'.

To help create the values of the Boo.com brand, Boom, a lavish online fashion magazine, was created, which required substantial staff for different language versions. The magazine wasn't a catalogue which directly supported sales, rather it was a publishing venture competing with established fashion titles. For existing customers the Look Book, a 44-page print catalogue, was produced which showcased different products each month.

The challenges of building a global brand in months

The challenges of creating a global brand in months are illustrated well by Malmsten *et al.* (2001). After an initial round of funding, including investment from JP Morgan, LMVH Investment and the Benetton family, which generated around $9 million, the founders planned towards launch by identifying thousands of individual tasks, many of which needed to be completed by staff yet to be recruited. These tasks were divided into 27 areas of responsibility familiar to many organisations, including office infrastructure, logistics, product information, pricing, front-end applications, call centres, packaging, suppliers, designing logos, advertising/PR, legal issues, and recruitment. At its zenith, Boo.com had 350 staff, with over one hundred in London and new offices in Munich, New York, Paris and Stockholm. Initially boo.com was available in UK English, US English, German, Swedish, Danish and Finnish, with localised versions for France, Spain and Italy added after launch. The website was tailored for individual countries using the local language and currency and also local prices. Orders were fulfilled and shipped out of one of two warehouses: one in Louisville, Kentucky and the other in Cologne, Germany. This side of the business was relatively successful with on-time delivery rates approaching 100% achieved.

Boo possessed classic channel conflicts. Initially, it was difficult getting fashion and sports brands to offer their products through Boo.com. Manufacturers already had a well-established distribution network through large high-street sports and fashion retailers and many smaller retailers. If clothing brands permitted Boo.com to sell their clothes online at discounted prices, then this would conflict with retailers' interests and would also portray the brands in a negative light if their goods were in an online 'bargain bucket'. A further pricing issue is where local or zone pricing in different markets exists, for example lower prices often exist in the US than Europe and there are variations in different European countries.

Making the business case to investors

Today, it seems incredible that investors were confident enough to invest $130 million in the company and, at the high point, the company was valued at $390 million. Yet much of this investment was based on the vision of the founders to be a global brand and achieve 'first-mover advantage'. Although there were naturally revenue projections, these were not always based on an accurate detailed analysis of market potential. Immediately before launch, Malmsten *et al.* (2001) explain, a meeting was held with would-be investor Pequot Capital, represented by Larry Lenihan who had made successful investments in AOL and Yahoo! The Boo.com management team were able to provide revenue forecasts, but unable to answer fundamental questions for modelling the potential of the business, such as 'How many visitors are you aiming for? What kind of conversion rate are you aiming for? How much does each customer have to spend? What's your customer acquisition cost? And what's your payback time on customer acquisition cost?' When these figures were obtained, the analyst found them to be 'far-fetched' and reputedly ended the meeting with the words. 'I'm not interested. Sorry for my bluntness, but I think you're going to be out of business by Christmas.'

When the site launched on 3 November 1999, around 50,000 unique visitors were achieved on the first day, but only 4 in 1,000 placed orders (a 0.25% conversion rate). This shows the importance of modelling conversion rates accurately. This low conversion rate was also symptomatic of problems with technology. It also gave rise to negative PR. One reviewer explained how he waited: '*Eighty-one minutes to pay too much money for a pair of shoes that I still have to wait a week to get?*' These rates did improve as problems were ironed out – by the end of the week 228,848 visits had resulted in 609 orders with a value of $64,000. In the 6 weeks from launch, sales of $353,000 were made and conversion rates had more than doubled to 0.98% before Christmas. However, a re-launch was required within

6 months to cut download times and to introduce a 'low-bandwidth version' for users using dial-up connections. This led to conversion rates of nearly 3% on sales promotion. Sales results were disappointing in some regions, with US sales accounting for 20% compared to the planned 40%.

The management team felt that further substantial investment was required to grow the business from a presence in 18 countries and 22 brands in November to 31 countries and 40 brands the following spring. Turnover was forecast to rise from $100 million in 2000/01 to $1,350 million by 2003/04 which would be driven by $102.3 million in marketing in 2003/04. Profit was forecast to be $51.9 million by 2003/4.

The end of Boo.com

The end of Boo.com came on 18 May 2000, when investor funds could not be raised to meet the spiralling marketing, technology and wage bills.

Source: Prepared by Dave Chaffey from original sources, including Malmsten *et al.* (2001) and *New Media Age* (1999).

Questions

1 Which strategic marketing assumptions and decisions arguably made Boo.com's failure inevitable? Contrast these with other dot-com-era survivors that are still in business, for example lastminute.com, Egg.com and Firebox.com.

2 Using the framework of the marketing mix, appraise the marketing tactics of Boo.com in the areas of Product, Pricing, Place, Promotion, Process, People and Physical evidence.

3 In many ways, the visions of Boo's founders were 'ideas before their time'. Give examples of e-retail techniques used to create an engaging online customer experience which Boo adopted that are now becoming commonplace.

Focus on　Aligning and impacting digital business strategies

An essential part of any digital business strategy is consideration of how information systems strategy supports change. The importance to digital business success of utilising information systems to manage information is highlighted by Willcocks and Plant (2000) who found in a study of 58 major corporations in the US, Europe and Australasia that the leading companies were astute at *distinguishing the contributions of information and technology, and considering them separately*. They make the point that competitive advantage *comes not from technology, but from how information is collected stored, analysed and applied*.

An established aspect of information systems strategy development is the focus of IS strategy on business impact or alignment. In the **business-alignment** approach, a top-down approach is used to review how information systems can be used to directly support a defined business strategy. Referring to digital business strategy, Pant and Ravichandran (2001) say:

Alignment models focus on aligning the information system's plans and priorities with organizational strategy and business goals.

The importance of alignment is stressed in the digital channel strategic initiative business-case prioritisation investment matrix (Figure 5.7). Linking information systems to objectives and critical success factors (CSF) (Table 5.6) is one approach for using the alignment approach. Another is the use of business systems planning methodology which focusses on deriving data and applications needs by analysis of existing business processes.

In the **business-impacting** approach, a bottom-up approach is used to determine whether there are new opportunities from deploying information systems that may impact positively on a business strategy. New hardware and software technologies are monitored by the IS manager and other managers to evaluate whether they can achieve competitive advantage. Pant and Ravichandran (2001) say:

impact models focus on the potential impact of information technology on organizational tasks and processes and use this as a basis to identify opportunities for deploying information systems.

Business-alignment IS strategy
The IS strategy is generated from the business strategy through techniques such as CSF analysis.

Business-impacting IS strategy
IS strategy analyses opportunities for new technologies and processes to favourably impact the business strategy.

The impacting approach may also involve redesigning business processes to integrate with partners. Sultan and Rohm (2004), based on a study of three organisations, identify different forms of aligning Internet strategies with business goals, with their framework identifying these strategic objectives:

- *Cost reduction and value chain efficiencies.* For example, B2B supplier AB Dick used the Internet to sell printer supplies via the Internet to reduce service calls.
- *Revenue generation.* Reebok uses the Internet for direct licensed sales of products such as treadmills which do not have strong distribution deals.
- *Channel partnership.* Partnering with distributors using extranets.
- *Communications and branding.* Car company Saturn developed the MySaturn site to foster close relationships with customers.

Value chain analysis (Chapter 6, p. 268) can be used for the impact approach. For example, this might identify the need for e-procurement which can be used as part of an effort to reduce costs and increase efficiency as part of business strategy. This technique has merit in that it not only considers internal use of information systems, but also how they can be used to integrate with external organisations such as suppliers, perhaps through innovative methods such as marketplace exchanges.

The impact and alignment techniques need not be mutually exclusive. During initial development of an digital business strategy, a business-alignment approach can be applied to ensure that IS strategy supports digital business strategy. A business-impacting approach is also useful to see which new opportunities IS produce. For instance, managers could consider how a relatively new technology such as workflow management software (Chapter 11, p. 524) can be used to improve efficiency and customer service.

Perhaps the ultimate expression of using IS to impact business performance is through business process re-engineering (considered in Chapter 10).

The application of an impacting or aligning strategy with respect to IS and business strategy is dependent on the importance attached to IS within an organisation.

> **Debate 5.2**
>
> **The influence of IS managers**
>
> *'Board-level representation for IS managers is essential in the digital business era.'*

Elements of IS strategy

Ward and Griffiths (1996) suggest that an IS strategy plan contains three elements:

1 **Business information strategy.** How information will support the business. This will include applications to manage particular types of business.
2 **IS functionality strategy.** Which services are provided?
3 **IS/IT strategy.** Providing a suitable technological, applications and process infrastructure (see Chapter 3).

The advent of digital business clearly increases the strategic importance of information systems resources of an organisation. However, developing an IS strategy to achieve digital business goals is complex because it can be viewed from many different perspectives (Table 5.12). This table is essentially a checklist of different aspects of IS strategy that have to be implemented by an IS manager in the digital business. Many of these aspects are solutions to business and technical problems that are described in Parts 2 and 3 of this book as summarised in the table. We will now consider one of the most important issues facing IS managers in more detail.

Investment appraisal

In the digital business context, investment appraisal can refer to:

1 Overall levels of spending on information systems to support digital business.
2 Decisions about which business applications to invest in (portfolio analysis).
3 Assessment of the cost/benefit for individual applications.

Table 5.12	Different elements of IS strategy		

IS strategy element	What needs to be specified	Approaches to aid selected tactics (applications)	Specification
1 Business contribution perspective (Chapter 5)	How applications achieve digital business objectives	Impact and alignment Portfolio analysis Investment types	Implementation of key systems
2 Information management strategy (Chapter 10)	Strategy for integrated information and knowledge management	Audit information management and knowledge management requirements by internal and external resources Security audit	Committee to standardise company information Enterprise resource planning, knowledge management, data warehousing, intranet and extranet projects
3 Applications perspective (Chapters 3 and 11)	Priorities for applications acquisition	Portfolio analysis Investment appraisal	As above
4 Process perspective (supply chain perspective to digital business) (Chapters 6 and 11)	How do applications and infrastructure support processes and value chain activities? Are new processes required?	Process mapping and analysis Value chain analysis	Enterprise resource planning integrated with transactional e-commerce
5 Departmental (functional) perspective (Chapters 3 and 10)	Which applications support different departments?	Portfolio analysis	Standardisation of applications
6 Infrastructure perspective (Chapters 3 and 11)	Network capacity and service levels	Cost/benefit feasibility study of applications	Managing total cost of ownership Outsourcing
7 Communications perspective (Chapter 9)	Using technology to improve process efficiency and customer service quality	Audit communications volume and complexity Prioritise	Email, groupware and workflow systems Knowledge management
8 User services perspective (Chapter 9)	Helpdesk services for internal and external system users	Audit service levels, impact on business and then prioritise	Outsourcing Enquiry management systems
9 Customer and partner relationship management perspective (Chapters 6 and 9)	Investment in systems for managing customer and partner relationships	Customer relationship management and partner relationship management systems Use of standards for integration: EDI and XML	CRM facilities on website Integration
10 Resourcing perspective (Chapter 10)	How are relevant IS skills acquired and developed?	Skills audit and industry comparison End-user computing	Technology partners Outsourcing Recruitment tactics E-learning and skills transfer
11 Change management perspective (Chapter 10)	How organisational culture and structure change to achieve digital business are managed	Apply existing change management approaches	Risk management Project management
12 Internal integration perspective (Chapters 3 and 11)	Overall applications architecture across the value chain	Analyse information access constraints, rekeying	Enterprise resource planning
13 External integration perspective (Chapters 3 and 11)	How are links between internal applications and partners managed?	Analyse ease of setting up links, prioritise	Outsourcing to systems integrator Standardisation through ERP Integration of IS systems with buy- and sell-side intermediaries
14 Legal constraints approach (Chapter 4)	How do we ensure company stays within international legal and ethical constraints?	Seek specialist advice	Specialist lawyers and privacy statements

Decisions about which business applications to invest in

A portfolio analysis such as that illustrated for a B2B company in Figure 5.7 can also be used to decide priorities for application by selecting those that fall within the strategic and turnaround categories for further investment. Relative priorities and the amount of investment in different applications can also be assisted if priorities for digital business objectives have been assigned, as is the case with Table 5.4.

Traditionally investments in information systems have been categorised according to their importance and contribution to the organisation. For example, Robson (1997) describes four types of BIS investment:

1 **Operational value investment.** These investments are in systems that are key to the day-to-day running of the organisation. Such systems are often valuable in increasing efficiency or reducing costs, but they do not contribute directly to the performance of the business.
2 **Strategic value investment.** Strategic investments will enhance the performance of a business and should help in developing revenue. A customer relationship management system would increase customer loyalty, resulting in additional sales from existing customers.
3 **Threshold investment.** These are investments in BIS that a company must make to operate within a business. They may have a negative return on investment but are needed for competitive survival.
4 **Infrastructure investment.** These can be substantial investments which result in gain in the medium-to-long term. Typically this includes investment in internal networks, electronic links and new hardware.

Companies can prioritise potential information systems investments in the above categories according to their impact on the business. A similar approach is to specify the applications portfolio described in the section on situation analysis. It is evident that priority should be given to applications that fall into the strategic and high-potential categories in Figure 5.7. Now complete Activity 5.4.

Activity 5.4	Digital business investment types

Purpose

To gain an appreciation of how to prioritise IS investments.

Questions

1 Referring to the four investment categories of Robson (1997), discuss in groups which category the following investments would fit into:

(a) E-procurement system.
(b) Transactional e-commerce website.
(c) Contract with ISP to host web server and provide Internet connectivity for staff.
(d) Workflow system to manage complex customer orders (e.g. processing orders).
(e) Upgrading a company network.

2 Assume you had sufficient funds to invest in only two of these options. Which two would you choose?

Answers to activities can be found at www.pearsoned.co.uk/chaffey

---

Productivity paradox
Research results indicating a poor correlation between organisational investment in information systems and organisational performance measured by return on equity.

The productivity paradox

All discussion of investment appraisals in information systems should acknowledge the existence of the **productivity paradox**. Studies in the late 1980s and 1990s summarised by Brynjolfsson (1993) and Strassman (1997) suggested that there is little or no correlation between a company's investment in information systems and its business performance measured in terms of profitability or stock returns. Strassman's work, based on a study of 468 major North American and European firms, showed a random relationship between IT spending per employee and return on equity.

To the present day, there has been much dispute about the reality of the productivity paradox. Carr (2003) suggested that information technology has become commoditised to such an extent that it no longer delivers a competitive advantage. Carr says:

> What makes a resource truly strategic – what gives it the capacity to be the basis for a sustained competitive advantage is not ubiquity, but scarcity. You only gain an edge over rivals by having something that they can't have or can't do. By now the core functions of IT – data storage, data processing and data transport have become available and affordable to all . . . They are becoming costs of doing business that must be paid by all but provide distinction to none.

Carr's argument is consistent with the productivity paradox concept, since although IT investments may help in increasing productivity, this does not necessarily yield a competitive advantage if all competitors are active in making similar IT investments.

Today, most authors, such as Brynjolfsson and Hitt (1998) and Mcafee and Brynjolfsson (2008), refute the productivity paradox and conclude that it results from mismeasurement, the lag occurring between initial investment and payback and the mismanagement of information systems projects. Mcafee and Brynjolfsson (2008) suggest that to use digital technology to support competition the mantra should be:

> 'Deploy, innovate, and propagate': First, deploy a consistent technology platform. Then separate yourself from the pack by coming up with better ways of working. Finally, use the platform to propagate these business innovations widely and reliably. In this regard, deploying IT serves two distinct roles – as a catalyst for innovative ideas and as an engine for delivering them.

More recent detailed studies such as that by Sircar *et al.* (2000) confirm the findings of Brynjolfsson and Hitt (1998). They state that:

> Both IT and corporate investments have a strong positive relationship with sales, assets, and equity, but not with net income. Spending on IS staff and staff training is positively correlated with firm performance, even more so than computer capital.

In conclusion they state:

> The value of IS staff and staff training was also quite apparent and exceeded that of computer capital. This confirms the positions of several authors, that the effective use of IT is far more important than merely spending on IT.

The disproportionate allocation of spend to implementation was highlighted by the *Financial Times* (2003), which said:

> Prof Brynjolfsson and colleagues found that of the $20m total cost of an enterprise resource planning (ERP) system, only about $3m goes to the software supplier and perhaps $1m towards the acquisition of new computers. The $16m balance is spent on business process redesign, external consultants, training and managerial time. The ratio between IT investment and this 'supporting' expenditure varies across projects and companies. But, over a range of IT projects, Prof Brynjolfsson believes that a 10:1 ratio is about right. Returns on these investments commonly take 5 years to materialise.

The 10:1 ratio between total investment in new information management practices and IT also shows that applying technology is only a relatively small part in achieving returns – developing the right approaches to process innovation, business models and change management are more important, and arguably more difficult and less easy to replicate. Some leading companies have managed to align investment in digital business with their business strategies to achieve these unique gains.

For example, Dell has used a range of IT-enabled techniques mentioned earlier in the chapter such as online ordering, the Dell Premier extranet for large purchasers, vendor-managed inventory, adaptive supply chains, and build-to-order to gain competitive advantage.

Research into the productivity paradox highlights the importance of considering the information, people and technology resources together when planning for digital business strategy and implementation. It also suggests that digital business contributes to productivity gains only when combined with investments in process redesign, organisational change management and innovation.

Summary

1 Digital business strategy process models tend to share the following characteristics:
   • Continuous internal and external environment scanning or analysis is required.
   • Clear statement of vision and objectives is required.
   • Strategy development can be broken down into formulation and selection, a key emphasis being assessing the differential benefits provided by e-channels for company and stakeholders and then selecting the most appropriate channels for different business activities and partners ('right-channelling').
   • After strategy development, enactment of the strategy occurs as strategy implementation.
   • Control is required to detect problems and adjust the strategy accordingly.
   • They must be responsive to changes in the marketplace.

2 In this chapter a four-stage model is used as a framework for digital business strategy development. Key digital business issues within this framework are outlined below.

3 **Strategic analysis.** Continuous scanning of the micro- and macro-environment of an organisation is required, with particular emphasis on the changing needs of customers, actions and business models of competitors, and opportunities afforded by new technologies.

4 **Strategic objectives.** Organisations must have a clear vision on whether digital media will complement or replace other media, and their capacity for change. Clear objectives must be defined and, in particular, goals for the online revenue contribution should be set.

5 **Strategy definition.** Six key elements of digital business strategy that were reviewed are:
   • Digital business priorities – significance to organisation (replace or complement) and emphasis on buy-side or sell-side.
   • Form of restructuring required.
   • Business and revenue models.
   • Marketplace restructuring.
   • Market and product development strategies.
   • Positioning and differentiation strategies.

6 **Strategy implementation.** Detailed in the remainder of Part 2 and in Part 3.

7 Information systems strategy should use a combination of impact and alignment techniques to govern digital business strategy. IS strategy can take a number of perspectives, of which those that focus on information or knowledge management and technological and applications infrastructure are most important.

Exercises

Self-assessment questions

1 What are the key characteristics of a digital business strategy model?

2 Select a retailer or manufacturer of your choice and describe what the main elements of its situation analysis should comprise.

3 For the same retailer or manufacturer, suggest different methods and metrics for defining digital business objectives.

4 For the same retailer or manufacturer, assess different strategic options to adopt for digital business.

Essay and discussion questions

1 Evaluate the range of restructuring options for an existing 'bricks-and-mortar' organisation to move to 'bricks-and-clicks' or 'clicks-only' contributing a higher online revenue.

2 Explain the main strategy definition options or decisions available to an organisation intending to become a digital business.

3 Between 1994 and 1999 Amazon lost more than $500m, but at the end of this period its valuation was still more than $20bn. At the start of 2000, Amazon.com underwent its first round of job cuts, sacking 150 staff or 2% of its worldwide workforce. Later in 2000 its valuation dropped to less than half.

   Write an essay on the strategy of Amazon.com exploring its history, different criteria for success and its future. See the *Wired Magazine* archive for profiles of Amazon (www.wired.com).

4 Analyse the reasons for the failure of the original boo.com. Research and assess the sustainability of the new boo.com business model.

5 What can existing businesses learn from the business approaches of the dot-com organisations?

6 What are the similarities and differences between the concepts of business process re-engineering (BPR) and digital business? Will the digital business concept face the same fate as BPR?

7 Discuss this statement by David Weymouth, Barclays Bank chief information officer (Simons, 2000b):

   There is no merit in becoming a dot-com business. Within five years successful businesses will have embraced and deployed at real-scale across the whole enterprise, the processes and technologies that we now know as dot-com.

8 Compare and contrast different approaches to developing digital business strategy.

Examination questions

1 Define the main elements of a digital business strategy.

2 You are the incumbent digital business manager for a domestic airline. What process would you use to create objectives for the organisation? Suggest three typical objectives and how you would measure them.

3 Explain the productivity paradox and its implications for managers.

4 What choices do executives have for the scope and timeframe of implementing digital business?

References

Aaker, D. and Joachimsthaler, E. (2000) *Brand Leadership*. Free Press, New York.

Ansoff, H. (1957) Strategies for diversification. *Harvard Business Review,* September–October, 113–24.

Atos Consulting (2008) Ebusiness maturity framework. Published 4 November at **www.maxx-online.nl/?p=273**.

Berthon, P., Lane, N., Pitt, L. and Watson, R. (1998) The World Wide Web as an industrial marketing communications tool: models for the identification and assessment of opportunities. *Journal of Marketing Management,* 14, 691–704.

Brewer, J. (2008) Analytics Meets Targeting Meets CRM. Presentation to eMetrics Marketing Optimization Summit. London, 20–21 May.

Brynjolfsson, E. (1993) The productivity paradox of information technology. *Communications of the ACM,* 36(12), 67–77.

Brynjolfsson, E. and Hitt, L. (1998) Beyond the productivity paradox. *Communications of the ACM,* 41(8), 49–55.

Carr, N. (2003) IT doesn't matter. *Harvard Business Review,* May, 5–12.

Chaffey, D. and Ellis-Chadwick, F. (2012) *Digital Marketing: Strategy, Implementation and Practice,* 5th edn. Financial Times Prentice Hall, Harlow.

Chaffey, D. and White, G. (2010) *Business Information Management: Improving Performance Using Information Systems*, 2nd edn. Financial Times Prentice Hall, Harlow.

Chaston, I. (2000) *E-Marketing Strategy*. McGraw-Hill, Maidenhead.

Daniel, E., Wilson, H., McDonald, M. and Ward, J. (2001) *Marketing Strategy in the Digital Age*. Financial Times Prentice Hall, Harlow.

Deise, M., Nowikow, C., King, P. and Wright, A. (2000) *Executive's Guide to Digital business. From Tactics to Strategy*. Wiley, New York.

de Kare-Silver, M. (2000) *EShock 2000. The Electronic Shopping Revolution: Strategies for Retailers and Manufacturers*. Macmillan, London.

der Zee, J. and de Jong, B. (1999) Alignment is not enough: integrating business and information technology management with the balanced business scorecard. *Journal of Management Information Systems*, 16(2), 137–57.

Doherty, N. and McAulay, L. (2002) Towards the formulation of a comprehensive framework for the evaluation of investments in sell-side e-commerce. *Evaluation and Program Planning*, 25, 159–65.

E-consultancy (2008a) Managing Digital Channels Research Report. Author: Dave Chaffey. Available from **www.econsultancy.com**.

E-consultancy (2008b) Digital business Briefing. Arena Flowers' Sam Barton on web design and development, E-newsletter interview, 12 March.

Episerver (2013). Mobile Commerce: What Consumers Really Want. Research published 16 April 2013. **www.episerver.com/Best-practices-on-the-web/7-Steps-to-the-Perfect-Mobile-Commerce-Strategy/**

Financial Times (2003) Buried treasure. Article by Simon London. *Financial Times,* 10 December.

Google (2010) New GfK ROPO study with Vodafone. Published on Google Barometer Blog October 20th. **http://googlebarometer.blogspot.com/2010/10/new-gfk-ropo-study-with-vodafone.html** (no longer available).

Guardian (2007) Beware when you compare Harriet Meyer, Friday 22 June, *Guardian,* **www.theguardian.com/money/2007/jun/22/insurance**.

Gulati, R. and Garino, J. (2000) Getting the right mix of bricks and clicks for your company. *Harvard Business Review,* May–June, 107–14.

Hitwise (2006) Paid and Organic Search: Profile of MoneySupermarket. *Hitwise blogposting*: **http://weblogs.hitwise.com/heather-hopkins/2006/09/paid** and organic search profil. html (no longer available).

Hughes, S. (2001) Market orientation and the response of UK financial services companies to changes in market conditions as a result of e-commerce. *International Journal of Bank Marketing,* 19(6), 222–31.

Jeffcoate, J., Chappell, C. and Feindt, S. (2002) Best practice in SME adoption of e-commerce. *Benchmarking: An International Journal,* 9, 122–32.

Jelassi, T. and Enders, A. (2008) *Strategies for digital business: Creating Value through Electronic and Mobile Commerce,* 2nd edn. Financial Times Prentice Hall, Harlow.

Johnson, G. and Scholes, K. (2006) *Exploring Corporate Strategy: Text and Cases,* 7th edn. Financial Times Prentice Hall, Harlow.

Kalakota, R. and Robinson, M. (2000) *Digital business. Roadmap for Success.* Addison-Wesley, Reading, MA.

Kaplan, R.S. and Norton, D.P. (1993) Putting the balanced scorecard to work. *Harvard Business Review,* September–October, 134–42.

Kumar, N. (1999) Internet distribution strategies: dilemmas for the incumbent. *Financial Times,* Special Issue on Mastering Information Management, no. 7, Electronic Commerce.

Levy, M. and Powell, P. (2003) Exploring SME Internet adoption: towards a contingent model. *Electronic Markets,* 13(2), 173–81, **www.electronicmarkets.org**.

Lynch, R. (2000) *Corporate Strategy.* Financial Times Prentice Hall, Harlow.

Mcafee, A. and Brynjolfsson, E. (2008) Investing in the IT that makes a competitive difference. *Harvard Business Review,* 7/8, 98–107.

McDonald, M. (1999) Strategic marketing planning: theory and practice. In *The CIM Marketing Book,* 4th edn, M. Baker (ed.). Butterworth-Heinemann, Oxford, pp. 50–77.

McDonald, M. and Wilson, H. (2002) *New Marketing: Transforming the Corporate Future.* Butterworth-Heinemann, Oxford.

McFarlan, F. and McKenney, J. (1993) *Corporate Information Systems Management.* Prentice Hall, London.

Malmsten, E., Portanger, E. and Drazin, C. (2001) *Boo Hoo. A Dot.com Story from Concept to Catastrophe.* Random House, London.

Marchand, D. (1999) Hard choices for senior managers. In *Mastering Information Management,* D. Marchand, T. Davenport and T. Dickson (eds). Financial Times Prentice Hall, Harlow, pp. 187–92.

Marchand, D., Kettinger, W. and Rollins, J. (2002) *Information Orientation: The Link to Business Performance.* Oxford University Press, Oxford, UK.

Miller, T. (2003) Top ten lessons from the Internet shakeout. Article on Webmergers.com, **www.webmergers.com/data/article.php?id=48** (no longer available).

Mintzberg, H. and Quinn, J. (1991) *The Strategy Process,* 2nd edn. Prentice-Hall, Upper Saddle River, NJ.

Myers, J., Pickersgill, A, and Van Metre, E. (2004) Steering customers to the right channels. *McKinsey Quarterly,* no. 4.

New Media Age (1999) Will boo.com scare off the competition? By Budd Margolis. *New Media Age,* 22 July. Online only, **www3.telus.net/kim_milnes/boo.com_case.pdf**.

New Media Age (2005) Delivering the goods. By Nic Howell. *New Media Age,* 5 May.

Nolan, R. (1979) Managing the crisis in data processing. *Harvard Business Review,* March–April, 115–26.

Olve, N., Roy, J. and Wetter, M. (1999) *Performance Drivers. A Practical Guide to Using the Balanced Scorecard.* Wiley, Chichester.

Pant, S. and Ravichandran, T. (2001) A framework for information systems planning for digital business. *Logistics Information Management,* 14(1), 85–98.

Perrott, B. (2005) Towards a manager's model of digital business strategy decisions. *Journal of General Management,* 30(4), 73–89.

Phillips, S. (2000) Retailer's crown jewel is a unique customer database. *Financial Times,* 4 December.

Picardi, R. (2000) *EBusiness Speed: Six Strategies for eCommerce Intelligence.* IDC Research Report. IDC, Framingham, MA.

Plant, R. (2000) *ECommerce: Formulation of Strategy*. Prentice-Hall, Upper Saddle River, NJ.

Porter, M. (1980) *Competitive Strategy*. Free Press, New York.

Porter, M. (2001) Strategy and the Internet. *Harvard Business Review,* March, 62–78.

Quelch, J. and Klein, L. (1996) The Internet and international marketing. *Sloan Management Review,* Spring, 60–75.

Revolution (2005) Campaign of the Month, by Emma Rigby. *Revolution,* October, 69.

Robson, W. (1997) *Strategic Management and Information Systems: An Integrated Approach.* Pitman, London.

Rowley, J. (2002) Synergy and strategy in e-commerce. *Marketing Intelligence and Planning,* 20(4), 215–20.

Simons, M. (2000a) Barclays gambles on web big bang. *Computer Weekly,* 13 July, p. 1.

Simons, M. (2000b) Setting the banks alight. *Computer Weekly,* 20 July, p. 6.

Sircar, S., Turnbow, J. and Bordoloi, B. (2000) A framework for assessing the relationship between information technology investments and firm performance. *Journal of Management Information Systems,* Spring, 16(4), 69–98.

Smith, P. (1999) *Marketing Communications: An Integrated Approach,* 2nd edn. Kogan Page, London.

Strassman, P. (1997) *The Squandered Computer.* Information Economics Press, New Canaan, CT.

Sultan, F. and Rohm, A. (2004) The evolving role of the Internet in marketing strategy. *Journal of Interactive marketing,* 19(2), 6–19.

Tjan, A. (2001) Finally, a way to put your Internet portfolio in order. *Harvard Business Review,* February, 78–85.

Tse, T. (2007) Reconsidering the source of value of digital business strategies. *Strategic Change,* 16, 117–26.

Ward, J. and Griffiths, P. (1996) *Strategic Planning for Information Systems.* Wiley, Chichester.

Willcocks, L. and Plant, R. (2000) Business Internet strategy – moving to the net. In *Moving to Digital business,* L. Willcocks and C. Sauer (eds). Random House, London, pp. 19–46.

Web links

Smart Insights.com (www.smartinsights.com/digital-marketing-strategy/) Updates by the author about all aspects of digital business, including strategy.

E-commerce Times (www.ecommercetimes.com) An online newspaper specific to e-commerce developments.

Knowledge@Wharton (http://knowledge.wharton.upenn.edu/www) Knowledge@ Wharton is an online resource that offers the latest business insights, information, and research from a variety of sources.

Financial Times Digital Business (http://news.ft.com/reports/digitalbusiness) Monthly articles based on case studies.

McKinseyQuarterly (www.mckinsey.com/insights) Articles regularly cover digital marketing strategy.

E-consultancy (www.econsultancy.com) Digital business portal with links to news and White Papers on other sites.

MIT Center for Digital Business (http://digital.mit.edu) in the MIT Sloan School of Management. Resources and papers from leading researchers into digital business including Professor Erik Brynjolfsson (http://digital.mit.edu/erik).

Mohansawney.com (http://mohansawhney.com/) Case studies and White Papers from one of the leading US authorities on e-commerce.

6

Supply chain management

Web support

The following additional case studies are available at
www.pearsoned.co.uk/chaffey

→ A short history of the Sainsbury's approach to e-fulfilment models

→ The telecoms supply chain

→ The site also contains a range of study material designed to help improve your results.

Scan code to find the latest updates for topics in this chapter

Learning outcomes

After completing this chapter the reader should be able to:

- Identify the main elements of supply chain management and their relationship to the value chain and value networks
- Assess the potential of information systems to support supply chain management and the value chain

Management issues

The issues for the manager:

- Which technologies should we deploy for supply chain management and how should they be prioritised?
- Which elements of the supply chain should be managed within and beyond the organisation and how can technology be used to facilitate this?
- What are the practical issues with online supply chain management?

Links to other chapters

The main related chapters are:

- *Chapter 1* introduces the supply chain as a key element of digital business
- *Chapter 7* considers the e-procurement part of the supply chain in more detail

Introduction

In the end business all comes down to supply chain vs supply chain.

(Robert Rodin, then CEO of Marshall Industries, one of the
largest global distributors of electronic components, 1999)

Supply chain management is essentially the optimisation of material flows and associated information flows involved with an organisation's operations. To manage these flows, digital business applications are today essential. Supply chain management is presented as the premier application of digital business in Part 2 of this book since it is a unifying concept that incorporates both e-procurement (Chapter 7) and sell-side e-commerce (Chapters 8 and 9). By applying information systems, companies can enhance or radically improve many aspects of the supply chain. In the context of Figure 1.4, which was used to introduce the concept of digital business, supply chain management can be enhanced through buy-side e-commerce, internal communications, relationships with partners and sell-side e-commerce. Digital business technologies enable information flows to be redefined to facilitate the sharing of information between partners, often at lower costs than were previously possible.

Supply chain management capabilities are best known for their importance in delivering profitability. For example, AMR (2008) reported that Nike, a company best known for its marketing, used improvements to its supply chain to increase operating margins of between 10 and 15% in each of the preceding four years. But for Nike and other companies which constantly innovate to renew products, selecting the right technology is important to *'orchestrate the constant collaboration between supply, demand, and product management groups that brings profitable new products to market'*. Managing distribution and returns from e-commerce sites is a further challenge. *Internet Retailing* (2010) reported that while the average rates of return to a high-street retailer can be as high as 10%, the average for UK e-commerce sites is 22%.

The importance of supply chain management capabilities to customer satisfaction and so repeat business for a digital business is highlighted by Mini case study 6.1.

Mini Case Study 6.1	Premier Farnell uses its global supply chain system to improve customer satisfaction	FT

Constant investment in technology is vital for electronics component distributor *Premier Farnell*, a growing business with a mission to deliver industry-leading customer service.

The FTSE-250 company, which supplies electronic components in North America, Europe and Asia, has a demanding group of valuable customers who need to know swiftly and accurately when their order will be shipped.

Most of them are design engineers building prototypes of high-tech goods, working for manufacturers of a wide range of equipment.

'For our customers, service is paramount,' explains Laurence Bain, chief operating officer. 'They are looking for a product and they are looking for it now.

'So we had to address the completeness of our product range, our stock levels, and ensure next-day delivery.' As a result, an efficient supply chain operation is essential.

Premier Farnell sets a tough target: 99.9% of shipments must arrive the next day. Shipments also need to be complete.

Add to this a move into China – Premier Farnell now offers next-day delivery to 90 cities for items in its Chinese distribution centre – and the company would seem a prime candidate for investing in a new supply chain management or ERP system.

This option was considered carefully, says Mr Bain. The company, however, decided to keep its existing technology. This allowed it to focus its resources on improving connections between the supply chain systems in North America, Europe and Asia, and critically, improving business processes.

This freed resources for investment in e-commerce and front-office systems, including a three-year project to install a Siebel-based customer relationship management system.

Forty per cent of European orders are now online and Mr Bain expects this to rise to 50%. In the US, all orders, save those placed by new customers, are handled without manual intervention.

'We did a review of our order processes, looking at the level of interconnectivity between our systems and our ability to transfer data,' says Mr Bain.

'We looked at the processes end to end. We used quality techniques to identify the gaps that created the greatest opportunity for error. It was not just about the cycle time [the time from taking an order to shipment] but the quality of the orders.'

As a result, Premier Farnell decided to maintain its existing supply chain management system, but improve the links between its parts, as well as its capacity.

'We looked at our supply chains holistically and identified the areas where we needed the systems to interface and talk to each other,' explains Mr Bain. 'Our supply chain group specified the enhancements needed to interface the systems and ensure data completeness.'

The task of updating the system fell to Premier Farnell's 200-strong in-house IT team. The project had to be managed in a way that ensured the supply chain targets were met, but without drawing too many resources away from the company's Siebel deployment or its expanding e-commerce operations.

'We have a fairly strong governance designed to ensure business strategy translates into IT priorities,' Mr Bain points out. 'We have an IT leadership group that meets quarterly to assess the evolution of that strategy and a global IT leadership group that signs off IT projects.'

This way, Premier Farnell has ensured customers can see orders placed across all channels, including the web, phone or, in the US, a branch, when they log in to their online accounts.

'We have to be able to capture all transactions,' says Mr Bain. 'You have to take the customer with you. For us, all roads lead to IT: we are a high-volume, high-service distributor dealing in massive numbers of transactions on a daily basis.

'The traffic on our website is growing strongly and we rely on IT to manage these transactions effectively and on a real-time basis.'

Premier Farnell also likes to differentiate itself by its speed in bringing new products to market.

The company recently added 55,000 products to its catalogue. These need to appear simultaneously in its ordering and back-office systems, as well as in the supply chain system so orders reach suppliers on time.

Other material, such as specifications and product data sheets, also have to be loaded before a new product is sold.

As well as the flexibility to handle new products, Premier Farnell relies on its supply chain management system to monitor key aspects of performance. 'In terms of the supply chain, the key metric is our distribution performance,' says Mr Bain.

'We compare it, and have targets, for each facility. We look at the cost of processing an order, the efficiency of goods in and out, and service measures.' Head office collates the data monthly, but operations managers in each distribution facility monitor the figures daily.

The result has been a tough set of targets for engineers tasked with updating a supply chain management system that many less prudent – or less confident – companies might have replaced.

But for Premier Farnell, the combination of clear objectives, a capable in-house team of developers and the lower risks of updating rather than replacing made it the most effective choice.

'Our overall services were good but not as good as they are now. We were confident we could enhance our systems and improve our processes,' says Mr Bain.

'We were comfortable we had the capacity. We had to invest, but it cost a lot less than replacing the back-office system, and that allowed us to prioritise our investments in CRM and our web channels.'

Source: Did IT work? Service was paramount when enhancing supply chain. Stephen Pritchard, *The Financial Times*, 30 January 2008. Reprinted with permission.

Much of the excitement generated by the digital business concept concerns the benefits that companies can achieve through increasing the efficiency of the whole supply chain. Companies such as Argos (Case Study 6.2), which have enthusiastically embraced technology to manage the supply chain, have been reaping the benefits for many years.

Digital business also potentially makes it easier to set up supply chains, as Mini case study 6.2 on the Pebble watch launch shows.

| Mini-case study 6.2 | Pebble watch launched without existing supply chain |

The Pebble watch gives an example both of the power of what has been called crowdfunding and the challenges of creating a new product and setting up the supply chain. Pebble is a 'smartwatch' that uses Bluetooth to communicate with a mobile phone, enabling calls, messages and notifications from apps to be displayed on its high-resolution e-ink display. Two-way communication is also possible, so for example, music played on the phone can be started and stopped. This watch was developed by just five engineers for five years and financed by crowdfunding.

Figure 6.1 shows how Pebble appealed to its backers through Kickstarter. Each paid between $99 and $150 to receive the watch when shipping started; 68,000 backers raised over $10 million in a period of a

| Figure 6.1 | The initial funding of the Pebble watch on Kickstarter |

Source: www.kickstarter.com, Kickstarter, Inc. and Pebble 2014.

year. Although the funding was a success, the challenges of such a project are shown by the product first shipping in 2013, several months after the original shipping date, which led to many complaints on the forum since refunds are not possible in the Kickstarter funding model. Orders shipped to American addresses were initially shipped from a US distribution centre using USPS and orders for other addresses will be sent from the Hong Kong distribution centre using Singapore Post and Sweden Post.

Launched in April 2009, Kickstarter is an innovative online brand that provides a forum to help creative start-up projects harness 'crowd power'; crowdsourcing, concept testing and benefit. The approach builds communities and generates funding to potentially help new creative businesses move forward quickly without external funding rounds. In its own words, the projects have been '*successfully funded by awesome people from around the world*'. Pebble failed to gain initial venture capital funding, but shortly after the product shipped it gained $15 million backing.

Problems of supply chain management

The challenge of managing inventory across the supply chain is shown by US Department of Commerce (2013) data which regularly catalogues the ratio between inventory held in different parts of the supply chain.

Their analysis shows that $1,660,000 million was held in inventory across all types of business broken down into:

- Manufacturers: $628,000 million
- Retailers: $522,000 million
- Merchant wholesales: $503,000 million

Increasing supply chain efficiency involves reducing the holding within inventory while maximising sales. This report shows that the total business inventories/sales ratio at the time was 1.31. Surprisingly, between 2004 and 2013 the inventory/sales ratio has remained relatively stable, suggesting that across business there is limited potential to reduce inventory in systems that are already optimised and that must avoid lost potential sales through out-of-stock items in-store.

Inventory turnover
An indication of efficiency of inventory turn calculated by the cost of goods sold divided by the average inventory.

In individual companies, **inventory turnover** is used as a measure of the number of times inventory is sold or used in a time period such as a year. It is calculated as the cost of goods sold divided by the average inventory. A low turnover rate may indicate overstocking or difficulty in selling products at an acceptable rate. A high turnover rate may suggest inadequate inventory levels, which may lead to a loss in business as the inventory is too low and sales are missed.

Using digital business technology to support SCM can help to avoid some problems that can occur in a supply chain (Table 6.1). This introduces many of the key concepts of technology-enabled supply chain management.

Table 6.1	A summary of the problems of supply chain management and how digital business technology can assist

Problems of supply chain management	How digital technology can reduce problems in SCM
Pressure to reduce costs of manufacturing and distributing products in order to remain competitive	Reduction in paperwork through electronic transmission of orders invoices and delivery notes. Reduced inventory holdings needed through better understanding of demand. Reduced time for information and component supply across the supply chain. Lower SCM system purchase and management costs through use of online services (SaaS)

Table 6.1	Continued

Problems of supply chain management	How digital technology can reduce problems in SCM
Demand forecasting	Sharing of demand by customers with suppliers as part of efficient consumer response (ECR)
Failure to deliver products on time consistently or lack of items on shelf in retailer	Supplier becomes responsible for item availability through vendor-managed inventory
Failure to deliver or ship correct product	Human error reduced. 'Checks and balances can be built into system'
High inventory costs	Inventory reduced throughout the supply chain through better demand forecasting and more rapid replenishment of inventory
Time for new product development	Improved availability of information about potential suppliers and components, for example through online marketplaces

What is supply chain management?

Supply chain management (SCM)
The coordination of all supply activities of an organisation from its suppliers and partners to its customers.

Supply chain management (SCM) involves the coordination of all supply activities of an organisation from its suppliers and delivery of products to its customers. Figure 6.2 introduces the main players in the supply chain. In Figure 6.2(a) the main members of the supply chain are the organisations that manufacture a product and/or deliver a service.

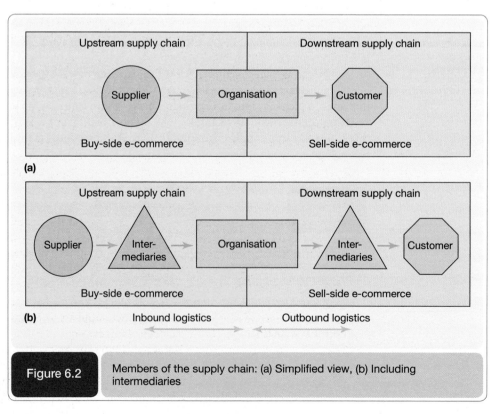

Figure 6.2	Members of the supply chain: (a) Simplified view, (b) Including intermediaries

Upstream supply chain

Transactions between an organisation and its suppliers and intermediaries, equivalent to buy-side e-commerce.

Downstream supply chain

Transactions between an organisation and its customers and intermediaries, equivalent to sell-side e-commerce.

Supply chain network

The links between an organisation and all partners involved in multiple supply chains.

Efficient consumer response (ECR)

Creating and satisfying customer demand by optimising product assortment strategies, promotions, and new product introductions.

For most commercial and not-for-profit organisations we can distinguish between **upstream supply chain** activities which are equivalent to buy-side e-commerce and **downstream supply chain** activities which correspond to sell-side e-commerce. In this chapter and the next we focus mainly on improving the efficiency of upstream supply chain activities, while in Chapters 8 and 9 the emphasis is on the marketing aspects of improving downstream supply chain activities.

Remember also from Figure 1.4 that supply chain management includes not only supplier and buyer, but also the intermediaries such as the supplier's suppliers and the customer's customers (Figure 6.2(b)). Indeed, some companies may have first-tier, second-tier and even third-tier suppliers or first-, second- and higher-tier customers. Because each company effectively has many individual supply chains for different products, the use of the term 'chain' is limiting and **supply chain network** is a more accurate reflection of the links between an organisation and its partners.

Technology is vital to supply chain management since managing relationships with customers, suppliers and intermediaries is based on the flow of information and the transactions between these parties. The main strategic thrust of enhancing the supply chain is to provide a superior value proposition to the customer, of which **efficient consumer response** (ECR, see Box 6.1) is important within the retail and packaged consumer goods market. Improving customer value involves improving product quality, customer service quality and/or reducing price and fulfilment times (as explained in Chapter 5). Increasing efficiency in obtaining resources from a supplier organisation or distributing products to customers reduces operational costs and so increases profitability.

Using technology to support supply chain management – an example

A good example of how the introduction of information systems can be used to improve supply chain management is provided by BHP Steel (now BlueScope Steel, www.bluescopesteel.com.au), an Australian firm. Its use of PC-based technology for supply chain management dates back to the 1980s and digital business represents a change of emphasis rather than a radically new approach. Chan and Swatman (2000) assess the stages in implementation of e-commerce for this company. The authors identify three phases:

1 **Early implementation: 1989–93.** This was a PC-based EDI purchasing system. At this stage, objectives were to (1) reduce data errors to 0, (2) reduce administration costs, (3) improve management control and (4) reduce order lead time. Benefits included rationalisation of suppliers to 12 major partnerships (accounting for 60% of invoices); 80% of invoices placed electronically by 1990; 7,000 items were eliminated from the warehouse, to be sourced directly from suppliers, on demand. Shorter lead times in the day-to-day process – from 10 days to 26 hours for items supplied through a standard contract and from 42 days to 10 days for direct-purchase items. At this stage the main barriers to the implementation were technological.

2 **Electronic trading gateway: 1990–4.** This was again EDI-based, but involved a wider range of parties both externally (from suppliers through to customers) and internally (from marketing, sales, finance, purchasing and legal). The aim was to provide a combined upstream and downstream supply chain solution to bring benefits to all parties. The main learning from this process was the difficulty of getting customers involved – only four were involved after 4 years, although an industry-standard method for data exchange was used. This was surprising since suppliers had been enthusiastic adopters. From 1994, there was no further uptake of this system.

3 **The move towards Internet commerce: 1996 onwards.** The Internet was thought to provide a lower-cost alternative to traditional EDI for smaller suppliers and customers, through using a lower-cost value-added network. So, one objective of the project was to extend the reach of electronic communications with supply chain partners. The second

Box 6.1	Efficient consumer response (ECR)

The ECR concept was developed for the food retailing business in the USA but since then it has been applied to other products and in other countries. It was originally developed by David Jenkins, then chairman of Shaw's supermarkets, to compete with other players such as Wal-Mart. Supply chain management had traditionally focussed on efficient product replenishment, whereas the focus of ECR is on demand management aimed at creating and satisfying customer demand by optimising product assortment strategies, promotions and new product introductions (Legner and Schemm, 2008). Figure 6.3 shows the complexity and lead times of

Figure 6.3	Inter-organisational process flow for introduction of a new product

Source: Excerpted from Towards the interorganisational product information supply chain: Evidence from the retail and consumer goods industry by C. Legner and J. Schemm © 2008. Used with permission from Association for Information Systems, Atlanta, GA, 404-713-7444, www.aisnet.org. All rights reserved.

a process where a new consumer product is introduced and then stocked. ECR focusses on improving this process.

Table 6.2 shows that some of the aims and strategic approaches generated by ECR can also apply to business customers.

Table 6.2	Objectives and strategies for effective consumer response (ECR)

Objective	Strategy
Timely, accurate, paperless information flow	Revision of organisation processes supported by information systems
Smooth, continual product flow matched to variations in consumption levels	See strategies below
Optimise productivity of retail space and inventory	Efficient store assortments
Optimise for time and cost in the ordering process	Efficient replacement
Maximise efficiency of promotions	Promotions are integrated into entire supply chain planning
Maximise effectiveness of new product development (NPD)	NPD process improved and better forward planning with other partners

was to broaden the type of communications to include catalogue ordering, freight forwarding and customer ordering. The strategy divided transactions into three types: (1) strategic (high volume, high value, high risk) – a dedicated EDI line was considered most appropriate; (2) tactical (medium volume, value and risk) – EDI or Internet EDI was used; (3) consumer transactions (low volume, value and risk) – a range of lower-cost Internet-based technologies could be used. The main barriers to implementation at this stage have been business issues, i.e. convincing third parties of the benefits of integration and managing the integration process.

More recently, BlueScope Steel has introduced bluescopesteelconnect.com (Figure 6.4) which is a secure Internet-based steel procurement solution which allows customers to order and confirm the status of products. It also offers users the ability to check statements and download invoices in real time, simplifying reconciliations.

The implementation of SCM at BlueScope Steel reflects changing developments in the wider industry which are summarised in Box 6.2.

A simple model of a supply chain

An organisation's supply chain can be viewed from a systems perspective as the acquisition of resources (inputs) and their transformation (process) into products and services (outputs). Such a perspective indicates that as part of moving to digital business, organisations can review the transformation process and optimise it in order to deliver products to customers with greater efficiency and lower cost. Note that the position of the systems boundary for SCM extends beyond the organisation – it involves improving not only internal processes, but also processes performed in conjunction with suppliers, distributors and customers. However, this process perspective misses the strategic importance of supply chain management – it also provides great opportunities to improve product performance and deliver superior value to the customer as suggested by Figure 6.1. As a result, supply chain management can dramatically have an impact on the profitability of a company.

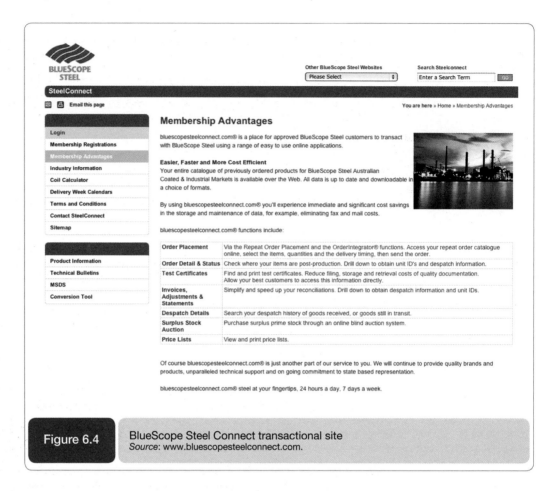

Figure 6.4	BlueScope Steel Connect transactional site
	Source: www.bluescopesteelconnect.com.

Box 6.2 The past, present and future of SCM

Professor Alan Braithwaite of LCP Consulting, writing in PMP (2008), identifies these developments in SCM technology:

The 70s were characterised by monster batch-processing mainframes, manual data entry and primarily custom programming. These systems were driven by finance and generated huge piles of printout with little useful management information.

The 80s were the time when the minicomputer and the PC emerged, computing power became more accessible and the debate was between packaged software or customised solutions. Custom code was still the preferred route for many, but information rather than data was emerging.

The 90s saw a huge 'Windows-based' expansion of computing power – with packages overtaking custom software as their functionality matured – and the emergence of ERP. The debate was about best-of-breed versus all-in-one integrated software.

The end of the 90s was focussed on the Y2K question as companies replaced their solutions wherever the risk of corruption in old legacy systems was too high – ERP was again a big winner from this.

In the first decade of the new century, the Internet has come of age as a transaction medium, with exponential growth in computing power and storage encouraging the introduction of more and more sophisticated supply chain solutions and management information.

Braithwaite goes on to make these predictions about the future of SCM:

A fundamental principle of supply chain management is to secure end-to-end visibility and a single version of the truth – one number for forecasts, inventory, orders, billings and commitments; ERP in principle seeks to achieve that goal.

A second fundamental principle is that end-to-end visibility includes inventory and processes that extend beyond the focal firm and its ERP. The Internet provides this capability in a way that was barely conceivable 10 years ago.

There are three key points from the growth of ERP and the Internet that form the basis for my prediction of the future of supply chain systems . . .

The first is that managing the extended supply chain with a requirement to continually optimise means integrated ERP versus best-of-breed is an irrelevant argument. Systems in the future will be more open and include core and extended supply chain integration and optimisation. ERP is less good at the smart stuff and the data structures are not organised to deal with the extended chain.

The second point is that most systems are not delivering business benefits to their full potential because supply chain business processes are not good enough and the systems are not set up right to handle good practice.

The third factor is that a surprising number of companies are still stranded with legacy systems that are so customised it is difficult to migrate to new more open architectures based on 'best practice' processes. These companies have to determine how they will reengineer their businesses and migrate their systems. At present they will not be able to access the smart optimisation and extended chain capabilities easily.

The implication of these trends is that the long-term direction for companies will be extended open system architectures with an ERP core. Application and data interchange maturity exist, and the industry now talks widely about service-oriented architecture (SOA). The real challenge now is process design and simplification and being able to represent that in supply chain systems.

So the future of supply chain systems will be about simply more of the same on the latest platforms, only this time better and more flexible. It will be up to management to provide better process clarity and execution, and work with the systems community to exploit the capabilities that exist. Anything new technically may be a bonus, but not if it distracts from the core concepts.

Source: PMP (2008).

Figure 6.5 shows the supply chain for a sample business-to-business company. Complete Activity 6.1 to consider the issues involved in modifying the supply chain in response to digital business. Note that although this example is based on a business-to-business scenario, supply chain management is also vital to the management of business-to-consumer and service companies. With service companies, the resources managed tend not to be physical but human, financial and information resources. However, the same principles can be applied.

Case study 6.1 shows how Shell Chemicals has developed a **vendor-managed inventory (VMI)** supply chain management system to enable delivery of supplies to be more responsive to customers' demands. VMI is a key concept in electronic supply chain and procurement management which shifts the day-to-day tasks of stock management, purchasing and order tracking from the customer to the supplier.

Vendor-managed inventory (VMI)
Supply chain partners manage the replenishment of parts or items for sale through sharing of information on variations in demand and stocking level for goods used for manufacture or sale.

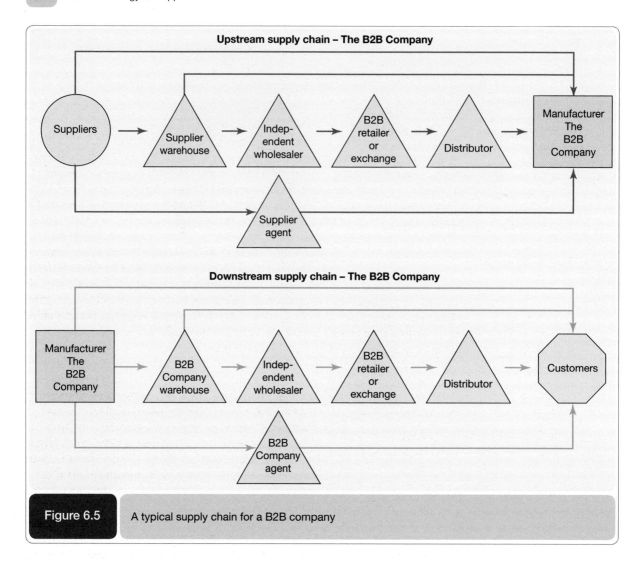

| Figure 6.5 | A typical supply chain for a B2B company |

Purpose

To examine the nature of a B2B supply chain and its potential for modification through restructuring and information systems as part of digital business development.

Questions

1 Referring to Chapter 2 and the section on disintermediation and reintermediation, discuss the opportunities for a B2B company to restructure its supply chain as part of the move to digital business, and the benefits this may bring.

2 How can information systems be used to accomplish the changes you have identified in question 1?

Answers to activities can be found at www.pearsoned.co.uk/chaffey

Shell Chemicals redefines its customers' supply chains

This case illustrates the evolution of a typical digital business application for supply chain management within one company. Shell Chemicals originally introduced SIMON, a bespoke system to manage their customers' inventory based on data shared by its customers about their usage and forecast demand for chemicals. SIMON was then used for upstream supply chain management. Ultimately, Shell Chemicals switched to using the Elemica marketplace portal for supply chain management since this was thought to be more cost-effective than maintaining an in-house system.

The introduction of SIMON

Shell Chemicals (www.shell.com/chemicals) manufactures the chemicals used by other manufacturers of many industrial and consumer products. Shell's customers use detergents, solvents, plastics, and epoxy resins to produce everything from automotive paints and aircraft structures to diapers and plastic bottles.

According to IBM (1998) who developed the SIMON system for Shell, their shared vision for creating SIMON was to:

Use customer production schedules so that we could maintain an adequate supply of on-site inventory and provide seamless product availability at the lowest possible cost, and achieve customer-driven service levels if a customer wants product today or next week, we can fulfil that request.

Source: IBM (1998) Shell Chemical re-defines Supply Chain Management with Notes. A customer case study, http://www-304.ibm.com/easyaccess/ukcomms/gclcontent/gcl_xmlid/91467, accessed June 28th, 2014.

Within such an organisation, supply chain management has a dramatic impact on customer satisfaction and profitability. Shell Chemicals have invested in SIMON, which stands for 'Shell Inventory Managed Order Network', for managing both upstream and downstream relationships.

SIMON was originally launched in 1995 using the IBM Lotus Notes Domino application server and is one of the earliest examples of a digital business application. This represented a change from the industry-standard practice of using electronic data interchange (EDI) forms, telephone orders and paper invoices. EDI didn't give Shell the flexibility it needed to accommodate data on exceptions and up-to-date information about dynamic processes.

The benefits of SIMON

Initially, Shell used SIMON to manage their downstream supply chain processes which involve distribution of chemical products for use by their customers. The system enabled Shell to assume the inventory management role on behalf of their customers. Once it was successful in this role it was then applied to the upstream processes of Shell acquiring raw materials from suppliers.

For customers, the benefits of the SIMON system are that responsibility for inventory management is transferred from customer to supplier. A Shell Chemicals customer doesn't need to place an order. Instead, SIMON manages the amount of inventory in stock at the customers' manufacturing locations.

Before the introduction of SIMON, there were a lot of manual, time-consuming transactions, often initiated by the customer, that required a lot of phone calls and faxes. There was also the danger that Shell's customers might run out of an essential chemical, so that plant time and then revenues would be lost. To avoid this, companies tend to maintain 'safety stock' levels. Re-ordering then occurs when inventory gets too close to these safety stock levels. The problem was that a typical re-supply order can take at least two weeks from the time the order is placed. This delay occurred since chemicals must be weighed at the plant, loaded on to railcars and then sent to the customer, who then weighs the materials at the other end before moving them into inventory. Miscalculations and errors can also occur.

For SIMON to enable a supplier to manage inventory, the customer needed to supply three types of information: the levels of current inventory; forecast demand for inventory; and the shipment details such as location, timing and quantities.

In addition to analysing inventory and consumption, SIMON also generates demand forecasts, calculates stock, tracks shipment status and generates a re-supply plan.

We can summarise the benefits of SIMON by considering the supply chain and logistics information about which it regularly extracts information. This includes:

- The amount of product consumed in the past 24 hours
- The amount of new product that arrived and was unloaded in the same period
- Current and anticipated production schedules, and
- Known changes to those schedules.

Web-based communications are used to synchronise information at different locations. So this information is replicated back to a customer service centre in Houston, TX, where Shell then automatically reconcile it with their SAP Material Requirement Planning (MRP) system. Shell Chemical customer service representatives then automatically present customers with a resupply plan. If the plan indicates that stocking levels at the customer site are low, the customer service representative completes an electronic purchase order and initiates a new shipment to the customer.

From a customer perspective, the benefits of the enhanced supply chain management system include:

- Elimination of expensive excess inventory, which means an increase in working capital
- Facilitation of timely, low-cost 're-synching' of supply chain
- Ensures product is on site whenever needed
- Ensures quicker response times to changing conditions
- Reduces transaction costs (for example, invoices and data entry)
- Eliminates erratic order patterns
- Reduces order processing overhead
- Streamlines financial statements and reconciliation processes

The customer is able to access the status of orders and shipments; estimated dates of arrival, shipment weights, receipt and unloading dates; and current stock and consumption levels. SIMON offers customers a 'Reconciliation' tab, which compares metered and calculated consumption, and a 'Site level agreements' tab, which shows the mutually agreed-upon plan for the management of their inventory. Once a month (not once per railcar load), an invoice is generated. The invoice is based on consumption figures, not shipments.

Integration with the Elemica marketplace portal

By 2005, the Elemica chemical industry portal (www.elemica.com, Figure 6.6) had became an important part of the digital business strategy for Shell Chemical. It was reported in the Shell Chemicals Magazine that 30% of Shell Chemical business was online with an ambition to increase this to 50% by 2008.

Elemica was originally founded in 1999 by 22 leaders of the global chemical industry and by 2005 had a network of 1,800 industry trading partners, so it offered benefits of standardisation.

Today, Elemica processes approximately $250 billion in annual transactions across more than 6,500 process industry trading partners. Clients include BASF, BP, Continental, The Dow Chemical Company, DuPont, The Goodyear Tire & Rubber Company, LANXESS, Michelin, Shell, Solvay, Sumitomo Chemical, and Wacker. Elemica has a simple, focused vision which is to:

Give customers total control over their global supply chains.

Their mission adds more detail to this:

As the leading Supply Chain Operating Network provider for the process industries, we enable a market driven supply chain through integrated messaging, applications, and analytics.

Elemica described the principles of its marketplace, now described as a Supply Chain Operating Network provider, as follows (www.elemica.com/about):

Elemica enables companies to achieve operational excellence by replacing complex approaches with automated systems and intelligent business processes. Utilizing leading-edge technology and in-depth process expertise, Elemica integrates disparate enterprise business systems and processes into one unified network across all customers, suppliers and third party service providers irrespective of company size or industry.

Elemica's innovative business process network (BPN) provides a fully connected operational framework that removes transactional and communication barriers and institutionalizes processes for integrating the information flow between global trading partners. With seamless access and visibility into the supply chain network, the enterprise can use fewer resources to do the same work more efficiently and release people, inventory, and assets that cover for these issues in the current process.

Elemica describes the benefits of their customer management suite, used by Shell and other customers, as:

- Touchless order processing
- Improved day to day supply chain service & reliability
- Increase the 'perfect order' percentage
- Lower the cost of errors
- Improved customer service
- Reduced invoice processing errors

These benefits are delivered across a series of modules covering a range of business processes essential for managing industrial processes like those of Shell Chemical. In the customer management suite of applications, these include:

- Sales Order Management
- Vendor Managed Inventory (VMI)

- Terminal Managed Inventory
- Repeat Order Entry
- Rail Car Fulfillment
- Delivery Schedule
- Invoice Management

Other applications available in the other Elemica modules are logistics management, supplier management and sourcing management.

Looking at Elemica in more detail, there are three key types of benefits

1 Global reach and connectivity
   Our founding member companies are among the industry leaders and represent a significant proportion of the industry's buy and sell transactions, creating substantial initial liquidity. This foundation provides financial stability and global reach for Elemica, and the proven ability to scale quickly. This combination will continue to attract many additional buyers and sellers, resulting in an ever-growing reservoir of potential connections for new customers.
2 Neutrality
   Elemica is an independent company with a dedicated management team. Our network is designed as an open network, embracing all industry buyers and sellers looking for a robust infrastructure, network and e-commerce solutions to improve core business processes. Elemica is not an 'aggregator' of material purchasing, nor a 'buyer', 'seller', or 'owner' of products – it is a facilitator of transactions.
3 Security
   Elemica has incorporated state-of-the-art security measures to safeguard the flow and accessibility of information so that participants' individual transaction data is not shared with any other company. We have state-of-the-art security features and processes, including highly visible firewalls and strong data protection policies, a policy of confidentiality regarding handling of customer data, encryption technology to safeguard confidential data and secured information with access limited by individual user and regular independent auditing of these policies and procedures.

Integration with marketplace portals such as Elemica, which were not in existence earlier in the life cycle of SIMON, became important to Shell.

Using an external, standardised supply chain management system meant that Shell did not have to create a bespoke approach through a systems developer and integrator such as IBM, but could use a more standardised approach at a lower cost with less specification of requirements.

Elemica could offer similar benefits to SIMON, i.e. it could:

- Reduce transaction costs through reduction of human input to transactions
- Standardise business processes
- Reduce error sources
- Improve response time
- Improve cash flow through faster payment
- Increase customer satisfaction

The article describes this example of the practical benefits the new system could bring. A company in Europe shipped products directly from a Shell Chemical plant to their customers. Shell Chemical make the product; the company markets it and manages pick-up from the plant and delivery to the customer. Before the application of Elemica, these additional process stages or 'hand-offs' were required while each truck waited after loading:

- Paperwork was developed at the plant
- Then faxed to the partner company
- Then entered manually into their system
- Then faxed back to the Shell company – where the truck had been all along

A further complication was that the partner's offices closed earlier than the Shell traffic office. So, truck drivers could sit for hours waiting at the plant until the documents were faxed through! After switching to Elemica, paperwork was automatically processed 24 hours a day. Average truck-waiting times were cut from two hours to 15 minutes.

In addition to the process benefits which would create better customer service, Shell Chemical switched from using SIMON to Elemica for supply chain management since SIMON would require continued investment in ongoing development and maintenance costs. Elemica, as an outsourced solution, was more favourable in terms of ongoing costs and development. Since Elemica is not company-specific it also helped exchange of data since formats could be standardised across companies.

Global positioning systems also enable details on the railcar carrying the chemicals including current location and estimated time of arrival. There are also links to road hauliers. For example, a link with Bertschi AG, one of the largest road transport logistics providers in Europe, enables thousands of transport instructions generated every month to be sent automatically, removing the need for manual faxing and reducing the potential for errors.

Bertschi transport planning manager, Stefan Bryner, explains the benefits as follows:

'It has reduced our paperwork and made the whole process more transparent. The potential for errors has been reduced and issues are easier to resolve.'

Questions

1 The SIMON system supports both 'upstream and downstream' business relationships. Explain how this relates to Figure 6.5 and whether you would consider it an e-commerce system or a digital business system.

2 Draw a table summarising the before and after implementation roles for Shell and their customers (downstream side).

3 This description of SIMON is explained from the Shell perspective. Using your answer to question 2, state whether you think the customer truly benefits, or is Shell transferring some of its workload to the customer?

4 Visit the Shell Chemicals website (www.shellchemicals.com). How are the benefits of these facilities explained?

Figure 6.6   Elemica trading platform
Source: www.elemica.com.

What is logistics?

Inbound logistics
The management of material resources entering an organisation from its suppliers and other partners.

Outbound logistics
The management of resources supplied from an organisation to its customers and intermediaries.

Logistics is a concept closely related to supply chain management. According to the Institute of Logistics and Transportation (www.iolt.org):

> Logistics is the time-related positioning of resource, or the strategic management of the total supply chain. The supply chain is a sequence of events intended to satisfy a customer. It can include procurement, manufacture, distribution, and waste disposal, together with associated transport, storage and information technology.

This definition of logistics is broad, reflecting its provenance. More typically, logistics is used to refer not to all supply chain activities, but specifically to the management of logistics or **inbound** and **outbound logistics** (Figure 6.2). Logistics is essential to the efficient management of the supply chain.

To understand why supply chain management plays an important role in modern management thinking, read Box 6.3.

Box 6.3   Developments in supply chain management

In order to understand how e-commerce can be used to enhance supply chain and logistics management it is useful to consider the historical context of management approaches to supply chain management and how information systems have been used to support them. The following stages can be identified.

1960s/70s: Physical distribution management (PDM)
PDM focussed upon the physical movement of goods by treating stock management, warehousing, order processing and delivery as related rather than separate activities. Although information systems were developed to manage these processes they were often paper-based and not integrated across different functions. However, some leading companies started using EDI at this time. EDI was mainly used on a point-to-point basis for document automation with electronic purchaser orders sent to suppliers who responded with shipping notes and invoices. PDM was essentially about the management of finished goods but not about the management of materials and processes that impacted upon the distribution process. PDM was superseded by logistics management which viewed manufacturing storage and transport from raw material to final consumer as integral parts of a total distribution process.

1970s/80s: Logistics management (materials requirement planning (MRP) and just-in-time – JIT)
The just-in-time philosophy (JIT) aims to make the process of raw materials acquisition, production and distribution as efficient and flexible as possible in terms of material supply and customer service. Minimum order quantities and stock levels were sought by the customer and therefore manufacturers had to introduce flexible manufacturing processes and systems that interfaced directly with the customer who could call an order directly against a prearranged schedule with a guarantee that it would be delivered on time. Materials requirement planning systems were important in maintaining resources at an optimal level. The design for manufacture technique was used

to simplify the number of components required for manufacture. An associated phenomenon is lean production and lean supply where supply chain efficiency is aimed at eliminating waste and minimising inventory and work in progress.

1980s/90s: Supply chain management and efficient consumer response (ECR)

Effective management of the supply chain involved much closer integration between the supplier, customer and intermediaries and in some instances involved one organisation in the channel taking over functions that were traditionally the domain of the intermediary. Bottlenecks or undersupply/oversupply can have a significant impact on an organisation's profitability. The two primary goals of supply chain management are to maximise the efficiency and effectiveness of the total supply chain for the benefit of all the players, not just one section of the channel, and to maximise the opportunity for customer purchase by ensuring adequate stock levels at all stages of the process. These two goals impact upon the sourcing of raw materials and stockholding. A recent phenomenon has been the rapid growth in global sourcing of supplies from preferred suppliers, particularly amongst multinational or global organisations. The Internet will provide increased capability for smaller players to globally source raw materials and therefore improve their competitiveness. Quelch and Klein (1996) argue that the Internet will revolutionise the dynamics of international commerce and in particular lead to the more rapid internationalisation of small and medium-sized enterprises. The web will reduce the competitive advantage of economies of scale in many industries, making it easier for smaller companies to compete on a worldwide basis.

New integrated information systems such as the SAP enterprise resource planning (ERP) system have helped manage the entire supply chain. ERP systems include modules which are deployed throughout the business and interface with suppliers through EDI or XML. These can potentially automate the requests for new orders. Technology has enabled the introduction of faster, more responsive and flexible ordering, manufacturing and distribution systems, which has diminished even further the need for warehouses to be located near to markets that they serve.

1990s/2000s: Technological interface management (TIM)

According to Hamill and Gregory (1997), the challenge facing suppliers, intermediaries and customers in the supply chain will shift from a focus on physically distributing goods to a process of collection, collation, interpretation and dissemination of vast amounts of information. Enterprise resource planning systems are continuously being updated to support direct data interfaces with suppliers and customers, for example to support EDI. A more recent development is interfacing of ERP systems with B2B intermediary sites or exchanges such as Elemica, referred to in Case study 6.1. (See the '*Focus on B2B marketplaces*' in Chapter 7 for further discussion of these.) SAP has also created the mySAP facility to help customers manage and personalise their interactions with these exchanges. XML (Chapter 3) is increasingly used as the technical means by which technological interface management is achieved. (The critical resource possessed by these new intermediaries will be information rather than inventory. Hagel and Rayport (1997) take this a stage further by suggesting that customer information capture will serve customers rather than vendors in future. Currently customers leave a trail of information behind them as they visit sites and make transactions. This data can be captured and then used by suppliers and agents to improve targeting of offers. However, as customers become more aware of the value of information and as technology on the Internet enables them to protect private information relating to site visits and transactions, then the opportunity grows for intermediaries to act as customer agents and not supplier agents.)

Push and pull supply chain models

Push supply chain
A supply chain that emphasises distribution of a product to passive customers.

A change in supply chain thinking, and also in marketing communications thinking, is the move from push models of selling to pull models or to combined push–pull approaches. The **push** model is illustrated by a manufacturer who perhaps develops an innovative product, identifies a suitable target market and creates a distribution channel to push the product to the market – Figure 6.7(a). The typical motivation for a push approach is to optimise the production process for cost and efficiency.

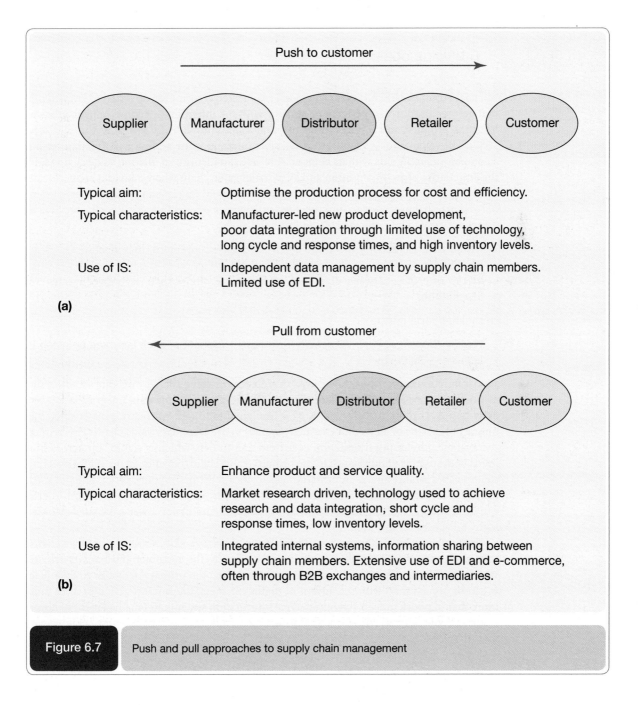

(a)

Push to customer

Supplier — Manufacturer — Distributor — Retailer — Customer

Typical aim:	Optimise the production process for cost and efficiency.
Typical characteristics:	Manufacturer-led new product development, poor data integration through limited use of technology, long cycle and response times, and high inventory levels.
Use of IS:	Independent data management by supply chain members. Limited use of EDI.

(b)

Pull from customer

Supplier — Manufacturer — Distributor — Retailer — Customer

Typical aim:	Enhance product and service quality.
Typical characteristics:	Market research driven, technology used to achieve research and data integration, short cycle and response times, low inventory levels.
Use of IS:	Integrated internal systems, information sharing between supply chain members. Extensive use of EDI and e-commerce, often through B2B exchanges and intermediaries.

Figure 6.7   Push and pull approaches to supply chain management

Pull supply chain
An emphasis on using the supply chain to deliver value to customers who are actively involved in product and service specification.

The alternative approach consistent with ECR is the **pull model**, which is focussed on the customer's needs and starts with analysis of their requirements through market research and close cooperation with customers and suppliers in new product development (Figure 6.7(b)). Here the supply chain is constructed to deliver value to the customer by reducing costs and increasing service quality. Figure 6.7(b) shows how there are much closer links between the elements of the supply chain through use of technology such as EDI to minimise document transfer and rekeying. The typical motivation for a pull approach is to optimise the production process for customer response, cost and efficiency. Such an approach is also consistent with management thinking about the similar concept of the value chain as illustrated in the '*Focus on* The value chain' section.

Focus on	The value chain

Value chain (VC)
A model that considers how supply chain activities can add value to products and services delivered to the customer.

Michael Porter's **value chain (VC)** is a well-established concept for considering key activities that an organisation can perform or manage with the intention of adding value for the customer as products and services move from conception to delivery to the customer (Porter, 1980). The value chain is a model that describes different value-adding activities that connect a company's supply side with its demand side. We can identify an *internal* value chain within the boundaries of an organisation and an *external* value chain where activities are performed by partners. By analysing the different parts of the value chain managers can redesign internal and external processes to improve their efficiency and effectiveness. Benefits for the customer are created by reducing cost *and* adding value:

- *within each* element of the value chain such as procurement, manufacture, sales and distribution;
- *at the interface between* elements of the value chain such as between sales and distribution.

In equation form this is:

Value = (Benefit of each VC activity – Its cost) + (Benefit of each interface between VC activities – Its cost)

Electronic communications can be used to enhance the value chain by making activities such as procurement more efficient (see Chapter 7) and also enabling data integration between activities. According to IBF (2008), BT's implementation of e-procurement enabled 95% online purchasing of all its office-related supplies in the secondary value chain. This reduced the average purchasing transaction cost from £56 to £40, which is significant across hundreds of thousands of purchases. In the primary value chain, benefits can be even greater; for example, if a retailer shares information electronically with a supplier about demand for its products, this can enhance the value chain of both parties since the cycle time for ordering can be reduced, resulting in lower inventory holding and hence lower costs for both. Case study 6.1 illustrates this point.

Traditional value chain analysis (Figure 6.8(a)) distinguishes between *primary activities* that contribute directly to getting goods and services to the customer and *support activities* which provide the inputs and infrastructure that allow the primary activities to take place. It can be argued that, with the advent of digital business, the support activities offer much more than support; indeed, having effective information systems and management of human resources contributes critically to the primary activities. Michael Porter now acknowledges that this is the case.

Internet technologies can reduce production times and costs by increasing the flow of information as a way to *integrate* different value chain activities. Rayport and Sviokla (1996) contend that the Internet enables value to be created by gathering, organising, selecting, synthesising and distributing information. They refer to a separate parallel virtual value chain

Figure 6.8	Two alternative models of the value chain: (a) Traditional value chain model, (b) Revised value chain model *Source*: Adapted from Deise *et al*. (2000) Figure 6.4(b).

mirroring the physical value chain. The *virtual value chain* involves electronic commerce used to mediate traditional value chain activities such as market research, procurement, logistics, manufacture, marketing and distribution. The processing is machine-based or 'virtual' rather than paper-based. Human intervention is still required in many activities but the 'virtuality' of the value chain will increase as software agents increasingly perform these activities.

Restructuring the internal value chain

Traditional models of the value chain (such as Figure 6.8(a)) have been re-evaluated with the advent of global electronic communications. It can be suggested that there are some key weaknesses in the traditional value chain model:

- It is most applicable to manufacturing of physical products as opposed to providing services.
- It is a one-way chain involved with pushing products to the customer; it does not highlight the importance of understanding customer needs.
- The internal value chain does not emphasise the importance of value networks (although Porter (1980) did produce a diagram that indicated network relationships).

A revised form of the value chain has been suggested by Deise *et al.* (2000); an adaptation of this model is presented in Figure 6.8(b). This value chain starts with the market research process, emphasising the importance of real-time environment scanning made possible through electronic communications links with distributors and customers. For example, leading e-tailers now monitor, on an hourly basis, how customers are responding to promotional offers on their website and review competitors' offers and then revise them accordingly. Similarly, manufacturers such as Cisco have feedback forms and forums on their site that enable them to collect information from customers and channel partners that can feed through to new product development. As new product development occurs the marketing strategy will be refined and at the same time steps can be taken to obtain the resources and production processes necessary to create, store and distribute the new product. Through analysis of the value chain and looking at how electronic communications can be used to speed up the process, manufacturers have been able to significantly reduce time to market from conception of a new product idea through to launch on the market. At the same time the use of technology increases value chain efficiency.

Electronic commerce also has implications for whether value chain activities are achieved internally or externally. These changes have been referred to as value chain *disaggregation* (Kalakota and Robinson, 2000) or *deconstruction* (Timmers, 1999) and value chain *reaggregation* (Kalakota and Robinson, 2000) or *reconstruction* (Timmers, 1999). Disaggregation can occur through deconstructing the primary activities of the value chain and approaching the elements in a new way. In reaggregation the value chain is streamlined to increase efficiency between each of the stages. Indeed, Timmers (1999) notes that the conventional wisdom of the value chain as a separate series of discrete steps may no longer be tenable as steps such as inbound logistics and operations become more tightly integrated through technology. We have only touched upon changes to the structure of the value chain here, since there is great similarity with the changes possible in the structure of the supply chain. This is evaluated in more depth in the sections on vertical integration and models for redefining the value chain.

The value stream

Value stream
The combination of actions required to deliver value to the customer as products and services.

The **value stream** is a concept closely related to the value chain. The difference is that it considers different types of tasks that are involved with adding value and looks at how the efficiency of these tasks can be improved. Womack and Jones (1998) define the value stream as:

> *the set of all the specific actions required to bring a specific product through the three critical management tasks of any business:*
>
> 1 the problem-solving task [the processes of new product development and production launch]
> 2 the information management task [the processes of order taking, scheduling to delivery]
> 3 the physical transformation task [the processes of transforming raw materials to finished product delivered to customers].

Tasks 2 and 3 are traditional value chain activities (Figure 6.8(a)), but task 1 is not.

Returning to the definition of customer value from Deise *et al.* (2000) shown in the equation below, we can see that the lean thinking approach proposed by Womack and Jones is aimed at adding value by cutting out waste in each of these three management tasks. By reducing new product development and production times and costs, organisations can then either increase customer value by decreasing fulfilment time or price, and/or increasing product and service quality. Clearly e-commerce plays a key role in decreasing time to market and production times and costs.

$$Customer\ value\ (brand\ perception) = \frac{Product\ quality \times Service\ quality}{Price \times Fulfilment\ time}$$

Value chain analysis

This is an analytical framework for decomposing an organisation into its individual activities and determining value added at each stage. In this way the organisation can then assess how effectively resources are being used. It may be possible to use information systems to increase the efficiency of resource usage for each element in the value chain and even *between* activities.

How can an organisation positively impact on its value chain by investing in new or upgraded information systems? Porter and Millar (1985) propose the following five-step process.

1 **Step 1** Assess the information intensity of the value chain (i.e. the level and usage of information within each value chain activity and between each level of activity). The higher the level of intensity and/or the higher the degree of reliance on good-quality information, the greater the potential impact of new information systems.
2 **Step 2** Determine the role of IS in the industry structure. It is also important here to understand the information linkages between buyers and suppliers within the industry and how they and competitors might be affected by and react to new information technology.
3 **Step 3** Identify and rank the ways in which IS might create competitive advantage. High-cost or critical activity areas present good targets.
4 **Step 4** Investigate how IS might spawn new businesses.
5 **Step 5** Develop a plan for taking advantage of IS, which is business-driven rather than technology-driven. The plan should assign priorities to the IS investments (which of course should be subjected to an appropriate cost–benefit analysis).

This process can also be applied to an organisation's external value chain. Womack and Jones (1998) refer to *value stream analysis*, which considers how the whole production and delivery process can be made more efficient. They suggest that companies should map every activity that occurs in creating new products and delivering products or services to customers and then categorise them as:

1 Those that create value as perceived by the customer.
2 Those which create no value, but are required by product development or production systems and so cannot immediately be eliminated.
3 Those that don't add value, so can be immediately eliminated.

Having performed this analysis, plans can be made for removing the category 3 activities and then eliminating category 2 activities and enhancing category 1 activities. Womack and Jones give the example of the value stream for a cola can. Even a superficially simple product such as canned cola can have many activities involved in its production. Indeed there are several value streams: that in producing the can itself, those to produce the contents from beet field to sugar and corn field to caramel and those to produce the packaging. Taking the example of the can itself, value stream analysis can be performed to identify the stages in production as follows:

1 Mine bauxite.
2 Reduction mill.
3 Smelter.
4 Hot rolling mill.
5 Cold rolling mill.
6 Can maker.
7 Bottler.
8 Regional distribution centre (RDC).
9 Retail unit storage.
10 Home storage.

In value stream analysis, efficiency for each of the stages above will be calculated. For example, at stage 7, the bottler (adding the drink to the can), Womack and Jones (1998) give times of incoming storage four days, processing time one minute, finished storage five weeks. The need for such analysis is shown by the delays in the whole process which give incoming storage of five months, finished storage of six months, but processing time of only three hours. This gives a total cycle time of nearly a year from mine to home. Clearly, if information management can be used to reduce these storage times, it can create large savings in terms of reduced storage capacities. The benefits are evident for a retailer such as Tesco that has already undertaken value stream analysis and deployed e-commerce in the Tesco Information Exchange to reduce its storage in the RDC and in-store to only two and three days respectively. It has also been able to move to a system of continuous replenishment in 24 hours. Orders made by a Tesco store on a Monday night are delivered from suppliers via the RDCs to arrive before the store opens Wednesday morning!

At a practical level, improvements in the value chain are implemented through iterative improvements planning implemented through Sales and Operations Planning (S&OP) systems. Kjellsdotter and Jonsson (2010) have identified these benefits of digital business throughout the stages of an iterative planning cycle:

1 **Creating a consensus forecast.** Using statistical forecast methods, demand planning tools are able to integrate different departments and companies for improved decision support.

2 **Creating a preliminary delivery plan.** Reducing planning effort through applying the insights from the forecast.

3 **Creating a preliminary production plan.** Possibility to integrate several entities, coordination of different functions, possibility to use optimisation models to find the most feasible solution.

4 **Adjusting delivery and production plan.** Visibility of information, scenario analysis, for example what-if analyses of the impact in resource availability and customer demands.

5 **Settle delivery and production plan.** Overall benefits of tangible cost savings and the intangible benefit of improved confidence in planning and scheduling.

Value networks

Reduced time to market and increased customer responsiveness are not simply the result of reviewing the efficiency of internal processes and how information systems are deployed, but also result through consideration of how partners can be involved to outsource some processes. Porter's original work considered not only the internal value chain, but also the **external value chain or value network**. As companies outsource more and more activities, management of the links between the company and its partners becomes more important. Deise *et al.* (2000) describe value network management as:

> *the process of effectively deciding what to outsource in a constraint-based, real-time environment based on fluctuation.*

Electronic communications have enabled the transfer of information necessary to create, manage and monitor outsourcing partnerships. These links are also mediated through intermediaries known as 'value chain integrators' or directly between partners. As a result the concept of managing a value network of partners has become commonplace.

Figure 6.9, which is adapted from the model of Deise *et al.* (2000), shows some of the partners of a value network that characterises partners as:

1 Supply-side partners (upstream supply chain) such as suppliers, business-to-business exchanges, wholesalers and distributors.

2 Partners that fulfil primary or core value chain activities. In some companies the management of inbound logistics may be outsourced, in others different aspects of the manufacturing process. In the virtual organisation all core activities may be outsourced.

3 Sell-side partners (downstream supply chain) such as business-to-business exchanges, wholesalers, distributors and customers (not shown, since conceived as distinct from other partners).

4 Value chain integrators or partners who supply services that mediate the internal and external value chain. These companies typically provide the electronic infrastructure for a company.

External value chain or value network
The links between an organisation and its strategic and non-strategic partners that form its external value chain.

Strategic core VC partners

| Inbound logistics | Manufacturing | Product warehousing |

Value chain integrators*

Upstream VC partners

Suppliers

Buy-side intermediaries

Core value chain activities

Downstream VC partners

Fulfilment

Sell-side intermediaries

Value chain integrators*

*includes IS partners, for example:
- Strategic outsourcer
- System integrator
- ISP/WAN provider
- ASP provider

| Finance | Human resources | Admin e.g. travel |

Non-strategic service partners

| **Figure 6.9** | Members of the value network of an organisation
Source: Adapted from Deise *et al*. (2000). |

The similarity between elements of the value network of Figure 6.9 and the supply chain of a typical B2B company of Figure 6.5 will be apparent. But the value network offers a different perspective that is intended to emphasise:

- The electronic interconnections between partners and the organisation and directly between partners that potentially enables real-time information exchange between partners.
- The dynamic nature of the network. The network can be readily modified according to market conditions or in response to customer demands. New partners can readily be introduced into the network and others removed.
- Different types of links can be formed between different types of partners.

Wholesale outsourcing to third parties is not the only option. The different types of partnership that can be formed are described in more detail in the later section on 'Managing partnerships'. Remember also that outsourcing does imply cost reduction. Michael Dell relates that Dell do not see outsourcing as getting rid of a process that does not add value; rather they see it as a way of '*coordinating their activity to create the most value for customers*' (Magretta, 1998). Dell has improved customer service by changing the way it works with both its suppliers and distributors to build a computer to the customer's specific order within just six days.

Towards the virtual organisation

Davidow and Malone (1992) describe a virtual corporation as follows:

To the outside observer, it will appear almost edgeless, with permeable and continuously changing interfaces between company, supplier and customer. From inside the firm, the view will be no less amorphous, with traditional offices, departments, and operating divisions constantly reforming according to need. Job responsibilities will regularly shift.

Virtual organisation

An organisation which uses information and communications technology to allow it to operate without clearly defined physical boundaries between different functions.

An implication of increasing outsourcing of core activities is that companies will move towards the **virtual organisation**. Benjamin and Wigand (1995) state that '*it is becoming increasingly difficult to delineate accurately the borders of today's organisations*'. Electronic networks make it easier to outsource aspects of the production and distribution of goods to third parties (Kraut *et al.*, 1998). This can lead to the boundaries between supplier and organisation becoming blurred. Employees may work in any time zone and customers are able to purchase tailored products from any location. The absence of any rigid boundary or hierarchy within the organisation should lead to a more responsive and flexible company with greater market orientation.

Virtual organisations can also be viewed as a way of transforming existing organisations. Malcolm Warner has defined a virtual organisation, in this context, as follows:

> *Put simply, it is an organisational form that enables companies to reduce their physical assets (large headquarters, centralised plants and so on), relying instead on small decentralised units linked by a strong communications network. In other words, the old physical constraints of the plant and office building are broken down, and activities of co-ordination and control, which used to take place face-to-face, are now handled remotely 'over the wire'. (Warner, 2001)*

He suggests that companies are experimenting with different characteristics of virtual organisations, including:

- *Lack of physical structure*: virtual organisations have little or no physical existence.
- *Reliance on knowledge*: the lack of physical facilities and contacts means that knowledge is the key driving force of the virtual organisation.
- *Use of communications technologies*: it follows that virtual organisations tend to rely on information technology.
- *Mobile work*: the reliance on communications technologies means that the traditional office or plant is no longer the only site where work is carried out.
- *Boundaryless and inclusive*: virtual companies tend to have fuzzy boundaries.
- *Flexible and responsive*: virtual organisations can be pulled together quickly from disparate elements, used to achieve a certain business goal and then dismantled again.

An alternative viewpoint on features of a virtual organisation (Kraut *et al.*, 1998) is:

1 Processes transcend the boundaries of a single firm and are not controlled by a single organisational hierarchy.
2 Production processes are flexible with different parties involved at different times.
3 Parties involved in the production of a single product are often geographically dispersed.
4 Coordination is heavily dependent on telecommunications and data networks.

Virtualisation

The process of a company developing more of the characteristics of the virtual organisation.

Here, all companies tend to have some elements of the virtual organisation. As these characteristics increase this is known as **virtualisation**. Malone *et al.* (1987) argued that the presence of electronic networks tends to lead to virtualisation since the governance and coordination of business transactions can be conducted effectively at lower costs.

Mini-case study 6.1 on the Pebble watch and the PwC (2013) research at the end of this chapter give further examples of virtualisation through outsourcing.

Options for restructuring the supply chain

As part of strategy definition for digital business, managers will consider how the structure of the supply chain can be modified. These are mainly choices that have existed for many years but Internet technology provides a more efficient enabler and lower-cost communications.

Vertical integration
The extent to which supply chain activities are undertaken and controlled within the organisation.

Virtual integration
The majority of supply chain activities are undertaken and controlled outside the organisation by third parties.

Supply chain management options can be viewed as a continuum between internal control ('**vertical integration**') and external control through outsourcing ('**virtual integration**'). The intermediate situation is sometimes referred to as 'vertical disintegration' or 'supply chain disaggregation'. This continuum is illustrated in Figure 6.10.

There was a general trend during the second half of the twentieth century from vertical integration through vertical disintegration to virtual integration. In the car manufacturing industry traditionally car plants would be located near to a steelworks so that the input would be raw materials, with finished cars as the output. Other components of the car would also be manufactured by the company and other value chain activities such as marketing would largely be performed in-house. There has been a gradual move to sourcing more and more components such as lights, upholstery and trim and even engines to third parties. Marketing activities are now largely outsourced to marketing agencies. Another example is the purchase by pharmaceutical companies of pharmacy benefit managers (companies that manage drug distribution with private and company health schemes). By acquiring these companies which are part of a pharmaceutical company's downstream supply chain the aim is to 'get closer to the customer' while at the same time favourably controlling the distribution of the company's own drugs.

Hayes and Wheelwright (1994) provide a useful framework that summarises choices for an organisation's vertical integration strategy. The three main decisions are:

1 **The direction of any expansion.** Should the company aim to direct ownership at the upstream or downstream supply chain? The pharmaceuticals companies referred to above have decided to buy into the downstream part of the supply network (downstream vertical integration). This is sometimes referred to as an offensive strategic move since it enables the company to increase its power with respect to customers. Alternatively, if the pharmaceuticals company purchased other research labs this would be upstream-directed vertical integration which is strategically defensive.

2 **The extent of vertical integration.** How far should the company take downstream or upstream vertical integration? Originally car manufacturers had a high degree of vertical integration, but more recently they have moved from a wide process span to a narrow process span.

Figure 6.10 The characteristics of vertical integration, vertical disintegration and virtual integration

3 **The balance amongst the vertically integrated stages.** To what extent does each stage of the supply chain focus on supporting the immediate supply chain? For example, if a supplier to a motor manufacturer also produced components for other industries this would be an unbalanced situation.

Debate 6.2

Virtual integration and outsourcing of core processes

'The success of companies such as Dell in outsourcing core business processes and in virtual integration suggests that all companies need to adopt this model in order to be competitive.'

Combining these concepts, we can refer to a typical B2B company (Figure 6.5). If it owned the majority of the upstream and downstream elements of the supply chain and each element was focussed on supporting the activities of a B2B company, its strategy would be to follow upstream and downstream directions of vertical integration with a wide process span and a high degree of balance. Alternatively, if the strategy were changed to focus on core competencies it could be said to have a narrow process span.

How, then, can electronic communications support these strategies? Through increasing the flow of information between members of the supply chain, a strategy of narrower process span can be supported by e-commerce. However, this relies on all members of the supply chain being e-enabled. Companies undertaking offensive or defensive strategies will be in a better position to stipulate adoption of e-commerce, and so increase the overall efficiency of the supply chain. As we saw in Case study 6.1, a company such as Shell helps e-enable the supply chain by sharing information in its own databases with customers to increase the efficiency of the supply chain.

Our next example in the manufacture of personal computers also illustrates the concept of the two different supply chain products. Complete Activity 6.2 to review the benefits of each approach.

Activity 6.2 | **Supply chain models in personal computer manufacture**

Activity

1 Review the approaches of the two companies illustrated below. Which tends to vertical integration and which tends to virtual integration?

2 Produce a table summarising the benefits and disadvantages of each approach. Which do you think is the better approach?

3 How can information systems facilitate each approach?

Approach 1 IBM during the 1980s and early 1990s

Manufacture of many components by IBM plants in different locations including IBM processors, IBM hard disks, IBM cases and IBM monitors and even IBM mice. Distribution to companies by IBM logistics.

Approach 2 Dell during the 1990s and 2000s

Manufacture of all components by third parties in different locations including Intel processors, Seagate hard disks, Sony monitors and Microsoft mice. Assembly of some components in final product by third parties, e.g. adding appropriate monitor to system unit for each order.

Answers to activities can be found at www.pearsoned.co.uk/chaffey

Using digital business to restructure the supply chain

Information supply chain

An information-centric view of the supply chain which addresses the organisational and technological challenges of achieving technology-enabled supply chain management efficiency and effectiveness.

Using digital communications to improve supply chain efficiency is dependent on effective exchange and sharing of information. The challenges of achieving standardised data formats and data exchange have given rise to the study of optimisation of the **information supply chain** (ISC) as suggested by Marinos (2005) and Sun and Yen (2005). March *et al.* (2007) describe the ISC as:

> *an information-centric view of physical and virtual supply chains where each entity adds value to the chain by providing the right information to the right entity at the right time in a secure manner. ISCs create value for the collaborating entities by gathering, organizing, selecting, synthesizing, and distributing information. The challenges to cultivating an ISC arise from both organizational and technological perspectives. Agility and flexibility in both internal and inter-organizational business processes are required to benefit from technology investments in ISCs.*

This definition shows the scope and challenges of managing the ISC. Research by Legner and Schemm (2008) suggests two different types of information sharing and coordination problems in the retail and consumer goods industries: (1) the transactional information flow that allows for coordinating the physical demand and supply chain (demand signals, forecasts, orders, shipping, notifications, or invoices), and (2) the contextual information flow that ensures that retailers and manufacturers interpret data in the same way. They explain that a well-established problem is the 'bullwhip effect' or **information asymmetry** which results in amplification of the demand signal and fluctuation of inventory level along a supply chain. The ECR concept introduced earlier in this chapter is an attempt to reduce information asymmetry. Although information asymmetry can be reduced through the use of technology, technical barriers such as the lack of standards, expertise or the cost of implementation will prevent it. Organisational issues such as the level of trust of supply chain partners and the competitive advantage that may result from keeping information are equally significant.

Information asymmetry

Imperfect information sharing between members of a supply chain which increases uncertainty about demand and pricing.

In this section we review efforts to optimise the ISC and describe the benefits of implementing ISC support technologies. We then consider how companies can use technologies to support the management of the upstream and downstream supply chain.

Technology options and standards for supply chain management

Some of the data transfer options and standards which enable e-SCM were introduced in Chapter 3. These include:

- EDI which is an established and relatively simple method of exchanging orders, delivery notes and invoices.
- XML- or XML-EDI-based data transfer enables more sophisticated one-to-many data transfers such as a request for orders being transmitted to potential suppliers.
- Middleware or software used to integrate or translate requests from external systems in real time so they are understood by internal systems and follow-up events will be triggered.
- Manual email orders or online purchase through a traditional web-based e-commerce store for B2B.

These mechanisms enable data to be transferred to suppliers from clients using enterprise resource planning (ERP) systems which include material requirements planning modules which are used to model future demand for products, create a bill of materials of the relevant components needed to manufacture the products and then order them.

A rise in popularity of Software as a Service (SaaS, see Chapter 3) web applications has supported the growth of e-SCM systems as shown by Mini case study 6.3. (In Chapter 3 we discuss some of the advantages and disadvantages of SaaS and in particular the single- or multi-tenancy decision.)

Mini Case Study 6.3	E2open prospers through e-SCM as SaaS

E2open (Figure 6.11) is a leading provider of multi-enterprise value chain solutions delivered on demand as a working business process in a pay-as-you-go model. Benefits of E2open according to the company include *'end-to-end visibility, collaboration and responsiveness over global value networks with faster time-to-value, lower total cost of ownership, a continuous value roadmap, and easier integration between internal enterprise applications and trading partners, including suppliers, customers, distributors and logistics providers'*. Over 45,000 companies worldwide currently use E2open which offers the choice of single-tenancy or multi-tenancy.

Companies that use E2open to support supply chain management include the Boeing Company, Celestica, Cisco Systems, Flextronics, Hitachi, IBM, LG Electronics, LSI, Matsushita Electric Industrial (Panasonic), Motorola, Seagate Technology, Spansion, Vodafone, Wistron and YRC Worldwide.

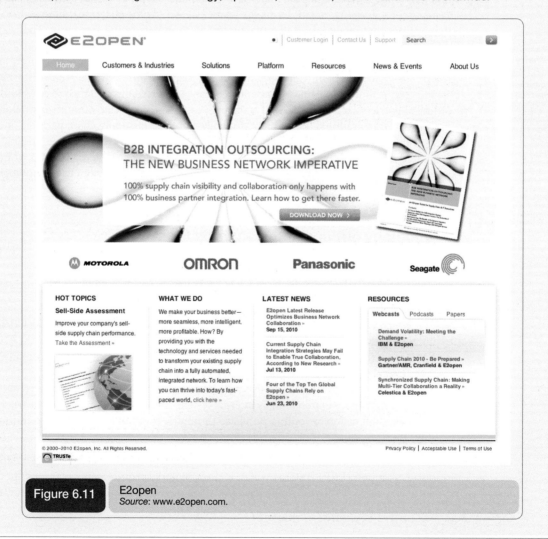

Figure 6.11	E2open *Source*: www.e2open.com.

Adoption rates of digital business applications

How popular are the digital business technologies for supply chain management? The European Commission Information Society report (European Commission, 2008) showed that the majority of businesses surveyed have Internet access; the proportion actively buying, selling or sharing information with partners online is much lower.

In 2006, the UK launched the Supplier Route to Government Portal (www.supply2.gov. uk) as part of its e-government initiative; this was an online marketplace for public-sector procurement valued at less than £100,000. Registered users could receive daily email alerts about contracts appropriate to them, search for contracts online and post details of their offerings. This service is no longer available, showing the difficulty in encouraging and sustaining adoption of these types of procurement services.

A European Union report (European Commission, 2008) also shows surprisingly low rates of adoption of different types of digital business applications. Figure 6.12 shows the popularity of different digital business applications. Despite the benefits of these applications, adoption is surprisingly low, particularly amongst smaller companies that use manual systems.

Benefits of e-supply chain management

Given the relative lack of adoption of e-SCM, particularly in SMEs, which opportunities are being missed that are available to adopters? Research by IDC (2004) into the challenges facing manufacturers in one sector (electronic component manufacture) showed that their main challenges (scored out of 5) were:

- Reduce order-to-delivery time (4.3).
- Reduce costs of manufacturing (4.1).
- Manage inventory more effectively (4.0).
- Improve demand forecasting (3.9).
- Reduce time to introduce new products (3.7).
- Improve after-market/post-sales operations (3.2).

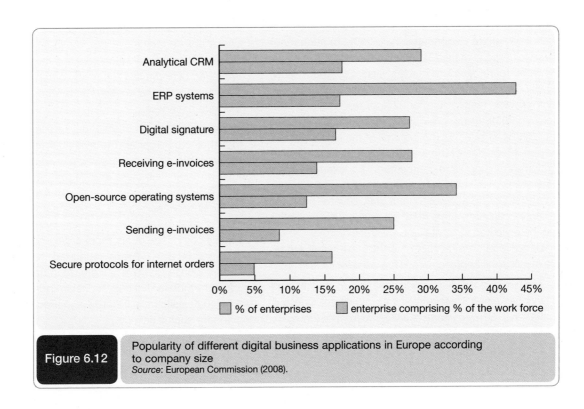

Figure 6.12   Popularity of different digital business applications in Europe according to company size
Source: European Commission (2008).

Typical benefits with respect to a B2B company include:

1 **Increased efficiency of individual processes.** If the B2B company adopts e-procurement this will result in a faster cycle time and lower cost per order (as described in Chapter 7). Benefit: reduced cycle time and cost per order (as described in Chapter 7).

2 **Reduced complexity of the supply chain.** This is the process of disintermediation referred to in Chapter 2. Here the B2B company will offer the facility to sell direct from its e-commerce site rather than through distributors or retailers. Benefit: reduced cost of channel distribution and sale.

3 **Improved data integration between elements of the supply chain.** The B2B company can share information with its suppliers on the demand for its products to optimise the supply process. Case study 6.2 on the Argos multichannel retail strategy shows the online sales growth that can be achieved through good integration of systems and data. Benefit: reduced cost of paper processing.

4 **Reduced cost through outsourcing.** The company can outsource or use virtual integration to transfer assets and costs such as inventory holding costs to third-party companies. Benefits: lower costs through price competition and reduced spend on manufacturing capacity and holding capacity.

5 **Innovation.** E-SCM should make it possible to be more flexible in delivering a more diverse range of products and to reduce time to market.

Benefit: better customer responsiveness.

Case Study 6.2	Argos uses e-supply chain management to improve customer convenience

Retailer Argos is a leading proponent of using supply chain management to improve multichannel sales. The transactional Argos website was launched in 2000 when they were pioneers in implementing a reservation service. Sales have grown significantly since the launch over 10 years ago.

According to E-consultancy (2010), multichannel sales for Argos reached £1.9bn in 2009. Its 'Check and Reserve' feature, which enables visitors to check store availability and then order from a specific store for later pick-up, was responsible for 22% of the retailer's total sales in 2009, growing by 36%. Internet sales account for 32% of all sales. Some features of the system which rely on integration of the website with different logistics systems are superior to competitors'. For example, real-time stock availability information is shown and while some retailers make customers wait several days for in-store collection, items reserved on the Argos website can be collected straightaway.

David Tarbuck is head of multichannel retail at Argos. He explains the approach Argos has used for its fulfilment:

The way Argos is built is unique in the UK market, and this has made it easier for us to implement Check & Reserve. Since customers are in the front of the store, and the stock is held in the back, we have a clear picture of stock levels in our stores. This means we can be confident that, if we ask our systems about stock levels at any store, this information will be accurate.

Check & Reserve gained immediate adoption with customers, and this has accelerated over the last two or three years, with this channel growing by 36% for a second year in a row. People have caught on to it, and appreciate the convenience of being able to check before they leave the house and save themselves a wasted journey. While our model has been improved over the last ten years, other retailers have a more difficult and costly process for implementing this kind of service.

A further benefit for multichannel retailers like Argos is that they can broaden the available range of products available to shoppers by providing extended ranges on their websites, and Argos planned to add 10,000 online-only products in 2010. Argos also provides kiosk services in-store to help customers arrange home delivery.

Mobile commerce offers more order choice for Argos customers. In 2010, Argos launched its first iPhone app, in response to a 600% increase in traffic to Argos. co.uk from mobile devices. In December 2009, Argos had 750,000 visits from iPhones and iPods, suggesting demand for such a service.

The iPhone app initially asks you to set your home store to make subsequent reservations smoother. The app can also find the local store via GPS, or by entering the town name or postcode. Results of local stores are shown via Google Maps, and details are provided on opening hours, as well as driving directions, and the option to set this as your store. You can then use the search icon to search for stock held at that store. The stock checker works just like the machines in the Argos stores. Each product page comes with some detailed review information, which makes the app very useful for people to do some extra product research while in the store. Once a product is selected, the reservation process is straightforward.

Argos is well known for catalogues, which are also part of retail multichannel strategy since products featured can encourage purchase both in-store and on the web. Argos release two catalogues every year, each with a print run of 18 million. David Tarbuck explains how the catalogue fits into the multichannel strategy works:

We have large numbers of people who have our catalogue in their lounges, on their coffee tables, and this gives us a presence in people's homes.

Catalogues are often the starting point for customers shopping with Argos, they will flick through the catalogue, or browse the website at the same time.

We have over 11,000 products online that aren't in the catalogue, so people will come online to check this and for latest offers, so catalogues are used in conjunction with other channels. With catalogues or any other

channel, it's all about talking to customers and working with them in whichever way they want to interact with us.

Tarbuck believes that the structure and focus of the team has also been important to success. He says:

We have a multichannel team, and I head up the development team and the operation of the website, overseeing online strategy.

We have e-commerce, marketing and commercial teams who respond to the trading side of the business, and make sure the various promotional campaigns are joined up, and there is consistency across channels. We've had a self-contained Internet-focussed team in place for the last ten years, and this dedicated team has been very closely related to marketing and other areas of the business.

Questions

1 Explain how Argos uses supply chain management to improve the proposition for its customers.
2 What do you think are the factors that have made Argos successful within its multichannel retail strategy?

Flexibility in adapting to new business requirements is a key capability of e-SCM systems. For example, in 2006, digital business system supplier and integrator SAP (www.sap.com) explained the three key capabilities of its SCM solution as:

- *Synchronise supply to demand* – Balance push and pull network planning processes. Replenish inventory and execute production based on actual demand.
- *Sense and respond with an adaptive supply chain network* – Drive distribution, transportation, and logistics processes that are integrated with real-time planning processes.
- *Provide network-wide visibility, collaboration, and analytics* – Monitor and analyse your extended supply chain.

Source: www.sap.com/solutions/business-suite/scm (no longer available).

An alternative perspective is to look at the benefits that technology can deliver to customers at the end of the supply chain. For the B2B company these could include:

- Increased convenience through 24 hours a day, 7 days a week, 365 days a year ordering.
- Increased choice of supplier leading to lower costs.
- Faster lead times and lower costs through reduced inventory holding.
- The facility to tailor products more readily.
- Increased information about products and transactions.

There are two alternative, contradictory implications of supply chains becoming electronically mediated networks. Malone *et al.* (1987) and Steinfield *et al.* (1996) suggest that networks may foster electronic marketplaces that are characterised by more *ephemeral* relationships. In other words, since it is easier to form an electronically mediated relationship, it is also easier for the customer to break it and choose another supplier. Counter to this is the suggestion that electronic networks may *lock in* customers to a particular supplier because of the overhead or risk in changing to another supplier.

The conception that the introduction of the Internet will tend to lead to more ephemeral relationships may yet prove to be the case as more intermediaries evolve and this becomes an accepted way of buying. However, the review by Steinfield *et al.* (1996) seems to suggest that EDI and the Internet tend to cement existing relationships. Furthermore, research indicates that the use of networks for buying may actually reduce outcomes such as quality, efficiency and satisfaction with suppliers. If the findings of Steinfield *et al.* (1996) are confirmed in practice, then this calls into doubt the future of many B2B marketplaces (Chapter 7, p. 314). Personal relationships between the members of the buying unit and the supplier still seem to be important.

IS-supported upstream supply chain management

The key activities of upstream supply chain management are procurement and upstream logistics. The way in which information systems can be used to support procurement in the digital business is of such importance that a whole chapter is devoted to this (Chapter 7). However, in the current chapter we look at some examples of how technologies are used to improve upstream supply chain management.

Many grocery retailers have been at the forefront of using technology to manage their upstream supply chain. For example, Tesco created the Tesco Information Exchange and other UK retailers have developed services such as 'Sainsbury Information Direct' and 'Safeway Supplier Information Service'. The Tesco Information Exchange (TIE) was developed in conjunction with GE Information Services (GEIS), and is an extranet solution that allows Tesco and its suppliers to collaboratively exchange trading information. TIE is linked to Tesco's key systems to give suppliers access to relevant and up-to-date information such as electronic point of sale (EPOS) data, to track sales and access the internal telephone/mail directory, so that suppliers can quickly find the right person to talk to.

RFID and The Internet of Things

Radio-frequency identification (RFID)
Microchip-based electronic tags are used for monitoring anything they are attached to, whether inanimate products or animate (people).

The Internet of Things
Objects are uniquely identified and tagged through technologies such as RFID and made accessible through Internet-like addresses.

Machine-to-machine (M2M) applications
Objects are uniquely identified and tagged through technologies such as RFID and made accessible through Internet-like addresses.

RFID tags are a relatively recent innovation in e-SCM that are already widely used for logistics purposes. They can be attached to individual product items in a warehouse or in a retail location. With appropriate RFID reader technology they can then be used to assess stock levels. With the possibility of the RFID reader being connected to a system to upload item location and status to the Internet, this approach is referred to as **The Internet of Things**, although the term was proposed in 1999 originally. Innovation is still continuing, with software companies such as Thingworx.com and wireless hardware services such as KORE collaborating to develop what are known as **Machine-to-Machine (M2M) applications**. According to ThingWorx (2013), in the mobile phone sector a solution will enable companies to order and manage SIM inventory more readily and access data about device location and last data session. For customers, they will be able to create custom bills and use more location-based services.

The approach is already used in simple systems like vending machines where data is exchanged with readers on stock availability. In the house of the future, appliances and devices will be located and activated using similar approaches.

RFID is still in a relatively early phase of its adoption, with PMP (2008) reporting that only 3% of UK companies are using RFID extensively while 19% are deploying it in some areas. A further 3% only use it if mandated by their customers, while 16% are planning to use it in a few areas. The main disadvantage of RFID technology is still seen as its cost, cited by 42% of respondents to PMP (2008), while a lack of technology standards is mentioned by 32% and a lack of consumer understanding or distrust by 23%.

Fisher (1997) makes the distinction between two strategies that manufacturers can follow according to the type of product and the nature of its demand. For functional products, particularly those with easily predictable demand, the product does not need to be modified frequently in response to consumer demand. Here the implication is that the supply chain should be directed at cost reduction and efficiency. For more complex products, including those with less predictable demand, Fisher (1997) gives the example of two contrasting products, skiwear from Sport Obermayer and soup from Campbell. Each year, 95% of Sport Obermayer's products are new designs and demand forecasts may err by over 200%. In contrast, 95% of Campbell's products are similar each year, with predictable demand levels. The strategic response for these products is to develop a physically efficient supply chain in the former case and a market-responsive supply chain in the latter case.

In a company such as Campbell the biggest cost savings are possible by reviewing the structure of the supply chain as a whole. In 1991 the company operationalised what it referred to as a 'continuous replenishment programme'. It set up EDI links with major retailers and each morning retailers electronically inform Campbell of their demand for all products. Campbell then uses this information to determine which products require replenishment. Trucks leave Campbell's shipping plants and then arrive at the retailers' distribution centres each day. This approach reduced the inventory of participating retailers from about four weeks to two weeks, with the associated cost reductions. This is the equivalent of a 1% increase in sales. This does not sound like a large improvement, but retailers' margins are thin, so this translates to a large increase in profitability on these product lines. The problem that Campbell encountered was that when it ran price promotions this could lead to up to five times the demand. This cannot be fulfilled on a short timescale so manufacture and retailer have to cooperate on advanced buying to meet these peaks in demand.

IS-supported downstream supply chain management

The key activities of downstream supply chain management are outbound logistics and fulfilment. In a B2B context the benefits for downstream customers are, of course, similar to the benefits that the organisation receives through automating its upstream supply chain. These issues are considered from a marketing perspective in Chapters 8 and 9, but in this chapter we review the importance of fulfilment in achieving e-commerce success.

We also use the grocery retail market to illustrate the implications of e-commerce for management of the downstream supply chain. Tesco is one of the leaders in using e-commerce for downstream supply chain management. Tesco's downstream supply chain involves selling direct to customers, in other words it is operating a strategy of disintermediation (Chapter 2, p. 53) by reducing the role of its branches. Through being an early adopter, Tesco.com has developed as the world's largest online grocery site.

Outbound logistics management

The importance of outbound logistics relates to the expectations of offering direct sales through a website. In a nutshell, logistics is crucial to delivering the service promise established on the website.

A different angle on the importance of logistics and how it relates to the bottom line is illustrated by the fortunes of Amazon. Phillips (2000) reported that the fulfilment mechanism was adding to Amazon's costs because of split shipments, where multiple deliveries of items are necessary from a single order. This is a particular problem in the USA, which is the source of 86% of Amazon's revenue. Here the distance between population centres requires a network of seven distribution centres for shipments. Phillips (2000) explains that the need to fulfil a single order by shipping items from multiple locations increases costs for postage and the labour to assemble and dispatch goods. The alternative situation of stocking all distribution centres with every product is financially prohibitive. Some analysts suggest that Amazon should change its logistics strategy by separating out its distribution operation as a separate revenue source and outsourcing fulfilment to reduce costs.

An indication of the scale of the challenge for distribution companies to deliver on time and provide services to enable customers to track shipment of products ordered online is shown by Mini case study 6.4.

Mini Case Study 6.4	Optimising the performance of the online sales channel at 3 Suisses France

Founded in 1932 in France, 3 Suisses originally ran a mail-order service for woollen knitting yarn manufactured at a spinning plant owned by the Toulemonde-Destombes family. 3 Suisses has since become one of France's leading multi-channel 'distance retailers', offering customers a wide range of goods, including clothing and household items, all of which can be bought via the Internet, by mail-order or over the phone.

Annually, 3 Suisses delivers more than 5 million consignments to its customers, representing a total of more than 15 million individual items. Having had a web presence since 1996, 3 Suisses' online business has experienced exponential growth, with, 80% of its turnover now generated online. The proprietary supply chain system the company previously relied on was not scalable enough, could not provide real-time inventory visibility and did not offer 3 Suisses the necessary flexibility to run a catalogue and digital commerce order fulfilment operation. This factor is underlined by 3 Suisses' strategy to become a pure-player and stop printed catalogues at the end of 2014.

In this context, the 3SI Group (the mother company of 3 Suisses) decided to reorganise its activities by mutualising the logistic expertise of its digital commerce brands, subsidiarising this activity and investing more than €250 million in new IT, new logistics processes, equipment and personnel training.

Dispeo, the new 3SI Group's subsidiary dedicated to supply chain and e-fulfilment, now works for in-house brands but also for external digital commerce competitors as a pure sub-contractor. It has been specifically designed to meet the essential needs of digital commerce - speed, reliability, cost and volume.

At the heart of Dispeo's logistics system is France's largest order-processing centre for digital commerce companies, opened in 2013. The centre is able to deliver 8 items a second, and prepare orders in just two hours, with 400,000 items dispatched each day.

Objectives of SCM

To optimise the performance of its online sales channel, which now generates 80% of the multi-channel retailer's revenues, 3 Suisses France set several key objectives. Firstly, the company wanted to improve product availability and inventory accuracy, and rationalise the order preparation process. Secondly, the

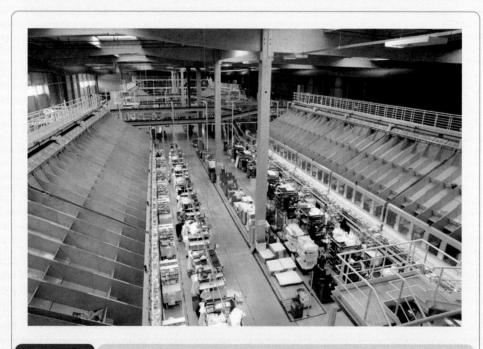

| Figure 6.13 | The Dispeo centre in Hem, France. |

company needed to support its multi-channel sales strategy by increasing its stock- keeping unit (SKU) range from 100,000 to 150,000 individual products, as well as improving visibility of inventory. Finally, 3 Suisses France sought to increase productivity levels and reduce operational costs.

By contracting its logistics and fulfilment operations to Dispeo, 3 Suisses has managed to render these costs variable and achieve its objectives.

Implementation of a new approach

Dispeo deployed Manhattan Associates' Warehouse Management solution for Open Systems and Supply Chain Intelligence solution at two distribution centres in Northern France, with a combined floor area of almost 1.5 million sq. ft. and a total storage capacity of over 1 million box spaces.

These solutions were implemented in three phases over a period of five months. The implementation required a complete change in the company's standard operating procedures (SOPs) in a very short period of time. Dispeo developed, with the Manhattan Associates, a well-defined and pragmatic training programme. A series of workshops in which Dispeo replicated processes from the warehouse floor and the introduction of a pilot zone within the warehouse where the company would train managers and operators in a 'real' environment culminated in the delivery of more than 13,000 hours of training.

Results of the implementation

A few months after the solutions' go-live, 3 Suisses France recorded these tangible results. Dispeo, using Manhattan Associates' solutions and a unique automated processing system, helped the company experience a 50% productivity improvement in the inventory receiving process, achieve significant improvement in overall service quality and obtain a real-time view of warehouse and outbound inventory. This real-time view, complemented by sales forecasts, enables 3 Suisses to optimise merchandise allocation when stock arrives in the warehouse. As a result, Dispeo's picking operations are more efficient and order fulfilment rates have improved, reducing the proportion of inaccurately prepared orders to historically low levels.

In addition, Dispeo benefits from improved productivity and has also reduced the warehouse area needed to process goods received by 50%, making better use of existing capacity. From storage to the flow transit zone and sorting equipment, everything has been designed for fast, reliable, high-capacity processing, enabling Dispeo to provide bespoke essential solutions for its digital commerce customers.

IS infrastructure for supply chain management

Supply chain visibility
Access to up-to-date, accurate, relevant information about supply chain processes to different stakeholders.

Information systems need to deliver **supply chain visibility** to different parties who need to access the supply chain information of an organisation, whether they be employees, suppliers, logistics service providers or customers. Users need to be able to personalise their view of the information according to their needs – customers want to see the status of their order, suppliers want to access the organisation's database to know when their customer is next likely to place a major order. Security is also important – if a company has differential pricing, it will not want customers to see price differences.

These requirements for delivering supply chain information imply the need for an integrated supply chain database with different personalised views for different parties. A typical integrated information systems infrastructure for delivering supply chain management is illustrated in Figure 6.14. It can be seen that applications can be divided into those for planning the supply chain and those to execute the supply chain processes. Case studies 6.1 and 6.2 are both good examples of how new technologies are used to collect demand data and transfer data between different databases and applications. A key feature of a modern supply chain infrastructure is the use of a central operational database that enables information to be shared between supply chain processes and applications. This operational database is usually part of an enterprise resource planning system such as SAP, Baan or Prism and is usually purchased with the applications for supply chain planning and execution. Some of the planning applications such as network simulation and optimisation are more likely to be supplied by separate software suppliers. The use of Internet technologies to deliver information over

Figure 6.14 A typical IS infrastructure for supply chain management

a TCP/IP protocol is becoming standard to reduce the costs of proprietary leased-line networks (Chapter 3). Information needed by managers to intervene in the supply chain process when problems occur is delivered as alerts or through continuous monitoring across secure private intranets or extranets used to link to partners.

Supply chain management implementation

The difficulties facing managers who are responsible for managing supply chains is indicated by these quotes from Conspectus (2000). When asked 'How difficult do you find it coordinating distribution and logistic plans at your sites?' a respondent from a UK mobile phone operator described his company's distribution and logistics process as 'an absolute nightmare'. Another commented:

> Everything is moving so quickly within our industry at the moment that sourcing suppliers and changing our processes to fit with them is a constant battle. We are hoping our SCM software and the roll-out of our extranet will grow end-to-end ROI but it is easy to forget that we must constantly examine the business model to ensure we are doing things right.

Data standardisation and exchange

The difficulties of exchanging information between incompatible systems has been a barrier limiting the adoption of SCM. Successful online marketplaces such as Elemica within the chemical industry have been based on collaboration between a limited number of partners within a vertical sector. But for markets with a more diverse range of products, standardisation is more difficult. GDSN is a more recent development which should help accelerate adoption of e-SCM (see Box 6.4).

Some of the benefits of this approach for retailers identified by Schemm *et al.* (2007) include:

- Order and item administration improved by 50%.
- Coupon rejection at the checkout reduced by 40%.
- Data management efforts reduced by 30%.
- Improvement of on-shelf availability, with out-of-stock items reduced from 8% to 3%.

The supply chain management strategy process

A strategic approach for supply chain management can also be defined using the SOSTAC™ approach(referred to in Chapters 5 and 8). Table 6.3 summarises a SOSTAC™ approach to supply chain management strategy development based on the guidance of Hughes *et al.* (1998). Table 6.3 implies a linear approach to strategic thinking, but, as was pointed out in Chapters 4 and 5, an iterative approach is called for in which there is a joint development between the organisation, the suppliers and other third parties.

Strategies for supply chain improvement have been categorised by Hughes *et al.* (1998) according to the scope of change and the speed of change. Figure 6.15 illustrates four strategic options for the supply chain. The two strategies that are relatively limited in scope apply to individual processes such as procurement or outbound logistics and can be thought of as delivering improvement at an operational level. These may give short-term benefits while minimising the risk of more radical change. Conversely, where the scope of change is more extensive there is a greater risk, but also greater potential reward. These changes include complete re-engineering of processes or major changes to the supply chain.

Box 6.4	Standardising the world's data with GDSN

Every commercial organisation has databases or catalogues containing information about the products they make, or sell, or buy. But, and it is a big but, the way in which they describe the information differs according to internal terminology, country, competing industry standards and when the database was last updated. This is one of the reasons for the development of barcodes and this principle has been developed further by supply chain trade organisation Global Standards One (GS1) into the Electronic Product Code (EPC) and GDSN.

The Global Data Synchronisation Network (GDSN) was launched in 2005 to create standards for sharing information about retail products. By 2008 there were over 2 million items registered. G1, the organisation that manages this standard, explains that there are five simple steps that allow trading partners to synchronise item, location and price data with each other:

1 **Load Data.** The seller registers product and company information in its data pool.
2 **Register Data.** A small subset of this data is sent to the GS1 Global Registry.
3 **Request Subscription.** The buyer, through its own data pool, subscribes to receive a seller's information.
4 **Publish Data.** The seller's data pool publishes the requested information to the buyer's data pool.
5 **Confirm & Inform.** The buyer sends a confirmation to the seller via each company's data pool, which informs the supplier of the action taken by the retailer using the information.

Table 6.3	A SOSTAC™ approach to supply chain management

Strategy element	SCM approach of Hughes *et al.* (1998)
Situation analysis	Gather the data: • Internal assessment of current approaches to the supply chain • External analysis of marketplace trends and customer opportunities
Objective setting	Set the objectives • Definition of required target returns and release of shareholder value
Strategy	Frame the strategies: • Development of supply chain strategies to achieve these goals (actions)
Tactics	Prioritisation of operational improvement strategies and quick wins
Actions	Implement the change and challenge the thinking: • Formation of a supply chain strategy forum to assess the needs • Analysis of value-added, cost and cycle time of supply chain activities • Cascade of executive-led project groups to scrutinise key processes • Allocation of business development strategies to sponsor executives
Control	Measure the outcome: • Integration of supply chain measurement in corporation-wide reviews • Baselining to maintain pressure for performance delivery

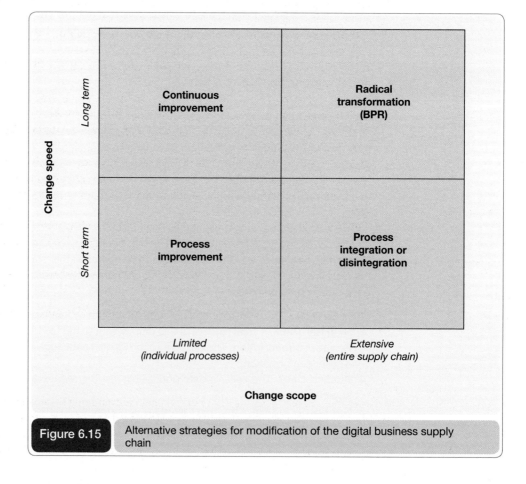

Figure 6.15	Alternative strategies for modification of the digital business supply chain

Goal-setting and performance management for e-SCM

In an earlier section we discussed the benefits of e-supply chain management. To manage e-SCM effectively, the type of benefits such as time and cost savings and an improved service to customers should be developed into a performance management framework. Sambasivan *et al.* (2009) have consolidated performance measures described by other supply chain management researchers. In their measurement framework, they identified these categories of measures and gave examples of metrics within each:

1 **Cost in supply chain:** Total cost, distribution cost, manufacturing cost, inventory cost.
2 **Profitability:** ROI.
3 **Customer responsiveness:** Time required to produce, number of orders delivered on time, number of units produced, fill rate, stockout probability, number of back-orders, number of stockouts, customer response time, average lead time, shipping errors, customer complaints.
4 **Flexibility:** Volume flexibility, delivery flexibility, mix flexibility, new product flexibility, planned order procedures, order lead time, customer order path.
5 **Supply chain partnership:** Level and degree of information sharing, buyer–vendor cost-saving initiatives, extent of mutual cooperation leading to improved quality, extent of mutual assistance in problem-solving efforts, the entity and stage at which supplier is involved.
6 **Production level metric:** Range of products and services, effectiveness of scheduling techniques, capacity utilisation.
7 **Delivery performance:** Delivery-to-request data, delivery-to-commit date, order fill lead time, number of faultless notes invoiced, flexibility of delivery systems to meet customer needs, total distribution cost, delivery lead time.
8 **Customer service and satisfaction:** Flexibility, customer query time, post-transaction measures of customer service, customer perception of service.
9 **Supply chain finance and logistics cost:** Cost associated with assets and ROI, total inventory cost, total cash flow time.
10 **Cost performance:** Material cost, labour cost, machinery energy cost, machinery material consumption, inventory and WIP level, total productivity, direct labour productivity, fixed capital productivity, indirect labour productivity, working capital productivity, value-added productivity.
11 **Internal and external time performance:** Time to market, distribution lead time, delivery reliability, supplier lead time, supplier reliability, manufacturing lead time, standard run time, set-up time, wait time, move time, inventory turnover, order carrying-out time.
12 **Quality performance:** SPC measures, machine reliability, rework, quality system cost, inbound quality, vendor quality rating, customer satisfaction, technical assistance, returned goods.
13 **Customer relationship management:** Supplier relationship management and order fulfilment process: measures not discussed in paper.

To think about how e-SCM can assist in improving performance in this area, complete Activity 6.3.

Managing partnerships

A key element of restructuring of the supply chain is examining the form of relationships with partners such as suppliers and distributors. This need to review the form of partnership has been accentuated with the globalisation enabled by e-commerce. In this section we consider what forms these partnerships should take and how technology can be used to facilitate them.

| Activity 6.3 | An e-SCM performance management framework |

Purpose

To highlight the benefits of e-SCM and how improvements in performance and operational management of e-SCM can be achieved.

Questions

In a large group, each pair of students should take one of the categories of measures and then discuss:

1 How information systems can help improve performance.

2 The constraints that may limit performance improvements.

Stuart and McCutcheon (2000) state that typically low cost is the main driver for partnership management in supply management (mainly upstream). According to these authors, the modification of supply chain partnerships usually follows what they describe as the 'received wisdom which many practitioners are rigidly following'. This approach requires companies to:

1 Focus on core competencies.
2 Reduce their number of suppliers.
3 Develop strong partnership relationships built on shared information and trust with the remaining suppliers.

Stuart and McCutcheon (2000) suggest that this approach may not suit all needs and the type of relationship required will be dependent on the ultimate objective. When reviewing partnerships, companies need to decide the options for the extent of their control of the supply chain process. Table 6.4 presents some strategic options for partnerships in order of increasing control and ownership over the process by the organisation. Option 1 is total insourcing of a particular process while 2 to 9 give varying degrees of outsourcing. There is also a continuum between collaborative partnerships where risks are shared (options 1 to 5) and competitive sourcing where market competition is used to achieve the best combination of price and value. Note that although an organisation may lose control of the *process* through outsourcing, a contractual arrangement will still enable them to exert a strong control over the *outputs* of the process.

From Table 6.4 it can be seen that as the depth of relationship between partners increases, the volume and complexity of information exchange requirements will increase. For a long-term arrangement information exchange can include:

• Short-term orders.
• Medium-to-long-term capacity commitments.
• Long-term financial or contractual agreement.
• Product design, including specifications.
• Performance monitoring, standard of product and service quality.
• Logistics.

For a short-term relationship simple information on transactions only, such as the EDI purchase order example in Chapter 3, is all that is required.

Stuart and McCutcheon (2000) present a more simplified set of partnership choices. They suggest that the partnering option chosen should be dependent on the core objective. If this is cost reduction, then a relationship with competitive tension is required (equivalent to options 6 to 9 in Table 6.4). Alternatively, if the core objective is value-added benefits such as improved delivery speed, additional design features or the need for customisation, then the

Table 6.4	Strategic options for partnerships

Partnering arrangement	Technical infrastructure integration	Examples
1 Total ownership (more than 51% equity in company)	Technical issues in merging company systems	Purchase of Booker (distribution company) by Iceland (retailer). Since 1993 Cisco has made over 30 acquisitions (not all SCM related)
2 Investment stake (less than 49% equity)	Technical issues in merging company systems	Cisco has also made over 40 investments in hardware and software suppliers
3 Strategic alliance	Collaboration tools and groupware for new product development	Cable and Wireless, Compaq and Microsoft new digital business solution called a-Services
4 Profit-sharing partnership	As above	Arrangement sometimes used for IS outsourcing
5 Long-term contract	See above. Tools for managing service level agreements important	ISPs have performance and availability SLAs with penalty clauses
6 Preferred suppliers	Permanent EDI or Internet EDI links set up with preferred partners	Tesco Information Exchange
7 Competitive tendering	Tenders issued at intermediary or buyer's website	Buyer-arranged auctions (see Chapter 2)
8 Short-term contracts	As above	As above
9 Spot markets and auctions	Auctions at intermediary or buyer's website	Business-to-business marketplaces, e.g. www.freemarkets.com (no longer available)

'arm's-length' approach of options 6 to 9 may not be appropriate. In this case they suggest that a strategic alliance or cooperative partnership is the best option. Stuart and McCutcheon point out that the competitive advantages achieved through cost reduction are likely to be short-lived so companies will increasingly need to turn to value-added benefits. Each supplier has to be considered for whichever type of partnership is most appropriate.

Managing global distribution

Arnold (2000) suggests action that manufacturers should follow as they enter new overseas markets enabled by the Internet. The seven actions are:

1 Select distributors. Do not let them select you.
2 Look for distributors capable of developing markets rather than those with new customer contacts.
3 Treat the local distributors as long-term partners, not temporary market entry vehicles.
4 Support market entry by committing money, managers and proven marketing ideas.
5 From the start, maintain control over marketing strategy.
6 Make sure distributors provide you with detailed market and financial performance data.
7 Build links amongst national distributors at the earliest opportunity.

A Global Supply Chain Survey published by PwC (2013) gives a good summary of the current challenges and opportunities of improving competitiveness through supply chain management. The survey assesses the views of 500 supply chain experts in Europe, North America and Asia from across a range of industries. The next-generation supply chain is described as '*Efficient, Fast and Tailored, with speed and adaptability necessary to drive success*'. However, only 45% of the participants agreed that supply chain is seen as a strategic asset in their company. The survey is useful since it reviews, for different industries, the geographical organisation for different supply chain functions. For example, in retail and consumer goods the pattern of global and local management of the supply chain is shown in Figure 6.16. In this sector, companies outsource about 7% of their planning, sourcing and enabling activities; only 30% of their manufacturing activities; and 10–55% of their delivery activities. This industry has the highest number of inventory turns (18.2) amongst 'leaders' and a better delivery performance than companies in any other industry. 'Laggards' in this industry have an average number of industry turns of 3.3.

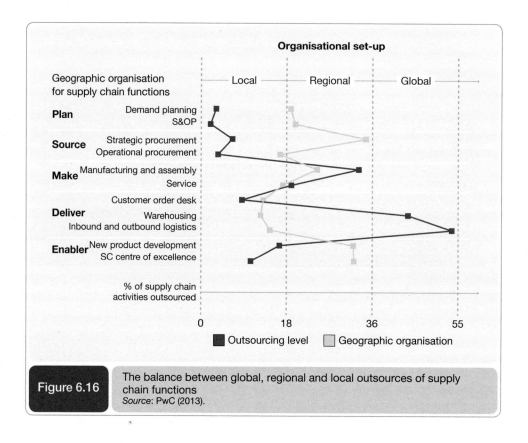

Figure 6.16	The balance between global, regional and local outsources of supply chain functions *Source*: PwC (2013).

RFID: keeping track starts its move to a faster track

Over the years many techniques and technologies have been developed to make supply chains more efficient, but they often fail for the simple reason that it is notoriously difficult to get sufficient accurate information to be useful.

Radio frequency identification (RFID) technology tackles this problem using small radio tags to keep track of goods as they move through the supply chain.

Demand for these tags, which cost around 40 cents each, has soared because of mandates from US and European retailers – Wal-Mart is the best known – and

the US Department of Defense which require large suppliers to put tags on pallets and cases as of 2005.

A clear sign that RFID is coming of age is that Nokia recently unveiled a kit to transform one of its phones into a mobile RFID reader. Despite the current hype, RFID is not a new technology. It was first used to identify aircraft in the Second World War and has been employed to tag cattle, collect road tolls and open doors for many years.

What is new is the application of RFID to supply chains.

The combination of RFID hardware with a unique number, called the electronic product code (EPC), enables businesses to associate a wealth of information with each tagged object. Not only is the information more detailed than a barcode, it can be read and updated using radio readers.

Early RFID technologies often delivered disappointing performance, but today's tags can be read reliably as packing cases are on a conveyor belt or even if the case is hidden behind others.

'RFID is a barcode on steroids,' says Lyle Ginsburg, RFID specialist at Accenture, the management consultancy. 'It promises tremendous productivity gains because you do not have the human intervention and line-of-sight issues that you get with barcodes.'

Many experts believe the combination of RFID and EPC has the potential to transform supply chains: no more inventory counts, no more lost or misdirected shipments, and no more guessing how much is in the supply chain or on the store shelves.

'Just by knowing what is in the store and what is still in the back room, you can get much greater visibility on inventory,' says Peter Regen, vice president of global visible commerce at Unisys, the US IT company.

Visibility is sorely lacking from real-world supply chains, which is why companies hold buffer stocks and build warehouses. This lessens the chance of running out, but the annual cost of holding all this inventory – in warehousing, opportunity cost and obsolescence – adds up to $300bn, just in the US.

AMR Research estimates around $3 trillion of inventory is locked in US and European supply chains, which suffer order error rates of 20%. 'There is just too much waste in the supply chain,' says Michael Witty, an analyst with Manufacturing Insights, part of the IDC research group.

Even if RFID only manages to reduce inventory levels or error rates by a few percentage points, the benefits to the economy in terms of extra working capital are substantial. In the case of an emerging economy such as China, RFID's potential is even greater.

China's supply chains have not kept pace with the country's rapid rise as a manufacturing nation and bottlenecks now threaten its export-led growth. The Chinese government is keeping a close eye on RFID and officials recently attended a big RFID trade fair in the US.

'In China, there is a lot of interest in RFID, which has really surprised us,' says Amar Singh, VP of global RFID initiatives at SAP, the German software giant. In part, this interest is driven by Chinese manufacturers' need to fall into line with the RFID mandates of western customers, most notably Wal-Mart, which accounts for more than 10% of all US imports from China.

But the Chinese government also sees RFID as a strategic technology that will bring the country's supply chains up to the standards of developed nations. Several projects are under way to test the use of RFID in Chinese port and logistics operations.

In the past three years, ports have become more conscious about security. Shipping companies know they face delays and may be refused entry if they are carrying suspect containers. 'Before 9/11, there was not much concern about what was inside the container,' says Scott Brown, general manager for cargo security at GE, the US engineering giant.

GE has developed a 'smart box' that uses RFID to track the movements of maritime containers when they enter ports and sensors to detect if the containers have been opened. The smart box technology has been tested in GE's domestic appliance business, which imports most of its products from China.

'The impetus for doing this was security, but there are also potential supply chain benefits,' says Mr Brown. However, he admits that it is difficult to make a case for using RFID on these benefits alone.

This problem affects most RFID initiatives, according to Accenture's Mr Lyle. Unless forced to comply with an RFID mandate, many potential users prefer to wait. Standards are still evolving and the cost of the technology is still too high for many applications. Data security is another big issue.

Burt Kaliski, chief scientist at RSA Laboratories, a US security software firm, fears thieves could quickly discover how to destroy or change the information on RFID tags, while hackers could launch 'denial-of-service' attacks with the potential to create chaos in RFID-equipped supply chains.

But the main reason not to jump in yet is that, mandates aside, there are too many hurdles that need to be overcome before RFID can show a clear return on investment.

'The business case for RFID is very challenging,' admits Mr Lyle.

Source: Geoffrey Nairn, Keeping track starts its move to a faster track, *The Financial Times*, 20 April 2005. Reprinted with permission.

Question

Select a manufacturing sector and then evaluate the benefits and risks of applying RFID in this sector.

Summary

1. Supply chain management involves the coordination of all supply activities of an organisation from its suppliers and partners to its customers. Upstream supply chain activities (procurement and inbound logistics) are equivalent to buy-side e-commerce and downstream supply chain activities (sales, outbound logistics and fulfilment) correspond to sell-side e-commerce.

2. There has been a change in supply chain management thinking from a push-oriented supply chain that emphasises distribution of a product to passive customers to a pull-oriented supply chain that utilises the supply chain to deliver value to customers who are actively involved in product and service specification.

3. The value chain concept is closely allied to supply chain management. It considers how value can be added both between and within elements of the supply chain and at the interface between them.

4. Electronic communications enable value networks to be created that enable the external value chain to be dynamically updated in response to marketplace variables.

5. Supply chains and value chains can be revised by disaggregation or re-aggregation. Disaggregation may involve outsourcing core supply chain activities to external parties. As more activities are outsourced a company moves towards becoming a virtual organisation.

6. Electronic communications have played a major role in facilitating new models of supply chain management. Technology applications that have facilitated supply chain management are:
   - Email
   - Web-based ordering
   - EDI of invoices and payment
   - Web-based order tracking.

7. Benefits of deploying these technologies include:
   - More efficient, lower-cost execution of processes
   - Reduced complexity of the supply chain (disintermediation)
   - Improved data integration between elements of the supply chain
   - Reduced costs through ease of dynamic outsourcing
   - Enabling innovation and customer responsiveness.

8. Intranets connecting internal business applications such as operational enterprise resource planning systems and decision-support-oriented data warehouses enable supply chain management. Such systems increasingly support external links to third parties such as suppliers.

9. Key strategic issues in supply chain management include:
   - Redesigning supply chain activities
   - Restructuring partnerships which support the supply chain through outsourcing or ownership.

Exercises

Self-assessment questions

1 Define supply chain management; how does it relate to:
   - logistics;
   - the value chain concept;
   - value networks?

2 What is the difference between a push orientation to the value chain and pull orientation?

3 How can information systems support the supply chain?

4 What are the key strategic options in supply chain management?

Essay and discussion questions

1 How does electronic communications enable restructuring of the value chain network?

2 'The concept of a linear value chain is no longer tenable with the advent of electronic commerce.' Discuss.

3 Select an industry of your choice and analyse how business-to-business exchanges will change the supply chain.

4 'In the end business all comes down to supply chain vs supply chain.' Discuss.

5 Select a retailer of your choice and analyse their strategy for management of the upstream and downstream supply chain.

Examination questions

1 Explain how the concepts of disintermediation, reintermediation and countermediation apply to the supply chain.

2 You have recently been appointed as supply chain manager for a pharmaceutical company. Summarise the main Internet-based applications you would consider for communicating with your suppliers.

3 How has the increase in electronic communications contributed to the development of value networks?

4 What are the characteristics of a virtual organisation? Using examples, explain how e-commerce can support the virtual organisation.

5 Explain how information technologies can be employed for different elements of a purchaser–supplier relationship.

6 Using industry examples, summarise three benefits of using e-commerce to streamline the supply chain.

7 How can electronic commerce be used to support restructuring of the supply chain?

8 What are the differences and similarities of using information technology to support:

(a) the upstream supply chain;

(b) the downstream supply chain?

References

AMR (2008) The AMR Research Supply Chain Top 25 for 2008. Value Chain Report: **www.amrresearch.com.**

Arnold, D. (2000) Seven rules of international distribution. *Harvard Business Review,* November–December, 131–7.

Benjamin, R. and Wigand, R. (1995) Electronic markets and virtual value-chains on the information superhighway. *Sloan Management Review*, Winter, 62–72.

Chan, C. and Swatman, P. (2000) From EDI to Internet commerce – the BHP Steel experience. *Internet Research Electronic Networks: Applications and Policy*, 10(1), 77–82.

Conspectus (2000) Supply chain management software issue. Prime Marketing Publications, June. PMP Research. **www.conspectus.com**.

Davidow, W.H. and Malone, M.S.C. (1992) *The Virtual Corporation: Structuring and Revitalising the Corporation for the 21st Century*. HarperCollins, London.

Deise, M., Nowikow, C., King, P. and Wright, A. (2000) *Executive's Guide to Digital business. From Tactics to Strategy*. John Wiley & Sons, New York.

E-consultancy (2010) Multichannel accounts for 43% of Argos sales. By Graham Charlton, 4 May 2010: **http://econsultancy.com/blog/5850-multichannel-accounts-for-43-of-argos-sales**.

European Commission (2008) i2010 Annual Information Society Report 2008, mid-term report published at **http://ec.europa.eu/information_society/eeurope/i2010/mid_ term_ review_2008/index_en.htm** (no longer available at current address).

Fisher, M. (1997) What is the right supply chain for your product? *Harvard Business Review*, March–April, 105–16.

Hagel, J. III and Rayport, J. (1997) The new infomediaries. *McKinsey Quarterly*, no. 4, 54–70.

Hamill, J. and Gregory, K. (1997) Internet marketing in the internationalisation of UK SMEs. *Journal of Marketing Management*, 13, 1–3.

Hayes, R. and Wheelwright, S. (1994) *Restoring our Competitive Edge*. John Wiley & Sons, New York.

Hughes, J., Ralf, M. and Michels, B. (1998) *Transform Your Supply Chain*. International Thomson Business Press, London.

IBF (2008) *12 Ways to Use Your Intranet to Cut Your Costs*. Member Briefing Paper August 2008. Published by the Intranet Benchmarking Forum (**www.ibforum.com**).

IDC (2004) Increasing Supply Chain Responsiveness among Configured Electronic Systems Manufacturers, IDC White paper. Author: Meredith Whalen, January.

Internet Retailing (2010) Taking cost out of the reverse supply chain. *Internet Retailing*, 4 (6), September 2010.

Kalakota, R. and Robinson, M. (2000) *Digital Business. Roadmap for Success*. Addison-Wesley, Reading, MA.

Kjellsdotter, L. and Jonsson, P. (2010) The potential benefits of advanced planning and scheduling systems in sales and operations planning, *Industrial Management & Data Systems*, 110(5), 659–81.

Kraut, R., Chan, A., Butler, B. and Hong, A. (1998) Coordination and virtualisation: the role of electronic networks and personal relationships. *Journal of Computer Mediated Communications*, 3(4).

Legner, C. and Schemm, J. (2008) Towards the inter-organizational product information supply chain – evidence from the retail and consumer goods industries. *Journal of the Association for Information Systems*, 9(3/4), 119–50, Special Issue.

Magretta, J. (1998) The power of virtual integration. An interview with Michael Dell. *Harvard Business Review*, March–April, 72–84.

Malone, T., Yates, J. and Benjamin, R. (1987) Electronic markets and electronic hierarchies: effects of information technology on market structure and corporate strategies. *Communications of the ACM*, 30(6), 484–97.

March, S., Raghu, T. and Vinze, A. (2007) Cultivating and securing the information supply chain. *Journal of the Association for Information Systems*, 9, pp. 95–7, Special Issue.

Marinos, G. (2005). The information supply chain: achieving business objectives by enhancing critical business processes. *DM Review,* **www.dmreview.com/article_sub. cfm? articleId=1023896** (no longer available at current address).

Phillips, S. (2000) Retailer's crown jewel is a unique customer database. *Financial Times,* 4 December.

PMP (2008) Supply Chain and Manufacturing Systems Report. PMP Research Report published at **www.conspectus.com**, March.

PwC (2013) Global Supply Chain Survey. Report published at: **www.pwc.com/ GlobalSupplyChainSurvey2013.**

Porter, M. (1980) *Competitive Strategy.* Free Press, New York.

Porter, M. and Millar, V. (1985) How information gives you competitive advantage. *Harvard Business Review,* July–August, 149–60.

Quelch, J. and Klein, L. (1996) The Internet and international marketing. *Sloan Management Review,* Spring, 60–75.

Rayport, J. and Sviokla, J. (1996) Exploiting the virtual value-chain. *McKinsey Quarterly,* no. 1, 20–37.

Sambasivan, M., Tamizarasu, N. and Zainal, A. (2009) Consolidation of performance measures in supply chain environment. *Journal of Enterprise Information Management,* 22(6), 660–89.

Schemm, J. Legner, C. and Otto, B. (2007) Global Data Synchronisation, Current Status and Future Trends. University of Gallen, Institute of Information Management, Research Report: **www.gsl.org/productssolutions/gdsn/ds/retailers.html** (no longer available at current address).

Steinfield, C., Kraut, R. and Plummer, A. (1996) The impact of inter-organisational networks on buyer–seller relationships. *Journal of Computer Mediated Communication,* 1(3).

Stuart, F. and McCutcheon, D. (2000) The manager's guide to supply chain management. *Business Horizons,* March–April, 35–44.

Sun, S. and Yen, J. (2005). Information supply chain: a unified framework for information-sharing, in *Intelligence and Security Informatics,* P. Kantor, G. Muresan, F. Roberts, D. Zeng, F.-Y. Wang, H. Chen and R. Merkle (eds). Springer, Berlin, pp. 422–9.

Timmers, P. (1999) *Electronic Commerce Strategies and Models for Business-to-Business Trading.* John Wiley Series in Information Systems. John Wiley& Sons, Chichester.

ThingWorx (2013). Press release, 21 May 2013. KORE Telematics and ThingWorx Partner to Enable Rapid, Network-Ready M2M Solution Delivery. Published at: **www.thingworx. com/2013/05/kore-thingworx-partner-m2m-solutions/.**

US Department of Commerce (2013) Manufacturing and Trade Inventories and Sales, April 2013. Published at **www.census.gov/mtis/www/data/pdf/mtis_current.pdf** (no longer available at current address).

Warner, M. (2001) Managing in virtual space. FT Mastering Management: **www.ftmaster ing.com/mmo/mmo03_1.htm** (no longer available at current address).

Womack, J. and Jones, D. (1998) *Lean Thinking.* Touchstone, Simon and Schuster, London.

Web links

Supply Chain Digital (www.supplychaindigital.com) A portal dedicated to supply chain enhancement.

GS1 (www.gs1.org) Information on global standards for data exchange to support SCM.

Toolbox for IT (http://erp.ittoolbox.com) Specialist portal containing news and articles about ERP (enterprise resource planning systems), one application of which is supply chain management.

Manhattan Associates (www.manh.com/resources) Whitepapers and thought leadership from specialist SCM consultants.

Oracle SCM introduction (www.oracle.com/applications/scm/) Oracle is one of the biggest providers of SCM applications; here they introduce the benefits of their approach.

7

E-procurement

Web support

The following additional case studies
are available at
www.pearsoned.co.uk/chaffey

→ Worldwide oil exchange – the
   Shell perspective
→ E-procurement in the aerospace
   industry

The site also contains a range of study
materials designed to help improve
your results.

**Scan code
to find the
latest updates
for topics in
this chapter**

Learning outcomes

After reading this chapter the reader should be able to:

● Identify the benefits and risks of e-procurement
● Analyse procurement methods to evaluate cost savings
● Assess different options for integration of organisations'
  information systems with e-procurement suppliers

Management issues

Managers will be concerned with the following e-procurement
issues:

● What benefits and risks are associated with e-procurement?
● Which method(s) of e-procurement should we adopt?
● What organisational and technical issues are involved in
  introducing e-procurement?

Links to other chapters

The main related chapters are:

● *Chapter 2* – introduces business-to-business marketplaces,
  models of electronic trading and B2B auctions
● *Chapter 6* – covers the role of purchasing within supply chain
  management

Introduction

Procurement has not traditionally been a significant topic for management study in comparison with other areas such as marketing, operations or strategy. The transformation to digital business has, however, highlighted its importance as a strategic issue since introducing electronic procurement or e-procurement can achieve significant savings and other benefits which directly impact upon the customer.

In this chapter we review the benefits and risks of e-procurement together with techniques that can be used to assess these benefits and risks. We also consider the selection and management of the different types of e-procurement, including the hyped business-to-business marketplaces.

Read Mini case study 7.1 which gives an example of how one UK business has created a solution to help its customers worldwide with e-procurement.

Mini Case Study 7.1	Proactis deliver E-procurement for Boehringer Ingelheim

Proactis (2013), an example of an e-procurement solution company that describes itself as *The Spend Control Company*, summarises the benefits of using a flexible e-procurement solution as giving:

- **The right balance** of consistent organisation-wide policies and processes with appropriate levels of local autonomy when it comes to daily operations.
- **The right combination** of centralised, decentralised and virtual business functions.
- **The ability to leverage your full buying power** without losing the advantages of local sources where they best fit the need.
- **Rapid, incremental performance improvement** at the pace that works best for your particular environment.
- **The ability to evolve** smoothly as your organisation responds to market changes, and as it experiences mergers, acquisitions and restructuring that may occur over time.

One of the examples Proactis gives of a customer it assists is the Boehringer Ingelheim group, which is one of the world's 20 leading pharmaceutical companies. Headquartered in Ingelheim, Germany, it operates globally with 137 affiliates in 47 countries and more than 38,000 employees. Jack Smith, Head of Purchasing at Boehringer Ingelheim UK, was looking for a solution that would automate and streamline the complete purchase-to-pay cycle while supporting the company's existing policies and procedures.

Not only did we want to eliminate the paper chase and improve efficiencies, we also needed a system that would help us to enforce our policies and procedures to give us the level of financial control and visibility of spend we needed.

Reasons for adopting the new e-procurement system included:

- **Support for the organisation's cost coding systems.** Every item/service purchased has to be allocated with a cost centre code, account code and purchasing code. These need to be consistent across the organisation's international offices because HQ needs a global view of spending. The complexity of the coding systems can leave these open to inaccuracies, so Boehringer needed a system which could allow users to cross-reference different combinations of codes, to help it reduce and identify any coding errors.
- **Adherence to the organisation's purchasing policy.** Boehringer's procurement approval hierarchy spans up to eight different levels of authority across eight divisions, governing who has the authority to approve purchases in specific categories and at various value thresholds. Added to this, for purchases above £20k/year the purchasing department has to be involved. Boehringer needed a solution that could

not only mirror and ensure compliance with the approval tree, but that could also provide an audit trail to record every stage of the purchase and payment processes.

- **Corporate governance.** Boehringer needed a solution that would enable it to securely store purchase orders, quotations and invoices, all held as computer records accessible only to those with the appropriate authority.
- **Spend visibility and data compatibility.** The software needed to enable Boehringer to capture data easily, and in a format that would be compatible with other procurement and financial systems in use across the global organisation.

Source: www.proactis.com/resources/case-studies/pharmaceutical-spend-under-management-at-boehringer-ingelheim.aspx

What is e-procurement?

The terms 'purchasing' and 'procurement' are sometimes used interchangeably, but as Kalakota and Robinson (2000) point out, 'procurement' generally has a broader meaning. 'Procurement' refers to all activities involved with obtaining items from a supplier; this includes purchasing, but also inbound logistics such as transportation, goods-in and warehousing before the item is used. The use of e-procurement is sometimes considered as part of 'strategic sourcing' where it is used to deliver commercially significant benefits to the company.

The key procurement activities and associated information flows within an organisation are shown in Figure 7.1. In this chapter we focus on these activities, which include searching and specification of product by the end-user, purchasing by the buyer, payment by an account, and receipt and distribution of goods within a warehouse.

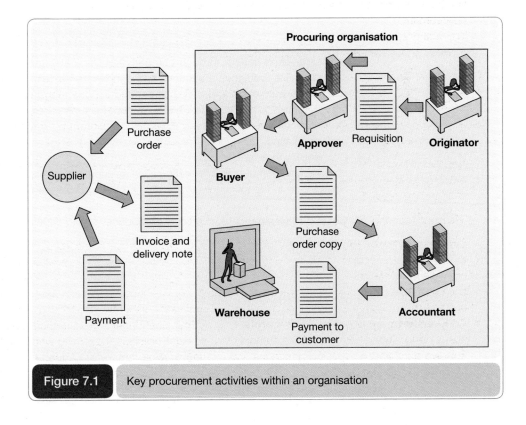

| Figure 7.1 | Key procurement activities within an organisation |

Electronic procurement (e-procurement)

The electronic integration and management of all procurement activities, including purchase request, authorisation, ordering, delivery and payment, between a purchaser and a supplier.

E-procurement should be directed at improving performance for each of the 'five rights of purchasing' (Baily *et al.*, 1994), which are sourcing items:

1 at the right price
2 delivered at the right time
3 of the right quality
4 of the right quantity
5 from the right source.

Box 7.1 gives an additional perspective on e-purchasing.

E-procurement is not new; there have been many attempts to automate the process of procurement for the buyer using **electronic procurement systems (EPS)**, workflow systems and links with suppliers through EDI (Chapter 3). These involved online entry, authorisation and placing of orders using a combination of data entry forms, scanned documents and email-based workflow. It is convenient to refer to these as 'first-generation e-procurement'.

Electronic procurement systems (EPS)

An electronic system used to automate all or part of the procurement function.

Box 7.1	What is e-purchasing?

This is how the Chartered Institute of Purchasing and Supply (CIPS, www.cips.org) explains e-purchasing to its members:

> *The combined use of information and communications technology through electronic means to enhance external and internal purchasing and supply management processes. These tools and solutions deliver a range of options that will facilitate improved purchasing and supply management.*

The range of potential options for improving purchasing processes are indicated by these benefits described by CIPS:

1 Evaluation of end-to-end trading cycles, e.g. evaluation and possible re-engineering of trading cycles leading to reduced cycle times; improved workflow of the internal procurement process enabling end-user self-service and decentralisation with centralised control through company-specific catalogues; new functionality such as online bidding in e-auctions and e-requests for quotations (RFQs).
2 Use of more efficient and cheaper connectivity methods such as the Internet and XML. XML is not, however, a requirement for e-procurement.
3 Connectivity to external sources of information, e.g. portals, e-hubs, e-marketplaces.
4 Connectivity to external supply chains, e.g. extranets, EDI, e-hubs, e-marketplaces – allowing shared real-time information such as suppliers accessing real-time sales.
5 Sourcing, e.g. identifying new sources via the Internet, use of intelligent search engines.
6 Content management, e.g. private catalogues, public catalogues, internal inventory management, maintenance management.
7 Connectivity to internal systems and sources of information such as inventory management, maintenance management, materials resource planning (MRP) systems.
8 Payment systems, e.g. purchasing cards.
9 Multimedia (although e-procurement does not necessarily contain multimedia elements).
10 Improvements in localised supply chain mechanisms and consortia etc. leading to mutual benefit.

Source: CIPS (2008).

Understanding the procurement process

Before the advent of e-procurement, organisational purchasing processes had remained similar for decades. Table 7.1 highlights the paper-based process. It can be seen that it involves the end-user selecting an item by conducting a search and then filling in a paper requisition form that is sent to a buyer in the purchasing department (often after authorisation by a manager, which introduces further delay). The buyer then fills in an order form that is dispatched to the supplier. After the item is delivered, the item and a delivery note are usually reconciled with the order form and an invoice and then payment occurs. Procurement also includes the transport, storage and distribution of goods received within the business – this is referred to as 'inbound logistics'.

IFO-Basware (2012) published a study of the global adoption of e-invoicing in businesses of all sizes in key markets, surveying 908 finance professionals from the US, UK, Sweden, Norway, Germany and Finland. Amongst the respondents, an average of around 5,000 invoices are received and sent each month.

The report shows a continuing increased adoption and use of e-invoicing and automated payment processing, with 73% of respondents using electronic invoicing to some degree in 2012, compared with 59% in 2011. Sixty-seven per cent of respondents believed that e-invoicing can help to achieve the goal of improving operational efficiencies, compared with 50% in 2011. Faster invoicing cycles and reduced invoice costs are the top two e-invoice benefits experienced by respondents.

However, the challenges of implementing e-invoicing solutions are highlighted by a continued reliance on rudimentary 'electronic documents' and manual processes, with 58% of respondents receiving invoices as PDF attachments, with a further 13% avoiding automated processes altogether. There is a lack of focus on invoice scan and capture deployment; 53% of respondents still scan and capture physical invoices in-house, with an additional 26% opting not to scan invoices at all. Overall, levels of fully automated e-invoicing are increasing but are in need of improvement. Only 15% of respondents state that the majority of e-invoices are sent out electronically (up from 9% in 2011).

Activity 7.1 explains how the procurement process can be simplified through e-procurement.

Table 7.1	Process flow analysis for traditional procurement (typical cycle time, 5½ days)	
Task description	**Chart symbols**	**Time**
1 Search for goods	●⇨□D▽	1 hour
2 Fill in paper requisition	●⇨□D▽	10 min
3 Send to buyer	○➔□D▽	1 day
4 In buyer's in-tray	○⇨□◗▽	½ day
5 Buyer enters order number	●⇨□D▽	10 min
6 Buyer authorises order	●⇨□D▽	10 min
7 Buyer prints order	●⇨□D▽	10 min
8 Order copies to supplier and goods-in	○➔□D▽	1 day
9 Delivery from supplier	○⇨□D▼	1 day
10 Order copy to accounts	○➔□D▽	1 day
11 Three-way invoice match	●⇨□D▽	1 day
12 Cheque payment	●⇨□D▽	10 min

Note: see Table 7.2 on p.302 for key to symbols.

| Activity 7.1 | Evaluating the benefits of the e-procurement process for a typical B2B company |

Purpose

To highlight the tasks involved in organisational purchasing and to indicate the potential time savings from e-procurement.

Introduction

Table 7.1 illustrates a typical traditional procurement process using the flow process chart symbols explained in more detail in Chapter 11. It is based on the actual procurement process for Cambridge Consultants described in Case study 7.1. Note that this process is for relatively low-value items that do not need authorisation by senior managers. The timings are for a new item rather than a repeat buy for which searching would not be required. Table 7.2 summarises the new procurement process.

Questions

1 Identify inefficiencies in the traditional procurement process (Table 7.1).

2 Identify process benefits to Table 7.1 that would be possible through the automation of a system through an email-based workflow system.

3 Summarise why the e-procurement process in Table 7.2 is more efficient.

Answers to activities can be found at www.pearsoned.co.uk/chaffey

| Table 7.2 | Process flow analysis for new procurement (typical cycle time, $1\frac{1}{2}$ days) |

	Chart symbols	Time
1 Search for goods	●⇨□D▽	20 min
2 Order on web	●⇨□D▽	10 min
3 Delivery from supplier	○⇨□D▼	1 day
4 Generate invoice	●⇨□D▽	10 min
5 Cheque payment	●⇨□D▽	10 min

Key to flow process chart symbols
○ Process
⇨ Transport
□ Inspection
D Delay
▽ Inbound goods

Types of procurement

To understand the benefits of e-procurement, and also to highlight some of the practical considerations with introducing e-procurement, we need to briefly consider the different types of items that are obtained by procurement (what is bought?) and types of ordering (how is it bought?).

Let us start us by reviewing what is bought by businesses. A B2B company might buy everything from steel for manufacturing products, through equipment to help machine products, to paper clips and pens for office use. There are two broad categories of procurement: those that relate to manufacturing of products (production-related procurement) and operating or non-production-related procurement that supports the operations of the whole business and includes office supplies, furniture, information systems, **MRO** goods and a range of services from catering to buying travel, and professional services such as consulting and training. Raw materials for the production of goods and MRO goods are particularly important since they are critical to the operation of a business. For the B2B company, they would include manufacturing equipment, network cables and computers to control the process.

Businesses tend to buy by one of two methods:

- *Systematic sourcing* – negotiated contracts with regular suppliers.
- *Spot sourcing* – fulfilment of an immediate need, typically of a commoditised item for which it is less important to know the credibility of the supplier.

Often items such as stationery are purchased repeatedly, either for identical items (straight rebuy) or with some changes (modified rebuy). E-procurement systems can make rebuys more straightforward.

MRO
Maintenance, repairs and operations of manufacturing facilities.

Participants in different types of e-procurement

In Chapter 2 we showed how different types of online intermediaries, such as price comparison sites, changed the marketplace options for consumers. A similar understanding of new potential participants or actors in e-procurement is helpful. Riggins and Mitra (2007) identify eight types of intermediary that need to be reviewed to understand options for changes to procurement as part of developing an e-procurement strategy:

- *Traditional manufacturers* which produce physical goods that are generally sold to other corporate customers.
- *Direct sales manufacturers,* similar to traditional manufacturers except that they bypass intermediaries and sell direct to end consumers via web or phone channels. These can include services companies. Direct sales manufacturer can be a cost-effective option for companies procuring business services such as flight bookings for staff.
- *Value-added procurement partners* act as intermediaries to sell products and services to other businesses; examples include travel agents and office solutions companies.
- *Online hubs* are industry-specific vertical portals such as Elemica (www.elemica.com) that generate revenues via B2B exchanges.
- *Knowledge experts* who produce information goods, for example E-consultancy.com and Experian Hitwise have subscription services with innovation alerts, best practice and statistics of Internet usage.
- *Online information services* provide unique information to end users that is either original in its development or provides a unique editorial perspective. From an e-procurement perspective, as we saw in Chapter 6, SaaS services such as E2open (Figure 6.11) are available to manage the information supply chain.
- *Online retailers* include start-up digital businesses and more traditional multichannel retailers. Euroffice (www.euroffice.co.uk) is an Internet pureplay providing office goods at lower prices than traditional providers. Traditional providers in this space with a network of stores include Staples (www.staples.co.uk/).
- *Portal communities* seek to aggregate different online information services into an integrated customer experience, for example personalised news stories, online bill presentment and payment, and community discussion features. These overlap with the online information services and knowledge experts.

Knudsen (2003) and Smart (2010) have reviewed a simple classification of different types or applications of e-procurement. These are the main types:

1 **E-sourcing.** Finding potential new suppliers using the Internet during the information-gathering step of the procurement process.
2 **E-tendering.** The process of screening suppliers and sending suppliers requests for information (RFI) or requests for price (RFP).
3 **E-informing.** Qualification of suppliers for suitability. It doesn't involve transactions but instead handles information about the supplier's quality, financial status or delivery capabilities.
4 **E-reverse auctions.** Enable the purchasing company to buy goods and services that have the lowest price or combination of lowest price and other conditions via Internet technology.
5 **E-MRO and web-based ERP.** These involve the purchase and supply of products which are the core of most e-procurement applications. The software used manages the process of creating and approving purchasing requisitions, placing orders and receiving the goods or service ordered.

Drivers of e-procurement

Smart (2010) has completed a review of the business benefits of e-procurement through case studies of three companies. He identifies five key drivers or supplier selection criteria for e-procurement adoption related to improving:

- *Control* – improving compliance, achieving centralisation, raising standards, optimising sourcing strategy and improved auditing of data. Enhanced budgetary control is achieved through rules to limit spending and improved reporting facilities.
- *Cost* – improved buying leverage through increased supplier competition, monitoring savings targets and transactional cost reduction.
- *Process* – rationalisation and standardisation of e-procurement processes giving reduced cycle time, improved visibility of processes for management and efficient invoice settlement.
- *Individual performance* – knowledge sharing, value-added productivity and productivity improvements.
- *Supplier management* – reduced supplier numbers, supplier management and selection and integration.

Direct cost reductions are achieved through efficiencies in the process, as indicated by Tables 7.1 and 7.2. Process efficiencies result in less staff time spent in searching and ordering products and reconciling deliveries with invoices. Savings also occur due to automated validation of pre-approved spending budgets for individuals or departments, leading to fewer people processing each order, and in less time. It is also possible to reduce the cost of physical materials such as specially printed order forms and invoices.

There are also indirect benefits from e-procurement; Tables 7.1 and 7.2 show how the cycle time between order and use of supplies can be reduced. In addition e-procurement may enable greater flexibility in ordering goods from different suppliers according to best value. E-procurement also tends to change the role of buyers in the purchasing department. By removing administrative tasks such as placing orders and reconciling deliveries and invoices with purchase orders, buyers can spend more time on value-adding activities. Such activities may include more time spent with key suppliers to improve product delivery and costs or analysis and control of purchasing behaviour.

A useful framework for evaluating the benefits of e-procurement and e-SCM has been created by Riggins and Mitra (2007, Figure 7.2). This can also be used to review strategy since

Value Creation Dimension	Efficiency	Effectiveness	Strategic
Planning	Implement rich media for company-wide interaction	Provide online executive Information systems	Facilitate knowledge management between partners
Development	Standardise platform for cross-functional design	Share detailed requirements between partners	Enable concurrent design across virtual organisation
Inbound	Support electronic transactions with supply partners	Generate supply flexibility through e-hub communities	Offload replenishment responsibility to supply partners
Production	Integrate internal systems	Exchange production data between partners	Optimise utilization of global capacity
Outbound	Support electronic transactions with customers	Furnish customised instantaneous order status	Institute direct fulfilment via logistics partners

Figure 7.2	Digital business e-value grid
	Source: Riggins and Mitra (2007).

Vendor-managed inventory (VMI)
Supply chain partners manage the replenishment of parts or items for sale through sharing of information on variations in demand and stocking level for goods used for manufacture or sale.

Efficient consumer response (ECR)
ECR is focussed on demand management aimed at creating and satisfying customer demand by optimising product assortment strategies, promotions and new product introductions. It creates operational efficiencies and cost savings in the supply chain through reducing inventories and deliveries.

it highlights potential benefits in terms of process efficiency and effectiveness and strategic benefits to the company. Some of the main dimensions of value highlighted by the approach include:

- *Planning* – this shows the potential for an e-procurement system to increase the quality and dissemination of management information about e-procurement.
- *Development* – e-procurement systems can potentially be incorporated early in new product development to identify manufacturing costs; this can help accelerate development.
- *Inbound* – this is the main focus of e-procurement with efficiency gains from paperless transactions and more cost-effective sourcing possible through hubs or marketplaces. A strategic benefit is **vendor-managed inventory (VMI)**, where supply chain partners will manage the replenishment of parts or items for sale as described in Case Study 6.1.
- *Production* – the integration of systems managing manufacture with the procurement systems used to ensure that manufacturing is not limited by poor availability of parts.
- *Outbound* – this is management of fulfilment of products to customers. It is not usually managed by the e-procurement system, but demand must be evaluated by linking through these systems to achieve **efficient consumer response (ECR)**.

Examples of the benefits of e-procurement

Case study 7.1 is a classic example illustrating many of the reasons why many companies are now introducing e-procurement. The primary driver is cost reduction, in this case from an average of £60 per order to £10 per order. In many cases the cost of ordering exceeds the value of the product purchased. In another example, BT's implementation of e-procurement enabled 95% of all its goods – including desktop computing, stationery, clothing, travel and agency staff – and so reduced the average purchasing transaction cost from £56 to £40 inside a year (IBF, 2008). Finally, Mini case study 7.2 gives a video example of the benefits of e-procurement according to the purchasing manager at a law firm.

Mini Case Study 7.2	IT procurement at a law firm

Mark Rowley, the head of purchasing at Herbert Smith, one of the ten largest law firms in the UK, explains how they use e-procurement systems to manage recurring orders and gain budget control. As a client-facing service, project managers at a law firm need to react straight away to a client's needs, and the system provides real-time visibility of their budget and spend at every stage so they maintain full control.

Video Explanation: www.proactis.com/resources/videos/herbert-smith-freehills-llp-video-case-study.aspx

---

Case Study 7.1	Cambridge Consultants reduces costs through e-procurement

Illustrates the potential benefits of e-procurement by reviewing the original and revised process and costs. The e-procurement system in this case is a direct link between the purchaser, Cambridge Consultants, and the web-based catalogue of one its major suppliers, RS Components.

Cambridge Consultants is a manufacturer offering technical product design and development services to commerce and industry. With hundreds of projects in hand at any one time, Cambridge needs a diverse range of components every day.

Purchasing is centralised across the company and controlled by its Purchasing Manager, Francis Pullen. Because of its varied and often unique requirements, Cambridge has a supplier base of nearly 4,000 companies, with 20 new ones added each month. Some of these companies are providing items so specialised that Cambridge purchases from them no more than twice a year. Of the total, only 400 are preferred suppliers. Of those, just 10% – 1% of the overall supplier base – have been graded key supplier by Cambridge. That number includes RS Components. Francis Pullen says, 'We charge our clients by the hour, so if a product is faulty or late we have engineers waiting for new parts to arrive. This doesn't align with our fast time to market business proposition. RS Components' guarantee of service and range of products fits in with our business ethos.'

The existing purchasing process

Pullen has seen many changes and improvements in the company's purchasing process as its suppliers have used new technology to introduce new services. The first was moving to CD-ROM from the paper-based catalogue. Next was an online purchasing card – an account card with detailed line item billing, passwords and controls. Using industry-standard guidelines from the Chartered Institute of Purchasing and Supply (CIPS), Francis Pullen analysed the internal cost of raising an order. This took into account every step, from the engineer raising a paper requisition, through processing by purchasing, the cost of handling the delivery once it arrived, invoice matching and clearance and even the physical cost of a four-part purchase order form. The whole process involved between eight and ten people and cost the company anywhere from £60 to £120, depending on the complexity of the order.

The main cost is in requisitioning, when engineers and consultants spend their revenue-producing time in identifying their needs and raising paperwork. (Centralised purchasing, by contrast, is very efficient, costing around £50 an order.)

Using the RS purchase card removes the need for engineers and consultants to raise a paper requisition. This makes low-value ordering much more cost-efficient. Invoice matching costs are also reduced, since the purchase-card statement lists all purchases made each month.

Although the purchase card is undoubtedly an advance, on its own it does not allow costs to be assigned to jobs in the system each day. The purchase-card statement takes a month to arrive, giving rise to an equivalent lag in showing the real costs on internal project accounts.

The e-procurement process

To enable the company to order online immediately, RS put Cambridge's pre-Internet trading records on the web server. Purchasing agreements and controls were thus automatically set up on the Internet order form, including correct pricing and special payment terms.

The benefit was instantly apparent. The use of the RS purchase card when ordering from the website meant that the complete order was automatically collated, with all controls in place. Accuracy was assured and the purchase process was speeded up, with the cost per transaction reduced significantly.

Pullen describes the change this has had on Cambridge's purchasing process:

For the first time in our purchasing history, our financial controllers saw the benefit of distributed purchasing because of the cost savings, reassured by the central purchasing controls as back-up.

This has benefited us enormously. We have allowed three department heads to have their own purchasing cards, so that they can order independently from the website.

We have implemented a very efficient electronic workflow requisition system which is initiated by the purchase card holders and mailed to central purchasing. The orders are held in a mailbox and checked against physical delivery. This has cut out two layers of order activity.

In purchasing, we no longer spend our time passing on orders that they have raised, and there is no generation of paper during the order process. It doesn't just save time and money – it's also far more environmentally friendly. Passing on low-value orders each day adds very little value, so devolving this function back to our internal customers frees up our time in purchasing to work on higher-value tasks.

Benefits for staff

Francis Pullen continues: 'Our internal customers are also much happier. We leave at 6 p.m. but the engineers will often work late if they are on a deadline.

Because they can order off the website from their desks (everyone at Cambridge has Internet access), they can add items to the order right up until RS's 8 p.m. deadline without our involvement. We maintain control because of the reporting functions on the site.'

Phase 2 of the rswww.com design has also made it possible for multiple orders to be opened during the day and then put against different cost centres internally.

Results

In the year to June 1999, Cambridge Consultants placed 1,200 orders with RS Components, totalling more than £62,000 in value. Of those transactions, 95% went via the Internet. Average order value over the Internet was £34 and accounted for £43,000 of the total business done. The remaining 60 orders were placed through traditional channels but had an average value of £317.

The cost to Cambridge of raising a paper-based order was identified as being £60. Using the combination of the RS purchasing card and rswww.com, this has been reduced to £10 an order. Over a year, this represents a saving of £57,000 to Cambridge. The net effect, therefore, is that its purchases from RS Components now cost it a mere £5,000 a year!

Francis Pullen again: 'RS has demonstrated its commitment to its customers in spending time and investing money in developing a world-class purchasing system that delivers tangible customer cost savings and benefits. We have welcomed their innovative approach to purchasing and believe they are way ahead of their competition in this sector.'

Source: RS Components White Paper (www.rswww.com), courtesy of RS Components Ltd © RS Components Ltd.

Questions

1 Given the scale of the purchasing operation at Cambridge Consultants, what benefits do you think e-procurement has brought?

2 Why are procurement costs currently as high as £60 to £100 per order?

3 How are procurement costs reduced through e-procurement?

4 What staff benefits accrue to Cambridge Consultants as a result of e-procurement?

Focus on   ## Estimating e-procurement costs

The general approach to estimating procurement costs is straightforward. First, we calculate the average procurement cost per item, then we multiply by the average number of requisitions. A Tranmit (1999) report provides some illustrations – typical medium-to-large companies issue between 1,000 and 5,000 requisitions a month and are spending between £600,000 and £3 million annually on the procurement process, based on the £50 median cost per item. In exceptional cases, the number of requisitions was between 30,000 and 40,000 per month. In these cases, the annual cost of procurement could be between £18 million and £43 million!

To calculate cost savings from e-procurement we perform the following calculation:

Savings = No. of requisitions × (Original cost − New cost)

For Cambridge Consultants (Case study 7.1) cost savings from orders placed with RS Components alone are as follows:

Savings = 1,300 × (£90 − £10) = £104,000

These are relative to a typical order value of £70, i.e. savings of £104,000 on purchase item costs of £91,000.

The impact of cost savings on profitability

A study by Kluge (1997) suggested that cost savings achieved through e-procurement may have a significant effect on profitability. Activity 7.2 illustrates how the savings will vary between companies according to their buying characteristics. The largest savings and impact on profitability will typically be for manufacturing companies in which procurement is a major cost element and there are many requisitions for relatively low-value items. Service industries have lower potential for savings. The consequence for this is that there will be a wide variation in potential savings according to industry, as illustrated in Table 7.3.

To conclude this *Focus on* topic, a note of caution should be struck. Many of the models used to calculate savings and return on investment are, of course, only as good as the assumptions they use.

Debate 7.1

E-procurement cost savings

'The cost-saving benefits of e-procurement are theoretical rather than actual since only reduced headcount in procurement can result in savings.'

Table 7.3	Procurement as a percentage of cost of goods sold for different industry sectors (estimates from Kluge, 1997)

Industry	Procurement costs as a percentage of cost of goods sold
Consumer electronics	60–70%
Mini and personal computers	50–70%
Consumer goods	50–70%
Automotive	50–60%
Pharmaceuticals	25–50%
Service industry	10–40%

Activity 7.2	Modelling cost savings and profitability arising from e-procurement

Purpose

To explore the different characteristics of purchasing in organisations that will govern the scale of savings made through e-procurement.

Activity

Imagine you are a procurement manager, IS manager or consultant who needs to demonstrate the cost savings of e-procurement to a senior management team in order to obtain approval for investment in an e-procurement system. Develop a spreadsheet model for each of two hypothetical companies to demonstrate the case as follows:

1 **Cost-saving calculations.** Using the input parameters for the two companies in Table 7.4, develop a spreadsheet model to calculate traditional overall purchasing cost, new overall purchasing cost, percentage change in cost per order and percentage change in overall purchasing cost.

2 **Profitability calculations.** Using input parameters of turnover, traditional purchasing costs, other costs and a 5% reduction in purchasing costs, as shown in Table 7.5, develop a model that calculates the profitability before and after introduction of e-procurement and also shows the change in profitability as an absolute (£) and as a percentage.

3 Analyse the sensitivity of the models to differences in volume of orders and values of purchases (Table 7.4) and the balance between traditional purchasing costs and other costs such as salaries and capital by using the parameters (Table 7.5). Explain to the managers the typical characteristics of a company that will make significant changes to profitability from introducing e-procurement.

Table 7.4	Input parameters for cost-saving calculations for two companies

Input parameters (Company A)		Input parameters (Company B)	
Number of orders	25,000	Number of orders	2,500
Traditional cost per order (average)	£50	Traditional cost per order (average)	£50
New cost per order (average)	£10	New cost per order (average)	£10
Average value of order	£150	Average value of order	£1,500

Table 7.5	Input parameters for profitability calculations for two companies

Parameter	Company X	Company Y
Turnover	£10,000,000	£10,000,000
Traditional purchasing costs	£5,000,000	£1,000,000
Other costs	£4,000,000	£8,000,000
Reduction in purchasing costs	20%	20%

Answers to activities can be found at www.pearsoned.co.uk/chaffey

Barriers and risks of e-procurement adoption

Of course, there are also barriers to adoption of e-procurement. CIPS (2008) identifies the following issues for suppliers:

- Competition issues, e.g. in exchanges using collaborative purchasing.
- Possible negative perception from suppliers, e.g. their margins reduced further from e-auctions.
- Negotiated procurement benefits may be shared with other exchange users who may be competitors.
- Creation of catalogues can be a long process and costly to suppliers.
- Culture profile within organisations, e.g. resistance to change.

These barriers are specific to e-procurement. There are also more general limitations to digital business adoption mentioned in Chapters 1 and 4, such as the cost of implementation and managing change.

If the cost savings referred to earlier in the chapter are to be achieved it may be necessary to redeploy staff, or in the worst case make them redundant. For a medium-sized company such as Cambridge Consultants the purchasing team of five people was reduced to four. The threat of redundancy or redeployment is likely to lead to resistance to the introduction of the system and this needs to be managed. The purchasing manager will have to carefully explain the reasons for introducing the new system, emphasising the benefits to the company as a whole and how it should enable more variety to be introduced to the buying role.

Since the cost savings of e-procurement are achieved through empowerment of originators throughout the business to directly purchase their own items, there is a risk that some originators may take advantage of this. 'Maverick or off-contract purchasing' occurs when items are ordered that are unnecessary or too expensive. Complete Activity 7.3 to review the mechanisms that can be used to reduce this risk.

Activity 7.3	Avoiding maverick purchasing

Purpose

To identify responses to problems of maverick purchasing.

Activity

To avoid maverick purchasing, businesses introducing e-procurement need to put safeguards into the e-procurement system. Think about the type of rules that could be written into an e-procurement system.

Answers to activities can be found at www.pearsoned.co.uk/chaffey

Implementing e-procurement

Implementing e-procurement has the challenges of change management associated with any information system (which are discussed in Chapter 10). If the implementation can mirror existing practices, then it will be most straightforward, but many of the benefits will not be gained and the use of new technology often forces new processes to be considered. CIPS (2008) forcefully makes the case that some re-engineering will be required:

Organisations should not simply automate existing procurement processes and systems but should consider improving ways of working and re-engineering business processes

prior to the implementation of eSourcing/eProcurement. Purchasing and supply management professionals should challenge established procurement practices to test whether these have evolved around a paper-based system and as such can be replaced. CIPS strongly recommends that, wherever possible, processes should be re-engineered prior to implementing ePurchasing.

To introduce e-procurement the IS manager and procurement team must work together to find a solution that links together the different people and tasks of procurement shown in Figure 7.1. Figure 7.3 shows how different types of information system cover different parts of the procurement cycle. The different type of systems are as follows.

- *Stock control system* – this relates mainly to production-related procurement; the system highlights that reordering is required when the number in stock falls below reorder thresholds.
- *CD or web-based catalogue* – paper catalogues have been replaced by electronic forms that make it quicker to find suppliers.
- *Email- or database-based workflow systems* integrate the entry of the order by the originator, approval by manager and placement by buyer. The order is routed from one person to the next and will wait in their inbox for actioning. Such systems may be extended to accounting systems.
- *Order-entry on website* – the buyer often has the opportunity to order directly on the supplier's website, but this will involve rekeying and there is no integration with systems for requisitioning or accounting.
- *Accounting systems* – networked accounting systems enable staff in the *buying department to enter* an order which can then be used by accounting staff to make payment when the invoice arrives. The IFO-Basware (2012) global e-invoicing report that automation is still

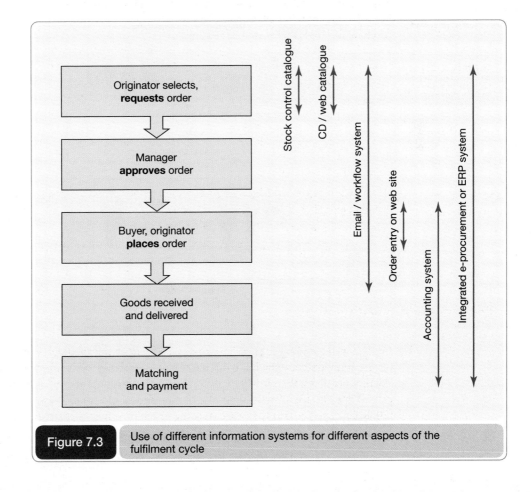

| Figure 7.3 | Use of different information systems for different aspects of the fulfilment cycle |

limited with around half of companies receiving email invoices with PDF attachments. Around a half receive XML e-invoices using a service provider and 14% with their own system.

- *Integrated e-procurement or ERP systems* – these aim to integrate all the facilities above and will also include integration with suppliers' systems.

Companies face a difficult choice in achieving full-cycle e-procurement since they have the option of trying to link different systems or purchasing a single new system that integrates the facilities of the previous systems. Purchasing a new system may be the simplest technical option, but it may be more expensive than trying to integrate existing systems and it also requires retraining in the system.

Integrating company systems with supplier systems

We saw from the Shell case study in Chapter 6 the cost and cycle-time benefits that a company can achieve through linking its systems with those of its suppliers. If integrating systems within a company is difficult, then linking with other companies' systems is more so. This situation arises since suppliers will use different types of systems and different models for integration. There are three fundamental models for location of B2B e-commerce: sell-side, buy-side and marketplace-based (as explained in Chapter 2). These are summarised in Figure 7.4 and the advantages and disadvantages of each are summarised in Table 7.6.

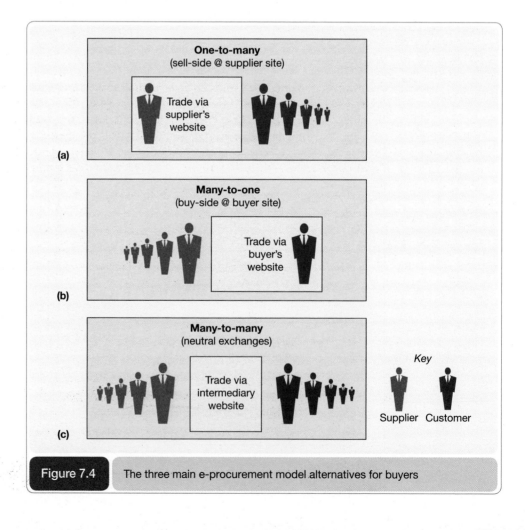

Figure 7.4 The three main e-procurement model alternatives for buyers

Table 7.6	Assessment of the procurement model alternatives for buyers

Procurement model	Advantages to buyer	Disadvantages to buyer
Sell-side e.g. many catalogue-based B2B suppliers such as www.rswww.com	• Searching • Onus of maintaining data on supplier	• Different interface on each site (catalogue and ordering) • Restricted choice • Poor integration with ERP/ procurement systems • Limited purchase control
Buy-side Private exchanges hosted by manufacturers and major suppliers to these manufacturers, e.g. solutions developed by www.covisint.com and ERP suppliers such as SAP and Oracle	• Simplicity – single interface • Wider choice than sell-side • Integration with ERP/procurement systems • Good purchase control	• Onus of maintaining data is on buyer • Software licence costs • Retraining
Independent marketplace e.g. www.ec21.com	• Simplicity – single interface • Potentially widest choice of suppliers, products and prices • Often unified terms and conditions and order forms	• Difficult to know which marketplace to choose (horizontal and vertical) • Poor purchase controls* • Uncertainty on service levels from unfamiliar suppliers • Interfacing with marketplace data format* • Relatively poor integration with ERP*

*Note that these disadvantages of the marketplace will disappear as marketplaces develop ERP integration.

Chapter 2 explained that companies supplying products and services had to decide which combination of these models would be used to distribute their products. From the buyer's point of view, they will be limited by the selling model their suppliers have adopted.

Figure 7.5 shows options for a buyer who is aiming to integrate an internal system such as an ERP system with external systems. Specialised e-procurement software may be necessary to interface with the ERP system. This could be a special e-procurement application or

| Figure 7.5 | Integration between e-procurement systems and catalogue data |

it could be middleware to interface with an e-procurement component of an ERP system. The e-procurement system can access price catalogues in two ways. Choice (a) is to house electronic catalogues from different suppliers inside the company and firewall. This traditional approach has the benefit that the data are housed inside the company and so can be readily accessed. However, electronic links beyond the firewall will be needed to update the catalogues, or this is sometimes achieved via delivery of a CD with the updated catalogue. Choice (b) is to use a **punchout catalogue** where access through the firewall is used to access catalogues either on a supplier site or at an intermediary site, ideally within a standard format. One of the benefits of linking to an intermediary site such as a B2B exchange is that this has done the work of collecting data from different suppliers and producing it in a consistent format.

Punchout catalogue
A purchasing company accesses a dynamic real-time catalogue hosted by a supplier or intermediary containing detailed product information, pricing and product images.

Focus on	**B2B marketplaces**

Before 2000, B2B marketplaces were heralded as transforming B2B purchases; however, many have had difficulty in achieving sustainable business models, although we will see that there are examples of successful marketplaces in vertical industries such as Elemica (www. elemica.com) within the chemicals industry which we referenced in Case study 6.1. Perhaps the prime example of a general digital marketplace is Alibaba.com, which is discussed in Mini case study 7.3.

Mini Case Study 7.3	Alibaba provides a global market for SMEs

The Alibaba Group is one of the leading B2B e-commerce companies. It was founded in 1999 by 18 people led by Jack Ma, a former English teacher from Hangzhou, China who has aspired to help make the Internet accessible, trustworthy and beneficial for everyone. The privately held Alibaba Group, including its affiliated entities, employs some 24,000 people around the world and has more than 70 offices in Greater China, India, the United Kingdom and the United States.

Alibaba.com is a marketplace connecting small and medium-sized buyers and suppliers from China and around the world. Its web presence includes an international marketplace (www.alibaba.com) focussing on global importers and exporters. As of 31 December 2012, the platform had around 36.7 million registered users from more than 240 countries and regions and showcased more than 2.8 million supplier storefronts.

In addition to many consumer marketplaces, payment systems and search engines for its primary audience in China, it also runs a China marketplace (www.1688.com) which focuses on suppliers and buyers trading domestically in China. As of 31 December 2012, the platform had around 77.7 million registered users and showcased more than 8.5 million supplier storefronts.

From a launch in 1999 the marketplaces have a community of more than 24 million registered users and over 255,000 paying members. In November 2007, Alibaba launched on the Hong Kong stock exchange and raised HK$13.1 billion (US$1.7 billion) in gross proceeds before offering expenses, making it the largest Internet IPO (initial public offering) in Asia and the second largest globally.

Jack Ma, the founder of Alibaba (Figure 7.6), first saw the Internet in 1995 when he went to Seattle as an interpreter for a trade delegation and a friend showed him the Internet. They searched for the word 'beer' on Yahoo and discovered that there was no data about China. They decided to launch a website and registered the name China Pages.

Mr Ma borrowed $2,000 to set up his first company and at the time knew nothing about personal computers or emails and had never touched a keyboard before. He described the experience as a 'blind man riding on the back of a blind tiger'.

Initially, the business did not fare well, since it was a part of China Telecom and Jack Ma reflects that 'everything we suggested, they turned us down; it was like an elephant and an ant'.

He resigned, but in 1999, he gathered 18 people in his apartment and spoke to them for two hours about his vision. Everyone put their money on the table, and he got $60,000 to start Alibaba. He chose Alibaba as the name since it was easy to spell and associated with 'Open, Sesame', the command that Ali Baba used to open doors to hidden treasures in *The Thousand and One Nights*.

During the dot-com bubble, there were lay-offs, such that by 2002 there was only enough cash to survive for 18 months. They had a lot of free members using the site, and didn't know how they could make money. But they then developed a product for China exporters to meet US buyers online, which Ma said saved the company. By the end of 2002, Alibaba made $1 in profits! Each year since it has improved in profitability to the position where it was launched on the stock market.

Today, Jack Ma's vision is to build an e-commerce ecosystem that allows consumers and businesses to do all aspects of business online. They are partnering with Yahoo and have launched online auction and payment businesses. His vision is expansive, he says: 'I want to create one million jobs, change China's social and economic environment, and make it the largest Internet market in the world.'

You can view the video of CEO Jack Ma talking about the business on FT.com.

Source: Ali Baba Press releases Alibaba.com Limited Trading Debut, 7 November 2007: http://resources.alibaba.com/article/225276/ Alibaba_com_Limited_Trading_Debut_.htm.

Riding the Blind Tiger: The Unlikely Rise of Alibaba CEO, Jack Ma, 8 January 2008: http://resources.alibaba.com/article/246718/ Riding_the_Blind_Tiger_The_Unlikely_Rise_of_Alibaba_CEO_Jack_MA.htm.

Web Explanation: Interview with Jack Ma (search on Jack Ma): www.ft.com/cms/8a38c684-2a26-11dc-9208-000b5df10621.html.

Figure 7.6   Jack Ma, CEO Alibaba.com
Source: FT.com.

B2B electronic marketplaces, exchanges and hubs
Virtual locations with facilities to enable trading between buyers and sellers.

Electronic B2B marketplaces are variously known as 'marketplaces, exchanges or hubs'. Typically they are intermediaries that are part of the *reintermediation* (Chapter 2, p. 54) phenomenon and are independent of buyers and suppliers.

Why did so many B2B marketplaces fail?

After a great deal of hype at the turn of the millennium, many B2B marketplaces have closed. Examples of independent B2B exchanges mentioned in the previous edition are Chemdex (www.chemdex.com), Vertical Net (www.vertical.net), CommerceOne Marketsite (www.commerceone.com) and Covisint (www.covisint.net), none of which now exists in its original form. In January 2001, Dell shut down one of its B2B online marketplaces, called Dell Marketplace, only four months after it opened, citing the lack of a mature e-commerce marketplace. *Computer World* (2001a) reported that of an estimated 900 business-to-business websites that were functioning worldwide in mid-2000, a little more than 400 were left by end-2000. Despite this, enthusiasm for the B2B marketplace concept still seems quite strong. Today, Googling 'B2B Exchanges' shows that just a handful are still active.

The B2B exchange intermediaries that remain seem to be mainly for commodities or simple services (for example, EC21 (www.ec21.com), Elance (www.elance.com) and eBay Business (http://business.ebay.com)). One of the top categories on eBay Business is for tractors, with bids of between $10,000 and $20,000 common; another is photocopiers with over 3,000 listed, with a maximum price of $65,000.

Reasons for limited adoption of e-marketplaces

Johnson (2010) has investigated the reasons for limited adoption. Based on interviews with purchasing managers in a range of sectors, he believes the most significant are potentially misguided perceptions of the benefits, risks and trust in partners. However, these perceptions may be valid. He gives one example of a marketplace servicing the aerospace and defence industry where it couldn't recruit sufficient small suppliers because the e-market charged the same fee to all suppliers regardless of their size. The e-market charged suppliers $4,000 per year to use its catalogue software tool to create their own electronic catalogues, and a yearly subscription fee of $390. Although most small suppliers could afford the subscription, many could not afford to pay $4,000 per year in order to create electronic catalogues on the e-market.

From neutral to private B2B exchanges

So, these new online trading arrangements have not developed as open, neutral marketplaces as predicted by many analysts. This seems to be due to the complexity of business purchase decisions and negotiations and their destabilising nature on markets. The *Computer World* (2001b) article gives these reasons why what it terms 'private exchanges' are proving successful:

> *First, owners of private exchanges regulate supplier and customer access – and exclude competitors – making the sharing of sensitive information more likely.*

> *Second, owners can direct suppliers and customers to use the exchange through price incentives or by mandating changes in the way to conduct business.*

> *Third, private exchanges can be secured and tailored to serve specific projects and customers, unlike public exchanges, which must be generic so as to accommodate everyone.*

The article gives the example of IBM which has well-established private marketplaces. IBM has saved about $1.7 billion since 1993 by being able to divulge sensitive price and inventory information over a private exchange built for 25,000 suppliers and customers. As host of the exchange, the company helped defray the cost of connecting suppliers. As a result, on-time delivery of systems to customers increased from around 50% to 90%.

Private B2B exchanges

A manufacturer or major supplier to different manufacturers creates a portal which is used for managing all aspects of procurement.

The approach that has evolved is that **private B2B exchanges** have developed. These are the buy-side exchanges referred to in Table 7.1. These are usually created by an individual manufacturer or supplier and include a 'walled garden of suppliers', i.e. everyone has to be approved as a member, although the forms to register as a supplier to bid in response to a particular Request for Quotation (RFQ) or to participate in a reverse auction are open to all, but with each vetted to avoid competitor involvement.

Case Study 7.2 | **Covisint – a typical history of a B2B marketplace?**

This case studies a successful marketplace to prompt learning about what makes such a marketplace effective. It also illustrates the importance of online bidding in some industries.

The Covisint marketplace was originally created by Ford, GM and DaimlerChrysler (www.covisint.com). Today, Covisint is not a marketplace, but is described by its owners Compuware as a 'connectivity solution'. Its service is still used by motor manufacturers, although they now don't use a single marketplace, rather each manufacturer uses technology to access its suppliers direct.

2002: Covisint used extensively for bidding

Covisint (2002) describes a high-level of activity on the exchange. Taking the example of DaimlerChrysler AG, 512 online bidding events were processed through Covisint over a twelve-month period from 2001 to 2002. In total, this amounted to €10 billion. In May 2001, DaimlerChrysler staged the largest online bidding event ever, with an order volume of €3.5 billion in just four days. In total, 43% of the total value of the parts for a future Chrysler model series was negotiated online, with over 50 online bidding events in the third quarter of 2001 alone. As well as savings in material purchasing prices, DaimlerChrysler succeeded in reducing throughput times in purchasing by approximately 80%, thus saving on process costs. According to Dr Rüdiger Grube, Deputy Member of the Board of Management responsible for corporate development,

the economic effects achieved with e-Procurement in the first year of implementation have already covered the costs of previous investment in e-Business and hold great potential for the future, too. Therefore, we will continue to pursue our e-Business activities to the fullest extent in 2002 as well.

With the online catalogue system 'eShop' which was part of the Covisint service at that time, DaimlerChrysler would be able to reduce process costs by 50% after the completion of the blanket roll-out, which will give approximately 15,000 users the possibility of ordering several million articles. By the end of 2002 about 1,500 business partners would be connected to the electronic document exchange system 'eDocs', which would enable them to process approximately 500,000 document transmissions per year. Initial results using the 'FastCar' program for networking change management in automotive development at Chrysler show cuts in communication processes by 60–90%. In 2001, over 600 managers connected to the system developed over 300 product improvement suggestions online with the 'New Product Change Management' used in the development department of Mercedes-Benz.

'e-Business activities are already closely intertwined from development through procurement, logistics, sales and marketing. To a great extent, they are already a part of everyday business,' says Olaf Koch, Vice President of Corporate e-Business. Dr Grube: 'We're a good deal closer to our goal of making DaimlerChrysler the first automotive company to be networked throughout the entire value chain.'

2004: Covisint purchased by Compuware

Line56 (2004) summarises the acquisition of Covisint by B2B software company Compuware. The article quotes Compuware CEO Pete Karmanos as predicting that the messaging and portal part of Covisint will contribute $20 million in 2005, and will eventually become a $100 million-plus business in the automotive industry alone. The primary e-procurement offering of Covisint is as a method of managing purchasing across the many different electronic business document formats including traditional EDI formats like ANSI X12 and EDIFACT along with XML purchasing formats such as OAGIS, STAR, RosettaNet and others. Different suppliers tend to have adopted different exchange formats, so a solution that integrates them is helpful. Covisint continues to offer a portal solution both for manufacturers and their suppliers, who in turn have tier 2 or 3 suppliers. A study for Covisint by AMR Research suggested that the Covisint Communicate service was found to help a company reduce the cost of developing and deploying a portal by up to 80% and reduce the annual cost of maintenance by 50%. You can see the portal solutions at www.covisint.com.

2008: Covisint used by more than 80,000 organisations in 96 countries

Today, Covisint technology is used by over 3,000 global customers across multiple industries, with more than 18 million users connecting to over 80,000 organizations, and processing over 1 billion transactions per year (www.covisint.com/about). Many of its customers are still in the automotive industry, but now also in diverse industries including manufacturing, healthcare, aerospace, public-sector and financial services. The scale of operations is evident from these figures:

- Translation and secure transportation of over 40 million messages annually.
- Hosted infrastructure boasts 99.997% uptime.
- Provides critical portal, messaging and/or security services for users at over 45,000 organisations worldwide.

For each industry it has developed specific services particular to data exchange within these industries. Covisint Connect offers EDI and web EDI facilities for e-procurement. Covisint Communicate has over

300 applications available, some typical modules of which are used by DaimlerChrysler AG, including:

- **Accounts payable** – enables suppliers to research past and future payment/information, resolve issues prior to payment due dates and download document information to the desktop for further analysis.
- **Cooperative raw material acquisition** – provides suppliers with access to a cooperative raw material supply program to leverage customers' purchasing power and maximise operational savings.
- **Product catalogue compilation tool** – collects and distributes information required to produce and update the company's catalogue of products.
- **Request for quote application** – enables customers to issue an online request for quotation process.
- **Supplier profile** – enables customers to maintain an accurate profile consisting of key information about the supplier.

Sources: Covisint website (www.covisint.com), Covisint (2002) and Line56 (2004).

Question

By reviewing the case study and examples of the different supplier portals available on Covisint (www.covisint.com), explain why Covisint has prospered as a supplier of e-procurement portals and business document data exchange rather than as a neutral marketplace.

Types of marketplace

Kaplan and Sawhney (2000) developed a taxonomy of B2B marketplaces by applying existing classifications of corporate purchasing, namely *how* businesses buy (systematic purchasing or spot purchasing) and *what* businesses buy (manufacturing inputs or operating resource inputs). They identify the types of marketplace shown in Table 7.7. Note that manufacturing-input marketplaces tend to be vertical marketplaces set up for a particular industry such as steel, construction or chemicals, while operating resources tend to be horizontal marketplaces offering a range of products to differing industries.

Kaplan and Sawhney introduce another variation in the way marketplaces differ. This is according to whether the marketplace is direct between buyer and seller or whether some degree of aggregation occurs. In the same way that, for consumer products, volume discounts can be achieved through combining the purchasing power of individuals, this can also occur for small and medium businesses. Kaplan and Sawhney refer to this type of aggregation as 'reverse aggregation' since aggregation is back through the supply chain from customers to suppliers. They also identify 'forward aggregation' in which the supply chain operates through distributors in a traditional way. A distributor

Debate 7.2

The future for independent B2B marketplaces

'There is no future for independent B2B marketplaces, exchanges or hubs; instead those sponsored by buyers in the industry (for example, Covisint in the car industry) will be dominant.'

Table 7.7	Types of B2B marketplaces identified by Kaplan and Sawhney (2000) with examples

How businesses buy	What businesses buy	
	Operating resources	**Manufacturing resources**
Systematic sourcing	MRO hubs www.barclaysb2b.com	Catalogue hubs www.sciquest.com
Spot sourcing	Yield managers www.elance.com	Exchanges www.e-steel.com www.plasticsnet.com

Source: Adapted and reprinted by permission of *Harvard Business Review* from table on p. 99 from 'E-hubs: the new B2B marketplaces', by Kaplan, S. and Sawhney, M., in *Harvard Business Review*, May–June 2000. Copyright © 2000 by the Harvard Business School Publishing Corporation, all rights reserved.

of PCs from different manufacturers aggregates supply from the different manufacturers. Marketplaces can also act as value chain integrators when they combine supply chain functions (referred to in Chapter 6).

According to Sawhney (1999) companies looking to create exchanges typically specialise in one of the four sectors of Table 7.7, although some B2B marketplaces do offer both catalogue hubs and exchanges.

Metamediaries
Third parties that provide a single point of contact and deliver a range of services between customers and suppliers.

Some marketplaces also differ in the range of services they offer – some may go beyond procurement to offer a range of services that integrate the supply chain. Sawhney (1999) refers to these marketplaces as '**metamediaries**'. An example of a metamediary is Plastics Net (www.plasticsnet.com). This provides services of supplier evaluation, procurement, tracking, marketplace information, certification monitoring, auctions and catalogues.

The future of e-procurement

Software (intelligent) agents
Software programs that assist humans by automatically gathering information from the Internet or exchanging data with other agents based on parameters supplied by the user.

In the future, some suggest that the task of searching for suppliers and products may be taken over by **software agents** which have defined rules or some degree of intelligence that replicates intelligence in humans. On the Internet, agents can already be used for marketing research by performing searches using many search engines and in the future they may also be used to search for products or even purchase products. Agents work using predetermined rules or may learn rules using neural network techniques. Such rules will govern whether purchases should be made or not.

Some of the implications of agent technology on marketing are explored by Gatarski and Lundkvist (1998). They suggest that agent technology may create artificial consumers who will undertake supplier search, product evaluation and product selection functions. The authors suggest that such actors in a supplier-to-consumer dialogue will behave in a more rational way than their human equivalents and existing marketing theories may not apply.

Tucker and Jones (2000) also review the use of intelligent agents for sourcing. They foresee agents undertaking evaluation of a wide range of possible alternative suppliers based on predefined quantitative selection criteria including price, availability and delivery. They believe the technology is already available – indeed, similar intelligent software is used for making investments in financial markets. What is not clear is how the software will assess trustworthiness of a supplier or their competence as a business partner or associate.

Summary

1 Procurement activities involved with purchasing items from a supplier include purchasing, but also transportation, goods-in and warehousing before the item is used.

2 E-procurement involves the electronic integration of all procurement activities.

3 The numbers of staff and stages involved in procurement are reduced through e-procurement by empowering the originator of orders and changing the role of buying staff.

4 E-procurement is intended to achieve reduced purchasing cycle time and cost savings, principally through reduced staff time spent in procurement and lower inventory.

5 Options for introducing e-procurement include:
- Sell-side e-procurement – purchase direct from a seller's website that is typically not integrated with the buyer's procurement system.
- Buy-side e-procurement – integration of sellers' catalogues with the buyer's procurement system.
- Marketplace procurement – trading through an intermediary with many suppliers (may or may not be integrated with buyer's procurement system).

6 The main types of electronic marketplace in the terminology of Kaplan and Sawhney (2000) are combinations of:
- Systematic sourcing of operating resources (MRO hubs)
- Systematic sourcing of manufacturing resources (catalogue hubs)
- Spot sourcing of operating resources (yield managers)
- Spot sourcing of manufacturing resources (exchanges).

7 Organisational hurdles involved with the introduction of e-procurement include redeployment or redundancy of staff and overcoming fears of trust in suppliers.

8 The main technical challenges are the integration or replacement of a range of existing purchasing systems with a variety of supplier or marketplace systems.

Exercises

Self-assessment questions

1 Outline the two main methods by which companies purchase supplies and the two broad divisions of supplies needed.

2 Taking your answer from 1, give examples of B2B exchanges that have been created to meet these purchasing needs.

3 Draw a sketch that shows the main stages and people involved in traditional and e-procurement.

4 Outline the main reasons for e-procurement.

5 What is maverick purchasing? What safeguards need to be introduced into e-procurement to avoid this?

6 Explain the differences between the buy-side, sell-side and marketplace options for e-procurement.

7 Outline the benefits and disadvantages of each of the options in 6.

8 What are the organisational implications of introducing e-procurement?

Essay and discussion questions

1   Chris Miller of Shell Chemical has been quoted as saying:

'E-procurement is not about screwing suppliers. It's about taking cost out for both suppliers and buyers and reducing institutionalized inefficiencies. Plus it supports smaller buyers and suppliers just as much as larger ones. It's not a big boys' club.'

Discuss this statement through reviewing the benefits and disadvantages of e-procurement to both buyers and suppliers.

2   For an industry sector of your choice review the current alternative options for, and business adoption of B2B marketplaces available to, purchasing and IS professionals and attempt to forecast the situation in five years.

3   Critically assess the claims made for cost savings and increased profitability available from e-procurement.

4   Analyse the procurement process for an organisation with which you are familiar. Explain the changes and possible problems involved with introducing e-procurement.

5   'Fully automated end-to-end procurement is not practical.' Discuss.

Examination questions

1   Draw a diagram explaining four types of B2B exchanges that are dependent on the type of purchasing and what is purchased. Give one example of a product that could be purchased at each, and the name of an exchange offering this service.

2   Describe the different elements of an e-procurement system.

3   Draw a diagram that summarises the main differences in processes within an organisation for traditional procurement and e-procurement.

4   Outline the main benefits of e-procurement.

5   Explain the differences between buy-side and sell-side e-procurement. Give an advantage for each type for the purchasing company.

6   Current adoption levels of e-procurement are low. Identify the main reasons for this.

7   Explain how cost savings may arise from e-procurement.

8   Why do some commentators suggest real cost savings from e-procurement may be nearer to 10% than higher figures suggested by e-procurement solutions providers?

References

Baily, P., Farmer, D., Jessop, D. and Jones, D. (1994) *Purchasing Principles and Management.* Pitman, London.

CIPS (2008) E-commerce/ E-purchasing CIPS Knowledge Summary. **www.cips.org/documents/e-commerce.pdf**. Accessed September 2008.

Computer World (2001a) B2B outlook still ominous. By Gary Kadet, 23 April: **www.computerworld.com**.

Computer World (2001b) Private exchanges drive B2B success. By Pimm Fox, 7 May: **www.computerworld.com**.

Covisint (2002) Press release, 4 February. Covisint.com.

Gatarski, R. and Lundkvist, A. (1998) Interactive media face artificial customers and marketing theory must rethink. *Journal of Marketing Communications*, 4, 45–59.

IBF (2008) 12 ways to use your intranet to cut your costs. Member Briefing Paper, August. Published by the Intranet Benchmarking Forum (**www.ibforum.com**).

IFO-Basware (2012) 2012 Global E-invoicing study: A shift towards e-invoicing ecosystems. Joint research by the Institute of Financial Operations and Basware. Available from: **www.basware.com/knowledge-center/2012-global-e-invoicing**.

Johnson, M. (2010) Barriers to innovation adoption: a study of e-markets. *Industrial Management & Data Systems*, 110(2), 157–74.

Kalakota, R. and Robinson, M. (2000) *E-Business: Roadmap for Success*. Addison-Wesley, Reading, MA.

Kaplan, S. and Sawhney, M. (2000) E-hubs: the new B2B marketplaces. *Harvard Business Review*, May–June, 97–103.

Kluge, J. (1997) Reducing the cost of goods sold: role of complexity, design relationships. *McKinsey Quarterly*, 2, 212–15.

Knudsen, D. (2003) Aligning corporate strategy, procurement strategy and e-procurement tools. *International Journal of Physical Distribution and Logistics Management*, 33(8), 720–34.

Line56 (2004). Compuware buys last of Covisint. Article by Jim Ericson, *Line56* (**www.line56.com**), 6 February.

Proactis (2013) *Spend Control. Spend control for the multi-location, multi-business unit organisation*. Whitepaper accessed June 2013: **www.proactis.com/resources/white-papers/spend-control-for-the-multi-location,-multi-business-unit-organisation.aspx**.

Riggins, F. and Mitra, S. (2007) An e-valuation framework for developing net-enabled business metrics through functionality interaction. *Journal of Organizational Computing and Electronic Commerce*, 17(2), 175–203.

Sawhney, M. (1999) Making new markets. *Business 2.0*, May, 116–21.

Smart, A. (2010) Exploring the business case for e-procurement. *International Journal of Physical, Distribution and Logistics Management*, 40(3), 181–201.

Tranmit (1999) *Procurement Management Systems: A Corporate Black Hole. A survey of technology trends and attitudes in British industry*. Tranmit plc, UK. Survey conducted by Byline Research. Report originally available at **www.rswww.com/purchasing**.

Tucker, D. and Jones, L. (2000) Leveraging the power of the Internet for optimal supplier sourcing. *International Journal of Physical Distribution and Logistics Management*, 23 May, 30(3/4), 255–67.

Web links

Ariba.com (**www.ariba.com**) Guidelines on B2B e-commerce procurement from this 'spend management provider' which is now part of SAP.

The Chartered Institute of Purchasing and Supply (CIPS) (**www.cips.org**) Industry body in UK. Has research and best-practice advice on e-procurement including a 2006 survey on SME attitudes to e-commerce.

The Logistics web guide on About.com (**http://logistics.about.com**) Also has collection of links on the benefits and disadvantages of e-procurement.

8

Digital marketing

Web support

The following additional case studies are available at
www.pearsoned.co.uk/chaffey

→ Personalised 'cybercycles' from DBS Oegland, Norway
→ Hamley's e-tail

The site also contains a range of study materials designed to help improve your results.

Scan code to find the latest updates for topics in this chapter

Learning outcomes

After completing this chapter the reader should be able to:

• Assess the need for separate digital business and digital marketing strategies
• Create an outline digital marketing plan intended to implement the digital marketing strategy
• Distinguish between marketing communication characteristics of traditional and new media

Management issues

The issues for managers raised in this chapter include:

• How do we integrate traditional marketing approaches with digital marketing?
• How can we use electronic communications to differentiate our products and services?
• How do we redefine our marketing and communications mixes to incorporate new media?

Links to other chapters

The main related chapters are:

• *Chapter 4* – e-environment provides underpinning on the macro-economic factors that support digital marketing planning
• *Chapter 5* – on digital business strategy acts as an introduction to Part 2 and the chapters that follow; in particular, the section on eight strategic decisions is relevant to this chapter
• *Chapter 9* – CRM details practical implementation of digital marketing plans through promotional techniques and customer relationship management
• *Chapter 10* – discusses the change management issues associated with introducing multichannel marketing within an organisation

Introduction

In Chapter 5 we explored approaches to developing digital business strategies. In this chapter we examine digital marketing strategy and planning separately since, in many organisations, a distinct digital marketing plan integrated with other marketing plans will often be developed by the marketing or e-commerce team. The digital marketing plan will help define specific digital marketing objectives and develop strategies to ensure that resources are deployed to take advantage of the marketing opportunities provided by the Internet, and to counter its threats. Digital marketing is focussed on how a company and its brands use its website together with other digital platforms and media such as mobile sites and apps, search and social media and email marketing to interact with its audiences in order to add value to its brand and so meet its marketing goals. The Real-world case study on Dunelm shows the range of activities that need to be managed in marketing for an e-commerce site offering consumer retail.

Figure 8.1 shows that there are three main operational processes involved in digital marketing. These are:

- **Customer acquisition.** Attracting visitors to a website or promoting a brand through reaching them via search engines or advertising on other sites.

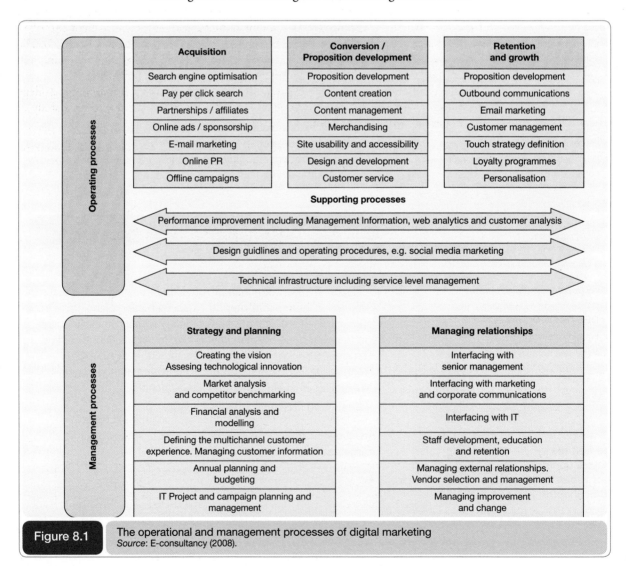

Figure 8.1 The operational and management processes of digital marketing
Source: E-consultancy (2008).

- **Customer conversion.** Engaging site visitors to achieve the outcomes the site owner seeks such as leads, sales or browsing of other content.
- **Customer retention and growth.** Encouraging repeat usage of digital channels and, for transactional sites, repeat sales.

RACE (Figure 9.3) is a similar framework we have developed at SmartInsights.com to help marketers manage and improve the commercial value that their organisations gain from digital marketing. In this chapter we focus on the management issues involved in developing a strategy for digital marketing. The digital marketing strategy will naturally be informed by the wider business and marketing objectives and digital business strategy to ensure it supports the goals of the organisation. Figure 8.2 shows that typically there is a hierarchy of plans in an organisation with the corporate or business plan informing the marketing plan and this then informing specific market plans for different products or geographical markets. There is usually a separate communications plan that details the marketing campaigns that need to be executed to achieve the marketing objectives from the marketing plan.

Chapter structure

This chapter assumes limited previous knowledge of marketing, so we start with an introduction to the marketing and digital marketing concept and explain its relationship to digital business. A structured approach to developing a digital marketing plan is then described (which is based on a similar strategy process model to that introduced in Chapter 5). The chapter also reviews how marketing concepts such as target marketing, the marketing mix and branding may require different treatment when we are using digital media.

Examples of typical ways in which organisations align their digital marketing strategy with business strategy are provided by Sultan and Rohm (2004) who, based on a study of three organisations, identify these strategic objectives:

- *Cost reduction and value chain efficiencies.* For example, B2B supplier AB Dick used the Internet to sell printer supplies to reduce service calls.

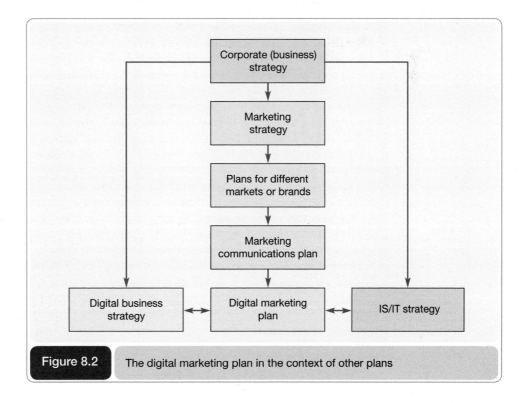

Figure 8.2 The digital marketing plan in the context of other plans

- *Revenue generation.* Reebok uses the Internet for direct licensed sales of products such as treadmills which do not have strong distribution deals.
- *Channel partnership.* Partnering with distributors using extranets.
- *Communications and branding.* Car company Saturn developed the MySaturn site to foster close relationships with customers.

Real-world Digital Business   **The Smart Insights interview**

Digital strategy development at Dunelm

Dunelm Mill is the UK's largest homewares retailer with a portfolio of established out-of-town superstores with the 'Simply Value for Money' proposition. Its online store features over 17,500 products under the brand name Dunelm Mill.

In this interview, *Sajjad Bhojani*, Head of Dunelm Direct Trading at Dunelm, explains their approach to digital marketing.

The interview

Q. What is your process for creating a digital marketing strategy?

Sajjad Bhojani, Dunelm: The business has an ongoing three-year plan, which is revised every 18 months or so. It has the standard Profit and Loss projections for the online sales part of the business. Project P&L is based on estimates of growth in traffic and sales based on conversion models. These targets stay fairly fixed within that period, but are re-reviewed as part of the annual planning process.

For introducing new features to the site and improving our digital marketing we have a 12-month cycle for development of new features.

Q. How do you define your e-commerce strategy?

Sajjad Bhojani, Dunelm: I see the 4Ps of the marketing mix as still vital to take strategic decisions for multichannel retailers. Product relates to the range of products we offer on our site compared to the stores and how we prioritise them through merchandising such as featured offers on the home page or different categories.

With Price, multichannel retailers need to consider whether they have consistent pricing with stores; this is the approach we have. The right approach will vary by market. For example, I don't believe that in our sector, channel-specific pricing such as online discounts is right. But it may be in other sectors such as Electrical where price checking can be important. That's less relevant for us since we offer own-branded products.

We aim to have competitive pricing, but don't tend to offer web exclusives – these were more relevant earlier on in the development of e-commerce to encourage use of the web, but we don't want to erode margin now. There's also the risk that differential channel pricing can be confusing. Customers are multichannel so they don't see Dunelm as two different companies. We offer free delivery for consistency too, although this is currently for orders over £50 or £150 for furniture.

For me, Place online is about offering the right experience, but also offering the right product for each search visitor. Merchandising as people search ('searchandising') the first listings page is really important. You have to decide the combination of featuring offers or best sellers which will vary as our brand runs different promotions. With our Websphere platform we also have the flexibility for offers such as BOGOF – buy one, get one free.

Place today also involves mobile access to our site. This has grown significantly so that it is now 20% of our traffic. But it is a browsing channel, so conversion rates will be lower. It's used for different applications depending where the consumer is. If you look at our target audience of busy females, they are always on the go and are increasingly using their smartphones and tablets for research and store location while shopping. We try to encourage use of mobile through in-store features like point-of-sale posters and shelf-ticket labels explaining the benefits of mobile.

We use different forms of qualitative and quantitative research both online and in-store about usage of website. However, it is difficult to have a complete 'single view of channel', since it's not possible to collect email address consistently across channels, for example.

Place also relates to how you combine online and in-store experiences. We want to provide a service that fits around the varied needs of our customers, that's why we've expanded our delivery options to include Reserve and Collect where customers can reserve products online for free and then collect in-store at a convenient time.

Promotion is about driving visitors using the channels available to all, such as search, affiliate and display. There is also promotion to existing customers using email marketing where we look to encourage increases in average order frequency and breadth of categories purchased, those are our KPIs here. Many customers will have bought in a single category, so the CRM programme will encourage that, for example by offering free delivery in a category. This is another area we're looking to refine and we have a specific role for this.

Q. How do you manage conversion rate improvements and the implementation of new features on the site?

Sajjad Bhojani, Dunelm: We're not that advanced at this stage in our use of conversion rate optimisation since we're currently updating our e-commerce platform to IBM Websphere. For example, we're not yet using AB or multivariate testing. We see it as more of a priority to introduce better personalisation features onto the site. We do have basic product recommendations based on wisdom of crowd, but human intervention is required to implement the rules.

We're around 12 months from an active customer experience improvement programme, but the intention is to implement a tool to help use these approaches. It's not simply a case of choosing the right tool, resource is a big challenge too; we need a specific analytics resource and content/copy creation resource to make the updates.

Instead, what we currently do when we introduce new features is that we involve users to check that the experience is effective. This is typically a two-phase process where we review the experience with customers based on an initial working version of the page. For example, we may be improving our product page template, so we will create working wireframes for review before building the full template. We will then test again to make minor changes when in User Acceptance Testing (UAT).

Q. What is your process for getting the right investment in marketing channels?

Sajjad Bhojani, Dunelm: How we assign our online marketing budget overall is simple - it's based on Return on investment (ROI); for every £1 of investment we have to return £X either through the site or in-store, although we need to understand contribution to in-store better. Within this you have to think about different types of investment, for example brand investments such as display advertising and direct response elements such as paid search (Google AdWords). Direct response is directed at hitting the sales target, with investment re-reviewed each month. What's important is how you test and learn. It's an evolving strategy, with separate budgets identified for each and different KPIs for search and display since the intent is different.

Search is hugely important, it's core to most retailers including us, but you have to separate investments and analysis for brand and non-search behaviour. Brand searches are where people know about us already and they search for Dunelm on its own or with a product name or category. It's important to connect these searchers with the right product, but even more important to attract visitors searching more generally. To help here, we have invested in a non-brand SEO strategy, which has involved improvements to site content and architecture, on-site optimisation and off-site optimisation looking at linking patterns. This is a fixed-line investment, which has seen significant improvements year-on-year.

Have a 12-months sales and profit target, then build in flexibility to change brand and direct response marketing activities within this, separated into brand and direct response.

It can vary between test and responsibility – we have a display retargeting budget where we conduct different trials each month. We are reviewing budget for prospecting – attracting new customers via Ad networks too.

We also have an affiliate programme set up within the last 12 months. At the same time we need to review investment.

As we review the effectiveness of our media spend we review relative return on investment from different categories, for example focussing on higher average order items. With the breadth of our product range we need to! For each category we review brand, non-brand, direct response and email sales for the current year against the previous year.

With the importance of branded search, non-branded search visits are separated out as a separate channel in our analysis. The team has a weekly visit and sales target to hit. Year-on-year performance weekly review is a key part of setting performance targets and spend analysis. We also have separate targets for Reserve and Collect against home delivery linking through to profitability of these channels.

What is digital marketing?

Digital marketing has been described simply as '*achieving marketing objectives through applying digital technologies*' (Chaffey and Ellis-Chadwick, 2012). This succinct definition helps remind us that it is the results delivered by technology that should determine investment in Internet marketing, not the adoption of the technology!

Marketing defined

We need to return to an original definition of the topic to more fully understand what digital marketing involves. The definition of marketing by the UK's Chartered Institute of Marketing is:

Marketing is the management process responsible for identifying, anticipating and satisfying customer requirements profitably.

This definition emphasises the focus of marketing on the customer, while at the same time implying a need to link to other business operations to achieve this profitability. In this chapter, and in Chapter 9, we will focus on how the Internet can be used to achieve the processes implied by this statement:

- *Identifying* – how can the Internet be used for marketing research to find out customers' needs and wants?

- *Anticipating* – we have seen that anticipating the demand for digital services (the online revenue contribution) is key to governing the resource allocation to digital business (Chapter 5).
- *Satisfying* – a key issue for digital marketing is how to achieve customer satisfaction through the electronic channel; this raises issues such as: is the site easy to use, does it perform adequately, what is the standard of associated customer service and how are physical products dispatched?

Mini case study 8.1 gives a great example of how companies can use digital techniques to fulfil marketing aims. We introduced crowdsourcing in Chapter 4 where we defined it as '*Utilising a network of customers or other partners to gain insights for new product or process innovations and to potentially help promote a brand*'.

Mini Case Study 8.1	Crowdsourcing – Penguin recruits teenagers to appeal to teenagers

Penguin used crowdsourcing to cover both the creation and management of Spinebreakers (Figure 8.3), a new site proposition to enable them to interact with teenagers. In an interview with the *Marketer* (2009), Anna Rafferty, Managing Director of the Digital Division at Penguin Books, described the process. During the website development Penguin recruited hundreds of teenagers from every area and background for focus groups and usability testing. The teenagers made every decision, choosing the URL and the nature of the brand themselves. 'We decided not to make any assumptions,' says Rafferty.

The site is now run by three tiers of teenagers, or 'crews' as they elected to be called, who have varying levels of control over the site. The core crew of 12 teenagers write all of the website copy and come into the Penguin offices every month to discuss strategy; the second crew of 70 deputy editors are based all over the country and have back-end access to the site; while the third tier consists of the hundreds of teenage bloggers who participate on the site.

Figure 8.3	Spinebreakers *Source*: www.spinebreakers.co.uk.

Smart Insights (2010) identifies five different classes of interactive online feedback tools at http://bit.ly/smartfeedback, which digital businesses can use to understand and identify customer needs and perceptions as part of marketing:

1 **Website feedback tools.** Provide a permanent facility for customers to feed back by prompts on every page. They are run continuously to enable continuous feedback, including ratings on page content, but also products and services. On SmartInsights.com we use Kamyple (www.kampyle.com, Figure 8.4).

2 **Site user intent-satisfaction surveys.** These tools measure the gap between what the user had hoped to do on the site and what they actually achieved. (We give the example of iPerceptions in Chapter 11 which covers four questions to assess site effectiveness but also see www.kampyle.com.)

3 **Crowdsourcing product opinion software.** This is broader than web feedback, enabling customers to comment about potential new services. This is the approach used by Dell in the IdeaStorm (www.ideastorm.com) and similar forums are available through Uservoice (www.uservoice.com). Some customers will also feed back on the website experience or customer experience off-site in a forum, of which GetSatisfaction (www.getsatisfaction.com) is the best known.

4 **Simple page or concept feedback tools.** Again a form of crowdsourcing, these tools give feedback from an online panel about page layout, messaging or services. On SmartInsights.com we use Qualaroo (www.qualaroo.com) to ask specific questions on what people are looking for from our services.

5 **General online survey tools.** These tools, such as Zoomerang (www.zoomerang.com) and SurveyMonkey (www.surveymonkey.com), enable companies to survey their audience at a low cost.

Digital marketing defined

The term 'Internet marketing' was widely used to refer to an external perspective of how the Internet can be used in conjunction with traditional media to acquire and deliver services to customers. An alternative term is 'e-marketing' (for example, McDonald and

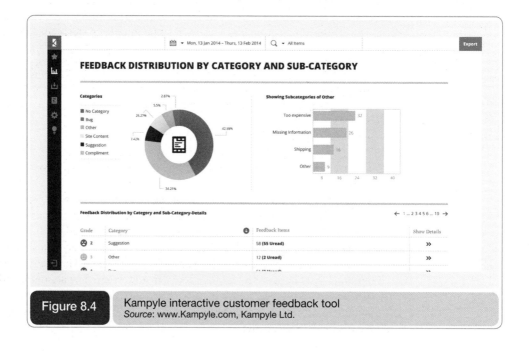

Figure 8.4	Kampyle interactive customer feedback tool
	Source: www.Kampyle.com, Kampyle Ltd.

Digital marketing
Achieving marketing objectives through use of electronic communications technology.

Wilson, 1999), more commonly described now as **digital marketing**, which can be considered to have a broader scope since it refers to any use of technology to achieve marketing objectives and has an external and an internal perspective. This is more consistent with the concept of digital business, which involves managing both internal and external digital communications.

Inbound marketing

Inbound marketing
The consumer is proactive in actively seeking out information for their needs and interactions with brands are attracted through content, search and social media marketing.

Marketing professionals commonly refer to this new approach to marketing based on digital media as **inbound marketing** (introduced in Chapter 1). Inbound marketing is powerful since advertising wastage is reduced. Content and search marketing can be used to target prospects with a defined need – they are proactive and self-selecting. But this is a weakness since marketers may have less control than in traditional communications where the message is pushed out to a defined audience and can help generate awareness and demand. Advocates of inbound marketing such as Dharmesh Shah and Brian Halligan argue that content, social media and search marketing do have a role to play in generating demand.

Content marketing

Content marketing
The management of text, rich media, audio and video content aimed at engaging customers and prospects to meet business goals published through print and digital media, including web and mobile platforms, which is repurposed and syndicated to different forms of web presence such as publisher sites, blogs, social media and comparison sites.

Success in inbound marketing requires exceptional, compelling content to attract visitors to a site and then engage them. Different content types such as videos and buyers guides on e-commerce sites can help attract visitors through search engines and, since engaging content is more likely to be shared within social media, encouraging visitors to a site. To emphasise the importance of content marketing to gaining permission to communicate through email, encouraging sharing and ongoing engagement through websites and social media, the concepts of **content marketing** and content strategy have developed to describe best practice approaches. Today, by content we refer to the combination of static content forming web pages, but also dynamic rich-media content which encourages interaction. Videos, podcasts, user-generated content and interactive product selectors should also be considered as content which should be refined to engage issues.

You can see the challenge that content strategy presents since today there are so many different types of content delivered in different forms to different places on different access platforms, yet it is increasingly important to engage customers in social media.

The definition suggests these elements of content management that need to be planned and managed:

1 **Content engagement value.** Which types of content will engage the audience – is it simple product or services information, a guide to buying product, or a game to engage your audience? Examples of content to engage leading to sale are shown by the resources section of e-procurement company Proactis (Figure 8.5).
2 **Content media.** Plain text, rich media such as Flash or rich Internet applications or mobile apps (see Chapter 3), audio (podcasts) and hosted and streamed video. Even plain text offers different format options, from HTML text to ebook formats and PDFs.
3 **Content syndication.** Content can be syndicated to different type of sites through feeds, APIs, microformats or direct submission by email. Content can be embedded in sites through widgets displaying information delivered by a feed.
4 **Content participation.** Effective content today is not simply delivered for static consumption, it should enable commenting, ratings and reviews. These also need to be monitored and managed both in the original location and where they are discussed elsewhere.
5 **Content access platform.** The different digital access platforms such as desktops and laptops of different screen resolution and mobile devices. Paper is also a content access platform for print media.

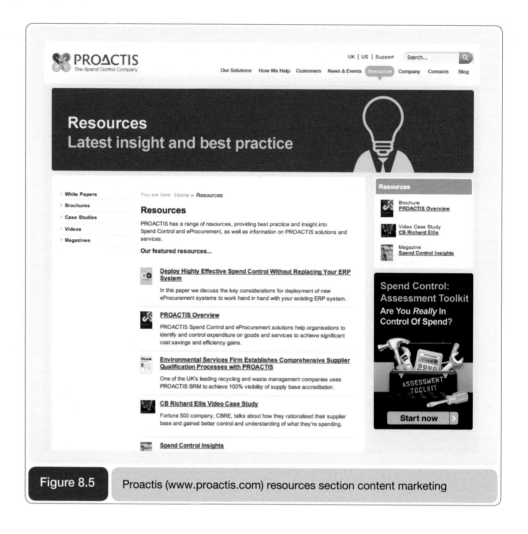

Figure 8.5   Proactis (www.proactis.com) resources section content marketing

To review how content can best support digital marketing, I developed the Content Marketing Matrix with Dan Bosomworth of Smart Insights (Figure 8.6). Activity 8.1 explains how this can be used to identify the right content types.

Activity 8.1   Using the Content Marketing Matrix to audit and improve content effectiveness

We recommend the Content Marketing Matrix as a key technique to review current use of content marketing and to identify new types of content.

The matrix is structured to help you think through the dimensions of different content based on how an audience could find content valuable and what you're trying to achieve as a business.

Activity

Complete this process to review a company's use of different types of content to support marketing:

1   Review current use of content within the company through plotting different content types on the grid.

2 Repeat this review for 2 to 3 competitors (direct or indirect), again plotting on the grid.

3 Brainstorm future content types possible.

4 Define criteria for investing in content (e.g. generating reach, helping conversion, existing customers).

5 Use your criteria from Step 4 to prioritise the 2 or 3 types of content needed to trial in content campaigns.

No answer provided.

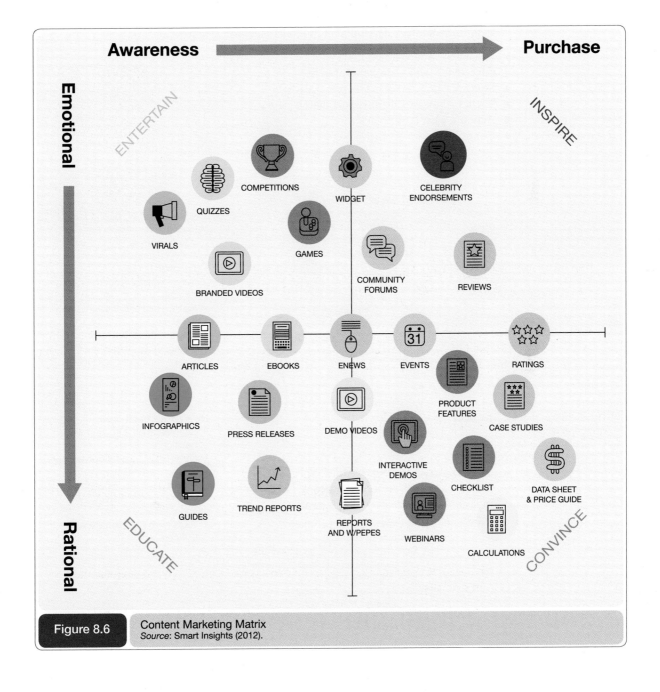

Figure 8.6	Content Marketing Matrix
	Source: Smart Insights (2012).

Digital marketing planning

Digital marketing plan

A plan to achieve the marketing objectives of the digital business strategy.

A digital marketing plan is needed in addition to a broader digital business strategy to detail how the sell-side specific objectives of the digital business strategy will be achieved through marketing activities such as research and communications. Since a digital marketing plan is based on the objectives of the marketing strategy, there is overlap between the elements of each approach, particularly for environment analysis, objective setting and strategic analysis. Figure 8.2 shows how digital marketing activities will inform the digital business strategy which, in turn, will inform the digital marketing plan.

We will use a strategy process model for digital marketing planning (similar to that introduced in Chapter 5). In this chapter we use the SOSTAC™ framework developed by Paul Smith (1999), which summarises the different stages that should be involved in a marketing strategy, from strategy development to implementation (Figure 8.7):

- Situation – where are we now?
- Objectives – where do we want to be?
- Strategy – how do we get there?
- Tactics – how exactly do we get there?
- Action – what is our plan?
- Control – did we get there?

Where are we now?
- Goal performance (5Ss)
- Customer insight
- Digital marketplace SWOT
- Brand perception
- Internal capabilities and resources

Where do we want to be?
5Ss objectives:
- Sell – customer acquisition and retention targets
- Serve – customer satisfaction targets
- Sizzle – site stickiness, visit duration
- Speak – trialogue; number of engaged customers
- Save – quantified efficiency gains

How do we monitor performance?
- 5Ss + web analytics – KPIs
- Usability testing/mystery shopper
- Customer satisfaction surveys
- Site visitor profiling
- Frequency of reporting
- Process of reporting and actions

The details of tactics, who does what and when
- Responsibilities and structures
- Internal resources and skills
- External agencies

How do we get there?
- Segmentation, targeting and positioning
- OVP (online value proposition)
- Sequence (credibility before visibility)
- Integration (consistent OVP) and database
- Tools (web functionality, email, IPTV etc.)

How exactly do we get there?
(the details of strategy)
- Digital marketing mix, including: the communications mix, social networking, what happens when?
- Details of contact strategy
- E-campaign initiative schedule

Control → Situation analysis → Objectives → Strategy → Tactics → Actions → Control

Figure 8.7	SOSTAC® – a generic framework for digital marketing planning
	Source: PR Smith's SOSTAC® Planning Model (1990).

Measurement of the effectiveness of digital marketing is an integral part of the strategy process in order to assess whether objectives have been achieved. The loop is closed by using the analysis of web analytics data (Chapter 12) metrics collected as part of the control stage to continuously improve digital marketing through making enhancements to the website and associated marketing communications.

We will now review the six elements of the SOSTAC™ approach to digital marketing planning. (Overlap between this coverage and that in Chapter 5 is minimised by cross-referencing between these chapters.)

Is a separate digital marketing plan required?

If there is a specific resource for digital marketing activities such as a digital marketing or e-commerce manager, then he or she will be responsible for the digital marketing plan. However, where there is no identified responsibility for digital marketing, which is still the case in many small and medium organisations, there is likely to be no digital marketing plan. This often occurs when marketing managers have limited resources or other priorities and a lack of recognition that a separate digital marketing plan is valuable.

> **Debate 8.1**
>
> **Is a distinct digital marketing plan necessary?**
>
> 'A separate digital marketing plan is not necessary as part of the marketing planning process – digital marketing can and should be integrated into existing marketing plans.'

These problems are typical and commonplace when there is no clear planning or control for digital marketing:

1 Customer demand for online services will be underestimated if this has not been researched and it is under-resourced and no or unrealistic objectives are set to achieve online marketing share.

2 Existing and start-up competitors will gain market share if insufficient resources are devoted to digital marketing and no clear strategies are defined.

3 Duplication of resources will occur, for example different parts of the marketing organisation purchasing different tools or using different agencies for performing similar online marketing tasks.

4 Insufficient resource will be devoted to planning and executing digital marketing and there is likely to be a lack of specific specialist digital marketing skills which will make it difficult to respond to competitive threats effectively.

5 Insufficient customer data are collected online as part of relationship-building and these data are not integrated well with existing systems.

6 Efficiencies available through online marketing will be missed, for example lower communications costs and enhanced conversion rates in customer acquisition and retention campaigns.

7 Opportunities for applying online marketing tools such as search marketing or email marketing will be missed or the execution may be inefficient if the wrong resources are used or marketers don't have the right tools.

8 Changes required to internal IT systems by different groups will not be prioritised accordingly.

9 The results of online marketing are not tracked adequately on a detailed or high-level basis.

10 Senior management support of digital marketing is inadequate to drive what often needs to be a major strategic initiative.

However, managers responsible for a substantial investment in an Internet website and associated digital marketing communications will naturally want to ensure that the correct amount of money is invested and that it is used effectively. For these reasons and to avoid the 10 problems noted above, many leading adopters of e-commerce do have a distinct or integrated digital marketing plan

For smaller organisations, the digital plan need not be exhaustive – a two-page summary aligning objectives and outlining strategies may be sufficient. The important thing is to set clear objectives and strategies showing how the digital presence should contribute to the sales and marketing process. Specific initiatives that are required such as search marketing, email marketing or features of a website redesign can be specified.

In the longer term, once an organisation has successfully defined its approaches to Internet marketing, it is likely that a separate Internet marketing strategy or digital marketing plan *will not* need to be developed each year since the Internet can be considered as any other communications medium and integrated into existing communications plans.

Situation analysis

Situation analysis
Environment analysis and review of internal processes and resources to inform strategy.

The aim of situation analysis is to understand the current and future environment in which the company operates in order that the strategic objectives are realistic in light of what is happening in the marketplace. Figure 8.8 shows the inputs from situation analysis that inform the digital marketing plan. These mainly refer to a company's external environment.

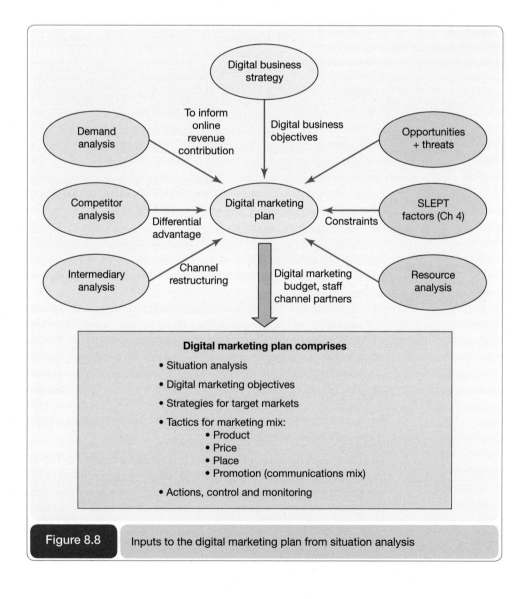

| Figure 8.8 | Inputs to the digital marketing plan from situation analysis |

The study of an organisation's online environment was introduced in Figure 2.1 and Figure 2.3 where it was noted that there was the immediate (micro-)environment of customers, competitors, suppliers and intermediaries and a broader (macro-)environment of social, legal, political, economic and technological characteristics. Situation analysis will involve consideration of all of these factors and will form the basis for defining objectives, strategies and tactics. Consideration of the SLEPT or macro-environment factors is a major topic (covered in Chapter 4). In this chapter we will concentrate on what needs to be analysed about the more immediate marketplace in terms of customers, competitors, intermediaries and market structure. An internal audit of the capability of the resources of the company such as its people, processes and technology also needs to take place.

SWOT analysis (introduced in Chapter 5 for an organisation's digital channels) can be used to summarise the range of analyses covered in this section. Figure 8.9 gives an example of a typical Internet SWOT.

The organisation	Strengths – S 1 Existing brand 2 Existing customer base 3 Existing distribution	Weaknesses – W 1 Brand perception 2 Intermediary use 3 Technology/skills (poor web experience) 4 Cross-channel support 5 Churn rate
Opportunities – O 1 Cross-selling 2 New markets 3 New services 4 Alliances/co-branding	SO strategies Leverage strengths to maximise opportunities = attacking strategy **Examples:** 1 Migrate customers to web strategy 2 Refine customer contact strategy across customer life cycle or ccmmitment segmentation (email, web) 3 Partnership strategy (co-branding, linking) 4 Launch new web-based products or value-adding experiences, e.g. video streaming	WO strategies Counter weaknesses through exploiting opportunities = build strengths for attacking strategy **Examples:** 1 Countermediation strategy (create or acquire) 2 Search marketing acquisition strategy 3 Affiliate-based acquisition strategy 4 Refine customer contact strategy (email, web)
Threats – T 1 Customer choice (price) 2 New entrants 3 New competitive products 4 Channel conflicts 5 Social network	ST strategies Leverage strengths to minimise threat = defensive strategy **Examples:** 1 Introduce new Internet-only products 2 Add value to web services – refine OVP 3 Partner with complementary brand 4 Create own social network/customer reviews	WT strategies Counter weaknesses and threats: = build strengths for defensive strategy **Examples:** 1 Differential online pricing strategy 2 Acquire/create pure-play company with lower cost-base 3 Customer engagement strategy to increase conversion, average order value and lifetime value 4 Online reputation management strategy/E-PR

Figure 8.9   Example SWOT analysis

Customer demand analysis

A key factor driving digital marketing and digital business strategy objectives is the current level and future projections of customer demand for e-commerce services in different market segments (see Strategic analysis, Chapter 5, p. 192). This will influence the demand for products online and this, in turn, should govern the resources devoted to different online channels. **Demand analysis** examines current and projected customer use of each digital channel and different services within different target markets. It can be determined by asking for each market:

Demand analysis for digital business
Assessment of the demand for e-commerce services amongst existing and potential customer segments.

- What percentage of customer businesses have access to the Internet?
- What percentage of members of the buying unit in these businesses have access to the Internet?
- What percentage of customers are prepared to purchase your particular product online?
- What percentage of customers with access to the Internet are not prepared to purchase online, but are influenced by web-based information to buy products offline?
- What is the popularity of different online customer engagement devices such as Web 2.0 features such as blogs, online communities and video?
- What are the barriers to adoption amongst customers of different channels and how can we encourage adoption?

Savvy digital marketers use tools provided by search engine services such as Google to evaluate the demand for their products or services based on the volume of different search terms typed in by search engine users. Table 8.1 shows the volume of searches for these generic, broad keywords. Most users also narrow their searches using qualifiers like 'free', 'cheap' or 'compare' which gives opportunities for comparison sites to attract visitors and to gain commission through affiliate marketing. Online retailers can target their messages to consumers looking for these products through advertising services such as Google AdWords and Bing.

Through evaluating the volume of phrases used to search for products in a given market it is possible to calculate the total potential opportunity and the current share of search terms for a company. 'Share of search' can be determined from web analytics reports from the company site which indicate the precise key phrases used by visitors to actually reach a site from different search engines.

Thus the situation analysis as part of digital marketing planning must determine levels of access to the Internet in the marketplace and propensity to be influenced by the Internet to buy either offline or online. In a marketing context, the propensity to buy is an aspect of buyer behaviour (The online buying process, Chapter 9).

Figure 8.10 summarises the type of picture the digital marketing planner needs to build up. For each geographic market the company intends to serve, research needs to establish:

1 Percentage of customers with Internet (or mobile) access.
2 Percentage of customers who access the website (and choose to use different types of services and channels such as mobile or social media options such as Facebook or Twitter).
3 Percentage of customers who will be favourably influenced.
4 Percentage of customers who buy online.

Now refer to Activity 8.2 where this analysis is performed for the car market. This picture will vary according to different target markets, so the analysis will need to be performed for each of these. For example, customers wishing to buy 'luxury cars' may have web access and a higher propensity to buy than those for small cars.

Table 8.1	Volume of searches for single keywords in a single month		

Keyword	Total global searches	Total estimated UK searches on Google	Cost-per-click
[samsung tv]	201,000	22,200	£0.58
[television]	246,000	14,800	£0.65
[led tv]	165,000	12,100	£0.77
[lg tv]	90,500	9,900	£0.53
[panasonic tv]	40,500	8,100	£0.58
[flat screen tv]	49,500	6,600	£0.50
[lcd tv]	90,500	6,600	£0.67
[samsung led tv]	90,500	4,400	£0.68
[lcd]	135,000	4,400	£0.65
[plasma tv]	33,100	3,600	£0.73
[hd tv]	33,100	3,600	£0.67
[samsung televisions]	8,100	2,400	£0.57
[samsung tvs]	9,900	2,400	£0.79
[buy tv]	6,600	2,400	£0.75
[cheap lcd tv]	4,400	1,900	£0.55
[sharp tv]	40,500	1,900	£0.55
[led tvs]	6,600	1,600	£0.81
[blu ray players]	6,600	1,600	£0.40
[compare tv prices]	2,400	1,600	£0.46
[led tv reviews]	9,900	1,600	£0.54

Note: Estimates are baswed on the Google keyword tool in June 2013 based on LCD related exact-match search phrases.

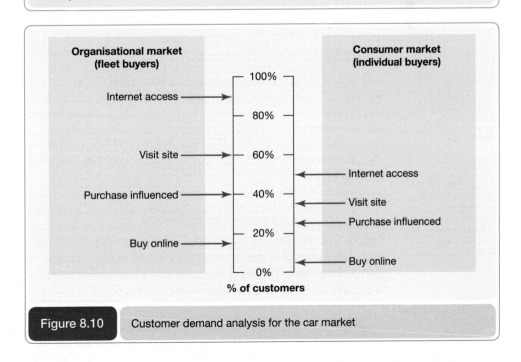

Figure 8.10	Customer demand analysis for the car market

| Activity 8.2 | Customer activity in the car market in your country |

Purpose

To illustrate the type of marketing research needed to inform demand analysis for digital marketing planning and approaches to finding this information.

Activity

For your country update Figure 8.10 to reflect current and future projections:

A For corporate buyers (known as the 'fleet market') where a specialist manager coordinates the purchase and management of company cars for efficiency purposes:

1 Percentage of customers with Internet access.

2 Percentage of customers who access the website.

3 Percentage of customers who will be favourably influenced (may be difficult to determine).

4 Percentage of customers who buy online.

If possible, try to gauge how these figures vary according to companies of different sizes and different members of the buying unit.

B For individual buyers (consumers):

1 Percentage of customers with Internet access.

2 Percentage of customers who access the website or social media services via web or mobile channels.

3 Percentage of customers who will be favourably influenced.

4 Percentage of customers who buy online or use other services such as brochure download, book a test drive or service.

If possible, try to gauge how these figures vary according to age, sex and social class.

Government sources and trade associations for car purchasing can be used to research the data.

No suggested answer supplied.

Qualitative customer research

Persona
A summary of the characteristics, needs, motivations and environment of typical website users.

Customer scenario
Alternative tasks or outcomes required by a visitor to a website. Typically accomplished in a series of stages of different tasks involving different information needs or experiences.

It is important that customer analysis not be restricted to quantitative demand analysis. Variani and Vaturi (2000) point out that qualitative research provides insights that can be used to inform strategy. They suggest using graphic profiling, which is an attempt to capture the core characteristics of target customers, not only demographics, but also their needs and attitudes and how comfortable they are with the Internet. (In Chapter 11 we will review how customer **personas** and **scenarios** are developed to help inform understanding of online buyer behaviour.)

A summary of the categories of different sources of customer insight that an organisation can tap into and their applications is shown in Table 8.2. The challenge within organisations seems to be selecting which paid-for and free services to select and then ensure sufficient time is spent reviewing and actioning the data to create value-adding insights. My experience shows that often data are only used by the digital team and not utilised more widely since in large organisations, staff are unaware of the existence of the data or service provider supplying it. There is also the significant issue of privacy; organisations need to be transparent about how they collect and use these data and give customers choice (as discussed in Chapter 4).

Table 8.2	Categories of suppliers of digital customer insight and sample suppliers	

Insight type	Description	Sample suppliers
Voice of customer	Customer perceptions of online and multichannel experience including advocacy and Net Promoter Score. Online reputation (buzz) management tools	www.iperceptions.com www.opinionlab.com www.foreseeresults.com www.bazaarvoice.com
Customer profile data	Characteristics of customers in line with segments	Internal databases
Purchase behaviour	Transaction history including product category, recency, frequency and monetary value	Internal databases
Visitor behaviour from web analytics	Customer journeys on-site and referral sources. Popularity of landing pages, content and products	www.google.com/analytics www.adobe.com/solutions/digital-analytics.html www.getclicky.com
Audience panel data	Audience volume/reach and profile on third-party sites	www.experian.com/hitwise/ www.comscore.com www.nielsen-online.com/intlpage.html
Competitive benchmarking	Independent review of website functionality and features from independent review team or customers (mystery shoppers)	www.globalreviews.com www.psyma.com www.edigitalresearch.com
Campaign response	Combination of digital media touchpoints leading to website visits and conversion. Ad network behavioural targeting.	www.atlassolutions.com www.doubleclick.com www.lynchpin.com
Experimentation	AB and multivariate testing. On-site behavioural targeting. On-site merchandising solutions	www.autonomy.com/products/optimost www.adobe.com/solutions/testing-targeting/testandtarget.html www.maxymiser.com

As well as external sources, many online businesses are now harnessing customer viewpoints or innovation through their own programmes. Well-known examples from business and consumer fields include:

- Dell IdeaStorm (www.ideastorm.com)
- MyStarbucks Idea (http://mystarbucksidea.com)
- Proctor and Gamble Innocentive (www.innocentive.com)
- Lego MindStorm (http://mindstorms.lego.com/community/default.aspx)
- Oracle Mix.

You can see how web-savvy companies use the web for marketing research, as a listening channel. They use the web and email channels as means of soliciting feedback and suggestions which contribute to shaping future services.

Competitor analysis

Competitor analysis for digital business
Review of digital business services offered by existing and new competitors and adoption by their customers.

Competitor analysis or the monitoring of competitor use of e-commerce to acquire and retain customers is especially important in the digital marketplace due to the dynamic nature of the Internet medium. This enables new services to be launched and promotions changed much more rapidly than through print communications. The implications of this dynamism are that competitor benchmarking is not a one-off activity while developing a strategy, but needs to be continuous.

Benchmarking of competitors' online services and strategy is a key part of planning activity and should also occur on an ongoing basis in order to respond to new marketing approaches such as price or promotions. According to Chaffey *et al.* (2009), competitor benchmarking has different perspectives which serve different purposes:

1 **Review of internal capabilities:** such as resourcing, structure and processes vs external customer-facing features of the sites.

2 **From core proposition through branding to online value proposition (OVP).** The core proposition will be based on the range of products offered, price and promotion. The OVP describes the type of web services offered which add to a brand's value. We cover proposition more in the sections on OVP and the marketing mix later in this chapter.

3 **Different aspects of the customer life cycle:** customer acquisition, conversion to retention. Competitor capabilities should be benchmarked for all the digital marketing activities of each competitor, as shown in Figure 8.1. These should be assessed from the viewpoint of different customer segments or personas, possibly through usability sessions. Performance in search engines (using the tools mentioned in Chapter 2) should be reviewed as a key aspect of customer acquisition and brand strength. In addition to usability, customer views should be sought on different aspects of the marketing mix such as pricing and promotions mentioned later in the chapter.

4 **Qualitative to quantitative:** from qualitative assessments by customers through surveys and focus groups through to quantitative analysis by independent auditors of data across customer acquisition (e.g. number of site visitors or reach within market, cost of acquisition, number of customers, sales volumes and revenues and market share); conversion (average conversion rates) and retention such as repeat conversion and number of active customers.

5 **In-sector and out-of-sector:** benchmarking against similar sites within sector and reviewing sectors which tend to be more advanced, e.g. online publishers, social networks and brand sites. Benchmarking services are available from analysts such as Bowen Craggs & Co (www.bowencraggs.com). An example of one of their benchmark reports is shown in Figure 8.11. You can see that this is based on the expert evaluation of the suitability of the site for different audiences as well as measures under the overall construction (which includes usability and accessibility), message (which covers key brand messages and suitability for international audiences) and contact (which shows integration between different audiences). The methodology states: 'it is not a "tick box": every metric is judged by its existence, its quality and its utility to the client, rather than "Is it there or is it not?"'

6 **Financial to non-financial measures.** Through reviewing competitive intelligence sources such as company reports or tax submissions additional information may be available on turnover and profit generated by digital channels. But other forward-looking aspects of

Pos	Company	Construction	Message	Contact	Serving society	Serving investors	Serving the media	Serving job seekers	Serving customers	Total	URL	Country
	maximum score	60	48	12	32	32	32	32	32	280		
1	Siemens	47	40	10	27	21	28	24	24	221	www.siemens.com	Germany
2	Royal Dutch Shell	46	41	7	26	22	21	24	22	209	www.shell.com	Netherlands
3	BP	41	39	10	28	27	18	19	25	207	www.bp.com	UK
4	Nokia	44	36	8	26	24	24	16	25	203	www.nokia.com	Finland
5	AstraZeneca	48	33	9	20	20	27	16	27	200	www.astrazeneca.com	France
	Total	44	39	11	25	27	12	22	21	200	www.total.com	UK/Sweden
7	IBM	41	36	11	23	26	26	12	24	199	www.ibm.com	US
8	ING	43	40	8	22	25	21	16	22	197	www.ing.com	Netherlands
9	UBS	37	36	6	20	27	22	26	20	194	www.ubs.com	Switzerland
10	General Electric	42	37	10	25	17	19	17	24	191	www.ge.com	US

Figure 8.11 Benchmark comparison of corporate websites
Source: Bowen Craggs & Co (www.bowencraggs.com).

the company's capability which are incorporated on the balanced scorecard measurement framework (see Chapter 4) should also be considered, including resourcing, innovation and learning.

7 **From user experience to expert evaluation.** Benchmarking research should take two alternative perspectives, from actual customer reviews of usability to independent expert evaluations.

Now complete Activity 8.3 to gain an appreciation of how benchmarking competitor digital business services can be approached.

Activity 8.3	Competitor benchmarking

Purpose

To understand the services of a competitor website it is useful to benchmark and to assess the value of benchmarking.

Activity

You have been commissioned by a major company to evaluate the *marketing effectiveness* of their online services in comparison with their competitors'. You have to present your findings on their services and how they can be improved in a ten-minute PowerPoint presentation.

Choose a B2C industry sector such as airlines, book retailers, book publishers, CDs or clothing or for B2B a sector such as oil companies, chemical companies or construction industry companies.

Work individually or in groups to identify the type of information that should be available from the website (and which parts of the site you will access it from) which will be useful in terms of competitor benchmarking. Once your criteria have been developed, you should then benchmark companies and summarise which you feel is making best use of the Internet medium.

Table 5.10 may also prove useful.

Answers to activities can be found at www.pearsoned.co.uk/chaffey

---

Intermediary or influencer analysis

Chapter 2 highlighted the importance of web-based intermediaries such as publisher or media sites in driving traffic to an organisation's website or influencing visitors while they consume content. Situation analysis will also involve identifying relevant intermediaries for a particular marketplace. These will be different types of publisher such as horizontal and vertical portals which will be assessed for suitability for advertising, PR or partnership. This activity can be used to identify strategic partners or will be performed by a media planner or buyer when executing an online advertising campaign.

For example, an online electronics retailer needs to assess which comparison or aggregator services such as Kelkoo (www.kelkoo.com) and Shopsmart (www.shopsmart.com) it and its competitors are represented on. Questions which are answered by analysis of intermediaries are do competitors have any special sponsorship arrangements and are microsites created with intermediaries? The other main aspect of situation analysis for intermediaries is to consider the way in which the marketplace is operating. To what extent are competitors using disintermediation or reintermediation? How are existing channel arrangements being changed?

Internal marketing audit

An internal audit will assess the capability of the resources of the company such as its people, processes and technology to deliver digital marketing compared with its competitors. (In Chapter 10 we discuss how teams should be restructured and new resources used to deliver competitive online marketing and customer experience.) The internal audit will also review the way in which a current website or e-commerce service performs. The audit is likely to review the following elements of an e-commerce site (which are described in more detail in 'Focus on Web analytics: measuring and improving performance of digital business services' in Chapter 12):

1 **Business effectiveness.** This will include the contribution of the site to revenue, profitability and any indications of the corporate mission for the site. The costs of producing and updating the site will also be reviewed, i.e. cost–benefit analysis.
2 **Marketing effectiveness.** These measures may include:
   - leads;
   - sales;
   - cost of acquiring new customers;
   - retention;
   - market share;
   - brand engagement and loyalty;
   - customer service.

   These measures will be assessed for each of the different product lines delivered through the website. The way in which the elements of the marketing mix are utilised will also be reviewed.
3 **Internet effectiveness.** These are specific measures that are used to assess the way in which the website is used, and the characteristics of the audience. Such measures include specialist measures such as unique visitors and page impressions that are collected through web analytics, and also traditional research techniques such as focus groups and questionnaires to existing customers. From a marketing point of view, the effectiveness of the value proposition of the site for the customer should also be assessed.

Objective setting

Effective digital marketing plans are based on clearly defined objectives since these will inform the strategies and tactics and help in communicating the strategic aims to the workforce and investors.

Strategies are agreed to be most effective when they support specific business objectives. A useful technique to help align strategies and objectives is to present them together in a table together with the insight developed from situation analysis which may have informed the strategy. Table 8.3 gives an example which also shows the links between strategies of customer acquisition, conversion and retention and the tactics used to fulfil them, such as email marketing and search engine marketing, which we discuss in Chapter 9.

We also discussed the importance of SMART digital business objectives in Chapter 5. We noted the value of using metrics which combined efficiency and effectiveness and could be applied in the context of the balanced scorecard. Table 8.4 presents detailed digital marketing metrics in this way.

Table 8.3	The relationship objectives, strategies and performance indicators for a B2B company (in order of priority)

Objectives	Substantiation (informed by situation analysis or insight, example)	Strategies to achieve goals	Key performance indicators (critical success factors)
1 *Acquisition objective.* Acquire 50,000 new online customers this financial year at an average cost per acquisition (CPA) of £30 with an average profitability of 5%	Based on growth forecast based on current sales of 40,000 sales per year, but with incremental sales arising from new affiliate programme and SEO development	Start affiliate marketing programme and improve SEO. Existing media mix based on pay-per-click and display advertising supported by offline media	Overall CPA for online sales. Incremental number and % of sales from affiliate marketing programme Number of strategic keywords ranked in top positions in natural search results page
2 *Acquisition (or conversion) objective.* Migrate 40% of existing customers to using online 'paperless' bill payment services and email communications within 3 years	Extrapolation of current natural migration coupled with increased adoption from offline direct marketing campaign	Direct marketing campaign using direct mail, phone prompts and online persuasion to encourage adoption. Use of incentive to encourage change	Number and percentage of existing customers registering to use online services Number and percentage of customers actively using online services at different points after initially registering
3 *Conversion objective.* Increase the average order value of online sales to £42 per customer	Growth estimated based on current AOV of £35 plus model suggesting 20% increase in AOV	Use of new merchandising system to show users related 'next-best product' for different product categories	% of site visitors responding to merchandising/cross-selling messages
4 *Conversion objective.* Increase site conversion rate to 3.2%	Model showing separate increase in conversion for new and existing customers based on strategies shown on the right	Combination of strategies: • Incentivised email follow-up on checkout abandonments for new customers • Introduction of more competitive pricing strategy on best sellers • AB and multivariate messaging improvement of landing pages • Refinement to quality of traffic purchased through pay-per-click programme	Variations in conversion rates for new and existing customers in different product categories
5 *Retention objective.* Increase annual repeat new customer conversion rate by 20%	Business case based on limited personalisation of offers to encourage repeat purchases via email.	• Delivery of personalised product offers by email • 5% second purchase discount voucher	• Increased conversion rate of retention email contact programme • Conversion to sale for second purchase discount campaigns
6 *Growth objective.* Increase new prospects recommended by friends (viral marketing or 'member get member') by 10,000 per annum	Model based on encouraging 2% of customers to recommend friends annually (based on trial scheme)	Supported by direct mail and email recommendation programme	• Response rate to direct mail campaign

Table 8.4	Example Internet marketing objectives within the balanced scorecard framework for a transactional e-commerce site

Balanced scorecard sector	Efficiency	Effectiveness
Financial results (business value)	• Channel costs • Channel profitability	• Online contribution (direct) • Online contribution (indirect) • Profit contributed
Customer value	• Online reach (unique visitors as % of potential visitors) • Cost of acquisition or cost per sale (CPA or CPS) • Customer satisfaction ratings	• Sales and sales per customer • New customers • Online market share • Customer propensity to defect • Customer loyalty index
Operational processes	• Conversion rates • Average order value • List size and quality • Email-active %	• Fulfilment times • Support response times
Innovation and learning (people and knowledge)	• Novel approaches tested • Internal digital marketing education • Internal satisfaction ratings	• Novel approaches deployed • Performance appraisal review

Online revenue contribution

An assessment of the direct contribution of the Internet or other digital media to sales, usually expressed as a percentage of overall sales revenue.

In Chapter 5, we also mentioned the importance of defining the **online revenue contribution** as a target to improve performance. Figure 8.12 gives an example combining the online revenue contribution and the online promotion contribution as a forecast based on marketing research of demand analysis and competitor analysis. Complete Case study 8.1 to review how easyJet increased their online revenue contribution.

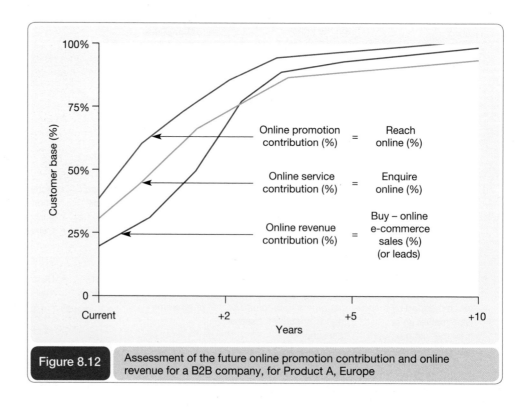

Figure 8.12	Assessment of the future online promotion contribution and online revenue for a B2B company, for Product A, Europe

Case Study 8.1 | The evolution of easyJet's online revenue contribution

This historical case shows how the easyJet website (Figure 8.13) became the main sales channel for easyJet from its launch in the 1990s. How the Internet was used for service delivery and marketing communications is also described. This case study has been retained since it is a popular case illustrating the benefits of management commitment to a planned, well-resourced strategy to help grow digital channels and to trial new online products. By 2013, over 98% of seats were sold online and easyJet still incentivises people to book their cheap flights online through a £7.50 discount for each leg of a journey.

easyJet was founded by Stelios Haji-Ioannou, the son of a Greek shipping tycoon who reputedly used to 'hate the Internet'. In the mid-1990s Haji-Ioannou reportedly denounced the Internet as something 'for nerds', and swore that it wouldn't do anything for his business. This is no longer the case, since by August 1999 the site accounted for 38% of ticket sales or over 135,000 seats. This was past the company's original Internet contribution target at launch of 30% of sales by 2000. In the period from launch, the site had taken more than 800,000 bookings since it was set up in April 1998 after a shaky start of two sales in the first week and one thousand within the first month. In March 2000 easyJet increased its online discount to £2.50 for a single trip – a higher level of permanent discount than any other airline. By September 2000, Internet sales reached 85% of total sales. Since this time, the growth in proportion of online sales has decreased. By 2003, over 90% of all sales were online.

Figure 8.13 | easyJet website
Source: www.easyjet.com.

The company was originally set up in 1994. As a low-cost airline, looking to undercut traditional carriers such as British Airways, it needed to create a lean operation. To achieve this, Haji-Ioannou decided on a single sales channel in order to survive. He chose the phone. At the time this was ground-breaking, but the owner was encouraged by companies such as Direct Line insurance, and the savings which direct selling would bring.

Although Haji-Ioannou thought at the time that there was no time to worry about the Internet and that one risk was enough, he was adaptable enough to change. When a basic trial site was launched, he kept a close eye on how popular the dedicated information and booking phone line was (having a web-specific phone number advertised on the site can be used to trace the volume of users on the site). A steady rise in the number of calls occurred every week. This early success coincided with the company running out of space at its call centre due to easyJet's growth. Haji-Ioannou related, 'We either had to start selling over the Internet or build a new call centre. So our transactional site became a £10 million decision.'

Although the success of easyJet could be put down solely to the founder's adaptability and vision, the company was helped by the market it operated in and its chosen business model – it was already a 100% direct phone sales operation. This meant it was relatively easy to integrate the web into the central booking system. There were also no potential channel conflicts with intermediaries such as travel agents. The web also fitted in with the low-cost easyJet proposition of no tickets, no travel agents, no network tie-ups and no in-flight meals. Customers are given a PIN number for each order on the website which they give when they get to the airport.

Sales over the Internet began in April 1998, and although easyJet's new-media operations were then handled by Tableau, a few months later easyJet took them in-house.

The Internet is important to easyJet since it helps it to reduce running costs, important for a company where each passenger generates a profit of only £1.50. Savings to easyJet made through customers booking online enable it to offer at least £1 off to passengers who book online – this is part of the online proposition.

The owner says that 'the savings on the Internet might seem small compared to not serving a meal on a plane, which saves between £5 and £10, but when you think how much it would cost to build a new call centre, pay every easyJet reservation agent 80 pence for each seat sold – not to mention all the middlemen – you're talking much more than the £1 off we give online buyers'.

What about the risks of alienating customers who don't want to book online? This doesn't worry the owner. He says 'I'm sure there are people who live in the middle of nowhere who say they can't use the Internet and will fly Ryanair instead. But I'm more worried about keeping my cost base down, and finding enough people to fill my aeroplanes. I only need 6 million people a year, not all 56 million.'

Promotion

The Internet marketing gurus say 'put the company URL everywhere'; easyJet has taken this literally with its web address along the side of its Boeing 737s.

easyJet frequently varies the mix by running Internet-only promotions in newspapers. easyJet ran its first Internet-only promotion in a newspaper in *The Times* in February 1999, with impressive results. Some 50,000 seats were offered to readers and 20,000 of them were sold on the first day, rising to 40,000 within three days. And, according to the marketing director, Tony Anderson, most of these were seats that otherwise would have been flying along at 600 mph – empty. The scalability of the Internet helped deal with demand since everyone was directed to the website rather than the company needing to employ an extra 250 telephone operators. However, risk management did occur with a micro-site built for *Times* readers (www.times.easyjet.com) to avoid putting a strain on easyJet's main site.

Anderson says, 'The airline promotions are basically designed to get rid of empty seats.' He adds, 'If we have a flight going to Nice that's leaving in 20 minutes' time, it costs us very little to put some extra people on board, and we can get, say, £15 a head for it.' Flight promotions are intended to avoid attracting people who would fly with easyJet, so advanced booking schemes are intended to achieve that.

A later five-week promotion within *The Times* and *The Sunday Times* newspapers offered cheap flights to a choice of all easyJet destinations when 18 tokens were collected. In total, 100,000 seats were sold during the promotion, which was worth more than £2 million to the airline. Thirty per cent of the seats were sold online, with the rest of the transactions being completed by phone; 13,000 orders were taken over the Internet in the first day alone with over 15,000 people on the site at one point.

The website also acts as a PR tool. Haji-Ioannou uses its immediacy to keep newspapers informed about new promotions and offers.

The website is also used as an aggressive tool in what is a very competitive marketplace. Haji-Ioannou says, 'Once we had all these people coming to our site, I asked myself: Why pay a PR company to publicise what we think when we have a captive audience on the site?' For example, easyJet ran a competition in which people had to guess what BA's losses would be on 'Go', its budget rival to easyJet (the figure turned out to be £20 million). Within minutes of the BA results being announced on 7 September, the easyJet site had the 50 flight-ticket winners from an incredible 65,000 people who had entered.

In a similar vein a section of the site was entitled 'Battle with Swissair', giving easyJet's view that Swissair's head had persuaded the Swiss government to stop easyJet being granted a commercial scheduled licence on the Geneva–Barcelona route. easyJet also called itself 'The web's favourite airline', in 1999, a direct counterpoint to British Airways' slogan of 'The world's favourite airline' for which it enjoyed a court battle.

The creation of a mobile site

In an interview with Peter Duffy, the easyJet Marketing Director, the potential of mobile marketing was emphasised (*Marketer*, 2013):

> 'Mobile was clearly a huge growth area. In some Mediterranean countries mobile is often leapfrogging broadband as a way to get online. So we set about making a mobile website where you could do all the things you can do on easyJet.com: buy from a website, cancel a flight, shift a flight, and do all those things in six languages. We have seen tremendous demand for it. The app has been downloaded 4.3m times. Today 5 per cent of revenue comes through mobile – that's not insignificant for a £4bn company.'

Peter Duffy has also introduced a conversion rate optimisation programme. He says:

> 'When I arrived, my first observation was that we had 400 million people going to the website; 90 per cent of sales come through it. If we could improve conversion by just a small amount it was probably the most effective thing we could do commercially.
>
> At any point in time a dozen to 20 tests can be running based on a series of ideas for how the company can do things better, inspired either by watching our customers or looking at where customers are dropping out of the process, or where there is a new feature like allocated seating.'

easyEverything

easyJet has used the 'easy' prefix to trial additional services as part of the easyGroup. Trials include:

- easyEverything, a chain of 400-seat-capacity Internet cafés originally offering access at £1 an hour. This is run as an independent company and will charge easyJet for banner ads, but clearly the synergy will help with clickthrough between 2 and 3%. The only concession easyEverything makes towards easyJet is that café customers can spend time on the easyJet site for free.
- easyRentacar, a low-cost car rental business offering car rental at £9 a day. These costs are possible through offering a single car type and being an Internet-only business.

Today, most non-flight services such as holidays, car rental and insurance are directly related to travel, often provided by partners.

Implementation

The articles report that Russell Sheffield, head of new-media agency Tableau, which initially worked with easyJet had an initial problem of colour! 'He says there was a battle to stop him putting his favourite colour all over the site.' The site was intended to be highly functional, simply designed and without any excess baggage. He says, 'The home page (orange) only had four options – buy online, news, info, and a topic of the moment such as BA "GO" losses – and the site's booking system is simpler to use than some of its competitors'. He adds: 'Great effort was put into making the navigation intuitive – for example, users can move directly from the timetables to the booking area, without having to go via the home page.'

The site was designed to be well integrated into easyJet's existing business processes and systems. For example, press releases are fed through an electronic feed into the site, and new destinations appear automatically once they are fed into the company's information system.

Measurement of the effectiveness of the site occurred through the dedicated phone number on the site which showed exactly how many calls the site generated, and the six-month target was met within six weeks. Website log file analysis showed that people were spending an average of eight minutes a time on the site, and better still, almost everyone who called bought a ticket, whereas with the normal phone line, only about one in six callers buys. Instead of having to answer questions, phone operators were doing nothing but sell tickets.

Source: Based on *Revolution* articles: EasyJet site a success in first month, 1 August 1998; EasyJet promotion sells 30,000 seats, 1 November 1998; Say hello to Mr e-Everything, 13 October 1999. *Marketer* (2013).

Questions

1 To what extent was the Internet revenue contribution of around 90% achieved 'more by luck than judgement'?
2 Explain the proposition of using the Internet for the customer and define the benefits for the company.
3 Explain how easyJet uses the website to vary the different elements of the marketing mix and as a marketing communications tool.
4 Use a news source such as www.ft.com or review its investors' relations site to find out how easyJet has extended its Internet applications.

Strategy

The strategy element of a digital marketing plan defines how digital marketing objectives will be achieved. Strategy definition has to be tightly integrated into the digital marketing planning process since digital marketing planning is an iterative process from situation analysis to objective setting to strategy definition (Figure 8.7). (Key decisions in strategy definition for digital business were described in Chapter 5.) To avoid significant overlap here, the reader is referred to that section. Another perspective on digital marketing strategy is provided by my evaluation in the E-consultancy (2008) report, which explains that the output from the digital strategy will often be a series of strategic e-commerce initiatives in the key areas of customer acquisition, conversion or retention such as those shown in Table 8.5. These e-commerce initiatives will typically be prioritised and placed as part of a long-term e-commerce 'roadmap' defining required developments over a longer period of 18 months to three years.

The amount invested on the Internet should be based on the anticipated contribution the Internet will make to a business, as explained in the sections on objectives. The Electronic

Table 8.5	Summary of typical focus for main types of e-commerce-related strategic initiatives

Type of digital marketing strategy initiative	Commentary	Examples of strategy implementation
1 **New customer proposition (Product, Place and Pricing)**	These are new site features or other online communications which are directly related to offering new products or services, potentially from new locations that will generate revenue.	• Bank – introduce new product requiring different quotes • Portal – introduce comparison service • Service company – introduce new functionality acquired through takeover of company • Magazine or music service offering new pricing options • See also channel integration initiatives
2 **Customer acquisition strategic initiatives**	These are strategic projects to enhance a site's capability to deliver new prospects on a continuous basis through different online marketing techniques. They may involve investment in the site itself (e.g. SEO) or the back-end, integrating with affiliates.	• SEO • PPC • Affiliate marketing • Aggregators • Enhance page type (to help increase conversion rate), e.g. category or product landing pages
3 **Customer conversion and customer experience strategic initiatives**	Investments in new customer features on the site. These will be based on a business case of increased conversion rate and average order value. May include major new functionality such as that for a new online store or more specific functionality integrated into existing site functionality. Many strategic initiatives are aimed at improving the customers' experience of a brand.	• Implement online shop / secure payment • Introduce customer reviews and ratings • Merchandising capability to offer tailored promotions • Interactive tools to help product selection • Refine on-site search engine • Buyers guides consisting of in-depth content about products or rich media (e.g. videos showcasing products)

Type of digital marketing strategy initiative	Commentary	Examples of strategy implementation
4 Customer development and growth strategic initiatives	Investments to improve the experience and delivery of offers to existing customers.	• Personalised recommendations for existing customers • Development of email welcome strategy for new online customers as part of development of an integrated contact or e-CRM strategy delivered through personalised web and email messages and traditional direct communications • Introduce blogs or RSS feeds to encourage return visitors • Introduce more participation through customer communities
5 Channel integration initiatives	These may reference any of the strategies above.	• Offline retailer launches 'click and reserve' service • Digital facilities introduced in-store • Integration of mobile marketing into direct mail or email campaigns
6 Enhance marketing capabilities through site infrastructure improvements	These typically involve 'back-end or back-office features' which won't be evident to users of the site, but will help in the management or administration of the site. Will often involve improving customer insight capabilities.	• CRM or personalisation • Content management system • Performance improvement – improve management information, web analytics systems including systems for multivariate and AB testing • Improve customer feedback or other customer survey facilities • Update development approach for introducing new functionality

Shopping Test (Box 8.1), for reviewing the likely strategic importance of the Internet to a company as developed by de Kare-Silver (2000), is still relevant today since the drivers for online against offline services remain similar.

Market and product positioning

The Internet offers new opportunities for selling new products into new markets. These present strategic alternatives that can be evaluated using the options first stated by Ansoff (1957). The risks involved with the four options of market penetration, market development, product development and both market and product development (diversification) vary (as shown in Figure 5.20 and explained in the commentary).

There may also be options for new digital products that could include information products that can be delivered over the web. Such products may not be charged for, but will add value to existing products. Ghosh (1998) suggested developing new products or adding 'digital value' to customers. Still relevant today for consideration as part of digital marketing strategy, he says companies should ask the following questions:

1 Can I offer additional information or transaction services to my existing customer base?
2 Can I address the needs of new customer segments by repackaging my current information assets or by creating new business propositions using the Internet?

| Box 8.1 | The Electronic Shopping or ES Test |

This test was developed by Michael de Kare-Silver to assess the extent to which consumers are likely to purchase a retail product using the Internet. De Kare-Silver suggests factors that should be considered in the ES Test:

1 **Product characteristics.** Does the product need to be physically tried or touched before it is bought?
2 **Familiarity and confidence.** Considers the degree the consumer recognises and trusts the product and brand.
3 **Consumer attributes.** These shape the buyer's behaviour – are they amenable to online purchases in terms of access to the technology skills available and do they no longer wish to shop for a product in a traditional retail environment?

In his book, de Kare-Silver describes a method for ranking products. Product characteristics, familiarity and confidence are each marked out of 10, and consumer attributes are marked out of 30. Using this method, he scores products as shown in Table 8.6.

De Kare-Silver states that any product scoring over 20 has good potential, since the score for consumer attributes is likely to increase through time. Given this, he suggests companies will regularly need to review the score for their products.

| Table 8.6 | Product scores in de Kare-Silver (2000), Electronic Shopping Potential Test |

Product	1 Product characteristics (10)	2 Familiarity and confidence (10)	3 Consumer attributes (30)	Total
Groceries	4	8	15	27
Mortgages	10	1	4	15
Travel	10	6	15	31
Books	8	7	23	38

3 Can I use my ability to attract customers to generate new sources of revenue such as advertising or sales of complementary products?
4 Will my current business be significantly harmed by other companies providing some of the value I currently offer?

In addition Ghosh (1998) suggested that companies should provide free digital value to help build an audience. He refers to this process as building a 'customer magnet'; today this would be known as a 'portal' or 'community'. There is good potential for customer magnets in specialised vertical markets served by business-to-business companies. For example, a customer magnet could be developed for the construction industry, agrochemicals, biotechnology or independent financial advisers. Today, this would be labelled as content marketing.

Target market strategies

We have seen that we need to review the options for using the digital media to reach new markets or develop existing markets. Within both of these markets we need to analyse the target market in more detail to understand their needs and potential and then develop a

Target marketing strategy
Evaluation and selection of appropriate segments and the development of appropriate offers.

Segmentation
Identification of different groups within a target market in order to develop different product offerings and communications for the groups.

strategy to satisfy these markets to maximise revenue. This is **target marketing strategy** and involves the four stages shown in Figure 8.14.

The first stage in Figure 8.14 is **segmentation**. Segmentation involves understanding the groupings of customers in the target market to understand their needs and potential as a revenue source in order to develop a strategy to satisfy these segments while maximising revenue. Dibb *et al.* (2000) say that:

> *Market segmentation is the key of robust marketing strategy development . . . it involves more than simply grouping customers into segments . . . identifying segments, targeting, positioning and developing a differential advantage over rivals is the foundation of marketing strategy.*

In a digital marketing planning context market segments will be analysed to assess:

1 Their current market size or value, future projections of size and the organisation's current and future market share within the segment.
2 Competitor market shares within the segment.
3 Needs of each segment, in particular unmet needs.
4 Organisation and competitor offers and proposition for each segment across all aspects of the buying process.

The targeting approaches used for online acquisition and retention campaigns will naturally depend on established segmentation. Table 8.7 summarises options for targeting customers online. The power of digital technology is that it makes it easier and more cost-effective to deliver targeted messages on a web page or in an email compared to traditional media.

Let's look at each targeting variable in a little more depth.

1 **Relationship with company.** Campaigns will often be intended to target new contacts or existing contacts. But remember, some communications will reach both. Marketers have

Informed by	Stage of target marketing	Informs
Market research and analysis of customer data	**Segmentation** Identify customer needs and segment market	• Market segment definition • Persona development • Customer experience requirements
Demand analysis	**Target marketing** Evaluate and select target segments	• Select online targeting • Target segments • Online revenue contribution for each segment • Customer life cycle targeting
Competitor analysis Internal analysis	**Positioning** Identify proposition for each segment	• Core brand proposition • Online value proposition • Online marketing mix • Life cycle brand development and proposition messaging
Evaluation of resources	**Planning** Deploy resources to achieve plan	• Online marketing mix • Restructuring • Automated online customer contact strategy

Figure 8.14   Stages in target marketing strategy development

Table 8.7	A range of targeting and segmentation approaches for a digital campaign

Targeting variable	Examples of segments and potential online targeting attributes
1 Relationship with company	New contacts (prospects), existing customers, lapsed customers
2 Demographic segmentation	B2C: Age, sex, social group, geographic location
	B2B: Company size, industry served, individual members of decision-making unit
3 Psychographic or attitudinal segmentation	Attitudes to risk and value when buying, e.g. early adopter, brand loyal or price conscious
4 Value	Assessment of current or historical value and future value. Valuable customers can be targeted and given special promotions as part of a VIP or customer club
5 Life cycle stage	Position in life cycle, related to value and behaviour, i.e. time since initial registration, number of products purchased, categories purchased in
6 Behaviour	(a) Search terms entered into search engine (Table 8.1) (b) Interests shown through content shared or liked on social networks. Companies can target users of Facebook, LinkedIn and Twitter with ads using this method. (c) Responsiveness to different types of offers (promotion or product type) (d) Responsiveness to campaigns in different channels (channel preference) (e) Purchase history in product categories including recency, frequency and monetary value (Chapter 9)

to consider whether it will be cost-effective to have separate communications for new, existing and lapsed contacts – or to target each of these groups in the same communications but using different content aimed at each.

When visitors click through to your website from online and offline campaigns, copy should be presented that recognises the relationship or, again, provide a range of content to recognise each different relationship. Visit Microstrategy (www.microstrategy.com) to see how its registration page establishes the relationship.

2 **Demographic segmentation.** This is typically based on age, sex or social group. Online demographics are often used as the basis for which sites to purchase display advertising or for renting email lists. Demographics can also be used to limit or focus who pay-per-click search ads are displayed to.

3 **Psychographic or attitudinal segmentation.** This includes attitudes to risk and value when buying. It is less straightforward to target on these attributes of a consumer since it is easier to buy media based on demographic breakdown. However, certain sites may be more suitable for reaching a particular psychographic audience. The psychographic characteristics of the audience are still an important part of the brief, to help develop particular messages.

It is possible to collect attitudinal information on a site and add it to the customer profile. For example, Wells Fargo asks investors to select:
- The type of investment preferred (individual stocks or mutual funds).
- What type of investor best describes you (aggressive growth to more cautious).

4 **Value.** The higher-value customers (indicated by higher average order value and higher modelled customer lifetime values) will often warrant separate communications with different offers. Sometimes digital channels are not the best approach for these customers – relationship managers will want direct contact with their most valuable customers, while digital channels are used to communicate more cost-effectively with lower-value customers. It is also worth considering reducing the frequency of emails to this audience.

5 **Life cycle stage.** This is very useful where customers follow a particular sequence in buying or using a service, such as online grocery shopping or online banking. Automated event-triggered email marketing can be developed for this audience (as explained in Chapter 9). For example, bank First Direct uses a six-month welcome strategy based on email and direct mail communications. For other campaigns, the status of a customer can be used for targeting, for example not purchased or used service, purchased once, purchased more than five times and active, purchased more than five times and inactive, etc.

6 **Behavioural.** Behavourial targeting is one of the big opportunities provided by digital marketing. It involves assessing customers' past actions in following links, reading content, using online services or buying products, and then follows up on these with a more relevant message based on the propensity to act based on the previous action.

Online options for behavioural targeting can be illustrated by a travel company such as lastminute.com:

- Pay-per-click search engine marketing such as Google AdWords makes targeting possible according to the type of keyphrase typed when a potential customer searches for information. A relevant ad specific to a holiday destination the prospect is looking for, e.g. 'Hotel New York' can then be shown.
- Display advertising makes behavioural targeting possible since cookies can be used to track visitors across a site or between sites and display relevant ads. If a site user visits the travel section of a newspaper site, then the ad about lastminute.com can be served as they visit other content on this site, or potentially on other sites.
- Email marketing can be targeted based on customer preferences indicated by links they have clicked on. For example, if a user has clicked a link about a holiday in North America, then a targeted email can be delivered relevant to this product or promotion. More sophisticated analysis based on RFM analysis (Chapter 9) can also be used.

When reviewing the options for which variables to use to target, the campaign planner must keep in mind that the variables selected for targeting should be those which are most likely to influence the level of response for the campaign. Figure 8.15 indicates the general improvement in campaign response dependent on the type of targeting variables used. This approach is used by travel company Travelocity in their email marketing. Speaking at the 2006 Internet Retailing Forum they described how they concentrate their efforts on behaviour suggesting purchase intent, i.e. when a visitor to their site clicks on a particular type of holiday, emails sent to the customer should be updated to reflect that.

Seybold (1999) identified five questions to help develop a customer-centric strategy for digital marketing (which are still relevant today; the questions apply equally to marketing). The questions are:

1 Who are our customers?

This involves identifying target segments that share certain characteristics and needs. Different criteria for identifying segments include demographics and geographical location for the B2C market and organisational characteristics and members of the buying unit for the B2B market (as seen in Chapter 4).

2 How are their needs changing?

Understanding the needs of different segments when they venture online is important to the next stages of delivering value to the customer. Some segments may have originally been

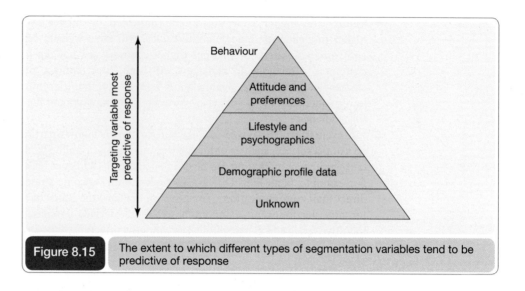

Figure 8.15	The extent to which different types of segmentation variables tend to be predictive of response

motivated by price, but customer service may become more important. This is closely related to buyer behaviour (Chapter 9).

3 Which do we target?

This is an important strategic decision in digital marketing (which we discussed in Chapter 5 under the strategic decision Decision 2: Market and product development strategies).

4 How can we add value?

We have seen (in Chapters 5 and 6) that customer value is mainly dependent on the combination of product quality, customer service quality, fulfilment time and price. Companies need to decide for each segment which of these is most important and then seek to adjust these elements accordingly as part of the marketing mix described in the next section.

5 How do we become first choice?

Positioning
Influencing the customer's perception of a product within a marketplace.

Differential advantage
A desirable attribute of a product offering that is not currently matched by competitor offerings.

Online value proposition (OVP)
A statement of the benefits of e-commerce services that ideally should not be available in competitor offerings or offline offerings.

To decide on this it is necessary to know how to position within the marketplace relative to competitor offerings. **Positioning** is related to how a consumer perceives a product in terms of the elements of value described above. It is related to Positioning in Figure 8.14. A positioning statement is often developed to encapsulate this. Companies then need to decide how to highlight the benefits as a **differential advantage** over rivals' products.

Having a clear, powerful positioning is crucial online, since it is so easy for customers to compare service providers when initially selecting a product. It is also important to customer retention since the first experience of a brand will determine whether the customer naturally returns to the supplier as first choice or initiates another search to find alternatives.

In a digital marketing context (as mentioned in Chapter 5), the differential advantage and positioning can be clarified and communicated by developing an **online value proposition (OVP)**. This is similar to a unique selling proposition, but is developed for e-commerce services. It *builds on the core proposition* for the company's services. In developing a proposition managers should identify:

- A clear differentiation of the proposition from competitors' based on product features or service quality.
- Target market segment(s) that the proposition will appeal to.
- How the proposition will be communicated to site visitors and in all marketing communications. Developing a tagline can help this.

- How the proposition is delivered across different parts of the buying process.
- How the proposition will be delivered and supported by resources.

Ideally, the e-commerce site should have an additional value proposition to further differentiate the company's products or services. The site design will also need to communicate the core proposition of the brand or products.

Having a clear online value proposition has several benefits:

- it helps distinguish an e-commerce site from its competitors' (this should be a website design objective);
- it helps provide a focus to marketing efforts and enables company staff to be clear about the purpose of the site;
- if the proposition is clear it can be used for PR and word-of-mouth recommendations;
- it can be linked to the normal product propositions of a company or its product.

Variani and Vaturi (2000) have conducted a review of failures in B2C dot-com companies. They believe that many of the problems have resulted from a failure to apply established marketing orientation approaches. They summarise their guidelines as follows:

> *First identify customer needs and define a distinctive value proposition that will meet them, at a profit. The value proposition must then be delivered through the right product and service and the right channels and it must be communicated consistently. The ultimate aim is to build a strong, long-lasting brand that delivers value to the company marketing it.*

Conversely, Agrawal *et al.* (2001) suggest that the success of leading e-commerce companies is often due to matching value propositions to segments successfully.

Some of the best taglines have been developed by the start-up companies, for which the OVP is particularly important. For example:

> *'Compare. Buy. Save.' Kelkoo (www.kelkoo.com)*
> *'Earth's biggest selection.' Amazon (www.amazon.com)*

The Citibank site design (www.citibank.com) uses a range of techniques to illustrate its core proposition and OVP. For example, when the site was first included in this book, the main messages were:

> *Welcome to Citibank: The one-stop solution for all your financial needs.*
> *Look for a product or service; Learn about a financial product; Find a location.*

Different OVPs can be developed for different products or different segments. For Citibank UK, the OVP for its Internet banking service is:

> *Bank whenever you want, from wherever you are. Citibank Internet Banking gives you the freedom and flexibility to manage your day-to-day finances. It's secure, convenient and very easy to use.*

Many strategic digital marketing planning decisions are based around the OVP and the quality of online customer experience delivered by a company. Interactive Web 2.0 features can be particularly important for transactional sites in that they may enhance the user's experience and so encourage conversion and repeat sales. Examples of how companies have developed their OVP through interactive features include customer reviews and ratings, podcast product reviews, a blog with customer comments enabled, buyers' guide and video reviews.

Content strategy

It is evident that a compelling OVP demands exceptional, compelling content and a compelling experience provided for customers through the website and other online presence on blogs, social networking sites and through mobile platforms. Today, by content we not only refer to the combination of static content forming web pages, but also dynamic rich media content which encourages interaction. Videos, podcasts, user-generated content and interactive product selectors should also be considered as content which should be refined to engage issues.

You can see the challenge **content strategy** presents since today there are so many different types of content delivered in different forms to different places on different access platforms, yet it is increasingly important to engage customers in social media.

It can be seen that managing the creation of quality content is part of a broader customer engagement strategy which looks at delivering effective content across the whole customer life cycle. As such it is an integral part of the CRM strategy development which we cover in more detail in the next chapter.

To help deliver a compelling OVP requires a change of mindset for many companies. They need to think more like a publisher and so invest in quality content that is superior to that of their competitors. This requires:

- Quality, compelling content – content is still king!
- Quality writers to create quality content who may be internal staff or external freelance writers.
- An editorial calendar and appropriate process to schedule and deliver the content.
- Investment in software tools to facilitate the process.
- Investment in customer research to determine the content their different audiences will engage with.
- Careful tracking of which content engages and which does not.

Content strategy

The management of text, rich media, audio and video content aimed at engaging customers and prospects to meet business goals published through print and digital media including web and mobile platforms which is repurposed and syndicated to different forms of web presence such as publisher sites, blogs, social media and comparison sites.

Focus on	**Characteristics of digital media communications**

In this section, we explore the main differences between marketing communications in the traditional media such as TV, print and radio and new digital media such as websites, interactive TV and mobile commerce. This section is based on the summary presented in Chaffey (2000). Recognising the differences between the Internet and other media is important to achieving success in channel promotion and channel satisfaction, and will lead in turn to positive channel outcomes and profitability.

A useful summary of the differences between the new media and traditional media has been developed by McDonald and Wilson (1999) as the '6 Is' of digital marketing. These highlight factors that apply to practical aspects of Internet marketing such as personalisation, direct response and marketing research, but also strategic issues of industry restructuring and integrated channel communications. By considering each of these facets of the new media, marketing managers can develop marketing plans that accommodate the characteristics of the new media. This presentation of the '6 Is' is a new interpretation of these factors using new examples and diagrams to illustrate these concepts.

1 Interactivity

Deighton (1996) was one of the first authors to explain that interactivity is a key characteristic of the Internet which enables companies to communicate with customers in a new way. Figure 8.16(a) shows how traditional media are predominantly *push media* where the marketing message is broadcast from company *to* customer and other stakeholders. During this process, there is limited interaction with the customer. On the Internet, it is usually a customer who initiates contact and is *seeking* information on a website. In other words it is a **pull marketing communications** technique (but email can be considered as a **push marketing communications** technique). Figure 8.16(b) shows how the Internet should be used to encourage two-way communication; these may be extensions of the direct-response

Pull marketing communications

The consumer is proactive in interacting with companies through actively seeking information or entertainment on company websites or social media sites through search engines, comparison intermediaries or direct navigation.

Push marketing communications

Communications are broadcast from an advertiser to consumers of the message, who are passive recipients.

| Figure 8.16 | Summary of communication models for (a) traditional media, (b) new media |

approach. For example, FMCG (fast-moving consumer goods) suppliers such as Nestlé (www.nescafe.co.uk) use their website and social media presence as a method of generating interaction by providing incentives such as competitions and sales promotions to encourage the customer to respond with their names, addresses and profile information such as age and sex.

Hoffman and Novak (1997) realised early in the development of the web that interactivity was significant enough to represent a new model for marketing or a new marketing paradigm. They suggest that the facilities of the Internet represent a computer-mediated environment in which the interactions are not between the sender and receiver of information, but with the medium itself. They said:

> consumers can interact with the medium, firms can provide content to the medium, and in the most radical departure from traditional marketing environments, consumers can provide commercially-oriented content to the media.

The user-generated content customers can provide may be directly commercial such as auctioning of their possessions such as via eBay (www.ebay.com) or can include comments on products or suppliers on a neutral site (e.g. www.kelkoo.com) or a destination site (www.firebox.com). (The *Focus on* Social media and social CRM strategy section in Chapter 9 covers techniques for harnessing the interactivity of the web in more detail.)

2 Intelligence

The Internet can be used as a relatively low-cost method of collecting marketing research, particularly about customer perceptions of products and services. In the competitions referred to above, Nestlé is able to profile its customers on the basis of the information received in questionnaires. The Internet can be used to create two-way feedback which does not usually occur in other media. Financial services provider Egg (www.egg.com, which has now been transferred to Yorkshire Building Society) collected information about its online service levels through a questionnaire that was continuously available in the customer service part of its site. What was significant was that the company responded via the website to the main concerns of the customer; if the length of time it took to reply to customer service emails was seen as a problem it would explain what the organisation was trying to do to resolve this problem.

A wealth of marketing research information is also available from the website itself, since every time a user clicks on a link this is recorded and can be analysed with web analytics tools (described in Chapter 12). Potentially companies can respond in real time to buyer behaviour. For example, banks such as HSBC (www.hsbc.co.uk) and Lloyds (www.lloyds-bank.com) use a service from Adobe Marketing Cloud (www.adobe.com/solutions/digital-marketing.html) to serve messages according to an evaluation of which offers they are most likely to respond to.

3 Individualisation

Another important feature of interactive marketing communications is that they can be tailored to the individual (Figure 8.17(b)), unlike traditional media where the same message tends to be broadcast to everyone (Figure 8.17(a)). The process of tailoring is also referred to as *personalisation* and is an important aspect of achieving customer relationship management online. Personalisation is often achieved through extranets which are set up with key accounts to manage the buying and after-sales processes. Dell (www.dell.com/premier) set up 'Dell Premier' for key accounts such as the Abbey where special offers and bespoke customer support are delivered. Another example of personalisation is that achieved by

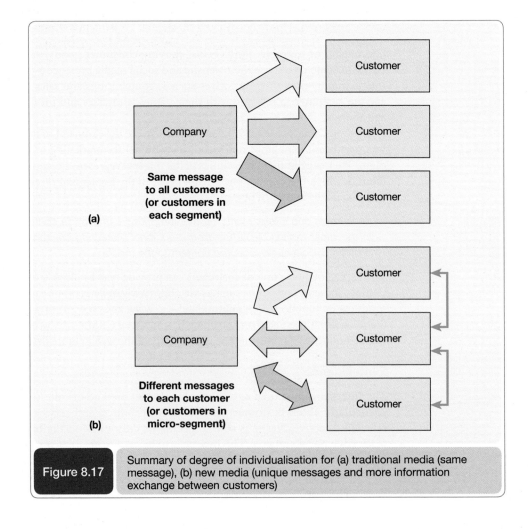

| Figure 8.17 | Summary of degree of individualisation for (a) traditional media (same message), (b) new media (unique messages and more information exchange between customers) |

business-to-business e-tailer RS Components (www.rswww.com). Every customer who accesses their system is profiled according to their area of product interest and information describing their role in the buying unit. When they next visit the site information will be displayed relevant to their product interest. This is an example of what is known as *mass customisation* where generic customer information is supplied for particular segments, i.e. the information is not unique to individuals, but to those with a common interest. Amazon (www.amazon.com) is well known for using a *collaborative filtering* approach or Amazon's 'Customers Who bought X . . . also bought . . . Y'. Amazon also has two other personalisation features, 'Customers who shopped for X also SHOPPED for . . .' and 'Customers who searched for X also BOUGHT . . .' You can read about the approach that they use to achieve this in IEE (2003).

4 Integration

The Internet provides further scope for integrated marketing communications. Figure 8.18 shows how it is just one of many different media channels (these channels are also offered by intermediaries). When assessing the success of a website, the role of the Internet in communicating with customers and other partners can best be considered from two perspectives. First, organisation-to-customer direction: how does the Internet complement other channels in communication of proposition for the company's products and services to new and existing customers with a view to generating new leads and retaining existing customers? Second, customer-to-organisation: how can the Internet complement other channels to deliver customer service to these customers? Many companies are now considering how they integrate email response and website call-back into their existing call-centre or customer service operation. This may require a substantial investment in training and new software.

Some practical examples of how the Internet can be used as an integrated communications tool are as shown by Figure 8.19 and Activity 8.4.

| Figure 8.18 | Channels requiring integration as part of integrated digital marketing strategy |

Figure 8.19	Channel integration required for digital marketing and mixed-mode buying

Integrating online and offline communications

Purpose

To highlight differences in marketing communications introduced through the use of the Internet as a channel and the need to integrate these communications with existing channels.

Activity

List communications between a PC vendor and a home customer over the lifetime of a product such as a PC. Include communications using both the Internet and traditional media. Refer to channel swapping alternatives in the buying decision shown in Figure 8.19 to develop your answer.

Answers to activities can be found at www.pearsoned.co.uk/chaffey

- The Internet can be used as a direct-response tool enabling customers to respond to offers and promotions publicised in other media. Dell uses 'e-value codes' which it publishes in magazines and offline material to direct people to specific pages (via a search) when they visit the website. CapitalOne uses a similar approach. These codes include a media code to assess which offline communications were most effective in driving sales on the website.
- The website can have a direct-response or call-back facility built into it. The Automobile Association has a feature where a customer service representative will contact a customer by phone when the customer fills in their name, phone number and a suitable time to ring.
- The Internet can be used to support the buying decision even if the purchase does not occur via the website. For example, Dell has a prominent web-specific phone number on

their website that encourages customers to ring a representative in the call centre to place their order. This has the benefits that Dell is less likely to lose the business of customers who are anxious about the security of online ordering and Dell can track sales that result partly from the website according to the number of callers on this line. This is alternative 3 in Figure 8.19. Changing from one channel to another during the buying process is referred to as **mixed-mode buying** or channel switching. It is a key aspect of devising online marketing communications since the customer should be supported in changing from one channel to another. Bazett *et al.* (2005) give the example of a high-street chain that estimated (through credit card tracking) that for every £1 of revenue it takes on the web, £3 are spent in-store after browsing online – so it has objectives for this and works equally hard to help these customers through facilities such as store locators and information on stock availability for that store.

- Customer information delivered on the website must be integrated with other databases of customer and order information such as those accessed via staff in the call centre to provide what Seybold (1999) calls a '360 degree view of the customer'.
- The Internet can be used to support customer service. For example, easyJet (www.easyjet.com), which receives over half its orders electronically, encourages users to check a list of frequently asked questions (FAQs) compiled from previous customer enquiries before contacting customer support via phone.

5 Industry restructuring

Disintermediation, reintermediation and countermediation are key concepts of industry restructuring that should be considered by any company developing a digital marketing strategy (see Chapters 2 and 4). For the marketer defining their company's communications strategy it becomes very important to consider the company's representation on these intermediary sites by answering questions such as 'Which intermediaries should we be represented on?' and 'How do our offerings compare to those of competitors in terms of features, benefits and price?'

6 Independence of location

Electronic media also introduce the possibility of increasing the reach of company communications to the global market. This gives opportunities to sell into international markets that may not have been previously accessible. Scott Bader (www.scottbader.com), a business-to-business supplier of polymers and chemicals for the paints and coatings industry, can now target countries beyond the forty or so it has traditionally sold to via a network of local agents and franchises. The Internet makes it possible to sell to a country without a local sales or customer service force. Strategists also need to carefully consider channel conflicts that may arise. If a customer is buying direct from a company in another country rather than via the agent, this will marginalise the business of the local agent who may want some recompense for sales efforts or may look to partner with competitors.

(A further appraisal of using the characteristics of new media for effective communications is presented in Chapter 9.)

Tactics

Marketing tactics to implement strategies and objectives are traditionally based around the elements of the marketing mix and models of how to engage customers throughout their life cycle as part of customer relationship management. In this chapter we focus on the marketing mix. (In Chapter 9, we will review the life cycle-based approach.)

The marketing mix – the 4Ps of Product, Price, Place and Promotion originally proposed by Jerome McCarthy (1960) – is still used as an essential part of implementing marketing

---

Mixed-mode buying
The process by which a customer changes between online and offline channels during the buying process.

strategy by many practitioners. The 4Ps have been extended to the 7Ps by including three further elements that better reflect service delivery: People, Processes and Physical evidence (Booms and Bitner, 1981), although others argue that these are subsumed within the 4Ps. The marketing mix is applied frequently when developing marketing strategies since it provides a simple framework like that shown in Figure 8.20 for varying different elements of the offering to influence the demand for products within target markets. For example, to increase sales of a product the price can be decreased or the amount or type of promotion changed, or there can be some combination of these elements.

E-commerce provides new opportunities for the marketer to vary the marketing mix which have been summarised well by Allen and Fjermestad (2001).

There are some well-known criticisms of applying the marketing mix as a solitary tool for marketing strategy. First, the marketing mix is symptomatic of a push approach to marketing and does not explicitly acknowledge the needs of customers. As a consequence, the marketing mix tends to lead to a product rather than a customer orientation. To mitigate this effect, Lautenborn (1990) suggested the 4Cs framework, which considers the 4Ps from a customer perspective. In an e-commerce context the 4Cs can be interpreted as follows:

- Customer needs and wants (from the product) – the website is a mechanism for explaining how the product proposition meets these needs and wants.
- Cost to the customer (price) – online the customer is likely to be comparing prices to other websites and traditional purchasing sources.
- Convenience (relative to place) – online this is the quality of customer experience in terms of the ordering process and fulfilment.
- Communication (promotion) – the website itself coupled with the methods of driving traffic to the site, such as search engine marketing and email marketing (as described in Chapter 9).

It follows that the selection of the marketing mix is based on detailed knowledge of buyer behaviour collected through market research. Furthermore, it should be remembered that the mix is often adjusted according to different target markets or segments. An increased focus on 'one-to-one marketing' which means tailoring of the offer for specific customers also sits uncomfortably within the 7Ps framework.

The **long-tail concept** is useful for considering the role of Product, Place, Price and Promotion online as explained in Box 8.2.

The long-tail concept

A frequency distribution suggesting the relative variation in popularity of items selected by consumers.

Using the Internet to vary the marketing mix						
Product	**Promotion**	**Price**	**Place**	**People**	**Process**	**Physical evidence**
• Quality	• Marketing communications	• Positioning	• Trade channels	• Individuals on marketing activities	• Customer focus	• Sales/staff contact experience of brand
• Image	• Personal promotion	• List	• Sales support	• Individuals on customer contact	• Business-led	• Product packaging
• Branding	• Sales promotion	• Discounts	• Channel number	• Recruitment	• IT-supported	• Online experience
• Features	• PR	• Credit	• Segmented channels	• Culture/ image	• Design features	
• Variants	• Branding	• Payment methods		• Training and skills	• Research and development	
• Mix	• Direct marketing	• Free or value-added elements		• Remuneration		
• Support						
• Customer service						
• Use occasion						
• Availability						
• Warranties						

Figure 8.20   The elements of the marketing mix

Box 8.2	Applying the long-tail concept

The phenomenon now referred to as the 'long tail', following an article by Anderson (2004), was arguably first applied to human behaviour by George Kingsley Zipf, professor of linguistics at Harvard, who observed the phenomenon in word usage (see http://en.wikipedia.org/wiki/Zipf%27s_law). He found that if the variation in popularity of different words in a language is considered, there is a systematic pattern in the frequency of usage or popularity. Zipf's 'law' suggests that if a collection of items is ordered or ranked by popularity, the second item will have around half the popularity of the first one and the third item will have about a third of the popularity of the first one and so on. In general:

The kth item is 1/k the popularity of the first.

Look at Figure 8.21 which shows how the 'relative popularity' of items is predicted to decline according to Zipf's law from a maximum count of 1,000 for the most popular item to 20 for the 50th item.

In an online context, application of this 'law' is now known as 'the long tail' thanks to Anderson (2004). It can be applied to the relative popularity of a group of websites or web pages or products on an individual site, since they tend to show a similar pattern of popularity. There are a small number of sites (or pages within sites) which are very popular (the head which may account for 80% of the volume) and a much larger number of sites or pages that are less popular individually, but still collectively important. Returning to the product context, Anderson (2004) argued that for a company such as Amazon, the long tail or Zipf's law can be applied to describe the variation in preferences for selecting or purchasing from a choice for products as varied as books, CDs, electronic items, travel or financial services. This pattern has also been identified by Brynjolfsson *et al.* (2003) who present a framework that quantifies the economic impact of increased product variety made available through electronic markets. They say:

> *One reason for increased product variety on the Internet is the ability of online retailers to catalog, recommend, and provide a large number of products for sale. For example, the number of book titles available at Amazon.com is more than 23 times larger than the number of books on the shelves of a typical Barnes & Noble*

Figure 8.21	Zipf's law, showing decrease in popularity of items within an ordered sequence

superstore, and 57 times greater than the number of books stocked in a typical large independent bookstore.

Looking at the issue from another perspective, they estimate that 40% of sales are from relatively obscure books with a sales rank of more than 100,000 (if you visit Amazon, you will see that every book has a sales rank from 1 for the most popular to over 1 million for the least popular). This indicates the importance of the long tail for online retailers like Amazon, since 40% of sales are from these less popular books which cannot be stocked in a conventional bookstore (a large real-world bookstore would typically hold 100,000 books). In a pricing context, another benefit for online retailers is that less popular products cannot be readily obtained in the real world, so Amazon can justify higher prices for these books. Brynjolfsson *et al.* (2003) estimated that average Amazon prices for an item in the top 100,000 is $29.26 and in less popular titles $41.60.

Product

Product variable
The element of the marketing mix that involves researching customers' needs and developing appropriate products.

Core product
The fundamental features of the product that meet the user's needs.

Extended product
Additional features and benefits beyond the core product.

Mass customisation
Using economies of scale enabled by technology to offer tailored versions of products to individual customers or groups of customers.

Bundling
Offering complementary services.

There are many alternatives for varying the product when a company is developing its online strategy. Internet-related product decisions can be usefully divided into decisions affecting the **core product** and the **extended product**. For some companies, there may be options for new digital products which will typically be information products that can be delivered over the web. In some cases, the core product offering has been replaced by information about the product. For example, a company providing oil-drilling equipment focussing instead on analysis and dissemination of information about drilling. In some cases, an online version of the product may be more valuable to customers in that it can be updated more regularly. The advertising directory BRAD (www.brad.co.uk) has been changed from a large paper-based document to an online version with searching facilities that were not available in the paper-based version. The Internet also introduces options for **mass customisation** of products. Levi's provided a truly personal service that dates back to 1994, when Levi Strauss initiated its 'Personal Pair' programme. Women who were prepared to pay up to $15 more than the standard price and wait for delivery could go to Levi's stores and have themselves measured.

Companies can also consider how the Internet can be used to change the range or combination of products offered. Some companies only offer a subset of products online; others may have a fuller catalogue available online than is available through offline brochures. **Bundling** is a further alternative. For example, easyJet has developed a range of complementary travel-related services including flights, packages and car hire.

For many companies, using the Internet to vary the extended product is most practical. Chaffey and Smith (2008) suggest these examples of how the Internet can be used to vary the extended product:

- Endorsements
- Awards
- Testimonies
- Customer lists
- Customer comments
- Warranties
- Guarantees
- Money-back offers
- Customer service (see People, Process and Physical evidence)
- Incorporating tools to help users during their use of the product. Options for digital products.

Companies such as publishers, TV companies and other media owners who can offer digital products such as published content, music or videos now have great flexibility to offer a range of product purchase options at different price points including:

- **Subscription.** This is a traditional publisher revenue model, but subscription can potentially be offered for different periods at different price points, e.g. 3 months, 12 months or 2 years.
- **Pay-per-view.** A fee for a single download or viewing session at a higher relative price than the subscription service. Music service Napster offers vouchers for download in a similar way to a mobile company 'pay as you go' model. Travel publisher Lonely Planet enables visitors to a destination to download an introduction for a fraction of the price of a full printed guide.
- **Bundling.** Different channels or content can be offered as individual products or grouped at a reduced price compared to pay-per-view.
- **Ad-supported content.** The publisher's main revenue source is through adverts on the site (CPM display advertising using banners ads and skyscrapers, a fixed sponsorship arrangement or CPC, which stands for 'cost-per-click'). Other options include affiliate revenue from sales on third-party sites or offering access to subscriber lists. The UK's most popular newspaper site, *The Guardian* (www.guardian.co.uk), once trialled an ad-free subscription service, but it, like many online publishers, has reverted to ad-supported content.

Also related to the product element of the mix is how the Internet can be used to assist in new product development by assessing product needs from website logs (Chapter 12), testing new concepts, online surveys and focus groups.

Quelch and Klein (1996) also noted that the implication of the Internet and globalisation is that to remain competitive, organisations will have to roll out new products more rapidly to international markets. More recently, Malcolm Gladwell in his book *The Tipping Point* (2000) has shown how word-of-mouth communication has a tremendous impact on the rate of adoption of new products and we can suggest this effect is often enhanced or facilitated through the Internet. The implications of the tipping point are discussed in Box 8.3.

Box 8.3	How does the tipping point apply to digital marketing?

Tipping point
Using the science of social epidemics explains principles that underpin the rapid spread of ideas, products and behaviours through a population.

Marsden (2004) provides a good summary of the implications of the tipping point for marketers. He says that 'using the science of social epidemics, *The Tipping Point* explains the three simple principles that underpin the rapid spread of ideas, products and behaviours through a population'. He advises how marketers should help create a 'tipping point' for a new product or service, the moment when a domino effect is triggered and an epidemic of demand sweeps through a population like a highly contagious virus.

There are three main laws that are relevant from *The Tipping Point*:

1 The law of the few

This suggests that the spread of any new product or service is dependent on the initial adoption by 'connectors' who are socially connected and who encourage adoption through word-of-mouth and copycat behaviour. In an online context, these connectors may use personal blogs, email newsletters and podcasts to propagate their opinions.

2 The stickiness factor

Typically, this refers to how 'glued' we are to a medium such as a TV channel or a website, but in this context it refers to attachment to the characteristics and attributes of a product or a brand. Gladwell stresses the importance of testing and market research to make the product effective. Marsden suggests that there are key cross-category attributes which are key drivers for product success and he commends the work of Morris and Martin (2000) which summarises these attributes as:

- *Excellence*: perceived as best of breed
- *Uniqueness*: clear one-of-a-kind differentiation
- *Aesthetics*: perceived aesthetic appeal
- *Association*: generates positive associations
- *Engagement*: fosters emotional involvement
- *Expressive value*: visible sign of user values
- *Functional value*: addresses functional needs
- *Nostalgic value*: evokes sentimental linkages
- *Personification*: has character, personality
- *Cost*: perceived value for money.

You can see that this list is also a useful prompt about the ideal characteristics of a website or online service.

3 The power of context

Gladwell suggests that like infectious diseases, products and behaviours spread far and wide only when they fit the physical, social and mental context into which they are launched. He gives the example of a wave of crime in the New York subway that came to an abrupt halt by simply removing the graffiti from trains and clamping down on fare-dodging. It can be suggested that products should be devised and tested to fit their context, situation or occasion of use.

Case study 8.2 shows how Dell has revised its marketing mix through deep customer understanding.

Case Study 8.2	Dell gets closer to its customers online

Dell is a technology company, offering a broad range of product categories, including desktop computer systems, storage, servers and networking products, mobility products, software and peripherals and services to manage IT infrastructure for large organisations. Dell are the number one supplier of personal computer systems in the United States, and the number two supplier worldwide.

Dell proposition

The main Dell product offerings are:

1 **Desktop PCs.** Five lines of desktop computer systems are produced for different markets. For example, the OptiPlex line is designed to help business, government, and institutional customers manage their total cost of ownership by offering stability, security, and managed product transitions; the Dimension line is designed for small

businesses and home users requiring the latest features for their productivity and entertainment needs. The XPS™ and Alienware lines are targeted at customers who require the highest-performance gaming or entertainment experience available. In July 2007, Dell introduced the Vostro™ line, which is designed to provide technology and services to suit the specific needs of small businesses.

2 **Servers and networking.** The PowerEdge™ line of servers is designed to offer customers affordable performance, reliability, and scalability. Again different options are available for different markets including high-performance rack, blade, and tower servers for enterprise customers and lower-priced tower servers for small organisations, networks, and remote offices.

3 **Storage.** For example, storage area networks, network-attached storage, direct-attached storage,

disk and tape back-up systems, and removable disk back-up.

4 **Mobility.** Notebook computers are targeted at customers who require the highest-performance gaming or entertainment experience available.

5 **Software and peripherals.** Office software and hardware including printers, televisions, notebook accessories, networking and wireless products, digital cameras, power adapters, scanners, and other products.

6 **Enhanced services.** Tailored solutions that help customers lower the cost of their services environment and maximise system performance, efficiency, and return on investment. These include: Infrastructure Consulting Services; Deployment Services to instal and integrate new systems; Asset Recovery and Recycling Services; Training Services; Enterprise Support Services and Managed Life Cycle Services (outsourced IT management).

7 **Financial services** for business and consumer customers in the US through a joint venture between Dell and CIT Group, Inc.

Dell business strategy

Dell's vision is to:

strive to provide the best possible customer experience by offering superior value; high-quality, relevant technology; customized systems; superior service and support; and differentiated products and services that are easy to buy and use.

The core elements of the strategy which are evident in Dell's marketing communications are:

- *'We simplify information technology for customers.* Making quality personal computers, servers, storage, and services affordable is Dell's legacy. We are focused on making information technology affordable for millions of customers around the world. As a result of our direct relationships with customers, or "customer intimacy", we are best positioned to simplify how customers implement and maintain information technology and deliver hardware, services, and software solutions tailored for their businesses and homes.

- *We offer customers choice.* Customers can purchase systems and services from Dell via telephone, kiosks, and our website, www.dell.com, where they may review, configure, and price systems within our entire product line; order systems online; and track orders from manufacturing through shipping. We have recently launched a retail initiative and plan to expand that initiative by adding new distribution channels to reach additional consumers and small

businesses through retail partners and value-added resellers globally.

- *Customers can purchase custom-built products and custom-tailored services.* Historically our flexible, build-to-order manufacturing process enabled us to turn over inventory every five days on average, thereby reducing inventory levels, and rapidly bring the latest technology to our customers. The market and our competition has evolved, and we are now exploring the utilization of original design manufacturers and new distribution strategies to better meet customer needs and reduce product cycle times. Our goal is to introduce the latest relevant technology more quickly and to rapidly pass on component cost savings to a broader set of our customers worldwide.

- *We are committed to being environmentally responsible in all areas of our business.* We have built environmental consideration into every stage of the Dell product life cycle – from developing and designing energy-efficient products, to reducing the footprint of our manufacturing and operations, to customer use and product recovery.'

Dell's sales and marketing

Dell sells products and services directly to customers through dedicated sales representatives, telephone-based sales, and online at www.dell.com.

Customer segments include large corporate, government, healthcare, and education accounts, as well as small-to-medium businesses and individual consumers.

Dell stresses the importance of its direct business model in providing direct and continuous feedback from customers, thereby allowing them to develop and refine their products and marketing programs for specific customer groups.

In its SEC filing Dell emphasises how it listens to customers to develop relevant innovative technology and services they trust and value. Evidence for using the participative nature of Web 2.0 is that customers can offer suggestions for current and future Dell products, services, and operations on an interactive portion of the Dell website called Dell IdeaStorm. It says: 'This constant flow of communication, which is unique to our direct business model, also *allows us to rapidly gauge customer satisfaction and target new or existing products*.'

For large business and institutional customers, Dell maintains a field sales force throughout the world. Dedicated account teams, which include field-based system engineers and consultants, form long-term relationships to provide their largest customers with a single source of assistance and develop specific tailored solutions for these customers. Dell also maintains specific sales and marketing programmes targeted at federal, state, and local governmental agencies as well as specific healthcare and educational markets.

Dell Premier

For its large organisational customers, Dell offers Premier (http://premier.dell.com) which is a secure, customisable procurement and support site or extranet designed to save organisations time and money through all phases of IT product ownership. The main benefits of Dell Premier are described as:

- *Easy Ordering* – A custom online store ensures access to your products at your price.
- *Easy Tracking* – View real-time order status, online invoices and purchase history details.
- *Easy Control* – Custom access groups define what users can see and do within Premier.

Marketing communications

Dell markets its products and services to small-to-medium businesses and consumers primarily by advertising on television and the Internet, advertising in a variety of print media, and by mailing a broad range of direct marketing publications, such as promotional pieces, catalogues, and customer newsletters. In certain locations, they also operate Dell stores or kiosks, typically located within shopping centres, that allow customers to view their products in person and purchase online with the assistance of a Dell expert.

Dell online communications

The management of the consumer site was presented to E-consultancy (2008). Dell has a three-stage order funnel:

- Marketing communications execution measured by site visits
- Site merchandising measured by *consideration* % (site visits to e-store visits)
- Store merchandising measured by *conversion* % (e-store visits to e-receipts).

The presenter explained how Dell aims to understand and act on customer behaviour based on identification of a series of consideration drivers, for example, the quality of online advertising; path quality through site; merchandising/offers and conversion drivers, for example, configurator 'ease of use'; accessibility of decision support tools and consistency of message through entire path.

Dell will invest in strategic improvements to the site to improve these levers; examples mentioned included new merchandising approaches such as customer ratings and reviews, videos, major 'path' or customer journey changes created through decision support tools to 'help me choose'. There are also more tactical initiatives to help deliver the right message to each customer including customisation/personalisation, real estate optimisation and message balancing.

More tactical persuasion of site visitors is based on price moves/optimised price position to market and the mix of product features. A wide range of different offers need to be managed. Tactical promotions are driven by promotional 'end dates' which are weekly or bi-weekly and include varying:

- Free shipping
- Money off discounts
- Free upgrades (e.g. memory)
- Free accessories
- Finance offers
- Service upgrades.

The presenter also noted how across Europe, the promotional mix has to vary to reflect the differences in buying psychology. He summarises the main differences between customers as follows:

- UK – all about price
- CH – add value over price
- DE – all about high-end products in mix
- IT – design is important (!)
- DK – cheap is good
- NO – added value is key
- FR – tailored for France.

Dell's use of digital media channels

The main digital media channels used by Dell.com in Europe are:

- Paid search through programmes such as Google AdWords is used to promote value through time limited offers related to the phrase searched upon.
- Display advertising – for example advertising on technology websites is particularly important for the corporate market.
- Affiliate marketing – used to protect the Dell brand by enabling affiliates to bid on terms such as 'Dell laptops' and to target niche audiences such as owners of gaming machines.
- Email marketing – an e-newsletter is used to keep in touch with existing customers and deliver targeted offers when their hardware may be renewed.

Dell and indirect channels

Although the focus of Dell's business strategy has been selling directly to its customers, it also uses some indirect sales channels when there is a business need. In the US it sells products indirectly through third-party solution providers, system integrators, and third-party resellers. During financial year 2008, Dell began offering Dimension desktop computers and Inspiron notebook computers in retail stores in the Americas and announced partnerships with retailers in the UK, Japan, and China. Dell says: '*These actions represent the first steps in our retail strategy, which will allow us to extend our business model and reach customers that we have not been able to reach directly.*'

Source: Security Exchange Commission filing 10-K for Dell, 2007.

> **Question**
>
> Describe approaches used by Dell within their site design and promotion to deliver relevant offers for different types of online customers.

Price

Price variable

The element of the marketing mix that involves defining product prices and pricing models.

Pricing models

Describe the form of payment such as outright purchase, auction, rental, volume purchase and credit terms.

The price element of the marketing mix refers to an organisation's pricing policies which are used to define **pricing models** and, of course, to set prices for products and services. The Internet has dramatic implications for pricing in many sectors and there is a lot of literature in this area. Baker *et al.* (2001) and more recently Xing *et al.* (2006) have noted two approaches that have been commonly adopted for pricing on the Internet. Start-up companies have tended to use low prices to gain a customer base, while many existing companies have transferred their existing prices to the web. However, Case study 8.1 showed how easyJet discounted online prices in an effort to meet its objectives of online revenue contribution. In this case, price reduction was possible because of the lower overhead of processing a customer transaction online in comparison with on the phone. Similarly, to acquire customers online booksellers may decide to offer a discount of 50% on the top 25 best-selling books in each category, for which no profit is made, but offer a relatively small discount on the less popular books of the long tail to give a profit margin.

The main implications of the Internet for the Price aspect of the mix are as follows.

1 Increased price transparency and its implications on differential pricing

Quelch and Klein (1996) describe two contradictory effects of the Internet on price that are related to price transparency. First, a supplier can use the technology for differential pricing, for example customers in different countries. However, if precautions are not taken about price, the customers may be able to quickly find out about the price discrimination and they will object to it. So, customer knowledge of pricing is enhanced through the Internet. This is particularly the case for standardised goods sold through online retailers. Not only can customers visit sites of rival suppliers, they can visit sites of price-comparison engines. It is difficult to retain price differentials if all customers are aware of these differences. Currently, this is probably not the case. However, research quoted by Baker *et al.* (2001) suggests that only around 8% of active online consumers are 'aggressive price shoppers'. Furthermore, they note that Internet price brands have remained quite broad. Online booksellers' prices varied by an average of 33% and CD sellers' by 25%.

There appear to be two main reasons for this: first, pricing is only one variable – consumers also decide on suppliers according to other aspects about the brand such as familiarity, trust and perceived service levels. Secondly, consumers often display **satisficing behaviour**. The term 'satisfice' was coined by Herbert Simon in 1957 when he said that people are only 'rational enough' and that they suspend or relax their rationality if they feel it is no longer required. This is called 'bounded rationality' by cognitive psychologists. In other words, although consumers may seek to minimise some variable (such as price) when making a product or supplier selection, most may not try too hard. Online, this is supported by research by Johnson *et al.* (2004) who showed that by analysing panel data from over 10,000 Internet households and three commodity-like products (books, CDs and air travel services) the amount of online search is actually quite limited. On average, households visit

Satisficing behaviour

Consumers do not behave entirely rationally in product or supplier selection. They will compare alternatives, but then may make their choice given imperfect information.

only 1.2 book sites, 1.3 CD sites and 1.8 travel sites during a typical active month in each category. Of course, these averages will reflect a range of behaviour.

A compromise approach used by many companies is to use differential pricing with lower prices or Internet offers for some of their products online. This has been the approach followed by online electrical retailers such as Comet (www.comet.co.uk), travel companies such as Thomson (www.thomson.co.uk) and companies with e-savings products.

Pricing online has to take into account the concept of **price elasticity of demand**. This is a measure of consumer behaviour based on economic theory that indicates the change in demand for a product or service in response to changes in price. Price elasticity of demand is determined by the price of the product, availability of alternative goods from alternative suppliers (which tends to increase online) and consumer income. A product is said to be 'elastic' (or responsive to price changes) if a small change in price increases or reduces the demand substantially. A product is 'inelastic' if a large change in price is accompanied by a small amount of change in demand. More details on price elasticity of demand are given in Box 8.4.

Price elasticity of demand
Measure of consumer behaviour that indicates the change in demand for a product or service in response to changes in price.

2 Downward pressure on price (including commoditisation)

For business commodities, auctions on business-to-business exchanges (e.g. Emiliani, 2001) can also have a similar effect of driving down price. Many companies, such as GlaxoSmithKline (pharmaceuticals), Whitbread (entertainment and leisure) and DaimlerChrysler (automotive), have reported that price has been decreased by 10% or more using reverse auctions.

Box 8.4	Price elasticity of demand

Price elasticity of demand assesses the extent to which a change in price will influence the demand for a product. It is calculated as the change in quantity demanded (expressed as a percentage divided by the change in price as a percentage). Different products will naturally have different coefficients of price elasticity of demand depending on where they lie on the continuum of consumer tastes from relatively undifferentiated commodities to luxury, highly differentiated products where the brand perception is important.

The formula for the price elasticity of demand is:

$$\text{Price Elasticity of Demand coefficient} = \frac{\% \text{ Change in Quantity Demanded}}{\% \text{ Change in Price}}$$

Price elasticity for products is generally described as:

- Elastic (*coefficient of price elasticity > 1*). Here, the percentage change in quantity demanded is greater than the percentage change in price. In elastic demand, the demand curve is relatively shallow and a small percentage increase in price leads to a reduction in revenue. On balance overall, when the price is raised, the total revenue of producers or retailers falls since the rise in revenue does not compensate for the fall in demand and when the price is decreased total revenue rises because the income from additional customers compensates in the decrease in revenue from reduced prices. Figure 8.22 shows the demand curve for a relatively elastic product (price elasticity = 1.67).
- Inelastic demand (*coefficient of price elasticity < 1*). Here, the percentage change in quantity demanded is smaller than the percentage change in price. In inelastic demand, the demand curve is relatively steep and a small percentage increase in price causes a small decrease in demand. On balance overall revenue increases as the price increases and falls as the price falls. Figure 8.23 shows the demand curve for a relatively inelastic product (price elasticity = 0.3125).

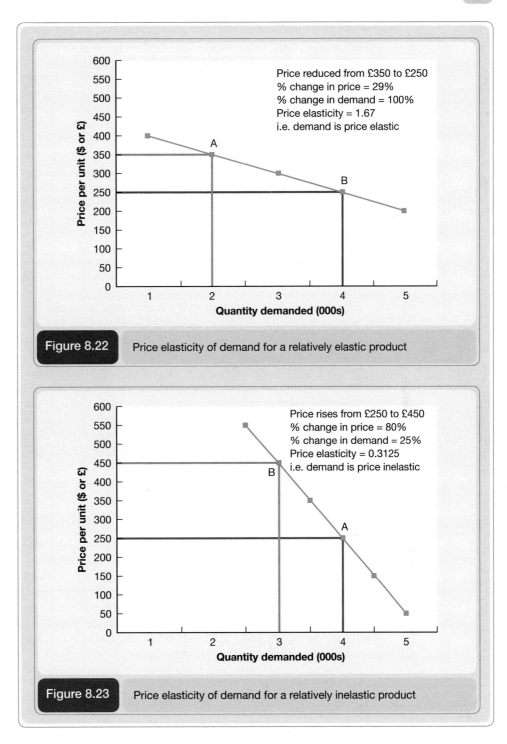

Figure 8.22	Price elasticity of demand for a relatively elastic product

Figure 8.23	Price elasticity of demand for a relatively inelastic product

Commoditisation
The process whereby product selection becomes more dependent on price than on differentiating features, benefits and value-added services.

Purchase of some products that have not traditionally been thought of as commodities may become more price-sensitive. This process is known as 'commoditisation'. Goods that are becoming commoditised include electrical goods and cars.

3 New pricing approaches (including dynamic pricing and auctions)

Dynamic pricing
Prices can be updated in real time according to the type of customer or current market conditions.

In addition to the auctions described above, the Internet introduces new opportunities for **dynamic pricing**, for example new customers could be automatically given discounted purchases for the first three items. Care has to be taken with differential pricing since established customers will be unhappy if significant discounts are given to new customers. Amazon trialled such a discounting scheme in 2000 and it received negative press and had to be withdrawn when people found out that their friends or colleagues had paid less. If the scheme had been a clear introductory promotion this problem might not have arisen.

A further approach is aggregated buying. This approach was promoted by LetsBuyit.com, but the business model did not prove viable – the cost of creating awareness for the brand and explaining the concept was not offset by the revenue from each transaction.

Aggregated buying
A form of customer union where buyers collectively purchase a number of items at the same price and receive a volume discount.

Baye *et al.* (2007) reported that European electronics online retailer Pixmania (www.pixmania.com) used price experimentation to learn about its customers' price sensitivity. They noted that for a PDA, Pixmania adjusted its product price 11 times in a 14-week period, from a low of £268 to a high of £283 as part of a series of small experiments that enabled it to learn about the price sensitivities of its customers. This pricing strategy also provides an additional strategic benefit – unpredictability.

Baye *et al.* (2007) recommend that online retailers should ask the following questions when reviewing pricing online:

1 **How many competitors are there at a point in time?** They suggest a product's mark-up should be increased when the number of rivals falls and decreased when the number of rivals increases. They also recommend that since the identity of competitors online will differ from traditional offline rivals it is important to include key online competitors.
2 **What is the position in the product life cycle?** A product's mark-up should be decreased over its life cycle or when new versions are introduced.
3 **What is the price sensitivity or elasticity of a product?** They suggest continuously experimenting to learn changes in the price sensitivity of a product.
4 **At what level is pricing set?** The optimal mark-up factor should be applied at the product rather than category or firm level based on price testing at the product level. They also note the variation of conversion rates and clickthrough fees from paid search engines and aggregators at the category or product level, which makes it important to have micro-management of pricing.
5 **Are rivals monitoring my price?** Be unpredictable if rivals are watching. Exploit 'blind spots' if rivals are not watching.
6 **Are we stuck in the middle?** A middle pricing point is sub-optimal particularly if prices can be set to target the lowest point in the market.

4 Alternative pricing structure or policies

Different types of pricing may be possible on the Internet, particularly for digital, downloadable products. Software and music have traditionally been sold for a continuous right to use. The Internet offers new options such as payment per use, rental at a fixed cost per month or a lease arrangement. Bundling options may also be more possible. The use of Software as a Service (SaaS) (Chapter 3) providers to deliver services such as website traffic monitoring also gives new methods of volume pricing. Web analytics companies such as Omniture (www.omniture.com) and ClickTracks (www.clicktracks.com) charge in price bands based on the number of visitors to the purchaser's site.

Further pricing options which could be varied online include:

- Basic price
- Discounts
- Add-ons and extra products and services
- Guarantees and warranties
- Refund policies
- Order cancellation terms.

Place
The element of the marketing mix that involves distributing products to customers in line with demand and minimising cost of inventory, transport and storage.

Place

Allen and Fjermestad (2001) argue that the Internet has the greatest implications for place in the marketing mix since the Internet has a global reach. However, due to cost and time of international fulfilment together with issues of trust in the local country and the availability of phone support, most products are still sourced locally. The exception to this is digital products where there is no physical limitation on fulfilment, so for example Apple iTunes has proved successful in offering this service worldwide. The main implications of the Internet for the place aspect of the mix, which we will review in this section, are:

1 Place of purchase

In a B2B context, e-commerce is conducted on the manufacturer's own site, at an intermediary or is procured on a customer's site.

2 New channel structures

New channel structures such as changes introduced by disintermediation, reintermediation and countermediation (referred to in Chapter 2).

3 Channel conflicts

A significant threat arising from the introduction of an Internet channel is that while disintermediation gives a company the opportunity to sell direct and increase profitability on products, it can also threaten distribution arrangements with existing partners. Such channel conflicts are described by Frazier (1999), and need to be carefully managed. Frazier (1999) identifies some situations when the Internet should only be used as a communications channel. This is particularly the case where manufacturers offer an exclusive, or highly selective, distribution approach. To take an example, a company manufacturing expensive watches costing thousands of pounds will not in the past have sold direct, but will have used a wholesaler to distribute watches via retailers. If this wholesaler is a major player in watch distribution, then it is powerful, and will react against the watch manufacturer selling direct. The wholesaler may even refuse to act as distributor and may threaten to distribute only a competitor's watches, which are not available over the Internet.

Further channel conflicts involve other stakeholders including sales representatives and customers. Sales representatives may see the Internet as a direct threat to their livelihood. In some cases, such as Avon cosmetics and *Encyclopaedia Britannica,* this has proved to be the case with this sales model being partly or completely replaced by the Internet. For many B2B purchases, sales representatives remain an essential method of reaching the customer to support them in the purchase decision. Here, the Internet can be used as a sales support and customer education tool. Customers who do not use the online channels may also respond negatively if lower prices are available to their online counterparts. This is less serious than other types of channel conflict.

Internet channels can take these forms:

- a communication channel only;
- a distribution channel to intermediaries;
- a direct sales channel to customers;
- any combination of the above.

To avoid channel conflicts, the appropriate combination of channels must be arrived at.

Internet channel strategy will, of course, depend on the existing arrangements for the market. If a geographical market is new and there are no existing agents or distributors, there is unlikely to be channel conflict, in that there is a choice of distribution through the Internet only or appointments of new agents to support Internet sales, or a combination of the two. Often SMEs will attempt to use the Internet to sell products without appointing agents, but this strategy will only be possible for retail products that need limited pre-sales and after-sales support. For higher-value products such as engineering equipment, which will require skilled sales staff to support the sale and after-sales servicing, agents will have to be appointed.

For existing geographical markets in which a company already has a mechanism for distribution in the form of agents and distributors, the situation is more complex, and there is the threat of channel conflict.

4 Virtual organisations

The concept of virtual organisations was introduced in Chapter 6. From a digital marketing perspective, the Internet provides new options for forming partnerships to mutually benefit all parties.

Referring to small and medium businesses, Azumah *et al.* (2005) indicate three levels of development towards what they term an e-organisation:

1 Half-fusion organisations (minimum use of the Internet and network technologies);
2 Fusion organisation (committed and intensive use of the Internet and network technologies).
3 E-organisation (uses technologies as the core of the business for managing the entire business processes).

Place tactics will have to review all the types of opportunities and threats described above and decide which are appropriate. (Issues in distribution and fulfilment are described in Chapter 6.)

Promotion

Promotion

The element of the marketing mix that involves communication with customers and other stakeholders to inform them about the product and the organisation.

Specification of the **promotion** is usually part of a communications strategy. This will include selection of target markets, positioning and integration of different communications tools. The Internet offers a new marketing communications channel to inform customers of the benefits of a product and assist in the buying decision. The main elements of the promotional or communications mix and their online equivalents summarised by Chaffey and Smith (2008) are shown in Table 8.8.

One approach for developing promotion tactics is to specify the communications techniques required for different stages of the buying. Another approach is to look at how the Internet can supplement the range of promotional activities such as advertising, sales promotions, PR and direct marketing. (These approaches are discussed in Chapter 9, where we also look at how customers can be persuaded to return to a site for future purchases.)

The promotion element of the marketing plan also requires three important decisions about investment:

1 **Investment in promotion compared to site creation and maintenance.** Since there is often a fixed budget for site creation, maintenance and promotion, the digital marketing plan should specify the budget for each to ensure there is a sensible balance.

Table 8.8	The main elements of the promotional mix

Communications tool	Online implementation
1 Advertising	Interactive display ads, pay-per-click search advertising
2 Selling	Virtual sales staff, site merchandising, chat and affiliate marketing
3 Sales promotion	Incentives such as coupons, rewards, online loyalty schemes
4 Public relations	Online editorial, blogs, feeds, e-newsletters, newsletters, social networks, links and viral campaigns
5 Sponsorship	Sponsoring an online event, site or service
6 Direct mail	Opt-in email using e-newsletters and e-blasts (stand-alone emails)
7 Exhibitions	Virtual exhibitions and White Paper distribution
8 Merchandising	Promotional ad serving on retail sites, personalised recommendations and e-alerts
9 Packaging	Virtual tours, real packaging is displayed online
10 Word-of-mouth	Viral, affiliate marketing, email a friend, links

2 **Investment in online promotion techniques in comparison to offline promotion.** A balance must be struck between these techniques. Figure 8.24 summarises the tactical options that companies have. Which do you think would be the best option for an established company as compared to a dot-com company? It seems that in both cases, offline promotion investment often exceeds that for online promotion investment.

There will naturally be a variation in spend on online marketing tools depending upon level of adoption of e-commerce by a company and its customers. Factors that will affect the proportion of online media spend in any organisation include:

- Proportion of customers in a segment that can be reached through traditional or digital media.
- Proportion of customers in target market in researching and purchasing products online.
- Propensity of customers to purchase products using traditional channels.
- The relative cost-effectiveness of different online media (see Chapter 9) in comparison with traditional media such as TV and print.

There is a delicate balance to be struck between driving visitors to a website where they may be less likely to convert, but the cost of sale will be lower. With any medium there is a point of diminishing returns where more spend on that medium will not result in improved results. It seems that many companies are following a strategy of gradually increasing their digital spend since they want to find this inflexion point without overstepping it too far.

3 **Investment in different online promotion techniques.** For example, how much to pay for banner advertising as against online PR; how much to pay for search engine registration. (These and other traffic-building techniques are described in Chapter 9.)

People, process and physical evidence

People, process and **physical evidence** are particularly important for service delivery. Since service delivery is an important aspect of e-commerce sites this is referred to in the 'Focus on Excelling in e-commerce service quality' in Chapter 9; managing organisational change is the focus of Chapter 10; and user-centred design is in Chapter 11. Enhancing service is also an important element of online branding which is described in the next *Focus on* section. Physical evidence could be applied to site design or the accompanying packaging when products are delivered. Alternatively, these could be interpreted as part of the extended product.

Smith and Chaffey (2001) suggest that online, part of the consideration for the people element of the mix is the consideration of the tactics by which people can be replaced or their work automated. These are some of the options:

- *Autoresponders.* These automatically generate a response when a company emails an organisation, or submits an online form.
- *Email notification.* Automatically generated by a company's systems to update customers on the status of their order, for example, order received, item now in stock, order dispatched.

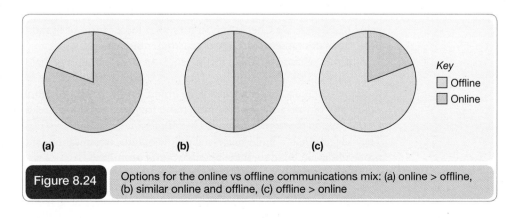

Key
☐ Offline
☐ Online

(a)   (b)   (c)

Figure 8.24 Options for the online vs offline communications mix: (a) online > offline, (b) similar online and offline, (c) offline > online

- *Call-back facility.* Customers fill in their phone number on a form and specify a convenient time to be contacted.
- *Frequently asked questions* (FAQs). For these, the art is in compiling and categorising the questions so customers can easily find (a) the question and (b) a helpful answer.
- *On-site search engines.* These help customers find what they are looking for quickly and are popular when available. Site maps are a related feature.
- *Virtual assistants* come in varying degrees of sophistication and usually help to guide the customer through a maze of choices.

Focus on	Online branding

What comprises a successful online brand? Is it an e-commerce site with high levels of traffic? Is it a brand with good name recognition? Is it a profitable brand? Or is it a site with more modest sales levels, but one that customers perceive as providing good service? Although sites meeting only some of these criteria are often described as successful brands, we will see that a successful brand is dependent on a wide range of factors.

Erdem *et al.* (2002) noted, in their study into the impact of brand credibility on consumer price sensitivity, that a credible brand signal helps to generate customer value by: (i) reducing perceived risk, (ii) reducing information search costs, and (iii) creating a favourable, trustworthy perception of the organisation. This shows the importance of online branding since websites must give the impression of trust and deliver a favourable experience to encourage first-time and repeat sales.

Branding

The process of creating and evolving successful brands.

Brand

The sum of the characteristics of a product or service perceived by a user.

Many think of branding only in terms of aspects of the brand identity such as the name or logo associated with a company or products, but branding gurus seem agreed that it is much more than that – it is dependent on a customer's psychological affinity for a product. A brand is described by Leslie de Chernatony and Malcolm McDonald in their classic 1992 book *Creating Powerful Brands* as:

an identifiable product or service augmented in such a way that the buyer or user perceives relevant unique added values which match their needs most closely. Furthermore, its success results from being able to sustain these added values in the face of competition.

This definition highlights three essential characteristics of a successful brand which we need to relate to the online environment:

- brand is dependent on customer perception;
- perception is influenced by the added-value characteristics of the product;
- the added-value characteristics need to be sustainable.

De Chernatony (2001) has evaluated the relevance of the brand concept on the Internet. He also believes that the main elements of brand values and brand strategy are the same in the Internet environment. However, he suggests that consumers on the Internet become active co-producers of value where they can contribute feedback through discussion groups to add value to a brand. De Chernatony argues for a looser form of brand control where the company facilitates rather than controls customer discussion.

A further method by which the Internet can change branding that was suggested by Jevons and Gabbot (2000) is that online, '*the first-hand experience of the brand is a more powerful token of trust than the perception of the brand*'. In the online environment, the customer can experience or interact with the brand more frequently and to a greater depth. As Dayal *et al.* (2000) say, '*on the world wide web, the brand is the experience and the experience is the brand*'. They suggest that to build successful online brands, organisations should consider how their proposition can build on these possible brand promises:

- *the promise of convenience* – making a purchase experience more convenient than the real-world one, or that with rivals;

- *the promise of achievement* – to assist consumers in achieving their goals, for example supporting online investors in their decision or supporting business people in their day-to-day work;
- *the promise of fun and adventure* – this is clearly more relevant for B2C services;
- *the promise of self-expression and recognition* – provided by personalisation services such as Yahoo! Geocities where consumers can build their own website;
- *the promise of belonging* – provided by online communities.

De Chernatony (2001) suggests successful online branding requires delivering three aspects of a brand: rational values, emotional values and promised experience (based on rational and emotional values).

An alternative perspective on branding is provided by Aaker and Joachimsthaler (2000) who refer to '**brand equity**' which they define as:

> *a set of brand assets and liabilities linked to a brand, its name and symbol, that add to or subtract from the value provided by a product or service to a firm and/or to that firm's customers.*

So, brand equity indicates the value provided to a company, or its customers, through a brand. Assessing brand equity on the web needs to address the unique characteristics of computer-mediated environments, as Christodoulides and de Chernatony (2004) have pointed out. These researchers set out to explore whether additional measures of brand equity were required online. Based on expert interviews they have identified the additional measures of brand equity which are important online, as summarised in Table 8.9. As we would expect, this includes attributes of the digital medium such as interactivity and customisation which combine to form relevance and a great online **brand experience**. Content is not stressed separately, which is surprising, although they do mention its importance under site design and it is also a key aspect of other attributes such as customisation, relevance and the overall experience. (Their work on the need for rational, emotional appeal together with the promised experience of the website is presented in Figure 11.8.)

Brand identity

Aaker and Joachimsthaler (2000) also emphasise the importance of developing a plan to communicate the key features of the **brand identity** and increase brand awareness. Brand identity is again more than the name. These authors refer to it as a set of brand associations

Brand equity

The assets (or liabilities) linked to a brand's name and symbol that add to (or subtract from) a service.

Brand experience

The frequency and depth of interactions with a brand can be enhanced through the Internet.

Brand identity

The totality of brand associations including name and symbols that must be communicated.

Table 8.9	Traditional measures of brand equity and online measures of brand equity

Traditional measures of brand equity (Aaker and Joachimsthaler, 2000)	Online measures of brand equity (from Christodoulides and de Chernatony, 2004)
Price premium	Online brand experience
Satisfaction/loyalty	Interactivity
Perceived quality	Customisation
Leadership popularity	Relevance
Perceived value	Site design
Brand personality	Customer service
Organisational associations	Order fulfilment
Brand awareness	Quality of brand relationships
Market share	Communities
Market price and distribution coverage	Website logs (see Chapter 9)

Mini Case Study 8.2   Napster.com's brand identity

Aaker and Joachimsthaler (2000) suggest that the following characteristics of identity need to be defined at the start of a brand-building campaign. Marketing communications can then be developed that create and reinforce this identity. Here, we will apply them to Napster.

- Brand essence (a summary of what the brand represents)
  This is not necessarily a tagline, but Napster has been described as an 'All you can eat music service which is fun and affordable'.
- Core identity (its key features)
  choice – millions of tracks
  value for money – under £10 per month subscription for as many tracks as you can listen to
  easy to use – Napster runs as a separate application built for purpose
  listen anywhere – on a PC or other computer, MP3 player or mobile phone
  listen on anything – unlike iPod, Napster is compatible with most MP3 players rather than being tied in to a specific hardware manufacturer.
- Extended identity
  personality – flouts what is standard for existing music providers thanks to its heritage as a peer-to-peer file-sharing service
  personalisation – Napster Radio based on particular genres or based on other songs you have downloaded
  community – facility to share tracks with friends or other Napster members
  symbols – Napster cat logo.
- Value proposition
  functional benefits – ease of use and personalisation
  emotional benefits – community, non-conformist
  self-expressive benefit – build your own collection of your tastes.
- Relationship
  customers value and will be loyal to a company that isn't stuffy.

that imply a promise to customers from an organisation. See 'Napster.com's brand identity', Mini case study 8.2, to see the different elements of brand identity which are effectively a checklist of what many e-tailers are looking to achieve.

Ries and Ries (2000) suggest two rules for naming brands: (a) The Law of the Common Name – 'The kiss of death for an Internet brand is a common name.' This argues that common names such as Art.com or Advertising.com are poor since they are not sufficiently distinctive; (b) The Law of the Proper Name – 'Your name stands alone on the Internet, so you'd better have a good one.' This suggests that proper names are to be preferred to generic names, e.g. Handbag.com against Woman.com or Moreover.com against Business.com. The authors suggest that the best names will follow most of these eight principles: (1) short, (2) simple, (3) suggestive of the category, (4) unique, (5) alliterative, (6) speakable, (7) shocking and (8) personalised. Although these are cast as 'immutable laws' there will of course be exceptions!

The importance of brand online

The Internet presents a 'double-edged sword' to existing brands. A consumer who already has knowledge of a brand is more likely to trust it, but loyalty can be decreased because the Internet encourages consumers to trial other brands.

The activity illustrates the importance of building brand awareness for an e-commerce service in a cost-effective manner at the same time as achieving good levels of service quality. (Success factors for building a brand online are described further in Chapter 9.) Key aspects of creating a positive customer experience are:

- Content quality (Can the customer easily find relevant, up-to-date content? Are there errors?).
- Adequate performance of website infrastructure in terms of availability and download speed.
- Ease of contacting a company for support.
- Quality of response to email enquiries and fulfilment quality.
- Acknowledgement of customer privacy.
- Reflecting and supporting the characteristics of the offline brand.

Managing the technology and customer database necessary to deliver service is a key aspect of digital marketing and requires close interaction between marketers and the IS department or external consultants.

Actions

The actions component of digital marketing planning refers to activities conducted by managers to execute the plan. Questions that need to be resolved when specifying actions include:

- What level of investment in the Internet channel is sufficient to deliver these services? What will be the payback?
- What training of staff is required?
- What new responsibilities are required for effective Internet marketing?
- Are changes in organisational structure required to deliver Internet-based services?
- What activities are involved in creating and maintaining the website?

At this stage a digital marketing plan will be finalised to summarise actions that need to occur. An example of what appears in a typical digital marketing plan is presented in Box 8.5. This also acts as a summary for the chapter.

Box 8.5   **A typical digital marketing plan framework**

1 Situation analysis

Internal audits

- Current Internet marketing audit (business, marketing and Internet marketing effectiveness)
- Audience composition and characteristics
- Reach of website, contribution to sales and profitability
- Suitability of resources to deliver online services in face of competition.

External audits

- Macro-economic environment (Chapter 4)
- Micro-environment – new marketplace structures, predicted customer activity
- Competition – threats from existing rivals, new services, new companies and intermediaries.

Assess opportunities and threats (SWOT analysis)

- Market and product positioning
- Methods of creation of digital value and detailed statement of customer value proposition

- Marketplace positioning (buyer, seller and neutral marketplaces)
- Scope of marketing functions.

2 Objectives statement

- Corporate objectives of online marketing (mission statement)
- Detailed objectives: tangible and intangible benefits, specific critical success factors
- Contribution of online marketing to promotional and sales activities
- Online value proposition.

3 Strategy definition

- Investment and commitment to online channels (mixture of bricks and clicks)
- Market and product positioning – aims for increasing reach, new digital products and new business and revenue models
- Target market strategies – statement of prioritised segments, new segments, online value proposition and differential advantage. Significance of non-customer audiences?
- Change management strategy (Which new processes, structures and responsibilities will be required? Chapter 10).

4 Tactics

- *Product*. Creating new core and extended value for customers, options for migrating brand online
- *Promotion*. Specify balance of online and offline promotion methods. Role of CRM (see Chapter 9)
- *Price*. Discounting online sales, options for setting pricing, new pricing options, e.g. auctions
- *Place*. Disintermediation and reintermediation, seller, buyer or neutral sales
- *People, process and physical evidence*. Online service delivery through support and characteristics of website.

5 Actions

Specify:

- Tasks
- Resources
- Partnering and outsourcing
- Budget including costs for development, promotion and maintenance
- Timescale
- Staff.

Implementation

- Key development tasks (Chapters 11 and 12): analysis of business and audience needs, scenario-based design, development of content, integration of databases, migration of data, testing and changeover
- Project and change management (Chapter 10)
- Team organisation and responsibilities
- Risk assessment (identify risks, measures to counter risks)
- Legal issues
- Development and maintenance process.

6 Control

Identify a measurement process and metrics (Chapter 12) covering:

- Business contribution (channel profitability – revenue, costs, return on investment)
- Marketing effectiveness (channel outcomes – leads, sales, conversion rate, channel satisfaction)
- Online marketing effectiveness (channel behaviour – page impressions, visitors, repeat visits, conversion rates).

Control

The control element of the digital marketing plan can be achieved through a combination of traditional techniques such as marketing research to obtain customer views and opinions and novel techniques such as analysis of web-server log files that use technology to monitor whether objectives are achieved. (These techniques are reviewed in detail in Chapter 12.) Intranets can be used to share information amongst marketers and consultants within an organisation.

Summary

1 Digital marketing is the application of technology to achieve marketing objectives, defined by the Chartered Institute of Marketing as: 'the management process responsible for identifying, anticipating and satisfying customer requirements profitably.'

2 Digital marketing can be considered a subset of digital business and is equivalent to sell-side e-commerce.

3 A digital marketing plan is often developed separately from a digital business strategy. The SOSTAC™ framework is used to introduce the elements of a digital marketing plan.

4 Situation analysis – involves a consideration of the external environment with the emphasis on levels of customer access to the Internet, benchmarking of competitors and new entrants.

5 Objective setting – a key objective is setting the online revenue contribution or the percentage of sales that will be achieved online. For companies where direct sales are not practical because of the nature of the product companies may set objectives for how the web will affect marketing communications, customer service and cost reductions.

6 Strategies – through evaluating the suitability of product for direct sale a company may define a replacement (product suitable for direct sale, e.g. airline tickets) or complementary strategy (product unsuitable for direct sale, e.g. FMCG or consultancy services). Replacement strategies may involve changing distribution networks. Complementary strategies will involve using the Internet as an additional marketing communications channel.

7 Tactics – digital marketing tactics can be reviewed through varying the elements of the marketing mix: Price, Place, Product, Promotion, People, Processes and Physical evidence.

8 Actions – the planning of digital marketing strategy by identifying resources and timescales.

9 Control – control can be achieved through monitoring customer satisfaction and channel performance via the website and traditional channels.

Exercises

Self-assessment questions

1 Explain the link between digital marketing and digital business and why they may be considered separately.

2 Outline the stages in a strategic digital marketing planning process, for each stage noting two aspects that are of particular importance for digital marketing.

3 What is the Internet contribution and what is its relevance to digital marketing strategy?

4 What factors will govern the Internet contribution that is set for a given organisation?

5 Why and how should a company approach benchmarking of online competitors?

6 Describe what is meant by a complementary and replacement Internet channel strategy and give examples of products for which companies follow a particular approach.

7 Summarise new opportunities to vary the marketing mix that arise through deploying the Internet.

8 How can online and offline techniques be used in the control stage of strategy?

Essay and discussion questions

1 Select a particular market sector and assess the past, current and future customer use of the Internet as a medium to select and buy products.

2 Develop an outline strategic digital marketing plan for an organisation with which you are familiar.

3 'Traditional strategic planning has no relevance for the start-up company given the dynamism of the marketplace.' Discuss.

4 Assess the value and importance of the Internet contribution in setting digital marketing objectives in relation to other possible objectives.

5 Explain how the digital business can make use of technology to monitor and control its operations.

Examination questions

1 Outline the stages involved in developing a strategic digital marketing plan.

2 Explain what is meant by the Internet contribution and outline how companies will decide on a realistic objective.

3 What opportunities may there be to vary the Price and Place components of the marketing mix when delivering services through the Internet?

4 What is a complementary Internet channel strategy and for which companies will this be most appropriate?

5 What different aspects of digital marketing should be monitored as part of controlling digital marketing? Name three examples of how technology can be used to assist monitoring.

6 Explain the strategic options available for a company currently selling the majority of its products in a single country for product and marketplace positioning.

7 What do the concepts of reintermediation and disintermediation imply for the tactics a company employs for the Promotion and Place elements of the marketing mix?

8 Outline how the electronic medium requires different tactics for effective marketing communications.

References

Aaker, D. and Joachimsthaler, E. (2000) *Brand Leadership*. Free Press, New York.

Agrawal, V., Arjona, V. and Lemmens, R. (2001) E-performance: the path to rational exuberance. *McKinsey Quarterly*, no. 1, 31–43.

Allen, E. and Fjermestad, J. (2001) E-commerce marketing strategies: a framework and case analysis. *Logistics Information Management*, 14(1/2), 14–23.

Anderson, C. (2004) The Long Tail. *Wired*. 12(10), October.

Ansoff, H. (1957) Strategies for diversification. *Harvard Business Review*, September–October, 113–24.

Azumah, G., Loh, S. and McGuire, S. (2005) E-organisation and its future implication for SMEs. *Production Planning and Control*, 16(6), September, 555–62.

Baker, W., Marn, M. and Zawada, C. (2001) Price smarter on the Net. *Harvard Business Review*, February, 2–7.

Baye, M., Gatti, J., Kattuman, P. and Morgan, J, (2007) Dashboard for online pricing. *The California Management Review*, Fall, 50(1), 202–16.

Bazett, M., Bowden, I., Love, J., Street, R. and Wilson, H. (2005) Measuring multichannel effectiveness using the balanced scorecard. *Interactive Marketing*, 6(3), 224–31.

Booms, B. and Bitner, M. (1981) Marketing strategies and organization structure for service firms. In *Marketing of Services*, eds J. Donelly and W. George, American Marketing Association, New York.

Brynjolfsson, E., Smith, D. and Hu, Y. (2003) Consumer surplus in the digital economy: estimating the value of increased product variety at online booksellers, *Management Science*, 49(11), 1580–96: **http://ebusiness.mit.edu/research/papers/176_ErikB_OnlineBooksellers2.pdf**.

Chaffey, D. (2000) Achieving success in Internet marketing. *Marketing Review*, 1, 1–23.

Chaffey, D. and Ellis-Chadwick, F. (2012) *Digital Marketing: Strategy, Implementation and Practice*, 5th edn. Financial Times Prentice Hall, Harlow.

Chaffey, D. and Smith, P. (2008) *EMarketing Excellence. Planning and Optimising Your Digital Marketing*, 3rd edn. Butterworth-Heinemann, Oxford.

Chaffey, D., Mayer, R., Johnston, K. and Ellis-Chadwick, F. (2009) *Internet Marketing: Strategy, Implementation and Practice*, 4th edn. Financial Times Prentice Hall, Harlow.

Christodoulides, G. and de Chernatony, L. (2004) Dimensionalising on- and offline brands' composite equity. *Journal of Product and Brand Management*, 13(3), 168–79.

Dayal, S., Landesberg, H. and Zeissberg, M. (2000) Building digital brands. *McKinsey Quarterly*, no. 2.

de Chernatony, L. (2001) Succeeding with brands on the Internet. *Journal of Brand Management*, 8(3), 186–95.

de Chernatony, L. and McDonald, M. (1992) *Creating Powerful Brands*. Butterworth-Heinemann, Oxford.

Deighton, J. (1996) The future of interactive marketing. *Harvard Business Review*, November–December, 151–62.

de Kare-Silver, M. (2000) *EShock 2000. The Electronic Shopping Revolution: Strategies for Retailers and Manufacturers*. Macmillan, London.

Dibb, S., Simkin, L., Pride, W. and Ferrell, O. (2000) *Marketing. Concepts and Strategies*, 4th edn. Houghton Mifflin, Boston.

E-consultancy (2008) Managing Digital Teams. Integrating digital marketing into your organisation. 60-page report. Author: Dave Chaffey. Available from **www.econsultancy.com**.

Emiliani, V. (2001) Business-to-business online auctions: key issues for purchasing process improvement. *Supply Chain Management: An International Journal*, 5(4), 176–86.

Erdem, T., Swait, J. and Louviere, J. (2002) The impact of brand credibility on consumer price sensitivity, *International Journal of Research in Marketing*, 19(1), 1–19.

Frazier, G. (1999) Organising and managing channels of distribution. *Journal of the Academy of Marketing Science*, 27(2), 222–40.

Ghosh, S. (1998) Making business sense of the Internet. *Harvard Business Review*, March–April, 126–35.

Gladwell, M. (2000) *The Tipping Point: How Little Things can Make a Big Difference*. Little, Brown, New York.

Hoffman, D.L. and Novak, T.P. (1997) A new marketing paradigm for electronic commerce. *The Information Society*, Special issue on electronic commerce, 13 (January–March), 43–54.

IEE (2003) Amazon.com recommendations: item-to-item collaborative filtering. *Internet Computing*, January–February, 76–80.

Jevons, C. and Gabbot, M. (2000) Trust, brand equity and brand reality in Internet business relationships: An interdisciplinary approach. *Journal of Marketing Management*, 16, 619–34.

Johnson, E., Moe, W., Fader, P., Bellman, S. and Lohse, G. (2004) On the depth and dynamics of online search behavior. *Management Science*, 50(3), 299–308.

Lautenborn, R. (1990) New marketing litany: 4Ps passes, 4Cs takeovers. *Advertising Age*, 1 October, 26.

Marketer (2009) Shelf Life, a profile of Anna Rafferty, October 2009. The Marketer CIM member magazine: **www.themarketer.co.uk/archives/interviews/profiles/shelf-life/**.

Marketer (2013) Mobilising the Fleet. Interview with Peter Duffy, published May 2013. **www.themarketer.co.uk/in-practice/profiles/mobilising-the-fleet/**.

McCarthy, J. (1960) *Basic Marketing: A Managerial Approach*. Irwin, Homewood, IL.

McDonald, M. and Wilson, H. (1999) *Digital marketing: Improving Marketing Effectiveness in a Digital World*. Financial Times Prentice Hall, Harlow.

Marsden, P. (2004) Tipping point marketing: a primer. *Brand strategy*, April.

Morris, R.J. and Martin, C.L. (2000) Beanie Babies: a case study in the engineering of a high involvement/relationship-prone brand. *Journal of Product and Brand Management*, 9(2), 78–98.

Quelch, J. and Klein, L. (1996) The Internet and international marketing. *Sloan Management Review*, Spring, 60–75.

Ries, A. and Ries, L. (2000) *The 11 Immutable Laws of Internet Branding*. HarperCollins Business, London.

Seybold, P. (1999) *Customers.com*. Century Business Books, Random House, London.

Simon, Herbert A. (1957) *Models of Man*. Wiley, New York.

Smart Insights (2010) Website Feedback Tools Review. Author, Dave Chaffey. Available from **http://bit.ly/smartfeedback**.

Smart Insights (2012) The Content Marketing Matrix. Blog post by Danyl Bosomworth published 16th May 2013. Available from **http://bit.ly/smartercontent**.

Smith, P. (1999) *Marketing Communications: An Integrated Approach*, 2nd edn. Kogan Page, London.

Smith, P. and Chaffey, D. (2001) *Digital Marketing Excellence at the Heart of E-Business*. Butterworth-Heinemann, Oxford.

Sultan, F. and Rohm, A. (2004) The evolving role of the Internet in marketing strategy. *Journal of Interactive Marketing*, 19(2), Spring.

Variani, V. and Vaturi, D. (2000) Marketing lessons from e-failures. *McKinsey Quarterly*, no. 4, 86–97.

Xing, X., Yang, S. and Tang, F. (2006) A comparison of time-varying online price and price dispersion between multichannel and dotcom DVD retailers. *Journal of Interactive Marketing* 20(2), 3–20.

Web links

Clickz (www.clickz.com) US site of statistics and advice about all aspects of digital marketing.

Content Marketing Institute (www.contentmarketinginstitute.com) A publisher advising on content marketing.

Marketing Sherpa (www.marketingsherpa.com) Articles and links on Internet marketing communications including email and online advertising.

SmartInsights.com (www.smartinsights.com) A blog of links and articles about developments in digital marketing and digital communications managed by Dave Chaffey.

9

Customer relationship management

Web support

The following additional case studies are available at **www.pearsoned.co.uk/chaffey**

→ Variations in online buyer behaviour and loyalty
→ Worldwide demand for CRM applications
→ Digital loyalty networks

The site also contains a range of study material designed to help improve your results.

Scan code to find the latest updates for topics in this chapter

Learning outcomes

After completing this chapter the reader should be able to:

- Outline different methods of reaching and acquiring new customers via digital media
- Evaluate different buyer behaviour amongst online customers
- Describe techniques for retaining customers and cross- and up-selling using digital media communications

Management issues

Customer relationship management involves these management issues:

- Which digital media should we invest in to reach new audiences?
- What are the practical success factors for using digital media need to make customer acquisition more effective?
- What technologies can be used to build and maintain the online relationship?
- How do we deliver superior service quality to build and maintain relationships?

Links to other chapters

The main related chapters are:

- *Chapter 4* – CRM techniques are constrained by social, legal and ethical factors
- *Chapter 5* – CRM supports digital business strategy
- *Chapter 8* – CRM is one of the tactics aimed at fulfilling the objectives defined in the digital marketing plan

Introduction

Customer relationship management (CRM)
An approach to building and sustaining long-term business with customers.

The application of technology to support **customer relationship management (CRM)** is a key element of digital business. Building long-term relationships with customers is essential for any sustainable business. Failure to build relationships largely caused the failures of many dot-coms following huge expenditure on customer acquisition (as explained in Chapters 2 and 5). The importance of customer retention to long-term profitability is well known from modelling of the type referred to in Chapter 4. But research summarised by Reichheld and Schefter (2000) showed that acquiring online customers in the retail sector is so expensive (20–30% higher than for traditional businesses) that such start-up companies may remain unprofitable for at least two to three years. The research also shows that by retaining just 5% more customers, online companies can boost their profits by 25% to 95%. These authors say:

> but if you can keep customers loyal, their profitability accelerates much faster than in traditional businesses. It costs you less and less to service them.

Note that the relationship between customer loyalty and profitability has been questioned, notably by Reinartz and Kumar (2002), who discovered through analysis of four company databases that:

> there was little or no evidence to suggest that customers who purchase steadily from a company over time are necessarily cheaper to serve, less price sensitive, or particularly effective at bringing in new business.

They have suggested that companies that base their marketing focus on the simple assumption that loyal customers are the most profitable will miss opportunities in targeting other potentially profitable customers.

This chapter evaluates different digital communications techniques such as search and social media marketing to reach new audiences and then initiate and build relationships with them as

Customer life cycle
The stages each customer will pass through in a long-term relationship through acquisition, retention and extension.

customers. The chapter is structured around the different stages of the classic **customer life cycle** of Select, Acquire, Retain, Extend, as is shown in Figure 9.1. The figure emphasises the importance of integrating customer relationship management activities across the appropriate channels.
The four marketing activities that comprise CRM involve the following:

1 **Customer selection** means defining the types of customers that a company will market to. It means identifying different groups of customers for which to develop offerings and to target during acquisition, retention and extension. Different ways of segmenting customers by value and by their detailed life cycle with the customer are reviewed. From an digital business perspective (as we see in Chapter 5), we may want to selectively target customer types who have adopted e-channels.

Customer extension
- 'Sense and Respond'
- Cross-selling and up-selling
- Optimise service quality
- Use the right channels

Customer selection
- Who do we target?
- What is their value?
- What is their life cycle?
- Where do we reach them?

Customer retention
- Understand individual needs
- Relevant offers for continued usage of online services
- Maximise service quality
- Use the right channels

Customer acquisition
- Target the right segments
- Minimise acquisition costs
- Optimise service quality
- Use the right channels

Extend · Select · Customers · Retain · Acquire

Figure 9.1 | The four classic marketing activities of customer relationship management

2 **Customer acquisition** refers to marketing activities intended to form relationships with new customers while minimising acquisition costs and targeting high-value customers. Service quality and selecting the right channels for different customers are important.

3 **Customer retention** refers to the marketing activities taken by an organisation to keep its existing customers. Identifying relevant offerings based on their individual needs and detailed position in the customer life cycle (e.g. number or value of purchases) is key.

4 **Customer extension** refers to increasing the depth or range of products that a customer purchases from a company. This is often referred to as 'customer development'.

There are a range of customer extension techniques for CRM that are particularly important to online retailers:

(a) **Re-sell.** Selling similar products to existing customers – particularly important in some B2B contexts as re-buys or modified re-buys.

(b) **Cross-sell.** Sell additional products which may be closely related to the original purchase.

(c) **Up-sell.** A subset of cross-selling, but in this case, selling more expensive products.

(d) **Reactivation.** Customers who have not purchased for some time, or have lapsed, can be encouraged to purchase again.

(e) **Referrals.** Generating sales from recommendations from existing customers.

Note that although the concept of CRM is prevalent in current marketing thinking and provides a valuable framework for tactics to increase loyalty and profitability, it may not accurately reflect the way the customer views their dealings with a company. Consumers may simply see their dealings with an organisation as an exchange relationship and will not believe that they are tied to any company, i.e. they may say 'I don't want a relationship'. O'Malley and Tynan (2001) note that the concept of a long-term relationship or partnership may be more readily applied to B2B marketing than consumer marketing. They say consumers:

> do not consider this false intimacy an interpersonal relationship. It is not driven primarily by trust, commitment, communication and shared values, but by convenience and self-interest.

It is useful to remember this consumer perspective on relationships when considering tactics to employ to help build and maintain relationships.

Marketing applications of CRM

A CRM system to support the four activities is made up of different marketing applications:

1 **Salesforce automation (SFA).** Sales representatives are supported in their account management and phone-based sales through tools to arrange and record customer enquiries and visits.

2 **Customer service management.** Representatives in contact centres respond to customer requests for information by using an intranet to access databases containing information on the customer, products and previous queries.

3 **Managing the sales process.** This can be achieved through e-commerce sites, or in a B2B context by supporting sales representatives by recording the sales process (SFA).

4 **Campaign management.** Managing ad, direct mail, email and other campaigns.

5 **Analysis.** Through technologies such as data warehouses and approaches such as data mining, which are explained later in the chapter, customers' characteristics, their purchase behaviour and campaigns can be analysed in order to optimise the marketing mix.

Vision Express

Kate Webb, Online Marketing Manager at Vision Express, explains how the multichannel retailer prioritises its use of social media to meet business goals. Her LinkedIn profile explains that at the time of the interview she was managing a budget of over £750,000, increasing online sales by 12% year-on-year 2010–2011 and by 16% year-on-year 2011–2012 while improving the online eye-exam booking conversion rate by 28%.

Q. How big an impact has the increase in popularity of social media with consumers had on Vision Express?

Kate Webb, Vision Express: It's had quite an impact in terms of time and resource, especially in the early days.

As a company we're relatively new to social media, we've only been active for just over a year. We spent a lot of time during the first 3–6 months listening, watching and learning what consumers were saying about our brand/looking for from our brand, in order to decide on how we should communicate, and where – which platforms.

During this time we have seen both our follower and fan numbers grow, but more importantly the engagement with our customers is increasing and we feel that our customers are really starting to converse with us as a brand.

Since being involved in social media we have seen an increase in the number of customers who mention us directly, or seek us out, rather than simply mentioning our brand name in passing conversation. To us this is an important development in building our customer relationship.

At Vision Express our social media activities are based on engaging with our existing customer base; we want to improve on relationships, or continue offline relationships, with our customers, online. In the optical industry we have a long purchase cycle – on average our customers come back to us every 2 years – so it is a long period during which to maintain our social media relationships.

We have found that for probably about 1–2% of our customer base, social media is their main point of contact with us. The type of communication varies between the different social media platforms, for example we find that Twitter is more of a customer service tool, while Facebook is a fun and engaging platform, suitable for promotional outreach.

There is still progress to be made, especially as social media grows and platforms are developed/changed, but we're confident we're on the right track to providing the same high level of service that our customers get in our stores, online.

Q. What do you see as the key parts of a social media strategy that require management?

Kate Webb, Vision Express: I find that too often businesses think that social media is just about posting messages about the company on Twitter or Facebook, or getting an agency in to handle everything for them. But the key to making social media work, for me, is to have a strong strategy behind it, and to manage that strategy.

For me the key areas of focus in this strategy should be:

Brand/Business persona: I feel it's key to define a persona or personality for your business and to identify how you want to position your brand on social media; is the brand/business fun/funky, calm/serious, sensitive/nurturing or brash/loud? You need flexibility to evolve this over time as your relationship with customers grows.

Which Platforms: There are hundreds of social media platforms that we could all be involved in, so it's key to identify which platforms support your business objectives, and which ones you are going to get involved with. Otherwise resources and communication will simply be spread too thinly.

Goals/Objectives: It is important to ensure that your social media objectives or goals are aligned with that of your organisation. What is it that you want to achieve via social media? For Vision Express, our three critical goals are to:

- Add value and service to our online customers, via informative dialogue, responsive customer service and feedback. This also works as a two-way path, in that we then pass on to our store network all/any feedback we have received from our online customers.

- Engage with our online customers, and build relationships with them. In order to do this effectively, we are working towards a one customer view database, which will enable us to match social media activity to in-store activity by our customers, thus enabling us to provide a tailored approach in our conversations.

- Build brand awareness and consumer knowledge about our service offering. We want our customers to understand our company, and to recognise our values, ethics and personality, online and offline.

Analytics/Results: Be this sentiment or engagement levels, reporting on results/analytics needs to be regular, managed and analysed in order to adapt future strategy.

Technology advancements: Social media platforms are changing all the time; because of this it is imperative that we understand and gain knowledge of how these advancements/changes will affect our business's social media presence going forward. For example, the development of Facebook's iframes in March this year [2013] opened up a great opportunity for us to integrate our website's core offers into our Facebook page.

Q. How should a company assess the relevance of different social media opportunities to prioritise their focus?

Kate Webb, Vision Express: Having clear objectives and a clear strategy will help – enabling you, on a case-by-case basis, to identify what social media opportunities work for which promotion/aspect of the business.

It's important for any business/brand not to spread their actions/activities too thinly. Identify where the majority of your customers are and focus on engaging well with your customers on a few platforms.

As well as identifying which platforms to be active on, it's important to also understand to what extent you work with these platforms. Does your business need/require interactive apps or games? Or is simple communication the key to your social media engagement?

I feel it is also important to identify where social media fits in with your overall online and offline presence, and ensure that it complements your other activities. Recently I have seen an increase in brands advertising both online and on TV their Facebook and Twitter presences, but not their website. To me, a brand's website should take precedence, and social media presences should complement the website messaging and be aimed at engaging customers with the website.

If through doing these engagement activities we acquire customers, then great, but this isn't our primary focus.

Q. What advice would you give to a company starting a social media listening/reputation management initiative?

Kate Webb, Vision Express: Listen, listen and listen some more. Social media isn't about who shouts the loudest, it's about engaging in conversation with your customers/prospective customers and about keeping them informed.

There are some free tools which you can use at the very beginning, such as Tweetdeck or Hootsuite, but bear in mind these are often limited to either one platform, or to scheduling outreach messages only.

If you are really serious about social media, and I think companies need to be these days, you need to enlist a social media monitoring platform, which will enable you to listen to what consumers are saying about your brand across micromedia (Twitter/Facebook), blogs and forums.

You won't be able to respond to all consumer mentions, due to forum rules, but you can at least listen and feed this back into the business, so you can modify activities, or continue doing popular ones!

Start small, don't overstretch your resources, and be realistic about the amount of time/resource and money that social media can take up.

A few key things to remember are that once you start talking, you need to continue the commitment to maintain the conversations, and ensure you gain intercompany awareness; there is nothing worse than talking to a customer via Twitter, and then having them go into store to be presented with 'We're on Twitter? I didn't know that'.

You will also need to get to know your customers; the ideal solution here is to integrate social media activities into your core customer database, so you have one customer view, but this can take time, money and resource. In the interim, the better social media monitoring tools these days are offering engagement platforms, which allow you to add notes and assign tasks, so you can build up a reasonable knowledge of your social media customers.

Q. Where do you think the responsibilities for managing social media marketing in a company should lie? How is it managed at Vision Express?

Kate Webb, Vision Express: By spending our first 3 to 6 months listening to what our customers were saying about our brand/looking for from our brand, we managed to identify that our social media activities needed to be part of the whole business, not just an 'add-on' to our marketing activities.

It is important that social media activities have management 'buy-in' in any business. It needs to be integrated into core business activities if it is going to work properly.

To integrate these activities into different departments correctly requires management support; the management structure needs to understand why/how/who social media impacts on and affects both internally and within our customer base.

As a result, so far, we've integrated social media into a couple of key departments within the business, with the Online Marketing team as social media 'owners', in that we will identify the next strategic steps, bring in agency support, provide understanding of new developments and report on analytics and progress.

We have involvement from our Customer Care team, who respond on a day-to-day basis to customer enquiries/queries and feedback. We integrate social media into our marketing planning activities from the outset, identifying whether a promotion is suitable for social media and if so, which platform it suits best, and we have our Product Department involved to provide a great level of product information and advice.

To have social media as purely a marketing tool/activity will restrict a business in providing the right level of customer care, and will lead to sporadic/untimely and unfocussed outreach.

What is e-CRM?

The interactive nature of the web combined with email communications provides an ideal environment in which to develop customer relationships, and databases provide a foundation for storing information about the relationship and providing information to strengthen it by improved, personalised services. This online approach to CRM is often known as 'e-CRM', and it is on this we focus in this chapter. Although Figure 9.1 refers to the whole customer life cycle, typically it is used to refer to customer retention and extension activities.

It is difficult to state where CRM ends and e-CRM starts, since today they both make extensive use of digital technology and media. This is what Chaffey and Smith (2008) say:

> *What is e-CRM? Customer Relations Management with an 'e'? Ultimately, e-CRM cannot be separated from CRM, it needs to be integrated and seamlessly. However, many organisations do have specific e-CRM initiatives or staff responsible for e-CRM. Both CRM and e-CRM are not just about technology and databases, it's not just a process or a way of doing things, it requires, in fact, a complete customer culture.*

Digital marketing activities which are within the scope of e-CRM and which we will cover in this chapter include:

- Using the *website and online social presences for customer development* from generating leads through to conversion to an online or offline sale using email and web-based content to encourage purchase.
- *Managing customer profile information and email list quality* (coverage of email addresses and integration of customer profile information from other databases to enable targeting).
- Managing customer contact options through mobile, *email and social networks* to support up-sell and cross-sell.
- *Data mining* to improve targeting.
- Providing online **personalisation** or **mass customisation** facilities to automatically recommend the 'next-best product'.
- Providing *online customer service facilities* (such as frequently asked questions, call-back and chat support).
- Managing *online service quality* to ensure that first-time buyers have a great customer experience that encourages them to buy again.
- Managing the *multichannel customer experience* as they use different media as part of the buying process and customer life cycle.

To help understand the scope of e-CRM, you may also find Figure 8.1 useful. This summarises different marketing activities that need to be completed by an online retailer, structured according to customer acquisition, conversion and retention activities.

From e-CRM to social CRM

In previous chapters, we have seen the growing popularity of social media with consumers and as a marketing technique. It's natural that a new marketing approach, **social CRM,** has developed to determine how social media can be applied to develop customer relationships and customer value.

(We discuss this further in Chapter 10 where we look at the rise of social business.) Areas that overlap with e-CRM are customer research, identifying new customers through social media and managing customer service through social media.

Sharma and Sheth (2004) have stressed the importance of a trend from mass marketing to what is now widely known as 'one-to-one' or **'customer-centric marketing'**. They note that

---

Electronic customer relationship management (e-CRM)
Using digital communications technologies to maximise sales to existing customers and encourage continued usage of online services.

Personalisation
Delivering customised content for the individual through web pages, email or push technology.

Mass customisation
The creation of tailored marketing messages or products for individual customers or groups of customers typically using technology to retain the economies of scale and the capacity of mass marketing or production.

Social CRM
The process of managing customer-to-customer conversations to engage existing customers, prospects and other stakeholders with a brand and so enhance customer-relationship management.

Customer-centric marketing
This is based on customer behaviour within the target audience and then seeks to fulfil the needs and wants of each individual customer.

e-channels can have advantages in terms of delivering relevant messages and offers to customers at relatively low cost. It can also be used to support customisation of products. These authors give the example of the Dell model where each PC is manufactured and distributed 'on demand' according to the need of a specific customer. This is an example of what they refer to as 'reverse marketing' with the change on marketing execution from product supply to customer need. Another aspect of this transformation is that online, web marketers can track the past and current behaviours of customers in order to customise communications to encourage future purchases. This approach, which is another aspect of reverse marketing and also a key concept with e-CRM, can be characterised as '**sense and respond communications**'. The classic example of this is the personalisation facilities provided by Amazon. Companies can also arrange triggered or follow-up email activity after a customer event such as a quote (as used by insurer MORE TH>N, www.morethan.com) or an abandoned shopping basket (as used by Tesco.com) to encourage purchase.

Sense and respond communications
Delivering timely, relevant communications to customers as part of a contact strategy based on assessment of their position in the customer life cycle and monitoring specific interactions with a company's website, emails and staff.

Benefits of e-CRM

Using the Internet for relationship marketing involves integrating the customer database with websites to make the relationship targeted and personalised. Through doing this marketing can be improved as follows:

- *Targeting more cost-effectively*. Traditional targeting, for direct mail for instance, is often based on mailing lists compiled according to criteria that mean that not everyone contacted is in the target market. For example, a company wishing to acquire new affluent consumers may use postcodes to target areas with appropriate demographics, but within the postal district the population may be heterogeneous. The result of poor targeting will be low response rates, perhaps less than 1%. The Internet has the benefit that the list of contacts is *self-selecting* or pre-qualified. A company will only aim to build relationships with those who have visited a website and expressed an interest in its products by registering their name and address. The act of visiting the website and browsing indicates a target customer. Thus the approach to acquiring new customers with whom to build relationships is fundamentally different, as it involves attracting the customers to the website, where the company provides an offer to make them register.
- *Achieve mass customisation of the marketing messages* (and possibly the product). This tailoring process is described in a subsequent section. Technology makes it possible to send tailored emails at much lower costs than is possible with direct mail and also to provide tailored web pages to smaller groups of customers (micro-segments).
- *Increase depth, breadth and nature of relationship*. The nature of the Internet medium enables more information to be supplied to customers as required. The nature of the relationship can be changed in that contact with a customer can be made more frequently. The frequency of contact with the customer can be determined by customers – whenever they have the need to visit their personalised pages – or they can be contacted by email by the company according to their communications preferences.
- *A learning relationship can be achieved using different tools throughout the customer life cycle*. For example, tools on Amazon and other retailers summarise products purchased on-site and the searching behaviour that occurred before these products were bought; online feedback forms about the site or products are completed when a customer requests free information; questions asked through forms or emails to the online customer service facilities; online questionnaires asking about product category interests and opinions on competitors; new product development evaluation – commenting on prototypes of new products.
- *Lower cost*. Contacting customers by email or through their viewing web pages costs less than using physical mail, but perhaps more importantly, information only needs to be sent to those customers who have expressed a preference for it, resulting in fewer mail-outs. Once personalisation technology has been purchased, much of the targeting and communications can be implemented automatically.

Customer engagement strategy

Customer engagement
Repeated interactions that strengthen the emotional, psychological or physical investment a customer has in a brand.

This difficulty in finding opportunities to achieve attention online on all types of sites has led to the emergence of the concept of **customer engagement** as a key challenge with which digital marketers are increasingly concerned. cScape (2008) describe customer engagement as:

> *Repeated interactions that strengthen the emotional, psychological or physical investment a customer has in a brand.*

while for Haven (2007) customer engagement is:

> *the level of involvement, interaction, intimacy, and influence an individual has with a brand over time.*

Arguably the biggest difference in communications introduced by the growth of digital media and the web is that customers' conversations are an integral part of communications (as we noted in Chapter 8). Today, proactively managing consumer participation through social media is seen as essential. The '*Focus on* Social media' section discusses this challenge.

Permission marketing

Permission marketing
Customers agree (opt in) to be involved in an organisation's marketing activities, usually as a result of an incentive.

Permission marketing is an established approach which should form a practical foundation for CRM and online customer engagement. 'Permission marketing' is a term coined by Seth Godin. Godin (1999) noted that while research used to show we were bombarded by 500 marketing messages a day, with the advent of the web and digital TV this has now increased to over 3,000 a day! From an organisation's viewpoint, this leads to a dilution in the effectiveness of the messages – how can the communications of any one company stand out? From the customer's viewpoint, time is seemingly in ever-shorter supply, customers are losing patience and expect reward for their attention, time and information. Godin refers to the traditional approach as '**interruption marketing**'. Despite the growth in social media marketing, permission marketing is still a core concept within digital media today which works well when integrated with social media. Companies from consumer brands, to retailers, to travel companies and business-to-business start-ups all want visitors to their site to sign up to email and then deepen the relationship with them through e-CRM. Today, it's more likely to be known as inbound marketing (which we introduced in Chapter 8); this describes how permission marketing fits in with digital marketing techniques like search engine optimisation and social media. It's about seeking the customer's permission before engaging them in a relationship and providing something in exchange. The classic exchange is based on information or entertainment – a B2B site can offer a free report in exchange for a customer sharing their email address, while a B2C site can offer a newsletter with valuable content and offers.

Interruption marketing
Marketing communications that disrupt customers' activities.

Opt-in
A customer proactively agrees to receive further information.

From an e-commerce perspective, a customer agrees to engage in a relationship when they check a box on a web form to indicate that they agree to receiving further communications from a company. This is referred to as '**opt-in**'. This is preferable to **opt-out**, the situation where a customer has to consciously agree not to receive further information. You may recall (from Chapter 4) that in many countries data protection laws requiring opt-in before customers receive communications and mandatory inclusion of opt-out have now been introduced in an attempt to stop spamming. Effectively, the law is mandating permission marketing as best practice!

Opt-out
A customer declines the offer to receive further information.

The importance of incentivisation in permission marketing has been emphasised by Seth Godin who likens the process of acquisition and retention to dating someone. Godin (1999) suggests that dating the customer involves:

1 Offering the prospect an incentive to volunteer.
2 Using the attention offered by the prospect, offer a curriculum over time, teaching the consumer about your product or service.

3 Reinforce the incentive to guarantee that the prospect maintains the permission.

4 Offer additional incentives to get even more permission from the consumer.

5 Over time, use the permission to change consumer behaviour towards profits.

Notice the importance of incentives at each stage. The use of incentives at the start of the relationship and throughout it is key to successful relationships. As we shall see in a later section, email is very important in permission marketing to maintain the dialogue between company and customer.

Figure 9.2 summarises the process of permission marketing in an online context. It shows how different methods are used to drive visitors to a website (1); incentives are then used to profile the customer (2). Subsequent email or social network communications (3) and direct mail (4) are used to encourage repeat visits to the website for future purchase or to learn more about the customer and increase the information in the profile (5).

Customer profiling

To engage a customer in an online relationship, the minimum information that needs to be collected in an online form such as in Figure 9.2 is an email address. This was an initial approach taken by the Peppers and Rogers site (www.1to1.com). What we really need,

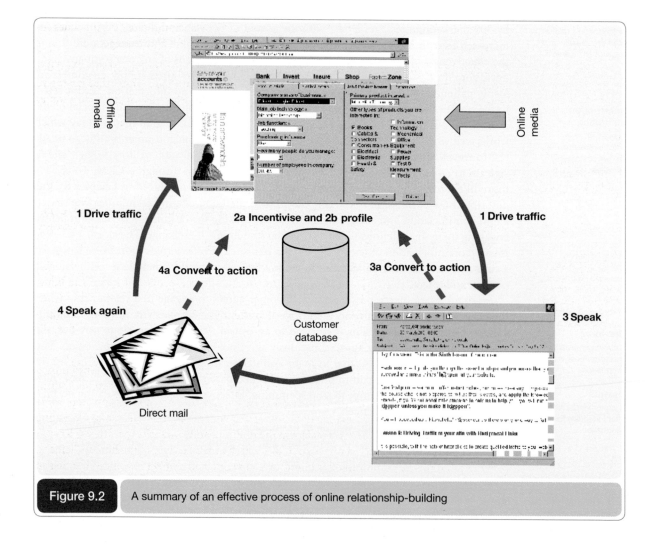

| Figure 9.2 | A summary of an effective process of online relationship-building |

Qualified lead
Contact information for a customer and an indication of his or her propensity to purchase different products.

Customer profile
Information that can be used to segment a customer.

particularly for B2B sites, is a **qualified lead** that provides us with more information about the customer to help us decide whether that customer is a good prospect who should be targeted with further communications. For B2B this could mean a visit by field sales staff or a follow-up email to arrange this. The Peppers and Rogers site has now been updated to reflect this approach.

To continue the relationship it is essential to build a **customer profile** that details each customer's product interest, demographics or role in the buying decision. This will affect the type of information and services delivered at the retention stage. For the customer to give this information a company will have to offer an incentive, establish trust and demonstrate credibility. Data protection and privacy law sets constraints on what can be collected from the customer (as described in Chapter 4. p. 141).

Peppers and Rogers (1999) were amongst the first commentators to explain how to use technology to build a *one-to-one* relationship. They suggested the IDIC approach as a framework for using the web effectively to form and build relationships:

1 **Customer identification.** This stresses the need to identify each customer on their first visit and subsequent visits. Common methods for identification are use of cookies or asking the customer to log on to a site.
2 **Customer differentiation.** This refers to building a profile to help segment customers. (Characteristics for differentiating customers are described in Chapter 4 (p. 142).)
3 **Customer interactions.** These are interactions provided on-site, such as customer service questions or creating a tailored product.
4 **Customisation.** This refers to personalisation or mass customisation of content or emails according to the segmentation achieved at the acquisition stage. Approaches for personalisation are explained in the section on customer retention management.

Note that although we are suggesting it is vital to capture the registration information, this should not be too 'up-front' since studies reported by Nielsen (2000) show that having to register acts as a barrier to entering sites. So the advice is to delay customer registration as late as possible.

Conversion marketing

Conversion marketing
Using marketing communications to maximise conversion of potential customers to actual customers and existing customers to repeat customers.

For managers to assess and improve the effectiveness of their CRM implementation, evaluation using the **conversion marketing** concept is useful. In an online context, this assesses how effective marketing communications are in converting:

- web browsers or offline audiences to site visitors;
- site visitors to engaged site visitors who stay on the site and progress beyond the home page;
- engaged site visitors to prospects (who are profiled for their characteristics and needs);
- prospects into customers;
- customers into repeat customers.

We referenced a high-level model based on this approach which can be used for planning purposes in Figure 5.14. This shows the acquisition part of the process and gives an indication of how the different channels can support each other. At each conversion step, some visitors will switch from one channel to the other, dependent on preferences and marketing messages. The dilemma for marketers is that the online channels are cheapest to service, but tend to have a lower conversion rate than traditional channels because of the human element. It follows that it is important to offer phone, live chat or email contact in online channels to help convert customers who need further information or persuading to purchase. Box 9.1 shows how a framework covering all marketing activities to develop relationships online can be used to manage online customer relationships.

| Box 9.1 | Using the RACE marketing value framework to increase sales |

RACE (Figure 9.3) is a practical framework designed to help marketers manage and improve the commercial value that their organisations gain from digital marketing. RACE is an evolution of the REAN (Reach Engage Activate Nurture) framework originally developed by Xavier Blanc and popularised by Steve Jackson in his book *Cult of Analytics* (Jackson, 2009). It is intended to help create a simplified approach to reviewing the performance of online marketing and taking actions to improve its effectiveness. (The measures in the figure are covered in more depth in Chapter 12 where we explore the power of using web analytics for improving marketing performance.)

RACE consists of four steps designed to help engage prospects, customers and fans with brands throughout the customer life cycle:

- *Step 1 Reach* – Build awareness of a brand, its products and services on other sites and in offline media and build traffic by driving visits to web presences.
- *Step 2 Act* – Engage audience with brand on its website or other online presence to encourage them to act or interact with a company or other customers.

REACH
Build awareness on other sites and in offline media and drive to web presences
KPIs:
- Unique visitors and fans
- Audience share
- Revenue or goal value per visit

ACT
Engage audience with brand on its website or other online presence
KPIs:
- Bounce rate
- Pages per visit
- Product page conversion

CONVERT
Achieve conversion to marketing goals such as fans, leads or sales on web presences and offline
KPIs:
- Conversion rates
- Leads and sales
- Revenue and margin

ENGAGE
Build customer and fan relationships through time to achieve retention goals
KPIs:
- % active hurdle rates
- Fan engagement
- Repeat conversion

| Figure 9.3 | Reach–Act–Convert–Engage model |

Source: Smart Insights (2010) Introducing RACE = A practical framework to improve your digital marketing. Dave Chaffey, 15 July 2010. www.smartinsights.com/blog/digital-marketing-strategy/race-a-practical-framework-to-improve-your-digital-marketing.

- *Step 3 Convert* – Achieve conversion to marketing goals such as new fans, leads or sales on web presences and offline.
- *Step 4 Engage* – Build customer relationships through time to achieve retention goals.

Integrating RACE
Digital channels always work best when they are integrated with other channels, so where appropriate digital channels should be combined with the traditional offline media and channels. The most important aspects of integration are, first, using traditional media to raise awareness of the value of the online presences at the Reach and Act stages. Second, at the Convert and Engage steps, customers may prefer to interact with customer representatives.

Digital marketing – it's not just about the website
Today, the popularity of participation in social media means that how to reach, interact, convert and maintain ongoing engagement of customers through social networks is vital to the success of a brand. At each step in RACE you need to think how social media can help achieve your goals and how you can measure the effectiveness.

Performance drivers
Critical success factors that govern whether objectives are achieved.

RACE is a development of the work by Agrawal *et al.* (2001) who created a scorecard for effective conversion marketing, assessed using a longitudinal study analysing hundreds of e-commerce sites in the USA and Europe. The scorecard is based on the **performance drivers** or critical success factors for e-commerce, such as the costs for acquisition and retention, conversion rates of visitors to buyers to repeat buyers, together with churn rates. Note that to maximise retention and minimise churn, service-quality-based drivers need to be evaluated.

There are three main parts to this scorecard:

1 **Attraction.** Size of visitor's base, visitor acquisition cost and visitor advertising revenue (e.g. media sites).
2 **Conversion.** Customer base, customer acquisition costs, customer conversion rate, number of transactions per customer, revenue per transaction, revenue per customer, customer gross income, customer maintenance cost, customer operating income, customer churn rate, customer operating income before marketing spending.
3 **Retention.** This uses similar measures to those for conversion customers.

The survey performed by Agrawal *et al.* (2001) shows that:

companies were successful at luring visitors to their sites, but not at getting these visitors to buy or at turning occasional buyers into frequent ones.

Agrawal *et al.* (2001) performed a further analysis where they modelled the theoretical change in net present value contributed by an e-commerce site in response to a 10% change in these performance drivers. This shows the relative importance of these drivers, or 'levers' as they refer to them:

Attraction
- Visitor acquisition cost: 0.74% change in net present value (NPV)
- Visitor growth: 3.09% change in NPV.

Conversion
- Customer conversion rate: 0.84% change in NPV
- Revenue per customer: 2.32% change in NPV.

Retention

- Cost of repeat customer: 0.69% change in NPV
- Revenue per repeat customer: 5.78% change in NPV
- Repeat-customer churn rate: 6.65% change in NPV
- Repeat-customer conversion rate: 9.49% change in NPV.

This modelling highlights the importance of on-site marketing communications and the quality of service delivery in converting browsers to buyers and buyers into repeat buyers. It also highlights the need to balance investment between customer acquisition and retention. Many start-up companies invest primarily in customer acquisition. For failed dot-com retailers such as LetsBuyit.com this was a strategic error since customer retention through repeat purchases is vital to the success of the online service.

The online buying process

Companies that understand how customers use the new media in their purchase decision-making can develop integrated communications strategies that support their customers at each stage of the buying process. Considering mixed-mode buying is a key aspect of devising online marketing communications since the customer should be supported in changing from one channel to another.

The simple model of the buying process shown in Figure 9.4 is valuable in developing the right online marketing tactics to support each stage of the process for each business.

Individual preferences for using the web will also differ. Lewis and Lewis (1997) identified five different types of web users who exhibit different **searching behaviours** according to the purpose of using the web:

Searching behaviours
Approaches to finding information vary from directed to undirected.

- *Directed information-seekers.* Will be looking for product, market or leisure information. This type of user tends to be experienced in using the web and is proficient in using search engines and directories.
- *Undirected information-seekers.* These are the users usually referred to as 'surfers', who like to browse and change sites by following hyperlinks. This group tends to be novice users (but not exclusively so) and they may be more likely to click on banner advertisements. The research in Figure 9.6 suggests that this behaviour is now less common.
- *Directed buyers.* These buyers are online to purchase specific products. For such users, brokers or intermediaries who compare product features and prices will be important locations to visit.
- *Bargain hunters.* These users want to use the offers available from sales promotions such as free samples or prizes.
- *Entertainment seekers.* Users looking to interact with the web for enjoyment through entering contests such as quizzes.

These different types of behaviour could be exhibited by the same person in different sessions online, or, less likely, in the same session.

Differences in buyer behaviour in target markets

There is great variation in the proportion of user access in different countries (as explained in Chapter 4, in the section Understanding users' access requirements). This gives rise to differences in buyer behaviour between different countries or between different segments according to how sophisticated customers are in their use of the Internet.

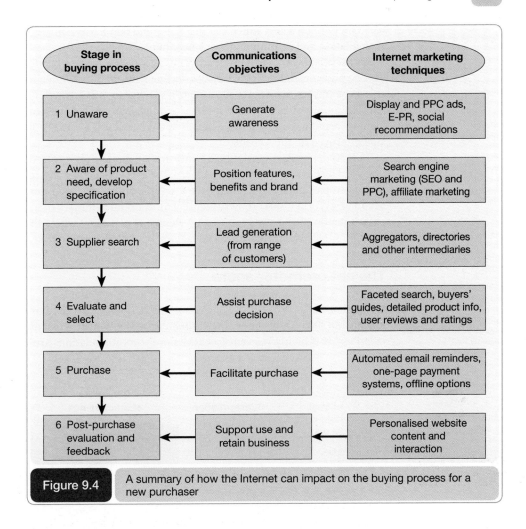

Stage in buying process	Communications objectives	Internet marketing techniques
1 Unaware	Generate awareness	Display and PPC ads, E-PR, social recommendations
2 Aware of product need, develop specification	Position features, benefits and brand	Search engine marketing (SEO and PPC), affiliate marketing
3 Supplier search	Lead generation (from range of customers)	Aggregators, directories and other intermediaries
4 Evaluate and select	Assist purchase decision	Faceted search, buyers' guides, detailed product info, user reviews and ratings
5 Purchase	Facilitate purchase	Automated email reminders, one-page payment systems, offline options
6 Post-purchase evaluation and feedback	Support use and retain business	Personalised website content and interaction

Figure 9.4 A summary of how the Internet can impact on the buying process for a new purchaser

Differences between B2C and B2B buyer behaviour

Major differences in buyer behaviour exist between the B2B and B2C markets, and these must be accommodated in digital marketing communications. The main differences are:

1 Market structure
2 Nature of the buying unit
3 Type of purchase
4 Type of buying decision
5 Communication differences.

One of the main differences between business-to-business and business-to-consumer is the number of buyers. As Kotler (1997) points out, in B2B there tend to be *far fewer but larger buyers*. This means that the existence of suppliers tends to be well known, so efforts to promote the website using methods such as banner advertising or listing in search engines are less important than for consumer brands.

Influences on purchase

In the online environment, purchasers lack the physical reassurance we have when purchasing from a store or talking to someone over the phone. This is compounded because of stories of fraud and security problems. It follows that consumers are looking for cues of trust when they are on a site, which can include brand familiarity, site design, the type of content, accreditation and recommendations by other customers.

Bart *et al.* (2005) have developed a useful, widely referenced conceptual model that links website and consumer characteristics, online trust, and behaviour based on 6,831 consumers across 25 sites from 8 website categories including retail, travel, financial services, portals and community sites. We have summarised the eight main drivers of trust from the study in Figure 9.5 and have added some details about how these elements of trust can be substantiated or proved on the website.

The model of Bart *et al.* (2005) and similar models are centred on a site, but perceptions of trust are also built from external sources including the role of social media and friends, in particular, which can have a significant influence on purchase as research from BrandNewWorld (2004) shows (Figure 9.6). A useful summary of influences on online purchase intention has been proposed by Dennis *et al.* (2009) where they do stress the importance of 'subjective norms' or 'social factors' in influencing purchase.

Net promoter score (NPS)

A measure of the number of advocates a company (or website) has who would recommend it compared to the number of detractors.

The net promoter score

Net promoter score (NPS) is a measure of customer advocacy originally popularised by Reichheld (2006) in his book *The Ultimate Question* which is essentially '*would you recommend us?*' It is highly relevant to CRM since recommendations are important to acquiring

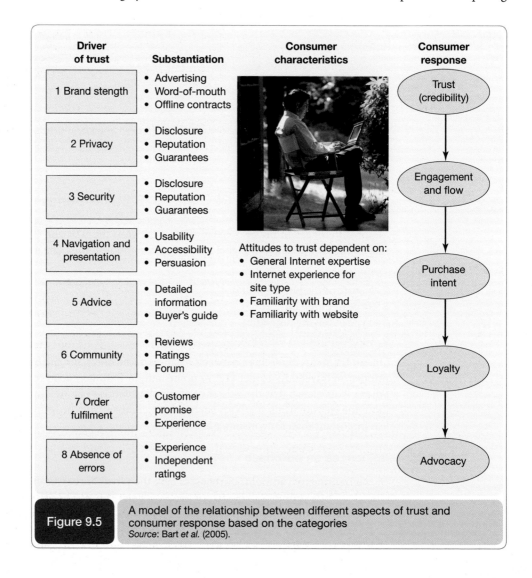

Figure 9.5	A model of the relationship between different aspects of trust and consumer response based on the categories

Source: Bart *et al.* (2005).

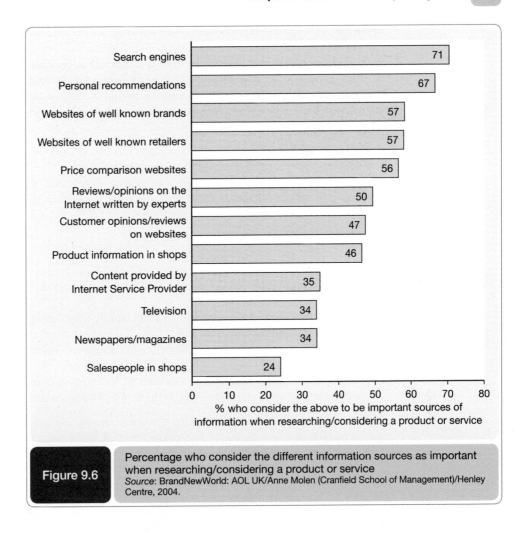

| **Figure 9.6** | Percentage who consider the different information sources as important when researching/considering a product or service
Source: BrandNewWorld: AOL UK/Anne Molen (Cranfield School of Management)/Henley Centre, 2004. |

customers, but it is also the ultimate measure of customer satisfaction which is needed to drive retention.

Reichheld explains the main process for NPS as follows:

1 Systematically categorise customers into promoters, passives, or detractors. If you prefer, you can call them loyal advocates, fair-weather friends, and adversaries.
2 Creating closed-loop processes so that the right employees will directly investigate the root causes that drive customers into these categories.
3 Making the creation of more promoters and fewer detractors a top priority so employees up and down the organisation take actions based on their findings from these root-cause investigations.

In practice, consumers are asked 'Would you recommend [Brand/Company X] to a friend or colleague', answered on a scale between 0 (not at all likely) and 10 (extremely likely). The actual score is calculated by subtracting the percentage of detractors (those giving 0–6 answers) from promoters (9–10s). The middle section, between 7 and 8, is the so-called passives.

The concept of NPS is based on economic analysis of the customer base of a company. For Dell, Reichheld estimates that the average consumer is worth $210 (based on a lifetime-value calculation of future value over a five-year period calculated as net present value (NPV)), whereas a detractor costs the company $57 and a promoter generates $328. Online Dell uses software from Opinion Labs (www.opinionlabs.com) to both gather feedback and follow up on negative experiences and so reduce the number of detractors with major negative sentiment.

So, the idea is that after surveying as many customers as possible (to make it representative) and show you are listening, you then work backwards to determine which aspects of the experience of interacting with a brand creates 'promoters' or 'detractors'. Some specific approaches that can be used to help manage NPS in the online environment are:

Facilitating online advocacy:

- Page template contains 'forward/recommend to a friend' options.
- Email templates contain 'forward to a friend option'.
- Facilitate customer feedback through a structured programme of emailing customers for their opinions and NPS evaluations and by making it easy for site owners to comment.
- Showcase positive experiences, for example, e-retail sites often contain options for rating and commenting on products.
- Involve customers more in shaping your web services and core product offerings.

Managing online detractors:

- Use online reputation management tools for notification of negative (and positive) comments.
- Develop a process and identify resource for rapidly responding to negative comments using a natural and open approach.
- Assess and manage the influence of negative comments within the natural listings of search engines.
- Practise fundamental marketing principles of listening to customer comments about products and services and aim to rectify them to win back the situation!

Kirby and Samson (2008) have critiqued the use of the NPS in practice. For example, they ask: 'Is an NPS of 40, consisting of 70% promoters and 30% detractors, the same as the same NPS consisting of 40% promoters and 0% detractors?' They also quote research by Kumar *et al.* (2007) which shows that while about three-quarters of US telecoms and financial service customers may intend to recommend when asked, only about one-third actually follow through and only about 13% of those referrals actually generate new customers. Keiningham *et al.* (2007) have assessed the value of recommendation metrics as determinants of customer lifetime value and also believe that the use of NPS could be misleading. They say the consequences of a simple focus on NPS are:

> *the potential misallocation of customer satisfaction and loyalty resources due to flawed strategies that are guided by a myopic focus on customers' recommend intentions.*

Customer acquisition management

Customer acquisition
Techniques used to gain new prospects and customers.

In an online context, '**customer acquisition**' can have two meanings. First, it may mean the use of the website to acquire new customers for a company as qualified leads that can hopefully be converted into sales. Second, it may mean encouraging existing customers to *migrate* to using online for purchase or service. Many organisations concentrate on the former, but where acquisition is well managed, campaigns will be used to achieve online conversion. For example, American Express developed a '*Go Paperless*' campaign to persuade customers to receive and review their statements online rather than by post. Phone bank First Direct used call centre representatives to persuade customers of the benefits of bypassing them by reviewing their statements online. They also encourage 'e-advocacy' amongst employees, i.e. encourage them to use the online services so they can better empathise with customer needs.

Before an organisation can acquire customers through the content on its site, it must, of course, develop marketing communications strategies to attract visitors to the website.

Marketing communications for customer acquisition, including search engine marketing, online PR, online partnerships, interactive advertising, email marketing and social media marketing

Offline marketing communications
Traditional techniques such as print and TV advertising used to generate website traffic.

Online marketing communications
Internet-based techniques used to generate website traffic.

Digital media channels
Online communications techniques used to achieve goals of brand awareness, familiarity, favourability and to influence purchase intent.

Push media
Communications are broadcast from an advertiser to consumers of the message who are passive recipients.

Pull media
The consumer is proactive in selection of the message through actively seeking out a website responding to inbound marketing cues.

Interactivity
The medium enables a dialogue between company and customer.

E-commerce managers constantly strive to deliver the most effective mix of communications to drive traffic to their e-commerce sites. The different techniques can be characterised as traditional **offline marketing communications** or rapidly evolving **online marketing communications** which are also referred to as **digital media channels**. The objective of employing these techniques is often to acquire new visitors or 'build traffic' using the diverse marketing communications techniques summarised in Figure 1.8. Some additional techniques to promote repeat visits are considered in the section on *Customer retention management*.

The characteristics of interactive marketing communications

To best exploit the characteristics of digital media, it is important to understand the different communications characteristics of traditional and new media. In this section, we look at eight key differences.

1 From push to pull

Traditional media such as print, TV and radio are **push media**, a one-way street where information is mainly unidirectional, from company to customer. In contrast, the web is an example of **pull media**, more idely known today as inbound marketing. It means that as prospects and customers only visit a website when it enters their head to do so – when they have a defined need – they are proactive and self-selecting. But online pull means marketers have less control than in traditional communications where the message is pushed out to a defined audience. What are the digital marketing implications of the pull medium? First, we need to provide the physical stimuli to encourage visits to websites. This may mean traditional ads, direct mail or physical reminders. Second, we need to ensure our site is optimised for search engines. Third, email is an online push medium, so it should be a priority objective of website design to capture customers' email addresses in order that opt-in email can be used to push relevant and timely messages to customers.

2 From monologue to dialogue

Creating a dialogue through **interactivity** is important. Since the Internet is a digital medium and communications are mediated by software on the web server that hosts the web content, this provides the opportunity for two-way interaction with the customer. This is a distinguishing feature of the medium (Peters, 1998). For example, if a registered customer requests information, or orders a particular product, it will be possible for the supplier to contact them in future using email with details of new offers related to their specific interest. Deighton (1996) proclaimed the interactive benefits of the Internet as a means of developing long-term relationships with customers.

A website, interactive digital TV and mobile phones all enable marketers to enter dialogue with customers. But digital dialogues have a less obvious benefit also – intelligence. Interactive tools for customer self-help can help collect intelligence – clickstream analysis recorded in web analytics can help us build up valuable pictures of customer preferences and help marketers 'sense and respond'.

3 From one-to-many to one-to-some and one-to-one

Traditional push communications such as TV and print are one-to-many: from one company to many customers, often the same message to different segments and often poorly targeted.

With new media 'one-to-some' – reaching a niche or micro-segment becomes more practical – e-marketers can afford to tailor and target their message to different segments. We can even move to one-to-one communications where personalised messages can be delivered.

4 From one-to-many to many-to-many communications

New media also enable many-to-many communications. Hoffman and Novak (1996) noted that new media are many-to-many media. Here customers can interact with other customers via your website or in independent communities. The success of online auctions such as eBay also shows the power of many-to-many communications.

5 From 'lean-back' to 'lean-forward'

New media are also intense media – they are lean-forward media in which the website usually has the visitor's undivided attention. This intensity means that the customer wants to be in control and wants to experience flow and responsiveness to their needs. First impressions are important.

TV is more lean-back – the TV may be on, but its audience is not necessarily watching it. An article in *The Guardian* (2003) entitled 'TV ads "a waste of money"' summarises research observing the reaction of consumers to ads. It supports those who argue that many consumers do not regularly watch TV ads. The study found people who watched television with family or friends were far more likely to talk to each other during the commercial breaks than to focus on the ads. Others spent the commercial break doing housework, reading or channel hopping.

6 The medium changes the nature of standard marketing communications tools such as advertising

In addition to offering the opportunity for one-to-one marketing, the Internet can be, and still is, widely used for one-to-many advertising. On the Internet the overall message from the advertiser becomes less important, and typically it is detailed information the user is seeking. The website itself can be considered as similar in function to an advertisement (since it can inform, persuade and remind customers about the offering, although it is not paid for in the same way as a traditional advertisement). Berthon *et al.* (1996) consider a website as a mix between advertising and direct selling since it can also be used to engage the visitor in a dialogue. Constraints on advertising in traditional mass media such as paying for time or space become less important.

Peters (1998) suggested that communication via the new media is differentiated from communication using traditional media in four different ways. First, *communication style* is changed, with *immediate* or synchronous transfer of information through online customer service being possible. Asynchronous communication, where there is a time delay between sending and receiving information as through email, also occurs. Second, *social presence* or the feeling that a communications exchange is sociable, warm, personal and active may be lower if a standard web page is delivered, but can be enhanced, perhaps by personalisation. Third, the consumer has more *control of contact*, and finally the user has control of *content*, through selection or through personalisation facilities.

7 Increase in communications intermediaries

If we consider advertising and PR, with traditional media this occurs through a potentially large number of media owners for TV, radio and print publications. In the Internet era there is a vastly increased range of media owners or publishers through which marketers can promote their services and specifically gain links to their website. Publishers also include individual influencers such as celebrities, industry commentators, bloggers and anyone actively using social media! Traditional radio channels, newspapers and print titles have migrated online, but in addition there are a vast number of online-only publishers including horizontal portals (Chapter 2) such as search engines and specialist sites such as industry-specific sites. The online marketer needs to select the most appropriate of this plethora of sites to drive traffic to their website.

8 Integration remains important

Although new media have distinct characteristics compared to traditional media, this does not mean we should necessarily concentrate our communications solely on new media. Rather we should combine and integrate new and traditional media according to their strengths. We can then achieve synergy – the sum is greater than its parts. Most of us still spend most of our time in the real world rather than the virtual world, so offline promotion of the proposition of a website is important. It is also important to support mixed-mode buying.

Similarly, inbound communications to a company need to be managed. Consider what happens if the customer needs support for an error with their system. They may start by using the on-site diagnostics but these do not solve the problem. They then ring customer support. This process will be much more effective if support staff can access the details of the problem as previously typed in by the customer to the diagnostics package.

Referrer
The source of a website visit, e.g. paid search, affiliate marketing, online advertising or recorded as 'no referrer', i.e. when a URL is typed in directly.

Cost per acquisition (CPA)
The cost of acquiring a new customer. Typically limited to the communications cost and refers to cost per sale for new customers.

Allowable cost per acquisition
A target maximum cost for generating leads or new customers profitably.

Assessing marketing communications effectiveness

A campaign will not be successful if it meets its objectives of acquiring site visitors and customers but the cost of achieving this is too high. This constraint is usually imposed simply by having a campaign budget. However, it is also essential to have specific objectives for the cost of getting the visitor to the site using different **referrers** combined with the cost of achieving the outcomes during their visit. This is stated as the **cost per acquisition (CPA)** (sometimes cost per action). Depending on context and market of a site, CPA may refer to different outcomes – the acquisition of a visitor, a lead or a sale.

To control costs, it is important for managers to define a target **allowable cost per acquisition** such as £30 for generating a business lead or £50 for achieving sign-up to a credit card.

Figure 9.7 shows the full range of measures used by digital marketers to control communications expenditure from least sophisticated to more sophisticated. To help remember, the key measures use the VQVC mnemonic which stands for Volume, Quality, Value and Cost of interactions such as website visits or social media interactions. Common measures used to assess digital media include.

| Figure 9.7 | Measures used for setting campaign objectives or assessing campaign success increasing in sophistication from bottom to top |

0 **Volume or number of visitors.** This is usually measured as thousands of unique visitors. It is preferable to using page views or hits (see Chapter 12) as a measure of effectiveness, since it is opportunities to communicate with individuals. A more sophisticated measure is reach (%) or online audience share. This is only possible using panel data or audience data tools such as www.netratings.com or www.hitwise.com.

Example: An online bank has 1 million unique visitors per month.

1 **Quality or conversion rates to action.** This shows what proportion of visitors from different sources take specific marketing outcomes on the web such as lead, sale or subscription. **Bounce rates** can also be used to assess the relevance and appeal of the page that the visitor arrives on.

Example: Of these visitors 10% convert to an outcome such as logging in to their account or asking for a quote for a product.

Bounce rate
Percentage of visitors entering a site who leave immediately after viewing one page only (known as 'single-page visits').

2 **Cost (cost per click).** The cost of visitor acquisition is usually measured specific to a particular online marketing tool such as paid search-engine marketing since it is difficult to estimate for an entire site with many visitors referred from different sources.

Example: £2 CPC.

3 **Cost (cost per action or acquisition).** When cost of visitor acquisition is combined with conversion to outcomes this is the cost of (customer) acquisition.

Example: £20 CPA (since only one in ten visitors take an action).

4 **Return on investment (ROI).** Return on investment is used to assess the profitability of any marketing activity or indeed any investment. There are different forms of ROI, depending on how profitability is calculated. Here we will assume it is just based on sales value or profitability based on the cost per click and conversion rate.

$$ROI = \frac{Profit\ generated\ from\ referrer}{Amount\ spent\ on\ advertising\ with\ referrer}$$

A related measure, which does not take profitability into account, is return on advertising spend (ROAS) which is calculated as follows:

$$ROI = \frac{Total\ sales\ revenue\ generated\ from\ referrer}{Amount\ spent\ on\ advertising\ with\ referrer}$$

5 **Branding metrics.** These tend to be only relevant to interactive advertising or sponsorship. They are the equivalent of offline advertising metrics, i.e. brand awareness (aided and unaided), ad recall, brand favourability and purchase intent. Recorded using tools such as Dynamic Logic (www.dynamiclogic.com).

6 **Lifetime-value-based ROI.** Here the value of gaining the customer is not just based on the initial purchase, but the lifetime value (and costs) associated with the customer. This requires more sophisticated models which can be most readily developed for online retailers and online financial services providers.

Example: A bank uses a net present value model for insurance products which looks at the value over 10 years but the main focus is on a 5-year result and takes into account:
- acquisition cost
- retention rates
- claims
- expenses.

This is valuable since it helps give them a realistic 'allowable cost per sale' from different communications tools which is needed to get return over 5 years.

Figure 9.8 shows an example of effectiveness measures for an online ad campaign for an insurance product. Here an opportunity or lead is when a quote is requested. Note that the cost of acquisition is high, but this does not take into account the synergies of online

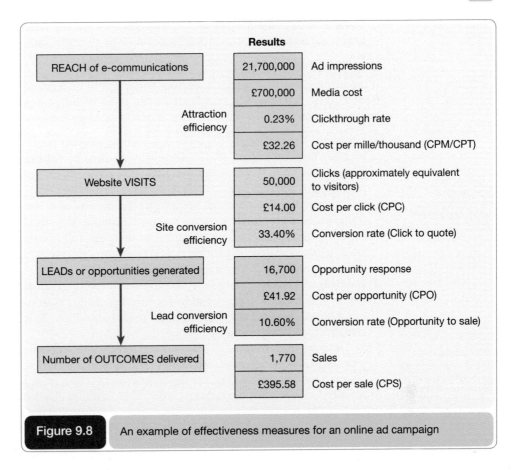

		Results	
REACH of e-communications		21,700,000	Ad impressions
		£700,000	Media cost
	Attraction efficiency	0.23%	Clickthrough rate
		£32.26	Cost per mille/thousand (CPM/CPT)
Website VISITS		50,000	Clicks (approximately equivalent to visitors)
		£14.00	Cost per click (CPC)
	Site conversion efficiency	33.40%	Conversion rate (Click to quote)
LEADs or opportunities generated		16,700	Opportunity response
		£41.92	Cost per opportunity (CPO)
	Lead conversion efficiency	10.60%	Conversion rate (Opportunity to sale)
Number of OUTCOMES delivered		1,770	Sales
		£395.58	Cost per sale (CPS)

Figure 9.8 An example of effectiveness measures for an online ad campaign

advertising with offline campaigns, i.e. those who are influenced by the ad, but do not click through immediately.

Online marketing communications

In this section we will review approaches to online promotion using the different tools of Figure 1.8 from 1 to 6. These techniques are often combined in what is known as a 'traffic-building campaign'; this is a method of increasing the audience of a site using different online (and offline) techniques.

A company's investment in the techniques in Figure 1.8 for customer acquisition should be based on the metrics discussed in the previous section. Most important is minimising the cost of acquisition against volume required.

1 Search engine marketing (SEM)

Search engines are a primary way of finding information about a company and its products (as explained in Chapter 2). We all now naturally turn to a search engine when we are seeking a new product, service of entertainment. The main options include Google, Bing or a regional search engine popular in one country such as Baidu in China, Naver in South Korea or Yandex in Russia. It follows that if an organisation is not prominent in the search engines, then many potential sales could be lost since otherwise, a company is dependent on the strength of its brand and offline communications to drive visitors to the website.

Consequently, Chaffey and Smith (2011) stress the importance of timing for traffic-building. They say:

Some e-marketers may consider traffic building to be a continuous process, but others may view it as a specific campaign, perhaps to launch a site or a major enhancement.

Traffic-building campaign
The use of online and offline promotion techniques to increase the audience of a site (both new and existing customers).

Search engines
Provide an index of content on registered sites that can be searched by keyword.

Some methods tend to work best continuously; others are short term. Short-term campaigns will be for a site launch or an event such as an online trade show.

How does Google work?

It can help managers of search marketing campaigns to understand the technology behind Google which it discloses in many patents and in its Webmaster guidelines (www.google.com/webmasters). Figure 9.9 shows that search technology involves these main processes:

Spiders or robots

Spiders are software processes, technically known as robots, employed by search engines to index web pages of registered sites on a regular basis.

1 **Crawling.** The purpose of the crawl is to identify relevant pages for indexing and assess whether they have changed. Crawling is performed by **robots** (bots), which are also known as **spiders**. These access web pages and retrieve a reference URL of the page for later analysis and indexing.

  Although the terms 'bot' and 'spider' give the impression of something physical visiting a site, the bots are simply software processes running on a search engine's server which request pages, follow the links contained on that page and so create a series of page references with associated URLs. This is a recursive process, so each link followed will find additional links which then need to be crawled.

2 **Indexing.** An index is created to enable the search engine to rapidly find the most relevant pages containing the query typed by the searcher. Rather than searching each page for a query phrase, a search engine 'inverts' the index to produce a look-up table of documents containing particular words.

Link anchor text

The text used to form the blue underlined hyperlink viewed in a web browser defined in the HTML source.

  The index information consists of phases stored within a document and also other information characterising a page such as the document's title, meta description, page rank, trust or authority, and spam rating. For the keywords in the document additional attributes will be stored such as semantic markup (<h1>, <h2> headings denoted within HTML), occurrence in **link anchor text**, proximity, frequency or density and position in document.

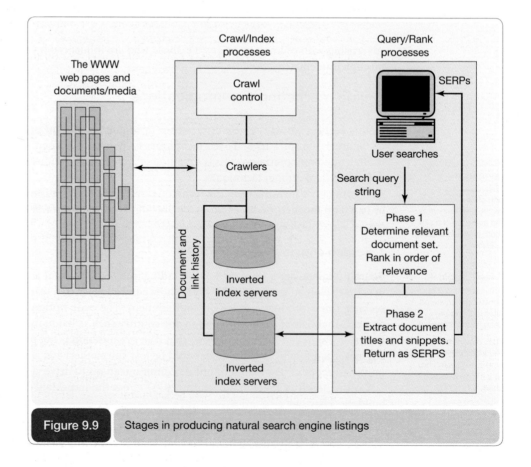

| Figure 9.9 | Stages in producing natural search engine listings |

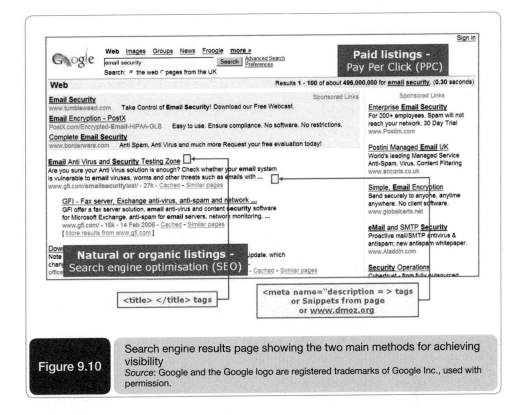

Figure 9.10	Search engine results page showing the two main methods for achieving visibility *Source*: Google and the Google logo are registered trademarks of Google Inc., used with permission.

3 **Ranking or scoring.** The indexing process has produced a lookup of all the pages that contain particular words in a query, but they are not sorted in terms of relevance. Ranking of the document to assess the most relevant set of documents to return in the SERPs (search engine results pages, Figure 9.10) occurs in real time for the search query entered. First, relevant documents will be retrieved from a run-time version of the index at a particular data centre, then a rank in the SERPs for each document will be computed based on many ranking factors of which we highlight the main ones in later sections.

4 **Query request and results serving.** The familiar search engine interface accepts the searcher's query. The user's location is assessed through their IP address and the query is then passed to a relevant data centre for processing. Ranking then occurs in real time for a particular query to return a sorted list of relevant documents and these are then displayed on the search results page.

Google has stated that it uses more than 200 factors or signals within its search ranking algorithms. These include positive ranking factors which help boost position and negative factors or filters which are used to remove search engine spam from the index. (Further details (on ranking factors) can be found in Box 12.2, p. 605.)

Keyphrase analysis

Keyphrase (keyword phrase)
The combination of words users of search engines type into a search box which form a search query.

The starting point to successful search engine marketing is target the right keyphrases. Notice that I say '**keyphrase**' (short for 'keyword phrase') rather than 'keyword' since search engines such as Google attribute more relevance when there is a phrase match between the keywords that the user types and a phrase on a page. Companies should complete a 'gap analysis' which will identify keyphrases to target by showing, for each phrase, the number of visitors they could potentially attract compared to the actual positions or number of visitors they are receiving.

Key sources for identifying the keyphrases customers are likely to type when searching for products include your market knowledge, competitors' sites, keyphrases from visitors who arrive at the site (from web analytics), the internal site search tool and the Google Keyword analysis tool. It is also useful to understand customer searching behaviour (Box 9.2).

Box 9.2

How do we search?

How do consumers respond when they search and are presented with a search results page containing natural and paid links? Research by GroupeM of 28 million people searching across 1.4 billion terms reported by Smart Insights showed that the behaviour depends upon whether the search term contains a brand term. For these terms 94% clicked on natural rather than paid results, which accounted for just 6%. Note though that many of these search terms would be non-commercial and there may not be a choice of paid results for a search term.

As you would expect, if users are looking for a specific brand then more people will click on the top few results.

Overall:

- **Result 1:** 48%
- **Result 2:** 12%
- **Result 3:** 8%
- **Remainder:** 32%

Branded:

- **Result 1:** 80%
- **Result 2:** 6%
- **Result 3:** 4%
- **Remainder:** 10%

Non-branded:

- **Result 1:** 35%
- **Result 2:** 15%
- **Result 3:** 11%
- **Remainder:** 39%

Source: Smart Insights (2012).

Search engine optimisation (SEO)

Search engine optimisation (SEO)
A structured approach used to improve the position of a company or its products in search engine natural or organic results listings for selected keyphrases.

Search engine optimisation (SEO) involves a structured approach used to increase the position of a company or its products in search engine natural or organic results listings (shown in Figure 9.10) for selected keyphrases. It also involves controlling index inclusion or ensuring that as many pages of a site as possible are included within the search engine. There may be technical difficulties with this with some content management or e-commerce systems which need to be corrected.

Although each search engine has its own evolving algorithm with hundreds of weighting factors only known to the search engineers they employ, fortunately there are common factors that influence search engine rankings. These are, in approximate order of importance:

1 **Frequency of occurrence in body copy.** The number of times the keyphrase is repeated in the text of the web page is a key factor in determining the position for a keyphrase. Copy can be written to increase the number of times a word or phrase is used (technically, its 'keyphrase density') and ultimately boost position in the search engine. Note, though, that search engines make checks that a phrase is not repeated too many times such as 'cheap flights...cheap flights...cheap flights...cheap flights...cheap flights...cheap flights...cheap flights...cheap flights...' or the keyword is hidden using the same colour text and background and will not list the page if this keyphrase density is too high or it believes the page creator has tried to mislead the search engine ('search engine

spamming'). Relevance is also increased by a gamut of legitimate 'tricks' such as including the keyphrase in headings (<H1>, <H2>), linking anchor text in hyperlinks and using a higher density towards the start of the document.

2 **Number of inbound links (page rank).** The more links you have from good-quality sites, the better your ranking will be. Evaluation of inbound links or backlinks to determine ranking is one of the key reasons Google became popular. Google uses an assessment called '**page rank**' to deliver relevant results since it counts each link from another site as a vote. However, not all votes are equal – Google gives greater weight to links from pages which themselves have high page rank and which have the same context or topical content as the page they link to. Weighting is also given where hyperlink anchor text or adjacent text contains text relevant to the keyphrase, i.e. the linking page must have context.

Inclusion in directories such as Yahoo! or Business.com (for which a fee is payable) or the Open Directory (www.dmoz.org, which is currently free) is important since it can assist in boosting page rank. Another key aspect of linking is the architecture of internal links within the site. Keyphrases that occur within the hypertext of different forms of navigation are important to Google in indicating the context of a page.

3 **Title HTML tag.** The keywords in the title tag of a web page that appears at the top of a browser window are indicated in the HTML code by the <Title> keyword. For example, for my site (<title>E-business and Internet marketing articles – DaveChaffey.com </title>). This is significant in search engine listings since if a keyphrase appears in a title it is more likely to be listed high than if it is only in the body text of a page. It follows that each page on a site should have a specific title giving the name of a company and the product, service or offer featured on a page. Greater weighting is given to keyphrases at the left of the title tag and those with a higher keyphrase density. The Title HTML tag is also vital in search marketing since this is typically the text underlined within the search results page which forms a hyperlink through to your website. If the Title tag appearing on the search results page is a relevant call to action that demonstrates relevance, you will receive more clicks, which equals more visits (incidentally, Google will monitor click-throughs to a site and will determine that your content is relevant too and boost position accordingly).

4 **Meta-tags.** Meta-tags are part of the HTML source file, typed in by web page creators, which is read by the search engine spider or robot. They are effectively hidden from users, but are used by some search engines when robots or spiders compile their index. In the past, search engines assigned more relevance to a site containing keyphrases in its meta-tags than one that didn't. Search engine spamming of meta-tags resulted in this being an inaccurate method of assessing relevance and Google has reported that it assigns no relevance to meta-tags. However, other search engines such as 'Yahoo! Search' do assign some relevance to meta-tags, so it is best practice to incorporate these and to change them for each page with distinct content. There are two important meta-tags which are specified at the top of an HTML page using the <meta name="content=" > HTML keyword:

(i) The 'keywords' meta-tag highlights the key topics covered on a web page. Example: <meta name="keywords" content="E-business, E-commerce, E-marketing">

(ii) The 'description' meta-tag denotes the information which will be displayed in the search results page so is very important to describe what the website offers to encourage searchers to click through to the site.

Example: <meta name="description" content="Your guide to E-business and Internet marketing – DaveChaffey.com">.

5 **Alternative graphic text.** A site that uses a lot of graphical material and/or plug-ins is less likely to be listed highly. The only text on which the page will be indexed will be the <Title> keyword. To improve on this, graphical images can have hidden text associated with them that is not seen by the user (unless graphical images are turned off), but will be seen and indexed by the search engine. For example, text about a company name and products

Page rank

A scale of 0 to 10 used by Google to assess the importance of websites according to the number of inbound links (link popularity).

Meta-tags

Keywords that are part of an HTML page that result in a higher search listing if they match the typed keyword.

can be assigned to a company logo using the 'ALT' tag as follows: <IMG NAME="Logo" SRC= "logo.gif" ALT="Internet marketing links and articles – DaveChaffey.com">.

Again, due to search engine spamming this factor is assigned less relevance than previously (unless the image is also a link), but it is best practice to use this since it is also required by accessibility law (screen-readers used by the blind and visually impaired read out the text assigned through ALT tags).

Paid search marketing

Paid search marketing or paid listings are similar to conventional advertising; here a relevant text ad with a link to a company page is displayed when the user of a search engine types in a specific phrase. A series of text ads usually labelled as 'sponsored links' are displayed on the right and/or above and below the natural search engine listings. Unlike conventional advertising, the advertiser doesn't pay when the ad is displayed, but only when the ad is clicked on which then leads to a visit to the advertiser's website – hence this is often known as 'pay-per-click marketing'! The relative ranking of these 'paid performance placements' is typically based on the highest bid cost-per-click value for each keyphrase. The variation in bid amounts for clients of one search bid management tool are shown in Table 9.1.

But it is not a simple case that the company which is prepared to pay the most per click gets top spot as many think. The search engines also take the relative clickthrough rates of the ads dependent on their position (lower positions naturally have lower clickthrough rates) into account when ranking the sponsored links, so ads which do not appear relevant, because fewer people are clicking on them, will drop down or may even disappear off the listing. The analysis of CTR to determine position is part of the **quality score**, a concept originally developed by Google, but now integrated as part of the Microsoft Live and Yahoo! search networks.

As well as paid search ads within the search engines, text ads are also displayed on third-party sites (for example, the ads on www.davechaffey.com) which form a **contextual 'display network'** such as Google Adsense (http://adsense.google.com) or Content Match on Yahoo! Search where 'contextual ads' are displayed automatically according to the type of content. These are typically paid for on a cost-per-click (CPC) basis but ads can also be paid for on a **CPM** basis. The search networks and publishers share the fees. They account for around 30% of Google's revenue. They enable marketers to reach a wider audience on

Quality score
An assessment in paid search by Google AdWords (and now other search engines) of an individual ad triggered by a keyword which, in combination with the bid amount, determines the ranking of the ad relative to competitors.

Contextual display network
Contextual ads are automatically displayed according to the type of content on partner publisher sites by the search engine.

Cost per thousand (CPM)
Cost per 1,000 ad impressions for a banner advert.

Table 9.1	Variation in cost per click in campaigns, January 2008 different categories for US paid search
Category	**CPC ($)**
All finance	2.70
Credit	2.95
Mortgage	2.61
Auto finance	1.68
Travel	0.65
Automotive	0.57
Retail	0.36
Dating	0.40

Source: Efficient Frontier.

selectable third-party sites, but they need to decide how to use these to deliver different messages.

Facebook pay-per-click advertising

Facebook has adopted the successful pay-per-click model from Google in an effort to monetise its audience. Mini case study 9.1, below, summarises the benefits. The case study shows how you can target effectively in Facebook and increase awareness of a service beyond Google, while limiting your exposure through a CPC investment. But it also shows a much lower response rate than Google Adwords. This is to be expected since customers aren't in research or buy mode – they're socialising! So it's worth remembering that although not disclosed in this case study, conversion rates are likely to be lower too.

Mini Case Study 9.1	Saxo Bank uses Facebook to reach its audience

Saxo Bank is a global investment bank with headquarters in Denmark specialising in online trading and investment across international financial markets.

Saxo Bank uses Facebook's standard advertising units to advertise three products: Forex Trading, CFD Trading and Saxo Premium Account. It uses targeting by finance-related, sporting and luxury keywords which may be used in people's profiles when they express their interest and passion. It also targets by their demographics. Using both of these targeting characteristics enables them to reach around 600,000 people on Facebook.

Head of marketing at Saxo Bank UK, Stuart Rice, describes the advantages:

Facebook ads have a tremendous advantage over Google (which we also use) because we can target people who perhaps use words like 'Rolex', 'yachting' or 'shooting' in their profiles. It enables me to target to a better degree than Google.

Ads are bought on a cost-per-click (CPC) basis because it makes them easier to monitor; according to Rice:

I just know with CPC what it has cost me when someone clicks there. If I bought 100,000 impressions I'd have to spend a lot of time going through the data to see what I got for my money.

Campaign results

Average CPC paid is £1.31 and the CTR is 0.05%. The total clicks for the period 1 June to 1 September for the three Saxo Bank campaigns on Facebook was 4,344, giving a cost of c£6,000, with 7,439,276 impressions.

Source: New Media Age article Facebook Bidding, by Nicola Smith, 7 October 2010: www.nma.co.uk/features/facebook-bidding/3019000.article.

Beware of the fake clicks!

Whenever the principle of PPC marketing is described to marketers, very soon a light bulb comes on and they ask, 'So we can click on competitors and bankrupt them?' Well, actually no. The PPC ad networks detect multiple clicks from the same computer (IP address) and say they filter them out. However, there are techniques to mimic multiple clicks from different locations such as software tools to fake clicks and even services where you can pay a team of people across the world to click on these links. It is estimated that in competitive markets one in five of the clicks may be fake. While fake clicks can be monitored for and refunds obtained if proved, ultimately this could destroy PPC advertising.

In Mini case study 5.2 we saw how Arena Flowers defines KPIs to control its marketing spend. In Mini case study 9.2 Arena provides insights into its communications strategy and in particular the role of search engine and social marketing.

| Mini Case Study 9.2 | Arena Flowers online communications |

Although we are florists in the traditional sense, at the heart of our business model is a website which makes shopping an enjoyable experience for our customers. Arena Flowers (www.arenaflowers.co.uk) has always prided itself in offering unique customer-focussed experiences and believes that technology plays a significant role in achieving this. Since its inception we have envisaged customer needs and requirements and tailored our website accordingly. We have continually sought customer feedback and worked extensively to make improvements to make ordering flowers and gifts an incredible experience for the customer. Everything from the website interface to product display, shopping cart and the checkout is an intuitive process.

We have leveraged the features of Web 2.0 to make Arena Flowers website an enjoyable experience while ensuring the highest security standards to protect our customers from Internet fraud.

However, that represents one dimension of our website. Like all other online businesses, it is vital for Arena Flowers to be found by customers and we rely extensively on Internet marketing to achieve this. The Internet has changed the way we interact with our stakeholders. It is a vibrant and rich advertising medium full of opportunities despite being multi-faceted. It requires a variety of strategies to be woven together to succeed. The significant aspect of Internet marketing is the ability to deliver relevant content to consumers at the right time. On the web, marketing and communications has shifted from the one-size-fits-all approach of traditional advertising to delivering the right information at the right time to help consumers in making a decision.

The crux of our Internet marketing strategy is marketing for search engines. Search is an intrinsically buyer-led medium, which is flexible and responsive to consumer tastes. Research indicates that Internet users rarely type website addresses into the browser bars – they locate them through search engines such as Google, Yahoo, Ask or Live.

Therefore it is necessary for Arena Flowers to promote search rankings by improving our website's structure and content. It is important for us to appear as near as possible to the top of search engine results for a set of keywords. We achieve this by investing in considerable time and resources to research and identify a number of measures including keywords, on-site content, external link partners etc. while ensuring that the structure of our website is search engine friendly to warrant a listing.

Apart from search engines, we focus on other broader Internet marketing strategies to insulate our reliance on search. Online mediums such as **blogs**, **podcasts**, **streaming video**, etc. are changing the way consumers research and buy products and services, necessitating Arena's presence on such mediums.

Furthermore, we also have a number of additional systems in place including affiliate marketing, social networking such as Facebook, Twitter, Squidoo etc., comparison shopping, newsletters etc. We constantly evolve with the Web 2.0 medium to strengthen our web presence. These initiatives help in getting prospective customers to Arena Flowers.

From the beginning, we have strived to strike the right balance between technology and design to benefit from the important and powerful marketing channel – the Internet. Through the Internet, we are committed to engage in a personal relationship with our customers to provide them value added service. We regularly measure our Internet marketing efforts internally and we feel happy to see an increase in the number of visitors to our website, conversions, sales, customer feedback etc. But we certainly feel privileged when we get appreciated by an unexpected quarter – to be cited by an academic text on Internet marketing. It highlights the success of our Internet marketing efforts and motivates us further to take it to the next level.

Source: Blog posting, 9 September 2008, www.arenaflowers.com/blog/2008 ÷ 09/09/wiser-about-web-from-a-flowers-website-to-academic-text/#comment-4361.

2 Online PR

The UK Institute of PR (IPR) defines PR as:

> *the management of reputation – the planned and sustained effort to establish and maintain goodwill and mutual understanding between an organisation and its publics.*

Online PR
Maximising favourable mentions of your company, brands, products or websites on third-party websites which are likely to be visited by your target audience.

Online PR or e-PR leverages the network effect of the Internet. Remember, Internet is a contraction of 'interconnected networks'! Mentions of a brand or site on other sites are powerful in shaping opinions and driving visitors to your site. The main element of online PR is maximising favourable mentions of an organisation, its brands, products or websites on third-party websites which are likely to be visited by its target audience. Furthermore, as we noted in the topic on search engine optimisation, the more links there are from other sites to your site, the higher your site will be ranked in the natural or organic listings of the search engines. Minimising unfavourable mentions through online reputation management is also an aspect of online PR.

Activities which can be considered to be online PR include the following:

(a) Communicating with media (journalists) online

This uses the Internet as a new conduit to disseminate press releases (SEO-optimised) through email and on-site and on third-party sites. Options include: setting up a press-release area on the website; creating email alerts about news that journalists and other third parties can sign up to; submitting your news stories or releases to online news feeds.

(b) Link-building

Link-building
A structured activity to include good-quality hyperlinks to your site from relevant sites with a good page rank.

Reciprocal links
Links which are agreed between your and another's organisation.

Link-building is a key activity for search engine optimisation. It can be considered to be an element of online PR since it is about getting your brand visible on third-party sites. Link-building needs to be a structured effort to achieve as many links into a website as possible from referring websites (these commonly include **reciprocal links**), which will also improve your position in the search engine results pages.

McGaffin (2004) provides a great introduction to implementing a structured link-building programme. He says: '*Create great content, link to great content and great content will link to you*'. He describes how you should review existing links to your site and links to competitors, set targets and then proactively enquire to suitable site owners for links.

You can use the syntax 'link:site' in Google to see a sample of quality links into a page on your site as judged by Google, e.g. 'link:www.davechaffey.com'.

Note that this also includes internal links. To gain a more comprehensive view of links, search marketing specialists use tools that are listed at http://bit.ly/smartlinkcheck.

(c) Blogs, podcasting and RSS

Blog
An online diary or news source prepared by an individual or a group of people.

Podcasts
Individuals and organisations post online media (audio and video) which can be accessed in the appropriate players including the iPod which first sparked the growth of this technique.

'**Blogs**' (introduced in Chapter 2) give an easy method of regularly publishing web pages which are best described as online journals, diaries or news or events listings. They may include feedback (traceback) comments from other sites or contributors to the site. Frequency can be hourly, daily, weekly or less frequently, but daily updates are typical.

Podcasts are related to blogs since they can potentially be generated by individuals or organisations to voice an opinion either as audio (typically MP3) or video. They have been successfully used by media organisations like the BBC, which has used them for popular programmes such as film reviews or discussions and for live recording such as the Beethoven symphonies that received over 600,000 downloads in June 2005 alone. A big challenge for achieving visibility for podcasts is that contents can only currently be recognised by tags and it is difficult to assess quality without listening to the start of a podcast. Podcasts have decreased in popularity with the growth of streamed media services from media publishers such as the BBC iPlayer. Likewise the use of RSS feeds (chapter 2) has descreased with the growth in social media updates.

(d) Online communities and social networks

The power of the Internet to facilitate peer-to-peer interactions was evident from the mid-1990s (as we explained in Chapter 8). However, it is only relatively recently that this power to transform the way companies and customers interact has been apparent. The human need to socialise and share experiences is the real reason behind the popularity of online communities and social networks. In most countries, social networks are amongst the most popular sites due to this need. It follows that marketers will want to 'swim with the fishes' or try to communicate with customers in this environment. Certainly there are opportunities to advertise on social networks, as shown in the Saxo Bank Mini case study, above. But if marketers perceive social media simply as an opportunity to push messages from a brand to passive recipients, then the opportunity to engage with customers to develop a deeper relationship is missing. Facebook aims to facilitate this through its ads which typically lead through to a brand page or company page within Facebook where brands can collect feedback.

So it is important for organisations to determine how their audiences use social networks and assess the opportunities to reach and interact with them. Dee *et al.* (2007) also note the importance of social networks in influencing perceptions about brands, products and suppliers. Their research shows large differences in gender and age on the types of products discussed, but recommendations on restaurants, computers, movies and vehicles being popular in all categories.

While many Facebook applications have been developed (www.facebook.com/apps/), the majority of well-known apps were not created by brands. Companies can also set up brand pages within Facebook, but these tend not to reach large numbers. Box 9.3 (see later) describes further advice on the use of social networks for marketing.

| Focus on | Social media and social CRM strategy |

Social media marketing

Monitoring and facilitating customer-customer interaction, participation and sharing through digital media to encourage positive engagement with a company and its brands leading to commercial value. Interactions may occur on a company site, social networks and other third-party site.

Social media marketing is an important category of digital marketing which involves encouraging customer communications on a company's own site, or social presences such as Facebook or Twitter or in specialist publisher sites, blogs and forums. It can be applied as a traditional broadcast medium, for example companies can use Facebook or Twitter to send messages to customers or partners who have opted in. However, to take advantage of the benefits of social media it is important to start and participate in customer conversations. These can be related to products, promotions or customer service and are aimed at learning more about customers and providing support so improving the way a company is perceived.

The growth of social networks has been documented by Boyd and Ellison (2007) who describe social networking sites (SNS) as:

> *Web-based services that allow individuals to (1) construct a public or semi-public profile within a bounded system, (2) articulate a list of other users with whom they share a connection, and (3) view and traverse their list of connections and those made by others within the system.*

The interactive capabilities to post comments or other content and rate content are surprisingly missing from this definition.

We've seen throughout this book that the opportunities of communicating with customers through social network sites, online communities and interactions on company sites are so great today that a social media strategy has become a core element of digital business strategy. Yet creating a social media or customer engagement strategy is challenging since it requires a change in mindset for the company since they may have to give up some control on their messaging to enable them to communicate with customers effectively. The change in approach required is clear from a movement that originated in the USA in 1999, known as the Cluetrain manifesto (www.cluetrain.com). The authors, Levine *et al.* (2000), say:

> *Conversations among human beings sound human. They are conducted in a human voice. Most corporations, on the other hand, only know how to talk in the soothing, humorless monotone of the mission statement, marketing brochure, and your-call-is-important-to-us busy signal. Same old tone, same old lies. No wonder networked markets have no respect for companies unable or unwilling to speak as they do. Corporate firewalls have kept smart employees in and smart markets out. It's going to cause real pain to tear those walls down.*

But the result will be a new kind of conversation. And it will be the most exciting conversation business has ever engaged in.

Of course, more than a change in mindset is required – to achieve change on this scale requires senior management sponsorship, investment and changes to processes and tools, as described in the next chapter on change management.

You can see that the Cluetrain manifesto is a call to action, encouraging managers to change their culture and provide processes and tools to enable employees of an organisation to interact with and listen to customer needs in a responsible way.

Developing a social media strategy

When developing a social media strategy there seems to be a tendency for managers to turn straight to the tools they'll be using – should we start with Twitter or Facebook, or should we create a blog? This is the worst possible way to develop strategy; indeed, it's not strategy, it's tactics! Strategy development for social media should be informed by demand analysis of customer channel adoption and the commercial potential of the approach.

Customer adoption of social media tools will vary according to customer segments and markets. So it's important to start by completing a marketplace analysis (as described in Chapter 2), to see which social tools and engagement techniques are most effective for the target audience.

Next, the commercial benefits of social media need to be reviewed and goals defined. Some marketers will see social media primarily as a way of gaining new customers through the viral effect of social media as existing customers or contacts discuss or recommend your content or products. For others, the benefits may be centred more on how recommendations, reviews and ratings can increase conversion rate. Public relations specialists will want to listen to the conversations for positive and negative sentiment about brand and then seek to manage this by increasing the positives and managing the negatives. Finally, social media can be viewed as a customer engagement and retention tool. Here social media are used to deliver customer service or are used as alternative channels to email marketing to inform customers about new product launches or promotions.

Mini Case Study 9.3	Best Buy offers, listens and responds in multiple channels

Best Buy is a multinational retailer of technology and entertainment products operating in the United States, Canada, Europe, China and Mexico. The Best Buy family of brands and partnerships collectively generates more than $45 billion in annual revenue and includes brands such as Best Buy; Audiovisions; The Carphone Warehouse; Future Shop; Geek Squad, Jiangsu Five Star; Magnolia Audio Video; Napster; Pacific Sales; The Phone House; and Speakeasy. Providing quality customer service is a large part of the customer experience. Best Buy explains:

Approximately 155,000 employees apply their talents to help bring the benefits of these brands to life for customers through retail locations, multiple call centers and websites, in-home solutions, product delivery and activities in our communities.

Figure 9.11 shows the customer support page for Bestbuy.com. You can see that there are a wide range of choices of customer service including:

- The Twelpforce (http://twitter.com/twelpforce). Immediate Twitter response followed by around 30,000 customers.
- Geek Squad Online Support. 'A live agent can fix your PC now! Prices starting at $49.99'.
- Discussion in communities.
- Standard email and Click To Call options.

Video explanation: www.bby.com/about/.

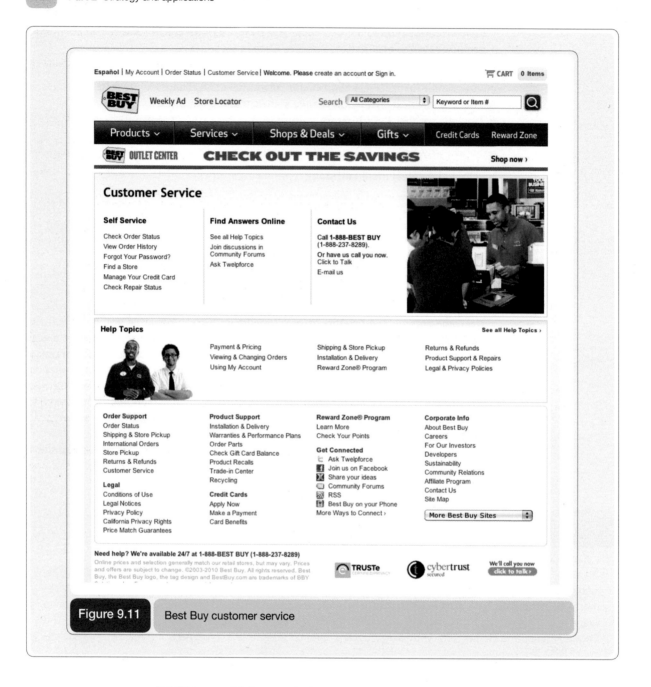

Figure 9.11 Best Buy customer service

POST is a useful framework for businesses to apply to help them develop a social media strategy, as summarised by Forrester (2007). POST is a simplified version of the SOSTAC framework introduced at the start of this chapter:

- *People.* Understanding the adoption of social media within an audience is an essential starting-point. The Forrester social media profiling tool shows how usage varies for different demographic groups: www.forrester.com/Groundswell/profile_tool.html.
- *Objectives.* Set different goals for different options to engage customers across different aspects of the customer life cycle from customer acquisition to conversion to retention. Josh Bernoff of Forrester recommends: '*decide on your objective before you decide on a technology. Then figure out how you will measure it.*'
- *Strategy.* How to achieve your goals. Bernoff suggests that because social media are a disruptive approach you should imagine how social media will support change. He says:

'Imagine you succeed. How will things be different afterwards? Imagine the endpoint and you'll know where to begin.'

- *Technology.* Finally, decide on the best social media platforms to achieve your goals; we'll review these in a moment.

Social CRM strategy

Social CRM

The process of managing customer-to-customer conversations to engage existing customers, prospects and other stakeholders with a brand and so enhance customer relationship management.

We have seen that there are a diverse range of goals of applying social media within an organisation, which is a significant challenge, particularly in larger organisations since success will require collaboration across different roles and functions. **Social CRM** is a relatively new term which helps define the broad scope of social media across the customer life cycle and value chain.

Conversations can occur across a range of site types, including 'social networks' such as Facebook and Twitter, but also in a company's own blog, third-party blogs, reviews-and-ratings sites or in neutral web self-service forums like Get Satisfaction. Many organisations have developed a social media governance policy to ensure that conversations are listened to and responded to accordingly. You can read examples at http://socialmediagovernance.com/policies.php.

The scope of social CRM is well illustrated as grouped within the six business application areas in Figure 9.12, which is presented by Altimeter (2010). The scope of each area is:

1 **Marketing.** Monitoring, analysis and response of customer conversations through social listening tools. I think the report misses a discussion on integration of social marketing into other campaign tactics such as email marketing.

2 **Sales.** Understanding where prospects are discussing selection of products and services offered by you and competitors and determining the best way to get involved in the conversation to influence sales and generate leads. Within B2B, Linked In is an obvious location that should be monitored.

3 **Service and support.** Customer self-help through forums provided by you and neutral sites.

4 **Innovation.** Using conversations to foster new product development or enhance online offerings is one of the most exciting forms of social CRM.

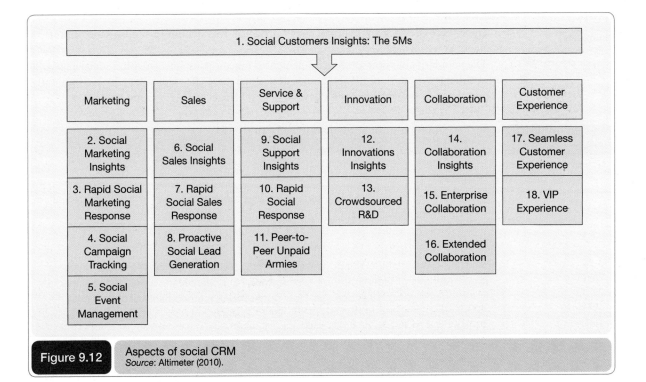

| **Figure 9.12** | Aspects of social CRM
Source: Altimeter (2010). |

5 **Collaboration.** This is digital business collaboration within an organisation through an intranet and other software tools to encourage all forms of collaboration which support business processes.

6 **Customer experience.** This references the use of social CRM to enhance the customer experience and add value to a brand which is implied by many of the other aspects above. It gives the examples of using VIP programmes, offering collaboration between customers with shared characteristics to add value and create advocacy.

A social CRM strategy can be developed by reviewing and prioritising options in each of the six business applications above.

The 5Ms provide another useful framework within the Altimeter (2010) report which can be used for reviewing strategy implementation. The 5Ms are:

1 **Monitoring.** Reviewing the method of social listening and deriving insights from these.
2 **Mapping.** Finding relationships between individual customers or grouped segments using different social platforms, e.g. Facebook and Twitter or email marketing.
3 **Management.** Processes for implementing and reviewing strategy. More report detail on campaign management would be helpful here.
4 **Middleware.** The software tools and APIs used to monitor and gather insight.
5 **Measurement.** The measures used to assess social marketing effectiveness and ROI.

Categories of social media

There are many, many sites and tools which provide an environment for social media; to gain an idea of just how many, complete Activity 9.1 which lists hundreds of tools in 25 categories.

A social media site is much more than simply a website. From a technology viewpoint most of these sites can be considered as software applications or web services which give access to users at different levels of permission and then enable management and storage of different forms of user-generated content. Messaging is also an important feature of many of these sites, particularly the main social networks which will alert users when new content related to their content or connections is published. APIs for exchanging data with other web services interfaces are also a key feature of social networks which enable them and their members to extend their reach and influence by being incorporated into other sites.

Community
A customer-to-customer interaction delivered via email groups, web-based discussion forums or chat.

Since there are so many types of social presence, it is helpful to simplify the options to manage (as we introduced in Chapter 1).

The popularity of **communities** implemented on company sites or within social networks means that it is important for companies to manage these effectively. But why is community important and how can companies best manage it? Hagel and Armstrong (1997) say:

Activity 9.1   Understanding the range of social media marketing platforms

Purpose

To explore the range of social media sites and tools, to categorise them and assess their business applications.

Activity

Visit the Conversation Prism (www.conversationprism.com) or the Smart Insights Digital Marketing Radar (http://bit.ly/smartradar) and identify the types of social media sites you and your colleagues use. How do you think the popularity of tools would differ for different types of B2B and B2C sites? Discuss how businesses should decide on the most important to invest in to achieve their goals.

The rise of virtual communities in online networks has set in motion an unprecedented shift from vendors of goods and services to the customers who buy them. Vendors who understand this transfer of power and choose to capitalize on it by organizing virtual communities will be richly rewarded with both peerless customer loyalty and impressive economic returns.

Depending on market sector, an organisation has a choice of developing different types of community for B2C, and communities of purpose, position, interest and profession for B2B.

1 **Purpose** – people who are going through the same process or trying to achieve a particular objective. Examples include those researching cars, such as Autotrader (www.autotrader.co.uk), or stocks online, such as the Motley Fool (www.motleyfool.co.uk). Price or product comparison services such as MySimon, Shopsmart and Kelkoo serve this community.

2 **Position.** Communities set up specifically for people who are in a certain circumstance, such as having a health disorder or being at a certain stage of life. Examples are teenage chat site Dobedo (www.dobedo.co.uk), Cennet (www.cennet.co.uk) offering 'New horizons for the over 50s', www.babycenter.com and www.parentcentre.com for parents, and the Pet Channel (www.thepetchannel.com).

3 **Interest.** This community is for people who share an interest or passion such as sport (www.football365.com), music (www.pepsi.com), leisure (www.walkingworld.com) or any other interest (www.deja.com).

4 **Profession.** These are important for companies promoting B2B services.

These B2B vertical portals can be thought of as 'trade papers on steroids'. In fact, in many cases they have been created by publishers of trade papers, for example Emap Business Communications has created Construction Plus for the construction industry. Each has industry and company news and jobs, as expected, but they also offer online storefronts and auctions for buyers and sellers and community features such as discussion topics. Of course, the trade papers such as Emap's *Construction Weekly* are responding by creating their own portals.

Today social networks provide a low-cost method for companies to create a community. You will notice that most of these examples of community are intermediary sites that are independent of a particular manufacturer or retailer. A key question to ask before embarking on a community-building programme is: '*Can customer interests be best served through a company-independent community?*'

If the answer to this question is 'yes', then it may be best to form a community that is a brand variant, differentiated from its parent. For example, Boots the Chemist created Handbag.com as a community for its female customers. Another and less costly alternative is to promote your products through sponsorship or co-branding on an independent community site or portal or to get involved in the community discussions.

Alternatively, companies can create their own forums although successful examples are relatively rare since there is a fear that a brand may be damaged if customers criticise products, so some moderation is required. Honda UK (www.honda.co.uk/car) provide a good example of a community created by their brand on their site. Rather than having a separate community section, the community is integrated within the context of each car as 'second opinions' menu options. Interestingly, some negative comments are permitted to make the discussion more meaningful.

A potential problem with a company-hosted forum is that it may be unable to get sufficient people to contribute to a company-hosted community. But initial recruitment of contributors and moderation has been used to grow the forum by software services company SAP, which has successfully created several niche communities to support its business with over 1 million software engineers, partners and business people (www.sap.com/community). Contributions are rewarded through donations to international aid charities.

What tactics can organisations use to foster community? Parker (2000) suggests eight questions organisations should ask when considering how to create a customer community:

1 What interests, needs or passions do many of your customers have in common?
2 What topics or concerns might your customers like to share with each other?
3 What information is likely to appeal to your customers' friends or colleagues?
4 What other types of business in your area appeal to buyers of your products and services?
5 How can you create packages or offers based on combining offers from two or more affinity partners?
6 What price, delivery, financing or incentives can you afford to offer to friends (or colleagues) which your current customers recommend?
7 What types of incentives or rewards can you afford to provide customers who recommend friends (or colleagues) who make a purchase?
8 How can you best track purchases resulting from word-of-mouth recommendations from friends?

A good approach to avoiding problems is to think about the difficulties you may have with your community-building efforts. Typical problems are:

1 **Empty communities.** A community without any people is not a community. The traffic-building techniques mentioned earlier need to be used to communicate the proposition of the community.
2 **Silent communities.** A community may have many registered members, but a community is not a community if the conversation flags. How do you get people to participate? Here are some ideas:
    - **Seed the community.** Use a moderator to ask questions or have a weekly or monthly question written by the moderator or sourced from customers. Have a resident independent expert to answer questions.
    - **Make it select.** Limit it to key account customers or set it up as an extranet service that is only offered to valued customers as a value-add. Members may be more likely to get involved.
3 **Critical communities.** Many communities on manufacturer or retailer sites can be critical of the brand, for example an early community from the bank Egg (www.egg.com) was closed due to negative comments.

Finally, remember the *lurkers* – those who read the messages but do not actively contribute. There may be ten lurkers for every active participant. The community can also positively influence these people and build brand.

Box 9.3	Social networks – success factors for social network marketing

Research by Microsoft (2007) based on interviews and surveys with social networkers found these human motivations for using social networks:

- 59% To keep in touch with friends and family
- 57% I like looking at other people's spaces
- 47% I want to meet people with similar interests
- 46% To express my opinions and views on topics
- 20% It is a good way to date
- 17% Using it for a specific reason, e.g. wedding, job networking.

In the same report, Microsoft, which part-owns Facebook, has developed these approaches for taking advantage of social networking either through buying ad space, or creating a brand space or brand channels that enable consumers to interact with or promote a brand:

1 **Understand consumers' motivations for using social networks.** Ads will be most effective if they are consistent with the typical life stage of networkers or the topics that are being discussed.

2 **Express yourself as a brand.** Use the web to show the unique essence of your brand, but think about how to express a side of the brand that it is not normally seen.

3 **Create and maintain good conversations.** Advertisers who engage in discussions are more likely to resonate with the audience, but once conversations are started they must be followed through.

4 **Empower participants.** Social network users use their space and blogs to express themselves. Providing content or widgets to associate themselves with a brand may be appealing.

5 **Identify online brand advocates.** Use reputation management tools to identify influential social network members who are already brand advocates. Approach the most significant ones directly. Consider using contextual advertising such as Microsoft content ads or Google Adsense to display brand messages within their spaces when brands are discussed.

6 **The golden rule:** behave like a social networker. This means:
  - Being creative
  - Being honest and courteous (ask permission)
  - Being individual
  - Being conscious of the audience
  - Updating regularly.

Members of a community or social network will differ in the extent to which they are connected with others. The most influential network members will be highly connected and will discuss issues of interests with a wider range of contacts than those who are less connected

It is generally believed by PR professionals seeking to influence marketplace perceptions that it is important to target the highly connected individuals since they are typically trusted individuals who other members of the community may turn to for advice. But there is much discussion about the influence of the influencers online. Researchers of community interactions believe that it is the collective interactions between typical network members (known as the '*moderately connected majority*') that are equally important. For example, Watts and Dodds (2007) argue that the 'influential hypothesis' is based on untested assumptions and in most cases does not match how diffusion operates in the real world. They comment that '*most social change is driven not by influentials, but by easily influenced individuals influencing other easily influenced individuals*'.

Although there is a clear wish to socialise online, site owners need to remember that it is not straightforward to engage an online audience as they move between different sites. Only a relatively small proportion will engage. Mini case study 9.4 shows that only a relatively small number of site visitors will actively participate.

Mini Case Study 9.4	Nielsen's 90-9-1 rule of participation inequality: encouraging more users to contribute

To encourage online community participation is a challenge since the majority of visitors to a community lurk or don't participate. Usability expert Jakob Nielsen gives examples of participation on Wikipedia (just 0.2% of visitors are active) and Amazon (fewer than 1% post reviews). He explains:

- 90% of users are lurkers (i.e. read or observe, but don't contribute).
- 9% of users contribute from time to time, but other priorities dominate their time.
- 1% of users participate a lot and account for most contributions: it can seem as if they don't have lives because they often post just minutes after whatever event they're commenting on occurs.

(e) Managing how your brand is presented on third-party sites

As part of online PR it is useful to set up monitoring services. It is also necessary to have the resources to deal with negative PR as part of online reputation management. Microsoft's PR agency reputedly has a 'rapid response unit' that can respond to online PR. Examples of alerting services include Googlealert (www.googlealert.com) and the other tools listed at www.davechaffey.com/online-reputation-management-tools.

(f) Creating a buzz – online viral marketing

From a functional point of view, online viral marketing often involves generating word-of-mouth and links through to a website (as outlined in Chapter 4), so it can be considered part of online PR.

To summarise the section on online PR, see Figure 9.13. This highlights the importance of activities involving participation and how all online PR activities feed back into SEO through the links generated.

3 Online partnerships

Partnerships are an important part of today's marketing mix. Smith and Chaffey (2005) say that they are the eighth 'P' (Chapter 8). The same is true online. There are three key types of online partnerships: link building (covered in the previous section, this can also be considered to be part of online PR), affiliate marketing and online sponsorship. All should involve a structured approach to managing links through to a site. The important types of partner arrangement are as follows.

(a) Affiliate marketing

Affiliate marketing
A commission-based arrangement where an e-retailer pays sites that link to it for sales leads (CPA-based) or, less commonly, visitors (CPC-based).

Affiliate marketing has become very popular with e-retailers since many achieve over 20% of their online sales through affiliates (also known as 'aggregators' since they aggregate offers from different providers). The great thing about affiliate marketing for the e-retailer is that they, the advertiser, do not pay until the product has been purchased or a lead generated. It is sometimes referred to as 'zero-risk advertising' (Figure 9.14).

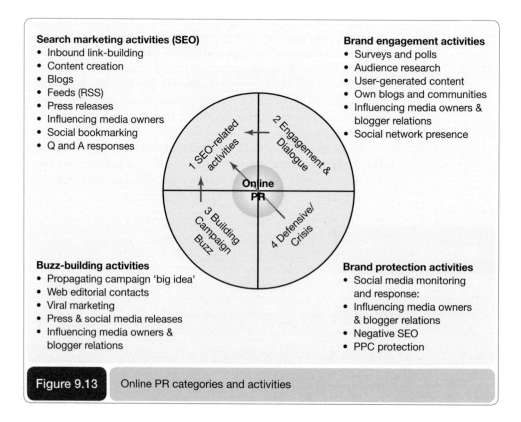

Search marketing activities (SEO)
- Inbound link-building
- Content creation
- Blogs
- Feeds (RSS)
- Press releases
- Influencing media owners
- Social bookmarking
- Q and A responses

Brand engagement activities
- Surveys and polls
- Audience research
- User-generated content
- Own blogs and communities
- Influencing media owners &
  blogger relations
- Social network presence

Buzz-building activities
- Propagating campaign 'big idea'
- Web editorial contacts
- Viral marketing
- Press & social media releases
- Influencing media owners &
  blogger relations

Brand protection activities
- Social media monitoring
  and response:
- Influencing media owners
  & blogger relations
- Negative SEO
- PPC protection

1 SEO-related activities

2 Engagement & Dialogue

Online PR

3 Building Campaign Buzz

4 Defensive/ Crisis

Figure 9.13 Online PR categories and activities

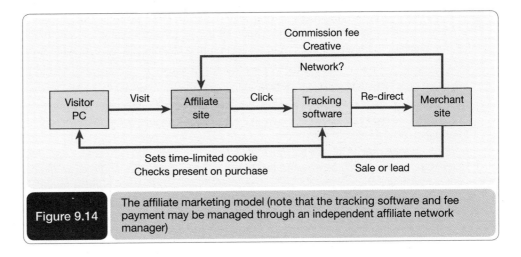

| Figure 9.14 | The affiliate marketing model (note that the tracking software and fee payment may be managed through an independent affiliate network manager) |

Amazon was one of the earliest adopters of affiliate marketing and it now has hundreds of thousands of affiliates that drive visitors to Amazon through links in return for commission on products sold. Internet legend records that Jeff Bezos, the creator of Amazon, was chatting at a cocktail party to someone who wanted to sell books about divorce via her website. Subsequently, Amazon.com launched its Associates Program in July 1996 and it is still going strong. To manage the process of finding affiliates, updating product information, tracking clicks and making payments, many companies use an affiliate network or affiliate manager such as Commission Junction (www.cj.com) or Trade Doubler (www.tradedoubler.com).

Some of the issues with balancing spend between affiliate marketing and other online communications techniques and offline communications techniques are illustrated by Mini case study 9.5.

| Mini Case Study 9.5 | Electronic retailers cut back on their e-communications spend |

Technology e-retailer dabs.com has traditionally used these as their main communications tools:

- Search engine marketing (the main investment)
- Referrals from affiliates (this has been reduced)
- Online display advertising on third-party sites (limited)
- PR.

Jonathan Wall, Dabs marketing director, explains (New Media Age, 2005a) how dabs.com reappraised their use of e-communications tools. He said:

We stopped all our affiliate and price-comparison marketing in February because we wanted to see what effect it had on our business and if we were getting value for money. It was proving a very expensive channel for us and we've found [stopping] it has had virtually no effect, because we're seeing that people will still go to Kelkoo to check prices and then come to our site anyway. It's like they're having a look around first and then coming to a brand they know they can trust. We're continuing with paid-for search on Google, but that's all we're doing with online marketing at the moment.

New Media Age (2005a) also reported that Empire Direct had adopted a similar approach to its communication mix, reporting that its co-founder and sales and marketing director, Manohar Showan, had revealed that the company has significantly moved from online to offline advertising. He said:

We've moved a lot more into national papers and specialist magazines. Two years ago, if you'd asked me where we marketed and advertised ourselves, I would have said the majority was online. But now it's turned right round and online's the minority.

New Media Age (2005a) believes that the reason for this is not a mistrust of the very medium it's using to take sales but, instead, the result of a growing realisation that its acquisition costs were swelling online. Showan says:

We were very keen advocates of affiliate marketing and pay-per-click search. The trouble was we had to pay for every click and we were finding that the cost of acquiring each new customer was getting more and more. One big issue was that we were finding people would come to us through affiliates just to check information on a product they'd already bought, so we were basically paying for customers to find out how to hook up their new VCR. We still have affiliates – our main one is Kelkoo – and we still bid for clicks on Google, but not as much as we used to. One of the things we were finding with the search engines is that, with our own search optimisation and because so many people were coming to our site, we were normally very high up the list just through normal searching. In our experience, particularly with Google, if people can see what they want in the main list, they don't look to the right-hand side of the page.

(b) Online sponsorship

Online sponsorship is not straightforward. It's not just a case of mirroring existing 'real-world' sponsorship arrangements in the 'virtual world' although this is a valid option. There are many additional opportunities for sponsorship online which can be sought out, even if you don't have a big budget at your disposal.

Ryan and Whiteman (2000) define online sponsorship as:

the linking of a brand with related content or context for the purpose of creating brand awareness and strengthening brand appeal in a form that is clearly distinguishable from a banner, button, or other standardized ad unit.

For the advertiser, online sponsorship has the benefit that their name is associated with an online brand that the site visitor is already familiar with. Sponsorship builds on this existing relationship and trust. Closely related is online 'co-branding' where there is an association between two brands.

4 Interactive advertising

How positively do you view interactive advertising as a communications tool? Even today, there are relatively few advertisers who have used interactive advertising. The first 468 by 68 pixels banner ad was placed on Hotwired in 1995 and the call to action 'Click here!' generated a clickthrough of 25%. Since then, the clickthrough rate (CTR) has fallen dramatically as many consumers suffer from 'banner blindness' – they ignore anything on a website that looks like an ad. The Doubleclick compilation of ad response (www.doubleclick.com) shows that today the average CTR is typically less than 0.1%, although video ads can receive a higher response rate. This low response rate, combined with relatively high costs of over £20 per thousands of ads served, has seemingly made some marketers prejudiced against interactive advertising. But we will see that there are many innovative approaches to interactive advertising which are proved to increase brand awareness and purchase intent. Given these limitations to banner ads, most media owners, digital marketing agencies and industry bodies now refer to 'interactive or display advertising', which is more suggestive of the range of options.

Media multiplier or halo effect
The role of one media channel on influencing sale or uplift in brand metrics. Commonly applied to online display advertising, where exposure to display ads may increase clickthrough rates when the consumer is later exposed to a brand through other media.

Online ads also seem to provide a **media multiplier or halo effect** which can help increase the response rates from other online media. For example, if a web user has been exposed to banner ads, this may increase their response to paid search ads and may also increase their likelihood of converting on a site since brand awareness and trust may be higher.

This effect is suggested by research reported by MAD (2007) in the travel market which involved asking respondents what their response to an online ad that appealed to them would be. Surely it would be a click? In fact, the results broke down as follows:

- Search for a general term relating to the advertisement (31%)
- Go straight to advertiser's site (29%)
- Search for the advertiser's name (26%)
- Click on banner to respond (26%)
- Visit a retail store (4%).

Of course, this methodology shows us reported behaviour rather than actual behaviour, but it is still significant that more than twice as many people are being driven to a search engine by banner advertising than by clicking directly on the banner! The research concludes that paid-search marketing needs to be optimised to work with banner advertising, by anticipating searches that are likely to be prompted by the banner and ensure a higher rank for search results. For example, a brand featuring a Cyprus holiday offer will generate generic search terms like 'package holiday Cyprus' rather than brand searches.

Abraham (2008) has also shown that online ads can stimulate offline sales. For one retailer with a turnover of $15 billion, their research showed that over a three-month period sales increased (compared to a control group) by 40% online and by 50% offline amongst people exposed to an online search marketing and display-ad campaign promoting the entire company. Because its baseline sales volumes are greater in physical stores than on the Internet, this retailer derived a great deal more revenue benefit offline than the percentages suggest.

Fundamentals of online advertising

Advertising on the web takes place when an advertiser pays to place advertising content on another website. The process usually involves **ad serving** from a different server from that on which the page is hosted (ads can be served on destination sites in a similar way).

Advertising is possible on a range of sites in order to drive traffic to an organisation's **destination site** or alternatively a **microsite** or nested ad-content on the media owner's site or on the destination site.

The purpose of interactive advertising

Robinson *et al.* (2007) have noted that the two primary goals of online display advertising are, first, using display adverts as a form of marketing communication used to raise brand awareness and, second, as a direct-response medium focussed on generating a response. Cartellieri *et al.* (1997) identify the following objectives:

- *Delivering content.* This is the typical case where a clickthrough on a banner advertisement leads through to a destination site giving more detailed information on an offer. This is where a direct response is sought.
- *Enabling transaction.* If a clickthrough leads through to a merchant such as a travel site or an online bookstore this may lead directly to a sale. A direct response is also sought here.
- *Shaping attitudes.* An advertisement that is consistent with a company brand can help build brand awareness. Building awareness is a key aspect of online advertising.
- *Soliciting response.* An advertisement may be intended to identify new leads or as a start for two-way communication. In these cases an interactive advertisement may encourage a user to type in an email address or other information.
- *Encouraging retention.* The advertisement may be placed as a reminder about the company and its service and may link through to on-site sales promotions such as a prize draw.

Interactive ad targeting options

Online ads can be targeted through placing ads:

1 **On a particular type of site (or part of site)** which has a specific visitor profile or type of content. So a car manufacturer can place ads on the home page of Handbag.com to appeal to a young female audience. A financial services provider can place an ad in the money section of the site to target those interested in these products. To reach large mass-market audiences, place an ad on a large portal home page such as MSN which has millions of

---

Ad serving

The term for displaying an advertisement on a website. Often the advertisement will be served from a web server different from the site on which it is placed.

Destination site

The site reached on clickthrough.

Microsite

A small-scale destination site reached on clickthrough which is part of the media owner's site.

visitors each day (sometimes known as a 'road-block' or 'takeover' if they take all ad inventory).

2 **To target a registered user's profile.** A business software provider could advertise on FT. com to target finance directors or IT managers.

3 **At a particular time of day or week.**

4 **Online behaviour. Behavioural ad targeting** is all about relevance – dynamically serving relevant content, messaging or an ad which matches the interests of a site visitor according to inferences about their characteristics. These inferences are made by anonymously tracking the different types of pages visited by a site user during a single visit to a site or across multiple sessions. Other aspects of the environment used by the visitor can also be determined, such as their location, browser and operating system.

Interactive ad formats

As well as the classic 468 by 60 pixel rotating GIF banner ad, which is decreasing in popularity, media owners now provide a choice of larger, richer formats which web users are more likely to notice. Research has shown that message association and awareness building are much higher for flash-based ads, rich-media ads and larger-format rectangles (multipurpose units, MPUs) and skyscrapers. Specific ad formats are available within the social networks, for example Facebook Engagement Ads, Twitter Promoted Tweets and YouTube Promoted videos.

Other online ad terms you will hear include '**interstitials**' (intermediate adverts before another page appears); the more common '**overlays**' which appear above content; and of course pop-up windows that are now less widely used because of their intrusion. Online advertisers face a constant battle with users who deploy pop-up blockers or less commonly ad-blocking software, but they will persist in using rich-media formats where they generate the largest response.

Robinson *et al.* (2007) conducted research on the factors which increased clickthrough response to banner ads. The main variables they (and previous studies they reference) include are:

- Banner size
- Message length
- Promotional incentive
- Animation
- Action phrase (commonly referred to as a call to action)
- Company brand/logo.

Media planning – deciding on the online/offline mix for advertising

This decision is typically taken by the media planner. The mix between online and offline spend should reflect consumers' media consumption and the cost-response effectiveness of each medium. But, depending on the agency used, they may play it safe by putting the ad spend into what they are familiar with and what may be most rewarding in terms of commission – offline media. Many **cross-media optimisation studies (XMOS)** have shown that the optimal online spend for low-involvement products is surprisingly high at 10–15% of total spend. Although this is not a large amount, it compares to previous spend levels below 1% for many organisations.

XMOS research is designed to help marketers and their agencies answer the (rather involved) question, 'What is the optimal mix of advertising vehicles across different media, in terms of frequency, reach and budget allocation, for a given campaign to achieve its marketing goals?'

The mix between online and offline spend is varied to maximise campaign metrics such as reach, brand awareness and purchase intent. Table 9.2 summarises the optimal mix identified for four famous brands. For example, Dove found that increasing the level of interactive advertising to 15% would have resulted in an increase in overall branding metrics of 8%. The proportion of online is small, but remember that many companies are spending less than 1% of their ad budgets online, meaning that offline frequency is too high and they may not be reaching many consumers.

Behavioural ad targeting

Enables an advertiser to target ads at a visitor as they move elsewhere on the site or return to the site, thus increasing the frequency or number of impressions served to an individual in the target market.

Interstitial ads

Ads that appear between one page and the next.

Overlay

Typically an animated ad that moves around the page and is superimposed on the website content.

Cross-media optimisation studies (XMOS)

Studies to determine the optimum spend across different media to produce the best results.

Table 9.2	Optimum media mix suggested by XMOS® studies		
Brand	**TV**	**Magazine**	**Online**
Colgate	75%	14%	11%
Kleenex	70%	20%	10%
Dove	72%	13%	15%
McDonald's	71%	16% (radio)	13%

Source: Interactive Advertising Bureau (www.iab.net). XMOS is a registered trademark of the IAB.

The reasons for using and increasing the significance of online in the media mix are similar to those for using any media mix as described by Sissors and Baron (2002):

- Extend reach (adding prospects not exposed by a single medium or other media).
- Flatten frequency distribution (if audience viewing TV ads is exposed too many times, there is a law of diminishing returns and it may be better to reallocate that budget to other media).
- To reach different kinds of audiences.
- To provide unique advantages in stressing different benefits based on the different characteristics of each medium.
- To allow different creative executions to be implemented.
- To add gross impressions if the other media are cost-efficient.
- Reinforce message by using different creative stimuli.

All of these factors, and the first three in particular, provide the explanation of why XMOS shows it is worthwhile to put double-digit percentages into online media.

5 Email marketing

When devising plans for email marketing communications, marketers need to plan for:

Outbound email marketing

Emails are sent to customers and prospects from an organisation.

- **outbound email marketing**, where email campaigns are used as a form of direct marketing to encourage trial and purchases and as part of a CRM dialogue;

Inbound email marketing

Management of emails from customers by an organisation.

- **inbound email marketing**, where emails from customers such as support enquiries are managed. These are often managed today in conjunction with chat and co-browsing sessions.

Despite the increase in spam such that the vast majority of emails are spam or viruses (most estimates exceed 80%), email can still drive good response levels; this is particularly the case with in-house lists, so email communications to customers through e-newsletters or periodic email blasts are today a vital communications technique for companies.

The main measures for evaluating email marketing are:

- *Delivery rate* – this excludes email 'bounces' – emails will bounce if the email address is no longer valid or a spam filter blocks the email. So, online marketers check their 'deliverability' to make sure their messages are not identified as 'false positives' by spam prevention software. Web-based email providers such as Hotmail and Yahoo! Mail have introduced standard authentication techniques known as Sender ID and Domain Keys which make sure the email broadcaster is who they say they are and doesn't spoof their address as many spammers do.
- *Open rate* – this is measured for HTML messages through downloaded images. It is an indication of how many customers open an email, but is not accurate since some users have preview panes in their email readers which load the message even if it is deleted without reading and some email readers such as Outlook Express now block images by default (this has resulted in a decline in open rates through time).

- *Clickthrough rate* – this is the number of people who click through on the email of those delivered (strictly unique clicks rather than total clicks). You can see that response rates are quite high at around 10%.

Mini case study 9.6 shows how an online intermediary has been able to launch a revolutionary service which now operates in several countries in Europe. It shows the importance of using strategic email communications effectively to engage customers as part of its retention strategy by targeting them more closely through a defined contact strategy and then integrating with the website booking system.

Opt-in email options for customer acquisition

For acquiring new visitors and customers to a site, there are three main options for email marketing. From the point of view of the recipient, these are:

1 **Cold email campaign.** In this case, the recipient receives an opt-in email from an organisation that has rented an email list from a consumer or a business email list provider. Although they have agreed to receive offers by email, the email is effectively cold.

2 **Co-branded email.** Here, the recipient receives an email with an offer from a company they have a reasonably strong affinity with. For example, the same credit card company could partner with a mobile service provider such as Vodafone and send out the offer to their customer (who has opted in to receive emails from third parties). Although this can be considered a form of cold email, it is warmer since there is a stronger relationship with one of the brands and the subject line and creative will refer to both brands.

3 **Third-party e-newsletter.** In this visitor acquisition option, a company publicises itself in a third-party e-newsletter. This could be in the form of an ad, sponsorship or PR (editorial) which links through to a destination site. These placements may be set up as part of an interactive advertising ad buy since many e-newsletters also have permanent versions on the website. Since e-newsletter recipients tend to engage with them by scanning the headlines or reading them if they have time, e-newsletter placements can be relatively cost-effective.

Viral marketing, which is discussed in the next section, also uses email as the mechanism for transferring messages. Email is most widely used as a prospect conversion and customer

---

Mini Case Study 9.6   Toptable uses CRM and email to engage customers online

Launched in February 2000, Toptable (toptable.co.uk, Figure 9.15) is now Europe's largest online restaurant booking and advisory service – a free service for customers to research, plan and book anything from a romantic dinner for two to a large corporate event. Toptable receives a fee for every booking and is on course to seat 3 million diners in 2008.

Challenges and objectives of email usage

While Toptable was already utilising an established industry solution for delivering and tracking its email campaigns, expert input was required to help achieve its aggressive CRM sales targets.

The existing CRM programme consisted of two weekly email sends that contained minimal segmentation and tailoring of content. As a result, in some cases open rates had fallen to as low as 10% and all the signs pointed to list fatigue as users lost interest in the communications.

Toptable chose to partner with Emailcenter in August 2007 to help them develop an industry-leading CRM programme and to move the communications strategy away from a mass broadcast model.

Key objectives included:

- Increase the frequency of bookings from regular customers
- Reactivate defected customers
- Encourage those users who had yet to make a booking to do so.

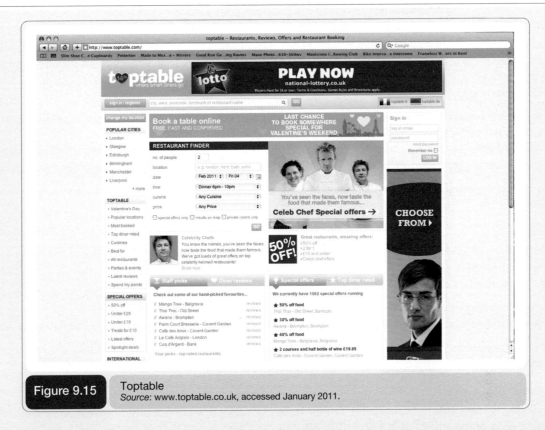

Figure 9.15 Toptable
Source: www.toptable.co.uk, accessed January 2011.

Emailcenter put a plan in place around their ROAD methodology to achieve these goals and continues to work closely with Toptable to project manage their entire CRM programme. ROAD is a model developed by Emailcenter that covers the four key areas that need to be addressed for a successful email marketing programme:

Applying ROAD to the Toptable CRM programme

Relevance

Prior to working with Emailcenter Toptable emails contained minimal personalisation. Each recipient received the same restaurant offers and reviews no matter where they lived or worked in the UK.

Using existing RSS feeds from the Toptable site Emailcenter automated the production of content containing offers, reviews and news items for each of their 300 locations. All Toptable have to do now for each email is change global elements such as subject lines, intro messages and advertising.

Not only did this see increases in performance (tailored emails have generated conversion rates over twice that of the generic versions), it enabled Toptable to offer a highly relevant email to all of their customers no matter where they are based in the UK.

Increasing the relevance of the content always improves the performance of an email programme. However, an additional tactic is to be relevant with the timing of the email.

An effective tactic was put in place that sent targeted triggered messages that replaced the newsletter to a number of segments including:

- Defectors – customers that made their last booking 6 weeks ago
- Lookers – customers that registered a month ago but have yet to make a booking.

Each segment had a series of emails that were delivered a week apart, each with ever improving offers. If a customer makes a booking from one of these emails they do not get any further emails in future weeks and resume receipt of the newsletter.

These emails were over 17 times more effective at reactivating customers and changing their booking behaviour than the newsletter. These triggered emails also helped increase the number of paid bookings from email activity by 26% per week, despite being less than 5% of the emails sent each week.

Optimisation

Continually reviewing the email campaigns and testing variables such as subject lines, from names, styles, content or timing enables Toptable to learn what works best for them and helps them maximise email performance.

Two main areas of testing are run:

- **Subject line tests** – 3 to 4 variants on subject lines are sent to a test file the night before, enabling them to identify the best-performing subject line for the next day's send.
- **Ad-hoc tests** – testing any variant that may have an impact on performance from changing the type of content, the number of offers, position of content, automated content vs manual content, frequency of send and timing.

The subject line tests alone show a deviation of around 2% points between the best and worst subject lines open rates.

Analysis

In order to identify whether progress towards the sales targets is being met and to isolate areas within the email programme which either require improvement or are succeeding, a range of custom reporting is carried out. These reports include:

- How does frequency of send impact on long-term booking rates?
- Analysis of generic newsletters versus tailored content and the impact on defection and reactivation rates

Other standard reports Toptable utilise from within Maxemail include the Heatmap report that shows visually where clients are clicking and comparison reports that make it easy to identify trends over time.

Deliverability

While deliverability was not considered a major issue previously it was discovered upon analysis that only around 65% of the emails were being delivered into the inbox due to their incumbent suppliers' sending reputation. More worrying, it was found that the bounce list contained a large number of addresses that were falsely classified as invalid due to a black listing bouncing them. Upon analysis of this bounce list and subsequent test sends the overall list size was increased by 25% by reactivating the emails.

For future sends through Maxemail Emailcenter took full ownership of deliverability issues. This involved:

- Set-up of SPF/Sender ID records
- Dedicated IP range for corporate domains and use of a shared IP for Hotmail for the ultimate IP configuration
- Using spam-checking tools and running test sends to major ISPs such as Hotmail and AOL using 'Inbox Seeding'
- White-listing and feedback loops set up with major ISPs.
- Within one month of the first delivery an inbox placement rate of 99.87% was achieved which has remained in place since.

Results

Since partnering with Emailcenter on their CRM activity Toptable have seen the following year-on-year performance increases across the board.

Bookings	Open rates	Click-thru rates	Delivery rates
+60%	+28.3%	+49.4%	+53.6%

Source: Adapted from Emailcenter (2008).

House list
A list of prospect and customer names, email addresses and profile information owned by an organisation.

retention tool using an opt-in or **house list** of prospects and customers who have given permission to an organisation to contact them. For example, Lastminute.com has built a house list of over 10 million prospects and customers across Europe. Successful email marketers adopt a strategic approach to email and develop a contact or touch strategy which plans the frequency and content of email communications (as explained in Chapters 4 and 6). For customer retention, a house list is built where email is used to communicate to existing customers.

Social media marketing

Social media marketing
Monitoring and facilitating customer–customer interaction and participation throughout the web to encourage positive engagement with a company and its brands. Interactions may occur on a company site, social networks and other third-party sites.

Viral marketing
Email is used to transmit a promotional message to another potential customer.

Social media marketing, covered in the 'Focus on' section earlier in this chapter, can often be assisted through **viral marketing** approaches which harness the network effect of the Internet and can be effective in reaching a large number of people rapidly in the same way as a natural virus or a computer virus. It is effectively an online form of word-of-mouth communications. Smith and Chaffey (2005) say ideally viral marketing is a clever idea, a game, a shocking idea, or a highly informative idea which makes compulsive viewing. It can be a video clip, TV ad, cartoon, funny picture, poem, song, political message, or news item. It is so amazing, it makes people want to pass it on. This is a challenge for commercial companies since, to be successful, it will need to challenge convention and this may not fit well with the brand.

To make a viral campaign effective, Justin Kirby of viral marketing specialists DMC (www.dmc.co.uk) suggests that three things are needed (Kirby, 2003):

1 **Creative material – the 'viral agent'.** This includes the creative message or offer and how it is spread (text, image, video).
2 **Seeding.** Identifying websites, blogs or people to send email to start the virus spreading.
3 **Tracking.** To monitor the effect, to assess the return from the cost of developing the viral agent and seeding.

With the widespread adoption of high-speed broadband in many countries, rich media experiences are increasingly used to engage customers with the hope they will have a 'viral effect', i.e. they will be discussed online or offline and more people will become aware of or interact with the brand campaign.

Offline marketing communications

Offline communications will never disappear – they are effective at reaching an audience to encourage them to visit a site, but are also useful as a way of having an impact or explaining a complex proposition, as Mini case study 9.7 shows.

| Mini Case Study 9.7 | Offline communications vital for finding the perfect partner at Match.com |

UK-based online dating company Match.com has over 1.5 million members and in 2004 was responsible for 200,000 marriages around the world. Match.com and partner company uDate.com compete against Yahoo! Personals, Dating Direct, traditional players and a host of smaller players. Given the intense competition, Samantha Bedford, UK MD believes it is essential to invest in offline communications for continued growth. In Autumn 2005, Match.com spent over £3 million on a TV advertising campaign since they wanted to generate brand awareness, given that they estimated that by 2008 the value of the online dating market would double. In addition to achieving reach and brand awareness, offline advertising is important because it enables Match.com to communicate a fairly complex message to potential customers. Focus groups showed that many singles felt they didn't need an online dating service and didn't realise how Match.com could help as part of the overall dating experience.

Source: New Media Age (2005b).

Table 9.3	Summary of the strengths and weaknesses of different communications channels for promoting an online presence	

Promotion technique	Main strengths	Main weaknesses
1a Search engine optimisation (SEO)	Highly targeted, relatively low cost of PPC. High traffic volumes if effective. Considered credible by searchers	Intense competition, may compromise look of site. Complexity of changes to ranking algorithm
1b Pay-per-click (PPC) marketing	Highly targeted with controlled cost of acquisition. Extend reach through content network	Relatively costly in competitive sectors and low volume compared with SEO
1c Trusted feed	Update readily to reflect changes in product lines and prices	Relatively costly, mainly relevant for e-retailers
2 Online PR	Relatively low cost and good targeting. Can assist with SEO through creation of backlinks	Identifying online influencers and setting up partnerships can be time-consuming. Need to monitor comments on third-party sites
3a Affiliate marketing	Payment is by results (e.g. 10% of sale or leads goes to referring site)	Costs of payments to affiliate networks for set-up and management fees. Changes to ranking algorithm may affect volume from affiliates
3b Online sponsorship	Most effective if low-cost, long-term co-branding arrangement with synergistic site	May increase awareness, but does not necessarily lead directly to sales
4 Interactive advertising	Main intention to achieve visit, i.e. direct-response model. But also role in branding through media multiplier effect	Response rates have declined historically because of banner blindness
5 Email marketing	Push medium – can't be ignored in user's inbox. Can be used for direct-response link to website. Integrates as a response mechanism with direct mail	Requires opt-in for effectiveness. Better for customer retention than for acquisition? Inbox cut-through – message diluted amongst other emails. Limits on deliverability
6 Social media and viral marketing	With effective viral agent possible to reach a large number at relatively low cost. Influencers in social networks significant	Difficult to create powerful viral concepts and control targeting. Risks damaging brand since unsolicited messages may be received
Traditional offline advertising (TV, print, etc.)	Larger reach than most online techniques. Greater creativity possible, leading to greater impact	Targeting arguably less easy than online. Typically high cost of acquisition

Table 9.3 gives a summary of the strengths and weaknesses of the digital media channels discussed in this chapter (numbers reference the different boxes in Figure 1.8).

Customer retention management

For an e-commerce site, customer retention has two distinct goals:

1 To retain customers of the organisation (repeat customers).
2 To keep customers using the online channel (repeat visits).

These are similar to the two aims of customer acquisition as described in a previous section. Ideally marketing communications should address both aims.

Maintaining online customer relationships is difficult. Laurie Windham (2001) says:

> *That's what's so scary about customer retention in the online space. We've created this empowered, impatient customer who has a short attention span, a lot of choices, and a low barrier to switching.*

To create long-term online customer relationships that build on acquisition, to retain and extend, we need to analyse the drivers of satisfaction amongst these e-customers, since satisfaction drives loyalty and loyalty drives profitability. The relationship is shown in Figure 9.16. The objective of marketers is to drive customers up the curve towards the zone of affection. However, it is worth remembering that the majority are not in that zone and to achieve retention marketers must understand why customers defect or are indifferent.

It follows from Figure 9.16 that we need to understand different factors that affect loyalty. The type of approach that can be taken is highlighted by Reichheld and Schefter (2000). They reported that Dell Computer has created a customer experience council that has researched key loyalty drivers, identified measures to track these and put in place an action plan to improve loyalty (Table 9.4).

Since quality of service is so crucial in determining satisfaction and loyalty, see the '*Focus on* Excelling in e-commerce service quality' section later in this chapter.

Now let us consider key digital marketing tools that help retain customers. Repeat visits can be generated by a variety of means and brainstorming sessions can help generate these. Often it may simply be the expedient of regularly updated market and product or technical information that helps customers perform their day-to-day work. Such information can be delivered through extranets such as Dell Premier or through personalisation services such as that described for RS Components. Information to help people perform their work is the proposition of the vertical portals such as industry-specific sites. Online communities are popular for both consumer and business markets since users can discuss topical issues or ask for answers to their queries. For example, the UK Net Marketing Group at www.chinwag.com discusses

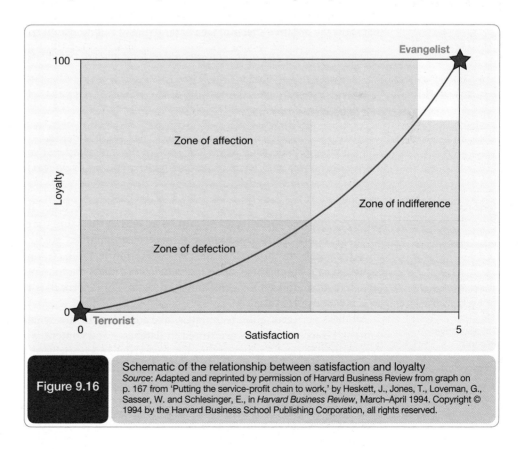

Figure 9.16	Schematic of the relationship between satisfaction and loyalty
	Source: Adapted and reprinted by permission of Harvard Business Review from graph on p. 167 from 'Putting the service-profit chain to work,' by Heskett, J., Jones, T., Loveman, G., Sasser, W. and Schlesinger, E., in *Harvard Business Review*, March–April 1994. Copyright © 1994 by the Harvard Business School Publishing Corporation, all rights reserved.

Table 9.4	Relationship between loyalty drivers and measures to assess their success at Dell Computer

Loyalty drivers	Summary metric
1 Order fulfilment	Ship to target. Percentage that ship on time exactly as the customer specified.
2 Product performance	Initial field incident rate – the frequency of problems experienced by customers.
3 Post-sale service and support	On-time, first-time fix – the percentage of problems fixed on the first visit by a service rep who arrives at the time promised.

Source: Adapted and reprinted by permission of *Harvard Business Review* from information on pp. 105–13 from 'Your secret weapon on the web', by Reichheld, F. and Schefter, P., in *Harvard Business Review*, July–August 2000. Copyright © 2000 by the Harvard Business School Publishing Corporation, all rights reserved.

the benefits of new technologies such as mobile commerce and recommends suppliers of Internet services. Many such communities work because they are independent of suppliers, so it may be difficult to introduce these types of facilities on to a corporate site. Finally, traditional sales promotion techniques translate well to the Internet. RS Components use Product of the Week or Month to discount some items and offer competitions and prize draws to encourage repeat visits. These are often publicised in offline mail-outs to encourage repeat visits.

Personalisation and mass customisation

The potential power of personalisation is suggested by these quotes from Evans *et al.* (2000) that show the negative effects of lack of targeting of traditional direct mail:

Don't like unsolicited mail…haven't asked for it and I'm not interested.

(Female, 25–34)

Most isn't wanted, it's not relevant and just clutters up the table…you have to sort through it to get to the 'real mail'.

(Male, 45–54)

It's annoying to be sent things that you are not interested in. Even more annoying when they phone you up…If you wanted something you would go and find out about it.

(Female, 45–54)

Personalisation
Delivering individualised content through web pages or email.

Mass customisation
Delivering customised content to groups of users through web pages or email.

Collaborative filtering
Profiling of customer interest coupled with delivery of specific information and offers, often based on the interests of similar customers.

Personalisation and mass customisation can be used to tailor information and opt-in email can be used to deliver it to add value and at the same time remind the customer about a product. 'Personalisation' and 'mass customisation' are terms that are often used interchangeably. In the strict sense, personalisation refers to customisation of information requested by a site customer at an *individual* level. **Mass customisation** involves providing tailored content to a *group* with similar interests. This approach is sometimes also referred to as '**collaborative filtering**'.

All these personalisation techniques take advantage of the dynamic possibilities of web content. Users' preferences are stored in databases and content is taken from a database. Personalisation can be achieved through several dynamic variables including:

- the customers' preferences
- the date or time
- particular events
- the location.

Personalisation can also be used to offer innovative services. Online bookseller BOL (www.bol.com) allows customers to choose their favourite parts from different types of travel guides, perhaps history from the Rough Guides and maps from Lonely Planet, but excluding night clubs and restaurants. The personalised book can then be printed on demand on the customer's printer.

A more typical personalisation service is that provided by the portals such as Google, Yahoo! and NetVibes. These enable users to configure their home page so that it delivers the information they are most interested in: perhaps their regional weather, the results from their soccer team and the prices of shares they have purchased.

Turning to negative aspects of personalisation, there are two chief difficulties. First, cost, for the reasons explained in the next section and, second, it may act as a barrier to users. For example, some personalisation requires the user to log in. This may be a problem if a customer has mislaid a password. Equally, for a new visitor to the site the need to apply for a password can be offputting and a customer may disappear, never to return. Effective personalisation will still enable a new visitor to view a good deal of content even if they do not have a password. Use of *cookies* can avoid the need for the customer to actively log in, with this occurring automatically.

Creating personalisation

Personalisation of web content is much more expensive than developing static content, since it requires database integration and specialised software tools such as Omniture Test and Target (now part of Adobe Marketing Cloud), which recognises visitors when they return and then accesses and displays the relevant information from a database.

Mini case study 9.8 shows how implementation of personalisation can result in more relevant messages and improved response rates.

Extranets

Extranets were introduced in Chapter 3. Since they require a user to log in they signify differential services through premium content and services. Many options are possible. A dynamic example of using an extranet is the use of the web to host online events that mirror traditional events such as seminars, trade shows and user group conferences, virtual seminars with a guest speaker by webcast, virtual trade shows where exhibitors, seminar speakers and

---

Mini Case Study 9.8	HSBC uses personalisation to deliver tailored propositions

When HSBC Bank International (HBIB) refined its website it wanted to use personalisation with the goal of delivering specific offers and servicing to different customer segments and encourage customers to move into more valuable segments. This would enable it to capitalise on sales opportunities that would otherwise be missed. *New Media Age* (2007) reported that this was a challenge since '60% of total weekly visitors to offshore.hsbc.com log on to the internet banking service, HSBC wanted to market to them effectively while they were engaged in this task, disrupting their banking experience without infuriating them'. Business rules were created to serve promotions dependent on the type of content accessed and the level of balance in the customer's account.

HSBC was successful in meeting its goals and the results show the benefit of personalised, targeted banners. On average, *New Media Age* (2007) reported that the new banners had an 87.5% higher clickthrough rate than non-personalised banners (6.88% versus 3.67%). The number of savings accounts opened via Internet banking increased by 30% (based on six months pre- and post-launch). And the number of non-Premier customers upgrading to Premier accounts (requiring a balance of £60,000 or more) increased by 86% (based on four weeks pre- and post-launch of the targeted banners).

delegates are linked by the web. Dell Computer has a special brand variant known as Dell Premier that can be used to provide value-added services for key accounts. Other traditional retention methods such as loyalty schemes and sales promotions translate well to the online environment.

The use of extranets presents a barrier to entry, particularly if users lose their passwords. To limit this effect RS Components sends out password reminders to help retention. A Dutch insurer combined online and offline techniques to use an extranet to deliver mass customisation. Existing customers were divided into six segments and then contacted through a direct mail campaign. Members of each segment were given one of six passwords, so that when they accessed the extranet there were six different versions of content for the website giving product suggestions and offers consistent with the segment. Extranets provide good traceability of marketing outcomes and tagging of visitors. In this case the effectiveness of the campaign in terms of response rate from the email and conversion to sales could also be monitored for different segments.

Opt-in email

Opt-in email is vital in communicating the retention offers either through regular email communications such as a newsletter or higher-impact irregular email communications such as details of a product launch. Remember that email has the power of traditional push communication. It enables a targeted message to be pushed out to a customer to inform and remind and they are certain to view it within their email inbox; even if it is only deleted, it cannot be ignored.

Spam
Unsolicited email
(usually bulk-mailed and
untargeted).

Despite its potential, use of email for marketing has negative connotations due to **spam** and privacy concerns (as discussed in Chapter 3), so it's essential that email marketing is permission-based.

Once an email address has been collected, managers must plan the frequency of email communications. Options include:

- *Regular newsletter type.* For example, once a day, once a week, once a month. It is best if customers are given choice about the frequency.
- *Event-related.* These tend to be less regular and are sent out perhaps every three or six months when there is news of a new product launch or an exceptional offer.
- *Email sequence.* Software can be purchased to send out a series of emails. For example, after subscription to a trial version of an online magazine, emails will be sent out at 3, 10, 25 and 28 days to encourage a subscription before the trial lapses.

Techniques for managing customer activity and value

Within the online customer base of an organisation, there will be customers who have different levels of activity in usage of online services or in sales. A good example is a bank – some customers may use the online account once a week, others much less frequently and some not at all. Figure 9.17 illustrates the different levels of activity.

To improve the adoption of 'web self-service' which helps reduce costs it is important to define measures which indicate activity levels and then develop tactics to increase activity levels through more frequent use. Objectives and corresponding tactics can be set for:

- Increasing number of *new users per* month and annually (separate objectives will be set for existing bank customers and new bank customers) through promoting online services to drive visitors to the website.
- Increasing % of *active users* (an appropriate threshold can be used – for some other organisations it could be set at 7, 30 or 90 days). Using direct communications such as email, personalised website messages, direct mail and phone communications to new, dormant and inactive users increases the percentage of active users.

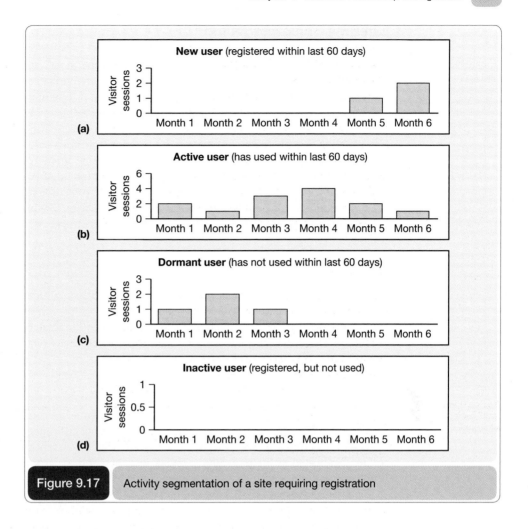

Figure 9.17 | Activity segmentation of a site requiring registration

- Decreasing % of *dormant users* (were once new or active, could be sub-categories), but have not used within a time period to be classified as active.
- Decreasing % of *inactive users* (or non-activated) users. These are those who signed up for a service such as online banking and username was issued, but they have not used the service.

You can see that corresponding strategies can be developed for each of these strategies.

Another key metric, in fact the key retention metric for e-commerce sites, refers to repeat business. The importance of retention rate metrics was highlighted by Agrawal *et al.* (2001). The main retention metrics they mention and show the impact on profitability are:

- *Repeat-customer conversion rate* – how many first-time customers purchase a second product?
- *Repeat-customer base* – the proportion of the customer base who have made repeat purchases.
- *Number of transactions per repeat customer* – this indicates the stage of development of the customer in the relationship (another similar measure is number of product categories purchased).
- *Revenue per transaction of repeat customer* – this is a proxy for lifetime value since it gives average order value.

Lifetime-value modelling

Lifetime value (LTV)
Lifetime value is the total net benefit that a customer or group of customers will provide a company over their total relationship with the company.

An appreciation of **lifetime value (LTV)** is also key to the theory and practice of customer relationship management. However, while the term is often used, calculation of LTV is not straightforward, so many organisations do not calculate it. Lifetime value is defined as the total net benefit that a customer or group of customers will provide a company over their total relationship with a company. Modelling is based on estimating the income and costs associated with each customer over a period of time and then calculating the net present value in current monetary terms using a discount rate value applied over the period.

There are different degrees of sophistication in calculating LTV. These are indicated in Figure 9.18. Option 1 is a practical way or approximate proxy for future LTV, but the true LTV is the future value of the customer at an individual level. Lifetime-value modelling at a segment level (4) is vital within marketing since it answers the question:

How much can I afford to invest in acquiring a new customer?

Lifetime-value analysis enables marketers to:

- Plan and measure investment in customer acquisition programmes
- Identify and compare critical target segments
- Measure the effectiveness of alternative customer retention strategies
- Establish the true value of a company's customer base
- Make decisions about products and offers
- Make decisions about the value of introducing new e-CRM technologies.

Figure 9.19 gives an example of how LTV can be used to develop a CRM strategy for different customer groups. Four main types of customers are indicated by their current and future value as bronze, silver, gold and platinum. Distinct customer groupings (circles) are identified according to their current value (as indicated by current profitability) and future value as indicated by lifetime-value calculations. Each of these groups will have a customer profile signature based on their demographics, so this can be used for customer selection. Different strategies are developed for different customer groups within the four main value groupings. Some bronze customers such as Groups A and B realistically do not have development potential and are typically unprofitable, so the aim is to reduce costs in communications and if they do not remain as customers, this is acceptable. Some bronze customers such as Group C may have potential for growth, so for these the strategy is to extend their purchases. Silver customers are targeted with customer extension offers and gold customers are extended where possible although these have relatively little growth potential. Platinum

Figure 9.18   Different representations of lifetime-value calculation

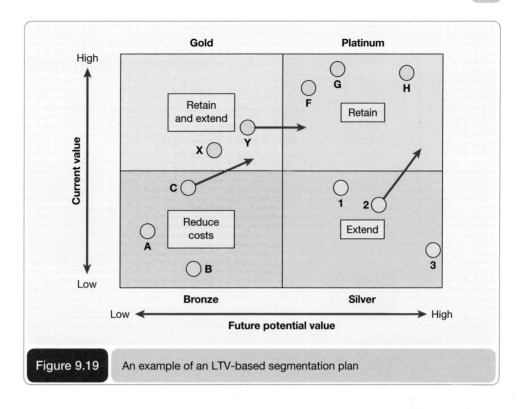

Figure 9.19 An example of an LTV-based segmentation plan

customers are the best customers, so it is important to understand the communication preferences of these customers and not to over-communicate unless there is evidence that they may defect.

Excelling in e-commerce service quality

In the virtual world customer service is a key difference between brands. Jevons and Gabbot (2000) explain: '*the first-hand experience of the brand is a more powerful token of trust than the perception of the brand*'.

Research across industry sectors suggests that the quality of service is a key determinant of loyalty. Feinberg *et al.* (2000) report that if reasons why customers leave a company are considered, over 68% leave because of 'poor service experience', with other factors such as price (10%) and product issues (17%) less significant.

Mini Case Study 9.9 Zappos delivers customer happiness

Zappos is a US online clothing retailer often referred to as a pioneer in online marketing. Tony Hsieh, CEO of Zappos, puts its success down to a customer-centric approach. He says simply: '*We pay more attention to our customers*'. He explains, '*People may not remember exactly what you did or what you said, but they will always remember how you made them feel*'. Tony's summary of the evolution of the Zappos brand has seen it go from simply having a strong customer focus to being really passionate about how it makes their customers feel (Figure 9.20):

1999 Selection

2003 Customer Service

Figure 9.20	Zappos Family Core Values *Source*: www.zappos.com, Zappos IP, Inc.

2005 Culture and Core Values as our platform

2007 Personal Emotional Connection

2009 Delivering Happiness

Overall, the approach seems to be successful. In 2009, Amazon purchased Zappos for $1.2bn. Here is our summary of the five success factors we can take from Zappos' success which can be applied to other businesses:

1 Customers come back, order more and more often.
    On any given day, about 75% of purchases from Zappos are from returning customers.
    ● Repeat customers order >2.5x more in the following 12 months.
    ● Repeat customers spend more.
2 Make it easy for customers to build your brand.
    ● Superior experience drives word-of-mouth, so do the unexpected.
    ● Remove the risk of purchase and make it easy to return product for free.
    ● Fast, accurate fulfilment is worth talking about.
    ● Deliver an 'above and beyond' customer service.
    ● Drive people to the phone, be contactable and be open.
3 Talk to people!
    ● 'The telephone is one of the best branding devices available.'
    ● Take time to talk to people properly.
    ● At Zappos there are no call times and no sales-based performance goals for sales reps.
    ● Zappos will also pay you $2,000 to quit, so only the best people who enjoy the job stay.
    ● The Culture Book makes it clear how Zappos does business and even underpins performance management.
4 Build a culture that envelops customers and internal staff.
    Zappos has 'committable core values' that are clear, exciting and simple.
    ● It doesn't matter what your core values are as long as you commit to them and get internal alignment.
    ● Commit to a culture of transparency: 'An Ask Anything Culture'.
    ● Zapposinsights.com focusses on lifting the lid for customers and future employees.

5 Have a vision . . .

   'Whatever you're thinking, think bigger', comments Tony.

   ● Does your company vision have real meaning? Without it, there little chance of achieving any of the above.

   ● 'What would you be passionate about doing for 10 years even if you never made a dime?'

Source: Hsieh (2010).

Improving online service quality

Delivering service quality in e-commerce can be assessed through reviewing existing frameworks for determining levels of service quality. Those most frequently used are based on the concept of a 'service-quality gap' that exists between the customers' *expected* level of service (from previous experience and word-of-mouth communication) and their perception of the *actual* level of service delivery.

Parasuraman *et al.* (1985) suggested that these dimensions of service quality on which consumers judge expected and delivered service-quality levels are:

● tangibles – the physical appearance and visual appeal of facilities;
● reliability – the ability to perform the service consistently and accurately;
● responsiveness – a willingness to help customers and provide prompt service;
● assurance – the knowledge and courtesy of employees and their ability to convey trust and confidence;
● empathy – providing caring, individualised attention.

Note that there has been heated dispute about the validity of this SERVQUAL instrument framework (Parasuraman *et al.*, 1985) in determining service quality, see for example Cronin and Taylor (1992). Despite this it is still instructive to apply these dimensions of service quality to customer service on the web. We will now review each dimension of SERVQUAL.

Tangibles

It can be suggested that the tangibles dimension is influenced by ease of use and visual appeal based on the structural and graphic design of the site. The importance of these factors to consumers is indicated by a 1999 study by Forrester Research of 8,600 US consumers that found that the main reason for returning to a site were high-quality content (75%), ease of use (66%), speed to download (58%) and frequency of update (54%); these were the most important aspects of website quality mentioned.

Reliability

The reliability dimension is dependent on the availability of the website, or in other words, how easy it is to connect to the website as a user.

Reliability of email response is also a key issue; Chaffey and Edgar (2000) report on a survey of 361 UK websites across different sectors. Of those in the sample, 331 (or 92%) were accessible at the time of the survey and, of these, 299 provided an email contact point. Email enquiries were sent to all of these 299 websites; of these, 9 undeliverable mail messages were received. It can be seen that at the time of the survey, service availability is certainly not universal.

Responsiveness

The same survey showed that responsiveness was poor overall: of the 290 successfully delivered emails, a 62% response rate occurred within a 28-day period. For over a third of companies there was zero response!

Of the companies that did respond, there was a difference in responsiveness (excluding immediately delivered automated responses) from 8 minutes to over 19 working days! While the mean overall was 2 working days, 5 hours and 11 minutes, the median across all sectors (on the basis of the fastest 50% of responses received) was 1 working day and 34 minutes. The median result suggests that response within one working day represents best practice and could form the basis for consumer expectations.

Responsiveness is also indicated by the performance of the website – the time it takes for a page request to be delivered to the user's browser as a page impression. Since there is a wide variability in the delivery of information and hence service quality from web servers hosted at ISPs, companies should be careful to monitor this and specify levels of quality with suppliers in service level agreements (SLAs). Zona Research (1999) conducted an analysis that suggests that \$4.35 billion may be lost in e-commerce revenues due to customer 'bailout' when customers are unwilling to wait for information to download. The report notes that many customers may not be prepared to wait longer than eight seconds!

Effective fulfilment is also an essential part of responsiveness (as explained in Chapter 7).

Assurance

In an email context, assurance can best be considered as the quality of response. In the survey reported by Chaffey and Edgar (2000), of 180 responses received, 91% delivered a personalised human response with 9% delivering an automated response which did not address the individual enquiry; 40% of responses answered or referred to all three questions with 10% answering two questions, and 22% one. Overall, 38% did not answer any of the specific questions posed!

A further assurance concern of e-commerce websites is the privacy and security of customer information. A company that subscribes to the Internet Shopping Is Safe – ISIS (www. imrg.org/is) – merchant accreditation or TRUSTe principles (www.truste.org) will provide better assurance than one that does not. The following actions can be suggested to achieve assurance in an e-commerce site:

1 Provide clear and effective privacy statements
2 Follow privacy and consumer protection guidelines in all local markets
3 Make security of customer data a priority
4 Use independent certification bodies
5 Emphasise the excellence of service quality in all communications.

Empathy

Although it might be considered that empathy requires personal human contact, it can still be achieved, to an extent, through email. Chaffey and Edgar (2000) report that of the responses received, 91% delivered a personalised human response, with 29% passing on the enquiry within their organisation. Of these 53, 23 further responses were received within the 28-day period and 30 (or 57%) of passed-on queries were not responded to further.

Provision of personalisation facilities is also an indication of the empathy provided by the website, but more research is needed as to customers' perception of the value of web pages that are dynamically created to meet a customer's information needs.

An alternative approach for considering how service quality can be delivered through e-commerce is to consider how the site provides customer service at the different stages of the buying decision shown in Figure 9.4. Thus quality service is not only dependent on how well the purchase itself is facilitated, but also on how easy it is for customers to select products and on after-sales service, including fulfilment quality. The Epson UK site (www. epson.co.uk) illustrates how the site can be used to help in all stages of the buying process. Interactive tools are available to help users select a particular printer, diagnose and solve faults, and technical brochures can be downloaded. Feedback is solicited on how well these services meet customers' needs.

These SERVQUAL elements have been applied to online banking by Jun and Cai (2001) in a detailed study. This supports the importance of the original SERVQUAL elements in an online setting. For example, it highlights the importance of a timely, accurate response to customer queries. It also uncovers a particular feature of online service – that customers expect to see a continuous improvement to site services, and suggests their satisfaction will be reduced if positive changes are not made.

In summary, it can be suggested that for managers wishing to apply a framework such as SERVQUAL in an e-commerce context there are three stages appropriate to managing the process.

1 **Understanding expectations.** The SERVQUAL framework can be used with market research and benchmarking of other sites (as described in Chapter 12), to understand customer requirements such as responsiveness and empathy. Scenarios can also be used to identify the customer expectations of using services on a site.

2 **Setting and communicating the service promise.** Once expectations are understood, marketing communications can be used to inform the customers of the level of service. This can be achieved through customer service guarantees or promises. It is better to under-promise than over-promise. A book retailer that delivers the book in two days when three days were promised will earn the customer's loyalty better than the retailer that promises one day, but delivers in two! The enlightened company may also explain what it will do if it does not meet its promises – will the customer be recompensed? The service promise must also be communicated internally and combined with training to ensure that the service is delivered.

3 **Delivering the service promise.** Finally, commitments must be delivered through on-site service, support from employees and physical fulfilment. If not, online credibility is destroyed and a customer may never return.

Debate 9.2

Will software replace 'humanware'?

'Some remote customer service contacts will always require personal, human interaction rather than automated electronic responses.'

As a conclusion to this section review Mini case study 9.10, which shows how one company delivers service quality online.

Mini Case Study 9.10　Online customer service at Barclays

In 2005, Barclays deployed web self-service to answer customers' question online and reduce the 100,000 monthly calls to its helpdesk. Accessible on every page, via 'Ask a question', the Barclays solution allows customers to ask questions and receive meaningful, accurate answers on any subject from credit card offers to information about how the company credit scores.

In the first 12 months, 'Ask a question' was used by 350,000 customers and answered more than half a million questions. Only 8% of customers escalated through to the call centre, pointing to high levels of customer satisfaction and resulting in improvements to call-centre efficiency and quality of service. In 2007, more than 2 million customers used 'Ask a question' to find answers to their questions.

'Ask a question' is providing invaluable insight at the critical decision-making process about what concerns customers have and what products are of interest. For example, it identified a higher demand from personal banking customers for making foreign currency payments than was previously known to Barclays. This information is being used to inform the bank about customer trends and requirements, and for creating customer-driven website content.

It was apparent that website visitors who ask questions through web self-service were more than casual browsers but customers with genuine buying requirements. There was potential to increase sales conversion by putting the right information and product offer in front of these customers based on what they were asking about. 'Ask a question' was enhanced to incorporate ad-serving, which serves up targeted advertising and sales promotions in response to questions asked by customers via the bank's website. The adverts change automatically depending on their relevance to customer questions, or to products and services Barclays wants to promote. For example, when customers ask questions about foreign currency accounts, 'Ask a question' will provide a specific answer and display adverts for travel insurance, the use of debit cards abroad and foreign mortgages. As well as promoting products directly relevant to the customers' search, ad serving is used to cross-promote related products and services. These ads provide customers with an appealing call to action that speeds sales completion and increases response rates.

Advertising products alongside search results is producing high conversion rates with 12% of customers responding to a product advertisement. 'Ask a question' is also improving usability, allowing customers to access all of the content relevant to them from a single click or question. By integrating ad serving with 'Ask a question', Barclays have been able to achieve high levels of behavioural targeting that have previously only been available through expensive and complicated website analytic tools. Because advertisements and promotions are served in response to customer enquiries, there is no need for the system to log or track vast amounts of historical customer data to analyse and predict customer behaviour in order to deliver targeted information. This cuts the complexity of delivering targeted information and increases sales.

Source: Transversal (2008) UK companies fail the multichannel customer service test. Research report, March.

Customer extension

Customer extension
Deepening the relationship with the customer through increased interaction and product transactions.

Customer extension has the aim of increasing the lifetime value of the customer to the company by encouraging cross-sales, for example an Egg credit card customer may be offered the option of a loan or a deposit account. When a customer returns to a website this is an opportunity for cross-selling and such offers can be communicated. Direct email is also an excellent way for informing a customer about other company products and it is also useful in encouraging repeat visits by publicising new content or promotions. Email is vitally important to achieving online CRM as it is a push medium where the customer can be reminded why they should visit the website.

Share of wallet or share of customer
The proportion of customer expenditure in a particular category that belongs to a single customer.

Many companies are now only proactively marketing to favoured customers. Seth Godin (1999) says, *'Focus on share of customer, not market share – fire 70 per cent of your customers and watch your profits go up!'* One UK financial services provider has analysed characteristics of high-churn-rate customers, and when a new prospect fitting this profile contacts the call centre they are actively discouraged. Using these techniques it is possible to increase share of customer.

Advanced online segmentation and targeting techniques

The most sophisticated segmentation and targeting (see Chapter 8 for an introduction) schemes for extension are often used by e-retailers, who have detailed customer profiling information and purchase history data as they seek to increase customer lifetime value through encouraging increased use of online services over time. However, the general principles of this approach can also be used by other types of companies online. The segmentation and targeting approach used by e-retailers is based on five main elements which in effect are layered on top of each other. The number of options used, and so the sophistication of the approach, will depend on resources available, technology capabilities and opportunities afforded by the list:

1 **Identify customer life cycle groups.** Figure 9.21 illustrates this approach. As visitors use online services they can potentially pass through seven or more stages. Once companies

Figure 9.21   Customer life cycle segmentation

have defined these groups and set up the customer relationship management infrastructure to categorise customers in this way, they can then deliver targeted messages, either by personalised on-site messaging or through emails that are triggered automatically due to different rules.

2 **Identify customer profile characteristics.** This is a traditional segmentation based on the type of customer. For B2C e-retailers it will include age, sex and geography. For B2B companies, it will include size of company and the industry sector or application they operate in.

3 **Identify behaviour in response and purchase.** As customers progress through the life cycle shown in Figure 9.21, though analysis of the database, they will be able to build up a detailed response and purchase history which considers the details of recency, frequency, monetary value and category of products purchased. This approach, which is known as 'RFM or FRAC analysis', is reviewed below. See Case study 9.1 for how Tesco target their online customers.

4 **Identify multichannel behaviour (channel preference).** Regardless of the enthusiasm of the company for online channels, some customers will prefer using online channels and others will prefer traditional channels. This will, to an extent, be indicated by RFM and response analysis since customers with a preference for online channels will be more responsive and will make more purchases online. Customers that prefer online channels can be targeted mainly by online communications such as email, while customers who prefer traditional channels can be targeted by traditional communications such as direct mail or phone. This is 'right-channelling' (introduced in Chapter 5).

5 **Tone and style preference.** In a similar manner to channel preference, customers will respond differently to different types of message. Some may like a more rational appeal, in which case a detailed email explaining the benefits of the offer may work best. Others will prefer an emotional appeal based on images and with warmer, less formal copy. Sophisticated companies will test for this in customers or infer it using profile characteristics and response behaviour and then develop different creative treatments accordingly. Companies that use polls can potentially use this to infer style preferences.

To summarise this section, read Mini case study 9.11, which illustrates the combination of these different forms of communication.

Mini Case Study 9.11	Euroffice segment office supplies purchasers using 'touch marketing funnel' approach

Euroffice (www.euroffice.co.uk) targets small and mid-sized companies. According to George Karibian, CEO, 'getting the message across effectively required segmentation' to engage different people in different ways. The office sector is fiercely competitive, with relatively little loyalty since company purchasers will often simply buy on price. However, targeted incentives can be used to reward or encourage buyers' loyalty. Rather than manually developing campaigns for each segment, which is time-consuming, Euroffice mainly uses an automated event-based targeting approach based on the system identifying the stage at which a consumer is in the life cycle, i.e. how many products they have purchased and the types of product within their purchase history. Karibian calls this a 'touch marketing funnel approach', i.e. the touch strategy is determined by customer segmentation and response. Three main groups of customers are identified in the life cycle and these are broken down further according to purchase category. Also layered on this segmentation is breakdown into buyer type – are they a small home-user, an operations manager at a mid-size company or a purchasing manager at a larger company? Each will respond to different promotions.

The first group, at the top of the funnel and the largest are 'Group 1: Trial customers' who have made one or two purchases. For the first group, Euroffice believes that creating impulse-buying through price promotions is most important. These will be based on categories purchased in the past. The second group, 'Group 2: The nursery', have made three to eight purchases. A particular issue, as with many e-retailers, is encouraging customers from the third to fourth purchase; there is a more significant drop-out at this point which the company uses marketing to control. Karibian says: '*When they get to group two, it's about creating frequency of purchase to ensure they don't forget you*'. Euroffice sends a printed catalogue to Group 2 separately from their merchandise as a reminder about the company. The final group, 'Group 3: Key accounts or Crown Jewels', have made nine or more orders. They also tend to have a higher basket value. These people are the Crown Jewels and will spend an average of £135 per order compared to an average of £55 for trial customers. They have a 90% probability of re-ordering within a six-month period. For this group, tools have been developed on the site to make it easier for them to shop. The intention is that these customers find these tools help them in making their orders and they become reliant on them, so achieving 'soft lock-in'.

Source: Adapted from the company website press releases and Revolution (2005).

Sense, Respond, Adjust – delivering relevant e-communications through monitoring customer behaviour

To be able to identify customers in the categories of value, growth, responsiveness or defection risk we need to characterise them using information which indicates their purchase and campaign-response *behaviour*. Past and current actual behaviour is often the best predictor of future behaviour so we can then seek to influence this future behaviour.

Digital marketing enables marketers to create a cycle of:

- Monitoring customer actions or behaviours and then . . .
- Reacting with appropriate messages and offers to encourage desired behaviours
- Monitoring response to these messages and continuing with additional communications and monitoring.

Or, if you prefer, simply:

Sense → Respond → Adjust

The sensing is done through using technology to monitor visits to particular content on a website or clicking on particular links in an email. Purchase history can also be monitored, but since purchase information is often stored in a legacy sales system it is important to integrate this with systems used for communicating with customers. The response can be done through messages on-site, or in email, and then adjustment occurs through further sensing and responding.

This 'Sense and Respond' technique has traditionally been completed by catalogue retailers such as Argos or Littlewoods Index using a technique known as 'RFM analysis'. This technique tends to be little known outside retail circles, but e-CRM gives great potential to applying it in a range of techniques since we can use it not only to analyse purchase history, but also visit or log-in frequency to a site or online service and response rates to email communications.

Recency, Frequency, Monetary value (RFM) analysis

RFM is sometimes known as 'FRAC', which stands for: Frequency, Recency, Amount (obviously equivalent to monetary value), Category (types of product purchased – not included within RFM). We will now give an overview of how RFM approaches can be applied, with special reference to online marketing. We will also look at the related concepts of latency and hurdle rates.

Recency

This is the recency of customer action, e.g. purchase, site visit, account access, email response, e.g. 3 months ago. Novo (2004) stresses the importance of recency when he says:

> *Recency, or the number of days that have gone by since a customer completed an action (purchase, log-in, download, etc.) is the most powerful predictor of the customer repeating an action... Recency is why you receive another catalogue from the company shortly after you make your first purchase from them.*

Online applications of analysis of recency include: monitoring through time to identify vulnerable customers and scoring customers to preferentially target more responsive customers for cost savings.

Frequency

Frequency is the number of times an action is completed in the period of a customer action, e.g. purchase, visit, email response, e.g. five purchases per year, five visits per month, five log-ins per week, five email opens per month, five email clicks per year. Online applications of this analysis include combining with recency for RF targeting.

Monetary value

The monetary value of purchase(s) can be measured in different ways, e.g. average order value of £50, total annual purchase value of £5,000. Generally, customers with higher monetary values tend to have a higher loyalty and potential future value since they have purchased more items historically. One example application would be to exclude these customers from special promotions if their RF scores suggested they were actively purchasing. Frequency is often a proxy for monetary value per year since the more products purchased, the higher the overall monetary value. It is possible then to simplify analysis by just using recency and frequency. Monetary value can also skew the analysis for high-value initial purchases.

Latency

Latency is related to frequency, being the average time between customer events in the customer life cycle. Examples include the average time between website visits, second and third purchase and email clickthroughs. Online applications of latency include putting in place triggers that alert companies to customer behaviour outside the norm, for example increased interest or disinterest, then managing this behaviour using e-communications or traditional communications. For example, a B2B or B2C organisation with a long interval between purchases would find that if the average latency decreased for a particular customer, then they may be investigating an additional purchase (their recency and frequency would likely increase also). Emails, phone calls or direct mail could then be used to target this person with relevant offers according to what they were searching for.

Hurdle rate

According to Novo (2004), hurdle rate refers to the percentage of customers in a group (such as in a segment or on a list) who have completed an action. It is a useful concept, although the terminology doesn't really describe its application. Its value is that it can be used to compare the engagement of different groups or to set targets to increase engagement with online channels as the examples below show:

- 20% of customers have visited in the past 6 months
- 5% of customers have made three or more purchases in the year
- 60% of registrants have logged on to the system in the year
- 30% have clicked through on email in the year.

Grouping customers into different RFM categories

In the examples above, each division for recency, frequency and monetary value is placed in an arbitrary position to place a roughly equal number of customers in each group. This approach is also useful since the marketer can set thresholds of value relevant to their understanding of their customers.

RFM analysis involves two techniques for grouping customers:

1 **Statistical RFM analysis.** This involves placing an equal number of customers in each RFM category using quintiles of 20% (10 deciles can also be used for larger databases), as shown in Figure 9.22. The figure also shows one application of RFM with a view to using communications channels more effectively. Lower-cost e-communications can be used to communicate with customers who use online services more frequently since they prefer these channels and more expensive communications can be used for customers who seem to prefer traditional channels. This process is sometimes known as 'right-channelling' or 'right-touching'.

2 **Arbitrary divisions of customer database.** This approach is also useful since the marketer can set thresholds of value relevant to their understanding of their customers.

For example, RFM analysis can be applied for targeting using email according to how a customer interacts with an e-commerce site. Values could be assigned to each customer as follows:

Recency:
    1 – Over 12 months
    2 – Within last 12 months
    3 – Within last 6 months
    4 – Within last 3 months
    5 – Within last 1 month

Note here boundaries are arbitrary in order to place an equal number into each group

Figure 9.22 RFM analysis

Frequency:
1 – More than once every 6 months
2 – Every 6 months
3 – Every 3 months
4 – Every 2 months
5 – Monthly

Monetary value:
1 – Less than £10
2 – £10–£50
3 – £50–£100
4 – £100–£200
5 – More than £200

Simplified versions of this analysis can be created to make it more manageable, for example a theatre group uses these nine categories for its direct marketing:

Oncers (attended theatre once)
- Recent oncers   attended <12 months
- Rusty oncers   attended >12, <36 months
- Very rusty oncers   attended 36+ months

Twicers:
- Recent twicer   attended <12 months
- Rusty twicer   attended >12, <36 months
- Very rusty twicer   attended in 36+ months

2+ subscribers:
- Current subscribers   booked 2+ events in current season
- Recent   booked 2+ last season
- Very rusty   booked 2+ more than a season ago

Product recommendations and propensity modelling

<table>
<tr><td>

Propensity modelling

A name given to the approach of evaluating customer characteristics and behaviour and then making recommendations for future products.

</td><td>

Propensity modelling is one name given to the approach of evaluating customer characteristics and behaviour, in particular previous products or services purchased, and then making recommendations for the next suitable product. However, it is best known as 'recommending the "next-best product" to existing customers'.

A related acquisition approach is to target potential customers with similar characteristics through renting direct mail or email lists or advertising online in similar locations.

</td></tr>
</table>

The following recommendations are based on those in van Duyne *et al.* (2002):

1 Create automatic product relationships (i.e. next-best product). A low-tech approach to this is, for each product, to group together products previously purchased together. Then for each product, rank product by number of times purchased together to find relationships.

2 Cordon off and minimise the 'real estate' devoted to related products. An area of screen should be reserved for 'next-best product prompts' for up-selling and cross-selling. However, if these can be made part of the current product they may be more effective.

3 Use familiar 'trigger words'. This is familiar from using other sites such as Amazon. Such phrases include:

'Related products', 'Your recommendations', 'Similar', 'Customers who bought…'
'Top 3 related products'.

4 Editorialise about related products, i.e. within copy about a product.

5 Allow quick purchase of related products.

6 Sell related products during checkout. And also on post-transaction pages, i.e. after one item has been added to basket or purchased.

Note that techniques do not necessarily require an expensive recommendations engine except for very large sites.

Technology solutions for CRM

Database technology is at the heart of delivering CRM applications. Often the database is accessible through an intranet website accessed by employees, or an extranet accessed by customers or partners provides an interface with the entire customer relationship management system. Today, on-demand web services such as Siebel CRM On Demand (www.crmondemand .com) and Salesforce.com (www.salesforce.com) are becoming increasingly popular.

Email is used to manage many of the inbound, outbound and internal communications managed by the e-CRM system. Using email for communications is a service provided by e-CRM systems such as Salesforce (www.salesforce.com) or Oracle (www.oracle.com), or smaller businesses can use an email marketing ASP service such as MailChimp (www. mailchimp.com).

A workflow system is often used for automating CRM processes. For example, a workflow system can remind sales representatives about customer contacts or can be used to manage service delivery such as the many stages of arranging a mortgage. The three main types of customer data held as tables in customer databases for CRM are typically:

1 **Personal and profile data.** These include contact details and characteristics for profiling customers such as age and sex (B2C) and business size, industry sector and individual's role in the buying decision (B2B).
2 **Transaction data.** A record of each purchase transaction including specific product purchased, quantities, category, location, date and time, and channel where purchased.
3 **Communications data.** A record of which customers have been targeted by campaigns, and their response to them (outbound communications). Also includes a record of inbound enquiries and sales representative visits and reports (B2B).

The behavioural data available through 2 and 3 are very important for targeting customers to more closely meet their needs.

Research completed by Stone *et al.* (2001) illustrates how customer data collected through CRM applications can be used for marketing. The types of data that are held, together with the frequency of their usage, are:

Basic customer information	75%
Campaign history	62.5%
Purchase patterns (sales histories)	50%
Market information	42.5%
Competitor information	42.5%
Forecasts	25%

The data within CRM systems that were reported to be used for marketing applications were as follows:

Targeted marketing	80%
Segmentation	65%
Keeping the right customers	47.5%
Trend analysis	45%
Increased loyalty	42.5%
Customised offers	32.5%
Increase share of customer	27.5%

The Hewson Consulting Group (www.hewson.co.uk) identifies the following benefits of CRM systems to customers:

- Improved response times to customer requests for information.
- Delivered product meets customer requirements.
- Reduced costs of buying and using a product or service.
- Immediate access to order status and more responsive technical support.

It is apparent that while many of these benefits could be achieved by phoning customer support staff who then access a CRM system, it may increase customer convenience, and reduce costs to the company, if they can access this information through a web interface. This approach is referred to as 'customer self-service'.

Despite the benefits of CRM described in this chapter, it must be stressed that failure rates are high. Research conducted independently in 2000 by analysts Gartner and the Butler Group suggested that around 60 to 70% of CRM projects fail (Mello, 2001). This is not necessarily indicative of weaknesses in the CRM concept, rather it indicates the difficulty of implementing a complex information system that requires substantial changes to organisations' processes and has major impacts on the staff. Such failure rates occur in many other information systems projects. In addition to the change management issues (discussed in Chapter 10), key technical issues for managers selecting e-CRM systems are:

1 Type of applications.
2 Integration with back-office systems.
3 The choice of single-vendor solutions or a more fragmented choice.
4 Data quality.

Types of CRM applications

Figure 9.23 is intended to convey the complexity of providing CRM solutions. The aim of CRM technology is to provide an interface between the customer and the employee that replaces or facilitates direct interaction. From both customer and employee perspectives,

Customer self-service
Customers perform information requests and transactions through a web interface rather than contact with customer support staff.

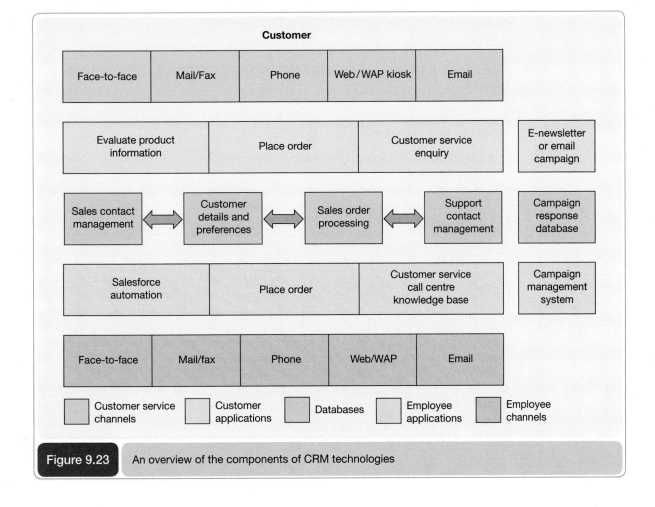

Figure 9.23   An overview of the components of CRM technologies

the ultimate aim of CRM systems is to enable contact regardless of the communications channel that the customer wants to use, whether this is traditional methods such as phone or fax or newer digital technologies. Thus the ideal CRM system will support multichannel communication or the customer-preferred channel. Regardless of channel, the customer will have different needs depending on their stage in the buying process (see section on 'Differences in buyer behaviour in target markets'). In the figure, we identify three core needs for the customer – to find out more information about a product, to place an order and to receive post-sales support. Applications must be provided to support each of these needs. Likewise, the employee will have applications requirements to support the customer and the sales and marketing objectives of the organisation; in the figure these are sales force automation, to place an order received by phone, by fax or in person and to answer customers' questions via a support system and knowledge base. At the heart of the system is the database storage needed to support these applications. The IT infrastructure (described in Chapter 3) such as servers, middleware and networking is not shown in the figure.

Integration with back-office systems

When introducing a CRM system to an organisation, a company will have previously invested in systems for other key business functions such as sales order processing or customer support. These existing, legacy systems appear at both the applications and database levels in Figure 9.23. It will not be financially viable to discard these applications, but integration with them is vital to give visibility of the customer information to everyone in the organisation and provide excellent customer support. Thus integration of legacy systems is a vital part of deciding on and implementing CRM systems.

The choice of single-vendor solutions or a more fragmented choice

Figure 9.23 highlights the key issues in deciding on and designing a system to support CRM. Think about the ideal situation; it would be:

- A single customer-facing and employee-facing application that supports all the communications channels.
- A single integrated database such that any employee has total visibility about a customer – they can access all visit, sales and support histories.
- From a single vendor for ease of implementation and support.

Now think about the reality in organisations you are familiar with: in all probability the system will have different applications for different communications channels, separate databases in different functional areas and multiple vendors. E-commerce systems are often separate from traditional systems. Such fragmentation makes implementation and maintenance of such systems a headache for managers and will often result in poor levels of service for the customer. The solution that many companies are looking to move to is close to the situation above. This need has been the reason for the growth in importance of enterprise resource planning systems from companies such as SAP and Oracle. However, the difficulty is that no single company can provide best-of-breed applications in all areas. To gain competitive edge, companies may need to turn to solutions from innovators who, for example, support new channels such as WAP, and provide knowledge management solutions or sales management solutions. Thus managers are faced with a precarious balancing act between selecting standardised products or integrating more leading systems for each CRM capability.

Data quality

All CRM systems are critically dependent on the currency, completeness and accuracy of their databases. One of the biggest challenges after installation is maintaining data quality. The importance of this was recognised in a survey of CRM and marketing managers in 120 medium–large UK B2C organisations (QAS, 2002). Of these, 86% rated accurate data as 'crucial' to their CRM system. However, the majority rated their data quality as falling short of their objectives. It can be suggested that for data quality to be managed successfully, the following are important:

1 **Establish a business owner.** This issue is too important to be managed solely by technologists and it requires management at customer contact points, which are part of the responsibility of marketing. All staff involved with managing customer data should be made clear about their responsibilities.
2 **Optimise quality on capture.** Validation checks can be built in at data entry to check that fields such as postcode are complete and accurate.
3 **Continuously improve quality.** Customer contact details constantly change. Changes of email address are even more difficult to manage than changes of physical address. As a consequence, all contact points should be used to help maintain data quality.
4 **Work towards a single view of customer.** Many errors result because different data are stored in different databases so unifying the data in a single database is the aim for many organisations.
5 **Adopt a data quality policy.** Of the sample in the QAS (2002) survey 40% had no data quality policy, but this is essential to help achieve the four steps above.

As a conclusion to this chapter, read Case study 9.1 as an example of how Tesco has used CRM technology to improve their customers' 'share of wallet'. It is estimated that for every £8 spent on groceries in the UK £1 is spent at Tesco, which is now seeking its share of all retail category sales.

Case Study 9.1	Tesco.com increases product range and uses triggered communications to support CRM

Context

Tesco, well known as Britain's leading food retail group with a presence in Europe and Asia, has also been a pioneer online.

Product ranges

The Tesco.com site acts as a portal to most of Tesco's products, including various non-food ranges, Tesco Personal Finance and the telecoms businesses, as well as services offered in partnership with specialist companies, such as clothing, dieting clubs, flights and holidays, music downloads, gas, electricity and DVD rentals.

Competitors

Tesco currently leads the UK's other grocery retailers in terms of market share. This pattern is repeated online. The compilation below is from Hitwise (2005) and the figures in brackets show market share for traditional offline retail formats from the Taylor Nelson Softres Super Panel (see http://superpanel.tns-global.com).

1 Tesco Superstore, 27.28% (29% of retail trade)
2 ASDA, 13.36%
3 ASDA@t Home, 10.13% (17.1%)
4 Sainsburys, 8.42%
5 Tesco Wine Warehouse, 8.19%
6 Sainsburys to You, 5.86% (15.9%)
7 Waitrose.com, 3.42% (3.6%)
8 Ocado, 3.32% (owned by Waitrose, 3.6%)
9 Lidl, 2.49% (1.8%)
10 ALDI-UK, 2.10% (2.3%).

Some companies are repeated since their main site and the online shopping site are reported on separately. Asda.com now seems to be performing in a consistent manner online to its offline presence. However, Sainsburys' online performance seems to be significantly lower compared to its offline performance.

Some providers such as Ocado which originally just operated within the London area have a strong local performance.

Notably, some of Tesco.com's competitors are absent from the Hitwise listing since their strategy has been to focus on retail formats. These are Morrisons (12.5% retail share), Somerfield (5.5%) and Co-op (5.0%).

Promotion of service

As with other online retailers, Tesco.com relies on in-store advertising and marketing to the supermarket's Clubcard loyalty scheme's customer base to persuade customers to shop online. *New Media Age* (2005c) quotes Nigel Dodd, marketing director at Tesco.com, as saying: 'These are invaluable sources as we have such a strong customer base.' However, for non-food goods the supermarket does advertise online using keyword targeted ads.

For existing customers, email marketing and direct mail marketing to provide special offers and promotions to customers are important.

According to Humby and Hunt (2003), e-retailer Tesco.com uses what they describe as a 'commitment-based segmentation' or 'loyalty ladder', which is based on recency of purchase, frequency of purchase and value which is used to identify six life cycle categories which are then further divided to target communications:

- 'Logged-on'
- 'Cautionary'
- 'Developing'
- 'Established'
- 'Dedicated'
- 'Logged-off' (the aim here is to win back).

Tesco then uses automated event-triggered messaging to encourage continued purchase. For example, Tesco.com has a touch strategy which includes a sequence of follow-up communications triggered after different events in the customer life cycle. In the example given below, communications after event 1 are intended to achieve the objective of converting a website visitor to action; communications after event 2 are intended to move the customer from a first-time purchaser to a regular purchaser and for event 3 to reactivate lapsed purchasers.

- *Trigger event 1: Customer first registers on site (but does not buy)*
  Auto-response (AR) 1: 2 days after registration email sent offering phone assistance and £5 discount off first purchase to encourage trial.
- *Trigger event 2: Customer first purchases online*
  AR1: Immediate order confirmation.

AR2: Five days after purchase email sent with link to online customer satisfaction survey asking about quality of service from driver and picker (e.g. item quality and substitutions).
AR3: Two weeks after first purchase – direct mail offering tips on how to use service and £5 discount on next purchases intended to encourage reuse of online services.
AR4: Generic monthly e-newsletter with online exclusive offers encouraging cross-selling.
AR5: Bi-weekly alert with personalised offers for customer.
AR6: After two months – £5 discount for next shop.
AR7: Quarterly mailing of coupons encouraging repeat sales and cross-sales.
- *Trigger event 3: Customer does not purchase for an extended period*
  AR1: Dormancy detected – reactivation email with survey of how the customer is finding the service (to identify any problems) and a £5 incentive.
  AR2: A further discount incentive is used in order to encourage continued usage to shop after the first shop after a break.

Tesco's online product strategy

New Media Age (2005c) ran a profile of Laura Wade-Gery, CEO of Tesco.com since January 2004, which provides an interesting insight into how the business has run. In her first year, total sales were increased 24% to £719 million. Laura is 40 years old, a keen athlete and has followed a varied career developing through an MA in History at Magdalen College, Oxford, and an MBA from Insead; Manager and partner in Kleinwort Benson; Manager and senior consultant, Gemini Consulting; Targeted marketing director (Tesco Clubcard), and Group strategy director, Tesco Stores.

The growth overseen by Wade-Gery has been achieved through a combination of initiatives. Product range development is one key area. In early 2005, Tesco.com fulfilled 150,000 grocery orders a week but now also offers more intangible offerings, such as e-diets and music downloads.

Wade-Gery has also focussed on improving the customer experience online – the time it takes for a new customer to complete their first order has been decreased from over an hour to 35 minutes through usability work culminating in a major site revision.

To support the business as it diversifies into new areas, Wade-Gery's strategy was 'to make home delivery part of the DNA of Tesco', according to *New Media Age* (2005c). She continues: 'What we offer is delivery to your home of a Tesco service – it's an obvious extension of the home-delivered groceries concept.' By

May 2005, Tesco.com had 30,000 customers signed up for DVD rental, through partner Video Island (which runs the rival Screenselect service). Over the next year, Wade-Gery's target is to treble this total, while also extending home-delivery services to the likes of bulk wine and white goods.

Wade-Gery looks to achieve synergy between the range of services offered. For example, its partnership with eDiets can be promoted through the Tesco Clubcard loyalty scheme, with mailings to 10 million customers a year. In July 2004, Tesco.com Limited paid £2 million for the exclusive licence to eDiets.com in the UK and Ireland under the URLs www.eDietsUK.com and www.eDiets.ie. Through promoting the services through the URLs, Tesco can use the dieting business to grow use of the Tesco.com service and in-store sales.

To help keep focus on home retail delivery, Wade-Gery sold women's portal iVillage (www.ivillage.co.uk) back to its US owners for an undisclosed sum in March 2004. She explained to *New Media Age*:

It's a very different sort of product to the other services that we're embarking on. In my mind, we stand for providing services and products that you buy, which is slightly different to the world of providing information.

The implication is that there was insufficient revenue from ad sales on iVillage and insufficient opportunities to promote Tesco.com sales. However, iVillage was a useful learning experience in that there are some parallels with iVillage, such as message boards and community advisers.

Wade-Gery is also director of Tesco Mobile, the joint 'pay-as-you-go' venture with O$_2$ which is mainly serviced online, although promoted in-store and via direct mail. Tesco also offers broadband and dial-up ISP services, but believes the market for Internet telephony (provided through Skype and Vonage, for example) is not sufficiently developed. Tesco.com have concentrated on more traditional services which have the demand, for example Tesco Telecom fixed-line services attracted over a million customers in their first year.

However, this is not to say that Tesco.com will not invest in relatively new services. In November 2004, Tesco introduced a music download service, and just six months later Wade-Gery estimates they have around 10% market share – one of the benefits of launching relatively early. Again, there is synergy, this time with hardware sales. *New Media Age* (2005c) reported that as MP3 players were unwrapped, sales went up – even on Christmas Day! She says:

The exciting thing about digital is where can you take it in the future. As the technology grows, we'll be able to turn Tesco.com into a digital download store of all sorts, rather than just music. Clearly, film [through video on demand] would be next.

But it has to be based firmly on analysis of customer demand. Wade-Gery says: 'The number one thing for us is whether the product is something that customers are saying they want; has it reached a point where mass-market customers are interested?' There also has to be scope for simplification. *New Media Age* (2005c) notes that Tesco is built on a core premise of convenience and value and Wade-Gery believes what it's already done with mobile tariffs, broadband packages and music downloads are good examples of the retailer's knack for streamlining propositions. She says: 'We've actually managed to get people joining broadband who have never even had a dial-up service.'

Source: Humby and Hunt (2003), *New Media Age* (2005c), Hitwise (2005), Wikipedia (2005).

Questions

Based on the case study and your own research on competitors, summarise the strategic approaches which have helped Tesco.com achieve success online.

Summary

1   The objective of customer relationship management (CRM) is to increase customer loyalty in order to increase profitability. CRM is aimed at improving all aspects of the level of customer service.

2   CRM tactics can be based around the acquisition–retention–extension model of the ideal relationship between company and customer.

3   In an e-commerce context, acquisition refers to gaining new customers to a company and converting existing customers to online services. To enable an online

relationship it is important to profile customers to find out their needs and expectations and obtain an opt-in email agreement to continue the dialogue.

4   Marketing communications techniques to achieve acquisition, retention and extension include traditional online mass-media techniques and specialised online techniques such as search engine registration, link-building, email marketing and banner advertising.

5   Techniques for customer retention include the use of extranets, online communities, online sales promotions and email marketing.

6   Customer extension involves better understanding of the customer through feedback on new product development and encouraging customers to increase the depth of their relationship by offering complementary products for purchase or increasing purchase frequency.

7   Knowledge of online buyer behaviour, and in particular, the differing needs of the customer through the different stages of the buying decision can be used to improve CRM management.

8   Customer service quality is important in achieving loyalty and the SERVQUAL framework can be used to consider how to use the Internet to achieve this.

9   Technology solutions for CRM are aimed at providing interaction between employees and customers across multiple communications channels with all customer information stored in a single database to provide complete visibility of the customer by employees. Managers look to minimise the number of solutions partners they work with to achieve these goals.

10 Specific technology application requirements for CRM are salesforce automation (contact management) and call-centre applications which integrate workflow to manage queries and a knowledge base from which queries can be reviewed.

Exercises

Self-assessment questions

1   What are the goals of acquisition and retention in an online context?
2   Outline the differences between permission marketing and interruption marketing including reference to the terms 'opt-in' and 'opt-out'.
3   Summarise the main types of online marketing communications for traffic-building.
4   Explain why mixed-mode buying needs to be understood by those managing an e-commerce site.
5   Explain a range of techniques for attracting repeat visits to a website.
6   What is the difference between personalisation and mass customisation?
7   How can an e-commerce site be used to achieve extension in CRM?
8   What are the management issues in managing data and applications integration in CRM?

Essay and discussion questions

1   On what basis should marketing managers decide on the communications mix for an e-commerce site?
2   Evaluate the current communications mix for an online e-tailer and make recommendations for future communications to achieve customer acquisition and retention.

3 Show how an understanding of the online buying process can be used to revise marketing communications.

4 Explain, using examples, typical differences between a traffic-building campaign for a B2B and a B2C company.

5 Examine the relationship between customer satisfaction, loyalty and sales in relation to a pureplay e-commerce site.

6 Examine the benefits and disadvantages of personalisation, community-building and direct email. For an organisation of your choice recommend a suitable balance between these e-marketing tools.

7 Assess whether a multi-vendor or single (limited number) vendor strategy is best for the implementation of e-CRM systems.

8 Recommend a social CRM data and application architecture for a B2C company that provides integration with related legacy systems.

Examination questions

1 Explain the concept of mixed-mode buying with reference to a pureplay e-commerce bookseller.

2 You are the e-commerce manager for a B2C site. Write an explanation to be included in a report to the managing director of why a permission marketing approach is required.

3 What different types of searching behaviour are exhibited by online users and what are the implications for someone responsible for traffic-building on a site?

4 With reference to customer acquisition and retention, explain two goals for each required by an e-commerce site manager.

5 Outline four different methods of building website traffic.

6 Explain three factors that will influence the balance of online and offline website promotion for an organisation.

7 How can an e-commerce site be used to inform new product development?

8 What is a legacy system and what is its relevance to CRM?

References

Abraham, M. (2008) The off-line impact of online ads. *Harvard Business Review*, 86(4), 28.

Agrawal, V., Arjona, V. and Lemmens, R. (2001) E-performance: the path to rational exuberance. *McKinsey Quarterly*, no. 1, 31–43.

Altimeter (2010) Social CRM: The New Rules of Relationship Management. White Paper published April 2010, Editor Charlene Li. Published online at **www.altimeter-group.com/2010/03/altimeter-report-the-18-use-cases-of-social-crm-the-new-rules-of-relationship-management.html**.

Bart, Y., Shankar, V., Sultan, E. and Urban, G. (2005) Are the drivers and role of online trust the same for all web sites and consumers? A large-scale exploratory empirical study. *Journal of Marketing*, October, 133–52.

Berthon, B., Pitt, L. and Watson, R. (1996) Resurfing W3: research perspectives on marketing communication and buyer behaviour on the World Wide Web. *International Journal of Advertising*, 15, 287–301.

Boyd, D. and Ellison, N. (2007) Social network sites: definition, history and scholarship, *Journal of Computer-Mediated Communication*, 13(1), 210–230.

BrandNewWorld (2004) AOL Research, originally published at **www.brandnewworld.co.uk**.

Cartellieri, C., Parsons, A., Rao, V. and Zeisser, M. (1997) The real impact of Internet advertising. *McKinsey Quarterly*, no. 3, 44–63.

Chaffey, D. and Edgar, M. (2000) Measuring online service quality. *Journal of Targeting, Analysis and Measurement for Marketing*, 8(4), 363–78.

Chaffey, D. and Smith, P. (2008) *EMarketing Excellence: Planning and Optimising Your Digital Marketing*, 3rd edn. Butterworth-Heinemann, Oxford.

Chaffey, D. and Smith, P.R. (2012). *Emarketing Excellence: Planning and Optimizing your Digital Marketing*, 4th edn. Routledge, London.

Cronin, J. and Taylor, S. (1992) Measuring service quality: a re-examination and extension. *Journal of Marketing*, 56, 55–63.

cScape (2008) Second Annual Online Customer Engagement Report (2008). Produced by E-consultancy in association with cScape. Published online at **www.cscape.com** (no longer available).

Dee, A., Bassett, B. and Hoskins, J. (2007) Word-of-mouth research: principles and applications. *Journal of Advertising Research*, 47(4), 387–97.

Deighton, J. (1996) The future of interactive marketing. *Harvard Business Review*, November–December, 151–62.

Dennis, C., Merrilees, B., Jayawardhena, C. and Wright, L.T. (2009) E-consumer behaviour. *European Journal of Marketing*, 43(9/10), 1121–39.

Emailcenter (2008) Toptable. Utilising Maxemail ROAD to increase bookings by 60%. Case study published at: **www.emailcenteruk.com/case%20studies/toptable.php** (no longer available).

Evans, M., Patterson, M. and O'Malley, L. (2000) Bridging the direct marketing-direct consumer gap: some solutions from qualitative research. *Proceedings of the Academy of Marketing Annual Conference*, Derby.

Feinberg, R., Trotter, M. and Anton, J. (2000) At any time – from anywhere – in any form. In D. Renner (ed.) *Defying the Limits, Reaching New Heights in Customer Relationship Management*. Report from Montgomery Research Inc, San Francisco, CA: **http://feinberg.crmproject.com** (no longer available).

Forrester (2007) Consumer Trends Survey North America – leveraging user-generated content. January 2007. Brian Haven.

Forrester Research (1999) Strong content means a loyal audience. Forrester Research report. 27 January.

Guardian (2003) TV ads 'a waste of money', Claire Cozens. Tuesday 4 February.

Godin, S. (1999) *Permission Marketing*. Simon& Schuster, New York.

Hagel, J. and Armstrong, A. (1997) *Net Gain: Expanding Markets through Virtual Communities*. Harvard Business School Press, Cambridge, MA.

Haven, B. (2007) Marketing's New Key Metric: Engagement, 8 August, Forrester.

Heskett, J., Jones, T., Loveman, G., Sasser, W. and Schlesinger, E. (1994) Putting the service-profit chain to work. *Harvard Business Review*, March–April, 164–74.

Hitwise (2005) Press release: The top UK Grocery and Alcohol websites, week ending 1 October, ranked by market share of website visits, from Hitwise.co.uk. **www.hitwise.co.uk** (no longer available).

Hoffman, D.L. and Novak, T.P. (1996) Marketing in Hypermedia computer-mediated environments: conceptual foundations. *Journal of Marketing*, 60 (July), 50–68.

Hsieh (2010) Delivering customer happiness. A presentation by Zappos CEO Tony Hsieh with Tony Robbins. **www.slideshare.net/zappos/zappos-tony-robbins-business-mastery-011610**.

Humby, C. and Hunt, T. (2003) *Scoring Points. How Tesco is Winning Customer Loyalty*. Kogan Page, London.

Jevons, C. and Gabbot, M. (2000) Trust, brand equity and brand reality in Internet business relationships: an interdisciplinary approach. *Journal of Marketing Management*, 16(6), 619–34.

Jun, M. and Cai, S. (2001) The key determinants of banking service quality: a content analysis. *International Journal of Bank Marketing*, 19(7), 276–91.

Keiningham, T., Cooil, B., Aksoy, L., Andreassen, T. and Weiner, J. (2007) The value of different customer satisfaction and loyalty metrics in predicting customer retention, recommendation and share-of-wallet. *Managing Service Quality*, 17(4), 172–81.

Kirby, J. (2003) Online viral marketing: next big thing or yesterday's fling? *New Media Knowledge*. Published online at **www.newmediaknowledge.co.uk** (no longer available).

Kirby, K. and Samson, A. (2008) Customer advocacy metrics: the NPS theory in practice, *AdMap*, February, 17–19.

Kotler, P. (1997) *Marketing Management – Analysis, Planning, Implementation and Control.* Prentice-Hall, Englewood Cliffs, NJ.

Kumar, V., Peterson, J. and Leone, R. (2007) How valuable is word of mouth? *Harvard Business Review*, 85(10), 139–46.

Levine, R., Locke, C., Searls, D. and Weinberger, D. (2000) *The Cluetrain Manifesto.* Perseus Books, Cambridge, MA.

Lewis, H. and Lewis, R. (1997) Give your customers what they want. *Selling on the Net. Executive Book Summaries*, 19(3).

McGaffin, K. (2004) Linking matters: how to create an effective linking strategy to promote your website. Published at **www.linkingmatters.com** (no longer available).

MAD (2007) How online display advertising influences search volumes. Published 4 June 2007. MAD Network (*Marketing Week*), Centaur Communications.

Mello, A. (2001) Watch out for CRM's hidden costs. ZdNet online, 15 October.

Microsoft (2007) Word of the web guidelines for advertisers: understanding trends and monetising social networks. Research report.

New Media Age (2005a) Product placement. By Sean Hargrave. *New Media Age*, 12 May, **www.nma.co.uk.**

New Media Age (2005b) Perfect match. By Greg Brooks. *New Media Age*, 29 September.

New Media Age (2005c) Delivering the goods. By Nic Howell. *New Media Age*, 5 May.

New Media Age (2007) Impulse buying. By Emma Rubach. *New Media Age*, 30 August.

Nielsen, J. (2000) Web research: believe the data. *Jakob Nielsen's Alertbox*, 11 July 1999: **www.useit.com/alertbox/990711.html.**

Novo, J. (2004) Drilling Down: Turning customer data into profits with a spreadsheet. Available from **www.jimnovo.com.**

O'Malley, L. and Tynan, C. (2001) Reframing relationship marketing for consumer markets. *Interactive Marketing*, 2(3), 240–46.

Parasuraman, A., Zeithaml, V. and Berry, L. (1985) A conceptual model of service quality and its implications for future research. *Journal of Marketing*, 49, Fall, 41–50.

Parker, R (2000) *Relationship Marketing on the Web.* Adams Streetwise, Avon, MA.

Peppers, B. and Rogers, P. (1999) *One-to-One Field Book.* Currency/Doubleday, New York.

Peters, L. (1998) The new interactive media: one-to-one but to whom? *Marketing Intelligence and Planning*, 16(1), 22–30.

QAS (2002) Data Quality – the Reality Gap. Executive summary of a report commissioned by QAS.

Reichheld, F. (2006) *The Ultimate Question: Driving Good Profits and True Growth.* Harvard Business School Press, Boston.

Reichheld, F. and Schefter, P. (2000) E-loyalty, your secret weapon on the web. *Harvard Business Review*, July–August, 105–13.

Reinartz, W. and Kumar. V. (2002) The mismanagement of customer loyalty. *Harvard Business Review*, July, 4–12.

Revolution (2005) Email marketing report. By Justin Pugsley. *Revolution*, September, 58–60.

Robinson, H., Wysocka, A. and Hand, C. (2007) Internet advertising effectiveness: the effect of design on click-through rates for banner ads. *International Journal of Advertising*, 26(4), 527–41.

Ryan, J. and Whiteman, N. (2000) Online Advertising Glossary: Sponsorships. ClickZ Media Selling Channel, 15 May.

Sharma, A. and Sheth, J. (2004) Web-based marketing: the coming revolution in marketing thought and strategy. *Journal of Business Research*, 57(7), 696–702.

Sissors, J. and Baron, R. (2002) *Advertising Media Planning*, 6th edn. McGraw-Hill, Chicago.

Smart Insights (2010) Introducing RACE = A practical framework to improve your digital marketing. Blog post by Dave Chaffey, 15 July. Available from: **www.smartinsights. com/digital-marketing-strategy**.

Smart Insights (2012) Comparison of Google Clickthrough rate by position. Blog post by Dave Chaffey published September 24th 2012. **www.smartinsights. com/search-engine-optimisation-seo/seo-analytics/comparison-of-google-clickthrough-rates-by-position/**.

Smith, P.R. and Chaffey, D. (2005) *EMarketing Excellence – at the Heart of EBusiness*, 2nd edn. Butterworth-Heinemann, Oxford.

Stone, M., Abbott, J. and Buttle, E (2001) Integrating customer data into CRM strategy. In B. Foss and M. Stone (eds) *Successful Customer Relationship Marketing*. Wiley, Chichester.

Transversal (2008) UK companies fail the multi-channel customer service test. Research report, March.

van Duyne, D., Landay, J. and Hong, J. (2002) *The Design of Sites: Patterns, Principles, and Processes for Crafting a Customer-centered Web Experience*. Addison-Wesley, Reading, MA.

Watts, D. and Dodds, S. (2007) Influentials, networks, and public opinion formation. *Journal of Consumer Research*, 34(4), 441–58.

Wikipedia (2005) Tesco. Wikipedia, the free encyclopaedia: http://en.wikipedia.org/wiki/Tesco.

Windham, L. (2001) *The Soul of the New Consumer: The Attitudes, Behaviors and Preferences of E-Customers*. Allworth Press, New York.

Zona Research (1999) The economic impacts of unacceptable website download speeds. White Paper, April.

Further reading

Chaffey, D., Mayer, R., Johnston, K. and Ellis-Chadwick, F. (2009) *Internet Marketing: Strategy, Implementation and Practice*, 4th edn. Financial Times Prentice Hall, Harlow.

Chapter 6 covers online relationship building and Chapters 8 and 9 interactive communications.

Chatterjee, P. (2010) Multiple-channel and cross-channel shopping behavior: Role of consumer shopping orientations. *Marketing Intelligence & Planning*, 28(1), 9–24.

This paper explores buyer behaviour implications for multi-channel transactions.

Dennis, C., Merrilees, B., Jayawardhena, T. and Wright, L.T. (2009) E-consumer behaviour. *European Journal of Marketing*, 43(9/10), 1121–39.

A good overview of consumer behaviour.

Jackson, S. (2009) *Cult of Analytics: Driving Online Marketing Strategies Using Web Analytics*. Elsevier, Oxford.

Møller, K. and Halinen, A. (2000) Relationship marketing theory: its roots and direction. *Journal of Marketing Management*, 16, 29–54.

Sargeant, A. and West, D. (2001) *Direct and Interactive Marketing*. Oxford University Press, Oxford.

An excellent coverage of traditional direct marketing, although the specific chapter on digital marketing is brief.

Winer, R. (2001) A framework for customer relationship management. *California Management Review*, 43(4).

A good overview of CRM and e-CRM.

Web links

Direct Marketing Association (www.dma.org.uk) Best-practice guidelines and benchmarks of response rates.

DoubleClick (www.doubleclick.net) An email broadcaster and advertising network worldwide, with offices in many countries. Its site provides research of ad and email marketing response rates across its clients.

Internet-advertising-related links

ClickZ (www.clickz.com/experts/) An excellent collection of articles on online marketing communications. US-focussed. Relevant sections for this chapter include: affiliate marketing, advertising technology, email marketing, media buying.

eMarketer (www.emarketer.com) Includes reports on media spend based on compilations of other analysts.

iMediaConnection (www.imediaconnection.com) Media site reporting on best practice in online advertising.

Internet Advertising Bureau (www.iab.net) The widest range of studies about Internet advertising effectiveness. In UK: **www.iabuk.net**. Internet Advertising Bureau XMOS microsite (**www.iab.net/xmos**).

Search-engine-related links

ClickZ (www.clickz.com/) An excellent collection of articles on online marketing communications. US-focussed. Relevant sections for this chapter include: affiliate marketing, advertising technology, email marketing, media buying.

Searchenginewatch (www.searchenginewatch.com) A complete resource on SEO and PPC marketing.

Webmasterworld (www.webmasterworld.com) A forum where search practitioners discuss best practice.

CRM and database marketing

CRM Today (www.crm2day.com) A portal with articles about the practical aspects of deploying CRM technology.

Direct Marketing Association UK (www.dma.org.uk) Source of up-to-date data protection advice and how-to guides about online direct marketing.

Jim Novo (www.jimnovo.com) A site by a US consultant that has a lot of detail on techniques to profile customers online.

MyCustomer.com (www.mycustomer.com) A media site focussing on customer relationship marketing techniques and tools.

Peppers and Rogers One-to-one marketing website (**www.1to1.com**) A site containing a lot of information on the techniques and tools of relationship marketing.

Permission marketing (www.permission.com) Site supporting book by Seth Godin of Yahoo! on permission marketing. No content, but four sample chapters.

Part 3

Implementation

Management of digital business implementation is described in Part 3 of the book in which we examine practical management issues involved with creating and maintaining digital business solutions.

10 Change management p. 468

- The challenges of digital business transformation
- Different types of change in business
- Planning change
- Human resource requirements
- Revising organisational structures

- Approaches to managing change
- Towards the social business
- Risk management

Focus on . . .
- Knowledge management

11 Analysis and design p. 517

- Analysis for digital business
- Process modelling
- Data modelling
- Design for digital business

Focus on . . .
- User-centred site design
- Security design for digital business

12 Digital business service implementation and optimisation p. 597

- Alternatives for acquiring digital business systems
- Testing
- Changeover
- Content management and maintenance

Focus on . . .
- Web analytics: measuring and improving performance of digital business services

Web support

The following additional case studies are available at **www.pearsoned.co.uk/chaffey**

→ Orange evolves customer services to achieve 12,000 visitors to site each week
→ Staff acquisition and retention at Netdecisions
→ Managing global change at Guinness

The site also contains a range of study material designed to help improve your results.

Scan code to find the latest updates for topics in this chapter

Learning outcomes

After completing this chapter the reader should be able to:

● Identify the different types of change that need to be managed for e-commerce
● Develop an outline plan for implementing e-commerce change
● Describe alternative approaches to organisational structure resulting from organisational change

Management issues

The issues for managers raised in this chapter include:

● What are the success factors in managing change?
● Should we change organisational structure in response to digital business? If so, what are the options?
● How do we manage the human aspects of the implementation of organisational change?
● How do we share knowledge between staff in the light of high staff turnover and rapid changes in market conditions?

Links to other chapters

The main related chapters are:

● Chapters in *Part 2* on strategy development should be read before this chapter since they explain the reasons for change. *Chapter 5* describes structural change for digital business
● *Chapters 11* and *12* on strategy implementation which follow this chapter describe how the change management approach is implemented through analysis, design and implementation

Introduction

What we anticipate seldom occurs: what we least expect generally happens.

(Benjamin Disraeli)

Disraeli's quote, referring to changes that need to be responded to in government, could equally be applied to the responses that are necessary from an organisation applying digital business practices.

However, for managing **digital business transformation** within a particular organisation it is possible to anticipate many of the changes that will be required by learning lessons from the pioneers of digital business. Through applying best practice and adopting risk management, it is possible to be proactive and manage change successfully. However, achieving this is not straightforward, as suggested by Mini case study 10.1.

Approaches to managing changes to organisational processes and structures and their impact on organisation staff and culture are known as **change management**.

The introduction of digital business often requires company staff to learn how to use new internal information systems, but more significantly it will require new methods of working. The changes experienced by staff tend to be greatest for large-scale projects which are intended to assist digital business transformation. For example, the introduction of a digital system to support online sales or online procurement may introduce major changes for staff working in these areas. Both types of systems represent a potential threat to existing staff. Some staff may have been working face-to-face with customers or suppliers for many years and they are now asked to use technology which decreases the human element of contact. They may consider this reduces the efficiency of the work, they may feel their jobs are less interesting or even that their jobs are under threat.

Digital business transformation

Significant changes to organisational processes, structures and system implemented to improve organisational performance through increasing the use of digital media and technology platforms.

Change management

Managing process, structural, technical, staff and culture change within an organisation.

Mini Case Study 10.1	The reasons behind a failed digital business project

McLaughlin (2010) has reviewed a case study of a project where, after significant financial investment (approximately US$300m) and three years of development, a digital transformation project was deemed a failure. The initiative was designed to link the sales, marketing, fulfilment, manufacturing and distribution systems together in order to reduce supply chain stock levels, increase responsiveness to customer demands and increase profit margins by providing a direct link to customers (circumventing business partners for some product lines).

The project was managed centrally from the North American headquarters, with input sought from the other geographies (Europe/Middle East/Africa, Asia Pacific, and Latin America). The geographies had responsibility to respond to the central team on local aspects of the e-CRM project. The central team had responsibility for the overall scope of the project and the back office, or the e-CRM 'engine', while the geographies had responsibility to ensure that the system, once deployed, considered local and cultural aspects of how the organisation interacted with customers and business partners.

In this study, McLaughlin surveyed the level of employee awareness of the e-CRM system; employee buy-in; employee confidence in an e-CRM system; and employee awareness of barriers to successful implementation. Although most employees had heard of the e-CRM project, the depth of awareness was not consistent across the organisation. From the surveyed population, 24% had heard of e-CRM but were unaware of what the project would deliver; 28% understood the deliverables and received regular communications on the project's progress. But 48% of the surveyed workforce, while understanding what e-CRM was about and what it was trying to achieve, did not receive any communications on a regular basis updating them on the project's progress. In effect, 72% of the workforce was not aware of how e-CRM was progressing, and how the objectives and deliverables were changing.

Note that this is one example behind project failure in digital business where lack of education and buy-in from staff was a major issue. Examples from the end of Chapter 2, such as that for Ecomum, show that failure can also commonly occur when accounting fundamentals are forgotten.

We start this chapter by reviewing some of the challenges of implementing and managing e-commerce. We then go on to consider different aspects of change management and the chapter is structured around the different aspects of change we need to plan for; these include:

- *Scheduling* – what are the suitable stages for introducing change?
- *Budgeting* – how do we cost investment in digital business systems and projects?
- *Resources needed* – what type of resources do we need, what are their responsibilities and where do we obtain them?
- *Organisational structures* – do we need to revise organisational structure?
- *Managing the human impact of change* – what is the best way to introduce large-scale digital business change to employees?
- *Technologies to support digital business change* – the roles of knowledge management, groupware and intranets are explored.
- *Risk management* – approaches to managing risk in digital business projects.

The Smart Insights interview below shows that many companies who have made a transformation to digital marketing are continuing to change, but continuously through optimisation.

Real-world Digital Business | The Smart Insights interview

Ben Jesson and Karl Blanks of agency Conversion Rate Expert on conversion rate optimisation

The interview

Q. We're seeing a lot more companies working now on CRO. What is it and why is its use increasing?

Ben Jesson, Conversion Rate Expert: Yes, it should be. Landing page optimisation focusses on one page. We coined the term conversion rate optimisation ('CRO') in 2007 to describe the process of optimising the business itself. It's really commercial optimisation. A proper job of CRO includes the review of the entire process, from the initial lead-generation ad all the way through to the post-sale follow-up. The real goal is to identify which parts of the sales funnel will yield the greatest wins with the least work.

That means it's necessary to bring a lot of disciplines to the party, including understanding traffic sources, visitor psychology and the company's position in the marketplace, including its core strengths and weaknesses. On top of that there's usability testing, copywriting and web design factors to look at.

All these elements go into creating hypotheses for testing. We're maniacal about testing, because we've seen too many businesses merely throw a series of 'best practices' against the wall to see if anything sticks. Best practices should not be the answer to optimising a website, but merely one starting point for formulating a test strategy.

Once we determine what truly works for a particular website, then we examine how our findings might be used in other media channels. For instance, a better series of benefit statements might be transferrable to direct mail or email autoresponder campaigns – subject to testing in those media, of course.

Q. How do you help companies build a business case for returns from CRO?

Karl Blanks, Conversion Rate Expert: It's easy, we explain that CRO allows companies to generate more revenue without spending more on advertising. It's about getting a higher return from the existing ad spend. Unlike certain industries like public relations, the entire foundation of CRO is based on data, measurement and testing. You don't need to present arguments when the data can do the talking for you. Once you measure the value of visitors, conversions and sales, then it's simple arithmetic to show how, say, a 10% boost in conversions would help the bottom line.

Here's another powerful side-benefit: when you optimise your funnel and bring in more revenues, you then have earned a luxury: you get to decide whether to pocket those profits or plough them back into even more advertising, thus distancing yourself even further from your competitors. It's a nice problem to have.

Q. Which approaches do you use to decide which part of a site needs most urgent attention?

Ben Jesson, Conversion Rate Expert: Fortune magazine called what we do 'a combination of multivariate statistical analysis and good old-fashioned detective work' and that pretty well describes our approach.

It's often very useful to map out your entire sales/conversion funnel and make sure it's being comprehensively measured in whatever web analytics package you prefer.

Then you should look for the biggest drop-offs from one step to the next. We like to say that we look for the 'blocked arteries' (that is, pages – or page elements – that get loads of visitors but are underperforming). How do you know if something is underperforming? Clues come from a range of feedback mechanisms: the analytics data, usability tests, surveys, customer support feedback . . . and, of course, gut feel. Of course, we have the advantage of having been engaged by companies on several continents and in many industries, so we have a good knowledgebase of what's good and what's bad. See our list of effective tactics and strategies.

Q. What can limit conversion? Give some examples of the most common 'conversion rate killers' you see.

Karl Blanks, Conversion Rate Expert: These are some of the most common mistakes we see:

Killer #1: Not split testing. Many people think they're done if they take action to make changes to their site. In reality they're only 'done' when tests show that the changes in fact improved conversions. Installing a 'best practice' magic button that another site swears by might actually lower conversions. Despite the popularity of video, Google once discovered through tests that video reduced conversions on one of its pages. You simply must test to find out.

Not long ago, multivariate testing software cost more than £5,000 per month. Now you can use Google Website Optimizer and other software packages for free, so there's really no excuse. We created a tool, called Which Multivariate, which helps you to select the best software for multivariate testing.

Killer #2 is 'meek tweaking' – in other words, making changes that are never likely to have a significant effect.

Killer #3 is asking for the sale on the first visit. It's often a good idea to test the creation of a multi-step conversion funnel, in which you provide great value before you ask for the order. Comparison charts, forums, special reports and email marketing are examples of elements that allow you to provide good information, ask for names, cultivate a relationship and thereby improve the chances of a sale.

We recently gave a talk on '15 Common Causes of Conversion Death'.

Q. Could you share some tools that readers could use on their sites?

Ben Jesson, Conversion Rate Expert: Excellent design is a prerequisite for conversion, but the biggest breakthroughs tend to be the new tools and techniques for gathering insights into the visitor's mindset.

For determining how visitors interact with a site we often use both ClickTale and CrazyEgg for this.

KISSInsights and Ethnio are both good for asking your visitors to give you immediate feedback on your site. GazeHawk enables you to conduct an eyetracking study on your site for a tiny fraction of the traditional cost.

Many of your readers will already know about how wireframing is important in order to get agreement on functional aspects before you take the time to make a site look good. We like Balsamiq for that purpose.

The challenges of digital business transformation

Figure 10.1 shows key aspects or levers of change that need to be assessed in order to maximise the benefits of digital business:

1 Market and business model (described in Chapter 2).
2 Business process (described in Chapter 4).
3 Organisational structure, culture and staff responsibilities (described in this chapter).
4 Technology infrastructure changes (described in Chapters 3, 9 and 11).

These are all major changes that are required in order for an organisation to be agile enough to respond to marketplace changes and deliver competitive customer service. To help achieve these different aspects of change, a series of success factors seem to be required. These include:

- management buy-in and ownership;
- effective project management;

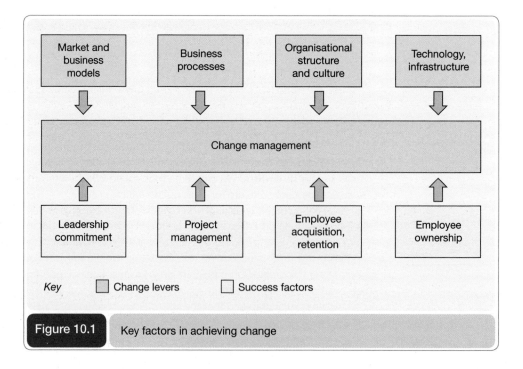

Figure 10.1   Key factors in achieving change

- action to attract and keep the right staff to achieve change;
- employee ownership of change.

This chapter focuses on how to best achieve these success factors. Activity 10.1 introduces some of the changes required by digital business.

Some of these challenges for smaller business in a start-up phase are similar, but many different challenges are raised by their scale. These challenges are explored in Box 10.1.

Activity 10.1	Managing change at a B2C company

Purpose

To investigate the impacts of change on employees associated with digital business.

Activity

Speculate how the introduction of changes by a CEO or managing director such as those illustrated by the top four boxes of Figure 10.1 would affect different employees at a B2C company. Imagine you are each of the following people. What would your reaction be on a professional and a personal level? What would be your role in affecting change?

- Marketing manager
- Warehouse manager
- HR manager
- IS manager
- Employee in call centre.

Answers to activities can be found at www.pearsoned.co.uk/chaffey

---

The challenges of sell-side e-commerce implementation

A useful framework for reviewing an organisation's capabilities to manage digital business-related transformation is shown in Table 10.1. This 7S framework was developed by McKinsey consultants in the 1970s and summarised by Waterman *et al.* (1980). It can be readily applied to businesses of all sectors and sizes.

Table 10.1 summarises some of the main issues which need management, but what are the main challenges in implementing strategy? E-consultancy (2005) surveyed UK e-commerce managers to assess their views on the main challenges of managing e-commerce within an organisation. In the context of the 7Ss, we can summarise the main challenges as follows:

- *Strategy* – Limited capabilities to integrate Internet strategy into core marketing and business strategy as discussed in Chapter 5 is indicated by frustration on gaining appropriate budgets.
- *Structure* – Structural and process issues are indicated by the challenges of gaining resource and buy-in from traditional marketing and IT functions.
- *Skills and staff* – These issues were indicated by difficulties in finding specialist staff or agencies.

Research for E-consultancy that I completed in 2005 and updated in 2008 highlighted some of the main challenges of implementing e-commerce. My initial sample for interviews was e-commerce managers for transactional sites – for example, mobile phones (Orange, The Carphone Warehouse), travel (Tui and MyTravel), financial services (Lloyds TSB and Bradford and Bingley) and direct marketers such as BCA.

Table 10.1	The 7S strategic framework and its application to digital business management

Element of 7S mode	Relevance to digital business management	Key issues
Strategy	The contribution of digital business in influencing and supporting organisations' strategy	• Gaining appropriate budgets and demonstrating/delivering value and ROI from budgets. Annual planning approach • Techniques for using digital business to impact organisation strategy • Techniques for aligning digital business strategy with organisational and marketing strategy
Structure	The modification of organisational structure to support digital business	• Integration of e-commerce team with other management, marketing (corporate communications, brand marketing, direct marketing) and IT staff • Use of cross-functional teams and steering groups • Insourcing *vs* outsourcing
Systems	The development of specific processes, procedures or information systems to support Internet marketing	• Campaign planning approach-integration • Managing/sharing customer information • Managing content quality • Unified reporting of digital marketing effectiveness • In-house *vs* external best-of-breed *vs* external integrated technology solutions
Staff	The breakdown of staff in terms of their background, age and sex and characteristics such as IT vs marketing, use of contractors/consultants	• Insourcing *vs* outsourcing • Achieving senior management buy-in/involvement with digital marketing • Staff recruitment and retention. Virtual working • Staff development and training
Style	Includes both the way in which key managers behave in achieving the organisation's goals and the cultural style of the organisation as a whole	• Relates to role of the e-commerce team in influencing strategy – is it dynamic and influential or conservative and looking for a voice?
Skills	Distinctive capabilities of key staff, but can be interpreted as specific skill-sets of team members	• Staff skills in specific areas: supplier selection, project management, content management, specific digital marketing approaches (search engine marketing, affiliate marketing, email marketing, online advertising)
Superordinate	The guiding concepts of the e-commerce organisation which are also part of shared values and culture. The internal and external perception of these goals may vary	• Improving the perception of the importance and effectiveness of the e-commerce team amongst senior managers and staff it works with (marketing generalists and IT)

One of the aims of the research was to gain a picture of the organisational processes and activities that need to be managed as part of sell-side e-commerce and the organisational structures that had been created to manage this. Figure 10.2 gives an indication of the number of operational e-CRM processes that need to be managed across the three core e-CRM areas (acquisition, conversion, retention) which we reviewed in Chapter 9. It also shows the management activities needed to support these. Some large organisations in the study had between 10 and 50 specialist staff managing these activities. For smaller companies, there is also the challenge that only 1 or 2 people are responsible for these activities, so they will need to work smart and outsource many of the activities!

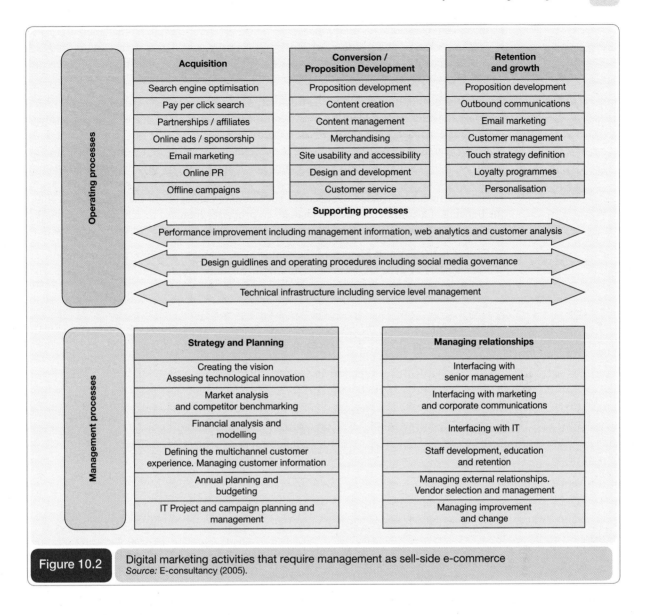

Figure 10.2	Digital marketing activities that require management as sell-side e-commerce
	Source: E-consultancy (2005).

As part of the research, respondents were asked what their main challenges were and these highlighted the issues of gaining sufficient resources for Internet marketing. Their key challenges included:

- *Gaining buy-in and budget* consistent with audience media consumption and value generated.
- *Conflicts of ownership and tensions* between a digital marketing team, traditional marketing, IT, and finance and senior management.
- *Coordination with different channels* in conjunction with teams managing marketing programmes elsewhere in the business.
- *Managing and integrating customer information* about characteristics and behaviours collected online.
- *Achieving a unified reporting* and performance improvement process throughout the business including reporting, analysis and actioning suggested changes.
- *Structuring the specialist digital team* and integrating into the organisation by changing responsibilities elsewhere in the organisation.

- *Insourcing vs outsourcing online marketing tactics,* i.e. search, affiliate, email marketing, PR.
- *Staff recruitment and retention* since there is a shortage of digital marketing skills given the rapid growth in demand for these skills, which gives great opportunities for everyone reading this book!

After initial qualitative interviews, identifying the type of challenges faced by an e-commerce manager, a wider survey identified how common these problems were. The responses of e-commerce managers are summarised in Figure 10.3.

The research showed that managing the interfaces between the e-commerce team and other parts of the organisation was a major challenge for many organisations. Managing these interfaces is a key role of the head of e-commerce and managers within their team. Every respondent articulated the need for education of colleagues in the organisation about the benefits of e-commerce and the changes in processes required to achieve these benefits. This need for education was mentioned with respect to three main parts of the organisation:

1 Senior management. Managing the senior management team interface was mainly an issue for less-evolved adopters of e-commerce. Leading adopters mentioned it had been a

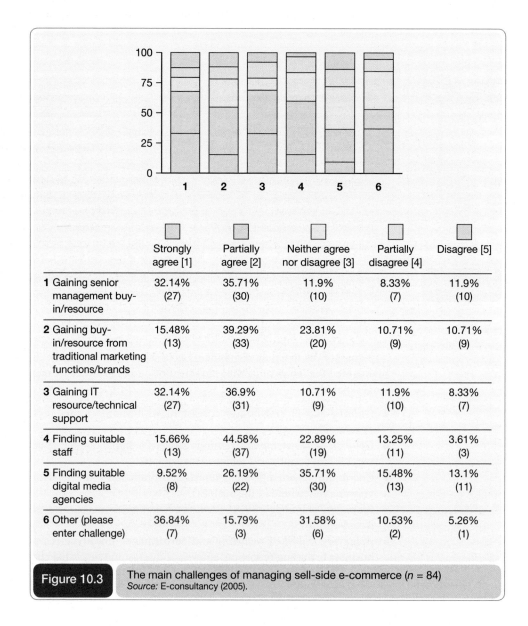

	Strongly agree [1]	Partially agree [2]	Neither agree nor disagree [3]	Partially disagree [4]	Disagree [5]
1 Gaining senior management buy-in/resource	32.14% (27)	35.71% (30)	11.9% (10)	8.33% (7)	11.9% (10)
2 Gaining buy-in/resource from traditional marketing functions/brands	15.48% (13)	39.29% (33)	23.81% (20)	10.71% (9)	10.71% (9)
3 Gaining IT resource/technical support	32.14% (27)	36.9% (31)	10.71% (9)	11.9% (10)	8.33% (7)
4 Finding suitable staff	15.66% (13)	44.58% (37)	22.89% (19)	13.25% (11)	3.61% (3)
5 Finding suitable digital media agencies	9.52% (8)	26.19% (22)	35.71% (30)	15.48% (13)	13.1% (11)
6 Other (please enter challenge)	36.84% (7)	15.79% (3)	31.58% (6)	10.53% (2)	5.26% (1)

Figure 10.3   The main challenges of managing sell-side e-commerce (*n* = 84)
Source: E-consultancy (2005).

problem, but they now felt they had achieved understanding of the strategic importance of online channels and this was matched by financial resources and sufficient input into planning to achieve alignment between business objectives and e-commerce initiatives.

2 **Marketing, different brands, businesses or countries.** Similarly, this was more of an issue for the less-evolved organisations. Others had created processes for collaboration between e-commerce and marketing teams and defined responsibilities for e-commerce within these marketing teams.

3 **Information technology.** This interface was mentioned as a challenge by nearly every respondent – there was a belief that insufficient resource for applications development was limiting the potential of e-commerce to deliver value to customers and the organisation. Where this was less of an issue, companies had either incorporated some development function within the e-commerce function, or had outsourced parts of development.

Growth hacking
An approach to improving the commercial results from online services through structured testing and optimisation of marketing approaches.

Smaller business and start-up business face a different set of challenges in using digital technologies to make their business a success, particularly if their business is based on using digital technology to see their services only as a pureplay retailer of Software as a Service (SaaS) business, introduced in Chapter 3. Recently, the concept of **growth hacking** has developed as a way of supporting the profitable growth of these businesses.

Box 10.1	Growth hacking

Andrew Chen, an entrepreneur who is an adviser and investor to many start-ups, describes a growth hacker as follows in his post *Growth Hacker is the new VP Marketing* (Chen, 2012).

Growth hackers are a hybrid of marketer and coder, one who looks at the traditional question of "How do I get customers for my product?" and answers with A/B tests, landing pages, viral factor, email deliverability, and Open Graph. On top of this, they layer the discipline of direct marketing, with its emphasis on quantitative measurement, scenario modeling via spreadsheets, and a lot of database queries.

This quote shows that many of the features such as a focus on testing and learning through conversion rate optimisation (CRO) are not new – indeed, they have been featured in this book for several editions – but it shows a change in mindset in how business transformation can be achieved. Another key feature of growth hacking is examining techniques for getting viral growth through encouraging users to share their experience. The growth of Hotmail from 0 to 12 million users before it was bought by Microsoft is a favourite anecdote of growth hackers. For Hotmail the sharing was rapid due to the email signature: 'PS I love you. Get your free email at Hotmail. Signature.' Today, encouraging sharing through social sign-on and social sharing is more an approach sought by growth hackers. These techniques have helped companies like LinkedIn grow from 13 million to 175 million users, according to Schranz (2012), who explained that Facebook's Growth team started by establishing a simple framework of things to measure and improve to make it easier for everyone to understand what to focus on and why it matters:

- Acquisition – Get people in front of your product . . .
- Activation – Provide a great initial experience . . .
- Engagement – Keep people engaged, deliver value . . .
- (Virality) – Get people to recommend your product . . .

Some of the principles of growth hacking are being adopted by existing businesses, looking to enhance the sales of their digital channels. For example, publisher

The Guardian's advertising for a Head of Growth Hacking . . . describing the growth in the role as:

> 'The Guardian is committed to a "digital-first" strategy and in order to support this, we are seeking a Head of Growth Hacking to manage a virtual, cross functional team focussed on GNM's growth hacking plan. This role is responsible for finding innovative ways to accelerate adoption, use, and retention to drive up audiences to the Guardian's digital product portfolio.'

Different types of change in business

Incremental change
Relatively small adjustments required by an organisation in response to its business environment.

Discontinuous change
Change involving a major transformation in an industry.

Organisational change
Includes both incremental and discontinuous change to organisations.

Anticipatory change
An organisation initiates change without an immediate need to respond.

Reactive change
A direct response by an organisation to a change in its environment.

Viewed at a large scale across an entire industry, change takes two forms. **Incremental change** involves relatively small adjustments required by changes in the business environment (Chapter 4). Organisations scan their environment and make adjustments according to the introduction of new products from competitors, new laws or long-term changes in customer behaviour. Organisations also make changes to improve the efficiency of their processes. More significant discontinuous change or transformational change involves a major change in the business environment which changes the basis for competition. The opportunities and threats presented by widespread availability of low-cost Internet connectivity is a **discontinuous change**.

Organisational change mirrors that at industry level. It can occur on a continuous or incremental basis or on a discontinuous basis. The introduction of digital business requires organisations to manage both types of change.

Nadler *et al.* (1995) developed a useful way of classifying types of organisational change. This uses the concepts of incremental and discontinuous change together with anticipatory or reactive change. **Anticipatory change** occurs when an organisation makes proactive changes in order to improve its efficiency or to create an advantage within the competitive environment. **Reactive change** is a direct response to a change in the external environment. The four different forms of organisational change identified by Nadler *et al.* (1995) are:

1 **Tuning.** This is an incremental form of change when there is no immediate need for change. It can be categorised as 'doing things better'. New procedures or policies may be used to improve process efficiency, e.g. to reduce time to market or reduce costs of doing business. Digital business involves 'tuning' as Internet technologies are applied to improve efficiency.

2 **Adaptation.** Also an incremental form of change, but in this case it is in response to an external threat or opportunity. It can also be categorised as 'doing things better'. For example, a competitor may introduce a new product or there may be a merger between two rivals. A response is required, but it does not involve a significant change in the basis for competition. Managing digital business-related change also requires adaptation.

3 **Re-orientation.** A significant change or transformation to the organisation is identified as a priority in the short-to-medium term. There is not an immediate need for change, but a significant change is anticipation of change. When IBM was one of the first organisations to introduce the concept of 'digital business' in the mid-1990s, this was a re-orientation in the way it delivered its service (with an increased focus on consultancy services rather than hardware and software) which helped to spark a wider change in the way businesses worked. Successful adoption of digital business also requires re-orientation for many organisations.

4 **Re-creation.** In re-creation, the senior management team of an organisation decides that a fundamental change to the way it operates is required to compete effectively. In the airline industry, established airlines have had to establish change programmes to respond

to the low-cost carriers, for example by emphasising service quality or introducing rival low-cost services. Both re-orientation and re-creation can be categorised as 'doing things differently'. Digital business has also caused 're-creation' in the airline industry, with the low-cost airlines now gaining more than 90% of bookings online. However, as we saw in Chapter 4, such dramatic change has not been caused in every industry.

Business process management

So, some forms of digital business initiative related to internal processes such as the introduction of a human resources management system are simply about improving efficiency – they involve incremental change. The practice of improving the efficiency of business processes with the assistance of information systems is an important activity in many organisations as is shown by Case study 10.1. It can be seen that the label in vogue at the time of writing is 'business process management' (BPM). This encompasses different scales of improving business process that are introduced above.

The BPM concept has been defined by Gartner (2003) as follows:

BPM is a methodology, as well a collection of tools that enables enterprises to specify step-by-step business processes. Proper analysis and design of BPM flows require a strong understanding of the atomic business steps that must be performed to complete a business process. As BPM executes a business process, these atomic steps will often correspond to well-known business activities, such as checking credit ratings, updating customer accounts and checking inventory status. In effect, the BPM process flow is often just a sequence of well-known services, executed in a coordinated fashion.

Classic document workflow, which was BPM's predecessor, focused on humans performing the services. Fueled by the power of application integration, BPM focuses on human and automated agents doing the work to deliver the services.

Discontinuous process change

Although BPM often refers to continuous, incremental change, other forms of information-management-related applications such as e-ticketing for an airline will be associated with discontinuous change – with low-cost airlines such as easyJet and Ryanair now selling over 90% of their tickets online this has had a fairly significant impact on the airline industry. The introduction of digital business applications or enterprise resource planning systems described in Chapter 2 are also often related to transformational change programmes. Three degrees of business process change are shown in Table 10.2.

In the early to mid-1990s organisation-wide transformational change was advocated under the label of 'business process re-engineering' (BPR). It was popularised through

Business process management (BPM)
An approach supported by software tools intended to increase process efficiency by improving information flows between people as they perform business tasks.

Business process re-engineering (BPR)
Identifying radical, new ways of carrying out business operations, often enabled by new IT capabilities.

Table 10.2	Alternative terms for using IS to enhance company performance		
Term	**Involves**	**Intention**	**Risk of failure**
Business process re-engineering	Fundamental redesign of all main company processes through organisation-wide initiatives	Large gains in performance (>100%?)	Highest
Business process improvement	Targets key processes in sequence for redesign	(<50%)	Medium
Business process automation	Automating existing process. Often uses workflow software (Chapter 2)	(<20%)	Lowest

the pronouncements of Hammer and Champy (1993) and Davenport (1993). The essence of BPR is the assertion that business processes, organisational structures, team structures and employee responsibilities can be fundamentally altered to improve business performance. Hammer and Champy (1993) defined BPR as:

> *the fundamental rethinking and radical redesign of business processes to achieve dramatic improvements in critical, contemporary measures of performance, such as cost, quality, service, and speed.*

The key terms from this definition that encapsulate the BPR concept are:

- *Fundamental rethinking* – re-engineering usually refers to changing of significant business processes such as customer service, sales order processing or manufacturing.
- *Radical redesign* – re-engineering involves a complete rethinking about the way business processes operate.
- *Dramatic improvements* – the aim of BPR is to achieve improvements measured in tens or hundreds of per cent. With automation of existing processes only single-figure improvements may be possible.
- *Critical contemporary measures of performance* – this point refers to the importance of measuring how well the processes operate in terms of the four important measures of cost, quality, service and speed.

In *Re-engineering the Corporation* (1993) Hammer and Champy have a chapter giving examples of how IS can act as a catalyst for change (disruptive technologies). These technologies are familiar from applications of digital business such as those described in Chapter 2 and include tracking technology, decision support tools, telecommunications networks, teleconferencing and shared databases. Hammer and Champy label these as 'disruptive technologies', a term still used today, which suggests how new digital technologies can force companies to reconsider their processes and find new ways of operating. It is arguable, though, whether technology is commonly disruptive in the sense of achieving major changes such as those in the re-orientation and re-creation categories.

Many re-engineering projects were launched in the 1990s and failed due to their ambitious scale and the problems of managing large information systems projects. Furthermore, BPR was also often linked to downsizing in many organisations, leading to an outflow of staff and knowledge from businesses. As a result BPR as a concept has fallen out of favour and more caution in achieving change is advocated.

Business process improvement (BPI)
Optimising existing processes, typically coupled with enhancements in information technology.

Less radical approaches to organisational transformation are referred to as **business process improvement (BPI)** or by Davenport (1993) as 'business process innovation'. Taking the example of a major digital business initiative for supply chain management, an organisation would have to decide on the scope of change. For instance, do all supply chain activities need to be revised simultaneously or can certain activities such as procurement or outbound logistics be targeted initially? Modern thinking would suggest that the latter approach is preferable.

Business process automation (BPA)
Automating existing ways of working manually through information technology.

If a less radical approach is adopted, care should be taken not to fall into the trap of simply using technology to automate existing processes which are sub-optimal – in plain words, using information technology 'to do bad things faster'. This approach of using technology to support existing procedures and practices is known as **business process automation (BPA)**. Although benefits can be achieved through this approach, the improvements may not be sufficient to generate a return on investment.

A staged approach to the introduction of BPR has been suggested by Davenport (1993). This can also be applied to digital business change. He suggests the following stages that can be applied to digital business:

- *Identify the process for innovation* – these are the major business processes from the organisation's value chain which add most to the value for the customer or achieve the largest efficiency benefits for the company. Examples include customer relationship management, logistics and procurement.

- *Identify the change levers* – these can encourage and help achieve change. The main change levers are innovative technology and, as we have seen, the organisation's culture and structure.
- *Develop the process vision* – this involves communication of the reasons for changes and what can be achieved in order to help achieve buy-in throughout the organisation.
- *Understand the existing processes* – current business processes are documented. This allows the performance of existing business processes to be benchmarked and so provides a means for measuring the extent to which a re-engineered process has improved business performance.
- *Design and prototype the new process* – the vision is translated into practical new processes which the organisation is able to operate. Prototyping the new process operates on two levels. First, simulation and modelling tools can be used to check the logical operation of the process. Second, assuming that the simulation model shows no significant problems, the new process can be given a full operational trial. Needless to say, the implementation must be handled sensitively if it is to be accepted by all parties.

Cope and Waddell (2001) assessed approaches managers in manufacturing industry in Australia use to introduce e-commerce services. They tested for different stages of transformation from fine-tuning through incremental adjustment, modular transformation and corporate transformation. They found that in this particular industry at the time of the survey, a relatively conservative approach of 'fine-tuning' was predominant.

Case Study 10.1	Process management: making complex business simpler	**FT**

This case gives a modern perspective on approaches to improve business processes using information systems. It summarises the tools, benefits and some of the problems associated with business process management.

Steven S. Smith, chief technology officer for the US bank Wells Fargo Financial, introduced his company to business process management last year.

Note how he did it: 'I didn't go to our divisional chief executive and say: "We are going to invest in this tool." Instead, we brought the technology in and worked together with the business on a specific issue. It was the business manager who presented to the divisional CEO. He said: "Look at the benefits of this new technology."

'All the IT people were sitting in the room with big smiles on their faces. They didn't have to say a word. It was the business bragging about how wonderful it is,' he says.

When the business side of an organisation has good things to say, unprompted, about a new technology, something unusual is happening and, for many companies, that something is business process management.

It is a methodology underpinned by a technology and it is a hot ticket.

Accenture, the world's largest consultancy, already has a global director for BPM, Jim Adamczyk.

He describes it as a mindset: 'It is something that has mostly been going on for a long time. What has changed is the convergence of the business need for process engineering with the evolution of technology that lets people build systems flexible enough to supply the need.'

In a new book, Kiran Garimella, Michael Lees and Bruce Williams (2008) of Software AG, the European consultancy, say that BPM represents a culmination of all the collective experience, thinking and professional development in business management over the past several decades.

'It's customer first. It's business focused, it empowers people in all corners of a business to be more successful. It brings people and systems together. BPM is where all the lofty goals and best strategies are coming home to roost,' they say.

It sounds too good to be true and it has already attracted the attention of a string of software houses and consultancies from the 'pure play' vendors such as Pegasystems, Savvion and Lombardi at one end to the big 'stack' vendors including Oracle and IBM at the other.

It is easy to see why Mr Adamczyk worries: 'I fear that this is being hyped as one of our endless series of silver bullets, but at core we are trying to align the domain of the business – what the business needs – with what IT can understand and build.'

What is driving the adoption of BPM? Ram Menon, head of worldwide marketing for the pure play vendor Tibco, argues that increasing business complexity is the chief cause: 'At the core, it's about agility, efficiency and productivity. Businesses are continually under pressure to get more work done with fewer resources.

'Regulatory compliance is another driver. Rules such as the European Union's Markets in Financial Instruments directive (MiFID) and Sarbanes–Oxley in the US have a significant process dimension. In healthcare, it's HIPAA. Almost every industry has its list of compliance requirements.

'Used appropriately, BPM helps companies streamline processes, reduce cycle times and get things done faster. This frees employees to focus on areas where they can add real value.'

BPM provides the tools to enable organisations to examine, analyse and improve their processes, with a process being anything that transforms resources and materials into products or services.

'This transformation is how a business works; it's the magic elixir of the enterprise,' say the Software AG authors. 'The more effective this transformation, the more successfully you create value.'

BPM software provides the technological underpinning that facilitates communication and mobility of data across applications. Only in the past few years has the software become mature enough to be used reliably for this purpose.

There are four main phases: process analysis, process design, process automation and business activity monitoring – which provides the feedback for further improvements.

Here are two examples of BPM in action.

University College London Hospitals comprises seven large hospitals in central London treating hundreds of thousands of in and out-patients each year through a bewilderingly large number of specialisms.

Government targets demand that no more than 18 weeks elapse between first referral and the start of treatment. James Thomas, UCLH IT director, knew the existing manual methods of tracking patients through what are known as 'care pathways' could not cope.

He wanted to introduce technology that would enable tracking by exception. Only if a staging post on the care pathway failed – a missing laboratory report, for example – would a warning flag be raised. The UCLH system sends an email to the individual responsible to alert them to the deficiency.

In conjunction with Logica CMG, the consultancy, Mr Thomas used BPM software from Lombardi to map the care pathway for a single specialism, discovering in the process that the first and last thirds of the process are identical. The middle third depends on the particular specialism involved.

Business activity monitoring (BAM) software was used to monitor the progress of the patient along the pathway. 'It's your conscience. It's an incredibly good policeman,' Mr Thomas says.

The system will be live across one hospital in the group by the end of this month; the whole of UCLH by the end of the year. But it has not been easy: 'Getting people to acknowledge that they work to processes and to document those processes and then work through harmonising those processes is not easy. You're talking about administrative and clinical staff in different hospital buildings.

'Potentially, people might see this as a form of electronic Big Brother that sends them emails when they haven't done something. We have to turn that on its head and say the task facing us is too big for our current way of working – this is something to help us break up and digest the problem.'

At Wells Fargo Financial, Mr Smith was concerned that it was taking too long to complete certain business processes. The test bed for the BPM software that he brought in was the process that tracked the answers the bank gave customers who asked for a loan.

'The specific issue was: how to track the salesperson's response to the customer after a decision had been made on a loan. If the customer failed to take up the loan even if it was approved, what was the reason,' Mr Smith says.

Tracking the process manually would have required hiring another 20 staff across the US; four were already in place.

The BPM software took four months to install – Mr Smith blames the delay on his team's reluctance to use 'agile' development methods rather than the tried and tested 'waterfall' technique – but it resulted in automating the process for the whole of North America using three rather than the four existing staff.

The bank has implemented a number of BPM systems after that first deployment. In one, the process for adding a new merchant to the bank's private label credit card product, which used to take weeks now takes only a day or so.

Mr Smith says that, with so many BPM vendors, it is important to choose the most appropriate by bringing them into the facility and asking them to interface with the existing systems.

These two examples demonstrate important principles of BPM deployment.

First, the need to start in a small way – a single process such as Mr Thomas's patient care pathway or Mr Smith's loan agreement is enough for proof of concept.

Second, the need to capture the hearts and the minds of the people who have to use the system. Mr Thomas insisted, for example, that hospital staff would not have to use new techniques or undergo extra training to make full use of the system.

Rod Favaron, chief executive of Lombardi, says companies will see three kinds of benefits from BPM, properly deployed: efficiency, effectiveness and agility.

'In the era of Service Oriented Architecture and on-demand market messages, agility is a well understood concept. In the world of process management, the ability to change quickly is essential,' he says.

'Customers on average change their key processes between four and seven times a year. New opportunities can arise. New partners or customers need you to support a different way of doing business.'

'Government regulations can require companies to change their processes. BPM provides the platform they need to be able to change processes faster and in a more controlled fashion than any other option.'

Source: Alan Cane, Process Management: Making complex business a lot simpler? *The Financial Times,* 14 May 2008. Reprinted with permission.

Questions

1 How does the article suggest that business thinking and practice has evolved since the exhortations for business process re-engineering in the 1990s?
2 Summarise the benefits for BPM discussed in the article.
3 Discuss the need for a concept such as BPM when all new information systems and digital business initiatives are ultimately driven by process improvement.

Planning change

Our starting point for managing change is when the objectives, strategy and tactics for introducing digital business change have already been specified as outlined in Part 2. Here, we are concerned with how to implement the strategy to achieve the objectives through the activities performed by the project management team as part of project planning.

The imperative for project governance?

A recent survey of the challenges of managing digital business implementation projects is indicated by a survey of over 600 European and US businesses involved in management of web-related projects (E-consultancy, 2007). The research found that:

- Only 58% of respondents say that their projects always achieve their goals, and yet only 21% of them say they always achieve deadlines.
- Only 39% always achieve budget and a positive ROI.
- Over 8% of respondents never meet their project deadlines and nearly 6% never deliver their projects within budget.
- Nearly half of all respondents (45.5%) do *not* have a structured approach to managing their web projects.

Respondents to the E-consultancy (2007) research believed that web-related projects are different from other projects because of their need to be responsive to:

- changing customer requirements and market conditions;
- the breadth of people and skills involved;
- the raft of stakeholders;
- frequently tight or fixed deadlines;
- a degree of uncertainty;
- and the need for interaction with real customers.

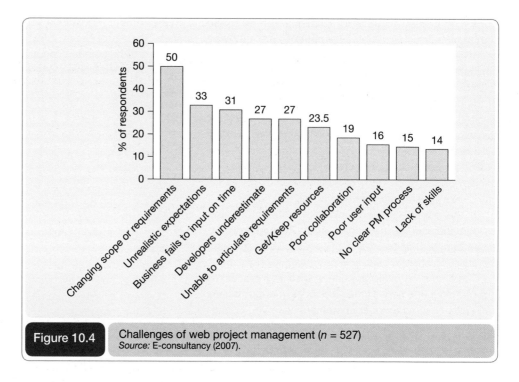

| Figure 10.4 | Challenges of web project management (*n* = 527)
Source: E-consultancy (2007). |

E-consultancy (2007) also looked at the main challenges of web project management which are shown in Figure 10.4 and corresponding approaches to overcome these challenges in Figure 10.5.

The research concluded that web projects require a project management approach that helps with:

- evolving requirements;
- putting focus on the end-customer;

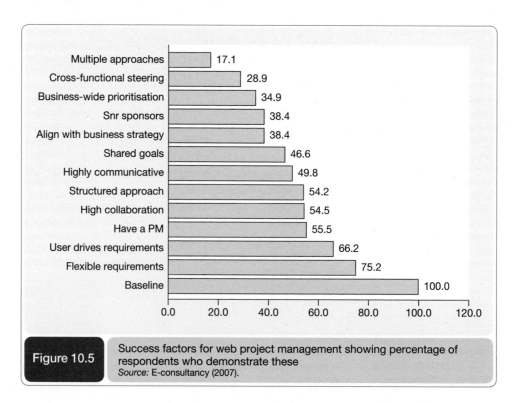

| Figure 10.5 | Success factors for web project management showing percentage of respondents who demonstrate these
Source: E-consultancy (2007). |

- collaboration between different skill sets;
- managing stakeholder expectations.

Further research by the Standish Group summarised by Clarety (2009) reveals further insights into the reasons for project failure. It identifies the top five reasons for 'challenged projects' mentioned by respondents:

1 Lack of user input (12.8%)
2 Incomplete requirements and specifications (12.3%)
3 Changing requirements and specifications (11.8%)
4 Lack of executive support (7.5%)
5 Technology incompetence (7%)

The top five success factors were identified as:

1 User involvement (15.9%)
2 Executive management support (13.9%)
3 Clear statement of requirements (13.0%)
4 Proper planning (9.6%)
5 Realistic expectations (8.2%)

You can see that a focus on user requirements and senior management support are common to many of these factors.

It follows that the project governance of digital business projects, like that of other major information systems, is essential to success. The COBIT framework provides a good summary of the requirements from a governance approach. COBIT is the widely adopted IT governance model for Control Objectives for Information and related Technology. This definition is also helpful since it highlights some of the success factors in project management which we will cover later in this chapter. Project management is one of the key processes COBIT identifies for the effective governance of IT. It defines its control objective PO10 (COBIT, 2001) as follows.

Managing projects should satisfy the business requirement:

to set priorities and to deliver on time and within budget

and be enabled by

the organisation identifying and prioritising projects in line with the operational plan and the adoption and application of sound project management techniques for each project undertaken and takes into consideration:

- *business management sponsorship for projects*
- *program management*
- *project management capabilities*
- *user involvement*
- *task breakdown, milestone definition and phase approvals*
- *allocation of responsibilities*
- *rigorous tracking of milestones and deliverables*
- *cost and manpower budgets, balancing internal and external resources*
- *quality assurance plans and methods*
- *program and project risk assessments*
- *transition from development to operations.*

For effective project management the following elements need to be incorporated as part of the project management process as described, for example, by Chaffey and Wood (2005):

- *Estimation* – identifying the activities involved in the project, sometimes referred to as a 'work breakdown structure' (WBS). The sequence of activities for implementation of a typical digital business system is shown in Figure 10.6.

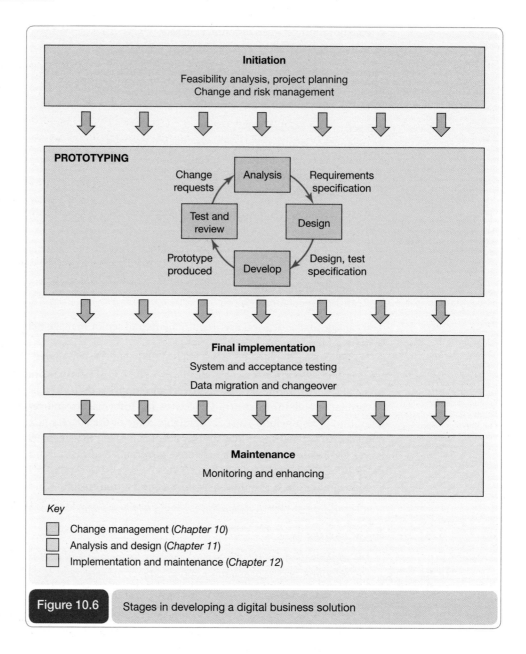

Figure 10.6 Stages in developing a digital business solution

- *Resource allocation* – after the initial WBS, appropriate resources can be allocated to the tasks.
- *Schedule/plan* – after resource allocation, the amount of time for each task can be determined according to the availability and skills of the people assigned to the tasks. Effort time is the total amount of work that needs to occur to complete a task. Elapsed time indicates how long in time (such as calendar days) the task will take, and is dependent on the number of people working on the task, and their skills.
- *Monitoring and control* – monitoring involves ensuring the project is working to plan once it has started. Control is taking corrective action if the project deviates from the plan. In particular the project manager will want to hit **milestones** – events that need to happen on a particular date are defined for which performance against objectives can be measured.

Milestone
Key deadline to be achieved during project, usually with defined deliverable.

The project plan and schedule for a digital business system

The project plan for a digital business system will involve all of the stages shown in Figure 10.6. This diagram also shows how the final part of the book is structured.

Initiation

The start-up phase of the project.

- In this chapter we review the activities needed during the **initiation** phase of a project that involves the creation of a change management programme including project planning, managing organisational change and risk management. In this chapter we do not consider feasibility analysis since assessment of the costs and benefits of the digital business system have already been considered as an aspect of strategy as described in Part 2.
- In Chapter 11 the analysis and design phases are described. In these the requirements of the organisation and users of the system are defined and translated into a design from which the system can be built. Analysis and design occur in an iterative fashion through prototyping as described in the section that follows.
- In Chapter 12 the final stages of developing the digital business system are described. These include writing the program code, building the databases, migrating data, testing the system and managing the changeover to the live system. Chapter 12 also describes the maintenance of the system once it is live. This is monitoring the system and enhancing it as bugs and opportunities arise.

These stages in developing a digital business system use well-established approaches to building IS based on the **systems development life cycle**. But significant differences project managers need to take into account are:

Systems development life cycle

The sequence in which a system is created from initiation, analysis, design, implementation, build and maintenance.

- The timescales for delivery of the system are compressed compared to traditional applications – the system needs to be developed in 'Internet time'. Prototyping and making activities such as analysis, design and testing which occur in parallel are used to achieve tight deadlines, as is the use of off-the-shelf systems perhaps hosted with an ASP (Chapter 3).
- The e-commerce system may be hosted outside of an organisation so we need to consider the constraints imposed by hosting the site externally with an ISP and integrating external components of the system with data stored and processes occurring inside the organisation.
- The focus of the project is on content and services rather than on application; this means that delivery of information is the key. Linking different information sources and different applications through APIs is also becoming more important.
- Because the system is customer-facing and on the public Internet, speed and availability are crucial, as is securing the system from malicious hackers and spammers.
- Analysis and design are arguably more closely related in an e-commerce implementation since the usability of the site is critically dependent on the needs of the user and the prototyping approach is used to achieve users' needs.
- Once launched the site or service should be more dynamic than a traditional application: an effective site will be updated continuously in response to customer demands and testing. The solution is never complete. Mini case study 10.2 illustrates how continuous improvements to a site can improve performance.

With increasing use of the SaaS services introduced in Chapter 3, the analysis, design and build stages tend to be different from bespoke IS implementation. The analysis stage is equally important, but will focus on mapping the facilities of the off-the-shelf software with the existing business practices. A vital decision is the extent to which the company will change or adapt its practices and processes to match the software or web services or the extent it will be possible to tailor the system to match the processes. The degree of customisation to a company's needs also becomes a key issue.

Mini Case Study 10.2	Conversion optimisation leads to increased sales for one of Europe's leading hip hop stores

Def-Shop.com provides Europe's largest selection of hip hop clothing. Most of its sales are to the German market.

In April 2009, Def-Shop began working with Conversion Rate Experts to help increase its profits. Early tests on key pages have resulted in increases in conversion rate of 20%, 63% and 115%.

Here are some of the activities that Def-Shop and Conversion Rate Experts have collaborated on:

- E-commerce sites have several core functions, one of which is 'matchmaking' – the site needs to show products that the visitor is most likely to be interested in. There are several ways of doing this, such as product recommendation engines, search boxes, information architecture and navigation. An analysis of Def-Shop's site revealed great opportunities for improving the information architecture and navigation.
- It's important to give visitors reasons to buy from your site rather than from your competitors. Conversations with Def-Shop's staff revealed ten compelling advantages to ordering from Def-Shop; for example, Def-Shop has the largest selection, it has a great returns policy, and it has great credibility, in the form of associations with MTV and hip hop celebrities. This information was made prominent at key points in the conversion funnel.

Many successful businesses are based around a community of customers that share the same passions, values and interests. Def-Shop's CEO, Alexander Buchler, is passionate about hip hop culture, and feels that hip hop lacks a cultural focus in Europe. Conversion Rate Experts have encouraged Alex to invest in creating a whole community around Def-Shop, so the company becomes a focus for hip hop culture, rather than being just a web store.

The design phase will require much less input than for a bespoke system. It will focus on issues of how to tailor the user interface, database structures and security of the off-the-shelf package to the needs of the digital business solution. The build and implementation phases will still be involved and, as for any implementation, the project manager will have to schedule software and database configuration, data migration, testing and training.

An illustration of a typical project schedule for a sell-side e-commerce system is illustrated in Box 10.2.

Box 10.2	Example task breakdown and schedule

This case illustrates the different tasks that need to be performed as part of a sell-side e-commerce implementation for a company that does not have a website presence.

The schedule can be structured as followed:

1 **Pre-development tasks.** These include domain name registration and deciding on the company to host the website. It is important to register the domain name for the site as early as possible. It also includes preparing a brief of the aims and objectives of the site, then, if intending to outsource, presenting this to rival companies to bid.
2 **Content planning.** This is the detailed analysis and design of the site, including prototyping.
3 **Content development and testing.** Writing the HTML pages, producing the graphics and testing.
4 **Publishing the site.** This is a relatively short stage.
5 **Pre-launch promotion.** This is the marketing communications techniques described in Chapter 9.
6 **Ongoing promotion.** The schedule should also allow for periodic promotion which might involve discount promotions or competitions. These are often reused.

Figure 10.7 gives an indication of the relationship between these tasks, and how long they may take for a typical initial e-commerce site.

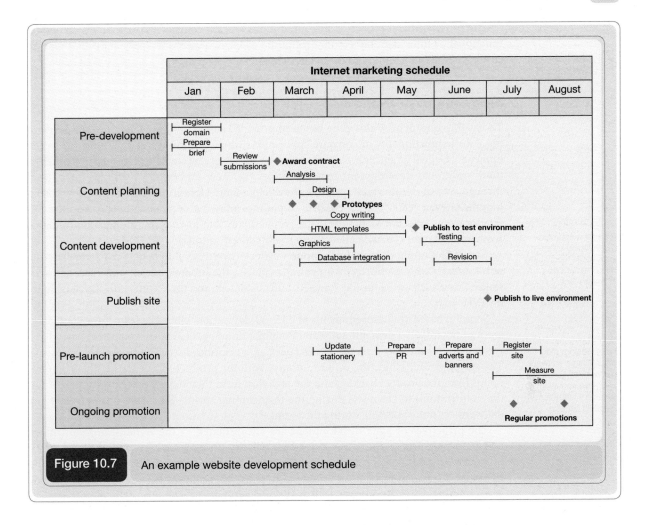

| Figure 10.7 | An example website development schedule |

Prototyping

Prototyping

An iterative process in which website users suggest modifications before further prototypes and the live version of the site are developed.

RAD – Rapid Application Development

An approach to information systems development that includes incremental development using prototypes.

Prototype

A preliminary version of part or all of an information system reviewed by its users and business sponsors.

Prototyping is a common approach to the development of digital business systems; its essence is that it is:

- *Rapid* – Prototyping is part of a systems development approach known as '**RAD – Rapid Application Development**' since the time from inception to completion is reduced to months rather than years. More rapid development is achieved through reducing the length of time of the analysis, design and build stages by combining them in conjunction with the use of graphical software tools with which applications can be built quickly from pre-assembled components.
- *Simple* – Skeleton applications are produced as prototypes that do not contain all the functions of a system but are a framework which gives a good indication to users of the information available and the look and feel of an application. They can then comment on it and say, for example, 'this information is missing' or 'we like that feature, but it would be nice to do that also' or 'that feature isn't necessary, it's not what we meant'.
- *Iterative* – Prototypes are produced often at a frequency of one every few days or weeks so that the comments from the last review can be fed into the evolving system.
- *Incremental* – Each prototype incorporates the feedback from the previous review, so each version of the application has a limited number of new features.
- *User-centred* – Users are involved at all stages of development, in describing the existing system, reviewing the **prototypes** and testing the system.

The prototyping approach is now ubiquitous since it reduces the risk of major design, functional or informational errors during the construction of the application that may be costly and time-consuming to fix at a later stage in development.

Agile software development

Today, the concept of prototyping has been extended across the whole life cycle for developing website functionality or software applications where it is known as agile software development. The goal of agile development is to be able to create stable releases more frequently than traditional development methodologies, i.e. new functionality will be introduced through several releases each month rather than a more significant release every few weeks, months or even years. The approach is sometimes known as 'permanent beta'. Another difference from agile development is the emphasis on face-to-face communication to define requirements rather than detailed requirements specifications.

Scrum is a methodology that supports agile software development. Scrum involves the *scrum master* who is effectively a project manager, the *product owner* who represents the stakeholders such as the business owners and customers, and the scrum *team* which includes the developers.

Scrum is based on focussed sprints of a 15–30-day period where the team creates an increment of potentially releasable software. Potential functionality for each sprint is agreed at a *sprint planning meeting from the product backlog*, a prioritised set of high-level requirements. The sprint planning meeting is itself iterative with the product owner stating their requirements from the product backlog and the technical team then determining how much of this they can commit to complete during the forthcoming sprint. The term 'scrum' refers to a daily project status meeting during the sprint.

The principles of agile development are encapsulated in the *Agile Manifesto* (http://agilemanifesto.org/), which was agreed in 2001 by proponents of previous rapid development methodologies, including the Dynamic Systems Development Methodology and Extreme Programming. The Agile Manifesto is useful in illustrating the principles of agile programming which it contrasts with traditional approaches. The text of the manifesto is:

> *We are uncovering better ways of developing software by doing it and helping others do it.*
>
> *Through this work we have come to value:*
>
> - *Individuals and interactions over processes and tools*
> - *Working software over comprehensive documentation*
> - *Customer collaboration over contract negotiation*
> - *Responding to change over following a plan*
>
> *That is, while there is value in the items on the right, we value the items on the left more.*

Agile development
An iterative approach to developing software and website functionality with the emphasis on face-to-face communications to elicit, define and test requirements.

Scrum
A methodology that supports agile software development based on 15–30-day sprints to implement features from a product backlog.

Human resource requirements

Digital business implementation requires specialist skills that may not be present within an organisation. The range of specialist skill requirements is indicated in Figure 10.8. The E-consultancy (2005) research showed that over half of respondents felt it was a challenge, although there were more pressing challenges.

Digital business project managers have a choice of building a new skills set within their organisation or outsourcing and partnering with other organisations.

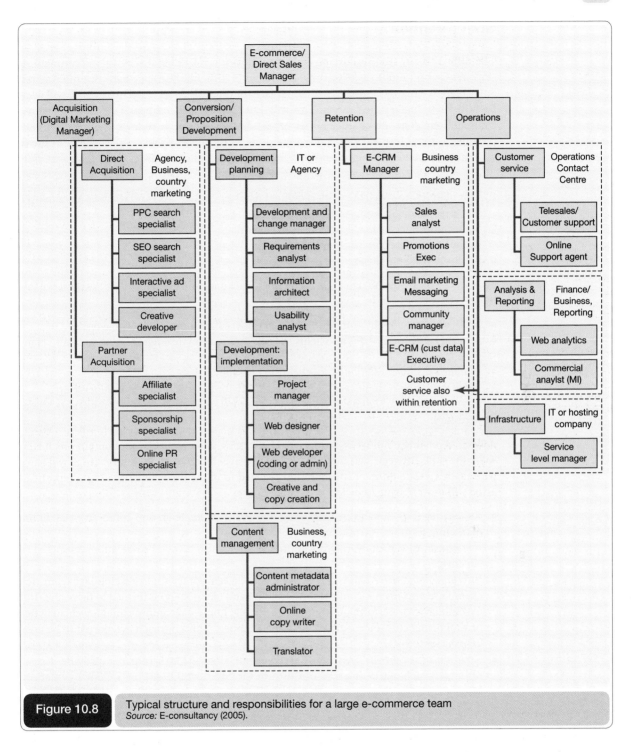

| Figure 10.8 | Typical structure and responsibilities for a large e-commerce team
Source: E-consultancy (2005). |

Even more problematic than selecting the right type of staff is attracting and retaining digital business staff. If we want effective, experienced staff then these will demand high salaries. We will be competing for these staff with dot-com companies that are trying to recruit and also other established medium-to-large companies that are looking to build a digital business capability. Smaller companies will have an even trickier problem of needing to find all of these skills rolled into one person!

Staff retention

The difficulties in staff resourcing for digital business do not end with the recruitment of staff. As Crush (2000) says, 'Getting good staff is difficult, keeping them is a nightmare!' Since there is a highly competitive marketplace for digital business staff, many staff will want to move on to further their career. This will often be after the company has spent some time training them. The job characteristics model developed by Hackman and Oldham (1980) provides a useful framework for designing jobs that provide a good experience to improve staff motivation and so help retention. The five intrinsic characteristics of a job are:

1 Skill variety.
2 Task identity, how well the work is defined relative to other tasks and whether an employee sees a job through 'from start to finish'.
3 Task significance or the importance of the work.
4 Autonomy or freedom in completing work.
5 Feedback from employer.

To enhance these psychological characteristics Hackman and Oldham (1980) suggest the following approaches can be used:

● *Task combination* – by combining tasks employees see more of the whole task.
● *Natural workgroups* – this also helps in task combination through creating a team to complete tasks.
● *Establish customer relations* – this helps in task significance.
● *Vertical loading* – employees take responsibility for tasks completed by supervisors.
● *Opening feedback channel* – from internal or external customers, via managers where necessary.

As well as making employees' roles more challenging and enjoyable, another approach is to share the skills between staff, so that if key staff leave, then not all their knowledge will leave with them. Certain types of collaboration referred to in the E-consultancy (2005) report can assist with staff sharing knowledge and experience:

● *Co-locating staff* – including marketing staff in the digital team or e-commerce staff in the marketing team was mentioned.
● *Job-swapping* – a slightly different approach, which also involves co-location, was noted as effective.
● *Interim collaborative teams ('SWAT' teams)* – a temporary multi-disciplinary team (for example, teams from e-commerce, marketing and technology) is formed to drive a particular initiative or performance improvement, e.g. home page improvement, web analytics or supporting customer journeys between channels. This approach is reported to be used by Amazon.
● *Creation of a central 'Centre of Excellence for Digital Marketing'* can provide a clear resource which marketing staff can turn to for advice and best-practice documentation. Members of this team can also be involved in proactively 'spreading the word' through involvement in training or operational campaign planning.
● *Combined planning sessions* – rather than the digital team developing a plan and then discussing with the marketing team who may then incorporate it into their plan, a more collaborative approach is used with both working on creating an integrated plan.

Outsourcing

Given the difficulties of recruiting new business staff referred to above, many companies turn to third parties to assist with their digital business implementation. However, there is a bewildering series of supplier choices. Complete Activity 10.2 to help understand the choices required.

Activity 10.2	Options for outsourcing different digital business activities

Purpose

To highlight the outsourcing available for digital business implementation and to gain an appreciation of how to choose suppliers.

Activity

A B2C company is trying to decide which of its sell-side digital business activities it should outsource. Select a single supplier (single tick for each function) that you think can best deliver each of these services indicated in Table 10.3. Justify your decision.

Table 10.3	Options for outsourcing different digital business activities

Digital marketing function	Traditional marketing agency	New media agency	ISP or traditional IT supplier	Management consultant
1 Strategy				
2 Design				
3 Content and service development				
4 Online promotion				
5 Offline promotion				
6 Infrastructure				

Answers to activities can be found at www.pearsoned.co.uk/chaffey

We are seeing a blurring between the types of supplier shown in Table 10.3 as they recruit expertise so as to deliver a 'one-stop shop' service, though they still tend to be strongest in particular areas. Companies need to decide whether to partner with the best of breed in each, or to compromise and choose the one-stop shop that gives the best balance; this would argu-ably be the new media agency or perhaps a traditional marketing agency that has an estab-lished new media division. Which approach do you think is best?

The increased use of outsourcing marks a move towards the virtual organisation. With the introduction of electronic networks such as the Internet it becomes easier to outsource aspects of the production and distribution of goods to third parties. Hallowell (2001) notes that the degree to which businesses can automate or outsource their human resources is strongly dependent on the type and level of service expected for a particular type of product. This can be significant in governing their **scalability** or capacity for growth without taking on additional staff. He says that customer services in e-commerce are:

Scalability
The ability of an organisation or system to adapt to increasing demands being placed on it.

described as 'virtual' (either pure information or automated) and 'physical' (requiring some degree of human intervention) . . . because the nature and quantity of physical ser-vice necessary to deliver value to customers influences the quantity of human interven-tion required, it also influences a firm's ratio of variable to fixed costs, which alters its 'scalability'. The paradox comes in that while reduced scalability is viewed negatively by many venture capitalists and proponents of ecommerce, the cause of that reduction in scalability, human intervention, may help a firm to differentiate its offering to customers, thus providing a source of competitive advantage.

He concludes:

For firms that are very high on the scalability continuum, the need for physical service does not present a 'scalability' problem. At these firms, information is the core service offering. Physical service is relatively insignificant, both from customers' perspectives (use of physical service is infrequent, if at all) and from the firm's perspective (it represents a very small portion of total costs). Thus, these firms do not rely on physical service (and the employees it requires) to differentiate their offering; their differentiation tends to come from the quality of their content and the ease with which users can access it.

In contrast, firms that sell non-information services such as travel, or goods such as books, toys, or antiques require significantly more complex physical service operations. The degree to which they need more physical service is inversely proportional to the degree to which they are 'scalable'.

Case study 10.1 explores the extent to which outsourcing of core business processes is possible.

Revising organisational structures

When a company first embarks on digital business, perhaps through creating a new website to promote its products, it will normally operate within the existing company structure, perhaps using outsourcing to make good a resource deficit. However, as the contribution of the website to the company increases, the work involved increases and more staff from different parts of the organisation are involved in digital business, it may be necessary to adopt new organisational structures and working practices. This issue has been considered by Parsons *et al.* (1996) from a sell-side e-commerce perspective. They recognise four stages in the growth of what they refer to as 'the digital marketing organisation':

- **Ad hoc activity.** At this stage there is no formal organisation related to e-commerce and the skills are dispersed around the organisation. It is likely that there is poor integration between online and offline marketing communications. The website may not reflect the offline brand, and the website services may not be featured in the offline marketing communications. Maintenance of the website will be informal and errors may occur as information becomes out of date.
- **Focussing the effort.** At this stage, efforts are made to introduce a controlling mechanism for Internet marketing. Parsons *et al.* (1996) suggest that this is often achieved through a senior executive setting up a steering group which may include interested parties from marketing and IT and legal experts. At this stage the efforts to control the site will be experimental with different approaches being tried to build, promote and manage the site. This approach is useful for specific digital business initiatives which involve stakeholders across an organisation, for example, CRM or Social media.
- **Formalisation.** At this stage the authors suggest that Internet marketing will have reached a critical mass and there will be a defined group or separate business unit within the company which manages all digital marketing.
- **Institutionalising capability.** This stage also involves a formal grouping within the organisation, with formal links created between digital marketing and a company's core activities.

Although this is presented as a stage model with evolution implying all companies will move from one stage to the next, many companies will find that true formalisation with the creation of a separate e-commerce or digital business department is unnecessary. For small and medium companies with a marketing department numbering a few people and an IT department perhaps consisting of two people, it will not be practical to have a separate group. Even large companies may find it is sufficient to have a single person or small team responsible for e-commerce with their role being to coordinate the different activities within the company using a matrix management approach.

Activity 10.3 reviews different types of organisational structures for e-commerce. Table 10.4 reviews some of the advantages and disadvantages of each.

Activity 10.3   Which is the best organisational structure for e-commerce?

Purpose

To review alternative organisational structures for e-commerce.

1 Match the four types of companies and situations to the structures (a) to (d) in Figure 10.9.

(a) Distributed   (b) Matrix control

(c) New division   (d) Autonomous company

Figure 10.9   Summary of alternative organisational structures for e-commerce suggested in Parsons *et al*. (1996)

(a) A separate operating company. Examples: Prudential and Egg (www.egg.com).
(b) A separate business unit with independent budgets. Examples: RS Components Internet Trading Company (www.rswww.com).
(c) A separate committee or department manages and coordinates e-commerce. Example: Nationwide Building Society (www.nationwide.co.uk).
(d) No formal structure for e-commerce. Examples: many small businesses.

2 Under which circumstances would each structure be appropriate?
3 Summarise the advantages and disadvantages of each approach.

Answers to activities can be found at www.pearsoned.co.uk/chaffey

Table 10.4	Advantages and disadvantages of the organisational structures shown in Figure 10.9

Organisational structure	Circumstances	Advantages	Disadvantages
(a) No formal structure for e-commerce	Initial response to e-commerce or poor leadership with no identification of need for change	Can achieve rapid response to e-commerce service responses (email, phone). Priorities not decided logically. Insufficient resources	Poor-quality site in terms of content quality and customer
(b) A separate committee or department manages and coordinates e-commerce	Identification of problem and response in (a)	Coordination and budgeting and resource allocation possible	May be difficult to get different departments to deliver their input due to other commitments
(c) A separate business unit with independent budgets	Internet contribution (Chapter 6) is sizeable (>20%)	As for (b), but can set own targets and not be constrained by resources. Lower-risk option than (d)	Has to respond to corporate strategy. Conflict of interests between department and traditional business
(d) A separate operating company	Major revenue potential or flotation. Need to differentiate from parent	As for (c), but can set strategy independently. Can maximise market potential	High risk if market potential is overestimated due to start-up costs

Where the main e-commerce function is internal, the E-consultancy (2005) research suggested that it was typically located in one of four areas (see Figure 10.10) in approximate decreasing order of frequency:

(a) Main e-commerce function in separate team.
(b) Main e-commerce function part of operations or direct channel.
(c) Main e-commerce function part of marketing, corporate communications or other central marketing function.
(d) Main e-commerce function part of information technology (IT).

There is also often one or several secondary areas of e-commerce competence and resource. For example, IT may have a role in applications development and site build and each business, brand or country may have one or more e-commerce specialists responsible for managing e-commerce in their unit. Consider which of the options would be preferable for organisations you are familiar with. The research suggested that the approach which was appropriate depended strongly on the market(s) the company operated in and their existing channel structures.

Approaches to managing change

Change agents
Managers involved in controlling change transitions.

Hayes (2002) notes that for external forces of change, it may be difficult for those in an organisation to manage and control the impact of change – the deterministic view. However, the voluntarist view is that managers can make an important difference to managing the impact of change. In the case of information systems management, it is clear that much can be done to reduce the impact of change. Change management is conducted by **change agents** who are the managers responsible for controlling change. In the context of digital business, the change agent could be the project manager responsible for implementing a new information

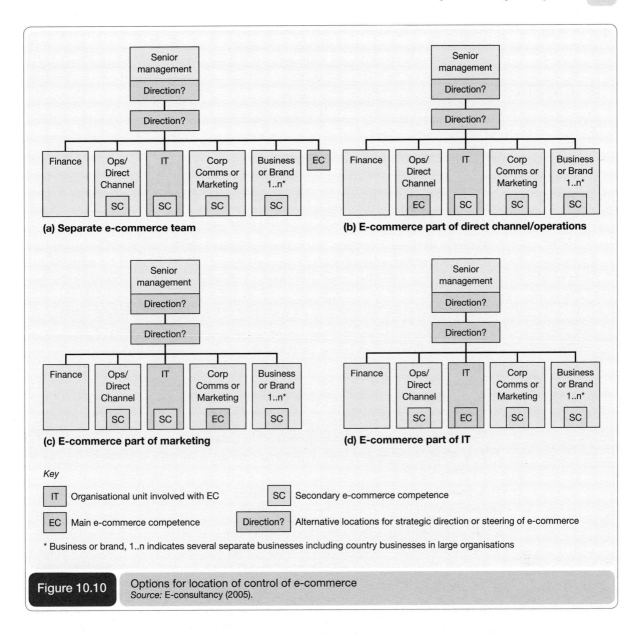

(a) Separate e-commerce team

(b) E-commerce part of direct channel/operations

(c) E-commerce part of marketing

(d) E-commerce part of IT

Key

| IT | Organisational unit involved with EC |

| SC | Secondary e-commerce competence |

| EC | Main e-commerce competence |

| Direction? | Alternative locations for strategic direction or steering of e-commerce |

* Business or brand, 1..n indicates several separate businesses including country businesses in large organisations

Figure 10.10	Options for location of control of e-commerce
	Source: E-consultancy (2005).

system, a digital business manager responsible for increasing adoption of digital business by an organisation, or specialist digital marketing or supply chain managers seeking to increase adoption of e-channels.

Senior management involvement

Cope and Waddell (2001) have assessed the role of leadership style in e-commerce implementations. They assessed the most common approaches to e-commerce implementation, distinguishing between these approaches:

- *Collaborative* – widespread participation of employees occurs to define the changes required and techniques to achieve them.
- *Consultative* – management takes the final decision, after calling on some employees for input.

- *Directive* – the management team takes the decisions, with the employees generally trusting them to do so and being generally informed.
- *Coercive* – the management team takes the decision with very limited recourse to employees.

Of these approaches, the consultative approach was, as might be expected, most common, but other statements used in the research suggested that there were elements of other approaches.

Models for achieving change

There are many process models for achieving change which can be usefully applied to managing digital business-related change. A classic model for achieving organisational change was suggested by Lewin and Schein. It involves three stages:

1 Unfreeze the present position by creating a climate of change by education, training and motivation of future participants.
2 Quickly move from the present position by developing and implementing the new system.
3 Refreeze by making the system an accepted part of the way the organisation works.

Note that Lewin and Schein did not collaborate on developing this model of personal and organisational change. Kurt Lewin developed the model in unpublished work and this was then extended by Edgar Schein (1956) who undertook research into psychology based on Lewin's ideas. More recently, Lewin (1972) summarised some of his ideas. Later, Schein (1992) concluded that three variables are critical to the success of any organisational change:

1 The degree to which the leaders can break from previous ways of working.
2 The significance and comprehensiveness of the change.
3 The extent to which the head of the organisation is actively involved in the change process.

To achieve the unfreeze stages different staff can be identified for different roles by the project manager:

- *System sponsors* are senior managers or board members who have bought into the digital business initiative, are committed to major change and want to achieve success. The sponsors will try to fire up staff with their enthusiasm and stress why introducing the system is important to the business and its workers.
- *System owners* are managers in the organisation of key processes such as a procurement manager or marketing manager who will use the digital business system to achieve benefits in their area.
- *System users*. These are staff in the different areas of the business who are actively involved in making the process happen. They could be a buyer in procurement or a brand manager within the marketing department.

Special types of system users can be identified, and it is important for the change manager to try to influence these staff to help achieve commitment amongst other staff. The three main types of system users that should be influenced are as follows:

- *Stakeholders* should be identified for each of the process areas where change will be introduced. These will be staff who are respected by their co-workers and will again act as a source of enthusiasm for the system. The user representatives used in specification, testing and sign-off are key stakeholders.
- *The legitimiser* protects the norms and values of the system; they are experienced in their job and regarded as the experts by fellow workers; they may initially be resistant to change and therefore need to be involved early.

- *Opinion leaders* are people whom others watch to see whether they accept new ideas and changes. They usually have little formal power, but are regarded as good ideas people who are receptive to change and again need to be involved early in the project.

For digital business implementation these roles will need to be identified for each implementation project as well as the overall change.

A more detailed change model proposed by Jay and Smith (1996) identifies four phases:

1 **Initial orientation.** In the orientation phase, it is necessary that there be a clear understanding of the reasons for bringing about change. This should be identified as part of the digital business, digital marketing or SCM strategies. A change strategy must be developed that includes an indication of how results will be measured, the project milestones, and how objectives would be measured and the change project organised. A skilled change team should be established and committed change sponsors identified.

2 **Preparation.** The preparation phase will involve an analysis of the environment within which the change is to take place. This includes an identification of the critical success factors for change along with a threat analysis. A work-plan for the change process must also be developed that includes detailed tasks and timings. The change direction must be announced to those affected and there should be an emphasis on maximising communication effectiveness. The final step in this phase is to provide direction, particularly through strong communication of the goals and how they will be achieved.

3 **Change implementation.** In the third phase, Jay and Smith suggest that the changes are implemented by piloting the change, introducing the new procedures, conducting training and finally rolling out the change. Choosing a pilot department or site may be difficult. However, the organisational aspects as they relate to reporting relationships, job definitions, training schedules, working procedures and reward systems must be still be defined and communicated.

4 **A supportive phase.** In the final phase, the change must be stabilised. This means that management must openly commit itself to the change and fine-tune or adjust procedures where necessary. Measuring acceptance and new behaviour and producing a formal report can be used to evaluate the effectiveness of the change. There must be prevention of a relapse, such as an attempt to revert to old systems and practices or even bypassing the new system altogether. Conducting regular review meetings along with continual training and procedure reviews can help this.

Hayes (2002) has summarised how change managers can facilitate progress through the overall change process and progress through the transitions an individual makes during change. He notes the following general implications of the transition model for change managers:

- The overall form of the transition curve will take different forms – individual stages may be longer or shorter and the degree of mood change at each stage can vary considerably.
- There will often be a time lag between the announcement of a change and a reaction to it. It is possible to mistake initial shock and denial for acceptance of the change.
- Different people and different parts of the organisation will pass through the change cycle at different rates and in different ways.
- Change managers will typically be out of step with other staff since they are involved earlier and deeper.
- The cycle cannot be avoided, but there is much that change managers can do to facilitate people's progress through it.

Hayes (2002) gives specific advice about how change managers can facilitate change through different change transitions. This advice is summarised in Table 10.5 together with typical implications for digital business initiatives and applications.

Table 10.5	Facilitating organisational change through a transition model	

Transition phase	Typical actions by change managers	Implications for digital business implementation
1 Shock/ awareness	Create a climate of receptivity to change. Announcement sufficiently in advance in involving senior managers.	Pre-announcement and involvement are readily practicable for digital business. Announcement and ownership by a senior manager is important.
2 Denial	Diagnosis of the reason for denial is important. Gently support the staff through denial. Repeat message of reason for change and justify. Find ways to get staff involved in change early.	Involvement is typically a requirement of digital business projects, so this is usually practical for some staff; for others communication of the benefits and progress of the project and the implications for them should be considered.
3 Depression	Providing support and listening are required at this stage rather than ignoring complaints.	This stage can be accommodated through prototyping and recording feedback in the live system.
4 Letting go	Continued explanation of the benefits of the new system without denigrating the past approach. Setting targets associated with the new system.	Around this stage prototypes of the new system will be available which will help with the process of letting go since tangible evidence of the new system and, hopefully, its benefits will be available.
5 Testing	Testing is encouraged by encouraging experimentation without blame where problems occur.	Testing corresponds to the testing phase of the system or adoption of the new system dependent on involvement. Positive or negative feedback on the new system should be encouraged, discussed and acted upon where appropriate.
6 Consolidation	This is facilitated by reviewing performance and learning and recognising, rewarding and communicating benefits.	Improvements achieved through the system should be assessed and communicated.
7 Reflection and learning	This is achieved through structured learning about the change through reviews and encouraging unstructured learning such as feedback about the system.	Post-implementation reviews should occur at this stage, since this acknowledges that no system can be perfect first time and future improvements are planned for. The use of a structured system to log problems with the system or process can also help.

Source: The middle column is based on a summary of the commentary in Hayes (2002).

Organisational culture

Culture
This concept includes shared values, unwritten rules and assumptions within the organisation as well as the practices that all groups share.

Bocij *et al.* (2005) suggest that social relationships in an organisation that are part of its **culture** are important. They say '*the efficiency of any organisation is dependent on the complex formal and informal relationships that exist within it*'. Formal relationships include the hierarchical work relationships within and between functional business areas. Informal relationships are created through people working and socialising with each other on a regular basis and will cut across functional boundaries. Digital business-led change has the capacity to alter both types of relationships as it brings about change within and between functional business areas.

Boddy *et al.* (2001) summarise four different types of cultural orientation that may be identified in different companies:

1 Survival (outward-looking, flexible) – the external environment plays a significant role (an open system) in governing company strategy. The company is likely to be driven by customer demands and will be an innovator. It may have a relatively flat structure.

2 Productivity (outward-looking, ordered) – interfaces with the external environment are well structured and the company is typically sales-driven and is likely to have a hierarchical structure.

3 Human relations (inward-looking, flexible) – this is the organisation as family, with interpersonal relations more important than reporting channels, a flatter structure and staff development, and empowerment is thought of as important by managers.

4 Stability (inward-looking, ordered) – the environment is essentially ignored, with managers concentrating on internal efficiency and again management is through a hierarchical structure.

Now complete Activity 10.4 to investigate how companies may need to realign their culture to succeed in digital business.

Activity 10.4	Changing the culture for digital business

Purpose

To identify appropriate cultural changes that may be necessary for digital business success.

Activity

Review the four general categories of organisational cultural orientation summarised by Boddy *et al*. (2001) and take each as characterising four different companies and then suggest which is most appropriate for digital business. State whether you think they are most likely to occur in a small or a larger organisation.

Answers to activities can be found at www.pearsoned.co.uk/chaffey

Focus on	Knowledge management

Knowledge management (KM)
Techniques and tools disseminating knowledge within an organisation.

Business Intelligence
Methodology, process and technologies used to support the transformation of different data sources to improve strategic, tactical and operational decision-making to improve business performance.

Knowledge management (KM) still has an important role within digital business since business success is critically dependent on staff knowledge about all aspects of the microenvironment such as customers, suppliers, intermediaries, competitors and how to shape internal processes to best deliver customer service. These help inform strategic, tactical and operational decisions. That said, today KM is often referenced as part of broader **Business Intelligence** or Business Insight initiatives or as an aspect of managing Big Data (Chapter 11) and content marketing (Chapter 12). See, for example, the coverage by the KM World (www.kmworld.com) portal, which also commonly features these broader issues.

KM is only introduced here. A more detailed coverage of how KM can support business processes is available in Chaffey and White (2011).

With the move towards globalisation and responding more rapidly to changing market conditions, knowledge transfer is a key to competitiveness. KM is also a change management response to the problems of staff retention referred to earlier. As Saunders (2000) puts it:

Every day, knowledge essential to your business walks out of your door, and much of it never comes back. Employees leave, customers come and go and their knowledge leaves with them. This information drain costs you time, money and customers.

What is knowledge?

The concept of knowledge is more difficult to state than that of data or information. However, knowledge can be regarded as the next level of sophistication or business value in the cycle from data through information to **knowledge**. KM seeks to share this experience within a company. Useful summaries have been produced by Mekhilef *et al.* (2004):

Knowledge *Applying experience to problem solving.*

> **Knowledge** *is the combination of data and information, to which is added expert opinion, skills and experience, to result in a valuable asset which can be used to aid decision making. Knowledge may be explicit and/or tacit, individual and/or collective.*
>
> **Knowledge Management** *is the management of activities and processes for leveraging knowledge to enhance competitiveness through better use and creation of individual and collective knowledge resources.*

Theorists have identified two different types of knowledge, and different approaches can be used to disseminate each type of knowledge within an organisation:

Explicit knowledge *Knowledge that can be readily expressed and recorded within information systems.*

1 **Explicit** – details of processes and procedures. Explicit knowledge can be readily detailed in procedural manuals and databases.
2 **Tacit** – less tangible than explicit knowledge, this is experience on how to react to a situation when many different variables are involved. It is more difficult to encapsulate this knowledge, which often resides in the heads of employees. Techniques for sharing this knowledge include learning stories and histories. To acquire tacit knowledge may rely on sharing knowledge with partners outside the company or others in different sectors. So knowledge management should not be considered solely as confining corporate knowledge within the firewalls.

Tacit knowledge *Mainly intangible knowledge that is typically intuitive and not recorded since it is part of the human mind.*

It follows that one goal of knowledge management is to turn tacit knowledge into explicit knowledge which can then be shared between employees and used to train new employees.

A framework for the different activities that comprise knowledge management is given in Figure 10.11. The main activities are:

1 **Identify knowledge.** This is an analysis of the availability of existing knowledge to support the activities forming existing processes and a gap analysis showing what is missing.
2 **Create new knowledge.** This reviews methods to create new knowledge. At the personal and team levels, recommended techniques are through training, process problem improvement sessions or brainstorming. At the departmental or organisational levels, knowledge creation can occur through benchmarking against other organisations and through establishing expert groups known as 'communities of practice' or use of consultants or other companies to acquire new knowledge.
3 **Store knowledge.** Mekhilef *et al.* (2004). point out that much knowledge is typically 'stored' in people's brains and so will often remain there as 'tacit knowledge'. Knowledge can also be embedded or become part of the 'organisational memory' through revising processes that form team routines. Storing explicit knowledge requires a structured approach to selecting, updating, organising or categorising knowledge within information systems.
4 **Share knowledge.** This increases knowledge availability to ensure it is available in the right context – i.e. for the right person, at the right time to support their current activity. Mekhilef *et al.* (2004) identify the stock method of distribution where knowledge is made available through databases and the flow method where knowledge is transferred directly from person to person through collaboration, workshops or mentoring.

These authors also say that approaches to support knowledge sharing include: intranets or portals, databases, collaboration, communities of practice, job rotation, coaching, seminars and training. Technology can be used to assist this through making information available through an intranet which enables browsing and searching

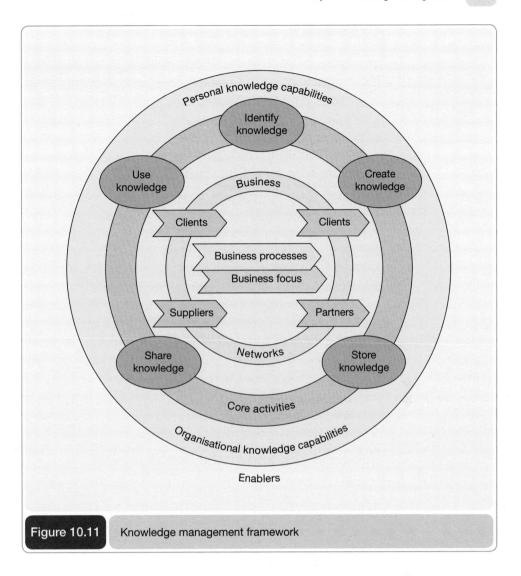

Figure 10.11	Knowledge management framework

of document databases or more collaborative approaches such as 'wikis' (web-based discussions which can be authored by several people) or 'webinars' (staff learn through dialling into a presentation or discussion hosted by an expert member of staff).

5 **Use knowledge.** Since a lot of knowledge remains under-utilised, the authors suggest that the purpose of this stage is to ensure that all effort that is spent in the previous activities pays off! It also involves managing further additions to the knowledge base.

Sveiby (1997–2000) suggests that one of the best ways to understand knowledge management is by looking at how people use the term 'knowledge management'. This includes academic researchers, consultants and industry practitioners. The two different views of knowledge management are:

- IT-based view – knowledge can be stored as objects within databases and information systems.
- People-track view – knowledge management is about trying to improve individual skills and behaviour.

Objectives of knowledge management

The reasons for moving to knowledge management are highlighted by a 1999 IDC survey from when the approach first came to prominence. The main reasons, which you can see are still relevant today, given by 355 US IS manager respondents were:

- Improving profit/growing revenue (67%)
- Retaining key talent/expertise (54%)
- Increasing customer retention and/or satisfaction (52%)
- Defending market share against new entrants (44%)
- Gaining faster time to market with products (39%)
- Penetrating new market segments (39%)
- Reducing costs (38%)
- Developing new products/services (35%).

It is evident that although employee retention is important, knowledge management is also seen as a competitive force for acquiring and retaining customers. Unlike other digital business initiatives cost reduction is relatively unimportant.

Sveiby (1997–2000) identifies an evolution of knowledge management objectives through time starting with a realisation around 1992 that many companies were reinventing the wheel by not applying the experience acquired through previous, similar projects. Sharing knowledge was achieved by using best-practice databases using groupware such as Lotus Notes. Later the database was again the focus as companies aimed to learn more about their customers through data warehousing and data mining. The third phase is, he says, associated with sell-side e-commerce and learning more about *interactions* with customers through web-based forms and online purchases.

Implementing knowledge management

The reasons for difficulties in moving to knowledge management (KM) are also highlighted by the 1999 IDC survey. The main problems, which are again still relevant, are:

- Lack of understanding of KM and its benefits (55%)
- Lack of employee time for KM (45%)
- Lack of skill in KM techniques (40%)
- Lack of encouragement in the current culture for sharing (35%)
- Lack of incentives/rewards to share (30%)
- Lack of funding for KM initiatives (24%)
- Lack of appropriate technology (18%)
- Lack of commitment from senior management (15%).

Note that lack of the appropriate technology is not a major issue, although selecting the right technology may be important. All the main barriers relate to organisational structure and culture. A key finding seems to be the need to explain the benefits of knowledge management, develop skills and encourage sharing. Marianne Hedin, Research Manager at IDC Research (IDC, 2000) says:

> It is impossible to achieve full benefits from knowledge management unless individuals are willing and motivated to share their knowledge or unless organizations lose their structural rigidity to permit information and knowledge flow.

David Snowden (2002) puts it more simply when he says:

> Knowledge can only be volunteered – it cannot be conscripted.

Hansen *et al.* (1999) suggest that incentives are required to encourage staff to share knowledge such as making knowledge sharing a factor in the employees' performance review.

For example, with ShareNet, a knowledge management system at Siemens, contributors could collect points called ShareNet shares, similar to frequent-flier miles. Users earned shares for entering knowledge objects into the library (20 shares for a success story), answering urgent requests (3 shares), reusing knowledge and rating one another's contributions (single shares). In May 2000, the top 50 point collectors were invited to New York for a conference on ShareNet. Redemption of shares was possible against prizes such as textbooks, mobile phones, computers, PDAs and business trips. One share was roughly equivalent to one euro at the time. Different countries and business units were then compared on their success in generating shares.

Technologies for implementing knowledge management

The implementation of digital business applications can support knowledge management through providing different applications which support the five different steps of knowledge management described above. Binney (2001) identifies six different classes of KM applications as follows:

1 **Transactional.** Helpdesk and customer service applications.
2 **Analytical.** Data warehousing and data mining for CRM applications.
3 **Asset management.** Document and content management.
4 **Process support.** Total quality management, benchmarking, BPR, Six Sigma (see www.isixsigma.com for further information).
5 **Developmental.** Enhancing staff skills and competencies – training and e-learning.
6 **Innovation and creation.** Communities, collaboration and virtual teamwork.

Today, there is much discussion about the opportunities for using collaborative tools like Yammer, which we introduced in Chapter 2, to enable sharing of information using social networking approaches. Collectively this approach and these tools is often referred to as Enterprise 2.0. You can see that these are potentially applicable across all six stages identified above and can help share tacit and explicit knowledge.

Vendors now offer many tools for knowledge management, but it must be recognised that these tools only facilitate knowledge management. Major changes to knowledge creation and dissemination processes within the organisation are likely to be required to reap the benefits of this technology.

Alternative tools for managing knowledge include:

- Knowledge capture tools such as software for devising knowledge maps and mind maps.
- Knowledge sharing techniques such as chat, discussion groups, wikis, webinars and video-conferencing.
- Knowledge delivery tools such as intranets and email.
- Knowledge storage in document databases or knowledge bases such as Lotus Notes/ Domino and content management systems.
- Electronic document management systems such as Interleaf publisher.
- Expert systems used to capture specific task-based knowledge and deliver a solution.

Chaffey and Wood (2005) point out that intranets tend to have three stages of sophistication for knowledge management:

1 **Static.** Basic web pages stored on a web server. Information publishing is centrally controlled. Employees browse and search for information but do not interact. Content is refreshed on an irregular basis. The danger is that the intranet will become a silo of underused and untrustworthy information.
2 **Interaction.** The intranet evolves into a dynamic environment developing around the knowledge needs of employees. Publishing becomes a regular process that many employees are involved with. Discussion boards and bulletin boards are introduced. Employees start to develop trust in using the intranet to share and locate knowledge.

3 **Collaborative electronic workspace.** The intranet becomes a 'self-service' environment where all employees are empowered to share knowledge via publishing mechanisms and collaborative tools. It becomes the starting point for discovering explicit knowledge. All core business processes will take place across the intranet platform.

Hansen *et al.* (1999) identify two contrasting approaches for implementing knowledge management which they illustrate through case studies of management consultancies. They refer to these approaches as 'codification' and 'personalisation'. They found that companies tend to focus on one approach or the other, although there was some overlap. In the codification approach, used by Andersen Consulting and Ernst & Young, knowledge is codified or translated into a form suitable for searching using a database. Hansen *et al.* (1999) give the example of a partner in the Los Angeles office of Ernst & Young who needed assistance in creating a bid for implementation of an ERP system. Since he did not have this type of implementation he tapped into the knowledge management repository to find similar bids completed by others in the past. The reuse of a previous bid made it possible to complete the bid in half the normal period of four to six weeks, even though the partner was relatively inexperienced in this area. The codification process has been a major initiative at Ernst & Young with over 250 employed at the Center for Business Knowledge to codify information and help others perform searches. In addition, each of Ernst & Young's 40 practice areas has a specialist in codifying documents.

The personalisation approach has been adopted more by strategy consulting firms such as Bain and McKinsey. Hansen *et al.* (1999) relate the case of a partner in the London office of Bain who had to advise a UK financial institution how to solve a particular strategy dilemma. This assignment required knowledge of different market and geographical sectors and creative input. She used the Bain people-finder system to find those with suitable information, then convened a meeting in Europe that involved video-conferencing with others in Singapore and Sydney. Over the next four months, the partner then consulted regularly through email, video-conferencing and phone. As well as using these technological approaches, McKinsey also fosters knowledge transfer by moving staff between offices, by having directories of experts and by having a culture that encourages prompt return of calls.

Knowledge management has been beset by difficulties of project implementation. Storey and Barnett (2000) review the literature on project failure and report on a detailed case study. They highlight six key learnings:

1 *Listen very carefully to the expectations, agendas and wants of all parties involved. They may appear to be using the same language and to be supporting the programme but in fact their understandings and plans may be very different.*

2 *Check continuously that top management support is continuing and is delivered in a practical and public way.*

3 *Be alert to the potential differences between a paradigm based on knowledge management which is IT-led and infused with priorities relating to knowledge capture, archiving and mining, and one based on the learning organization concept which may be inspired by wider developmental values. If handled with extraordinary skill the two approaches may reinforce each other but this cannot be expected simply to occur by happenchance.*

4 *It will be found useful to ensure that the purpose and reason for expending effort on knowledge sharing is clarified and understood by everyone involved. It needs to be seen to be useful to those who are, in effect, being asked to behave differently.*

5 *The interrelationship between knowledge sharing, knowledge creation and organizational change needs to be understood and realized. Reversal to traditional ways of operating based on low trust and direct command are too easily adopted when problems arise as our case demonstrates.*

6 *If knowledge is to be more widely shared and more readily created and used, there is an implication that innovation in process and probably service or products will also ensue and indeed should be sought. There are different types or levels of organizational KM systems: at the lower level, expert practitioners simply make available their operating routines and information. At the second level, the new knowledge is used as a basis for the shift in the kind of products and services offered to customers.*

Using collaborative approaches for knowledge management

Throughout this book we have discussed the power of social media approaches in digital communications. As we highlighted in the case study on Suncorp in Chapter 1, these approaches are increasingly used within business. Here are some approaches:

- Use of content management systems such as Microsoft Sharepoint Server for managing intranet content.
- Use of internal blogs where staff can blog about project work in different categories.
- Use of microblogging using tools like Yammer, which has been dubbed Twitter for business.
- Use of social networks within a business. Google+ is increasingly used for this since it can be limited to external staff.
- Use of wikis, as shown by Case study 10.2.

Case Study 10.2	Using collaborative tools to support knowledge management at Janssen-Cilag Australia

About Janssen-Cilag

Janssen-Cilag is one of the fastest growing, research based pharmaceutical companies in Australia. It has more than 300 employees, split across Australia and New Zealand with around half based in the field. It is one of 250 Johnson & Johnson operating companies, which total about 121,000 employees across 57 countries.

Intranet history

In 2006, Janssen-Cilag completely replaced our simple, static HTML intranet with a Wiki solution. Over the 16 months since its launch, it has dramatically transformed internal communication and continues to increase in both visits and content contributions each month.

Intranet requirements gathering

The culture at Janssen-Cilag is highly consultative and relationship based. As such, gathering information and buy-in is often achieved through a series of conversations and discussions, building a coalition of support.

Requirements for a new intranet site were collected through 27 interviews with a variety of people from all levels of the business. Three themes emerged:

1 We need a trusted source of information
2 Whatever we do has to be simple
3 Just do something!

Each conversation varied widely in focus, but the format usually went as follows:

1 The floodgates open with a dump of information the user considers vital for the intranet, which lasts about 15 minutes. (What can I get?)
2 They highlight search as a key requirement.
3 I would steer the conversation to questions about how content should be maintained. (What can you give?)

Pitching a Wiki to the business

With many years of experience building one of the first large scale completely open collaboration platforms ▶

for the web and then building heavyweight enterprise CMS systems for large organisations, I've personally come full-circle to the idea that the best collaboration systems are incredibly simple and open. Wikis are a powerful starting point for any organisation, but latent demand at Janssen-Cilag created the perfect environment.

As such, I used the requirements gathering session as a chance to pitch the idea of a Wiki as the solution to our intranet problem. After bringing the conversation to understand our content maintenance requirements, I'd talk through the Wiki approach and how it may work for Janssen-Cilag. My sales pitch went as follows:

1 We need a system where editing is immediate and very simple.
2 Getting people to contribute at all is hard, so we need to concentrate on letting people do things rather than worrying about what they shouldn't do.
3 The risk of letting anyone change anything is low, since we'll keep a complete history of changes so we can quickly undo mistakes and we can hold irresponsible individuals accountable for anything improper. (Reactive moderation rather than Proactive moderation.)

In general, the response was incredibly positive. Predictably, the main argument against this system was fear of improper changes to content, particularly for information subject to regulatory control. I would counter this argument in two ways:

1 There are two ways to control people's behaviour: social forces and technical forces. Currently, we successfully rely on social forces to control a wide range of things like who calls or emails the CEO with their latest crazy idea. Technical forces are powerful, but with each technical feature we increase training and raise the bar against collaboration. Surely, we can see if social forces will be enough for all but the most critical of content?
2 Anyone can choose to monitor any content that they are concerned about (e.g. automatic email alert with changes). So, they can quickly jump in and correct any mistakes.
3 For exceptional cases, we may choose to lock down critical content and define clear ownership and responsibility for its maintenance.

At the end, showing people around Wikipedia was an incredibly powerful way to seal the deal, particularly since they have often used it to find information in the past.

There were no major objections to trying a Wiki-style concept.

Implementing a Wiki for your Enterprise Intranet

We purchased, customised and launched a pilot Wiki intranet within two weeks and with a budget of $11,000 AUD. This included all graphic design and single sign on integration.

After evaluating a wide range of alternatives including MediaWiki, Twiki and FlexWiki, we selected Confluence by Atlassian. Our main concerns were support for a hierarchy of pages, strong attachment capabilities, news features, LDAP integration, high-quality search and a decent rich text editor.

Our customisation focussed almost completely on usability. People shouldn't know or care that they are using a Wiki. All that matters is that they can easily browse, search and contribute content. (In fact, after 16 months, only a small set of Janssen-Cilag staff would think of our intranet as a Wiki. To them, it just seems natural that intranet software would have evolved to something this simple to use.)

Here were our implementation decisions:

Integration with LDAP and use of NTLM for automatic single sign-on is essential. We even hacked someone's starting point and open sourced our improved version.

Rich text editing must be available and as Word-like as possible.

Users like hierarchy and structure, the Wiki should not feel disorganised or completely free-form. (Confluence supports this with an exact page hierarchy capability.)

Sacrifice power and flexibility for simplicity. For example, our page design is fixed into a title, alphabetical list of subpages, page content, alphabetical list of attachments. While it would be nice to be able to change this at times, or order the attachments, or change the look and feel, it's far more important that everyone can contribute and clearly understands how things work.

Remove as many unnecessary features as possible. For example, labels are a great idea, but we already have hierarchy and most users don't really know what labels are.

Launch & user training

We started the new site as a pilot, launching as the source of information for a relocation of our head office. (Nothing drives traffic like the seating plan for a new office!) Information around the relocation was fast moving and changing daily for the two weeks between announcement of the move and our actual relocation.

Building on that success, we obtained executive approval to replace the existing intranet. Over the next two weeks we worked with key content owners (most particularly HR) to show them how to create pages and migrate appropriate information. We made the decision to not automatically migrate any content, mostly because it was so old and trust in the existing intranet information was so low.

Our launch was timed with an informal head office monthly meeting, where around 100 people stand and listen to an update from senior management. We switched the site to live during the meeting, and had 5 minutes to present:

1 1 min: Highlight the desire for a trusted source of information that was simple to use.
2 3 mins: Full training that showed how easy it was to view, search, edit & maintain.
3 1 min: Point out that responsibility for building that trusted source is now in your hands!

That launch presentation remains the only formal training we've ever provided on how to use the system.

Continuing training has been provided through short one-on-one demonstrations (we only show, we never do) and a detailed help section (I'm happy to show you now, but for future reference here is the help page).

Adoption, statistics & business impact

The adoption of JCintra has been remarkable. After only 3 months, 111 people had contributed more than 5,000 changes. After 12 months, we had 18,000 contributions from 184 people within the business.

Most significantly, our contributions per month has continued to grow since launch. People are engaging and collaborating more with time, they are not losing steam as you might expect.

To drive adoption, we've primarily focussed on owning the flow of new information. Early on, we established a policy that all announcements must be on JCintra. When necessary, they may be sent via email in addition to posting as news on the intranet. Today, announcements ranging from major restructures to new babies

for employees flow through the news page without clogging up email inboxes.

Owning the flow of news has established JCintra as a trusted source for the latest information. This translates into an expectation that the stocks of information (e.g. policies) will be available and up to date. Own the flow and the stock will come.

Business information that was previously scattered in email (e.g. Business Planning presentations) is now collected into a permanent, secure online space. We have a growing reference and history of information to build on and make available to newcomers. Knowledge management, previously a big concern, has moved off the agenda for the time being.

Content ownership model

For many intranet owners, the model for content ownership is a key point of focus. With JCintra, our philosophy (successfully so far) has been:

1 If someone isn't willing to maintain a piece of content, it can't be that important to the business.
2 We happily show people how to do things with the site, but we don't do it for them.
3 Occasionally we highlight sections of the site on the home page, which is a great way to drive the de facto owners to clean it up a little.
4 We encourage people to have high expectations for content on the intranet. If something is missing, please report it to the appropriate area of the business, or better still, add it for them.
5 The answer to verbal queries for many departments has become, 'it's on JCintra'. This reminds people to search first and ask later.
6 In the end, the quality of content in an area is a reflection on the de facto department owner, not the intranet itself.

As a result, we've seen some departments embrace the intranet in a big way, while others don't update content as much as we'd like. As expected, service areas of the business have been strong adopters, which means the main areas of intranet content have been well maintained.

We've not yet adopted a formal content review process, but believe this will become more important in the next year of the site's life.

Keeping momentum & next steps

The primary barrier to continued success of JCintra remains the same as our initial barrier: encouraging a culture of collaboration and transparency. Some areas of JCintra have been highly successful in this regard, while other sections have never gained clear ownership or momentum.

JCintra works best when it is established as the source of truth for information and becomes the place where the work is done on a day-to-day basis. While the intranet is a place that has to hold a published copy, it will remain as 'extra work' and struggle in the competition for people's time.

Source: (Janssen-Cilag): e-gineer.com blog by Nathan Wallace, Associate Director – Information Technology (i.e. CIO) for Janssen-Cilag Australia, a pharmaceutical subsidiary of Johnson & Johnson. www.e-gineer.com/v2/blog/2007/08/our-intranet-wiki-case-study-of-wiki.htm.

Questions

1 What does this case study suggest are the main challenges for different stages of introducing a wiki or other Enterprise 2.0 approaches in a large organisation?
2 Which solutions does Nathan Wallace describe as being effective for overcoming these problems?

Towards the social business

With the increasing consumer usage of social media, leading social media commentators such as Chris Brogan (www.chrisbrogan.com), Brian Solis (www.briansolis.com) and Charlene Li (www.charleneli.com) have advocated that businesses need to change their organisational setup to get closer to customers to provide better services and enhance their brands.

What is social business?

Social business specialist Hamill (2012) says that these two quotes show its essence. Dion Hinchcliffe and Peter Kim, authors of *Social Business by Design*, say:

> *Social media touches the entire organisation, every department and every business process, every channel, every customer interaction, every investor and supplier relationship. Social is too important to be left to the Marketing Department.*

Social media guru Brian Solis says:

> *A social business . . . embraces introspection and extrospection to reevaluate internal and external processes, systems, and opportunities to transform into a living, breathing entity that adapts to market conditions and opportunities.*

Debate 10.2

Creating a social business

'*Creating a social business is impractical for most organisations since the types of changes needed are likely to be opposed by managers of different functional areas of the organisation.*'

Jim Hamill uses a simple '4Cs Model' to explain the potential business benefits of 'being social'. The key question to address is how can your organisation best use social technologies to build relationships and derive tangible business benefits from four main customer groups which we have discussed through this book: existing customers; potential customers; internal customers (staff); and external customers (business partners).

The scope of social business across an organisation is illustrated well by the Altimeter (2010) model shown in Figure 9.12 (p. 421), which crosses many business processes.

Many businesses are not yet at this level of sophistication since social media marketing is still new to many companies. Many seem to use social media as another broadcasting channel for talking *at* rather than *with* customers. Very few organisations have developed an integrated and coordinated social media strategy fully aligned with, and supportive of, core business goals and objectives.

Risk management

To conclude this chapter and act as a bridge to the final two chapters we review the problems associated with change when managing a digital business implementation. Risk management is intended to identify potential risks in a range of situations and then take actions to minimise the risks. We all unconsciously perform risk management throughout our lives. For example, when crossing a country road we will assess the likely risk of a car approaching, or a silent cyclist approaching around the blind bend, and perhaps increase our pace accordingly. Activity 10.5 is intended to illustrate these risks. **Risk management** involves these stages:

Risk management
Evaluating potential risks, developing strategies to reduce risks and learning about future risks.

1 Identify risks, including their probabilities and impacts.
2 Identify possible solutions to these risks.
3 Implement the solutions, targeting the highest-impact, most likely risks.
4 Monitor the risks to learn for future risk assessment.

Activity 10.5	Digital business risk management

Purpose

To highlight risks that are part of a digital business implementation and suggest solutions. This activity acts as a summary of many of the change management concepts reviewed in this chapter.

Activity

Review this chapter with reference to Chapters 4 and 5 and produce a grid with four columns describing the risk for a company with which you are familiar, or for a typical B2C company, assessing its probability on a scale of 0 (no risk) to 10 (very high risk), its impact from a scale of 0 (no impact) to 10 (catastrophic), and possible solutions.

Answers to activities can be found at www.pearsoned.co.uk/chaffey

As an alternative view of risks with a wider organisation context, Simon (1999) presents a simple risk calculator based on different types of risks faced at a company level (Table 10.6). This calculator can be usefully applied to digital business change or a high-growth dot-com company since significant change may accentuate these risks.

Table 10.6	Organisational risk exposure factors (from Simon, 1999)

Growth risks	Culture risks	Information management risks
Pressures for performance (over-ambitious targets due to external demands)	Rewards for entrepreneurial risk-taking	Transaction complexity and velocity (a particularly high risk for companies having to purchase or sell raw materials in bulk)
Rate of expansion (expansion difficult to control and recruit new employees)	Executive resistance to bad news (and lack of action)	Gaps in diagnostic performance measures (poor reporting capabilities)
Inexperience of key employees	Levels of internal competition (Is the culture cooperative or too competitive?)	Degree of decentralised decision-making (lack of central control and management of other risks)

Source: Adapted and reprinted by permission of *Harvard Business Review* from table on p. 87 from 'How risky is your company?' by Simon, R., in *Harvard Business Review,* May–June 1999. Copyright © 1999 by the Harvard Business School Publishing Corporation, all rights reserved.

Summary

1   Change as a result of digital business needs to be managed on two levels. First, the change that needs to be managed as part of projects to introduce digital business. Second, organisation-wide change is required for digital business. We focus on this change in this chapter.

2   Sound project management is required to achieve change. Traditional project management activities such as estimation, resource allocation, scheduling, planning and monitoring are all important here. A project manager also needs to facilitate change by communicating the need for change.

3   Traditional life cycle stages – analysis, design and build – can be used to estimate the tasks required for a digital business implementation. Since most digital business solutions will be based on tailoring off-the-shelf packages, there will be a change in balance between the analysis, design, build and implementation phases in comparison with a bespoke solution. Prototyping is essential to achieve the fast timescales required by digital business.

4   Building a team for digital business will require technical, marketing and project management skills. This will be difficult in the face of a competitive marketplace for these skills and high staff turnover. Tactics should be developed to help retain staff in this environment.

5   To implement digital business, a company will need to partner with a variety of companies. The digital business manager will need to decide whether to outsource activities such as strategy, content development and site promotion at the outset of a digital business project and whether it may be necessary to bring these activities back in-house at a later stage.

6   Changes to organisational structures are likely to be required to build the digital business. Coordination of digital business-related activities can be achieved through a working party, digital business manager or separate department. Companies may also spin off sell-side e-commerce to a completely separate business.

7 Managing staff responses to change is an important aspect of change. Managers will need to consider how to achieve commitment and action from senior managers and also how to gain staff acceptance of the new system and new working practices. Techniques that may be used are user education, user involvement and achieving support from respected staff. Companies with an outward-looking cultural orientation will be predisposed to digital business-led change while others that have an inward-facing, inflexible cultural orientation may have to consider changes in culture.

Exercises

Self-assessment questions

1 Summarise the main types of change that need to be managed during introduction of digital business.
2 What approaches must managers take to achieve change management successfully?
3 Outline the main stages of a sell-side e-commerce implementation.
4 Explain the role of prototyping in developing a sell-side e-commerce solution.
5 Describe four different approaches to retaining staff.
6 What alternative approaches are there to structuring e-commerce within an organisation?
7 Which type of organisational culture is most amenable to digital business-related change?
8 What are some of the risks of digital business change, and how can they be managed?

Essay and discussion questions

1 Write an essay on approaches to managing digital business change.
2 'Total outsourcing of digital business operations is the best method to overcome the skills shortage.' Discuss.
3 Contrast the project management stages involved with sell-side and buy-side e-commerce implementations (referring to Chapters 11 and 12 will help with this question).
4 'High turnover of technical staff is a fact of life in a buoyant job market and there is little that can be done to reduce turnover.' Discuss.
5 Develop a change management plan for a company you are familiar with.
6 You are the HR manager at a new-media design agency and are evaluating the use of overseas contract workers to help on projects. Write a report summarising the feasibility of this approach.
7 Write a report on how the knowledge within a company can be better managed. Refer to particular technologies and procedures for managing explicit and tacit knowledge.
8 Assess the merits of virtualisation in an organisation of your choice.

Examination questions

1 Explain what prototyping is and why it may be used on an e-commerce implementation.

2 Summarise the main human resource requirements for an e-commerce implementation.

3 A company has implemented a brochureware site without any changes to managerial or organisational structure. They are now seeking to achieve one-third of their revenues via the website. What changes to managerial and organisational structure would you suggest?

4 Explain how knowledge management differs from information management.

5 Explain the concept of the virtual organisation. What are the advantages over a traditional organisation?

6 Name four approaches a company can take to increase retention of technical staff.

7 Prioritise, with justification, your recommendations for outsourcing these functions: e-commerce strategy, e-commerce hosting, e-commerce content updating.

8 You are project manager of an e-procurement implementation. How would you maximise acceptance of the new system amongst staff?

References

Altimeter (2010) Social CRM: The New Rules of Relationship Management, White Paper published April 2010, Editor Charlene Li.

Bocij, P., Chaffey, D., Greasley, A. and Hickie, S. (2005) *Business Information Systems. Technology, Development and Management,* 3rd edn. Financial Times Prentice Hall, Harlow.

Boddy, D., Boonstra, A. and Kennedy, G. (2001) *Managing the Information Revolution.* Financial Times Prentice Hall, Harlow.

Chaffey, D. and White, S. (2011) *Business Information Management: Improving Performance Using Information Systems,* 2nd edn. Financial Times Prentice Hall, Harlow.

Chaffey, D. and Wood, S. (2005) *Business Information Management.* Pearson Education, Harlow.

Chen, A. (2012) Growth Hacker is the new VP Marketing. Blog post by Andrew Chen, published 27 April.

Clarety (2009) Project and programme failure rates, posted by Kevin Bradyon Sat 27 June 2009, **www.claretyconsulting.com/it/comments/project-and-programme-failure-rates/2009-06-27/**.

COBIT (2001) Control Objectives. COBIT (3rd edn). Released by the COBIT Steering Committee and the IT Governance Institute: **www.isacf.org/cobit** (no longer available).

Cope, O. and Waddell, D. (2001) An audit of leadership styles in e-commerce. *Managerial Auditing Journal,* 16(9), 523–9.

Crush, P. (2000) What's my motivation? *Revolution,* 2 August, 34–6.

Davenport, T.H. (1993) *Process Innovation: Re-engineering Work through Information Technology.* Harvard Business School Press, Boston.

E-consultancy (2005) Managing an E-commerce team. Integrating digital marketing into your organisation. 60-page report by Dave Chaffey. Available from **www.econsultancy.com.**

E-consultancy (2007) Web Project Management. The practices behind successful web projects. Research report by Sonia Kay. Available from E-consultancy (**www.econsultancy.com**).

Garimella, K., Lees, M. and Williams, B. (2008) *BPM Basics for Dummies.* Wiley, New York.

Gartner (2003) Gartner Application Integration and Middleware Strategies Research Note T-19-4751, J. Sinur, D. McCoy and J. Thompson, 14 April. The Gartner Group (**www.gartner.com**).

Hackman, J. and Oldham, G. (1980) *Work Redesign.* Addison-Wesley, Reading, MA.

Hallowell, R. (2001) 'Scalability': the paradox of human resources in e-commerce. *International Journal of Service Industry Management,* 12(1), 34–43.

Hammer, M. and Champy, J. (1993) *Re-engineering the Corporation: A Manifesto for Business Revolution.* HarperCollins, New York.

Hamill, J. (2012). What is social business. Blog post, August 29th 2012. **www.smartinsights.com/social-media-marketing/social-media-governance/what-is-social-business/.**

Hansen, M., Nohria, N. and Tierney, T. (1999) What's your strategy for measuring knowledge? *Harvard Business Review,* May–June, 106–16.

Hayes, J. (2002) *The Theory and Practice of Change Management.* Palgrave, Basingstoke.

IDC (1999) Knowledge Management Survey. IDC Research (**www.idcresearch.com**).

IDC (2000) Capitalizing on Knowledge Management. IDC Research Report: **www.idcresearch.com#W18864** (no longer available).

Jay, K.E. and Smith, D.C. (1996) A generic change model for the effective implementation of information systems. *South African Journal of Business Management,* 27(3).

Lewin, K. (1972) Quasi-stationary social equilibrium and the problems of permanent change. In *Organizational Development: Values, Process, and Technology,* N. Margulies and A. Raia (eds). McGraw-Hill, New York, pp. 65–72.

McLaughlin, S. (2010) Dangerous solutions: case study of a failed e-project. *Journal of Business Strategy,* 31(2).

Mekhilef, M., Kelleher, D. and Oleson, A. (2004) *European Guide to Good Practice in Knowledge Management* – Chapter 5, Terminology. Published by European Committee for Standardization at **www.cenorm.be** (no longer available).

Nadler, D., Shaw, R. and Walton, E. (1995) *Discontinuous Change.* Jossey-Bass, San Francisco.

Parsons, A., Zeisser, M. and Waitman, R. (1996) Organizing for digital marketing. *McKinsey Quarterly,* no. 4, 183–92.

Saunders, R. (2000) Managing knowledge. *Harvard Management Communication Letter,* June, 3–5.

Schein, E. (1956) The Chinese indoctrination program for prisoners of war. *Psychiatry,* 19, 149–72.

Schein, E. (1992) *Organizational Culture and Leadership.* Jossey-Bass, San Francisco.

Schranz, T. (2012) Growth Hackers Conference: Lessons Learned. Blog post, 1 November 2012 by Thomas Schranz, published at **https://www.blossom.io/blog/2012/11/01/growth-hackers-conference-lessons-learned.html.**

Simon, R. (1999) How risky is your company? *Harvard Business Review,* May–June, 85–94.

Snowden, D. (2002) Complex acts of knowing – paradox and descriptive self awareness. IBM Global Services, July: **www-1.ibm.com/services/files/complex.pdf** (no longer available).

Storey, J. and Barnett, E. (2000) Knowledge management initiatives: learning from failure. *Journal of Knowledge Management,* 4(2), 145–56.

Sveiby, K.E. (1997–2000) *The New Organizational Wealth: Managing and Measuring Knowledge-Based Assets.* Berrett-Koehler, San Francisco. Updated on author's website: **www.sveiby.com.au/KnowledgeManagement.html** (no longer available).

Waterman, R.H., Peters, T.J. and Phillips, J.R. (1980) Structure is not organization. *McKinsey Quarterly,* in-house journal. McKinsey& Co., New York.

Web links

David Snowden's Cognitive Edge (www.cognitive-edge.com) Blog by ex-IBM knowledge management expert.

Information Research – an International Journal (http://informationr.net) An open online journal focussing on information and knowledge management moderated by staff at the Department of Information Studies, University of Sheffield.

KMWorld (www.kmworld.com) A portal focussing on Knowledge Management and Business Intelligence.

11

Analysis and design

Web support

The following additional case studies are available at
www.pearsoned.co.uk/chaffey

→ Legacy data integration
→ User interface enhancements at Waterstones
→ Additional activity – creating a database for a B2C company

The site also contains a range of study material designed to help improve your results.

Scan code to find the latest updates for topics in this chapter

Learning outcomes

After completing this chapter the reader should be able to:

- Summarise approaches for analysing requirements for digital business systems
- Identify key elements of approaches to improve the interface design and security design of e-commerce systems

Management issues

Analysis and design of digital business systems raises these issues for management:

- What are the critical success factors for analysis and design of digital business systems?
- What is the balance between requirements for usable and secure systems and the costs of designing them in this manner?

Links to other chapters

The main related chapters are:

- *Chapter 10* places analysis and design into the context of change management for digital business as shown in Figure 10.6
- *Chapter 12* – the sections on measurement and marketing research show how the effectiveness of analysis and design are evaluated

Introduction

Analysis and design
Analysis of system requirements and design for creation of a system.

This chapter reviews new approaches to analysis and design required for **digital business systems**. It does not aim to explain how to follow well-established techniques for analysis and design such as data flow diagramming, information flow diagrams and entity relationship diagramming. These have been described many times before, for example in Bocij *et al.* (2008).

The chapter is intended to provide managers with an appreciation of some analysis and design techniques for digital business, in particular customer experience management through user interface design for desktop and mobile platforms. This familiarity should aid collaboration when the managers are involved in discussing the requirements of the system with technical staff. It is in two main parts. In the first part we review analysis techniques and in particular process analysis for re-engineering which is important in many digital business implementations. We also touch on data modelling and how to manage 'Big Data'.

The second part looks at the design of digital business systems. The techniques described are aimed at improving the information quality of end-users of digital business systems – ensuring information is timely and secure, has the correct content in terms of accuracy, relevance and completeness, and is in a form that is easy to interpret. The section on architectural design looks at how systems are integrated to improve flow of information and also to achieve timely delivery of information. '*Focus on* User-centred site design and customer experience management' demonstrates how using use-case analysis and interface design guidelines can be applied to produce usable sell-side or buy-side e-commerce systems with good information quality. '*Focus on* Security design for digital business' reviews security requirements for the digital business, reviews generic approaches to security and finally looks at the current usage of e-commerce security techniques.

The importance of analysis and design is such that even if an effective strategy has been developed, its execution can be destroyed by ineffectual analysis and design. Complete Activity 11.1 to review some of the consequences of poor analysis and design.

Activity 11.1 | **The consequences of poor analysis and design**

Purpose

To highlight the impact of poor analysis and design on customer satisfaction and business performance.

Activity

Form a focus group and discuss your own experiences of online purchasing. What have been your problems and frustrations? Refer to a particular example such as purchasing a book – what are your expectations? Alternatively, visit GetSatisfaction.com to see the types of complaints about different brands.

Answers to activities can be found at www.pearsoned.co.uk/chaffey

An interview with Matt Lawson of ao.com on how they develop their customer experience

Matt Lawson is Head of Conversion at ao.com. In this interview he describes how they have grown their business through keeping the web experience focussed on the customer through constant feedback, review and testing. Today ao.com (Figure 11.1) is the UK's largest online kitchen retailer, with over 4,000 large appliances ready for Next Day Delivery.

Their About Us promise page is one of the best I've seen for showcasing the proposition and integrating customer feedback and social networking. Taking such care with the About page may not be essential for established high-street retailers, but is important for online pureplays and start-ups. We also like the way their masthead below the navigation showcases their proposition.

ao.com can no longer be called a start-up, with annual turnover of more than £50 million. In fact, it was formed as part of DRL Limited in 2000, as an online kitchen appliance retailer, by John Roberts, who remains CEO of the company today. Today DRL also provides white label kitchen appliance websites for its big brand clients like Boots, Marks and Spencer, Next, House of Fraser, Debenhams, Screw Fix, Empire Direct, Argos and B&Q, including supply, distribution and customer care.

Q. How often do you review strategy?

Matt Lawson, ao.com: Our overall approach to strategy is that our actions focus on our objectives. The world and the way we work changes all the time so you must be dynamic and flexible. If you are not dynamic and flexible, then you are going to fail; the world is changing all the time so always keep as up to date and savvy as possible and I think you can apply that to any decent business.

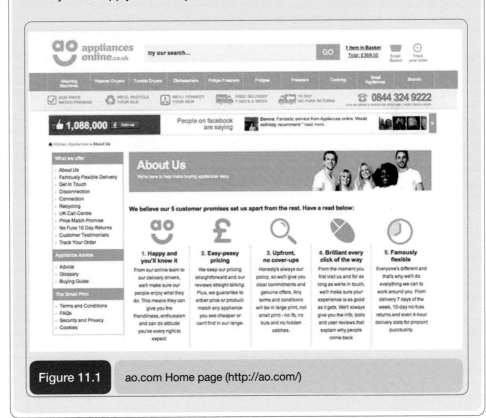

| Figure 11.1 | ao.com Home page (http://ao.com/) |

In essence, at ao.com, we put the customer first: 'We strive to deliver what they want in everything we do; from our proposition to the content the see on our site'.

Q. What and how often do you review your marketplace?

Matt Lawson, ao.com: Honestly? We very, very rarely look at what our competitors are doing. We always get our customers' feedback and work towards what is right for them. It is not about staying one step ahead of the game and always trying to edge out the competition – what's the point in that? We listen to the customers and reverse-engineer our strategy to what is right for them.

Q. How do you set your goals each year? What are the KPIs?

Matt Lawson, ao.com: The one common goal across our business is gut feelings. It is actions that deliver results and if someone presents an idea and it feels right then we try to run with it. In terms of KPIs, we look at profit and website experience.

Q. The business growth is impressive. What are the strategic success factors for entering this marketplace?

Matt Lawson, ao.com: Simple: Understanding the customer.

Q. How do you set the right levels of investment?

Matt Lawson, ao.com: People often ask why we have such a large team (400+) for an online-only retailer and I always relate this back to a physical store – one store could have hundreds of customers a day across the nation dealing with customers – if we were a physical chain of stores then we would need much more staff.

It is about context and we see that in our business.

Q. How important is content marketing for you?

Matt Lawson, ao.com: Massive! Sixty per cent of the market buy online, do their research online, etc. The only reason people would need to go into a physical store is to ask a question and we can still engage the customer and get exactly the same results without that.

Q. What steps have you taken to develop a mobile experience?

Matt Lawson, ao.com: We have an extremely dedicated team who focus purely on mobile experience; we have appointed these people to concentrate solely on making this work for us and the customer. We've also been getting increased revenue from tablet devices too.

Q. How do you manage conversion rate improvements and the implementation of new features on the site?

Matt Lawson, ao.com: We use a range of testing (multivariate, AB testing, etc.). It may not seem groundbreaking but what we do is focus on customers and what they are addicted to, and then we simplify it.

Designers design out not in. It's a simple methodology.

One example of this is testing our customer interaction with our online video testimonials, and we found that when they watch our video, they are 120.5% more like to buy and spend 9.1% more on their order. So the action is to simply, encourage more customers to watch more videos!

Q. What is the process for trading review of analytics and sales?

Matt Lawson, ao.com: Aside from our analytics and testing tools we have no business reporting in the digital team, all reporting is in commercial. We don't believe in marking our own homework.

Q. What has surprised you when reviewing consumer preferences and the results of tests?

Matt Lawson, ao.com: It's important to remember that sometimes, what you think will work, and when you really invest in an idea, it can bomb and just go completely wrong.

Always be aware that what you think can work, sometimes just doesn't for whatever reason. It's something to always remember and try and be prepared for.

Q. What would you recommend other E-commerce site owners test?

Matt Lawson, ao.com: Just give customer a perfect proposition and then reverse-engineer it so it works for them.

Try and get as much feedback as you can consistently and then work around it, so it can apply to your business.

Q. What would you recommend for someone new in a role like yours – what are the top issues/areas of the site they should focus on?

Matt Lawson, ao.com: Collaboration and people are the most important things to remember, no matter what position you are in in the business, I can't stress that enough. Always remember the customer.

Q. What is your vision for the future of your service?

Matt Lawson, ao.com: I do not want an awesome website. I just want a website that works. It sounds weird, but if someone tells me that they enjoyed our website because of all the cool, wizzy features and apps, then I'll know I have failed.

I want people to use the website and for everything to just fit and be perfect, they don't always know why it works, but it just does, it's like the iPhone. That's success.

Source: Case study: Managing CRO at ao.com (formerly Appliances Online).

Blog post by Susanne Colwyn, 14 May 2013. www.smartinsights.com/conversion-optimisation/ab-multivariate-testing/managing-cro-appliances-online/.

Analysis for digital technology projects

Analysis for digital systems
Using analytical techniques to capture and summarise business and user requirements.

Analysis for digital systems is concerned with understanding the business and user requirements for a new system. Typical analysis activity can be broken down into: understanding the current process and then reviewing possible alternatives for implementing the digital business solution. In the following sections we will review different techniques. In this section we focus on using diagrams to demonstrate the business processes. User requirements capture techniques that help determine the function required by a system are described in the '*Focus on* User-centred site design' section.

Analysts recognise that delivering quality information to employees and partners, or exchanging it between processes, is the key to building information systems that improve efficiency and customer service. Pant and Ravichandran (2001) say:

> *Information is an agent of coordination and control and serves as a glue that holds together organisations, franchises, supply chains and distribution channels. Along with material and other resource flows, information flows must also be handled effectively in any organisation.*

We retain this quote since we like the analogy of information as 'glue'. Others have called it 'the New Oil' with reference to Big Data which we cover later! This shows that in the era of digital business analysis should be used as a tool to optimise the flow of information both inside and outside organisations. In this chapter we start by looking at how workflow management is a key to managing time-based information flows. We then review how process modelling is used to analyse information flows to optimise business processes and then look at information storage analysis through a brief review of data modelling.

Process modelling

Traditional approaches to process analysis use established systems analysis and design methods that are part of methodologies such as Structured Systems Analysis and Design Methodology (SSADM), like the data flow diagram technique outlined in Bocij *et al.* (2008). Such approaches often use a hierarchical method of establishing

- the processes and their constituent sub-processes
- the dependencies between processes
- the inputs (resources) needed by the processes and the outputs.

Activity-based process definition methods
Analysis tools used to identify the relationship between tasks within a business process.

The processes and sub-processes are essentially the activities or tasks that need to be performed by the business information system, so these are sometime referred to as 'Activity-based process definition methods'. A process can be defined at the business level in terms of the main activities of a business. Each process can be broken down further as explained in the section on 'Task analysis and task decomposition'. Significant business processes are elements of the value chain; they include inbound logistics (including procurement), manufacture, outbound logistics or distribution, and customer relationship management or sales and marketing activity. Davenport (1993) notes that even for large multinational organisations the number of main processes will rarely exceed ten.

Process
Part of a system that has a clearly defined purpose or objective and clearly defined inputs and outputs.

Note that in addition to the approaches shown here, use-case analysis to assist in defining interface requirements is described in the '*Focus on* User-centred site design' section.

Process mapping

Process mapping
Identification of location and responsibilities for processes within an organisation.

Existing business processes often overlap different functional areas of a business. So, before detailed activities are identified the analyst needs to identify where in the organisation processes occur and who is responsible for them. This procedure is often known as 'process mapping'. Such process mapping is clearly important for identifying potential users of a digital business system. Table 11.1 shows an outline process map that might be used for a B2B company to prepare a proposal for a new major account.

Table 11.1 Process map for activities with process 'prepare proposal'

Process activity	Marketing	Engineering	Finance	Senior management
1 Cost estimation		M		
2 Assess financial risk		m	M	
3 Publicity presentation	M	m		
4 Review	M	M	M	m
5 Authorisation			M	M

M = major role in function, m = minor role in function

Task analysis and task decomposition

Task analysis

Identification of different tasks, their sequence and how they are broken down.

Before a process such as 'prepare proposal' can be designed and implemented, a more detailed breakdown is required. This is usually referred to as '**task analysis**'.

Noyes and Baber (1999) point out that a difficulty with this type of process or task decomposition is that there are no set rules for what to call the different levels of decomposition or how far to decompose the process. The number of levels and the terminology used for the different levels will vary according to the application you are using and the consultant you may be working with. Georgakoupoulos *et al.* (1995) talk about 'task nesting' of tasks broken down into sub-tasks as part of the activity-based method for describing workflows. They give the example of a workflow process for procurement where the task 'procure materials' is broken down further into the sub-tasks of 'verify status', 'get bids' and 'place order'. Curtis *et al.* (1992) provide a useful framework, referring to *process units* or *elements* at each process level as follows:

Level 1 *business processes* are decomposed into:
　　Level 2 *activities* which are further divided to:
　　　　Level 3 *tasks* and finally:
　　　　　　Level 4 *sub-tasks*.

An example of a four-level task decomposition is presented in Figure 11.2. Attempts to standardise the meanings of these terms have been produced by the Workflow Management

Level 1. Business process:
Obtain listings

　　　　Level 2. Activities
　　　　1. Register vendor
　　　　2. Inspection preparation
　　　　3. Inspection appointment
　　　　4a. Follow up inspection – IF listing instructions obtained
　　　　4b. Follow up inspection – IF listing instructions NOT obtained (exception)
　　　　5. Ensure listing obtained

　　　　　　Level 3. Tasks for 'ensure listing obtained'
　　　　　　1. Prepare initial property particulars (48hours)
　　　　　　2. Remind negotiator to handle sale to contact vendor
　　　　　　3. Send property particulars
　　　　　　4. Instruction to sell with draft PMA
　　　　　　　　(Property Misdescriptions Act 1991) details
　　　　　　5. Contact vendor to obtain PMA on particulars

　　　　　　Level 4. Subtasks
　　　　　　1. PMA chase
　　　　　　2. Tenure details
　　　　　　3. Amended details

Key
　Reminder required for negotiator
　Record information (data input)
　Retrieve information (data output)
　IT system used to perform activity
　Letter or form produced (level4)

Figure 11.2	An example task decomposition for an estate agency
	Source: Adapted from Chaffey (1998).

Coalition, an industry standards body (WfMC, 1996), which describes the different process elements as follows:

1 **Business process.** A set of one or more linked procedures or activities which collectively realise a business objective or policy goal, normally within the context of an organisational structure defining functional roles and relationships.
2 **Activity.** A description of a piece of work that forms one logical step within a process. An activity may be a manual activity, which does not support computer automation, or a workflow (automated) activity. A workflow activity requires human and/or machine resource(s) to support process execution; where human resource is required an activity is allocated to a workflow participant.
3 **Work item.** The representation of the work to be processed (by a workflow participant) in the context of an activity within a process instance. An activity typically generates one or more work items which together constitute the task to be undertaken by the user (a workflow participant) within this activity.

Process dependencies

Process dependencies summarise the order in which activities occur according to the business rules that govern the processes. Normally, activities occur in a sequence and are serial; sometimes activities can occur simultaneously, when they are known as parallel. Data flow diagrams and flow charts are widely used as diagramming techniques to show process dependencies. In this section we will review three techniques for showing dependencies that are more commonly applied in digital business analysis. These are flow process charts and network diagrams including the EPC (event-driven process chain) standard used by the SAP product.

Workflow management

Workflow management (WFM)
The automation of information flows; provides tools for processing the information according to a set of procedural rules.

Process dependencies are a core part of analysing and revising an organisation's workflow as part of **workflow management (WFM)**, a concept that is integral to many digital business applications, so before we look at process analysis techniques, let us look at why workflow is integral to digital business.

WFM was defined by the Workflow Management Coalition (WfMC, 1996) as

the automation of a business process, in whole or part during which documents, information or tasks are passed from one participant to another for action, according to a set of procedural rules.

Workflow systems automate digital business processes by providing a *structured* framework to support a process. Applications of workflow in digital business include actioning queries from external customers or handling internal support queries. Email enquiries can be analysed and routed to the right person depending on their subject. Letters may need to be scanned before being added to the workflow queue. Workflow helps manage business processes by ensuring that tasks are prioritised to be performed:

→ as soon as possible
→ by the right people
→ in the right order.

The workflow approach gives a consistent, uniform approach for improved efficiency and better customer service. Workflow software provides functions to:

- assign tasks to people
- remind people about their tasks which are part of a workflow queue
- allow collaboration between people sharing tasks

- retrieve information needed to complete the task such as a customer's personal details
- provide an overview for managers of the status of each task and the team's performance.

What type of workflow applications will exist in a company? For a B2B company, digital business applications of workflow might include:

1 **Administrative workflow.** Internal administrative tasks such as managing purchase orders for procurement and booking holidays and training.
2 **Production workflows.** Customer-facing or supplier-facing workflows such as an intranet- or extranet-based customer support database and stock management system integrated with a supplier's system.

Flow process charts

A simple flow chart is a good starting point for describing the sequence of activities of a workflow. Despite their simplicity, flow charts are effective in that they are easy to understand by non-technical staff and also they highlight bottlenecks and inefficiencies. Flow process charts are used commonly when solving digital business problems, whether in the front office or the back office. Each symbol in the chart refers to a particular operation within the overall process. An explanation of the symbols used in flow process chart analysis is shown in Figure 11.3. Box 11.1 and Figure 11.4 show one way of laying out flow process charts. Another example of how flow process charts are applied in practice using a tabular arrangement is presented in Activity 11.2. An example of how tabular flow process charts can be applied to e-procurement analysis is given in Chapter 7 (p. 301).

Box 11.1	Use of flow process charts for design of workflow systems

In this example mortgage (loan) applications are received by post. It is then necessary to identify *new applications* and supporting documentation for applications already received. (This is a decision point indicated by a diamond-shaped decision box.) New applications are keyed into the workflow system as a new case and the original form is scanned in for reference (these are processes shown as circles on the chart). Supporting material such as ID (driving licences) and letters from employers are also scanned in. A team member will then assign or associate all scanned images of material which has been scanned in to a particular case. Assigning new documents (*assignment tasks*) is always the most important task, so these need to be automatically placed by the software at the head of the workflow queue. Once assigned the documents will need to be actioned (*action tasks*) by the operator, so according to the type of document and when it needs to be chased the workflow system will assign a priority to the task and place it in the workflow queue. Team members will then have to action tasks from the workflow queue which are prioritised according to date. Processing an action task will usually involve phoning the customer for clarification or writing a letter to request additional information. After this has been achieved the operator will mark the item as complete and a new workflow task will be created if necessary: for example, to follow up if a letter is not received within ten days.

This diagram is also useful for summarising system design since it can identify different modules of a system and the hardware and software necessary to support these modules. In this case some of the modules are:

- Scan document (scanner and scanning software)
- Associate document to customer case (link to customer database)
- Prioritise document (specialised workflow module)
- Review document (link to customer database)
- Contact customer (link to phone system and letter printer).

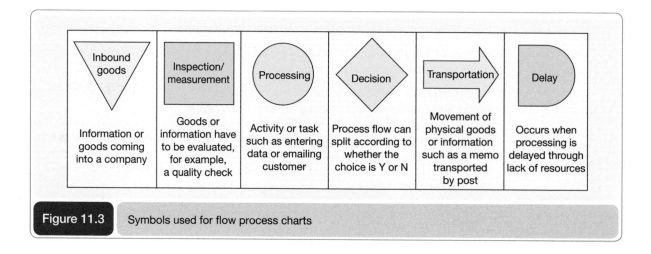

Figure 11.3 Symbols used for flow process charts

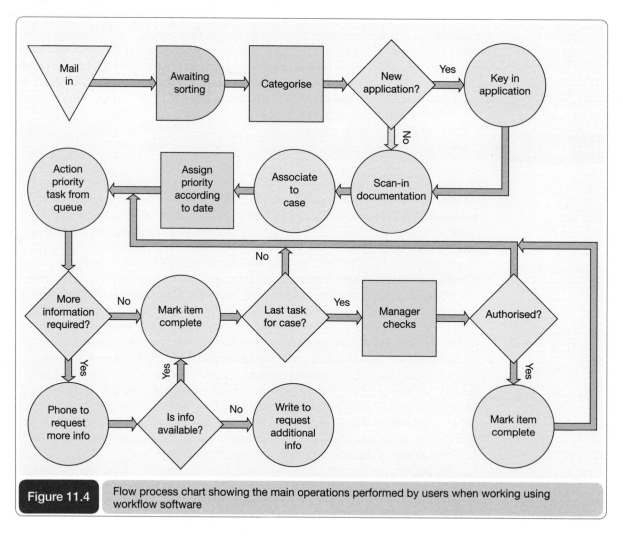

Figure 11.4 Flow process chart showing the main operations performed by users when working using workflow software

Effort duration analysis

Effort duration analysis is an analytical tool that can be used to calculate the overall efficiency of a process when we have performed a detailed analysis such as that in Activity 11.2. To do this, we sum the average time it takes workers to complete every activity making up the overall process, then divide this by the total length of time the whole process takes to occur. The

Activity 11.2	Transforming invoice processing at a B2B company

Purpose

To illustrate how the flow process chart can be used to simplify a business process.

Background

Table 11.2 has been drawn up following observation of tasks performed during a systems analysis project at a B2B company. The main problem is the delay currently occurring when the MD has to authorise an invoice of £10,000. The company can obtain a discount of 10% if payment is made in 10 days. This is not achievable currently and the MD wants to use IT to make this possible. As part of this re-engineering, restructuring may be required also – the MD believes that fewer staff are needed for invoice payment.

Table 11.2	Flow process chart for invoice processing – original situation

No.	Task description	Chart symbols	Distance (m)	Average time (hours)
1	Receive invoice, stamp date	○⇨□D▼	–	–
2	To first payable clerk	○➡□D▽	50	5
3	On first payable clerk's desk	○⇨□◗▽	–	1
4	Write and attach purchase order	●⇨□D▽	–	0.1
5	To cost accountant	○➡□D▽	20	5
6	On cost accountant's desk	○⇨□◗▽	–	5
7	Code to appropriate job number	●⇨□D▽	–	0.1
8	Return to first payable clerk	○➡□D▽	20	5
9	On first payable clerk's desk	○⇨□◗▽	–	1
10	Make copies	●⇨□D▽	–	0.1
11	To Managing Director	○➡□D▽	200	5
12	On Managing Director's desk	○⇨□◗▽	–	48
13	Reviewed and approved by MD	●⇨□D▽	–	0.1
14	To second payable clerk	○➡□D▽	200	5
15	On second payable clerk's desk	○⇨□◗▽	–	1
16	Add vendor number and due date	●⇨□D▽	–	0.1
17	Write to accounts payable ledger in accounting systems	●⇨□D▽	–	0.5
18	Pay invoice – write cheque	●⇨□D▽	–	0.1
19	To file clerk	○➡□D▽	20	5
20	On file clerk's desk	○⇨□◗▽	–	1
21	File invoice	●⇨□D▽	–	0.1

Activity

As a business analyst you have to produce a more efficient way of working. You should restructure the workflow by filling in a blank table. You should also write down assumptions about changed roles and give details of new software needed to support the new workflow. You can assume each member of staff has access to a networked PC and the MD has access to a notebook with fax/modem that they use twice daily.

See Table 11.3.

Table 11.3	Flow process chart for invoice processing – re-engineered process			
No.	**Task description**	**Chart symbols**	**Distance (m)**	**Average time (hours)**
1	Receive invoice, stamp and scan	●⇨□D▼	–	0.1
2	Email to first payable clerk	○➜□D▽	–	0.1
3	In worklist of first payable clerk	○⇨□▶▽	–	5
4	Fill in purchase order, code job number	●⇨□D▽	–	0.5
5	Email to MD	○➜□D▽	–	0.1
6	In MD's worklist	○⇨□▶▽	–	12
7	Review and approval by MD	●⇨□D▽	–	0.1
8	Email to second payable clerk	○➜□D▽	–	0.1
9	In worklist of second payable clerk	○⇨□▶▽	–	5
10	Add vendor number and due date	●⇨□D▽	–	0.1
11	Key into accounting system	●⇨□D▽	–	0.1
12	Pay invoice and mark task as complete	●⇨□D▽	–	0.1

Answers to activities can be found at www.pearsoned.co.uk/chaffey

total process time is often much longer since this includes time when the task is not being worked on. Here this is during transport of the forms, and when they are waiting in out-trays and in-trays. The efficiency relationship can be given as:

$$Efficiency = \frac{\sum (T(effort\,on\,tasks))}{T(total\,process\,time)}$$

If we apply effort duration analysis to the first scenario in Activity 11.2, with delays and transport not contributing to the overall process, we can see that the efficiency is barely 2%! This measure can be extended by noting the activities that add value to the customer rather than simply being administrative.

Network diagrams

While data flow diagrams and flow process charts may give a good indication of the sequence in which activities and tasks occur, they often do not give a sufficiently tight, formal definition of the process sequence necessary for input into a digital business, workflow or ERP system. To do this we can use a network diagram known as a GAN (generalised activity network). Here, nodes are added between the boxes representing the tasks, to define precisely the alternatives that exist following completion of a task. The most common situation is that one activity must follow another, for example a check on customer identity must be followed by a credit check. Where alternatives exist, the logic is defined at the node as follows: where a single pathway is taken from two or more alternatives, the node is defined as an OR node, and when several pathways may be followed this is an AND node. Join nodes combine previous activities, and splits determine which activities occur next. Where there are alternatives, business rules are defined as pre-conditions or post-conditions. A summary of the alternative dependencies is given in Table 11.4.

Event-driven process chain (EPC) model

One of the most widely used methods for describing business events and processes is the event-driven process chain method (EPC). This has been popularised by its application to re-engineering of enterprises performed using the SAP R/3 ERP product which accounts for worldwide sales of several billion dollars. Over 800 standard business EPCs are defined to support the SAP R/3 system; they are intended to illustrate business rules clearly for interpretation by business users before enactment in the software. The different elements of the EPC model are shown in Table 11.5; these include the different types of dependencies previously reviewed in Table 11.4. Figure 11.5 is an EPC meta-model illustrating how the different elements relate

Table 11.4	Workflow dependencies at a node on a network diagram

Node type	Description	Summary
AND-SPLIT	Workflow splits into two or more parallel activities which all execute	
OR-SPLIT	Workflow splits into multiple branches of which only one is followed	
AND-JOIN	Multiple executing activities join into a single thread of control	
OR-JOIN	An exclusive alternative activity joins into a single thread of execution	
Iteration	Repetition of one or more workflow activities until a condition is met	
Must follow	No alternative paths exist	

Table 11.5	Elements of the event-driven process chain (EPC) model

EPC symbol	Description of EPC element
Business Event	An event occurs when there is a change in the status of a process. It occurs in response to completion of a function

Table 11.5	Continued

EPC symbol	Description of EPC element
Business Function	A function is an activity or task that is usually completed by a person in the organisational unit responsible for the function. Alternatively it can be completed automatically through the workflow system
xor and or logical operations	Control flow logic between processes is denoted by joins/splits as follows: xor – a single activity follows the completed process(es) and – an and-split gives rise to multiple subsequent functions or – an or-split gives a multiple-choice split
⟹	Control flow forming the process network used to link other elements
Information object	Data needed for completion of a function and acting as input to subsequent functions (workflow relevant data in the WfMC definition). Also known as entity
Organisational unit	The unit responsible for the execution of a function

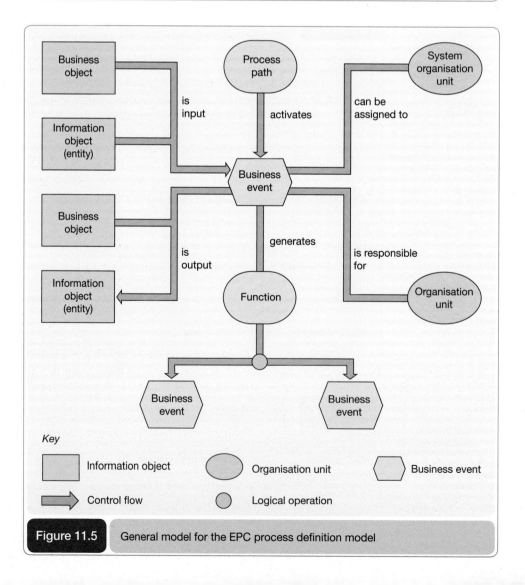

Key

▭ Information object	⬭ Organisation unit	⬡ Business event
⟹ Control flow	◯ Logical operation	

Figure 11.5	General model for the EPC process definition model

to one another. This figure shows how business functions are triggered through transactions on *business objects* which also lead to a *business event*. *Control flows* link the activities, events and logical operators. Entities or information objects are items such as sales orders or invoices.

Validating a new process model

Whichever method has been used to arrive at the process definition, we need to check that the process definition is realistic. When developing a wish list of process capabilities and corresponding business rules the stages described by David Taylor in his book on concurrent engineering (Taylor, 1995) may be useful. He suggests that once new processes have been established they are sanity checked by performing a 'talk-through, walk-through and run-through'. Here, the design team will describe the proposed business process as a model in which different business objects interact. Once the model has been adjusted, the walk-through stage involves more detail in the scenario and the design team will role-play the services the objects provide. The final run-through stage is a quality check in which no on-the-spot debugging occurs – just the interactions between the objects are described.

Data modelling

Data modelling of digital business and e-commerce systems uses well-established techniques such as normalisation that are used for relational database analysis and design. As a consequence, this section is brief in comparison with that on process modelling which introduces some novel techniques. See Bocij *et al.* (2008, Chapter 11) for an introduction to normalisation and relational database design. Some basic definitions are given in this section as a reminder of key terms. Before we start it is worth mentioning that the advent of data mining and object-oriented approaches has meant increasing use of non-relational database design. These are outlined further in Chapters 6 and 11 of Bocij *et al.* (2008). The approach we use to explore data modelling for e-commerce is to use examples that identify typical elements of data modelling for a sell-side e-commerce system. We will use ER (entity relationship) modelling to review typical structures for these databases. In simple ER modelling there are three main stages.

1 Identify entities

Entity
A grouping of related data, such as customer entity, implemented as a table.

Database table
Each database comprises several tables.

Attribute
A property or characteristic of an entity, implemented as a field.

Field
Attributes of products, such as date of birth.

Record
A collection of fields for one instance of an entity, such as Customer Smith.

Social sign-in
Users or members of sites can sign-in with their social network accounts such as Google+, Facebook or LinkedIn through use of APIs exchanging data between different web services.

Relationship
Describes how different tables are linked.

Entities define the broad groupings of information such as information about different people, transactions or products. Examples include customer, employee, sales orders, purchase orders. When the design is implemented each design will form a **database table**.

2 Identify attributes for entities

'**Attributes**' describe the characteristics of any single instance of an entity. For example, the customer entity has attributes such as name, phone number and email address. When the design is implemented each attribute will form a **field**, and the collection of fields for one instance of the entity such as a particular customer will form a **record**.

With the growth in use of social media services, there is a need for businesses to link customer data from different sources. The development of APIs from social networks to enable **social sign-in** has helped with this (Box 11.2).

3 Identify relationships between entities

The **relationships** between entities require identification of which fields are used to link the tables. For example, for each order a customer places we need to know which customer has placed the order and which product they have ordered. As is evident from Figure 11.6, the fields 'customer ID' and 'product ID' are used to relate the order information between the

Box 11.2	The growth in social sign-in

Smart Insights (2013) explain that this is an approach that was first seen mainly on publishers' sites, but is being used more widely on other types of site like retailer sites such as ao.com (Figure 11.1) and Sears Shopyourway.com. You've almost certainly seen this on technology publisher sites like Mashable, Stackoverflow or TechCrunch which enable commenting through logging in/authentication through Facebook, Twitter, LinkedIn or OpenID.

The approach has the benefit that it can reduce the barriers to sign-in, which can reduce the effectiveness of permission marketing (Chapter 8). It has the disadvantage that if simple social sign-in is used, then no data will be collected about the user for profiling. This can, however, be used. Smart Insights (2013) reports on research that says that although 87% have seen social sign-in, only 25% use it regularly. The share of social sign-in at this time was:

- Facebook 46%
- Google 34%
- Yahoo! 7%
- Twitter 6%

The growth in social sign-in shows how it should be considered by all businesses that need to provide log-in to their services.

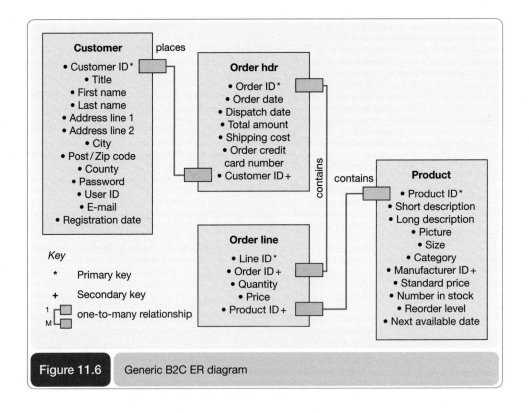

Figure 11.6	Generic B2C ER diagram

Primary key

The field that uniquely identifies each record in a table.

three tables. The fields that are used to relate tables are referred to as 'key fields'. A **primary key** is used to uniquely identify each instance of an entity and a **secondary key** is used to link to a primary key in another table. In Figure 11.6 the primary key of the customer table is customer ID, but the field customer ID in the order table is here a secondary key that links

Secondary key
A field that is used to link tables, by linking to a primary key in another table.

back to the customer table. This relationship is an example of a one-to-many relationship since each customer may place many orders over the lifetime of the relationship.

Normalisation is an additional stage, not covered here, used to optimise the database to minimise redundancy or duplication of information. If you have previous experience in analysis and design for databases, complete Activity 11.3 to develop an ER diagram for a typical B2C company. If you do not have this experience then refer to the generic answers to gain an appreciation of how databases are structured.

Big Data
Within marketing, this concept describes the opportunity to harness customer data from different touchpoints, including as point-of-sale transactions, desktop and mobile sites and apps, and social media.

Big Data and data warehouses

Digital business systems manage a vast number of transactions with data recorded for each. In 2012/2013 it became commonplace for businesses managing this issue to reference this issue as 'Big Data' rather than 'Data warehouse', a term that dates back to the 1990s. We introduce this concept in Box 11.3, showing how it reflects the opportunities to gain value from the increased volumes of data collected in today's digital business.

Activity 11.3 | **ER modelling for a B2C company**

Purpose

To gain an understanding of the generic structure for transactional e-commerce databases.

Activity

Create a normalised ER diagram for the B2C company, or a B2C consumer transactional site.

For answers see Figure 11.6.

Comments

- Customer. May also have a separate delivery address.
- Order. Many items may be required on each order, so each order header can have many line items.
- Product. Includes catalogue information, such as description and a picture.
- Product. Informs the customer the number in stock and when they will be available.
- There will be a separate manufacturer table not shown here.

Box 11.3 | **Analysis of the business applications of Big Data**

What is Big Data?

Big Data has developed as a concept describing a business issue that needs to be managed to make the most of the opportunities available from the increasing volumes of data collected by business today. Managing Big Data also provides challenges of securing data and protecting customer privacy. IBM (2013), which has been one of the leaders in defining the scope and application of Big Data and has developed services for this, has defined the 4Vs characterising Big Data. The 4Vs show that the challenges of managing Big Data not only relate to volume:

1 **Volume.** IBM estimated in 2013 that every day, we create 2.5 quintillion bytes of data. This rate of growth means that 90% of the data in the world today has been created in the past two years alone! By comparison, all of Earth's oceans contain

352 quintillion gallons of water; if bytes were buckets, it would only take about 20 weeks of information-gathering to fill the seas.

2 **Variety.** That's variety in formats of data from structured and unstructured data such as text, sensor data, audio, video, click streams, log files and more. New insights are found when analysing these data types together.

3 **Velocity.** Velocity refers to exploiting data in real time. For example, catching online fraud requires that data must be reviewed rapidly to detect problems. For time-sensitive processes such as catching fraud, Big Data must be used as it streams into your enterprise in order to maximise its value.

4 **Veracity.** Companies need to be able to trust the information used to make decisions in terms of source, accuracy and relevance. With Big Data involving data from different sources, often presented as models, there is a danger that it may not be believed and so not be in the right format to support decisions.

The growth in volume of data enabled by Big Data has become possible through more forms of *instrumentation* that captures 'events' through time, according to Eaton *et al.* (2012), which can be integrated into systems. This instrumentation can be simply data collection where the events are a sequence of customer interactions with a business through its desktop or mobile site or social media, for example through web analytics or social analytics. From an e-commerce and online marketing perspective, understanding the sequence of events is important to understand whether investments in media investments or building multichannel experiences is important. Machine-to-machine *interconnection* is also commonly involved in data collection; for example, sensors on cars or GPS tracking of items in supply chain systems are collated centrally. Eaton *et al.* (2012) note that Big Data systems such as Hadoop tend to be more likely to process unstructured data which doesn't need to be cleansed in comparison with traditional data warehouses which are highly structured with data integrity enforced.

What, then, is the scope of Big Data applications? Andy Mendelsohn, Senior VP of Database Server Technologies at Oracle, explains it this way:

> Today, we have our information systems for business intelligence, and people call them data marts and data warehouses, and they're loaded with all this transactional information from our transaction processing systems like E-Business Suite and other application vendors. And that information is really valuable, the crown jewels of the company, that transactional data. It's not going away. So what's really important about Big Data is to understand there's a lot of this data, most of it's completely worthless to the business, but there are these gems, these nuggets of information, like the fact that a customer just had a baby. You want to take that information, you want to integrate it to your existing transactional data that you've got in your data warehouse and really use that to make better business decisions and make more money for your company.

Example applications of Big Data

IBM gives these simple examples of transformation of different types of real-time data that can be harnessed in digital business:

- Turn 12 terabytes of Tweets created each day into improved product sentiment analysis.
- Convert 350 billion annual meter readings to better predict power consumption.
- For time-sensitive processes such as catching fraud, Big Data must be used as it streams into your enterprise in order to maximise its value.
- Analyse 500 million daily call detail records in real time to predict customer churn faster.

Mendelsohn, quoted in Smart Insights (2013), gives three more detailed examples of Big Data applications. These show that Big Data applications often build on existing data about customer purchase transactions stored in data warehouses, but introduce additional types of data.

1. Car Insurance sector example

This business already has an Exadata data warehouse, and it's already capturing all its transactional insurance information about its customers, their accidents, their policy information, etc., says Mendelsohn.

> *What they would like to do is enhance that data with a new kind of data that you can get from cars. Cars are now loaded with sensors that are capturing your every movement of what's going on out there and it's called car telematics data. What they would like to do is use that information to actually study the actual driving behaviour of their customers and use that to better understand maybe what their insurance rates should be, what their driving habits are and maybe even help customers be better drivers. This is actually a very classic-use case. So they're interested in augmenting their Exadata system with a BDA, Big Data Appliance.*

2. Travel insurance sector example

This company is an online business comparing and providing holidays of different types. It's already capturing all the transactional data about its customers, what are the trips they're buying.

> *What they would like to do is augment that information with what's going on in their websites. They want to capture the web logs, they want to get social media data to better understand what their customers are up to, what are the trips they're antici-pating maybe going on and combine that information with their existing information about their customers' previous transactions and use that to help make better pro-motional offers to the customers and grow their business.*

3. Gaming sector example

This company is in the business of selling game consoles of various sorts and Internet games, and it also has a big Exadata data warehouse that's analysing that information. It is looking to augment its Exadata data warehouse with business decision analysis, and want to use it for what you might expect: better understand what the customers are doing out in the games. '*They want to understand relationships between custom-ers. One of the really interesting things in games is that people play games with each other. And you want to understand the social networks of people who are playing with each other because it's likely that if one person in that network wants to do something, the others will want to do the same thing. So they can use that information to better upsell information in this game space.*' According to the company, integrating data alone does not generate value. Analytic modelling and tools to interpret the output is needed. They say '*Advanced analytic models are needed to enable data-driven opti-mization (for example, of employee schedules or shipping networks) or predictions (for instance, about flight delays or what customers will want or do given their buying histo-ries or Web-site behavior)*'. A plan is also needed to identify where models will create additional business value, who will need to use them, and how to avoid inconsisten-cies and unnecessary proliferation as models are scaled up across the enterprise. They also note the importance of decision support tools. They say:

> *the output of modeling may be strikingly rich, but it's valuable only if managers and, in many cases, frontline employees understand and use it. Output that's too com-plex can be overwhelming or even mistrusted. What's needed are intuitive tools that integrate data into day-to-day processes and translate modeling outputs into*

> *tangible business actions: for instance, a clear interface for scheduling employees, fine-grained cross-selling suggestions for call-center agents, or a way for marketing managers to make real-time decisions on discounts.*
>
> A key design issue is how the information about these transactions can usefully be applied to improve the effectiveness and business contribution of these systems. In Chapter 12 we describe how web analytics systems are used to analyse and improve the effectiveness of sell-side e-commerce systems.
>
> While independent analytics systems are available, larger companies are increasingly finding that to apply the insights available they have to integrate web analytics information with internal sales and ordering systems to form data warehouses.

Design for digital technology projects

System design
Defines how an information system will operate.

The **design** element of creating a digital business system involves specifying how the system should be structured and how the end-user functionality and 'back-end' integration with other projects will be implemented.

In the two *Focus on* sections that follow we look at two aspects of design that are of great importance to how digital business systems are perceived by customers – security and interface design. Before that, we consider the overall architectural design of digital business systems.

Architectural design of digital business systems

The starting point for design of digital business systems is to ensure that a common architecture exists across the company in terms of hardware and software technology, applications and business processes. This goal is summarised in Figure 3.5(b).

Client–server model
A system architecture in which end-user machines such as PCs, known as 'clients', run applications while accessing data and possibly programs from a server.

Digital business systems follow the same **client–server model** architecture of many business information systems created in the 1990s. For the digital business, the clients were traditionally employees, suppliers or customers' desktop PCs which gave the 'front-end' access point to digital business applications. Today increasingly, they are mobile devices such as smartphones and tablets as shown by the trends in increasing mobile usage described in Chapters 3 and 4. These client devices are connected to a 'back-end' server computer via an intranet, extranet or Internet. In Chapters 3 and 6 we have discussed the management issues involved with selecting 'Software as a Service' (SaaS) digital business systems, which are client–server systems where the client is a web browser on a computer or mobile device and the server is located outside the organisation and the application process is commonly shared with many other companies in a 'multi-tenancy' model.

A key design decision in client–server systems is how different tasks involved in delivering a working application to the users are distributed between client and server. The typical situation for these tasks in a digital business system is:

Debate 11.1

Digital business vs ERP architectures

'Designing an appropriate architecture for digital business is effectively the same as the architecture for enterprise resource planning systems.'

- *Data storage.* Predominantly on server. Client storage is ideally limited to cookies, which are then related to the data for the user which are stored on database servers. SaaS systems often use a cloud of multiple servers in different locations to deliver these services more efficiently, as again described in Chapter 3.
- *Query processing.* Predominantly on the server, although some validation can be performed on the client.

- *Display.* Traditionally this is largely a client function, but with the increasing importance of mobile usage, responsive and adaptive mobile approaches are used as described later in Chapter 11 on design.
- *Application logic.* Traditionally, in early PC applications this has been a client function, but for digital business systems the design aim is to maximise the application logic processing, including the business rules on the server.

Three-tier client–server

The first tier is the client that handles display, second is application logic and business rules, third is database storage.

Thin client

An end-user access device (terminal) where computing requirements such as processing and storage (and so cost), are minimised.

A typical digital business architecture uses a **three-tier client–server** model where the client is mainly used for display with application logic and the business rules partitioned on a server, which is the second tier, and the database server is the third tier. Since most of the processing is executed on the servers rather than the client, this architecture is sometimes referred to as a '**thin client**', because the size of the executable program is smaller. The application server provider (ASP) described in Chapter 3 is typically based upon the three-tier model. This is shown in Figure 11.7.

Although the three-tier model of a digital business system suggests a relatively simple architectural design, the reality is more complex. Different servers are needed which combine applications logic and database storage for different requirements. These may be physically separate servers or may be combined. Figure 11.8 shows a typical digital business architecture. The purpose of each of the servers is as follows:

- *Web server.* Manages http requests from client and acts as a passive broker to other servers. Returns or serves web pages.
- *Merchant server.* This is the main location of the application logic and integrates the entire application by making requests to the other server components.
- *Personalisation server.* Provides tailored content – may be part of commerce server functionality.
- *Payment commerce server.* Manages payment systems and secure transactions.
- *Catalogue server.* A document management server used to display detailed product information and technical specifications.
- *CRM server.* Stores information on all customer contacts.
- *ERP server.* Required for information on stock availability and pricing from the customer. Will need to be accessed for sales order processing and histories, and logistics for distribution.

It is evident that designing the method of integration between different components is not straightforward – creating a fully integrated digital business is not straightforward! As was discussed in Chapter 9, the best approach to simplifying the design is to reduce the number of suppliers of components to improve the ease of data and applications integration.

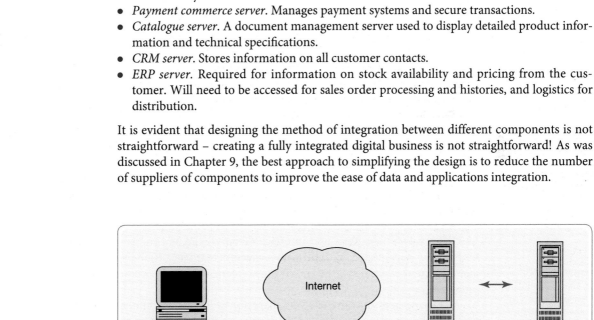

Tier 1 — Web browser | Internet | Tier 2 — Applications server | Tier 3 — Database server

Figure 11.7 Three-tier client–server in a digital business environment

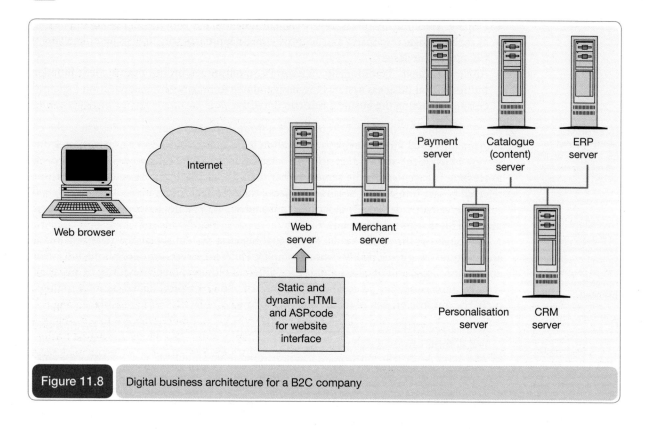

Figure 11.8   Digital business architecture for a B2C company

---

User-centred site design and customer experience management

User-centred design (UX)

Design based on optimising the user experience according to all factors, including the user interface, which affect this.

Since digital business systems are often customer- or employee-facing systems, the importance of human–computer interaction in the design of web applications is high. Referring to website design, Nigel Bevan says:

Unless a web site meets the needs of the intended users it will not meet the needs of the organization providing the web site. Web site development should be user-centred, evaluating the evolving design against user requirements. (Bevan, 1999a)

Noyes and Baber (1999) explain that **user-centred design** (now commonly abbreviated to UX) involves more than user interface design. It can be conceived of as centring on the human, but surrounded concentrically by factors that affect usability such as user interface, computers, workplace and the environment. Here we will be specifically looking at the user interface.

Customer experience management (CXM)

User experience improvements are broadened to consider the context of use to different physical locations or customer touchpoints across different digital platforms including desktop, mobile sites, apps, social networks and email marketing. Context of use includes device type, location and interactions with customer service.

As digital platforms have evolved, there are an increasing number of online brand presences, from company websites accessed over desktop computers to mobile sites and apps accessed via tablets and mobile phone to social presences on the major social networks like Facebook, Google+, LinkedIn and Twitter. Consequently, improvements to the UX of systems have been extended to consider the context of access of systems within the location of the user. This is known as **customer experience management (CXM)**. The development of UX to CXM has been prompted by:

- The use of smartphone and mobile devices.
- Dual or multiscreening where a smartphone or tablet may be used alongside other devices, including TVS.

- Multichannel shopping behaviour where mobile devices may be used in-store as part of the purchase decision, or the decision to purchase offline is prompted by online experiences and vice versa.
- The website experience being closely integrated to other online company platforms, including company social network pages and email communications.
- The integration of offline customer service with online customer service through services such as livechat and call-back integrated into websites.

The range of platforms that must be controlled as part of CXM is shown in Figure 11.9.

CXM is particularly important to multichannel or omnichannel transactional sites such as those for travel, retail and financial services. Forrester (2011) describes CXM in terms of different systems that can be used to deliver customer experience. These include web content management, personalisation, marketing automation, commerce platforms, customer service interaction management, on-site search, merchandising and combining analytics with test and optimisation. This description suggests the design challenge of creating an effective customer experience based on integration of different systems or services that form the overall experience. It also shows that CXM is not a one-off activity during creation of a new site, but an ongoing process of improvement using analytics and structured testing as part of a **conversion rate optimisation (CRO)** programme. CRO is increasingly being used by companies to improve the commercial contribution of online presence to a business, as the Smart Insights interview introducing this chapter shows. So design for digital business should not be considered as a one-off investment when a new site or service is created, but as a continuous investment.

User-centred design starts with understanding the nature and variation within the user groups. According to Bevan (1999a), issues to consider include:

- Who are the important users?
- What is their purpose in accessing the site?

Conversion rate optimisation (CRO)

Improving the commercial returns from a transactional site through increasing conversion to key goals such as sales, quotes, bookings or leads. CRO combines customer and competitor research with evaluation of customer behaviour using web analytics and AB and multivariate testing. (See Chapter 12 for details.)

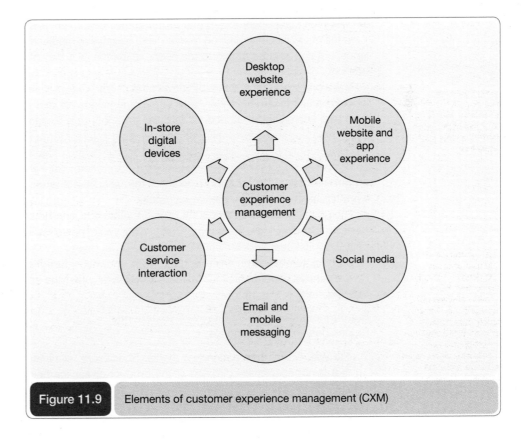

| Figure 11.9 | Elements of customer experience management (CXM) |

- How frequently will they visit the site?
- What experience and expertise do they have?
- What nationality are they? Can they read English?
- What type of information are they looking for?
- How will they want to use the information: read it on the screen, print it or download it?
- What type of browsers will they use? How fast will their communication links be?
- How large a screen/window will they use, with how many colours?

Box 11.4 gives a modern perspective on mistakes companies continue to make with their websites and suggests how companies can be persuaded to invest in usability initiatives.

Before we study best practice in user-centred design, it should be noted that usability and accessibility are only one part of the overall experience which determines a visitor's experience. In Chapter 5, in the section on competitor analysis, we explained how it is important to provide a promise of what the online representation of the brand will deliver to customers. The concept of online brand promise is closely related to that of delivering online customer experience. In this chapter, we will explore different practical actions that companies can take to create and maintain satisfactory online experiences. An indication of the effort

Online customer experience
The combination of rational and emotional factors of using a company's online services that influences customers' perceptions of a brand online.

Box 11.4	Why do websites torture their visitors?

Bruce Tognazzini was Apple's 66th employee, developing the company's first usability guidelines and founding its Human Interface team. Almost 30 years later, he's a principal at Nielsen Norman Group and still making his feelings known when companies commit design errors.

The main web usability/user experience mistakes
The level of open hostility that websites display is breathtaking. For every Bed, Bath & Beyond, with its smooth, comfortable user experience, there are a thousand amateurish websites that appear to feel that torturing their customers is a really good idea.

In the main, this has resulted from striving to achieve mediocrity, rather than excellence, but it is as devastating to the user experience as if they had set out to achieve hostility.

The worst single fault is throwing away the user's work. You see this in travel sites, where the user spends an hour selecting airline tickets for dates five months hence, then tries searching for a hotel for that same period, only to find the site has thrown away the dates and is assuming the user wants a hotel for tomorrow night.

The customer playing 'what if' with different airlines and different hotels may have to enter the same group of dates as many as a dozen times during these transactions – often resulting in their making a mistake the last, fateful time, and ending up with worthless airline tickets for the wrong dates.

Then there's the worst single bit of information that can be discarded: the user's decision to uncheck the box saying, 'Yes! I want you to spam me 14 times a day for the rest of my life!' that appears embedded in the order page.

Go back to change anything on that page, and they'll turn the checkbox back on. How do these people imagine customers feel later when the spam they specifically rejected starts rolling in?

Recommendations on a faster web experience
Bruce Tognazzini recommends:

1 Rid your site of time-dependent media. Specifically, eliminate all Flash and video that is not specifically directed at the product or service being sold or discussed and that is not under the direct and voluntary control of the user.

2   Support tabbed browsing.

3   Limit the number of pages and interactions necessary for a user to accomplish his or her task.

4   Do 'boredom testing', where you observe new and experienced users and see where they fidget, their mind and eyes wander, or they sit back with arms crossed.

5   Work out solutions so that when you must do some work 'behind the scenes', the user is engaged in decision-making and doesn't miss your presence. Use Firefox's ability to pre-fetch pages, for example, so when the user is ready to go, you are ready to go, too.

Will all companies have grasped the importance of user experience in another 12 years?

If you look back at my 1980 guidelines, above, and compare them with what is out there in 2007, you will see that the vast majority of companies don't yet grasp even the rudiments of human–computer interaction (HCI).

We still see, for example, most websites demanding that users enter difficult-to-check data, such as phone and credit card numbers, without spaces, all to save the programmer five minutes and a single line of code.

Such ignorance and laziness ensures full employment for HCI designers for the foreseeable future, and also ensures that the original promise of the web, with its sweeping aside of 'bricks-and-mortar stores', will continue unfulfilled.

Persuade senior management to buy in to usability/user experience?

Pore over your log files [web analytics] and be prepared to point out the places where users are 'bailing out', along with cogent arguments as to why, mentioning things like your lovely, design-award-winning Flash animated-splash screen that takes a minute to load and does nothing towards selling the product.

Then, convert those bail-outs into dollars:

We are losing 20% of our customers before they ever even enter the site because of our splash screen. Last year, our sales were $140,000,000. If we hadn't lost all these people, we could have realised an additional $11,420,000. Total lost profit: Around $750,000. A single HCI designer could have prevented that, at a savings of around $700,000 dollars. We also will no longer have to put out release x.01, x.1, and x.2 every time we come out with a new design, because the design will be right. That would save us millions more in engineering resources.

Companies not only save millions by having HCI talent available to them; they often move back from the brink of extinction.

HCI can be a no-brainer to senior management if the case is made clearly and expressed in terms they understand – money.

Failing buy-in, do it anyway. All that's needed is a broom closet and a couple of tables.

Forget about video. Just see if people can use your site. A single test with a single user in a broom closet can be such an eye-opener, it can change the course of a whole project. (Of course, even with qualitative testing, 20 or 30 users, over time, are better.)

Even a really bad designer, with sufficient user-testing, will eventually be able to cobble together a decent design – the infinite number of monkeys theory – the worst crime is to not test at all.

Also consider becoming an HCI designer yourself. If you're concerned enough to petition management, you have the most important prerequisite – you care.

Source: E-consultancy (2007).

required to produce a customer-centric online presence is given by Alison Lancaster, at the time the head of marketing and catalogues at John Lewis Direct and currently Marketing Director at Charles Tyrrwhitt (www.ctshirts.co.uk), who says:

A good site should always begin with the user. Understand who the customer is, how they use the channel to shop, and understand how the marketplace works in that category. This includes understanding who your competitors are and how they operate online. You need continuous research, feedback and usability testing to continue to monitor and evolve the customer experience online. Customers want convenience and ease of ordering. They want a site that is quick to download, well-structured and easy to navigate.

You can see that creating effective online experiences is a challenge since there are many practical issues to consider which we present in Figure 11.10. This is based on a diagram by de Chernatony (2001), who suggested that delivering the online experience promised by a brand requires delivering rational values, emotional values and promised experience (based on rational and emotional values). The factors that influence the online customer experience can be presented in a pyramid form of success factors as is shown in Figure 11.10 (the different success factors reflect current best practice and differ from those of de Chernatony). The diagram also highlights the importance of delivering service quality online, as has been indicated by Trocchia and Janda (2003). Research by Christodoulides *et al.* (2006) has tested the importance of a range of indicators of online brand equity for online retail and

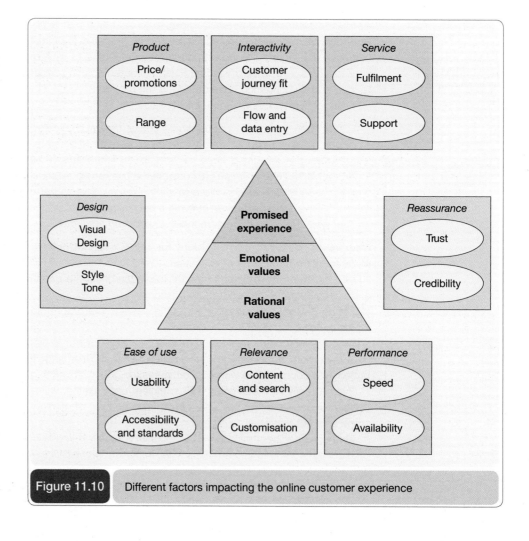

| Figure 11.10 | Different factors impacting the online customer experience |

service companies. This analysis was performed across these five dimensions of brand equity assessed by asking the questions which are listed below:

1 Emotional connection

Q1: I feel related to the type of people who are [X]'s customers
Q2: I feel like [X] actually cares about me
Q3: I feel as though [X] really understands me

2 Online experience

Q4: [X]'s website provides easy-to-follow search paths
Q5: I never feel lost when navigating through [X]'s website
Q6: I was able to obtain the information I wanted without any delay

3 Responsive service nature

Q7: [X] is willing and ready to respond to customer needs
Q8: [X]'s website gives visitors the opportunity to 'talk back' to [X]

4 Trust

Q9: I trust [X] to keep my personal information safe
Q10: I feel safe in my transactions with [X]

5 Fulfilment

Q11: I got what I ordered from [X]'s website
Q12: The product was delivered by the time promised by [X]

Usability

Usability
An approach to website design intended to enable the completion of user tasks.

Usability is a key concept within user-centred design that is applied to the analysis and design for a range of products which defines how easy they are to use. The British Standards Institute ISO Standard: Human-centred Design Processes for Interactive Systems (1999) defined usability as the:

extent to which a product can be used by specified users to achieve specified goals with effectiveness, efficiency and satisfaction in a specified context of use.

You can see how the concept can be readily applied to website design – web visitors often have defined *goals* such as finding particular information or completing a particular action. In Jakob Nielsen's classic book, *Designing Web Usability* (Nielsen, 2000a), he describes usability as follows:

An engineering approach to website design to ensure the user interface of the site is learnable, memorable, error free, efficient and gives user satisfaction. It incorporates testing and evaluation to ensure the best use of navigation and links to access information in the shortest possible time. A companion process to information architecture.

Expert review
An analysis of an existing site or prototype, by an experienced usability expert who will identify deficiencies and improvements to a site based on their knowledge of web design principles and best practice.

In practice, usability involves two key project activities. **Expert reviews** are often performed at the beginning of a redesign project as a way of identifying problems with a previous design. **Usability testing** involves:

1 Identifying representative users of the site and typical tasks.
2 Asking them to perform specific tasks such as finding a product or completing an order.
3 Observing what they do and how they succeed.

For a site to be successful, the user tasks or actions need to be completed:

Usability/user-testing
Representative users are observed performing representative tasks using a system.

- Effectively – web usability specialists measure task completion, for example, only 3 out of 10 visitors to a website may be able to find a telephone number or other piece of information.
- Efficiently – web usability specialists also measure how long it takes to complete a task on-site, or the number of clicks it takes.

Jakob Nielsen explains the imperative for usability best in his 'Usability 101' (www.useit. com/alertbox/20030825.html – now unavailable). He says:

> On the Web, usability is a necessary condition for survival. If a website is difficult to use, people leave. If the homepage fails to clearly state what a company offers and what users can do on the site, people leave. If users get lost on a website, they leave. If a website's information is hard to read or doesn't answer users' key questions, they leave. Note a pattern here?

For these reasons, Nielsen suggests that around 10% of a design project budget should be spent on usability, but often actual spend is significantly less.

Evaluating designs

A test of effective design for usability is, according to Bevan (1999b), dependent on three areas:

1 Effectiveness – can users complete their tasks correctly and completely?
2 Productivity (efficiency) – are tasks completed in an acceptable length of time?
3 Satisfaction – are users satisfied with the interaction?

User involvement is vital to assess the effectiveness of design and focus groups have traditionally been used as part of a website prototyping approach described in Chapter 10.

E-consultancy (2009) describes how insurance company Hiscox (www.hiscox.co.uk) approached a site redesign using three different models of user interaction which were prototyped:

- A distribution model in which visitors pick the type of customer they are, then choose their product.
- A retail model, where customers pick the product they want, then choose how to buy it.
- A needs-based model to help customers choose products.

Eyetracking
A usability testing technique that provides a visual overlay of where visitors most commonly look at on the screen (heatmaps) and individual or common paths (gaze trails).

Eyetracking is an effective technique for assessing design effectiveness. Eyetracking of prospects is offered by many usability agencies as part of a focus group (see, for example, the Video Explanation at: www.etre.com/blog/ and Eyetracking examples at www.youtube.com/user/ SimpleUsability) or through remote testing through services such as WhatUsersDo.com.

Traditionally usability tests have been completed during analysis and design, but many businesses now gain feedback continuously via tools. Smart Insights (2010) identifies five types of tools:

1 **Website feedback tools.** Sometimes described as 'Voice of Customer', these provide a permanent facility for customers to feed back by prompts on every page.
2 **Crowdsourcing product opinion software.** Feedback on new features or service delivery.
3 **Simple page or concept feedback tools.** These give basic feedback from other site users.
4 **Site exit survey tools.** These tools rate intent (reason to visit site) against satisfaction. Some companies use for redesign, others for permanent tracking of site effectiveness.
5 **General online survey tools.** Many companies use generic low-cost or free survey tools to research audience opinions.

Use-case modelling
A user-centred approach to modelling system requirements.

Unified Modelling Language (UML)
A language used to specify, visualise and document the artefacts of an object-oriented system.

Use-case analysis

The **use-case method** of process analysis and modelling was developed in the early 1990s as part of the development of object-oriented techniques. It is part of a methodology known as **Unified Modelling Language (UML)** that attempts to unify the approaches that preceded it such as the Booch, OMT and Objectory notations. Jacobsen *et al.* (1994) give an accessible introduction and describe how object modelling can be applied to workflow analysis.

Persona and scenario analysis

Website designers and marketers use a similar model, but using different terminology. Marketers create **web design personas** for typical site visitors; this is a powerful technique for influencing the planning of online campaigns and the usability and customer-centricity of a website. Forrester (2005) researched the use of personas and found that ethnographic researchers averaged 21 interviews with typical users per project to create with an average of between four and eight personas and this cost between \$47,000 and \$500,000! Ford uses three buyer personas at Ford.com, Staples.com has seven personas for shoppers and Microsoft had seven for Windows XP.

Personas are essentially a 'thumbnail' description of a type of person. They have been used for a long time in research for segmentation and advertising, but in recent years have also proved effective for improving website design by companies that have applied this technique.

Customer scenarios are developed for different personas. Patricia Seybold in the book *The Customer Revolution* (Seybold and Marshak, 2001) explains them as follows:

> *A customer scenario is a set of tasks that a particular customer wants or needs to do in order to accomplish his or her desired outcome.*

You will see that scenarios can be developed for each persona. Each scenario is split up into a series of steps or tasks, which can be best thought of as a series of questions a visitor asks. By identifying questions website designers identify the information needs of different customer types at different stages in the buying process.

The use of scenarios is a simple, but very powerful web design technique that is still relatively rare in website design. They can also be used when benchmarking competitor sites as part of situation analysis. The following are some guidelines and ideas on what can be included when developing a persona. The start or end point is to give each persona a name. The detailed stages are:

1 Build personal attributes into personas:
   - Demographic: age, sex, education, occupation and for B2B, company size, position in buying unit
   - Psychographic: goals, tasks, motivation
   - Webographics: web experience (months), usage location (home or work), usage platform (dial-up, broadband), usage frequency, favourite sites.
2 Remember that personas are only models of characteristics and environment:
   - Design targets
   - Stereotypes
   - Three or four usually suffice to improve general usability, but more are needed for specific behaviours
   - Choose one primary persona which, if satisfied, means others are likely to be satisfied.
3 Different scenarios can be developed for each persona as explained further below. Write three or four, for example:
   - Information-seeking scenario (leads to site registration)
   - Purchase scenario – new customer (leads to sale)
   - Purchase scenario – existing customer (leads to sale).

Once different personas have been developed that are representative of key site-visitor types or customer types, a **primary persona** is sometimes identified. Wodtke (2002) says:

> *Your primary persona needs to be a common user type who is both important to the business success of the product and needy from a design point of view – in other words, a beginner user or a technologically challenged one.*

She also says that secondary personas can also be developed such as super-users or complete novices. Complementary personas are those that don't fit into the main categories which display unusual behaviour. Such complementary personas help 'out-of-box thinking' and offer choices or content that may appeal to all users.

For another example of the application of personas, see Mini case study 11.1 about paint manufacturer Dulux.

Mini Case Study 11.1   Dulux paints a picture of consumers with personas

Campaign aims

The aims behind this brand initiative were to reposition Dulux from a paint brand to a colour help brand by meeting customer needs in a way competitors don't to help differentiate the Dulux brand. The aim was to position Dulux.co.uk (Figure 11.11) as 'the online destination for colour scheming and visualisation to help you achieve your individual style from the comfort of your home'. Specific outcomes on the site are to browse colours, add colours to a personal scrapbook, use the paint calculator and find a stockist. Further aims were to 'win the war before the store', i.e. to provide colour help tools that can help develop a preference for Dulux before consumers are in-store and to prompt other ideas to sell more than one colour at a time.

Specific SMART objectives were to increase the number of unique visitors from 1m p.a. in 2003 to 3.5m p.a. in 2006 and to drive 12% of visitors to a desired outcome (e.g. ordering swatches).

Target audience

Based on research, it was found that the main audience for the site was female with these typical demographics and psychographics:

- Would-be adventurous 25–44 women, online
- Lack of confidence with previous site:
  - Gap between inspiration (TV, magazines, advertising) and lived experience (large DIY retail premises, nervous discomfort)
  - No guidance or reassurance previously available currently on their journey

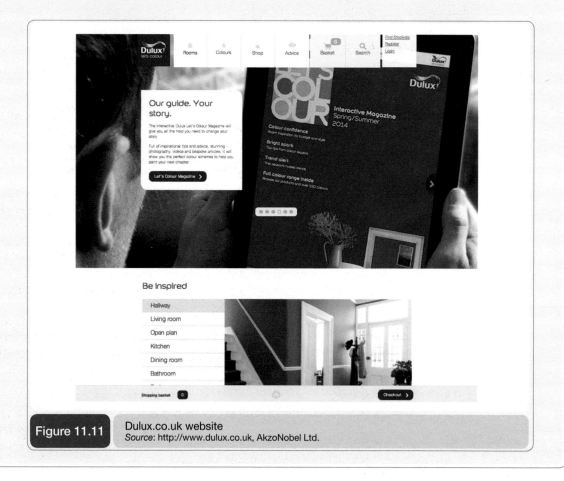

Figure 11.11   Dulux.co.uk website
Source: http://www.dulux.co.uk, AkzoNobel Ltd.

- Colours and colour combining are key
- Online is a well-used channel for help and guidance on other topics
- 12-month decorating cycle
- Propensity to socialise
- Quality, technical innovation and scientific proficiency of Dulux are given.

Specific personas were developed as follows:

- First-time buyer. Penny Edwards, Age: 27, Partner: Ben, Location: North London, Occupation: Sales Assistant
- *Part-time mum*. Jane Lawrence, Age: 37, Husband: Joe, Location: Manchester, Occupation: Part-time PR consultant
- *Single mum*. Rachel Wilson, Age: 40, Location: Reading, Occupation: Business Analyst

Each has a different approach to interacting with the brand. For Penny it is summarised by the statement:

I've got loads of ideas and enthusiasm, I just don't know where to start.

Each persona was also characterised by their media consumption and preferences such as types of website, TV, magazines and radio channels and their favourite hobbies and socialising activities.

A storyboard was developed to illustrate the typical 'customer journey' for each persona, and these informed the final site design.

Brand campaign

To support the re-launch of the site, digital channels such as online banner advertising and interactive TV, with traditional channels such as press, in-store and PR. The main theme of the ads was 'colour chemistry', which was developed through featuring personas in the ads such as Candy Love, Forest Lake and Treacle Tart. The ads had a clear call to action to visit the website to find the right match for the consumer's personality and style.

Source: Case study developed by Agency.com available through the IAB (www.iabuk.net) and presented at the Engage 2007 Online Marketing conference.

Stages in use-case analysis

The following stages are identified by Schneider and Winters (1998) for analysis using the use-case method.

1 Identify actors

Actors

People, software or other devices that interface with a system.

Actors are those objects which are involved in using or interacting with a system. They are not part of the system. The obvious actors are the users of a system. In a customer service application the actors may be a customer and the customer service person at the company. When performing process analysis to define use-cases we ask questions such as 'Who are the actors for this process?' 'What services do these actors provide?' 'What are the actors' tasks?' and 'What changes do they make to the status of the overall process?' Actors may add information to the system or receive it through reporting facilities. Note that an employee who has several roles would be represented by two different actors.

Schneider and Winters (1998) point out that other actors include software and hardware control devices that change the state of the process and external systems that interface with the system under consideration. These are effectively human actors who have been automated. Actors are denoted using the straightforward approach shown in Figure 11.12.

2 Identify use-cases

Use-case

The sequence of transactions between an actor and a system that supports the activities of the actor.

Use-cases are the different things users of a system want it to perform. These can be described as activities or tasks that are part of a dialogue between an actor and the system. They summarise the requirements of a system from each actor since they describe the functionality that will be provided by the system. Common use-cases are:

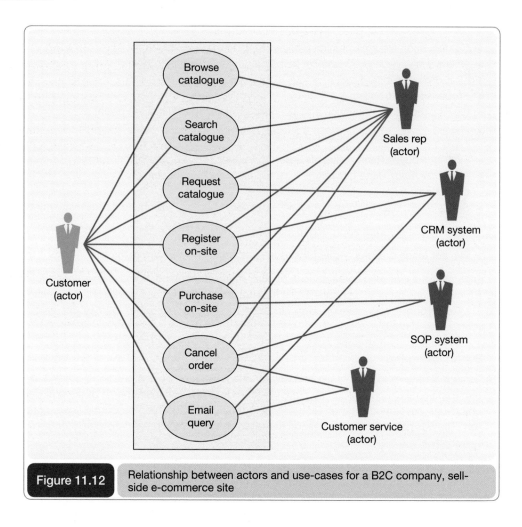

| Figure 11.12 | Relationship between actors and use-cases for a B2C company, sell-side e-commerce site |

- Starting up, shutting down or amending a system.
- Adding or amending information on a system. Examples include placing an e-commerce order or recording a complaint via email.
- Using a system for reporting or decision support.

Some use-cases for a B2C company are shown in Figure 11.12.

Bevan (1999b) also notes the importance of defining key scenarios of use. This stage, often known as 'knowledge elicitation', involves interviewing users and asking them to talk through their current or preferred way of working. Once the scenarios have been established, card sorting techniques, as described by Noyes and Baber (1999), can be used. They describe how after interviewing users, typical tasks or actions were written down on cards. These were then used to identify the sequence of actions users required from a menu system. They explain that the menu system devised was quite different from that envisaged by the software engineers. Card sorting techniques can also be used to check that no stages have been missed during the **talk-through** – a **walk-through** of the cards is performed.

Talk-through
A user verbally describes their required actions.

Walk-through
A user executes their actions through using a system or mock-up.

3 Relate actors to use-cases

Figure 11.12 also shows how actors relate to use-cases. It can be used to identify responsibilities and check for missing activities. For example, 'Check order status' is a use-case that is missing and the company would have to discuss whether it was acceptable for a customer service rep to place an order for a customer who was complaining about a particular product.

4 Develop use-case scenarios

Scenario

A particular path or flow of events or activities within a use-case.

A detailed **scenario** is then developed to detail the different paths of events and activities for each use-case. The primary scenario describes the typical case where nothing goes wrong. The use-case includes detail of activities or functions, what happens when there is an alternative or decision, or if there is an error. Pre-conditions for entering and post-conditions for exiting the use-case are also specified.

Figure 11.13 shows a primary scenario for the complete e-commerce purchase cycle. A more detailed primary scenario for the particular use-case 'Register' written from the point of view of the customer actor from Figure 11.14 is as follows:

Pre-condition: A user is active on the website.
Scenario: Register.
Basic path:

1 Use-case starts when customer presses 'register'.
2 Customer enters name, postal address and email.
3 The post/postcode and email address (@ symbol) will be checked for validity after entry and the user prompted if there is an error.
4 The customer will select 'submit'.
5 The system will check all fields are present and the customer information will be passed to the CRM system.

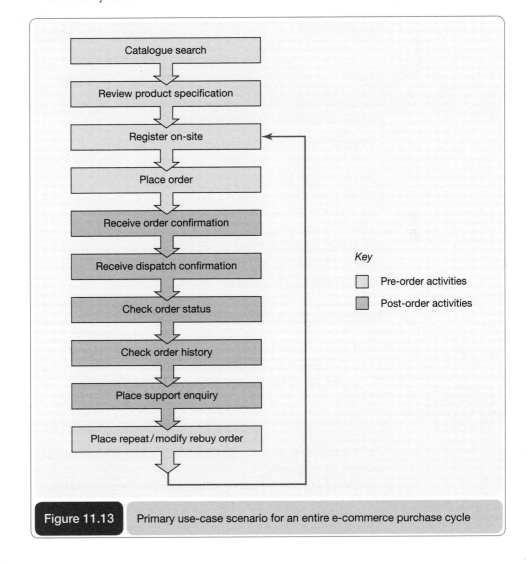

| Figure 11.13 | Primary use-case scenario for an entire e-commerce purchase cycle |

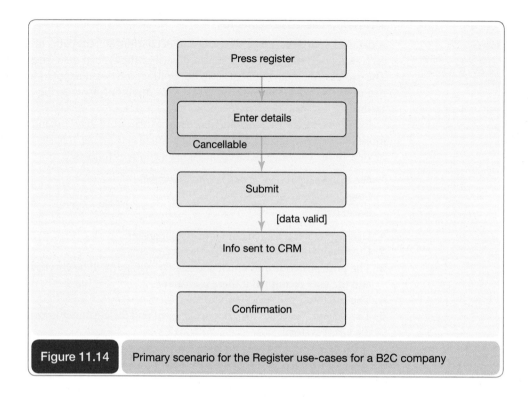

Figure 11.14 Primary scenario for the Register use-cases for a B2C company

6 A redirect page will be displayed to thank the customer for registering and provide an option to return to the home page, and the use-case ends.

Post-condition: The customer details have been saved.
Alternative paths: The customer can cancel at stages 2 to 4 before pressing 'submit' and the use-case ends.

It can be seen that by stating the use-case in this way different issues can be clarified. After the primary scenario is complete, second or alternative scenarios can be developed and added to the primary scenarios as alternatives. For the register scenario, cancel is a secondary scenario; others could include error conditions such as whether the postcode is invalid. Figure 11.15 illustrates an e-commerce site with clear menu options which is consistent with use-case analysis.

Designing the information architecture

Information architecture

The combination of organisation, labelling and navigation schemes composing an information system.

Rosenfeld and Morville (2002) emphasise the importance of information architecture to an effective website design. In their book, they give alternative definitions of an information architecture.

They say it is:

1 *The combination of organisation, labelling, and navigation schemes within an information system.*
2 *The structural design of an information space to facilitate task completion and intuitive access to content.*
3 *The art and science of structuring and classifying web sites and intranets to help people find and manage information.*
4 *An emerging discipline and community of practice focused on bringing principles of design and architecture to the digital landscape.*

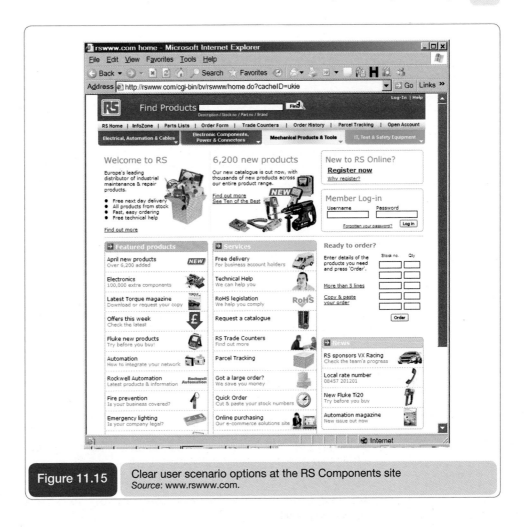

Figure 11.15	Clear user scenario options at the RS Components site

Source: www.rswww.com.

Essentially, in practice, creation of an information architecture involves creating a plan to group information logically – it involves creating a site structure which is often represented as a **site map**. Note, though, that whole books have been written on information architecture, so this is necessarily a simplification! A well-developed information architecture is very important to usability since it determines navigation options. It is also important to search engine optimisation (Chapter 9), since it determines how different types of content that users may search for are labelled and grouped.

A planned information architecture is essential to large-scale websites that include a large volume of product or support documentation. Information architectures are less important to small-scale websites and brand sites, but even here, the principles can be readily applied and can help make the site more visible to search engines and usable. The benefits of creating an information architecture include:

- A defined structure and categorisation of information will support user and organisation goals, i.e. it is a vital aspect of usability.
- It helps increase 'flow' on the site – a user's mental model of where to find content should mirror that of the content on the website.
- Search engine optimisation – a higher listing in the search rankings can often be used through structuring and labelling information in a structured way.
- Applicable for integrating offline communications – ads or direct mail can link to a product or campaign landing page to help achieve direct response. A sound URL strategy as explained in Chapter 8 can help this.

Site map
A graphical or text depiction of the relationship between different groups of content on a website.

- Related content can be grouped to measure the effectiveness of a website as part of design for analysis which is also explained below.

Card sorting

Card sorting or web classification

The process of arranging a way of organising objects on the website in a consistent manner.

Websites are frequently designed from the perspective of the designer rather than the information user, leading to labels, subject grouping and categories that are not intuitive to the user. **Card sorting or web classification** should categorise web objects (e.g. documents) in order to facilitate information task completion or information goals the user has set.

Robertson (2003) identifies the following questions when using card sorting to aid the process of modelling web classification systems:

- Do the users want to see the information grouped by: subject, task, business or customer groupings, or type of information?
- What are the most important items to put on the main menu?
- How many menu items should there be, and how deep should it go?
- How similar or different are the needs of the users throughout the organisation?

Selected groups of users or representatives will be given index cards with the following written on them depending on the aim of the card sorting process:

- Types of document
- Organisational key words and concepts
- Document titles
- Descriptions of documents
- Navigation labels.

The user groups may then be asked to:

- group together cards that they feel relate to each other;
- select cards that accurately reflect a given topic or area;
- organise cards in terms of hierarchy – high-level terms (broad) to low-level terms.

At the end of session the analyst must take the cards away and map the results into a spreadsheet to find out the most popular terms, descriptions and relationships. If two or more different groups are used the results should be compared and reasons for differences should be analysed.

Blueprints

Blueprints

Show the relationships between pages and other content components.

According to Rosenfeld and Morville (2002), **blueprints**:

> *Show the relationships between pages and other content components, and can be used to portray organization, navigation and labelling systems.*

They are often thought of, and referred to, as site maps or site structure diagrams and have much in common with these, except that they are used as a design device clearly showing grouping of information and linkages between pages, rather than a page on the website to assist navigation.

Refer to Figure 11.16 for an example of a site structure diagram for a toy manufacturer website which shows the groupings of content and an indication of the process of task completion also.

Wireframes

Wireframes

Also known as 'schematics', a way of illustrating the layout of an individual web page.

A related technique to blueprints is **wireframes**, which are used by web designers to indicate the eventual layout of a web page. Figure 11.17 shows that the wireframe is so called because it just consists of an outline of the page with the 'wires' of content separating different areas of content or navigation shown by white space.

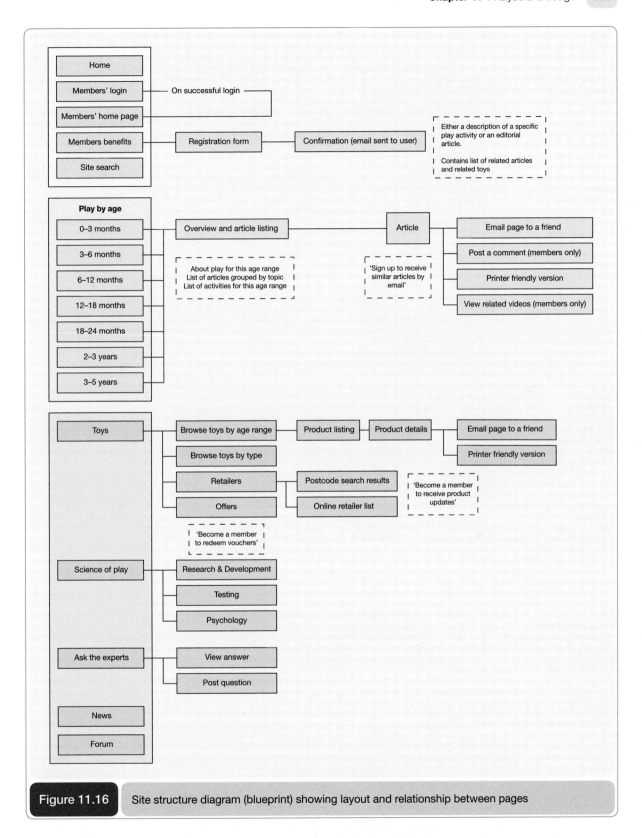

Figure 11.16 Site structure diagram (blueprint) showing layout and relationship between pages

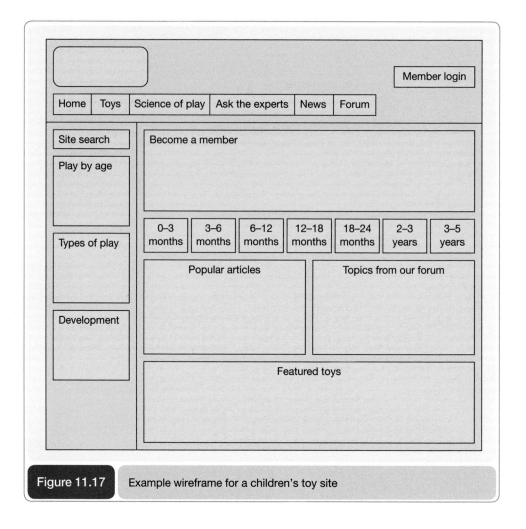

| Figure 11.17 | Example wireframe for a children's toy site |

Wodtke (2002) describes a wireframe (sometimes known as a 'schematic') as:

a basic outline of an individual page, drawn to indicate the elements of a page, their relationships, and their relative importance.

A wireframe will be created for all types of similar page groups, identified at the blueprint (site map) stage of creating the information architecture. A wireframe focusses on individual pages; the navigation focus becomes where it will be placed on the page.

Storyboarding
The use of static drawings or screenshots of the different parts of a website to review the design concept with user groups.

The process of reviewing wireframes is sometimes referred to as '**storyboarding**', although the term is often applied to reviewing creative ideas rather than formal design alternative. Early designs are drawn on large pieces of paper, or mock-ups are produced using a drawing or paint program.

At the wireframe stage, emphasis is not placed on use of colour or graphics, which will be developed in conjunction with branding or marketing teams and graphic designers and integrated into the site towards the end of the wireframe process. According to Chaffey and Wood (2005), the aim of a wireframe will be to:

- Integrate consistently available components on the web page (e.g. navigation, search boxes).
- Order and group key types of components together.
- Develop a design that will focus the user on to core messages and content.
- Make correct use of white space to structure the page.
- Develop a page structure that can be easily reused by other web designers.

Common wireframe or template features you may come across are:

- Navigation in columns on left or right and at top or bottom.
- Header areas and footer areas.
- 'Slots' or 'portlets' – these are areas of content such as an article or list of articles placed in boxes on the screen. Often slots will be dynamically populated from a content management system.

Slots on the home page may be used to:

- Summarise the online value proposition
- Show promotions
- Recommend related products
- Feature news, etc.
- Contain ads.

Page template

A standard page layout format which is applied to each page of a website. Typically defined for different page categories (e.g. category page, product page, search page).

Cascading Style Sheets (CSS)

A simple mechanism for adding style (e.g. fonts, colours, spacing) to web documents. CSS enables different style elements to be controlled across an entire site or section of site.

Wireframes are then transformed into physical site design **page templates** which are now created using standardised **Cascading Style Sheets (CSS)** which enable a standard look and feel to be enforced across different sections of the site.

The standards body W3C (www.w3.org) defines cascading style sheets (CSS) as

a simple mechanism for adding style (e.g. fonts, colors, spacing) to Web documents.

CSS enables different style elements to be controlled across an entire site or section of site. Style elements that are commonly controlled include:

- Typography
- Background colour and images
- Borders and margins.

A style sheet consists of a series of rules that controls the way selected elements should be displayed. For example:

```
body {font-family: Verdana, Arial, Helvetica, Sans Serif, Sans; font-
size: 0.7em; text-align:center; margin: 0; background-color: white;
color: black;}
```

In this example, the HTML 'body' tag is the *selector* and the required style for text defined between the curly brackets is the *declaration*. The benefits of CSS are:

- *Bandwidth* – pages download faster after initial page load since style definitions only need to be downloaded once as a separate file, not for each page.
- *More efficient development* – through agreeing site style and implementing in CSS as part of page templates, it is more efficient to design a site.
- *Reduces updating and maintenance time* – presentational mark-up is stored in one place separate from the content, making it quicker to update the site globally.
- *Increased interoperability* – adhering to W3C recommendations helps with support of multiple browsers.
- *Increases accessibility* – users can more readily configure the way a site looks or sounds using browsers and other accessibility support tools. Site is more likely to render on a range of access platforms like PDAs and Smartphones and appear well formatted on printers.

Customer orientation

Customer orientation

Developing site content and services to appeal to different customer segments or other members of the audience.

A well-designed site will have been developed to achieve **customer orientation** or customer-centricity. This involves the difficult task of trying to provide content and services to appeal to a wide range of audiences. For a B2B company the three main types of audience are customers, other companies and organisations, and staff. The detailed breakdown of these audiences is illustrated in Figure 11.18. Visit the Dell website (www.dell.com) to see how Dell segments its customer base on the home page into:

- Small office and home users
- Small businesses
- Medium businesses
- Large businesses
- Corporates
- Government organisations.

Think about how well this approach works. What would be your reaction to being classified as a mere small business or home owner? Do you think this is a valid approach? A similar approach, by Microsoft, is to offer specialised content for IS managers to help them in their investment decisions. Is a more straightforward product-centric structure to the website appropriate?

Marketing-led site design

Site design elements are developed to achieve customer acquisition, retention and communication of marketing messages.

Marketing-led or commercial-led site design is informed by marketing objectives and customer needs rather than a restricted view of information architecture or structuring a site simply around products, services or offer.

Some key business requirements from a site design based on this commercial approach are:

- *Customer acquisition* – the online value proposition must be clear. Appropriate incentives for customer acquisition and permission marketing such as those described in Chapter 9 must be devised.
- *Customer conversion* – the site must engage first-time visitors. Call to action for customer acquisition and retention offers must be prominent with benefits clearly explained. The fulfilment of the offer or purchase must be as simple as possible to avoid attrition during this process.
- *Customer retention* – appropriate incentives, content and customer service information to encourage repeat visits and business must be available.
- *Branding* – the brand offer must be clearly explained and interaction with the brand must be possible.

Persuasion marketing

Using design elements such as layout, copy and typography together with promotional messages to encourage site users to follow particular paths and specific actions rather than giving them complete choice in their navigation.

Marketing-led site design is also known as **persuasion marketing**.

Consultant Bryan Eisenberg of Future Now (www.bryaneisenberg.com) is an advocate of persuasion marketing alongside other design principles such as usability and accessibility. He said:

during the wireframe and storyboard phase we ask three critical questions of every page a visitor will see:

1 *What action needs to be taken?*
2 *Who needs to take that action?*
3 *How do we persuade that person to take the action we desire?*

Figure 11.18   Different types of audience for a typical B2B website

BJ Fogg (Fogg, 2009) has developed a model to inform persuasive design. The FBM asserts that for a person to perform a target behaviour, he or she must (1) be sufficiently motivated, (2) have the ability to perform the behaviour, and (3) be triggered to perform the behaviour. These three factors must occur at the same moment, else the behaviour will not happen.

Before we review user-centred design processes consider Mini case study 11.2, which shows how one company has developed a site that blends marketing-led and user-centric design.

Mini Case Study 11.2   Ultralase

Ultralase is one of the UK's largest laser eye treatment companies. The first Ultralase clinic was opened in January 1991 and there are now 31 locations in the UK. Its growth has been supported through its website and digital media since the content available online is a key part of the consumer decision-making process and for company lead generation.

Figure 11.19 shows how Ultralase combines persuasion, usability and accessibility within its home page to help meet business needs.

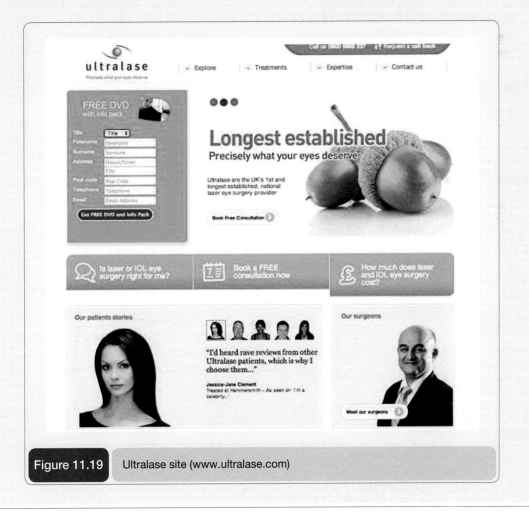

Figure 11.19   Ultralase site (www.ultralase.com)

These are some of the design elements used by Ultralase to help it achieve its goals:

1 **Carousel area (centre top of page).** Use to deliver key brand messages and position the brand through imagery.

2 **Customer journey highlighted (buttons below carousel).** The 'call-to-action' buttons for 'book a consultation', 'request a brochure' and 'find your local clinic' help highlight what the customer can do on the site and its goals.

3 **Intro text.** This helps show relevance for users, communicates key brand messages and is used for search engine optimisation to target the keyphrases laser eye surgery and treatment.

4 **Incentivised response-form (left sidebar).** Multiple incentives and prominent position consistent with eyetracking studies.

5 **Clear calls-to-action.** Again, prominent on the left-hand side, these are likely set up as conversion goals in Google Analytics. Containers blend image and text to avoid banner blindness. These containers all highlight the site Online Value Proposition.

6 **Common questions answered (centre panel).** These 'points of resolution' are often hidden in an FAQ, interesting that Ultralase highlights them on the home page. Key concerns are also highlighted in the main navigation.

7 **Prominent phone response (top right).** Vital for high-value, complex products since conversion tends to be higher via the phone channel. Unique web number can be used for tracking online influence.

8 **Social proof (right sidebar).** The right sidebar is used for the map to show the scale of the company through number of clinics and engaging containers for customer testimonials.

9 **MyUltralase (top right and right sidebar).** This site registration facility again shows the online value proposition. This is intended to encourage a deeper relationship and return visits.

Elements of site design

Once the requirements of the user are established we can turn our attention to the design of the human–computer interface. Nielsen (2000a) structures his book on web usability according to three main areas, which can be interpreted as follows:

- Site design and structure.
- Page design.
- Content design.

Today, the increasing importance of mobile design means that designing for mobile devices is a key consideration, so we have added a separate section on design for mobile platforms.

Site design and structure

The structures created by designers for websites will vary greatly according to their audience and the site's purpose, but we can make some general observations about design and structure. We will review the factors designers consider in designing the style, organisation and navigation schemes for the site.

Debate 11.2

Whither website design?

'Website design is too complex, and too important, to be left to marketers and IT staff untrained in its principles. Specialist usability professionals and psychologists should be present in every large e-commerce team.'

Site style

An effective website design will have a style that is communicated through use of colour, images, typography and layout. This should support the way a product is positioned or its brand.

Site personality

The style elements can be combined to develop a personality for a site. We could describe site personalities in the same way we can describe people, such as 'formal' or 'fun'. This personality has to be consistent with the needs of the target audience. A business audience often requires detailed information and prefers an information-intensive style such as that of the Cisco site (www.cisco.com). A consumer site is usually more graphically intensive. Designers need to consider the constraints on the user experience, such as screen resolution and colour depth, the browser used and download speed. The list of constraints which must be tested is illustrated in Chapter 12. Rosen and Purinton (2004) have assessed the relative importance of design factors which influence a consumer (based on questionnaires of a group of students). They believe there are some basic factors that determine the effectiveness of an e-commerce site:

(i) Coherence – simplicity of design, easy to read, use of categories (for browsing products or topics), absence of information overload, adequate font size, uncrowded presentation.
(ii) Complexity – different categories of text.
(iii) Legibility – use of 'mini home page' on every subsequent page, same menu on every page, site map.

You can see that these authors suggest that simplicity in design is important. Another example of research into website design factors supports the importance of design. Fogg *et al.* (2003) asked students to review sites to assess the credibility of different suppliers based on the website design. They considered these factors most important:

Design look	46.1%
Information design/structure	28.5%
Information focus	25.1%
Company motive	15.5%
Usefulness of information	14.8%
Accuracy of information	14.3%
Name recognition and reputation	14.1%
Advertising	13.8%
Bias of information	11.6%
Tone of the writing	9.0%
Identity of site sponsor	8.8%
Functionality of site	8.6%
Customer service	6.4%
Past experience with site	4.6%
Information clarity	3.7%
Performance on a test	3.6%
Readability	3.6%
Affiliations	3.4%

However, it should be borne in mind that such generalisations can be misleading based on the methodology used. Reported behaviour may be quite different from actual observed behaviour.

Site organisation

Information organisation schemes
The structure chosen to group and categorise information.

In their book on information architectures for the web, Rosenfeld and Morville (2002) identify several different **information organisation schemes**. These can be applied for different aspects of e-commerce sites, from the whole site through to different parts of the site.

Rosenfeld and Morville (2002) identify the following information organisation schemes:

1 **Exact.** Here information can be naturally indexed. If we take the example of books, these can be alphabetical – by author or title; chronological – by date; or for travel books, for example, geographical – by place. Information on an e-commerce site may be presented alphabetically, but this is not suitable for browsing.

2 **Ambiguous.** Here the information requires classification; again taking the examples of books, the Dewey decimal system is an ambiguous classification scheme since the librarians classify books into arbitrary categories. Such an approach is common on an

e-commerce site since products and services can be classified in different ways. Content can also be broken down by topic, by task or by audience. The use of metaphors is also common, where the website corresponds to a familiar real-world situation. The Microsoft Windows Explorer, where information is grouped according to Folders, Files and Trash, is an example of a real-world metaphor. The use of the shopping basket metaphor is widespread within e-commerce sites. It should be noted, though, that Nielsen (2000a) believes that metaphors can be confusing if the metaphor is not understood immediately or is misinterpreted.

3 **Hybrid.** Here there will be a mixture of organisation schemes, both exact and ambiguous. Rosenfeld and Morville (2002) point out that using different approaches is common on websites but this can lead to confusion, because the user is not clear what mental model is being followed. It is probably best to minimise the number of information organisation schemes.

Site navigation schemes

Devising a site that is easy to use is critically dependent on the design of the site navigation scheme. Hoffman and Novak (1997) stress the importance of the concept of 'flow', which essentially describes how easy it is for the users to find the information they need as they move from one page of the site to the next, but also includes other interactions such as filling in on-screen forms. Rettie (2001) summarises the meaning of flow and gives guidelines on how this concept can be used to enhance the visitor experience. These statements describing flow were used originally by Csikszentmihalyi (1990) and more recently by Rettie's research to test for a flow experience on a website:

1 *My mind isn't wandering. I am not thinking of something else. I am totally involved in what I am doing. My body feels good. I don't seem to hear anything. The world seems to be cut off from me. I am less aware of myself and my problems.*

2 *My concentration is like breathing. I never think of it. I am really oblivious to my surroundings after I really get going. I think that the phone could ring, and the doorbell could ring, or the house burn down or something like that. When I start, I really do shut out the whole world. Once I stop, I can let it back in again.*

3 *I am so involved in what I am doing, I don't see myself as separate from what I am doing.*

Rettie (2001) suggests that the following factors limit flow: long download times, delays to download plug-ins, long registration forms, limited stimulation, boring sites, slow responses, sites which are not intuitive, navigation links that fail, challenge greater than skill, irrelevant advertising. Conversely, reversing these factors can improve flow: quick download times, alternative versions (e.g. text and graphics), automatic completion of forms, opportunities for interaction, rapid responses, navigation which creates choices, predictable navigation for control, segmentation by Internet experience. Most navigation systems are based upon a hierarchical site structure. When creating the structure, designers have to compromise between the two approaches shown in Figure 11.20. The narrow and deep approach has the benefit of fewer choices on each page, making it easier for the user to make their selection, but more clicks are required to reach a particular piece of information (see Figure 11.20(a)). The broad and shallow approach requires fewer clicks to reach the same piece of information, but the design of the screen potentially becomes cluttered (Figure 11.20(b)). These approaches are appropriate for the non-technical and technical audiences respectively. A rule of thumb is that site designers should ensure it only takes three clicks to reach any piece of information on a site. This implies the use of a broad and shallow approach on most large sites. This may also be beneficial for SEO purposes. Lynch and Horton (1999) recommend a broad and shallow approach and note that designers should not conceive of a single home page where customers arrive on the site, but of different home pages according to different audience types. Each of the pages in the second row of Figure 11.20(b) could be thought of as

---

Site navigation scheme

Tools provided to the user to move between different information on a website.

Flow

Flow describes how easy it is for users of a site to move between the different pages of content of the site.

Narrow and deep navigation

Fewer choices, more clicks to reach required content.

Broad and shallow navigation

More choices, fewer clicks to reach required content.

Figure 11.20 (a) Narrow and deep and (b) broad and shallow organisation schemes

Deep linking

Jakob Nielsen's term for a user arriving at a site deep within its structure.

an example of a home page which the visitors can bookmark. Nielsen (2000a) points out that many users will not arrive on the home page, but may be referred from another site or advert to a particular page. He calls this process 'deep linking' and site designers should ensure that navigation and context are appropriate for users arriving on these pages.

As well as compromises on depth of links within a site it is also necessary to compromise on the amount of space devoted to menus. Nielsen (2000b) points out that some sites devote so much space to navigation bars that the space available for content is limited. Nielsen (2000b) suggests that the designer of navigation systems should consider the following information that a site user wants to know:

- *Where am I?* The user needs to know where they are on the site and this can be indicated by highlighting the current location and clear titling of pages. Chaffey *et al.* (2009) refer to this as *context*. *Consistency* of menu locations on different pages is also required to aid cognition. Users also need to know where they are on the web. This can be indicated by a logo, which by convention is at the top or top left of a site.
- *Where have I been?* This is difficult to indicate on a site, but for task-oriented activities such as purchasing a product, the display can show the user that they are at the *n*th stage of an operation, such as making a purchase.
- *Where do I want to go?* This is the main navigation system which gives options for future operations.

To answer these questions, clear succinct labelling is required. Widely used standards such as Home, Main page, Search, Find, Browse, FAQ, Help and About Us are preferable. But for other particular labels it is useful to have what Rosenfeld and Morville (2002) call 'scope notes' – an additional explanation. These authors also argue against the use of iconic labels or pictures without corresponding text since they are open to misinterpretation and take longer to process. Since using the navigation system may not enable the user to find the information they want rapidly, alternatives have to be provided by the site designers. These alternatives include search, advanced search, browse and site map facilities.

Page design

The page design involves creating an appropriate layout for each page. The main elements of a particular page layout are the title, navigation and content. Standard content such as copyright may be added to every page as a footer. Issues in page design include:

- *Page elements.* The proportion of page devoted to content compared to all other content such as headers, footers and navigation elements. The location of these elements also needs to be considered. It is conventional for the main menu to be at the top or on the left. The use of a menu system at the top of the browser window enables more space for content below.
- *The use of frames.* This is generally discouraged for the reasons given in Chapter 12.
- *Resizing.* A good page layout design should allow for the user to change the size of text or work with different monitor resolutions.
- *Consistency.* Page layout should be similar for all areas of the site unless more space is required, for example for a discussion forum or product demonstration.
- *Printing.* Layout should allow for printing or provide an alternative printing format.

Content design

Copywriting for the web is an evolving art form, but many of the rules for good copywriting are as for any medium. Common errors we see on websites are:

- too much knowledge assumed of the visitor about the company, its products and services;
- using internal jargon about products, services or departments – using undecipherable acronyms.

Web copywriters also need to take account of the user reading the content on-screen. Approaches to deal with the limitations imposed by the customer using a monitor include:

- writing more concisely than in brochures;
- chunking or breaking text into units of 5–6 lines at most; this allows users to scan rather than read information on web pages;
- using lists with headline text in larger font;
- never including too much on a single page, except when presenting lengthy information such as a report which may be easier to read on a single page;
- using hyperlinks to decrease page sizes or help achieve flow within copy, either by linking to sections further down a page or linking to another page.

Hofacker (2001) describes five stages of human information processing when a website is being used. These can be applied to both page design and content design to improve usability. Each of the five stages summarised in Table 11.6 acts as a hurdle, since if the site design or content is too difficult to process, the customer cannot progress to the next stage.

Using these layers we can map content across different access levels to produce a site which is integrated across the needs of its audiences. This also relates to the section on security since different access levels may be given for different information.

Mobile design

In Chapter 3 we explained the increasing adoption of mobile sites. The challenge of the many options for mobile site design has been nicely summarised by ex-eBay designer Luke Wroblewski (Wroblewski, 2011), who when lead designer at start-up BagCheck said:

> *As use of mobile devices continues to skyrocket across the globe, we're seeing more ways to tackle the challenge of creating great web experiences across multiple devices. But which approach is right for any given project?*

Table 11.6	A summary of information web stages described by Hofacker (2001)	
Stage	**Description**	**Applications**
1 Exposure	Content must be present for long enough to be processed.	Content on banner ads may not be on-screen long enough for processing and cognition.
2 Attention	User's eyes will be drawn towards headings and content, not graphics and moving items on a web page (Nielsen, 2000a).	Emphasis and accurate labelling of headings is vital to gain a user's attention. Evidence suggests that users do not notice banner adverts, suffering from 'banner blindness'.
3 Comprehension and perception	The user's interpretation of content.	Designs that use common standards and metaphors and are kept simple will be more readily comprehended.
4 Yielding and acceptance	Is the information (copy) presented accepted by customers?	Copy should reference credible sources and present counter-arguments as necessary.
5 Retention	As for traditional advertising, this describes the extent to which the information is remembered.	An unusual style or high degree of interaction leading to flow and user satisfaction is more likely to be recalled.

Source: Adapted from Hofacker (2001).

For us site performance and speed of development were crucial. So many of the decisions we made were designed to make both of these as fast as possible. As part of our focus on performance, we also had a philosophy of 'just what's necessary'. This meant sending things to devices (and people) that didn't actually need them made us squeamish. We liked to optimize. With a dual template system we felt we had more optimization of: source order, media, URL structure, and application design.

We will now review five common options for mobile site development identified by Thurner (2013):

A Simple mobile site (different content).
B Screen-scrape (same content).
C Responsive design (same content, different mobile styling).
D HTML5 site (same content, different mobile styling).
E Adaptive design (potentially different content, different styling on different mobile devices)

These are not mutually exclusive, so an HTML5 site can typically offer adaptive and responsive design too.

Mobile site design option A. Simple mobile site

The quickest method of creating a mobile site is to create a completely separate mobile site on a domain http://m.company.com which has a different design, build, hosting and content. This option may be appropriate for very small businesses looking for a simple mobile site which they don't update frequently, but we would advise that this not a viable long-term option for most companies for these reasons:

- Updates to content have to be duplicated across each site.
- Different tools and resources often needed to manage each site.
- Future updates to styling have to be duplicated too.
- May not give a consistent brand experience for users.

Mobile site design option B. Screen-scrape

Although it's not an option we can recommend as best practice, it's worth noting that a number of high-profile retail brands like ASOS and John Lewis opted for a temporary 'screen-scrape' approach, which involves dropping existing web content into a basic mobile site template without opting for back-end integration. The advantage of the screen-scrape approach is that it presents a quick route to market, and avoids contact potential conflict between PC web and mobile web developers.

Think through the widespread disadvantages of screen-scraping when compared with the fully integrated approach, which provides the better long-term solution.

- The screen-scrape option incurs additional time and cost to manage the site, as changes to the back-end CMS will need to be updated manually on the mobile site, rather than benefiting from automatic updates.
- A review of 'screen-scrape' sites reveals an alarming degree of standardisation across the sites, and lacks the differentiation that brands demand across their PC websites.

Mobile site design option C. Responsive design

Responsive design
Layout and formatting of website content is modified at the point of rendering to suit different screen resolutions and capabilities to produce a better experience to users of a range of desktop, tablet and smartphone devices using web development methods like CSS and image scaling.

Today's multiple-device-using consumers need content in the right format in real time, which presents challenges as the form factor and operating system varies across most of their devices. Enter **responsive design**, which automates the overlay of contextually relevant content matching the profiles of mobile users – allowing you to access social media feeds, loyalty offers and other data feeds triggered by your preferences to maximise engagement and to optimise sales conversion.

First introduced as a concept in 2010, responsive design is the principle that web developers deploy to design website styling that changes the display layout to suit users of a range of mobile devices using modern web development methods like CSS3 and image scaling. Blocks of content are moved and rescaled based on screen resolution, as shown in Figure 11.21.

Figure 11.21 Responsive design showing updated layout for different content blocks
Source: Author.

Responsive design is an increasingly popular approach to building mobile sites since it enables a single version of the site and content to be maintained which adapts for different resolutions. It was formerly called a 'fluid design' since the layout 'flows' as resolution is changed (as you change the size of a browser, for instance). Contrast this to what we often see when browsing using a smartphone on a non-responsive site: tiny text and difficult to select buttons and navigation which require us to zoom in to select the next page.

Media Queries
A styling approach within Cascading Style Sheets (CSS3) enabling the layout to change based on type of device at its scale.

Technically speaking, responsive design uses cascading style sheets, in particular an approach called **Media Queries** (Worldwide Web Consortium, 2013) to specify how the page is laid out based on device type and resolution. See, for example, Knight (2011) for an introduction to the technical approaches. This will produce an improved experience for users across a range of devices, but there are limitations such as break points where less common devices may not be supported or sites which aren't 'upwardly responsive', i.e. high-resolution displays, may be less well supported than lower resolution. Responsive design disadvantages include its being more technically complex to implement and test, which leads to higher costs and a larger codebase (particularly of style sheets) to load, which can harm page load times. Despite this, it is now implemented for many new sites and site redesigns. The disadvantages of responsive design can be overcome at cost through adaptive design.

Mobile site design option D. HTML5

HTML5 blurs the line between sites and apps, and challenges the prominence and cash flow of the appstore hosts. Companies operating in the main sectors who were enthusistic adopters of mobile – such as retail, packaged goods, travel, financial services, publishing – are turning to HTML5 'web apps' in order to build once and target all mobile platforms at once. This is more cost-effective and less labour-intensive than building different native apps for iOS, Android, Windows Phone and BlackBerry.

As Mini case study 11.3 shows, HTML5 web apps allows developers and publishers to circumnavigate the 30% commission charged by Apple and Google on app download costs and a further 30% on products and subscriptions sold 'in-app'. Both costs can be eliminated with HTML5-based sites.

From the technical perspective, HTML5 apps have some problems that native apps do not. HTML5 apps are typically slower than native apps and it is more costly to support a range of apps. FT.com still uses native apps for Android and Windows platforms.

Mini Case Study 11.3	FT.com adopts HTML5 for its iOS Web App

FT.com proves that HTML5 web apps are now providing clear benefits over OS-specific apps.

The success of the FT.com web app for iOS shows that developing mobile platform-specific apps isn't the only option; in future, the dependence on app stores for each mobile native OS may seem quaint. The figures on digital publishing by FT.com a year after the app was launched certainly show the importance of mobile platforms for publishers:

- Digital subscriptions to the title, which operate behind a metered paywall, increased 31% year-on-year to more than 300,000.
- The number of registered users climbed 29% to 4.8 million.
- Mobile devices account for 25% of traffic to FT.com, while there are 2.7 million FT web app users.

Figure 11.22	FT.com mobile app proposition *Source*: www.app.ft.com Financial Times, © The Financial Times Limited. All Rights Reserved.

FT.com HTML5 mobile site, it's not a native mobile app

The FT does a great job in explaining the benefits of non-OS apps (Figure 11.22). Under the heading, '*a better, faster app*', the FT explains these benefits:

- **Web browser access** – No app store download needed.
- **Automatic enhancements** – No need to visit an app store for the latest version.
- **Reading offline** – The latest edition is automatically stored for offline access (this is possible with native OS apps).
- **Speed** – Improved performance on most connections.
- **Greater range of content** – Including video on iPhone – this gets around the problem of Flash players.
- **Use your existing account** – no additional registration required.

Of course, the other big benefit for publishers, not mentioned here, is that they can take a bigger share of subscription revenues. The app was launched in June 2011 in response to Apple's introduction of new rules governing subscription-based iOS apps – Apple is looking for a 30% cut of subscription revenues for people signing up from its native app and keeping access to those subscribers.

Rob Grimshaw of FT.com told *The Guardian* (2013) that switching to HTML5 wasn't just about a spat with Apple, but was an attempt to ensure that the FT could scale quickly across different devices and platforms: 'The origins of the web app come from thinking more broadly about our mobile strategy, and particularly how we are going to cope with developing for numerous different platforms,' he said. 'There are at least five [native mobile platforms] out there that you reasonably have to cover, and a web app is the obvious solution. We just accelerated it because of some of the things Apple did with their subscriptions.'

	Approach	Advantages	Disadvantages
Responsive Web Design (RWD)	CSS Media Queries modify presentation for device resolution	Single template for all devices gives speed and cost benefits	Bigger page weight Compromises experience for higher resolutions?
Client-side Adaptive	JavaScript on the user's device loads different templates based on device resolution	• Complete rebuild of CSS not needed • Only resources needed loaded onto client • Experience customised for devices	Maintenance of additional code
Server-side Adaptive	Dynamic serving of styles based on device detection	Smaller mobile pages than other approaches	Multiple templates must be maintained

Mobile site design option E. Adaptive design

Adaptive mobile web design

Generally a more sophisticated approach than Responsive web design that involves delivering an experience optimised for the handsets targeted and splits the code and processing to render on different devices between the client and the server.

The **adaptive mobile web design** is a hybrid approach combining different client and server-based logic to give the best performance with the best experience on priority devices without the speed limitations of the responsive approach. The approach is contrasted with responsive web design in the table above. You can see that by only serving code and styling needed for a specific mobile device the approach can result in a faster experience, although development times and costs can be higher, so it is an approach best suited to the largest businesses.

Consider personalisation options

Q. *Have mobile personalisation options been considered?*

Mobile sites featuring personalisation are still relatively unusual. This is surprising if you consider that one phone has one user. Ask a group of strangers to pass their phones round the room and you'll detect a potent sense of anxiety. We don't share our phones, with anyone. We don't want others seeing the texts we send and receive, the photos we've taken, our social media pages, the sites we've browsed or the apps we've downloaded.

This means that we can develop highly personalised and customised sites. Back-end integration, with application programming interfaces (APIs) exposing individual customer records, can be used to build bespoke sites which match the profile of each user. Look no further than Amazon to see how brands can use purchase history data and apply intelligence to develop sites with highly targeted product offers. To make your sites highly relevant to users, you can apply behavioural targeting, with time and location sensitive messaging.

A personalised mobile-optimised site has the benefit that specific features can be developed for mobile users. This is not the case with a basic responsive design approach. Back-end integration enabling linkage to individual customer records can be used to build bespoke sites which match the profile of each user. Amazon is well known for integrating purchase history data and applying intelligence to its desktop site with highly targeted product offers. Of course, it now also does this for its mobile site.

Accessibility

An approach to site design intended to accommodate site usage using different browsers and settings particularly required by the visually impaired.

Web accessibility

Web accessibility is another core requirement for websites. It is about allowing all users of a website to interact with it regardless of disabilities they may have or the web browser or platform they are using to access the site. The visually impaired are the main audience that designing an accessible website can help. However, increased usage of mobile or wireless access devices make consideration of accessibility important.

The quote below shows the importance of the accessibility to a visually impaired user of a website who uses a screen-reader which reads out the navigation options and content.

For me being online is everything. It's my hi-fi, it's my source of income, it's my super-market, it's my telephone. It's my way in.

(Lynn Holdsworth, screen-reader user, web developer and programmer, RNIB, www.rnib.org.uk)

Accessibility legislation
Legislation intended to protect users of websites with disabilities, including those with visual disability.

Remember that many countries now have specific accessibility legislation to which website owners are subject. This is often contained within disability and discrimination acts. In the UK, the relevant act is the Disability and Discrimination Act (DDA) 1995. Recent amendments to the DDA makes it unlawful to discriminate against disabled people in the way in which a company recruits and employs people, provides services or provides education. Providing accessible websites is a requirement of Part II of the Disability and Discrimination Act published in 1999 and required by law from 2002. This is most important for sites which provide a service; the 2002 code of practice gives this example:

An airline company provides a flight reservation and booking service to the public on its website. This is a provision of a service and is subject to the Act.

Although there is a moral imperative for accessibility, there is also a business imperative. The main arguments in favour of accessibility are:

1 Number of visually impaired people – in many countries there are millions of visually impaired people varying from 'colour blind' to partially sighted to blind.
2 Number of users of less popular browsers or variation in screen display resolution. Microsoft Internet Explorer is now the dominant browser, but other browsers have a loyal following amongst the visually impaired (for example screen-readers and Lynx, a text-only browser) and early adopters (for example Mozilla Firefox, Safari and Opera). If a website does not display well in these browsers, then you may lose these audiences. Complete Activity 11.4 to review variation in access rate.
3 More visitors from natural listings of search engines. Many of the techniques used to make sites more usable also assist in search engine optimisation. Clearer navigation, text alternatives for images and site maps can all help improve a site's position in the search engine rankings.
4 Legal requirements. In many countries it is a legal requirement to make websites accessible.

Guidelines for creating accessible websites are produced by the governments of different countries and non-government organisations such as charities. Internet standards organisations such as the World Wide Web Consortium have been active in promoting guidelines for web accessibility through its Website Accessibility Initiative (WAI), see www.w3.org/WAI.

There are three different priority levels which it describes as follows:

- *Priority 1 (Level A).* A Web content developer must satisfy this checkpoint. Otherwise, one or more groups will find it impossible to access information in the document. Satisfying this checkpoint is a basic requirement for some groups to be able to use Web documents.
- *Priority 2 (Level AA).* A Web content developer should satisfy this checkpoint. Otherwise, one or more groups will find it difficult to access information in the document. Satisfying this checkpoint will remove significant barriers to accessing Web documents.

Activity 11.4	Allowing for the range in access devices

One of the benefits of accessibility requirements is that it helps website owners and web agencies consider the variation in platforms used to access websites.

Questions

1 Update the compilation in Table 11.7 to the latest values using Onestat.com or other data from web analytics providers.

2 Explain the variations. Which browsers and screen resolutions do you think should be supported?

Table 11.7	Summary of the range in browsers and screen resolutions used at the time of writing

Web browser popularity			Screen resolution popularity		
1	Chrome	48.9%	1	1366 × 768	22.5%
2	Firefox	14.9%	2	1920 × 1080	11.1%
3	Safari	12.1%	3	1280 × 800	9.8%
4	Internet Explorer	10.9%	4	1440 × 900	9.1%
5	Android Browser	1.0%	5	1280 × 1024	5.3%

Source: Visitors to SmartInsights.com, September 2008, used by students and professionals worldwide. Note that the formerly standard resolution of 800 by 600 is now less than 3%.

- *Priority 3 (Level AAA)*. A Web content developer may address this checkpoint. Otherwise, one or more groups will find it somewhat difficult to access information in the document. Satisfying this checkpoint will improve access to Web documents.

So, for many companies the standard is to meet Priority 1 and Priority 2 or 3 where practical.Some of the most important Priority 1 elements are indicated by these 'Quick Tips' from the WAI:

ALT tags

Alt tags (alternative tags) appear after an image tag and contain a phrase associated with that image.

- Images and animations. Use **ALT tags** to describe the function of each visual.
- Image maps. Use the client-side map and text for hotspots.
- Multimedia. Provide captioning and transcripts of audio, and descriptions of video.
- Hypertext links. Use text that makes sense when read out of context. Avoid 'click here'.
- Page organisation. Use headings, lists and consistent structure. Use CSS for layout and style where possible.
- Graphs and charts. Summarise or use the longdesc attribute.
- Scripts, applet and plug-ins. Provide alternative content in case active features are inaccessible or unsupported.
- Frames. Use the noframes element and meaningful titles.
- Tables. Make line-by-line reading sensible. Summarise.
- Check your work. Validate. Use the tools, checklist and guidelines at www.w3.org/TR/WCAG.

Figure 11.23 is an example of a site which meets brand and business objectives while supporting accessibility through resizing of screen resolution, text resizing and alternative image text.

Figure 11.23   HSBC Global home page
Source: www.hsbc.com.

Case Study 11.1   Providing an effective online experience for local markets

This case is about specialist travel and education company i-to-i, focussing on its online TEFL (Teaching English as a Foreign Language) courses. Their site (Figure 11.24) combines many of the features we have described in this chapter blending accessibility, usability and persuasion. This case considers the challenges of delivering an effective design across different markets for different audiences.

i-to-i background

i-to-i (www.i-to-i.com) is an international organisation with offices in the UK, USA, Ireland and Australia. Twenty thousand people have selected i-to-i as they travel on ventures to support 500 worthwhile projects on five continents and it has also trained a further 80,000 people as TEFL teachers. This service is offered

through the main site and also through a specialist Online TEFL site (www.onlinetefl.com) on which this case focusses.

The history of i-to-i

The founder of i-to-i, Deirdre Bounds, was inspired to create the company following a career break which took her to teach English in Japan, China and Greece and drive a backpackers' bus in Sydney. The company initially started through creating TEFL courses, eventually leading to organising volunteer projects.

Since 2003 the company has supported the i-to-i Foundation, a registered charity committed to providing funds to the most needy community and ecological projects in the i-to-i family. In 2007, i-to-i became part of the TUI travel group.

Figure 11.24	i-to-i website *Source*: www.i-to-i.com

Proposition

The main features of the i-to-i TEFL proposition communicated through its site are:

- International Accreditation: i-to-i is externally accredited by the ODLQC in order to ensure that its courses are rigorously monitored and always meet the highest industry standards.
- World-class reputation: i-to-i has four offices worldwide and it has over 12 years' experience teaching TEFL.
- Partnership: i-to-i is preferred TEFL course provider for STA Travel, Opodo and Lonely Planet.
- Complete student support: Students receive advice on how to get work abroad, how best to prepare for their time away and up-to-the-minute advice on current job opportunities.
- Highly experienced tutors: All i-to-i tutors have at least three years overseas teaching experience.

This proposition is backed up by 'the i-to-i TEFL Promise' which is communicated on the site:

- We will beat any equivalent and cheaper course by 150%.
- If you're not entirely satisfied after the first seven days, we'll give you a full refund.

- Our experience, our high academic standards and the quality of our courses means that i-to-i TEFL certificates are recognised by thousands of language schools worldwide.
- Additionally i-to-i can offer to help students find TEFL jobs abroad.

Audience segmentation

The main segmentation used by i-to-i is geographic:

- UK
- North America
- Europe
- Australia and New Zealand
- Rest of world (same as UK)

Different brochures are also available for each geographical area.

Information is also collected on an optional basis about prospects' age and status, although these are not used for targeting emails. Status categories are:

- Student
- Employed
- Self-employed
- Career break
- Unemployed
- Retired

Since optional information is restricted to certain lead tools it is not used to target emails. For weekend TEFL – post code/city is used to target courses to prospects.

Competitors

Some of the main competitors for online TEFL courses based in the UK and Australia include:
www.cactustefl.com
www.teflonline.com
www.eslbase.com

In the US, competitors who also operate in the UK and other countries include:www.teflcorp.com/

ITTP (International Tefl-Tesol-Online) www.tefl-tesol-online.com

Media mix

i-to-i uses a combination of these digital media channels to drive visits, leads and sales:

- Pay per click (PPC) (mainly Google AdWords)
- Social media marketing using Facebook, Twitter and i-to-i's own traveller community
- Natural search
- Affiliate marketing
- Display advertising
- Email marketing

Customer experience and conversion process

Detailed content to help visitors decide on purchasing a course is available on the site. This includes module outlines, and videos. Specific landing pages are used to convert visitors from paid search or affiliates, for example.

A number of engagement devices are blended into the design used to generate leads, including brochures, 'TEFL tasters', an email guide and campaign promotions such as winning a course. Customers have the choice of requesting a brochure (post or download), requesting a call-back or a live chat.

Such leads are followed up through a series of welcome emails. Results are monitored, but emails are not proactively followed up on. There is no phone follow-up of leads due to the relative low value of the products, but site visitors are encouraged to ring or set up a call-back which often leads to higher conversion rates.

Marketplace challenges

The main marketplace challenges faced by i-to-i are:

Increasing its presence and conversion effectiveness in a competitive market in different geographies:

i-to-i has good exposure in the UK, its primary market, but operates in a cluttered marketplace with price being the main differentiator (products are similar and some competitors are just as established etc.).

Research suggests that there is good opportunity within the US, but exposure is more limited because of the cost of pay-per-click advertising and because presence in natural search favours the US.

Rest-of-world sales (outside of UK, USA, Canada, Ireland/Europe, Australia, New Zealand) are increasing and this is believed to be a growing market. i-to-i seeks to penetrate these markets, but in a cost-effective way that will not distract attention from main markets.

Increasing demand through reaching and educating those considering travel who are not aware of TEFL courses and the opportunities they unlock. For example, many will look for casual work in other countries, e.g. in bars or in agriculture, but will be unaware of TEFL.

Questions

1 Select one country that i-to-i operates in closest to the area where you live. Define a persona based on their age and product needs and then identify the main customer journeys that form the customer for this persona. Which routes through the site would this user follow?

2 Review the range of engagement devices on the i-to-i website to engage the audience to generate leads.

3 Identify key areas for improvement for i-to-i based on your use of the site.

| Focus on | **Security design for digital business** |

Security is a prime concern of digital business managers. The principal concern is the security of information: both about customers and internal company data about finance, logistics, marketing and employees. Indeed, we saw in Chapter 4 that securing customer information is a legal requirement under data protection laws in many countries. These risks apply to all companies, but larger companies tend to be more at risk from targeted attacks. Information used within digital business systems must be safeguarded from a range of hazards. The range of risks faced by organisations is summarised in Box 11.5.

Box 11.5	Common security threats and solutions for the digital business

The BERR (2013) Information Security Breaches Survey highlights the extent of the security problem for digital businesses. Companies that had a security incident are shown in Table 11.8.

Figure 11.25 shows the most common security incidents. You can see that internal security problems are an increasing issue.

Table 11.8	Security incidents

	Small < 50 staff	Large > 250 staff
Any security incident	87%	93%
Accidental incident	59%	91%
Malicious incident	76%	69%
Serious incident	32%	31%

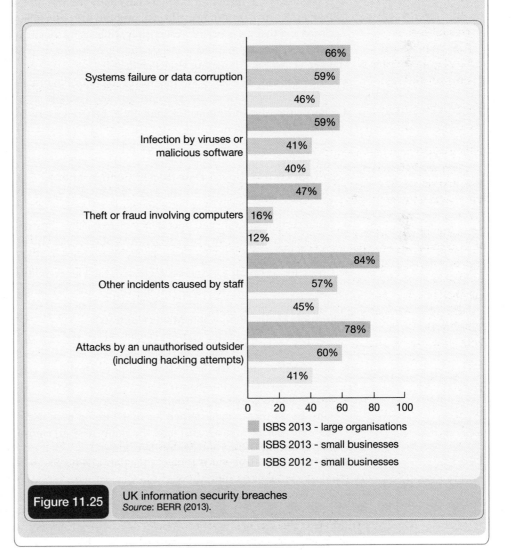

Figure 11.25	UK information security breaches *Source*: BERR (2013).

BERR (2013) has recommended 11 steps to help companies of all sizes improve security in business. We have included some simple, extra ideas reflecting use of personal devices (BYOD), cloud services, social media, etc., which are becoming more common in small businesses. The 11 steps are:

1 **Protect your Network (Network Security)**
   - Find out if your device which connects the organisation to the Internet – most commonly a router supplied by the Internet Service Provider (ISP) – has a firewall built in. If not then instal a proprietary firewall (for example, from mainstream suppliers like Symantec, Sophos, Kaspersky, etc., which is often included in a suite of software) on your PC or laptop. Follow the instructions to keep it properly configured and updated.
   - Take note of any warning messages and follow the guidance offered.
   - Consult an expert if you think your network has been compromised – you might know this has happened if you notice unusual activity, such as unusually high activity or no activity.

2 **Teach Good Practice (User Education and Awareness)**
   - Make knowledge of your Security Policy part of your induction process for new staff and make compliance with the Policy part of staff contracts.
   - Remind staff regularly about good security practices, especially when the risk or the policy changes. Make sure they know not to click on links in emails from unknown sources.
   - If you use social media for business purposes, you should ensure that all staff know that no sensitive material, intellectual property (IP) or similar material should be disclosed and that users behave responsibly while using social media for business or personal use, bearing in mind that they directly or indirectly represent the business.

3 **Manage IT Access (Managing User Privileges)**
   - Employ usernames and good passwords to control log-in. Good passwords contain upper and lower case characters, numbers and symbols.
   - Don't write passwords down or share them between users. Limit admin privileges to those who need them.
   - Ensure staff have access only to the folders they need to see. Keep sensitive data separate.

4 **Keep Your Own IT Up-To-Date (Secure Configuration)**
   - Document your IT assets so you know what you've got. IT assets will include hardware, software and even key IT staff.
   - Instal current software and operating system patches, firmware updates etc. immediately they are issued. You usually get this option when you instal the software or you should find it in the configuration menu. Ensure all software is licensed.
   - Check for technical weaknesses regularly (e.g. vulnerability or penetration testing). Regularly would mean when you update the risk assessment, perhaps annually or after major change of hardware or software.

5 **Removable Media (Removable Media Controls)**
   - If you transfer data using CD, DVD, USB, SD or any type of flash memory drive:
   - Only permit devices issued and controlled by your business in your business systems.
   - Issue, retrieve and track the devices – know where they all are, who has them and, ideally, what software is on each.
   - Ensure they are encrypted (some removable media devices already have encryption software on them) and scanned for **malware** on each use. Many commercial anti-malware packages (anti-virus) have the ability to scan removable media.

6 **Mobile Working (Home and Mobile Working)**
   - Use of mobile devices for business purposes (privately or business owned) should require board-level approval. Such devices must at a minimum have:
     - anti-malware software installed and updated daily (this can be set to happen automatically);

Malware
Malicious software or toolbars, typically downloaded via the Internet, which acts as a 'Trojan horse' by executing unwanted activities such as keylogging of user passwords or viruses which may collect email addresses

- pin, password or other authentication installed;
- be encrypted wherever possible; and
- be capable of being remotely tracked and wiped.
- All of the above can usually be done at little or no cost, without technical expertise. Many of the mobile devices, particularly the newer models, can do this and you can set it up through the options or set-up screens.
- Staff should inform the board-level risk owner (see above) immediately if the device is lost or stolen, and the device must be remotely wiped.

7 Use Anti-malware Defences (Malware Protection)

- Use a proprietary anti-malware or security package (one you can buy from a mainstream supplier like Symantic, Sophos, Kaspersky, etc.). Use this across the whole business.
- Use all the facilities of the anti-malware package even if you have to modify your business practices a little. Ensure 'sweeping' is done automatically.
- Update the protection as often as possible. Providers usually offer automatic free updates – ensure updates occur at least daily.

8 Understand Your Risk (Information Risk Management Regime)

- Decide who on your board (or senior manager in your company if you have no board) is responsible for managing the risk. Work out how much risk you face and how much risk you want to take. The IASME self-assessment questionnaire can help you do this. If you would like to be sent this questionnaire free of charge then please contact us.
- Identify your most valuable information in the company and mark documents containing this data clearly as 'confidential' or similar.
- Create a Security Policy describing what you want to do to manage the risk and include all the steps here. Distribute the Policy to your staff. Review the Policy regularly to ensure it meets your needs.
- Allocate security responsibilities clearly to other staff and ensure staff understand the importance.

9 Monitoring (Monitoring)

- Monitoring can detect potential hardware faults and unusual activity on your network or Internet-connected devices. Modern laptops often come with the former installed and some anti-malware packages also have the latter.
- If your business has a large network you should use network management tools to detect unusual activity. This includes monitoring traffic flow, IP usage, etc.
- Ensure that your staff report unusual activity to a central point and that you have sufficient plans and expertise on hand to react quickly.

10 Incident Management and Business Continuity (Incident Management)

Firewall

A specialised software application mounted on a server at the point where the company is connected to the Internet to prevent unauthorised access.

- Spotting an incident – an attack should be flagged by the **firewall** or security package. Anything which interferes with the business is an incident.
- Decide what to do (and who does it) if you have an incident such as a malware attack, loss or corruption of data, laptop theft, etc. and document it with the approval of the board.
- Get in-house or outsourced expertise ready to deal with your incidents. Just knowing of a company with the relevant skills so you can call them quickly is important.
- Document any incident and decide what caused it, how much it cost to fix and whether there is anything you could do better in future.
- You should ensure that you know what to do (and document the actions to be taken) on the catastrophic failure of anything critical to your business, such as information, applications, systems or network. Don't wait for an incident to try out the plan.

11 Using the Cloud

- Where you use data storage, applications or other services which are provided by another business (e.g. a 'cloud provider') you should choose one that has security which has been independently audited (e.g. certified to ISO 27001 or IASME). You can find this out by looking for details of accreditation on their website or contact them and ask. Do make sure to ask the scope of the certification, as some companies will accredit a small aspect of their business and then it may appear that the whole business is accredited.

- The use of the cloud should be treated like any other outsourced provision and (ideally) be subject to service level agreements. You can contact them and ask for a service level agreement.
- Do ensure that you know where and how your data is stored on the cloud and who is liable/responsible for that data. A particular issue is the country where the data are stored, which will have repercussions legally as anything stored outside Europe requires different procedures. The cloud company may be based in the UK but have data stored anywhere and could even sub-contract your data out to a third party. Even though the content of a website can be seen worldwide, it is the location of the storage that is the legal requirement.

Given the extent of the security risks described in Figure 11.25, many organisations now implement a formal **information security management system**.

Information security management system
An organisational process to protect information assets.

The information management strategy will mandate that there is an **information security policy**. This may be a policy developed in-house, or adoption of a security standard such as British Standard BS 7799, which has now been upgraded and ratified as international standard ISO/IEC 17799.

Information security policy
A definition of the organisational approaches to information security and the responsibilities of employees in protecting information.

ISO 17799 has comprehensive coverage of different risks and approaches to management of security. It recommends the following processes:

1 Plan – perform business risk analysis
2 Do – internal controls to manage the applicable risks
3 Check – a management review to verify effectiveness
4 Act – action changes required as part of the review as necessary.

ISO 17799/BS 7799 helps give a framework by which to manage the risks to the information evident from Figure 11.25. It requires the following areas of information security management to be defined:

- *Section 1: Security policy.* Describes the organisation's requirements and scope of security for different business areas and sites. It also should demonstrate the support of senior management in controlling and owning security.
- *Section 2: Organisational security.* Describes how the company manages security including different staff responsibilities for security, how security incidents are reported, actioned and reviewed as a standard business activity to improve security.
- *Section 3: Asset classification and control.* BSc 7799 recommends that an **information asset register (IAR)** be created, detailing every information asset within the organisation such as databases, personnel records, contracts, software licences, publicity material. For each asset, responsibility is defined. The value of each asset can then be determined to ensure appropriate security is in place.

Information asset register (IAR)
A repository for the types, value and ownership of all information within an organisation.

- *Section 4: Personnel security.* This ensures there is clarity within job definitions and employment contracts, to reduce the risk of human error leading to information loss and to ensure that staff understand what their rights and responsibilities are concerning information security. Staff training is also important to achieve this.
- *Section 5: Physical and environmental security.* This defines physical access to buildings. It also considers how information can be protected from threats such as fire and flood.
- *Section 6: Communications and operations management.* Guidelines on the day-to-day operation of information systems is the largest section of BS 7799. It covers acceptance criteria for new or updated systems, virus defence software, email and website usage, network access and back-up and restore systems.
- *Section 7: Access control.* This defines how to protect access to information systems through access control mechanisms (username and password procedures with different security clearance for different applications and types of information).

Business continuity management or disaster recovery

Measures taken to ensure that information can be restored and accessed if the original information and access method are destroyed.

- *Section 8: System development and maintenance.* This specifies how new systems must be designed and procured with security in mind.
- *Section 9: Business continuity management.* **Business continuity management or disaster recovery** specifies how the organisation will be able to continue to function in the event of a major event such as a fire or flood or other damage to information systems. Use of off-site back-ups and alternative systems is key to this.
- *Section 10: Compliance.* This specifies how an organisation will comply with the relevant UK and EU law related to information security management. Implementing BS 7799 is a good way of helping ensure that a business does comply with these requirements. Regular audit and review needs to occur to ensure the organisation remains compliant.

We will now cover some of the main threats to security in the digital business which need to be managed.

Managing computer viruses

Computer virus

A program capable of self-replication, allowing it to spread from one machine to another. It may be malicious and delete data, or benign.

Computer viruses are a significant threat to company and personal information since it is estimated that there are now over 100,000 of them.

Types of virus

There are many different mechanisms by which computer viruses reproduce or 'self-replicate' and spread from one machine to another. The main different types are:

Boot-sector virus

Occupies boot record of hard and floppy disks and is activated during computer start-up.

Worm

A small program that self-replicates and transfers across a network from machine to machine. A form of virus.

1 **Boot-sector virus. Boot-sector viruses** were most important when floppy disks were widely used.
2 **Worms.** A **worm** is a small computer program that replicates itself and then transfers itself from one machine to the next. Since no human interaction is required, worms can spread very rapidly. For example, the 'Code Red' worm replicated itself over 250,000 times in just nine hours on 19 July 2001. In 2003, the 'Slammer' worm exploited a security loophole in the Microsoft SQL server database product and rapidly infected 75,000 machines. Each infected machine sent out so much traffic that many other servers failed also. This was one of the fastest spreading viruses of all time, as Figure 11.26 shows. In future it seems such worms will bring the Internet to a complete standstill.
3 **Macro-viruses.** Macro-viruses are piggybacked on documents created by office applications such as Microsoft Word and Excel. Office software such as this has a macro-facility to help users record common actions. One of the best-known macro-viruses is 'Melissa'. This struck in March 1999 and it marked a new trend as it combined a macro-virus with one that accessed the address book of Microsoft Outlook to email itself to new victims. This was one of the fastest spreading viruses in history and it is estimated that it affected over a million PCs. In 2002, the author of the 'Melissa' virus, David L. Smith, was sentenced to 20 months in prison in the US.
4 **Email attachment viruses.** These viruses are activated when a user of an email program opens an attachment. 'Melissa' is an example of such a virus. The 'Love Bug' virus contains the subject line 'I love you', while the message contains the text 'kindly check the attached LOVELETTER from me' which is an attached file called LOVE-LETTER-FOR-YOU.TXT.VBS. The virus deleted image and audio files and accessed Internet servers to send out different versions of itself. According to ClickZ (2003), it was estimated that nearly $9 billion damage was done through this virus. Much of the cost is not the loss of data, but the cost of hiring specialists to rectify the problem or staff time lost.

Trojan

A virus that masquerades as a bona fide application.

5 **Trojan viruses.** A **Trojan** is a virus that masquerades as a bona fide application. They are named after the Greek myth of the giant wooden horse used by attackers to gain access to Troy. Examples include utilities such as a file-sharing program, a screen saver, upgrades to some system components and even imitation anti-virus programs. The advantage for

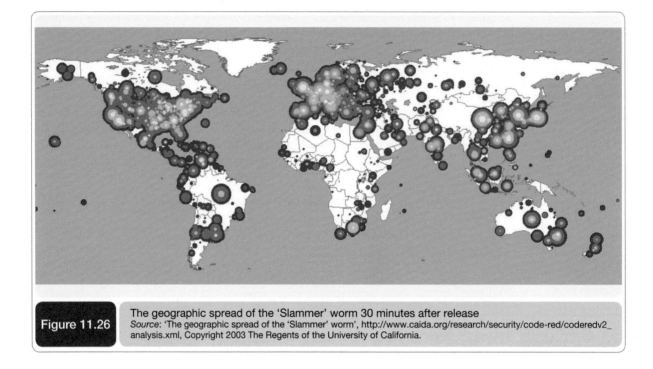

Figure 11.26   The geographic spread of the 'Slammer' worm 30 minutes after release
Source: 'The geographic spread of the 'Slammer' worm', http://www.caida.org/research/security/code-red/coderedv2_analysis.xml, Copyright 2003 The Regents of the University of California.

virus writers is that the programs can be much larger. One of the most famous Trojans is 'Back Orifice', reputedly developed by a hacking group known as 'Cult of the Dead Cow'. This could be attached to other larger files and gave complete access to a machine for a hacker.

6 **Hoax email viruses.** These are warnings about non-existent viruses which ask the recipient to send the warning on to their friends. They are usually malicious, but can contain instructions on how to remove the virus by deleting files which could cause damage. They cause disruption through time lost.

Protecting computer systems against viruses

All organisations and individuals require a policy to combat the potential impact of viruses given the frequency with which new, damaging viruses are released. Even individual computer users at home should think through the steps they can take to counter viruses. There are two approaches that can be combined to counter viruses. These are using the right tools and educating staff to change practices.

Anti-virus software
Software to detect and eliminate viruses.

Anti-virus software is well known as a tool to protect systems from viruses. Many businesses and homes now use products such as McAfee Virus Scan and Symantec Norton Anti-Virus to protect themselves against the threat of viruses. Unfortunately, a lot more action is required than initial purchase for the anti-virus software to be effective. New viruses are continually released so it is essential that regular updates be obtained.

Managed email service
Receipt and transmission of emails is managed by a third party.

Companies also need to decide on the frequency of scanning memory and computer files, since a full scan on start-up can take a long time. Most anti-virus software now seeks to identify viruses when they first arrive (real-time scanning). A further issue is how good the anti-virus tool is at identifying email and macro-viruses, since it is less straightforward for these types of virus to be identified. Another approach is to use an external **managed email service** which scans emails before they arrive in the organisation and then scans emails for viruses when they are sent. For example, Symantec (www.symantec.com/en/uk/products-solutions/

families/?fid=symantec-cloud) scans 2.7 billion emails a day for 7,500 companies worldwide. In August 2008 it reported that:

- 78% of messages were spam
- 1 in 88 contained a virus
- 1 in 522 was a **phishing** attempt.

Phishing
Obtaining personal details online through sites and emails masquerading as legitimate businesses.

Managed email services are likely to be more effective than using internal anti-virus software since the service providers are experts in this field. They will also be able to identify and respond to email worm attacks more rapidly. To summarise, organisations need a policy to be developed for use of anti-virus software. This should specify:

1 The preferred anti-virus software to be used on all machines.
2 The frequency and mechanism for updating anti-virus software.
3 The frequency with which the whole end-user PC is system-scanned for viruses.
4 Organisational blocking of attachments with uncommon extensions.
5 Organisational disabling of macros in office applications.
6 Scanning to be performed on mail servers when emails are first received and before viruses are sent.
7 Recommendations on use of spam-filtering software.
8 Back-up and recovery mechanisms.

Education of staff in identifying and then acting upon the different types of virus can also limit the impact of viruses. Some general instructions include the following:

1 Do not open attachments to emails from people you don't know (reduce transmission of email attachment viruses). Only open attachments which look legitimate, for example Word documents with relevant names. Some viruses use file extensions that are not commonly used such as .pif, .scr or .vbs. Viewing documents rather than opening them for editing can also reduce the risk of transmission.
2 Download software only from the official source, and always check for viruses before installing the software (reduces risk of Trojan horse viruses).
3 Disable or turn off macros in Word or Excel unless you use them regularly (reduces risk of macro-viruses).
4 Back up important files daily if this function is not performed by a system administrator.

Controlling information service usage

Issues in controlling information service typically involve one of two problems from the employer's perspective. First, hardware and software resources provided for work purposes are used for personal purposes, thus reducing productivity. Secondly, monitoring the use of information introduces legal issues of surveillance. Monitoring of information service usage includes checking for:

- Use of email for personal purposes.
- Inappropriate use of email, possibly leading to legal action against the company.
- Use of Internet or websites for personal use.

The problems in email usage are covered in the later section on email management. The extent of these issues, particularly in larger organisations, is apparent from Figure 11.27.

Employee communications monitoring
Companies monitor staff emails and web sites they access.

Monitoring of electronic communications

Employee communications monitoring or surveillance is used by organisations to reduce productivity losses through time wasting.

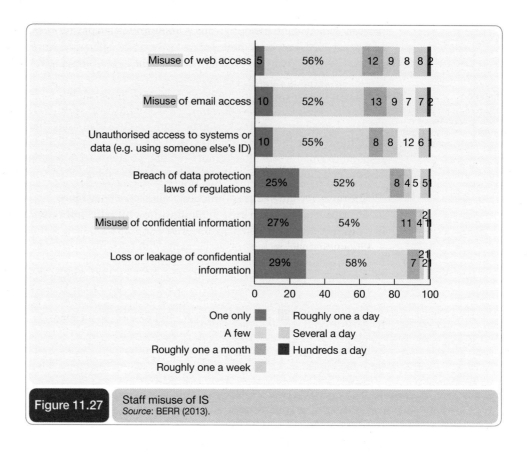

Figure 11.27	Staff misuse of IS
	Source: BERR (2013).

Simple calculations highlight the wastage when staff time is spent on non-productive work. If an employee earning £25,000 per year spends 30 minutes each day of a 5-day week answering personal emails or visiting non-work-related websites, this will cost the company over £1,500 per year. Activities such as using streaming media to view the news or download audio clips can also place strain on the company networks. A typical example of alleged time wasting where the company dismissed the employee involved Lois Franxhi, a 28-year-old IT manager who was sacked in July 1998 for making nearly 150 searches over four days in office hours for a holiday. She claimed unfair dismissal – she was pregnant at the time of the dismissal. As with many unfair dismissals, the case was not clear-cut, with Mrs Franxhi claiming the company sacked her because of sex discrimination. The tribunal dismissed these claims, finding that the employee had lied about the use of the Internet, saying she had only used it for one lunchtime when in fact records showed she had used it over four days. More recently DTI (2006) reported on a member of staff at a small services company who accessed adult websites at work. He used someone else's computer to conceal his activity. Communications monitoring of employees may also be warranted if it is felt they are sending or receiving emails or accessing websites which contain content the organisation deems unacceptable. Typical examples of such content are pornography or racist material. However, some organisations even block access to news, sports or web-based email sites because of the amount of time staff spend in accessing them. To define permissible content, many organisations now have an '**acceptable-use policy**'. This will describe the types of material it is not acceptable to access and is also a means of explaining monitoring procedures.

Scanning and filtering are the two most common forms of monitoring. **Scanning software** identifies the content of emails sent or received and web pages accessed. Tools such as WebSense or MailMarshal SMTP from Marshal or Web Marshal will look for the occurrence of particular words or images – pornography is indicated by skin colour tones for

Acceptable-use policy
Statement of employee activities involving use of networked computers that are not considered acceptable by management.

Scanning software
Identifies email or web-page access that breaches company guidelines or acceptable-use policies.

example. Rules will also be set up, for example to ban email attachments over a particular size or containing swearing, as indicated by Figure 11.28. Such tools can also give a picture of the most popular types of site or content. This might show, for example, how much time is being wasted accessing news and sports sites.

Such software usually also has blocking or filtering capabilities. **Filtering software** such as Websense (www.websense.com) can detect and block other activities such as:

Filtering software
Software that blocks specified content or activities.

- Peer-to-peer (P2P) file-sharing, for example of MP3 audio files.
- Instant messaging using Yahoo! Messenger or Microsoft Instant Messenger.
- The use of streaming media (e.g. audio and video) and other high-bandwidth applications.
- Accessing specified sites, e.g. social networks, news sites or personal email programs, since analysis has shown that staff spend so much time using them.
- Spyware which seeks to send out information collected from computers.
- Adware programs which place adverts or pop-ups.
- Employee hacking.

Websense and similar products can block sites in different categories, for different types of staff, according to the acceptable-use policy of the organisation using a database (www.websense.com/products/about/database/categories.cfm) that contains over 1.5 million websites in many categories of which we list just some to illustrate the degree of control available to the employer. Examples of the categories include:

- Abortion or Pro-Choice or Pro-Life
- Adult Material
- Parent category that contains the categories: Adult Content, Lingerie and Swimsuit, Nudity, Sex, Sex Education
- Adult Content
- Advocacy Groups
- Business and Economy
- Financial Data and Services
- Drugs.

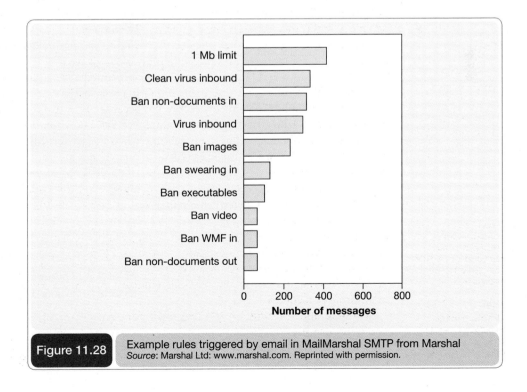

| Figure 11.28 | Example rules triggered by email in MailMarshal SMTP from Marshal
Source: Marshal Ltd: www.marshal.com. Reprinted with permission. |

Consider how many of those listed above you may visit when studying, at business or at home. It will be apparent that if an employer wishes, they can block virtually every site. When search engines are blocked, management-grade employees are likely to be restricted in their understanding of the business environment and are restricted from self-development! Employees are likely to view negatively an employer who does not trust them to use their time judiciously. The popularity of different methods of monitoring and blocking is shown in Figure 11.29.

Employee monitoring legislation

In June 2003, the Office of the Information Commissioner published *Monitoring at Work,* to provide practical guidance for employers on how they should approach monitoring of employees in the workplace. These guidelines seek to achieve a balance between employees' wishes for privacy and the need for employers to run their businesses efficiently. The code does not prevent monitoring, but is based on the concept of proportionality. Proportionality means that any adverse impacts from monitoring must be justified by the benefits to the employer and others. This addresses an apparent anomaly in that data protection law refers to individual consent for processing of personal data being 'freely given' and it is not normal for employees to give this consent. The code makes it clear that individual consent is not required provided that an organisation has undertaken an 'impact assessment' of monitoring activities.

Impact assessment
An assessment of the employee monitoring process in the workplace to identify improvements to minimise infringement of employee privacy.

According to the code, an impact assessment involves:

- identifying clearly the **purpose(s)** behind the monitoring arrangement and the benefits it is likely to deliver
- identifying any likely **adverse impact** of the monitoring arrangement
- considering **alternatives** to monitoring or different ways in which it might be carried out

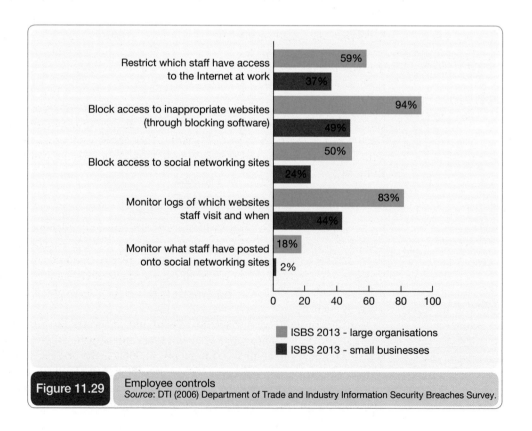

	Figure 11.29	Employee controls

Figure 11.29 Employee controls
Source: DTI (2006) Department of Trade and Industry Information Security Breaches Survey.

- *taking into account the **obligations** that arise from monitoring*
- *judging whether monitoring is **justified.***

The code does not make specific recommendations about monitoring of emails or web traffic, but it does refer to them as typical monitoring activities which it suggests may be acceptable if staff are informed of them and an impact assessment has been conducted. The code does ask employers to consider whether alternatives may be better than systematic monitoring. Alternatives may include training or clear communication from managers and analysis of stored emails where it is thought an infringement has taken place rather than continuous monitoring. For example, automated monitoring is preferred to IT staff viewing personal emails of staff. The code also makes clear that the company should not undertake any **covert monitoring**. An 'acceptable-use policy' will describe the types of material it is not acceptable to access and is also a means of explaining monitoring procedures. It does appear that if an employee was disciplined or dismissed for sending too many personal emails for instance, they would have legitimate grounds to appeal if they had not been informed that monitoring was occurring and their managers had not made it clear that this was acceptable practice.

Other European countries have different laws on monitoring. Some, such as Germany, are much more restrictive than the UK in terms of the level of monitoring that organisations are able to perform. Organisations opening offices abroad clearly need to be aware of local variations in legal constraints on employee monitoring and data protection.

Covert monitoring
Monitoring which the employer undertakes without notification of staff.

Email management

Email is now an essential business communication tool and is also widely used for personal use. Billions of messages are sent each day. Four main controls need to be considered to reduce the amount of time effectively wasted by staff reading email by minimising the volume of:

1 Spam (unsolicited email).
2 Internal business email.
3 External business email.
4 Personal email (friends and family).

Despite the potential time loss through email misuse an AMA (2003) survey suggested that only 34% of employers had a written email retention and deletion policy in place. Furthermore, there are issues of legal liability about what employees say in their email which also need to be considered. We will look at the risk and controls of each email risk in turn.

1 Minimising spam (unsolicited email)

Spam
Unsolicited email (usually bulk-mailed and untargeted).

Spam is now a potential problem for every company and individual using the Internet. At the time of writing over 75% of emails were spam or virus-related in some countries and individuals whose inboxes are unprotected can receive hundreds of spam emails each day. The spammers rely on sending out millions of emails often from **botnets** of infected PCs in the hope that even if there is only a 0.01% response they may make some money, if not necessarily get rich.

Botnet
Independent computers, connected to the Internet, are used together, typically for malicious purposes through controlling software. For example, they may be used to send out spam or for a denial-of-service attack.

Legal measures to combat spam have had limited success. So, many information services managers are now using a range of methods to control spam. Figure 11.30 summarises alternative techniques to combat spam. Figure 11.30(a) is the original situation where all mail is allowed into an inbox. Figure 11.30(b) uses different techniques to reduce the volume of email through identification and blocking of spam. Figure 11.30(c) is a closed inbox where only known, trusted emails are allowed into an organisation.

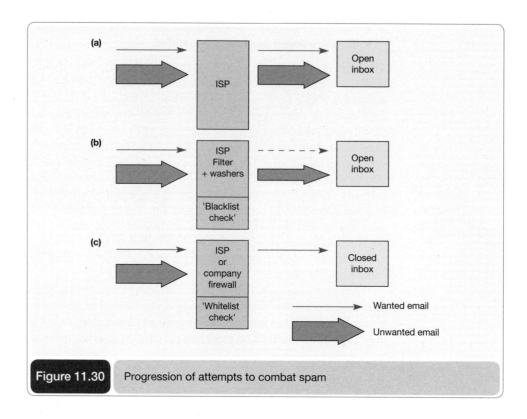

Figure 11.30   Progression of attempts to combat spam

The full range of techniques that can be used in combination to combat spam include:

1 **Avoid harvesting of addresses.** Spammers harvest emails from email addresses published on web pages and even the program code used to convert online form content to an email to a company. By reducing the number of email addresses published, or changing their format, the number of email addresses can be reduced.

2 **Educate staff not to reply to spam.** The worst thing an individual can do on receiving spam is to reply to it to complain or to attempt to unsubscribe. This merely confirms to the spammer that the address is valid and they are likely to send more junk email and sell your address on to other spammers.

3 **Use filters.** Filtering software can identify spam from key words and phrases such as 'For Free', 'Sex' or 'Viagra'. **Email filters** are provided for users of web-based email. Microsoft Outlook Express has its own filter. Filtering software such as Mailwasher (www.mailwasher.net) or Mcaffee Spamkiller (www.mcaffee.com) can also be installed. Unfortunately, many spammers know how to avoid the keywords in the filters. The problem with filters and other services is that there can be 'false positives' or valid emails that are classified as junk. Additionally, spammers find ways to work around filters by putting 'gobbeldy gook' in the footer of their messages that is not recognised by the filters or using variants of words such as V1agra, or Via-gra. Review of these may still be necessary. This technique is represented by Figure 11.30(b).

4 **Use 'peer-to-peer' blocking services.** These take advantage of humans being good at identifying spam and then notifying a central server which keeps an index of all spam. CloudMark (www.cloudmark.com), a peer-to-peer solution, requires users to identify spam by pressing a 'Block' button in Outlook Express which then updates a central server, so when others download the same message at a later time, it is automatically identified as spam. This technique is represented by Figure 11.30(b).

5 **Use blacklist services.** **Blacklists** are lists of known spammers such as those reported to Spamhaus Project (www.spamhaus.org/) or SpamCop (www.spamcop.net). They

Email filter
Software used to identify spam according to its characteristics such as keywords.

Blacklist
A compilation of known sources of spam that are used to block email.

are often used in conjunction with filters to block emails. Brightmail (now Symantec Enterprise, www.symantec.com/products-solutions/families/?fid=email-security) uses a global network of email addresses set up to trap and identify spam. Brightmail is increasingly used by ISPs such as BT OpenWorld to block spam, but it is not a cheap service, costing $5 to $15 per year. This price could easily be justified by the time staff save over the year. This technique is also represented by Figure 11.30(b).

6 **Use whitelist services.** The whitelist approach has not been adopted widely since it is difficult to set up, but it probably offers the best opportunity for the future. A **whitelist** gives a list of bona fide email addresses that are likely to want to contact people within an organisation. It will include all employees, partners, customers and suppliers who have obtained opt-in from employees to receive email. Email from anyone not on the list will be blocked. However, maintaining such a list will require new software and new procedures for keeping it up to date.

7 **Ensure anti-virus software and blocking is effective.** Email viruses are increasingly perpetrated by spammers since they are a method of harvesting email addresses. Virus protection needs to be updated daily.

Whitelist

A compilation of trusted sources of email that is permitted to enter an inbox.

2 Minimising internal business email

The ease and low cost of sending emails to a distribution list or copying people in on a message can lead to each person in an organisation receiving many messages each day from colleagues within the organisation. This problem tends to be worse in large organisations, simply because each individual has a larger address book of colleagues. A press release from the British Computer Society summarising research conducted by the Henley Management College in 2002 suggested that a lot of time is wasted by managers when processing irrelevant emails:

● Of seven common management tasks, meetings took up 2.8 hours on average, dealing with email came second with an average of 1.7 hours and accessing information from the Internet accounted for a further 0.75 hour.

● Respondents reported receiving on average 52 emails per day while 7% received 100 emails per day or more.

● Managers reported that less than half of emails (42%) warranted a response, 35% were read for information only and nearly a quarter were deleted immediately. On average only 30% of emails were classified as essential, 37% as important and 33% as irrelevant or unnecessary.

● Despite the reservations about the quality and volume of emails received, the majority of respondents (81%) regarded email as the communications technology which has had the most positive impact on the way they carried out their job, alongside the Internet and the mobile phone.

To overcome this type of business email overuse, companies are starting to develop email policies which explain best practice. For example, Chaffey and Wood (2005) devised these guidelines:

● Only send the email to employees who must be informed or who must act upon it.

● Banning certain types of email, such as the classic 'email to the person who sits next to you' or individuals in the same office.

● Avoid 'flaming' – these are aggressive emails which often put voice to feelings that wouldn't be said face-to-face. If you receive an annoying email it is best to wait 10 minutes to cool down rather than 'flaming' the sender.

● Avoid 'trolls' – these are a species of email closely related to flame mails. They are postings to a newsgroup deliberately posted to 'wind up' the recipient.

● Combine items from separate emails during the day or week into a single email for the day/week.

● Write clear subject lines.

- Structure emails so that they can be scanned quickly using sub-heads and numbered and bulleted lists.
- Make follow-up actions clear.
- When reading email, use folders to categorise emails according to content and priority.
- Perform email reading and checking in batches, e.g. once per morning or afternoon rather than being alerted to and opening every email that arrives.
- Delete emails which are not required for future reference (large volumes are taken up on servers through staff not deleting emails and their attachments).
- And so on – all common-sense guidelines, but often common sense isn't common!

3 Minimising external business email

People within an organisation can receive many emails from legitimate suppliers. For example, an IT manager might receive emails from hardware and software manufacturers, service providers, event or conference organisers and e-newsletters from magazines. It is usually left to the judgement of the individual employee to select appropriate e-newsletters. Spam filters will not usually block such messages, but primitive filters may. The challenge/respond system will still enable such emails to be received. If certain websites are blocked, e-newsletters will be less effective since images are not downloaded from blocked sites. Many individuals use a separate email address from the main inbox when opting in. This means the e-newsletter can be read at the office or at home and is also available when the individual changes jobs.

4 Minimising personal email (friends and family)

Although there are many surveys about the volume of spam and amount of time spent processing email at work, there is relatively little data published on the amount of time spent writing personal emails. To minimise this problem and some of the problems of over-using email for business use, the following steps can be taken:

1 Create written guidelines defining the policy on acceptable email use and disciplinary procedures for when guidelines are breached.
2 Use increasing levels of control or sanctions for breaches including performance reviews, verbal warnings, removal of email privileges, termination and legal action.
3 Providing training for staff on acceptable and efficient email use.
4 Monitor emails for signatures of personal use and any breaches of the policy, e.g. swearing, and take action accordingly.

Hacking

Hacking
The process of gaining unauthorised access to computer systems, typically across a network.

'Hacking' refers to the process of gaining unauthorised access to computer systems, typically across a network. Hacking can take different forms. Hacking for monetary gain is usually aimed at identity theft where personal details and credit card details are accessed for the purpose of fraud. Hacking could also occur with malicious intent. For example, a former employee might gain access to a network with a view to deleting files or passing information on to a competitor. Notorious hackers who have been prosecuted, but often seem to have ultimately gained from their misdemeanours, include:

- *Robert Morris* – The son of the chief scientist at the US National Computer Security Center, this graduate student created a destructive Internet worm in 1988 which took advantage of a security flaw in the Unix operating system. When unleashed it caused thousands of computers to crash. The disruption was partly accidental and he released instructions to system administrators on how to resolve the problem. He was sentenced to three years of probation, 400 hours of community service and a fine of $10,050. He is now an assistant professor at MIT, where he originally released his worm to disguise its creation at Cornell University.

- *Kevin Poulsen* – In 1990 Poulsen took over all telephone lines into the Los Angeles radio station KIIS-FM, assuring that he would be the 102nd caller. Poulsen won a Porsche 944 S2. This was one of many hacks conducted while he worked for hi-tech company SRI International by day and hacked at night. He was eventually traced and, in June 1994, he pleaded guilty to seven counts of mail, wire and computer fraud, money laundering and obstruction of justice, and was sentenced to 51 months in prison and ordered to pay $56,000 in restitution. It was the longest sentence ever given for hacking. He is now a computer security journalist.

- *Kevin Mitnick* – The first hacker to be featured on an FBI 'Most wanted' poster, Mitnick was arrested in 1995. He later pleaded guilty to four counts of wire fraud, two counts of computer fraud and one count of illegally intercepting a wire communication. He admitted that he broke into computer systems and stole proprietary software belonging to Motorola, Novell, Fujitsu, Sun Microsystems and other companies. He was sentenced to 46 months. Following his sentence he became a security consultant and is now a leading commentator on security and has made many TV appearances and written books and articles.

Gaining access to a system may be perceived by the hacker as simply a technical challenge. The term 'hacking' traditionally refers to the process of creating program code, another form of technical challenge. This can almost be considered as a pastime, albeit an unethical one. The BBC (2003) reported that TruSecure, a US hacking monitoring organisation, currently tracks more than 11,000 individuals in about 900 different hacking groups and gangs.

Three main forms of gaining unauthorised access to computer systems can be identified. First, the normal entry points to systems through usernames and passwords can be used. Tools are available to try different alternative log-ins, although most modern systems will refuse access after several attempts. Hacking can be combined with identity theft to gain an idea of the passwords used.

The second form of hacking exploits known vulnerabilities in systems. Although these vulnerabilities are publicly known and will be posted on the vendor's website and specialist security websites, there will be many system administrators who have not updated their systems with the latest security update or 'patch'. This is partly because there are so many security vulnerabilities, with new ones being announced every week.

Social engineering
Exploiting human behaviour to gain access to computer security information from employees or individuals.

Thirdly, Kevin Mitnick refers to 'social engineering', which typically involves impersonating employees of an organisation to access security details. One example of this, given in Mitnick and Simon (2002), is when the attacker contacts a new employee and advises them of the need to comply with security policies. The attacker then asks the user for their password to check it is in line with the policy of choosing a difficult-to-guess password. Once the user reveals their password, the caller makes recommendations to construct future passwords in such a way that the attacker will be able to guess them.

Protecting computer systems against hackers

Protecting computer systems against hackers involves creating counter-measures to the three main types of hacking outlined above. For gaining access to systems via passwords, policies can be developed to reduce the risk of access. One simple approach is to mandate that new passwords are required every month and that they contain at least one number and a mix of upper and lower case. This prevents users using simple passwords which are easily guessed. Education is required to reduce the risk of passwords falsely obtained through 'social engineering', but this will never completely remove the threat.

Firewall

A specialised software application typically mounted on a server at the point where the company is connected to the Internet. Its purpose is to prevent unauthorised access into the company.

Computer systems can also be protected by limiting access at the point the external network enters the company. **Firewalls** are essential to prevent outside access to confidential company information, particularly where an extranet has been set up. Firewall software can then be configured to only accept links from trusted domains representing other offices in the company.

Measures must also be put in place to stop access to systems through published security vulnerabilities. The BBC (2003) reported that in 2003 there were 5,500 security vulnerabilities that could be used. A policy on updating operating systems and other software with the latest versions is also required. It is not practical to make all updates, but new vulnerabilities must be monitored and patches applied to the highest-risk categories. This is a specialist task and is often outsourced. TruSecure (www.trusecure.com) is an example of a specialist company that monitors security vulnerabilities and advises organisations on prevention. They also employ a team of people who attempt to infiltrate hacker groups to determine the latest techniques. TruSecure gave the FBI over 200 documents about the 'Melissa' virus author. Although they did not know his real name, they knew his three aliases and had built a detailed profile of him. '**Ethical hackers**' are former hackers who now apply their skills to test the vulnerabilities of existing systems.

Ethical hacker

Hacker employed legitimately to test the quality of system security.

Sometimes 'low-tech' techniques can be used too. The *Guardian* (2003) reported cases where criminals had impersonated call-centre staff in order to gain access to customer accounts!

Secure e-commerce transactions

For digital businesses offering online sales there are also additional security risks from the customer or merchant perspective:

(a) Transaction or credit card details stolen in transit.
(b) Customer's credit card details stolen from merchant's server.
(c) Merchant or customer is not who they claim to be.

In this section we assess the measures that can be taken to reduce the risk of these breaches of e-commerce security. We start by reviewing some of the theory of online security and then review the techniques used.

Principles of secure systems

Before we look at the principle of secure systems, it is worth reviewing the standard terminology for the different parties involved in the transaction:

- *Purchasers.* These are the consumers buying the goods.
- *Merchants.* These are the retailers.
- *Certification authority (CA).* This is a body that issues digital certificates that confirm the identity of purchasers and merchants.
- *Banks.* These are traditional banks.
- *Electronic token issuer.* A virtual bank that issues digital currency.
- The basic requirements for security systems from these different parties to the transaction are as follows:

1 Authentication – are parties to the transaction who they claim to be (risk (c) above)?
2 Privacy and confidentiality – are transaction data protected? The consumer may want to make an anonymous purchase. Are all non-essential traces of a transaction removed from the public network and all intermediary records eliminated (risks (b) and (c) above)?
3 Integrity – checks that the message sent is complete, i.e. that it is not corrupted.
4 Non-repudiability – ensures sender cannot deny sending message.

5 Availability – how can threats to the continuity and performance of the system be eliminated?

Kesh *et al.* (2002) explore the security requirements for e-commerce in more detail.

Approaches to developing secure systems

Digital certificates

Digital certificates (keys)
Consist of keys made up of large numbers that are used to uniquely identify individuals.

Symmetric encryption
Both parties to a transaction use the same key to encode and decode messages.

There are two main methods of encryption using **digital certificates**.

1 Secret-key (symmetric) encryption

Symmetric encryption involves both parties having an identical (shared) key that is known only to them. Only this key can be used to encrypt and decrypt messages. The secret key has to be passed from one party to the other before use in much the same way as a copy of a secure attaché case key would have to be sent to a receiver of information. This approach has traditionally been used to achieve security between two separate parties, such as major companies conducting EDI. Here the private key is sent out electronically or by courier to ensure it is not copied.

This method is not practical for general e-commerce, as it would not be safe for a purchaser to give a secret key to a merchant since control of it would be lost and it could not then be used for other purposes. A merchant would also have to manage many customer keys.

2 Public-key (asymmetric) encryption

Asymmetric encryption
Both parties use a related but different key to encode and decode messages.

Asymmetric encryption is so called since the keys used by the sender and receiver of information are different. The two keys are related by a numerical code, so only the pair of keys can be used in combination to encrypt and decrypt information. Figure 11.31 shows how public-key encryption works in an e-commerce context. A customer can place an order with a merchant by automatically looking up the public key of the merchant and then using this key to encrypt the message containing their order. The scrambled message is then sent across the Internet and on receipt by the merchant is read using the merchant's private key. In this way only the merchant who has the only copy of the private key can read the order. In the reverse case the merchant could confirm the customer's identity by reading identity information such as a digital signature encrypted with the private key of the customer using their public key.

Pretty Good Privacy (PGP) is a public-key encryption system used to encrypt email messages.

| Figure 11.31 | Public-key or asymmetric encryption |

Digital signatures

Digital signatures can be used to create commercial systems by using public-key encryption to achieve authentication: the merchant and purchaser can prove they are genuine. The purchaser's digital signature is encrypted before sending a message using their private key and, on receipt, the public key of the purchaser is used to decrypt the digital signature. This proves the customer is genuine. Digital signatures are not widely used currently due to the difficulty of setting up transactions, but they will become more widespread as the public-key infrastructure (PKI) stabilises and use of certificate authorities increases.

The public-key infrastructure (PKI) and certificate authorities (CAs)

In order for digital signatures and public-key encryption to be effective it is necessary to be sure that the public key intended for decryption of a document actually belongs to the person you believe is sending you the document. The developing solution to this problem is the issuance by a trusted third party (TTP) of a message containing owner identification information and a copy of the public key of that person. The TTPs are usually referred to as **certificate authorities (CAs)**, and various bodies such as banks and the Post Office are likely to fulfil this role. That message is called a certificate. In reality, as asymmetric encryption is rather slow, it is often only a sample of the message that is encrypted and used as the representative digital signature.

Example certificate information could include:

- user identification data;
- issuing authority identification and digital signature;
- user's public key;
- expiry date of this certificate;
- class of certificate;
- digital identification code of this certificate.

It is proposed that different classes of certificates would exist according to the type of information contained. For example:

- name, email address
- driver's licence, national insurance number, date of birth
- credit check
- organisation-specific security clearance data.

Virtual private networks

A **virtual private network (VPN)** is a private wide-area network that runs over the public network, rather than a more expensive private network. The technique by which VPN operates is sometimes referred to as 'tunnelling', and involves encrypting both packet headers and content using a secure form of the Internet Protocol known as IPSec. As explained in Chapter 3, VPNs enable the global organisation to conduct its business securely, but using the public Internet rather than more expensive proprietary systems.

Current approaches to e-commerce security

In this section we review the approaches used by e-commerce sites to achieve security using the techniques described above.

Secure Sockets Layer Protocol (SSL)

SSL is a security protocol used in the majority of B2C e-commerce transactions since it is easy for the customer to use without the need to download additional software or a certificate.

When a customer enters a secure checkout area of an e-commerce site SSL is used and the customer is prompted that 'you are about to view information over a secure connection' and a key symbol is used to denote this security. When encryption is occurring they will see that the web address prefix in the browser changes from 'http://' to 'https://' and a padlock appears at the bottom of the browser window.

The main facilities it provides are security and confidentiality. SSL enables a private link to be set up between customer and merchant. Encryption is used to scramble the details of an e-commerce transaction as it is passed between sender and receiver and also when the details are held on the computers at each end. It would require a determined attempt to intercept such a message and decrypt it. SSL is more widely used than the rival S-HTTP method. Since, with enough computing power, time and motivation, it is possible to decrypt messages encrypted using SSL, much effort is being put into finding more secure methods of encryption such as **SET**. From a merchant's point of view there is also the problem that authentication of the customer is not possible without resorting to other methods such as credit checks.

Secure Electronic Transaction (SET)
A standard for public-key encryption intended to enable secure e-commerce transactions; lead-development by MasterCard and Visa.

Certificate authorities (CAs)

For secure e-commerce, there is a requirement for the management of the vast number of public keys. This management involves procedures and protocols necessary throughout the lifetime of a key – generation, dissemination, revocation and change – together with the administrative functions of time/date stamping and archiving. The successful establishment of a CA is an immense challenge of trust building and complex management. There are two opposing views on how that challenge should be met:

- *Decentralised*: market driven, creating brand-name-based 'islands of trust' such as the Consumers Association. There is a practical need for a local physical office to present certificates of attestable value, e.g. passports, drivers' licences. Banks and the Post Office have a huge advantage.
- *Centralised*: in the UK, the Department of Trade and Industry (DTI) has proposed a hierarchical tree leading ultimately to the government.

The best-known commercial CA is Verisign (www.verisign.com) and this is commonly used for merchant verification. Post Offices and telecommunications suppliers are also acting as CAs. Examples in the UK include BT (Trust Wise) and the Post Office (ViaCode).

Reassuring the customer

Once the security measures are in place, content on the merchant's site can be used to reassure the customer, for example Amazon (www.amazon.com) takes customer fears about security seriously, judging by the prominence and amount of content it devotes to this issue. Some of the approaches used indicate good practice in allaying customers' fears. These include:

- use of customer guarantee to safeguard purchase;
- clear explanation of SSL security measures used;
- highlighting the rarity of fraud ('ten million customers have shopped safely without credit card fraud');
- the use of alternative ordering mechanisms such as phone or fax;
- the prominence of information to allay fears – the guarantee is one of the main menu options.

Companies can also use independent third parties that set guidelines for online privacy and security. The best-known international bodies are TRUSTe (www.truste.org) and Verisign for payment authentication (www.verisign.com). Within particular countries there may be other bodies such as, in the UK, the ISIS or Internet Shopping Is Safe scheme (http://isis.imrg.org).

Summary

1   Analysis of business and user requirements for digital business systems is important in delivering usable and relevant systems.

2   Process modelling is used to assess existing business processes and suggest revised processes. Techniques such as task analysis and flow process charts from workflow design are useful in understanding tasks that must be supported by the system and weaknesses in the current process.

3   Data modelling for digital business systems mainly involves traditional entity relationship approaches.

4   Architectural designs involve assessing appropriate integration between legacy systems and new e-commerce systems. Such designs are based on the client–server approach.

5   User interface design can be improved through using structured approaches such as use-case and following evolving standards for site structure, page structure and content.

6   Security design is important to maintain trust amongst the customer base. Security solutions target protecting servers from attack and prevent interception of messages when they are in transit.

Exercises

Self-assessment questions

1   What are the risks if analysis and design are not completed adequately?

2   Distinguish between process analysis and data analysis.

3   What are workflow analysis and workflow management systems?

4   What are legacy data and what are the options for their incorporation into an e-commerce system?

5   What are the four requirements of a secure e-commerce site?

6   Explain the concepts of digital keys and digital signatures and how they relate.

7   Explain the notation used for use-case analysis.

8   Summarise the characteristics of a usable website according to Jakob Nielsen (www.useit.com).

Essay and discussion questions

1   Write a plan for the analysis and design of an e-commerce site, recommending which aspects of process and data analysis should be conducted and explaining how they should be integrated.

2   Write an essay on the significance of workflow systems to digital business, illustrating your answer with examples of organisations of your choice.

3   Write a report summarising the characteristics of a website with good usability.

4   How can the concept of customer orientation be translated into e-commerce site design?

5   Assess the success of e-tailers in designing secure e-commerce systems.

Examination questions

1   Summarise the purpose of process analysis.

2   What is meant by 'user-centred design'?

3 Explain the concept of task analysis with reference to a customer placing an order online.

4 Explain the stages involved in use-case analysis with reference to a customer placing an order online.

5 Describe the stages of data modelling with reference to a database for an e-procurement system.

6 Outline the different types of services that need to be provided by different servers on an e-commerce site based on the three-tier client–server system.

7 How do the attributes of a secure e-commerce site differ from customer and company viewpoints?

8 Explain the relationship between analysis, design and implementation for an e-commerce site.

References

AMA (2003) American Management Association 2003 E-mail Rules, Policies and Practices Survey: **www.amanet.org/research/pdfs/Email_Policies_Practices.pdf**.

BBC (2003) Cracking the hacker underground. BBC News Online: **http://news.bbc.co.uk/1/hi/technology/3246375.htm** (no longer available).

BERR (2013) Information Security Breaches Survey 2013, managed by PricewaterhouseCooper for UK Department of Business, Enterprise and Regulatory Reform (BERR), published at **www.pwc.co.uk/audit-assurance/publications/2013-information-security-breaches-survey.jhtml**.

Bevan, N. (1999a) Usability issues in web site design. *Proceedings of the 6th Interactive Publishing Conference,* November: **www.usability.serco.com** (no longer available).

Bevan, N. (1999b) Common industry format usability tests. *Proceedings of UPA 98,* Usability Professionals Association, Scottsdale, AZ, 29 June–2 July: **www.usability.serco.com** (no longer available).

Bocij, P., Greasley, A. and Hickie, S. (2008) *Business Information Systems. Technology, Development and Management,* 4th edn. Financial Times Prentice Hall, Harlow.

British Standards Institute (1999) BS 13407 Human-centred Design Processes for Interactive Systems.

Chaffey, D. (1998) *Groupware, Workflow and Intranets – Re-engineering the Enterprise with Collaborative Software.* Digital Press, Woburn, MA.

Chaffey, D. and Wood, S. (2005) *Business Information Management: Improving Performance using Information Systems.* Financial Times Prentice Hall, Harlow.

Chaffey, D., Mayer, R., Johnston, K. and Ellis-Chadwick, F. (2009) *Internet Marketing: Strategy, Implementation and Practice,* 3rd edn. Financial Times Prentice Hall, Harlow.

Christodoulides, G., de Chernatony, L., Furrer, O., Shiu, E and Temi, A. (2006) Conceptualising and measuring the equity of online brands. *Journal of Marketing Management,* 22(7/8), 799–825.

ClickZ (2003) Virus damage worst on record for August 2003. By Sharon Gaudin. News alert published online at ClickZ Stats, 2 September: **www.clickz.com/stats**.

Csiksczentmihaly, M. (1990) *Flow: the Pyschology of Optimal Experience.* Harper Collins, New York.

Curtis, B., Kellner, M. and Over, J. (1992) Process modeling. *Communications of the ACM,* 35(9), 75–90.

Davenport, T.H. (1993) *Process Innovation: Re-engineering Work through Information Technology*. Harvard Business School Press, Boston.

de Chernatony, L. (2001) Succeeding with brands on the Internet. *Journal of Brand Management*, 8(3), 186–95.

DTI (2006) Identity access and E-mail and Web Usage factsheets. A survey of UK business practice, managed by PricewaterhouseCoopers on behalf of the Department of Trade and Industry (DTI). Published at DTI Information Security Breaches Survey.

Eaton, C., Deroos, D., Deutsch, T., Lapis, G. and Zikopoulos, P. (2012). *Understanding Big Data: Analytics for Enterprise Class Hadoop and Streaming Data*. McGraw Hill, New York.

E-consultancy (2007) Digital business briefing interview. Bruce Tognazzini on human–computer interaction. Interview published November: **www.econsultancy.com/news-blog/newsletter/link_track.asp?id=3515&link_id=#1** (no longer available).

E-consultancy (2009) Q&A: Hiscox's Mike Beddington on selling financial services online, Posted 16 July 2009: **http://econsultancy.com/blog/4227-q-a-hiscox-on-selling-financial-services-online**.

Fogg, B. (2009) In *Proceedings of the 4th International Conference on Persuasive Technology* (2009), pp. 1–7. Available from **www.behaviormodel.org**.

Fogg, B., Soohoo, C., Danielson, D., Marable, L., Stanford, J. and Tauber, E. (2003) How do people evaluate a web site's credibility? A Consumer WebWatch research report, prepared by Stanford Persuasive Technology Lab.

Forrester (2005) Site Design Personas: How Many, How Much. By Harley Manning, 3 June. Forrester Research publication.

Forrester (2011) The Forrester Wave™: Web Content Management For Online Customer Experience, Q3 2011. Research report by Stephen Powers. Summarised at: **http://blogs.perficient.com/portals/2011/07/20/forrester-releases-new-wcm-wave-and-welcome-to-a-new-acronym**.

Georgakoupoulos, D., Hornick, M. and Sheth, A. (1995) An overview of workflow management: from process modeling to workflow automation infrastructure. *Distributed and Parallel Databases*, 3, 119–53.

Guardian (2003) Hijacked your bank balance, your identity, your life. *The Guardian*, 25 October).

Guardian (2103) Financial Times: There is no drawback to working in HTML5. Interview with Stuart Dredge, *The Guardian*, 29 April.

Hofacker, C. (2001) *Internet Marketing*. John Wiley & Sons, New York.

Hoffman, D.L. and Novak, T.P. (1997) A new marketing paradigm for electronic commerce. *The Information Society,* Special issue on electronic commerce, 13 (January–March), 43–54.

IBM (2013) What is Big Data? Service solutions page. **www.ibm.com/software/data/bigdata**. Accessed 20 July 2013. No publication date (no longer available).

Jacobsen, I., Ericsson, M. and Jacobsen, A. (1994) *The Object Advantage. Business Process Re-engineering with Object Technology*. Addison-Wesley, Wokingham.

Kesh, S., Ramanujan, S. and Nerur, S. (2002) A framework for analyzing e-commerce security. *Information Management and Computer Security*, 10(4), 149–58.

Knight, K. (2011). Responsive Web Design: What It Is and How To Use It. Smashing Magazine blog post, 12 January 2011. **http://coding.smashingmagazine.com/2011/01/12/guidelines-for-responsive-web-design/**.

Lynch, P. and Horton, S. (1999) *Web Style Guide. Basic Design Principles for Creating Web Sites*. Yale University Press, New Haven, CT. Available online at: **http://info.med.yale.edu/caim/manual/contents.html**.

Messagelabs (2008) Threat Statistics, published monthly at **www.messagelabs.com**.

Mitnick, K. and Simon, W. (2002) *The Art of Deception: Controlling the Human Element of Security*. John Wiley & Sons, New York.

Nielsen, J. (2000a) *Designing Web Usability*. New Riders, San Francisco.

Nielsen, J. (2000b) Details in Study Methodology Can Give Misleading Results. Jakob Nielsen's Alertbox, 21 February: **www.nngroup.com/articles/details-in-study-methodology-can-give-misleading-results/**.

Noyes, J. and Baber, C. (1999) *User-Centred Design of Systems*. Springer-Verlag, Berlin.

Pant, S. and Ravichandran, T. (2001) A framework for information systems planning for digital business. *Logistics Information Management*, 14(1), 85–98.

Rettie, R. (2001) An exploration of flow during Internet use. *Internet Research: Electronic Networking Applications and Policy*, 11(2), 103–13.

Robertson, J. (2003) Information design using card sorting. Step Two. Available online at **www.steptwo.com.au/papers/cardsorting/index.html**.

Rosen, D. and Purinton, E. (2004) Website design: viewing the web as a cognitive landscape, *Journal of Business Research*, 57(7), 787–94.

Rosenfeld, L. and Morville, P. (2002) *Information Architecture for the World Wide Web*, 2nd edn. O'Reilly, Sebastopol, CA.

Schneider, G. and Winters, J. (1998) *Applying Use Cases. A Practical Guide*. Addison-Wesley, Reading, MA.

Seybold, P. and Marshak, R. (2001) *The Customer Revolution*. Crown Business, London.

Smart Insights (2010) Website Feedback Tools review, published 7 April 2010: **www.smartinsights.com/digital-marketing-software/website-feedback-tools-review/**.

Smart Insights (2013) Social Sign-on: the implications for Ecommerce sites. Article by Dave Chaffey, 9 July 2013: **www.smartinsights.com/social-media-marketing/social-media-platforms/social-sign-on-the-implications-for-ecommerce-sites/**.

Taylor, D. (1995) *Business Engineering with Object Technology*. John Wiley & Sons, New York.

Thurner, R. (2013). *Winning with Mobile. Creating a strategy for Mobile marketing, Mobile commerce and Mobile CRM*. Published by Smart Insights. Available from Amazon.

Trocchia, P. and Janda, S. (2003) How do consumers evaluate Internet retail service quality? *Journal of Services Marketing*, 17(3), 243–53.

Wodtke, C. (2002) *Information Architecture: Blueprints for the Web*. New Riders, Indianapolis, IN.

Workflow Management Coalition (WfMC) (1996) Reference model. Version 1. In *The Workflow Management Coalition Specification. Terminology and Glossary*. Workflow Management Coalition, Brussels.

Worldwide Web Consortium (2013) Media Queries specification/recommendation. **www.w3.org/TR/css3-mediaqueries**. Updated June 2012.

Wroblewski, L. (2011) Why separate mobile and desktop web design. Blog Post, 1 September 2011. **www.lukew.com/ff/entry.asp?1390**.

Web links

British web site trade association BIMA (**www.bima.co.uk**) has good resources for the specialist in this area.

Big Data Hub (**www.ibmbigdatahub.com/**) A collection of case study and research from IBM.

DTI Information Security Breaches Survey (**www.infosec.co.uk/About/PWC-Survey/**) A survey of security in UK businesses.

Royal National Institute for the Blind (**www.rnib.org.uk/accessibility**) Web accessibility guidelines.

User Interface Engineering (**www.uie.com**) Articles on usability which often provide a counterpoint to those of Nielsen.

Smashing Magazine (**www.smashingmagazine.com**). A site for web developers and web managers explaining site design approaches.

UI Access (**www.uiaccess.com/access_links.html**) Resources on website accessibility.

Web Design References (**www.d.umn.edu/itss/support/Training/Online/webdesign**) A collection from the University of Minnesota, Duluth, including articles and references on accessibility, information architecture and usability.

Web Style Guide (**www.webstyleguide.com**) Supporting site for the style guide book of P. Lynch and S. Horton of Yale Medical School. Complete text online.

Worldwide Web Consortium Web accessibility guidelines (see **www.w3.org/WAI**).

12

Digital business service implementation and optimisation

Web support

The following additional case studies are available at
www.pearsoned.co.uk/chaffey

→ Change management at the Woolwich Group
→ Guide to smarter searching

The site also contains a range of study materials designed to help improve your results.

Scan code to find the latest updates for topics in this chapter

Learning outcomes

After completing this chapter the reader should be able to:

● Produce a plan to minimise the risks involved with the launch phase of an digital business application
● Define a process for the effective optimisation of an digital business system
● Create a plan to measure and improve the effectiveness of sell-side digital business applications using web analytics tools

Management issues

Implementation and optimisation of digital business systems raises these issues for management:

● What actions can we take to minimise the risks of implementation?
● How do we select the most appropriate systems?
● How do we achieve transition from previous systems to a new digital business system?
● What techniques are available to measure and optimise our services?

Links to other chapters

● This chapter follows naturally from *Chapters 10* and *11*. The context is given in Figure 10.6. The change management plan defined in *Chapter 10* will be enacted in the implementation phase. The coding, testing and changeover aspects of implementation will be based on the analysis and design documentation produced using the techniques described in *Chapter 11*

Introduction

Implementation
The creation of a system based on analysis and design documentation.

Maintenance phase
Commences after the system is live.

Dynamic digital business application
The application is continuously updated in response to competitive forces.

Maintenance activities
Involve measurement of an information system's effectiveness and updating to correct errors or introduce new features necessary to improve its value to the organisation.

In the traditional software development life cycle the **implementation** and **maintenance phases** are well-defined steps involved with the transition of new software application or system from the production to live environment. The increasing usage of web-based digital business services has rendered the concept of maintenance less useful since this suggests changes are limited to improving performance and bug fixing. Instead, a **dynamic digital business application** requires that content and services will be continuously updated in response to marketplace forces. As competitors introduce new services and offers, and as marketing research reveals problems or opportunities with the site from a customer perspective, ongoing **maintenance activities** will be required for the digital business to remain competitive. Consider the services of Google (Case study 3.1) which are continually updated to improve the user experience, performance and monetisation of the service. For example, Google has stated that it makes over 300 changes a year to its search algorithm to combat search spam and deliver more relevant results.

We saw in Chapter 10 how agile development methodologies such as scrum promote continuous development in what is sometimes referred to as a 'permanent beta'. So today there is generally less distinction between development and live phases, and many pureplay digital businesses seek a model of '*continuous release project*' to enable more regular, incremental releases to web functionality. This approach is shown in Figure 12.1.

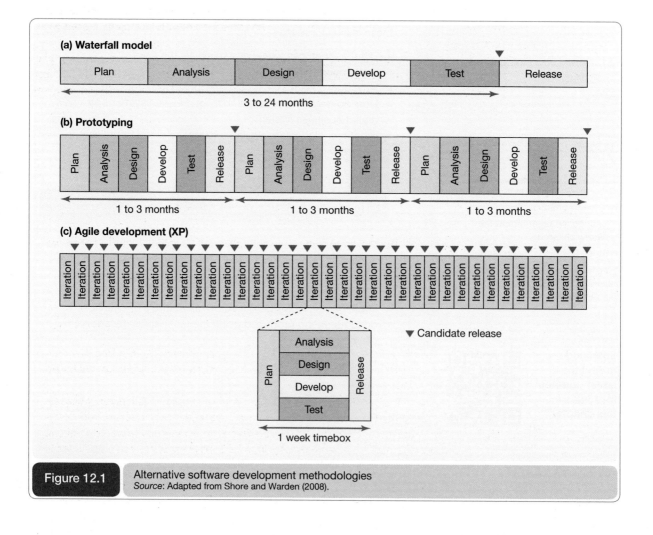

Figure 12.1	Alternative software development methodologies
	Source: Adapted from Shore and Warden (2008).

While analysis of requirements is occurring, design and implementation will be occurring simultaneously in order to produce storyboards and prototypes. This prototyping may occur in timeboxes of a certain duration, perhaps 30 days or 60 days, with a prototype produced at the end of each timebox. It is evident that implementation activities such as testing and review follow analysis and design and occur for each increment.

Optimisation of digital business services

Optimisation suggests a rigorous, ongoing approach to improving the effectiveness and efficiency of digital business services. When we reviewed goals for effectiveness and efficiency in Chapter 5, we explained the importance of defining both type of goals. Managers of digital business services need to continually revisit these questions:

- *Service effectiveness.* Is the service meeting business goals? Is the experience and service delivered satisfactory for users? Are new technology approaches or information available that could improve the experience?
- *Service efficiency.* Is the operation of the system measured through speed of response, usability and cost appropriate to lead to an effective service? Are new technology approaches available that could improve the system efficiency?

Web analytics is the discipline which helps answer the questions about experience and service levels for sell-side e-commerce. We see that through techniques like AB and multivariate testing many companies are optimising through continuous reviews of their sites and services. Producing quality content is also important to an effective experience and requires a sound process to keep content up to date and we cover methods of developing a good workflow for this.

In this chapter we also explore criteria for selecting key digital business technology platforms such as content management systems and web analytics. The 'Real-world digital business experiences' interview below introduces some of the issues involved with selecting and managing a CMS.

Real-world Digital Business   **The Smart Insights interview**

Avinash Kaushik, Google's analytics evangelist

Overview and main concepts covered

Avinash Kaushik is Google's Digital Marketing evangelist, well known for his books *Web Analytics: An Hour a Day*, *Web Analytics 2.0* and his Occam's Razor blog.

Q. Some have criticised online customer engagement as an abstract concept that can't be readily applied in the real world. Can you give some practical examples of how a site owner can apply the engagement concept to get better results?

Avinash Kaushik, Google: Engagement is a nice goal to have. Create sites that customers will find engaging and they'll stick around or come back again or maybe do business with you.

But that term has been manipulated to a point where it means nothing any more (or everything to everyone) and is often used as an excuse to know do the hard work of figuring out what the real outcomes of the site are for the company and the website visitors.

My encouragement to website owners is to be initially sceptical when someone is trying to pawn off 'engagement' on them and ask the tough question: 'What do you really mean by engagement and how does it specifically apply to my business?'

Secondly, I encourage people to realise that on the most glorious spring day when the birds are chirping the right song, web analytics tools can measure the Degree of engagement but they fall quite a bit short of measuring the Kind of engagement. So they can report that Visitors saw 19 pages on your site (Degree) but they can't tell you if that was because the Visitors were frustrated with your crappy navigation or thrilled with your content.

People use Google Analytics (or other tools) to easily measure various elements of the Degree of engagement. Perhaps the simplest example is using the bounce rate for the core landing pages to identify pages that won't even entice Visitors to make one click!

In two clicks you can also get Loyalty (recency), Frequency, Length of Visit and Depth of Visit to get a solid feel for if Visitors are making repeat visits to the site or if they do it more frequently and marry that up with content consumption. Doing this by looking at trends over time is a fantastic way to understand if the site is delivering value for your customers.

For many 'social' websites, website owners also measure the number of people who sign up and then contribute by writing reviews or comments, etc.

All really good examples of (1) measuring the degree of engagement and (2) not confusing the real metric being measured by calling it engagement.

Q. Which are the best measures or reports you could point to which help marketers understand how well an E-commerce site is performing for retention?

Avinash Kaushik, Google: I touched on some of the obvious ones above, the Loyalty metrics (specifically Recency and Frequency). They immediately tell you if you are acquiring traffic that comes back again and again, and since GA will tell you Recency by going as far back in history as you have data, that is a great way to know when customers come back (and perhaps also understand why).The other obvious thing to do for shorter time periods is to look at the trends for percentage of New Visits, especially by the sources of your traffic.

Some retailers want to do retention analysis by looking at repeat purchases. For this, Google Analytics, like pretty much every tool out there, provides a very strong complement of e-commerce reports that allow you to segment the data by the types of purchasers (new or returning), which will help you understand their purchase behaviour, and by applying filters to your data you can dig deeper into sources of traffic, trends in number of visits, content consumed etc.

This in conjunction with using even simple on-exit website surveys can give you a great picture of what is happening on your website and where you are missing the boat.

Q. Conversion optimisation. Today there is a lot more talk in large organisations about using techniques like AB or multivariate testing. How would you advise a small business owner to set out on this journey?

Avinash Kaushik, Google: This might surprise you, but I am seeing a lot more traction in using optimisation techniques with smaller companies than with larger companies. There are a couple of interesting reasons:

1 A/B or MVT is now free with tools like Google Website Optimizer, so you can dispense with RFPs and all that 'stuff' and just go try the tool.
2 Smaller companies are much more willing to try new things and have less politics and entrenched opinions (and HiPPO's) that are hard to overcome.

This is of course a tad bit sad because given the traffic and the sheer opportunities it really is a crime for larger companies to leave so much more revenue on the table, or the chance to optimise the customer experience which will improve loyalty and satisfaction.

My recommendations for any company are perhaps similar:

1 **Start with A/B testing.** In my experience, starting simple will ensure that you will get of the gates fast and be able to start the critical process of cultural shift with

easily understandable experiments. Then you can move to the 1.8 billion combination page test.

2 **For the highest impact, try dramatic differences in your test versions.** Trying shades of blue might sound interesting but the test might take a very, very long time to provide you with statistically significant differences. But trying a page with only text and one with text and images might get you on the path to understanding your customers faster.

3 **Run a report for your top 25 landing pages** (entry pages) on your site, then look at the bounce rates for each of them. Pick three with the highest bounce rates, these are the pages letting you down the most. You'll win big by testing these first.

4 **Have an active 'customer listening channel'.** Remote usability testing, market research, customer call centres or surveys (even a free excellent solution like 4Q, which I helped create with iPerceptions). The best focus points about what is not working on your site come from your customers (sadly not you) and likewise the greatest ideas on how to improve your site (and hence test) also come from your customers. Listen and you will prosper.

Q. What excites you most about potential developments in web analytics into the future?

Avinash Kaushik, Google: The thing that excites me most is that no one has a clue where this is all headed. We have no idea what 'web analytics' will look like in five years. That is exciting because there is a ton of change and growth to come and being a part of helping play a small part in that change is simply fantastic.

There are new data collection methods to come, there are new ways of doing superior analysis of data, there is so much more we could do with Artificial Intelligence in optimising customer experiences, there are opportunities to bridge the various islands of data (on the web or outside) to create something amazing, there are . . . it goes on and on.

They are going to get a lot better about what you should look at.

Visualisation is great and tables are good but what is killing Analysts right now is their ability to figure out, from megabytes and megabytes of data, what is actually worth looking at. Most tools still simply spew data out, relying on the Analyst (or the Data Consumer) to figure things out. That is a bad strategy, yet most tools follow it.

Visualisation has gotten a lot better – but I'm not seeing any form of intelligent recommendations – it's very tricky and the web analytics companies are too busy copying other functionality! It's good you mention that ClickTracks features, though.

Recently I talked about one specific example on my blog about how tools are getting smarter, 'Actionable Web Analytics: Focus on What's Changed'.

Using ClickTracks as an example, I demonstrated how to look at only the data that has shifted in importance by a statistically significant amount. Your top twenty of anything never changes, but using this type of report, What's Changed, you can look at just the data that really matters. Now it is easier to take action.

I expect all tools to get much, much better at applying advanced mathematics and statistics to help their users identify where to focus their attention.

The other thing I would highlight as an evolution for web analytics tools is that they are going to do a lot more than page view reporting on your site. I don't mean doing clever things like Event Logging to measure Web 2.0 experiences, that is cool, of course. I am referring to their ability to measure content no matter how it is distributed (widgets, RSS, etc.) and where it is consumed (websites, feed readers, mobile phones, your home refrigerator or washing machine!).

Opportunity is, I suppose, what I find most exciting about the future of web analytics!

Alternatives for acquiring digital business systems

The basic alternative **acquisition methods** for digital business systems are similar to those for traditional business information systems:

1 **Bespoke development.** With a **bespoke development**, the application is developed from 'scratch' through programming of a solution by an in-house or external development team or systems integrator.
2 **Off-the-shelf.** In a **packaged implementation** a standard existing system is purchased from a solution vendor and installed on servers and clients located within the organisation. Alternatively, free or low-cost open-source software may be used. A web design tool such as Dreamweaver is a simple example of an off-the-shelf packaged implementation.
3 **Hosted Software as a Service (SaaS) solution.** With a **hosted solution**, a standard system is used, but it is managed using a third-party applications service provider variously known as 'on-demand', 'web services' or a 'managed solution'. The merits and examples of the SaaS approach have been discussed in Chapters 3 and 6.
4 **Tailored development.** In a **tailored development**, an off-the-shelf system or SaaS solution is tailored according to the organisation's needs. This form of project is often based on integrating components from one or several vendors.

Chaffey and Wood (2005) demonstrated that the prevalent approach is the tailored off-the-shelf or hosted approach, which is often the best compromise between meeting an organisation's specific needs and reliability while minimising cost and development time. Decisions also have to be taken as to whether bespoke development or tailoring occurs in-house or using a consultant who is familiar with the latest e-commerce development tools.

Regardless of the source of the system, the main criteria used to select the solution are common. They are:

1 **Functionality.** The features of the application. Describes how well the digital business application meets the business need.
2 **Ease of use.** Systems should be intuitive to minimise the time needed to learn how to use them. A well-constructed piece of software will make it fast to conduct common tasks.
3 **Performance.** The speed of the application to perform different functions. This is measured by how long the user has to wait for individual functions to be completed such as data retrieval, calculation and screen display.
4 **Scalability.** Scalability is related to performance; it describes how well a system can adapt to higher workloads which arise as a company grows. For example, an ERP system will require more customer details, suppliers and products to be held on it as the company grows. The workload will also be higher as the number of internal and external users of the system increases.
5 **Compatibility or interoperability.** This refers to how easy it is to integrate the application with other applications. For example, does it have import and export facilities, does it support transfer of data using XML?
6 **Extensibility.** This describes how easy it is to add new functions or features to a package by adding new modules from the original vendor or other vendors.
7 **Stability or reliability.** All applications have errors or bugs and applications vary in the number of times they fail depending on how well they have been tested since they were first introduced.
8 **Security.** Capabilities for restricting access to applications should be assessed. This is particularly important for hosted solutions.
9 **Support.** Levels of support and the cost of support from the software vendor will vary. There is a risk that small companies may cease trading and the product may no longer be supported.

Now complete Activity 12.1 to consider how these different factors are balanced.

Activity 12.1	Selecting applications software for a small business

Purpose

To aid understanding of the different factors to assess when selecting applications software and the relative importance of them.

Activity

A start-up office supplies business which specialises in supply of printers is reviewing its alternatives for different types of digital business system. Form groups with each group selecting one type of digital business service from the list below and then discussing the importance of the nine criteria for selecting software described above. A ranked list of the criteria in order of importance should be produced. These can be put on a whiteboard, with one type of software in each column to assess the commonality in requirements.

Digital business service types:

1 Customer relationship management application.
2 Supply chain management application.
3 Employee management system.
4 Web analytics software (see later in chapter).

In this section we briefly introduce how simple static web pages can be developed using HTML and how scripts and databases can be used in conjunction with HTML to produce dynamic content.

Managing web content

Managers need to be aware of some aspects of managing content through content management systems:

1 **Standards compliance.** The World Wide Web Consortium (www.w3.org) has been prominent in defining web standards. Promoting standards has been taken up by other advocacy groups such as the WaSP, the Web Standards Project (www.webstandards.org/about/mission/) and many web design agencies. The use of web standards affects the quality of service and accessibility levels of sites.

   In his seminal reference on web standards, Jeffrey Zeldman says that the best way to view web standards is as 'a continuum, not a set of inflexible rules'. In practice a combination of the standards shown in Box 12.1 will be required. In particular the use of plug-ins and Ajax should be carefully discussed prior to implementation since this may exclude some site users or force them to use another plug-in.

2 **Cross-browser support.** Dependent on the standards used and how they are implemented, the site may appear different in different browsers since they may have interpreted some of the W3.org standards differently. This can result in a site rendering (appearing) differently in different browsers. Prior to implementation a list of browsers and versions should be targeted and then subsequently tested using tools such as BrowserShots.

   Increases accessibility – users can more readily configure the way a site looks or sounds using browsers and other accessibility support tools. Site is more likely to render on a range of access platforms like PDAs and smartphones.

Which web standards should the site support?

The main standards typically followed with current versions are:

1 Structural and semantic standards:
HTML (www.w3.org/TR/html401)
XHTML (www.w3.org/TR/xhtml1)
XML (www.w3.org/TR/2000/REC-xml-20001006)

2 Presentation languages:
Cascading Style Sheets (CSS) (www.w3.org/TR/css21)

3 Object models:
The Document Object Model (DOM), which describes the structural relationship between objects within an HTML or XML document enabling them to be accessed and updated, for example for form validation www.w3.org/DOM/DOMTR#dom2.

4 Scripting languages:
ECMA Script (the standard to which JavaScript has evolved) which is used for form validation, for example www.ecma-international.org/publications/standards/Ecma-262.htm.

5 Plug-in technology for rich Internet applications:
- Adobe Flash and Shockwave (a proprietary standard) for building interactive applications and displaying video http://en.wikipedia.org/wiki/Macromedia_Flash.
- Adobe Acrobat (www.adobe.com/acrobat), the de facto document display standard.
- Adobe Flex (www.adobe.com/products/flex) and Microsoft Silverlight (www.microsoft.com/Silverlight/) for building rich internet applications (RIA).
- Streaming media (proprietary standards for audio and video such as Real Networks.rm and Microsoft.wma).
- Java for rich Internet applications (www.java.com).

6 Ajax:
Ajax is based on other standards, notably JavaScript and XML supported by the DOM and CSS. A key feature of Ajax is that the XMLHttpRequest object is used to exchange data asynchronously with the web server without requiring new browser page loads. http://en.wikipedia.org/wiki/AJAX.

Cascading Style Sheets (CSS)

A simple mechanism for adding style (e.g. fonts, colours, spacing) to web documents. CSS enables different style elements to be controlled across an entire site or section of site.

Web accessibility

An approach to website design that enables sites and web applications to be used by people with visual impairment or other disabilities such as motor impairment. Accessibility also demands that web users should be able to use websites and applications effectively regardless of the browser or access platform they use and its settings.

3 **Use of style sheets for different platforms.** We introduced Cascading Style Sheets (CSS) in Chapter 11 as a mechanism for enabling different style elements such as typography and layout to be controlled across an entire site or section of site.

Managers need to check with designers that the CSS will be designed to be flexible for making minor changes to presentation (for example in the case of a re-branding) and that it supports different platforms such as mobile access or print output.

4 **Accessibility support.** We saw in the section on user-centred design in Chapter 11 that web accessibility is about allowing all users of a website to interact with it regardless of disabilities they may have or the web browser or platform they are using to access the site. The level of accessibility support provided (Level A, AA and AAA) should be defined before implementation and then validated as part of implementation.

5 **SEO support.** We saw in Chapter 9 that different on-page optimisation techniques are important to indicate to search engine algorithms the context of the page. Box 12.2 highlights some of the main standards. Unless SEO support is strictly defined as part of a site redesign it may be difficult to change these attributes of a page through a content management system. The on-page factors should be uniquely defined for each page within the site to avoid a 'duplicate content penalty' meaning that the search engine does not index a page since it is considered similar to another page.

Box 12.2	Key search engine optimisation (SEO) requirements

This compilation of the main factors that affect the position of a site within the search engines is taken from SEOMoz (www.seomoz.org), a resource created for webmasters and online marketers to help them achieve better rankings in the search engines.

This compilation shows an assessment of the most important ranking success factors by 30 experts in SEO where they rate each factor out of 5 and then the average is presented. Terms such as <title> and meta description are described in more detail in Chapter 9.

1 Key on-page optimisation factors:
These are attributes of the page which are defined through HTML tags with the exception of keyword frequency and density (the number of times a word is repeated on the page in relation to its length) and document name.
- <title> tag = 4.9 ÷ 5
- Keyword frequency and density = 3.7/5
- Keyword in headings = <h1> = 3.1, <h2> = 2.8
- Keyword in document name = 2.8
- Alt tags and image titles = 2.6 (particularly when linked to destination page)
- Meta name description = 2/5
- Meta name keywords = 1/5

2 Key off-page optimisation factors:
Off-page optimisation describes the characteristics of links to a page from within the site and most importantly from external sites:
- More backlinks (higher page rank) = 4/5
- Link anchor text contains keyword = 4.4/5
- Page assessed as a hub = 3.5/5
- Page assessed as an authority = 3.5/5
- Link velocity (rate at which changes) = 3.5/5

The importance of keyword text in anchor links means that sites which have a linking system based on text rather than image links will perform better for SEO. Another issue to consider when obtaining links from other sites is the use of the nofollow tag on a link, e.g. <a href= www.domain.com rel="nofollow">Link anchor text</a>. This indicates to search engines that the link should not be counted in the index and the destination page not indexed (unless it is linked to from another source). This means that many links in social networks and forums are effectively worthless for SEO since their owners have implemented the 'nofollow' to reduce 'SEO spamming'.

Source: SEOMoz (2013).

It is also important that staff creating and reviewing content are aware of these factors and can then modify the way their site is described through the content management system. So SEO mark-up needs to be part of a page creation and review process.

6 **Form validation.** Forms are vital pages in a site since they create value from a visit through leads (via a contact us form for example), forum postings or the shopping trolley and checkout. It is vital that they use cross-browser web standards and that they use an appropriate approach to check user inputs are valid.

Web application frameworks
A standard programming framework based on reusable library functions for creating dynamic websites through a programming language.

Web application frameworks and application servers

Web application frameworks provide a foundation for building dynamic interactive websites and web services. They use standard programming conventions or Application Programming Interface (APIs) in combination with data storage to achieve different tasks such as simply adding a user to a system or rendering the different page elements of a site. They provide standard functions in libraries to make it quicker to develop functionality than starting from lower-level coding. Functions in the web application framework are executed by **web application servers** which are software processes running on the server which accept and action requests via the principal web server software (e.g. Apache or Microsoft Information Server). The Common Gateway Interface (CGI) was a forerunner of this concept since it enabled standard functions to be accessed on a server, for example to perform form validation.

Web application server

Software processes which are accessed by a standard programming interface (API) of a web application framework to serve dynamic website functionality in response to requests received from browsers.

A technical discussion of the issues involved with selection of application frameworks and servers is outside the scope of this text. Essentially all of the solutions above have been successfully used to develop enterprise web services and what is most important to successful project delivery is finding the right level of skills for implementation and a project methodology or development process which is effective. The open-source alternatives have lower costs associated, but there may be difficulty in obtaining the right in-house or third-party resources to create applications of some of the less widely used frameworks and servers. This is indicated by Figure 12.2, which shows a survey of the application frameworks used by Fortune 1000 companies in 2007.

Content management systems

Content management system (CMS)

A software tool for creating, editing and updating documents accessed by intranet, extranet or Internet.

A **content management system (CMS)** provides a method for non-specialists to update website pages. This is an efficient method of publishing content since the facility can be made available to people throughout the company. Today there are two main forms of CMS, both of which are delivered as web services which can be accessed through a web browser. Enterprise CMSs can be used for large, complex sites (and other corporate documents) and as well as the standard page creation and editing facilities offer version control and review of documents through workflow systems which notify reviewers when new documents are ready for editing. CMS for smaller companies traditionally lack workflow or multi-author facilities, but offer many of the other features to create content. But blogging platforms such as Wordpress and Moveable Type are increasingly used by smaller businesses for managing their entire site since they have enterprise features.

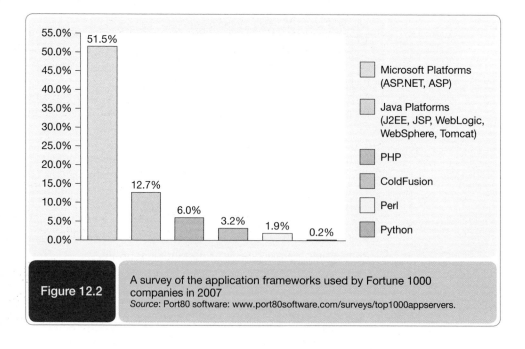

Figure 12.2   A survey of the application frameworks used by Fortune 1000 companies in 2007
Source: Port80 software: www.port80software.com/surveys/top1000appservers.

Criteria for selecting a content management system

A professional content management system should provide these facilities:

- *Easy authoring system.* Editing of new and existing documents should be possible through a WYSIWYG (what you see is what you get) facility similar to a word processor which makes it easy to embed images and supports a range of markup necessary for SEO.
- *Search engine robot crawling.* The content must be stored and linked such that it can be indexed by search engine crawlers to add it to their index. Sometimes URL rewriting to a search-engine-friendly format without many parameters is required. The Google Webmaster pages describe the requirements: www.google.com/webmasters.
- *Search-engine-optimisation-friendly markup.* Some bespoke content management systems created by design agencies do not enable easy editing of the key fields shown in Box 12.2, such as <title>, <h1> and <meta name= "description" content="page description">.
- *Different page templates.* The design and maintenance of content structure (sub-components, templates, etc.), web-page structure and website structure. It should be possible to create different layouts and designs for different site sections or categories of pages.
- *Link management.* The maintenance of internal and external links through content change and the elimination of dead links.
- *Input and syndication.* The loading (spidering) of externally originating content and the aggregation and dissemination of content from a variety of sources.
- *Versioning.* The crucial task of controlling which edition of a page, page element or the whole site is published. Typically this will be the most recent, but previous editions should be archived and it should be possible to roll back to a previous version.
- *Security and access control.* Different permissions can be assigned to different roles of users and some content may only be available through log-in details. In these cases, the CMS maintains a list of users.
- *Use of plug-ins and widgets.* Mashups are possible through embedding widgets such as links to social networks or third-party applications. But a content management system may not readily support embedding within the main content or sidebars.
- *Publication workflow.* Content destined for a website needs to pass through a publication process to move it from the management environment to the live delivery environment. The process may involve tasks such as format conversion (e.g. to PDF, or to WAP), rendering to HTML, editorial authorisation and the construction of composite documents in real time (personalisation and selective dissemination).
- *Tracking and monitoring.* Providing logs and statistical analysis of use to provide performance measures, tune the content according to demand and protect against misuse. It should also be possible to rapidly add tags to the page templates for web analytics tools such as Google Analytics.
- *Navigation and visualisation.* Providing an intuitive, clear and attractive representation of the nature and location of content using colour, texture, 3D rendering or even virtual reality.

Selecting e-commerce servers

E-commerce servers provide many of the capabilities of a CMS, but they focus on the needs of promoting product information and supporting the purchase process. The basic facilities of display of product content in different categories will be similar, so many of the most important requirements will relate to integration with other internal and external systems. Specific requirements of e-commerce servers include integration with:

- *Product catalogue systems* to import the latest products.
- *Feeds* to support shopping comparison engines such as Google Product Search or Shopzilla.
- *Advanced shopping search* or faceted browsing systems such as Endeca (www.endeca.com), Mercado and Google Mini Search appliance (www.google.com/enterprise).

- *Merchandising systems* which recommend appropriate products and promotions to visitors, for example ATG (www.atg.com).
- *Customer service solutions* including click-to-call or click-to-chat systems (e.g. www.atg.com).
- *Customer reviews and ratings systems*, for example BazaarVoice (www.bazaarvoice.com) and Feefoo (www.feefo.com).
- *Payment systems*, for example Netbanx (www.netbanx.com), Verisign (www.verisign. com), Worldbank (www.worldbank.com) and consumer systems Google Checkout (www. google.com/checkout) and PayPal (www.paypal.com).
- *Enterprise resource management systems* for supply chain management and order fulfilment, for example SAP (www.sap.com).
- *Testing and web analytics systems* since retailers will want to optimise their pages by trialling different versions to increase conversion rates.

Testing

Testing
Aims to identify non-conformance in the requirements specification and errors.

Testing has two main objectives: first, to check for non-conformance with the business and user requirements, and, second, to identify bugs or errors. In other words, it checks that the site does what users need and is reliable. Testing is an iterative process that occurs throughout development. As non-conformances are fixed by the development team, there is a risk that the problem may not have been fixed and that new problems have been created. Further testing is required to check that solutions to problems are effective.

The testing process

Test specification
A description of the testing process and tests to be performed.

A structured testing process is necessary in order to identify and solve as many problems as possible before the system is released to users. This testing is conducted in a structured way by using a **test specification** which is a comprehensive specification of testing in all modules of the system. If the use-case method of analysis described in Chapter 11 is used then it will specify the different use-cases or scenarios to be tested in detailed test scripts. The comprehensive testing specification will also cover all the different types of test outlined in Table 12.1.

Testing in the web environment requires new constraints. Unfortunately the list of constraints is long and sometimes neglected, to disastrous effect. Retailer Boo.com used a complex graphic to display clothes that was too time-consuming to use for visitors to the site. If there are a thousand potential users of an e-commerce site, all of the following constraints on design may exclude a proportion:

- *Speed of access* – everyone has used sites with huge graphics that take minutes to download. Good designers will optimise graphics for speed and then test using a slow modem across phone lines. Yahoo! downloads in just one second, so this is the performance that users expect from other sites.
- *Screen resolutions* – designing for different screen resolutions is necessary since some users with laptops may be operating at low resolution such as 640 by 480 pixels, the majority at 800 by 600 pixels, a few at higher resolutions of 1064 by 768 pixels or greater. If the designers have designed the site using PCs with high resolutions, they may be difficult to read for the majority.
- *Number of colours* – some users may have monitors capable of displaying 16 million colours giving photo-realism while others may only have the PC set up to display 256 colours.
- *Changing font size* – choosing large fonts on some sites causes unsightly overlap between the different design elements – depends on the type of web browser used.
- *Different browsers* and different versions of browsers may display graphics or text slightly differently or process JavaScript differently, so it is essential to test on a range of browser platforms.

Table 12.1	Types of testing required for an e-commerce site

Type of testing	Description
Developer tests	Code-level tests performed by developers of modules
Feasibility testing	Tests a new approach, often near the start of a project to make sure it is acceptable in terms of user experience
Module (component) tests	Checks individual modules have the correct functionality, i.e. correct outputs are produced for specified inputs (black-box testing)
Integration testing	Checks interactions between groups of modules
System testing	Checks interactions between all modules in the system
Database transaction taken	Can the user connect to the database and are transactions executed correctly?
Performance/capacity testing	Tests the speed of the system under high load
Usability and accessibility testing	Check that the system is easy to use, follows the conventions of user-centred design and meets accessibility requirements described in Chapter 11
Acceptance tests	Checks the system is acceptable for the party that commissioned it
Content or copy testing	Tests the acceptability of copy from a marketing view

- *Plug-ins such as Macromedia Flash and Shockwave* – if a site requires plug-ins, then a business will be cutting down its audience by the number of people who are unable or unprepared to download these plug-ins.

Testing environments

Development environment
Software and hardware used to create a system.

Test environment
Separate software and hardware used to test a system.

Production or live environment
Software and hardware used to host operational system.

Testing occurs in different environments during the project. Prototypes are tested in a **development environment** which involves programmers' testing data across a network on a shared server. In the implementation phase a special **test environment** may be set up which simulates the final operating environment for the system. This test environment will be used for early user training and testing and for system testing. Finally, the **production or live environment** is that in which the system will be used operationally. This will be used for user acceptance testing and when the system becomes live.

Changeover

Changeover
The term used to describe moving from the old to the new information system.

Soft launch
A preliminary site launch with limited promotion to provide initial feedback and testing of an e-commerce site.

Migration or changeover from a previous information system to a new system is particularly important for mission-critical digital business systems where errors in management of **changeover** will result in a negative customer experience or disruption to the supply chain.

When introducing a new sell-side e-commerce system there are two basic choices. First, the company can fully test the system in a controlled environment before it goes live and thus minimise the risk of adverse publicity due to problems with the site. Second, the company can perform what is known as a '**soft launch**'. Here, after initial testing, the site will be tested in a live environment where customers can use it.

Table 12.2	Advantages and disadvantages of the different methods of implementation

Method	Main advantages	Main disadvantages
1 **Immediate cutover.** Straight from old system to new system on a single date	Rapid, lowest cost	High risk. Major disruption if serious errors with system
2 **Parallel running.** Old system and new system run side-by-side for a period	Lower risk than immediate cutover	Slower and higher cost than immediate cutover
3 **Phased implementation.** Different modules of the system are introduced sequentially	Good compromise between methods 1 and 2	Difficult to achieve technically due to interdependencies between modules
4 **Pilot system.** Trial implementation occurs before widespread deployment	Essential for multinational or national roll-outs	Has to be used in combination with the other methods
5 **'Perpetual beta'**	Used by on-demand service providers such as the search engines to introduce new functionality in modules	Errors not identified in testing may impact large numbers of users, but can be updated to users rapidly

The alternatives for migrating from different versions of a system are reviewed in Bocij *et al.* (2005) and summarised in Table 12.2. Complete Activity 12.2 to review the relative merits of these approaches.

Activity 12.2	Understanding e-commerce and digital business

Purpose

Highlight the most suitable techniques for changeover.

Activity

1 Identify the variables which will determine the choice of changeover method.

2 Which changeover alternative would you recommend for a B2B company if it introduces a new intranet-based virtual helpdesk?

3 Justify your answer by analysing in a table the degree of risk, from high to low for each factor across each approach.

Answers to activities can be found at www.pearsoned.co.uk/chaffey

Database creation and data migration

Data migration

Transfer of data from old systems to new systems.

A final aspect of changeover that should be mentioned, and is often underestimated, is **data migration**. For an e-commerce system for a bank, for example, this would involve transferring or exporting data on existing customers and importing them to the new system. This is sometimes also referred to as 'populating the database'. Alternatively, a middleware layer may be set up such that the new system accesses customers from the original legacy database. Before migration occurs it is also necessary for a member of the development team known as 'the database administrator' to create the e-commerce databases. This can be time-consuming since it involves:

- Creating the different tables by entering the field definitions arising from the data modelling described in Chapter 11.
- Creating the different roles of users such as their security rights or access privileges. These need to be created for internal and external users.
- Creating stored procedures and triggers, which is effectively server-side coding to implement business rules.
- Optimising the database for performance.

Supporting search engines is significant where companies migrate their content to a new domain name or use a different CMS or commerce server which uses different document names. There is a risk that the search engine will lose the history of previous ranking based on backlinks to the site and its pages. To manage this a mapping can be provided to redirect from the old to the new pages known as a '301 redirect' on Apache servers.

Deployment planning

Deployment plan

A schedule which defines all the tasks that need to occur in order for changeover to occur successfully. This includes putting in place all the infrastructure such as cabling and hardware.

A **deployment plan** is needed to put in place the hardware and software infrastructure in time for user acceptance testing. This is not a trivial task since often a range of equipment will be required from a variety of manufacturers. Although the project manager is ultimately responsible for deployment planning, many companies employ **systems integrators** to coordinate these activities, particularly where there is a national roll-out.

Systems integrator

A company that organises the procurement and installation of hardware and software needed for implementation.

Content management and maintenance

Sell-side e-commerce sites are continuously under development, even when they become live. The sites need to be dynamic to deal with errors reported by customers and in response to innovations by competitors. Additionally the content, such as information about different events or new product launches and price promotions, will need to be updated if the site is to generate repeat visits from customers.

Buy-side e-commerce sites are less dynamic and are more akin to traditional business information systems, so in this section we will focus on maintenance of e-commerce sites, although this description will also apply to digital business implementations of intranets and extranets.

What are the management issues involved with maintenance? These are some of the challenges:

- Deciding on the frequency and scope of content updating.
- Processes for managing maintenance of the site and responsibilities for updating.
- Selection of content management system (covered in the previous section).
- Testing and communicating changes made.
- Integration with monitoring and measurement systems.
- Managing content in the global organisation.

As realisation of content as a strategic asset grows, more senior roles are being created to manage content quality. See Box 12.3.

Managing a content marketing strategy

Content marketing strategy

Selecting, sourcing, scheduling and encouraging sharing of the most relevant types of content to meet your business goals.

Halvorson (2010) describes how these content marketing activities can be managed. It can be seen that managing the creation of quality content is part of a broader customer engagement.

We saw in Chapter 8 how developing a **content marketing strategy** to support inbound marketing through sharing in social media is a key technique of modern marketing. This is a continuous activity that needs to be managed efficiently using a defined process, responsibilities and tools.

Box 12.3   Logitech appoint a content strategist

Computer peripheral provider Logitech advertised for a content strategist. This job description for a content strategist in a large company helps show us the key aspects of content strategy. These requirements summarise the essence of a sound content strategy:

- Senior management must understand the importance of content strategy to invest in good-quality resources with high-profile roles.
- Content must be of exceptional quality to be most effective – the job description says: '*useful, compelling and meaningful*'.
- Involves a strategy for syndication – not limited to company's own site.
- Blends improving customer experience, customer engagement and SEO.
- Requires an editorial calendar to manage creation of content.
- Content quality improved through a continuous process applying analytics and customer satisfaction.
- Integrates copywriting, web platform design and implementation, marketing communications, PR and SEO resources or teams.
- Supports goals and essence of company brand.

Content strategist responsibilities

- Drive the development and organisation of content that is useful, compelling and meaningful – directly on Logitech.com and indirectly through distributed content.
- Create user flows, information hierarchies, wireframes and content strategy for Logitech.com in support of campaigns, product launches and ongoing improvement.
- Determine content requirements for Logitech.com, inventory existing content, identify gaps, evaluate possible sources for additional material, and manage the process of getting that content into production.
- Creatively look for opportunities to improve content, consumer experience and SEO performance.
- Manage the Logitech.com editorial calendar to proactively keep content useful and up to date.
- Use analytics, consumer and usability testing and business requirements to help improve the experience and the content of Logitech.com in the long and short term.
- Work with the web, writing, PR and marcomm teams to determine the most effective ways to support campaigns and product launches on the web.
- Lead projects that make our web and component communication more intuitive and useful to consumers and internal partners.
- Work with brand architecture and terminology to guide the effective organisation of products and activities on Logitech.com.
- Drive the architecture of and improvements to the internal product content management system (worldwide product database) to fit the needs of the organisation.
- Occasionally write or edit content – particularly metadata, titles, alt text and edit general content to optimise for natural search.

Content strategist requirements

- 4-year college degree in a relevant field required, Masters degree preferred.
- 5–7 years of experience in an information architecture role, with 2–3 years working on complex websites.
- 2–3 years of experience being directly responsible for content strategy on a dynamic, complex or ever-evolving website.

- Experience with web content management systems, component content management systems (DITA or otherwise) and authoring systems (XML or other).
- Strong strategic, analytical skills with a solid ability to articulate information requirements clearly.
- A creative and collaborative approach that elevates the creative and communication opportunities – rather than straight analysis.
- Expertise in content strategy – including strong experience in SEO and keyword analysis as well as planning flexible approaches to keep content accurate and fresh.
- Accomplishments in the effective use of syndication (in and out) and user-generated content as well as working collaboratively with writers and designers.
- The ability to be measured by hard metrics – views, time on-site, consumer feedback – as well as soft metrics – support of the brand vision and architecture, consumer perception.
- Demonstrated ability to visualise and communicate complex information using Microsoft Visio or similar software.
- Deep experience with all levels of UX strategy and testing – but the ability to act quickly on consumer insights and best practices.
- Solid work ethic, ability to perform under pressure, meet deadlines, prioritise and deliver multiple tasks on time.
- Willing to learn and contribute to a strong team environment.
- Enthusiastic about the products and the possibilities of Logitech.

Other information

Logitech knows the value of strategic communication and content and now we're expanding our team to make the most of it. The global marketing team needs an expert who is ready to add his or her brain, talent and creativity to the cause of making our content work smarter, harder and around the globe. This is an opportunity for an IA/content strategy professional to put both strategy and executional excellence into practice every day and make an immediate and visible impact on the efficacy of a global organisation.

This role reports directly into the Global Director of Writing and Brand Architecture, with a direct and ongoing relationship with the Director of Global Web Marketing.

Source: Job description, Information Architect/ Content Strategist for Logitech, posted 29 September 2010: http://jobs.mashable.com/a/jbb/job-details/379895.

To help implement a content strategy requires a change of mindset for many companies (Pulizzi, 2010). They need to think more like a publisher and so invest in quality content that's superior to that of their competitors. This requires:

Quality, compelling content – content is still king!

- Quality writers to create quality content who may be internal staff or external freelance writers.
- An editorial calendar and appropriate process to schedule and deliver the content.
- Investment in software tools to facilitate the process.
- Investment in customer research to determine the content their different audiences will engage with.
- Careful tracking of which content engages and is effective for SEO and which doesn't.

Pulizzi and Barrett (2010) recommend creating a content marketing roadmap which is underpinned by the BEST principles. BEST stands for:

- *Behavioural.* Does everything you communicate with customers have a purpose? What do you want them to do as a result of interacting with content?

- *Essential.* Deliver information that your best prospects need if they are to succeed at work or in life.
- *Strategic.* Your content marketing efforts must be an integral part of your overall business strategy.
- *Targeted.* You must target your content precisely so that it's truly relevant to your buyers. Different forms of content will need to be delivered through different social platforms.

Frequency and scope of content and site updating

The frequency and scope of site updating will vary for different types of content and services.

The moment an e-commerce system is live it will require updates to the content and services. Different types of content will need to be updated at different frequencies, and a different approach will be required for each. It's most important that product and service information is kept up to date, particularly for transactional sites where pricing and availability change. Integration of systems is required to achieve this, with the ideal approach being automated update of availability information and single entry of new products and pricing shared across different platforms.

Content to support content marketing will need to be updated regularly to encourage return visits to the site, and amplified through social media, thus helping to increase visibility of a brand within the search engines. Companies that manage this effectively have a content or editorial calendar similar to that a magazine would use. They also use different tools to share content across different social networks to maximise the impact. Figure 12.3 shows the approach we use on Smart Insights to support content sharing across the main social networks while minimising the resource needed. We aim to publish two to three posts daily as a target, balancing advice and updates on major developments in digital marketing. These

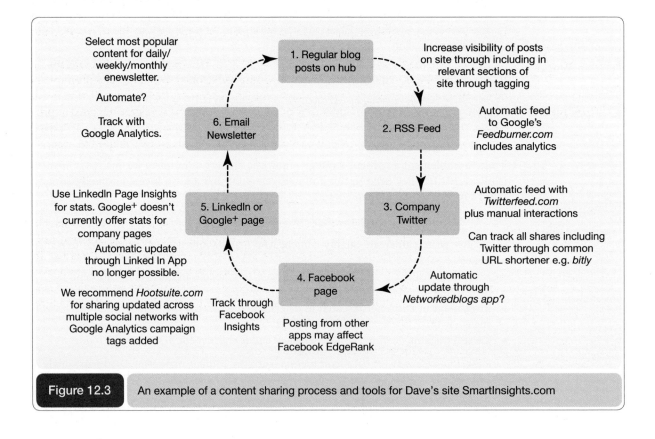

Figure 12.3   An example of a content sharing process and tools for Dave's site SmartInsights.com

are posted to our blog www.smartinsights.com/blog and then we use tagging of topics in different categories to surface the advice in relevant sections of the site. Each post is syndicated to Google's Feedburner service using RSS feeds which can then be automatically posted to Twitter. We use Hootsuite to post to other social networks like Facebook, Google+ and LinkedIn so that a more conversational tone can be used to recommend content or ask questions than is possible simply through updating a social network automatically. Hootsuite can also be set to automatically track posts and the impact of sharing using social media, using campaign tracking to add parameters to the URL of the post. The end of the cycle is where email is used to share content weekly with an editorial written to recommend the most useful posts or major updates for our readers to be aware of.

Feedback from users and analytics will reveal different types of errors and ideas across a website. A change request system is needed to prioritise and manage these, so that the highest-priority issues are corrected first. We can apply the fault taxonomy of Jorgensen (1995) to an e-commerce site to decide on the timing of the action required according to the type of problem. We can see that the approach is quite different from that for a traditional information system or packaged software that is distributed to thousands of customers. For example, with a mild problem such as a spelling mistake within software, it would be too costly to update and redistribute the software. With the e-commerce site, a spelling mistake, although trivial, can be updated immediately by correcting it on the web page or in the database or content management system where it is stored. Indeed, minor problems need to be corrected because they reduce the credibility of the site.

For more major errors, it is essential to fix the problems as soon as possible since revenue will be lost, both from customers who are unable to complete their current purchases and from users who will be unprepared to use the site in future because of their bad experience. Data from transactional e-commerce sites show that very few have continuous availability. If the site revenue for a 24-hours, 7-days-a-week site is £10 million per week then if availability falls to 95% this is the equivalent of losing £500,000, before the loss of future revenues from disgruntled customers is taken into account. A modular or component-based approach to e-commerce systems should enable the location of the problem module or cartridge to be identified rapidly and the problem in the module to be fixed, or possibly to revert to the previous version.

As well as fixing the problems shown in Table 12.3, companies will also wish to update the functionality of the e-commerce system in response to customer demands, sales promotions or competitor innovations. Again, a component-based approach can enable self-contained, discrete, new modules or cartridges to be plugged into the system which are designed to provide new functionality with only minimal changes to existing modules. For each such update, a small-scale prototyping process involving analysis, design and testing will need to occur.

Maintenance process and responsibilities

For efficient updating of an e-commerce system, it is vital to have a clearly defined process for content and service changes. Different processes will apply depending on the scope of the change, as described in the previous section. We can identify two different types of changes – routine content changes such as updates to documents on the site or new documents and major changes where we make changes to the structure, navigation or services on the site.

Process for routine content changes

The process for routine content changes should be communicated to all staff providing content to the site, with responsibilities clearly identified in their job descriptions. The main stages involved in producing an updated web page are to design it, write it, test it and publish

	Table 12.3	Fault taxonomy described in Jorgensen (1995) applied to an e-commerce site

Category	Example	Action – traditional BIS or packaged software	Action – e-commerce site
1 Mild	Misspelt word	Ignore or fix when next major release occurs	Fix immediately
2 Moderate	Misleading or redundant information. Problem with font readability	Ignore or defer to next major release	Fix immediately
3 Annoying	Truncated text, failed JavaScript, but site still usable	Defer to next major release	Fix immediately
4 Disturbing	Some transactions not processed correctly, intermittent crashes in one module	Defer to next maintenance release	Urgent patch required for module
5 Serious	Lost transactions	Defer to next maintenance release. May need immediate fix and release	Urgent patch required for module
6 Very serious	Crash occurs regularly in one module	Immediate solution needed	Urgent patch required for module, revert to previous version
7 Extreme	Frequent very serious errors	Immediate solution needed	Urgent patch required for module, revert to previous version
8 Intolerable	Database corruption	Immediate solution needed	Urgent patch required for module, revert to previous version
9 Catastrophic	System crashes, cannot be restarted – system unusable	Immediate solution needed	Urgent patch required for module, revert to previous version
10 Infectious	Catastrophic problem also causes failure of other systems	Immediate solution needed	Revert to previous version

Source: Copyright © 1995 from *Software Testing: A Craftsman's Approach* by Paul C. Jorgensen. Reproduced by permission of Routledge/Taylor & Francis Group, LLC.

it. A more detailed process is indicated here which distinguishes between review of the content and technical testing of the completed web page.

According to Chaffey *et al.* (2009), the different tasks involved in the maintenance process for new copy are as follows:

1 **Write.** This stage involves writing copy and, if necessary, designing the layout of copy and associated images.
2 **Review.** An independent review of the copy is necessary to check for errors before a document is published. Depending on the size of organisation, review may be necessary by one person or several people covering different aspects of site quality such as corporate image, marketing copy, branding and legality.
3 **Correct.** This stage is straightforward and involves updates necessary as a result of stage 2.

4 **Publish (to test environment).** The publication stage involves putting the corrected copy on a web page which can be checked further. This will be in a test environment that can only be viewed from inside the company.

5 **Test.** Before the completed web page is made available over the World Wide Web a final test will be required for technical issues such as whether the page loads successfully on different browsers.

6 **Publish (to live environment).** Once the material has been reviewed and tested and is signed off as satisfactory it will be published to the main website and will be accessible by customers.

The difficulty is that all these stages are required for quality control, but if different people are involved, then rapid, responsive publication is not possible. Activity 12.3 illustrates a

---

Activity 12.3 | **Optimising the content review process at a B2C company**

Purpose

Assess how quality control and efficiency can be balanced for revisions to web content.

Activity

The extract below and Figure 12.4 illustrate a problem of updating encountered by a B2C company. How can they solve this problem?

Problem description

From when the brand manager identifies a need to update copy for their product, the update might happen as follows: brand manager writes copy (1–2 days), one day later the web manager reviews copy, three days later the marketing manager checks the copy, seven days later the legal department checks the copy, two days later the revised copy is implemented on the test site, two days later the brand manager reviews the test site, the next day the web manager reviews the website followed by updating and final review before the copy is added to the live site two days later and over a fortnight from when a relatively minor change to the site was identified!

Answers to activities can be found at www.pearsoned.co.uk/chaffey

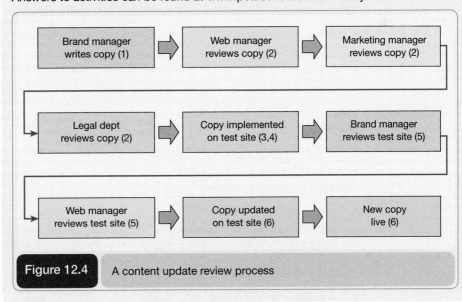

Figure 12.4   A content update review process

typical problem of content maintenance, involving the six stages described above, and assesses changes that could be made to improve the situation.

Frequency of content updates

Since the web is perceived as a dynamic medium, customers expect new information to be posted to a site straightaway. If material is inaccurate or 'stale' then the customer may not return to the site.

As information on a web page becomes outdated and will need to be updated, it is important to have a mechanism defining what triggers this update process. Trigger procedures should be developed such that when price changes, PR release or product specifications are updated in promotional leaflets or catalogues, these changes are also reflected on the website. Without procedures of this type, it is easy for there to be mismatches between online and offline content.

As part of defining a website update process and standards, a company may want to issue guidelines which suggest how often content is updated. This may specify that content is updated as follows:

- within two days of a factual error being identified;
- a new 'news' item is added at least once a month;
- when product information has been static for two months.

Process for major changes

For major changes to a website, such as changing the menu structure, adding a new section of content or changing the services for users, a different process is required. Such changes will involve a larger investment and there will be limited funds, so priorities must be agreed. The approach that is usually used is to set up a steering committee to ratify proposed changes. Such a decision usually needs an independent chair such as the e-commerce manager or marketing manager to make the final decision. The typical structure of such a committee is shown in Figure 12.5(a). It is made up of both technical and business staff and is useful for encouraging integration between these roles. Typical roles of some members of the committee who may also be involved in update of the site are shown in Figure 12.5(b). Figure 12.5(a), which could apply to Internet, extranet or intranet content, shows how a pyramid arrangement is used to ensure content quality on the site.

The committee will typically have a range of responsibilities such as:

- Defining agreed update process and responsibilities for different types of changes.
- Specifying site standards for structure, navigation and look and feel (Table 12.4).
- Specifying the tools that are used to update and manage content.
- Assessing proposals for major changes to site standards, content and services.
- Reviewing quality of service in terms of customer service and security.
- Specifying online promotion methods for the site (e.g. search engine registration) and evaluating the business contribution delivered via the site.
- Managing the budget for the site.

Initiatives to keep content fresh

It is often said that up-to-date content is crucial to site 'stickiness', but fresh content will not happen by accident, so companies have to consider approaches that can be used to control the quality of documents and in particular to keep them up to date and relevant. Generic approaches that can work well are:

- Assign responsibility for particular content types or site sections to individuals.
- Make the quality of web content produced part of employees' performance appraisal.
- Produce a target schedule for publication of content.

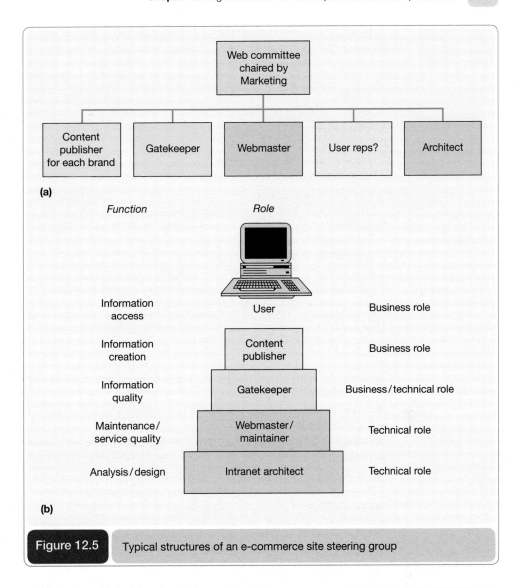

Figure 12.5   Typical structures of an e-commerce site steering group

Table 12.4	Website standards	
Standard	**Details**	**Applies to**
Site structure	Will specify the main areas of the site, e.g. products, customer service, press releases, how to place content and who is responsible for each area.	Content developers
Navigation	May specify, for instance, that the main menu must always be on the left of the screen with nested (sub) menus at the foot of the screen. The home button should be accessible from every screen at the top-left corner of the screen.	Website designer/webmaster usually achieves these through site templates
Copy style	General guidelines, for example, reminding those writing copy that copy for the web needs to be briefer than its paper equivalent. Where detail is required, perhaps with product specifications, it should be broken up into chunks that are digestible on-screen.	Individual content developers

Table 12.4	Continued	

Standard	Details	Applies to
Testing standards	Check site functions for: • different browser types and versions • plug-ins and invalid links • speed of download of graphics • spellchecking each page.	Website designer/webmaster
Corporate branding and graphic design	Specifies the appearance of company logos and the colours and typefaces used to convey the brand message.	Website designer/webmaster
Process	The sequence of events for publishing a new web page or updating an existing page. Who is responsible for reviewing and updating?	All
Performance	Availability and download speed figures.	Webmaster and designers

- Identify events which trigger the publication of new content, e.g. a new product launch, price change or press release.
- Identify stages and responsibilities in updating – who specifies, who creates, who reviews, who checks, who publishes.
- Measure the usage of content through web analytics or get feedback from site users.
- Publish a league table of content to highlight when content is out of date.
- Audit and publish content to show which is up to date.

Managing content for a global site

The issues in developing content management policies that are described above are complicated for a large organisation with many lines of business and particularly for a multinational company. Centralisation can give economies of scale and can achieve consistency in the way brand values are communicated nationally and internationally. However, content will need to be developed locally for regional audiences and this may require variations from central guidelines. Some regional autonomy needs to be allowed to enable buy-in from the different regions. It can be suggested that the following are required at an international level:

1 **Technology platform.** A common software system (CMS) will reduce costs of purchase, update and training. Integration with common software for customer relationship management (Chapter 9) and evaluation and measurement systems (see later in this chapter) will also be most efficient.
2 **System architecture.** A consistent architecture will avoid 'reinventing the wheel' in each country and will enable staff, partners and customers who need to access the CMS in different countries to be immediately familiar with it. Standards include:
   - Common page layout and navigation through templates.
   - Common directory structures and consistent URL structure.
   - Programming standard and languages and version control systems.
3 **Process/standards.** Update procedures for review of content for marketing, data protection and legal reasons as described in previous sections. Back-up and archiving policies will also be required.

Web analytics: measuring and improving performance of digital business services

We review measuring and improving the effectiveness of e-commerce system in detail since it is a key part of optimising e-commerce. We focus on measurement of sell-side e-commerce, since the approach is most advanced for this sector, but the principles and practice can be readily applied to other types of digital business system such as intranets and extranets.

Companies that have a successful approach to e-commerce often seem to share a common characteristic. They attach great importance and devote resources to monitoring the success of their online marketing and putting in place the processes to continuously improve the performance of their digital channels. This culture of measurement is visible in the UK bank Alliance and Leicester (Santander). Stephen Leonard, head of e-commerce, described their process as 'Test, Learn, Refine' (*Revolution*, 2004). Graeme Findlay, senior manager, customer acquisition of e-commerce at A&L, explains further: '*Our online approach is integrated with our offline brand and creative strategy, with a focus on direct, straightforward presentation of strong, value-led messages. Everything we do online, including creative, is driven by an extensive and dynamic testing process.*'

Seth Romanow, Director of Customer Knowledge at Hewlett-Packard, speaking at the 2004 E-metrics summit, described their process as 'Measure, Report, Analyse, Optimise'. Amazon refers to its approach as 'The Culture of Metrics' (see Case study 12.1). Jim Sterne, who convenes an annual event devoted to improving online performance (www.emetrics.org), has summarised his view on the required approach in his book *Web Metrics* (Sterne, 2002) as 'TIMITI', which stands for 'Try It! Measure It! Tweak It!', i.e. online content should be reviewed and improved continuously rather than as a periodic or ad hoc process. The importance of defining an appropriate approach to measurement and improvement is such that the term '**web analytics**' has developed to describe this key Internet marketing activity. A web analytics association (www.webanalyticsassociation.org) has been developed by vendors, consultants and researchers in this area. Eric Petersen (2004), an analyst specialising in web analytics, defines it as follows:

Web analytics is the assessment of a variety of data, including web traffic, web-based transactions, web server performance, usability studies, user submitted information [i.e. surveys], and related sources to help create a generalised understanding of the visitor experience online.

Web analytics

Techniques used to assess and improve the contribution of digital marketing to a business including reviewing traffic volume, referrals, clickstreams, online reach data, customer satisfaction surveys, leads and sales.

You can see that in addition to what are commonly referred to as 'site statistics' about web traffic, sales transactions, usability and researching customers' views through surveys are also included. However, this suggests analysis for the sake of it – whereas the business purpose of analytics should be emphasised. The definition could also refer to comparison of site-visitor volumes and demographics relative to competitors using panels and ISP collected data. Our definition is:

Web analytics is the customer-centred evaluation of the effectiveness of Internet-based marketing in order to improve the business contribution of online channels to an organisation.

A more recent definition from the Web Analytics Association (WAA, www. webanalyticsassociation.org) in 2005 is:

Web Analytics is the objective tracking, collection, measurement, reporting and analysis of quantitative Internet data to optimize websites and web marketing initiatives.

Principles of performance management and improvement

To improve results for any aspect of any business, performance management is vital. As Bob Napier, Chief Information Officer, Hewlett-Packard, was reported to have said back in the 1960s:

You can't manage what you can't measure.

The processes and systems intended to monitor and improve the performance of an organisation and specific management activities such as Internet marketing are widely known as 'performance management systems' and are based on the study of performance measurement systems.

Measurement is often neglected when a website is first created. Measurement is often highlighted as an issue once early versions of a site have been 'up and running' for a few months or even years, and employees start to ask questions such as '*How many customers are visiting our site, how many sales are we achieving as a result of our site and how can we improve the site to achieve a return on investment?*' The consequence of this is that performance measurement is often built into an online presence retrospectively. If measurement is built into site management, a more accurate approach can be developed and it is more readily possible to apply a technique known as 'design for analysis' (DFA). Here, the site is designed so companies can better understand the types of audience and their decision points. For example, for Dell (www.dell.com), the primary navigation on the home page is by business type. This is a simple example of DFA since it enables Dell to estimate the proportion of different audiences to their site and at the same time connect them with relevant content. Other examples of DFA include:

- Breaking up a long page or form into different parts, so you can see which parts people are interested in.
- A URL policy used to recommend entry pages for printed material.
- Group content by audience type or buying decision and setting up content groups of related content within web analytics systems.
- Measure attrition at different points in a customer journey, e.g. exit points on a five-page buying cycle.

In this section, we will review approaches to performance management by examining three key elements of an e-commerce performance improvement system. These are, first, the *process* for improvement, secondly, the measurement framework which specifies groups of relevant internet marketing metrics and, finally, an assessment of the suitability of tools and techniques for collecting, analysing, disseminating and actioning results.

Stage 1: Creating a performance management system

The essence of performance *management* is suggested by the definition for performance *measurement* used by Andy Neely of Cranfield School of Management's Centre for Business Performance. He defines (Neely *et al.*, 2002) performance measurement as:

> the process of quantifying the efficiency and effectiveness of past actions through acquisition, collation, sorting, analysis, interpretation and dissemination of appropriate data.

Performance management extends this definition to the process of analysis and actioning change in order to drive business performance and returns. Online marketers can apply many of the approaches of business performance management to Internet marketing. As you can see from the definition, performance is measured primarily through information on process effectiveness and efficiency as introduced in Chapter 5 in the section on objective setting where we noted that it is important to include both effectiveness and efficiency measures.

The need for a structured performance management process is clear if we examine the repercussions if an organisation does not have one. These include: poor linkage of measures with strategic objectives or even absence of objectives; key data not collected; data inaccuracies; data not disseminated or analysed; or no corrective action. Many of the barriers to improvement of measurement systems reported by respondents in Adams *et al.* (2000) also indicate the lack of an effective process. The barriers can be grouped as follows:

- *senior management myopia* – performance measurement not seen as a priority, not understood or targeted at the wrong targets – reducing costs rather than improving performance;
- *unclear responsibilities for delivering and improving the measurement system;*

Sidebar definitions:

Performance management system
A process used to evaluate and improve the efficiency and effectiveness of an organisation and its processes.

Performance measurement system
The process by which metrics are defined, collected, disseminated and actioned.

Design for analysis (DFA)
The required measures from a site are considered during design to better understand the audience of a site and their decision points.

Internet marketing metrics
Measures that indicate the effectiveness of Internet marketing activities in meeting customer, business and marketing objectives.

Effectiveness
Meeting process objectives, delivering the required outputs and outcomes. 'Doing the right thing.'

Efficiency
Minimising resources or time needed to complete a process. 'Doing the thing right.'

- *resourcing issues* – lack of time (perhaps suggesting lack of staff motivation), the necessary technology and integrated systems;
- *data problems* – data overload or of poor-quality, limited data for benchmarking.

To avoid these pitfalls, a coordinated, structured measurement process such as that shown in Figure 12.6 is required. Figure 12.6 indicates four key stages in a measurement process. These were defined as key aspects of annual plan control by Kotler (1997). Stage 1 is a goal-setting stage where the aims of the measurement system are defined – this will usually take the strategic Internet marketing objectives as an input to the measurement system. The aim of the measurement system will be to assess whether these goals are achieved and specify corrective marketing actions to reduce variance between target and actual key performance indicators. Stage 2, performance measurement, involves collecting data to determine the different metrics that are part of a measurement framework as discussed in the next section. Stage 3, performance diagnosis, is the analysis of results to understand the reasons for variance from objectives (the 'performance gap' of Friedman and Furey, 1999) and selection of marketing solutions to reduce variance. The purpose of Stage 4, corrective action, according to Wisner and Fawcett (1991), is:

> to identify competitive position, locate problem areas, assist the firm in updating strategic objectives and making tactical decisions to achieve these objectives and supply feedback after the decisions are implemented.

In an Internet marketing context, corrective action is the implementation of these solutions as updates to website content, design and associated marketing communications. At this stage the continuous cycle repeats, possibly with modified goals. Bourne *et al.* (2000) and Plant (2000) suggest that in addition to reviewing objectives, the suitability of the metrics should also be reviewed and revised.

Measurement is not something that can occur on an ad hoc basis because if it is left to the individual they may forget to collect the data needed. A 'measurement culture' is one in which each employee is aware of the need to collect data on how well the company is performing and on how well it is meeting its customers' needs.

Stage 2: Defining the performance metrics framework

Measurement for assessing the effectiveness of Internet marketing can be thought of as answering these questions:

1 Are corporate objectives identified in the Internet marketing strategy being met?
2 Are marketing objectives defined in the Internet marketing strategy and plan achieved?

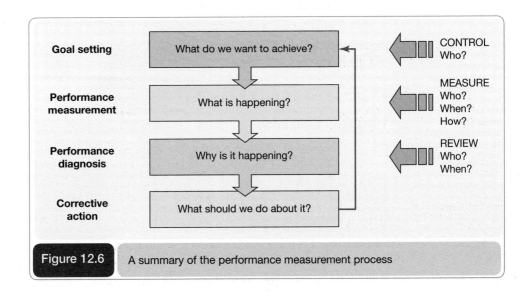

| Figure 12.6 | A summary of the performance measurement process |

3 Are marketing communications objectives identified in the Internet marketing plan achieved?

4 How efficient are the different promotional techniques used to attract visitors to a site?

Efficiency measures are more concerned with minimising the costs of online marketing while maximising the returns for different areas of focus such as acquiring visitors to a website, converting visitors to outcome or achieving repeat business.

Chaffey (2000) suggests that organisations define a measurement framework which defines groupings of specific metrics used to assess Internet marketing performance. He suggests that suitable measurement frameworks will fulfil these criteria:

A Include both macro-level effectiveness metrics which assess whether strategic goals are achieved and indicate to what extent e-marketing contributes to the business (revenue contribution and return on investment).

B Include micro-level metrics which assess the efficiency of e-marketing tactics and implementation. Wisner and Fawcett (1991) note that typically organisations use a hierarchy of measures and they should check that the lower-level measures support the macro-level strategic objectives. Such measures are often referred to as *performance drivers*, since achieving targets for these measures will assist in achieving strategic objectives. E-marketing performance drivers help optimise e-marketing by attracting more site visitors and increasing conversion to desired marketing outcomes.

C Assess the impact of the e-marketing on the satisfaction, loyalty and contribution of key stakeholders (customers, investors, employees and partners) as suggested by Adams *et al.* (2000).

D The framework must be flexible enough to be applied to different forms of online presence whether business-to-consumer, business-to-business, not-for-profit or transactional e-tail, CRM-orientated or brand-building. Adams *et al.* (2000) note that a 'one-size-fits-all' framework is not desirable.

E Enable comparison of performance of different e-channels with other channels as suggested by Friedman and Furey (1999).

F The framework can be used to assess e-marketing performance against competitors' or out-of-sector best practice.

When identifying metrics it is common practice to apply the widely used SMART mnemonic and it is also useful to consider three levels – business measures, marketing measures and specific Internet marketing measures (see objective setting section in Chapter 5).

Chaffey (2000) presented a framework of measures, shown in Figure 12.7, which can be applied to a range of different companies. Metrics for the categories are generated as objectives from Internet marketing planning which then need to be monitored to assess the success of strategy and its implementation. Objectives can be devised in a top-down fashion, starting with strategic objectives for business contribution and marketing outcomes leading to tactical objectives for customer satisfaction, behaviour and site promotion. An alternative perspective is bottom-up – success in achieving objectives for site promotion, on-site customer behaviour and customer satisfaction lead sequentially to achieving objectives for marketing outcomes and business contribution.

1 Channel promotion

Channel promotion
Measures that assess why customers visit a site – which adverts they have seen, which sites they have been referred from.

Referrer
The site that a visitor previously visited before following a link.

Channel promotion measures evaluate the volume, quality, value and cost of where the website, social presence or mobile site visitors originate – online or offline, and what are the sites or offline media that prompted their visit. Web analytics can be used to assess which intermediary sites customers are referred from and which keywords they typed into search engines when trying to locate product information. Similar information on **referrer** is not typically available for visits to social media sites. Promotion is successful if traffic is generated that meets objectives of volume and quality. Quality will be determined by whether visitors are in the target market and have a propensity for the service offered (conversion rates, bounce rate and cost of acquisition for different referrers).

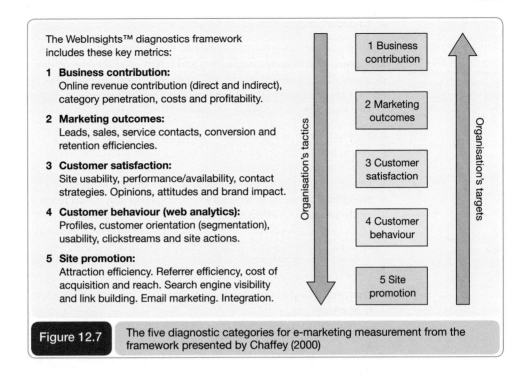

The WebInsights™ diagnostics framework includes these key metrics:

1 **Business contribution:**
Online revenue contribution (direct and indirect), category penetration, costs and profitability.

2 **Marketing outcomes:**
Leads, sales, service contacts, conversion and retention efficiencies.

3 **Customer satisfaction:**
Site usability, performance/availability, contact strategies. Opinions, attitudes and brand impact.

4 **Customer behaviour (web analytics):**
Profiles, customer orientation (segmentation), usability, clickstreams and site actions.

5 **Site promotion:**
Attraction efficiency. Referrer efficiency, cost of acquisition and reach. Search engine visibility and link building. Email marketing. Integration.

Figure 12.7 The five diagnostic categories for e-marketing measurement from the framework presented by Chaffey (2000)

Key measure: referral mix. For each referral source such as offline or banner ads online it should be possible to calculate:

- % of all referrals (or visitors);
- cost of acquisition (CPA) or cost per sale (CPS);
- revenue per visit generated;
- contribution to sales or other outcomes.

2 Channel buyer behaviour

Channel buyer behaviour
Describes which content is visited, time and duration.

Once customers have been attracted to the site we can monitor content accessed, when they visit and how long they stay, and whether this interaction with content leads to satisfactory marketing outcomes such as new leads or sales. If visitors are incentivised to register on-site it is possible to build up profiles of behaviour for different segments. It is also important to recognise return visitors for whom cookies or log-in are used.

Key measures are:

Bounce rates for different pages, i.e. proportion of single-page visits:

Home page views/all page views, e.g.	20%	= (2,358/11,612)
Stickiness: Page views/visitor sessions, e.g.	6	= 11,612/2,048
Repeats: Visitor sessions/visitors, e.g.	2	= 2,048/970.

Stickiness
An indication of how long a visitor stays on-site.

3 Channel satisfaction

Channel satisfaction
Evaluation of the customer's opinion of the service quality on the site and supporting services such as email.

Channel satisfaction with the online experience is vital in achieving the desired channel outcomes, although it is difficult to set specific objectives. However, it is not directly reported through web analytics, so is often not reported. Online methods such as online questionnaires, focus groups and interviews can be used to assess customers' opinions of the website content and customer service and how it has affected overall perception of brand. We reviewed five classes of website feedback tools in Chapter 11 in the section on user-centred design.

Key measure: channel satisfaction indices. These are discussed in Chapter 8 and include ease of use, site availability and performance, and email response. To compare customer satisfaction with other sites, benchmarking services can be used.

4 Channel outcomes

Conversion rate

Percentage of site visitors who perform a particular action such as making a purchase.

Traditional marketing objectives such as number of sales, number of leads, **conversion rates** and targets for customer acquisition and retention should be set and then compared to other channels. Dell Computer (www.dell.com) records on-site sales and also orders generated as a result of site visits, but placed by phone to a specific number unique to the site.

Key marketing outcomes include:

- registration to site or subscriptions to an email newsletter;
- requests for further information such as a brochure or a request for a call-back from a customer service representative;
- responding to a promotion such as an online competition;
- an offline (phone or store)lead or sale influenced by a visit to the site;
- a sale on-site.

Channel outcomes

Record customer actions taken as a consequence of a site visit.

A widely used method of assessing **channel outcomes** is to review the conversion rate, which gives an indication of the percentage of site visitors who take a particular outcome. For example:

> *Conversion rate, visitors to purchase = 2% (10,000 visitors, of which 200 make purchases).*
> *Conversion rate, visitors to registration = 5% (10,000 visitors, of which 500 register).*

Attrition rate

Percentage of site visitors who are lost at each stage in making a purchase.

A related concept is the **attrition rate** which describes how many visitors are lost at each stage of visiting a site. Figure 12.8 shows that for a set time period, only a proportion of site visitors will make their way to product information, a small proportion will add an item to a basket and a smaller proportion still will actually make the purchase. A key feature of e-commerce sites is that there is a high attrition rate between a customer's adding an item to a basket and subsequently making a purchase. Online marketers work to decrease this 'shopping basket abandonment rate' through improving usability and modifying messaging to persuade visitors to continue the 'user journey'.

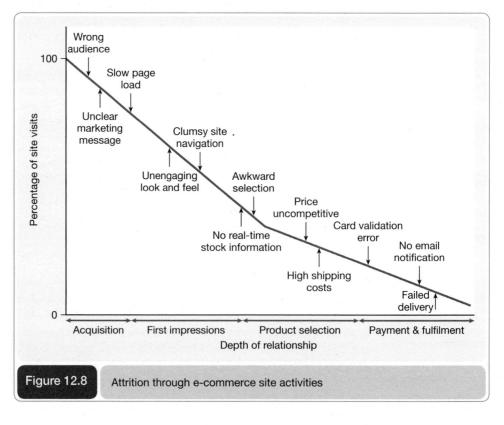

| **Figure 12.8** | Attrition through e-commerce site activities |

5 Channel profitability

Channel profitability
The profitability of the website, taking into account revenue and cost and discounted cash flow.

A contribution to business **profitability** is always the ultimate aim of e-commerce. To assess this, leading companies set an Internet contribution target of achieving a certain proportion of sales via the channel. When easyJet (www.easyjet.com) launched its e-commerce facility in 1998, it set an Internet contribution target of 30% by 2000. They put the resources and communications plan in place to achieve this and their target was reached in 1999. Assessing contribution is more difficult for a company that cannot sell products online, but the role of the Internet in influencing purchase should be assessed. Discounted cash flow techniques are used to assess the rate of return over time. Service contribution from e-channels should also be assessed.

Multichannel evaluation

The frameworks we have presented in this chapter are explained in the context of an individual channel. But, as Wilson (2008) has pointed out, there is a need to evaluate how different channels support each other.

He suggests the most important aspect of multichannel measurement is to measure 'channel cross-over effects'. This involves asking, for example: 'How can the impact of a paid search campaign be measured if it is as likely to generate traffic to a store, salesforce or call centre as to a website? How can the impact of a direct mail campaign be tracked if it generates website traffic as well as direct responses?'

1to1 Media (2008) summarises recommendations by Forrester, which are:

1 **Total number of hybrid customers.** These include the number and proportion who research online and purchase offline.
2 **Distribution and spend levels of those hybrid customers.** Proportion, average order value and type of category spend for these customers.
3 **Cross-channel conversion.** For example, online researchers who buy offline and potentially vice versa.
4 **Customer spend with competitors by channel.** This would have to be established by primary research for each brand. Audience measurement services such as Hitwise will give information on share of search, share of visitors and upstream/downstream patterns of visitors.

An example of a balanced scorecard-style dashboard developed to assess and compare channel performance for a retailer is presented in Figure 12.9.

Results (6)	**Customers & stakeholders (5)**
• Revenue	• Overall customer satisfaction
• Multichannel contribution	• Customer propensity to defect
• Degree multichannel sells up	• Customer propensity to purchase
• Costs per channel	• Customer perception of added value
• Degree of sweating assets	• Integration of customer experience
• Multichannel infrastructure costs	
Core processes (3)	**People and knowledge (4)**
• Productive multichannel usage	• Staff satisfaction
• Price (relative to competitors/other channels)	• Appropriate behaviours 'Living the brand'
• Quality of integrated customer view	• Willingness to diversify/extend the brand
	• Knowledge of target customer

Figure 12.9 Multichannel performance scorecard for a retailer

Focus on	Measuring social media marketing

Social media marketing has its own range of specialist measures, which can appear confusing, but are best understood in the context of a combination of website and PR measures. These show the volume, quality, sentiment and value of interactions. Analyst Altimeter (2011) has created a useful framework, shown in Figure 12.10, which helps map out different social media measures in the context of level of business management.

You can see that there are three levels of KPIs:

- *Business-level KPIs to measure contribution from social media.* These KPIs include contribution to revenue through direct sales attributed to social media. Softer measures include reputation and customer satisfaction (CSAT).
- *Reach and influence KPIs to review reach, share-of-voice and sentiment.* These show the relative comparison of a brand's reach.
- *Engagement KPIs to manage social media.* These are the easiest measures to collect, but the least valuable since they don't directly show contribution to business value. Although easy to collect, data is on interaction with social sites is often supplied separately by the owners of the different social presence and tools for managing social interaction. A new class of social analytics tools have been created to bring this data together. Figure 12.11 shows an example from the social media management tool Hootsuite where sharing of shortened URLs linking to different social media sites has driven traffic back to a main website. Direct traffic is where visitors click directly through from a social media messaging application like Hootsuite or Tweetdeck to the site.

A common question within social media is how to assess the value of a consumer connecting with a brand, by liking on Facebook, following on Twitter or placing a brand in a circle on Google+. Since the tracking of social media can't show what an individual does on the network, specific value is difficult to establish. Instead, what we can assess is the relative purchase rates of visitors from social media sites to websites compared to other channels, using measures like conversion rate and revenue per visitor.

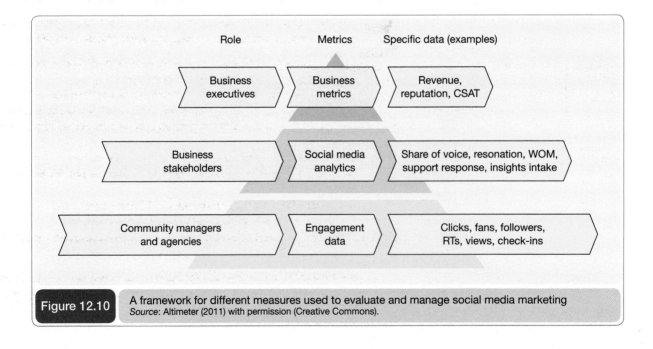

Figure 12.10	A framework for different measures used to evaluate and manage social media marketing

Source: Altimeter (2011) with permission (Creative Commons).

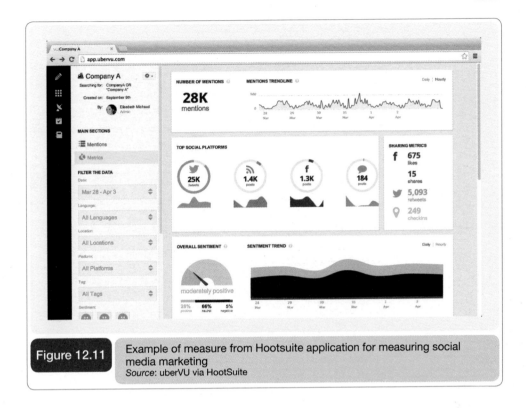

Figure 12.11	Example of measure from Hootsuite application for measuring social media marketing

Source: uberVU via HootSuite

Stage 3: Tools and techniques for collecting metrics and summarising results

Techniques to collect metrics include the collection of **site-visitor activity data** such as that collected from site log-files, the collection of metrics about outcomes such as online sales or email enquiries and traditional marketing research techniques such as questionnaires and focus groups which collect information on the customer's experience on the website.

Collecting site-visitor activity data

Site-visitor activity data captured in web analytics systems records the number of visitors on the site and the paths or clickstreams they take through the site as they visit different content. There is a wide variety of technical terms to describe these activity data which Internet marketers need to be conversant with.

Traditionally this information has been collected using a log-file analysis web analytics tool. The server-based log file is added to every time a user downloads a piece of information (a **hit**) and is analysed using a **log-file analyser**. Examples of transactions within a log file are:

www.davechaffey.com – [05/Oct/2012:00:00:49 -000] "GET/index.html HTTP/1.0" 200 33362

www.davechaffey.com – [05/Oct/2012:00:00:49 -000] "GET/logo.gif HTTP/1.0" 200 54342

Despite their wide use in the media, hits are not a useful measure of website effectiveness since if a page consists of 10 graphics, plus text, this is recorded as 11 hits. **Page impressions** or page views and **unique visitors** are better measures of site activity.

An example of visitor volume to a website using different measures based on real, representative data for one month is presented in Figure 12.12. You can see how hits are much higher than page views and unique visitors and are quite misleading in terms of the 'opportunities to

Site-visitor activity data
Information on content and services accessed by e-commerce site visitors.

Hit
Recorded for each graphic or text file requested from a web server. It is not a reliable measure for the number of people viewing a page.

Log-file analyser
A separate program such as Webtrends that is used to summarise the information on customer activity in a log file.

Page impression
A more reliable measure than a hit, denoting one person viewing one page.

Unique visitors
Individual visitors to a site measured through cookies or IP addresses on an individual computer.

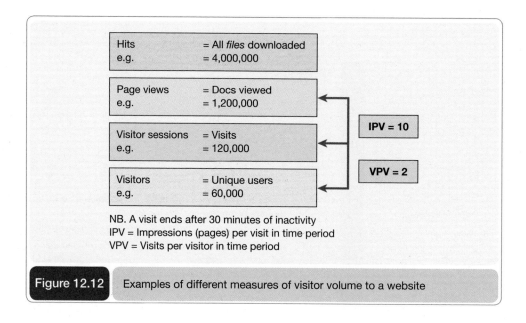

NB. A visit ends after 30 minutes of inactivity
IPV = Impressions (pages) per visit in time period
VPV = Visits per visitor in time period

| Figure 12.12 | Examples of different measures of visitor volume to a website |

see' a message. We can also learn from the ratio between some of these measures – the figure indicates:

- *Pages per visit (PPV)* – the average number of pages viewed per visitor to a site (this is indicative of engagement with a site since the longer a visitor stays on a 'sticky site', the higher this value will be). Duration on a site in minutes is inaccurate since this figure is skewed upwards by visitors who arrive on a site and are inactive before their session times out at 30 minutes.
- *Visits per (unique) visitor (VPV)* – this suggests the frequency of site visits. These data are reported for a month, during which time one would not expect many returning visitors. So it is often more relevant to present these data across a quarter or a year.

Other information giving detailed knowledge of customer behaviour that can be reported by any web analytics package include:

- Top pages.
- Entry and exit pages.
- Path or clickstream analysis showing the sequence of pages viewed.
- Country of visitor's origin (actually dependent on the location of their ISP).
- Browser and operating system used.
- Referring URL and domain (where the visitor came from).

Comparing apples to oranges?

With many different web analytics tools being used on different sites, it is important that there be standards for measuring visitor volumes. In particular, there are different techniques for measuring unique visitors which can be measured through IP addresses, but this is more accurate if it is combined with cookies and browser types. International standards bodies such as the IFABC (www.ifabc.org) and Web Analytics Association (www.webanalyticsassociation.org) and UK organisations such as ABC electronic (www.abce.org.uk) and JICWEBS (www.jicwebs.org) have worked to standardise the meaning of and data collection methods for different measures. See Table 12.5 or visit these sites for the latest precise definition of the terms in this section. Media buyers are particularly interested in accurate audited figures of media sites and organisations such as ABC electronic are important for this.

Table 12.5	Terminology for key website volume measures	

Measure	Measure	Definition
1 How many? (Audience reach)	Unique users	A unique and valid identifier [for a site visitor]. Sites may use (i) IP + user-agent, (ii) cookie and/or (iii) registration ID
2 How often? (Frequency metric)	Visit	A series of one or more PAGE IMPRESSIONS, served to one USER, which ends when there is a gap of 30 minutes or more between successive PAGE IMPRESSIONS for that USER
3 How busy? (Volume metric)	Page impression	A file, or combination of files, sent to a valid USER as a result of that USER's request being received by the server
4 What see?	Ad impressions	A file or a combination of files sent to a valid USER as an individual advertisement as a result of that USER's request being received by the server
5 What do?	Ad clicks	An AD IMPRESSION clicked on by a valid USER

Source: ABC electronic (www.abce.org.uk).

Collecting site outcome data

Site outcome data refer to a customer performing a significant action which is of value to the marketer. This is usually a transaction that is recorded. It involves more than downloading of a web page, and is proactive. Key marketing outcomes include:

- registration to site or subscriptions to an email newsletter;
- requests for further information such as a brochure or a request for a call-back from a customer service representative;
- responding to a promotion such as an online competition;
- a sale influenced by a visit to the site;
- a sale on-site.

When reviewing the efficiency of different e-communications tools referred to in Chapter 9, it is important to assess the outcomes generated. Measuring quantity of clickthroughs to a site is simplistic, it is conversion to these outcomes which should be used to assess the quality of traffic.

An important aspect of measures collected offline is that the marketing outcomes may be recorded in different media according to how the customer has performed mixed-mode buying. What we are really interested in is whether the website influenced the enquiry or sale. For all contact points with customers staff need to be instructed to ask how they found out about the company, or made their decision to buy. Although this is valuable information it is often intrusive, and a customer placing an order may be annoyed to be asked such a question. To avoid alienating the customer, these questions about the role of the website can be asked later, perhaps when the customer is filling in a registration or warranty card. Another device that can be used to identify use of the website is to use a specific phone number for customers coming from the website.

It will be apparent that to collect some of these measures we may need to integrate different information systems. Where customers provide details such as an email address and name in response to an offer, these are known as 'leads' and they may need to be passed on to a direct-sales team or recorded in a customer relationship management system. For full visibility of customer behaviour, the outcomes from these systems need to be integrated with the site-visitor activity data.

Selecting a web analytics tool

There is a bewildering range of hundreds of web analytics tools varying from shareware packages with often primitive reporting through to complex systems which may cost hundreds of thousands of dollars a year for a popular site. You can gain an idea of the range of tools by visiting the Web Analytics Demystified 'Vendor Discovery Tool' (www.webanalytics demystified.com/vendor_discovery_tool.asp) to find the tools used to monitor your sites or competitors' sites.

Given this, it is difficult for the Internet marketer to select the best tool or tools to meet their needs. One of the first issues to consider is the different types of measures that need to be integrated within the performance management system. Figure 12.13 gives an indication of the types of data that need to be integrated which include:

1 **Operational data.** Data would be ideally collected and reported within a single tool at this level, but unfortunately to obtain the best reporting it is often necessary to resort to four different types of tools or data source:
   - Referrer data from acquisition campaigns such as search marketing or online advertising. Separate tools are often also required for retention email marketing.
   - Site-centric data about visitor volume and clickstream behaviour.
   - Customer response and profile data.
   - Transactional data about leads and sales which are often obtained from separate legacy systems.
2 **Tactical data.** These data are typically models of required response such as:
   - Reach models with online audience share data for different demographic groupings from sources such as Hitwise and Netratings.
   - Lifetime-value models which are created to assess profitability of visitors to the site from different sources and so need to integrate with operational data.
3 **Strategic data.** Performance management systems for senior managers will give the big picture presented as scorecards or dashboards showing the contribution of digital channels to the organisation in terms of sales, revenue and profitability for different products. These data indicate trends and relative performance within the company and to competitors such that the Internet marketing strategy can be reviewed for effectiveness.

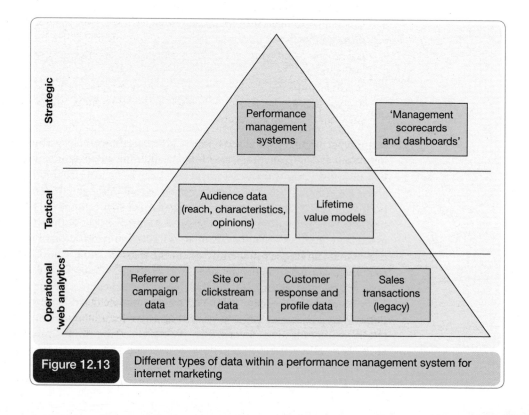

Figure 12.13 Different types of data within a performance management system for internet marketing

So an important requirement of a web analytics tool is that it should seek to integrate all these different data sources. The other main requirements of a web analytics tool to consider include:

- Reporting of marketing performance (many are technical tools which do not clearly report on results from a marketing perspective).
- Accuracy of technique.
- Analysis tools.
- Integration with other marketing information systems (export).
- Ease of use and configuration.
- Cost, which often varies according to site-visitor volumes and number of system users.
- Suitability for reporting on digital marketing campaigns.

Many online tracking tools were originally developed to report on the performance of the site and the pages accessed rather than specifically to report on digital marketing campaigns. It is therefore important that companies have an excellent campaign reporting capability, such as:

1 Can the tool track through from point of entry to site through to outcome such as site registration or sale? Integration with data to reflect actual leads or sales in a legacy system should also be reported.
2 Can the tool track and compare a range of online media types? For example, interactive (banner) ads, affiliates, email marketing, natural and paid search, explained in Chapter 8.
3 Can return-on-investment models be constructed? For example, by entering costs and profitability for each product?
4 Can reports be produced at both a detailed level and a summary level? This enables comparison of performance for different campaigns and different parts of the business.
5 Capability to track clickthroughs at an individual respondent level for email campaigns. This is important for follow-up marketing activities after an email list member has expressed interest in a product through clicking on a promotion link.
6 Are post-view responses tracked for ads? Cookies can be used to assess visitors who arrive on the site at a later point in time, rather than immediately.
7 Are post-click responses tracked for affiliates? Similarly, visitors from affiliates may buy the product not on their first visit, but on a later visit.
8 Do email campaign summaries give unique clicks as well as total clicks? If an email communication such as a newsletter contains multiple links, then total clicks will be higher.
9 Is real-time reporting available? Is immediate access to campaign performance data available?
10 Is cross-campaign and cross-product or content reporting available? Is it readily possible to compare campaigns and sales levels across different products or different parts of the site rather than an aggregate?

Accuracy is another an important aspect of web analytics tool. Perhaps the worst problems of log-file analysis are the problems of under-counting and over-counting. These are reviewed in Table 12.6.

A relatively new approach is to use the alternative *browser-based* or *tag-based* measurement system that records access to web pages every time a page is loaded into a user's web browser through running a short script, program or tag inserted into the web page. Potentially it is more accurate than server-based approaches for the reasons explained in Table 12.7. This approach usually runs as a hosted solution with the metrics recorded on a remote server. An example of the output reporting from a web analytics service is shown in Figure 12.14.

Internet-based market research
The use of online questionnaires and focus groups to assess customer perceptions of a website or broader marketing issues.

In addition to the quantitative web analytics measurement approaches discussed, traditional **marketing research** can be used to help determine the influence of the website and related communications on customer perception of the company and its products and services. The options for conducting survey research include interviews, questionnaires, focus groups and mystery shoppers. Each of these techniques can be conducted offline or online. The advantages and disadvantages of the different approaches are shown in Table 12.7.

Table 12.6   Inaccuracies caused by server-based log-file analysis

Sources of under-counting	Sources of over-counting
Caching in user's web browsers (when a user accesses a previously accessed file, it is loaded from the memory of the user's computer on a server-based cache on their PC)	Frames (a user viewing a framed page with three frames will be recorded as three page impressions or page views)
Caching on proxy servers (proxy servers are used within organisations or ISPs to reduce Internet traffic by storing copies of frequently used pages)	Spiders and robots (traversing of a site by spiders from different search engines is recorded as page impressions. These spiders can be excluded, but this is time-consuming)
Firewalls (these do not usually exclude page impressions, but they usually assign a single IP address for the user of the page, rather than referring to an individual's PC)	Executable files (these can also be recorded as hits or page impressions unless excluded)
Dynamically generated pages, generated 'on-the-fly', are difficult to assess with server-based log files	

Table 12.7   A comparison of different online metrics collection methods

Technique	Strengths	Weaknesses
1 **Server-based log-file analysis of site activity**	Directly records customer behaviour on-site plus where they were referred from Low cost	Not based around marketing outcomes such as leads, sales Size, even summaries may be over 50 pages long Doesn't directly record channel satisfaction Under-counting and over-counting Misleading unless interpreted carefully
2 **Browser-based site activity data**	Greater accuracy than server-based analysis Count all users, cf. panel approach	Relatively expensive method Similar weaknesses to server-based technique apart from accuracy Limited demographic information
3 **Panel activity and demographic data**	Provide competitor comparisons Give demographic profiling Avoid under-counting and over-counting	Depend on extrapolation from limited sample that may not be representative
4 **Outcome data**, e.g. enquiries, customer service emails	Record marketing outcomes	Difficulty of integrating data with other methods of data collection when collected manually or in other information systems
5 **Online questionnaires** Customers are prompted randomly – every nth customer or after customer activity or by email	Can record customer satisfaction and profiles Relatively cheap to create and analyse	Difficulty of recruiting respondents who complete accurately Sample bias – tend to be advocates or disgruntled customers who complete
6 **Online focus groups** Synchronous recording	Relatively cheap to create	Difficult to moderate and coordinate No visual cues, as from offline focus groups
7 **Mystery shoppers** Customers are recruited to evaluate the site, e.g. www. emysteryshopper.com	Structured tests give detailed feedback Also tests integration with other channels such as email and phone	Relatively expensive Sample must be representative

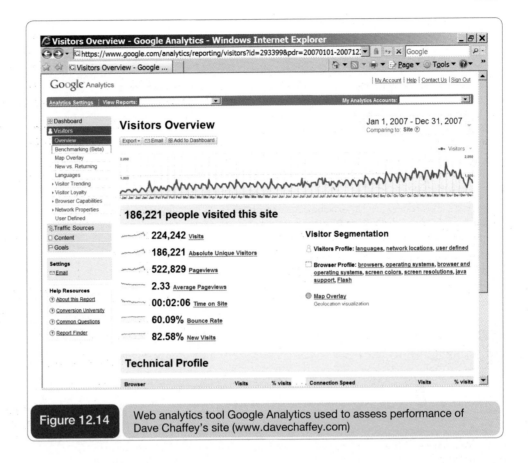

Figure 12.14	Web analytics tool Google Analytics used to assess performance of Dave Chaffey's site (www.davechaffey.com)

AB and multivariate testing

Often site owners and marketers reviewing the effectiveness of a site will disagree and the only method to be certain of the best-performing design or creative alternatives is through designing and running experiments to evaluate the best to use. Matt Round, then director of personalisation at Amazon, speaking at the E-metrics summit in 2004, said the Amazon philosophy, described further in Case study 12.1, is:

> **Data trumps intuition.**

AB testing and multivariate testing are two measurement techniques that can be used to review design effectiveness to improve results.

AB testing

A/B or AB testing
Refers to testing two different versions of a page or a page element such as a heading, image or button for effectiveness.

Control page
The page against which subsequent optimisation will be assessed. Typically a current landing page.

In its simplest form, **A/B or AB testing** refers to testing two different versions of a page or a page element such as a heading, image or button. Some members of the site are served alternately with the visitors to the page randomly split between the two pages. Hence it is sometimes called 'live split testing'. The goal is to increase page or site effectiveness against key performance indicators including clickthrough rate, conversion rates and revenue per visit.

When completing AB testing it is important to identify a realistic baseline or **control page** (or audience sample) to compare against. This will typically be an existing landing page. Two new alternatives can be compared to previous control, which is known as an ABC test. Different variables are then applied as in Table 12.8.

An example of the power of AB testing is an experiment Skype performed on their main topbar navigation, where they found that changing the main menu options 'Call Phones', to 'Skype Credit' and 'Shop' to 'Accessories' gave an increase of 18.75% revenue per visit (Skype were speaking at the 2007 E-metrics summit). That's significant when you have hundreds of millions of visitors! It also shows the importance of being direct with navigation and simply describing the offer available rather than the activity.

Table 12.8	AB test example	
Test	**A (Control)**	**B (Test page)**
Test 1	Original page	New headline, existing button, existing body copy
Test 2	Original page	Existing headline, new button, existing body copy
Test 3	Original page	Existing headline, existing button, new body copy

Multivariate testing

Multivariate testing is a more sophisticated form of AB testing which enables simultaneous testing of pages for different combinations of page elements that are being tested. This enables selection of the most effective combination of design elements to achieve the desired goal.

An example of a multivariate test is shown in Mini case study 12.1.

Mini Case Study 12.1   **Multivariate testing at National Express Group increases conversion rate**

The National Express Group is the leading provider of travel solutions in the UK. Around 1 billion journeys a year are made worldwide on National Express Group's bus, train, light rail and express coach and airport operations. A significant proportion of ticket bookings are made online through the company's website at www.nationalexpress.com.

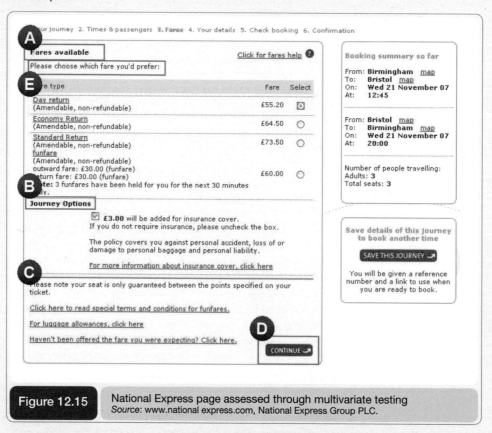

Figure 12.15	National Express page assessed through multivariate testing
	Source: www.national express.com, National Express Group PLC.

The company used multivariate testing provider Maxymiser to run an experiment to improve conversion rate of a fare selection page which was the penultimate step in booking (Figure 12.15). The analysis team identified a number of subtle alterations to content (labelled A to E) and calls to action on the page with the aim of stimulating visitor engagement and driving a higher percentage of visitors through to successful conversion without changing the structure of the page or National Express brand identity. In order to aid more effective up-sell to insurance add-ons, changes to this call to action were also proposed.

It was decided that a multivariate test would be the most effective approach to determine the best-performing combination of content. The variants jointly developed by Maxymiser and the client were tested with all live site visitors and the conversion rate of each combination monitored. They tried 3,500 possible page combinations and during the live test the underperforming combinations were taken out to maximise conversion rates at every stage.

At the end of the testing period, after reaching statistical validity, results showed that the best combination of elements showed a 14.11% increase in conversion rates for the page, i.e. 14.11% more visitors were sent through to the fourth and final step in the registration process, immediately hitting bottom line revenue for National Express (Figure 12.16).

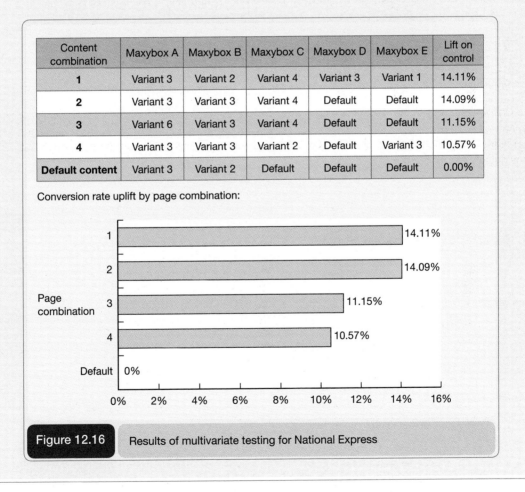

Content combination	Maxybox A	Maxybox B	Maxybox C	Maxybox D	Maxybox E	Lift on control
1	Variant 3	Variant 2	Variant 4	Variant 3	Variant 1	14.11%
2	Variant 3	Variant 3	Variant 4	Default	Default	14.09%
3	Variant 6	Variant 3	Variant 4	Default	Default	11.15%
4	Variant 3	Variant 3	Variant 2	Default	Variant 3	10.57%
Default content	Variant 3	Variant 2	Default	Default	Default	0.00%

Conversion rate uplift by page combination:

- 1 — 14.11%
- 2 — 14.09%
- 3 — 11.15%
- 4 — 10.57%
- Default — 0%

Page combination (0% 2% 4% 6% 8% 10% 12% 14% 16%)

Figure 12.16   Results of multivariate testing for National Express

Clickstream analysis and visitor segmentation

Clickstream analysis refers to detailed analysis of visitor behaviour in order to diagnose problems and opportunities. Table 12.9 gives an indication of the type of questions asked by web analyst Dave Chaffey (www.davechaffey.com) when reviewing clients' sites.

Table 12.9	A summary of how an analyst will interpret web analytics data. GA is terminology for Google Analytics (www.google.com/analytics), one of the most widely used tools

Analyst question	Typical web analytics report terminology	Diagnosis of analyst used to improve performance
How successful is the site at achieving engagement and outcomes?	Conversion goals (GA) Bounce rates (GA) Pages/visit (GA)	• Is engagement and conversion consistent with other sites in the sector? • What are maximum engagement and conversion rates from different referrers?
Where are visitors entering the site?	Top entry pages Top landing pages (GA)	• How important is home page compared to other page categories and landing pages? Does page popularity reflect product popularity? • Check that messaging and calls to action are effective on these pages • Assess source of traffic, in particular keywords from search engines and apply elsewhere
What are sources of visitors (referrers)?	Referrers Traffic sources Filters set up to segment visitors	• Are the full range of digital media channels relevant for a company represented? • Is the level of search engine traffic consistent with the brand reputation? • What are the main link partners driving free traffic (potential for more)?
What is the most popular content?	Top content (GA)	• Is page popularity as expected? Are there problems with findability caused by navigation labelling? • Which content is most likely to influence visitors to outcome? • Which content is most popular with returning visitors segment?
Which are the most popular findability methods?	Site search (GA)	• How popular are different forms of navigation, e.g. top menu, sidebar menus? • What are the most popular searches? Where do searches tend to start? Are they successfully finding content or converting to sale?
Where do visitors leave the site?	Top exit pages (GA)	• Are these as expected (home page, About Us page, transaction completion)? • Are there error pages (e.g. 404 not found) which cause visitors to leave?
Which clickstreams are taken?	Path analysis Top paths (GA)	• How can attrition in conversion funnels be improved? • What does forward path analysis show are the most effective calls to action? • What does reverse path analysis indicate about the pages which influence sale?

Path analysis

Aggregate clickstreams are usually known within web analytics software as 'forward' or 'reverse' paths. This is a fairly advanced form of analysis, but the principle is straightforward – you seek to learn from the most popular paths.

Viewed at an aggregate level across the site through 'top paths' type reports, this doesn't appear particularly useful as the top paths are often:

- Home page: Exit
- Home page: Contact Us: Exit
- News page: Exit

Forward path analysis

Reviews the combinations of clicks that occur from a page. This form of analysis is most beneficial from important pages such as the home page, product and directory pages. Use this technique to identify: messaging/navigation combinations which work best to yield the most clicks from a page.

Reverse path analysis

Indicates the most popular combination of pages and/or calls to action which lead to a page. This is particularly useful for transactional pages such as the first checkout page on a consumer site; a lead-generation or 'contact us' page on a business-to-business site; an email subscription page or a call-me-back option.

Clickstream analysis becomes more actionable when the analyst reviews clickstreams in the context of a single page – this is **forward path analysis** or **reverse path analysis**.

On-site search effectiveness

On-site search is another crucial part of clickstream analysis since it is a key way of finding content, so a detailed search analysis will pay dividends. Key search metrics to consider are:

- Number of searches.
- Average number of searches per visitor or searcher.
- % of searches returning zero results.
- % of site exits from search results.
- % of returned searches clicked.
- % of returned searches resulting in conversion to sale or other outcome.
- Most popular search terms – individual keyword and keyphrases.

Visitor segmentation

Segmentation is a fundamental marketing approach, but it is often difficult within web analytics to relate customer segments to web behaviour because the web analytics data aren't integrated with customer or purchase data, although this is possible in the most advanced systems such as Omniture, Visual Sciences and WebTrends.

However, all analytics systems have a capability for segmentation and it is possible to create specific filters or profiles to help understand one type of site visitor behaviour. Examples include:

- First-time visitors or returning visitors
- Visitors from different referrer types including:
  - Google natural
  - Google paid
  - Strategic search keyphrases, brand keyphrases, etc.
  - Display advertising
- Converters against non-converters
- Geographic segmentation by country or region (based on IP addresses)
- Type of content accessed, e.g. are some segments more likely to convert? For example, speaking at Ad Tech London '06, MyTravel reported that they segment visitors into:
  - Site flirt (2 pages or less)
  - Site browse (2 pages or more)
  - Saw search results
  - Saw quote
  - Saw payment details
  - Saw booking confirmation details.

Budgeting

To estimate profitability and return on investment of e-channels as part of budgeting, companies need to consider both tangible and intangible costs and benefits. A suggested checklist of these is shown in Box 12.4.

A similar approach can be used to calculating the ROI of enhancements to an e-commerce site. Hanson (2000) suggests an approach to this which requires identification of revenue from the site, costs from site and costs from supporting it via a call centre. These are related to profit as follows:

Operating profit = Net income from sales − E-commerce site costs − Call-centre costs

Net income from sales = (Product price − Unit cost) × Sales − Fixed product costs

$$E\text{-}commerce\ site\ costs = Site\ fixed\ costs + ((\%\ site\ support\ contacts) \times$$
$$Cost\ site\ support\ contact \times Sales)$$

$$Call\text{-}centre\ (CC)\ costs = CC\ fixed\ costs + ((\%\ CC\ support\ contacts) \times$$
$$Cost\ CC\ support\ contact \times Sales)$$

Box 12.4	Suggested worksheet for calculating return on investment for an e-commerce site

Tangible business benefits

1 Reduced costs
   (a) Promotional materials, including catalogues – creative, printing, paper, distribution
   (b) Product support materials – creation, printing, paper, distribution
   (c) Lower infrastructure or communication costs – fewer outbound calls required
   (d) Support staff savings
   (e) Sales staff savings
   (f) Order inaccuracies
   (g) Lower cost of supporting channel
2 Increased revenue
   (a) New sales to new geo-demographic segments
   (b) Penetration/retention/repeat orders
   (c) Cross-sales to existing purchasers
   (d) Penetration/cross-sales to new purchasers in an organisation

Intangible business benefits

3 Faster time to market
   • Reduce product introduction by n weeks
4 Improved customer satisfaction/brand equity
   • How does this affect retention?

Tangible costs

1 Physical costs
   (a) Hardware, software
   (b) Network costs
2 Planning costs
3 Implementation costs
   (a) Project management
   (b) Software development, testing
   (c) Data migration
   (d) Training
   (e) Promotion (online and offline)
4 Operational costs
   (a) Hardware and software maintenance
   (b) Network maintenance
   (c) Technical staff costs
   (d) Content maintenance staff costs
   (e) Support staff costs
   (f) Management staff costs
   (g) Ongoing promotional costs (online and offline)

Source: This worksheet was originally based on White Paper 'A Return on Investment Guide for Business-to-Business Internet Commerce' provided by e-commerce solution provider Openmarket (www.openmarket.com).

Different approaches for estimating costs are recommended by Bayne (1997):

- *Last year's Internet marketing budget.* This is assuming the site has been up and running for some time.
- *Percentage of company sales.* It is again difficult to establish this for the first iteration of a site.
- *Percentage of total marketing budget.* This is a common approach. Typically the percentage will start small (less than 5%, or even 1%), but will rise as the impact of the Internet increases.
- *Reallocation of marketing dollars.* The money for digital marketing will often be taken by cutting back other marketing activities.
- *What other companies in your industry are spending.* This is definitely necessary in order to assess and meet competitive threats, but competitors may be over-investing.
- *Creating an effective online presence.* In this model of 'paying whatever it takes', a company spends sufficient money to create a website which is intended to achieve their objectives. This may be a costly option, but for industries in which the Internet is having a significant impact, it may be the wise option. A larger than normal marketing budget will be necessary to achieve this.
- *A graduated plan tied into measurable results.* This implies an ongoing programme in which investment each year is tied into achieving the results established in a measurement programme.
- *A combination of approaches.* Since the first budget will be based on many intangibles it is best to use several methods and present high, medium and low expenditure options for executives with expected results related to costs.

As a summary to this section, complete Activity 12.4.

Activity 12.4	Creating a measurement plan for a B2C company

Purpose

To develop skills in selecting appropriate techniques for measuring digital business effectiveness.

Activity

This activity acts as a summary to this section on digital business measurement. Review Table 12.10 and assess the frequency with which metrics in each of the following categories should be reported for a sell-side e-commerce site and acted upon. For each column, place an R in the column for the frequency with which you think the data should be recorded.

Table 12.10	Alternative timescales for reporting e-commerce site performance

	Promotion	Behaviour	Satisfaction	Outcomes	Profitability
Hour					
Day					
Week					
Month					
Quarter					
Re-launch					

Answers to activities can be found at www.pearsoned.co.uk/chaffey

In Chapter 1, we started this book with a case study of the world's largest digital business retailer. We conclude with a case of the world's second largest e-retailer, showing how the culture of test, learn, refine is key to their success.

Context

Why a case study on Amazon? Surely everyone knows about who Amazon are and what they do? Yes, well, that may be true, but this case goes beyond the surface to review innovations in Amazon's business and revenue model based on a historical review from their published annual reports (United States SEC filings).

Like eBay, Amazon.com was born in 1995. The name reflected the vision of Jeff Bezos to produce a large-scale phenomenon like the River Amazon. This ambition has proved justified since, just 8 years later, Amazon passed the $5 billion sales mark – it took Wal-Mart 20 years to achieve this.

Vision and strategy

On their investor relations site Amazon describe their current mission:

We seek to be Earth's most customer-centric company for four primary customer sets: consumers, sellers, enterprises, and content creators.

This is now a generic statement, but previous statements such as that from SEC filings in 2008 are more specific:

Relentlessly focus on customer experience by offering our customers low prices, convenience, and a wide selection of merchandise.

Consider how these core marketing messages summarising the Amazon online value proposition are communicated both on-site and through offline communications.

Of course, achieving customer loyalty and repeat purchases has been key to Amazon's success. Many dot-coms failed because they succeeded in achieving awareness, but not loyalty. Amazon achieved both. In their latest SEC filing for their 2013 Annual Report they stress how they seek to achieve this by reiterating a comment in a letter made by Jeff Bezos to shareholders in 1997 when it first became a publicly quoted company:

We will continue to measure our programs and the effectiveness of our investments analytically, to jettison those that do not provide acceptable returns, and to step up our investment in those that work best. We

will continue to learn from both our successes and our failures.

More recently, this approach has been applied to a range of business model innovations including: Fire TV, smartphone and tablets, grocery delivery in the West coast of the United States, Prime Instant Video, Amazon Fashion and expansion to Amazon Web services (AWS).

In practice, as is the case for many online retailers, the lowest prices are for the most popular products, with less popular products commanding higher prices and a greater margin for Amazon. Free shipping offers are used to encourage increase in basket size since customers have to spend over a certain amount to receive free shipping. The level at which free shipping is set is critical to profitability and Amazon has changed it as competition has changed and for promotional reasons.

Amazon communicates the fulfilment promise in several ways including presentation of latest inventory availability information, delivery date estimates, and options for expedited delivery, as well as delivery shipment notifications and update facilities.

This focus on the customer has translated to excellence in service with the 2004 American Customer Satisfaction Index giving Amazon.com a score of 88, which was at the time the highest customer satisfaction score ever recorded in any service industry, online or offline.

Round (2004) notes that Amazon focuses on customer satisfaction metrics. Each site is closely monitored with standard service availability monitoring (for example, using Keynote or Mercury Interactive) site availability and download speed. Interestingly, it also monitors per-minute site revenue upper/lower bounds – Round describes an alarm system rather like a power plant where if revenue on a site falls below $10,000 per minute, alarms go off! There are also internal performance service level agreements for web services where T% of the time, different pages must return in X seconds.

Competition

In its SEC (2005) filing Amazon describes the environment for its products and services as 'intensely competitive'. It views its main current and potential competitors as: (1) physical-world retailers, catalogue retailers, publishers, vendors, distributors and manufacturers of products, many of which possess significant brand awareness, sales volume and customer bases, and some of which currently sell, or may sell, products or services through the Internet, mail-order or direct marketing; (2) other online e-commerce sites; (3) a number of indirect competitors, including media companies, web portals, comparison shopping websites, and web search engines, either directly or in collaboration with other retailers; and (4) companies that provide e-commerce services, including website development, third-party fulfilment and customer service.

It believes the main competitive factors in its market segments include 'selection, price, availability, convenience, information, discovery, brand recognition, personalised services, accessibility, customer service, reliability, speed of fulfillment, ease of use, and ability to adapt to changing conditions, as well as our customers' overall experience and trust in transactions with us and facilitated by us on behalf of third-party sellers'.

For services offered to business and individual sellers, additional competitive factors include the quality of their services and tools, their ability to generate sales for third parties they serve, and the speed of performance for their services.

From auctions to marketplaces

Amazon auctions (known as zShops) were first launched in March 1999, in large part as a response to the success of eBay. They were promoted heavily from the home page, category pages and individual product pages. Despite this, a year after launch they had only achieved a 3.2% share of the online auction compared to 58% for eBay and it only declined from this point.

Today, competitive prices of products are available through third-party sellers in the 'Amazon Marketplace' which are integrated within the standard product listings. The strategy to offer such an auction facility was initially driven by the need to compete with eBay, but now the strategy has been adjusted such that Amazon describes it as part of the approach of low pricing.

Although it might be thought that Amazon would lose out on enabling its merchants to sell products at lower prices, in fact Amazon makes greater margin on these sales since merchants are charged a commission on each sale and it is the merchant who bears the cost of storing inventory and fulfilling the product to customers. As with eBay, Amazon is just facilitating the exchange of bits and bytes between buyers and sellers without the need to distribute physical products.

How 'the culture of metrics' started

A common theme in Amazon's development is the drive to use a measured approach to all aspects of the business,

beyond the finance. Marcus (2004) describes an occasion at a corporate 'boot-camp' in January 1997 when Amazon CEO Jeff Bezos 'saw the light':

> 'At Amazon, we will have a Culture of Metrics,' he said while addressing his senior staff. He went on to explain how web-based business gave Amazon an 'amazing window into human behavior.' Marcus says: 'Gone were the fuzzy approximations of focus groups, the anecdotal fudging and smoke blowing from the marketing department. A company like Amazon could (and did) record every move a visitor made, every last click and twitch of the mouse. As the data piled up into virtual heaps, hummocks and mountain ranges, you could draw all sorts of conclusions about their chimerical nature, the consumer. In this sense, Amazon was not merely a store, but an immense repository of facts. All we needed were the right equations to plug into them.'

James Marcus then goes on to give a fascinating insight into a breakout group discussion of how Amazon could better use measures to improve its performance. Marcus was in the Bezos group, brainstorming customer-centric metrics. Marcus (2004) summarises the dialogue, led by Bezos:

> 'First, we figure out which things we'd like to measure on the site,' he said. 'For example, let's say we want a metric for customer enjoyment. How could we calculate that?'
>
> There was silence. Then somebody ventured: 'How much time each customer spends on the site?'
>
> 'Not specific enough,' Jeff said.
>
> 'How about the average number of minutes each customer spends on the site per session,' someone else suggested. 'If that goes up, they're having a blast.'
>
> 'But how do we factor in purchase?' I [Marcus] said feeling proud of myself. 'Is that a measure of enjoyment?'
>
> 'I think we need to consider frequency of visits, too,' said a dark-haired woman I didn't recognize. 'Lot of folks are still accessing the web with those creepy-crawly modems. Four short visits from them might be just as good as one visit from a guy with a T-1. Maybe better.'
>
> 'Good point,' Jeff said. 'And anyway, enjoyment is just the start. In the end, we should be measuring customer ecstasy.'

It is interesting that Amazon was having this debate about the elements of RFM analysis (described in Chapter 9) in 1997, after already having achieved $16 million of revenue in the previous year. Of course, this is a miniscule amount compared with today's billions of dollar turnover. The important point was that this was the start of a focus on metrics which can be seen through the description of Matt Round's work later in this case study.

In their 2013 Annual report Amazon explained their ongoing approach to experimentation. They explain how they have created their own internal experimentation platform called 'Weblab' which they use to evaluate improvements to their websites and products. In 2013 they ran 1,976 Weblabs worldwide, up from 1,092 in 2012, and 546 in 2011. One recent example of how they are applied is a new feature called 'Ask an owner'. From a product page, customers can ask any question related to the product, and Amazon route these questions to owners of the product who then supply an answer.

From human to software-based recommendations

Amazon has developed internal tools to support this 'culture of metrics'. Marcus (2004) describes how the 'Creator Metrics' tool shows content creators how well their product listings and product copy are working. For each content editor such as Marcus, it retrieves all recently posted documents including articles, interviews, booklists and features. For each one it then gives a conversion rate to sale plus the number of page views, adds (added to basket) and repels (content requested, but the back button then used). In time, the work of editorial reviewers such as Marcus was marginalised since Amazon found that the majority of visitors used the search tools rather than read editorials and they responded to the personalised recommendations as the matching technology improved (Marcus likens early recommendation techniques to 'going shopping with the village idiot').

Experimentation and testing at Amazon

The 'culture of metrics' also led to a test-driven approach to improving results at Amazon. Matt Round, speaking at E-metrics 2004 when he was director of personalisation at Amazon, describes the philosophy as '*data trumps intuitions*'. He explained how Amazon used to have a lot of arguments about which content and promotion should go on the all-important home page or category pages. He described how every category VP wanted top-centre and how the Friday meetings about placements for next week were getting 'too long, too loud, and lacked performance data'.

But today 'automation replaces intuitions' and real-time experimentation tests are always run to answer these questions since actual consumer behaviour is the best way to decide upon tactics.

Marcus (2004) also notes that Amazon has a culture of experiments, of which A/B tests are key components. Examples where A/B tests are used include new home page design, moving features around the page, different algorithms for recommendations, changing search relevance rankings. These involve testing a new treatment against a previous control for a limited time of a few days or a week. The system will randomly show one or more treatments to visitors and measure a range of parameters such as units sold and revenue by category (and total), session time, session length, etc. The new features will usually be launched if the desired metrics are statistically significantly better. Statistical tests are a challenge though, as distributions are not normal (they have a large mass at zero, for example, of no purchase). There are other challenges since multiple A/B tests are running every day and A/B tests may overlap and so conflict. There are also longer-term effects where some features are 'cool' for the first two weeks and the opposite effect where changing navigation may degrade performance temporarily. Amazon also finds that as its users evolve in their online experience the way they act online has changed. This means that Amazon has to constantly test and evolve its features.

Technology

It follows that the Amazon technology infrastructure must readily support this culture of experimentation and this can be difficult to achieve with standardised content management. Amazon has achieved its competitive advantage through developing its technology internally and with a significant investment in this which may not be available to other organisations without the right focus on the online channels.

Round (2004) describes the technology approach as 'distributed development and deployment'. Pages such as the home page have a number of content 'pods' or 'slots' which call web services for features. This makes it relatively easy to change the content in these pods and even change the location of the pods on-screen. Amazon uses a flowable or fluid page design, unlike many sites, which enables it to make the most of real estate on-screen.

Data-driven automation

Round (2004) said that 'data is king at Amazon'. He gave many examples of data-driven automation including customer channel preferences, managing the way content is displayed to different user types such as new releases and top-sellers, merchandising and recommendation (showing related products and promotions) and also advertising through paid search (automatic ad generation and bidding).

The automated search advertising and bidding system for paid search has had a big impact at Amazon. Sponsored links were initially done by humans, but this was unsustainable due to the range of products at Amazon. The automated programme generates keywords, writes ad creative, determines best landing page, manages bids, and measures conversion rates, profit per converted visitor and updates bids. Again the problem of volume is there: Matt Round described how the book *How to Make Love Like a Porn Star* by Jenna Jameson received tens of thousands of clicks from pornography-related searches, but few actually purchased the book. So the update cycle must be quick to avoid large losses.

There is also an automated email measurement and optimisation system. The campaign calendar used to be manually managed with relatively weak measurement and it was costly to schedule and use. A new system:

- automatically optimises content to improve customer experience;
- avoids sending an email campaign that has low clickthrough or high unsubscribe rate;
- includes inbox management (avoid sending multiple emails/per week);
- has a growing library of automated email programmes covering new releases and recommendations;
- but there are challenges if promotions are too successful and inventory isn't available.

Your recommendations

'Customers Who Bought X . . . also bought Y' is Amazon's signature feature. Round (2004) describes how Amazon relies on acquiring and then crunching a massive amount of data. Every purchase, every page viewed and every search is recorded. So there are now two new versions: 'Customers who shopped for X also shopped for Y' and 'Customers who searched for X also bought Y'. They also have a system codenamed 'Goldbox' which is a cross-sell and awareness-raising tool. Items are discounted to encourage purchases in new categories!

He also describes the challenge of techniques for sifting patterns from noise (sensitivity filtering) and clothing and toy catalogues change frequently so recommendations become out of date. The main challenges though are the massive data size arising from millions of customers, millions of items and recommendations made in real time.

Partnership strategy

As Amazon grew, its share price growth enabled partnership or acquisition with a range of companies in different sectors. Marcus (2004) describes how Amazon partnered with Drugstore.com (pharmacy), Living.com, Pets.com (pet supplies), Wineshopper.com (wines), HomeGrocer.com (groceries), Sothebys.com (auctions) and Kozmo.com (urban home delivery). In most cases, Amazon purchased an equity stake in these partners, so that it would share in their prosperity. It also charged them fees for placements on the Amazon site to promote and drive traffic to their sites. Similarly, Amazon charged publishers for prime position to promote books on its site which caused an initial hue and cry, but this abated when it was realised that paying for prominent placements was widespread in traditional booksellers and supermarkets. Many of these new online companies failed in 1999 and 2000, but Amazon had covered the potential for growth and was not pulled down by these partners, even though for some, such as Pets. com, it had an investment of 50%.

Analysts sometimes refer to 'Amazoning a sector', meaning that one company becomes dominant in an online sector such as book retail such that it becomes very difficult for others to achieve market share. In addition to developing, communicating and delivering a very strong proposition, Amazon has been able to consolidate its strength in different sectors through its partnership arrangements and through using technology to facilitate product promotion and distribution via these partnerships. The Amazon retail platform enables other retailers to sell products online using the Amazon user interface and infrastructure through their 'Syndicated Stores' programme. Similarly, in the US, Borders, a large book retailer, uses the Amazon merchant platform for distributing its products. Toy retailer Toys R Us has a similar arrangement. Such partnerships help Amazon extend its reach into the customer base of other suppliers, and of course, customers who buy in one category such as books can be encouraged to purchase from other areas such as clothing or electronics.

Another form of partnership referred to above is the Amazon Marketplace which enables Amazon customers and other retailers to sell their new and used books and other goods alongside the regular retail listings. A similar partnership approach is the Amazon 'Merchants@' programme which enables third-party merchants (typically larger than those who sell via the Amazon Marketplace) to sell their products via Amazon. Amazon earns fees either as fixed fees or as sales commissions per unit. This arrangement can help customers who get a wider choice of products from a range of suppliers with the convenience of purchasing them through a single checkout process.

Finally, Amazon has also facilitated formation of partnerships with smaller companies through its affiliates programme. Internet legend records that Jeff Bezos, the creator of Amazon, was chatting at a cocktail party to someone who wanted to sell books about divorce via her website. Subsequently, Amazon.com launched its Associates Program in July 1996 and it is still going strong. Amazon does not use an affiliate network, which would take commissions from sale, but, thanks to the strength of its brand, has developed its own affiliate programme. Amazon has created tiered performance-based incentives to encourage affiliates to sell more Amazon products.

Marketing communications

In their SEC filings Amazon typically states that the aims of their communications strategy are (unsurprisingly) to:

1　Increase customer traffic to their websites.
2　Create awareness of their products and services.
3　Promote repeat purchases.
4　Develop incremental product and service revenue opportunities.
5　Strengthen and broaden the Amazon.com brand name.

Amazon also believes that their most effective marketing communications are a consequence of their focus on continuously improving the customer experience. This then creates word-of-mouth promotion which is effective in acquiring new customers and may also encourage repeat-customer visits.

As well as this, Marcus (2004) describes how Amazon used the personalisation enabled through technology to reach out to a difficult-to-reach market which Bezos originally called 'the hard middle'. Bezos's view was that it was easy to reach 10 people (you called them on the phone) or the 10 million people who bought the most popular products (you placed a Super Bowl ad), but more difficult to reach those in between. The search facilities in the search engine and on the Amazon site, together with its product recommendation features, meant that Amazon could connect its products with the interests of these people.

Online advertising techniques include paid-search marketing, interactive ads on portals, email campaigns and search engine optimisation. These are automated as far as possible as described earlier in the case study. As previously mentioned, the affiliate programme is also important in driving visitors to Amazon and Amazon offers a wide range of methods of linking to its site to help improve conversion. For example, affiliates can use straight text links leading direct to a product page and they also offer a range of dynamic banners which feature different content such as books about Internet marketing or a search box.

Amazon also uses cooperative advertising arrangements, better known as 'contra-deals', with some vendors and other third parties. For example, a print advertisement in 2005 for a particular product such as a wireless router with a free wireless laptop card promotion was to feature a specific Amazon URL in the ad. In product fulfilment packs, Amazon may include a leaflet for a non-competing online company such as Figleaves. com (lingerie) or Expedia (travel). In return, Amazon leaflets may be included in customer communications from the partner brands.

Amazon's associates programme directs customers to its websites by enabling independent websites to make millions of products available to its audiences with fulfilment performed by Amazon or third parties. It pays commissions to hundreds of thousands of participants in its associates programme when its customer referrals result in product sales.

In addition, it offers everyday free shipping options worldwide and recently announced Amazon.com Prime in the US, its first membership programme in which members receive free two-day shipping and discounted overnight shipping. Although marketing expenses do not include the costs of free shipping or promotional offers, it views such offers as effective marketing tools.

Source: *Internet Retailer* (2004); Marcus (2004); Round (2004); SEC (2005) filings of Annual Reports from 2013.

Questions

1　By referring to the case study, Amazon's website for your country and your experience of Amazon offline communications, evaluate how well Amazon communicates its core proposition and promotional offers.
2　Using the case study, characterise Amazon's approach to marketing communications.
3　Explain what distinguishes Amazon in its uses of technology for competitive advantage.
4　How does the Amazon 'culture of metrics' differ from that in other organisations from your experience?

Summary

1   Implementation is an iterative process of managing changes involving analysis, design, testing and review as part of an evolutionary prototyping process.

2   Maintenance is a continuous process of monitoring, assessing required changes and then implanting them using evolutionary prototyping.

3   Simple web pages are developed in static HTML. Most digital business systems require dynamic pages that are implemented using client- and server-side scripting, of which the most popular are JavaScript and ASP.

4   Testing has two main objectives: first, to check for non-conformance with the business and user requirements and, second, to identify bugs or errors. There are many specialised techniques to test either part of the system (component testing) or all of the system (system testing).

5   Changeover has to be managed to include elements of piloting, phased implementation, immediate cutover and parallel running.

6   Content management requires a clearly defined update process and responsibilities according to different types of changes required.

7   Measurement also requires process and responsibilities and also a measurement framework. A suggested framework for sell-side e-commerce assesses channel promotion, channel behaviour, channel satisfaction, channel outcomes and channel profitability. Selection of appropriate web analytics tools is important to assess the effectiveness of e-commerce.

Exercises

Self-assessment questions

1   Summarise how the activities involved with implementation and maintenance relate to analysis and design activities in previous chapters.

2   What are the risks of launching a new e-commerce site if implementation is not conducted effectively?

3   Distinguish between static and dynamic content and methods of achieving them.

4   What are the objectives of testing? How do these relate to an e-commerce site?

5   Summarise the advantages and disadvantages of the different changeover methods.

6   What are the issues for managers of content management?

7   What are the main elements of an e-commerce site measurement plan?

8   What are the elements of a budget for an e-commerce site enhancement?

Essay and discussion questions

1   Write a report to a manager recommending particular techniques that should or should not be implemented on an e-commerce site. Examples may include frames, Flash or Shockwave plug-ins, JavaScript, Java and active server pages.

2   Develop a plan for measuring the marketing effectiveness of an e-commerce site.

3   Discuss the balance of using a website and traditional methods for marketing research.

4   Choose an example of a simple brochureware website. Develop an implementation plan for this site, recommending development techniques that will be used to enhance the site.

Examination questions

1 You are developing a testing plan for an e-commerce site. Outline five key aspects of the site you would test.

2 Data migration is often overlooked in implementation planning. Explain what data migration is and explain when it may need to occur for creation of an e-commerce site for an existing business.

3 Analyse the advantages and disadvantages of a soft versus hard website launch.

4 Explain the following terms and suggest which is the most useful in measuring the effectiveness of a website.

   (a) hit

   (b) page impression

   (c) site visit.

5 Why are conversion and attrition rates important in evaluating the performance of an e-commerce site?

6 Suggest three key measures that indicate the contribution of an e-commerce site to overall business performance for a company with online and offline presence.

References

1to1 Media (2008) The Time for Cross-Channel Measurement Is Now, Article by Kevin Zimmerman, 22 September.

Adams, C., Kapashi, N., Neely, A. and Marr, B. (2000) Managing with measures. Measuring ebusiness performance. *Accenture White Paper*. Survey conducted in conjunction with Cranfield School of Management.

Agrawal, V., Arjana, V. and Lemmens, R. (2001) E-performance: the path to rational exuberance. *McKinsey Quarterly*, no. 1, 31–43.

Altimeter (2011) Framework: The Social Media ROI Pyramid. By Jeremiah Owyang, 13 December, 2010: **www.web-strategist.com/blog/2010/12/13/framework-the-social-media-roi-pyramid**.

Bayne, K. (1997) *The Internet Marketing Plan*. John Wiley & Sons, New York.

Bocij, P., Chaffey, D., Greasley, A. and Hickie, S. (2005) *Business Information Systems: Technology, Development and Management*, 3rd edn. Financial Times Prentice Hall, Harlow.

Bourne, M., Mills, J., Willcox, M., Neely, A. and Platts, K. (2000) Designing, implementing and updating performance measurement systems. *International Journal of Operations and Production Management*, 20(7), 754–71.

Chaffey, D. (2000) Achieving Internet marketing success. *Marketing Review*, 1(1), 35–60.

Chaffey, D. and Wood, S. (2005) *Business Information Management: Improving Performance Using Information Systems*. Financial Times Prentice Hall, Harlow.

Chaffey, D., Mayer, R., Johnston, K. and Ellis-Chadwick, F. (2009) *Internet Marketing: Strategy, Implementation and Practice*, 4th edn. Financial Times Prentice Hall, Harlow.

Friedman, L. and Furey, T. (1999) *The Channel Advantage*. Butterworth-Heinemann, Oxford.

Halvorson, K. (2010) *Content Strategy for the Web*. New Riders, Berkeley, CA.

Hanson, W. (2000) *Principles of Internet Marketing*. South Western College Publishing, Cincinnati, OH.

Internet Retailer (2004) The New Wal-Mart? By Paul Demery. *Internet Retailer*, 1 May. **www.internetretailer.com/2004/05/05/the-new-wal-mart**.

Jorgensen, P. (1995) *Software Testing: A Craftsman's Approach*. CRC Press, Boca Raton, FL.

Kotler, P. (1997) *Marketing Management – Analysis, Planning, Implementation and Control*. Prentice-Hall, Englewood Cliffs, NJ.

Marcus, J. (2004) *Amazonia: Five Years at the Epicentre of the Dot-com Juggernaut*. The New Press, New York.

Neely, A., Adams, C. and Kennerley, M. (2002) *The Performance Prism: The Scorecard for Measuring and Managing Business Success*. Financial Times Prentice Hall, Harlow.

Petersen, E. (2004) *Web Analytics Demystified*. Self-published. **www.webanlyticsdemysti fied.com** (no longer available).

Plant, R. (2000) *ECommerce: Formulation of Strategy*. Prentice-Hall, Upper Saddle River, NJ.

Revolution (2004) Alliance and Leicester Banks on E-commerce. *Revolution*. Article by Philip Buxton, 28 July. **www.revolutionmagazine.com** (no longer available).

Round, M. (2004) Presentation to E-metrics, London, May. **www.emetrics.org**.

SEC (2005) United States Securities and Exchange Commission submission Form 10-K from Amazon. For the fiscal year ended 31 December 2004.

Pulizzi, J. and Barrett, T. (2010) *Get Content. Get Customers*, McGraw-Hill, Columbus, OH.

SmartInsights (2010) Website Feedback Tools Review. Author, Dave Chaffey. Available at **http://bit.ly/smartfeedback**.

SEOMoz (2013) Search engine ranking factors v2, 2 April, **www.seomoz.org/article/ search-ranking-factors**.

Shore, J. and Warden, S. (2008) *The Art of Agile Development*. O'Reilly, Sebastopol, CA.

Sterne, J. (2002) *Web Metrics: Proven Methods for Measuring Web Site Success*. John Wiley & Sons, New York.

Wilson, H. (2008) *The Multichannel Challenge*. Butterworth-Heinemann, Oxford.

Wisner, J. and Fawcett, S. (1991) Link firm strategy to operating decisions through performance measurement. *Production and Inventory Management Journal*, Third Quarter, 5–11.

Web links

Web analytics expertise

Avinash Kaushik's blog (www.kaushik.net) Avinash is an expert in web analytics who is the Google evangelist for digital marketing. His popular blog shows how web analytics can be managed to control and improve return on digital marketing investments.

Emetrics (www.emetrics.org) Jim Sterne's site has many resources for online marketing metrics.

Smart Insights Google Analytics (www.smartinsights.com/google-analytics) Practical advice on how to drive value from the most popular digital analytics system.

Social media marketing analytics

These are the blogs of three of the leading commentators on social media marketing who discuss how to measure return from social media marketing.

Baer (www.convinceandconvert.com)

Brian Solis (www.briansolis.com)

Jeremiah Owyang (www.web-strategist.com)

Web Analytics Demystified (www.webanalyticsdemystified.com) Analyst Eric Peterson on web analytics.

Web Analytics Association (www.webanalyticsassociation.org) The trade association site has definitions and advice.

Content management

Gerry McGovern New Thinking (www.gerrymcgovern.com) Resources about user-centric content management.

ReadWriteWeb (www.readwriteweb.com) Site focussing on trends and developments in content management, web applications and social media.

Glossary

A

AB testing A/B or AB testing refers to testing two different versions of a page or a page element such as a heading, image or button for effectiveness. The alternatives are served alternately with the visitors to the page randomly split between the two pages. Changes in visitor behaviour can then be compared using different metrics such as clickthrough rate on page elements like buttons or images or macro-conversion rates, such as conversion to sale or sign-up.

Acceptable-use policy Statement of employee activities involving use of networked computers that are not considered acceptable by management.

Accessibility An approach to website design that enables sites and web applications to be used by people with visual impairment or other disabilities such as motor impairment. Accessibility also demands that web users should be able to use websites and applications effectively regardless of the browser and access platform they use and its settings.

Accessibility legislation Legislation intended to protect users of websites with disabilities, including those with visual disability.

Acquisition method Defines whether the system is purchased outright or developed from scratch.

Activity-based process definition methods Analysis tools used to identify the relationship between tasks within a business process.

Actors People, software or other devices that interface with a system. See Use-case.

Ad serving The term for displaying an advertisement on a website. Often the advertisement will be served from a web server different from the site on which it is placed.

Adaptive mobile web design Generally a more sophisticated approach than Responsive web design that involves delivering an experience optimised for handsets targeted and splits the code and processing to render on different devices between the client and the server.

Affiliate A company promoting a merchant typically through a commission-based arrangement either directly or through an affiliate network.

Affiliate marketing A commission-based arrangement where an e-tailer pays sites that link to it for sales, leads (CPA-based) or less commonly visitors (CPC-based).

Affiliate networks An e-tailer pays commission on sales referred from other sites.

Agents Software programs that assist humans by automatically gathering information from the Internet or exchanging data with other agents based on parameters supplied by the user.

Aggregated buying A form of customer union where buyers collectively purchase a number of items at the same price and receive a volume discount.

Aggregators An alternative term for price comparison sites. Aggregators include product, price and service information, comparing competitors within a sector such as financial services, retail or travel. Their revenue models commonly include affiliate revenues (CPA), pay-per-click advertising (CPC) and display advertising (CPM).

Agile development An iterative approach to developing software and website functionality with the emphasis on face-to-face communications to elicit, define and test requirements. Each iteration is effectively a mini software project including stages of planning, requirements analysis, design, coding, testing and documentation.

Allowable cost per acquisition A target maximum cost for generating leads or new customers profitably.

ALT tags ALT tags appear after an image tag and contain a phrase associated with that image. For example: `<img src="logo.gif" alt="Company name, company products"/>`.

Analysis and design Analysis of system requirements and design for creation of a system.

Analysis for digital systems Using analytical techniques to capture and summarise business and user requirements.

Anticipatory change An organisation initiates change without an immediate need to respond.

Anti-virus software Software to detect and eliminate viruses.

Applications service provider (ASP) A provider of business applications such as email, workflow or groupware or any business application on a server remote from the user. A service often offered by ISPs.

Asymmetric encryption Both parties use a related but different key to encode and decode messages.

Attribute A property or characteristic of an entity, implemented as a field; see Database.

Attrition rate Percentage of site visitors that are lost at each stage in making a purchase.

Augmented reality Blends real-world digital data capture typically with a digital camera in a webcam or mobile phone to create a browser-based digital representation or experience mimicking that of the real world.

B

B2B electronic marketplaces, exchanges and hubs Virtual locations with facilities to enable trading between buyers and sellers.

Backbones High-speed communications links used to enable Internet communications across a country and internationally.

Balanced scorecard A framework for setting and monitoring business performance. Metrics are structured according to customer issues, internal efficiency measures, financial measures and innovation.

Bandwidth Indicates the speed at which data are transferred using a particular network media. It is measured in bits per second (bps).

Behavioural ad targeting Enables an advertiser to target ads at a visitor as they move within or between sites dependent on their viewing particular sites or types of content that indicate their preference. This approach increases ad relevance and the frequency or number of impressions served to an individual in the target market, so increasing response.

Bespoke development Information system development specifically for a purpose.

Big Data Within marketing, this concept describes the opportunity to harness customer data from different touchpoints including as point-of-sale transactions, desktop and mobile sites and apps, social media.

Blacklist A compilation of known sources of spam that is used to block email.

Blog An online diary or news source prepared by an individual or a group of people.

Blueprints Show the relationships between pages and other content components, and can be used to portray organisation, labelling and navigation systems.

Boot-sector virus Occupies boot record of hard and floppy disks and is activated during computer start-up.

Botnet Independent computers, connected to the Internet, are used together, typically for malicious purposes through controlling software. For example, they may be used to send out spam or for a denial-of-service attack where they repeatedly access a server to degrade its service. Computers are often initially infected through a virus when effective anti-virus measures are not in place.

Bounce rate Percentage of visitors entering a site who leave immediately after viewing one page only (known as 'single-page visits').

Brand The sum of the characteristics of a product or service perceived by a user.

Brand equity A brand's assets (or liabilities) linked to the brand's name and symbol that add to (or subtract from) a service.

Brand experience The frequency and depth of interactions with a brand can be enhanced through the Internet.

Brand identity The totality of brand associations including name and symbols that must be communicated.

Branding The process of creating and developing successful brands.

Bricks-and-mortar or multichannel business A traditional organisation with limited online presence.

Broad and shallow navigation More choices, fewer clicks to reach required content.

Broadband connection Access to the Internet via phone lines using a digital data transfer mechanism.

Brochureware Brochureware describes a website in which a company has migrated its existing paper-based promotional literature on to the Internet without recognising the differences required by this medium.

Bundling Offering complementary services.

Burn rate The speed at which dot-coms spend investors' money.

Business-alignment IS strategy The IS strategy is generated from the business strategy through techniques such as Critical Success Factor analysis.

Business continuity management or disaster recovery Measures taken to ensure that information can be restored and accessed if the original information and access method are destroyed.

Business-impacting IS strategy IS strategy analyses opportunities for new technologies and processes to favourably impact the business strategy.

Business Intelligence Methodology, process and technologies used to support the transformation of different data sources to improve strategic, tactical and operational decision-making to improve business performance.

Business model A summary of how a company will generate revenue identifying its product offering, value-added services, revenue sources and target customers.

Business process automation (BPA) Automating existing ways of working manually through information technology.

Business process improvement (BPI) Optimising existing processes typically coupled with enhancements in information technology.

Business process management (BPM) An approach supported by software tools intended to increase process efficiency by improving information flows between people as they perform business tasks.

Business process re-engineering (BPR) Identifying radical, new ways of carrying out business operations, often enabled by new IT capabilities.

Business-to-business (B2B) Commercial transactions between an organisation and other organisations.

Business-to-consumer (B2C) Commercial transactions between an organisation and consumers.

Buy-side e-commerce E-commerce transactions between a purchasing organisation, its suppliers and partners.

C

Card sorting or web classification The process of arranging a way of organising objects on a website in a consistent manner.

Cascading Style Sheets (CSS) A simple mechanism for adding style (e.g. fonts, colours, spacing) to web documents. By separating the presentation style of documents from the content of documents, CSS enables different style elements to be controlled across an entire site or section of site.

Certificate and certificate authorities (CAs) A certificate is a valid copy of a public key of an individual or organisation together with identification information. It is issued by a trusted third party (TTP) or certificate authority (CA). CAs make public keys available and also issue private keys.

Change agents Managers involved in controlling change transitions.

Change management Managing process, structural, technical, staff and culture change within an organisation.

Changeover The term used to describe moving from the old information system to the new information system.

Channel buyer behaviour Describes which content is visited, time and duration.

Channel outcomes Record customer actions taken as a consequence of a site visit.

Channel profitability The profitability of the website, taking into account revenue and cost and discounted cash flow.

Channel promotion Measures that assess why customers visit a site – which adverts they have seen, which sites they have been referred from.

Channel satisfaction Evaluation of the customer's opinion of the service quality on the site and supporting services such as email.

Churn rate The proportion of customers (typically subscribers) that no longer purchase a company's products in a time period.

Click ecosystem Describes the customer behaviour or flow of online visitors between search engines, media sites, other intermediaries to an organisation and its competitors.

Clicks-only or Internet pureplay An organisation with principally an online presence.

Client–server The client–server architecture consists of client computers, such as PCs, sharing resources such as a database stored on more powerful server computers.

Client–server model A system architecture in which end-user machines such as PCs known as clients run applications while accessing data and possibly programs from a server.

Cloud computing The use of distributed storage and processing on servers connected by the Internet, typically provided as software or data storage as a subscription service provided by other companies.

Cold list Data about individuals that are rented or sold by a third party.

Collaborative filtering Profiling of customer interests coupled with delivery of specific information and offers, often based on the interests of similar customers.

Commoditisation The process whereby product selection becomes more dependent on price than on differentiating features, benefits and value-added services.

Community A customer-to-customer interaction delivered via email groups, web-based discussion forums or chat.

Competitor analysis for digital business Review of digital business services offered by existing and new competitors and adoption by their customers.

Computer virus A program capable of self-replication allowing it to spread from one machine to another. It may be malicious and delete data, or benign.

Consumer-to-business (C2B) Customer is proactive in making an offer to a business, e.g. the price they are prepared to pay for an airline ticket.

Consumer-to-consumer (C2C) Interactions between customers on a website, e.g. posting and reading of topics on an electronic bulletin board.

Content Content is the design, text and graphical information which forms a web page. Good content is the key to attracting customers to a website and retaining their interest or achieving repeat visits.

Content management system (CMS) A software tool for creating, editing and updating documents accessed by intranet, extranet or Internet.

Content marketing The management of text, rich media, audio and video content aimed at engaging customers and prospects to meet business goals published through print and digital media including web and mobile platforms which is repurposed and syndicated to different forms of web presence such as publisher sites, blogs, social media and comparison sites.

Content marketing strategy Selecting, sourcing, scheduling and encouraging sharing of the most relevant types of content to meet your business goals.

Contextual display network Contextual ads are automatically displayed according to the type of content on partner publisher sites by the search engine.

Control page The page against which subsequent optimisation will be assessed. Typically a current landing page. When a new page performs better than the existing control page, it becomes your control page in subsequent testing. Also known as 'champion-challenger'.

Conversion marketing Using marketing communications to maximise conversion of potential customers to actual customers and existing customers to repeat customers.

Conversion rate Percentage of site visitors that perform a particular action such as making a purchase.

Conversion rate optimisation (CRO) Improving the commercial returns from a transactional site through increasing conversion to key goals such as sales, quotes or bookings or leads. CRO combines customer and competitor research with evaluation of customer behaviour using web analytics and AB and multivariate testing. (See Chapter 12 for details.)

Cookies Cookies are small text files stored on an end-user's computer to enable websites to identity them.

Co-opetition Interactions between competitors and marketplace intermediaries which can mutually improve the attractiveness of a marketplace.

Core competencies Resources, including skills or technologies, that provide a particular benefit to customers.

Core product The fundamental features of the product that meet the user's needs.

Cost per acquisition (CPA) The cost of acquiring a new customer. Typically limited to the communications cost and refers to cost per sale for new customers. May also refer to other outcomes such as cost per quote or enquiry.

Cost per click (CPC) The cost to the advertiser (or the revenue received by the publisher) of each click of a link to a third-party site.

Cost per thousand (CPM) Cost per 1,000 ad impressions for a banner advert.

Countermediation Creation of a new intermediary such as a publisher or comparison site by an established company. May be a new site or acquired through purchase or partnering.

Covert monitoring Monitoring which the employer undertakes without notification of staff.

Cross-media optimisation studies (XMOS) Studies to determine the optimum spend across different media to produce the best results.

Crowdsourcing Utilising a network of customers or other partners to gain insights for new product or process innovations.

Culture This concept includes shared values, i.e. cultures are created when a group of employees interact over time and are relatively successful in what they undertake.

Customer acquisition Techniques used to gain new prospects and customers.

Customer-centric marketing An approach to marketing based on detailed knowledge of customer behaviour within the target audience which seeks to fulfil the individual needs and wants of customers.

Customer engagement Repeated interactions that strengthen the emotional, psychological or physical investment a customer has in a brand.

Customer experience management (CXM) User experience improvements are broadened to consider the context of use to different physical locations or customer touchpoints across different digital platforms including desktop, mobile sites, apps, social networks and email marketing. Context of use includes device type, location and interactions with customer service.

Customer extension Techniques to encourage customers to increase their involvement with an organisation.

Customer insight Knowledge about customers' needs, characteristics, preferences and behaviours based on analysis of qualitative and quantitative data. Specific insights can be used to inform marketing tactics directed at groups of customers with shared characteristics.

Customer journey A description of modern multichannel behaviour as consumers use different media to select suppliers, make purchases and gain customer support.

Customer life cycle The stages each customer will pass through in a long-term relationship through acquisition, retention and extension. There are more detailed stages within this.

Customer orientation Developing site content and services to appeal to different customer segments or other members of the audience.

Customer profile Information that can be used to segment a customer.

Customer relationship management (CRM) An approach to building and sustaining long-term business with customers.

Customer scenario Alternative tasks or outcomes required by a visitor to a website. Typically accomplished in a series of stages of different tasks involving different information needs or experiences.

Customer self-service Customers perform information requests and transactions through a web interface rather than contact with customer support staff.

Customer value Value dependent on product quality, service quality, price and fulfilment time.

D

Data controller Each company must have a defined person responsible for data protection.

Data migration Transfer of data from old to new systems.

Data subject The individual whose privacy is protected through data protection legislation.

Database A database can be defined as a collection of related information. The information held in the database is stored in an organised way so that specific items can be selected and retrieved quickly. See Database management system.

Database management system (DBMS) The information held in an electronic database is accessed via a database management system. A DBMS can be defined as one or more computer programs that allow users to enter, store, organise, manipulate and retrieve data from a database. For many users, the terms *database* and *database management system* are interchangeable. A *relational database management system (RDBMS)* is an extension of a DBMS and allows data to be combined from a variety of sources.

Database table Each database comprises several tables.

Dedicated server Server only contains content and applications for a single company.

Deep linking Jakob Nielsen's term for a user arriving at a site deep within its structure.

Demand analysis Assessment of the demand for e-commerce services amongst existing and potential customer segments.

Deployment plan A deployment plan is a schedule which defines all the tasks that need to occur in order for changeover to occur successfully. This includes putting in place all the infrastructure such as cabling and hardware.

Design for analysis (DFA) The required measures from a site are considered during design to better understand the audience of a site and their decision points.

Destination site Typically a retailer or manufacturer site with sales and service information. Intermediaries such as media sites may be destination sites for some.

Development environment Software and hardware used to create a system.

Dial-up connection Access to the Internet via phone lines using analogue modems.

Differential advantage A desirable attribute of a product offering that is not currently matched by competitor offerings.

Digital business How businesses apply digital technology and media to improve the competitiveness of their organisation through optimising internal processes with online and traditional channels to market and supply.

Digital business applications infrastructure Applications that provide access to services and information inside and beyond an organisation.

Digital business infrastructure The architecture of hardware, software, content and data used to deliver digital business services to employees, customers and partners.

Digital business strategy Definition of the approach by which applications of internal and external electronic communications can support and influence business strategy.

Digital business transformation Significant changes to organisational processes, structures and system implemented to improve organisational performance through increasing the use of digital media and technology platforms.

Digital certificates (keys) Consist of keys made up of large numbers that are used to uniquely identify individuals.

Digital marketing This has a similar meaning to 'electronic marketing' – both describe the management and execution of marketing using electronic media such as the web, email, interactive TV and wireless media in conjunction with digital data about customers' characteristics and behaviour.

Digital marketing plan A plan to achieve the marketing objectives of the digital business strategy.

Digital media channels Online communications techniques used to achieve goals of brand awareness, familiarity and favourability and to influence purchase intent by encouraging users of digital media to visit a website to engage with the brand or product and ultimately to purchase online or offline through traditional media channels such as by phone or in-store.

Digital rights management (DRM) The use of different technologies to protect the distribution of digital services or content such as software, music, movies or other digital data.

Digital signatures A method of identifying individuals or companies using public-key encryption.

Discontinuous change Change involving a major transformation in an industry.

Disintermediation The removal of intermediaries such as distributors or brokers that formerly linked a company to its customers.

Disruptive digital technologies Technologies which offer opportunities for business for new products and services for customers and can transform internal business processes. Danneels (2004) defined disruptive technologies as 'a technology that changes the bases of competition by changing the performance metrics along which firms compete'. Customer needs drive customers to seek certain benefits in the products they use and form the basis for customer choices between competing products.

Domain name The domain name refers to the name of the web server and it is usually selected to be the same as the name of the company, e.g. www.<company-name>. com, and the extension will indicate its type.

Domain name registration The process of reserving a unique web address that can be used to refer to the company website.

Dot-coms Businesses whose main trading presence is on the Internet.

Downstream supply chain Transactions between an organisation and its customers and intermediaries, equivalent to sell-side e-commerce.

Dynamic digital business application The application is continuously updated in response to competitive forces.

Dynamic pricing Prices can be updated in real time according to the type of customer or current market conditions.

Dynamically created web page A page that is created in real time, often with reference to a database query, in response to a user request.

E

Early adopter Company or department that invests in new technologies and techniques.

Early (first) mover An early entrant into the marketplace.

Effectiveness Meeting process objectives, delivering the required outputs and outcomes: 'doing the right thing'.

Efficiency Minimising resources or time needed to complete a process: 'doing the thing right'.

Efficient consumer response (ECR) ECR is focussed on demand management aimed at creating and satisfying customer demand by optimising product assortment strategies, promotions, and new product introductions. It creates operational efficiencies and costs savings in the supply chain through reducing inventories and deliveries.

Electronic channel service contribution The proportion of service-type processes that are completed using electronic channels.

Electronic channel strategies Define how a company should set specific objectives and develop specific differential strategies for communicating with its customers and partners through electronic media such as the Internet, emails and wireless media.

Electronic commerce (e-commerce) All electronically mediated information exchanges between an organisation and its external stakeholders. See Sell-side and Buy-side e-commerce.

Electronic customer relationship management (e-CRM) Using digital communications technologies to maximise sales to existing customers and encourage continued usage of online services.

Electronic economy (e-economy) The dynamic system of interactions between a nation's citizens, businesses and government that capitalise upon online technology to achieve a social or economic good.

Electronic government (e-government) The use of Internet technologies to provide government services to citizens.

Electronic mail (email) filter Software used to identify spam according to its characteristics such as keywords.

Electronic marketplace A virtual marketplace such as the Internet in which no direct contact occurs between buyers and sellers.

Electronic procurement (e-procurement) The electronic integration and management of all procurement activities including purchase request, authorisation, ordering, delivery and payment between a purchaser and a supplier.

Electronic procurement system (EPS) An electronic system used to automate all or part of the procurement function by enabling the scanning, storage and retrieval of invoices and other documents; management of approvals; routeing of authorisation requests; interfaces to other finance systems; and matching of documents to validate transactions.

Emergent strategy Strategic analysis, strategic development and strategy implementation are interrelated and are developed together.

Employee communications monitoring Companies monitor staff emails and websites they access.

Encryption See Asymmetric encryption and Symmetric encryption.

Enterprise application integration (EAI) Software used to facilitate communications between business applications including data transfer and control.

Enterprise resource planning (ERP) applications Enterprise applications used to manage information about organisational resources such as raw materials, products, staff and customers as part of delivery of a product or service.

Enterprise social media software Systems used inside organisations to enable real-time collaboration between employees and other stakeholders such as customers and suppliers to support business processes such as customer service, supply chain management and new product development. Collectively these tools are sometimes referenced as Enterprise 2.0.

Entity A grouping of related data, such as a customer entity. Implemented as a table.

Environmental scanning and analysis The process of continuously monitoring the environment and events and responding accordingly.

Ethical hacker Hacker employed legitimately to test the quality of system security.

Ethical standards Practice or behaviour which is morally acceptable to society.

Expert review An analysis of an existing site or prototype by an experienced usability expert who will identify deficiencies and improvements to a site based on their knowledge of web design principles and best practice.

Explicit knowledge Knowledge that can be readily expressed and recorded within information systems.

Extended product Additional features and benefits beyond the core product.

External value chain or value network The links between an organisation and its strategic and non-strategic partners that form its external value chain.

Extranet A service provided through Internet and web technology delivered by extending an intranet beyond a company to customers, suppliers and collaborators.

Eyetracking A usability testing technique that provides a visual overlay of where visitors most commonly look on the screen (heatmaps) and individual or common paths (gaze trails).

F

Field Attributes of products, such as date of birth. See Database.

Filtering software Software that blocks specified content or activities.

Firewall A specialised software application mounted on a server at the point where the company is connected to the Internet. Its purpose is to prevent unauthorised access into the company from outsiders.

First-party cookies Served by the site you are currently using – typical for e-commerce sites.

Flow Flow describes how easy it is for users of a site to move between the different pages of content of the site.

Forward path analysis Reviews the combinations of clicks that occur from a page. This form of analysis is most beneficial from important pages such as the home page, product and directory pages. Use this technique to identify: messaging/navigation combinations which work best to yield the most clicks from a page.

G

Globalisation The increase of international trading and shared social and cultural values.

Growth hacking An approach to improving the commercial results from online services through structured testing and optimisation of marketing approaches.

H

Hacking The process of gaining unauthorised access to computer systems, typically across a network.

Hit Recorded for each graphic or text file requested from a web server. It is not a reliable measure for the number of people viewing a page.

Hosted solution Standard software which is managed externally on the supplier's server.

Hosting provider A service provider that manages the server used to host an organisation's website and its connection to the Internet backbones.

House list Data about existing customers used to market products to encourage future purchase.

Hype cycle A graphic representation of the maturity, adoption and business application of specific technologies.

I

Identity theft The misappropriation of the identity of another person, without their knowledge or consent.

Impact assessment An assessment of the Employee communications monitoring process in the workplace to identify improvements to minimise infringement of employee privacy.

Implementation The creation of a system based on analysis and design documentation.

Inbound email marketing Management of emails from customers by an organisation.

Inbound marketing The consumer is proactive in actively seeking out information for their needs, and interactions with brands are attracted through content, search and social media marketing.

Inbound logistics The management of material resources entering an organisation from its suppliers and other partners.

Incremental change Relatively small adjustments required by an organisation in response to its business environment.

Information architecture The combination of organisation, labelling and navigation schemes making up an information system.

Information asset register A repository for the types, value and ownership of all information within an organisation.

Information asymmetry Imperfect information sharing between members of a supply chain which increases uncertainty about demand and pricing.

Information organisation schemes The structure chosen to group and categorise information.

Information security management system An organisational process to protect information assets.

Information security policy A definition of the organisational approaches to information security and the responsibilities of employees in protecting information.

Information supply chain An information-centric view of the supply chain which addresses the organisational and technological challenges of achieving technology-enabled supply chain management efficiency and effectiveness.

Infrastructure as a Service (IaaS) Hardware used to provide support for end-user applications is outsourced and paid for according to level of usage. The hardware infrastructure used includes servers and networks.

Initiation The start-up phase of the project.

Intellectual property rights (IPR) Protect the intangible property created by corporations or individuals that is protected under copyright, trade secret and patent laws.

Interactivity The medium enables a dialogue between company and customer.

Intermediary An organisation or e-commerce site that typically brings buyers and sellers together.

Internet The Internet refers to the physical network that links computers across the globe. It consists of the infrastructure of network servers and communication links between them that are used to hold and transport information between the client PCs and web servers.

Internet-based market research The use of online questionnaires and focus groups to assess customer perceptions of a website or broader marketing issues.

Internet governance Control of the operation and use of the Internet.

Internet marketing metrics Measures that indicate the effectiveness of Internet marketing activities in meeting customer, business and marketing objectives.

Internet service provider (ISP) A provider enabling home or business users a connection to access the Internet. They can also host web-based applications.

Interruption marketing Marketing communications that disrupt customers' activities.

Interstitial ads Ads that appear between one page and the next.

Intranet A private network within a single company using Internet standards to enable employees to access and share information using web publishing technology.

Inventory turnover An indication of efficiency of inventory turn calculated by the cost of goods sold divided by the average inventory.

IPTV (Internet Protocol Television) Digital television service is delivered using Internet Protocol, typically by a broadband connection. IPTV can be streamed for real-time viewing or downloaded before playback.

K

Keyphrase (keyword phrase) The combination of words users of search engines type into a search box which form a search query.

Knowledge Applying experience to problem-solving.

Knowledge management (KM) Techniques and tools for disseminating knowledge within an organisation.

L

Lead See Qualified lead.

Lifetime value (LTV) Lifetime value is the total net benefit that a customer or group of customers will provide a company over their total relationship with the company.

Link anchor text The text used to form the blue underlined hyperlink viewed in a web browser defined in the HTML source.

Link-building A structured activity to include good-quality hyperlinks to your site from relevant sites with a good page rank.

Localisation Tailoring of website information for individual countries or regions.

Location-based marketing Location or proximity-based marketing is mobile marketing based on the GPS built into phones or based on interaction with other local digital devices.

Log-file analyser A log-file analyser is a separate program such as Webtrends that is used to summarise the information on customer activity contained in a log file.

Logistics See Inbound logistics and Outbound logistics.

Long tail concept A frequency distribution suggesting the relative variation in popularity of items selected by consumers.

M

Machine-to-machine (M2M) applications Objects are uniquely identified and tagged through technologies such as RFID and made accessible through Internet-like addresses.

Maintenance activities Involve measurement of an information system's effectiveness and updating to correct errors or introduce new features necessary to improve its value to the organisation.

Maintenance phase Commences after the system is live.

Malware Malicious software or toolbars, typically downloaded via the Internet, which acts as a 'Trojan horse' by executing other unwanted activities such as keylogging of user passwords or viruses which may collect email addresses.

Managed email service Receipt and transmission of emails is managed by a third party.

Marketing-led site design Site design elements are developed to achieve customer acquisition, retention and communication of marketing messages.

Marketing mix Different factors that summarise the customer propositions offered by a business. Marketing mix refers to the 4 core Ps of Price, Product (including branding, Place and Promotion and the 7Ps of the extending Marketing Mix which include People, Process and Physical evidence.

Marketplace See B2B electronic marketplaces, exchanges and hubs.

Mashups Websites, pages or widgets that combine the content or functionality of one website or data source with another to create something offering a different type of value to web users from the separate types of content or functionality.

Mass customisation The creation of tailored marketing messages or products for individual customers or groups of customers typically using technology to retain the economies of scale and the capacity of mass marketing or production.

Media multiplier or halo effect The role of one media channel on influencing sale or uplift in brand metrics. Commonly applied to online display advertising, where exposure to display ads may increase clickthrough rates when the consumer is later exposed to a brand through other media, for example sponsored links or affiliate ads. It may also refer to conversion rates on a destination site through higher confidence in the brand or familiarity with the offer.

Media Queries A styling approach within Cascading Style Sheets (CSS3) enabling the layout to change based on type of device at its scale.

Metamediaries Third parties that provide a single point of contact and deliver a range of services between customers and suppliers.

Meta-tags Text within an HTML file summarising the characteristics of the document. The most relevant to search engines are the meta-keywords tag used to list keywords relevant to the page and the content meta-tag, the description of which forms part of the listings snippet in the search results page. They are not used for ranking purposes in Google.

Middleware Software used to facilitate communication between business applications including data transfer control.

Microformats A simple set of formats based on XHTML for describing and exchanging information about objects including product and travel reviews, recipes and event information.

Microsite A small-scale destination site reached on clickthrough which is part of the media owner's site.

Milestone Key deadline to be achieved during project, usually with defined deliverable criteria.

Mission statement See Vision or mission statement.

Mixed-mode buying The process by which a customer changes between online and offline channels during the buying process.

Mobile apps A software application that is designed for use on a mobile phone, typically downloaded from an App store. iPhone Apps are best known, but all smartphones support the use of apps which can provide users with information, entertainment or location-based services such as mapping.

Mobile commerce (m-commerce) Electronic transactions and communications conducted using mobile devices such as laptops, PDAs and mobile phones, and typically with a wireless connection.

Mobile marketing Marketing to encourage consumer engagement when they're using mobile phones (particularly smartphones) or tablet devices.

MRO Maintenance, repairs and operations of manufacturing facilities.

Multichannel (omnichannel) digital business strategy Defines how different marketing and supply chain channels should integrate and support each other to drive business efficiency and effectiveness.

Multichannel and omnichannel marketing Customer communications and product distribution are supported by a combination of digital and traditional channels at different points in the buying cycle. Omnichannel references the importance of social media and mobile-based interactions in informing purchase.

Multichannel marketing strategy Defines how different marketing channels should integrate and support each other in terms of their proposition development and communications based on their relative merits for the customer and the company.

Multiscreening A term used to describe simultaneous use of devices such as digital TV and tablet.

Multi-tenancy SaaS A single instance of a web service is used by different customers (tenants) run on a single server or load-balanced across multiple servers. Customers are effectively sharing processor, disk usage and bandwidth with other customers.

N

Narrow and deep navigation Fewer choices, more clicks to reach required content.

Net neutrality The principle of provision of equal access to different Internet services by telecommunications service providers.

Net promoter score A measure of the number of advocates a company (or website) has who would recommend it compared to the number of detractors.

Notification The process whereby companies register with the data protection registrar to inform about their data holdings.

O

Offline marketing communications Traditional techniques such as print and TV advertising used to generate website traffic.

Online business model A summary of how a company will generate a profit identifying its core product or service value proposition, target customers in different markets, position in the competitive online marketplace or value chain and its projections for revenue and costs.

Online buyer behaviour An assessment of how consumers and business people use the Internet in combination with other communications channels when selecting and buying products and services.

Online customer experience The combination of rational and emotional factors of using a company's online services that influences customers' perceptions of a brand online.

Online intermediaries Websites which help connect web users with content they are seeking on destination sites. Include new online intermediaries such as search engines and shopping comparison sites and traditional brokers, directories and newspaper and magazine publishers that now have an online presence.

Online market ecosystem Describes the customer behaviour or flow of online visitors between search engines, media sites, other intermediaries to an organisation and its competitors.

Online marketing communications Internet-based techniques used to generate website traffic.

Online marketplace Exchanges of information and commercial transactions between consumers, businesses and governments completed through different forms of online presence such as search engines, social networks, comparison sites and destination sites.

Online PR Maximising favourable mentions of your company, brands, products or websites on third-party websites which are likely to be visited by your target audience.

Online or Internet revenue contribution (ORC) An assessment of the direct contribution of the Internet or other digital media to sales, usually expressed as a percentage of overall sales revenue.

Online value proposition (OVP) A statement of the benefits of online services reinforces the core proposition and differentiates from an organisation's offline offering and those of competitors.

Open-source software Software that is developed collaboratively, independent of a vendor, by a community of software developers and users.

Opt-in A customer proactively agrees to receive further information.

Opt-out A customer declines the offer to receive further information.

Organisational change Includes both incremental and discontinuous change to an organisation.

Outbound email marketing Emails are sent to customers and prospects from an organisation.

Outbound logistics The management of resources supplied from an organisation to its customers and intermediaries such as retailers and distributors.

Overlay Typically an animated ad that moves around the page and is superimposed on the website content.

P

PaaS (Platform as a Service) Provision of software services for application design, development, data storage, testing and hosting together with messaging tools for collaboration on the development project.

Packaged implementation Standard software is installed with limited configuration required.

Page impression (view) A more reliable measure than a hit, denoting one person viewing one page.

Page rank A scale of 0 to 10 used by Google to assess the importance of websites according to the number of inbound links (link popularity).

Page template A standard page layout format which is applied to each page of a website. Typically defined for different page categories (e.g. category page, product page, search page).

Path to purchase The different sites, channels and devices and information sources that consumers use to inform their purchase decision for a product or service. Also known as conversion pathways on a site.

Pay-per-click (PPC) search marketing A company pays for text adverts to be displayed on the search engine results pages when a specific keyphrase is entered by the search users. It is so called because the marketer pays each time the hypertext link in the ad is clicked on.

People variable The element of the marketing mix that involves the delivery of service to customers during interactions with customers.

Performance drivers Critical success factors that govern whether objectives are achieved.

Performance management system A process used to evaluate and improve the efficiency and effectiveness of an organisation and its processes.

Performance measurement system The process by which metrics are defined, collected, disseminated and actioned.

Permission marketing Customers agree (opt in) to be involved in an organisation's marketing activities, usually as a result of an incentive.

Persistent cookies Cookies that remain on the computer after a visitor session has ended. Used to recognise returning visitors.

Persona A summary of the characteristics, needs, motivations and environment of typical website users.

Personal data Any information about an individual stored by companies concerning their customers or employees.

Personalisation Delivering individualised content through web pages or email.

Persuasion marketing Using design elements such as layout, copy and typography together with promotional messages to encourage site users to follow particular paths and specific actions rather than giving them complete choice in their navigation.

Phishing Obtaining personal details online through sites and emails masquerading as legitimate businesses.

Physical evidence variable The element of the marketing mix that involves the tangible expression of a product and how it is purchased and used.

Place variable The element of the marketing mix that involves distributing products to customers in line with demand and minimising cost of inventory, transport and storage.

Podcasts Individuals and organisations post online media (audio and video) which can be accessed in the appropriate players including the iPod, which first sparked the growth of this technique.

Portal An intermediary site focussed on providing a gateway to other information on other sites, but often also providing its own content and services. Examples include search engines, ISPs and online newspapers and magazines.

Positioning Influencing the customer's perception of a product within a marketplace.

Prescriptive strategy The three core areas of strategic analysis, strategic development and strategy implementation are linked together sequentially.

Price elasticity of demand Measure of consumer behaviour that indicates the change in demand for a product or service in response to changes in price. Price elasticity of demand is used to assess the extent to which a change in price will influence demand for a product.

Price variable The element of the marketing mix that involves defining product prices and pricing models.

Pricing models Describe the form of payment such as outright purchase, auction, rental, volume purchase and credit terms.

Primary key The field that uniquely identifies each record in a table. See Database.

Primary persona A representation of the typical website user, who is strategically important to the effectiveness of the site, but one whose needs are challenging to fulfil.

Privacy The right of an individual to control the information held about them by third parties.

Privacy and Electronic Communications Regulations (PECR) Act A law intended to control the distribution of email and other online communications including cookies.

Privacy statement Information on a website explaining how and why an individual's data are collected, processed and stored.

Private B2B exchange A manufacturer or major supplier to different manufacturers creates a portal which is used for managing all aspects of procurement.

Private key See Encryption.

Process Part of a system that has a clearly defined purpose or objective and clearly defined inputs and outputs.

Process mapping Identification of location and responsibilities for processes within an organisation.

Process variable The element of the marketing mix that involves the methods and procedures companies use to achieve all marketing functions.

Product variable The element of the marketing mix that involves researching customers' needs and developing appropriate products.

Production or live environment Software and hardware used to host an operational system.

Productivity paradox Research results indicating a poor correlation between organisational investment in information systems and organisational performance measured by return on equity.

Promotion variable The element of the marketing mix that involves communication with customers and other stakeholders to inform them about the product and the organisation.

Propensity modelling A name given to the approach of evaluating customer characteristics and behaviour and then making recommendations for future products.

Prototype A preliminary version of part or all of an information system reviewed by its users and business sponsors.

Prototyping Prototyping is an iterative process whereby website users suggest modifications before further prototypes and the live version of the site are developed.

Psychographic segmentation A breakdown of customers according to different characteristics.

Public key See Encryption.

Pull marketing communications The consumer is proactive in interacting with companies through actively seeking information or entertainment on company websites or social media sites through search engines, comparison intermediaries or direct navigation.

Pull media The consumer is proactive in selection of the message through actively seeking out a website.

Pull supply chain An emphasis on using the supply chain to deliver value to customers who are actively involved in product and service specification.

Punchout catalogue A purchasing company accesses through its firewall a dynamic real-time catalogue hosted by a supplier or intermediary containing detailed product information, pricing and product images. These can be potentially integrated with their own purchasing systems.

Push marketing communications Communications are broadcast from an advertiser to consumers of the message who are passive recipients or may respond by visiting a website through direct navigation or clickthrough.

Push media Communications are broadcast from an advertiser to consumers of the message who are passive recipients.

Push supply chain A supply chain that emphasises distribution of a product to passive customers.

Q

Qualified lead Contact information for a customer and an indication of their propensity to purchase different products.

Quality score An assessment in paid search by Google AdWords (and now other search engines) of an individual ad triggered by a keyword which, in combination with the bid amount, determines the ranking of the ad relative to competitors. The primary factor is the clickthrough rate for each ad, but Quality Score also considers the match between the keyword and the occurrence of the keyword in the text, historical clickthrough rates, the engagement of the searcher when they click through to the site and the speed at which the page loads.

R

RAD – Rapid Application Development An approach to information systems development that includes incremental development using **prototypes**.

Radio-frequency identification (RFID) Microchip-based electronic tags are used for monitoring anything they are attached to, whether inanimate (products) or animate (people).

Reactive change A direct response by an organisation to a change in its environment.

Really Simple Syndication (RSS) feeds Blog, news or other content is published by an XML standard and syndicated for other sites or read by users in RSS reader software services. Now typically shortened to 'feed', e.g. news feed or sports feed.

Reciprocal links An exchange of links between two site owners.

Record A collection of fields for one instance of an entity, such as Customer Smith. See Database.

Referrer The source of a website visit, e.g. paid search, affiliate marketing, online advertising or recorded as 'no referrer', i.e. when a URL is typed in directly.

Reintermediation The creation of new intermediaries between customers and suppliers providing services such as supplier search and product evaluation.

Relationship Describes how different tables are linked. See Database.

Resource analysis Review of the technological, financial and human resources of an organisation and how they are utilised in business processes.

Responsive design Layout and formatting of website content is modified at the point of rendering to suit different screen resolutions and capabilities to produce a better experience to users of a range of desktop, tablet and smartphone devices using web development methods like CSS3 and image scaling.

Revenue models Describe methods of generating income for an organisation.

Reverse path analysis Indicates the most popular combination of pages and/or calls-to-action which lead to a page. This is particularly useful for transactional pages such as the first checkout page on a consumer site; a lead generation or contact us page on a business-to-business site; an email subscription page or a call-me back option.

Rich media Digital assets such as ads are not static images, but provide animation, audio or interactivity as a game or form to be completed.

Risk management Evaluating potential risks, developing strategies to reduce risks and learning about future risks.

ROPO Research Online Purchase Offline.

S

Satisficing behaviour Consumers do not behave entirely rationally in product or supplier selection. They will compare alternatives, but then may make their choice given imperfect information.

Scalability The ability of an organisation or system to adapt to increasing demands being placed on it.

Scanning software Identifies email or website access that breaches company guidelines or acceptable-use policies.

Scenario A particular path or flow of events or activities within a use-case.

Scenario-based analysis Models of the future environment are developed from different starting points.

Schematics See Wireframes.

Scrum Scrum is a methodology that supports agile software development based on 15–30-day sprints to implement features from a product backlog. 'Scrum' refers to a daily project status meeting during the sprint.

Search-engine optimisation (SEO) A structured approach used to increase the position of a company or its products in search-engine results according to selected keywords.

Search engines, spiders and robots Automated tools known as 'spiders' or 'robots' index registered sites. Users use search engines by typing keywords and are presented with a list of ranked pages from the index.

Search marketing Companies seek to improve their visibility in search engines for relevant search terms by increasing their presence in the search engine results pages.

Searching behaviours Approaches to finding information vary from directed to undirected.

Secondary key A field that is used to link tables, by linking to a primary key in another table. See Database.

Secure Electronic Transaction (SET) A standard for public-key encryption intended to enable secure e-commerce transactions, lead-developed by MasterCard and Visa.

Secure Sockets Layer (SSL) A commonly used encryption technique for scrambling data as they are passed across the Internet from a customer's web browser to a merchant's web server.

Segmentation Identification of different groups within a target market in order to develop different offerings for the groups.

Sell-side e-commerce E-commerce transactions between a supplier organisation and its customers.

Semantic web Interrelated content including data with defined meaning, enabling better exchange of information between computers and between people and computers.

Sense and respond communications Delivering timely, relevant communications to customers as part of a contact strategy based on assessment of their position in the customer life cycle and monitoring specific interactions with a company's website, emails and staff.

Servers See Web servers.

Service level agreement A contractual specification of service standards a contractor must meet.

Service-oriented architecture (SOA) A service-oriented architecture is a collection of services that communicate with each other as part of a distributed systems architecture comprising different services.

Session cookies Cookies used to manage a single visitor session.

Share of search The audience share of Internet searches achieved by a particular audience in a particular market.

Share of wallet or share of customer The proportion of customer expenditure in a particular category that belongs to a single customer.

Single-tenancy SaaS A single instance of an application (and/or database) is maintained for all customers (tenants) who have dedicated resources of processor, disk usage and bandwidth. The single instance may be load-balanced over multiple servers for improved performance.

Site map A graphical or text depiction of the relationship between different groups of content on a website.

Site navigation scheme Tools provided to the user to move between different information on a website.

Site-visitor activity data Information on content and services accessed by e-commerce site visitors.

Situation analysis Environment analysis and review of internal processes and resources to inform strategy.

SMS (short message services) The formal name for text messaging.

Social commerce Social commerce is a subset of e-commerce which encourages participation and interaction of customers in rating, selecting and buying products through group buying. This participation can occur on an e-commerce site or on third-party sites.

Social CRM The process of managing customer-to-customer conversations to engage existing customers, prospects and other stakeholders with a brand and so enhance customer-relationship management.

Social engineering Exploiting human behaviour to gain access to computer security information from employees or individuals.

Social media A category of media focussing on participation and peer-to-peer communication between individuals with sites providing the capability to develop user-generated content (UGC) and to exchange messages and comments between different users.

Social media marketing Monitoring and facilitating customer–customer interaction and participation throughout the web to encourage positive engagement with a company or its brands. Interactions may occur on a company site, social networks and other third-party sites.

Social network A site facilitating exchange of text, audio or video content.

Social network sites (SNS) A site that facilitates peer-to-peer communication within a group or between individuals through providing facilities to develop user-generated content (UGC) and to exchange messages and comments between different users.

Social sign-in Users or members of sites can sign-in with their social network accounts such as Google+, Facebook or LinkedIn through use of APIs exchanging data between different web services.

Soft launch A preliminary site launch with limited promotion to provide initial feedback and testing of an e-commerce site.

Soft lock-in Customers or suppliers continue to use online services because of the switching costs.

Software (intelligent) agents Software programs that assist humans by automatically gathering information from the Internet or exchanging data with other agents based on parameters supplied by the user.

Spam Unsolicited email (usually bulk mailed and untargeted).

Stage models Used to review how advanced a company is in its use of information and communications technology (ICT) to support different processes.

Static web content See Static web page.

Static web page A page on the web server that is invariant.

Stickiness An indication of how long a visitor stays on a site.

Storyboarding The use of static drawings or screenshots of the different parts of a website to review the design concept with user groups. It can be used to develop the structure – an overall 'map' with individual pages shown separately.

Strategic agility The capability to innovate and so gain competitive advantage within a marketplace by monitoring changes within an organisation's marketplace and then to efficiently evaluate alternative strategies and select, review and implement appropriate candidate strategies.

Strategic analysis Collection and review of information about an organisation's internal processes and resources and external marketplace factors in order to inform strategy definition.

Strategic objectives Statement and communication of an organisation's mission, vision and objectives.

Strategy Definition of the future direction and actions of a company defined as approaches to achieve specific objectives. See Prescriptive and Emergent strategy.

Strategy definition Formulation, review and selection of strategies to achieve strategic objectives.

Strategy implementation Planning, actions and controls needed to achieve strategic goals.

Strategy process model A framework for approaching strategy development.

Subject access request A request by a data subject to view personal data from an organisation.

Supply chain management (SCM) The coordination of all supply activities of an organisation from its suppliers and partners to its customers. See Upstream and Downstream supply chain.

Supply chain network The links between an organisation and all partners involved with multiple supply chains.

Supply chain visibility Access to up-to-date, accurate, relevant information about a supply chain's process to different stakeholders.

SWOT analysis Strengths, weaknesses, opportunities and threats.

Symmetric encryption Both parties to a transaction use the same key to encode and decode messages.

System design Defines how an information system will operate.

Systems development life cycle The sequence in which a system is created through initiation, analysis, design, implementation, build and maintenance.

Systems integrator A company that organises the procurement and installation of hardware and software needed for implementation.

T

Tacit knowledge Mainly intangible knowledge that is typically intuitive and not recorded since it is part of the human mind.

Tailored development The standard solution requires major configuration or integration of different modules.

Talk-through A user verbally describes his or her required actions.

Target marketing strategy Evaluation and selection of appropriate segments and the development of appropriate offers.

Task analysis Identification of different tasks, their sequence and how they are broken down.

Technology scouting A structured approach to reviewing technology innovations akin to football scouting.

Test environment Separate software and hardware used to test a system.

Test specification A description of the testing process and tests to be performed.

Testing Aims to identify non-conformance in the requirements specification and errors.

The Internet of Things Objects are uniquely identified and tagged through technologies such as RFID and made accessible through Internet-like addresses.

Thin client An end-user device (terminal) where computing requirements such as processing and storage (and so cost) are minimised.

Third-party cookies Served by another site to the one you are visiting – typical for portals where an ad network will track remotely or where the web analytics software places a cookie.

Three-tier client–server The first tier is the client that handles display, second is application logic and business rules, third is database storage.

Tipping point Using the science of social epidemics explains principles that underpin the rapid spread of ideas, products and behaviours through a population.

Total cost of ownership (TCO) The sum of all cost elements of managing information systems for end-users including purchase, support *and* maintenance.

Trademark A trademark is a unique word or phrase that distinguishes your company. The mark can be registered as plain or designed text, artwork or a combination. In theory, colours, smells and sounds can also be trademarks.

Traffic-building campaign The use of online and offline promotion techniques such as banner advertising, search engine promotion and reciprocal linking to increase the audience of a site (both new and existing customers).

Trojan A virus that masquerades as a bona fide application.

U

Unified Modelling Language (UML) A language used to specify, visualise and document the artefacts of an object-oriented system.

Unique visitors Individual visitors to a site measured through cookies or IP addresses on an individual computer.

Upstream supply chain Transactions between an organisation and its suppliers and intermediaries, equivalent to buy-side e-commerce.

URL (uniform or universal resource locator) A web address used to locate a web page on a web server.

URL strategy A defined approach to forming URLs including the use of capitalisation, hyphenation and sub-domains for different brands and different locations. This has implications for promoting a website offline through promotional or vanity URLs, search engine optimisation and findability. A clean URL which fits many of these aims is http://www.domain.com/folder-name/document-name. Care must be taken with capitalisation since Linux servers parse capitals differently from lower-case letters.

Usability An approach to website design intended to enable the completion of user tasks.

Usability/user testing Representative users are observed performing representative tasks using a system.

Use-case The sequence of transactions between an actor and a system that supports the activities of the actor.

Use-case modelling A user-centred approach to modelling system requirements.

User-centred design Design based on optimising the user experience according to all factors, including the user interface, which affect this.

Utility computing IT resources and in particular software and hardware are utilised on a pay-per-use basis and are managed externally as 'managed services'.

V

Value chain A model for analysis of how supply chain activities can add value to products and services delivered to the customer.

Value network The links between an organisation and its strategic and non-strategic partners that form its external value chain.

Value stream The combination of actions required to deliver value to the customer as products and services.

Vendor-managed inventory (VMI) Supply chain partners manage the replenishment of parts or items for sale through sharing of information on variations in demand and stocking level for goods used for manufacture or sale.

Vertical integration The extent to which supply chain activities are undertaken and controlled within the organisation.

Viral marketing In an online context, 'Forward to a Friend' email is used to transmit a promotional message from one person to another. 'Online word-of-mouth'.

Virtual integration The majority of supply chain activities are undertaken and controlled outside the organisation by third parties.

Virtual organisation An organisation which uses information and communications technology to allow it to operate without clearly defined physical boundaries between different functions. It provides customised services by outsourcing production and other functions to third parties.

Virtual private network (VPN) A secure, encrypted (tunnelled) connection between two points using the Internet, typically created by ISPs for organisations wanting to conduct secure Internet trading.

Virtual world An electronic environment which simulates interactions between online characters known as avatars. Also known as Massively Multiplayer Online Roleplaying Games (MMORPG).

Virtualisation (company) The process of a company developing more of the characteristics of the virtual organisation.

Virtualisation (technology) The indirect provision of technology services through another resource (abstraction). Essentially one computer is using its processing and storage capacity to do the work of another.

Vision or mission statement A concise summary defining the scope and broad aims of an organisation's digital channel in the future, explaining how they will contribute to the organisation and support customers and interactions with partners.

Voice over IP (VOIP) Voice data are transferred across the Internet – it enables phone calls to be made over the Internet.

W

Walk-through A user executes their actions through using a system or mock-up.

Web 2.0 concept Web 2.0 refers to a collection of web services which facilitate certain behaviours online such as community participation and user-generated content, rating and tagging.

Web 3.0 concept Next-generation web incorporating high-speed connectivity, complex cross-community interactions, full range of digital media (text, voice, video) and an intelligent or semantic web where automated applications can access data from different online services to assist searchers perform complex tasks of supplier selection.

Web accessibility An approach to website design that enables sites and web applications to be used by people with visual impairment or other disabilities such as motor impairment. Accessibility also demands that web users should be able to use websites and applications effectively regardless of the browser or access platform they use and its settings.

Web address See URL (uniform or universal resource locator).

Web analytics Techniques used to assess and improve the contribution of digital marketing to a business including reviewing traffic volume, referrals, clickstreams, online reach data, customer satisfaction surveys, leads and sales.

Web application frameworks A standard programming framework based on reusable library functions for creating dynamic websites through a programming language.

Web application server Software processes which is accessed by a standard programming interface (API) of a web application framework to serve dynamic website functionality in response to requests received from browsers. They are designed to manage multiple requests from multiple users and will provide load-balancing to support high volumes of usage.

Web classification See Card sorting or web classification.

Web design personas A summary of the characteristics, needs, motivations and environment of typical website users.

Web page See Static web page, Dynamically created web page and Web servers.

Web servers Store and present the web pages accessed by web browsers.

Web services Business applications and software services are provided through Internet and web protocols with the application managed on a separate server from where it is accessed.

Whitelist A compilation of trusted sources of email that is permitted to enter an inbox.

Widgets A badge or button incorporated into a site or social network space by its owner, with content or services typically served from another site making widgets effectively a mini-software application or web service. Content can be updated in real time since the widget interacts with the server each time it loads.

Wireframes Also known as 'schematics' – a way of illustrating the layout of an individual web page.

Wireless communications Electronic transactions and communications conducted using mobile devices such as laptops and mobile phones (and fixed access platforms) with different forms of wireless connection.

Workflow management (WFM) Workflow management is the automation of information flows; it provides tools for processing the information according to a set of procedural rules.

World Wide Web (WWW) The most common technique for publishing information on the Internet. It is accessed through web browsers which display web pages of embedded graphics and HTML- or XML-encoded text.

Worm A small program that self-replicates and transfers across a network from machine to machine. A form of virus.

Z

Zero Moment of Truth (ZMOT) A summary of today's multichannel consumer decision making for product purchase where they search, review ratings, styles, prices comments on social media before visiting a retailer.

Index

Note: Terms which feature in the Glossary have **emboldened** page numbers.